connect to learning, connect to their futures.

Connect Business Statistics Plus

McGraw-Hill Connect Business Statistics is also available with the interactive online version of the text—*Connect Business Statistics Plus*.

Like *Connect Business Statistics*, *Connect Business Statistics Plus* provides students with online assignments and assessments, plus 24/7 online access to an eBook—an identical, online edition of the printed text—to aid them in successfully completing their work, wherever and whenever they choose.

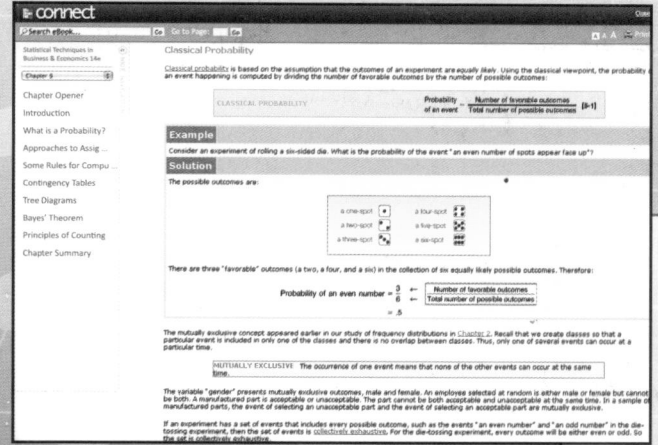

Integrated eBook with Connect Plus

By simply clicking on the eBook button while in Connect, Connect Plus users will be linked directly to the related textbook materials without additional login requirements. This feature makes it quick and convenient to study and complete assignments online.

Contact your local McGraw-Hill/Irwin representative to learn more about Connect Business Statistics. Visit www.mcgrawhillconnect.com or call 800-338-3987.

ALEKS®

Need assistance in learning business statistics concepts? ALEKS can help!

ALEKS is an assessment and learning system that provides individualized instruction in Business Statistics, Business Math, and Accounting. ALEKS is available from McGraw-Hill over the Internet. It delivers precise assessments of your knowledge, guides you in the selection of appropriate new study material, and records your progress toward mastery of goals.

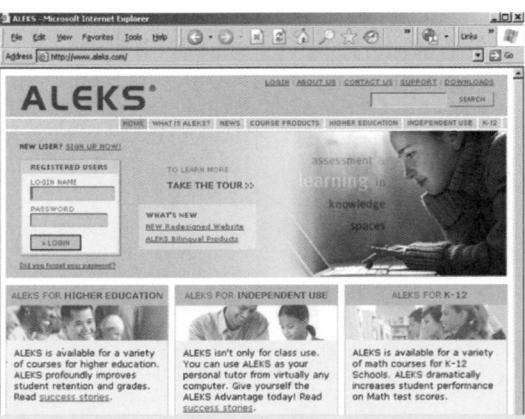

ALEKS interacts with you, much as a human tutor would, moving between explanation and practice as needed, correcting and analyzing errors, defining terms and changing topics on request. By accurately assessing your knowledge, ALEKS focuses precisely on what you are ready to learn next, helping you master the course content more quickly and easily.

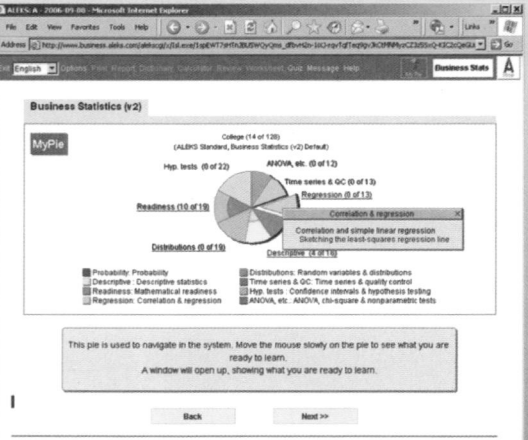

ALEKS is both comprehensive and flexible and can be used effectively in tandem with your business statistics text.

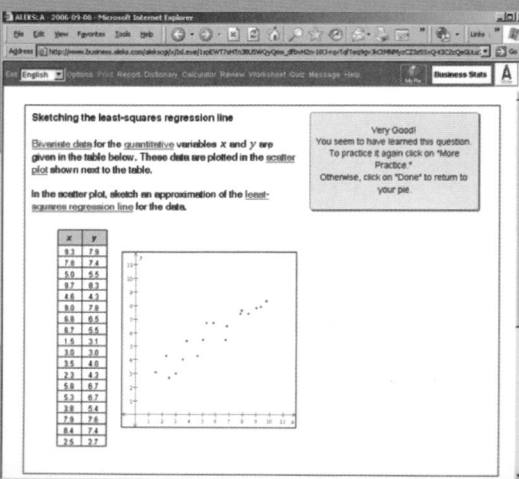

Statistical Techniques in
Business & Economics

Fourteenth Edition

Douglas A. Lind
Coastal Carolina University and The University of Toledo

William G. Marchal
The University of Toledo

Samuel A. Wathen
Coastal Carolina University

Boston   Burr Ridge, IL   Dubuque, IA   Madison, WI   New York   San Francisco   St. Louis
Bangkok   Bogotá   Caracas   Kuala Lumpur   Lisbon   London   Madrid   Mexico City
Milan   Montreal   New Delhi   Santiago   Seoul   Singapore   Sydney   Taipei   Toronto

McGraw-Hill
Irwin

STATISTICAL TECHNIQUES IN BUSINESS AND ECONOMICS

Published by McGraw-Hill/Irwin, a business unit of The McGraw-Hill Companies, Inc., 1221 Avenue of the Americas, New York, NY, 10020. Copyright © 2010, 2008, 2005, 2002, 1999, 1996, 1993, 1990, 1986, 1982, 1978, 1974, 1970, 1967 by The McGraw-Hill Companies, Inc. All rights reserved. No part of this publication may be reproduced or distributed in any form or by any means, or stored in a database or retrieval system, without the prior written consent of The McGraw-Hill Companies, Inc., including, but not limited to, in any network or other electronic storage or transmission, or broadcast for distance learning.

Some ancillaries, including electronic and print components, may not be available to customers outside the United States.

This book is printed on acid-free paper.

1 2 3 4 5 6 7 8 9 0 WCK/WCK 0 9

ISBN   978-0-07-340176-8 (student edition)
MHID   0-07-340176-5 (student edition)
ISBN   978-0-07-727006-3 (instructor's edition)
MHID   0-07-727006-1 (instructor's edition)

Vice president and editor-in-chief: *Brent Gordon*
Editorial director: *Stewart Mattson*
Publisher: *Tim Vertovec*
Executive editor: *Steve Schuetz*
Senior developmental editor: *Wanda J. Zeman*
Marketing manager: *Scott S. Bishop*
Senior project manager: *Bruce Gin*
Lead production supervisor: *Carol A. Bielski*
Lead designer: *Matthew Baldwin*
Senior photo research coordinator: *Jeremy Cheshareck*
Photo researcher: *Teri Stratford*
Senior media project manager: *Greg Bates*
Cover design: *Matthew Baldwin*
Typeface: *9.5/11 Helvetica Neue 55*
Compositor: *Aptara, Inc.*
Printer: *Quebecor World Versailles Inc.*

Library of Congress Cataloging-in-Publication Data

Lind, Douglas A.
    Statistical techniques in business & economics / Douglas A. Lind, William G. Marchal, Samuel A. Wathen. — 14th ed.
        p. cm. — (The McGraw-Hill/Irwin series operations and decision sciences)
    Includes index.
    ISBN-13: 978-0-07-340176-8 (student edition : alk. paper)
    ISBN-10: 0-07-340176-5 (student edition : alk. paper)
    ISBN-13: 978-0-07-727006-3 (instructor's edition : alk. paper)
    ISBN-10: 0-07-727006-1 (instructor's edition : alk. paper)
    1. Social sciences—Statistical methods. 2. Economics—Statistical methods. 3. Commercial statistics. I. Marchal, William G. II. Wathen, Samuel Adam. III. Title. IV. Title: Statistical techniques in business and economics.
HA29.M268 2010
519.5—dc22

                                                                        2008044486

www.mhhe.com

The McGraw-Hill/Irwin Series
Operations and Decision Sciences

Business Statistics

Aczel and Sounderpandian
Complete Business Statistics
Seventh Edition

ALEKS Corporation
ALEKS for Business Statistics
First Edition

Alwan
Statistical Process Analysis
First Edition

Bowerman, O'Connell, and Murphree
Business Statistics in Practice
Fifth Edition

Bowerman, O'Connell,
Orris, and Murphree
Essentials of Business Statistics
Third Edition

Bryant and Smith
Practical Data Analysis: Case Studies in Business Statistics, Volumes I, II, and III*

Cooper and Schindler
Business Research Methods
Tenth Edition

Doane, Mathieson, and Tracy
Visual Statistics
Second Edition, 2.0

Doane and Seward
Applied Statistics in Business and Economics
Second Edition

Doane and Seward
Essential Statistics in Business and Economics
Second Edition

Gitlow, Oppenheim, Oppenheim, and Levine
Quality Management
Third Edition

Kutner, Nachtsheim, Neter and Li
Applied Linear Statistical Models
Fifth Edition

Kutner, Nachtsheim, and Neter
Applied Linear Regression Models
Fourth Edition

Lind, Marchal, and Wathen
Basic Statistics for Business and Economics
Sixth Edition

Lind, Marchal, and Wathen
Statistical Techniques in Business and Economics
Fourteenth Edition

Merchant, Goffinet, and Koehler
Basic Statistics Using Excel for Office XP
Fourth Edition

Olson and Shi
Introduction to Business Data Mining
First Edition

Orris
Basic Statistics Using Excel and MegaStat
First Edition

Siegel
Practical Business Statistics
Fifth Edition

Wilson, Keating, and John Galt Solutions, Inc.
Business Forecasting
Fifth Edition

Zagorsky
Business Information
First Edition

Quantitative Methods and Management Science

Hillier and Hillier
Introduction to Management Science
Third Edition

Stevenson and Ozgur
Introduction to Management Science with Spreadsheets
First Edition

Kros
Spreadsheet Modeling for Business Decisions
First Edition

---

*Available only through McGraw-Hill's PRIMIS Online Assets Library.

Over the years, we have received many compliments on this text and have been told it's a favorite among students. We accept that as the highest compliment and continue to work very hard to maintain that status.

The objective of *Statistical Techniques in Business and Economics* is to provide students majoring in management, marketing, finance, accounting, economics, and other fields of business administration with an introductory survey of the many applications of descriptive and inferential statistics. While we focus on business applications, we also use many exercises and examples that are student oriented and do not require previous courses.

In this text we show beginning students every step needed to be successful in a basic statistics course. This step-by-step approach enhances performance, accelerates preparedness, and significantly improves motivation. Understanding the concepts, seeing and doing plenty of examples and exercises, and comprehending the application of statistical methods in business and economics are the focus of this book.

The first edition of this text was published in 1967. At that time locating relevant business data was difficult. That has changed! Today locating data is not a problem. The number of items you purchase at the grocery store is automatically recorded at the checkout counter. Phone companies track the time of our calls, the length of calls, and the number of the person called. Credit card companies maintain information on the number, time and date, and amount of our purchases. Medical devices automatically monitor our heart rate, blood pressure, and temperature. A large amount of business information is recorded and reported almost instantly. CNN, *USA Today,* and MSNBC, for example, all have websites where you can track stock prices with a delay of less than 20 minutes.

Today, skills are needed to deal with a large volume of numerical information. First, we need to be critical consumers of information presented by others. Second, we need to be able to reduce large amounts of information into a concise and meaningful form to enable us to make effective interpretations, judgments, and decisions.

All students have calculators and most have either personal computers or access to personal computers in a campus lab. Statistical software, such as Microsoft Excel and MINITAB, is available on these computers. The commands necessary to achieve the software results are available in a special section at the end of each chapter. We use screen captures within the chapters, so the student becomes familiar with the nature of the software output. Because of the availability of computers and software it is no longer necessary to dwell on calculations. We have replaced many of the calculation examples with interpretative ones, to assist the student in understanding and interpreting the statistical results. In addition we now place more emphasis on the conceptual nature of the statistical topics. While making these changes, we still continue to present, as best we can, the key concepts, along with supporting examples.

What's New in This Fourteenth Edition?

We have made several changes to this edition that we think you and your students will find useful.

- New exercises and examples using Excel 2007 screenshots and the latest version of MINITAB. We have also increased the size and clarity of these screenshots.

- There are also new Excel 2007 software commands and updated MINITAB commands at the ends of chapters.
- At the end of each Section Review, we have added a Practice Test. We think this will give the student an idea of what might appear on a test and how the test might be structured. Hopefully, this will reduce test anxiety. The test includes a section on vocabulary and a section of problems.
- We have carefully reviewed the Exercises within the chapters, those at the ends of chapters, and in the Review Section. We have revised or replaced those that were outdated. You can still find and assign your favorites that have worked well, or you can introduce fresh examples.
- There is new content on nominal-level data and its properties in Chapter 1.
- There are many new photos throughout with updated exercises in the chapter openers.
- Much of the relevant data and statistics within the text and exercises have been updated.

Dedication

To Jane, my wife and best friend, and our sons, their wives, and our grandchildren: Mike and Sue (Steve and Courtney), Steve and Kathryn (Kennedy and Jake), and Mark and Sarah (Jared, Drew, and Nate).

Douglas A. Lind

To Elizabeth and William, the most recent additions to our family.

William G. Marchal

To my wonderful family: Isaac, Hannah, and Barb.

Samuel A. Wathen

Chapter Goals

Each chapter begins with a set of goals, or learning objectives, designed to provide focus for the chapter and motivate student learning. These objectives indicate what the student should be able to do after completing the chapter.

Chapter Opening Exercise

A representative exercise opens the chapter and shows how the chapter content can be applied to a real world situation.

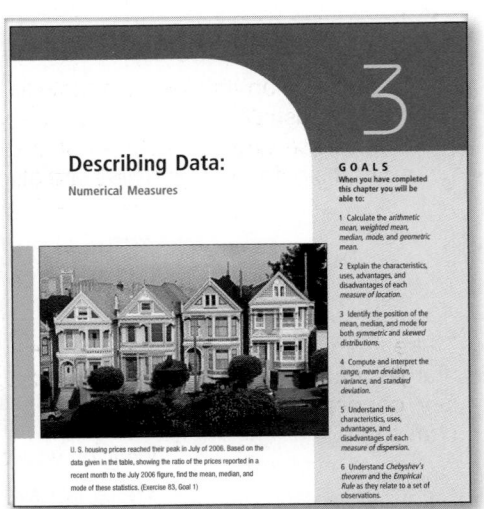

Describing Data:

Numerical Measures

3

GOALS
When you have completed this chapter you will be able to:

1 Calculate the arithmetic mean, weighted mean, median, mode, and geometric mean.

2 Explain the characteristics, uses, advantages, and disadvantages of each measure of location.

3 Identify the position of the mean, median, and mode for both symmetric and skewed distributions.

4 Compute and interpret the range, mean deviation, variance, and standard deviation.

5 Understand the characteristics, uses, advantages, and disadvantages of each measure of dispersion.

6 Understand Chebyshev's theorem and the Empirical Rule as they relate to a set of observations.

U. S. housing prices reached their peak in July of 2006. Based on the data given in the table, showing the ratio of the prices reported in a recent month to the July 2006 figure, find the mean, median, and mode of these statistics. (Exercise 83, Goal 1)

Introduction to the Topic

Each chapter starts with a review of the important concepts of the previous chapter and provides a link to the material in the current chapter. This step-by-step approach increases comprehension by providing continuity across the concepts.

Introduction

The highly competitive automotive retailing business has changed significantly over the past 5 years, due in part to consolidation by large, publicly owned dealership groups. Traditionally, a local family owned and operated the community dealership, which might have included one or two manufacturers, like Pontiac and GMC Trucks or Chrysler and the popular Jeep line. Recently, however, skillfully managed and well-financed companies have been acquiring local dealerships across large regions of the country. As these groups acquire the local dealerships, they often bring standard selling practices, common software and hardware technology platforms, and management reporting techniques. The goal is to provide an improved buying experience for the consumer, while increasing the profitability of

Example/Solution

After important concepts are introduced, a solved example is given to provide a how-to illustration for students and to show a relevant business or economics-based application that helps answer the question, "What will I use this for?" All examples provide a realistic scenario or application and make the math size and scale reasonable for introductory students.

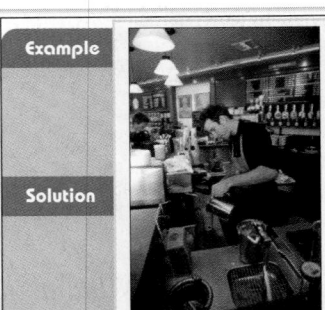

Example

Solution

The number of cappuccinos sold at the Starbucks location in the Orange County Airport between 4 and 7 p.m. for a sample of 5 days last year were 20, 40, 50, 60, and 80. In the LAX airport in Los Angeles, the number of cappuccinos sold at a Starbucks location between 4 and 7 p.m. for a sample of 5 days last year were 20, 49, 50, 51, and 80. Determine the mean, median, range, and mean deviation for each location. Compare the differences.

For the Orange County location the mean, median, and range are:

Mean	50 cappuccinos per day
Median	50 cappuccinos per day
Range	60 cappuccinos per day

The mean deviation is the mean of the absolute

Self-Reviews

Self-Reviews are interspersed throughout each chapter and closely patterned after the preceding Examples. They help students monitor their progress and provide immediate reinforcement for that particular technique.

Self-Review 3–2 Springers sold 95 Antonelli men's suits for the regular price of $400. For the spring sale the suits were reduced to $200 and 126 were sold. At the final clearance, the price was reduced to $100 and the remaining 79 suits were sold.
(a) What was the weighted mean price of an Antonelli suit?
(b) Springers paid $200 a suit for the 300 suits. Comment on the store's profit per suit if a salesperson receives a $25 commission for each one sold.

Statistics in Action

Statistics in Action articles are scattered throughout the text, usually about two per chapter. They provide unique and interesting applications and historical insights in the field of statistics.

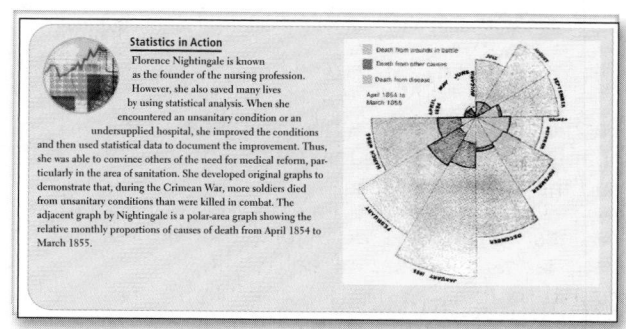

Margin Notes

There are more than 300 concise notes in the margin. Each is aimed at reemphasizing the key concepts presented immediately adjacent to it.

Definitions

Definitions of new terms or terms unique to the study of statistics are set apart from the text and highlighted for easy reference and review.

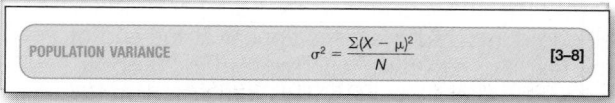

Formulas

Formulas that are used for the first time are boxed and numbered for reference. In addition, a formula card is bound into the back of the text, which lists these key formulas.

Exercises

Exercises are included after sections within the chapter and at the end of the chapter. Section exercises cover the material studied in the section.

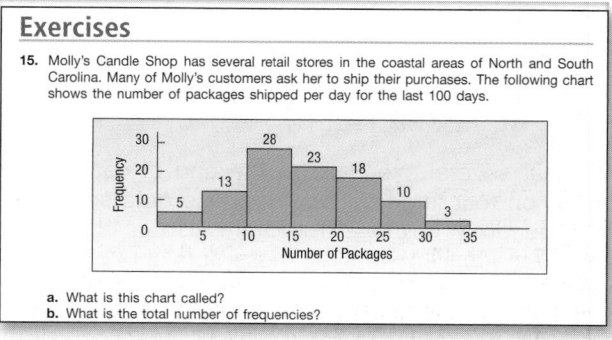

Computer Output

The text includes many software examples, using Excel, MegaStat®, and MINITAB. Screen captures are highlighted with either a MINITAB or Excel logo in the margin.

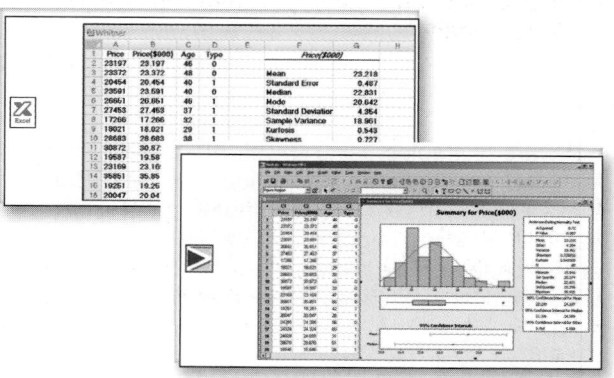

BY CHAPTER

Chapter Summary

Each chapter contains a brief summary of the chapter material, including the vocabulary and the critical formulas.

> **Chapter Summary**
> I. A frequency table is a grouping of qualitative data into mutually exclusive classes showing the number of observations in each class.
> II. A relative frequency table shows the fraction of the number of frequencies in each class.
> III. A bar chart is a graphic representation of a frequency table.
> IV. A pie chart shows the proportion each distinct class represents of the total number of frequencies.

Pronunciation Key

This tool lists the mathematical symbol, its meaning, and how to pronounce it. We believe this will help the student retain the meaning of the symbol and generally enhance course communications.

> **Pronunciation Key**
>
> | SYMBOL | MEANING | PRONUNCIATION |
> |---|---|---|
> | μ | Population mean | mu |
> | Σ | Operation of adding | sigma |
> | ΣX | Adding a group of values | sigma X |
> | $\bar{X}$ | Sample mean | X bar |

Chapter Exercises

Generally, the end of chapter exercises are the most challenging and integrate the chapter concepts. The answers and worked-out solutions for all odd-numbered exercises appear at the end of the text. For exercises with more than 20 observations, the data can be found on the Student CD and on the text's Web site. These files are in Excel and MINITAB formats.

> **Chapter Exercises**
> 23. Describe the similarities and differences of qualitative and quantitative variables. Be sure to include:
>   a. What level of measurement is required for each variable type?
>   b. Can both types be used to describe both samples and populations?

Data Set Exercises

The last several exercises at the end of each chapter are based on four large data sets. These data sets are printed in Appendix A in the text and are also on the Student CD and on the text's Web site. These data sets present the students with real-world and more complex applications.

> **Data Set Exercises**
> 46. Refer to the Real Estate data, which report information on the homes sold in the Denver, Colorado, area last year.
>   a. Compute the mean and the standard deviation of the distribution of the selling prices for the homes. Assume this to be the population. Develop a histogram of the data. Would it seem reasonable from this histogram to conclude that the population of selling prices follows the normal distribution?
>   b. Let's assume a normal population. Select a sample of 10 homes. Compute the mean and the standard deviation of the sample. Determine the likelihood of finding a sample mean this large or larger from the population.
> 47. Refer to the CIA data, which report demographic and economic information on 46 countries. Select a random sample of 10 countries. For this sample calculate the mean GDP/capita. Repeat this sampling and calculation process five more times. Then find the mean and standard deviation of your six sample means.
>   a. How do this mean and standard deviation compare with the mean and standard deviation of the original "population" of 46 countries?
>   b. Make a histogram of the six means and discuss whether the distribution is normal.
>   c. Suppose the population distribution is normal. For the first sample mean you computed, determine the likelihood of finding a sample mean this large or larger from the population.

Software Commands

Software examples using Excel, MegaStat®, and MINITAB are included throughout the text. But, the explanations of the computer input commands for each program are placed at the end of the chapter. This allows students to focus on the statistical techniques rather than how to input data.

> **Software Commands**
> 1. The Excel commands to select a simple random sample on page 261 are:
>   a. Select the **Data tab** on the top of the menu. Then on the far right select **Data Analysis**, then **Sampling** and **OK**.
>   b. For **Input Range** insert *B1:B31*. Since the column is named, click the **Labels** box. Select **Random**, and enter the sample size for the **Number of Samples**, in this case *5*. Click on **Output Range** and indicate the place in the spreadsheet you want the sample information. Note that your sample results will differ from those in the text. Also recall that Excel samples with replacement, so it is possible for a population value to appear more than once in the sample.

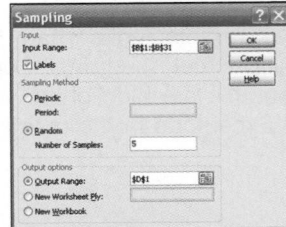

Reinforce Student Learning?

Answers to Self-Review

The worked-out solutions to the Self-Reviews are provided at the end of each chapter.

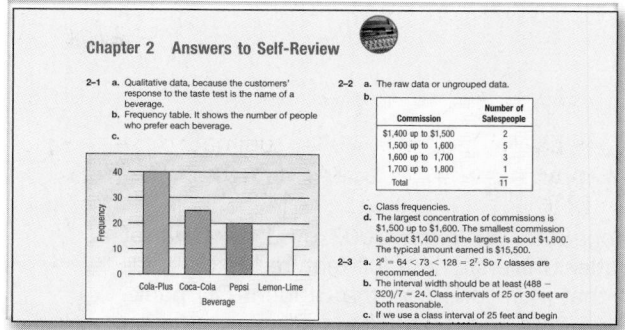

BY SECTION

Section Reviews

After selected groups of chapters (1–4, 5–7, 8 and 9, 10–12, 13 and 14, 15 and 16, and 17 and 18), a Section Review is included. Much like a review before an exam, these include a brief **overview** of the chapters, **glossary** of key terms, **multiple-choice questions,** and **problems for review.**

Cases

The review also includes continuing cases and several small cases that let students make decisions using tools and techniques from a variety of chapters.

Practice Test

The Practice Test is intended to give students an idea of content that might appear on a test and how the test might be structured. The Practice Test includes both objective questions and problems covering the material studied in the section.

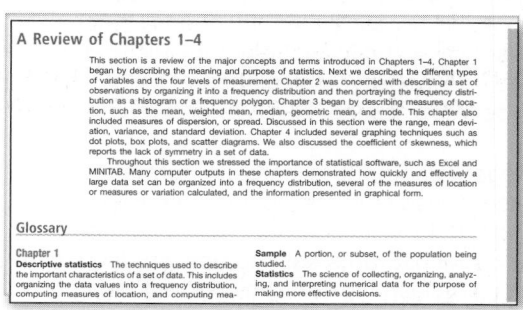

A Review of Chapters 1–4

This section is a review of the major concepts and terms introduced in Chapters 1–4. Chapter 1 began by describing the meaning and purpose of statistics. Next we described the different types of variables and the four levels of measurement. Chapter 2 was concerned with describing a set of observations by organizing it into a frequency distribution and then portraying the frequency distribution as a histogram or a frequency polygon. Chapter 3 began by describing measures of location, such as the mean, weighted mean, median, geometric mean, and mode. This chapter also included measures of dispersion, or spread. Discussed in this section were the range, mean deviation, variance, and standard deviation. Chapter 4 included several graphing techniques such as dot plots, box plots, and scatter diagrams. We also discussed the coefficient of skewness, which reports the lack of symmetry in a set of data.

Throughout this section we stressed the importance of statistical software, such as Excel and MINITAB. Many computer outputs in these chapters demonstrated how quickly and effectively a large data set can be organized into a frequency distribution, several of the measures of location or measures of variation calculated, and the information presented in graphical form.

Glossary

Chapter 1
Descriptive statistics The techniques used to describe the important characteristics of a set of data. This includes organizing the data values into a frequency distribution, computing measures of location, and computing mea-

Sample A portion, or subset, of the population being studied.
Statistics The science of collecting, organizing, analyzing, and interpreting numerical data for the purpose of making more effective decisions.

Cases

A. Century National Bank
The following case will appear in subsequent review sections. Assume that you work in the Planning Department of the Century National Bank and report to Ms. Lamberg. You will need to do some data analysis and prepare a short written report. Remember, Mr. Selig is the president of the bank, so you will want to ensure that your report is complete and accurate. A copy of the data appears in Appendix A.6.

Century National Bank has offices in several cities in the Midwest and the southeastern part of the United States. Mr. Dan Selig, president and CEO, would like to know the characteristics of his checking account customers. What is the balance of a typical customer?

How many other bank services do the checking account customers use? Do the customers use the ATM service and, if so, how often? What about debit cards? Who uses them, and how often are they used?

To better understand the customers, Mr. Selig asked Ms. Wendy Lamberg, director of planning, to select a sample of customers and prepare a report. To begin, she has appointed a team from her staff. You are the head of the team and responsible for preparing the report. You select a random sample of 60 customers. In addition to the balance in each account at the end of last month, you determine: (1) the number of ATM (auto-

B. Wildcat Plumbing Supply, Inc.: Do We Have Gender Differences?
Wildcat Plumbing Supply has served the plumbing needs of Southwest Arizona for more than 40 years. The company was founded by Mr. Terrence St. Julian and is run today by his son Cory. The company has grown from a handful of employees to more than 500 today. Cory is concerned about several positions within the company where he has men and women doing essentially the same job but at different pay. To investigate, he collected the information below. Suppose you are a student intern in the Accounting Department and have been given the task to write a report summarizing the situation.

Yearly Salary ($000)	Women	Men
Less than 30	2	0
30 up to 40	3	1
40 up to 50	17	4
50 up to 60	17	24
60 up to 70	8	21
70 up to 80	3	7
80 or more	0	3

Practice Test

There is a practice test at the end of each review section. The tests are in two parts. The first part contains several objective questions, usually in a fill-in-the-blank format. The second part is problems. In most cases it should take 30 to 45 minutes to complete the test. The problems require a calculator. Check the answers in the Answer Section in the back of the book.

Part I Objective
1. The science of collecting, organizing, presenting, analyzing, and interpreting data to assist in making effective decisions is called _____. 1. _____
2. Methods of organizing, summarizing, and presenting data in an informative way is called _____. 2. _____
3. The entire set of individuals or objects of interest or the measurements obtained from all individuals or objects of interest is called the _____. 3. _____
4. List the two types of variables. 4. _____
5. The number of bedrooms in a house is an example of a _____. (discrete variable, continuous variable, qualitative variable—pick one) 5. _____
6. The jersey numbers of Major League baseball players is an example of what level of measurement? 6. _____
7. The classification of students by eye color is an example of what level of measurement? 7. _____
8. The sum of the differences between each value and the mean is always equal to what value? 8. _____
9. A set of data contained 70 observations. How many classes would you suggest in order to construct a frequency distribution? 9. _____
10. What percent of the values in a data set are always larger than the median? 10. _____
11. The square of the standard deviation is the _____. 11. _____
12. The standard deviation assumes a negative value when _____. (All the values are negative, when at least half the values are negative, or never—pick one.) 12. _____
13. Which of the following is least affected by an outlier? (mean, median, or range—pick one) 13. _____

Part II Problems
1. The Russell 2000 index of stock prices increased by the following amounts over the last three years.

18%	4%	2%

What is the geometric mean increase for the three years?
2. The information below refers to the selling prices ($000) of homes sold in Warren, PA during 2007.

MegaStat® for Excel 2007

MegaStat® for Excel 2007 by J. B. Orris of Butler University is a full-featured Excel add-in that is included on the Student CD packaged with this text. The software performs statistical analyses within an Excel workbook. It does basic functions, such as descriptive statistics, frequency distributions, and probability calculations as well as hypothesis testing, ANOVA, and regression.

MegaStat output is carefully formatted and ease-of-use features include Auto Expand for quick data selection and Auto Label detect. Since *MegaStat* is easy to use, students can focus on learning statistics without being distracted by the software. *MegaStat* is always available from Excel's main menu. Selecting a menu item pops up a dialog box. *MegaStat* works with all recent versions of Excel including Excel 2007. Help files are built in and an introductory user's manual is also included.

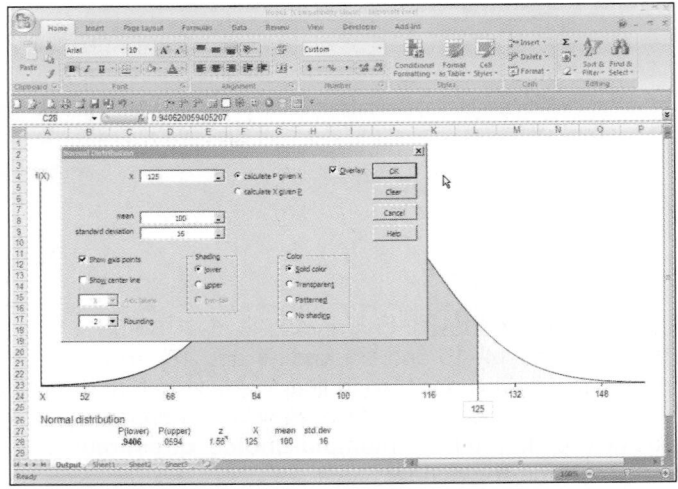

Visual Statistics

Visual Statistics 2.2 by Doane, Mathieson, and Tracy is a package of 21 software programs for teaching and learning statistics concepts. It is unique in that it allows students to learn the concepts through interactive experimentation and visualization. The software and worktext promote active learning through competency building exercises, individual and team projects, and built-in data bases. Over 400 data sets from business settings are included within the package as well as a worktext in electronic format.

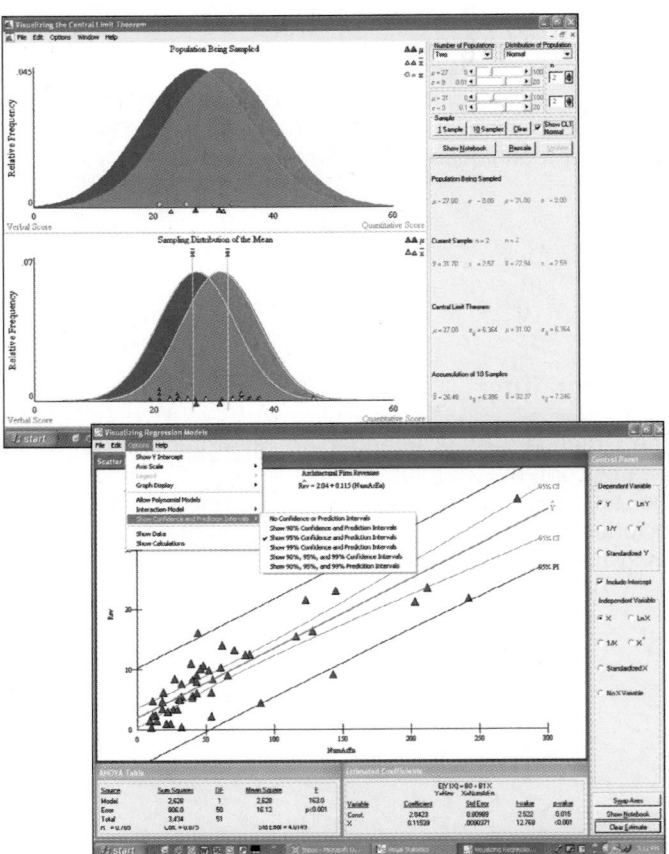

MINITAB®/SPSS®/JMP®

MINITAB® Student Version 14, SPSS® Student Version 15, and JMP® Student Edition 6 are software tools that are available to help students solve the business statistics exercises in the text. Each is available in the student version and can be packaged with any McGraw-Hill business statistics text.

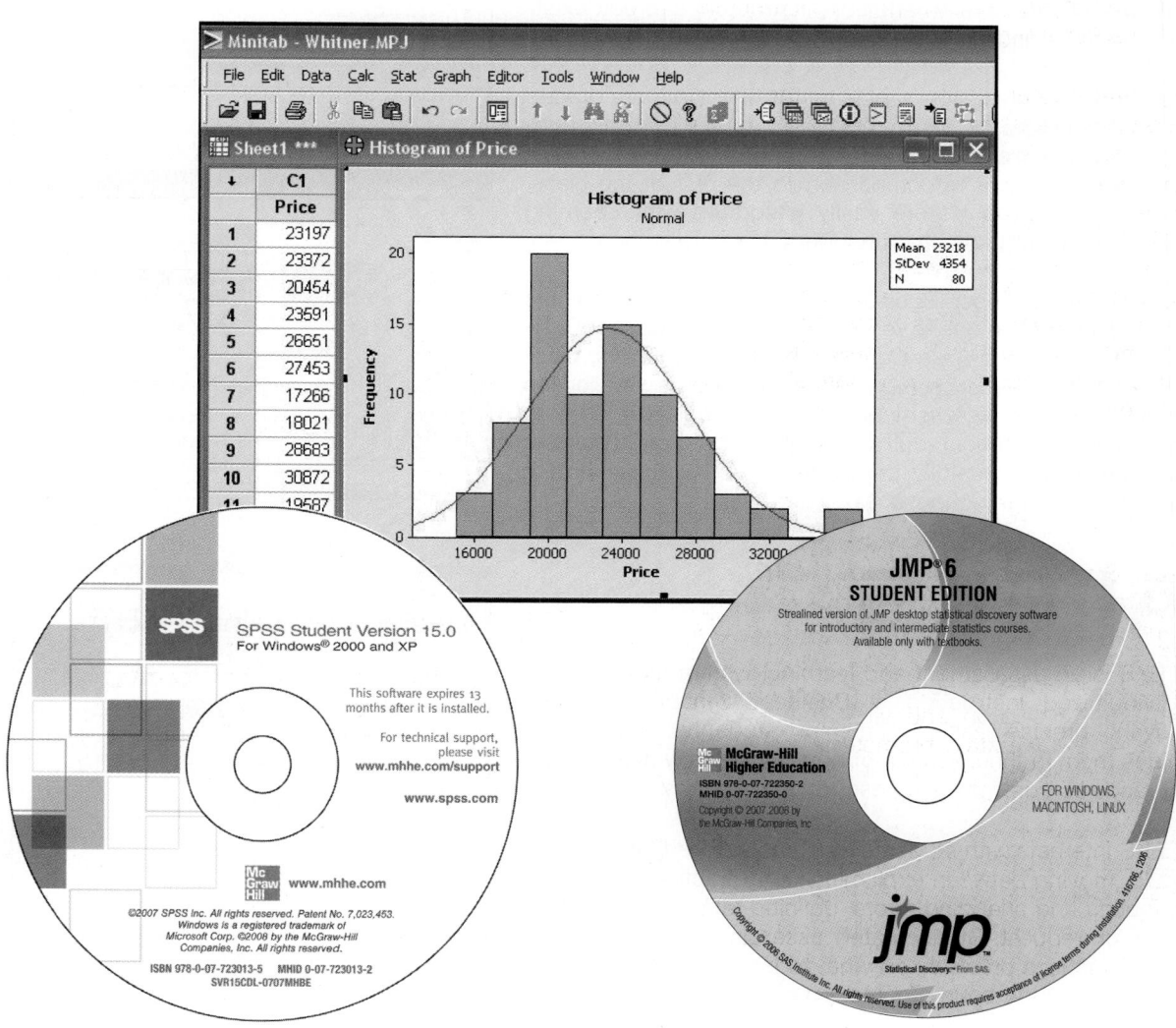

McGraw-Hill Connect™ Business Statistics

McGraw-Hill *Connect Business Statistics* is an online assignment and assessment system customized to the text and available as an option for students. With *Connect Business Statistics,* instructors can deliver assignments, quizzes, and tests online. The system utilizes the exercises from the text both in a static one-problem-at-a-time fashion as well as algorithmically where problems generate multiple data possibilities and answers. In addition, instructors can edit existing questions and author entirely new problems.

You choose or create the problems. Assignments are graded automatically, and the results are stored in your private gradebook. You can track individual student performance by question, assignment, or in comparison to the rest of the class. Detailed grade reports are easily integrated with Learning Management Systems, such as WebCT and Blackboard.

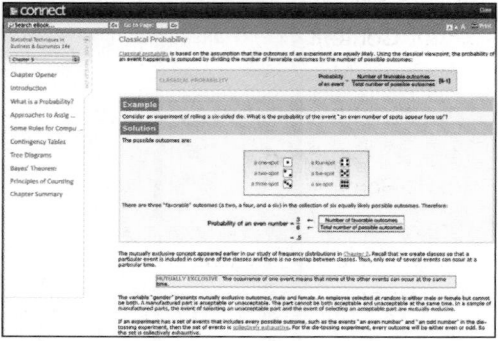

McGraw-Hill Connect Business Statistics is also available with the interactive online version of the text—*Connect Business Statistics Plus.* Like *Connect Business Statistics, Connect Business Statistics Plus* provides students with online assignments and assessments, plus 24/7 online access to an eBook, an identical, online edition of the printed text, to aid them in successfully completing their work, wherever and whenever they choose.

ALEKS®

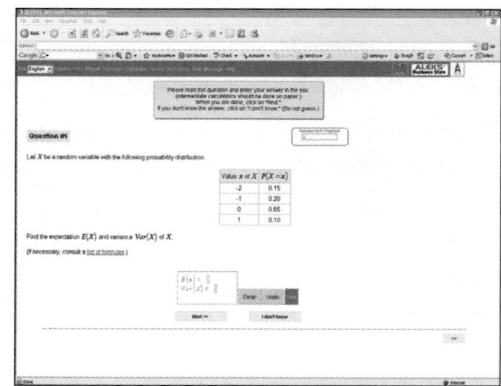

ALEKS is an assessment and learning system that provides individualized instruction in Business Statistics. ALEKS delivers precise assessments of students' knowledge, guides them in the selection of appropriate new study material, and records their progress toward mastery of goals.

ALEKS interacts with students much as a skilled human tutor would, moving between explanation and practice as needed, correcting and analyzing errors, defining terms and changing topics on request. By accurately assessing their knowledge, ALEKS focuses precisely on what to learn next, helping students master the course content more quickly and easily.

Aid Student Learning?

Save Money. Go Green. McGraw-Hill eBooks

Green . . . it's on everybody's mind these days. It's not only about saving trees, it's also about saving money. At 55 percent of the bookstore price, McGraw-Hill eBooks are an eco-friendly and cost-saving alternative to the traditional printed textbook. So, you do some good for the environment and . . . you do some good for your wallet.

CourseSmart

CourseSmart is a new way to find and buy eTextbooks. CourseSmart has the largest selection of eText-books available anywhere, offering thousands of the most commonly adopted textbooks from a wide variety of higher-education publishers. Course Smart eTextbooks are available in one standard online reader with full text search, notes and highlighting, and e-mail tools for sharing notes between classmates. Visit www.CourseSmart.com for more information on ordering.

Online Learning Center: www.mhhe.com/lind14e

The Online Learning Center (OLC) is the text Web site with online content for both students and instructors.

Instructor Content
- Solutions Manual
- Solutions to Study Guide
- Test Bank
- PowerPoint
- Image Library
- MegaStat User's Guide
- Instructor Updates and Errata

Student Content
- Quizzes
- PowerPoint
- Data Sets
- Data Files
- Appendices
- Updates and Errata
- Screencam Tutorials
- MegaStat User's Guide
- iPod® Content
- Chapter 20

WebCT/Blackboard/eCollege

All of the material in the Online Learning Center is also available in portable WebCT, Blackboard, or eCollege content "cartridges" provided free to adopters of this text.

Business Statistics Center (BSC): www.mhhe.com/bstat/

The BSC contains links to statistical publications and resources, software downloads, learning aids, statistical Web sites and databases, and McGraw-Hill/Irwin product Web sites and online courses.

Instructor's Resources CD-ROM (ISBN: 007727007X)

This resource allows instructors to conveniently access the Instructor's Solutions Manual, Test Bank in Word and EZ Test formats, Instructor PowerPoint slides, data files, and data sets.

Online Learning Center: www.mhhe.com/lind14e

The Online Learning Center (OLC) provides the instructor with a complete Instructor's Manual in Word format, the complete Test Bank in both Word files and computerized EZ Test format, Instructor PowerPoint slides, text art files, an introduction to ALEKS®, an introduction to McGraw-Hill Connect Business Statistics™, access to the eBook, and more.

All test bank questions are available in an EZ Test electronic format. Included are a number of multiple-choice, true/false, and short-answer questions and problems. The answers to all questions are given, along with a rating of the level of difficulty, chapter goal the question tests, Bloom's taxonomy question type, and AACSB knowledge category.

AACSB Statement

The McGraw-Hill Companies is a proud corporate member of AACSB International. Understanding the importance and value of AACSB accreditation, Lind, Marchal, and Wathen *Statistical Techniques in Business and Economics,* 14e, has connected questions in the Test Bank to the six general knowledge and skill guidelines found in the AACSB standards.

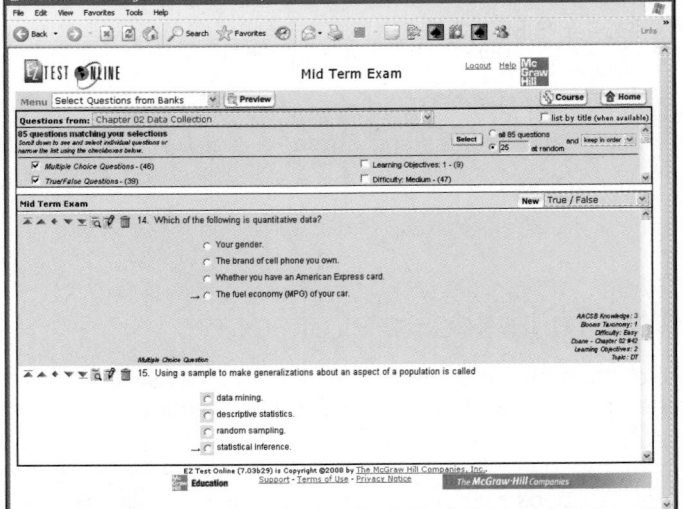

Student CD-ROM

The Student CD-ROM packaged with each copy of the text contains software resources for student self-study and tools for working the exercises in the text. These resources include:

- Visual Statistics
- MegaStat® for Excel 2007
- Data sets
- Data files
- Chapter 20
- Link to the Online Learning Center (OLC) for quizzes, PowerPoint, and other resources.

Student Study Guide (ISBN: 0077270134)

This supplement has been created to help students master the course content. It highlights the important ideas in the text and provides opportunities for students to review the worked-out solutions, review terms and concepts, and practice.

Basic Statistics Using Excel 2007 (ISBN: 0077270010)

This workbook introduces students to Excel and shows how to apply it to introductory statistics. This manual presumes no prior familiarity with Excel or statistics and provides step-by-step directions in a how-to style using Excel 2007 with text examples and problems.

Acknowledgments

This edition of *Statistical Techniques in Business and Economics* is the product of many people: students, colleagues, reviewers, and the staff at McGraw-Hill/Irwin. We thank them all. We wish to express our sincere gratitude to the survey and focus group participants, and the reviewers:

Reviewers

Sung K. Ahn
Washington State University–Pullman

Douglas Barrett
University of North Alabama

Pamela A. Boger
Ohio University–Athens

Giorgio Canarella
California State University–Los Angeles

James Carden
University of Mississippi

Anne Davey
Northeastern State University

Neil Desnoyers
Drexel University

Nirmal Devi
Embry Riddle Aeronautical University

David Doorn
University of Minnesota–Duluth

Clifford B. Hawley
West Virginia University

Lloyd R. Jaisingh
Morehead State University

Mark Kesh
University of Texas

John D. McGinnis
Pennsylvania State–Altoona

Mary Ruth J. McRae
Appalachian State University

Jackie Miller
Ohio State University

Carolyn Monroe
Baylor University

Elizabeth J. T. Murff
Eastern Washington University

Quinton Nottingham
Virginia Polytechnic Institute and State University

René Ordonez
Southern Oregon University

Robert Patterson
Penn State University

Joseph Petry
University of Illinois at Urbana-Champaign

Tammy Prater
Alabama State University

Michael Racer
University of Memphis

Darrell Radson
Drexel University

Steven Ramsier
Florida State University

Christopher W. Rogers
Miami Dade College

Stephen Hays Russell
Weber State University

Martin Sabo
Community College of Denver

Amar Sahay
Salt Lake Community College and University of Utah

Nina Sarkar
Queensborough Community College

Robert Smidt
California Polytechnic State University

Gary Smith
Florida State University

Stanley D. Stephenson
Texas State University–San Marcos

Bedassa Tadesse
University of Minnesota–Duluth

Lawrence Tatum
Baruch College

Elzbieta Trybus
California State University–Northridge

Daniel Tschopp
Daemen College

Jesus M. Valencia
Slippery Rock University

Joseph Van Matre
University of Alabama at Birmingham

Angie Waits
Gadsden State Community College

Kathleen Whitcomb
University of South Carolina

Blake Whitten
University of Iowa

Oliver Yu
San Jose State University

Zhiwei Zhu
University of Louisiana

Survey and Focus Group Participants

Nawar Al-Shara
American University

Charles H. Apigian
Middle Tennessee State University

Nagraj Balakrishnan
Clemson University

Philip Boudreaux
University of Louisiana at Lafayette

Nancy Brooks
University of Vermont

Qidong Cao
Winthrop University

Margaret M. Capen
East Carolina University

Robert Carver
Stonehill College

Jan E. Christopher
Delaware State University

James Cochran
Louisiana Tech University

Farideh Dehkordi-Vakil
Western Illinois University

Brant Deppa
Winona State University

Bernard Dickman
Hofstra University

Casey DiRienzo
Elon University

Erick M. Elder
University of Arkansas at Little Rock

Nicholas R. Farnum
California State University, Fullerton

K. Renee Fister
Murray State University

Gary Franko
Siena College

Maurice Gilbert
Troy State University

Deborah J. Gougeon
University of Scranton

Christine Guenther
Pacific University

Charles F. Harrington
University of Southern Indiana

Craig Heinicke
Baldwin-Wallace College

George Hilton
Pacific Union College

Cindy L. Hinz
St. Bonaventure University

Johnny C. Ho
Columbus State University

Shaomin Huang
Lewis-Clark State College

J. Morgan Jones
University of North Carolina at Chapel Hill

Michael Kazlow
Pace University

John Lawrence
California State University, Fullerton

Sheila M. Lawrence
Rutgers the State University of New Jersey

Jae Lee
State University of New York at New Paltz

Rosa Lemel
Kean University

Robert Lemke
Lake Forest College

Francis P. Mathur
California State Polytechnic University, Pomona

Ralph D. May
Southwestern Oklahoma State University

Richard N. McGrath
Bowling Green State University

Larry T. McRae
Appalachian State University

Dragan Miljkovic
Southwest Missouri State University

John M. Miller
Sam Houston State University

Cameron Montgomery
Delta State University

Broderick Oluyede
Georgia Southern University

Andrew Paizis
Queens College

Andrew L. H. Parkes
University of Northern Iowa

Paul Paschke
Oregon State University

Srikant Raghavan
Lawrence Technological University

Surekha K. B. Rao
Indiana University Northwest

Timothy J. Schibik
University of Southern Indiana

Carlton Scott
University of California, Irvine

Samuel L. Seaman
Baylor University

Scott J. Seipel
Middle Tennessee State University

Sankara N. Sethuraman
Augusta State University

Daniel G. Shimshak
University of Massachusetts, Boston

Robert K. Smidt
California Polytechnic State University

William Stein
Texas A&M University

Robert E. Stevens
University of Louisiana at Monroe

Debra Stiver
University of Nevada, Reno

Ron Stunda
Birmingham-Southern College

Edward Sullivan
Lebanon Valley College

Dharma Thiruvaiyaru
Augusta State University

Daniel Tschopp
Daemen College

Bulent Uyar
University of Northern Iowa

Lee J. Van Scyoc
University of Wisconsin–Oshkosh

Stuart H. Warnock
Tarleton State University

Mark H. Witkowski
University of Texas at San Antonio

William F. Younkin
University of Miami

Shuo Zhang
State University of New York, Fredonia

Zhiwei Zhu
University of Louisiana at Lafayette

Their suggestions and thorough reviews of the previous edition and the manuscript of this edition make this a better text.

Special thanks go to a number of people. Julia Norton of California State University–Hayward and Christopher Rogers of Miami Dade College reviewed the manuscript and page proofs, checking exercises for accuracy. Professor Kathleen Whitcomb of the University of South Carolina prepared the study guide. Dr. Samuel Wathen of Coastal Carolina University prepared the quizzes and the Test Bank. Professor René Ordonez of Southern Oregon University prepared the PowerPoint presentation and many of the screencam tutorials. Ms. Denise Heban and the authors prepared the Instructor's Manual.

We also wish to thank the staff at McGraw-Hill. This includes Steve Schuetz, Executive Editor; Wanda Zeman, Senior Development Editor; Bruce Gin, Senior Project Manager; and others we do not know personally, but who have made valuable contributions.

In addition we wish to personally acknowledge Richard T. Hercher, Jr., who served as our Sponsoring and Executive Editor for many editions of this book as well as *Basic Statistics for Business and Economics*. His insight and efforts made our texts better for students and instructors. It was always a pleasure to work with him. We wish him continued success in his new position at McGraw-Hill.

Brief Contents

Contents

Chapter

10 One-Sample Tests of Hypothesis   326

Chapter

11 Two-Sample Tests of Hypothesis   364

Chapter

12 Analysis of Variance   402

Contents

Chapter

13 Linear Regression and Correlation   454

Chapter

14 Multiple Regression and Correlation Analysis   505

Contents

What Is Statistics?

1

GOALS

When you have completed this chapter you will be able to:

1 Understand why we study statistics.

2 Explain what is meant by *descriptive statistics* and *inferential statistics.*

3 Distinguish between a *qualitative variable* and a *quantitative variable.*

4 Describe how a *discrete variable* is different from a *continuous variable.*

5 Distinguish among the *nominal, ordinal, interval,* and *ratio* levels of measurement.

A poll solicits a large number of college undergraduates for information on the following variables: the name of their cell phone provider, the number of minutes used last month, and their satisfaction with the service. What is the data scale for each of these three variables? (See Exercise 10, Goal 5)

Introduction

More than 100 years ago H. G. Wells, an English author and historian, suggested that one day quantitative reasoning will be as necessary for effective citizenship as the ability to read. He made no mention of business because the Industrial Revolution was just beginning. Mr. Wells could not have been more correct. While "business experience," some "thoughtful guesswork," and "intuition" are key attributes of successful managers, today's business problems tend to be too complex for this type of decision making alone.

One of the tools used to make decisions is statistics. Statistics is used not only by businesspeople; we all also apply statistical concepts in our lives. For example, to start the day you turn on the shower and let it run for a few moments. Then you put your hand in the shower to sample the temperature and decide to add more hot water or more cold water, or that the temperature is just right and to enter the shower. As a second example, suppose you are at Costco wholesale and wish to buy a frozen pizza. One of the pizza makers has a stand, and they offer a small wedge of their pizza. After sampling the pizza, you decide whether to purchase the pizza or not. In both the shower and pizza examples, you make a decision and select a course of action based on a sample.

Businesses face similar situations. The Kellogg Company must ensure that the mean amount of Raisin Bran in the 25.5-gram box meets label specifications. To do so, it sets a "target" weight somewhat higher than the amount specified on the label. Each box is then weighed after it is filled. The weighing machine reports a distribution of the content weights for each hour as well as the number "kicked-out" for being under the label specification during the hour. The Quality Inspection Department also randomly selects samples from the production line and checks the quality of the product and the weight of the contents of the box. If the mean product weight differs significantly from the target weight or the percent of kick-outs is too large, the process is adjusted.

Alan Greenspan, former chairman of the Federal Reserve Board, knows and understands the importance of statistical tools and techniques to provide accurate and timely information to make public statements that have the power to move global stock markets and influence political thinking. Dr. Greenspan, speaking before a National Skills Summit, stated: "Workers must be equipped not simply with technical know-how, but also with the ability to create, analyze, and transform information and to interact effectively with others. That is, separate the facts from opinions, and then organize these facts in an appropriate manner and analyze the information."

As a student of business or economics, you will need basic knowledge and skills to organize, analyze, and transform data and to present the information. In this text, we will show you basic statistical techniques and methods that will develop your ability to make good personal and business decisions.

Why Study Statistics?

If you look through your university catalog, you will find that statistics is required for many college programs. Why is this so? What are the differences in the statistics courses taught in the Engineering College, the Psychology or Sociology Departments in the Liberal Arts College, and the College of Business? The biggest difference is the examples used. The course content is basically the same. In the College of Business we are interested in such things as profits, hours worked, and wages. Psychologists are interested in test scores, and engineers are interested in how many units are manufactured on a particular machine. However, all three are interested in what is a typical value and how much variation there is in the data. There may also be a difference in the level of mathematics required. An engineering statistics course usually requires calculus. Statistics courses in colleges of business and education usually teach the course at a more applied level. You should be able to handle the mathematics in this text if you have completed high school algebra.

So why is statistics required in so many majors? The first reason is that numerical information is everywhere. Look in the newspapers *(USA Today)*, news magazines *(Time, Newsweek, U.S. News and World Report)*, business magazines *(BusinessWeek, Forbes)*, or general interest magazines *(People)*, women's magazines *(Ladies Home Journal or Elle)*, or sports magazines *(Sports Illustrated, ESPN The Magazine)*, and you will be bombarded with numerical information.

Examples of why we study statistics

Here are some examples:

- In 2006 the typical household income in the United States was $48,201. For households in the Northeast the typical income was $52,057, $47,836 in the Midwest, $43,884 in the South, and $52,249 in the West. You can check the latest information by going to http://www.census.gov/prod/2007pubs/p60-233.pdf.
- In 2006 Boeing, Inc., an aircraft manufacturer, built 1,057 aircraft and in 2007 they built 1,423. The table below summarizes the information by year and aircraft type.

Sales of Boeing Aircraft						
	Aircraft					
Year	737	747	767	777	787	Total
2006	738	72	10	77	160	1,057
2007	850	25	36	143	369	1,423

You can view the sales for the most recent periods by going to the Boeing website at www.boeing.com and searching for "Orders and Deliveries."
- *USA Today* (www.usatoday.com) prints "Snapshots" that are the result of surveys conducted by various research organizations, foundations, and the federal government. The following chart summarizes the increase in college courses taken online.

USA TODAY Snapshot

05/02/2008-Updated 12:40 AMET

Enrollment in online college courses keeps climbing. Among the reasons: convenience for students with jobs and families to support.

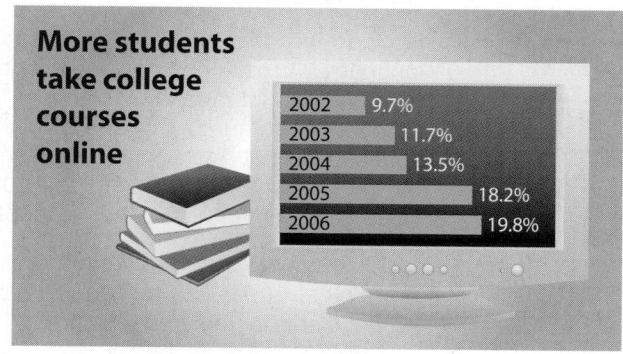

By David Stuckey and Keith Carter, USA Today
Source: National Association for College Admission Counselling

A second reason for taking a statistics course is that statistical techniques are used to make decisions that affect our daily lives. That is, they affect our personal welfare. Here are a few examples:

- Insurance companies use statistical analysis to set rates for home, automobile, life, and health insurance. Tables are available showing estimates that a 20-year-old female has 60.25 years of life remaining, an 87-year-old woman 4.56 years remaining, and a 50-year-old man 27.85 years remaining. Life insurance premiums are established based on these estimates of life expectancy. These tables

Statistics in Action

We call your attention to a feature title—*Statistics in Action*. Read each one carefully to get an appreciation of the wide application of statistics in management, economics, nursing, law enforcement, sports, and other disciplines.

- In 2007, *Forbes* published a list of the richest Americans. William Gates, founder of Microsoft Corporation, is the richest. His net worth is estimated at $59.0 billion. (www.forbes.com)

- In 2007, the four largest American manufacturing companies, ranked by revenue were ExxonMobil, Chevron, General Motors, and ConocoPhillips. (www. Industryweek.com)

- In the United States, a typical high school graduate earns $1.2 million in his or her lifetime, a typical college graduate with a bachelor's degree earns $2.1 million, and a typical college graduate with a master's degree earns $2.5 million. (usgovinfo.about. com/library/weekly /aa072602a.htm)

are available at www.ssa.gov/OACT/STATS/table4cb.html. [This site is sensitive to capital letters.]

- The Environmental Protection Agency is interested in the water quality of Lake Erie as well as other lakes. They periodically take water samples to establish the level of contamination and maintain the level of quality.
- Medical researchers study the cure rates for diseases using different drugs and different forms of treatment. For example, what is the effect of treating a certain type of knee injury surgically or with physical therapy? If you take an aspirin each day, does that reduce your risk of a heart attack?

A third reason for taking a statistics course is that the knowledge of statistical methods will help you understand how decisions are made and give you a better understanding of how they affect you.

No matter what line of work you select, you will find yourself faced with decisions where an understanding of data analysis is helpful. In order to make an informed decision, you will need to be able to:

1. Determine whether the existing information is adequate or additional information is required.
2. Gather additional information, if it is needed, in such a way that it does not provide misleading results.
3. Summarize the information in a useful and informative manner.
4. Analyze the available information.
5. Draw conclusions and make inferences while assessing the risk of an incorrect conclusion.

The statistical methods presented in the text will provide you with a framework for the decision-making process.

In summary, there are at least three reasons for studying statistics: (1) data are everywhere, (2) statistical techniques are used to make many decisions that affect our lives, and (3) no matter what your career, you will make professional decisions that involve data. An understanding of statistical methods will help you make these decisions more effectively.

What Is Meant by Statistics?

How do we define the word *statistics*? We encounter it frequently in our everyday language. It really has two meanings. In the more common usage, statistics refers to numerical information. Examples include the average starting salary of college graduates, the number of deaths due to alcoholism last year, the change in the Dow Jones Industrial Average from yesterday to today, and the number of home runs hit by the Chicago Cubs during the 2007 season. In these examples statistics are a value or a percentage. Other examples include:

- The typical automobile in the United States travels 11,099 miles per year, the typical bus 9,353 miles per year, and the typical truck 13,942 miles per year. In Canada the corresponding information is 10,371 miles for automobiles, 19,823 miles for buses, and 7,001 miles for trucks.
- The mean time waiting for technical support is 17 minutes.
- The mean length of the business cycle since 1945 is 61 months.

The above are all examples of **statistics. A collection of numerical information is called statistics** (plural).

We often present statistical information in a graphical form. A graph is often useful for capturing reader attention and to portray a large amount of information. For example, Chart 1–1 shows Frito-Lay volume and market share for the major snack and potato chip categories in supermarkets in the United States. It requires only a quick glance to discover there were nearly 800 million pounds of potato chips sold and that Frito-Lay sold 64 percent of that total. Also note that Frito-Lay has 82 percent of the corn chip market.

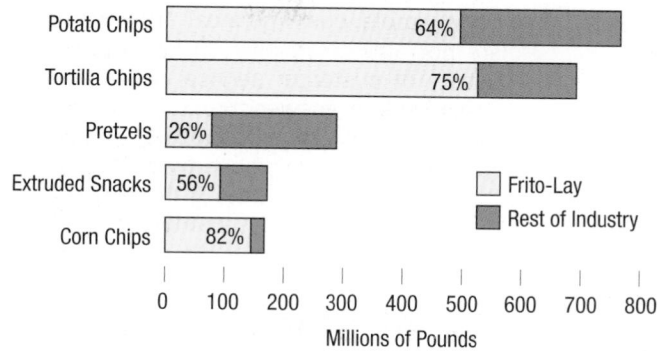

CHART 1–1 Frito-Lay Volume and Share of Major Snack Chip Categories in U.S. Supermarkets

The subject of statistics, as we will explore it in this text, has a much broader meaning than just collecting and publishing numerical information. We define statistics as:

> **STATISTICS** The science of collecting, organizing, presenting, analyzing, and interpreting data to assist in making more effective decisions.

As the definition suggests, the first step in investigating a problem is to collect relevant data. They must be organized in some way and perhaps presented in a chart, such as Chart 1–1. Only after the data have been organized are we then able to analyze and interpret them. Here are some examples of the need for data collection.

- Research analysts for Merrill Lynch evaluate many facets of a particular stock before making a "buy" or "sell" recommendation. They collect the past sales data of the company and estimate future earnings. Other factors, such as the projected worldwide demand for the company's products, the strength of the competition, and the effect of the new union–management contract, are also considered before making a recommendation.
- The marketing department at Colgate-Palmolive Co., a manufacturer of soap products, has the responsibility of making recommendations regarding the potential profitability of a newly developed group of face soaps having fruit smells, such as grape, orange, and pineapple. Before making a final decision, the marketers will test it in several markets. That is, they may advertise and sell it in Topeka, Kansas, and Tampa, Florida. On the basis of test marketing in these two regions, Colgate-Palmolive will make a decision whether to market the soaps in the entire country.
- The United States government is concerned with the present condition of our economy and with predicting future economic trends. The government conducts a large number of surveys to determine consumer confidence and the outlook of managers regarding sales and production for the next 12 months. Indexes, such as the Consumer Price Index, are constructed each month to assess inflation. Information on department store sales, housing starts, money turnover, and industrial production are just a few of the hundreds of items used to form the basis of the projections. These projections are used by banks to decide their

prime lending rate and by the Federal Reserve Board to decide the level of control to place on the money supply.

- Managers must make decisions about the quality of their product or service. For example, customers call software companies for technical advice when they are not able to resolve an issue regarding the software. One measure of the quality of customer service is the time a customer must wait for a technical consultant to answer the call. A software company might set a target of one minute as the typical response time. The company would then collect and analyze data on the response time. Does the typical response time differ by day of the week or time of day? If the response times are increasing, managers might decide to increase the number of technical consultants at particular times of the day or week.

Types of Statistics

The study of statistics is usually divided into two categories: descriptive statistics and inferential statistics.

Descriptive Statistics

The definition of statistics given earlier referred to "organizing, presenting, analyzing . . . data." This facet of statistics is usually referred to as **descriptive statistics.**

> **DESCRIPTIVE STATISTICS** Methods of organizing, summarizing, and presenting data in an informative way.

For instance, the United States government reports the population of the United States was 179,323,000 in 1960; 203,302,000 in 1970; 226,542,000 in 1980; 248,709,000 in 1990, and 265,000,000 in 2000. This information is descriptive statistics. It is descriptive statistics if we calculate the percentage growth from one decade to the next. However, it would **not** be descriptive statistics if we used these to estimate the population of the United States in the year 2010 or the percentage growth from 2000 to 2010. Why? Because these statistics are not being used to summarize past populations but to estimate future populations. The following are some other examples of descriptive statistics.

- There are a total of 46,837 miles of interstate highways in the United States. The interstate system represents only 1 percent of the nation's total roads but carries more than 20 percent of the traffic. The longest is I-90, which stretches from Boston to Seattle, a distance of 3,099 miles. The shortest is I-878 in New York City, which is 0.70 of a mile in length. Alaska does not have any interstate highways, Texas has the most interstate miles at 3,232, and New York has the most interstate routes with 28.
- According to the *Bureau of Labor Statistics,* the average hourly earnings of production workers were $17.90 for April 2008. You can review the latest information on wages and productivity of American workers by going to the Bureau of Labor Statistics website at: http://www.bls.gov/home.htm and selecting Average Hourly Earnings.

Masses of unorganized data—such as the census of population, the weekly earnings of thousands of computer programmers, and the individual responses of 2,000 registered voters regarding their choice for president of the United States—are of little value as is. However, statistical techniques are available to organize this type of data into a meaningful form. Data can be organized into a **frequency distribution.** (This procedure is covered in Chapter 2.) Various **charts** may be used to describe data; several basic chart forms are also presented in Chapter 4.

Specific measures of central location, such as the mean, describe the central value of a group of numerical data. A number of statistical measures are used to describe how closely the data cluster about an average. These measures of central tendency and dispersion are discussed in Chapter 3.

Inferential Statistics

The second type of statistics is **inferential statistics**—also called **statistical inference.** Our main concern regarding inferential statistics is finding something about a population from a sample taken from that population. For example, a recent survey showed only 46 percent of high school seniors can solve problems involving fractions, decimals, and percentages; and only 77 percent of high school seniors correctly totaled the cost of salad, a burger, fries, and a cola on a restaurant menu. Since these are inferences about a population (all high school seniors) based on sample data, we refer to them as inferential statistics. You might think of inferential statistics as a "best guess" of a population value based on sample information.

> **INFERENTIAL STATISTICS** The methods used to estimate a property of a population on the basis of a sample.

Note the words *population* and *sample* in the definition of inferential statistics. We often make reference to the population living in the United States or the 1.31 billion population of China. However, in statistics the word *population* has a broader meaning. A **population** may consist of *individuals*—such as all the students enrolled at Utah State University, all the students in Accounting 201, or all the CEOs from the Fortune 500 companies. A population may also consist of *objects,* such as all the Cobra G/T tires produced at Cooper Tire and Rubber Company in the Findlay, Ohio, plant; the accounts receivable at the end of October for Lorrange Plastics, Inc.; or auto claims filed in the first quarter of 2008 at the Northeast Regional Office of State Farm Insurance. The *measurement* of interest might be the scores on the first examination of all students in Accounting 201, the tread wear of the Cooper Tires, the dollar amount of Lorrange Plastics's accounts receivable, or the amount of auto insurance claims at State Farm. Thus, a population in the statistical sense does not always refer to people.

> **POPULATION** The entire set of individuals or objects of interest or the measurements obtained from all individuals or objects of interest.

To infer something about a population, we usually take a **sample** from the population.

> **SAMPLE** A portion, or part, of the population of interest.

Reasons for sampling

Why take a sample instead of studying every member of the population? A sample of registered voters is necessary because of the prohibitive cost of contacting millions of voters before an election. Testing wheat for moisture content destroys the wheat, thus making a sample imperative. If the wine tasters tested all the wine, none would be available for sale. It would be physically impossible for a few marine biologists to capture and tag all the seals in the ocean. (These and other reasons for sampling are discussed in Chapter 8.)

As noted, using a sample to learn something about a population is done extensively in business, agriculture, politics, and government, as cited in the following examples:

- Television networks constantly monitor the popularity of their programs by hiring Nielsen and other organizations to sample the preferences of TV viewers.

For example, in a sample of 800 prime-time viewers, 320, or 40 percent, indicated they watched "CSI: Crime Scene Investigation" on CBS last week. These program ratings are used to set advertising rates or to cancel programs.

- Gamous and Associates, a public accounting firm, is conducting an audit of Pronto Printing Company. To begin, the accounting firm selects a random sample of 100 invoices and checks each invoice for accuracy. There is at least one error on five of the invoices; hence the accounting firm estimates that 5 percent of the population of invoices contain at least one error.
- A random sample of 1,260 marketing graduates from four-year schools showed their mean starting salary was $42,694. We therefore estimate the mean starting salary for all marketing graduates of four-year institutions to be $42,694.

The relationship between a sample and a population is portrayed below. For example, we wish to estimate the mean miles per gallon of SUVs. Six SUVs are selected from the population. The mean MPG of the six is used to estimate MPG for the population.

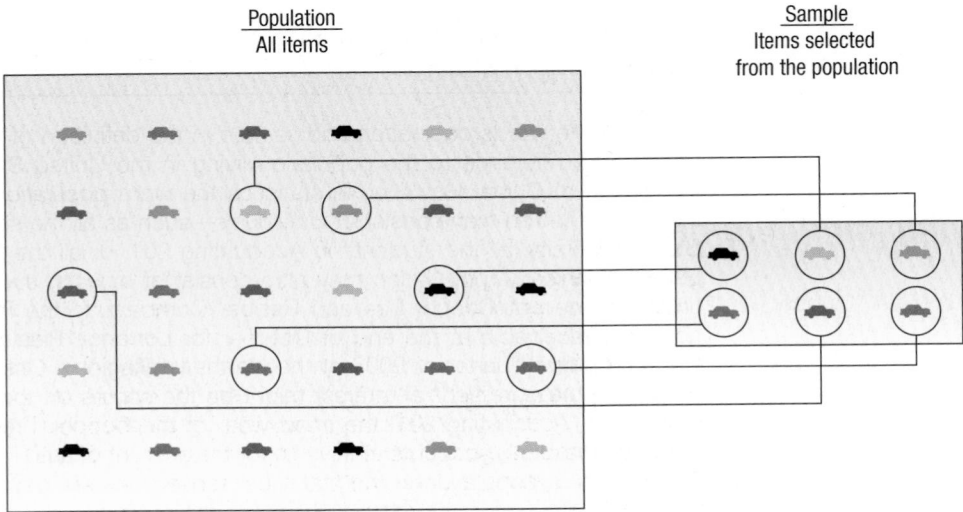

We strongly suggest you do the Self-Review exercise.

Following is a self-review problem. There are a number of them interspersed throughout each chapter. They test your comprehension of the preceding material. The answer and method of solution are given at the end of the chapter. You can find the answer to the following Self-Review on page 19. We recommend that you solve each one and then check your answer.

You can find the answer to the following Self-Review on page 19.

Self-Review 1–1

The answers are at the end of the chapter.

The Atlanta-based advertising firm, Brandon and Associates, asked a sample of 1,960 consumers to try a newly developed chicken dinner by Boston Market. Of the 1,960 sampled, 1,176 said they would purchase the dinner if it is marketed.

(a) What could Brandon and Associates report to Boston Market regarding acceptance of the chicken dinner in the population?
(b) Is this an example of descriptive statistics or inferential statistics? Explain.

Types of Variables

Qualitative variable

There are two basic types of variables: (1) qualitative and (2) quantitative (see Chart 1–2). When the characteristic being studied is nonnumeric, it is called a **qualitative variable** or an **attribute.** Examples of qualitative variables are gender, religious affiliation, type of automobile owned, state of birth, and eye color. When the data are qualitative, we are usually interested in how many or what percent fall in each category. For example, what percent of the population has blue eyes? How many Catholics and how many Protestants are there in the United States? What percent of the total number of cars sold last month were SUVs? Qualitative data are often summarized in charts and bar graphs (Chapter 2).

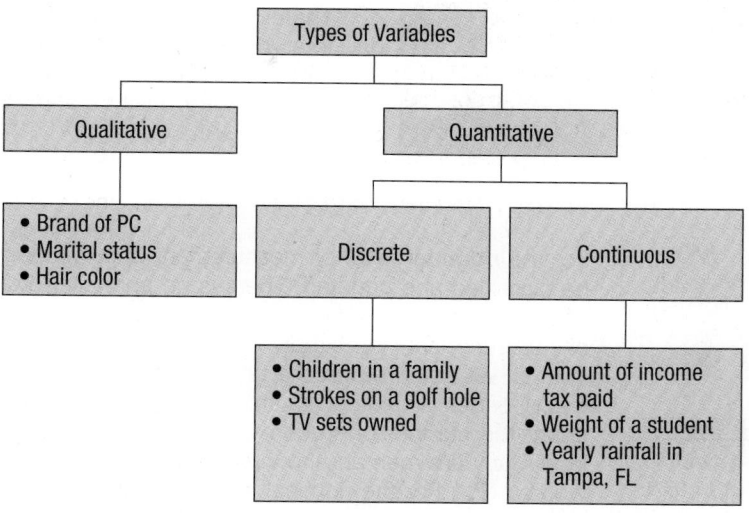

CHART 1–2   Summary of the Types of Variables

Quantitative variable

When the variable studied can be reported numerically, the variable is called a **quantitative variable.** Examples of quantitative variables are the balance in your checking account, the ages of company presidents, the life of an automobile battery (such as 42 months), and the number of children in a family.

Quantitative variables are either discrete or continuous. **Discrete variables** can assume only certain values, and there are "gaps" between the values. Examples of discrete variables are the number of bedrooms in a house (1, 2, 3, 4, etc.), the number of cars arriving at Exit 25 on I-4 in Florida near Walt Disney World in an hour (326, 421, etc.), and the number of students in each section of a statistics course (25 in section A, 42 in section B, and 18 in section C). We count, for example, the number of cars arriving at Exit 25 on I-4, and we count the number of statistics students in each section. Notice that a home can have 3 or 4 bedrooms, but it cannot have 3.56 bedrooms. Thus, there is a "gap" between possible values. Typically, discrete variables result from counting.

Observations of a **continuous variable** can assume any value within a specific range. Examples of continuous variables are the air pressure in a tire and the weight of a shipment of tomatoes. Other examples are the amount of raisin bran in a box and the duration of flights from Orlando to San Diego. Grade point average (GPA) is a continuous variable. We could report the GPA of a particular student as 3.2576952. The usual practice is to round to 3 places—3.258. Typically, continuous variables result from measuring.

Levels of Measurement

Data can be classified according to levels of measurement. The level of measurement of the data dictates the calculations that can be done to summarize and present the data. It will also determine the statistical tests that should be performed. For example, there are six colors of candies in a bag of M&M's. Suppose we assign brown a value of 1, yellow 2, blue 3, orange 4, green 5, and red 6. From a bag of candies, we add the assigned color values and divide by the number of candies and report that the mean color is 3.56. Does this mean that the average color is

blue or orange? Of course not! As a second example, in a high school track meet there are eight competitors in the 400-meter run. We report the order of finish and that the mean finish is 4.5. What does the mean finish tell us? Nothing! In both of these instances, we have not properly used the level of measurement.

There are actually four levels of measurement: nominal, ordinal, interval, and ratio. The lowest, or the most primitive, measurement is the nominal level. The highest, or the level that gives us the most information about the observation, is the ratio level of measurement.

Nominal-Level Data

For the **nominal level** of measurement observations of a qualitative variable can only be classified and counted. There is no particular order to the labels. The classification of the six colors of M&M's milk chocolate candies is an example of the nominal level of measurement. We simply classify the candies by color. There is no natural order. That is, we could report the brown candies first, the orange first, or any of the colors first. Gender is another example of the nominal level of measurement. Suppose we count the number of students entering a football game with a student ID and report how many are men and how many are women. We could report either the men or the women first. For the nominal level the only measurement involved consists of counts. Sometimes, for better reader understanding, we convert these counts to percentages. The following "Snapshot" from *USA Today* shows the results from a survey of workers. The variable of interest is "Perks" and there are five possible outcomes: "More money," "Better healthcare," "Better retirement," "Work/family balance," and, we will assume, "Other." The outcome "Other" is not shown on the chart, but is necessary to make the percent of respondents total 100 percent. There is no natural order to the outcomes, we could have put "Better healthcare" first instead of "More money."

To process the data, such as the information regarding worker perks, or information on gender, employment by industry, or state of birth of a student, we often numerically code the information. That is, we assign students from Alabama a code of 1, Alaska a code of 2, Arizona as 3, and so on. Using this procedure, Wisconsin is coded 49 and Wyoming 50. This coding facilitates counting by a computer. However, because we have assigned numbers to the various categories, this does not give us license to manipulate the numbers. To explain, 1 + 2 does not equal 3; that is, Alabama + Alaska does *not* yield Arizona.

To summarize, the nominal level has the following properties:

1. The variable of interest is divided into categories or outcomes.
2. There is no natural order to the outcomes.

USA TODAY Snapshot

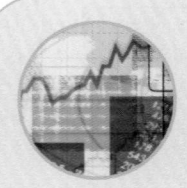

Statistics in Action

Where did statistics get its start? In 1662 John Graunt published an article called "Natural and Political Observations Made upon Bills of Mortality." The author's "observations" were the result of a study and analysis of a weekly church publication called "Bill of Mortality," which listed births, christenings, and deaths and their causes. Graunt realized that the Bills of Mortality represented only a fraction of all births and deaths in London. However, he used the data to reach broad conclusions about the impact of disease, such as the plague, on the general population. His logic is an example of statistical inference. His analysis and interpretation of the data are thought to mark the start of statistics.

03/15/2007-updated 11:51 PM ET

By Anne R. Carey and Chad Palmer, USA Today
Source: hudson-index.com

Ordinal-Level Data

The next higher level of data is the **ordinal level.** Table 1–1 lists the student ratings of Professor James Brunner in an Introduction to Finance course. Each student in the class answered the question "Overall, how did you rate the instructor in this class?" The variable rating illustrates the use of the ordinal scale of measurement. One classification is "higher" or "better" than the next one. That is, "Superior" is better than "Good," "Good" is better than "Average," and so on. However, we are not able to distinguish the magnitude of the differences between groups. Is the difference between "Superior" and "Good" the same as the difference between "Poor" and "Inferior"? We cannot tell. If we substitute a 5 for "Superior" and a 4 for "Good," we can conclude that the rating of "Superior" is better than the rating of "Good," but we cannot add a ranking of "Superior" and a ranking of "Good," with the result being meaningful. Further we cannot conclude that a rating of "Good" (rating is 4) is necessarily twice as high as a "Poor" (rating is 2). We can only conclude that a rating of "Good" is better than a rating of "Poor." We cannot conclude how much better the rating is.

TABLE 1–1 Rating of a Finance Professor

Rating	Frequency
Superior	6
Good	28
Average	25
Poor	12
Inferior	3

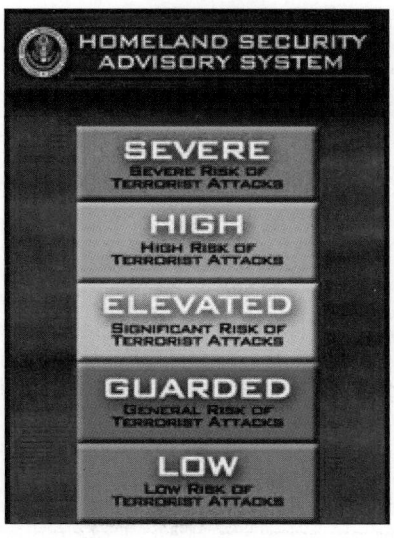

Another example of ordinal-level data is the Homeland Security Advisory System. The Department of Homeland Security publishes this information regarding the risk of terrorist activity to federal, state, and local authorities and to the American people. The five risk levels from lowest to highest, including a description and color codes, are shown to the left.

This is an example of the ordinal scale because we know the order or the ranks of the risk levels—that is, orange is higher than yellow—but the amount of the difference in risk is not necessarily the same. To put it another way, the difference in the risk level between yellow and orange is not necessarily the same as between green and blue. You can check the current risk level and read more about the various levels by going to: www.whitehouse.gov/homeland.

In summary the properties of the ordinal level of data are:

1. Data classifications are represented by sets of labels or names (high, medium, low) that have relative values.
2. Because of the relative values, the data classified can be ranked or ordered.

Interval-Level Data

The **interval level** of measurement is the next highest level. It includes all the characteristics of the ordinal level, but, in addition, the difference between values is a constant size. An example of the interval level of measurement is temperature. Suppose the high temperatures on three consecutive winter days in Boston are 28, 31, and 20 degrees Fahrenheit. These temperatures can be easily ranked, but we can also determine the difference between temperatures. This is possible because 1 degree Fahrenheit represents a constant unit of measurement. Equal differences between two temperatures are the same, regardless of their position on the scale. That is, the difference between 10 degrees Fahrenheit and 15 degrees is 5, the difference between 50 and 55 degrees is also 5 degrees. It is also important to note that 0 is just a point on the scale. It does not represent the absence of the condition. Zero degrees Fahrenheit does not represent the absence of heat, just that it is cold! In fact 0 degrees Fahrenheit is about -18 degrees on the Celsius scale.

Another example of the interval scale of measurement is women's dress sizes. Listed below is information on several dimensions of a standard U.S. women's dress.

Size	Bust (in)	Waist (in)	Hips (in)
8	32	24	35
10	34	26	37
12	36	28	39
14	38	30	41
16	40	32	43
18	42	34	45
20	44	36	47
22	46	38	49
24	48	40	51
26	50	42	53
28	52	44	55

Why is the "size" scale an interval measurement? Observe as the size changes by 2 units (say from size 10 to size 12 or from size 24 to size 26) each of the measurements increases by 2 inches. To put it another way, the intervals are the same.

There is no natural zero point for dress size. A "size 0" dress does not have "zero" material. Instead it would have a 24-inch bust, 16-inch waist and 27-inch hips. Moreover, the ratios are not reasonable. If you divide a size 28 by a size 14, you do not get the same answer as dividing a size 20 by 10. Neither ratio is equal to two as the "size" number would suggest. In short, if the distances between the numbers make sense, but the ratios do not, then you have an interval scale of measurement.

The properties of the interval-level data are:

1. Data classifications are ordered according to the amount of the characteristic they possess.
2. Equal differences in the characteristic are represented by equal differences in the measurements.

Ratio-Level Data

Practically all quantitative data is recorded on the ratio level of measurement. The **ratio level** is the "highest" level of measurement. It has all the characteristics of the interval level, but in addition, the 0 point is meaningful and the ratio between two numbers is meaningful. Examples of the ratio scale of measurement include wages, units of production, weight, changes in stock prices, distance between branch offices, and height. Money is a good illustration. If you have zero dollars, then you have no money. Weight is another example. If the dial on the scale of a correctly calibrated device is at 0, then there is a complete absence of weight. The ratio of two numbers is also meaningful. If Jim earns $40,000 per year selling insurance and Rob earns $80,000 per year selling cars, then Rob earns twice as much as Jim.

Table 1–2 illustrates the use of the ratio scale of measurement. It shows the incomes of four father-and-son combinations.

TABLE 1–2 Father–Son Income Combinations

Name	Father	Son
Lahey	$80,000	$ 40,000
Nale	90,000	30,000
Rho	60,000	120,000
Steele	75,000	130,000

Observe that the senior Lahey earns twice as much as his son. In the Rho family the son makes twice as much as the father.

In summary, the properties of the ratio-level data are:

1. Data classifications are ordered according to the amount of the characteristics they possess.
2. Equal differences in the characteristic are represented by equal differences in the numbers assigned to the classifications.
3. The zero point is the absence of the characteristic and the ratio between two numbers is meaningful.

Chart 1–3 summarizes the major characteristics of the various levels of measurement.

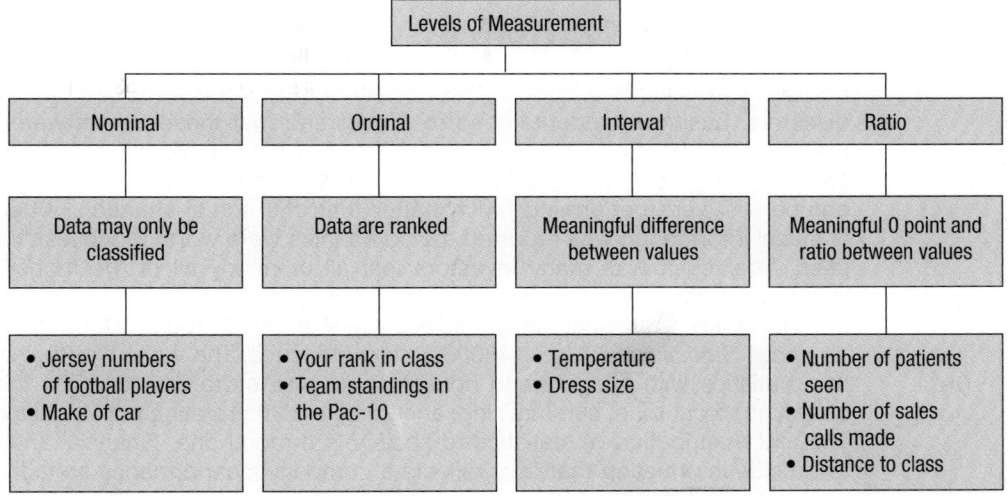

CHART 1–3 Summary of the Characteristics for Levels of Measurement

Self-Review 1–2   What is the level of measurement reflected by the following data?
(a) The age of each person in a sample of 50 adults who listen to one of the 1,230 talk radio stations in the United States is:

35	29	41	34	44	46	42	42	37	47
30	36	41	39	44	39	43	43	44	40
47	37	41	27	33	33	39	38	43	22
44	39	35	35	41	42	37	42	38	43
35	37	38	43	40	48	42	31	51	34

(b) In a survey of 200 luxury-car owners, 100 were from California, 50 from New York, 30 from Illinois, and 20 from Ohio.

Exercises

The answers to the odd-numbered exercises are at the end of the book.

1. What is the level of measurement for each of the following variables?
   a. Student IQ ratings.
   b. Distance students travel to class.
   c. The jersey numbers of a sorority soccer team.
   d. A classification of students by state of birth.

    e. A ranking of students as freshman, sophomore, junior, and senior.

    f. Number of hours students study per week.

2. What is the level of measurement for these items related to the newspaper business?

    a. The number of papers sold each Sunday during 2008.

    b. The departments, such as editorial, advertising, sports, etc.

    c. A summary of the number of papers sold by county.

    d. The number of years with the paper for each employee.

3. Look in the latest edition of *USA Today* or your local newspaper and find examples of each level of measurement. Write a brief memo summarizing your findings.

4. For each of the following, determine whether the group is a sample or a population.

    a. The participants in a study of a new cholesterol drug.

    b. The drivers who received a speeding ticket in Kansas City last month.

    c. Those on welfare in Cook County (Chicago), Illinois.

    d. The 30 stocks reported as a part of the Dow Jones Industrial Average.

Ethics and Statistics

Following the events of Enron, Tyco, HealthSouth, WorldCom, and other corporate disasters, business students need to understand that these events were based on the misrepresentation of business and financial data. In each case, people within each organization reported financial information to investors that indicated the companies were performing much better than the actual situation. When the true financial information was reported the companies were worth much less than advertised. The result was many investors lost all or nearly all of the money they put into these companies.

The article "Statistics and Ethics: Some Advice for Young Statisticians," in *The American Statistician* 57, no. 1 (2003), offers guidance. The authors advise us to practice statistics with integrity and honesty, and urge us to "do the right thing" when collecting, organizing, summarizing, analyzing, and interpreting numerical information. The real contribution of statistics to society is a moral one. Financial analysts need to provide information that truly reflects a company's performance so as not to mislead individual investors. Information regarding product defects that may be harmful to people must be analyzed and reported with integrity and honesty. The authors of *The American Statistician* article further indicate that when we practice statistics, we need to maintain "an independent and principled point-of-view."

As you progress through this text, we will highlight ethical issues in the collection, analysis, presentation, and interpretation of statistical information. We also hope that, as your learn about using statistics, you will become a more informed consumer of information. For example, you will question a report based on data that do not fairly represent the population, a report that does not include all relevant statistics, one that includes an incorrect choice of statistical measures, or a presentation that introduces the writer's bias in a deliberate attempt to mislead or misrepresent.

Computer Applications

Computers are now available to students at most colleges and universities. Spreadsheets, such as Microsoft Excel, and statistical software packages, such as MINITAB, are available in most computer labs. The Microsoft Excel package is bundled with many home computers. In this text we use both Excel and MINITAB for the applications. We also use an Excel add-in called MegaStat. This add-in gives Excel the capability to produce additional statistical reports.

The following example shows the application of computers in statistical analysis. In Chapters 2, 3, and 4 we illustrate methods for summarizing and describing data. An example used in those chapters refers to the price reported in thousands of dollars of 80 vehicles sold last month at Whitner Autoplex. The following Excel output reveals, among other things, that (1) 80 vehicles were sold last month, (2) the mean (average) selling price was $23,218, and (3) the selling prices ranged from a minimum of $15,546 to a maximum of $35,925.

	A	B	C	D	E	F	G	H
	Whitner							
	Price	Price($000)	Age	Type		*Price($000)*		
1								
2	23197	23.197	46	0				
3	23372	23.372	48	0		Mean	23.218	
4	20454	20.454	40	1		Standard Error	0.487	
5	23591	23.591	40	0		Median	22.831	
6	26651	26.651	46	1		Mode	20.642	
7	27453	27.453	37	1		Standard Deviation	4.354	
8	17266	17.266	32	1		Sample Variance	18.961	
9	18021	18.021	29	1		Kurtosis	0.543	
10	28683	28.683	38	1		Skewness	0.727	
11	30872	30.872	43	0		Range	20.379	
12	19587	19.587	32	0		Minimum	15.546	
13	23169	23.169	47	0		Maximum	35.925	
14	35851	35.851	56	0		Sum	1857.453	
15	19251	19.251	42	1		Count	80.000	
16	20047	20.047	28	1				

The following output is from the MINITAB system. It contains much of the same information.

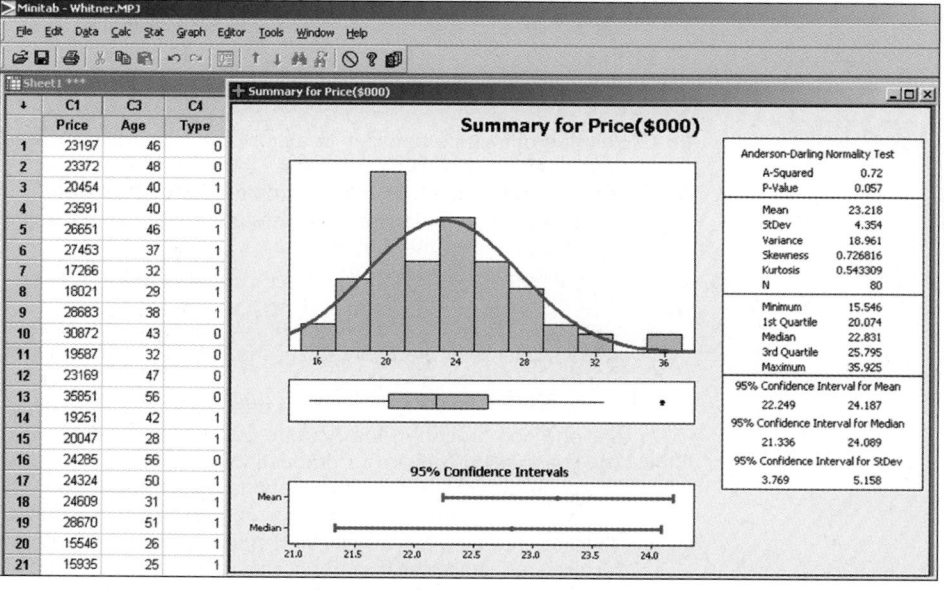

Had we used a calculator to arrive at these measures and others needed to fully analyze the selling prices, hours of calculation would have been required. The likelihood of an error in arithmetic is high when a large number of values are concerned. On the other hand, statistical software packages and spreadsheets can provide accurate information in seconds.

At the option of your instructor, and depending on the software system available, we urge you to apply a computer package to the exercises in the **Data Set Exercises** section in each chapter. It will relieve you of the tedious calculations and allow you to concentrate on data analysis.

Chapter Summary

I. Statistics is the science of collecting, organizing, presenting, analyzing, and interpreting data to assist in making more effective decisions.

II. There are two types of statistics.
  A. Descriptive statistics are procedures used to organize and summarize data.
  B. Inferential statistics involve taking a sample from a population and making estimates about a population based on the sample results.
    1. A population is an entire set of individuals or objects of interest or the measurements obtained from all individuals or objects of interest.
    2. A sample is a part of the population.

III. There are two types of variables.
  A. A qualitative variable is nonnumeric.
    1. Usually we are interested in the number or percent of the observations in each category.
    2. Qualitative data are usually summarized in graphs and bar charts.
  B. There are two types of quantitative variables and they are usually reported numerically.
    1. Discrete variables can assume only certain values, and there are usually gaps between values.
    2. A continuous variable can assume any value within a specified range.

IV. There are four levels of measurement.
  A. With the nominal level, the data are sorted into categories with no particular order to the categories.
  B. The ordinal level of measurement presumes that one classification is ranked higher than another.
  C. The interval level of measurement has the ranking characteristic of the ordinal level of measurement plus the characteristic that the distance between values is a constant size.
  D. The ratio level of measurement has all the characteristics of the interval level, plus there is a 0 point and the ratio of two values is meaningful.

Chapter Exercises

5. Explain the difference between qualitative and quantitative variables. Give an example of qualitative and quantitative variables.

6. Explain the difference between a sample and a population.

7. Explain the difference between a discrete and a continuous variable. Give an example of each not included in the text.

8. For the following questions, would you collect information using a sample or a population? Why?
  a. Statistics 201 is a course taught at a university. Professor A. Verage has taught nearly 1,500 students in the course over the past 5 years. You would like to know the average grade for the course.
  b. As part of a research project, you need to report the average profitability of the number one corporation in the Fortune 500 for the past 10 years.
  c. You are looking forward to graduation and your first job as a salesperson for one of five large pharmaceutical corporations. Planning for your interviews, you will need to know about each company's mission, profitability, products, and markets.
  d. You are shopping for a new MP3 music player such as the Apple iPod. The manufacturers advertise the number of music tracks that can be stored in the memory. Usually, the advertisers assume relatively short, popular music to estimate the number of tracks that can be stored. You, however, like Broadway musical tunes and they are much longer. You would like to estimate how many Broadway tunes will fit on your MP3 player.

9. Exits along interstate highways were formerly numbered successively from the western or southern edge of a state. However, the Department of Transportation has recently changed most of them to agree with the numbers on the mile markers along the highway.
  a. What level of measurement were data on the consecutive exit numbers?
  b. What level of measurement are data on the milepost numbers?
  c. Discuss the advantages of the newer system.

10. A review solicits a large number of college undergraduates for information on the following variables: the name of their cell phone provider (AT&T, Verizon, and so on), the numbers of minutes used last month (200, 400, for example), and their satisfaction with the service (Terrible, Adequate, Excellent, and so forth.). What is the data scale for each of these three variables?

11. Assume you have records of the daily sales receipts from the Gap store at Ridgedale Mall. Describe a condition in which this information could be considered a sample. Illustrate a second situation in which is same data would be regarded as a population.

12. Utilize the concepts of sample and population to describe how a presidential election is unlike an "exit" poll of the electorate.

13. Place these variables in the following classification tables. For each table, summarize your observations and evaluate if the results are generally true. For example, salary is reported as a continuous quantitative variable. It is also a continuous ratio scaled variable.
    a. Salary
    b. Gender
    c. Sales volume of MP3 players
    d. Soft drink preference
    e. Temperature
    f. SAT scores
    g. Student rank in class
    h. Rating of a finance professor
    i. Number of home computers

	Discrete Variable	**Continuous Variable**
Qualitative		
Quantitative		a. Salary

	Discrete	**Continuous**
Nominal		
Ordinal		
Interval		
Ratio		a. Salary

14. Using data from such publications as the *Statistical Abstract of the United States, The World Almanac, Forbes,* or your local newspaper, give examples of the nominal, ordinal, interval, and ratio levels of measurement.

15. The Struthers Wells Corporation employs more than 10,000 white collar workers in its sales offices and manufacturing facilities in the United States, Europe, and Asia. A sample of 300 of these workers revealed 120 would accept a transfer to a location outside the United States. On the basis of these findings, write a brief memo to Ms. Wanda Carter, Vice President of Human Services, regarding all white collar workers in the firm and their willingness to relocate.

16. AVX Stereo Equipment, Inc., recently began a "no-hassles" return policy. A sample of 500 customers who had recently returned items showed 400 thought the policy was fair, 32 thought it took too long to complete the transaction, and the rest had no opinion. On the basis of this information, make an inference about customer reaction to the new policy.

17. The table below reports the number of cars and light-duty trucks sold by the six largest automakers in January 2006 and in 2007.

	Units	
Company	**2007**	**2006**
General Motors	244,614	293,302
Toyota	175,850	160,594
Chrysler	173,407	168,030
Ford Motor	165,668	204,528
Honda	100,790	98,428
Nissan	82,644	75,890

   a. Compare the total sales in the two months. What would you conclude? Has there been an increase or a decrease in sales?

   b. Compare the percent change in sales for the six companies. Has there been a change in the size of the market or did one company gain sales at the expense of another?

18. The following chart depicts the average amounts spent by consumers on holiday gifts.

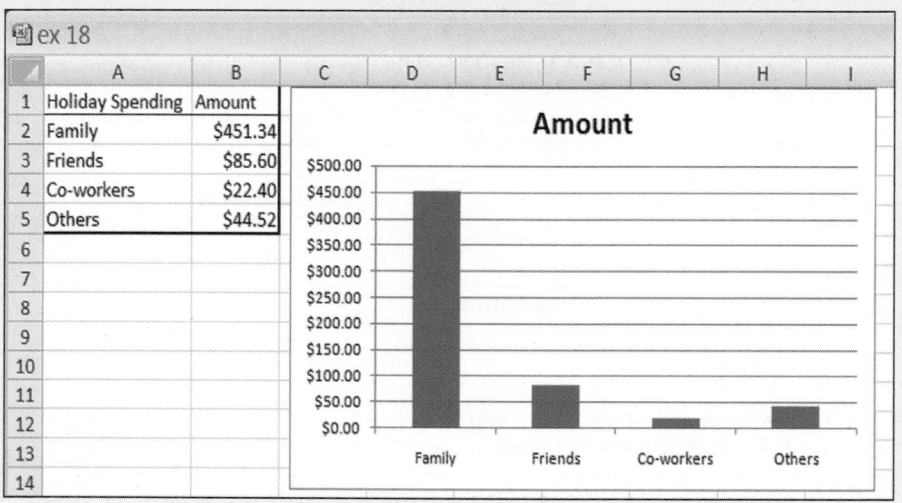

Write a brief report summarizing the amounts spent during the holidays. Be sure to include the total amount spent, and the percent spent by each group.

19. The following chart depicts the earnings in billions of dollars for ExxonMobil for the period 2003 to 2007. Write a brief report discussing earnings at ExxonMobil during the period. Did earnings increase or decrease over the period? Provide evidence to support your answer.

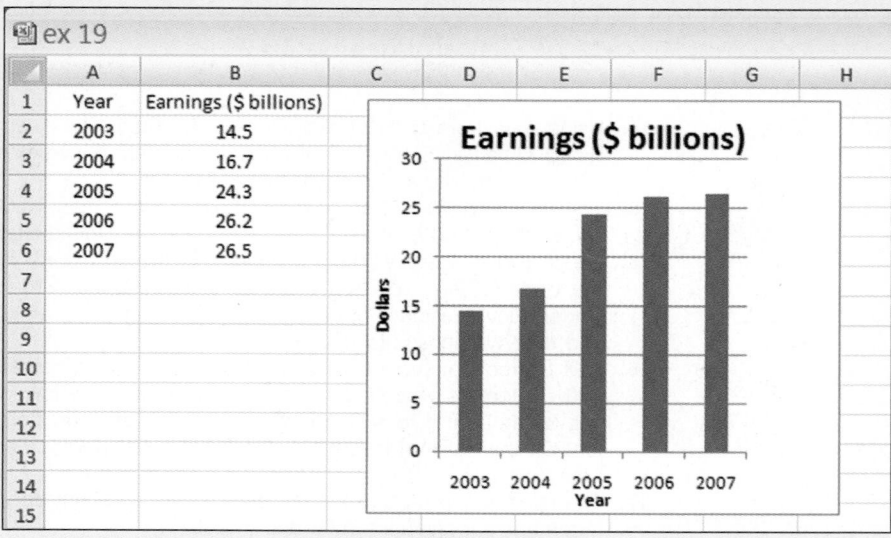

Data Set Exercises

20. Refer to the Real Estate data at the back of the text, which report information on homes sold in the Denver, Colorado, area last year. Consider the following variables: selling price, number of bedrooms, township, and distance from the center of the city.
   a. Which of the variables are qualitative and which are quantitative?
   b. Determine the level of measurement for each of the variables.

21. Refer to the Baseball 2007 data, which report information on the 30 Major League Baseball teams for the 2007 season. Consider the following variables: number of wins, team salary, season attendance, whether the team played its home games on a grass field or an artificial surface, and the number of home runs hit.
   a. Which of these variables are quantitative and which are qualitative?
   b. Determine the level of measurement for each of the variables.

22. Refer to the Wage data, which report information on annual wages for a sample of 100 workers. Also included are variables relating to industry, years of education, and gender for each worker.
   a. Which of the 12 variables are qualitative and which are quantitative?
   b. Determine the level of measurement for each variable.

23. Refer to the CIA data, which report demographic and economic information on 46 countries.
   a. Which of the variables are quantitative and which are qualitative?
   b. Determine the level of measurement for each of the variables.

Chapter 1   Answers to Self-Review

1–1 **a.** On the basis of the sample of 1,960 consumers, we estimate that, if it is marketed, 60 percent of all consumers will purchase the chicken dinner $(1,176/1,960) \times 100 = 60$ percent.

   b. Inferential statistics, because a sample was used to draw a conclusion about how all consumers in the population would react if the chicken dinner were marketed.

1–2 **a.** Age is a ratio-scale variable. A 40-year-old is twice as old as someone 20 years old.

   b. Nominal scale. We could arrange the states in any order.

2

(See Exercise 43 and Goal 4.)

GOALS

When you have completed this chapter you will be able to:

1 Organize qualitative data into a *frequency table*.

2 Present a frequency table as a *bar chart* or a *pie chart*.

3 Organize quantitative data into a *frequency distribution*.

4 Present a frequency distribution for quantitative data using *histograms, frequency polygons*, and *cumulative frequency polygons*.

Describing Data:

Frequency Tables, Frequency Distributions, and Graphic Presentation

Merrill Lynch recently completed a study of online investment portfolios for a sample of clients. For the 70 participants in the study, draw a histogram for the data. (See Exercise 43 and Goal 4.)

Introduction

The highly competitive automotive retailing business has changed significantly over the past 5 years, due in part to consolidation by large, publicly owned deal-

ership groups. Traditionally, a local family owned and operated the community dealership, which might have included one or two manufacturers, like Pontiac and GMC Trucks or Chrysler and the popular Jeep line. Recently, however, skillfully managed and well-financed companies have been acquiring local dealerships across large regions of the country. As these groups acquire the local dealerships, they often bring standard selling practices, common software and hardware technology platforms, and management reporting techniques. The goal is to provide an improved buying experience for the consumer, while increasing the profitability of the larger dealership organization. In many cases, in addition to reaping the financial benefits of selling the dealership, the family is asked to continue running the dealership on a daily basis. Today, it is common for these megadealerships to employ over 10,000 people, generate several billion dollars in annual sales, own more than 100 franchises, and be traded on the New York Stock Exchange or NASDAQ. Megadealerships include AutoNation (ticker symbol AN and the largest), Penske Auto Group (PAG and second largest), Asbury Automotive Group (ABG), and Hendrick Auto Group (which is privately held).

The consolidation has not come without challenges. With the acquisition of dealerships across the country, AutoUSA, one of the new megadealerships, now sells the inexpensive Korean import brands Kia and Hyundai, the high-line BMW and Mercedes Benz sedans, and a full line of Ford and Chevrolet cars and trucks.

Ms. Kathryn Ball is a member of the senior management team at AutoUSA. She is responsible for tracking and analyzing vehicle selling prices for AutoUSA. Kathryn would like to summarize vehicle selling prices with charts and graphs that she could review monthly. From these tables and charts, she wants to know the typical selling price as well as the lowest and highest prices. She is also interested in describing the demographics of the buyers. What are their ages? How many vehicles do they own? Do they want to buy or lease the vehicle?

Whitner Autoplex, which is located in Raytown, Missouri, is one of the AutoUSA dealerships. Whitner Autoplex includes Pontiac, GMC, and Buick franchises as well as a BMW store. General Motors is actively working with its dealer body to combine at one location several of its franchises, such as Chevrolet, Pontiac, or Cadillac. Combining franchises improves the floor traffic and a dealership has product offerings for all demographics. BMW, with its premium brand and image, wants to move away from calling its locations dealerships, instead calling them stores. Instead

Excel

	A	B	C	D
1	Price	Price($000)	Age	Type
2	23197	23.197	46	0
3	23372	23.372	48	0
4	20454	20.454	40	1
5	23591	23.591	40	0
6	26651	26.651	46	1
7	27453	27.453	37	1
8	17266	17.266	32	1
9	18021	18.021	29	1
10	28683	28.683	38	1
11	30872	30.872	43	0
12	19587	19.587	32	0
13	23169	23.169	47	0
14	35851	35.851	56	0
15	19251	19.251	42	1

Whitner

of offering a traditional automobile dealership experience, BMW wants to be more like Nordstrom, a U.S. retail store selling fine quality apparel. Like Nordstrom, BMW wants to offer customers superior service, great products, and a unique personalized shopping experience.

Ms. Ball decided to collect data on three variables at Whitner Autoplex: selling price ($000), buyer's age, and car type (domestic, coded as 1, or foreign, coded as 0). A portion of the data set is shown in the adjacent output. The entire data set is available on the student CD (included with the book), at the McGraw-Hill website, and in Appendix A.5 at the end of the text.

Constructing a Frequency Table

Recall from Chapter 1 that techniques used to describe a set of data are called descriptive statistics. To put it another way, descriptive statistics organize data to show the general pattern of the data and where values tend to concentrate and to expose extreme or unusual data values. The first procedure we discuss to organize and summarize a set of data is a **frequency table.**

> **FREQUENCY TABLE** A grouping of qualitative data into mutually exclusive classes showing the number of observations in each class.

In Chapter 1, we distinguished between qualitative and quantitative variables. To review, a qualitative variable is nonnumeric, that is, it can only be classified into distinct categories. There is no particular order to these categories. Examples of qualitative data include political affiliation (Republican, Democrat, Independent), state of birth (Alabama, . . . , Wyoming), and method of payment for a purchase at Barnes and Noble (cash, check, or charge). On the other hand, quantitative variables are numerical in nature. Examples of quantitative data relating to college students include the price of their textbooks, their age, and hours they spend studying each week.

In the Whitner Autoplex data, Ms. Ball observed three variables for each vehicle sale: selling price, age of the buyer, and car type. Selling price and age are quantitative variables, but vehicle type is a qualitative measure with two values, domestic or foreign. Suppose that Ms. Ball wanted to summarize last month's sales using vehicle type.

To summarize this qualitative data, we classify the vehicles as either domestic (coded as 1) or foreign (coded as 0) and count the number in each class. We use vehicle type to develop a frequency table with two mutually exclusive (distinctive) classes. This means that a particular vehicle cannot belong to both classes. The vehicle is either domestic or foreign and can never be both domestic and foreign. This frequency table is shown in Table 2–1. The number of observations in each class is called the **class frequency.** So the class frequency for domestic vehicles sold is 50.

TABLE 2–1 Frequency Table for Vehicles Sold at Whitner Autoplex Last Month

Car Type	Number of Cars
Domestic	50
Foreign	30

Relative Class Frequencies

You can convert class frequencies to **relative class frequencies** to show the fraction of the total number of observations in each class. So, a relative frequency captures the relationship between a class total and the total number of observations. In the vehicle sales example, we may want to know the percent of total cars sold that were domestic or foreign.

To convert a frequency distribution to a *relative* frequency distribution, each of the class frequencies is divided by the total number of observations. For example, 0.625, found by 50 divided by 80, is the fraction of domestic vehicles sold last month. The relative frequency distribution is shown in Table 2–2.

TABLE 2–2 Relative Frequency Table of Vehicles Sold by Type at Whitner Autoplex Last Month

Vehicle Type	Number Sold	Relative Frequency
Domestic	50	0.625
Foreign	30	0.375
Total	80	1.000

Graphic Presentation of Qualitative Data

The most common device to present a qualitative variable in graphic form is a **bar chart.** In most cases the horizontal axis shows the variable of interest and the vertical axis the amount, number, or fraction of each of the possible outcomes. A distinguishing characteristic of a bar chart is the distance or gap between the bars. That is, because the variable of interest is qualitative, the bars are not adjacent to each other. Thus, a bar chart graphically describes a frequency table using a series of uniformly wide rectangles, where the height of each rectangle is the class frequency.

> **BAR CHART** A graph in which the classes are reported on the horizontal axis and the class frequencies on the vertical axis. The class frequencies are proportional to the heights of the bars.

We use the Whitner Autoplex data as an example (Chart 2–1). The variable of interest is the vehicle type and the number of each type sold is the class frequency. We scale the vehicle type (domestic or foreign) on the horizontal axis and the number of each item on the vertical axis. The height of the bars, or rectangles, corresponds to the number of vehicles of each type sold. So for the number of foreign vehicles sold the height of the bar is 30. The order of foreign or domestic on the X-axis does not matter because the values of car type are qualitative.

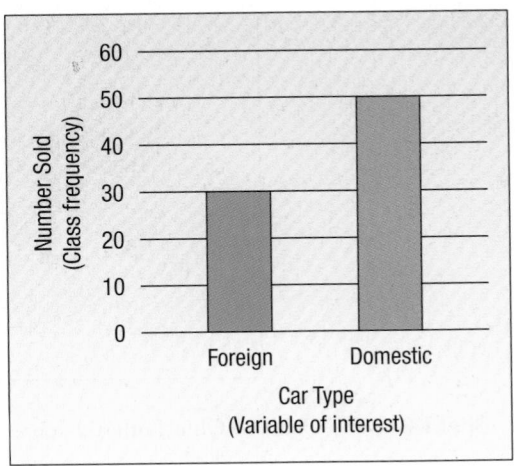

CHART 2–1 Vehicle Sold by Type Last Month at Whitner Autoplex

Another useful type of chart for depicting qualitative information is a **pie chart.**

> **PIE CHART** A chart that shows the proportion or percent that each class represents of the total number of frequencies.

We explain the details of constructing a pie chart using the information in Table 2–3, which shows a breakdown of the expenses for the Ohio State Lottery in 2007.

TABLE 2–3 Ohio State Lottery Expenses in 2007

Use of Sales	Amount ($ million)	Percent of Share
Prizes	1,311.1	65
Education	464.3	23
Bonuses	139.8	7
Expenses	109.8	5
Total	2,025.0	100

The first step to develop a pie chart is to record the percentages 0, 5, 10, 15, and so on evenly around the circumference of a circle (see Chart 2–2). To plot the 65 percent share awarded for prizes, draw a line from the center of the circle to 0 and another line from the center of the circle to 65 percent. The area in this "slice" represents the lottery proceeds that were awarded in prizes. Next, add the 65 percent of expenses awarded in prizes to the 23 percent payments to education; the result is 88 percent. Draw a line from the center of the circle to 88 percent, so the area between 65 percent and 88 percent depicts the payments made to education. Continuing, add the 7 percent for bonuses, which gives us a total of 95 percent. Draw a line from the center of the circle to 95, so the "slice" between 88 percent and 95 percent represents the payment of bonuses. The remainder, 5 percent, is for operating expenses.

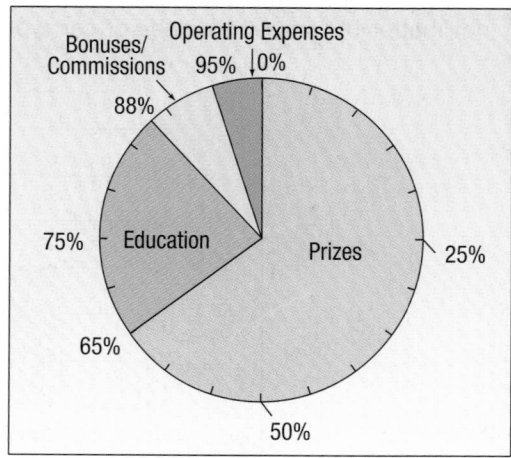

CHART 2–2 Pie Chart of Ohio Lottery Expenses in 2007

Because each slice of the pie represents the relative share of each component, we can easily compare them:

- The largest expense of the Ohio Lottery is for prizes.
- About one-fourth of the proceeds are transferred to education.
- Operating expenses account for only 5 percent of the proceeds.

The Excel system will develop a pie chart. See the following chart for the information in Table 2–3.

Excel

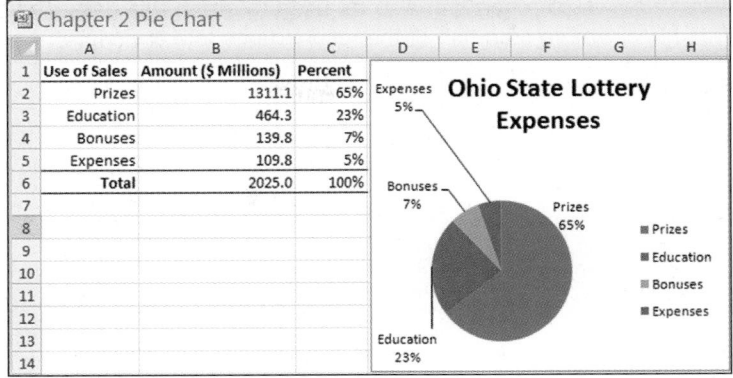

Example

SkiLodges.com is test marketing its new website and is interested in how easy its Web page design is to navigate. It randomly selected 200 regular Internet users and asked them to perform a search task on the Web page. Each person was asked to rate the relative ease of navigation as poor, good, excellent, or awesome. The results are shown in the following table:

Awesome	102
Excellent	58
Good	30
Poor	10

1. What type of measurement scale is used for ease of navigation?
2. Draw a bar chart for the survey results.
3. Draw a pie chart for the survey results.

Solution

The data are measured on an ordinal scale. That is, the scale is ranked in relative ease when moving from "poor" to "awesome." Also, the interval between each rating is unknown so it is impossible, for example, to conclude that a rating of good is twice the value of a poor rating.

We can use a bar chart to graph the data. The vertical scale shows the relative frequency and the horizontal shows the values of the ease of navigation scale.

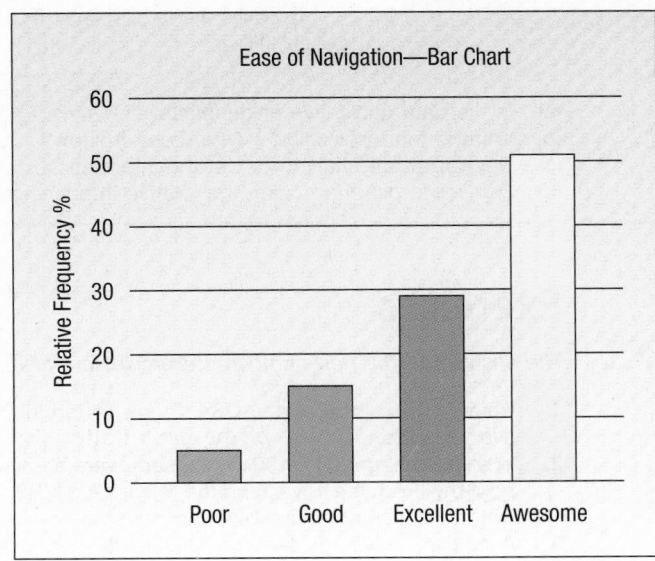

A pie chart can also be used to graph this data. The pie chart emphasizes the fact the more than half of the respondents rate the relative ease of using the website awesome.

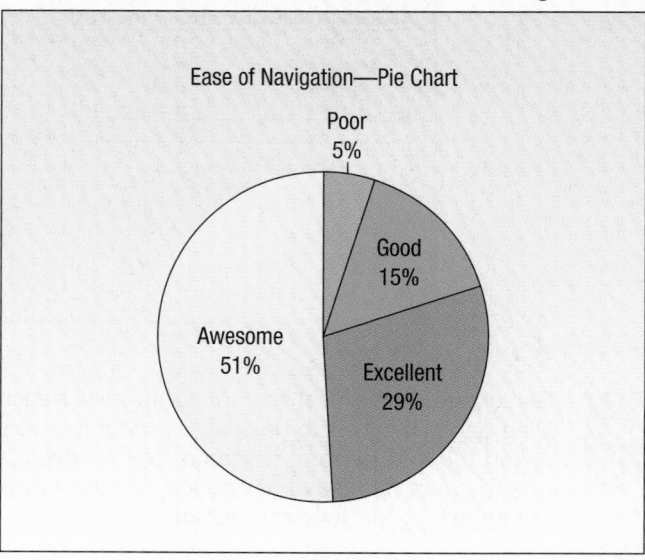

Ease of Navigation—Pie Chart

Poor 5%

Good 15%

Excellent 29%

Awesome 51%

Self-Review 2–1   *The answers are at the end of the chapter.*

DeCenzo Specialty Food and Beverage Company has been serving a cola drink with an additional flavoring, Cola-Plus, that is very popular among its customers. The company is interested in customer preferences for Cola-Plus versus Coca-Cola, Pepsi, and a lemon-lime beverage. They ask 100 randomly sampled customers to take a taste test and select the beverage they preferred most. The results are shown in the following table:

Beverage	Number
Cola-Plus	40
Coca-Cola	25
Pepsi	20
Lemon-Lime	15
Total	100

(a) Is the data qualitative or quantitative? Why?
(b) What is the table called? What does it show?
(c) Develop a bar chart to depict the information.
(d) Develop a pie chart using the relative frequencies.

Exercises

The answers to the odd-numbered exercises are at the end of the book.

1. Refer to your local paper, *USA Today,* or the Internet and find two examples of qualitative variables.
2. In a marketing study, 100 consumers were asked to select the best digital music player from the iPod, the iRiver, and the Magic Star MP3. To summarize the consumer responses with a frequency table, how many classes would the frequency table have?
3. A total of 1,000 residents in Minnesota were asked which season they preferred. The results were 100 liked winter best, 300 liked spring, 400 liked summer, and 200 liked fall. If the data were summarized in a frequency table, how many classes would be used? What would be the relative frequencies for each class?

4. Two thousand frequent Midwestern business travelers are asked which Midwest city they prefer: Indianapolis, Saint Louis, Chicago, or Milwaukee. The results were 100 liked Indianapolis best, 450 liked Saint Louis, 1,300 liked Chicago, and the remainder preferred Milwaukee. Develop a frequency table and a relative frequency table to summarize this information.

5. Wellstone, Inc., produces and markets replacement covers for cell phones in a variety of colors. The company would like to allocate its production plans to five different colors: bright white, metallic black, magnetic lime, tangerine orange, and fusion red. The company set up a kiosk in the Mall of America for several hours and asked randomly selected people which cover color was their favorite. The results follow:

Bright white	130
Metallic black	104
Magnetic lime	325
Tangerine orange	455
Fusion red	286

   a. What is the table called?
   b. Draw a bar chart for the table.
   c. Draw a pie chart.
   d. If Wellstone, Inc., plans to produce 1 million cell phone covers, how many of each color should it produce?

6. A small business consultant is investigating the performance of several companies. The fourth quarter sales for last year (in thousands of dollars) for the selected companies were:

Corporation	Fourth-Quarter Sales ($ thousands)
Hoden Building Products	$ 1,645.2
J & R Printing, Inc.	4,757.0
Long Bay Concrete Construction	8,913.0
Mancell Electric and Plumbing	627.1
Maxwell Heating and Air Conditioning	24,612.0
Mizelle Roofing & Sheet Metals	191.9

The consultant wants to include a chart in his report comparing the sales of the six companies. Use a bar chart to compare the fourth-quarter sales of these corporations and write a brief report summarizing the bar chart.

Constructing Frequency Distributions: Quantitative Data

In Chapter 1 and earlier in this chapter, we distinguished between qualitative and quantitative data. In the previous section using the Whitner Autoplex data, we summarized the qualitative variable, vehicle type, using a frequency table, a relative frequency table, a bar chart, and a pie chart.

The Whitner Autoplex data also includes two quantitative variables: selling price and age of the buyer. Suppose Ms. Ball wants to summarize last month's sales using selling price. We can describe selling price using a **frequency distribution.**

> **FREQUENCY DISTRIBUTION** A grouping of data into mutually exclusive classes showing the number of observations in each class.

How do we develop a frequency distribution? The first step is to tally the data into a table that shows the classes and the number of observations in each class. The steps in constructing a frequency distribution are best described by an example. Remember, our goal is to construct tables, charts, and graphs that will quickly reveal the concentration and shape of the data.

Example

We return to the situation where Ms. Kathryn Ball of AutoUSA wants tables, charts, and graphs to show the typical selling price on various dealer lots. Table 2–4 reports only the price of the 80 vehicles sold last month at Whitner Autoplex. What is the *typical* selling price? What is the *highest* selling price? What is the *lowest* selling price? Around what value do the selling prices tend to cluster?

TABLE 2–4 Prices of Vehicles Sold Last Month at Whitner Autoplex

Lowest

$23,197	$23,372	$20,454	$23,591	$26,651	$27,453	$17,266
18,021	28,683	30,872	19,587	23,169	35,851	19,251
20,047	24,285	24,324	24,609	28,670	15,546	15,935
19,873	25,251	25,277	28,034	24,533	27,443	19,889
20,004	17,357	20,155	19,688	23,657	26,613	20,895
20,203	23,765	25,783	26,661	32,277	20,642	21,981
24,052	25,799	15,794	18,263	35,925	17,399	17,968
20,356	21,442	21,722	19,331	22,817	19,766	20,633
20,962	22,845	26,285	27,896	29,076	32,492	18,890
21,740	22,374	24,571	25,449	28,337	20,642	23,613
24,220	30,655	22,442	17,891	20,818	26,237	20,445
21,556	21,639	24,296				

Highest

Solution

The steps for organizing data into a frequency distribution.

We refer to the unorganized information in Table 2–4 as **raw data** or **ungrouped data.** With a little searching, we can find the lowest selling price ($15,546) and the highest selling price ($35,925), but that is about all. It is difficult to determine a typical selling price. It is also difficult to visualize where the selling prices tend to cluster. The raw data are more easily interpreted if organized into a frequency distribution.

Step 1: Decide on the number of classes. The goal is to use just enough groupings or **classes** to reveal the shape of the distribution. Some judgment is needed here. Too many classes or too few classes might not reveal the basic shape of the data set. In the vehicle selling price example, three classes would not give much insight into the pattern of the data (see Table 2–5).

TABLE 2–5 An Example of Too Few Classes

Vehicle Selling Price ($)	Number of Vehicles
15,000 up to 24,000	48
24,000 up to 33,000	30
33,000 up to 42,000	2
Total	80

A useful recipe to determine the number of classes (k) is the "2 to the k rule." This guide suggests you select the smallest number (k) for the number of classes such that 2^k (in words, 2 raised to the power of k) is greater than the number of observations (n).

In the Whitner Autoplex example, there were 80 vehicles sold. So $n = 80$. If we try $k = 6$, which means we would use 6 classes, then $2^6 = 64$, somewhat less than 80. Hence, 6 is not enough classes. If we let $k = 7$, then $2^7 = 128$, which is greater than 80. So the recommended number of classes is 7.

Step 2: Determine the class interval or width. Generally the **class interval** or **width** should be the same for all classes. The classes all taken together

must cover at least the distance from the lowest value in the data up to the highest value. Expressing these words in a formula:

$$i \geq \frac{H - L}{k}$$

where i is the class interval, H is the highest observed value, L is the lowest observed value, and k is the number of classes.

In the Whitner Autoplex case, the lowest value is $15,546 and the highest value is $35,925. If we need 7 classes, the interval should be at least ($35,925 − $15,546)/7 = $2,911. In practice this interval size is usually rounded up to some convenient number, such as a multiple of 10 or 100. The value of $3,000 might readily be used in this case.

Unequal class intervals present problems in graphically portraying the distribution and in doing some of the computations, which we will see in later chapters. Unequal class intervals, however, may be necessary in certain situations to avoid a large number of empty, or almost empty, classes. Such is the case in Table 2–6. The Internal Revenue Service used unequal-sized class intervals to report the adjusted gross income on individual tax returns. Had they used an equal-sized interval of, say, $1,000, more than 1,000 classes would have been required to describe all the incomes. A frequency distribution with 1,000 classes would be difficult to interpret. In this case the distribution is easier to understand in spite of the unequal classes. Note also that the number of income tax returns or "frequencies" is reported in thousands in this particular table. This also makes the information easier to understand.

TABLE 2–6 Adjusted Gross Income for Individuals Filing Income Tax Returns

Adjusted Gross Income			Number of Returns (in thousands)
No adjusted gross income			178.2
$ 1 up to	$	5,000	1,204.6
5,000 up to		10,000	2,595.5
10,000 up to		15,000	3,142.0
15,000 up to		20,000	3,191.7
20,000 up to		25,000	2,501.4
25,000 up to		30,000	1,901.6
30,000 up to		40,000	2,502.3
40,000 up to		50,000	1,426.8
50,000 up to		75,000	1,476.3
75,000 up to		100,000	338.8
100,000 up to		200,000	223.3
200,000 up to		500,000	55.2
500,000 up to		1,000,000	12.0
1,000,000 up to		2,000,000	5.1
2,000,000 up to		10,000,000	3.4
10,000,000 or more			0.6

Step 3: Set the individual class limits. State clear class limits so you can put each observation into only one category. This means you must avoid overlapping or unclear class limits. For example, classes such as "$1,300–$1,400" and "$1,400–$1,500" should not be used because it is not clear whether the value $1,400 is in the first or second class. Classes stated as "$1,300–$1,400" and "$1,500–$1,600" are frequently used, but may also be confusing without the additional common convention of rounding all data at

or above $1,450 up to the second class and data below $1,450 down to the first class. In this text we will generally use the format $1,300 up to $1,400 and $1,400 up to $1,500 and so on. With this format it is clear that $1,399 goes into the first class and $1,400 in the second.

Because we round the class interval up to get a convenient class size, we cover a larger than necessary range. For example, 7 classes of width $3,000 in the Whitner Autoplex case result in a range of 7($3,000) = $21,000. The actual range is $20,379, found by $35,925 − $15,546. Comparing that value to $21,000 we have an excess of $621. Because we need to cover only the distance ($H − L$), it is natural to put approximately equal amounts of the excess in each of the two tails. Of course, we should also select convenient class limits. A guideline is to make the lower limit of the first class a multiple of the class interval. Sometimes this is not possible, but the lower limit should at least be rounded. So here are the classes we could use for this data.

$15,000 up to 18,000
18,000 up to 21,000
21,000 up to 24,000
24,000 up to 27,000
27,000 up to 30,000
30,000 up to 33,000
33,000 up to 36,000

Step 4: Tally the vehicle selling prices into the classes. To begin, the selling price of the first vehicle in Table 2–4 is $23,197. It is tallied in the $21,000 up to $24,000 class. The second selling price in the first column of Table 2–4 is $18,021. It is tallied in the $18,000 up to $21,000 class. The other selling prices are tallied in a similar manner. When all the selling prices are tallied, the table would appear as:

Class	Tallies
$15,000 up to $18,000	JHI III
$18,000 up to $21,000	JHI JHI JHI JHI III
$21,000 up to $24,000	JHI JHI JHI II
$24,000 up to $27,000	JHI JHI JHI III
$27,000 up to $30,000	JHI III
$30,000 up to $33,000	IIII
$33,000 up to $36,000	II

Step 5: Count the number of items in each class. The number of observations in each class is called the **class frequency.** In the $15,000 up to $18,000 class there are 8 observations, and in the $18,000 up to $21,000 class there are 23 observations. Therefore, the class frequency in the first class is 8 and the class frequency in the second class is 23. There is a total of 80 observations or frequencies in the entire set of data.

Often it is useful to express the data in thousands, or some convenient units, rather than the actual data. Table 2–7, for example, reports the vehicle selling prices in thousands of dollars, rather than dollars.

Now that we have organized the data into a frequency distribution, we can summarize the pattern in the selling prices of the vehicles for the AutoUSA lot of Whitner Autoplex in Raytown, Missouri. Observe the following:

1. The selling prices ranged from about $15,000 up to about $36,000.
2. The selling prices are concentrated between $18,000 and $27,000. A total of 58, or 72.5 percent, of the vehicles sold within this range.

TABLE 2–7 Frequency Distribution of Selling Prices at Whitner Autoplex Last Month

Selling Prices ($ thousands)	Frequency
15 up to 18	8
18 up to 21	23
21 up to 24	17
24 up to 27	18
27 up to 30	8
30 up to 33	4
33 up to 36	2
Total	80

3. The largest concentration, or highest frequency, is in the $18,000 up to $21,000 class. The middle of this class is $19,500. So we say that a typical selling price is $19,500.

By presenting this information to Ms. Ball, we give her a clear picture of the distribution of selling prices for last month.

We admit that arranging the information on selling prices into a frequency distribution does result in the loss of some detailed information. That is, by organizing the data into a frequency distribution, we cannot pinpoint the exact selling price, such as $23,197 or $26,237. Further, we cannot tell that the actual selling price for the least expensive vehicle was $15,546 and for the most expensive $35,925. However, the lower limit of the first class and the upper limit of the largest class convey essentially the same meaning. Likely, Ms. Ball will make the same judgment if she knows the lowest price is about $15,000 that she will if she knows the exact price is $15,546. The advantages of condensing the data into a more understandable and organized form more than offset this disadvantage.

Self-Review 2–2

The commissions earned for the first quarter of last year by the 11 members of the sales staff at Master Chemical Company are:

| $1,650 | $1,475 | $1,510 | $1,670 | $1,595 | $1,760 | $1,540 | $1,495 | $1,590 | $1,625 | $1,510 |

(a) What are the values such as $1,650 and $1,475 called?
(b) Using $1,400 up to $1,500 as the first class, $1,500 up to $1,600 as the second class, and so forth, organize the quarterly commissions into a frequency distribution.
(c) What are the numbers in the right column of your frequency distribution called?
(d) Describe the distribution of quarterly commissions, based on the frequency distribution. What is the largest concentration of commissions earned? What is the smallest, and the largest? What is the typical amount earned?

Class Intervals and Class Midpoints

We will use two other terms frequently: **class midpoint** and **class interval.** The midpoint is halfway between the lower limits of two consecutive classes. It is computed by adding the lower limits of consecutive classes and dividing the result by 2. Referring to Table 2–7, for the first class the lower class limit is $15,000 and the next limit is $18,000. The class midpoint is $16,500, found by ($15,000 + $18,000)/2. The midpoint of $16,500 best represents, or is typical of, the selling price of the vehicles in that class.

To determine the class interval, subtract the lower limit of the class from the lower limit of the next class. The class interval of the vehicle selling price data is $3,000, which we find by subtracting the lower limit of the first class, $15,000, from the lower limit of the next class; that is, $18,000 − $15,000 = $3,000. You can also determine the class interval by finding the difference between consecutive midpoints. The midpoint of the first class is $16,500 and the midpoint of the second class is $19,500. The difference is $3,000.

A Software Example

As we mentioned in Chapter 1, there are many software packages that perform statistical calculations. Throughout this text we will show the output from Microsoft Excel; from MegaStat, which is an add-in to Microsoft Excel; and from MINITAB. The commands necessary to generate the outputs are given in the **Software Commands** section at the end of each chapter.

The following is a frequency distribution, produced by MegaStat, showing the prices of the 80 vehicles sold last month at the Whitner Autoplex lot in Raytown, Missouri. The form of the output is somewhat different than the frequency distribution of Table 2–7, but the overall conclusions are the same.

Whitner Distribution

	A	B	C	D	E	F	G	H	I
1									
2	Frequency Distribution - Quantitative								
3									
4		Price						cumulative	
5	lower		upper	midpoint	width	frequency	percent	frequency	percent
6	15,000	<	18,000	16,500	3,000	8	10.0	8	10.0
7	18,000	<	21,000	19,500	3,000	23	28.8	31	38.8
8	21,000	<	24,000	22,500	3,000	17	21.3	48	60.0
9	24,000	<	27,000	25,500	3,000	18	22.5	66	82.5
10	27,000	<	30,000	28,500	3,000	8	10.0	74	92.5
11	30,000	<	33,000	31,500	3,000	4	5.0	78	97.5
12	33,000	<	36,000	34,500	3,000	2	2.5	80	100.0
14						80	100.0		
15									

Self-Review 2–3

Barry Bonds of the San Francisco Giants established a new single season home run record by hitting 73 home runs during the 2001 season. The longest of these home runs traveled 488 feet and the shortest 320 feet. You need to construct a frequency distribution of these home run lengths.
(a) How many classes would you use?
(b) What class interval would you suggest?
(c) What actual classes would you suggest?

Relative Frequency Distribution

A relative frequency distribution converts the frequency to a percent.

It may be desirable as we did earlier with qualitative data to convert class frequencies to relative class frequencies to show the fraction of the total number of observations in each class. In our vehicle sales example, we may want to know what percent of the vehicle prices are in the $21,000 up to $24,000 class. In another study, we may want to know what percent of the employees used 5 up to 10 personal leave days last year.

To convert a frequency distribution to a *relative* frequency distribution, each of the class frequencies is divided by the total number of observations. From the distribution of vehicle selling prices (Table 2–7, where the selling price is reported in thousands of dollars), the relative frequency for the $15,000 up to $18,000 class is 0.10, found by dividing 8 by 80. That is, the price of 10 percent of the vehicles sold at Whitner Autoplex is between $15,000 and $18,000. The relative frequencies for the remaining classes are shown in Table 2–8.

TABLE 2–8 Relative Frequency Distribution of the Prices of Vehicles Sold Last Month at Whitner Autoplex

Selling Price ($ thousands)	Frequency	Relative Frequency	Found by
15 up to 18	8	0.1000	8/80
18 up to 21	23	0.2875	23/80
21 up to 24	17	0.2125	17/80
24 up to 27	18	0.2250	18/80
27 up to 30	8	0.1000	8/80
30 up to 33	4	0.0500	4/80
33 up to 36	2	0.0250	2/80
Total	80	1.0000	

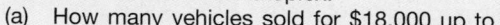
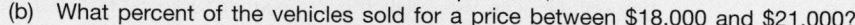

Self-Review 2–4

Refer to Table 2–8, which shows the relative frequency distribution for the vehicles sold last month at Whitner Autoplex.
(a) How many vehicles sold for $18,000 up to $21,000?
(b) What percent of the vehicles sold for a price between $18,000 and $21,000?
(c) What percent of the vehicles sold for $30,000 or more?

Exercises

connect™

7. A set of data consists of 38 observations. How many classes would you recommend for the frequency distribution?
8. A set of data consists of 45 observations between $0 and $29. What size would you recommend for the class interval?
9. A set of data consists of 230 observations between $235 and $567. What class interval would you recommend?
10. A set of data contains 53 observations. The lowest value is 42 and the largest is 129. The data are to be organized into a frequency distribution.
    a. How many classes would you suggest?
    b. What would you suggest as the lower limit of the first class?
11. Wachesaw Manufacturing, Inc., produced the following number of units in the last 16 days.

27	27	27	28	27	25	25	28
26	28	26	28	31	30	26	26

The information is to be organized into a frequency distribution.
    a. How many classes would you recommend?
    b. What class interval would you suggest?
    c. What lower limit would you recommend for the first class?
    d. Organize the information into a frequency distribution and determine the relative frequency distribution.
    e. Comment on the shape of the distribution.
12. The Quick Change Oil Company has a number of outlets in the metropolitan Seattle area. The daily number of oil changes at the Oak Street outlet in the past 20 days are:

65	98	55	62	79	59	51	90	72	56
70	62	66	80	94	79	63	73	71	85

The data are to be organized into a frequency distribution.
  a. How many classes would you recommend?
  b. What class interval would you suggest?
  c. What lower limit would you recommend for the first class?
  d. Organize the number of oil changes into a frequency distribution.
  e. Comment on the shape of the frequency distribution. Also determine the relative frequency distribution.

13. The manager of the BiLo Supermarket in Mt. Pleasant, Rhode Island, gathered the following information on the number of times a customer visits the store during a month. The responses of 51 customers were:

5	3	3	1	4	4	5	6	4	2	6	6	6	7	1
1	14	1	2	4	4	4	5	6	3	5	3	4	5	6
8	4	7	6	5	9	11	3	12	4	7	6	5	15	1
1	10	8	9	2	12									

  a. Starting with 0 as the lower limit of the first class and using a class interval of 3, organize the data into a frequency distribution.
  b. Describe the distribution. Where do the data tend to cluster?
  c. Convert the distribution to a relative frequency distribution.

14. The food services division of Cedar River Amusement Park, Inc., is studying the amount families who visit the amusement park spend per day on food and drink. A sample of 40 families who visited the park yesterday revealed they spent the following amounts:

$77	$18	$63	$84	$38	$54	$50	$59	$54	$56	$36	$26	$50	$34	$44
41	58	58	53	51	62	43	52	53	63	62	62	65	61	52
60	60	45	66	83	71	63	58	61	71					

  a. Organize the data into a frequency distribution, using seven classes and 15 as the lower limit of the first class. What class interval did you select?
  b. Where do the data tend to cluster?
  c. Describe the distribution.
  d. Determine the relative frequency distribution.

Graphic Presentation
of a Frequency Distribution

Sales managers, stock analysts, hospital administrators, and other busy executives often need a quick picture of the trends in sales, stock prices, or hospital costs. These trends can often be depicted by the use of charts and graphs. Three charts that will help portray a frequency distribution graphically are the histogram, the frequency polygon, and the cumulative frequency polygon.

Histogram

A **histogram** for a frequency distribution based on quantitative data is very similar to the bar chart showing the distribution of qualitative data. The classes are marked on the horizontal axis and the class frequencies on the vertical axis. The class frequencies are represented by the heights of the bars. However, there is one important difference based on the nature of the data. Quantitative data is usually measured using scales that are continuous, not discrete. Therefore, the horizontal axis represents all possible values, and the bars are drawn adjacent to each other to show the continuous nature of the data.

> **HISTOGRAM** A graph in which the classes are marked on the horizontal axis and the class frequencies on the vertical axis. The class frequencies are represented by the heights of the bars and the bars are drawn adjacent to each other.

We summarized the selling prices—a continuous variable—of the 80 vehicles sold last month at Whitner Autoplex with a frequency distribution. We construct a histogram to illustrate this frequency distribution.

Example

Below is the frequency distribution.

Selling Prices ($ thousands)	Frequency
15 up to 18	8
18 up to 21	23
21 up to 24	17
24 up to 27	18
27 up to 30	8
30 up to 33	4
33 up to 36	2
Total	80

Construct a histogram. What conclusions can you reach based on the information presented in the histogram?

Solution

The class frequencies are scaled along the vertical axis (Y-axis) and either the class limits or the class midpoints along the horizontal axis. To illustrate the construction of the histogram, the first three classes are shown in Chart 2–3.

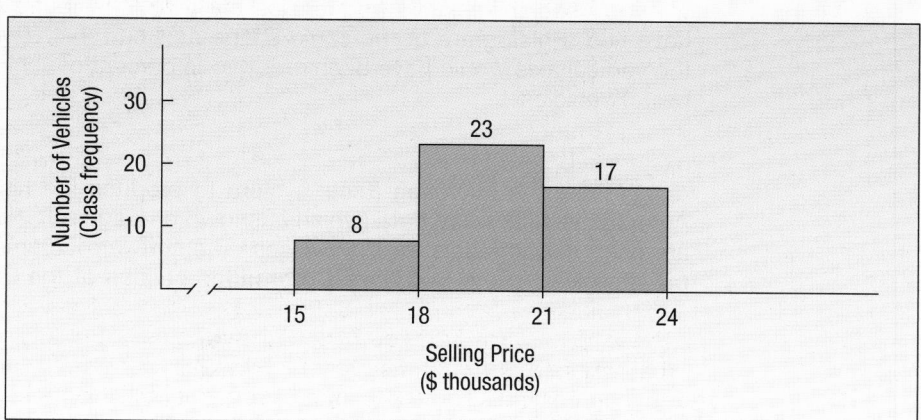

CHART 2–3 Construction of a Histogram

From Chart 2–3 we note that there are eight vehicles in the $15,000 up to $18,000 class. Therefore, the height of the column for that class is 8. There are 23 vehicles in the $18,000 up to $21,000 class. So, logically, the height of that column is 23. The height of the bar represents the number of observations in the class.

This procedure is continued for all classes. The complete histogram is shown in Chart 2–4. Note that there is no space between the bars. This is a feature of the histogram. Why is this so? Because the variable plotted on the horizontal axis is quantitative and of the interval, or in this case the ratio, scale of measurement. In bar charts, as described previously, the vertical bars are separated.

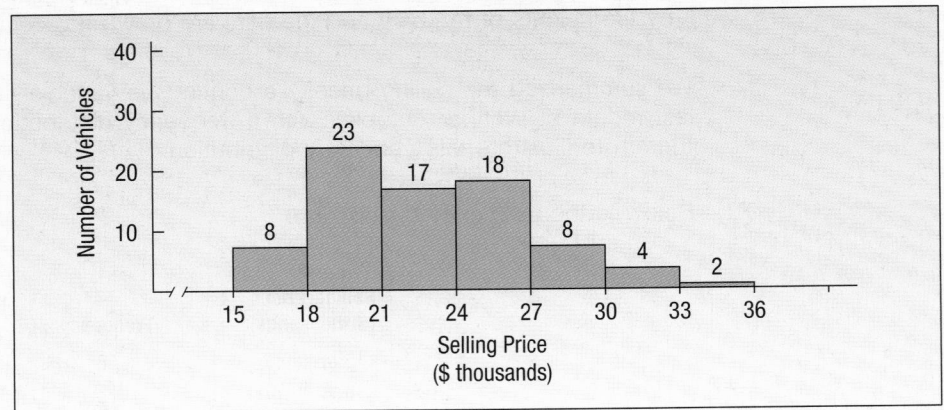

CHART 2–4 Histogram of the Selling Prices of 80 Vehicles at Whitner Autoplex

From the histogram in Chart 2–4, we conclude:

1. The lowest selling price is about $15,000, and the highest is about $36,000.
2. The largest class frequency is the $18,000 up to $21,000 class. A total of 23 of the 80 vehicles sold are within this price range.
3. Fifty-eight of the vehicles, or 72.5 percent, had a selling price between $18,000 and $27,000.

Thus, the histogram provides an easily interpreted visual representation of a frequency distribution. We should also point out that we would have reached the same conclusions and the shape of the histogram would have been the same had we used a relative frequency distribution instead of the actual frequencies. That is, if we had used the relative frequencies of Table 2–8, found on page 33, we would have had a histogram of the same shape as Chart 2–4. The only difference is that the vertical axis would have been reported in percent of vehicles instead of the number of vehicles.

We use the Microsoft Excel system to produce the histogram for the Whitner Autoplex vehicle sales data (which is shown on page 28). Note that class midpoints are used as the labels for the classes. The software commands to create this output are given in the **Software Commands** section at the end of the chapter.

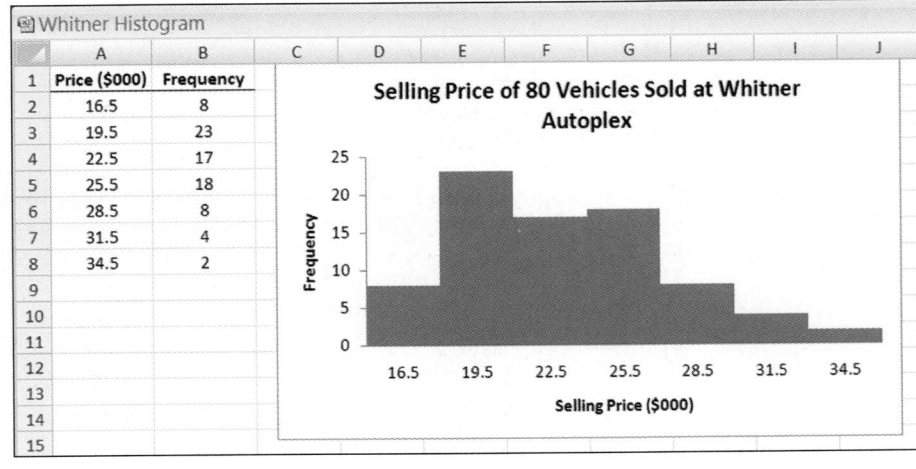

Frequency Polygon

In a frequency polygon the class midpoints are connected with a line segment.

A **frequency polygon** also shows the shape of a distribution and is similar to a histogram. It consists of line segments connecting the points formed by the intersections of the class midpoints and the class frequencies. The construction of a frequency polygon is illustrated in Chart 2–5 (on page 38). We use the vehicle prices for the cars sold last month at Whitner Autoplex. The midpoint of each class is scaled on the *X*-axis and the class frequencies on the *Y*-axis. Recall that the class midpoint is the value at the center of a class and represents the typical values in that class. The class frequency is the number of observations in a particular class. The vehicle selling prices at Whitner Autoplex are:

Selling Price ($ thousands)	Midpoint	Frequency
15 up to 18	16.5	8
18 up to 21	19.5	23
21 up to 24	22.5	17
24 up to 27	25.5	18
27 up to 30	28.5	8
30 up to 33	31.5	4
33 up to 36	34.5	2
Total		$\overline{80}$

Statistics in Action

Florence Nightingale is known as the founder of the nursing profession. However, she also saved many lives by using statistical analysis. When she encountered an unsanitary condition or an undersupplied hospital, she improved the conditions and then used statistical data to document the improvement. Thus, she was able to convince others of the need for medical reform, particularly in the area of sanitation. She developed original graphs to demonstrate that, during the Crimean War, more soldiers died from unsanitary conditions than were killed in combat. The adjacent graph by Nightingale is a polar-area graph showing the relative monthly proportions of causes of death from April 1854 to March 1855.

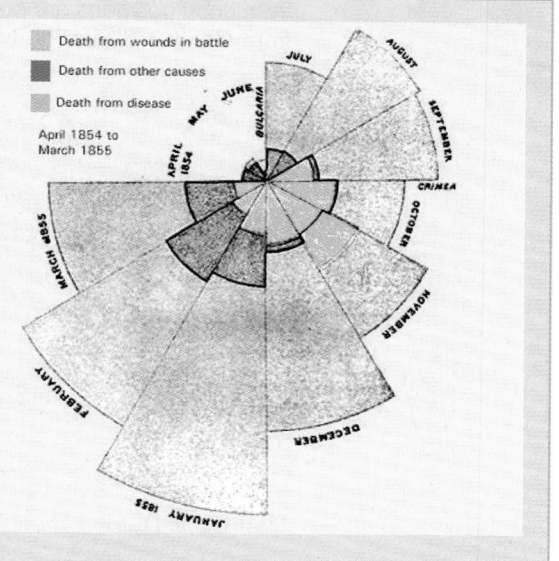

As noted previously, the $15,000 up to $18,000 class is represented by the midpoint $16,500. To construct a frequency polygon, move horizontally on the graph to the midpoint, $16.5, and then vertically to 8, the class frequency, and place a dot. The *X* and the *Y* values of this point are called the *coordinates*. The coordinates of the next point are *X* = $19.5 and *Y* = 23. The process is continued for all classes. Then the points are connected in order. That is, the point representing the lowest class is joined to the one representing the second class and so on.

Note in Chart 2–5 that, to complete the frequency polygon, midpoints of $13.5 and $37.5 are added to the *X*-axis to "anchor" the polygon at zero frequencies. These two values, $13.5 and $37.5, were derived by subtracting the class interval of $3.0 from the lowest midpoint ($16.5) and by adding $3.0 to the highest midpoint ($34.5) in the frequency distribution.

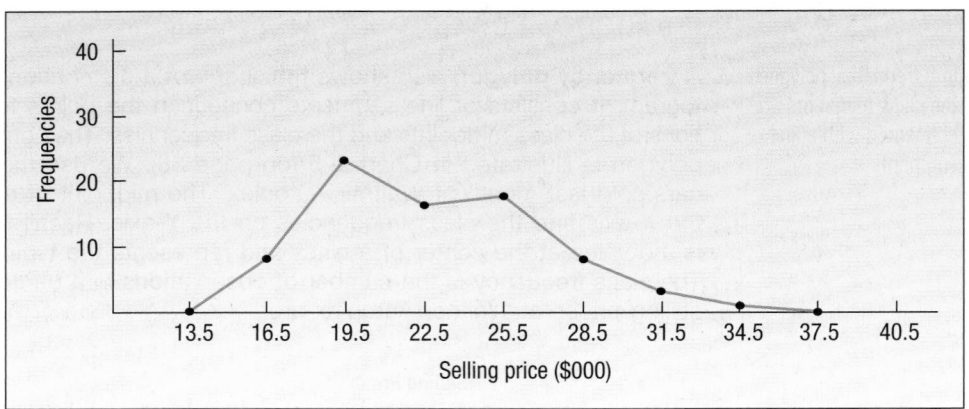

CHART 2–5 Frequency Polygon of the Selling Prices of 80 Vehicles at Whitner Autoplex

Both the histogram and the frequency polygon allow us to get a quick picture of the main characteristics of the data (highs, lows, points of concentration, etc.). Although the two representations are similar in purpose, the histogram has the advantage of depicting each class as a rectangle, with the height of the rectangular bar representing the number in each class. The frequency polygon, in turn, has an advantage over the histogram. It allows us to compare directly two or more frequency distributions. Suppose Ms. Ball of AutoUSA wants to compare the Whitner Autoplex lot in Raytown, Missouri, with a similar lot, Fowler Auto Mall in Grayling, Michigan. To do this, two frequency polygons are constructed, one on top of the other, as in Chart 2–6. It is clear from Chart 2–6 that the typical vehicle selling price is higher at the Fowler Auto Mall.

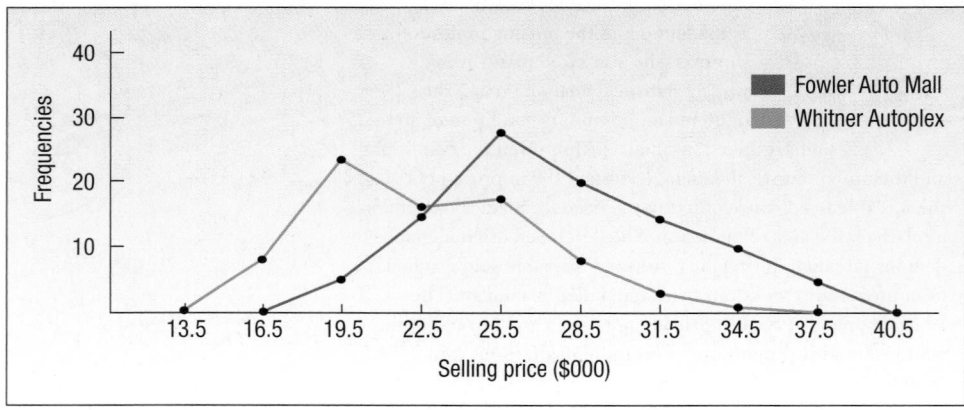

CHART 2–6 Distribution of Vehicle Selling Prices at Whitner Autoplex and Fowler Auto Mall

The total number of frequencies at the two dealerships is about the same, so a direct comparison is possible. If the difference in the total number of frequencies is quite large, converting the frequencies to relative frequencies and then plotting the two distributions would allow a clearer comparison.

Self-Review 2–5

The annual imports of a selected group of electronic suppliers are shown in the following frequency distribution.

Imports ($ millions)	Number of Suppliers	Imports ($ millions)	Number of Suppliers
2 up to 5	6	11 up to 14	10
5 up to 8	13	14 up to 17	1
8 up to 11	20		

(a) Portray the imports as a histogram.
(b) Portray the imports as a relative frequency polygon.
(c) Summarize the important facets of the distribution (such as classes with the highest and lowest frequencies).

Exercises

connect

15. Molly's Candle Shop has several retail stores in the coastal areas of North and South Carolina. Many of Molly's customers ask her to ship their purchases. The following chart shows the number of packages shipped per day for the last 100 days.

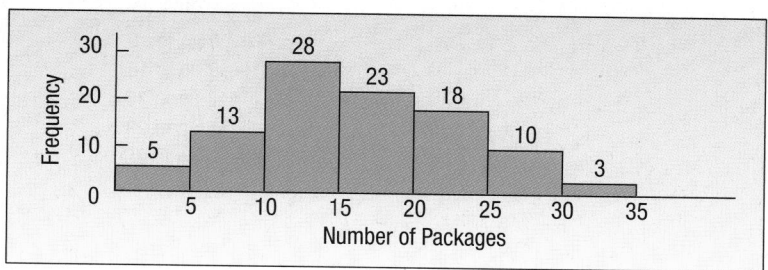

a. What is this chart called?
b. What is the total number of frequencies?
c. What is the class interval?
d. What is the class frequency for the 10 up to 15 class?
e. What is the relative frequency of the 10 up to 15 class?
f. What is the midpoint of the 10 up to 15 class?
g. On how many days were there 25 or more packages shipped?

16. The following chart shows the number of patients admitted daily to Memorial Hospital through the emergency room.

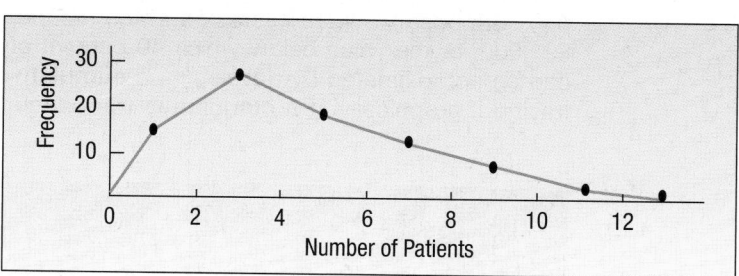

a. What is the midpoint of the 2 up to 4 class?
b. How many days were 2 up to 4 patients admitted?
c. Approximately how many days were studied?
d. What is the class interval?
e. What is this chart called?

17. The following frequency distribution reports the number of frequent flier miles, reported in thousands, for employees of Brumley Statistical Consulting, Inc., during the most recent quarter.

Frequent Flier Miles (000)	Number of Employees
0 up to 3	5
3 up to 6	12
6 up to 9	23
9 up to 12	8
12 up to 15	2
Total	50

  a. How many employees were studied?
  b. What is the midpoint of the first class?
  c. Construct a histogram.
  d. A frequency polygon is to be drawn. What are the coordinates of the plot for the first class?
  e. Construct a frequency polygon.
  f. Interpret the frequent flier miles accumulated using the two charts.
18. Ecommerce.com, a large Internet retailer, is studying the lead time (elapsed time between when an order is placed and when it is filled) for a sample of recent orders. The lead times are reported in days.

Lead Time (days)	Frequency
0 up to 5	6
5 up to 10	7
10 up to 15	12
15 up to 20	8
20 up to 25	7
Total	40

  a. How many orders were studied?
  b. What is the midpoint of the first class?
  c. What are the coordinates of the first class for a frequency polygon?
  d. Draw a histogram.
  e. Draw a frequency polygon.
  f. Interpret the lead times using the two charts.

Cumulative Frequency Distributions

Consider once again the distribution of the selling prices of vehicles at Whitner Auto-plex. Suppose we were interested in the number of vehicles that sold for less than $21,000, or the value below which 40 percent of the vehicles sold. These numbers can be approximated by developing a **cumulative frequency distribution** and portraying it graphically in a **cumulative frequency polygon.**

Example   The frequency distribution of the vehicle selling prices at Whitner Autoplex is repeated from Table 2–7.

Selling Price ($ thousands)	Frequency
15 up to 18	8
18 up to 21	23
21 up to 24	17
24 up to 27	18
27 up to 30	8
30 up to 33	4
33 up to 36	2
Total	80

Construct a cumulative frequency polygon. Fifty percent of the vehicles were sold for less than what amount? Twenty-five of the vehicles were sold for less than what amount?

Solution

As the name implies, a cumulative frequency distribution and a cumulative frequency polygon require *cumulative frequencies*. To construct a cumulative frequency distribution, refer to the preceding table and note that there were eight vehicles sold for less than $18,000. Those 8 vehicles, plus the 23 in the next higher class, for a total of 31, were sold for less than $21,000. The cumulative frequency for the next higher class is 48, found by 8 + 23 + 17. This process is continued for all the classes. All the vehicles were sold for less than $36,000. (See Table 2–9.)

To plot a cumulative frequency distribution, scale the upper limit of each class along the X-axis and the corresponding cumulative frequencies along the Y-axis. To provide additional information, you can label the vertical axis on the left in units and the vertical axis on the right in percent. In the Whitner Autoplex example, the vertical axis on the left is labeled from 0 to 80 and on the right from 0 to 100 percent. The value of 50 percent corresponds to 40 vehicles sold.

TABLE 2–9 Cumulative Frequency Distribution for Vehicle Selling Price

Selling Price ($ thousands)	Frequency	Cumulative Frequency	Found by
15 up to 18	8	8	
18 up to 21	23	31	◄── 8 + 23
21 up to 24	17	48	8 + 23 + 17
24 up to 27	18	66	8 + 23 + 17 + 18
27 up to 30	8	74	⋮
30 up to 33	4	78	
33 up to 36	2	80	
Total	80		

To begin the plotting, 8 vehicles sold for less than $18,000, so the first plot is at X = 18 and Y = 8. The coordinates for the next plot are X = 21 and Y = 31. The rest of the points are plotted and then the dots connected (see the green line) to form the chart below.

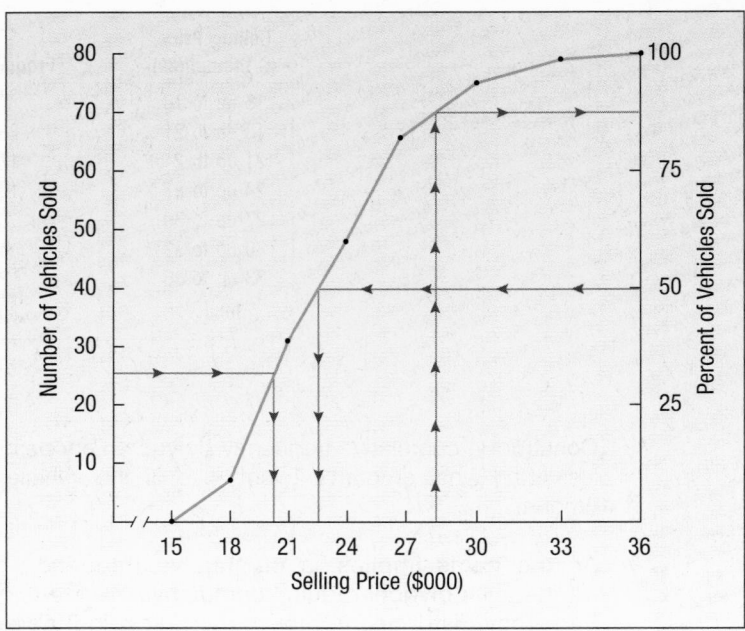

CHART 2–7 Cumulative Frequency Distribution for Vehicle Selling Price

To find the selling price below which half the cars sold, we draw a horizontal line from the 50 percent mark on the right-hand vertical axis over to the polygon, then drop down to the X-axis and read the selling price. The value on the X-axis is about 22.5, so we estimate that 50 percent of the vehicles sold for less than $22,500.

To find the price below which 25 of the vehicles sold, we locate the value of 25 on the left-hand vertical axis. Next, we draw a horizontal line from the value of 25 to the polygon, and then drop down to the X-axis and read the price. It is about 20.5, so we estimate that 25 of the vehicles sold for less than $20,500. We can also make estimates of the percent of vehicles that sold for less than a particular amount. To explain, suppose we want to estimate the percent of vehicles that sold for less than $28,500. We begin by locating the value of 28.5 on the X-axis, move vertically to the polygon, and then horizontally to the vertical axis on the right. The value is about 87 percent, so we conclude that 87 percent of the vehicles sold for less than $28,500.

Self-Review 2–6

A sample of the hourly wages of 15 employees at Home Depot in Brunswick, Georgia, was organized into the following table.

Hourly Wages	Number of Employees
$ 8 up to $10	3
10 up to 12	7
12 up to 14	4
14 up to 16	1

(a) What is the table called?
(b) Develop a cumulative frequency distribution and portray the distribution in a cumulative frequency polygon.
(c) On the basis of the cumulative frequency polygon, how many employees earn $11 an hour or less? Half of the employees earn an hourly wage of how much or more? Four employees earn how much or less?

Exercises

connect

19. The following chart shows the hourly wages of a sample of certified welders in the Atlanta, Georgia area.

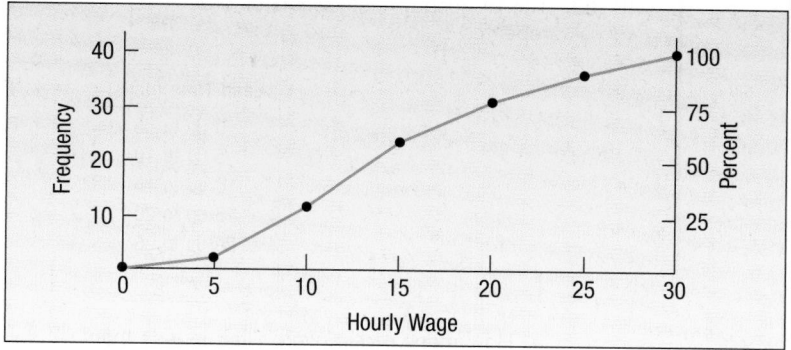

a. How many welders were studied?
b. What is the class interval?
c. About how many welders earn less than $10.00 per hour?
d. About 75 percent of the welders make less than what amount?
e. Ten of the welders studied made less than what amount?
f. What percent of the welders make less than $20.00 per hour?

20. The following chart shows the selling price ($000) of houses sold in the Billings, Montana area.

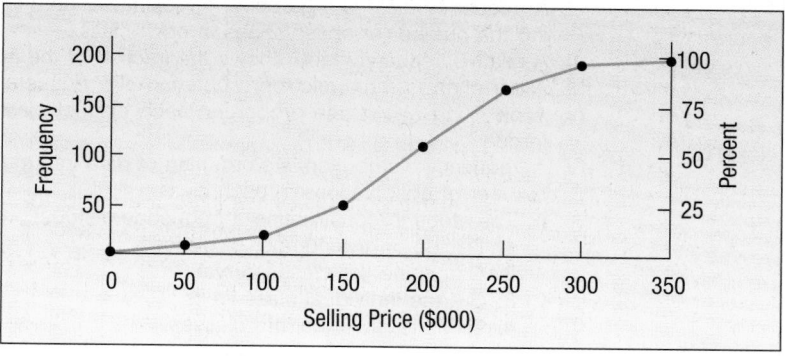

a. How many homes were studied?
b. What is the class interval?
c. One hundred homes sold for less than what amount?
d. About 75 percent of the homes sold for less than what amount?
e. Estimate the number of homes in the $150,000 up to $200,000 class.
f. About how many homes sold for less than $225,000?

21. The frequency distribution representing the number of frequent flier miles accumulated by employees at Brumley Statistical Consulting Company is repeated from Exercise 17.

Frequent Flier Miles (000)	Frequency
0 up to 3	5
3 up to 6	12
6 up to 9	23
9 up to 12	8
12 up to 15	2
Total	50

a. How many employees accumulated less than 3,000 miles?
b. Convert the frequency distribution to a cumulative frequency distribution.
c. Portray the cumulative distribution in the form of a cumulative frequency polygon.
d. Based on the cumulative frequency polygon, about 75 percent of the employees accumulated how many miles or less?

22. The frequency distribution of order lead time at Ecommerce.com from Exercise 18 is repeated below.

Lead Time (days)	Frequency
0 up to 5	6
5 up to 10	7
10 up to 15	12
15 up to 20	8
20 up to 25	7
Total	40

a. How many orders were filled in less than 10 days? In less than 15 days?
b. Convert the frequency distribution to a cumulative frequency distribution.
c. Develop a cumulative frequency polygon.
d. About 60 percent of the orders were filled in less than how many days?

Chapter Summary

I. A frequency table is a grouping of qualitative data into mutually exclusive classes showing the number of observations in each class.
II. A relative frequency table shows the fraction of the number of frequencies in each class.
III. A bar chart is a graphic representation of a frequency table.
IV. A pie chart shows the proportion each distinct class represents of the total number of frequencies.
V. A frequency distribution is a grouping of data into mutually exclusive classes showing the number of observations in each class.
  A. The steps in constructing a frequency distribution are:
   1. Decide on the number of classes.
   2. Determine the class interval.
   3. Set the individual class limits.
   4. Tally the raw data into classes.
   5. Count the number of tallies in each class.
  B. The class frequency is the number of observations in each class.
  C. The class interval is the difference between the limits of two consecutive classes.
  D. The class midpoint is halfway between the limits of consecutive classes.
VI. A relative frequency distribution shows the percent of observations in each class.
VII. There are three methods for graphically portraying a frequency distribution.
  A. A histogram portrays the number of frequencies in each class in the form of a rectangle.
  B. A frequency polygon consists of line segments connecting the points formed by the intersection of the class midpoint and the class frequency.
  C. A cumulative frequency distribution shows the number or percent of observations below given values.

Chapter Exercises

connect™

23. Describe the similarities and differences of qualitative and quantitative variables. Be sure to include:
a. What level of measurement is required for each variable type?
b. Can both types be used to describe both samples and populations?

24. Describe the similarities and differences of a frequency table and a frequency distribution. Be sure to include which requires qualitative data and which requires quantitative data.

25. Alexandra Damonte will be building a new resort in Myrtle Beach, South Carolina. She must decide how to design the resort based on the type of activities that the resort will offer to its customers. A recent poll of 300 potential customers showed the following results about customers' preferences for planned resort activities:

Like planned activities	63
Do not like planned activities	135
Not sure	78
No answer	24

a. What is the table called?
b. Draw a bar chart to portray the survey results.
c. Draw a pie chart for the survey results.
d. If you are preparing to present the results to Ms. Damonte as part of a report, which graph would you prefer to show? Why?

26. Speedy Swift is a package delivery service that serves the greater Atlanta, Georgia metropolitan area. To maintain customer loyalty, one of Speedy Swift's performance objectives is on-time delivery. To monitor its performance, each delivery is measured on the following scale: early (package delivered before the promised time), on-time (package delivered within 5 minutes of the promised time), late (package delivered more than 5 minutes past the promised time), lost (package never delivered). Speedy Swift's objective is to deliver 99 percent of all packages either early or on-time. Another objective is to never lose a package.

Speedy collected the following data for last month's performance:

On-time	On-time	Early	Late	On-time	On-time	On-time	On-time	Late	On-time
Early	On-time	On-time	Early	On-time	On-time	On-time	On-time	On-time	On-time
Early	On-time	Early	On-time	On-time	On-time	Early	On-time	On-time	On-time
Early	On-time	On-time	Late	Early	Early	On-time	On-time	On-time	Early
On-time	Late	Late	On-time	On-time	On-time	On-time	On-time	On-time	On-time
On-time	Late	Early	On-time	Early	On-time	Lost	On-time	On-time	On-time
Early	Early	On-time	On-time	Late	Early	Lost	On-time	On-time	On-time
On-time	On-time	Early	On-time	Early	On-time	Early	On-time	Late	On-time
On-time	Early	On-time	On-time	On-time	Late	On-time	Early	On-time	On-time
On-time	On-time	On-time	On-time	On-time	Early	Early	On-time	On-time	On-time

a. What scale is used to measure delivery performance? What kind of variable is delivery performance?
b. Construct a frequency table for delivery performance for last month.
c. Construct a relative frequency table for delivery performance last month.
d. Construct a bar chart of the frequency table for delivery performance for last month.
e. Construct a pie chart of on-time delivery performance for last month.
f. Analyze the data summaries and write an evaluation of last month's delivery performance as it relates to Speedy Swift's performance objectives. Write a general recommendation for further analysis.

27. A data set consists of 83 observations. How many classes would you recommend for a frequency distribution?

28. A data set consists of 145 observations that range from 56 to 490. What size class interval would you recommend?

29. The following is the number of minutes to commute from home to work for a group of automobile executives.

28	25	48	37	41	19	32	26	16	23	23	29	36
31	26	21	32	25	31	43	35	42	38	33	28	

a. How many classes would you recommend?
b. What class interval would you suggest?

    c. What would you recommend as the lower limit of the first class?
    d. Organize the data into a frequency distribution.
    e. Comment on the shape of the frequency distribution.

30. The following data give the weekly amounts spent on groceries for a sample of households.

$271	$363	$159	$ 76	$227	$337	$295	$319	$250
279	205	279	266	199	177	162	232	303
192	181	321	309	246	278	50	41	335
116	100	151	240	474	297	170	188	320
429	294	570	342	279	235	434	123	325

    a. How many classes would you recommend?
    b. What class interval would you suggest?
    c. What would you recommend as the lower limit of the first class?
    d. Organize the data into a frequency distribution.

31. A social scientist is studying the use of iPods by college students. A sample of 45 students revealed they played the following number of songs yesterday.

4	6	8	7	9	6	3	7	7	6	7	1	4	7	7
4	6	4	10	2	4	6	3	4	6	8	4	3	3	6
8	8	4	6	4	6	5	5	9	6	8	8	6	5	10

    Organize the above information into a frequency distribution.
    a. How many classes would you suggest?
    b. What is the most suitable class interval?
    c. What is the lower limit of the initial class?
    d. Create the frequency distribution.
    e. Describe the profile of the distribution.

32. David Wise handles his own investment portfolio, and has done so for many years. Listed below is the holding time (recorded to the nearest whole year) between purchase and sale for his collection of stocks.

8	8	6	11	11	9	8	5	11	4	8	5	14	7	12	8	6	11	9	7
9	15	8	8	12	5	9	8	5	9	10	11	3	9	8	6				

    a. How many classes would you propose?
    b. What class interval would you suggest?
    c. What quantity would you use for the lower limit of the initial class?
    d. Using your responses to parts (a), (b), and (c), create a frequency distribution.
    e. Identify the appearance of the frequency distribution.

33. You are exploring the music in your iTunes library. The total play counts over the past year for the songs on your "smart playlist" are shown below. Make a frequency distribution of the counts and describe its shape. It is often claimed that a small fraction of a person's songs will account for most of their total plays. Does this seem to be the case here?

128	56	54	91	190	23	160	298	445	50
578	494	37	677	18	74	70	868	108	71
466	23	84	38	26	814	17			

34. The *Journal of Finance* made its content available on the Internet starting in July of 2005. The table below shows the number of times a monthly version was downloaded and the number of articles that were viewed during each month. Suppose you wish to make a frequency distribution of the number of downloads.

312	2,753	2,595	6,057	7,624	6,624	6,362	6,575	7,760	7,085	7,272
5,967	5,256	6,160	6,238	6,709	7,193	5,631	6,490	6,682	7,829	7,091
6,871	6,230	7,253	5,507	5,676	6,974	6,915	4,999	5,689	6,143	7,086

    a. How many classes would you propose?
    b. What class interval would you suggest?
    c. What quantity would you use for the lower limit of the initial class?
    d. Using your responses to parts (a), (b), and (c), create a frequency distribution.
    e. Identify the appearance of the frequency distribution.

35. The following histogram shows the scores on the first exam for a statistics class.

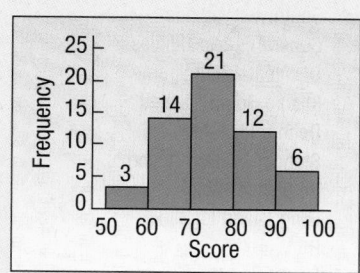

    a. How many students took the exam?
    b. What is the class interval?
    c. What is the class midpoint for the first class?
    d. How many students earned a score of less than 70?

36. The following chart summarizes the selling price of homes sold last month in the Sarasota, Florida, area.

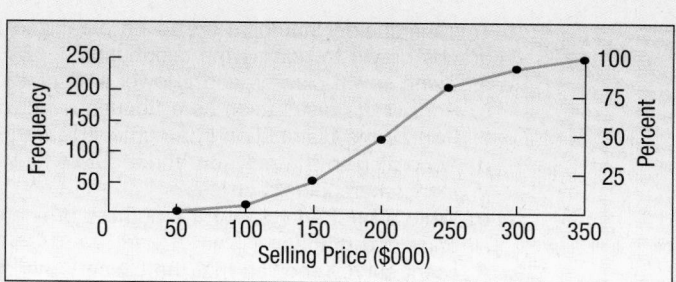

    a. What is the chart called?
    b. How many homes were sold during the last month?
    c. What is the class interval?
    d. About 75 percent of the houses sold for less than what amount?
    e. One hundred seventy-five of the homes sold for less than what amount?

37. A chain of sport shops catering to beginning skiers, headquartered in Aspen, Colorado, plans to conduct a study of how much a beginning skier spends on his or her initial purchase of equipment and supplies. Based on these figures, it wants to explore the possibility of offering combinations, such as a pair of boots and a pair of skis, to induce customers to buy more. A sample of cash register receipts revealed these initial purchases:

$140	$ 82	$265	$168	$ 90	$114	$172	$230	$142
86	125	235	212	171	149	156	162	118
139	149	132	105	162	126	216	195	127
161	135	172	220	229	129	87	128	126
175	127	149	126	121	118	172	126	

  a. Arrive at a suggested class interval. Use six classes, and let the lower limit of the first class be $70.

  b. What would be a better class interval?

  c. Organize the data into a frequency distribution using a lower limit of $80.

  d. Interpret your findings.

38. Following is the number of shareholders for a selected group of large companies (in thousands):

Company	Number of Shareholders (thousands)	Company	Number of Shareholders (thousands)
Southwest Airlines	144	Standard Oil (Indiana)	173
General Public Utilities	177	Home Depot	195
Occidental Petroleum	266	Detroit Edison	220
Middle South Utilities	133	Eastman Kodak	251
DaimlerChrysler	209	Dow Chemical	137
Standard Oil of California	264	Pennsylvania Power	150
Bethlehem Steel	160	American Electric Power	262
Long Island Lighting	143	Ohio Edison	158
RCA	246	Transamerica Corporation	162
Greyhound Corporation	151	Columbia Gas System	165
Pacific Gas & Electric	239	International Telephone & Telegraph	223
Niagara Mohawk Power	204	Union Electric	158
E. I. du Pont de Nemours	204	Virginia Electric and Power	162
Westinghouse Electric	195	Public Service Electric & Gas	225
Union Carbide	176	Consumers Power	161
BankAmerica	175		
Northeast Utilities	200		

The shareholder numbers are to be organized into a frequency distribution and several graphs drawn to portray the distribution.

  a. Using seven classes and a lower limit of 130, construct a frequency distribution.

  b. Portray the distribution as a frequency polygon.

  c. Portray the distribution in a cumulative frequency polygon.

  d. According to the polygon, three out of four (75 percent) of the companies have how many shareholders or less?

  e. Write a brief analysis of the number of shareholders based on the frequency distribution and graphs.

39. A recent survey showed that the typical American car owner spends $2,950 per year on operating expenses. Below is a breakdown of the various expenditure items. Draw an appropriate chart to portray the data and summarize your findings in a brief report.

Expenditure Item	Amount
Fuel	$ 603
Interest on car loan	279
Repairs	930
Insurance and license	646
Depreciation	492
Total	$2,950

40. Midland National Bank selected a sample of 40 student checking accounts. Below are their end-of-the-month balances.

$404	$ 74	$234	$149	$279	$215	$123	$ 55	$ 43	$321
87	234	68	489	57	185	141	758	72	863
703	125	350	440	37	252	27	521	302	127
968	712	503	489	327	608	358	425	303	203

    a. Tally the data into a frequency distribution using $100 as a class interval and $0 as the starting point.
    b. Draw a cumulative frequency polygon.
    c. The bank considers any student with an ending balance of $400 or more a "preferred customer." Estimate the percentage of preferred customers.
    d. The bank is also considering a service charge to the lowest 10 percent of the ending balances. What would you recommend as the cutoff point between those who have to pay a service charge and those who do not?

41. Residents of the state of South Carolina earned a total of $69.5 billion in adjusted gross income. Seventy-three percent of the total was in wages and salaries; 11 percent in dividends, interest, and capital gains; 8 percent in IRAs and taxable pensions; 3 percent in business income pensions; 2 percent in Social Security, and the remaining 3 percent from other sources. Develop a pie chart depicting the breakdown of adjusted gross income. Write a paragraph summarizing the information.

42. A recent study of home technologies reported the number of hours of personal computer usage per week for a sample of 60 persons. Excluded from the study were people who worked out of their home and used the computer as a part of their work.

9.3	5.3	6.3	8.8	6.5	0.6	5.2	6.6	9.3	4.3
6.3	2.1	2.7	0.4	3.7	3.3	1.1	2.7	6.7	6.5
4.3	9.7	7.7	5.2	1.7	8.5	4.2	5.5	5.1	5.6
5.4	4.8	2.1	10.1	1.3	5.6	2.4	2.4	4.7	1.7
2.0	6.7	1.1	6.7	2.2	2.6	9.8	6.4	4.9	5.2
4.5	9.3	7.9	4.6	4.3	4.5	9.2	8.5	6.0	8.1

    a. Organize the data into a frequency distribution. How many classes would you suggest? What value would you suggest for a class interval?
    b. Draw a histogram. Interpret your result.

43. Merrill Lynch recently completed a study regarding the size of online investment portfolios (stocks, bonds, mutual funds, and certificates of deposit) for a sample of clients in the 40- to 50-year-old age group. Listed following is the value of all the investments in thousands of dollars for the 70 participants in the study.

$669.9	$ 7.5	$ 77.2	$ 7.5	$125.7	$516.9	$ 219.9	$645.2
301.9	235.4	716.4	145.3	26.6	187.2	315.5	89.2
136.4	616.9	440.6	408.2	34.4	296.1	185.4	526.3
380.7	3.3	363.2	51.9	52.2	107.5	82.9	63.0
228.6	308.7	126.7	430.3	82.0	227.0	321.1	403.4
39.5	124.3	118.1	23.9	352.8	156.7	276.3	23.5
31.3	301.2	35.7	154.9	174.3	100.6	236.7	171.9
221.1	43.4	212.3	243.3	315.4	5.9	1,002.2	171.7
295.7	437.0	87.8	302.1	268.1	899.5		

    a. Organize the data into a frequency distribution. How many classes would you suggest? What value would you suggest for a class interval?
    b. Draw a histogram. Interpret your result.

44. A total of 5.9 percent of the prime time viewing audience watched shows on ABC, 7.6 percent watched shows on CBS, 5.5 percent on Fox, 6.0 percent on NBC, 2.0 percent on Warner Brothers, and 2.2 percent on UPN. A total of 70.8 percent of the audience watched shows on other cable networks, such as CNN and ESPN. You can find the latest information on TV viewing from the following website: http://tv.zap2it.com/news/ratings. Develop a pie chart or a bar chart to depict this information. Write a paragraph summarizing your findings.

45. The American Heart Association reported the following percentage breakdown of expenses. Draw a pie chart depicting the information. Interpret.

Category	Percent
Research	32.3
Public Health Education	23.5
Community Service	12.6
Fund Raising	12.1
Professional and Educational Training	10.9
Management and General	8.6

46. Annual revenues, by type of tax, for the state of Georgia are as follows. Develop an appropriate chart or graph and write a brief report summarizing the information.

Type of Tax	Amount ($000)
Sales	$2,812,473
Income (Individual)	2,732,045
License	185,198
Corporate	525,015
Property	22,647
Death and Gift	37,326
Total	$6,314,704

47. Annual imports from selected Canadian trading partners are listed below. Develop an appropriate chart or graph and write a brief report summarizing the information.

Partner	Annual Imports ($ millions)
Japan	$9,550
United Kingdom	4,556
South Korea	2,441
China	1,182
Australia	618

48. Farming has changed from the early 1900s. In the early 20th century, machinery gradually replaced animal power. For example, in 1910 U.S. farms used 24.2 million horses and mules and only about 1,000 tractors. By 1960, 4.6 million tractors were used and only 3.2 million horses and mules. In 1920 there were over 6 million farms in the United States. Today there are less than 2 million. Listed below is the number of farms, in thousands, for each of the 50 states. Write a paragraph summarizing your findings.

47	1	8	46	76	26	4	3	39	45
4	21	80	63	100	65	91	29	7	15
7	52	87	39	106	25	55	2	3	8
14	38	59	33	76	71	37	51	1	24
35	86	185	13	7	43	36	20	79	9

49. One of the most popular candies in the United States is M&M's, which are produced by the Mars Company. In the beginning M&M's were all brown; more recently they were produced in red, green, blue, orange, brown, and yellow. You can read about the history of the product, find ideas for baking, purchase the candies in the colors of your school or favorite team, and learn the percent of each color in the standard bags at www.m-ms.com. Recently the purchase of a 14-ounce bag of M&M's Plain had 444 candies with the following breakdown by color: 130 brown, 98 yellow, 96 red, 35 orange, 52 blue, and 33 green. Develop a chart depicting this information and write a paragraph summarizing the results.

50. The following graph shows the total wages paid by software and aircraft companies in the state of Washington from 1997 until 2005. Write a brief report summarizing this information.

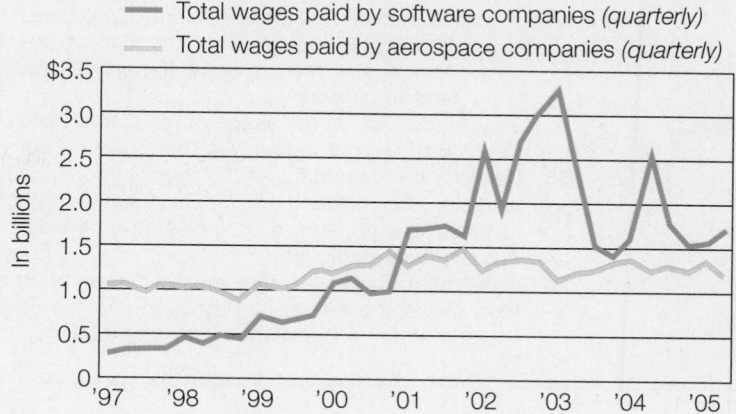

51. A pie chart shows the market shares of cola products. The "slice" for Pepsi-Cola has a central angle of 90 degrees. What is its market share?

52. The number of families who used the Minneapolis YWCA day care service was recorded over a 30-day period. The results are as follows: 31, 49, 19, 62, 24, 45, 23, 51, 55, 60, 40, 35, 54, 26, 57, 37, 43, 65, 18, 41, 50, 56, 4, 54, 39, 52, 35, 51, 63, and 42.
   a. Construct a cumulative frequency distribution of this data.
   b. Sketch a graph of the cumulative frequency polygon.
   c. How many days saw fewer than 30 families utilize the day care center?
   d. How busy were the highest 80 percent of the days?

Data Set Exercises

53. Refer to the Real Estate data at the end of the book, which reports information on homes sold in the Denver, Colorado, area during the last year.
   a. Organize the data on number of bedrooms into a frequency distribution.
      1. What is the typical number of bedrooms?
      2. What are the fewest and the most number of bedrooms offered in the market?
   b. Select an appropriate class interval and organize the selling prices into a frequency distribution.
      1. Around what values do the data tend to cluster?
      2. What is the largest selling price? What is the smallest selling price?
   c. Draw a cumulative frequency distribution based on the frequency distribution developed in part (b).
      1. How many homes sold for less than $200,000?
      2. Estimate the percent of the homes that sold for more than $220,000.
      3. What percent of the homes sold for less than $125,000?
   d. Write a report summarizing the selling prices of the homes.

54. Refer to the Baseball 2007 data, which reports information on the 30 Major League Baseball teams for the 2007 season.
   a. Organize the information on the team salaries into a frequency distribution. Select an appropriate class interval.
      1. What is a typical team salary? What is the range of salaries?
      2. Comment on the shape of the distribution. Does it appear that any of the team salaries are out of line with the others?

    b. Draw a cumulative frequency distribution based on the frequency distribution developed in part (a).

      1. Forty percent of the teams are paying less than what amount in total team salary?

      2. About how many teams have total salaries of less than $80,000,000?

      3. Below what amount do the lowest five teams pay in total salary?

    c. Organize the information on the size of the various stadiums into a frequency distribution.

      1. What is a typical stadium size? Where do the stadium sizes tend to cluster?

      2. Comment on the shape of the distribution. Does it appear that any of the stadium sizes are out of line with the others?

    d. Organize the information on the year in which the 30 major league stadiums were built into a frequency distribution. (You could also create a new variable called "age" by subtracting the year in which the stadium was built from the current year.)

      1. What is the year in which the typical stadium was built? Where do these years tend to cluster?

      2. Comment on the shape of the distribution. Does it appear that any of the stadium ages are out of line with the others? If so, which ones?

55. Refer to the Wage data, which reports information on annual wages for a sample of 100 workers. Also included are variables relating to industry, years of education, and gender for each worker. Draw a bar chart of the variable occupation. Write a brief report summarizing your findings.

56. Refer to the CIA data, which reports demographic and economic information on 46 countries. Develop a frequency distribution for the variable GDP per capita. Summarize your findings. What is the shape of the distribution?

Software Commands

1. The Excel commands for the pie chart on page 25 are:

    a. Set cell *A1* as the active cell and type the words *Use of Sales.* In cells *A2* through *A5* type *Prizes, Education, Bonuses, and Expense.*

    b. Set *B1* as the active cell and type *Amount ($ Millions)* and in cells *B2* through *B5* enter the data. When finished entering data in *B5*, hit the enter button.

    c. From the top row of tabs, select **Insert.** In the Chart tool bar, select **Pie.** Select the top-left **2-D** pie chart. A blank chart will appear.

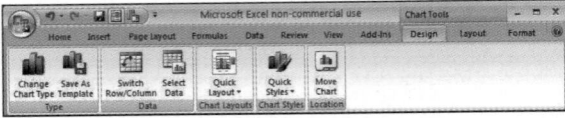

    d. In Excel's top row, a **Chart Tools** tab will appear. Select the **Design** option. Select the **Select Data** option from the tool bar. A **Select Data** window will appear. For the **Chart Data Range,** using the mouse, select all cells from A1 to B5. Click OK.

    e. Click on the pie chart. Right click for the options menu. Select **Add Data Labels.** Click on the pie chart again. Right click for the options menu. Select **Format Data Labels** then uncheck any boxes currently checked in the dialog box. Next select **Category, Percent,** and **Leader Lines.** Then click **Close.**

    f. Double-click on the chart title and rename **Ohio State Lottery Expenses**.

2. The MegaStat commands for the frequency distribution on page 32 are:

    a. Open Excel and from the CD provided, select **Data Sets,** and select the Excel format; go to

Chapter 2, and select **Whitner.** Click on **Mega-Stat, Frequency Distribution,** and select **Quantitative.**

    b. In the dialog box, input the range from *A1:A81,* select **Equal width intervals,** use *3,000* as the interval width, *15,000* as the lower boundary of the first interval, select **Histogram,** and then click **OK.**

3. The Excel commands for the histogram on page 36 are:

    a. In cell A1 indicate that the column of data is the selling price and in B1 that it is the frequency. In cells A2 to A8 insert the midpoints of the selling prices in $000. In B2 to B8 record the class frequencies. When finished entering data in cell B8, hit the enter key.

    b. With your mouse, highlight cells B2 through B8.

    c. From the tabs, select **Insert.** From the Charts, select **Column,** then **2-D column** and pick the first chart type. A graph will appear.

    d. When the graph area is active, a **Chart Tools** tab appears at the top of the screen. Select the **Design** tab, and then select **Data.** Under **Horizontal (Category) Axis Labels,** click **Edit,** then use the mouse to select cells A2 through A8 and click **OK** twice. The horizontal axis now shows the class midpoints.

    e. With the **Chart Tools** displayed at the top, select the **Design** tab. Select **Chart Layout.** Select the

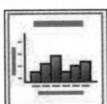

    layout:

    f. With **Chart Tools** displayed at the top, select the **Layout** tab. Double click on the **Chart Title** and type in *Selling price of 80 Vehicles Sold at the Whitner Autoplex Lot.* Next, under the same **Layout** tab, select **Axis Titles**. Using **Primary Vertical Axis Title,** name the vertical axis *Frequency* and delete the words *vertical axis*. Using the **Primary Horizontal Axis Title,** name the horizontal axis *Sales Dollars ($000)*. Next select **Legend** and select **None**.

g. Double click one of the columns in the graph. Then from the Tabs across the top select **Layout**. On the left-hand side of the tool bar click the words **Format Selection**. A dialog box will appear. Under *Series Option*, change the **Gap Width** to 0% by moving the arrow all the way to the left, and then click the **Close** button at the bottom of the dialog box.

Chapter 2   Answers to Self-Review

2–1 **a.** Qualitative data, because the customers' response to the taste test is the name of a beverage.
  b. Frequency table. It shows the number of people who prefer each beverage.
  c.

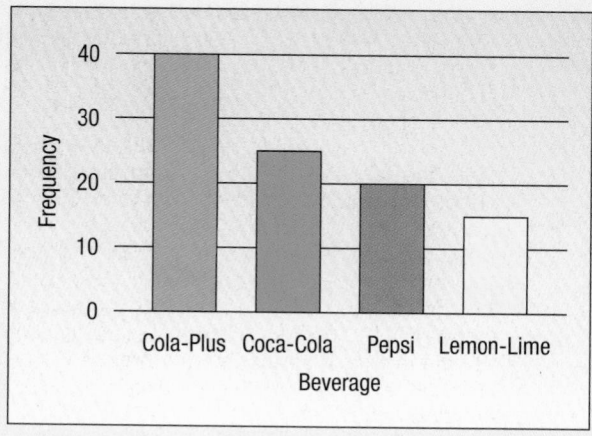

  d.

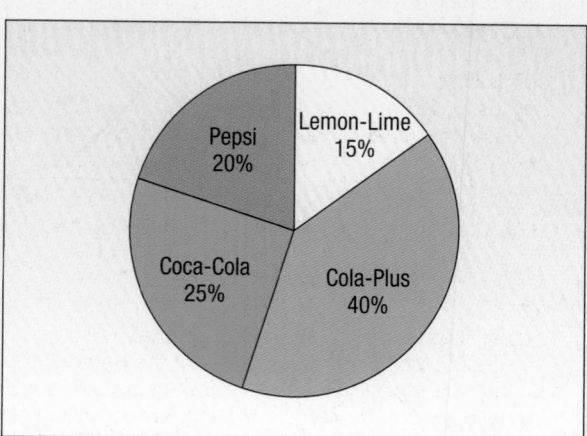

2–2 **a.** The raw data or ungrouped data.
  b.

Commission	Number of Salespeople
$1,400 up to $1,500	2
1,500 up to 1,600	5
1,600 up to 1,700	3
1,700 up to 1,800	1
Total	11

c. Class frequencies.

d. The largest concentration of commissions is $1,500 up to $1,600. The smallest commission is about $1,400 and the largest is about $1,800. The typical amount earned is $15,500.

2–3 **a.** $2^6 = 64 < 73 < 128 = 2^7$. So 7 classes are recommended.

b. The interval width should be at least $(488 - 320)/7 = 24$. Class intervals of 25 or 30 feet are both reasonable.

c. If we use a class interval of 25 feet and begin with a lower limit of 300 feet, eight classes would be necessary. A class interval of 30 feet beginning with 300 feet is also reasonable. This alternative requires only seven classes.

2–4 **a.** 23

b. 28.75%, found by $(23/80) \times 100$

c. 7.5%, found by $(6/80) \times 100$

2–5 **a.**

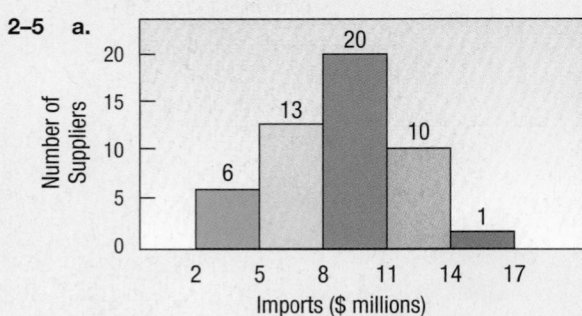

b.

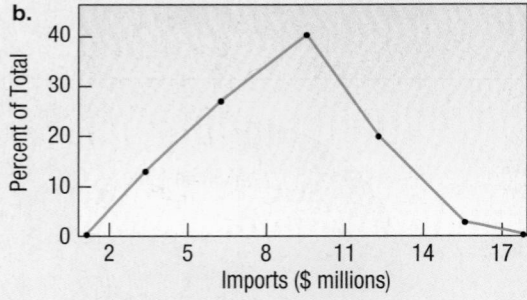

The plots are: (3.5, 12), (6.5, 26), (9.5, 40), (12.5, 20), and (15.5, 2).

c. The smallest annual volume of imports by a supplier is about $2 million, the largest about $17 million. The highest frequency is between $8 million and $11 million.

2–6 **a.** A frequency distribution.

b.

Hourly Wages	Cumulative Number
Less than $8	0
Less than $10	3
Less than $12	10
Less than $14	14
Less than $16	15

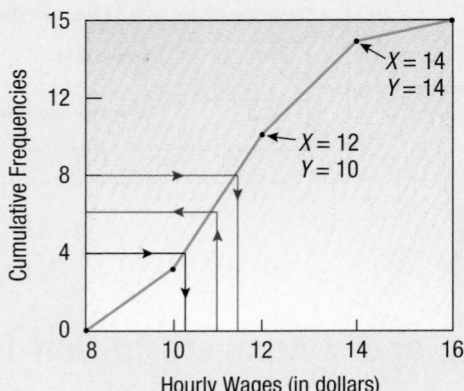

c. About seven employees earn $11.00 or less. About half the employees earn $11.25 or more. About four employees earn $10.25 or less.

Describing Data:

Numerical Measures

U. S. housing prices reached their peak in July of 2006. Based on the data given in the table, showing the ratio of the prices reported in a recent month to the July 2006 figure, find the mean, median, and mode of these statistics. (Exercise 83, Goal 1)

GOALS

When you have completed this chapter you will be able to:

1 Calculate the *arithmetic mean, weighted mean, median, mode,* and *geometric mean.*

2 Explain the characteristics, uses, advantages, and disadvantages of each *measure of location.*

3 Identify the position of the mean, median, and mode for both *symmetric* and *skewed distributions.*

4 Compute and interpret the *range, mean deviation, variance,* and *standard deviation.*

5 Understand the characteristics, uses, advantages, and disadvantages of each *measure of dispersion.*

6 Understand *Chebyshev's theorem* and the *Empirical Rule* as they relate to a set of observations.

Introduction

Chapter 2 began our study of descriptive statistics. To transform a mass of raw data into a meaningful form, we organized quantitative data into a frequency distribution and portrayed it graphically in a histogram. We also looked at other graphical techniques such as pie charts to portray qualitative data and frequency polygons to portray quantitative data.

This chapter is concerned with two numerical ways of describing quantitative data, namely, **measures of location** and **measures of dispersion.** Measures of location are often referred to as **averages.** The purpose of a measure of location is to pinpoint the center of a set of values.

You are familiar with the concept of an average. An average is a measure of location that shows the central value of the data. Averages appear daily on TV, in the newspaper, and other journals. Here are some examples:

- The average U.S. home changes ownership every 11.8 years.
- An American receives an average of 568 pieces of mail per year.
- The average American home has more TV sets than people. There are 2.73 TV sets and 2.55 people in the typical home.
- The average hourly earnings for civilian workers in the United States is $19.29 per hour.
- The average American couple spends $28,732 for their wedding, while their budget is 50 percent less. This does not include the cost of a honeymoon or engagement ring.
- In Chicago the mean high temperature is 84 degrees in July and 31 degrees in January. The mean amount of precipitation is 3.80 inches in July and 1.90 inches in January.

If we consider only the measures of location in a set of data, or if we compare several sets of data using central values, we may draw an erroneous conclusion. In addition to the measures of location, we should consider the **dispersion**—often called the *variation* or the *spread*—in the data. As an illustration, suppose the average annual income of executives for Internet-related companies is $80,000, and the average income for executives in pharmaceutical firms is also $80,000. If we looked only at the average incomes, we might wrongly conclude that the two salary distributions are identical or nearly identical. A look at the salary ranges indicates that this conclusion is not correct. The salaries for the executives in the Internet firms range from $70,000 to $90,000, but salaries for the marketing executives in pharmaceuticals range from $40,000 to $120,000. Thus, we conclude that although the average salaries are the same for the two industries, there is much more spread or dispersion in salaries for the pharmaceutical executives. To describe the dispersion we will consider the range, the mean deviation, the variance, and the standard deviation.

We begin by discussing measures of location. There is not just one measure of location; in fact, there are many. We will consider five: the arithmetic mean, the weighted mean, the median, the mode, and the geometric mean. The arithmetic mean is the most widely used and widely reported measure of location. We study the mean as both a population parameter and a sample statistic.

The Population Mean

Many studies involve all the values in a population. For example, there are 39 exits on I-75 through the state of Kentucky. The mean distance between these state exits is 4.76 miles. This is an example of a population parameter because we have studied the distance between *all* the exits. There are 12 sales associates employed at the Reynolds Road outlet of Carpets by Otto. The mean amount of commission they earned last month was $1,345. This is a population value because we considered the commission of *all* the sales associates. Other examples of a population mean would be: the mean closing price for Johnson & Johnson stock for the last 5 days is $61.75; the mean annual rate of return for the last 10 years for Berger Funds is 8.67 percent; and the mean number of hours of overtime worked last week by the six welders in the welding department of Butts Welding, Inc., is 6.45 hours.

For raw data, that is, data that has not been grouped in a frequency distribution, the population mean is the sum of all the values in the population divided by the number of values in the population. To find the population mean, we use the following formula.

$$\text{Population mean} = \frac{\text{Sum of all the values in the population}}{\text{Number of values in the population}}$$

Instead of writing out in words the full directions for computing the population mean (or any other measure), it is more convenient to use the shorthand symbols of mathematics. The mean of a population using mathematical symbols is:

POPULATION MEAN	$\mu = \dfrac{\Sigma X}{N}$	[3–1]

where:
μ represents the population mean. It is the Greek lowercase letter "mu."
N is the number of values in the population.
X represents any particular value.
Σ is the Greek capital letter "sigma" and indicates the operation of adding.
ΣX is the sum of the X values in the population.

Any measurable characteristic of a population is called a **parameter.** The mean of a population is a parameter.

PARAMETER A characteristic of a population.

Example

There are 12 automobile manufacturing companies in the United States. Listed below is the number of patents granted by the United States government to each company in a recent year.

Company	Number of Patents Granted	Company	Number of Patents Granted
General Motors	511	Mazda	210
Nissan	385	Chrysler	97
Daimler	275	Porsche	50
Toyota	257	Mitsubishi	36
Honda	249	Volvo	23
Ford	234	BMW	13

Is this information a sample or a population? What is the arithmetic mean number of patents granted?

Solution

This is a population because we are considering all the automobile manufacturing companies obtaining patents. We add the number of patents for each of the 12 companies. The total number of patents for the 12 companies is 2,340. To find the arithmetic mean, we divide this total by 12. So the arithmetic mean is 195, found by 2,340/12. From formula (3–1):

$$\mu = \frac{511 + 385 + \cdots + 13}{12} = \frac{2340}{12} = 195$$

How do we interpret the value of 195? The typical number of patents received by an automobile manufacturing company is 195. Because we considered all the companies receiving patents, this value is a population parameter.

The Sample Mean

As explained in Chapter 1, we often select a sample from the population to find something about a specific characteristic of the population. The quality assurance department, for example, needs to be assured that the ball bearings being produced have an acceptable outside diameter. It would be very expensive and time consuming to check the outside diameter of all the bearings produced. Therefore, a sample of five bearings is selected and the mean outside diameter of the five bearings is calculated to estimate the mean diameter of all the bearings.

For raw data, that is, ungrouped data, *the mean is the sum of all the sampled values divided by the total number of sampled values*. To find the mean for a sample:

Mean of ungrouped sample data

$$\text{Sample mean} = \frac{\text{Sum of all the values in the sample}}{\text{Number of values in the sample}}$$

The mean of a sample and the mean of a population are computed in the same way, but the shorthand notation used is different. The formula for the mean of a *sample* is:

SAMPLE MEAN	$\overline{X} = \dfrac{\Sigma X}{n}$	[3–2]

where:
    $\overline{X}$ is the sample mean. It is read "X bar."
    n is the number of values in the sample.

The mean of a sample, or any other measure based on sample data, is called a **statistic.** If the mean outside diameter of a sample of five ball bearings is 0.625 inches, this is an example of a statistic.

STATISTIC A characteristic of a sample.

Example

SunCom is studying the number of minutes used by clients in a particular cell phone rate plan. A random sample of 12 clients showed the following number of minutes used last month.

90	77	94	89	119	112
91	110	92	100	113	83

What is the arithmetic mean number of minutes used?

Solution	Using formula (3–2), the sample mean is:

$$\text{Sample mean} = \frac{\text{Sum of all values in the sample}}{\text{Number of values in the sample}}$$

$$\bar{X} = \frac{\Sigma X}{n} = \frac{90 + 77 + \cdots + 83}{12} = \frac{1170}{12} = 97.5$$

The arithmetic mean number of minutes used last month by the sample of cell phone users is 97.5 minutes.

Properties of the Arithmetic Mean

The arithmetic mean is a widely used measure of location. It has several important properties:

1. **Every set of interval- or ratio-level data has a mean.** Recall from Chapter 1 that ratio-level data include such data as ages, incomes, and weights, with the distance between numbers being constant.
2. **All the values are included in computing the mean.**
3. **The mean is unique.** That is, there is only one mean in a set of data. Later in the chapter we will discover an average that might appear twice, or more than twice, in a set of data.
4. **The sum of the deviations of each value from the mean is zero.** Expressed symbolically:

$$\Sigma(X - \bar{X}) = 0$$

As an example, the mean of 3, 8, and 4 is 5. Then:

$$\Sigma(X - \bar{X}) = (3 - 5) + (8 - 5) + (4 - 5)$$
$$= -2 + 3 - 1$$
$$= 0$$

Mean as a balance point

Thus, we can consider the mean as a balance point for a set of data. To illustrate, we have a long board with the numbers 1, 2, 3, ..., 9 evenly spaced on it. Suppose three bars of equal weight were placed on the board at numbers 3, 4, and 8, and the balance point was set at 5, the mean of the three numbers. We would find that the board is balanced perfectly! The deviations below the mean (−3) are equal to the deviations above the mean (+3). Shown schematically:

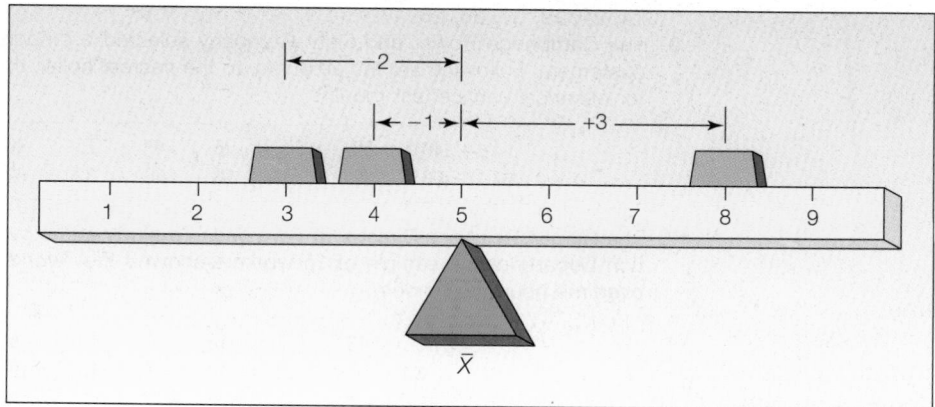

Mean unduly affected by unusually large or small values

The mean does have a weakness. Recall that the mean uses the value of every item in a sample, or population, in its computation. If one or two of these values are either extremely large or extremely small compared to the majority of data, the mean might not be an appropriate average to represent the data. For example, suppose the annual incomes of a small group of stockbrokers at Merrill Lynch are $62,900, $61,600, $62,500, $60,800, and $1,200,000. The mean income is $289,560. Obviously, it is not representative of this group, because all but one broker has an income in the $60,000 to $63,000 range. One income ($1.2 million) is unduly affecting the mean.

Self-Review 3–1

1. The annual incomes of a sample of middle-management employees at Westinghouse are: $62,900, $69,100, $58,300, and $76,800.
   (a) Give the formula for the sample mean.
   (b) Find the sample mean.
   (c) Is the mean you computed in (b) a statistic or a parameter? Why?
   (d) What is your best estimate of the population mean?
2. All the students in advanced Computer Science 411 are a population. Their course grades are 92, 96, 61, 86, 79, and 84.
   (a) Give the formula for the population mean.
   (b) Compute the mean course grade.
   (c) Is the mean you computed in (b) a statistic or a parameter? Why?

Exercises

connect™

The answers to the odd-numbered exercises are at the end of the book.

1. Compute the mean of the following population values: 6, 3, 5, 7, 6.
2. Compute the mean of the following population values: 7, 5, 7, 3, 7, 4.
3. a. Compute the mean of the following sample values: 5, 9, 4, 10.
   b. Show that $\Sigma(X - \bar{X}) = 0$.
4. a. Compute the mean of the following sample values: 1.3, 7.0, 3.6, 4.1, 5.0.
   b. Show that $\Sigma(X - \bar{X}) = 0$.
5. Compute the mean of the following sample values: 16.25, 12.91, 14.58.
6. Compute the mean hourly wage paid to carpenters who earned the following hourly wages: $15.40, $20.10, $18.75, $22.76, $30.67, $18.00.

For Exercises 7–10, (a) compute the arithmetic mean and (b) indicate whether it is a statistic or a parameter.

7. There are 10 salespeople employed by Midtown Ford. The number of new cars sold last month by the respective salespeople were: 15, 23, 4, 19, 18, 10, 10, 8, 28, 19.
8. The accounting department at a mail-order company counted the following numbers of incoming calls per day to the company's toll-free number during the first 7 days in May: 14, 24, 19, 31, 36, 26, 17.
9. The Cambridge Power and Light Company selected a random sample of 20 residential customers. Following are the amounts, to the nearest dollar, the customers were charged for electrical service last month:

54	48	58	50	25	47	75	46	60	70
67	68	39	35	56	66	33	62	65	67

10. The Human Relations Director at Ford began a study of the overtime hours in the Inspection Department. A sample of 15 workers showed they worked the following number of overtime hours last month.

13	13	12	15	7	15	5	12
6	7	12	10	9	13	12	

11. AAA Heating and Air Conditioning completed 30 jobs last month with a mean revenue of $5,430 per job. The president wants to know the total revenue for the month. Based on the limited information, can you compute the total revenue? What is it?

12. A large pharmaceutical company hires business administration graduates to sell its products. The company is growing rapidly and dedicates only one day of sales training for new salespeople. The company's goal for new salespeople is $10,000 per month. The goal is based on the current mean sales for the entire company, which is $10,000 per month. After reviewing the retention rates of new employees, the company finds that only 1 in 10 new employees stays longer than three months. Comment on using the current mean sales per month as a sales goal for new employees. Why do new employees leave the company?

The Weighted Mean

The weighted mean is a special case of the arithmetic mean. It occurs when there are several observations of the same value. To explain, suppose the nearby Wendy's Restaurant sold medium, large, and Biggie-sized soft drinks for $.90, $1.25, and $1.50, respectively. Of the last 10 drinks sold, 3 were medium, 4 were large, and 3 were Biggie-sized. To find the mean price of the last 10 drinks sold, we could use formula (3–2).

$$\overline{X} = \frac{\$.90 + \$.90 + \$.90 + \$1.25 + \$1.25 + \$1.25 + \$1.25 + \$1.50 + \$1.50 + \$1.50}{10}$$

$$\overline{X} = \frac{\$12.20}{10} = \$1.22$$

The mean selling price of the last 10 drinks is $1.22.

An easier way to find the mean selling price is to determine the weighted mean. That is, we multiply each observation by the number of times it happens. We will refer to the weighted mean as $\overline{X}_w$. This is read "X bar sub w."

$$\overline{X}_w = \frac{3(\$0.90) + 4(\$1.25) + 3(\$1.50)}{10} = \frac{\$12.20}{10} = \$1.22$$

In this case the weights are frequency counts. However, any measure of importance could be used as a weight. In general the weighted mean of a set of numbers designated $X_1, X_2, X_3, \ldots, X_n$ with the corresponding weights $w_1, w_2, w_3, \ldots, w_n$ is computed by:

WEIGHTED MEAN $$\overline{X}_w = \frac{w_1 X_1 + w_2 X_2 + w_3 X_3 + \cdots + w_n X_n}{w_1 + w_2 + w_3 + \cdots + w_n}$$ [3–3]

This may be shortened to:

$$\overline{X}_w = \frac{\Sigma(wX)}{\Sigma w}$$

Note that the denominator of a weighted mean is always the sum of the weights.

Example

The Carter Construction Company pays its hourly employees $16.50, $19.00, or $25.00 per hour. There are 26 hourly employees, 14 of which are paid at the $16.50 rate, 10 at the $19.00 rate, and 2 at the $25.00 rate. What is the mean hourly rate paid the 26 employees?

Solution

To find the mean hourly rate, we multiply each of the hourly rates by the number of employees earning that rate. From formula (3–3), the mean hourly rate is

$$\overline{X}_w = \frac{14(\$16.50) + 10(\$19.00) + 2(\$25.00)}{14 + 10 + 2} = \frac{\$471.00}{26} = \$18.1154$$

The weighted mean hourly wage is rounded to $18.12.

Springers sold 95 Antonelli men's suits for the regular price of $400. For the spring sale the suits were reduced to $200 and 126 were sold. At the final clearance, the price was reduced to $100 and the remaining 79 suits were sold.
(a) What was the weighted mean price of an Antonelli suit?
(b) Springers paid $200 a suit for the 300 suits. Comment on the store's profit per suit if a salesperson receives a $25 commission for each one sold.

Exercises

connect™

13. In June an investor purchased 300 shares of Oracle (an information technology company) stock at $20 per share. In August she purchased an additional 400 shares at $25 per share. In November she purchased an additional 400 shares, but the stock declined to $23 per share. What is the weighted mean price per share?
14. The Bookstall, Inc., is a specialty bookstore concentrating on used books sold via the Internet. Paperbacks are $1.00 each, and hardcover books are $3.50. Of the 50 books sold last Tuesday morning, 40 were paperback and the rest were hardcover. What was the weighted mean price of a book?
15. The Loris Healthcare System employs 200 persons on the nursing staff. Fifty are nurse's aides, 50 are practical nurses, and 100 are registered nurses. Nurse's aides receive $8 an hour, practical nurses $15 an hour, and registered nurses $24 an hour. What is the weighted mean hourly wage?
16. Andrews and Associates specialize in corporate law. They charge $100 an hour for researching a case, $75 an hour for consultations, and $200 an hour for writing a brief. Last week one of the associates spent 10 hours consulting with her client, 10 hours researching the case, and 20 hours writing the brief. What was the weighted mean hourly charge for her legal services?

The Median

We have stressed that, for data containing one or two very large or very small values, the arithmetic mean may not be representative. The center for such data can be better described by a measure of location called the **median.**

To illustrate the need for a measure of location other than the arithmetic mean, suppose you are seeking to buy a condominium in Palm Aire. Your real estate agent says that the typical price of the units currently available is $110,000. Would you still want to look? If you had budgeted your maximum purchase price at $75,000, you might think they are out of your price range. However, checking the prices of the individual units might change your mind. They are $60,000, $65,000, $70,000, and $80,000, and a superdeluxe penthouse costs $275,000. The arithmetic mean price is $110,000, as the real estate agent reported, but one price ($275,000) is pulling the arithmetic mean upward, causing it to be an unrepresentative average. It does seem that a price around $70,000 is a more typical or representative average, and it is. In cases such as this, the median provides a more valid measure of location.

MEDIAN The midpoint of the values after they have been ordered from the smallest to the largest, or the largest to the smallest.

The median price of the units available is $70,000. To determine this, we order the prices from low ($60,000) to high ($275,000) and select the middle value ($70,000). For the median, the data must be at least an ordinal level of measurement.

Prices Ordered from Low to High		Prices Ordered from High to Low
$ 60,000		$275,000
65,000		80,000
70,000	← Median →	70,000
80,000		65,000
275,000		60,000

Median less affected by extreme values

Note that there is the same number of prices below the median of $70,000 as above it. The median is, therefore, unaffected by extremely low or high prices. Had the highest price been $90,000, or $300,000, or even $1 million, the median price would still be $70,000. Likewise, had the lowest price been $20,000 or $50,000, the median price would still be $70,000.

In the previous illustration there is an *odd* number of observations (five). How is the median determined for an *even* number of observations? As before, the observations are ordered. Then by convention to obtain a unique value we calculate the mean of the two middle observations. So for an even number of observations, the median may not be one of the given values.

Example

The three-year annualized total returns of the six top-performing diversified mutual funds are listed below. What is the median annualized return?

Solution

Name of Fund	Annualized Total Return
Artisian Mid Cap	42.10%
Clipper	15.50
Fidelity Advisor Mid-Cap	27.58
Fidelity Mid-Cap Stock	28.64
Smith Barney Aggressive	41.77
Van Kampen Comstock	16.97

Note that the number of returns is *even* (6). As before, first order the returns from low to high. Then identify the two middle returns. The arithmetic mean of the two middle observations gives us the median return. Arranging from low to high:

Clipper	15.50%	
Van Kampen Comstock	16.97	
Fidelity Advisor Mid-Cap	27.58	56.22/2 =
Fidelity Mid-Cap Stock	28.64	28.11 percent
Smith Barney Aggressive	41.77	
Artisian Mid Cap	42.10	

Notice that the median is not one of the values. Also, half of the returns are below the median and half are above it.

The major properties of the median are:

1. **It is not affected by extremely large or small values.** Therefore the median is a valuable measure of location when such values do occur.

Median can be determined for all levels of data except nominal

2. **It can be computed for ordinal-level data or higher.** Recall from Chapter 1 that ordinal-level data can be ranked from low to high—such as the responses "excellent," "very good," "good," "fair," and "poor" to a question on a marketing survey. To use a simple illustration, suppose five people rated a new fudge bar. One person thought it was excellent, one rated it very good, one called it good, one rated it fair, and one considered it poor. The median response is "good." Half of the responses are above "good"; the other half are below it.

The Mode

The **mode** is another measure of location.

> **MODE** The value of the observation that appears most frequently.

The mode is especially useful in summarizing nominal-level data. As an example of its use for nominal-level data, a company has developed five bath oils. The bar chart in Chart 3–1 shows the results of a marketing survey designed to find which bath oil consumers prefer. The largest number of respondents favored Lamoure, as evidenced by the highest bar. Thus, Lamoure is the mode.

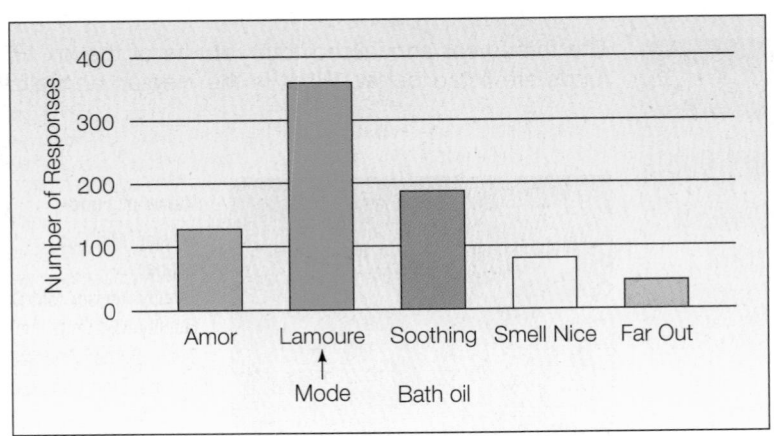

CHART 3–1 Number of Respondents Favoring Various Bath Oils

Example	The annual salaries of quality-control managers in selected states are shown below. What is the modal annual salary?

State	Salary	State	Salary	State	Salary
Arizona	$35,000	Illinois	$58,000	Ohio	$50,000
California	49,100	Louisiana	60,000	Tennessee	60,000
Colorado	60,000	Maryland	60,000	Texas	71,400
Florida	60,000	Massachusetts	40,000	West Virginia	60,000
Idaho	40,000	New Jersey	65,000	Wyoming	55,000

Solution	A perusal of the salaries reveals that the annual salary of $60,000 appears more often (six times) than any other salary. The mode is, therefore, $60,000.

In summary, we can determine the mode for all levels of data—nominal, ordinal, interval, and ratio. The mode also has the advantage of not being affected by extremely high or low values.

Disadvantages of the mode

The mode does have disadvantages, however, that cause it to be used less frequently than the mean or median. For many sets of data, there is no mode because no value appears more than once. For example, there is no mode for this set of price data: $19, $21, $23, $20, and $18. Since every value is different, however, it could be argued that every value is the mode. Conversely, for some data sets there is more than one mode. Suppose the ages of the individuals in a stock investment club are 22, 26, 27, 27, 31, 35, and 35. Both the ages 27 and 35 are modes. Thus, this grouping of ages is referred to as *bimodal* (having two modes). One would question the use of two modes to represent the location of this set of age data.

Self-Review 3–3

1. A sample of single persons in Towson, Texas, receiving Social Security payments revealed these monthly benefits: $852, $598, $580, $1,374, $960, $878, and $1,130.
   (a) What is the median monthly benefit?
   (b) How many observations are below the median? Above it?
2. The number of work stoppages in the automobile industry for selected months are 6, 0, 10, 14, 8, and 0.
   (a) What is the median number of stoppages?
   (b) How many observations are below the median? Above it?
   (c) What is the modal number of work stoppages?

Exercises

connect™

17. What would you report as the modal value for a set of observations if there were a total of:
    a. 10 observations and no two values were the same?
    b. 6 observations and they were all the same?
    c. 6 observations and the values were 1, 2, 3, 3, 4, and 4?

For Exercises 18–20, determine the (a) mean, (b) median, and (c) mode.

18. The following is the number of oil changes for the last 7 days at the Jiffy Lube located at the corner of Elm Street and Pennsylvania Avenue.

41	15	39	54	31	15	33

19. The following is the percent change in net income from last year to this year for a sample of 12 construction companies in Denver.

5	1	−10	−6	5	12	7	8	2	5	−1	11

20. The following are the ages of the 10 people in the video arcade at the Southwyck Shopping Mall at 10 A.M.

12	8	17	6	11	14	8	17	10	8

21. Several indicators of long-term economic growth in the United States are listed below.

Economic Indicator	Percent Change	Economic Indicator	Percent Change
Inflation	4.5%	Real GNP	2.9%
Exports	4.7	Investment (residential)	3.6
Imports	2.3	Investment (nonresidential)	2.1
Real disposable income	2.9	Productivity (total)	1.4
Consumption	2.7	Productivity (manufacturing)	5.2

a. What is the median percent change?
b. What is the modal percent change?

22. The total automobile sales (in millions of dollars) in the United States for the last 14 years are listed below. During this period, what was the median number of automobiles sold? What is the mode?

| 9.0 | 8.5 | 8.0 | 9.1 | 10.3 | 11.0 | 11.5 | 10.3 | 10.5 | 9.8 | 9.3 | 8.2 | 8.2 | 8.5 |

23. The accounting firm of Rowatti and Koppel specializes in income tax returns for self-employed professionals, such as physicians, dentists, architects, and lawyers. The firm employs 11 accountants who prepare the returns. For last year the number of returns prepared by each accountant was:

| 58 | 75 | 31 | 58 | 46 | 65 | 60 | 71 | 45 | 58 | 80 |

Find the mean, median, and mode for the number of returns prepared by each accountant. If you could report only one, which measure of location would you recommend reporting?

24. The demand for the video games provided by Mid-Tech Video Games, Inc., has exploded in the last several years. Hence, the owner needs to hire several new technical people to keep up with the demand. Mid-Tech gives each applicant a special test that Dr. McGraw, the designer of the test, believes is closely related to the ability to create video games. For the general population the mean on this test is 100. Below are the scores on this test for the applicants.

| 95 | 105 | 120 | 81 | 90 | 115 | 99 | 100 | 130 | 10 |

The president is interested in the overall quality of the job applicants based on this test. Compute the mean and the median score for the ten applicants. What would you report to the president? Does it seem that the applicants are better than the general population?

Software Solution

We can use a statistical software package to find many measures of location.

Example

Table 2–4 on page 28 shows the prices of the 80 vehicles sold last month at Whitner Autoplex in Raytown, Missouri. Determine the mean and the median selling price.

Solution

The mean and the median selling prices are reported in the following Excel output. (Remember: The instructions to create the output appear in the **Software Commands** section at the end of the chapter.) There are 80 vehicles in the study. So the calculations with a calculator would be tedious and prone to error.

Whitner Mean Median

	A	B	C	D	E	F	G	H
1	Price	Price($000)	Age	Type			Price	
2	23197	23.197	46	0				
3	23372	23.372	48	0		Mean	23218.1625	
4	20454	20.454	40	1		Standard Error	486.8409474	
5	23591	23.591	40	0		Median	22831	
6	26651	26.651	46	1		Mode	20642	
7	27453	27.453	37	1		Standard Deviation	4354.43781	
8	17266	17.266	32	1		Sample Variance	18961128.64	
9	18021	18.021	29	1		Kurtosis	0.5433087	
10	28683	28.683	38	1		Skewness	0.72681585	
11	30872	30.872	43	0		Range	20379	
12	19587	19.587	32	0		Minimum	15546	
13	23169	23.169	47	0		Maximum	35925	
14	35851	35.851	56	0		Sum	1857453	
15	19251	19.251	42	1		Count	80	
16	20047	20.047	28	1				

The mean selling price is $23,218 and the median is $22,831. These two values are less than $400 apart. So either value is reasonable. We can also see from the Excel output that there were 80 vehicles sold and their total price is $1,857,453. We will describe the meaning of standard error, standard deviation, and other measures later.

What can we conclude? The typical vehicle sold for about $23,000. Ms. Ball of AutoUSA might use this value in her revenue projections. For example, if the dealership could increase the number sold in a month from 80 to 90, this would result in an additional estimated $230,000 of revenue, found by 10 × $23,000.

The Relative Positions
of the Mean, Median, and Mode

For a symmetric, mound-shaped distribution, mean, median, and mode are equal.

Refer to the histogram in Chart 3–2. It is a symmetric distribution, which is also mound-shaped. This distribution *has the same shape on either side of the center*. If the polygon were folded in half, the two halves would be identical. For any symmetric distribution, the mode, median, and mean are located at the center and are always equal. They are all equal to 20 years in Chart 3–2. We should point out that there are symmetric distributions that are not mound-shaped.

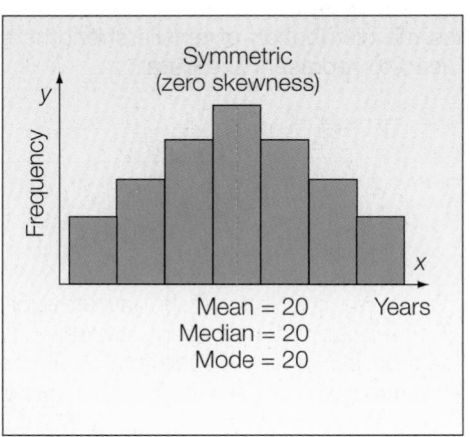

CHART 3–2 A Symmetric Distribution

The number of years corresponding to the highest point of the curve is the *mode* (20 years). Because the distribution is symmetrical, the *median* corresponds to the point where the distribution is cut in half (20 years). The total number of frequencies representing many years is offset by the total number representing few years, resulting in an *arithmetic mean* of 20 years. Logically, any of the three measures would be appropriate to represent the distribution's center.

A skewed distribution is not symmetrical.

If a distribution is nonsymmetrical, or **skewed,** the relationship among the three measures changes. In a **positively skewed distribution,** the arithmetic mean is the largest of the three measures. Why? Because the mean is influenced more than the median or mode by a few extremely high values. The median is generally the next largest measure in a positively skewed frequency distribution. The mode is the smallest of the three measures.

If the distribution is highly skewed, such as the weekly incomes in Chart 3–3, the mean would not be a good measure to use. The median and mode would be more representative.

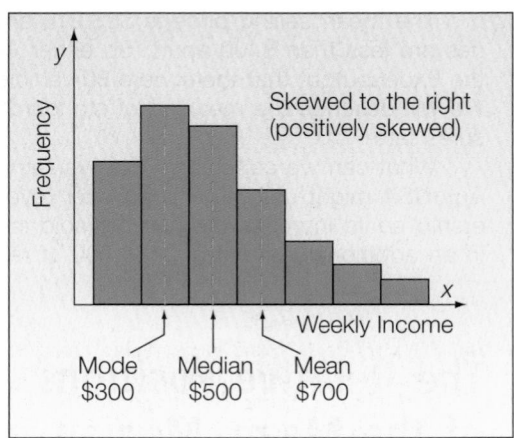

CHART 3–3 A Positively Skewed Distribution

Conversely, if a distribution is **negatively skewed,** the mean is the lowest of the three measures. The mean is, of course, influenced by a few extremely low observations. The median is greater than the arithmetic mean, and the modal value is the largest of the three measures. Again, if the distribution is highly skewed, such as the distribution of tensile strengths shown in Chart 3–4, the mean should not be used to represent the data.

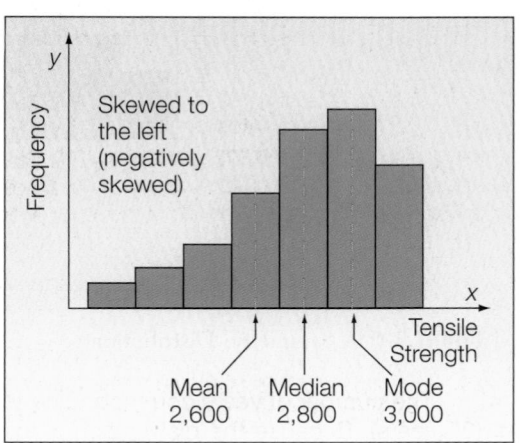

CHART 3–4 A Negatively Skewed Distribution

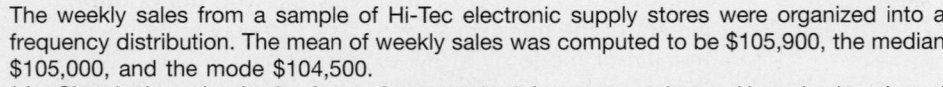

Self-Review 3–4   The weekly sales from a sample of Hi-Tec electronic supply stores were organized into a frequency distribution. The mean of weekly sales was computed to be $105,900, the median $105,000, and the mode $104,500.
(a) Sketch the sales in the form of a smoothed frequency polygon. Note the location of the mean, median, and mode on the X-axis.
(b) Is the distribution symmetrical, positively skewed, or negatively skewed? Explain.

Exercises

connect

25. The unemployment rate in the state of Alaska by month is given in the table below:

Jan	Feb	Mar	Apr	May	Jun	Jul	Aug	Sep	Oct	Nov	Dec
8.7	8.8	8.7	7.8	7.3	7.8	6.6	6.5	6.5	6.8	7.3	7.6

  a. What is the arithmetic mean of the Alaska unemployment rates?
  b. Find the median and the mode for the unemployment rates.
  c. Compute the arithmetic mean and median for just the winter (Dec–Mar) months. Is it much different?

26. Big Orange Trucking is designing an information system for use in "in-cab" communications. It must summarize data from eight sites throughout a region to describe typical conditions. Compute an appropriate measure of central location for each of the three variables shown in the table below:

City	Wind Direction	Temperature	Pavement
Anniston, AL	West	89	Dry
Atlanta, GA	Northwest	86	Wet
Augusta, GA	Southwest	92	Wet
Birmingham, AL	South	91	Dry
Jackson, MS	Southwest	92	Dry
Meridian, MS	South	92	Trace
Monroe, LA	Southwest	93	Wet
Tuscaloosa, AL	Southwest	93	Trace

The Geometric Mean

The geometric mean is never greater than the arithmetic mean.

The geometric mean is useful in finding the average change of percentages, ratios, indexes, or growth rates over time. It has a wide application in business and economics because we are often interested in finding the percentage changes in sales, salaries, or economic figures, such as the Gross Domestic Product, which compound or build on each other. The geometric mean of a set of n positive numbers is defined as the nth root of the product of n values. The formula for the geometric mean is written:

GEOMETRIC MEAN
$$GM = \sqrt[n]{(X_1)(X_2) \cdots (X_n)}$$ **[3–4]**

The geometric mean will always be less than or equal to (never more than) the arithmetic mean. Also all the data values must be positive.

As an example of the geometric mean, suppose you receive a 5 percent increase in salary this year and a 15 percent increase next year. The average annual percent increase is 9.886, not 10.0. Why is this so? We begin by calculating the geometric mean. Recall, for example, that a 5 percent increase in salary is 105 percent. We will write it as 1.05.

$$GM = \sqrt{(1.05)(1.15)} = 1.09886$$

This can be verified by assuming that your monthly earning was $3,000 to start and you received two increases of 5 percent and 15 percent.

$$Raise\ 1 = \$3,000\ (.05) = \$150.00$$
$$Raise\ 2 = \$3,150\ (.15) = \underline{472.50}$$
$$Total \qquad\qquad \$622.50$$

Your total salary increase is $622.50. This is equivalent to:

$$\$3,000.00 \ (.09886) = \$296.58$$

$$\$3,296.58 \ (.09886) = \underline{\ 325.90\ }$$

$622.48 is about $622.50

The following example shows the geometric mean of several percentages.

Example

The return on investment earned by Atkins Construction Company for four successive years was: 30 percent, 20 percent, −40 percent, and 200 percent. What is the geometric mean rate of return on investment?

Solution

The number 1.3 represents the 30 percent return on investment, which is the "original" investment of 1.0 plus the "return" of 0.3. The number 0.6 represents the loss of 40 percent, which is the original investment of 1.0 less the loss of 0.4. This calculation assumes the total return each period is reinvested or becomes the base for the next period. In other words, the base for the second period is 1.3 and the base for the third period is (1.3)(1.2) and so forth.

Then the geometric mean rate of return is 29.4 percent, found by

$$GM = \sqrt[n]{(X_1)(X_2) \cdots (X_n)} = \sqrt[4]{(1.3)(1.2)(0.6)(3.0)} = \sqrt[4]{2.808} = 1.294$$

The geometric mean is the fourth root of 2.808. So, the average rate of return (compound annual growth rate) is 29.4 percent.

Notice also that if you compute the arithmetic mean [(30 + 20 − 40 + 200)/4 = 52.5], you would have a much larger number, which would overstate the true rate of return!

A second application of the geometric mean is to find an average percent change over a period of time. For example, if you earned $30,000 in 1997 and $50,000 in 2007, what is your annual rate of increase over the period? It is 5.24 percent. The rate of increase is determined from the following formula.

RATE OF INCREASE OVER TIME	$$GM = \sqrt[n]{\dfrac{\text{Value at end of period}}{\text{Value at start of period}}} - 1$$	**[3–5]**

In the above box n is the number of periods. An example will show the details of finding the average annual percent increase.

Example

During the decade of the 1990s, and into the 2000s, Las Vegas, Nevada, was the fastest-growing city in the United States. The population increased from 258,295 in 1990 to 552,539 in 2007. This is an increase of 294,244 people or a 113.9 percent increase over the 17-year period. It has more than doubled over the period. What is the average *annual* percent increase?

Solution

There are 17 years between 1990 and 2007 so $n = 17$. Then formula (3–5) for the geometric mean as applied to this problem is:

$$GM = \sqrt[n]{\dfrac{\text{Value at end of period}}{\text{Value at start of period}}} - 1.0 = \sqrt[17]{\dfrac{552,539}{258,295}} - 1.0 = 1.0457 - 1.0 = .0457$$

The value of .0457 indicates that the average annual growth over the 17-year period was 4.57 percent. To put it another way, the population of Las Vegas increased at a rate of 4.57 percent per year from 1990 to 2007.

Self-Review 3–5

1. The percent increase in sales for the last 4 years at Combs Cosmetics were: 4.91, 5.75, 8.12, and 21.60.
   (a) Find the geometric mean percent increase.
   (b) Find the arithmetic mean percent increase.
   (c) Is the arithmetic mean equal to or greater than the geometric mean?
2. Production of Cablos trucks increased from 23,000 units in 1998 to 120,520 units in 2008. Find the geometric mean annual percent increase.

Exercises

connect

27. Compute the geometric mean of the following percent increases: 8, 12, 14, 26, and 5.
28. Compute the geometric mean of the following percent increases: 2, 8, 6, 4, 10, 6, 8, and 4.
29. Listed below is the percent increase in sales for the MG Corporation over the last 5 years. Determine the geometric mean percent increase in sales over the period.

| 9.4 | 13.8 | 11.7 | 11.9 | 14.7 |

30. In 1996 a total of 14,968,000 taxpayers in the United States filed their individual tax returns electronically. By the year 2005 the number increased to 68,476,000. What is the geometric mean annual increase for the period?
31. The Consumer Price Index is reported monthly by the U.S. Bureau of Labor Statistics. It reports the change in prices for a market basket of goods from one period to another. The index for 1994 was 148.2, by 2007 it increased to 210.2. What was the geometric mean annual increase for the period?
32. In 1976 the nationwide average price of a gallon of unleaded gasoline at a self-serve pump was $0.605. By 2008 the average price had increased to $3.23. What was the geometric mean annual increase for the period?
33. In 1985 there were 340,213 cell phone subscribers in the United States. By 2006 the number of cell phone subscribers increased to 233,000,000. What is the geometric mean annual increase for the period?
34. The information below shows the cost for a year of college in public and private colleges in 1992 and 2007. What is the geometric mean annual increase for the period for the two types of colleges? Compare the rates of increase.

Type of College	1992	2007
Public	$ 4,975	$ 11,354
Private	12,284	27,516

Why Study Dispersion?

A measure of location, such as the mean or the median, only describes the center of the data. It is valuable from that standpoint, but it does not tell us anything about the spread of the data. For example, if your nature guide told you that the river ahead averaged 3 feet in depth, would you want to wade across on foot without additional information? Probably not. You would want to know something about the variation in the depth. Is the maximum depth of the river 3.25 feet and the minimum 2.75 feet? If that is the case, you would probably agree to cross. What if you learned the river depth ranged from 0.50 feet to 5.5 feet? Your decision would probably be not to cross. Before making a decision about crossing the river, you want information on both the typical depth and the dispersion in the depth of the river.

A small value for a measure of dispersion indicates that the data are clustered closely, say, around the arithmetic mean. The mean is therefore considered representative of the data. Conversely, a large measure of dispersion indicates that the mean is not reliable. Refer to Chart 3–5. The 100 employees of Hammond Iron

Statistics in Action

The United States Postal Service has tried to become more "user friendly" in the last several years. A recent survey showed that customers were interested in more *consistency* in the time it takes to make a delivery. Under the old conditions, a local letter might take only one day to deliver, or it might take several. "Just tell me how many days ahead I need to mail the birthday card to Mom so it gets there on her birthday, not early, not late," was a common complaint. The level of consistency is measured by the standard deviation of the delivery times.

Works, Inc., a steel fabricating company, are organized into a histogram based on the number of years of employment with the company. The mean is 4.9 years, but the spread of the data is from 6 months to 16.8 years. The mean of 4.9 years is not very representative of all the employees.

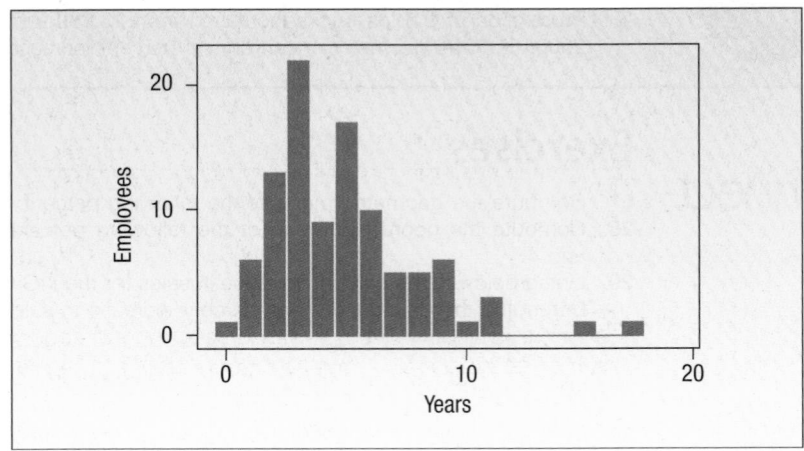

CHART 3–5 Histogram of Years of Employment at Hammond Iron Works, Inc.

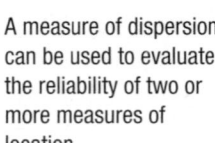

The average is not representative because of the large spread.

A second reason for studying the dispersion in a set of data is to compare the spread in two or more distributions. Suppose, for example, that the new Vision Quest LCD computer monitor is assembled in Baton Rouge and also in Tucson. The arithmetic mean hourly output in both the Baton Rouge plant and the Tucson plant is 50. Based on the two means, you might conclude that the distributions of the hourly outputs are identical. Production records for 9 hours at the two plants, however, reveal that this conclusion is not correct (see Chart 3–6). Baton Rouge production varies from 48 to 52 assemblies per hour. Production at the Tucson plant is more erratic, ranging from 40 to 60 per hour. Therefore, the hourly output for Baton Rouge is clustered near the mean of 50; the hourly output for Tucson is more dispersed.

A measure of dispersion can be used to evaluate the reliability of two or more measures of location.

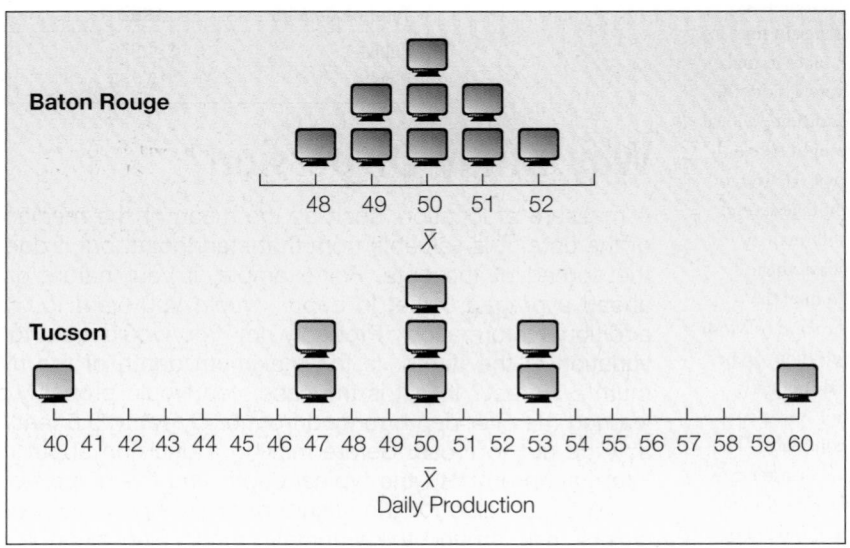

CHART 3–6 Hourly Production of Computer Monitors at the Baton Rouge and Tucson Plants

Measures of Dispersion

We will consider several measures of dispersion. The range is based on the largest and the smallest values in the data set, that is, only two values are considered. The mean deviation, the variance, and the standard deviation use all the values in a data set and are all based on deviations from the arithmetic mean.

Range

The simplest measure of dispersion is the **range.** It is the difference between the largest and the smallest values in a data set. In the form of an equation:

RANGE	Range = Largest value − Smallest value	[3–6]

The range is widely used in statistical process control (SPC) applications because it is very easy to calculate and understand.

Example

Refer to Chart 3–6 on the previous page. Find the range in the number of computer monitors produced per hour for the Baton Rouge and the Tucson plants. Interpret the two ranges.

Solution

The range of the hourly production of computer monitors at the Baton Rouge plant is 4, found by the difference between the largest hourly production of 52 and the smallest of 48. The range in the hourly production for the Tucson plant is 20 computer monitors, found by 60 − 40. We therefore conclude that (1) there is less dispersion in the hourly production in the Baton Rouge plant than in the Tucson plant because the range of 4 computer monitors is less than a range of 20 computer monitors, and (2) the production is clustered more closely around the mean of 50 at the Baton Rouge plant than at the Tucson plant (because a range of 4 is less than a range of 20). Thus, the mean production in the Baton Rouge plant (50 computer monitors) is a more representative measure of location than the mean of 50 computer monitors for the Tucson plant.

Mean Deviation

A defect of the range is that it is based on only two values, the highest and the lowest; it does not take into consideration all of the values. The **mean deviation** does. It measures the mean amount by which the values in a population, or sample, vary from their mean. In terms of a definition:

MEAN DEVIATION The arithmetic mean of the absolute values of the deviations from the arithmetic mean.

In terms of a formula, the mean deviation, designated *MD*, is computed for a sample by:

MEAN DEVIATION	$MD = \dfrac{\Sigma|X - \bar{X}|}{n}$	[3–7]

where:

X is the value of each observation.

$\overline{X}$ is the arithmetic mean of the values.

n is the number of observations in the sample.

$\|$ indicates the absolute value.

Why do we ignore the signs of the deviations from the mean? If we didn't, the positive and negative deviations from the mean would exactly offset each other, and the mean deviation would always be zero. Such a measure (zero) would be a useless statistic.

Example

The number of cappuccinos sold at the Starbucks location in the Orange County Airport between 4 and 7 p.m. for a sample of 5 days last year were 20, 40, 50, 60, and 80. In the LAX airport in Los Angeles, the number of cappuccinos sold at a Starbucks location between 4 and 7 p.m. for a sample of 5 days last year were 20, 49, 50, 51, and 80. Determine the mean, median, range, and mean deviation for each location. Compare the differences.

Solution

For the Orange County location the mean, median, and range are:

Mean	50 cappuccinos per day
Median	50 cappuccinos per day
Range	60 cappuccinos per day

The mean deviation is the mean of the absolute differences between individual observations and the arithmetic mean. For Orange County, the mean number of cappuccinos sold is 50, found by (20 + 40 + 50 + 60 + 80)/5. Next we find the differences between each observation and the mean. Then we sum these differences, ignoring the signs, and divide the sum by the number of observations. The result is the mean difference between the observations and the mean.

Number of Cappuccinos Sold Daily	$(X - \overline{X})$	Absolute Deviation
20	$(20 - 50) = -30$	30
40	$(40 - 50) = -10$	10
50	$(50 - 50) = 0$	0
60	$(60 - 50) = 10$	10
80	$(80 - 50) = 30$	30
		Total 80

$$MD = \frac{\Sigma |X - \overline{X}|}{n} = \frac{80}{5} = 16$$

The mean deviation is 16 cappuccinos per day and shows that the number of cappuccinos sold deviates, on average, by 16 from the mean of 50 cappuccinos per day.

The summary of the mean, median, range, and mean deviation for LAX follows. You should perform the calculations to verify the results.

Mean	50 cappuccinos per day
Median	50 cappuccinos per day
Range	60 cappuccinos per day
Mean Deviation	12.4 cappuccinos per day

Recall in the previous chapter that we described data using graphical methods. In this chapter, we describe data using numerical measures. When we use numerical measures, it is very important to always report measures of location and dispersion.

Let's interpret and compare the results of our measures for the Starbucks locations. The mean and median of the two locations are exactly the same, 50 cappuccinos per day. Therefore, the location of both distributions is the same. The range for both locations is also the same, 60. However, recall that the range provides limited information about the dispersion of the distribution.

Notice that the mean deviations are not the same because they are based on the differences between all observations and the arithmetic mean, which show the relative closeness or clustering of the data relative to the mean or center of the distribution. Compare the mean deviation for Orange County of 16 to the mean deviation for LAX of 12.4. Based on the mean deviation, we can say that the dispersion for the sales distribution of the LAX Starbucks is more concentrated near the mean of 50 than the Orange County location.

Advantages of mean deviation

The mean deviation has two advantages. First, it uses all the values in the computation. Recall that the range uses only the highest and the lowest values. Second, it is easy to understand—it is the average amount by which values deviate from the mean. However, its drawback is the use of absolute values. Generally, absolute values are difficult to work with and to explain, so the mean deviation is not used as frequently as other measures of dispersion, such as the standard deviation.

Self-Review 3–6

The weights of containers being shipped to Ireland are (in thousands of pounds):

| 95 | 103 | 105 | 110 | 104 | 105 | 112 | 90 |

(a) What is the range of the weights?
(b) Compute the arithmetic mean weight.
(c) Compute the mean deviation of the weights.

Exercises

connect

For Exercises 35–38, calculate the (a) range, (b) arithmetic mean, (c) mean deviation and (d) the range. Interpret your values.

35. There were five customer service representatives on duty at the Electronic Super Store during last weekend's sale. The numbers of HDTVs these representatives sold are: 5, 8, 4, 10, and 3.

36. The Department of Statistics at Western State University offers eight sections of basic statistics. Following are the numbers of students enrolled in these sections: 34, 46, 52, 29, 41, 38, 36, and 28.

37. Dave's Automatic Door installs automatic garage door openers. The following list indicates the number of minutes needed to install a sample of 10 door openers: 28, 32, 24, 46, 44, 40, 54, 38, 32, and 42.

38. A sample of eight companies in the aerospace industry was surveyed as to their return on investment last year. The results are (in percent): 10.6, 12.6, 14.8, 18.2, 12.0, 14.8, 12.2, and 15.6.

39. Ten randomly selected young adults living in California rated the taste of a newly developed sushi pizza topped with tuna, rice, and kelp on a scale of 1 to 50, with 1 indicating they did not like the taste and 50 that they did. The ratings were:

34	39	40	46	33	31	34	14	15	45

In a parallel study 10 randomly selected young adults in Iowa rated the taste of the same pizza. The ratings were:

28	25	35	16	25	29	24	26	17	20

As a market researcher, compare the potential markets for sushi pizza.

40. A sample of the personnel files of eight employees at the Pawnee location of Acme Carpet Cleaners, Inc., revealed that during the last six-month period they lost the following number of days due to illness:

2	0	6	3	10	4	1	2

A sample of eight employees during the same period at the Chickpee location of Acme Carpets revealed they lost the following number of days due to illness.

2	0	1	0	5	0	1	0

As the director of human relations, compare the two locations. What would you recommend?

Variance and Standard Deviation

Variance and standard deviation are based on squared deviations from the mean.

The **variance** and **standard deviation** are also based on the deviations from the mean. However, instead of using the absolute value of the deviations, the variance and the standard deviation square the deviations.

> **VARIANCE** The arithmetic mean of the squared deviations from the mean.

The variance is nonnegative and is zero only if all observations are the same.

> **STANDARD DEVIATION** The square root of the variance.

Population Variance   The formulas for the population variance and the sample variance are slightly different. The population variance is considered first. (Recall that a population is the totality of all observations being studied.) The **population variance** is found by:

> **POPULATION VARIANCE** $$\sigma^2 = \frac{\Sigma(X - \mu)^2}{N}$$ **[3–8]**

Where:

σ^2 is the population variance (σ is the lowercase Greek letter sigma). It is read as "sigma squared."

X is the value of an observation in the population.

μ is the arithmetic mean of the population.

N is the number of observations in the population.

Note the process of computing the variance.

- We begin by finding the mean.
- Next we find the difference between each observation and the mean, and square that difference.
- Then we sum all the squared differences.
- And finally we divide the sum of the squared differences by the number of items in the population.

So you might think of the population variance as the mean of the squared difference between each value and the mean. For populations whose values are near the mean, the variance will be small. For populations whose values are dispersed from the mean, the population variance will be large.

The variance overcomes the weakness of the range by using all the values in the population, whereas the range uses only the largest and the smallest. We overcome the issue where $\Sigma(X - \mu) = 0$ by squaring the differences, instead of using the absolute values. Squaring the differences will always result in non-negative values.

Example

The number of traffic citations issued last year by month in Beaufort County, South Carolina, is reported below.

Month	January	February	March	April	May	June	July	August	September	October	November	December
Citations	19	17	22	18	28	34	45	39	38	44	34	10

Determine the population variance.

Solution

Because we are studying all the citations for a year, the data is a population. To determine the population variance, we use formula [3-8]. The table below details the calculations.

Month	Citations (X)	X − μ	(X − μ)²
January	19	−10	100
February	17	−12	144
March	22	−7	49
April	18	−11	121
May	28	−1	1
June	34	5	25
July	45	16	256
August	39	10	100
September	38	9	81
October	44	15	225
November	34	5	25
December	10	−19	361
Total	348	0	1,488

1. We begin by determining the arithmetic mean of the population. The total number of citations issued for the year is 348, so the mean number issued per month is 29.

$$\mu = \frac{\Sigma X}{N} = \frac{19 + 17 + \cdots + 10}{12} = \frac{348}{12} = 29$$

2. Next we find the difference between each observation and the mean. This is shown in the third column of the table. Recall that earlier in the chapter (page 59) we indicated that the sum of the differences between each value and the mean is 0. From the spreadsheet, the sum of the differences between the mean and the number of citations each month is 0.
3. The next step is to square the difference between each monthly value. That is shown in the fourth column of the table. By squaring the differences, we convert both the positive and the negative values to a plus sign. Hence, each difference will be positive.
4. The squared differences are totaled. The total of the fourth column is 1,488. That is the term $\Sigma(X - \mu)^2$.
5. Finally, we divide the squared differences by N, the number of observations in the population.

$$\sigma^2 = \frac{\Sigma(X - \mu)^2}{N} = \frac{1488}{12} = 124$$

So, the population variation for the number of citations is 124.

Like the range and the mean deviation, the variance can be used to compare dispersion in two or more sets of observations. For example, the variance for the number of citations issued in Beaufort County was just computed to be 124. If the variance in the number of citations issued in Marlboro County, South Carolina, is 342.9, we conclude that (1) there is less dispersion in the distribution of the number of citations issued in Beaufort County than in Marlboro County (because 124 is less than 342.9); and (2) the number of citations in Beaufort County is more closely clustered around the mean of 29 than for the number of citations issued in Marlboro County. Thus the mean number of citations issued in Beaufort County is a more representative measure of location than the mean number of citations in Marlboro County.

Variance is difficult to interpret because the units are squared.

Population Standard Deviation   Both the range and the mean deviation are easy to interpret. The range is the difference between the high and low values of a set of data, and the mean deviation is the mean of the deviations from the mean. However, the variance is difficult to interpret for a single set of observations. The variance of 124 for the number of citations issued is not in terms of citations, but citations squared.

Standard deviation is in the same units as the data.

There is a way out of this difficulty. By taking the square root of the population variance, we can transform it to the same unit of measurement used for the original data. The square root of 124 citations-squared is 11.14 citations. The units are now simply citations. The square root of the population variance is the **population standard deviation.**

POPULATION STANDARD DEVIATION $\sigma = \sqrt{\dfrac{\Sigma(X - \mu)^2}{N}}$ [3–9]

Self-Review 3–7	The Philadelphia office of Price Waterhouse Coopers LLP hired five accounting trainees this year. Their monthly starting salaries were: $3,536; $3,173; $3,448; $3,121; and $3,622.

(a) Compute the population mean.
(b) Compute the population variance.
(c) Compute the population standard deviation.
(d) The Pittsburgh office hired six trainees. Their mean monthly salary was $3,550, and the standard deviation was $250. Compare the two groups.

Exercises

connect™

41. Consider these five values a population: 8, 3, 7, 3, and 4.
    a. Determine the mean of the population.
    b. Determine the variance.
42. Consider these six values a population: 13, 3, 8, 10, 8, and 6.
    a. Determine the mean of the population.
    b. Determine the variance.
43. The annual report of Dennis Industries cited these primary earnings per common share for the past 5 years: $2.68, $1.03, $2.26, $4.30, and $3.58. If we assume these are population values, what is:
    a. The arithmetic mean primary earnings per share of common stock?
    b. The variance?
44. Referring to Exercise 43, the annual report of Dennis Industries also gave these returns on stockholder equity for the same five-year period (in percent): 13.2, 5.0, 10.2, 17.5, and 12.9.
    a. What is the arithmetic mean return?
    b. What is the variance?
45. Plywood, Inc., reported these returns on stockholder equity for the past 5 years: 4.3, 4.9, 7.2, 6.7, and 11.6. Consider these as population values.
    a. Compute the range, the arithmetic mean, the variance, and the standard deviation.
    b. Compare the return on stockholder equity for Plywood, Inc., with that for Dennis Industries cited in Exercise 44.
46. The annual incomes of the five vice presidents of TMV Industries are: $125,000; $128,000; $122,000; $133,000; and $140,000. Consider this a population.
    a. What is the range?
    b. What is the arithmetic mean income?
    c. What is the population variance? The standard deviation?
    d. The annual incomes of officers of another firm similar to TMV Industries were also studied. The mean was $129,000 and the standard deviation $8,612. Compare the means and dispersions in the two firms.

Sample Variance The formula for the population mean is $\mu = \Sigma X/N$. We just changed the symbols for the sample mean; that is, $\overline{X} = \Sigma X/n$. Unfortunately, the conversion from the population variance to the sample variance is not as direct. It requires a change in the denominator. Instead of substituting n (number in the sample) for N (number in the population), the denominator is $n - 1$. Thus the formula for the **sample variance** is:

SAMPLE VARIANCE	$s^2 = \dfrac{\Sigma(X - \overline{X})^2}{n - 1}$	**[3–10]**

where:
    s^2 is the sample variance.
    X is the value of each observation in the sample.
    $\overline{X}$ is the mean of the sample.
    n is the number of observations in the sample.

Why is this change made in the denominator? Although the use of n is logical since $\overline{X}$ is used to estimate μ, it tends to underestimate the population variance, σ^2. The use of $(n-1)$ in the denominator provides the appropriate correction for this tendency. Because the primary use of sample statistics like s^2 is to estimate population parameters like σ^2, $(n-1)$ is preferred to n in defining the sample variance. We will also use this convention when computing the sample standard deviation.

Example

The hourly wages for a sample of part-time employees at Home Depot are: $12, $20, $16, $18, and $19. What is the sample variance?

Solution

The sample variance is computed by using formula (3–10).

$$\overline{X} = \frac{\Sigma X}{n} = \frac{\$85}{5} = \$17$$

Hourly Wage (X)	X − X̄	(X − X̄)²
$12	−$5	25
20	3	9
16	−1	1
18	1	1
19	2	4
$85	0	40

$$s^2 = \frac{\Sigma(X - \overline{X})^2}{n-1} = \frac{40}{5-1}$$

$$= 10 \text{ in dollars squared}$$

Sample Standard Deviation   The sample standard deviation is used as an estimator of the population standard deviation. As noted previously, the population standard deviation is the square root of the population variance. Likewise, the *sample standard deviation is the square root of the sample variance*. The sample standard deviation is most easily determined by:

SAMPLE STANDARD DEVIATION $$s = \sqrt{\frac{\Sigma(X - \overline{X})^2}{n-1}}$$ **[3–11]**

Example

The sample variance in the previous example involving hourly wages was computed to be 10. What is the sample standard deviation?

Solution

The sample standard deviation is $3.16, found by $\sqrt{10}$. Note again that the sample variance is in terms of dollars squared, but taking the square root of 10 gives us $3.16, which is in the same units (dollars) as the original data.

Software Solution

On page 66 we used Excel to determine the mean and median of the Whitner Autoplex sales data. You will also note that it outputs the sample standard deviation. Excel, like most other statistical software, assumes the data are from a sample.

Another software package that we will use in this text is MINITAB. This package uses a spreadsheet format, much like Excel, but produces a wider variety of statistical output. The information for the Whitner Autoplex selling prices follows. Note that a histogram (although the default is to use a class interval of $2,000 and 11 classes) is included as well as the mean, sample standard deviation and the number of observations. A graph of the normal curve is superimposed on the frequency distribution. We will explain the normal curve in Chapter 7.

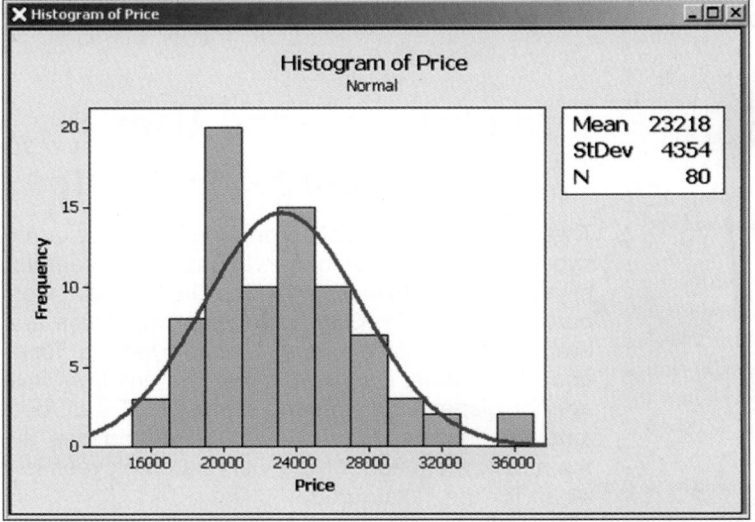

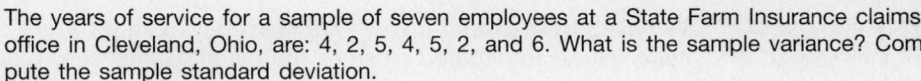

Self-Review 3–8

The years of service for a sample of seven employees at a State Farm Insurance claims office in Cleveland, Ohio, are: 4, 2, 5, 4, 5, 2, and 6. What is the sample variance? Compute the sample standard deviation.

Exercises

For Exercises 47–52, do the following:

    a. Compute the sample variance.
    b. Determine the sample standard deviation.

47. Consider these values a sample: 7, 2, 6, 2, and 3.
48. The following five values are a sample: 11, 6, 10, 6, and 7.

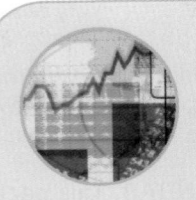
49. Dave's Automatic Door, referred to in Exercise 37, installs automatic garage door openers. Based on a sample, following are the times, in minutes, required to install 10 door openers: 28, 32, 24, 46, 44, 40, 54, 38, 32, and 42.

50. The sample of eight companies in the aerospace industry, referred to in Exercise 36, was surveyed as to their return on investment last year. The results are: 10.6, 12.6, 14.8, 18.2, 12.0, 14.8, 12.2, and 15.6.

51. The Houston, Texas, Motel Owner Association conducted a survey regarding weekday motel rates in the area. Listed below is the room rate for business-class guests for a sample of 10 motels.

| $101 | $97 | $103 | $110 | $78 | $87 | $101 | $80 | $106 | $88 |

52. A consumer watchdog organization is concerned about credit card debt. A survey of 10 young adults with credit card debt of more than $2,000 showed they paid an average of just over $100 per month against their balances. Listed below is the amounts each young adult paid last month.

| $110 | $126 | $103 | $93 | $99 | $113 | $87 | $101 | $109 | $100 |

Interpretation and Uses of the Standard Deviation

The standard deviation is commonly used as a measure to compare the spread in two or more sets of observations. For example, the standard deviation of the biweekly amounts invested in the Dupree Paint Company profit-sharing plan is computed to be $7.51. Suppose these employees are located in Georgia. If the standard deviation for a group of employees in Texas is $10.47, and the means are about the same, it indicates that the amounts invested by the Georgia employees are not dispersed as much as those in Texas (because $7.51 < $10.47). Since the amounts invested by the Georgia employees are clustered more closely about the mean, the mean for the Georgia employees is a more reliable measure than the mean for the Texas group.

Chebyshev's Theorem

We have stressed that a small standard deviation for a set of values indicates that these values are located close to the mean. Conversely, a large standard deviation reveals that the observations are widely scattered about the mean. The Russian mathematician P. L. Chebyshev (1821–1894) developed a theorem that allows us to determine the minimum proportion of the values that lie within a specified number of standard deviations of the mean. For example, according to **Chebyshev's theorem,** at least three of four values, or 75 percent, must lie between the mean plus two standard deviations and the mean minus two standard deviations. This relationship applies regardless of the shape of the distribution. Further, at least eight of nine values, or 88.9 percent, will lie between plus three standard deviations and minus three standard deviations of the mean. At least 24 of 25 values, or 96 percent, will lie between plus and minus five standard deviations of the mean.

Chebyshev's theorem states:

> **CHEBYSHEV'S THEOREM** For any set of observations (sample or population), the proportion of the values that lie within k standard deviations of the mean is at least $1 - 1/k^2$, where k is any constant greater than 1.

| Example | The arithmetic mean biweekly amount contributed by the Dupree Paint employees to the company's profit-sharing plan is \$51.54, and the standard deviation is \$7.51. At least what percent of the contributions lie within plus 3.5 standard deviations and minus 3.5 standard deviations of the mean? |

Solution   About 92 percent, found by

$$1 - \frac{1}{k^2} = 1 - \frac{1}{(3.5)^2} = 1 - \frac{1}{12.25} = 0.92$$

The Empirical Rule

The Empirical Rule applies only to symmetrical, bell-shaped distributions.

Chebyshev's theorem is concerned with any set of values; that is, the distribution of values can have any shape. However, for a symmetrical, bell-shaped distribution such as the one in Chart 3–7, we can be more precise in explaining the dispersion about the mean. These relationships involving the standard deviation and the mean are described by the **Empirical Rule,** sometimes called the **Normal Rule.**

> **EMPIRICAL RULE** For a symmetrical, bell-shaped frequency distribution, approximately 68 percent of the observations will lie within plus and minus one standard deviation of the mean; about 95 percent of the observations will lie within plus and minus two standard deviations of the mean; and practically all (99.7 percent) will lie within plus and minus three standard deviations of the mean.

These relationships are portrayed graphically in Chart 3–7 for a bell-shaped distribution with a mean of 100 and a standard deviation of 10.

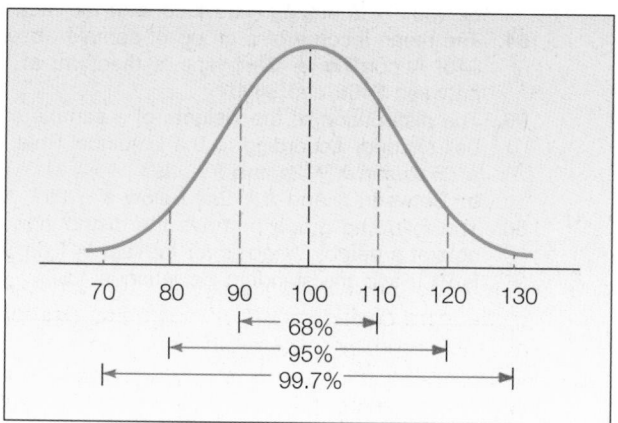

CHART 3–7 A Symmetrical, Bell-Shaped Curve Showing the Relationships between the Standard Deviation and the Observations

It has been noted that if a distribution is symmetrical and bell-shaped, practically all of the observations lie between the mean plus and minus three standard deviations. Thus, if $\overline{X} = 100$ and $s = 10$, practically all the observations lie between $100 + 3(10)$ and $100 - 3(10)$, or 70 and 130. The estimated range is therefore 60, found by $130 - 70$.

Conversely, if we know that the range is 60, we can approximate the standard deviation by dividing the range by 6. For this illustration: range ÷ 6 = 60 ÷ 6 = 10, the standard deviation.

Example

A sample of the rental rates at University Park Apartments approximates a symmetrical, bell-shaped distribution. The sample mean is $500; the standard deviation is $20. Using the Empirical Rule, answer these questions:

1. About 68 percent of the monthly food expenditures are between what two amounts?
2. About 95 percent of the monthly food expenditures are between what two amounts?
3. Almost all of the monthly expenditures are between what two amounts?

Solution

1. About 68 percent are between $480 and $520, found by $\overline{X} \pm 1s = \$500 \pm 1(\$20)$.
2. About 95 percent are between $460 and $540, found by $\overline{X} \pm 2s = \$500 \pm 2(\$20)$.
3. Almost all (99.7 percent) are between $440 and $560, found by $\overline{X} \pm 3s = \$500 \pm 3(\$20)$.

Self-Review 3–9

The Pitney Pipe Company is one of several domestic manufacturers of PVC pipe. The quality control department sampled 600 10-foot lengths. At a point 1 foot from the end of the pipe they measured the outside diameter. The mean was 14.0 inches and the standard deviation 0.1 inches.
(a) If the shape of the distribution is not known, at least what percent of the observations will be between 13.85 inches and 14.15 inches?
(b) If we assume that the distribution of diameters is symmetrical and bell-shaped, about 95 percent of the observations will be between what two values?

Exercises

connect

53. According to Chebyshev's theorem, at least what percent of any set of observations will be within 1.8 standard deviations of the mean?
54. The mean income of a group of sample observations is $500; the standard deviation is $40. According to Chebyshev's theorem, at least what percent of the incomes will lie between $400 and $600?
55. The distribution of the weights of a sample of 1,400 cargo containers is symmetric and bell-shaped. According to the Empirical Rule, what percent of the weights will lie:
    a. Between $\overline{X} - 2s$ and $\overline{X} + 2s$?
    b. Between $\overline{X}$ and $\overline{X} + 2s$? Below $\overline{X} - 2s$?
56. The following graph portrays the distribution of the number of Biggie-sized soft drinks sold at a nearby Wendy's for the last 141 days. The mean number of drinks sold per day is 91.9 and the standard deviation is 4.67.

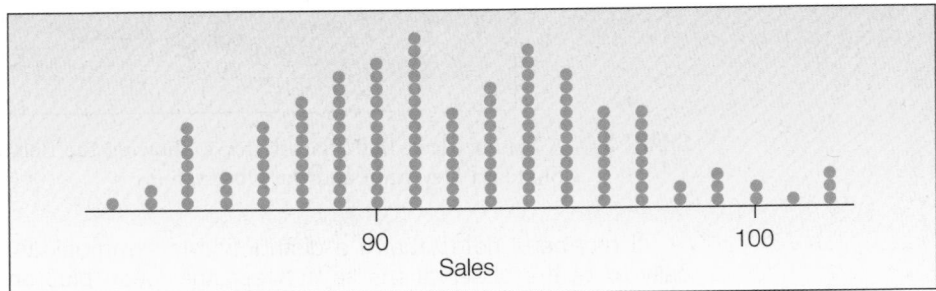

If we use the Empirical Rule, sales will be between what two values on 68 percent of the days? Sales will be between what two values on 95 percent of the days?

The Mean and Standard Deviation of Grouped Data

In most instances measures of location, such as the mean, and measures of dispersion, such as the standard deviation, are determined by using the individual values. Statistical software packages make it easy to calculate these values, even for large data sets. However, sometimes we are given only the frequency distribution and wish to estimate the mean or standard deviation. In the following discussion we show how we can estimate the mean and standard deviation from data organized into a frequency distribution. We should stress that a mean or a standard deviation from grouped data is an *estimate* of the corresponding actual values.

The Arithmetic Mean

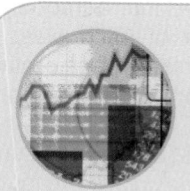

Statistics in Action

Magglio Ordonez of the Detroit Tigers had the highest batting average at .363 during the 2007 season. Tony Gwynn hit .394 in the strike-shortened season of 1994, and Ted Williams hit .406 in 1941. No one has hit over .400 since 1941. The mean batting average has remained constant at about .260 for more than 100 years, but the standard deviation declined from .049 to .031. This indicates less dispersion in the batting averages today and helps explain the lack of any .400 hitters in recent times.

To approximate the arithmetic mean of data organized into a frequency distribution, we begin by assuming the observations in each class are represented by the *midpoint* of the class. The mean of a sample of data organized in a frequency distribution is computed by:

$$\text{ARITHMETIC MEAN OF GROUPED DATA} \qquad \overline{X} = \frac{\Sigma fM}{n} \qquad\qquad [3\text{–}12]$$

where:

$\overline{X}$ is the designation for the sample mean.
M is the midpoint of each class.
f is the frequency in each class.
fM is the frequency in each class times the midpoint of the class.
ΣfM is the sum of these products.
n is the total number of frequencies.

Example

The computations for the arithmetic mean of data grouped into a frequency distribution will be shown based on the Whitner Autoplex data. Recall in Chapter 2, in Table 2–7 on page 31 we constructed a frequency distribution for the vehicle selling prices. The information is repeated below. Determine the arithmetic mean vehicle selling price.

Selling Price ($ thousands)	Frequency
15 up to 18	8
18 up to 21	23
21 up to 24	17
24 up to 27	18
27 up to 30	8
30 up to 33	4
33 up to 36	2
Total	80

Solution

The mean vehicle selling price can be estimated from data grouped into a frequency distribution. To find the estimated mean, assume the midpoint of each class is representative of the data values in that class. Recall that the midpoint of a class is halfway between the upper and the lower class limits. To find the midpoint of a particular class, we add the upper and the lower class limits and divide by 2. Hence, the midpoint of the first class is $16.5, found by ($15 + $18)/2. We assume that the value of $16.5 is representative of the eight values in that class. To put it another way, we assume the sum of the eight values in this class is $132, found by 8($16.5). We continue the process of multiplying the class midpoint by the class frequency for each class and then sum these products. The results are summarized in Table 3–1.

TABLE 3–1 Price of 80 New Vehicles Sold Last Month at Whitner Autoplex Lot

Selling Price ($ thousands)	Frequency (f)	Midpoint (M)	fM
15 up to 18	8	$16.5	$ 132.0
18 up to 21	23	19.5	448.5
21 up to 24	17	22.5	382.5
24 up to 27	18	25.5	459.0
27 up to 30	8	28.5	228.0
30 up to 33	4	31.5	126.0
33 up to 36	2	34.5	69.0
Total	80		$1,845.0

Solving for the arithmetic mean using formula (3–12), we get:

$$\overline{X} = \frac{\Sigma fM}{n} = \frac{\$1,845}{80} = \$23.1 \text{ (thousands)}$$

So we conclude that the mean vehicle selling price is about $23,100.

Standard Deviation

To calculate the standard deviation of data grouped into a frequency distribution, we need to adjust formula (3–11) slightly. We weight each of the squared differences by the number of frequencies in each class. The formula is:

STANDARD DEVIATION, GROUPED DATA $\qquad s = \sqrt{\dfrac{\Sigma f(M - \overline{X})^2}{n - 1}}$ **[3–13]**

where:
  s is the symbol for the sample standard deviation.
  M is the midpoint of the class.
  f is the class frequency.
  n is the number of observations in the sample.
  $\overline{X}$ is the designation for the sample mean.

<table>
<tr><td rowspan="2">**Example**</td></tr>
</table>

Example	Refer to the frequency distribution for the Whitner Autoplex data reported in Table 3–1. Compute the standard deviation of the vehicle selling prices.
Solution	Following the same practice used earlier for computing the mean of data grouped into a frequency distribution, f is the class frequency, M the class midpoint, and n the number of observations.

Selling Price ($ thousands)	Frequency (*f*)	Midpoint (*M*)	$(M - \bar{X})$	$(M - \bar{X})^2$	$f(M - \bar{X})^2$
15 up to 18	8	16.5	−6.6	43.56	348.48
18 up to 21	23	19.5	−3.6	12.96	298.08
21 up to 24	17	22.5	−0.6	0.36	6.12
24 up to 27	18	25.5	2.4	5.76	103.68
27 up to 30	8	28.5	5.4	29.16	233.28
30 up to 33	4	31.5	8.4	70.56	282.24
33 up to 36	2	34.5	11.4	129.96	259.92
	80				1,531.80

To find the standard deviation:

Step 1: Subtract the mean from the class midpoint. That is, find $(M - \bar{X})$. For the first class (16.5 − 23.1 = −6.6), for the second class (19.5 − 23.1 = −3.6), and so on.

Step 2: Square the difference between the class midpoint and the mean. For the first class it would be $(16.5 - 23.1)^2 = (-6.6)^2 = 43.56$, for the second class $(19.5 - 23.1)^2 = (-3.6)^2 = 12.96$, and so on.

Step 3: Multiply the squared difference between the class midpoint and the mean by the class frequency. For the first class the value is $8(16.5 - 23.1)^2 = 348.48$, for the second $23(19.5 - 23.1)^2 = 298.08$, and so on.

Step 4: Sum the $f(M - \bar{X})^2$. The total is 1,531.8.

To find the standard deviation we insert these values in formula (3–13).

$$s = \sqrt{\frac{\Sigma f(M - \bar{X})^2}{n - 1}} = \sqrt{\frac{1531.8}{80 - 1}} = 4.403.$$

The mean and the standard deviation calculated from the data grouped into a frequency distribution are usually close to the values calculated from raw data. The grouped data result in some loss of information. For the vehicle selling price problem the mean selling price reported in the Excel output on page 66 is $23,218 and the standard deviation is $4,354. The respective values estimated from data grouped into a frequency distribution are $23,100 and $4,403. The difference in the means is $118 or about 0.51 percent. The standard deviations differ by $49 or 1.1 percent. Based on the percentage difference, the estimates are very close to the actual values.

Self-Review 3–10 The net incomes of a sample of large importers of antiques were organized into the following table:

Net Income ($ millions)	Number of Importers	Net Income ($ millions)	Number of Importers
2 up to 6	1	14 up to 18	3
6 up to 10	4	18 up to 22	2
10 up to 14	10		

(a)   What is the table called?
(b)   Based on the distribution, what is the estimate of the arithmetic mean net income?
(c)   Based on the distribution, what is the estimate of the standard deviation?

Exercises

connect

57. When we compute the mean of a frequency distribution, why do we refer to this as an *estimated* mean?
58. Determine the mean and the standard deviation of the following frequency distribution.

Class	Frequency
0 up to 5	2
5 up to 10	7
10 up to 15	12
15 up to 20	6
20 up to 25	3

59. Determine the mean and the standard deviation of the following frequency distribution.

Class	Frequency
20 up to 30	7
30 up to 40	12
40 up to 50	21
50 up to 60	18
60 up to 70	12

60. SCCoast, an Internet provider in the Southeast, developed the following frequency distribution on the age of Internet users. Find the mean and the standard deviation.

Age (years)	Frequency
10 up to 20	3
20 up to 30	7
30 up to 40	18
40 up to 50	20
50 up to 60	12

61. The IRS was interested in the number of individual tax forms prepared by small accounting firms. The IRS randomly sampled 50 public accounting firms with 10 or fewer employees in the Dallas–Fort Worth area. The following frequency table reports the results of the study. Estimate the mean and the standard deviation.

Number of Clients	Frequency
20 up to 30	1
30 up to 40	15
40 up to 50	22
50 up to 60	8
60 up to 70	4

62. Advertising expenses are a significant component of the cost of goods sold. Listed below is a frequency distribution showing the advertising expenditures for 60 manufacturing companies located in the Southwest. Estimate the mean and the standard deviation of advertising expenses.

Advertising Expenditure ($ millions)	Number of Companies
25 up to 35	5
35 up to 45	10
45 up to 55	21
55 up to 65	16
65 up to 75	8
Total	60

Ethics and Reporting Results

In Chapter 1, we discussed the ethical and unbiased reporting of statistical results. While you are learning about how to organize, summarize, and interpret data using statistics, it is also important to understand statistics so that you can be an intelligent consumer of information.

In this chapter, we learned how to compute numerical descriptive statistics. Specifically, we showed how to compute and interpret measures of location for a data set: the mean, median, and mode. We also discussed the advantages and disadvantages for each statistic. For example, if a real estate developer tells a client that the average home in a particular subdivision sold for $150,000, we assume that $150,000 is a representative selling price for all the homes. But suppose that the client also asks what the median sales price is, and the median is $60,000. Why was the developer only reporting the mean price? This information is extremely important to a person's decision making when buying a home. Knowing the advantages and disadvantages of the mean, median, and mode is important as we report statistics and as we use statistical information to make decisions.

We also learned how to compute measures of dispersion: range, mean deviation, and standard deviation. Each of these statistics also has advantages and disadvantages. Remember that the range provides information about the overall spread of a distribution. However, it does not provide any information about how the data is clustered or concentrated around the center of the distribution.

As we learn more about statistics, we need to remember that when we use statistics we must maintain an independent and principled point of view. Any statistical report requires objective and honest communication of the results.

Chapter Summary

I. A measure of location is a value used to describe the center of a set of data.
 A. The arithmetic mean is the most widely reported measure of location.
  1. It is calculated by adding the values of the observations and dividing by the total number of observations.
   a. The formula for a population mean of ungrouped or raw data is

$$\mu = \frac{\Sigma X}{N} \qquad \text{[3–1]}$$

b. The formula for the mean of a sample is

$$\overline{X} = \frac{\Sigma X}{n} \qquad \text{[3–2]}$$

c. The formula for the sample mean of data in a frequency distribution is

$$\overline{X} = \frac{\Sigma fM}{n} \qquad \text{[3–12]}$$

   2. The major characteristics of the arithmetic mean are:
   a. At least the interval scale of measurement is required.
   b. All the data values are used in the calculation.
   c. A set of data has only one mean. That is, it is unique.
   d. The sum of the deviations from the mean equals 0.
B. The weighted mean is found by multiplying each observation by its corresponding weight.
   1. The formula for determining the weighted mean is

$$\overline{X}_w = \frac{w_1X_1 + w_2X_2 + w_3X_3 + \cdots + w_nX_n}{w_1 + w_2 + w_3 + \cdots + w_n} \qquad \text{[3–3]}$$

   2. It is a special case of the arithmetic mean.
C. The median is the value in the middle of a set of ordered data.
   1. To find the median, sort the observations from smallest to largest and identify the middle value.
   2. The major characteristics of the median are:
   a. At least the ordinal scale of measurement is required.
   b. It is not influenced by extreme values.
   c. Fifty percent of the observations are larger than the median.
   d. It is unique to a set of data.
D. The mode is the value that occurs most often in a set of data.
   1. The mode can be found for nominal-level data.
   2. A set of data can have more than one mode.
E. The geometric mean is the nth root of the product of n positive values.
   1. The formula for the geometric mean is

$$GM = \sqrt[n]{(X_1)(X_2)(X_3) \cdots (X_n)} \qquad \text{[3–4]}$$

   2. The geometric mean is also used to find the rate of change from one period to another.

$$GM = \sqrt[n]{\frac{\text{Value at end of period}}{\text{Value at beginning of period}}} - 1 \qquad \text{[3–5]}$$

   3. The geometric mean is always equal to or less than the arithmetic mean.
II. The dispersion is the variation or spread in a set of data.
A. The range is the difference between the largest and the smallest value in a set of data.
   1. The formula for the range is

$$\text{Range} = \text{Largest value} - \text{Smallest value} \qquad \text{[3–6]}$$

   2. The major characteristics of the range are:
   a. Only two values are used in its calculation.
   b. It is influenced by extreme values.
   c. It is easy to compute and to understand.
B. The mean absolute deviation is the sum of the absolute values of the deviations from the mean divided by the number of observations.
   1. The formula for computing the mean absolute deviation is

$$MD = \frac{\Sigma |X - \overline{X}|}{n} \qquad \text{[3–7]}$$

   2. The major characteristics of the mean absolute deviation are:
   a. It is not unduly influenced by large or small values.
   b. All observations are used in the calculation.
   c. The absolute values are somewhat difficult to work with.

C. The variance is the mean of the squared deviations from the arithmetic mean.
   1. The formula for the population variance is

$$\sigma^2 = \frac{\Sigma(X - \mu)^2}{N}$$

[3–8]

   2. The formula for the sample variance is

$$s^2 = \frac{\Sigma(X - \overline{X})^2}{n - 1}$$

[3–10]

   3. The major characteristics of the variance are:
      a. All observations are used in the calculation.
      b. It is not unduly influenced by extreme observations.
      c. The units are somewhat difficult to work with; they are the original units squared.
D. The standard deviation is the square root of the variance.
   1. The major characteristics of the standard deviation are:
      a. It is in the same units as the original data.
      b. It is the square root of the average squared distance from the mean.
      c. It cannot be negative.
      d. It is the most widely reported measure of dispersion.
   2. The formula for the sample standard deviation is

$$s = \sqrt{\frac{\Sigma(X - \overline{X})^2}{n - 1}}$$

[3–11]

   3. The formula for the standard deviation of grouped data is

$$s = \sqrt{\frac{\Sigma f(M - \overline{X})^2}{n - 1}}$$

[3–13]

III. We interpret the standard deviation using two measures.
   A. Chebyshev's theorem states that regardless of the shape of the distribution, at least $1 - 1/k^2$ of the observations will be within k standard deviations of the mean, where k is greater than 1.
   B. The Empirical Rule states that for a bell-shaped distribution about 68 percent of the values will be within one standard deviation of the mean, 95 percent within two, and virtually all within three.

Pronunciation Key

SYMBOL	MEANING	PRONUNCIATION
μ	Population mean	mu
Σ	Operation of adding	sigma
ΣX	Adding a group of values	sigma X
$\overline{X}$	Sample mean	X bar
$\overline{X}_w$	Weighted mean	X bar sub w
GM	Geometric mean	G M
ΣfM	Adding the product of the frequencies and the class midpoints	sigma f M
σ^2	Population variance	sigma squared
σ	Population standard deviation	sigma

Chapter Exercises

connect

63. The accounting firm of Crawford and Associates has five senior partners. Yesterday the senior partners saw six, four, three, seven, and five clients, respectively.
   a. Compute the mean number and median number of clients seen by the partners.
   b. Is the mean a sample mean or a population mean?
   c. Verify that $\Sigma(X - \mu) = 0$.

64. Owens Orchards sells apples in a large bag by weight. A sample of seven bags contained the following numbers of apples: 23, 19, 26, 17, 21, 24, 22.
   a. Compute the mean number and median number of apples in a bag.
   b. Verify that $\Sigma(X - \overline{X}) = 0$.

65. A sample of households that subscribe to United Bell Phone Company for land line phone service revealed the following number of calls received per household last week. Determine the mean and the median number of calls received.

52	43	30	38	30	42	12	46	39	37
34	46	32	18	41	5				

66. The Citizens Banking Company is studying the number of times the ATM located in a Loblaws Supermarket at the foot of Market Street is used per day. Following are the number of times the machine was used daily over each of the last 30 days. Determine the mean number of times the machine was used per day.

83	64	84	76	84	54	75	59	70	61
63	80	84	73	68	52	65	90	52	77
95	36	78	61	59	84	95	47	87	60

67. The Canadian government wants to know the relative age of its workforce. As the baby boom generation becomes older, the government is concerned about the availability of younger qualified workers. To become more informed, the government surveyed many industries regarding employee ages. The mean and median age for two industries, communication and retail trade, for six different job types are listed in the following table.

	Communication and Other Utilities		Retail Trade and Consumer Services	
	Mean	Median	Mean	Median
Managers	42.6	43	38.6	38
Professionals	40.8	40	40.0	39
Technical/Trades	41.4	42	37.1	37
Marketing/Sales	NA	NA	33.7	31
Clerical/Administrative	40.8	41	38.0	38
Production Workers	37.2	40	32.0	24

Comment on the distribution of age. Which industry appears to have older workers? Younger workers? In each industry, which job types show the greatest difference between mean and median age?

68. Trudy Green works for the True-Green Lawn Company. Her job is to solicit lawn-care business via the telephone. Listed below is the number of appointments she made in each of the last 25 hours of calling. What is the arithmetic mean number of appointments she made per hour? What is the median number of appointments per hour? Write a brief report summarizing the findings.

9	5	2	6	5	6	4	4	7	2	3	6	3
4	4	7	8	4	4	5	5	4	8	3	3	

69. The Split-A-Rail Fence Company sells three types of fence to homeowners in suburban Seattle, Washington. Grade A costs $5.00 per running foot to install, Grade B costs $6.50 per running foot, and Grade C, the premium quality, costs $8.00 per running foot. Yesterday, Split-A-Rail installed 270 feet of Grade A, 300 feet of Grade B, and 100 feet of Grade C. What was the mean cost per foot of fence installed?

70. Rolland Poust is a sophomore in the College of Business at Scandia Tech. Last semester he took courses in statistics and accounting, 3 hours each, and earned an A in both. He earned a B in a five-hour history course and a B in a two-hour history of jazz course. In addition, he took a one-hour course dealing with the rules of basketball so he could get his license to officiate high school basketball games. He got an A in this course. What was his GPA for the semester? Assume that he receives 4 points for an A, 3 for a B, and so on. What measure of location did you just calculate?

71. The table below shows the percent of the labor force that is unemployed and the size of the labor force for three counties in Northwest Ohio. Jon Elsas is the Regional Director of Economic Development. He must present a report to several companies that are considering locating in Northwest Ohio. What would be an appropriate unemployment rate to show for the entire region?

County	Percent Unemployed	Size of Workforce
Wood	4.5	15,300
Ottawa	3.0	10,400
Lucas	10.2	150,600

72. The American Automobile Association checks prices of gasoline before many holiday weekends. Listed below are the self-service prices for a sample of 15 retail outlets during the last Labor Day weekend in the Detroit, Michigan area.

3.44	3.42	3.35	3.39	3.49	3.49	3.41	3.46
3.41	3.49	3.45	3.48	3.39	3.46	3.44	

    a. What is the arithmetic mean selling price?
    b. What is the median selling price?
    c. What is the modal selling price?

73. The metropolitan area of Los Angeles–Long Beach, California, is the area expected to show the largest increase in the number of jobs between 1989 and 2010. The number of jobs is expected to increase from 5,164,900 to 6,286,800. What is the geometric mean expected yearly rate of increase?

74. A recent article suggested that, if you earn $25,000 a year today and the inflation rate continues at 3 percent per year, you'll need to make $33,598 in 10 years to have the same buying power. You would need to make $44,771 if the inflation rate jumped to 6 percent. Confirm that these statements are accurate by finding the geometric mean rate of increase.

75. The ages of a sample of Canadian tourists flying from Toronto to Hong Kong were: 32, 21, 60, 47, 54, 17, 72, 55, 33, and 41.
    a. Compute the range.
    b. Compute the mean deviation.
    c. Compute the standard deviation.

76. The weights (in pounds) of a sample of five boxes being sent by UPS are: 12, 6, 7, 3, and 10.
    a. Compute the range.
    b. Compute the mean deviation.
    c. Compute the standard deviation.

77. A southern state has seven state universities in its system. The numbers of volumes (in thousands) held in its libraries are 83, 510, 33, 256, 401, 47, and 23.
    a. Is this a sample or a population?
    b. Compute the standard deviation.

78. Health issues are a concern of managers, especially as they evaluate the cost of medical insurance. A recent survey of 150 executives at Elvers Industries, a large insurance and financial firm located in the Southwest, reported the number of pounds by which the executives were overweight. Compute the mean and the standard deviation.

Pounds Overweight	Frequency
0 up to 6	14
6 up to 12	42
12 up to 18	58
18 up to 24	28
24 up to 30	8

79. The Apollo space program lasted from 1967 until 1972 and included 13 missions. The missions lasted from as little as 7 hours to as long as 301 hours. The duration of each flight is listed below.

9	195	241	301	216	260	7	244	192	147
10	295	142							

    a. Explain why the flight times are a population.
    b. Find the mean and median of the flight times.
    c. Find the range and the standard deviation of the flight times.

80. Creek Ratz is a very popular restaurant located along the coast of northern Florida. They serve a variety of steak and seafood dinners. During the summer beach season, they do not take reservations or accept "call ahead" seating. Management of the restaurant is concerned with the time a patron must wait before being seated for dinner. Listed below is the wait time, in minutes, for the 25 tables seated last Saturday night.

28	39	23	67	37	28	56	40	28	50
51	45	44	65	61	27	24	61	34	44
64	25	24	27	29					

    a. Explain why the times are a population.
    b. Find the mean and median of the times.
    c. Find the range and the standard deviation of the times.

81. A sample of 25 undergraduates reported the following dollar amounts of entertainment expenses last year:

684	710	688	711	722	698	723	743	738	722	696	721	685
763	681	731	736	771	693	701	737	717	752	710	697	

    a. Find the mean, median and mode of this information.
    b. What are the range and standard deviation?
    c. Use the Empirical Rule to establish an interval which includes about 95 percent of the observations.

82. The EPA recently released the following air quality indexes for selected metropolitan areas.

Index	Metropolitan Area	Index	Metropolitan Area
41	Allentown–Bethlehem–Easton, PA	29	Monroe, LA
45	Athens, GA	48	New York, NY
44	Bergen–Passaic, NJ	34	Oakland, CA
39	Buffalo–Niagara Falls, NY	31	Pittsfield, MA
32	Cedar Rapids, IA	36	Reading, PA
42	Cleveland–Lorain–Elyria, OH	31	Rochester, NY
37	Florence, AL	38	San Antonio, TX
41	Fort Worth–Arlington, TX	42	Savannah, GA
37	Goldsboro, NC	35	Scranton–Wilkes Barre–Hazleton, PA
38	Huntsville, AL	36	Vineland–Millville–Bridgeton, NJ
38	Jacksonville, FL	54	Visalia–Tulare–Porterville, CA
33	Johnstown, PA	47	Wheeling, WV–OH
20	Mayaguez, PR		

    a. Find the mean, median, and mode of this data set.
    b. What are the range and standard deviation of the readings?
    c. Use the Empirical Rule to establish an interval which includes about 95 percent of the observations.

83. U.S. housing prices reached their peak in July of 2006. The following data shows the ratio of the prices reported in a recent month to the July 2006 figure. These are to be used to represent typical amounts of decline from that peak for 20 cities.

Phoenix	Los Angeles	San Diego	San Francisco	Denver	Washington	Miami	Tampa	Atlanta	Chicago
0.760	0.784	0.764	0.802	0.909	0.828	0.786	0.792	0.933	0.915

Boston	Detroit	Minneapolis	Charlotte	Las Vegas	New York	Cleveland	Portland	Dallas	Seattle
0.902	0.792	0.855	1.025	0.756	0.922	0.865	0.981	0.939	0.999

    a. Find the mean, median, and mode of these statistics.

    b. What are the range and standard deviation of the values? (Assume this to be sample information.)

    c. Use the Empirical Rule to determine an interval which contains approximately 95 percent of the observations.

84. The Kentucky Derby is held the first Saturday in May at Churchill Downs in Louisville, KY. The racing track is one and one-quarter miles. The following table shows the winners since 1990, their margin of victory, the winning time, and the payoff on a $2 bet.

Year	Winner	Margin (lengths)	Time (minutes)	Payoffs for $2 Bets
1990	Unbridled	3.5	2.03333	10.80
1991	Strike the Gold	1.75	2.05000	4.80
1992	Lil E. Tee	1	2.05000	16.80
1993	Sea Hero	2.5	2.04000	12.90
1994	Go For Gin	2	2.06000	9.10
1995	Thunder Gulch	2.25	2.02000	24.50
1996	Grindstone	Nose	2.01667	5.90
1997	Silver Charm	Head	2.04000	4.00
1998	Real Quiet	0.5	2.03667	8.40
1999	Charismatic	Neck	2.05333	31.30
2000	Fusaichi Pegasus	1.5	2.02000	2.30
2001	Monarchos	4.75	1.99667	10.50
2002	War Emblem	4	2.01667	20.50
2003	Funny Cide	1.75	2.01667	12.80
2004	Smarty Jones	2.75	2.06667	4.10
2005	Giacomo	0.5	2.04583	50.30
2006	Barbaro	6.5	2.03933	6.10
2007	Street Sense	2.25	2.03617	4.90
2008	Big Brown	4.75	2.03033	6.80

    a. Obtain the mean and median for the variables winning time and payoff on a $2 bet.

    b. Determine the range and standard deviation of the variables time and payoff.

    c. Refer to the variable winning margin. What is the level of measurement? What measure of location would be most appropriate?

85. The manager of the local Wal-Mart Super Store is studying the number of items purchased by customers in the evening hours. Listed below is the number of items for a sample of 30 customers.

15	8	6	9	9	4	18	10	10	12
12	4	7	8	12	10	10	11	9	13
5	6	11	14	5	6	6	5	13	5

    a. Find the mean and the median of the number of items.

    b. Find the range and the standard deviation of the number of items.

    c. Organize the number of items into a frequency distribution. You may want to review the guidelines in Chapter 2 for establishing the class interval and the number of classes.

    d. Find the mean and the standard deviation of the data organized into a frequency distribution. Compare these values with those computed in part (a). Why are they different?

86. The following frequency distribution reports the electricity cost for a sample of 50 two-bedroom apartments in Albuquerque, New Mexico during the month of May last year.

Electricity Cost	Frequency
$ 80 up to $100	3
100 up to 120	8
120 up to 140	12
140 up to 160	16
160 up to 180	7
180 up to 200	4
Total	50

   a. Estimate the mean cost.
   b. Estimate the standard deviation.
   c. Use the Empirical Rule to estimate the proportion of costs within two standard deviations of the mean. What are these limits?

87. Bidwell Electronics, Inc., recently surveyed a sample of employees to determine how far they lived from corporate headquarters. The results are shown below. Compute the mean and the standard deviation.

Distance (miles)	Frequency	M
0 up to 5	4	2.5
5 up to 10	15	7.5
10 up to 15	27	12.5
15 up to 20	18	17.5
20 up to 25	6	22.5

Data Set Exercises

88. Refer to the Real Estate data, which reports information on homes sold in the Denver, Colorado, area last year.
   a. Select the variable selling price.
      1. Find the mean, median, and the standard deviation.
      2. Write a brief summary of the distribution of selling prices.
   b. Select the variable referring to the area of the home in square feet.
      1. Find the mean, median, and the standard deviation.
      2. Write a brief summary of the distribution of the area of homes.

89. Refer to the Baseball 2007 data, which reports information on the 30 major league teams for the 2007 baseball season.
   a. Select the variable team salary and find the mean, median, and the standard deviation.
   b. Select the variable that refers to the age the stadium was built. (Hint: Subtract the year in which the stadium was built from the current year to find the stadium age and work with that variable.) Find the mean, median, and the standard deviation.
   c. Select the variable that refers to the seating capacity of the stadium. Find the mean, median, and the standard deviation.

90. Refer to the CIA data, which reports demographic and economic information on 46 countries.
   a. Select the variable life expectancy.
      1. Find the mean, median, and the standard deviation.
      2. Write a brief summary of the distribution of life expectancy.
   b. Select the variable GDP/cap.
      1. Find the mean, median, and the standard deviation.
      2. Write a brief summary of the distribution GDP/cap.

Software Commands

1. The Excel Commands for the descriptive statistics on page 66 are:
   a. From the CD retrieve the Whitner data file, which is called **Whitner.**
   b. From the menu bar select **Data** and then **Data Analysis.** Select **Descriptive Statistics** and then click **OK.**
   c. For the **Input Range,** type *A1:A81,* indicate that the data are grouped by column and that the labels are in the first row. Click on **Output Range,** indicate that the output should go in *H1* (or any place you wish), click on **Summary statistics,** then click **OK.**
   d. After you get your results, double-check the count in the output to be sure it contains the correct number of items.

2. The MINITAB commands for the descriptive summary on page 81 are:
   a. From the CD retrieve the Whitner data, which is called **Whitner.**
   b. Select **Stat, Basic Statistics,** and then **Display Descriptive Statistics.** In the dialog box select *Price* as the variable and then click on **Graphs** in the lower right-hand corner. Within the new dialog box select **Histogram of data, with normal curve** and click **OK.** Click **OK** in the next dialog box.

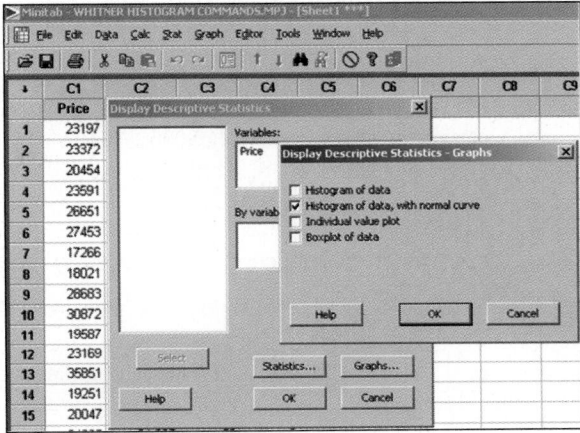

Descriptive Statistics

Input
Input Range: $A$1:$A$81
Grouped By: ⊙ Columns   ○ Rows
☐ Labels in first row

Output options
⊙ Output Range: $F$1
○ New Worksheet Ply:
○ New Workbook
☑ Summary statistics
☐ Confidence Level for Mean: 95 %
☐ Kth Largest: 1
☐ Kth Smallest: 1

OK   Cancel   Help

Chapter 3   Answers to Self-Review

3–1 1. a. $\bar{X} = \dfrac{\Sigma X}{n}$

   b. $\bar{X} = \dfrac{\$267,100}{4} = \$66,775$

   c. Statistic, because it is a sample value.
   d. $66,775. The sample mean is our best estimate of the population mean.

2. a. $\mu = \dfrac{\Sigma X}{N}$

   b. $\mu = \dfrac{498}{6} = 83$

   c. Parameter, because it was computed using all the population values.

3–2 a. $237, found by:
$$\frac{(95 \times \$400) + (126 \times \$200) + (79 \times \$100)}{95 + 126 + 79} = \$237.00$$

   b. The profit per suit is $12, found by $237 − $200 cost − $25 commission. The total profit for the 300 suits is $3,600, found by 300 × $12.

3–3 1. a. $878
   b. 3, 3

2. a. 7, found by (6 + 8)/2 = 7
   b. 3, 3
   c. 0

3–4 **a.**

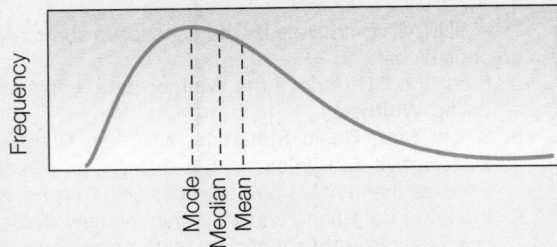

Weekly Sales

b. Positively skewed, because the mean is the largest average and the mode is the smallest.

3–5 **1. a.** About 9.9 percent, found by $\sqrt[4]{1.458602236}$, then $1.099 - 1.00 = .099$
  b. About 10.095 percent
  c. Greater than, because $10.095 > 9.9$

2. 8.63 percent, found by $\sqrt[20]{\dfrac{120,520}{23,000}} - 1 =$
  $1.0863 - 1$

3–6 **a.** 22 thousands of pounds, found by $112 - 90$
  b. $\overline{X} = \dfrac{824}{8} = 103$ thousands of pounds

c.

X	$|X - \overline{X}|$	Absolute Deviation
95	-8	8
103	0	0
105	$+2$	2
110	$+7$	7
104	$+1$	1
105	$+2$	2
112	$+9$	9
90	-13	13
		Total 42

$MD = \dfrac{42}{8} = 5.25$ thousands of pounds

3–7 **a.** $\mu = \dfrac{\$16,900}{5} = \$3,380$

b. $\sigma^2 = \dfrac{(3536 - 3380)^2 + \cdots + (3622 - 3380)^2}{5}$

$= \dfrac{(156)^2 + (-207)^2 + (68)^2 + (-259)^2 + (242)^2}{5}$

$= \dfrac{197,454}{5} = 39,490.8$

c. $\sigma = \sqrt{39,490.8} = 198.72$

d. There is more variation in the Pittsburgh office because the standard deviation is larger. The mean is also larger in the Pittsburgh office.

3–8 2.33, found by:

$$\overline{X} = \frac{\Sigma X}{n} = \frac{28}{7} = 4$$

X	$X - \overline{X}$	$(X - \overline{X})^2$
4	0	0
2	-2	4
5	1	1
4	0	0
5	1	1
2	-2	4
6	2	4
28	0	14

$s^2 = \dfrac{\Sigma(X - \overline{X})^2}{n - 1}$

$= \dfrac{14}{7 - 1}$

$= 2.33$

$s = \sqrt{2.33} = 1.53$

3–9 **a.** $k = \dfrac{14.15 - 14.00}{.10} = 1.5$

$k = \dfrac{13.85 - 14.0}{.10} = -1.5$

$1 - \dfrac{1}{(1.5)^2} = 1 - .44 = .56$

b. 13.8 and 14.2

3–10 **a.** Frequency distribution.
  b.

f	M	fM	$(M - \overline{X})$	$f(M - \overline{X})^2$
1	4	4	-8.2	67.24
4	8	32	-4.2	70.56
10	12	120	-0.2	0.40
3	16	48	3.8	43.32
2	20	40	7.8	121.68
20		244		303.20

$$\overline{X} = \frac{\Sigma fM}{M} = \frac{\$244}{20} = \$12.20$$

c. $s = \sqrt{\dfrac{303.20}{20 - 1}} = \$3.99$

Describing Data:

Displaying and Exploring Data

GOALS

When you have completed this chapter, you will be able to:

1 Develop and interpret a *dot plot.*

2 Develop and interpret a *stem-and-leaf display.*

3 Compute and understand *quartiles, deciles,* and *percentiles.*

4 Construct and interpret *box plots.*

5 Compute and understand the *coefficient of skewness.*

6 Draw and interpret a *scatter diagram.*

7 Construct and interpret a *contingency table.*

McGivern Jewelers recently ran an advertisement in the local newspaper reporting the shape, size, price, and cut grade for 33 of its diamonds in stock. Using the data provided in Exercise 37, develop a box plot of the variable price and comment on the result. (Goal 4)

Introduction

Chapter 2 began our study of descriptive statistics. In order to transform raw or ungrouped data into a meaningful form, we organize the data into a frequency distribution. We present the frequency distribution in graphic form as a histogram or a frequency polygon. This allows us to visualize where the data tends to cluster, the largest and the smallest values, and the general shape of the data.

In Chapter 3 we first computed several measures of location, such as the mean and the median. These measures of location allow us to report a typical value in the set of observations. We also computed several measures of dispersion, such as the range and the standard deviation. These measures of dispersion allow us to describe the variation or the spread in a set of observations.

We continue our study of descriptive statistics in this chapter. We study (1) dot plots, (2) stem-and-leaf displays, (3) percentiles, and (4) box plots. These charts and statistics give us additional insight into where the values are concentrated as well as the general shape of the data. Then we consider bivariate data. In bivariate data we observe two variables for each individual or observation selected. Examples include: the number of hours a student studied and the points earned on an examination; whether a sampled product is acceptable or not and the shift on which it is manufactured; and the amount of electricity used in a month by a homeowner and the mean daily high temperature in the region for the month.

Dot Plots

A histogram groups data into classes. Recall in the Whitner Autoplex data from Table 2–4 that 80 observations were condensed into seven classes. When we organized the data into the seven classes we lost the exact value of the observations. A **dot plot,** on the other hand, groups the data as little as possible and we do not lose the identity of an individual observation. To develop a dot plot we simply display a dot for each observation along a horizontal number line indicating the possible values of the data. If there are identical observations or the observations are too close to be shown individually, the dots are "piled" on top of each other. This allows us to see the shape of the distribution, the value about which the data tend to cluster, and the largest and smallest observations. Dot plots are most useful for smaller data sets, whereas histograms tend to be most useful for large data sets. An example will show how to construct and interpret dot plots.

Example

Recall in Table 2–4 on page 28 we presented data on the selling price of 80 vehicles sold last month at Whitner Autoplex in Raytown, Missouri. Whitner is one of the many dealerships owned by AutoUSA. AutoUSA has many other dealerships located in small towns throughout the United States. Reported below are the number of vehicles sold in the last 24 months at Smith Ford Mercury Jeep, Inc., in Kane, Pennsylvania, and Brophy Honda Volkswagen in Greenville, Ohio. Construct dot plots and report summary statistics for the two small-town AutoUSA lots.

Smith Ford Mercury Jeep, Inc.									
23	27	30	27	32	31	32	32	35	33
28	39	32	29	35	36	33	25	35	37
26	28	36	30						

Brophy Honda Volkswagen									
31	44	30	36	37	34	43	38	37	35
36	34	31	32	40	36	31	44	26	30
37	43	42	33						

Solution

The MINITAB system provides a dot plot and calculates the mean, median, maximum, and minimum values, and the standard deviation for the number of cars sold at each of the dealerships over the last 24 months.

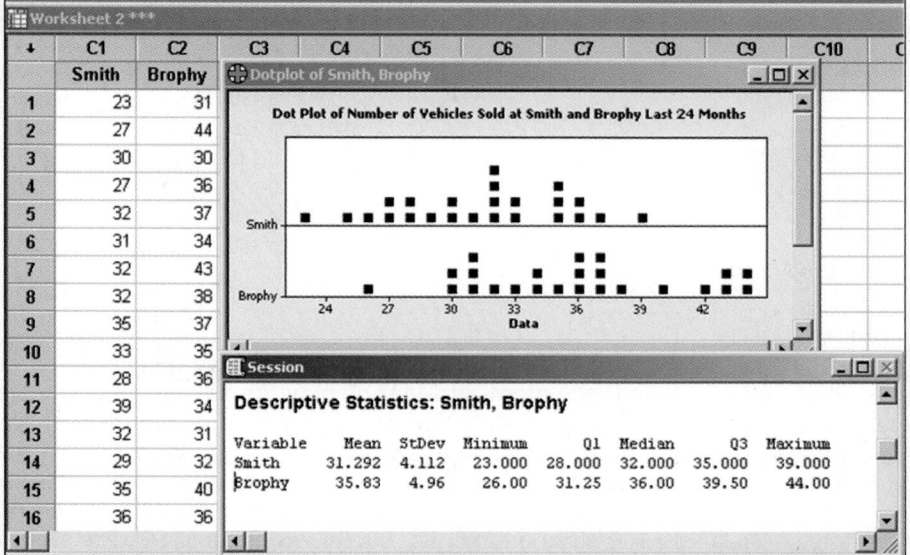

From the descriptive statistics we see that Brophy sold a mean of 35.83 vehicles per month and Smith a mean of 31.292. So Brophy typically sells 4.54 more vehicles per month. There is also more dispersion or variation in the monthly Brophy sales than in the Smith sales. How do we know this? The standard deviation is larger at Brophy (4.96 cars per month) than at Smith (4.112 cars per month).

The dot plot, shown in the center of the software output, graphically illustrates the distributions for both dealerships. The plots show the difference in the location and dispersion of the observations. By looking at the plots, we can see that Brophy's sales are more widely dispersed and have a larger mean than Smith's sales. Several other features of the monthly sales are apparent:

- Smith sold the fewest cars in any month, 23.
- Brophy sold 26 cars in its lowest month, which is 4 cars less than the next lowest month.
- Smith sold exactly 32 cars in four different months.
- The monthly sales cluster is around 32 for Smith and 36 for Brophy.

Stem-and-Leaf Displays

In Chapter 2, we showed how to organize data into a frequency distribution so we could summarize the raw data into a meaningful form. The major advantage to organizing the data into a frequency distribution is that we get a quick visual picture of the shape of the distribution without doing any further calculation. To put it another way, we can see where the data are concentrated and also determine whether there are any extremely large or small values. There are two disadvantages, however, to organizing the data into a frequency distribution: (1) we lose the exact identity of each value and (2) we are not sure how the values within each class are distributed. To explain, the following frequency distribution shows the number of advertising spots purchased by the 45 members of the Greater Buffalo Automobile Dealers Association in the year 2007. We observe that 7 of the 45 dealers purchased at least 90 but less than 100 spots. However, are the spots purchased within this class clustered about 90, spread evenly throughout the class, or clustered near 99? We cannot tell.

Number of Spots Purchased	Frequency
80 up to 90	2
90 up to 100	7
100 up to 110	6
110 up to 120	9
120 up to 130	8
130 up to 140	7
140 up to 150	3
150 up to 160	3
Total	45

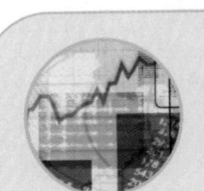

Statistics in Action

John W. Tukey (1915–2000) received a PhD in mathematics from Princeton in 1939. However, when he joined the Fire Control Research Office during World War II, his interest in abstract mathematics shifted to applied statistics. He developed effective numerical and graphical methods for studying patterns in data. Among the graphics he developed are the stem-and-leaf diagram and the box-and-whisker plot or box plot. From 1960 to 1980, Tukey headed the statistical division of NBC's election night vote projection team. He became renowned in 1960 for preventing an early call of victory for Richard Nixon in the presidential election won by John F. Kennedy.

One technique that is used to display quantitative information in a condensed form is the **stem-and-leaf display.** An advantage of the stem-and-leaf display over a frequency distribution is that we do not lose the identity of each observation. In the above example, we would not know the identity of the values in the 90 up to 100 class. To illustrate the construction of a stem-and-leaf display using the number of advertising spots purchased, suppose the seven observations in the 90 up to 100 class are: 96, 94, 93, 94, 95, 96, and 97. The **stem** value is the leading digit or digits, in this case 9. The **leaves** are the trailing digits. The stem is placed to the left of a vertical line and the leaf values to the right.

The values in the 90 up to 100 class would appear as follows:

> 9 | 6 4 3 4 5 6 7

It is also customary to sort the values within each stem from smallest to largest. Thus, the second row of the stem-and-leaf display would appear as follows:

> 9 | 3 4 4 5 6 6 7

With the stem-and-leaf display, we can quickly observe that there were two dealers that purchased 94 spots and that the number of spots purchased ranged from 93 to 97. A stem-and-leaf display is similar to a frequency distribution with more information, that is, the identity of the observations is preserved.

> **STEM-AND-LEAF DISPLAY** A statistical technique to present a set of data. Each numerical value is divided into two parts. The leading digit(s) becomes the stem and the trailing digit the leaf. The stems are located along the vertical axis, and the leaf values are stacked against each other along the horizontal axis.

The following example will explain the details of developing a stem-and-leaf display.

Example

Listed in Table 4–1 is the number of 30-second radio advertising spots purchased by each of the 45 members of the Greater Buffalo Automobile Dealers Association last year. Organize the data into a stem-and-leaf display. Around what values do the number of advertising spots tend to cluster? What is the fewest number of spots purchased by a dealer? The largest number purchased?

TABLE 4–1 Number of Advertising Spots Purchased by Members of the Greater Buffalo Automobile Dealers Association

96	93	88	117	127	95	113	96	108	94	148	156
139	142	94	107	125	155	155	103	112	127	117	120
112	135	132	111	125	104	106	139	134	119	97	89
118	136	125	143	120	103	113	124	138			

Solution

From the data in Table 4–1 we note that the smallest number of spots purchased is 88. So we will make the first stem value 8. The largest number is 156, so we will have the stem values begin at 8 and continue to 15. The first number in Table 4–1 is 96, which will have a stem value of 9 and a leaf value of 6. Moving across the top row, the second value is 93 and the third is 88. After the first 3 data values are considered, your chart is as follows.

Stem	Leaf
8	8
9	6 3
10	
11	
12	
13	
14	
15	

Organizing all the data, the stem-and-leaf chart looks as follows.

Stem	Leaf
8	8 9
9	6 3 5 6 4 4 7
10	8 7 3 4 6 3
11	7 3 2 7 2 1 9 8 3
12	7 5 7 0 5 5 0 4
13	9 5 2 9 4 6 8
14	8 2 3
15	6 5 5

The usual procedure is to sort the leaf values from the smallest to largest. The last line, the row referring to the values in the 150s, would appear as:

15	5 5 6

The final table would appear as follows, where we have sorted all of the leaf values.

Stem	Leaf
8	8 9
9	3 4 4 5 6 6 7
10	3 3 4 6 7 8
11	1 2 2 3 3 7 7 8 9
12	0 0 4 5 5 5 7 7
13	2 4 5 6 8 9 9
14	2 3 8
15	5 5 6

You can draw several conclusions from the stem-and-leaf display. First, the minimum number of spots purchased is 88 and the maximum is 156. Two dealers purchased less than 90 spots, and three purchased 150 or more. You can observe, for example, that the three dealers who purchased more than 150 spots actually purchased 155, 155, and 156 spots. The concentration of the number of spots is between 110 and 130. There were nine dealers who purchased between 110 and 119 spots and eight who purchased between 120 and 129 spots. We can also tell that within the 120 to 129 group the actual number of spots purchased was spread evenly throughout. That is, two dealers purchased 120 spots, one dealer purchased 124 spots, three dealers purchased 125 spots, and two purchased 127 spots.

We can also generate this information on the MINITAB software system. We have named the variable *Spots.* The MINITAB output is below. You can find the MINITAB commands that will produce this output at the end of the chapter.

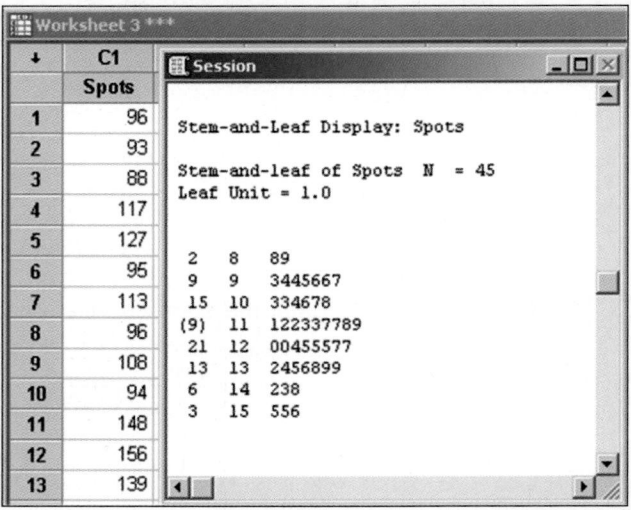

The MINITAB solution provides some additional information regarding cumulative totals. In the column to the left of the stem values are numbers such as 2, 9, 15, and so on. The number 9 indicates that there are 9 observations that have occurred before the value of 100. The number 15 indicates that 15 observations have occurred prior to 110. About halfway down the column the number 9 appears in parentheses. The parentheses indicate that the middle value or median appears in that row and that there are nine values in this group. In this case, we describe the middle value as the value below which half of the observations occur. There are a total of 45 observations, so the middle value, if the data were arranged from smallest to largest, would be the 23rd observation; its value is 118. After the median, the values begin to decline. These values represent the "more than" cumulative totals. There are 21 observations of 120 or more, 13 of 130 or more, and so on. The number 9 in parentheses also tells you there are 9 observations in the middle row.

This is really a matter of personal choice and convenience. For presenting data, especially with a large number of observations you will find dot plots are more frequently used. You will see dot plots in analytical literature, marketing reports and occasionally in annual reports. If you are doing a quick analysis for yourself, stem-and-leaf tallies are handy and easy, particularly on a smaller set of data.

Self-Review 4–1

1. The number of employees at each of the 142 Home Depot Stores in the Southeast region is shown in the following dot plot.

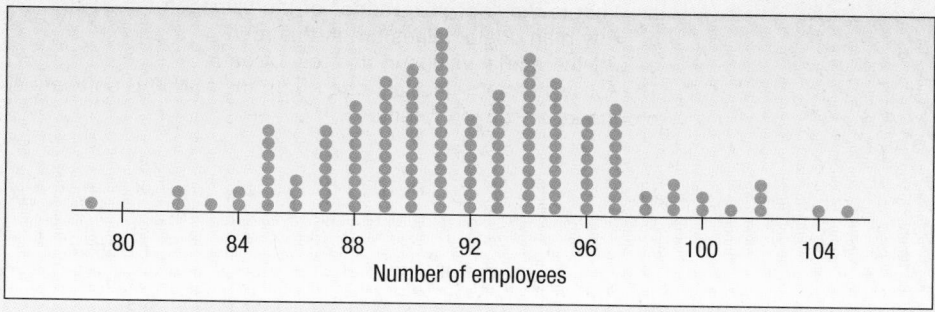

Number of employees

   (a)   What are the maximum and minimum numbers of employees per store?
   (b)   How many stores employ 91 people?
   (c)   Around what values does the number of employees per store tend to cluster?

2. The rate of return for 21 stocks is:

8.3	9.6	9.5	9.1	8.8	11.2	7.7	10.1	9.9	10.8
10.2	8.0	8.4	8.1	11.6	9.6	8.8	8.0	10.4	9.8	9.2

Organize this information into a stem-and-leaf display.
   (a)   How many rates are less than 9.0?
   (b)   List the rates in the 10.0 up to 11.0 category.
   (c)   What is the median?
   (d)   What are the maximum and the minimum rates of return?

Exercises

connect

1. Describe the differences between a histogram and a dot plot. When might a dot plot be better than a histogram?
2. Describe the differences between a histogram and a stem-and-leaf display.
3. Consider the following chart.

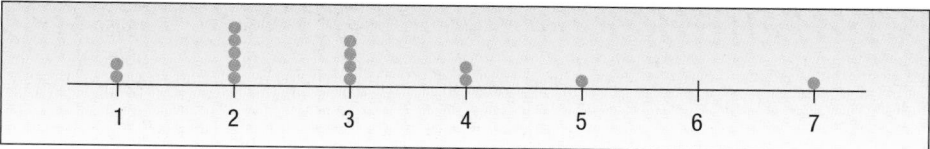

   a. What is this chart called?
   b. How many observations are in the study?
   c. What are the maximum and the minimum values?
   d. Around what values do the observations tend to cluster?

4. The following chart reports the number of cell phones sold at Radio Shack for the last 26 days.

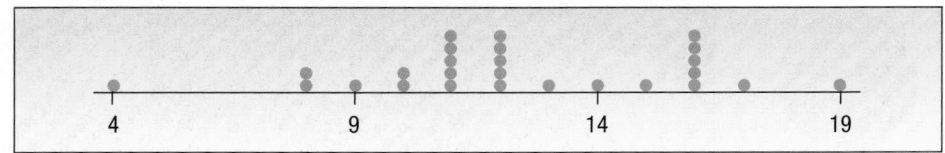

    a. What are the maximum and the minimum number of cell phones sold in a day?
    b. What is a typical number of cell phones sold?

5. The first row of a stem-and-leaf chart appears as follows: 62 | 1 3 3 7 9. Assume whole number values.
    a. What is the "possible range" of the values in this row?
    b. How many data values are in this row?
    c. List the actual values in this row of data.

6. The third row of a stem-and-leaf chart appears as follows: 21 | 0 1 3 5 7 9. Assume whole number values.
    a. What is the "possible range" of the values in this row?
    b. How many data values are in this row?
    c. List the actual values in this row of data.

7. The following stem-and-leaf chart from the MINITAB software shows the number of units produced per day in a factory.

1	3	8
1	4	
2	5	6
9	6	0133559
(7)	7	0236778
9	8	59
7	9	00156
2	10	36

    a. How many days were studied?
    b. How many observations are in the first class?
    c. What are the minimum value and the maximum value?
    d. List the actual values in the fourth row.
    e. List the actual values in the second row.
    f. How many values are less than 70?
    g. How many values are 80 or more?
    h. What is the median?
    i. How many values are between 60 and 89, inclusive?

8. The following stem-and-leaf chart reports the number of movies rented per day at Video Connection on the corner of Fourth and Main Streets.

3	12	689
6	13	123
10	14	6889
13	15	589
15	16	35
20	17	24568
23	18	268
(5)	19	13456
22	20	034679
16	21	2239
12	22	789
9	23	00179
4	24	8
3	25	13
1	26	
1	27	0

    a. How many days were studied?
    b. How many observations are in the last class?
    c. What are the maximum and the minimum values in the entire set of data?
    d. List the actual values in the fourth row.
    e. List the actual values in the next to the last row.
    f. On how many days were less than 160 movies rented?
    g. On how many days were 220 or more movies rented?
    h. What is the middle value?
    i. On how many days were between 170 and 210 movies rented?

9. A survey of the number of cell phone calls made by a sample of Alltel Wireless subscribers last week revealed the following information. Develop a stem-and-leaf chart. How many calls did a typical subscriber make? What were the maximum and the minimum number of calls made?

52	43	30	38	30	42	12	46	39
37	34	46	32	18	41	5		

10. Aloha Banking Co. is studying ATM use in suburban Honolulu. A sample of 30 ATMs showed they were used the following number of times yesterday. Develop a stem-and-leaf chart. Summarize the number of times each ATM was used. What was the typical, minimum, and maximum number of times each ATM was used?

83	64	84	76	84	54	75	59	70	61
63	80	84	73	68	52	65	90	52	77
95	36	78	61	59	84	95	47	87	60

Other Measures of Dispersion

The standard deviation is the most widely used measure of dispersion. However, there are other ways of describing the variation or spread in a set of data. One method is to determine the *location* of values that divide a set of observations into equal parts. These measures include **quartiles, deciles,** and **percentiles.**

    Quartiles divide a set of observations into four equal parts. To explain further, think of any set of values arranged from smallest to largest. In Chapter 3 we called the middle value of a set of data arranged from smallest to largest the median. That is, 50 percent of the observations are larger than the median and 50 percent are smaller. The median is a measure of location because it pinpoints the center of the data. In a similar fashion **quartiles** divide a set of observations into four equal parts. The first quartile, usually labeled Q_1, is the value below which 25 percent of the observations occur, and the third quartile, usually labeled Q_3, is the value below which 75 percent of the observations occur. Logically, Q_2 is the median. Q_1 can be thought of as the "median" of the lower half of the data and Q_3 the "median" of the upper half of the data.

    In a similar fashion **deciles** divide a set of observations into 10 equal parts and **percentiles** into 100 equal parts. So if you found that your GPA was in the 8th decile at your university, you could conclude that 80 percent of the students had a GPA lower than yours and 20 percent had a higher GPA. A GPA in the 33rd percentile means that 33 percent of the students have a lower GPA and 67 percent have a higher GPA. Percentile scores are frequently used to report results on such national standardized tests as the SAT, ACT, GMAT (used to judge entry into many master of business administration programs), and LSAT (used to judge entry into law school).

Quartiles, Deciles, and Percentiles

To formalize the computational procedure, let L_p refer to the location of a desired percentile. So if we want to find the 33rd percentile we would use L_{33} and if we wanted the median, the 50th percentile, then L_{50}. The number of observations is n, so if we want to locate the median, its position is at $(n + 1)/2$, or we could write this as $(n + 1)(P/100)$, where P is the desired percentile.

LOCATION OF A PERCENTILE	$L_p = (n + 1)\dfrac{P}{100}$	**[4–1]**

An example will help to explain further.

Example

Listed below are the commissions earned last month by a sample of 15 brokers at Salomon Smith Barney's Oakland, California office. Salomon Smith Barney is an investment company with offices located throughout the United States.

$2,038	$1,758	$1,721	$1,637	$2,097	$2,047	$2,205	$1,787	$2,287
1,940	2,311	2,054	2,406	1,471	1,460			

Locate the median, the first quartile, and the third quartile for the commissions earned.

Solution

The first step is to sort the data from the smallest commission to the largest.

$1,460	$1,471	$1,637	$1,721	$1,758	$1,787	$1,940	$2,038
2,047	2,054	2,097	2,205	2,287	2,311	2,406	

The median value is the observation in the center. The center value or L_{50} is located at $(n + 1)(50/100)$, where n is the number of observations. In this case that is position number 8, found by $(15 + 1)(50/100)$. The eighth largest commission is $2,038. So we conclude this is the median and that half the brokers earned commissions more than $2,038 and half earned less than $2,038.

Recall the definition of a quartile. Quartiles divide a set of observations into four equal parts. Hence 25 percent of the observations will be less than the first quartile. Seventy-five percent of the observations will be less than the third quartile. To locate the first quartile, we use formula (4–1), where $n = 15$ and $P = 25$:

$$L_{25} = (n + 1)\frac{P}{100} = (15 + 1)\frac{25}{100} = 4$$

and to locate the third quartile, $n = 15$ and $P = 75$:

$$L_{75} = (n + 1)\frac{P}{100} = (15 + 1)\frac{75}{100} = 12$$

Therefore, the first and third quartile values are located at positions 4 and 12, respectively. The fourth value in the ordered array is $1,721 and the twelfth is $2,205. These are the first and third quartiles.

In the above example the location formula yielded a whole number. That is, we wanted to find the first quartile and there were 15 observations, so the location formula indicated we should find the fourth ordered value. What if there were 20 observations in the sample, that is $n = 20$, and we wanted to locate the first quartile? From the location formula (4–1):

$$L_{25} = (n + 1)\frac{P}{100} = (20 + 1)\frac{25}{100} = 5.25$$

We would locate the fifth value in the ordered array and then move .25 of the distance between the fifth and sixth values and report that as the first quartile. Like the median, the quartile does not need to be one of the actual values in the data set.

To explain further, suppose a data set contained the six values: 91, 75, 61, 101, 43, and 104. We want to locate the first quartile. We order the values from smallest to largest: 43, 61, 75, 91, 101, and 104. The first quartile is located at

$$L_{25} = (n + 1)\frac{P}{100} = (6 + 1)\frac{25}{100} = 1.75$$

The position formula tells us that the first quartile is located between the first and the second value and that it is .75 of the distance between the first and the second values. The first value is 43 and the second is 61. So the distance between these two values is 18. To locate the first quartile, we need to move .75 of the distance between the first and second values, so .75(18) = 13.5. To complete the procedure, we add 13.5 to the first value and report that the first quartile is 56.5.

We can extend the idea to include both deciles and percentiles. To locate the 23rd percentile in a sample of 80 observations, we would look for the 18.63 position.

$$L_{23} = (n + 1)\frac{P}{100} = (80 + 1)\frac{23}{100} = 18.63$$

To find the value corresponding to the 23rd percentile, we would locate the 18th value and the 19th value and determine the distance between the two values. Next, we would multiply this difference by 0.63 and add the result to the smaller value. The result would be the 23rd percentile.

With a statistical software package, it is quite easy to sort the data from smallest to largest and to locate percentiles and deciles. Both MINITAB and Excel output summary statistics. Listed below is the MINITAB output. The data are reported in $000. It includes the first and third quartiles, as well as the mean, median, and standard deviation for the Whitner Autoplex data (see Table 2–4). We conclude that 25 percent of the vehicles sold for less than $20,074 and that 75 percent sold for less than $25,795.

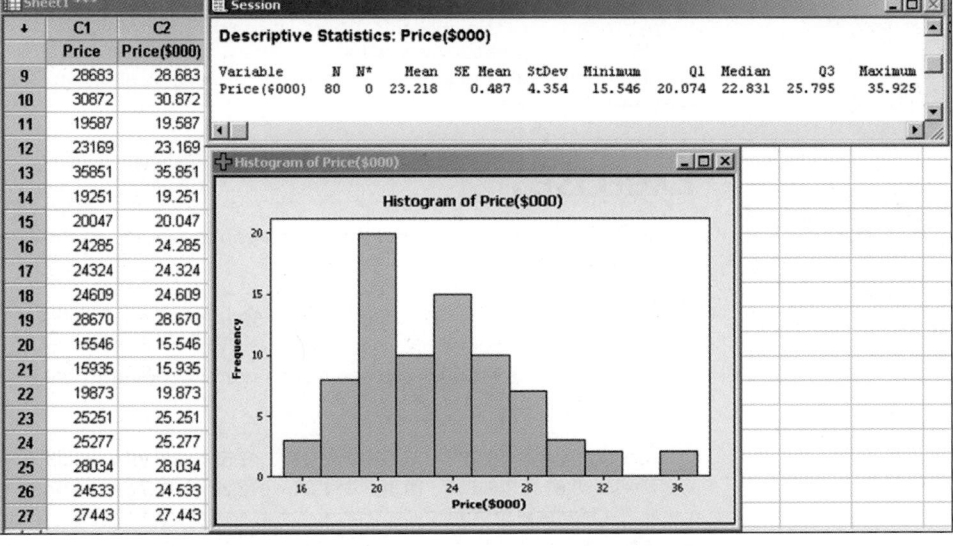

The following Excel output includes the same information regarding the mean, median, and standard deviation. It will also output the quartiles, but the method of calculation is not as precise. To find the quartiles, we multiply the sample size by the desired percentile and report the integer of that value. To explain, in the Whitner Autoplex data there are 80 observations, and we wish to locate the 25th percentile. We multiply $n + 1 = 80 + 1 = 81$ by .25; the result is 20.25. Excel will not allow us to enter a fractional value, so we use 20 and request the location of the largest 20 values and the smallest 20 values. The result is a good approximation of the 25th and 75th percentiles.

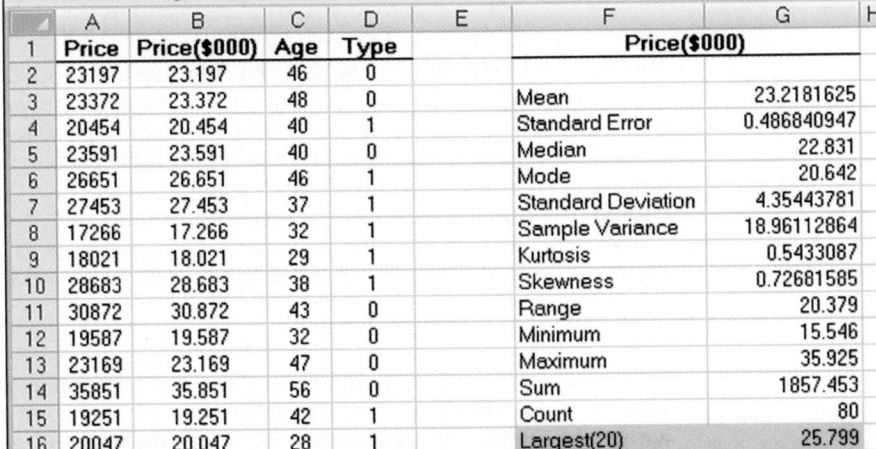

Whitner Quartiles

	A	B	C	D	E	F	G	H
1	Price	Price($000)	Age	Type		Price($000)		
2	23197	23.197	46	0				
3	23372	23.372	48	0		Mean	23.2181625	
4	20454	20.454	40	1		Standard Error	0.486840947	
5	23591	23.591	40	0		Median	22.831	
6	26651	26.651	46	1		Mode	20.642	
7	27453	27.453	37	1		Standard Deviation	4.35443781	
8	17266	17.266	32	1		Sample Variance	18.96112864	
9	18021	18.021	29	1		Kurtosis	0.5433087	
10	28683	28.683	38	1		Skewness	0.72681585	
11	30872	30.872	43	0		Range	20.379	
12	19587	19.587	32	0		Minimum	15.546	
13	23169	23.169	47	0		Maximum	35.925	
14	35851	35.851	56	0		Sum	1857.453	
15	19251	19.251	42	1		Count	80	
16	20047	20.047	28	1		Largest(20)	25.799	
17	24285	24.285	56	0		Smallest(20)	20.047	
18	24324	24.324	50	1				

Excel

Self-Review 4–2 The Quality Control department of Plainsville Peanut Company is responsible for checking the weight of the 8-ounce jar of peanut butter. The weights of a sample of nine jars produced last hour are:

7.69	7.72	7.8	7.86	7.90	7.94	7.97	8.06	8.09

(a) What is the median weight?
(b) Determine the weights corresponding to the first and third quartiles.

Exercises

connect

11. Determine the median and the values corresponding to the first and third quartiles in the following data.

46	47	49	49	51	53	54	54	55	55	59

12. Determine the median and the values corresponding to the first and third quartiles in the following data.

5.24	6.02	6.67	7.30	7.59	7.99	8.03	8.35	8.81	9.45
9.61	10.37	10.39	11.86	12.22	12.71	13.07	13.59	13.89	15.42

13. The Thomas Supply Company, Inc., is a distributor of gas-powered generators. As with any business, the length of time customers take to pay their invoices is important. Listed below, arranged from smallest to largest, is the time, in days, for a sample of The Thomas Supply Company, Inc., invoices.

13	13	13	20	26	27	31	34	34	34	35	35	36	37	38
41	41	41	45	47	47	47	50	51	53	54	56	62	67	82

  a. Determine the first and third quartiles.
  b. Determine the second decile and the eighth decile.
  c. Determine the 67th percentile.

14. Kevin Horn is the national sales manager for National Textbooks, Inc. He has a sales staff of 40 who visit college professors all over the United States. Each Saturday morning he requires his sales staff to send him a report. This report includes, among other things, the number of professors visited during the previous week. Listed below, ordered from smallest to largest, are the number of visits last week.

| 38 | 40 | 41 | 45 | 48 | 48 | 50 | 50 | 51 | 51 | 52 | 52 | 53 | 54 | 55 | 55 | 55 | 56 | 56 | 57 |
| 59 | 59 | 59 | 62 | 62 | 62 | 63 | 64 | 65 | 66 | 66 | 67 | 67 | 69 | 69 | 71 | 77 | 78 | 79 | 79 |

a. Determine the median number of calls.
b. Determine the first and third quartiles.
c. Determine the first decile and the ninth decile.
d. Determine the 33rd percentile.

Box Plots

A **box plot** is a graphical display, based on quartiles, that helps us picture a set of data. To construct a box plot, we need only five statistics: the minimum value, Q_1 (the first quartile), the median, Q_3 (the third quartile), and the maximum value. An example will help to explain.

Example

Alexander's Pizza offers free delivery of its pizza within 15 miles. Alex, the owner, wants some information on the time it takes for delivery. How long does a typical delivery take? Within what range of times will most deliveries be completed? For a sample of 20 deliveries, he determined the following information:

$$\text{Minimum value} = 13 \text{ minutes}$$

$$Q_1 = 15 \text{ minutes}$$

$$\text{Median} = 18 \text{ minutes}$$

$$Q_3 = 22 \text{ minutes}$$

$$\text{Maximum value} = 30 \text{ minutes}$$

Develop a box plot for the delivery times. What conclusions can you make about the delivery times?

Solution

The first step in drawing a box plot is to create an appropriate scale along the horizontal axis. Next, we draw a box that starts at Q_1 (15 minutes) and ends at Q_3 (22 minutes). Inside the box we place a vertical line to represent the median (18 minutes). Finally, we extend horizontal lines from the box out to the minimum value (13 minutes) and the maximum value (30 minutes). These horizontal lines outside of the box are sometimes called "whiskers" because they look a bit like a cat's whiskers.

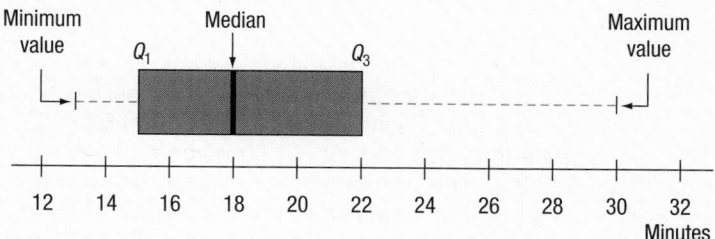

The box plot shows that the middle 50 percent of the deliveries take between 15 minutes and 22 minutes. The distance between the ends of the box, 7 minutes, is the **interquartile range.** The interquartile range is the distance between the first and the third quartile. It shows the spread or dispersion of the majority of deliveries.

The box plot also reveals that the distribution of delivery times is positively skewed. Recall from page 67 in Chapter 3 that we defined skewness as the lack of symmetry in a set of data. How do we know this distribution is positively skewed? In this case there are actually two pieces of information that suggest this. First, the dashed line to the right of the box from 22 minutes (Q_3) to the maximum time of 30 minutes is longer than the dashed line from the left of 15 minutes (Q_1) to the minimum value of 13 minutes. To put it another way, the 25 percent of the data larger than the third quartile is more spread out than the 25 percent less than the first quartile. A second indication of positive skewness is that the median is not in the center of the box. The distance from the first quartile to the median is smaller than the distance from the median to the third quartile. We know that the number of delivery times between 15 minutes and 18 minutes is the same as the number of delivery times between 18 minutes and 22 minutes.

Example

Refer to the Whitner Autoplex data in Table 2–4. Develop a box plot of the data. What can we conclude about the distribution of the vehicle selling prices?

Solution

The MINITAB statistical software system was used to develop the following chart.

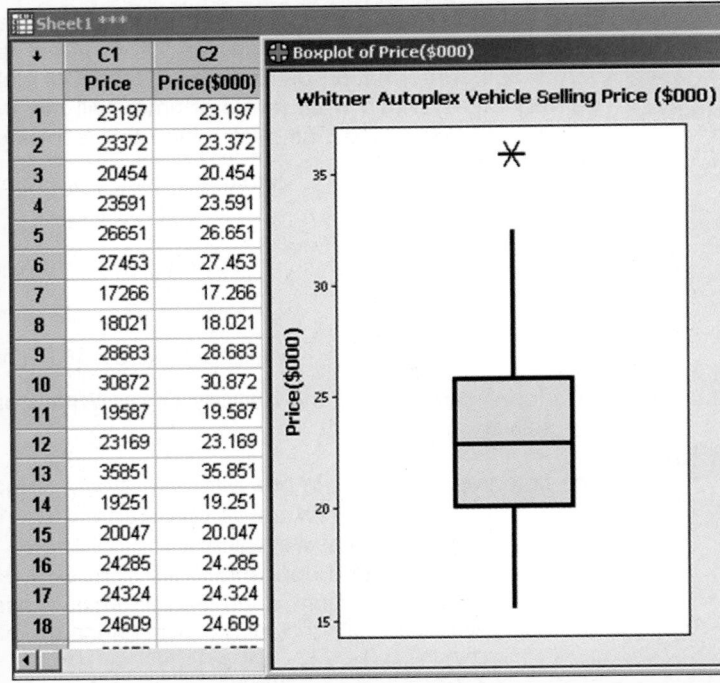

We conclude that the median vehicle selling price is about $23,000, that about 25 percent of the vehicles sell for less than $20,000, and that about 25 percent sell for more than $26,000. About 50 percent of the vehicles sell for between $20,000 and $26,000. The distribution is positively skewed because the solid line above $26,000 is somewhat longer than the line below $20,000.

There is an asterisk (*) above the $35,000 selling price. An asterisk indicates an **outlier.** An outlier is a value that is inconsistent with the rest of the data. An outlier is defined as a value that is more than 1.5 times the interquartile range smaller than Q_1 or larger than Q_3. In this example, an outlier would be a value larger than $35,000, found by

$$\text{Outlier} > Q_3 + 1.5(Q_3 - Q_1) = \$26,000 + 1.5(\$26,000 - \$20,000) = \$35,000$$

A value less than $11,000 is also an outlier.

Outlier $< Q_1 - 1.5(Q_3 - Q_1) = \$20,000 - 1.5(\$26,000 - \$20,000) = \$11,000$

The MINITAB box plot indicates that there is only one value larger than $35,000. However, if you look at the actual data in Table 2–4 on page 28 you will notice that there are actually two values ($35,851 and $35,925). The software was not able to graph two data points so close together, so it shows only one asterisk.

Self-Review 4–3

The following box plot shows the assets in millions of dollars for credit unions in Seattle, Washington.

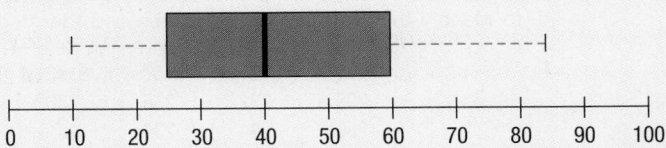

What are the smallest and largest values, the first and third quartiles, and the median? Would you agree that the distribution is symmetrical?

Exercises

connect™

15. The box plot below shows the amount spent for books and supplies per year by students at four-year public colleges.

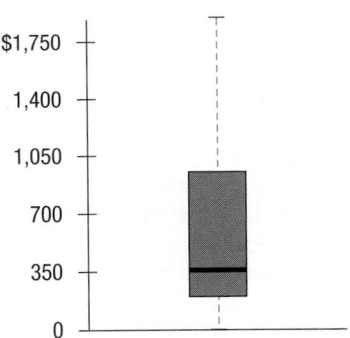

   a. Estimate the median amount spent.
   b. Estimate the first and third quartiles for the amount spent.
   c. Estimate the interquartile range for the amount spent.
   d. Beyond what point is a value considered an outlier?
   e. Identify any outliers and estimate their value.
   f. Is the distribution symmetrical or positively or negatively skewed?

16. The box plot shows the undergraduate in-state charge per credit hour at four-year public colleges.

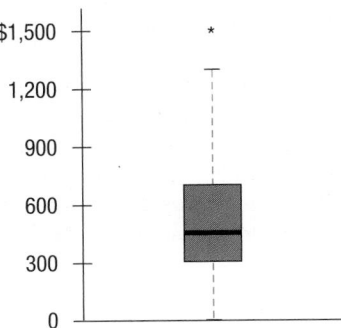

a. Estimate the median.
b. Estimate the first and third quartiles.
c. Determine the interquartile range.
d. Beyond what point is a value considered an outlier?
e. Identify any outliers and estimate their value.
f. Is the distribution symmetrical or positively or negatively skewed?

17. In a study of the gasoline mileage of model year 2007 automobiles, the mean miles per gallon was 27.5 and the median was 26.8. The smallest value in the study was 12.70 miles per gallon, and the largest was 50.20. The first and third quartiles were 17.95 and 35.45 miles per gallon, respectively. Develop a box plot and comment on the distribution. Is it a symmetric distribution?

18. A sample of 28 time shares in the Orlando, Florida, area revealed the following daily charges for a one-bedroom suite. For convenience the data are ordered from smallest to largest. Construct a box plot to represent the data. Comment on the distribution. Be sure to identify the first and third quartiles and the median.

$116	$121	$157	$192	$207	$209	$209
229	232	236	236	239	243	246
260	264	276	281	283	289	296
307	309	312	317	324	341	353

Skewness

In Chapter 3 we described measures of central location for a set of observations by reporting the mean, median, and mode. We also described measures that show the amount of spread or variation in a set of data, such as the range and the standard deviation.

Another characteristic of a set of data is the shape. There are four shapes commonly observed: symmetric, positively skewed, negatively skewed, and bimodal. In a **symmetric** set of observations the mean and median are equal and the data values are evenly spread around these values. The data values below the mean and median are a mirror image of those above. A set of values is **skewed to the right** or **positively skewed** if there is a single peak and the values extend much further to the right of the peak than to the left of the peak. In this case the mean is larger than the median. In a **negatively skewed** distribution there is a single peak but the observations extend further to the left, in the negative direction, than to the right. In a negatively skewed distribution the mean is smaller than the median. Positively skewed distributions are more common. Salaries often follow this pattern. Think of the salaries of those employed in a small company of about 100 people. The president and a few top executives would have very large salaries relative to the other workers and hence the distribution of salaries would exhibit positive skewness. A **bimodal distribution** will have two or more peaks. This is often the case when the values are from two or more populations. This information is summarized in Chart 4–1.

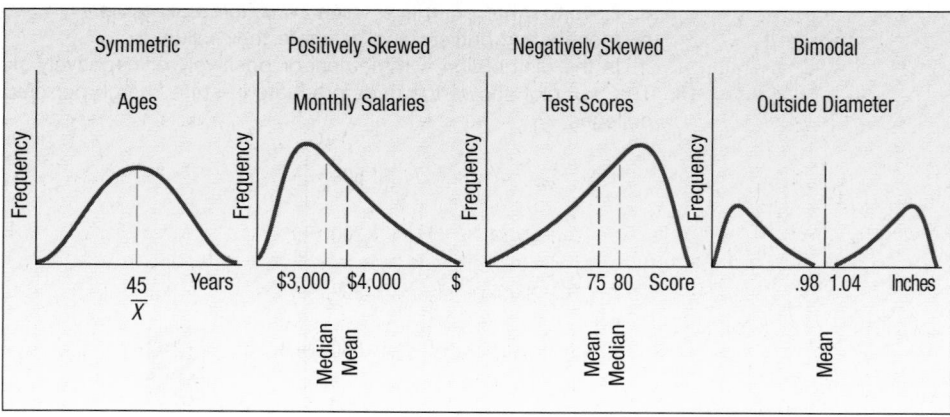

CHART 4–1 Shapes of Frequency Polygons

There are several formulas in statistical literature used to calculate skewness. The simplest, developed by Professor Karl Pearson (1857–1936), is based on the difference between the mean and the median.

PEARSON'S COEFFICIENT OF SKEWNESS	$sk = \dfrac{3(\overline{X} - \text{Median})}{s}$	**[4–2]**

Using this relationship the coefficient of skewness can range from −3 up to 3. A value near −3, such as −2.57, indicates considerable negative skewness. A value such as 1.63 indicates moderate positive skewness. A value of 0, which will occur when the mean and median are equal, indicates the distribution is symmetrical and that there is no skewness present.

In this text we present output from the statistical software packages MINITAB and Excel. Both of these software packages compute a value for the coefficient of skewness that is based on the cubed deviations from the mean. The formula is:

SOFTWARE COEFFICIENT OF SKEWNESS	$sk = \dfrac{n}{(n-1)(n-2)}\left[\sum\left(\dfrac{X - \overline{X}}{s}\right)^3\right]$	**[4–3]**

Formula (4–3) offers an insight into skewness. The right-hand side of the formula is the difference between each value and the mean, divided by the standard deviation. That is the portion $(X - \overline{X})/s$ of the formula. This idea is called **standardizing.** We will discuss the idea of standardizing a value in more detail in Chapter 7 when we describe the normal probability distribution. At this point, observe that the result is to report the difference between each value and the mean in units of the standard deviation. If this difference is positive, the particular value is larger than the mean; if the variation is negative, the standardized quantity is smaller than the mean. When we cube these values, we retain the information on the direction of the difference. Recall that in the formula for the standard deviation [see formula (3–11)] we squared the difference between each value and the mean, so that the result was all non-negative values.

If the set of data values under consideration is symmetric, when we cube the standardized values and sum over all the values the result would be near zero. If there are several large values, clearly separate from the others, the sum of the cubed differences would be a large positive value. Several values much smaller will result in a negative cubed sum.

An example will illustrate the idea of skewness.

Following are the earnings per share for a sample of 15 software companies for the year 2007. The earnings per share are arranged from smallest to largest.

$0.09	$0.13	$0.41	$0.51	$ 1.12	$ 1.20	$ 1.49	$3.18
3.50	6.36	7.83	8.92	10.13	12.99	16.40	

Compute the mean, median, and standard deviation. Find the coefficient of skewness using Pearson's estimate and the software methods. What is your conclusion regarding the shape of the distribution?

These are sample data, so we use formula (3–2) to determine the mean

$$\overline{X} = \frac{\sum X}{n} = \frac{\$74.26}{15} = \$4.95$$

The median is the middle value in a set of data, arranged from smallest to largest. In this case the middle value is \$3.18, so the median earnings per share is \$3.18.

We use formula (3–11) on page 80 to determine the sample standard deviation.

$$s = \sqrt{\frac{\Sigma(X - \overline{X})^2}{n - 1}} = \sqrt{\frac{(\$0.09 - \$4.95)^2 + \cdots + (\$16.40 - \$4.95)^2}{15 - 1}} = \$5.22$$

Pearson's coefficient of skewness is 1.017, found by

$$sk = \frac{3(\overline{X} - \text{Median})}{s} = \frac{3(\$4.95 - \$3.18)}{\$5.22} = 1.017$$

This indicates there is moderate positive skewness in the earnings per share data.

We obtain a similar, but not exactly the same, value from the software method. The details of the calculations are shown in Table 4–2. To begin we find the difference between each earnings per share value and the mean and divide this result by the standard deviation. Recall that we referred to this as standardizing. Next, we cube, that is, raise to the third power, the result of the first step. Finally, we sum the cubed values. The details for the first company, that is, the company with an earnings per share of \$0.09, are:

$$\left(\frac{X - \overline{X}}{s}\right)^3 = \left(\frac{0.09 - 4.95}{5.22}\right)^3 = (-0.9310)^3 = -0.8070$$

When we sum the 15 cubed values, the result is 11.8274. That is, the term $\Sigma[(X - \overline{X})/s]^3 = 11.8274$. To find the coefficient of skewness, we use formula (4–3), with $n = 15$.

$$sk = \frac{n}{(n - 1)(n - 2)} \Sigma\left(\frac{X - \overline{X}}{s}\right)^3 = \frac{15}{(15 - 1)(15 - 2)}(11.8274) = 0.975$$

TABLE 4–2 Calculation of the Coefficient of Skewness

Earnings per Share	$\dfrac{(X - \overline{X})}{s}$	$\left(\dfrac{X - \overline{X}}{s}\right)^3$
0.09	−0.9310	−0.8070
0.13	−0.9234	−0.7873
0.41	−0.8697	−0.6579
0.51	−0.8506	−0.6154
1.12	−0.7337	−0.3950
1.20	−0.7184	−0.3708
1.49	−0.6628	−0.2912
3.18	−0.3391	−0.0390
3.50	−0.2778	−0.0214
6.36	0.2701	0.0197
7.83	0.5517	0.1679
8.92	0.7605	0.4399
10.13	0.9923	0.9772
12.99	1.5402	3.6539
16.40	2.1935	10.5537
		11.8274

We conclude that the earnings per share values are somewhat positively skewed. The following chart, from MINITAB, reports the descriptive measures, such as the mean, median, and standard deviation of the earnings per share data. Also included are the coefficient of skewness and a histogram with a bell-shaped curve superimposed.

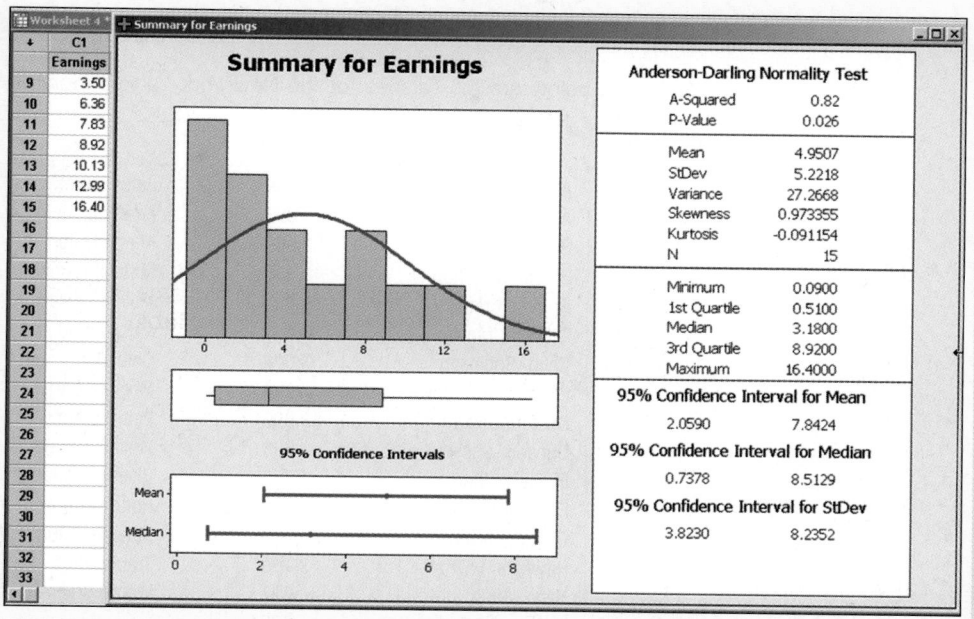

	C1
	Earnings
9	3.50
10	6.36
11	7.83
12	8.92
13	10.13
14	12.99
15	16.40
16	
17	
18	
19	
20	
21	
22	
23	
24	
25	
26	
27	
28	
29	
30	
31	
32	
33	

Summary for Earnings

Anderson-Darling Normality Test

A-Squared	0.82
P-Value	0.026
Mean	4.9507
StDev	5.2218
Variance	27.2668
Skewness	0.973355
Kurtosis	-0.091154
N	15
Minimum	0.0900
1st Quartile	0.5100
Median	3.1800
3rd Quartile	8.9200
Maximum	16.4000

95% Confidence Interval for Mean

2.0590   7.8424

95% Confidence Interval for Median

0.7378   8.5129

95% Confidence Interval for StDev

3.8230   8.2352

95% Confidence Intervals

Self-Review 4–4

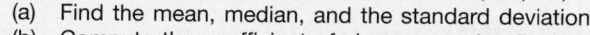

A sample of five data entry clerks employed in the Horry County Tax Office revised the following number of tax records last hour: 73, 98, 60, 92, and 84.
(a) Find the mean, median, and the standard deviation.
(b) Compute the coefficient of skewness using Pearson's method.
(c) Calculate the coefficient of skewness using the software method.
(d) What is your conclusion regarding the skewness of the data?

Exercises

connect

For Exercises 19–22:

a. Determine the mean, median, and the standard deviation.
b. Determine the coefficient of skewness using Pearson's method.
c. Determine the coefficient of skewness using the software method.

19. The following values are the starting salaries, in $000, for a sample of five accounting graduates who accepted positions in public accounting last year.

36.0	26.0	33.0	28.0	31.0

20. Listed below are the salaries, in $000, for a sample of 15 chief financial officers in the electronics industry.

$516.0	$548.0	$566.0	$534.0	$586.0	$529.0
546.0	523.0	538.0	523.0	551.0	552.0
486.0	558.0	574.0			

21. Listed below are the commissions earned ($000) last year by the sales representatives at Furniture Patch, Inc.

$ 3.9	$ 5.7	$ 7.3	$10.6	$13.0	$13.6	$15.1	$15.8	$17.1
17.4	17.6	22.3	38.6	43.2	87.7			

22. Listed below are the salaries for the New York Yankees for the year 2008.

Player	Salary ($000)	Player	Salary ($000)
Abreu, Bobby	$16,000	Jeter, Derek	$21,600
Albaladejo, Jon	393	Karstens, Jeffrey	393
Betemit, Wilson	1,165	Kennedy, Ian	394
Brackman, Andrew	1,185	Matsui, Hideki	13,000
Bruney, Brian	725	Molina, Jose	1,875
Cabrera, Melky	461	Mussina, Mike	11,071
Cano, Robinson	3,000	Ohlendorf, Ross	391
Chamberlain, Joba	390	Pavano, Carl	11,000
Damon, Johnny	13,000	Pettitte, Andy	16,000
Duncan, Shelley	398	Posada, Jorge	13,100
Ensberg, Morgan	1,750	Rivera, Mariano	15,000
Farnsworth, Kyle	5,917	Rodriguez, Alex	28,000
Giambi, Jason	23,429	Sanchez, Humberto	390
Hawkins, LaTroy	3,750	Traber, Billy	500
Henn, Sean	397	Wang, Chien-Ming	4,000
Hughes, Phil	406		

Describing the Relationship between Two Variables

In Chapter 2 and the first section of this chapter we presented graphical techniques to summarize the distribution of a single variable. We used a histogram in Chapter 2 to summarize the prices of vehicles sold at Whitner Autoplex. Earlier in this chapter we used dot plots and stem-and-leaf displays to visually summarize a set of data. Because we are studying a single variable we refer to this as **univariate** data.

There are situations where we wish to study and visually portray the relationship between two variables. When we study the relationship between two variables we refer to the data as **bivariate.** Data analysts frequently wish to understand the relationship between two variables. Here are some examples:

- Tybo and Associates is a law firm that advertises extensively on local TV. The partners are considering increasing their advertising budget. Before doing so, they would like to know the relationship between the amount spent per month on advertising and the total amount of billings for that month. To put it another way, will increasing the amount spent on advertising result in an increase in billings?
- Coastal Realty is studying the selling prices of homes. What variables seem to be related to the selling price of homes? For example, do larger homes sell for

more than smaller ones? Probably. So Coastal might study the relationship between the area in square feet and the selling price.

- Dr. Stephen Givens is an expert in human development. He is studying the relationship between the height of fathers and the height of their sons. That is, do tall fathers tend to have tall children? Would you expect Shaquille O'Neal, the 7'1", 335-pound professional basketball player, to have relatively tall sons?

One graphical technique we use to show the relationship between variables is called a **scatter diagram.**

To draw a scatter diagram we need two variables. We scale one variable along the horizontal axis (X-axis) of a graph and the other variable along the vertical axis (Y-axis). Usually one variable depends to some degree on the other. In the third example above, the height of the son *depends* on the height of the father. So we scale the height of the father on the horizontal axis and that of the son on the vertical axis.

We can use statistical software, such as Excel, to perform the plotting function for us. *Caution:* you should always be careful of the scale. By changing the scale of either the vertical or the horizontal axis, you can affect the apparent visual strength of the relationship.

Following are three scatter diagrams (Chart 4–2). The one on the left shows a rather strong positive relationship between the age in years and the maintenance cost last year for a sample of 10 buses owned by the city of Cleveland, Ohio. Note that as the age of the bus increases the yearly maintenance cost also increases. The example in the center, for a sample of 20 vehicles, shows a rather strong indirect relationship between the odometer reading and the auction price. That is, as the number of miles driven increases, the auction price decreases. The example on the right depicts the relationship between the height and yearly salary for a sample of 15 shift supervisors. This graph indicates there is little relationship between their height and yearly salary.

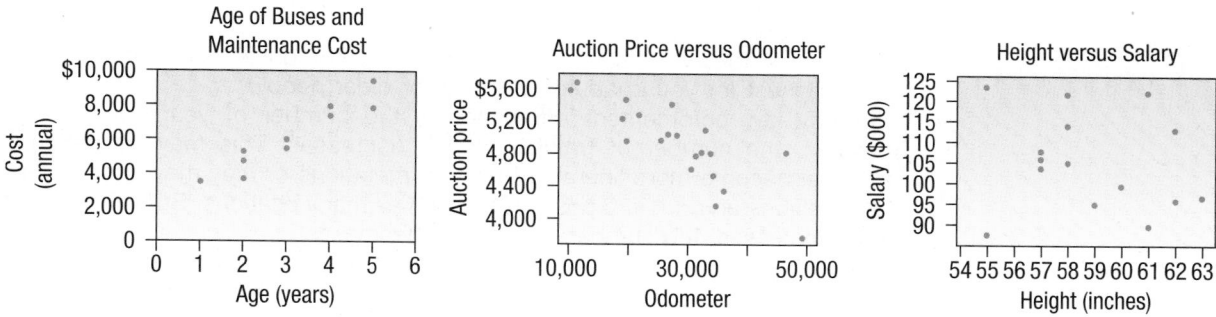

CHART 4–2 Three Examples of Scatter Diagrams.

Example

In the Introduction to Chapter 2 we presented data from AutoUSA. In this case the information concerned the prices of 80 vehicles sold last month at the Whitner Autoplex lot in Raytown, Missouri. The data shown on page 21 include the selling price of the vehicle as well as the age of the purchaser. Is there a relationship between the selling price of a vehicle and the age of the purchaser? Would it be reasonable to conclude that the more expensive vehicles are purchased by older buyers?

Solution

We can investigate the relationship between vehicle selling price and the age of the buyer with a scatter diagram. We scale age on the horizontal, or X-axis, and the selling price on the vertical, or Y-axis. We use Microsoft Excel to develop the scatter diagram. The Excel commands necessary for the output are shown in the **Software Commands** section at the end of the chapter.

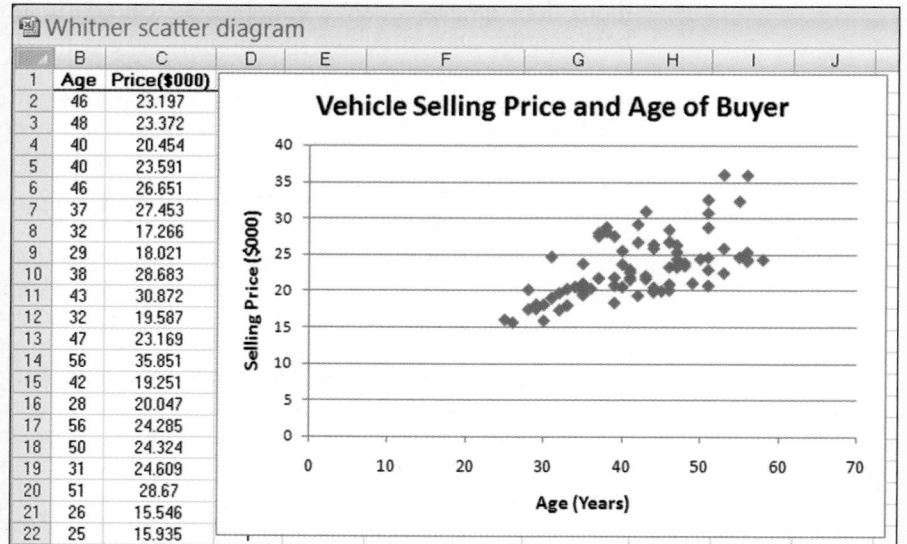

The scatter diagram shows a positive relationship between the variables. In fact, older buyers tend to buy more expensive cars. In Chapter 13 we will study the relationship between variables more extensively, even calculating several numerical measures to express the relationship between variables.

In the Whitner Autoplex example there is a positive or direct relationship between the variables. That is, as age increased, the vehicle selling price also increased. There are, however, many instances where there is a relationship between the variables, but that relationship is inverse or negative. For example:

- The value of a vehicle and the number of miles driven. As the number of miles increases, the value of the vehicle decreases.
- The premium for auto insurance and the age of the driver. Auto rates tend to be the highest for young adults and less for older people.
- For many law enforcement personnel as the number of years on the job increases, the number of traffic citations decreases. This may be because personnel become more liberal in their interpretations or they may be in supervisor positions and not in a position to issue as many citations. But in any event as age increases, the number of citations decreases.

A scatter diagram requires that both of the variables be at least interval scale. In the Whitner Autoplex example both age and selling price are ratio scale variables. Height is also ratio scale as used in the discussion of the relationship between the height of fathers and the height of their sons. What if we wish to study the relationship between two variables when one or both are nominal or ordinal scale? In this case we tally the results in a **contingency table.**

> **CONTINGENCY TABLE** A table used to classify observations according to two identifiable characteristics.

A contingency table is a cross-tabulation that simultaneously summarizes two variables of interest. For example:

- Students at a university are classified by gender and class rank.
- A product is classified as acceptable or unacceptable and by the shift (day, afternoon, or night) on which it is manufactured.

- A voter in a school bond referendum is classified as to party affiliation (Democrat, Republican, other) and the number of children that voter has attending school in the district (0, 1, 2, etc.).

Example

A manufacturer of preassembled windows produced 50 windows yesterday. This morning the quality assurance inspector reviewed each window for all quality aspects. Each was classified as acceptable or unacceptable and by the shift on which it was produced. Thus we reported two variables on a single item. The two variables are shift and quality. The results are reported in the following table.

	Shift			
	Day	**Afternoon**	**Night**	**Total**
Defective	3	2	1	6
Acceptable	17	13	14	44
Total	20	15	15	50

Compare the quality levels on each shift.

Solution

The level of measurement for both variables is nominal. That is, the variables shift and quality are such that a particular unit can only be classified or assigned into groups. By organizing the information into a contingency table we can compare the quality on the three shifts. For example, on the day shift, 3 out of 20 windows or 15 percent are defective. On the afternoon shift, 2 of 15 or 13 percent are defective and on the night shift 1 out of 15 or 7 percent are defective. Overall 12 percent of the windows are defective. Observe also that 40 percent of the windows are produced on the day shift, found by (20/50)(100). We will return to the study of contingency tables in Chapter 5 during the study of probability and in Chapter 17 during the study of nonparametric methods of analysis.

Self-Review 4–5

The rock group Blue String Beans is touring the United States. The following chart shows the relationship between concert seating capacity and revenue in $000 for a sample of concerts.

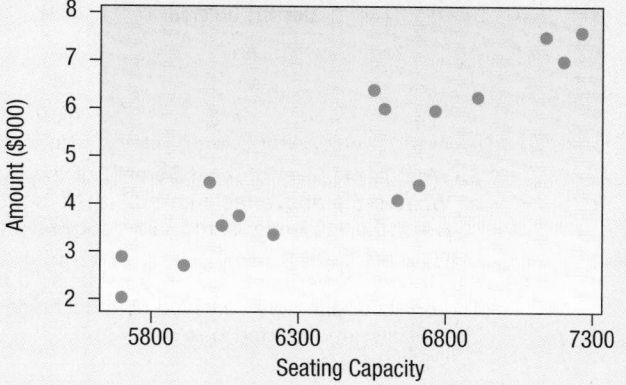

(a) What is the diagram called?
(b) How many concerts were studied?
(c) Estimate the revenue for the concert with the largest seating capacity.
(d) How would you characterize the relationship between revenue and seating capacity? Is it strong or weak, direct or inverse?

Exercises

connect

23. Develop a scatter diagram for the following sample data. How would you describe the relationship between the values?

X-Value	Y-Value	X-Value	Y-Value
10	6	11	6
8	2	10	5
9	6	7	2
11	5	7	3
13	7	11	7

24. Silver Springs Moving and Storage, Inc., is studying the relationship between the number of rooms in a move and the number of labor hours required for the move. As part of the analysis the CFO of Silver Springs developed the following scatter diagram.

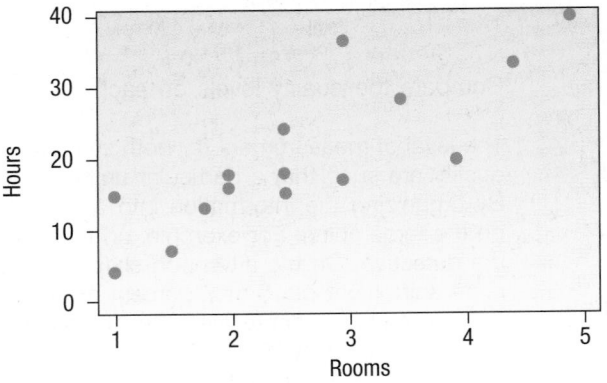

a. How many moves are in the sample?
b. Does it appear that more labor hours are required as the number of rooms increases, or do labor hours decrease as the number of rooms increases?

25. The Director of Planning for Devine Dining, Inc., wishes to study the relationship between the gender of a guest and whether the guest orders dessert. To investigate the relationship the manager collected the following information on 200 recent customers.

Dessert Ordered	Gender		Total
	Male	Female	
Yes	32	15	47
No	68	85	153
Total	100	100	200

a. What is the level of measurement of the two variables?
b. What is the above table called?
c. Does the evidence in the table suggest men are more likely to order dessert than women? Explain why.

26. Ski Resorts of Vermont, Inc., is considering a merger with Gulf Shores, Inc., of Alabama. The board of directors surveyed 50 stockholders concerning their position on the merger. The results are reported below.

Number of Shares Held	Opinion			Total
	Favor	Oppose	Undecided	
Under 200	8	6	2	16
200 up to 1,000	6	8	1	15
Over 1,000	6	12	1	19
Total	20	26	4	50

a. What level of measurement is used in this table?
b. What is this table called?
c. What group seems most strongly opposed to the merger?

Chapter Summary

I. A dot plot shows the range of values on the horizontal axis and a dot is placed above each of the values.
  A. Dot plots report the details of each observation.
  B. They are useful for comparing two or more data sets.
II. A stem-and-leaf display is an alternative to a histogram.
  A. The leading digit is the stem and the trailing digit the leaf.
  B. The advantages of a stem-and-leaf display over a histogram include:
    1. The identity of each observation is not lost.
    2. The digits themselves give a picture of the distribution.
    3. The cumulative frequencies are also shown.
III. Measures of location also describe the shape of a set of observations.
  A. Quartiles divide a set of observations into four equal parts.
    1. Twenty-five percent of the observations are less than the first quartile, 50 percent are less than the second quartile, and 75 percent are less than the third quartile.
    2. The interquartile range is the difference between the third and the first quartile.
  B. Deciles divide a set of observations into ten equal parts and percentiles into 100 equal parts.
  C. A box plot is a graphic display of a set of data.
    1. A box is drawn enclosing the regions between the first and third quartiles.
      a. A line is drawn inside the box at the median value.
      b. Dotted line segments are drawn from the third quartile to the largest value to show the highest 25 percent of the values and from the first quartile to the smallest value to show the lowest 25 percent of the values.
    2. A box plot is based on five statistics: the maximum and minimum values, the first and third quartiles, and the median.
IV. The coefficient of skewness is a measure of the symmetry of a distribution.
  A. There are two formulas for the coefficient of skewness.
    1. The formula developed by Pearson is:

$$sk = \frac{3(\overline{X} - \text{Median})}{s}$$ [4–2]

    2. The coefficient of skewness computed by statistical software is:

$$sk = \frac{n}{(n-1)(n-2)}\left[\sum\left(\frac{X-\overline{X}}{s}\right)^3\right]$$ [4–3]

V. A scatter diagram is a graphic tool to portray the relationship between two variables.
  A. Both variables are measured with interval or ratio scales.
  B. If the scatter of points moves from the lower left to the upper right, the variables under consideration are directly or positively related.
  C. If the scatter of points moves from the upper left to the lower right, the variables are inversely or negatively related.
VI. A contingency table is used to classify nominal-scale observations according to two characteristics.

Pronunciation Key

SYMBOL	MEANING	PRONUNCIATION
L_p	Location of percentile	L sub p
Q_1	First quartile	Q sub 1
Q_3	Third quartile	Q sub 3

Chapter Exercises

27. A sample of students attending Southeast Florida University is asked the number of social activities in which they participated last week. The chart below was prepared from the sample data.

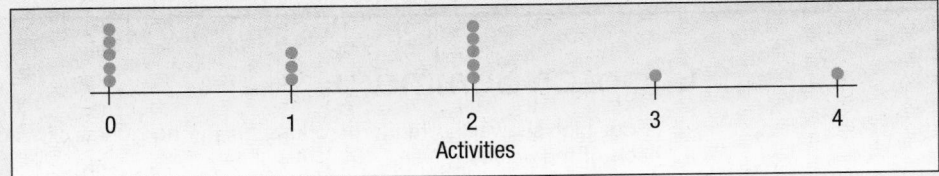

a. What is the name given to this chart?
b. How many students were in the study?
c. How many students reported attending no social activities?

28. Doctor's Care is a walk-in clinic, with locations in Georgetown, Monks Corners, and Aynor, at which patients may receive treatment for minor injuries, colds, and flu, as well as physical examinations. The following charts report the number of patients treated in each of the three locations last month.

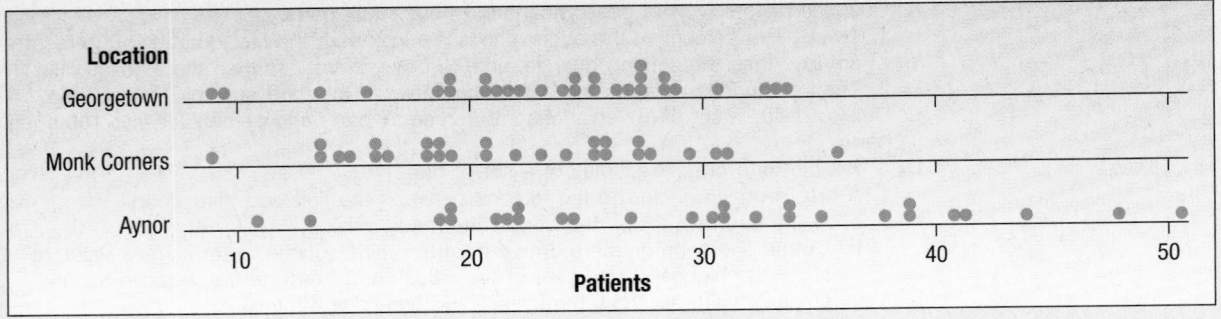

Describe the number of patients served at the three locations each day. What are the maximum and minimum numbers of patients served at each of the locations?

29. The screen size for 23 LCD televisions is given below. Make a stem-and-leaf display of this variable.

46	52	46	40	42	46	40	37	46	40	52	32	37	32	52
40	32	52	40	52	46	46	52							

30. The top 25 companies (by market capitalization) operating in the Washington, DC, area along with the year they were founded and the number of employees are given below. Make a stem-and-leaf display of each of these variables and write a short description of your findings.

Company Name	Year Founded	Employees
AES Corp.	1981	30000
American Capital Strategies Ltd.	1986	484
AvalonBay Communities Inc.	1978	1767
Capital One Financial Corp.	1995	31800
Constellation Energy Group Inc.	1816	9736
Coventry Health Care Inc.	1986	10250
Danaher Corp.	1984	45000
Dominion Resources Inc.	1909	17500
Fannie Mae	1938	6450
Freddie Mac	1970	5533
		(continued)

Company Name	Year Founded	Employees
Gannett Co.	1906	49675
General Dynamics Corp.	1952	81000
Genworth Financial Inc.	2004	7200
Harman International Industries Inc.	1980	11246
Host Hotels & Resorts Inc.	1927	229
Legg Mason Inc.	1899	3800
Lockheed Martin Corp.	1995	140000
Marriott International Inc.	1927	151000
MedImmune Inc.	1988	2516
NII Holdings Inc.	1996	7748
Norfolk Southern Corp.	1982	30594
Pepco Holdings Inc.	1896	5057
Sallie Mae	1972	11456
Sprint Nextel Corp.	1899	64000
T. Rowe Price Group Inc.	1937	4605
The Washington Post Co.	1877	17100

31. In recent years, due to low interest rates, many homeowners refinanced their home mortgages. Linda Lahey is a mortgage officer at Down River Federal Savings and Loan. Below is the amount refinanced for 20 loans she processed last week. The data are reported in thousands of dollars and arranged from smallest to largest.

59.2	59.5	61.6	65.5	66.6	72.9	74.8	77.3	79.2
83.7	85.6	85.8	86.6	87.0	87.1	90.2	93.3	98.6
100.2	100.7							

a. Find the median, first quartile, and third quartile.
b. Find the 26th and 83rd percentiles.
c. Draw a box plot of the data.

32. A study is made by the recording industry in the United States of the number of music CDs owned by senior citizens and young adults. The information is reported below.

Seniors									
28	35	41	48	52	81	97	98	98	99
118	132	133	140	145	147	153	158	162	174
177	180	180	187	188					

Young Adults									
81	107	113	147	147	175	183	192	202	209
233	251	254	266	283	284	284	316	372	401
417	423	490	500	507	518	550	557	590	594

a. Find the median and the first and third quartiles for the number of CDs owned by senior citizens. Develop a box plot for the information.
b. Find the median and the first and third quartiles for the number of CDs owned by young adults. Develop a box plot for the information.
c. Compare the number of CDs owned by the two groups.

33. The corporate headquarters of *Bank.com,* a new Internet company that performs all banking transactions via the Internet, is located in downtown Philadelphia. The director of human resources is making a study of the time it takes employees to get to work. The city is planning to offer incentives to each downtown employer if they will encourage their employees to use public transportation. Below is a listing of the time to get to work this morning according to whether the employee used public transportation or drove a car.

Public Transportation									
23	25	25	30	31	31	32	33	35	36
37	42								

Private									
32	32	33	34	37	37	38	38	38	39
40	44								

    a. Find the median and the first and third quartiles for the time it took employees using public transportation. Develop a box plot for the information.

    b. Find the median and the first and third quartiles for the time it took employees who drove their own vehicle. Develop a box plot for the information.

    c. Compare the times of the two groups.

34. The following box plot shows the number of daily newspapers published in each state and the District of Columbia. Write a brief report summarizing the number published. Be sure to include information on the values of the first and third quartiles, the median, and whether there is any skewness. If there are any outliers, estimate their value.

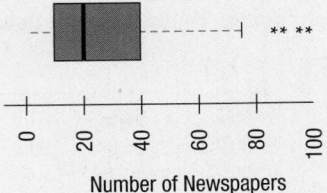

Number of Newspapers

35. Walter Gogel Company is an industrial supplier of fasteners, tools, and springs. The amounts of its invoices vary widely, from less than $20.00 to more than $400.00. During the month of January the company sent out 80 invoices. Here is a box plot of these invoices. Write a brief report summarizing the invoice amounts. Be sure to include information on the values of the first and third quartiles, the median, and whether there is any skewness. If there are any outliers, approximate the value of these invoices.

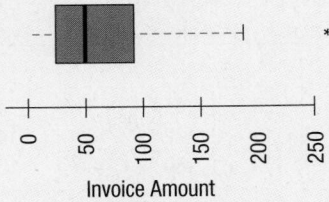

Invoice Amount

36. National Muffler Company claims it will change your muffler in less than 30 minutes. An investigative reporter for WTOL Channel 11 monitored 30 consecutive muffler changes at the National outlet on Liberty Street. The number of minutes to perform changes is reported below.

44	12	22	31	26	22	30	26	18	28	12
40	17	13	14	17	25	29	15	30	10	28
16	33	24	20	29	34	23	13			

    a. Develop a box plot for the time to change a muffler.

    b. Does the distribution show any outliers?

    c. Summarize your findings in a brief report.

37. McGivern Jewelers is located in the Levis Square Mall just south of Toledo, Ohio. Recently it ran an advertisement in the local newspaper reporting the shape, size, price, and cut grade for 33 of its diamonds currently in stock. The information is reported below.

Shape	Size (carats)	Price	Cut Grade	Shape	Size (carats)	Price	Cut Grade
Princess	5.03	$44,312	Ideal cut	Round	0.77	$ 2,828	Ultra ideal cut
Round	2.35	20,413	Premium cut	Oval	0.76	3,808	Premium cut
Round	2.03	13,080	Ideal cut	Princess	0.71	2,327	Premium cut
Round	1.56	13,925	Ideal cut	Marquise	0.71	2,732	Good cut
Round	1.21	7,382	Ultra ideal cut	Round	0.70	1,915	Premium cut
Round	1.21	5,154	Average cut	Round	0.66	1,885	Premium cut
Round	1.19	5,339	Premium cut	Round	0.62	1,397	Good cut
Emerald	1.16	5,161	Ideal cut	Round	0.52	2,555	Premium cut
Round	1.08	8,775	Ultra ideal cut	Princess	0.51	1,337	Ideal cut
Round	1.02	4,282	Premium cut	Round	0.51	1,558	Premium cut
Round	1.02	6,943	Ideal cut	Round	0.45	1,191	Premium cut
Marquise	1.01	7,038	Good cut	Princess	0.44	1,319	Average cut
Princess	1.00	4,868	Premium cut	Marquise	0.44	1,319	Premium cut
Round	0.91	5,106	Premium cut	Round	0.40	1,133	Premium cut
Round	0.90	3,921	Good cut	Round	0.35	1,354	Good cut
Round	0.90	3,733	Premium cut	Round	0.32	896	Premium cut
Round	0.84	2,621	Premium cut				

a. Develop a box plot of the variable price and comment on the result. Are there any outliers? What is the median price? What is the value of the first and the third quartile?
b. Develop a box plot of the variable size and comment on the result. Are there any outliers? What is the median price? What is the value of the first and the third quartile?
c. Develop a scatter diagram between the variables price and size. Be sure to put price on the vertical axis and size on the horizontal axis. Does there seem to be an association between the two variables? Is the association direct or indirect? Does any point seem to be different from the others?
d. Develop a contingency table for the variables shape and cut grade. What is most common cut grade? What is the most common shape? What is the most common combination of cut grade and shape?

38. Listed below is the amount of commissions earned last month for the eight members of the sales staff at Best Electronics. Calculate the coefficient of skewness using both methods. *Hint:* Use of a spreadsheet will expedite the calculations.

980.9	1,036.5	1,099.5	1,153.9	1,409.0	1,456.4	1,718.4	1,721.2

39. Listed below is the number of car thefts in a large city over the last week. Calculate the coefficient of skewness using both methods. *Hint:* Use of a spreadsheet will expedite the calculations.

3	12	13	7	8	3	8

40. The manager of Information Services at Wilkin Investigations, a private investigation firm, is studying the relationship between the age (in months) of a combination printer, copy, and fax machine and its monthly maintenance cost. For a sample of 15 machines the manager developed the following chart. What can the manager conclude about the relationship between the variables?

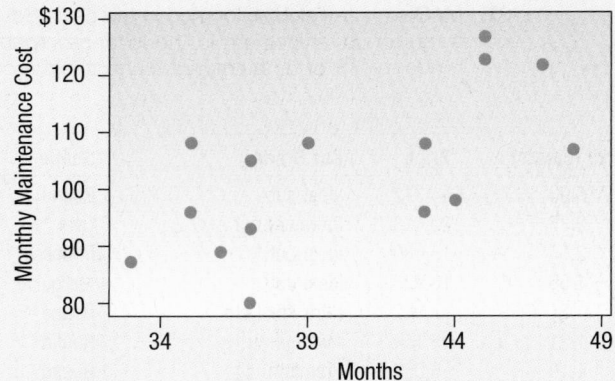

41. An auto insurance company reported the following information regarding the age of a driver and the number of accidents reported last year. Develop a scatter diagram for the data and write a brief summary.

Age	Accidents	Age	Accidents
16	4	23	0
24	2	27	1
18	5	32	1
17	4	22	3

42. Wendy's offers eight different condiments (mustard, catsup, onion, mayonnaise, pickle, lettuce, tomato, and relish) on hamburgers. A store manager collected the following information on the number of condiments ordered and the age group of the customer. What can you conclude regarding the information? Who tends to order the most or least number of condiments?

	Age			
Number of Condiments	**Under 18**	**18 up to 40**	**40 up to 60**	**60 or older**
0	12	18	24	52
1	21	76	50	30
2	39	52	40	12
3 or more	71	87	47	28

43. Listed below is a table showing the number of employed and unemployed workers 20 years or older by gender in the United States in 2006.

	Number of Workers (000)	
Gender	**Employed**	**Unemployed**
Men	70,415	4,209
Women	61,402	3,314

    a. How many workers were studied?
    b. What percent of the workers were unemployed?
    c. Compare the percent unemployed for the men and the women.

Data Set Exercises

44. Refer to the Real Estate data, which report information on homes sold in the Denver, Colorado, area last year. Select the variable selling price.
    a. Develop a box plot. Estimate the first and the third quartiles. Are there any outliers?
    b. Develop a scatter diagram with price on the vertical axis and the size of the home on the horizontal. Does there seem to be a relationship between these variables? Is the relationship direct or inverse?

   c. Develop a scatter diagram with price on the vertical axis and distance from the center of the city on the horizontal axis. Does there seem to be a relationship between these variables? Is the relationship direct or inverse?

45. Refer to the Baseball 2007 data, which report information on the 30 Major League Baseball teams for the 2007 season.

   a. Select the variable that refers to the year in which the stadium was built. (*Hint:* Subtract the year in which the stadium was built from the current year to find the age of the stadium and work with this variable.) Develop a box plot. Are there any outliers?

   b. Select the variable team salary and draw a box plot. Are there any outliers? What are the quartiles? Write a brief summary of your analysis. How do the salaries of the New York Yankees compare with the other teams?

   c. Draw a scatter diagram with the number of games won on the vertical axis and the team salary on the horizontal axis. What are your conclusions?

   d. Select the variable wins. Draw a dot plot. What can you conclude from this plot?

46. Refer to the Wage data, which report information on annual wages for a sample of 100 workers. Also included are variables relating to industry, years of education, and gender for each worker.

   a. Develop a stem-and-leaf chart for the variable annual wage. Are there any outliers? Write a brief summary of your findings.

   b. Develop a stem-and-leaf chart for the variable years of education. Are there any outliers? Write a brief summary of your findings.

   c. Draw a bar chart of the variable occupation. Write a brief report summarizing your findings.

47. Refer to the CIA data, which report demographic and economic information on 46 countries.

   a. Select the variable life expectancy. Develop a box plot. Find the first and third quartiles. Are there any outliers? Is the distribution skewed or symmetric? Write a paragraph summarizing your findings.

   b. Select the variable GDP/cap. Develop a box plot. Find the first and third quartiles. Are there any outliers? Is the distribution skewed or symmetric? Write a paragraph summarizing your findings.

   c. Develop a stem-and-leaf chart for the variable referring to the number of cell phones. Summarize your findings.

Software Commands

1. The MINITAB commands for the dot plot on page 101 are:

   a. Enter the vehicles sold at Smith Ford Mercury Jeep in column *C1* and Brophy Honda Volkswagen in *C2*. Name the variables accordingly.

   b. Select **Graph** and **Dotplot.** In the first dialog box select **Multiple Y's, Simple** in the lower left corner and click **OK.** In the next dialog box select **Smith** and **Brophy** as the variables to **Graph,** click on **Labels** and write an appropriate title. Then click **OK.**

   c. To calculate the descriptive statistics shown in the output select **Stat, Basic statistics,** and then **Display Descriptive statistics.** In the dialog box select **Smith** and **Brophy** as the **Variables,** click on **Statistics** and select the desired statistics to be output, and finally click **OK** twice.

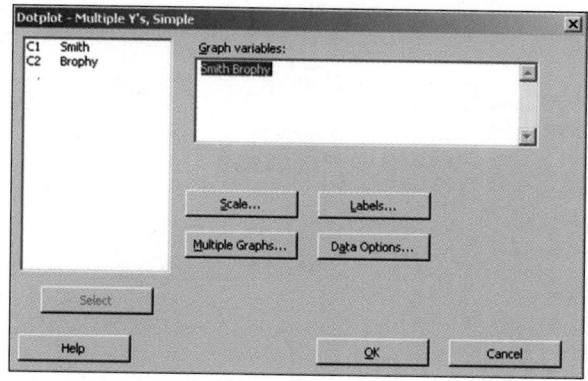

2. The MINITAB commands for the stem-and-leaf display on page 104 are:
  a. Import the data from the CD. The file name is **Table4–1.**
  b. Select **Graph,** and click on **Stem-and-Leaf.**
  c. Select the variable **Spots,** enter *10* for the **Increment,** and then click **OK.**

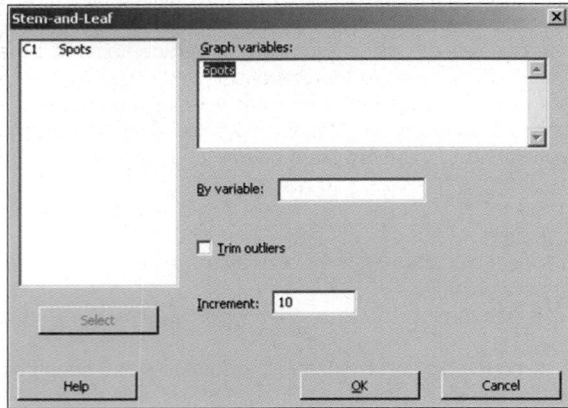

3. The MINITAB commands for the descriptive summary on page 109 are:
  a. Import the Whitner Autoplex data from the CD. The file name is **Whitner.** Select the variable **Price.**
  b. From the toolbar select **Stat, Basic Statistics,** and **Display Descriptive Statistics.** In the dialog box select **Price** as the **Variable,** in the lower right click on **Graphs.** In this box select **Graphs,** click on **Histogram of data,** and then click **OK** twice.

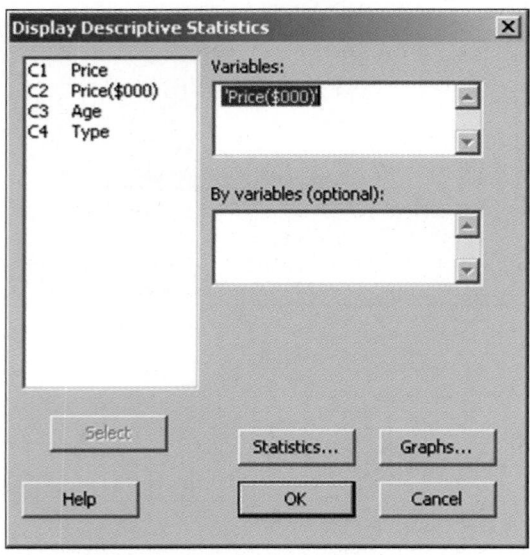

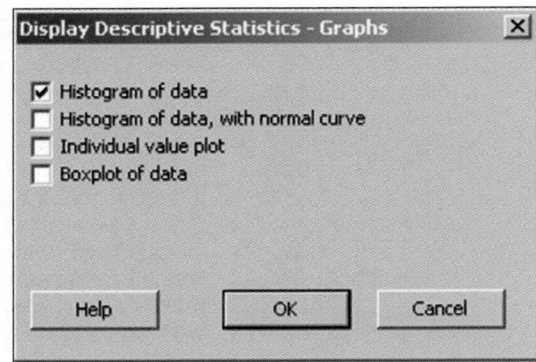

4. The Excel Commands for the descriptive statistics on page 110 are:
  a. From the CD retrieve the Whitner Autoplex data file, which is **Whitner.**
  b. From the menu bar select **Data,** and then **Data Analysis.** Select **Descriptive Statistics** and then click **OK.**
  c. For the **Input Range,** type *B1:B81,* indicate that the data are grouped by column and that the labels are in the first row. Click on **Output Range,** indicate that the output should go into *F1* (or any place you wish), and click on **Summary statistics.**
  d. In the lower left, click on **Kth Largest** and put *20* in the box and click on **Kth Smallest** and put *20* in that box.
  e. After you get your results, double-check the count in the output to be sure it contains the correct number of values.

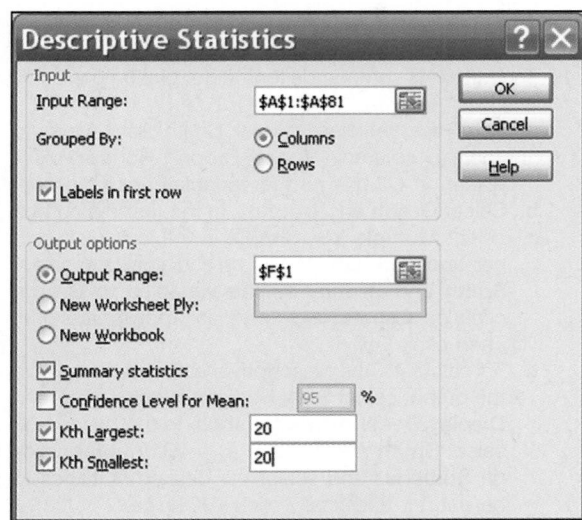

5. The MINITAB commands for the box plot on page 112 are:
  a. Import the data from the CD. The file name is **Table2–1.**

b. Select **Graph** and then **Boxplot.** In the dialog box select **Simple** in the upper left corner and click **OK.** Select **Price ($000)** as the **Graph variable,** click on **Labels** and include an appropriate heading, and then click **OK.**

6. The MINITAB commands for the descriptive summary on page 117 are:
   a. Enter the data in the first column. In the cell below C1, enter the variable *Earnings.*
   b. Select **Stat, Basic Statistics,** and then click on **Graphical Summary.** Select **Earnings** as the variable, and then click **OK.**

7. The Excel commands for the scatter diagram on page 120 are:
   a. Retrieve the data from **Whitner** on the CD.
   b. You will need to copy the variables to other columns on the spreadsheet with age in a column and price ($000) in the next column. This will allow you to place price on the vertical axis and age on the horizontal axis.
   c. Using the mouse, highlight the column of age and price ($000). Include the first row.
   d. Select the **Insert** tab. Select **Scatter** from the **Chart** options. Select the top left option. The scatter plot will appear.
   e. With **Chart Tools** displayed at the top, select the **Layout** tab. Select **Chart Title** and type in a title for the plot. Next, under the same **Layout** tab, select **Axis Titles.** Using **Primary Vertical Axis Title,** name the vertical axis *Price ($000).* Using the **Primary Horizontal Axis Title,** name the horizontal axis *Price ($000).* Next select **Legend** and select **None.**

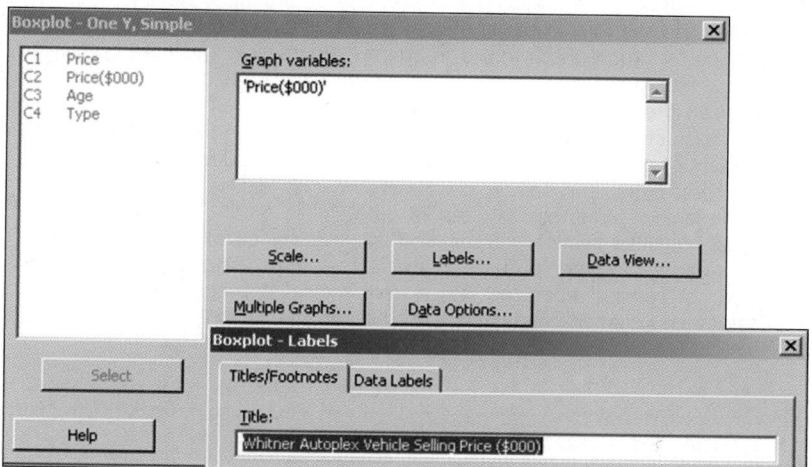

Chapter 4   Answers to Self-Review

4–1 **1. a.** 79, 105
  b. 15
  c. From 88 to 97; 75 percent of the stores are in this range.

2.

7	7
8	0013488
9	1256689
10	1248
11	26

  a. 8
  b. 10.1, 10.2, 10.4, 10.8
  c. 9.5
  d. 11.6, 7.7

4–2 **a.** 7.9
  b. $Q_1 = 7.76$, $Q_3 = 8.015$

4–3 The smallest value is 10 and the largest 85; the first quartile is 25 and the third 60. About 50 percent of the values are between 25 and 60. The median value is 40. The distribution is positively skewed.

4–4 **a.** $\overline{X} = \dfrac{407}{5} = 81.4$, Median = 84

  $$s = \sqrt{\dfrac{923.2}{5-1}} = 15.19$$

  b. $sk = \dfrac{3(81.4 - 84)}{15.19} = -0.51$

c.

X	$\dfrac{X - \overline{X}}{s}$	$\left[\dfrac{X - \overline{X}}{s}\right]^3$
73	−0.5530	−0.1691
98	1.0928	1.3051
60	−1.4088	−2.7962
92	0.6978	0.3398
84	0.1712	0.0050
		−1.3154

$$sk = \frac{5}{(4)(3)}[-1.3154]$$

$$= -0.5481$$

d. The distribution is somewhat negatively skewed.

4–5 a. Scatter diagram
b. 16
c. $7,500
d. Strong and direct

A Review of Chapters 1–4

This section is a review of the major concepts and terms introduced in Chapters 1–4. Chapter 1 began by describing the meaning and purpose of statistics. Next we described the different types of variables and the four levels of measurement. Chapter 2 was concerned with describing a set of observations by organizing it into a frequency distribution and then portraying the frequency distribution as a histogram or a frequency polygon. Chapter 3 began by describing measures of location, such as the mean, weighted mean, median, geometric mean, and mode. This chapter also included measures of dispersion, or spread. Discussed in this section were the range, mean deviation, variance, and standard deviation. Chapter 4 included several graphing techniques such as dot plots, box plots, and scatter diagrams. We also discussed the coefficient of skewness, which reports the lack of symmetry in a set of data.

Throughout this section we stressed the importance of statistical software, such as Excel and MINITAB. Many computer outputs in these chapters demonstrated how quickly and effectively a large data set can be organized into a frequency distribution, several of the measures of location or measures or variation calculated, and the information presented in graphical form.

Glossary

Chapter 1

Descriptive statistics   The techniques used to describe the important characteristics of a set of data. This includes organizing the data values into a frequency distribution, computing measures of location, and computing measures of dispersion and skewness.

Inferential statistics, also called **statistical inference** This facet of statistics deals with estimating a population parameter based on a sample statistic. For example, if 2 out of the 10 hand calculators sampled are defective, we might infer that 20 percent of the production is defective.

Interval measurement   If one observation is greater than another by a certain amount, and the zero point is arbitrary, the measurement is on an interval scale. For example, the difference between temperatures of 70 degrees and 80 degrees is 10 degrees. Likewise, a temperature of 90 degrees is 10 degrees more than a temperature of 80 degrees, and so on.

Nominal measurement   The "lowest" level of measurement. If data are classified into categories and the order of those categories is not important, it is the nominal level of measurement. Examples are gender (male, female) and political affiliation (Republican, Democrat, Independent, all others). If it makes no difference whether male or female is listed first, the data are nominal level.

Ordinal measurement   Data that can be ranked are referred to as ordinal measures. For example, consumer response to the sound of a new speaker might be excellent, very good, fair, or poor.

Population   The collection, or set, of all individuals, objects, or measurements whose properties are being studied.

Ratio measurement   If the distance between numbers is a constant size, there is a true zero point, and the ratio of two values is meaningful, then the data are ratio scale. For example, the distance between $200 and $300 is $100, and in the case of money there is a true zero point. If you have zero dollars, there is an absence of money (you have none). Also the ratio between $200 and $300 is meaningful.

Sample   A portion, or subset, of the population being studied.

Statistics   The science of collecting, organizing, analyzing, and interpreting numerical data for the purpose of making more effective decisions.

Chapter 2

Charts   Special graphical formats used to portray a frequency distribution, including histograms, frequency polygons, and cumulative frequency polygons. Other graphical devices used to portray data are line charts, bar charts, and pie charts. They are very useful, for example, for depicting the trend in long-term debt or percent changes in profit from last year to this year.

Class   The interval in which the data are tallied. For example, $4 up to $7 is a class; $7 up to $11 is another class.

Class frequency   The number of observations in each class. If there are 16 observations in the $4 up to $6 class, 16 is the class frequency.

Exhaustive   Each observation must fall into one of the categories.

Frequency distribution   A grouping of data into classes showing the number of observations in each of the mutually exclusive classes.

Histogram   A graphical display of a frequency or relative frequency distribution. The horizontal axis shows the classes. The vertical height of adjacent bars shows the frequency or relative frequency of each class.

Midpoint   The value that divides the class into two equal parts. For the classes $10 up to $20 and $20 up to $30, the midpoints are $15 and $25, respectively.

Mutually exclusive   A property of a set of categories such that an individual, object, or measurement is included in only one category.

Relative frequency distribution   A frequency distribution that shows the fraction or proportion of the total observations in each class.

Chapter 3

Arithmetic mean   The sum of the values divided by the number of values. The symbol for the mean of a sample is $\bar{X}$ and the symbol for a population mean is μ.

Geometric mean   The nth root of the product of all the values. It is especially useful for averaging rates of change and index numbers. It minimizes the importance of extreme values. A second use of the geometric mean is to find the mean annual percent change over a period of time. For example, if gross sales were $245 million in 1985 and $692 million in 2007, what is the average annual percent increase?

Mean deviation   The mean of the deviations from the mean, disregarding signs. It is abbreviated as *MD*.

Measure of dispersion   A value that shows the spread of a data set. The range, variance, and standard deviation are measures of dispersion.

Measure of location   A single value that is typical of the data. It pinpoints the center of a distribution. The arithmetic mean, weighted mean, median, mode, and geometric mean are measures of central location.

Median   The value of the middle observation after all the observations have been arranged from low to high. For example, if observations 6, 9, 4 are rearranged to read 4, 6, 9, the median is 6, the middle value.

Mode   The value that appears most frequently in a set of data. For grouped data, it is the *midpoint* of the class containing the largest number of values.

Range   It is a measure of dispersion. The range is found by subtracting the minimum value from the maximum value.

Standard deviation   The square root of the variance.

Variance   A measure of dispersion based on the average squared differences from the arithmetic mean.

Weighted mean   Each value is weighted according to its relative importance. For example, if 5 shirts cost $10 each and 20 shirts cost $8 each, the weighted mean price is $8.40: $[(5 \times \$10) + (20 \times \$8)]/25 = \$210/25 = \$8.40$.

Chapter 4

Box plot   A graphic display that shows the general shape of a variable's distribution. It is based on five descriptive statistics: the maximum and minimum values, the first and third quartiles, and the median.

Coefficient of skewness   A measure of the lack of symmetry in a distribution. For a symmetric distribution there is no skewness, so the coefficient of skewness is zero. Otherwise, it is either positive or negative, with the limits of ± 3.0.

Contingency table   A table used to classify observations according to two characteristics.

Deciles   Values of an ordered (minimum to maximum) data set that divide the data into ten equal parts.

Dot plot   A dot plot summarizes the distribution of one variable by stacking dots at points on a number line that shows the values of the variable. A dot plot shows all values.

Interquartile range   The absolute numerical difference between the first and third quartiles. Fifty percent of a distribution's values occur in this range.

Percentiles   Values of an ordered (minimum to maximum) data set that divide the data into one hundred intervals.

Quartiles   Values of an ordered (minimum to maximum) data set that divide the data into four intervals.

Scatter diagram   Graphical technique used to show the relationship between two variables measured with interval or ratio scales.

Stem-and-leaf display   A method to display a variable's distribution using every value. Values are classified by the data's leading digit. For example, if a dataset contains values between 13 and 84, eight classes based on the 10s digit would be used for the stems. The 1s digits would be the leaves.

Exercises

connect™   Part I—Multiple Choice

1. Patrons at a local restaurant are asked to rate the service as excellent, good, fair, or poor. The level of measurement is
   a. Nominal.
   b. Ordinal.
   c. Interval.
   d. Ratio.

2. A person's age, income, height, and weight are all examples of
   a. Population variables.
   b. Qualitative variables.
   c. Random variables.
   d. Quantitative variables.
3. Which of the following statements are true of a frequency table?
   a. It is based on qualitative data.
   b. The grouping must be mutually exclusive.
   c. The variable is nonnumeric.
   d. All of the above are correct.
4. In a bar chart
   a. The frequencies are always reported on the vertical axis.
   b. The classes are reported on the horizontal axis.
   c. The variable of interest is qualitative.
   d. All of the above are correct.
5. In a frequency distribution the number of observations in each class is called
   a. The class midpoint.
   b. The class frequency.
   c. The class interval.
   d. None of the above.
6. A set of data includes 75 observations. How many classes would you recommend?
   a. 2
   b. 7
   c. 9
   d. 8
7. Fine Furniture Inc. produced 2,460 desks in 1997 and 6,520 in 2007. What is the geo-metric mean annual rate of increase for the period? _____
8. A graph that shows the relationship between two interval or ratio variables is called a
   a. Contingency table.
   b. Scatter diagram.
   c. Stem-and-leaf display.
   d. Dot plot.
9. A summary of data measured on two nominal variables is called a
   a. Scatter diagram.
   b. Contingency table.
   c. Frequency distribution.
   d. Histogram.
10. The graph shown below is called a
    a. Frequency distribution.
    b. Cumulative frequency distribution.
    c. Frequency polygon.
    d. Histogram.

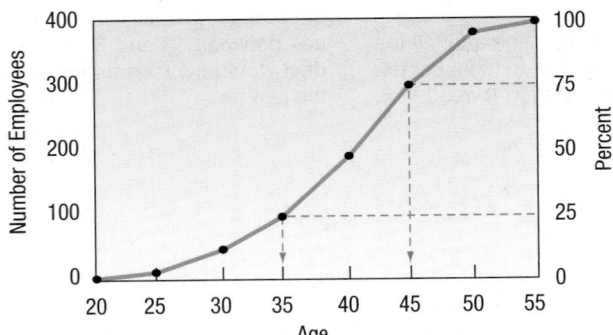

Part II—Problems

11. A sample of the funds deposited in First Federal Savings Bank's MCA (miniature check-ing account) revealed the following amounts.

$124	$14	$150	$289	$52	$156	$203	$82	$27	$248
39	52	103	58	136	249	110	298	251	157
186	107	142	185	75	202	119	219	156	78
116	152	206	117	52	299	58	153	219	148
145	187	165	147	158	146	185	186	149	140

Using the preceding raw data and a statistical package (such as MINITAB):
a. Organize the data into a frequency distribution.
b. Calculate the mean, median, and other descriptive measures. Include a dot plot, stem-and-leaf display, and a box plot. You decide on the class interval.
c. Interpret the computer output; that is, describe the central tendency, spread, skewness, and other measures.

12. A sample of 12 homes sold last week in St. Paul, Minnesota, revealed the following information. Draw a scatter diagram. Can we conclude that, as the size of the home (reported below in thousands of square feet) increases, the selling price (reported in $ thousands) also increases?

Home Size (thousands of square feet)	Selling Price ($ thousands)	Home Size (thousands of square feet)	Selling Price ($ thousands)
1.4	100	1.3	110
1.3	110	0.8	85
1.2	105	1.2	105
1.1	120	0.9	75
1.4	80	1.1	70
1.0	105	1.1	95

13. Following are the ages when the 43 U.S. presidents began their terms in office. Organize the data into a stem-and-leaf chart. Also construct a dot plot. Determine a typical age at the time of inauguration. Comment on the variation in age.

57	61	57	57	58	57	61	54	68	51
49	64	50	48	65	52	56	46	54	49
50	47	55	55	54	42	51	56	55	51
54	51	60	62	43	55	56	61	52	69
65	46	54							

14. Refer to the following diagram.

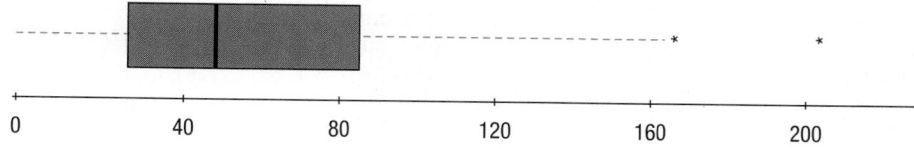

a. What is the graph called?
b. What are the median, and first and third quartile values?
c. Is the distribution positively skewed? Tell how you know.
d. Are there any outliers? If yes, estimate these values.
e. Can you determine the number of observations in the study?

15. The per capita personal income by state (including the District of Columbia), in thousands of dollars, follows.

11.1	17.7	13.2	10.7	16.8	15.1	19.2	15.1
18.9	14.3	13.2	14.7	11.4	15.4	12.9	13.2
14.4	11.1	11.2	12.7	16.6	17.5	14.1	14.7
9.5	13.6	11.9	13.8	15.1	15.9	18.3	11.1
17.1	12.2	12.3	13.7	12.4	12.2	13.9	14.7
11.1	11.9	11.8	13.5	10.7	12.8	15.4	14.5
10.5	13.8	13.2					

a. Organize these data into a frequency distribution.
b. What is a "typical" per capita income for a state?
c. How much variation in the income data is there?
d. Is the distribution symmetrical?
e. Summarize your findings.

Cases

A. Century National Bank

The following case will appear in subsequent review sections. Assume that you work in the Planning Department of the Century National Bank and report to Ms. Lamberg. You will need to do some data analysis and prepare a short written report. Remember, Mr. Selig is the president of the bank, so you will want to ensure that your report is complete and accurate. A copy of the data appears in Appendix A.6.

Century National Bank has offices in several cities in the Midwest and the southeastern part of the United States. Mr. Dan Selig, president and CEO, would like to know the characteristics of his checking account customers. What is the balance of a typical customer?

How many other bank services do the checking account customers use? Do the customers use the ATM service and, if so, how often? What about debit cards? Who uses them, and how often are they used?

To better understand the customers, Mr. Selig asked Ms. Wendy Lamberg, director of planning, to select a sample of customers and prepare a report. To begin, she has appointed a team from her staff. You are the head of the team and responsible for preparing the report. You select a random sample of 60 customers. In addition to the balance in each account at the end of last month, you determine: (1) the number of ATM (automatic teller machine) transactions in the last month; (2) the number of other bank services (a savings account, a certificate of deposit, etc.) the customer uses; (3) whether the customer has a debit card (this is a bank service in which charges are made directly to the customer's account); and (4) whether or not interest is paid on the checking account. The sample includes customers from the branches in Cincinnati, Ohio; Atlanta, Georgia; Louisville, Kentucky; and Erie, Pennsylvania.

1. Develop a graph or table that portrays the checking balances. What is the balance of a typical customer? Do many customers have more than $2,000 in their accounts? Does it appear that there is a difference in the distribution of the accounts among the four branches? Around what value do the account balances tend to cluster?

2. Determine the mean and median of the checking account balances. Compare the mean and the median balances for the four branches. Is there a difference among the branches? Be sure to explain the difference between the mean and the median in your report.

3. Determine the range and the standard deviation of the checking account balances. What do the first and third quartiles show? Determine the coefficient of skewness and indicate what it shows. Because Mr. Selig does not deal with statistics daily, include a brief description and interpretation of the standard deviation and other measures.

B. Wildcat Plumbing Supply, Inc.: Do We Have Gender Differences?

Wildcat Plumbing Supply has served the plumbing needs of Southwest Arizona for more than 40 years. The company was founded by Mr. Terrence St. Julian and is run today by his son Cory. The company has grown from a handful of employees to more than 500 today. Cory is concerned about several positions within the company where he has men and women doing essentially the same job but at different pay. To investigate, he collected the information below. Suppose you are a student intern in the Accounting Department and have been given the task to write a report summarizing the situation.

Yearly Salary ($000)	Women	Men
Less than 30	2	0
30 up to 40	3	1
40 up to 50	17	4
50 up to 60	17	24
60 up to 70	8	21
70 up to 80	3	7
80 or more	0	3

To kick off the project, Mr. Cory St. Julian held a meeting with his staff and you were invited. At this meeting it was suggested that you calculate several measures of location, draw charts, such as a cumulative frequency distribution, and determine the quartiles for both men and women. Develop the charts and write the report summarizing the yearly salaries of employees at Wildcat Plumbing Supply. Does it appear that there are pay differences based on gender?

C. Kimble Products: Is There a Difference In the Commissions?

At the January national sales meeting, the CEO of Kimble Products was questioned extensively regarding the company policy for paying commissions to its sales representatives. The company sells sporting goods to two major

markets. There are 40 sales representatives who call directly on large volume customers, such as the athletic departments at major colleges and universities and professional sports franchises. There are 30 sales representatives who represent the company to retail stores located in shopping malls and large discounters such as Kmart and Target.

Upon his return to corporate headquarters, the CEO asked the sales manager for a report comparing the commissions earned last year by the two parts of the sales team. The information is reported below. Write a brief report. Would you conclude that there is a difference? Be sure to include information in the report on both the central tendency and dispersion of the two groups.

Commissions Earned by Sales Representatives Calling on Athletic Departments ($)

354	87	1,676	1,187	69	3,202	680	39	1,683	1,106
883	3,140	299	2,197	175	159	1,105	434	615	149
1,168	278	579	7	357	252	1,602	2,321	4	392
416	427	1,738	526	13	1,604	249	557	635	527

Commissions Earned by Sales Representatives Calling on Large Retailers ($)

1,116	681	1,294	12	754	1,206	1,448	870	944	1,255
1,213	1,291	719	934	1,313	1,083	899	850	886	1,556
886	1,315	1,858	1,262	1,338	1,066	807	1,244	758	918

Practice Test

There is a practice test at the end of each review section. The tests are in two parts. The first part contains several objective questions, usually in a fill-in-the-blank format. The second part is problems. In most cases it should take 30 to 45 minutes to complete the test. The problems require a calculator. Check the answers in the Answer Section in the back of the book.

Part I—Objective

1. The science of collecting, organizing, presenting, analyzing, and interpreting data to assist in making effective decisions is called _____.   1. _____

2. Methods of organizing, summarizing, and presenting data in an informative way is called _____.   2. _____

3. The entire set of individuals or objects of interest or the measurements obtained from all individuals or objects of interest is called the _____.   3. _____

4. List the two types of variables.   4. _____

5. The number of bedrooms in a house is an example of a _____. (discrete variable, continuous variable, qualitative variable—pick one)   5. _____

6. The jersey numbers of Major League baseball players is an example of what level of measurement?   6. _____

7. The classification of students by eye color is an example of what level of measurement?   7. _____

8. The sum of the differences between each value and the mean is always equal to what value?   8. _____

9. A set of data contained 70 observations. How many classes would you suggest in order to construct a frequency distribution?   9. _____

10. What percent of the values in a data set are always larger than the median?   10. _____

11. The square of the standard deviation is the _____.   11. _____

12. The standard deviation assumes a negative value when _____. (All the values are negative, when at least half the values are negative, or never—pick one.)   12. _____

13. Which of the following is least affected by an outlier? (mean, median, or range—pick one)   13. _____

Part II—Problems

1. The Russell 2000 index of stock prices increased by the following amounts over the last three years.

| 18% | 4% | 2% |

   What is the geometric mean increase for the three years?

2. The information below refers to the selling prices ($000) of homes sold in Warren, PA, during 2007.

Selling Price ($000)	Frequency
120.0 up to 150.0	4
150.0 up to 180.0	18
180.0 up to 210.0	30
210.0 up to 240.0	20
240.0 up to 270.0	17
270.0 up to 300.0	10
300.0 up to 330.0	6

   a. What is the class interval?   _____
   b. How many homes were sold in 2007?   _____
   c. How many homes sold for less than $210,000?   _____
   d. What is the relative frequency of the 210 up to 240 class?   _____
   e. What is the midpoint of the 150 up to 180 class?   _____
   f. The selling prices range between what two amounts?   _____

3. A sample of eight college students revealed they owned the following number of CDs.

| 52 | 76 | 64 | 79 | 80 | 74 | 66 | 69 |

   a. What is the mean number of CDs owned?
   b. What is the median number of CDs owned?
   c. What is the 40th percentile?
   d. What is the range of the number of CDs owned?
   e. What is the standard deviation of the number of CDs owned?

4. An investor purchased 200 shares of the Blair Company for $36 each in July of 2007, 300 shares at $40 each in September 2007, and 500 shares at $50 each in January 2008. What is the investor's weighted mean price per share?

5. During the 2008 Super Bowl 30 million pounds of snack food was eaten. The chart below depicts this information.

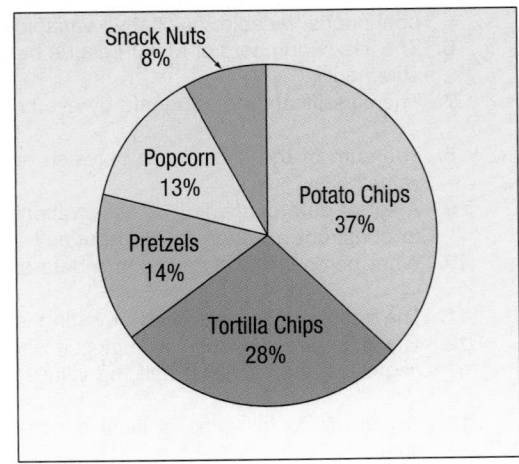

a. What is the name given to this graph? _____

b. Estimate, in millions, of pounds, the amount of potato chips eaten during the game.

_____

c. Estimate the relationship of potato chips to popcorn. (twice as much, half as much, three times, none of these—pick one) _____

d. What percent of the total do potato chips and tortilla chips comprise?

_____

5

A Survey of Probability Concepts

It was found that 60 percent of the tourists to China visited the Forbidden City, the Temple of Heaven, the Great Wall, and other historical sites in or near Beijing. Forty percent visited Xi'an and its magnificent terracotta soldiers, horses, and chariots, which lay buried for over 2,000 years. Thirty percent of the tourists went to both Beijing and Xi'an. What is the probability that a tourist visited at least one of these places? (Exercise 76, Goal 5)

Introduction

The emphasis in Chapters 2, 3, and 4 is on descriptive statistics. In Chapter 2 we organize the prices of 80 vehicles sold last month at the Whitner Autoplex location of AutoUSA into a frequency distribution. This frequency distribution shows the smallest and the largest selling prices and where the largest concentration of data occurs. In Chapter 3 we use numerical measures of location and dispersion to locate a typical selling price and to examine the variation in the data. We describe the variation in the selling prices with such measures of dispersion as the range and the standard deviation. In Chapter 4 we develop charts and graphs, such as a scatter diagram, to further describe the data graphically.

Descriptive statistics is concerned with summarizing data collected from past events. For example, we described the vehicle selling prices last month at Whitner Autoplex. We now turn to the second facet of statistics, namely, *computing the chance that something will occur in the future*. This facet of statistics is called **statistical inference** or **inferential statistics.**

Seldom does a decision maker have complete information to make a decision. For example:

- Toys and Things, a toy and puzzle manufacturer, recently developed a new game based on sports trivia. It wants to know whether sports buffs will purchase the game. "Slam Dunk" and "Home Run" are two of the names under consideration. One way to minimize the risk of making an incorrect decision is to hire a market research firm to select a sample of 2,000 consumers from the population and ask each respondent for a reaction to the new game and its proposed titles. Using the sample results the company can estimate the proportion of the population that will purchase the game.
- The quality assurance department of a Bethlehem Steel mill must assure management that the quarter-inch wire being produced has an acceptable tensile strength. Obviously, not all the wire produced can be tested for tensile strength because testing requires the wire to be stretched until it breaks—thus destroying

it. So a random sample of 10 pieces is selected and tested. Based on the test results, all the wire produced is deemed to be either acceptable or unacceptable.
- Other questions involving uncertainty are: Should the daytime drama "Days of Our Lives" be discontinued immediately? Will a newly developed mint-flavored cereal be profitable if marketed? Will Charles Linden be elected to county auditor in Batavia County?

Statistical inference deals with conclusions about a population based on a sample taken from that population. (The populations for the preceding illustrations are: all consumers who like sports trivia games, all the quarter-inch steel wire produced, all television viewers who watch soaps, all who purchase breakfast cereal, and so on.)

Because there is uncertainty in decision making, it is important that all the known risks involved be scientifically evaluated. Helpful in this evaluation is *probability theory,* which has often been referred to as the science of uncertainty. The use of probability theory allows the decision maker with only limited information to analyze the risks and minimize the gamble inherent, for example, in marketing a new product or accepting an incoming shipment possibly containing defective parts.

Because probability concepts are so important in the field of statistical inference (to be discussed starting with Chapter 8), this chapter introduces the basic language of probability, including such terms as *experiment, event, subjective probability,* and *addition* and *multiplication rules.*

What Is a Probability?

No doubt you are familiar with terms such as *probability, chance,* and *likelihood*. They are often used interchangeably. The weather forecaster announces that there is a 70 percent chance of rain for Super Bowl Sunday. Based on a survey of consumers who tested a newly developed pickle with a banana taste, the probability is .03 that, if marketed, it will be a financial success. (This means that the chance of the banana-flavor pickle being accepted by the public is rather remote.) What is a probability? In general, it is a number that describes the chance that something will happen.

> **PROBABILITY** A value between zero and one, inclusive, describing the relative possibility (chance or likelihood) an event will occur.

A probability is frequently expressed as a decimal, such as .70, .27, or .50. However, it may be given as a fraction such as 7/10, 27/100, or 1/2. It can assume any number from 0 to 1, inclusive. If a company has only five sales regions, and each region's name or number is written on a slip of paper and the slips put in a hat, the probability of selecting one of the five regions is 1. The probability of selecting from the hat a slip of paper that reads "Pittsburgh Steelers" is 0. Thus, the probability of 1 represents something that is certain to happen, and the probability of 0 represents something that cannot happen.

The closer a probability is to 0, the more improbable it is the event will happen. The closer the probability is to 1, the more sure we are it will happen. The relationship is shown in the following diagram along with a few of our personal beliefs. You might, however, select a different probability for Slo Poke's chances to win the Kentucky Derby or for an increase in federal taxes.

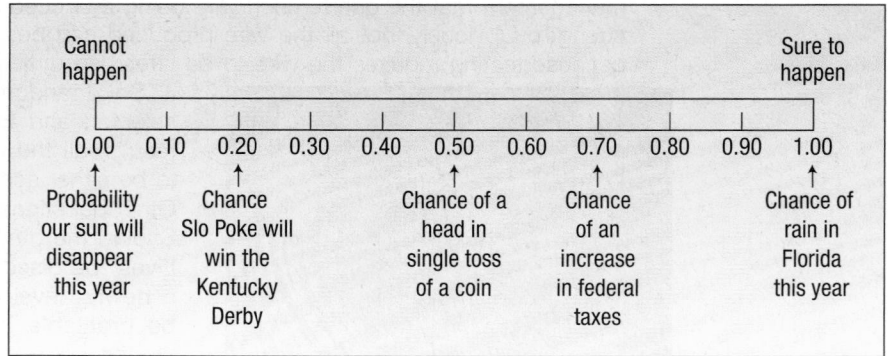

Three key words are used in the study of probability: **experiment, outcome,** and **event.** These terms are used in our everyday language, but in statistics they have specific meanings.

> **EXPERIMENT** A process that leads to the occurrence of one and only one of several possible observations.

This definition is more general than the one used in the physical sciences, where we picture someone manipulating test tubes or microscopes. In reference to probability, an experiment has two or more possible results, and it is uncertain which will occur.

> **OUTCOME** A particular result of an experiment.

For example, the tossing of a coin is an experiment. You may observe the toss of the coin, but you are unsure whether it will come up "heads" or "tails." Similarly, asking 500 college students whether they would purchase a new Dell computer system at a particular price is an experiment. If the coin is tossed, one particular outcome is a "head." The alternative outcome is a "tail." In the computer purchasing experiment, one possible outcome is that 273 students indicate they would purchase the computer. Another outcome is that 317 students would purchase the computer. Still another outcome is that 423 students indicate that they would purchase it. When one or more of the experiment's outcomes are observed, we call this an event.

> **EVENT** A collection of one or more outcomes of an experiment.

Examples to clarify the definitions of the terms *experiment, outcome,* and *event* are presented in the following figure.

In the die-rolling experiment there are six possible outcomes, but there are many possible events. When counting the number of members of the board of directors for Fortune 500 companies over 60 years of age, the number of possible outcomes can be anywhere from zero to the total number of members. There are an even larger number of possible events in this experiment.

Experiment	Roll a die	Count the number of members of the board of directors for Fortune 500 companies who are over 60 years of age
All possible outcomes	Observe a 1 Observe a 2 Observe a 3 Observe a 4 Observe a 5 Observe a 6	None are over 60 One is over 60 Two are over 60 ... 29 are over 60 ... ... 48 are over 60 ...
Some possible events	Observe an even number Observe a number greater than 4 Observe a number 3 or less	More than 13 are over 60 Fewer than 20 are over 60

Self-Review 5–1

Video Games, Inc., recently developed a new video game. Its playability is to be tested by 80 veteran game players.
(a) What is the experiment?
(b) What is one possible outcome?
(c) Suppose 65 players tried the new game and said they liked it. Is 65 a probability?
(d) The probability that the new game will be a success is computed to be −1.0. Comment.
(e) Specify one possible event.

Approaches to Assigning Probabilities

Two approaches to assigning probabilities to an event will be discussed, namely, the *objective* and the *subjective* viewpoints. **Objective probability** is subdivided into (1) *classical probability* and (2) *empirical probability*.

Classical Probability

Classical probability is based on the assumption that the outcomes of an experiment are *equally likely*. Using the classical viewpoint, the probability of an event happening is computed by dividing the number of favorable outcomes by the number of possible outcomes:

> **CLASSICAL PROBABILITY** $\dfrac{\text{Probability}}{\text{of an event}} = \dfrac{\text{Number of favorable outcomes}}{\text{Total number of possible outcomes}}$ **[5–1]**

Example

Solution

Consider an experiment of rolling a six-sided die. What is the probability of the event "an even number of spots appear face up"?

The possible outcomes are:

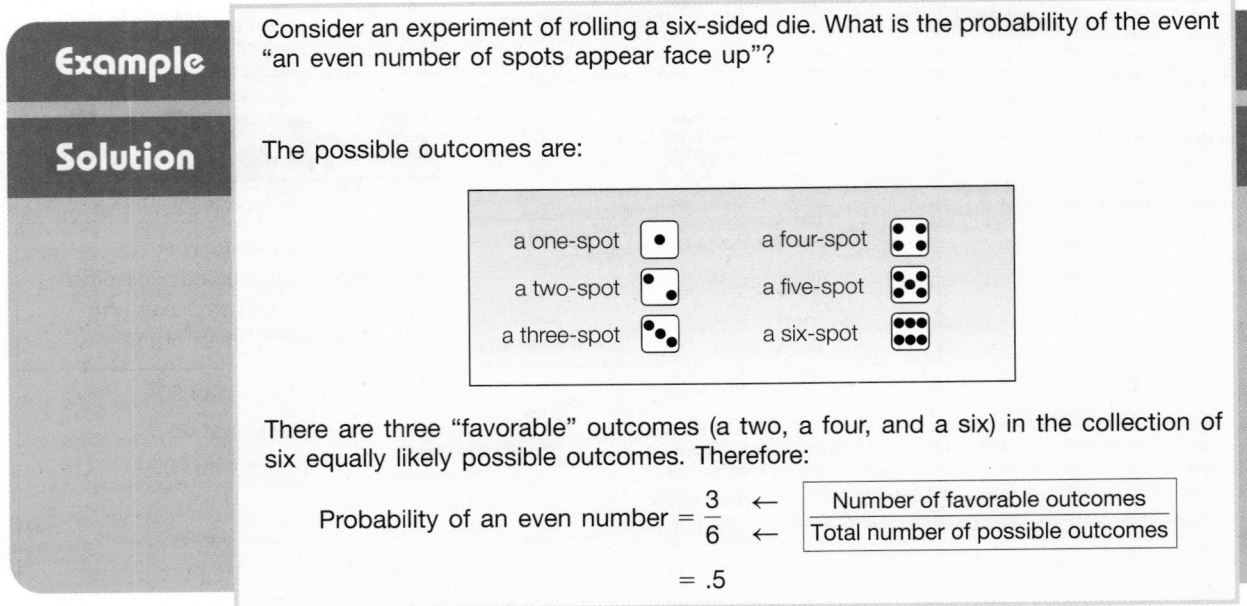

a one-spot	a four-spot
a two-spot	a five-spot
a three-spot	a six-spot

There are three "favorable" outcomes (a two, a four, and a six) in the collection of six equally likely possible outcomes. Therefore:

$$\text{Probability of an even number} = \frac{3}{6} \quad \leftarrow \quad \boxed{\begin{array}{l}\text{Number of favorable outcomes}\\ \hline \text{Total number of possible outcomes}\end{array}}$$

$$= .5$$

The mutually exclusive concept appeared earlier in our study of frequency distributions in Chapter 2. Recall that we create classes so that a particular value is included in only one of the classes and there is no overlap between classes. Thus, only one of several events can occur at a particular time.

> **MUTUALLY EXCLUSIVE** The occurrence of one event means that none of the other events can occur at the same time.

The variable "gender" presents mutually exclusive outcomes, male and female. An employee selected at random is either male or female but cannot be both. A manufactured part is acceptable or unacceptable. The part cannot be both acceptable and unacceptable at the same time. In a sample of manufactured parts, the event of selecting an unacceptable part and the event of selecting an acceptable part are mutually exclusive.

If an experiment has a set of events that includes every possible outcome, such as the events "an even number" and "an odd number" in the die-tossing experiment, then the set of events is **collectively exhaustive.** For the die-tossing experiment, every outcome will be either even or odd. So the set is collectively exhaustive.

> **COLLECTIVELY EXHAUSTIVE** At least one of the events must occur when an experiment is conducted.

Sum of probabilities = 1

If the set of events is collectively exhaustive and the events are mutually exclusive, the sum of the probabilities is 1. Historically, the classical approach to probability was developed and applied in the 17th and 18th centuries to games of chance, such as cards and dice. It is unnecessary to do an experiment to determine the probability of an event occurring using the classical approach because the total number of outcomes is known before the experiment. The flip of a coin has two possible outcomes; the roll of a die has six possible outcomes. We can logically arrive at the probability of getting a tail on the toss of one coin or three heads on the toss of three coins.

The classical approach to probability can also be applied to lotteries. In South Carolina, one of the games of the Education Lottery is "Pick 3." A person buys a lottery ticket and selects three numbers between 0 and 9. Once per week, the three numbers are randomly selected from a machine that tumbles three containers each with balls numbered 0 through 9. One way to win is to match the numbers and the order of the numbers. Given that 1,000 possible outcomes exist (000 through 999), the probability of winning with any three-digit number is 0.001, or 1 in 1,000.

Empirical Probability

Empirical or **relative frequency** is the second type of objective probability. It is based on the number of times an event occurs as a proportion of a known number of trials.

> **EMPIRICAL PROBABILITY** The probability of an event happening is the fraction of the time similar events happened in the past.

In terms of a formula:

$$\text{Empirical probability} = \frac{\text{Number of times the event occurs}}{\text{Total number of observations}}$$

The empirical approach to probability is based on what is called the law of large numbers. The key to establishing probabilities empirically is that more observations will provide a more accurate estimate of the probability.

> **LAW OF LARGE NUMBERS** Over a large number of trials the empirical probability of an event will approach its true probability.

To explain the law of large numbers, suppose we toss a fair coin. The result of each toss is either a head or a tail. With just one toss of the coin the empirical probability for heads is either zero or one. If we toss the coin a great number of times, the probability of the outcome of heads will approach .5. The following table reports the results of an experiment of flipping a fair coin 1, 10, 50, 100, 500, 1,000 and 10,000 times and then computing the relative frequency of heads. Note as we increase the number of trials the empirical probability of a head appearing approaches .5, which is its value based on the classical approach to probability.

Number of Trials	Number of Heads	Relative Frequency of Heads
1	0	.00
10	3	.30
50	26	.52
100	52	.52
500	236	.472
1,000	494	.494
10,000	5,027	.5027

What have we demonstrated? Based on the classical definition of probability the likelihood of obtaining a head in a single toss of a fair coin is .5. Based on the empirical or relative frequency approach to probability, the probability of the event happening approaches the same value based on the classical definition of probability.

This reasoning allows us to use the empirical or relative frequency approach to finding a probability. Here are some examples.

- Last semester 80 students registered for Business Statistics 101 at Scandia University. Twelve students earned an A. Based on this information and the empirical approach to assigning a probability, we estimate the likelihood a student will earn an A is .15.
- Kobe Bryant of the Los Angles Lakers made 623 out of 742 free throw attempts during the 2007–08 NBA season. Based on the empirical rule of probability the likelihood of him making his next free throw attempt is .840.

Life insurance companies rely on past data to determine the acceptability of an applicant as well as the premium to be charged. Mortality tables list the likelihood a person of a particular age will die within the upcoming year. For example, the likelihood a 20-year-old female will die within the next year is .00105.

The empirical concept is illustrated with the following example.

Example

On February 1, 2003, the Space Shuttle Columbia exploded. This was the second disaster in 123 space missions for NASA. On the basis of this information, what is the probability that a future mission is successfully completed?

Solution

To simplify, letters or numbers may be used. P stands for probability, and in this case $P(A)$ stands for the probability a future mission is successfully completed.

$$\text{Probability of a successful flight} = \frac{\text{Number of successful flights}}{\text{Total number of flights}}$$

$$P(A) = \frac{121}{123} = .98$$

We can use this as an estimate of probability. In other words, based on past experience, the probability is .98 that a future space shuttle mission will be successfully completed.

Subjective Probability

If there is little or no experience or information on which to base a probability, it may be arrived at subjectively. Essentially, this means an individual evaluates the available opinions and information and then estimates or assigns the probability. This probability is aptly called a **subjective probability.**

> **SUBJECTIVE CONCEPT OF PROBABILITY** The likelihood (probability) of a particular event happening that is assigned by an individual based on whatever information is available.

Illustrations of subjective probability are:

1. Estimating the likelihood the New England Patriots will play in the Super Bowl next year.
2. Estimating the likelihood you will be married before the age of 30.
3. Estimating the likelihood the U.S. budget deficit will be reduced by half in the next 10 years.

The types of probability are summarized in Chart 5–1. A probability statement always assigns a likelihood to an event that has not yet occurred. There is, of course, a considerable latitude in the degree of uncertainty that surrounds this probability, based primarily on the knowledge possessed by the individual concerning the underlying process. The individual possesses a great deal of knowledge about the toss of a die and can state that the probability that a one-spot will appear face up on the toss of a true die is one-sixth. But we know very little concerning the acceptance in the marketplace of a new and untested product. For example, even though a market research director tests a newly developed product in 40 retail stores and states that there is a 70 percent chance that the product will have sales of more than 1 million units, she has limited knowledge of how consumers will react when it is marketed nationally. In both cases (the case of the person rolling a die and the testing of a new product) the individual is assigning a probability value to an event of interest, and a difference exists only in the predictor's confidence in the precision of the estimate. However, regardless of the viewpoint, the same laws of probability (presented in the following sections) will be applied.

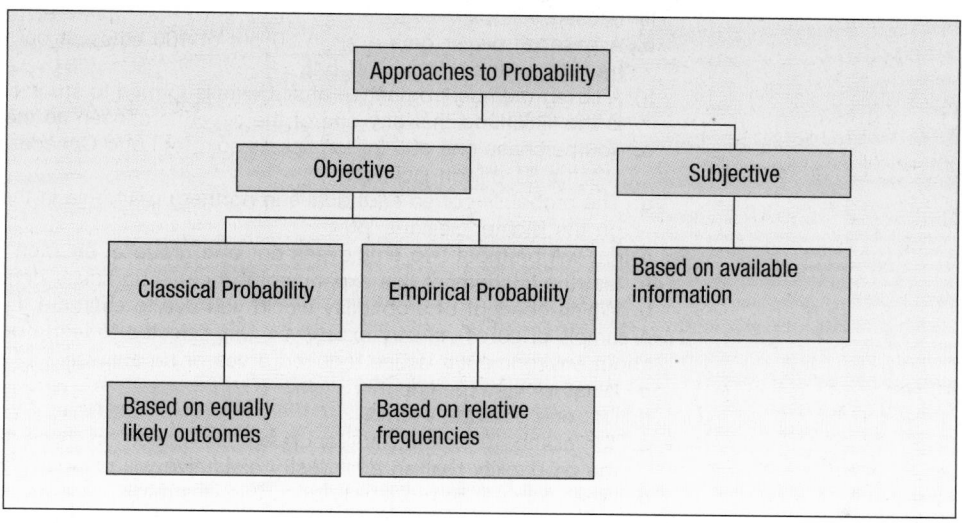

CHART 5–1 Summary of Approaches to Probability

Self-Review 5–2

1. One card will be randomly selected from a standard 52-card deck. What is the probability the card will be a queen? Which approach to probability did you use to answer this question?
2. The Center for Child Care reports on 539 children and the marital status of their parents. There are 333 married, 182 divorced, and 24 widowed. What is the probability a particular child chosen at random will have a parent who is divorced? Which approach did you use?
3. What is the probability that the Dow Jones Industrial Average will exceed 12,000 during the next 12 months? Which approach to probability did you use to answer this question?

Exercises

connect

1. Some people are in favor of reducing federal taxes to increase consumer spending and others are against it. Two persons are selected and their opinions are recorded. Assuming no one is undecided, list the possible outcomes.

2. A quality control inspector selects a part to be tested. The part is then declared acceptable, repairable, or scrapped. Then another part is tested. List the possible outcomes of this experiment regarding two parts.

3. A survey of 34 students at the Wall College of Business showed the following majors:

Accounting	10
Finance	5
Economics	3
Management	6
Marketing	10

   Suppose you select a student and observe his or her major.
   a. What is the probability he or she is a management major?
   b. Which concept of probability did you use to make this estimate?

4. A large company that must hire a new president prepares a final list of five candidates, all of whom are equally qualified. Two of these candidates are members of a minority group. To avoid bias in the selection of the candidate, the company decides to select the president by lottery.
   a. What is the probability one of the minority candidates is hired?
   b. Which concept of probability did you use to make this estimate?

5. In each of the following cases, indicate whether classical, empirical, or subjective probability is used.
   a. A baseball player gets a hit in 30 out of 100 times at bat. The probability is .3 that he gets a hit in his next at bat.
   b. A seven-member committee of students is formed to study environmental issues. What is the likelihood that any one of the seven is chosen as the spokesperson?
   c. You purchase one of 5 million tickets sold for Lotto Canada. What is the likelihood you win the $1 million jackpot?
   d. The probability of an earthquake in northern California in the next 10 years above 5.0 on the Richter Scale is .80.

6. A firm will promote two employees out of a group of six men and three women.
   a. List the chances of this experiment if there is particular concern about gender equity.
   b. Which concept of probability would you use to estimate these probabilities?

7. A sample of 40 oil industry executives was selected to test a questionnaire. One question about environmental issues required a yes or no answer.
   a. What is the experiment?
   b. List one possible event.
   c. Ten of the 40 executives responded yes. Based on these sample responses, what is the probability that an oil industry executive will respond yes?
   d. What concept of probability does this illustrate?
   e. Are each of the possible outcomes equally likely and mutually exclusive?

8. A sample of 2,000 licensed drivers revealed the following number of speeding violations.

Number of Violations	Number of Drivers
0	1,910
1	46
2	18
3	12
4	9
5 or more	5
Total	2,000

   a. What is the experiment?
   b. List one possible event.

    c. What is the probability that a particular driver had exactly two speeding violations?

    d. What concept of probability does this illustrate?

9. Bank of America customers select their own three-digit personal identification number (PIN) for use at ATMs.

    a. Think of this as an experiment and list four possible outcomes.

    b. What is the probability Mr. Jones and Mrs. Smith select the same PIN?

    c. Which concept of probability did you use to answer (b)?

10. An investor buys 100 shares of AT&T stock and records its price change daily.

    a. List several possible events for this experiment.

    b. Estimate the probability for each event you described in (a).

    c. Which concept of probability did you use in (b)?

Some Rules for Computing Probabilities

Now that we have defined probability and described the different approaches to probability, we turn our attention to computing the probability of two or more events by applying rules of addition and multiplication.

Rules of Addition

There are two rules of addition, the special rule of addition and the general rule of addition. We begin with the special rule of addition.

Mutually exclusive events cannot both happen.

Special Rule of Addition To apply the **special rule of addition,** the events must be *mutually exclusive*. Recall that mutually exclusive means that when one event occurs, none of the other events can occur at the same time. An illustration of mutually exclusive events in the die-tossing experiment is the events "a number 4 or larger" and "a number 2 or smaller." If the outcome is in the first group {4, 5, and 6}, then it cannot also be in the second group {1 and 2}. Another illustration is a product coming off the assembly line cannot be defective and satisfactory at the same time.

If two events *A* and *B* are mutually exclusive, the special rule of addition states that the probability of one *or* the other event's occurring equals the sum of their probabilities. This rule is expressed in the following formula:

| SPECIAL RULE OF ADDITION | $P(A \text{ or } B) = P(A) + P(B)$ | **[5–2]** |

For three mutually exclusive events designated *A*, *B*, and *C*, the rule is written:

$$P(A \text{ or } B \text{ or } C) = P(A) + P(B) + P(C)$$

An example will help to show the details.

Example

An automatic Shaw machine fills plastic bags with a mixture of beans, broccoli, and other vegetables. Most of the bags contain the correct weight, but because of the variation in the size of the beans and other vegetables, a package might be underweight or overweight. A check of 4,000 packages filled in the past month revealed:

Weight	Event	Number of Packages	Probability of Occurrence	
Underweight	A	100	.025	← $\frac{100}{4,000}$
Satisfactory	B	3,600	.900	
Overweight	C	300	.075	
		4,000	1.000	

Solution

What is the probability that a particular package will be either underweight or overweight?

The outcome "underweight" is the event *A*. The outcome "overweight" is the event *C*. Applying the special rule of addition:

$$P(A \text{ or } C) = P(A) + P(C) = .025 + .075 = .10$$

Note that the events are mutually exclusive, meaning that a package of mixed vegetables cannot be underweight, satisfactory, and overweight at the same time. They are also collectively exhaustive; that is, a selected package must be either underweight, satisfactory, or overweight.

English logician J. Venn (1834–1923) developed a diagram to portray graphically the outcome of an experiment. The *mutually exclusive* concept and various other rules for combining probabilities can be illustrated using this device. To construct a Venn diagram, a space is first enclosed representing the total of all possible outcomes. This space is usually in the form of a rectangle. An event is then represented by a circular area which is drawn inside the rectangle proportional to the probability of the event. The following Venn diagram represents the *mutually exclusive* concept. There is no overlapping of events, meaning that the events are mutually exclusive. In the following diagram assume the events *A*, *B*, and *C* are about equally likely.

> A Venn diagram is a useful tool to depict addition or multiplication rules.

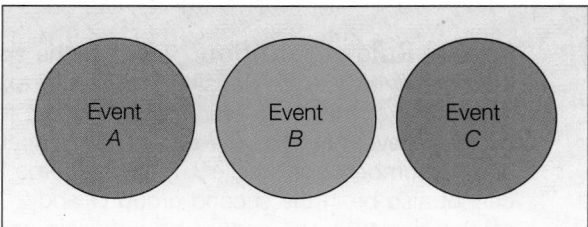

Complement Rule   The probability that a bag of mixed vegetables selected is underweight, *P*(*A*), plus the probability that it is not an underweight bag, written *P*(~*A*) and read "not *A*," must logically equal 1. This is written:

$$P(A) + P(\sim A) = 1$$

This can be revised to read:

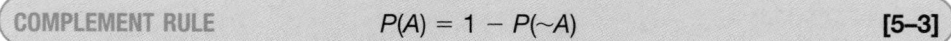

| COMPLEMENT RULE | $P(A) = 1 - P(\sim A)$ | [5–3] |

This is the **complement rule.** It is used to determine the probability of an event occurring by subtracting the probability of the event not occurring from 1. This rule is useful because sometimes it is easier to calculate the probability of an event happening by determining the probability of it not happening and subtracting the result from 1. Notice that the events *A* and ~*A* are mutually exclusive and collectively exhaustive. Therefore, the probabilities of *A* and ~*A* sum to 1. A Venn diagram illustrating the complement rule is shown as:

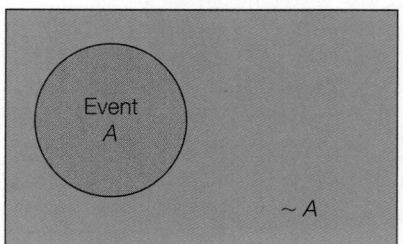

Example

Recall the probability a bag of mixed vegetables is underweight is .025 and the probability of an overweight bag is .075. Use the complement rule to show the probability of a satisfactory bag is .900. Show the solution using a Venn diagram.

Solution

The probability the bag is unsatisfactory equals the probability the bag is overweight plus the probability it is underweight. That is, $P(A \text{ or } C) = P(A) + P(C) = .025 + .075 = .100$. The bag is satisfactory if it is not underweight or overweight, so $P(B) = 1 - [P(A) + P(C)] = 1 - [.025 + .075] = 0.900$. The Venn diagram portraying this situation is:

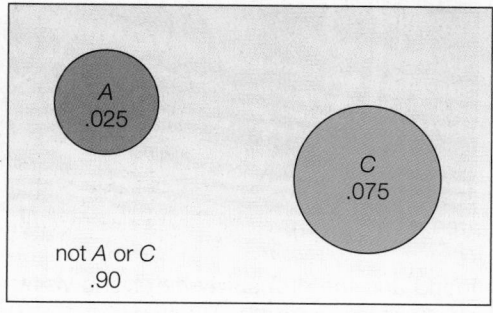

Self-Review 5–3

A sample of employees of Worldwide Enterprises is to be surveyed about a new health care plan. The employees are classified as follows:

Classification	Event	Number of Employees
Supervisors	A	120
Maintenance	B	50
Production	C	1,460
Management	D	302
Secretarial	E	68

(a) What is the probability that the first person selected is:
    (i)   either in maintenance or a secretary?
    (ii) not in management?
(b) Draw a Venn diagram illustrating your answers to part (a).
(c) Are the events in part (a)(i) complementary or mutually exclusive or both?

The General Rule of Addition The outcomes of an experiment may not be mutually exclusive. Suppose, for illustration, that the Florida Tourist Commission selected a sample of 200 tourists who visited the state during the year. The survey revealed that 120 tourists went to Disney World and 100 went to Busch Gardens near Tampa. What is the probability that a person selected visited either Disney World or Busch Gardens? If the special rule of addition is used, the probability of selecting a tourist who went to Disney World is .60, found by 120/200. Similarly, the probability of a tourist going to Busch Gardens is .50. The sum of these probabilities is 1.10. We know, however, that this probability cannot be greater than 1. The explanation is that many tourists visited both attractions and are being counted twice! A check of the survey responses revealed that 60 out of 200 sampled did, in fact, visit both attractions.

To answer our question, "What is the probability a selected person visited either Disney World or Busch Gardens?" (1) add the probability that a tourist visited Disney

World and the probability he or she visited Busch Gardens, and (2) subtract the probability of visiting both. Thus:

$$P(\text{Disney or Busch}) = P(\text{Disney}) + P(\text{Busch}) - P(\text{both Disney and Busch})$$
$$= .60 + .50 - .30 = .80$$

When two events both occur, the probability is called a **joint probability.** The probability that a tourist visits both attractions (.30) is an example of a joint probability.

The following Venn diagram shows two events that are not mutually exclusive.
The two events overlap to illustrate the joint event that some people have visited
both attractions.

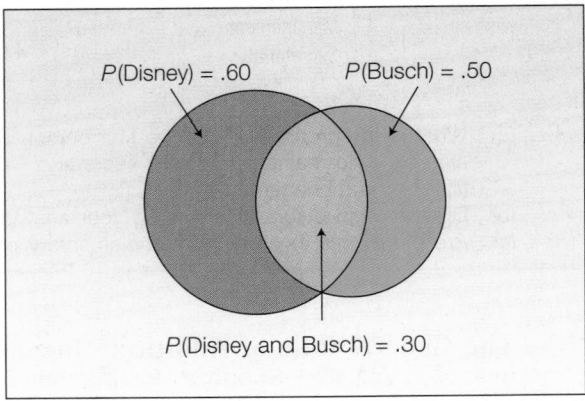

> **JOINT PROBABILITY** A probability that measures the likelihood two or more
> events will happen concurrently.

This rule for two events designated *A* and *B* is written:

GENERAL RULE OF ADDITION $P(A \text{ or } B) = P(A) + P(B) - P(A \text{ and } B)$ **[5–4]**

For the expression $P(A \text{ or } B)$, the word *or* suggests that A may occur or B may occur. This also includes the possibility that A and B may occur. This use of *or* is sometimes called an **inclusive.** You could also write $P(A \text{ or } B \text{ or both})$ to emphasize that the union of the events includes the intersection of A and B.

If we compare the general and special rules of addition, the important difference is determining if the events are mutually exclusive. If the events *are* mutually exclusive, then the joint probability $P(A \text{ and } B)$ is 0 and we could use the special rule of addition. Otherwise we must account for the joint probability and use the general rule of addition.

| Example | What is the probability that a card chosen at random from a standard deck of cards will be either a king or a heart? |

| Solution | We may be inclined to add the probability of a king and the probability of a heart. But this creates a problem. If we do that, the king of hearts is counted with the kings and also with the hearts. So, if we simply add the probability of a king (there are 4 in a deck of 52 cards) to the probability of a heart (there are 13 in a deck of 52 cards) and report that 17 out of 52 cards meet the requirement, we have counted the king of hearts twice. We need to subtract 1 card from the 17 so the king of hearts is counted only once. Thus, there are 16 cards that are either hearts or kings. So the probability is 16/52 = .3077. |

Card	Probability	Explanation
King	$P(A)$ = 4/52	4 kings in a deck of 52 cards
Heart	$P(B)$ = 13/52	13 hearts in a deck of 52 cards
King of Hearts	$P(A \text{ and } B)$ = 1/52	1 king of hearts in a deck of 52 cards

From formula (5–4):

$$P(A \text{ or } B) = P(A) + P(B) - P(A \text{ and } B)$$

$$= 4/52 + 13/52 - 1/52$$

$$= 16/52, \text{ or } .3077$$

A Venn diagram portrays these outcomes, which are not mutually exclusive.

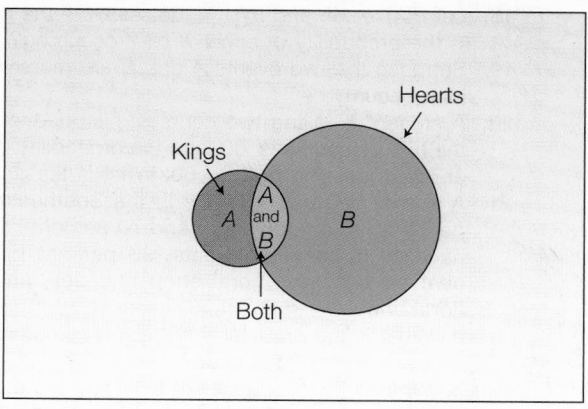

Routine physical examinations are conducted annually as part of a health service program for General Concrete, Inc., employees. It was discovered that 8 percent of the employees need corrective shoes, 15 percent need major dental work, and 3 percent need both corrective shoes and major dental work.
(a) What is the probability that an employee selected at random will need either corrective shoes or major dental work?
(b) Show this situation in the form of a Venn diagram.

Exercises

connect

11. The events *A* and *B* are mutually exclusive. Suppose *P(A)* = .30 and *P(B)* = .20. What is the probability of either *A* or *B* occurring? What is the probability that neither *A* nor *B* will happen?
12. The events *X* and *Y* are mutually exclusive. Suppose *P(X)* = .05 and *P(Y)* = .02. What is the probability of either *X* or *Y* occurring? What is the probability that neither *X* nor *Y* will happen?
13. A study of 200 advertising firms revealed their income after taxes:

Income after Taxes	Number of Firms
Under $1 million	102
$1 million to $20 million	61
$20 million or more	37

   a. What is the probability an advertising firm selected at random has under $1 million in income after taxes?
   b. What is the probability an advertising firm selected at random has either an income between $1 million and $20 million, or an income of $20 million or more? What rule of probability was applied?
14. The chair of the board of directors says, "There is a 50 percent chance this company will earn a profit, a 30 percent chance it will break even, and a 20 percent chance it will lose money next quarter."
   a. Use an addition rule to find the probability the company will not lose money next quarter.
   b. Use the complement rule to find the probability it will not lose money next quarter.
15. Suppose the probability you will get an A in this class is .25 and the probability you will get a B is .50. What is the probability your grade will be above a C?
16. Two coins are tossed. If *A* is the event "two heads" and *B* is the event "two tails," are *A* and *B* mutually exclusive? Are they complements?
17. The probabilities of the events *A* and *B* are .20 and .30, respectively. The probability that both *A* and *B* occur is .15. What is the probability of either *A* or *B* occurring?
18. Let *P(X)* = .55 and *P(Y)* = .35. Assume the probability that they both occur is .20. What is the probability of either *X* or *Y* occurring?
19. Suppose the two events *A* and *B* are mutually exclusive. What is the probability of their joint occurrence?
20. A student is taking two courses, history and math. The probability the student will pass the history course is .60, and the probability of passing the math course is .70. The probability of passing both is .50. What is the probability of passing at least one?
21. A survey of grocery stores in the Southeast revealed 40 percent had a pharmacy, 50 percent had a floral shop, and 70 percent had a deli. Suppose 10 percent of the stores have all three departments, 30 percent have both a pharmacy and a deli, 25 percent have both a floral shop and deli, and 20 percent have both a pharmacy and floral shop.
   a. What is the probability of selecting a store at random and finding it has both a pharmacy and a floral shop?
   b. What is the probability of selecting a store at random and finding it has both a pharmacy and a deli?

    c. Are the events "select a store with a deli" and "select a store with a pharmacy" mutually exclusive?

    d. What is the name given to the event of "selecting a store with a pharmacy, a floral shop, and a deli?"

    e. What is the probability of selecting a store that does *not* have all three departments?

22. A study by the National Park Service revealed that 50 percent of vacationers going to the Rocky Mountain region visit Yellowstone Park, 40 percent visit the Tetons, and 35 percent visit both.

    a. What is the probability a vacationer will visit at least one of these attractions?

    b. What is the probability .35 called?

    c. Are the events mutually exclusive? Explain.

Rules of Multiplication

When we use the rules of addition in the previous section we find the likelihood of combining two events. In this section we find the likelihood that two events both happen. For example, a marketing firm may want to estimate the likelihood that a person is 21 years old or older *and* buys a Hummer. Venn diagrams illustrate this as the intersection of two events. To find the likelihood of two events happening we use the rules of multiplication. There are two rules of multiplication, the special rule and the general rule.

Special Rule of Multiplication   The special rule of multiplication requires that two events A and B are independent. Two events are independent if the occurrence of one event does not alter the probability of the occurrence of the other event.

> **INDEPENDENCE** The occurrence of one event has no effect on the probability of the occurrence of another event.

One way to think about independence is to assume that events A and B occur at different times. For example, when event B occurs after event A occurs, does A have any effect on the likelihood that event B occurs? If the answer is no, then A and B are independent events. To illustrate independence, suppose two coins are tossed. The outcome of a coin toss (head or tail) is unaffected by the outcome of any other prior coin toss (head or tail).

For two independent events A and B, the probability that A and B will both occur is found by multiplying the two probabilities. This is the **special rule of multiplication** and is written symbolically as:

SPECIAL RULE OF MULTIPLICATION	$P(A \text{ and } B) = P(A)P(B)$	[5–5]

For three independent events, A, B, and C, the special rule of multiplication used to determine the probability that all three events will occur is:

$$P(A \text{ and } B \text{ and } C) = P(A)P(B)P(C)$$

Example

A survey by the American Automobile Association (AAA) revealed 60 percent of its members made airline reservations last year. Two members are selected at random. What is the probability both made airline reservations last year?

Solution

The probability the first member made an airline reservation last year is .60, written $P(R_1) = .60$, where R_1 refers to the fact that the first member made a reservation.

The probability that the second member selected made a reservation is also .60, so $P(R_2) = .60$. Since the number of AAA members is very large, you may assume that R_1 and R_2 are independent. Consequently, using formula (5–5), the probability they both make a reservation is .36, found by:

$$P(R_1 \text{ and } R_2) = P(R_1)P(R_2) = (.60)(.60) = .36$$

All possible outcomes can be shown as follows. R means a reservation is made, and NR means no reservation was made.

With the probabilities and the complement rule, we can compute the joint probability of each outcome. For example, the probability that neither member makes a reservation is .16. Further, the probability of the first or the second member (special addition rule) making a reservation is .48 (.24 + .24). You can also observe that the outcomes are mutually exclusive and collectively exhaustive. Therefore, the probabilities sum to 1.00.

Outcomes		Joint Probability	
R_1	R_2	(.60)(.60) =	.36
R_1	NR_2	(.60)(.40) =	.24
NR_1	R_2	(.40)(.60) =	.24
NR_1	NR_2	(.40)(.40) =	.16
	Total		1.00

Self-Review 5–5

From experience, Teton Tire knows the probability is .95 that a particular XB-70 tire will last 60,000 miles before it becomes bald or fails. An adjustment is made on any tire that does not last 60,000 miles. You purchase four XB-70s. What is the probability all four tires will last at least 60,000 miles?

General Rule of Multiplication If two events are not independent, they are referred to as **dependent.** To illustrate dependency, suppose there are 10 cans of soda in a cooler, seven are regular and three are diet. A can is selected from the cooler. The probability of selecting a can of diet soda is 3/10, and the probability of selecting a can of regular soda is 7/10. Then a second can is selected from the cooler, without returning the first. The probability the second is diet depends on whether the first one selected was diet or not. The probability that the second is diet is:

2/9, if the first can is diet. (Only two cans of diet soda remain in the cooler.)
3/9, if the first can selected is regular. (All three diet sodas are still in the cooler.)

The fraction 2/9 (or 3/9) is aptly called a **conditional probability** because its value is conditional on (dependent on) whether a diet or regular soda was the first selection from the cooler.

> **CONDITIONAL PROBABILITY** The probability of a particular event occurring, given that another event has occurred.

We use the general rule of multiplication to find the joint probability of two events when the events are not independent. For example, when event B occurs after event A occurs, and A has an effect on the likelihood that event B occurs, then A and B are not independent.

The general rule of multiplication states that for two events, A and B, the joint probability that both events will happen is found by multiplying the probability that event A will happen by the conditional probability of event B occurring given that A has occurred. Symbolically, the joint probability, $P(A \text{ and } B)$, is found by:

GENERAL RULE OF MULTIPLICATION	$P(A \text{ and } B) = P(A)P(B \mid A)$	[5–6]

Example

A golfer has 12 golf shirts in his closet. Suppose 9 of these shirts are white and the others blue. He gets dressed in the dark, so he just grabs a shirt and puts it on. He plays golf two days in a row and does not do laundry. What is the likelihood both shirts selected are white?

Solution

The event that the first shirt selected is white is W_1. The probability is $P(W_1) = 9/12$ because 9 of the 12 shirts are white. The event that the second shirt selected is also white is identified as W_2. The conditional probability that the second shirt selected is white, given that the first shirt selected is also white, is $P(W_2 \mid W_1) = 8/11$. Why is this so? Because after the first shirt is selected there are only 11 shirts remaining in the closet and 8 of these are white. To determine the probability of 2 white shirts being selected we use formula (5–6).

$$P(W_1 \text{ and } W_2) = P(W_1)P(W_2 \mid W_1) = \left(\frac{9}{12}\right)\left(\frac{8}{11}\right) = .55$$

So the likelihood of selecting two shirts and finding them both to be white is .55.

Incidentally, it is assumed that this experiment was conducted *without replacement*. That is, the first shirt was not laundered and put back in the closet before the second was selected. So the outcome of the second event is conditional or dependent on the outcome of the first event.

We can extend the general rule of multiplication to more than two events. For three events A, B, and C the formula is:

$$P(A \text{ and } B \text{ and } C) = P(A)P(B \mid A)P(C \mid A \text{ and } B)$$

In the case of the golf shirt example, the probability of selecting three white shirts without replacement is:

$$P(W_1 \text{ and } W_2 \text{ and } W_3) = P(W_1)P(W_2 \mid W_1)P(W_3 \mid W_1 \text{ and } W_2) = \left(\frac{9}{12}\right)\left(\frac{8}{11}\right)\left(\frac{7}{10}\right) = .38$$

So the likelihood of selecting three shirts without replacement and all being white is .38.

Self-Review 5–6

The board of directors of Tarbell Industries consists of eight men and four women. A four-member search committee is to be chosen at random to conduct a nationwide search for a new company president.
(a) What is the probability all four members of the search committee will be women?
(b) What is the probability all four members will be men?
(c) Does the sum of the probabilities for the events described in parts (a) and (b) equal 1? Explain.

Statistics in Action

In 2000 George W. Bush won the U.S. presidency by the slimmest of margins. Many election stories resulted, some involving voting irregularities, others raising interesting election questions. In a local Michigan election there was a tie between two candidates for an elected position. To break the tie the candidates drew a slip of paper from a box that contained two slips of paper, one marked "Winner" and the other unmarked. To determine which candidate drew first, election officials flipped a coin. The winner of the coin flip also drew the winning slip of paper. But was the coin flip really necessary? No, because the two events are independent. Winning the coin flip did not alter the probability of either candidate drawing the winning slip of paper.

Contingency Tables

Often we tally the results of a survey in a two-way table and use these results of this tally to determine various probabilities. We described this idea beginning on page 120 in Chapter 4. To review, we refer to a two-way table as a contingency table.

CONTINGENCY TABLE A table used to classify sample observations according to two or more identifiable characteristics.

A contingency table is a cross-tabulation that simultaneously summarizes two variables of interest and their relationship. The level of measurement can be nominal. Below are several examples.

- A survey of 150 adults classified each as to gender and the number of movies attended last month. Each respondent is classified according to two criteria—the number of movies attended and gender.

Movies Attended	Gender		Total
	Men	Women	
0	20	40	60
1	40	30	70
2 or more	10	10	20
Total	70	80	150

- The American Coffee Producers Association reports the following information on age and the amount of coffee consumed in a month.

Age (Years)	Coffee Consumption			Total
	Low	Moderate	High	
Under 30	36	32	24	92
30 up to 40	18	30	27	75
40 up to 50	10	24	20	54
50 and over	26	24	29	79
Total	90	110	100	300

According to this table each of the 300 respondents is classified according to two criteria: (1) age and (2) the amount of coffee consumed.

The following example shows how the rules of addition and multiplication are used when we employ contingency tables.

A sample of executives were surveyed about loyalty to their company. One of the questions was, "If you were given an offer by another company equal to or slightly better than your present position, would you remain with the company or take the other position?" The responses of the 200 executives in the survey were cross-classified with their length of service with the company. (See Table 5–1.)

TABLE 5–1 Loyalty of Executives and Length of Service with Company

	Length of Service				
Loyalty	Less than 1 Year, B_1	1–5 Years, B_2	6–10 Years, B_3	More than 10 Years, B_4	Total
Would remain, A_1	10	30	5	75	120
Would not remain, A_2	25	15	10	30	80
	35	45	15	105	200

What is the probability of randomly selecting an executive who is loyal to the company (would remain) and who has more than 10 years of service?

Note that two events occur at the same time—the executive would remain with the company, and he or she has more than 10 years of service.

1. Event A_1 happens if a randomly selected executive will remain with the company despite an equal or slightly better offer from another company. To find the probability that event A_1 will happen, refer to Table 5–1. Note there are 120 executives out of the 200 in the survey who would remain with the company, so $P(A_1) = 120/200$, or .60.

2. Event B_4 happens if a randomly selected executive has more than 10 years of service with the company. Thus, $P(B_4|A_1)$ is the conditional probability that an executive with more than 10 years of service would remain with the company despite an equal or slightly better offer from another company. Referring to the contingency table, Table 5–1, 75 of the 120 executives who would remain have more than 10 years of service, so $P(B_4|A_1) = 75/120$.

Solving for the probability that an executive randomly selected will be one who would remain with the company and who has more than 10 years of service with the company, using the general rule of multiplication in formula (5–6), gives:

$$P(A_1 \text{ and } B_4) = P(A_1)P(B_4|A_1) = \left(\frac{120}{200}\right)\left(\frac{75}{120}\right) = \frac{9,000}{24,000} = .375$$

To find the probability of selecting an executive who would remain with the company *or* has less than 1 year of experience we use the general rule of addition, formula (5–4).

1. Event A_1 refers to executives that would remain with the company. So $P(A_1) = 120/200 = .60$.

2. Event B_1 refers to executives that have been with the company less than 1 year. The probability of B_1 is $P(B_1) = 35/200 = .175$.

3. The events A_1 and B_1 are not mutually exclusive. That is, an executive can both be willing to remain with the company and have less than 1 year of experience.

We write this probability, which is called the joint probability, as $P(A_1 \text{ and } B_1)$. There are 10 executives who would both stay with the company and have less than 1 year of service, so $P(A_1 \text{ and } B_1) = 10/200 = .05$. These 10 people are in both groups, those who would remain with the company and those with less than 1 year with the company. They are actually being counted twice, so we need to subtract out this value.

4. We insert these values in formula (5–4) and the result is as follows.

$$P(A_1 \text{ or } B_1) = P(A_1) + P(B_1) - P(A_1 \text{ and } B_1)$$
$$= .60 + .175 - .05 = .725$$

So the likelihood that a selected executive would either remain with the company or has been with the company less than 1 year is .725.

Self-Review 5–7   Refer to Table 5–1 on page 159 to find the following probabilities.

(a) What is the probability of selecting an executive with more than 10 years of service?
(b) What is the probability of selecting an executive who would not remain with the company, given that he or she has more than 10 years of service?
(c) What is the probability of selecting an executive with more than 10 years of service or one who would not remain with the company?

Tree Diagrams

The **tree diagram** is a graph that is helpful in organizing calculations that involve several stages. Each segment in the tree is one stage of the problem. The branches of a tree diagram are weighted by probabilities. We will use the data in Table 5–1 to show the construction of a tree diagram.

Steps in constructing a tree diagram

1. To construct a tree diagram, we begin by drawing a heavy dot on the left to represent the root of the tree (see Chart 5–2).
2. For this problem, two main branches go out from the root, the upper one representing "would remain" and the lower one "would not remain." Their probabilities are written on the branches, namely, 120/200 and 80/200. These probabilities could also be denoted $P(A_1)$ and $P(A_2)$.
3. Four branches "grow" out of each of the two main branches. These branches represent the length of service—less than 1 year, 1–5 years, 6–10 years, and more than 10 years. The conditional probabilities for the upper branch of the tree, 10/120, 30/120, 5/120, and so on are written on the appropriate branches. These are $P(B_1|A_1)$, $P(B_2|A_1)$, $P(B_3|A_1)$, and $P(B_4|A_1)$, where B_1 refers to less than 1 year of service, B_2 1 to 5 years, B_3 6 to 10 years, and B_4 more than 10 years. Next, write the conditional probabilities for the lower branch.
4. Finally, joint probabilities, that the events A_1 and B_i or the events A_2 and B_i will occur together, are shown on the right side. For example, the joint probability of randomly selecting an executive who would remain with the company and who has less than 1 year of service, from formula (5–6), is:

$$P(A_1 \text{ and } B_1) = P(A_1)P(B_1|A_1) = \left(\frac{120}{200}\right)\left(\frac{10}{120}\right) = .05$$

Because the joint probabilities represent all possible outcomes (would remain, 6–10 years service; would not remain, more than 10 years of service; etc.), they must sum to 1.00 (see Chart 5–2).

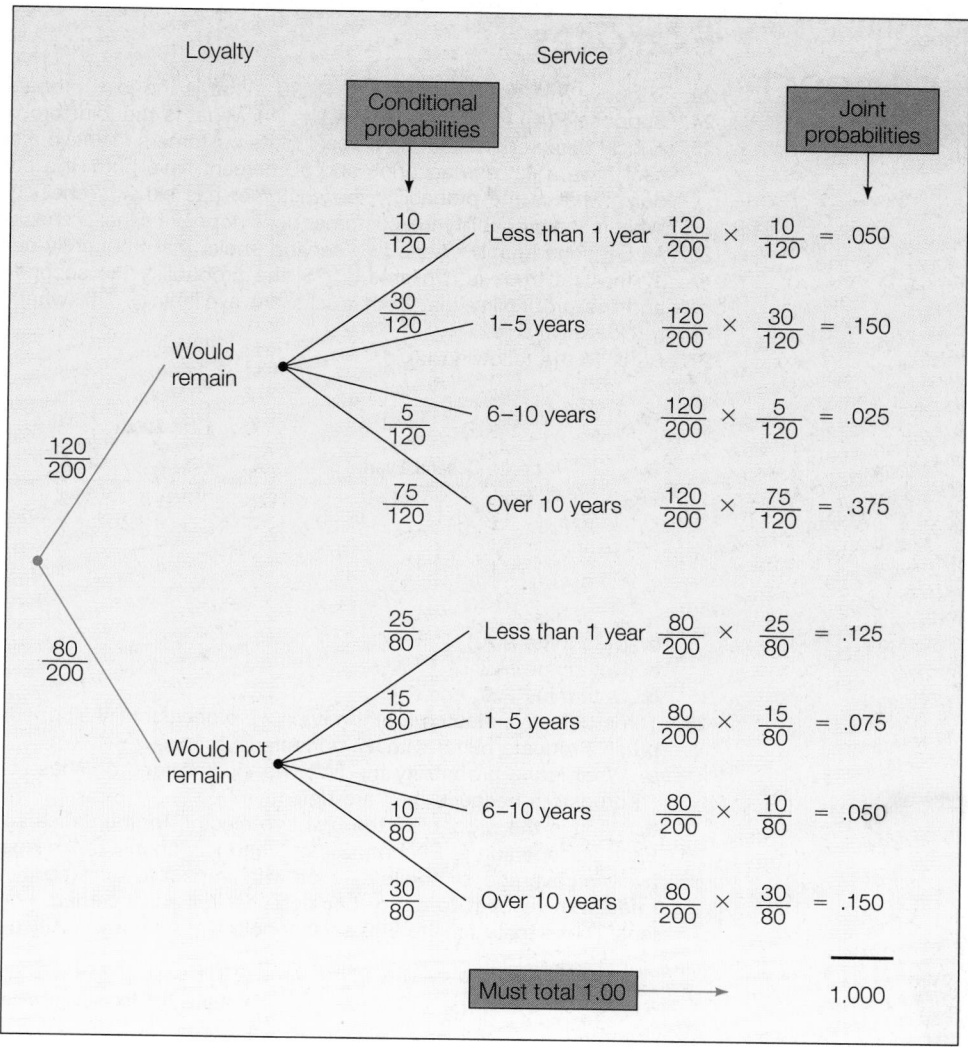

CHART 5–2 Tree Diagram Showing Loyalty and Length of Service

Self-Review 5–8

Consumers were surveyed on the relative number of visits to a Circuit City store (often, occasional, and never) and if the store was located in an enclosed mall (yes and no). When variables are measured nominally, such as these data the results are usually summarized in a contingency table.

	Enclosed Mall		
Visits	**Yes**	**No**	**Total**
Often	60	20	80
Occasional	25	35	60
Never	5	50	55
	90	105	195

(a) Are the number of visits and enclosed mall variables independent? Why? Interpret your conclusion.

(b) Draw a tree diagram and determine the joint probabilities.

Exercises

connect™

23. Suppose $P(A) = .40$ and $P(B|A) = .30$. What is the joint probability of A and B?
24. Suppose $P(X_1) = .75$ and $P(Y_2|X_1) = .40$. What is the joint probability of X_1 and Y_2?
25. A local bank reports that 80 percent of its customers maintain a checking account, 60 percent have a savings account, and 50 percent have both. If a customer is chosen at random, what is the probability the customer has either a checking or a savings account? What is the probability the customer does not have either a checking or a savings account?
26. All Seasons Plumbing has two service trucks that frequently need repair. If the probability the first truck is available is .75, the probability the second truck is available is .50, and the probability that both trucks are available is .30, what is the probability neither truck is available?
27. Refer to the following table.

	First Event			
Second Event	A_1	A_2	A_3	**Total**
B_1	2	1	3	6
B_2	1	2	1	4
Total	3	3	4	10

   a. Determine $P(A_1)$.
   b. Determine $P(B_1|A_2)$.
   c. Determine $P(B_2$ and $A_3)$.
28. Three defective electric toothbrushes were accidentally shipped to a drugstore by Cleanbrush Products along with 17 nondefective ones.
   a. What is the probability the first two electric toothbrushes sold will be returned to the drugstore because they are defective?
   b. What is the probability the first two electric toothbrushes sold will not be defective?
29. Each salesperson at Puchett, Sheets, and Hogan Insurance Agency is rated either below average, average, or above average with respect to sales ability. Each salesperson is also rated with respect to his or her potential for advancement—either fair, good, or excellent. These traits for the 500 salespeople were cross-classified into the following table.

	Potential for Advancement		
Sales Ability	**Fair**	**Good**	**Excellent**
Below average	16	12	22
Average	45	60	45
Above average	93	72	135

   a. What is this table called?
   b. What is the probability a salesperson selected at random will have above average sales ability and excellent potential for advancement?
   c. Construct a tree diagram showing all the probabilities, conditional probabilities, and joint probabilities.
30. An investor owns three common stocks. Each stock, independent of the others, has equally likely chances of (1) increasing in value, (2) decreasing in value, or (3) remaining the same value. List the possible outcomes of this experiment. Estimate the probability at least two of the stocks increase in value.
31. The board of directors of a small company consists of five people. Three of those are "strong leaders." If they buy an idea, the entire board will agree. The other "weak" members have no influence. Three salespeople are scheduled, one after the other, to make sales presentations to a board member of the salesperson's choice. The salespeople are convincing but do not know who the "strong leaders" are. However, they will know who the previous salespeople spoke to. The first salesperson to find a strong leader will win the account. Do the three salespeople have the same chance of winning the account? If not, find their respective probabilities of winning.

32. If you ask three strangers about their birthdays, what is the probability: (a) All were born on Wednesday? (b) All were born on different days of the week? (c) None were born on Saturday?

Bayes' Theorem

In the 18th century Reverend Thomas Bayes, an English Presbyterian minister, pondered this question: Does God really exist? Being interested in mathematics, he attempted to develop a formula to arrive at the probability God does exist based on evidence available to him on earth. Later Pierre-Simon Laplace refined Bayes' work and gave it the name "Bayes' theorem." In a workable form, **Bayes' theorem** is:

BAYES' THEOREM	$$P(A_i|B) = \frac{P(A_i)P(B|A_i)}{P(A_1)P(B|A_1) + P(A_2)P(B|A_2)}$$	**[5–7]**

Assume in formula 5–7 that the events A_1 and A_2 are mutually exclusive and collectively exhaustive, and A_i refers to either event A_1 or A_2. Hence A_1 and A_2 are in this case complements. The meaning of the symbols used is illustrated by the following example.

Suppose 5 percent of the population of Umen, a fictional Third World country, have a disease that is peculiar to that country. We will let A_1 refer to the event "has the disease" and A_2 refer to the event "does not have the disease." Thus, we know that if we select a person from Umen at random, the probability the individual chosen has the disease is .05, or $P(A_1) = .05$. This probability, $P(A_1) = P(\text{has the disease}) = .05$, is called the **prior probability.** It is given this name because the probability is assigned before any empirical data are obtained.

> **PRIOR PROBABILITY** The initial probability based on the present level of information.

The prior probability a person is not afflicted with the disease is therefore .95, or $P(A_2) = .95$, found by $1 - .05$.

There is a diagnostic technique to detect the disease, but it is not very accurate. Let B denote the event "test shows the disease is present." Assume that historical evidence shows that if a person actually has the disease, the probability that the test will indicate the presence of the disease is .90. Using the conditional probability definitions developed earlier in this chapter, this statement is written as:

$$P(B|A_1) = .90$$

Assume the probability is .15 that for a person who actually does not have the disease the test will indicate the disease is present.

$$P(B|A_2) = .15$$

Let's randomly select a person from Umen and perform the test. The test results indicate the disease is present. What is the probability the person actually has the disease? In symbolic form, we want to know $P(A_1|B)$, which is interpreted as: $P(\text{has the disease} \mid \text{the test results are positive})$. The probability $P(A_1|B)$ is called a **posterior probability.**

> **POSTERIOR PROBABILITY** A revised probability based on additional information.

With the help of Bayes' theorem, formula (5–7), we can determine the posterior probability.

Statistics in Action

A recent study by the National Collegiate Athletic Association (NCAA) reported that of 150,000 senior boys playing on their high school basketball team, 64 would make a professional team. To put it another way, the odds of a high school senior basketball player making a professional team are 1 in 2,344. From the same study:

1. The odds of a high school senior basketball player playing some college basketball are about 1 in 40.

2. The odds of a high school senior playing college basketball as a senior in college are about 1 in 60.

3. If you play basketball as a senior in college, the odds of making a professional team are about 1 in 37.5.

$$P(A_1 | B) = \frac{P(A_1)P(B|A_1)}{P(A_1)P(B|A_1) + P(A_2)P(B|A_2)}$$

$$= \frac{(.05)(.90)}{(.05)(.90) + (.95)(.15)} = \frac{.0450}{.1875} = .24$$

So the probability that a person has the disease, given that he or she tested positive, is .24. How is the result interpreted? If a person is selected at random from the population, the probability that he or she has the disease is .05. If the person is tested and the test result is positive, the probability that the person actually has the disease is increased about fivefold, from .05 to .24.

In the preceding problem we had only two mutually exclusive and collectively exhaustive events A_1 and A_2. If there are n such events, $A_1, A_2, \cdots, A_n$, Bayes' theorem, formula (5–7), becomes

$$P(A_i | B) = \frac{P(A_i)P(B|A_i)}{P(A_1)P(B|A_1) + P(A_2)P(B|A_2) + \cdots + P(A_n)P(B|A_n)}$$

With the preceding notation, the calculations for the Umen problem are summarized in the following table.

Event, A_i	Prior Probability, $P(A_i)$	Conditional Probability, $P(B|A_i)$	Joint Probability, $P(A_i$ and $B)$	Posterior Probability, $P(A_i | B)$
Disease, A_1	.05	.90	.0450	.0450/.1875 = .24
No disease, A_2	.95	.15	.1425	.1425/.1875 = .76
			$P(B)$ = .1875	1.00

Another illustration of Bayes' theorem follows.

Example

A manufacturer of DVD players purchases a particular microchip, called the LS-24, from three suppliers: Hall Electronics, Schuller Sales, and Crawford Components. Thirty percent of the LS-24 chips are purchased from Hall Electronics, 20 percent from Schuller Sales, and the remaining 50 percent from Crawford Components. The manufacturer has extensive histories on the three suppliers and knows that 3 percent of the LS-24 chips from Hall Electronics are defective, 5 percent of chips from Schuller Sales are defective, and 4 percent of the chips purchased from Crawford Components are defective.

When the LS-24 chips arrive at the manufacturer, they are placed directly in a bin and not inspected or otherwise identified by supplier. A worker selects a chip for installation in a DVD player and finds it defective. What is the probability that it was manufactured by Schuller Sales?

Solution

As a first step, let's summarize some of the information given in the problem statement.

- There are three mutually exclusive and collectively exhaustive events, that is, three suppliers.

    A_1 The LS-24 was purchased from Hall Electronics.
    A_2 The LS-24 was purchased from Schuller Sales.
    A_3 The LS-24 was purchased from Crawford Components.

- The prior probabilities are:

  $P(A_1) = .30$ The probability the LS-24 was manufactured by Hall Electronics.
  $P(A_2) = .20$ The probability the LS-24 was manufactured by Schuller Sales.
  $P(A_3) = .50$ The probability the LS-24 was manufactured by Crawford Components.

- The additional information can be either:

  B_1 The LS-24 appears defective, or
  B_2 The LS-24 appears not to be defective.

- The following conditional probabilities are given.

  $P(B_1|A_1) = .03$ The probability that an LS-24 chip produced by Hall Electronics is defective.
  $P(B_1|A_2) = .05$ The probability that an LS-24 chip produced by Schuller Sales is defective.
  $P(B_1|A_3) = .04$ The probability that an LS-24 chip produced by Crawford Components is defective.

- A chip is selected from the bin. Because the chips are not identified by supplier, we are not certain which supplier manufactured the chip. We want to determine the probability that the defective chip was purchased from Schuller Sales. The probability is written $P(A_2|B_1)$.

Look at Schuller's quality record. It is the worst of the three suppliers. Now that we have found a defective LS-24 chip, we suspect that $P(A_2|B_1)$ is greater than $P(A_2)$. That is, we expect the revised probability to be greater than .20. But how much greater? Bayes' theorem can give us the answer. As a first step, consider the tree diagram in Chart 5–3.

The events are dependent, so the prior probability in the first branch is multiplied by the conditional probability in the second branch to obtain the joint probability. The joint probability is reported in the last column of Chart 5–3. To construct the tree diagram of Chart 5–3, we used a time sequence that moved from the supplier to the determination of whether the chip was acceptable or unacceptable.

What we need to do is reverse the time process. That is, instead of moving from left to right in Chart 5–3, we need to move from right to left. We have a defective chip, and we want to determine the likelihood that it was purchased from Schuller Sales. How is that accomplished? We first look at the joint probabilities as relative frequencies out of 1,000 cases. For example, the likelihood of a defective LS-24 chip that was produced by Hall Electronics is .009. So of 1,000 cases we would expect to find 9 defective chips produced by Hall Electronics. We observe that in 39 of 1,000 cases the LS-24 chip selected for assembly will be defective, found by 9 + 10 + 20. Of these 39 defective chips, 10 were produced by Schuller Sales. Thus, the probability that the defective LS-24 chip was purchased from Schuller Sales is 10/39 = .2564. We have now determined the revised probability of $P(A_2|B_1)$. Before we found the defective chip, the likelihood that it was purchased from Schuller Sales was .20. This likelihood has been increased to .2564.

This information is summarized in the following table.

Event, A_i	Prior Probability, $P(A_i)$	Conditional Probability, $P(B_1|A_i)$	Joint Probability, $P(A_i \text{ and } B_1)$	Posterior Probability, $P(A_i|B_1)$
Hall	.30	.03	.009	.009/.039 = .2308
Schuller	.20	.05	.010	.010/.039 = .2564
Crawford	.50	.04	.020	.020/.039 = .5128
			$P(B_1) = .039$	1.0000

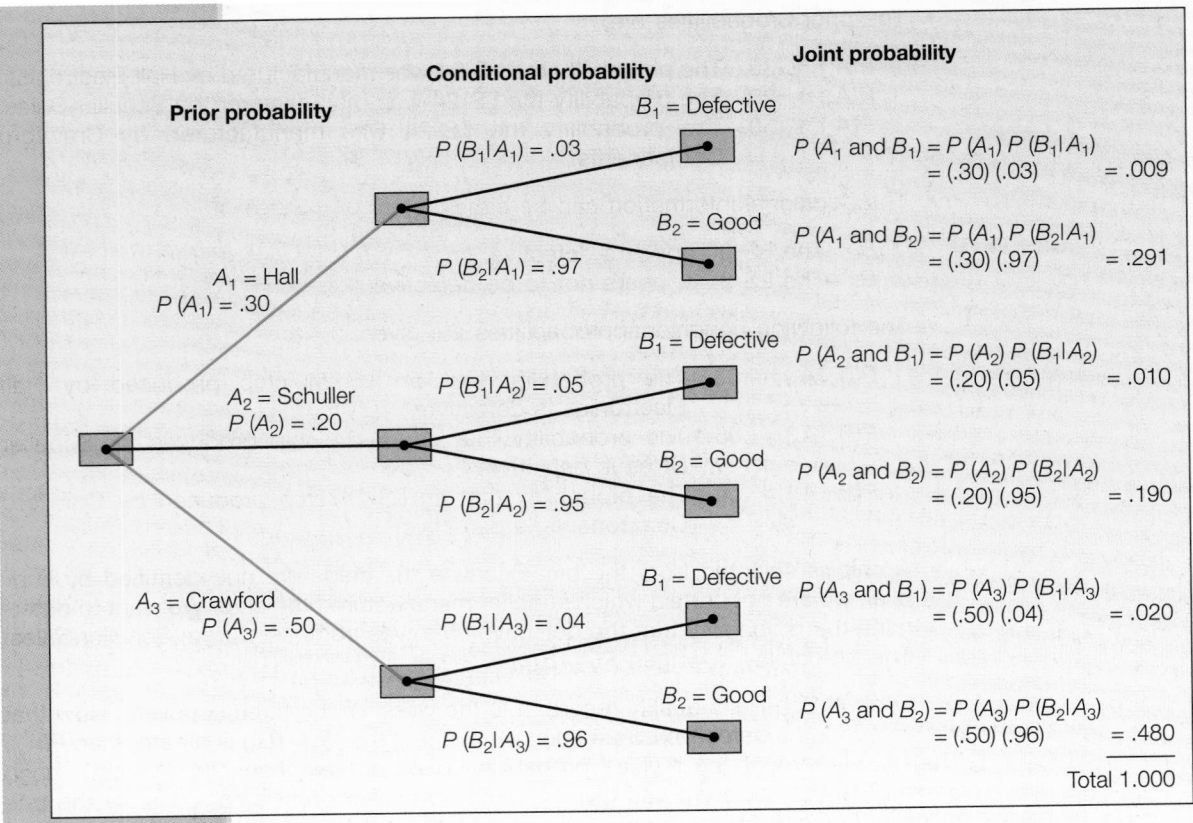

CHART 5–3 Tree Diagram of DVD Manufacturing Problem

The probability the defective LS-24 chip came from Schuller Sales can be formally found by using Bayes' theorem. We compute $P(A_2|B_1)$, where A_2 refers to Schuller Sales and B_1 to the fact that the selected LS-24 chip was defective.

$$P(A_2|B_1) = \frac{P(A_2)P(B_1|A_2)}{P(A_1)P(B_1|A_1) + P(A_2)P(B_1|A_2) + P(A_3)(B_1|A_3)}$$

$$= \frac{(.20)(.05)}{(.30)(.03) + (.20)(.05) + (.50)(.04)} = \frac{.010}{.039} = .2564$$

This is the same result obtained from Chart 5–3 and from the conditional probability table.

Self-Review 5–9

Refer to the preceding example and solution.
(a) Design a formula to find the probability the part selected came from Crawford Components, given that it was a good chip.
(b) Compute the probability using Bayes' theorem.

Exercises

connect

33. $P(A_1) = .60$, $P(A_2) = .40$, $P(B_1|A_1) = .05$, and $P(B_1|A_2) = .10$. Use Bayes' theorem to determine $P(A_1|B_1)$.
34. $P(A_1) = .20$, $P(A_2) = .40$, $P(A_3) = .40$, $P(B_1|A_1) = .25$, $P(B_1|A_2) = .05$, and $P(B_1|A_3) = .10$. Use Bayes' theorem to determine $P(A_3|B_1)$.

35. The Ludlow Wildcats baseball team, a minor league team in the Cleveland Indians organization, plays 70 percent of their games at night and 30 percent during the day. The team wins 50 percent of their night games and 90 percent of their day games. According to today's newspaper, they won yesterday. What is the probability the game was played at night?

36. Dr. Stallter has been teaching basic statistics for many years. She knows that 80 percent of the students will complete the assigned problems. She has also determined that among those who do their assignments, 90 percent will pass the course. Among those students who do not do their homework, 60 percent will pass. Mike Fishbaugh took statistics last semester from Dr. Stallter and received a passing grade. What is the probability that he completed the assignments?

37. The credit department of Lion's Department Store in Anaheim, California, reported that 30 percent of their sales are cash or check, 30 percent are paid with a credit card and 40 percent with a debit card. Twenty percent of the cash or check purchases, 90 percent of the credit card purchases, and 60 percent of the debit card purchases are for more than $50. Ms. Tina Stevens just purchased a new dress that cost $120. What is the probability that she paid cash or check?

38. One-fourth of the residents of the Burning Ridge Estates leave their garage doors open when they are away from home. The local chief of police estimates that 5 percent of the garages with open doors will have something stolen, but only 1 percent of those closed will have something stolen. If a garage is robbed, what is the probability the doors were left open?

Principles of Counting

If the number of possible outcomes in an experiment is small, it is relatively easy to count them. There are six possible outcomes, for example, resulting from the roll of a die, namely:

If, however, there are a large number of possible outcomes, such as the number of heads and tails for an experiment with 10 tosses, it would be tedious to count all the possibilities. They could have all heads, one head and nine tails, two heads and eight tails, and so on. To facilitate counting, we discuss three formulas: the **multiplication formula** (not to be confused with the multiplication *rule* described earlier in the chapter), the **permutation formula,** and the **combination formula.**

The Multiplication Formula

We begin with the multiplication formula.

> **MULTIPLICATION FORMULA** If there are *m* ways of doing one thing and *n* ways of doing another thing, there are *m* × *n* ways of doing both.

In terms of a formula:

> **MULTIPLICATION FORMULA**   Total number of arrangements = (*m*)(*n*)   **[5–8]**

This can be extended to more than two events. For three events *m*, *n*, and *o*:

$$\text{Total number of arrangements} = (m)(n)(o)$$

Example	An automobile dealer wants to advertise that for $29,999 you can buy a convertible, a two-door sedan, or a four-door model with your choice of either wire wheel covers or solid wheel covers. How many different arrangements of models and wheel covers can the dealer offer?
Solution	Of course the dealer could determine the total number of arrangements by picturing and counting them. There are six.

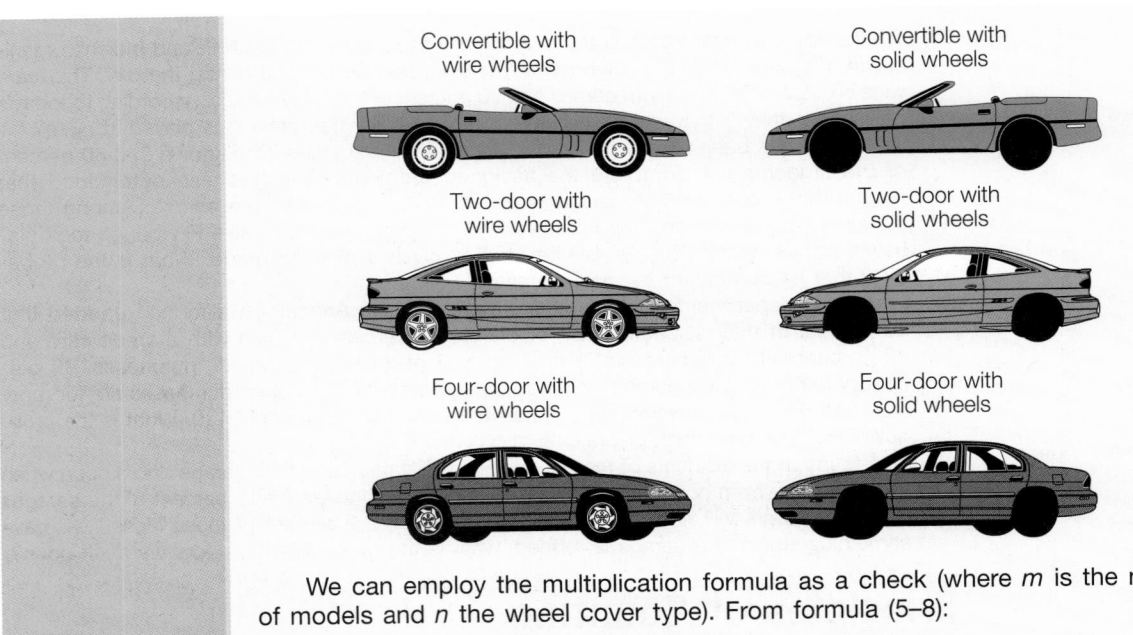

Convertible with wire wheels

Convertible with solid wheels

Two-door with wire wheels

Two-door with solid wheels

Four-door with wire wheels

Four-door with solid wheels

We can employ the multiplication formula as a check (where m is the number of models and n the wheel cover type). From formula (5–8):

$$\text{Total possible arrangements} = (m)(n) = (3)(2) = 6$$

It was not difficult to count all the possible model and wheel cover combinations in this example. Suppose, however, that the dealer decided to offer eight models and six types of wheel covers. It would be tedious to picture and count all the possible alternatives. Instead, the multiplication formula can be used. In this case, there are $(m)(n) = (8)(6) = 48$ possible arrangements.

Note in the preceding applications of the multiplication formula that there were *two or more groupings from which you made selections*. The automobile dealer, for example, offered a choice of models and a choice of wheel covers. If a home builder offered you four different exterior styles of a home to choose from and three interior floor plans, the multiplication formula would be used to find how many different arrangements were possible. There are 12 possibilities.

Self-Review 5–10

1. The Women's Shopping Network on cable TV offers sweaters and slacks for women. The sweaters and slacks are offered in coordinating colors. If sweaters are available in five colors and the slacks are available in four colors, how many different outfits can be advertised?
2. Pioneer manufactures three models of stereo receivers, two MP3 docking stations, four speakers, and three CD carousels. When the four types of components are sold together, they form a "system." How many different systems can the electronics firm offer?

The Permutation Formula

As noted, the multiplication formula is applied to find the number of possible arrangements for two or more groups. The **permutation formula** is applied to find the possible number of arrangements when there is only *one* group of objects. Illustrations of this type of problem are:

- Three electronic parts are to be assembled into a plug-in unit for a television set. The parts can be assembled in any order. The question involving counting is: In how many different ways can the three parts be assembled?
- A machine operator must make four safety checks before starting his machine. It does not matter in which order the checks are made. In how many different ways can the operator make the checks?

One order for the first illustration might be: the transistor first, the LEDs second, and the synthesizer third. This arrangement is called a **permutation.**

> **PERMUTATION** Any arrangement of r objects selected from a single group of n possible objects.

Note that the arrangements $a\ b\ c$ and $b\ a\ c$ are different permutations. The formula to count the total number of different permutations is:

> **PERMUTATION FORMULA** $$_nP_r = \frac{n!}{(n-r)!}$$ **[5–9]**

where:

    n is the total number of objects.

    r is the number of objects selected.

Before we solve the two problems illustrated, note that permutations and combinations (to be discussed shortly) use a notation called n *factorial*. It is written $n!$ and means the product of $n(n-1)(n-2)(n-3)\cdots(1)$. For instance, $5! = 5 \cdot 4 \cdot 3 \cdot 2 \cdot 1 = 120$.

Many of your calculators have a button with $x!$ that will perform this calculation for you. It will save you a great deal of time. For example the Texas Instrument TI-36X calculator has the following key: $x!$

$$\begin{array}{c} 10^x \\ \text{LOG} \end{array}$$

It is the "third function" so check your users' manual or the Internet for instructions.

The factorial notation can also be canceled when the same number appears in both the numerator and the denominator, as shown below.

$$\frac{6!3!}{4!} = \frac{6 \cdot 5 \cdot 4 \cdot 3 \cdot 2 \cdot 1(3 \cdot 2 \cdot 1)}{4 \cdot 3 \cdot 2 \cdot 1} = 180$$

By definition, zero factorial, written $0!$, is 1. That is, $0! = 1$.

Example

Referring to the group of three electronic parts that are to be assembled in any order, in how many different ways can they be assembled?

Solution

There are three electronic parts to be assembled, so $n = 3$. Because all three are to be inserted in the plug-in unit, $r = 3$. Solving using formula (5–9) gives:

$$_nP_r = \frac{n!}{(n-r)!} = \frac{3!}{(3-3)!} = \frac{3!}{0!} = \frac{3!}{1} = 6$$

We can check the number of permutations arrived at by using the permutation formula. We determine how many "spaces" have to be filled and the possibilities for each "space." In the problem involving three electronic parts, there are three locations in the plug-in unit for the three parts. There are three possibilities for the first place, two for the second (one has been used up), and one for the third, as follows:

$$(3)(2)(1) = 6 \text{ permutations}$$

The six ways in which the three electronic parts, lettered A, B, C, can be arranged are:

ABC	BAC	CAB	ACB	BCA	CBA

In the previous example we selected and arranged all the objects, that is $n = r$. In many cases, only some objects are selected and arranged from the n possible objects. We explain the details of this application in the following example.

Example

Betts Machine Shop, Inc., has eight screw machines but only three spaces available in the production area for the machines. In how many different ways can the eight machines be arranged in the three spaces available?

Solution

There are eight possibilities for the first available space in the production area, seven for the second space (one has been used up), and six for the third space. Thus:

$$(8)(7)(6) = 336,$$

that is, there are a total of 336 different possible arrangements. This could also be found by using formula (5–9). If $n = 8$ machines, and $r = 3$ spaces available, the formula leads to

$$_nP_r = \frac{n!}{(n-r)!} = \frac{8!}{(8-3)!} = \frac{8!}{5!} = \frac{(8)(7)(6)\cancel{5!}}{\cancel{5!}} = 336$$

The Combination Formula

If the order of the selected objects is *not* important, any selection is called a **combination.** The formula to count the number of r object combinations from a set of n objects is:

COMBINATION FORMULA	$_nC_r = \dfrac{n!}{r!(n-r)!}$	**[5–10]**

For example, if executives Able, Baker, and Chauncy are to be chosen as a committee to negotiate a merger, there is only one possible combination of these three; the committee of Able, Baker, and Chauncy is the same as the committee of Baker, Chauncy, and Able. Using the combination formula:

$$_nC_r = \frac{n!}{r!(n-r)!} = \frac{3 \cdot 2 \cdot 1}{3 \cdot 2 \cdot 1(1)} = 1$$

Example

The marketing department has been given the assignment of designing color codes for the 42 different lines of compact disks sold by Goody Records. Three colors are to be used on each CD, but a combination of three colors used for one CD cannot be rearranged and used to identify a different CD. This means that if green, yellow, and violet were used to identify one line, then yellow, green, and violet (or any other combination of these three colors) cannot be used to identify another line. Would seven colors taken three at a time be adequate to color-code the 42 lines?

Solution

According to formula (5–10), there are 35 combinations, found by

$$_7C_3 = \frac{n!}{r!(n-r)!} = \frac{7!}{3!(7-3)!} = \frac{7!}{3!4!} = 35$$

The seven colors taken three at a time (i.e., three colors to a line) would not be adequate to color-code the 42 different lines because they would provide only 35 combinations. Eight colors taken three at a time would give 56 different combinations. This would be more than adequate to color-code the 42 different lines.

When the number of permutations or combinations is large, the calculations are tedious. Computer software and handheld calculators have "functions" to compute these numbers. The Excel output for the location of the eight screw machines in the production area of Betts Machine Shop, Inc., is shown below. There are a total of 336 arrangements.

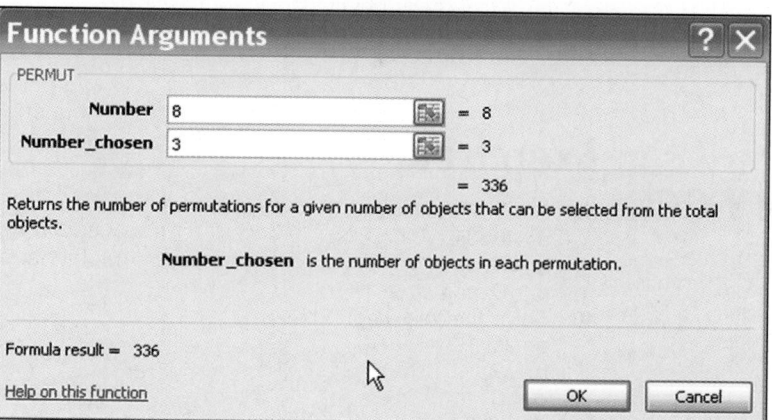

Below is the output for the color codes at Goody Records. Three colors are chosen from among seven possible. The number of combinations possible is 35.

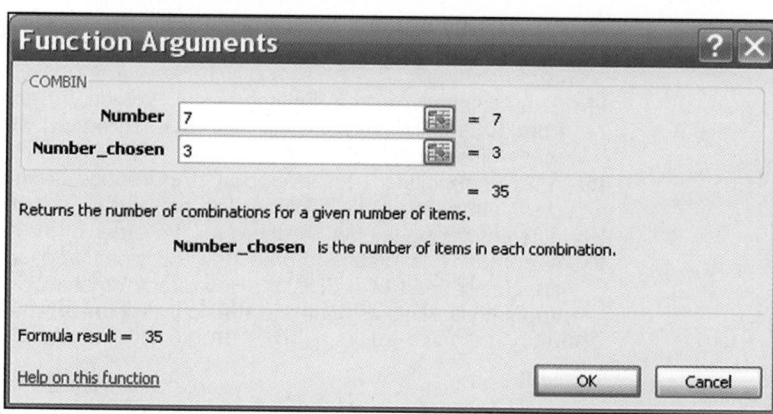

Self-Review 5–11

1. A musician wants to write a score based on only five chords: B-flat, C, D, E, and G. However, only three chords out of the five will be used in succession, such as C, B-flat, and E. Repetitions, such as B-flat, B-flat, and E, will not be permitted.
    (a) How many permutations of the five chords, taken three at a time, are possible?
    (b) Using formula (5–9), how many permutations are possible?
2. A machine operator must make four safety checks before machining a part. It does not matter in which order the checks are made. In how many different ways can the operator make the checks?
3. The 10 numbers 0 through 9 are to be used in code groups of four to identify an item of clothing. Code 1083 might identify a blue blouse, size medium; the code group 2031 might identify a pair of pants, size 18; and so on. Repetitions of numbers are not permitted. That is, the same number cannot be used twice (or more) in a total sequence. For example, 2256, 2562, or 5559 would not be permitted. How many different code groups can be designed?
4. In the above example involving Goody Records, we said that eight colors taken three at a time would give 56 different combinations.
    (a) Use formula (5–10) to show this is true.
    (b) As an alternative plan for color-coding the 42 different lines, it has been suggested that only two colors be placed on a disk. Would 10 colors be adequate to color-

code the 42 different lines? (Again, a combination of two colors could be used only once—that is, if pink and blue were coded for one line, blue and pink could not be used to identify a different line.)

5. In a lottery game, three numbers are randomly selected from a tumbler of balls numbered 1 through 50.
   (a) How many permutations are possible?
   (b) How many combinations are possible?

Exercises

connect

39. Solve the following:
   a. $40!/35!$
   b. $_7P_4$
   c. $_5C_2$
40. Solve the following:
   a. $20!/17!$
   b. $_9P_3$
   c. $_7C_2$
41. A pollster randomly selected 4 of 10 available people. How many different groups of 4 are possible?
42. A telephone number consists of seven digits, the first three representing the exchange. How many different telephone numbers are possible within the 537 exchange?
43. An overnight express company must include five cities on its route. How many different routes are possible, assuming that it does not matter in which order the cities are included in the routing?
44. A representative of the Environmental Protection Agency (EPA) wants to select samples from 10 landfills. The director has 15 landfills from which she can collect samples. How many different samples are possible?
45. A national pollster has developed 15 questions designed to rate the performance of the president of the United States. The pollster will select 10 of these questions. How many different arrangements are there for the order of the 10 selected questions?
46. A company is creating three new divisions and seven managers are eligible to be appointed head of a division. How many different ways could the three new heads be appointed? Hint: Assume the division assignment makes a difference.

Chapter Summary

I. A probability is a value between 0 and 1 inclusive that represents the likelihood a particular event will happen.
   A. An experiment is the observation of some activity or the act of taking some measurement.
   B. An outcome is a particular result of an experiment.
   C. An event is the collection of one or more outcomes of an experiment.
II. There are three definitions of probability.
   A. The classical definition applies when there are n equally likely outcomes to an experiment.
   B. The empirical definition occurs when the number of times an event happens is divided by the number of observations.
   C. A subjective probability is based on whatever information is available.
III. Two events are mutually exclusive if by virtue of one event happening the other cannot happen.
IV. Events are independent if the occurrence of one event does not affect the occurrence of another event.
V. The rules of addition refer to the union of events.

A. The special rule of addition is used when events are mutually exclusive.

$$P(A \text{ or } B) = P(A) + P(B)$$ [5–2]

B. The general rule of addition is used when the events are not mutually exclusive.

$$P(A \text{ or } B) = P(A) + P(B) - P(A \text{ and } B)$$ [5–4]

C. The complement rule is used to determine the probability of an event happening by subtracting the probability of the event not happening from 1.

$$P(A) = 1 - P(\sim A)$$ [5–3]

VI. The rules of multiplication refer to the product of events.
   A. The special rule of multiplication refers to events that are independent.

$$P(A \text{ and } B) = P(A)P(B)$$ [5–5]

   B. The general rule of multiplication refers to events that are not independent.

$$P(A \text{ and } B) = P(A)P(B \mid A)$$ [5–6]

   C. A joint probability is the likelihood that two or more events will happen at the same time.
   D. A conditional probability is the likelihood that an event will happen, given that another event has already happened.
   E. Bayes' theorem is a method of revising a probability, given that additional information is obtained. For two mutually exclusive and collectively exhaustive events:

$$P(A_1 \mid B) = \frac{P(A_1)P(B \mid A_1)}{P(A_1)P(B \mid A_1) + P(A_2)P(B \mid A_2)}$$ [5–7]

VII. There are three counting rules that are useful in determining the number of outcomes in an experiment.
   A. The multiplication rule states that if there are m ways one event can happen and n ways another event can happen, then there are mn ways the two events can happen.

$$\text{Number of arrangements} = (m)(n)$$ [5–8]

   B. A permutation is an arrangement in which the order of the objects selected from a specific pool of objects is important.

$${}_nP_r = \frac{n!}{(n-r)!}$$ [5–9]

   C. A combination is an arrangement where the order of the objects selected from a specific pool of objects is not important.

$${}_nC_r = \frac{n!}{r!(n-r)!}$$ [5–10]

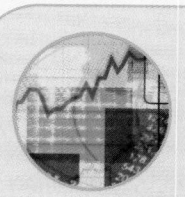

Statistics in Action

Government statistics show there are about 1.7 automobile-caused fatalities for every 100,000,000 vehicle-miles. If you drive 1 mile to the store to buy your lottery ticket and then return home, you have driven 2 miles. Thus the probability that you will join this statistical group on your next 2 mile round trip is $2 \times 1.7/100,000,000 = 0.000000034$. This can also be stated as "One in 29,411,765." Thus if you drive to the store to buy your Powerball ticket, your chance of being killed (or killing someone else) is more than 4 times greater than the chance that you will win the Powerball Jackpot, one chance in 120,526,770.
http://www.durangobill.com/Powerball Odds.html

Pronunciation Key

SYMBOL	MEANING	PRONUNCIATION
$P(A)$	Probability of A	P of A
$P(\sim A)$	Probability of not A	P of not A
$P(A \text{ and } B)$	Probability of A and B	P of A and B
$P(A \text{ or } B)$	Probability of A or B	P of A or B
$P(A \mid B)$	Probability of A given B has happened	P of A given B
${}_nP_r$	Permutation of n items selected r at a time	Pnr
${}_nC_r$	Combination of n items selected r at a time	Cnr

Chapter Exercises

47. The marketing research department at Vernors plans to survey teenagers about a newly developed soft drink. Each will be asked to compare it with his or her favorite soft drink.
  a. What is the experiment?
  b. What is one possible event?
48. The number of times a particular event occurred in the past is divided by the number of occurrences. What is this approach to probability called?
49. The probability that the cause and the cure for all cancers will be discovered before the year 2020 is .20. What viewpoint of probability does this statement illustrate?
50. Berdine's Chicken Factory has several stores in the Hilton Head, South Carolina, area. When interviewing applicants for server positions, the owner would like to include information on the amount of tip a server can expect to earn per check (or bill). A study of 500 recent checks indicated the server earned the following amounts in tips per 8-hour shift.

Amount of Tip	Number
$0 up to $ 20	200
20 up to 50	100
50 up to 100	75
100 up to 200	75
200 or more	50
Total	500

  a. What is the probability of a tip of $200 or more?
  b. Are the categories "$0 up to $20," "$20 up to $50," and so on considered mutually exclusive?
  c. If the probabilities associated with each outcome were totaled, what would that total be?
  d. What is the probability of a tip of up to $50?
  e. What is the probability of a tip of less than $200?
51. Winning all three "Triple Crown" races is considered the greatest feat of a pedigree race-horse. After a successful Kentucky Derby, Big Brown is a 1 to 2 favorite to win the Preakness Stakes.
  a. If he is a 1 to 2 favorite to win the Belmont Stakes as well, what is his probability of winning the Triple Crown?
  b. What do his chances for the Preakness Stakes have to be in order for him to be "even money" to earn the Triple Crown?
52. The first card selected from a standard 52-card deck is a king.
  a. If it is returned to the deck, what is the probability that a king will be drawn on the second selection?
  b. If the king is not replaced, what is the probability that a king will be drawn on the second selection?
  c. What is the probability that a king will be selected on the first draw from the deck and another king on the second draw (assuming that the first king was not replaced)?
53. Armco, a manufacturer of traffic light systems, found that under accelerated-life tests, 95 percent of the newly developed systems lasted 3 years before failing to change signals properly.
  a. If a city purchased four of these systems, what is the probability all four systems would operate properly for at least 3 years?
  b. Which rule of probability does this illustrate?
  c. Using letters to represent the four systems, write an equation to show how you arrived at the answer to part (a).
54. Refer to the following picture.

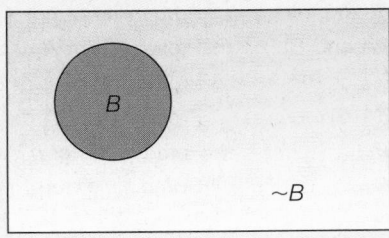

    a. What is the picture called?

    b. What rule of probability is illustrated?

    c. *B* represents the event of choosing a family that receives welfare payments. What does $P(B) + P(\sim B)$ equal?

55. In a management trainee program at Claremont Enterprises, 80 percent of the trainees are female and 20 percent male. Ninety percent of the females attended college, and 78 percent of the males attended college.

    a. A management trainee is selected at random. What is the probability that the person selected is a female who did not attend college?

    b. Are gender and attending college independent? Why?

    c. Construct a tree diagram showing all the probabilities, conditional probabilities, and joint probabilities.

    d. Do the joint probabilities total 1.00? Why?

56. Assume the likelihood that any flight on Northwest Airlines arrives within 15 minutes of the scheduled time is .90. We select four flights from yesterday for study.

    a. What is the likelihood all four of the selected flights arrived within 15 minutes of the scheduled time?

    b. What is the likelihood that none of the selected flights arrived within 15 minutes of the scheduled time?

    c. What is the likelihood at least one of the selected flights did not arrive within 15 minutes of the scheduled time?

57. There are 100 employees at Kiddie Carts International. Fifty-seven of the employees are production workers, 40 are supervisors, 2 are secretaries, and the remaining employee is the president. Suppose an employee is selected:

    a. What is the probability the selected employee is a production worker?

    b. What is the probability the selected employee is either a production worker or a supervisor?

    c. Refer to part (b). Are these events mutually exclusive?

    d. What is the probability the selected employee is neither a production worker nor a supervisor?

58. Magglio Ordonez of the Detroit Tigers had the highest batting average in the 2007 Major League Baseball season. His average was .363. So assume the probability of getting a hit is .363 for each time he batted. In a particular game assume he batted three times.

    a. This is an example of what type of probability?

    b. What is the probability of getting three hits in a particular game?

    c. What is the probability of not getting any hits in a game?

    d. What is the probability of getting at least one hit?

59. The probability that a cruise missile hits its target on any particular mission is .80. Four cruise missiles are sent after the same target. What is the probability:

    a. They all hit the target?

    b. None hit the target?

    c. At least one hits the target?

60. Ninety students will graduate from Lima Shawnee High School this spring. Of the 90 students, 50 are planning to attend college. Two students are to be picked at random to carry flags at the graduation.

    a. What is the probability both of the selected students plan to attend college?

    b. What is the probability one of the two selected students plans to attend college?

61. Brooks Insurance, Inc., wishes to offer life insurance to men age 60 via the Internet. Mortality tables indicate the likelihood of a 60-year-old man surviving another year is .98. If the policy is offered to five men age 60:

    a. What is the probability all five men survive the year?

    b. What is the probability at least one does not survive?

62. Forty percent of the homes constructed in the Quail Creek area include a security system. Three homes are selected at random:

    a. What is the probability all three of the selected homes have a security system?

    b. What is the probability none of the three selected homes have a security system?

    c. What is the probability at least one of the selected homes has a security system?

    d. Did you assume the events to be dependent or independent?

63. Refer to Exercise 62, but assume there are 10 homes in the Quail Creek area and four of them have a security system. Three homes are selected at random:

    a. What is the probability all three of the selected homes have a security system?

    b. What is the probability none of the three selected homes have a security system?

    c. What is the probability at least one of the selected homes has a security system?

    d. Did you assume the events to be dependent or independent?

64. There are 20 families living in the Willbrook Farms Development. Of these families 10 prepared their own federal income taxes for last year, 7 had their taxes prepared by a local professional, and the remaining 3 by H&R Block.

    a. What is the probability of selecting a family that prepared their own taxes?

    b. What is the probability of selecting two families both of which prepared their own taxes?

    c. What is the probability of selecting three families, all of which prepared their own taxes?

    d. What is the probability of selecting two families, neither of which had their taxes prepared by H&R Block?

65. The board of directors of Saner Automatic Door Company consists of 12 members, 3 of whom are women. A new policy and procedures manual is to be written for the company. A committee of 3 is randomly selected from the board to do the writing.

    a. What is the probability that all members of the committee are men?

    b. What is the probability that at least 1 member of the committee is a woman?

66. A recent survey reported in *BusinessWeek* dealt with the salaries of CEOs at large corporations and whether company shareholders made money or lost money.

	CEO Paid More Than $1 Million	CEO Paid Less Than $1 Million	Total
Shareholders made money	2	11	13
Shareholders lost money	4	3	7
Total	6	14	20

If a company is randomly selected from the list of 20 studied, what is the probability:

    a. the CEO made more than $1 million?

    b. the CEO made more than $1 million or the shareholders lost money?

    c. the CEO made more than $1 million given the shareholders lost money?

    d. of selecting 2 CEOs and finding they both made more than $1 million?

67. Althoff and Roll, an investment firm in Augusta, Georgia, advertises extensively in the *Augusta Morning Gazette,* the newspaper serving the region. The *Gazette* marketing staff estimates that 60 percent of Althoff and Roll's potential market read the newspaper. It is further estimated that 85 percent of those who read the *Gazette* remember the Althoff and Roll advertisement.

    a. What percent of the investment firm's potential market sees and remembers the advertisement?

    b. What percent of the investment firm's potential market sees, but does not remember the advertisement?

68. An Internet company located in Southern California has season tickets to the Los Angeles Lakers basketball games. The company president always invites one of the four vice presidents to attend games with him, and claims he selects the person to attend at random. One of the four vice presidents has not been invited to attend any of the last five Lakers home games. What is the likelihood this could be due to chance?

69. A computer-supply retailer purchased a batch of 1,000 CD-R disks and attempted to format them for a particular application. There were 857 perfect CDs, 112 CDs were usable but had bad sectors, and the remainder could not be used at all.

    a. What is the probability a randomly chosen CD is not perfect?

    b. If the disk is not perfect, what is the probability it cannot be used at all?

70. An investor purchased 100 shares of Fifth Third Bank stock and 100 shares of Santee Electric Cooperative stock. The probability the bank stock will appreciate over a year is .70. The probability the electric utility will increase over the same period is .60.

    a. What is the probability both stocks appreciate during the period?

    b. What is the probability the bank stock appreciates but the utility does not?

    c. What is the probability at least one of the stocks appreciates?

71. Flashner Marketing Research, Inc., specializes in providing assessments of the prospects for women's apparel shops in shopping malls. Al Flashner, president, reports that he assesses the prospects as good, fair, or poor. Records from previous assessments show that 60 percent of the time the prospects were rated as good, 30 percent of the time fair, and 10 percent of the time poor. Of those rated good, 80 percent made a profit the first year; of those rated fair, 60 percent made a profit the first year; and of those rated poor, 20 percent made a profit the first year. Connie's Apparel was one of Flashner's clients. Connie's Apparel made a profit last year. What is the probability that it was given an original rating of poor?

72. Two boxes of men's Old Navy shirts were received from the factory. Box 1 contained 25 mesh polo shirts and 15 Super-T shirts. Box 2 contained 30 mesh polo shirts and 10

Super-T shirts. One of the boxes was selected at random, and a shirt was chosen at random from that box to be inspected. The shirt was a mesh polo shirt. Given this information, what is the probability that the mesh polo shirt came from box 1?

73. With each purchase of a large pizza at Tony's Pizza, the customer receives a coupon that can be scratched to see if a prize will be awarded. The odds of winning a free soft drink are 1 in 10, and the odds of winning a free large pizza are 1 in 50. You plan to eat lunch tomorrow at Tony's. What is the probability:

   a. That you will win either a large pizza or a soft drink?
   b. That you will not win a prize?
   c. That you will not win a prize on three consecutive visits to Tony's?
   d. That you will win at least one prize on one of your next three visits to Tony's?

74. For the daily lottery game in Illinois, participants select three numbers between 0 and 9. A number cannot be selected more than once, so a winning ticket could be, say, 307 but not 337. Purchasing one ticket allows you to select one set of numbers. The winning numbers are announced on TV each night.

   a. How many different outcomes (three-digit numbers) are possible?
   b. If you purchase a ticket for the game tonight, what is the likelihood you will win?
   c. Suppose you purchase three tickets for tonight's drawing and select a different number for each ticket. What is the probability that you will not win with any of the tickets?

75. Several years ago Wendy's Hamburgers advertised that there are 256 different ways to order your hamburger. You may choose to have, or omit, any combination of the following on your hamburger: mustard, ketchup, onion, pickle, tomato, relish, mayonnaise, and lettuce. Is the advertisement correct? Show how you arrive at your answer.

76. It was found that 60 percent of the tourists to China visited the Forbidden City, the Temple of Heaven, the Great Wall, and other historical sites in or near Beijing. Forty percent visited Xi'an with its magnificent terracotta soldiers, horses, and chariots, which lay buried for over 2,000 years. Thirty percent of the tourists went to both Beijing and Xi'an. What is the probability that a tourist visited at least one of these places?

77. A new chewing gum has been developed that is helpful to those who want to stop smoking. If 60 percent of those people chewing the gum are successful in stopping smoking, what is the probability that in a group of four smokers using the gum at least one quits smoking?

78. Reynolds Construction Company has agreed not to erect all "look-alike" homes in a new subdivision. Five exterior designs are offered to potential home buyers. The builder has standardized three interior plans that can be incorporated in any of the five exteriors. How many different ways can the exterior and interior plans be offered to potential home buyers?

79. A new sports car model has defective brakes 15 percent of the time and a defective steering mechanism 5 percent of the time. Let's assume (and hope) that these problems occur independently. If one or the other of these problems is present, the car is called a "lemon." If both of these problems are present, the car is a "hazard." Your instructor purchased one of these cars yesterday. What is the probability it is:

   a. A lemon?
   b. A hazard?

80. The state of Maryland has license plates with three numbers followed by three letters. How many different license plates are possible?

81. There are four people being considered for the position of chief executive officer of Dalton Enterprises. Three of the applicants are over 60 years of age. Two are female, of which only one is over 60.

   a. What is the probability that a candidate is over 60 and female?
   b. Given that the candidate is male, what is the probability he is less than 60?
   c. Given that the person is over 60, what is the probability the person is female?

82. Tim Bleckie is the owner of Bleckie Investment and Real Estate Company. The company recently purchased four tracts of land in Holly Farms Estates and six tracts in Newburg Woods. The tracts are all equally desirable and sell for about the same amount.

   a. What is the probability that the next two tracts sold will be in Newburg Woods?
   b. What is the probability that of the next four sold at least one will be in Holly Farms?
   c. Are these events independent or dependent?

83. A computer password consists of four characters. The characters can be one of the 26 letters of the alphabet. Each character may be used more than once. How many different passwords are possible?

84. A case of 24 cans contains 1 can that is contaminated. Three cans are to be chosen randomly for testing.

   a. How many different combinations of 3 cans could be selected?
   b. What is the probability that the contaminated can is selected for testing?

85. A puzzle in the newspaper presents a matching problem. The names of 10 U.S. presidents are listed in one column, and their vice presidents are listed in random order in the second column. The puzzle asks the reader to match each president with his vice president. If you make the matches randomly, how many matches are possible? What is the probability all 10 of your matches are correct?

86. Two components, *A* and *B*, operate in series. Being in series means that for the system to operate, both components *A* and *B* must work. Assume the two components are independent. What is the probability the system works under these conditions? The probability *A* works is .90 and the probability *B* functions is also .90.

87. Horwege Electronics, Inc., purchases TV picture tubes from four different suppliers. Tyson Wholesale supplies 20 percent of the tubes, Fuji Importers 30 percent, Kirkpatricks 25 percent, and Parts, Inc., 25 percent. Tyson Wholesale tends to have the best quality, as only 3 percent of its tubes arrive defective. Fuji Importers' tubes are 4 percent defective, Kirkpatricks' 7 percent, and Parts, Inc. are 6.5 percent defective.
   a. What is the overall percent defective?
   b. A defective picture tube was discovered in the latest shipment. What is the probability that it came from Tyson Wholesale?

88. ABC Auto Insurance classifies drivers as good, medium, or poor risks. Drivers who apply to them for insurance fall into these three groups in the proportions 30 percent, 50 percent, and 20 percent, respectively. The probability a "good" driver will have an accident is .01, the probability a "medium" risk driver will have an accident is .03, and the probability a "poor" driver will have an accident is .10. The company sells Mr. Brophy an insurance policy and he has an accident. What is the probability Mr. Brophy is:
   a. A "good" driver?
   b. A "medium" risk driver?
   c. A "poor" driver?

89. You take a trip by air that involves three independent flights. If there is an 80 percent chance each specific leg of the trip is done on time, what is the probability all three flights arrive on time?

90. The probability a HP network server is down is .05. If you have three independent servers, what is the probability that at least one of them is operational?

91. Twenty-two percent of all liquid crystal displays (LCDs) are manufactured by Samsung. What is the probability that in a collection of three independent LCD purchases, at least one is a Samsung?

Data Set Exercises

92. Refer to the Real Estate data, which reports information on homes sold in the Denver, Colorado, area during the last year.
   a. Sort the data into a table that shows the number of homes that have a pool versus the number that don't have a pool in each of the five townships. If a home is selected at random, compute the following probabilities.
      1. The home is in Township 1 or has a pool.
      2. Given that it is in Township 3, that it has a pool.
      3. Has a pool and is in Township 3.
   b. Sort the data into a table that shows the number of homes that have a garage attached versus those that don't in each of the five townships. If a home is selected at random, compute the following probabilities:
      1. The home has a garage attached.
      2. Given that it is in Township 5, that it does not have a garage attached.
      3. The home has a garage attached and is in Township 3.
      4. Does not have a garage attached or is in Township 2.

93. Refer to the Baseball 2007 data, which reports information on the 30 Major League Baseball teams for the 2007 season. Set up a variable that divides the teams into two groups, those that had a winning season and those that did not. That is, create a variable to count the teams that won 81 games or more, and those that won 80 or less. Next create a new variable for attendance, using three categories: attendance less than 2.0 million, attendance of 2.0 million up to 3.0 million, and attendance of 3.0 million or more.
   a. Create a table that shows the number of teams with a winning season versus those with a losing season by the three categories of attendance. If a team is selected at random, compute the following probabilities:

       1. Having a winning season.

       2. Having a winning season or attendance of more than 3.0 million.

       3. Given attendance of more than 3.0 million, having a winning season.

       4. Having a losing season and drawing less than 2.0 million.

   b. Create a table that shows the number of teams that play on artificial surfaces and natural surfaces by winning and losing records. If a team is selected at random, compute the following probabilities:

       1. Selecting a team with a home field that has a natural surface.

       2. Is the likelihood of selecting a team with a winning record larger for teams with natural or artificial surfaces?

       3. Having a winning record or playing on an artificial surface.

94. Refer to the Wages data, which report information on annual wages for a sample of 100 workers. Also included are variables relating to industry, years of education, and gender for each worker. Develop a table showing the industry of employment by gender. A worker is randomly selected; compute the probability the person selected is:

   a. Female.

   b. Female or in manufacturing.

   c. Female, given that the selected person is in manufacturing.

   d. Female and in manufacturing.

Software Commands

1. The Excel Commands to determine the number of permutations shown on page 171 are:

   a. Click on the **Formulas** tab in the top menu, then, on the far left, select **Insert Function** *fx*.

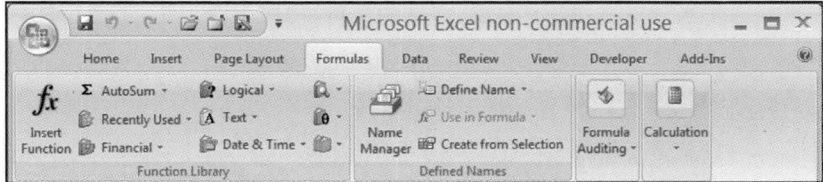

   b. In the **Insert Function** box select **Statistical** as the category, then scroll down to **PERMUT** in the **Select a function list.** Click **OK.**

   c. In the **PERM** box after **Number** enter *8* and the **Number_chosen** box enter *3*. The correct answer of *336* appears twice in the box.

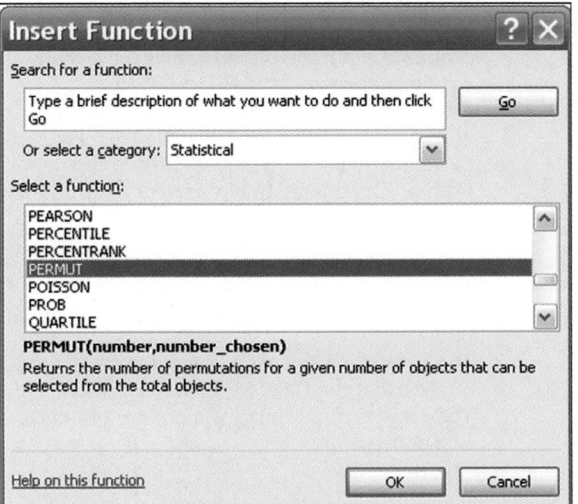

2. The Excel Commands to determine the number of combinations shown on page 171 are:

a. Click on the **Formulas** tab in the top menu, then, on the far left, select **Insert Function** *fx*.

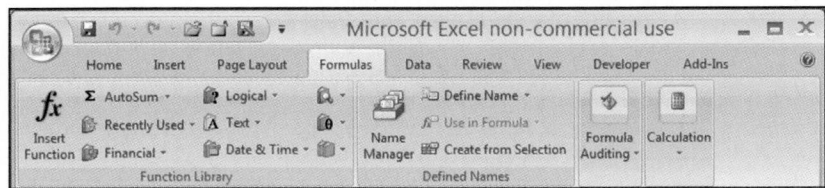

b. In the **Insert Function** box select **Math & Trig** as the category, then scroll down to **COMBIN** in the **Select a function list**. Click **OK**.

c. In the **COMBIN** box after **Number** enter *7* and the **Number_chosen** box enter *3*. The correct answer of *35* appears twice in the box.

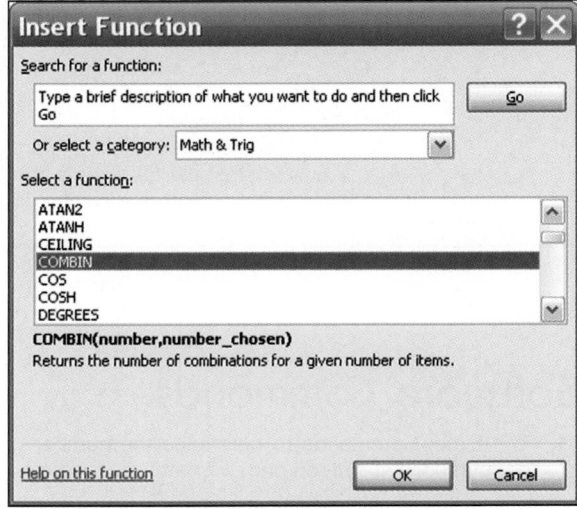

Chapter 5   Answers to Self-Review

5–1 **a.** Count the number who think the new game is playable.

b. Seventy-three players found the game playable. Many other answers are possible.

c. No. Probability cannot be greater than 1. The probability that the game, if put on the market, will be successful is 65/80, or .8125.

d. Cannot be less than 0. Perhaps a mistake in arithmetic.

e. More than half of the players testing the game liked it. (Of course, other answers are possible.)

5–2 **1.** $\dfrac{4 \text{ queens in deck}}{52 \text{ cards total}} = \dfrac{4}{52} = .0769$
Classical.

2. $\dfrac{182}{539} = .338$ Empirical.

3. The author's view when writing the text of the chance that the DJIA will climb to 12,000 is .25. You may be more optimistic or less optimistic. Subjective.

5–3 **a.** **i.** $\dfrac{(50 + 68)}{2,000} = .059$

ii. $1 - \dfrac{302}{2,000} = .849$

b.

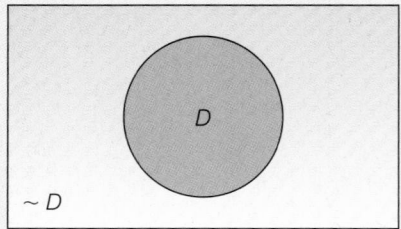

c. They are not complementary, but are mutually exclusive.

5–4 **a.** Need for corrective shoes is event A. Need for major dental work is event B.

$$P(A \text{ or } B) = P(A) + P(B) - P(A \text{ and } B)$$
$$= .08 + .15 - .03$$
$$= .20$$

b. One possibility is:

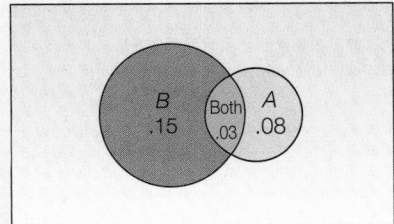

5–5 $(.95)(.95)(.95) = .86$

5–6 **a.** .002, found by:

$$\left(\frac{4}{12}\right)\left(\frac{3}{11}\right)\left(\frac{2}{10}\right)\left(\frac{1}{9}\right) = \frac{24}{11,880} = .002$$

b. .14, found by:

$$\left(\frac{8}{12}\right)\left(\frac{7}{11}\right)\left(\frac{6}{10}\right)\left(\frac{5}{9}\right) = \frac{1,680}{11,880} = .1414$$

c. No, because there are other possibilities, such as three women and one man.

5–7 **a.** $P(B_4) = \dfrac{105}{200} = .525$

b. $P(A_2 | B_4) = \dfrac{30}{105} = .286$

c. $P(A_2 \text{ or } B_4) = \dfrac{80}{200} + \dfrac{105}{200} - \dfrac{30}{200} = \dfrac{155}{200} = .775$

5–8 **a.** Independence requires that $P(A|B) = P(A)$. One possibility is:

$$P(\text{visit often} | \text{yes enclosed mall}) = P(\text{visit often})$$

Does $60/90 = 80/195$? No, the two variables are *not* independent.

Therefore, any joint probability in the table must be computed by using the general rule of multiplication.

b.

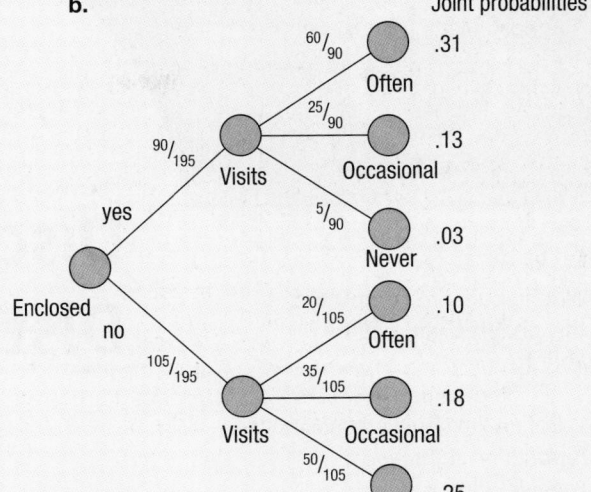

5–9 **a.** $P(A_3 | B_2) = \dfrac{P(A_3)P(B_2 | A_3)}{P(A_1)P(B_2 | A_1) + P(A_2)P(B_2 | A_2) + P(A_3)P(B_2 | A_3)}$

b. $= \dfrac{(.50)(.96)}{(.30)(.97) + (.20)(.95) + (.50)(.96)}$

$= \dfrac{.480}{.961} = .499$

5–10 **1.** $(5)(4) = 20$

2. $(3)(2)(4)(3) = 72$

5–11 **1.** **a.** 60, found by $(5)(4)(3)$.

b. 60, found by:

$$\frac{5!}{(5-3)!} = \frac{5 \cdot 4 \cdot 3 \cdot 2 \cdot 1}{2 \cdot 1}$$

2. 24, found by:

$$\frac{4!}{(4-4)!} = \frac{4!}{0!} = \frac{4!}{1} = \frac{4 \cdot 3 \cdot 2 \cdot 1}{1}$$

3. 5,040, found by:

$$\frac{10!}{(10-4)!} = \frac{10 \cdot 9 \cdot 8 \cdot 7 \cdot 6 \cdot 5 \cdot 4 \cdot 3 \cdot 2 \cdot 1}{6 \cdot 5 \cdot 4 \cdot 3 \cdot 2 \cdot 1}$$

4. **a.** 56 is correct, found by:

$$_8C_3 = \frac{n!}{r!(n-r)!} = \frac{8!}{3!(8-3)!} = 56$$

b. Yes. There are 45 combinations, found by:

$$_{10}C_2 = \frac{n!}{r!(n-r)!} = \frac{10!}{2!(10-2)!} = 45$$

5. **a.** $_{50}P_3 = \dfrac{50!}{(50-3)!} = 117,600$

b. $_{50}C_3 = \dfrac{50!}{3!\,(50-3)!} = 19,600$

6

GOALS

When you have completed this chapter, you will be able to:

1 Define the terms *probability distribution* and *random variable*.

2 Distinguish between *discrete* and *continuous* probability distributions.

3 Calculate the mean, variance, and standard deviation of a discrete probability distribution.

4 Describe the characteristics of and compute probabilities using the *binomial probability distribution*.

5 Describe the characteristics of and compute probabilities using the *hypergeometric probability distribution*.

6 Describe the characteristics of and compute probabilities using the *Poisson probability distribution*.

Discrete Probability Distributions

Recent statistics suggest that 15 percent of those who visit a retail site on the Web make a purchase. A retailer wished to verify this claim. To do so, she selected a sample of 16 "hits" to her site and found that 4 had actually made a purchase. What is the likelihood of exactly four purchases? How many purchases should she expect? What is the likelihood that four or more "hits" result in a purchase? (Exercise 49, Goal 4)

Introduction

Chapters 2 through 4 are devoted to descriptive statistics. We describe raw data by organizing it into a frequency distribution and portraying the distribution in tables, graphs, and charts. Also, we compute a measure of location—such as the arithmetic mean, median, or mode—to locate a typical value near the center of the distribution. The range and the standard deviation are used to describe the spread in the data. These chapters focus on describing *something that has already happened.*

Starting with Chapter 5, the emphasis changes—we begin examining *something that would probably happen.* We note that this facet of statistics is called *statistical inference.* The objective is to make inferences (statements) about a population based on a number of observations, called a sample, selected from the population. In Chapter 5, we state that a probability is a value between 0 and 1 inclusive, and we examine how probabilities can be combined using rules of addition and multiplication.

This chapter will begin the study of **probability distributions.** A probability distribution gives the entire range of values that can occur based on an experiment. A probability distribution is similar to a relative frequency distribution. However, instead of describing the past, it describes a likely future event. For example, a drug manufacturer may claim a treatment will cause weight loss for 80 percent of the population. A consumer protection agency may test the treatment on a sample of six people. If the manufacturer's claim is true, it is *almost impossible* to have an outcome where no one in the sample loses weight and it is *most likely* that 5 out of the 6 do lose weight.

In this chapter we discuss the mean, variance, and standard deviation of a probability distribution. We also discuss three frequently occurring probability distributions: the binomial, hypergeometric, and Poisson.

What Is a Probability Distribution?

A probability distribution shows the possible outcomes of an experiment and the probability of each of these outcomes.

> **PROBABILITY DISTRIBUTION** A listing of all the outcomes of an experiment and the probability associated with each outcome.

Below are the major characteristics of a probability distribution.

> **CHARACTERISTICS OF A PROBABILITY DISTRIBUTION**
> 1. The probability of a particular outcome is between 0 and 1 inclusive.
> 2. The outcomes are mutually exclusive events.
> 3. The list is exhaustive. So the sum of the probabilities of the various events is equal to 1.

How can we generate a probability distribution? The following example will explain.

Example

Suppose we are interested in the number of heads showing face up on three tosses of a coin. This is the experiment. The possible results are: zero heads, one head, two heads, and three heads. What is the probability distribution for the number of heads?

Solution

There are eight possible outcomes. A tail might appear face up on the first toss, another tail on the second toss, and another tail on the third toss of the coin. Or we might get a tail, tail, and head, in that order. We use the multiplication formula for counting outcomes (5–8). There are (2)(2)(2) or 8 possible results. These results are on the next page.

| Possible | Coin Toss | | | Number of |
Result	First	Second	Third	Heads
1	T	T	T	0
2	T	T	H	1
3	T	H	T	1
4	T	H	H	2
5	H	T	T	1
6	H	T	H	2
7	H	H	T	2
8	H	H	H	3

Note that the outcome "zero heads" occurred only once, "one head" occurred three times, "two heads" occurred three times, and the outcome "three heads" occurred only once. That is, "zero heads" happened one out of eight times. Thus, the probability of zero heads is one-eighth, the probability of one head is three-eighths, and so on. The probability distribution is shown in Table 6–1. Because one of these outcomes must happen, the total of the probabilities of all possible events is 1.000. This is always true. The same information is shown in Chart 6–1.

TABLE 6–1 Probability Distribution for the Events of Zero, One, Two, and Three Heads Showing Face Up on Three Tosses of a Coin

Number of Heads, x	Probability of Outcome, $P(x)$
0	$\frac{1}{8} = .125$
1	$\frac{3}{8} = .375$
2	$\frac{3}{8} = .375$
3	$\frac{1}{8} = .125$
Total	$\frac{8}{8} = 1.000$

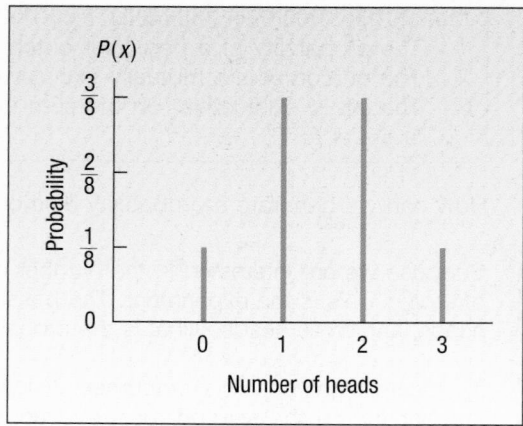

CHART 6–1 Graphical Presentation of the Number of Heads Resulting from Three Tosses of a Coin and the Corresponding Probability

Refer to the coin-tossing example in Table 6–1. We write the probability of *x* as *P(x)*. So the probability of zero heads is *P*(0 heads) = .125 and the probability of one head is *P*(1 head) = .375 and so forth. The sum of these mutually exclusive probabilities is 1; that is, from Table 6–1, 0.125 + 0.375 + 0.375 + 0.125 = 1.00.

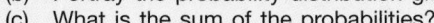

Self-Review 6–1

The possible outcomes of an experiment involving the roll of a six-sided die are a one-spot, a two-spot, a three-spot, a four-spot, a five-spot, and a six-spot.
(a) Develop a probability distribution for the number of possible spots.
(b) Portray the probability distribution graphically.
(c) What is the sum of the probabilities?

Random Variables

In any experiment of chance, the outcomes occur randomly. So it is often called a *random variable*. For example, rolling a single die is an experiment: any one of six possible outcomes can occur. Some experiments result in outcomes that are quantitative (such as dollars, weight, or number of children), and others result in qualitative outcomes (such as color or religious preference). Each value of the random variable is associated with a probability to indicate the chance of a particular outcome. A few examples will further illustrate what is meant by a **random variable.**

- If we count the number of employees absent from the day shift on Monday, the number might be 0, 1, 2, 3, . . . The number absent is the random variable.
- If we weigh four steel ingots, the weights might be 2,492 pounds, 2,497 pounds, 2,506 pounds, and so on. The weight is the random variable.
- If we toss two coins and count the number of heads, there could be zero, one, or two heads. Because the number of heads resulting from this experiment is due to chance, the number of heads appearing is the random variable.
- Other random variables might be the number of defective lightbulbs produced in an hour at the Cleveland Company, Inc., the grade level (9, 10, 11, or 12) of the members of the St. James girls' basketball team, the number of runners in the Boston Marathon for the 2008 race, and the daily number of drivers charged with driving under the influence of alcohol in Texas.

RANDOM VARIABLE A quantity resulting from an experiment that, by chance, can assume different values.

The following diagram illustrates the terms *experiment, outcome, event,* and *random variable.* First, for the experiment where a coin is tossed three times, there are eight possible outcomes. In this experiment, we are interested in the event that one head occurs in the three tosses. The random variable is the number of heads. In terms of probability, we want to know the probability of the event that the random variable equals 1. The result is *P*(1 head in 3 tosses) = 0.375.

Possible *outcomes* for three coin tosses

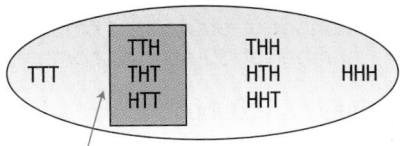

The *event* {one head} occurs and the *random variable x* = 1.

A random variable may be either *discrete* or *continuous.*

Discrete Random Variable

A discrete random variable can assume only a certain number of separated values. If there are 100 employees, then the count of the number absent on Monday can only be 0, 1, 2, 3, . . . , 100. A discrete random variable is usually the result of counting something. By way of definition:

> **DISCRETE RANDOM VARIABLE** A random variable that can assume only certain clearly separated values.

A discrete random variable can, in some cases, assume fractional or decimal values. These values must be separated, that is, have distance between them. As an example, the scores awarded by judges for technical competence and artistic form in figure skating are decimal values, such as 7.2, 8.9, and 9.7. Such values are discrete because there is distance between scores of, say, 8.3 and 8.4. A score cannot be 8.34 or 8.347, for example.

Continuous Random Variable

On the other hand, if the random variable is continuous, then the distribution is a continuous probability distribution. If we measure something such as the width of a room, the height of a person, or the pressure in an automobile tire, the variable is a *continuous random variable*. It can assume one of an infinitely large number of values, within certain limitations. As examples:

- The times of commercial flights between Atlanta and Los Angeles are 4.67 hours, 5.13 hours, and so on. The random variable is the time in hours.
- Tire pressure, measured in pounds per square inch (psi), for a new Chevy Trailblazer might be 32.78 psi, 31.62 psi, 33.07 psi, and so on. In other words, any values between 28 and 35 could reasonably occur. The random variable is the tire pressure.

Logically, if we organize a set of possible values from a random variable into a probability distribution, the result is a **probability distribution.** So what is the difference between a probability distribution and a random variable? A random variable reports the particular outcome of an experiment. A probability distribution reports all the possible outcomes as well as the corresponding probability.

The tools used, as well as the probability interpretations, are different for discrete and continuous probability distributions. This chapter is limited to the discussion and interpretation of discrete distributions. In the next chapter we discuss continuous distributions. How do you tell the difference between the two types of distributions? Usually a discrete distribution is the result of counting something, such as:

- The number of heads appearing when a coin is tossed 3 times.
- The number of students earning an A in this class.
- The number of production employees absent from the second shift today.
- The number of 30-second commercials on NBC from 8 to 11 P.M. tonight.

Continuous distributions are usually the result of some type of measurement, such as:

- The length of each song on the latest Linkin Park CD.
- The weight of each student in this class.

- The temperature outside as you are reading this book.
- The amount of money earned by each of the more than 750 players currently on Major League Baseball team rosters.

The Mean, Variance, and Standard Deviation of a Probability Distribution

In Chapter 3 we discussed measures of location and variation for a frequency distribution. The mean reports the central location of the data, and the variance describes the spread in the data. In a similar fashion, a probability distribution is summarized by its mean and variance. We identify the mean of a probability distribution by the lowercase Greek letter mu (μ) and the standard deviation by the lowercase Greek letter sigma (σ).

Mean

The mean is a typical value used to represent the central location of a probability distribution. It also is the long-run average value of the random variable. The mean of a probability distribution is also referred to as its **expected value.** It is a weighted average where the possible values of a random variable are weighted by their corresponding probabilities of occurrence.

The mean of a discrete probability distribution is computed by the formula:

MEAN OF A PROBABILITY DISTRIBUTION	$\mu = \Sigma[xP(x)]$	[6–1]

where $P(x)$ is the probability of a particular value x. In other words, multiply each x value by its probability of occurrence, and then add these products.

Variance and Standard Deviation

As noted, the mean is a typical value used to summarize a discrete probability distribution. However, it does not describe the amount of spread (variation) in a distribution. The variance does this. The formula for the variance of a probability distribution is:

VARIANCE OF A PROBABILITY DISTRIBUTION	$\sigma^2 = \Sigma[(x - \mu)^2 P(x)]$	[6–2]

The computational steps are

1. Subtract the mean from each value, and square this difference.
2. Multiply each squared difference by its probability.
3. Sum the resulting products to arrive at the variance.

The standard deviation, σ, is found by taking the positive square root of σ^2; that is, $\sigma = \sqrt{\sigma^2}$.

An example will help explain the details of the calculation and interpretation of the mean and standard deviation of a probability distribution.

Example

John Ragsdale sells new cars for Pelican Ford. John usually sells the largest number of cars on Saturday. He has developed the following probability distribution for the number of cars he expects to sell on a particular Saturday.

Number of Cars Sold, x	Probability, P(x)
0	.10
1	.20
2	.30
3	.30
4	.10
Total	1.00

1. What type of distribution is this?
2. On a typical Saturday, how many cars does John expect to sell?
3. What is the variance of the distribution?

Solution

1. This is a discrete probability distribution for the random variable called "number of cars sold." Note that John expects to sell only within a certain range of cars; he does not expect to sell 5 cars or 50 cars. Further, he cannot sell half a car. He can sell only 0, 1, 2, 3, or 4 cars. Also, the outcomes are mutually exclusive—he cannot sell a total of both 3 and 4 cars on the same Saturday. The sum of the possible outcomes total 1. Hence, these circumstance qualify as a probability distribution.

2. The mean number of cars sold is computed by weighting the number of cars sold by the probability of selling that number and adding or summing the products, using formula (6–1):

$$\mu = \Sigma[xP(x)]$$
$$= 0(.10) + 1(.20) + 2(.30) + 3(.30) + 4(.10)$$
$$= 2.1$$

These calculations are summarized in the following table.

Number of Cars Sold, x	Probability, P(x)	x · P(x)
0	.10	0.00
1	.20	0.20
2	.30	0.60
3	.30	0.90
4	.10	0.40
Total	1.00	$\mu = 2.10$

How do we interpret a mean of 2.1? This value indicates that, over a large number of Saturdays, John Ragsdale expects to sell a mean of 2.1 cars a day. Of course, it is not possible for him to sell *exactly* 2.1 cars on any particular Saturday. However, the expected value can be used to predict the arithmetic mean number of cars sold on Saturdays in the long run. For example, if John works 50 Saturdays during a year, he can expect to sell (50)(2.1) or 105 cars just on Saturdays. Thus, the mean is sometimes called the expected value.

3. Again, a table is useful for systemizing the computations for the variance, which is 1.290.

Number of Cars Sold, x	Probability, $P(x)$	$(x - \mu)$	$(x - \mu)^2$	$(x - \mu)^2 P(x)$
0	.10	0 − 2.1	4.41	0.441
1	.20	1 − 2.1	1.21	0.242
2	.30	2 − 2.1	0.01	0.003
3	.30	3 − 2.1	0.81	0.243
4	.10	4 − 2.1	3.61	0.361
				$\sigma^2 = 1.290$

Recall that the standard deviation, σ, is the positive square root of the variance. In this example, $\sqrt{\sigma^2} = \sqrt{1.290} = 1.136$ cars. How do we interpret a standard deviation of 1.136 cars? If salesperson Rita Kirsch also sold a mean of 2.1 cars on Saturdays, and the standard deviation in her sales was 1.91 cars, we would conclude that there is more variability in the Saturday sales of Ms. Kirsch than in those of Mr. Ragsdale (because 1.91 > 1.136).

Self-Review 6–2

The Pizza Palace offers three sizes of cola—small, medium, and large—to go with its pizza. The colas are sold for $0.80, $0.90, and $1.20, respectively. Thirty percent of the orders are for small, 50 percent are for medium, and 20 percent are for the large sizes. Organize the size of the colas and the probability of a sale into a probability distribution.
(a) Is this a discrete probability distribution? Indicate why or why not.
(b) Compute the mean amount charged for a cola.
(c) What is the variance in the amount charged for a cola? The standard deviation?

Exercises

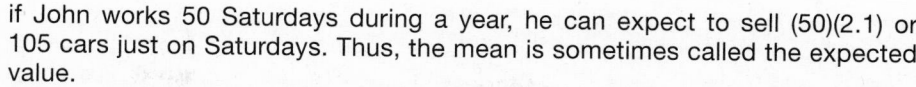

1. Compute the mean and variance of the following discrete probability distribution.

x	$P(x)$
0	.2
1	.4
2	.3
3	.1

2. Compute the mean and variance of the following discrete probability distribution.

x	$P(x)$
2	.5
8	.3
10	.2

3. Three tables listed at the top of page 190 show "random variables" and their "probabilities." However, only one of these is actually a probability distribution.

a. Which is it?

x	P(x)
5	.3
10	.3
15	.2
20	.4

x	P(x)
5	.1
10	.3
15	.2
20	.4

x	P(x)
5	.5
10	.3
15	−.2
20	.4

b. Using the correct probability distribution, find the probability that x is:
   (1) Exactly 15.   **(2)** No more than 10.   **(3)** More than 5.
c. Compute the mean, variance, and standard deviation of this distribution.

4. Which of these variables are discrete and which are continuous random variables?
   a. The number of new accounts established by a salesperson in a year.
   b. The time between customer arrivals to a bank ATM.
   c. The number of customers in Big Nick's barber shop.
   d. The amount of fuel in your car's gas tank.
   e. The number of minorities on a jury.
   f. The outside temperature today.

5. The information below is the number of daily emergency service calls made by the volunteer ambulance service of Walterboro, South Carolina, for the last 50 days. To explain, there were 22 days on which there were 2 emergency calls, and 9 days on which there were 3 emergency calls.

Number of Calls	Frequency
0	8
1	10
2	22
3	9
4	1
Total	50

a. Convert this information on the number of calls to a probability distribution.
b. Is this an example of a discrete or continuous probability distribution?
c. What is the mean number of emergency calls per day?
d. What is the standard deviation of the number of calls made daily?

6. The director of admissions at Kinzua University in Nova Scotia estimated the distribution of student admissions for the fall semester on the basis of past experience. What is the expected number of admissions for the fall semester? Compute the variance and the standard deviation of the number of admissions.

Admissions	Probability
1,000	.6
1,200	.3
1,500	.1

7. Belk Department Store is having a special sale this weekend. Customers charging purchases of more than $50 to their Belk credit card will be given a special Belk Lottery card. The customer will scratch off the card, which will indicate the amount to be taken off the total amount of the purchase. Listed below are the amount of the prize and the percent of the time that amount will be deducted from the total amount of the purchase.

Prize Amount	Probability
$ 10	.50
25	.40
50	.08
100	.02

a. What is the mean amount deducted from the total purchase amount?

b. What is the standard deviation of the amount deducted from the total purchase?

8. The Downtown Parking Authority of Tampa, Florida, reported the following information for a sample of 250 customers on the number of hours cars are parked and the amount they are charged.

Number of Hours	Frequency	Amount Charged
1	20	$ 3.00
2	38	6.00
3	53	9.00
4	45	12.00
5	40	14.00
6	13	16.00
7	5	18.00
8	36	20.00
	250	

a. Convert the information on the number of hours parked to a probability distribution. Is this a discrete or a continuous probability distribution?

b. Find the mean and the standard deviation of the number of hours parked. How would you answer the question: How long is a typical customer parked?

c. Find the mean and the standard deviation of the amount charged.

Binomial Probability Distribution

The **binomial probability distribution** is a widely occurring discrete probability distribution. One characteristic of a binomial distribution is that there are only two possible outcomes on a particular trial of an experiment.

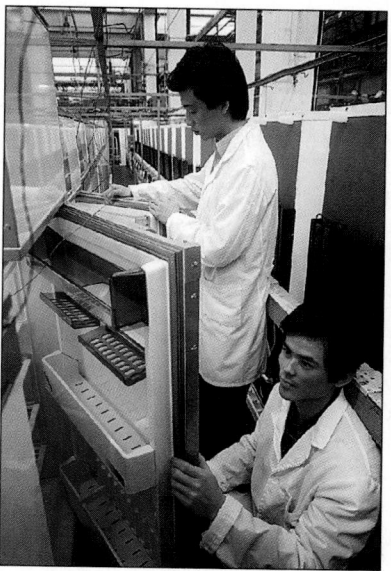

For example, the statement in a true/false question is either true or false. The outcomes are mutually exclusive, meaning that the answer to a true/false question cannot be both true and false at the same time. As other examples, a product is classified as either acceptable or not acceptable by the quality control department, a worker is classified as employed or unemployed, and a sales call results in the customer either purchasing the product or not purchasing the product. Frequently, we classify the two possible outcomes as "success" and "failure." However, this classification does *not* imply that one outcome is good and the other is bad.

Another characteristic of the binomial distribution is that the random variable is the result of counts. That is, we count the number of successes in the total number of trials. We flip a fair coin five times and count the number of times a head appears, we select 10 workers and count the number who are over 50 years of age, or we select 20 boxes of Kellogg's Raisin Bran and count the number that weigh more than the amount indicated on the package.

A third characteristic of a binomial distribution is that the probability of a success remains the same from one trial to another. Two examples are:

• The probability you will guess the first question of a true/false test correctly (a success) is one-half. This is the first "trial." The probability that you will guess correctly on the second question (the second trial) is also one-half, the probability of success on the third trial is one-half, and so on.

- If past experience revealed the swing bridge over the Intracoastal Waterway in Socastee was raised one out of every 20 times you approach it, then the probability is one-twentieth that it will be raised (a "success") the next time you approach it, one-twentieth the following time, and so on.

The final characteristic of a binomial probability distribution is that each trial is *independent* of any other trial. Independent means that there is no pattern to the trials. The outcome of a particular trial does not affect the outcome of any other trial.

Binomial characteristics

> **BINOMIAL PROBABILITY EXPERIMENT**
> 1. An outcome on each trial of an experiment is classified into one of two mutually exclusive categories—a success or a failure.
> 2. The random variable counts the number of successes in a fixed number of trials.
> 3. The probability of success and failure stay the same for each trial.
> 4. The trials are independent, meaning that the outcome of one trial does not affect the outcome of any other trial.

How Is a Binomial Probability Computed?

To construct a particular binomial probability, we use (1) the number of trials and (2) the probability of success on each trial. For example, if an examination at the conclusion of a management seminar consists of 20 multiple-choice questions, the number of trials is 20. If each question has five choices and only one choice is correct, the probability of success on each trial is .20. Thus, the probability is .20 that a person with no knowledge of the subject matter will guess the answer to a question correctly. So the conditions of the binomial distribution just noted are met.

A binomial probability is computed by the formula:

> **BINOMIAL PROBABILITY FORMULA** $P(x) = {}_nC_x \pi^x(1 - \pi)^{n-x}$ **[6–3]**

where:

     C denotes a combination.
     n is the number of trials.
     x is the random variable defined as the number of successes.
     π is the probability of a success on each trial.

We use the Greek letter π (pi) to denote a binomial population parameter. Do not confuse it with the mathematical constant 3.1416.

Example

There are five flights daily from Pittsburgh via US Airways into the Bradford, Pennsylvania, Regional Airport. Suppose the probability that any flight arrives late is .20. What is the probability that none of the flights are late today? What is the probability that exactly one of the flights is late today?

Solution

We can use Formula (6–3). The probability that a particular flight is late is .20, so let $\pi = .20$. There are five flights, so $n = 5$, and x, the random variable, refers to the number of successes. In this case a "success" is a flight that arrives late. Because there are no late arrivals $x = 0$.

$$P(0) = {}_nC_x(\pi)^x(1 - \pi)^{n-x}$$
$$= {}_5C_0(.20)^0(1 - .20)^{5-0} = (1)(1)(.3277) = .3277$$

The probability that exactly one of the five flights will arrive late today is .4096, found by

$$P(1) = {}_nC_x(\pi)^x(1 - \pi)^{n-x}$$
$$= {}_5C_1(.20)^1(1 - .20)^{5-1} = (5)(.20)(.4096) = .4096$$

The entire binomial probability distribution with $\pi = .20$ and $n = 5$ is shown in the following Excel bar chart. We can observe that the probability of exactly 3 late flights is .0512 and from the bar chart that the distribution of the number of late arrivals is positively skewed. The Excel instructions to compute these probabilities are the same as for the Excel output on page 196. These instructions are detailed in the Software Commands section on page 215 near the end of the chapter.

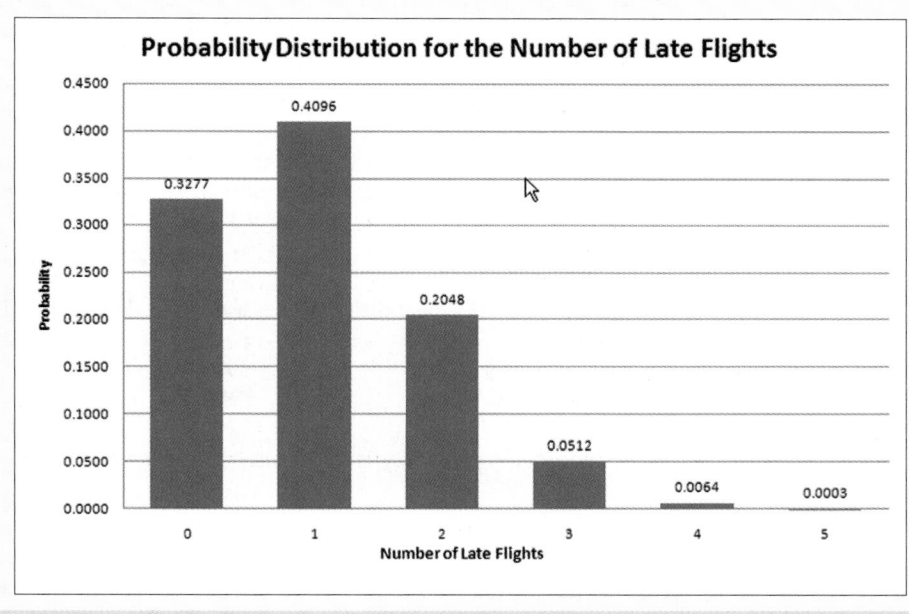

The mean (μ) and the variance (σ^2) of a binomial distribution can be computed in a "shortcut" fashion by:

MEAN OF A BINOMIAL DISTRIBUTION	$\mu = n\pi$	[6–4]

VARIANCE OF A BINOMIAL DISTRIBUTION	$\sigma^2 = n\pi(1 - \pi)$	[6–5]

For the example regarding the number of late flights, recall that $\pi = .20$ and $n = 5$. Hence:

$$\mu = n\pi = (5)(.20) = 1.0$$
$$\sigma^2 = n\pi(1 - \pi) = 5(.20)(1 - .20) = .80$$

The mean of 1.0 and the variance of .80 can be verified from formulas (6–1) and (6–2). The probability distribution from the Excel output on the previous page and the details of the calculations are shown below.

Number of Late Flights, x	P(x)	xP(x)	x − μ	(x − μ)²	(x − μ)²P(x)
0	0.3277	0.0000	−1	1	0.3277
1	0.4096	0.4096	0	0	0
2	0.2048	0.4096	1	1	0.2048
3	0.0512	0.1536	2	4	0.2048
4	0.0064	0.0256	3	9	0.0576
5	0.0003	0.0015	4	16	0.0048
		μ = 1.0000			σ² = 0.7997

Binomial Probability Tables

Formula (6–3) can be used to build a binomial probability distribution for any value of n and π. However, for a larger n, the calculations take more time. For convenience, the tables in Appendix B.9 show the result of using the formula for various values of n and π. Table 6–2 shows part of Appendix B.9 for $n = 6$ and various values of π.

TABLE 6–2 Binomial Probabilities for $n = 6$ and Selected Values of π

						n = 6 Probability					
x\π	.05	.1	.2	.3	.4	.5	.6	.7	.8	.9	.95
0	.735	.531	.262	.118	.047	.016	.004	.001	.000	.000	.000
1	.232	.354	.393	.303	.187	.094	.037	.010	.002	.000	.000
2	.031	.098	.246	.324	.311	.234	.138	.060	.015	.001	.000
3	.002	.015	.082	.185	.276	.313	.276	.185	.082	.015	.002
4	.000	.001	.015	.060	.138	.234	.311	.324	.246	.098	.031
5	.000	.000	.002	.010	.037	.094	.187	.303	.393	.354	.232
6	.000	.000	.000	.001	.004	.016	.047	.118	.262	.531	.735

Example

Five percent of the worm gears produced by an automatic, high-speed Carter-Bell milling machine are defective. What is the probability that out of six gears selected at random none will be defective? Exactly one? Exactly two? Exactly three? Exactly four? Exactly five? Exactly six out of six?

Solution

The binomial conditions are met: (a) there are only two possible outcomes (a particular gear is either defective or acceptable), (b) there is a fixed number of trials (6), (c) there is a constant probability of success (.05), and (d) the trials are independent.

Refer to Table 6–2 above for the probability of exactly zero defective gears. Go down the left margin to an x of 0. Now move horizontally to the column headed by a π of .05 to find the probability. It is .735.

The probability of exactly one defective in a sample of six worm gears is .232. The complete binomial probability distribution for $n = 6$ and $\pi = .05$ is:

Number of Defective Gears, x	Probability of Occurrence, P(x)	Number of Defective Gears, x	Probability of Occurrence, P(x)
0	.735	4	.000
1	.232	5	.000
2	.031	6	.000
3	.002		

Of course, there is a slight chance of getting exactly five defective gears out of six random selections. It is .00000178, found by inserting the appropriate values in the binomial formula:

$$P(5) = {}_6C_5(.05)^5(.95)^1 = (6)(.05)^5(.95) = .00000178$$

For six out of the six, the exact probability is .000000016. Thus, the probability is very small that five or six defective gears will be selected in a sample of six.

We can compute the mean or expected value of the distribution of the number defective:

$$\mu = n\pi = (6)(.05) = 0.30$$

$$\sigma^2 = n\pi(1 - \pi) = 6(.05)(.95) = 0.285$$

MegaStat software will also compute the probabilities for a binomial distribution. Below is the output for the previous example. In MegaStat p is used to represent the probability of success rather than π. The cumulative probability, expected value, variance, and standard deviation are also reported.

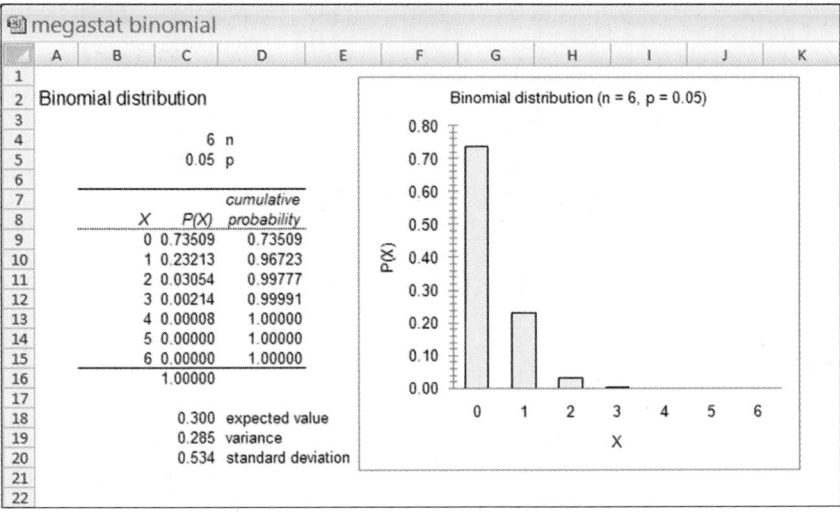

Self-Review 6–3

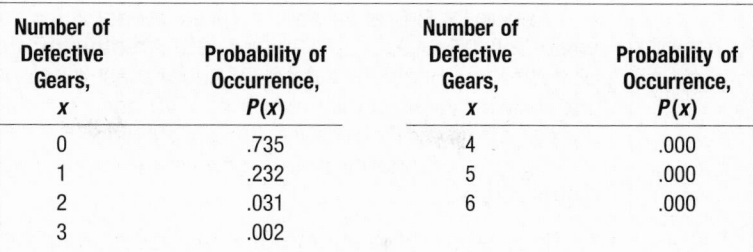

Eighty percent of the employees at the General Mills plant on Laskey Road have their bimonthly wages sent directly to their bank by electronic funds transfer. This is also called direct deposit. Suppose we select a random sample of seven recipients.
(a) Does this situation fit the assumptions of the binomial distribution?
(b) What is the probability that all seven employees use direct deposit?
(c) Use formula (6–3) to determine the exact probability that four of the seven sampled employees use direct deposit.
(d) Use Appendix B.9 to verify your answers to parts (b) and (c).

	A	B
1	Success	Probability
2	0	0.0230
3	1	0.0910
4	2	0.1754
5	3	0.2198
6	4	0.2011
7	5	0.1432
8	6	0.0826
9	7	0.0397
10	8	0.0162
11	9	0.0057
12	10	0.0017
13	11	0.0005
14	12	0.0001
15	13	0.0000
16	14	0.0000
17	15	0.0000

Excel

Appendix B.9 is limited. It gives probabilities for n values from 1 to 15 and π values of .05, .10, . . . , .90, and .95. A software program can generate the probabilities for a specified number of successes, given n and π. The Excel output to the left shows the probability when $n = 40$ and $\pi = .09$. Note that the number of successes stops at 15 because the probabilities for 16 to 40 are very close to 0.

Several additional points should be made regarding the binomial probability distribution.

1. If n remains the same but π increases from .05 to .95, the shape of the distribution changes. Look at Table 6–3 and Chart 6–2. The probabilities for a π of .05 are positively skewed. As π approaches .50, the distribution becomes symmetrical. As π goes beyond .50 and moves toward .95, the probability distribution becomes negatively skewed. Table 6–3 highlights probabilities for $n = 10$ and π of .05, .10, .20, .50, and .70. The graphs of these probability distributions are shown in Chart 6–2.

TABLE 6–3 Probability of 0, 1, 2, . . . Successes for a π of .05, .10, .20, .50, and .70 and an n of 10

$x \backslash \pi$	.05	.1	.2	.3	.4	.5	.6	.7	.8	.9	.95
0	.599	.349	.107	.028	.006	.001	.000	.000	.000	.000	.000
1	.315	.387	.268	.121	.040	.010	.002	.000	.000	.000	.000
2	.075	.194	.302	.233	.121	.044	.011	.001	.000	.000	.000
3	.010	.057	.201	.267	.215	.117	.042	.009	.001	.000	.000
4	.001	.011	.088	.200	.251	.205	.111	.037	.006	.000	.000
5	.000	.001	.026	.103	.201	.246	.201	.103	.026	.001	.000
6	.000	.000	.006	.037	.111	.205	.251	.200	.088	.011	.001
7	.000	.000	.001	.009	.042	.117	.215	.267	.201	.057	.010
8	.000	.000	.000	.001	.011	.044	.121	.233	.302	.194	.075
9	.000	.000	.000	.000	.002	.010	.040	.121	.268	.387	.315
10	.000	.000	.000	.000	.000	.001	.006	.028	.107	.349	.599

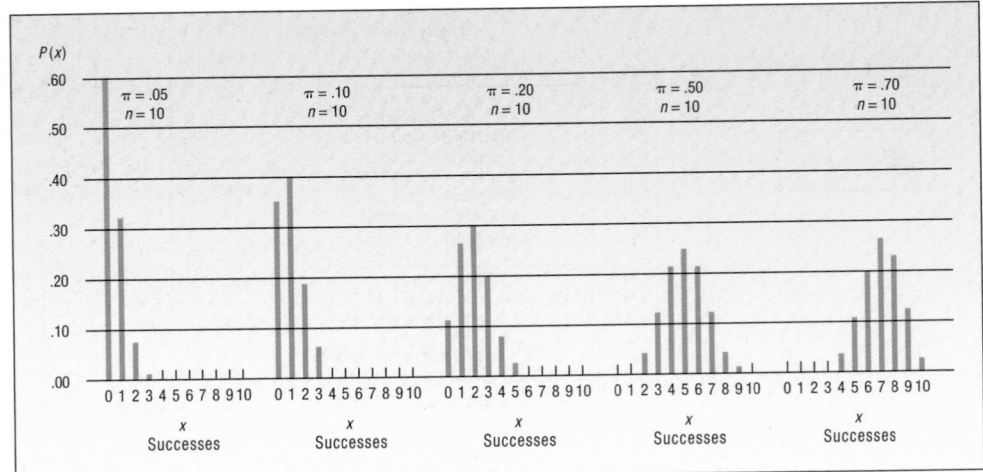

CHART 6–2 Graphing the Binomial Probability Distribution for a π of .05, .10, .20, .50, and .70 and an n of 10

2. If π, the probability of success, remains the same but n becomes larger, the shape of the binomial distribution becomes more symmetrical. Chart 6–3 shows a situation where π remains constant at .10 but n increases from 7 to 40.

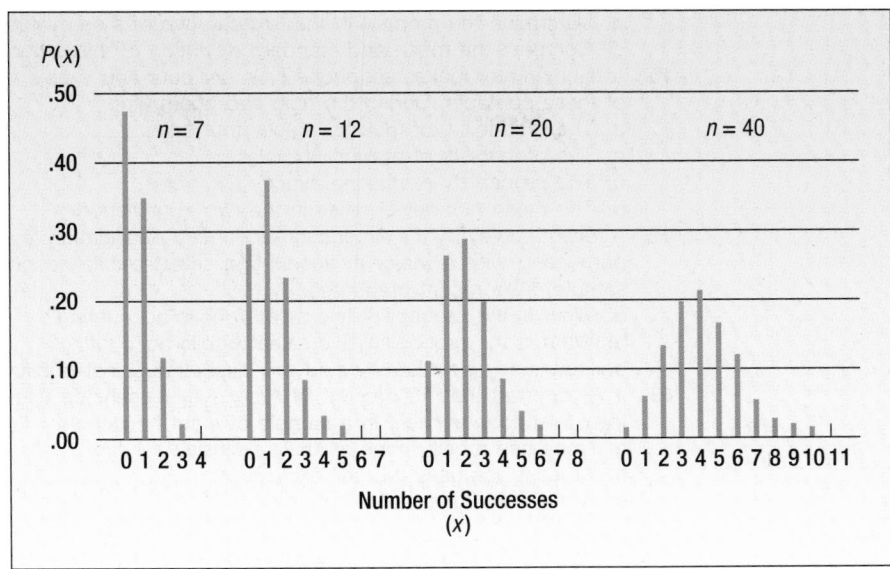

CHART 6–3 Chart Representing the Binomial Probability Distribution for a π of .10 and an n of 7, 12, 20, and 40

Exercises

9. In a binomial situation $n = 4$ and $\pi = .25$. Determine the probabilities of the following events using the binomial formula.
   a. $x = 2$
   b. $x = 3$
10. In a binomial situation $n = 5$ and $\pi = .40$. Determine the probabilities of the following events using the binomial formula.
    a. $x = 1$
    b. $x = 2$
11. Assume a binomial distribution where $n = 3$ and $\pi = .60$.
    a. Refer to Appendix B.9, and list the probabilities for values of x from 0 to 3.
    b. Determine the mean and standard deviation of the distribution from the general definitions given in formulas (6–1) and (6–2).
12. Assume a binomial distribution where $n = 5$ and $\pi = .30$.
    a. Refer to Appendix B.9, and list the probabilities for values of x from 0 to 5.
    b. Determine the mean and standard deviation of the distribution from the general definitions given in formulas (6–1) and (6–2).
13. An American Society of Investors survey found 30 percent of individual investors have used a discount broker. In a random sample of nine individuals, what is the probability:
    a. Exactly two of the sampled individuals have used a discount broker?
    b. Exactly four of them have used a discount broker?
    c. None of them have used a discount broker?
14. The United States Postal Service reports 95 percent of first class mail within the same city is delivered within two days of the time of mailing. Six letters are randomly sent to different locations.
    a. What is the probability that all six arrive within two days?
    b. What is the probability that exactly five arrive within two days?
    c. Find the mean number of letters that will arrive within two days.
    d. Compute the variance and standard deviation of the number that will arrive within two days.
15. Industry standards suggest that 10 percent of new vehicles require warranty service within the first year. Jones Nissan in Sumter, South Carolina, sold 12 Nissans yesterday.
    a. What is the probability that none of these vehicles requires warranty service?
    b. What is the probability exactly one of these vehicles requires warranty service?

connect

    c. Determine the probability that exactly two of these vehicles require warranty service.

    d. Compute the mean and standard deviation of this probability distribution.

16. A telemarketer makes six phone calls per hour and is able to make a sale on 30 percent of these contacts. During the next two hours, find:

    a. The probability of making exactly four sales.

    b. The probability of making no sales.

    c. The probability of making exactly two sales.

    d. The mean number of sales in the two-hour period.

17. A recent survey by the American Accounting Association revealed 23 percent of students graduating with a major in accounting select public accounting. Suppose we select a sample of 15 recent graduates.

    a. What is the probability two select public accounting?

    b. What is the probability five select public accounting?

    c. How many graduates would you expect to select public accounting?

18. It is reported that 16 percent of American households use a cell phone exclusively for their telephone service. In a sample of eight households, find the probability that:

    a. None use a cell phone as their exclusive service.

    b. At least one uses the cell exclusively.

    c. At least five use the cell phone.

Cumulative Binomial Probability Distributions

We may wish to know the probability of correctly guessing the answers to 6 *or more* true/false questions out of 10. Or we may be interested in the probability of *selecting less than two* defectives at random from production during the previous hour. In these cases we need cumulative frequency distributions similar to the ones developed in Chapter 2. See page 40. The following example will illustrate.

Example

A study by the Illinois Department of Transportation concluded that 76.2 percent of front seat occupants used seat belts. That means that both occupants of the front seat were using their seat belts. Suppose we decide to compare that information with current usage. We select a sample of 12 vehicles.

1. What is the probability the front seat occupants in exactly 7 of the 12 vehicles selected are wearing seat belts?
2. What is the probability the front seat occupants in at least 7 of the 12 vehicles are wearing seat belts?

Solution

This situation meets the binomial requirements.

- In a particular vehicle both the front seat occupants are either wearing seat belts or they are not. There are only two possible outcomes.
- There are a fixed number of trials, 12 in this case, because 12 vehicles are checked.
- The probability of a "success" (occupants wearing seat belts) is the same from one vehicle to the next: 76.2 percent.
- The trials are independent. If the fourth vehicle selected in the sample has all the occupants wearing their seat belts, this does not have any effect on the results for the fifth or tenth vehicle.

To find the likelihood the occupants of *exactly* 7 of the sampled vehicles are wearing seat belts we use formula 6-3. In this case $n = 12$ and $\pi = .762$.

$$P(x = 7 | n = 12 \text{ and } \pi = .762)$$
$$= {}_{12}C_7(.762)^7(1 - .762)^{12-7} = 792(.149171)(.000764) = .0902$$

So we conclude the likelihood that the occupants of exactly 7 of the 12 sampled vehicles will be wearing their seat belts is about 9 percent. We often use, as we did in this equation, a bar "|" to mean "given that." So in this equation we want to know the probability that x is equal to 7 "given that the number of trials is 12 and the probability of a success is .762."

To find the probability that the occupants in 7 or more of the vehicles will be wearing seat belts we use formula (6–3) from this chapter as well as the special rule of addition from the previous chapter. See formula (5–2) on page 149.

Because the events are mutually exclusive (meaning that a particular sample of 12 vehicles cannot have both a *total* of 7 and a *total* of 8 vehicles where the occupants are wearing seat belts), we find the probability of 7 vehicles where the occupants are wearing seat belts, the probability of 8 and so on up to the probability that occupants of all 12 sample vehicles are wearing seat belts. The probability of each of these outcomes is then totaled.

$P(x \geq 7 \mid n = 12$ and $\pi = .762)$

$$= P(x = 7) + P(x = 8) + P(x = 9) + P(x = 10) + P(x = 11) + P(x = 12)$$

$$= .0902 + .1805 + .2569 + .2467 + .1436 + .0383$$

$$= .9562$$

So the probability of selecting 12 cars and finding that the occupants of 7 or more vehicles were wearing seat belts is .9562. This information is shown on the following Excel spreadsheet. There is a slight difference in the software answer due to rounding. The Excel commands are similar to those detailed in the Software Commands section on page 215, number 2.

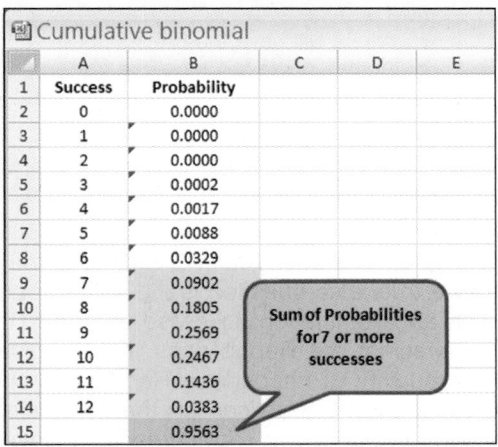

Self-Review 6–4

For a case where $n = 4$ and $\pi = .60$, determine the probability that:
(a) $x = 2$.
(b) $x \leq 2$.
(c) $x > 2$.

Exercises

connect

19. In a binomial distribution $n = 8$ and $\pi = .30$. Find the probabilities of the following events.
    a. $x = 2$.
    b. $x \leq 2$ (the probability that x is equal to or less than 2).
    c. $x \geq 3$ (the probability that x is equal to or greater than 3).

20. In a binomial distribution $n = 12$ and $\pi = .60$. Find the following probabilities.
   a. $x = 5$.
   b. $x \leq 5$.
   c. $x \geq 6$.

21. In a recent study 90 percent of the homes in the United States were found to have large-screen TVs. In a sample of nine homes, what is the probability that:
   a. All nine have large-screen TVs?
   b. Less than five have large-screen TVs?
   c. More than five have large-screen TVs?
   d. At least seven homes have large-screen TVs?

22. A manufacturer of window frames knows from long experience that 5 percent of the production will have some type of minor defect that will require an adjustment. What is the probability that in a sample of 20 window frames:
   a. None will need adjustment?
   b. At least one will need adjustment?
   c. More than two will need adjustment?

23. The speed with which utility companies can resolve problems is very important. GTC, the Georgetown Telephone Company, reports it can resolve customer problems the same day they are reported in 70 percent of the cases. Suppose the 15 cases reported today are representative of all complaints.
   a. How many of the problems would you expect to be resolved today? What is the standard deviation?
   b. What is the probability 10 of the problems can be resolved today?
   c. What is the probability 10 or 11 of the problems can be resolved today?
   d. What is the probability more than 10 of the problems can be resolved today?

24. It is asserted that 80 percent of the cars approaching an individual toll both in New Jersey are equipped with an E-ZPass transponder. Find the probability that in a sample of six cars:
   a. All six will have the transponder.
   b. At least three will have the transponder.
   c. None will have a transponder.

Hypergeometric Probability Distribution

For the binomial distribution to be applied, the probability of a success must stay the same for each trial. For example, the probability of guessing the correct answer to a true/false question is .50. This probability remains the same for each question on an examination. Likewise, suppose that 40 percent of the registered voters in a precinct are Republicans. If 27 registered voters are selected at random, the probability of choosing a Republican on the first selection is .40. The chance of choosing a Republican on the next selection is also .40, assuming that the sampling is done *with replacement,* meaning that the person selected is put back in the population before the next person is selected.

Most sampling, however, is done *without replacement.* Thus, if the population is small, the probability for each observation will change. For example, if the population consists of 20 items, the probability of selecting a particular item from that population is 1/20. If the sampling is done without replacement, after the first selection there are only 19 items remaining; the probability of selecting a particular item on the second selection is only 1/19. For the third selection, the probability is 1/18, and so on. This assumes that the population is **finite**—that is, the number in the population is known and relatively small in number. Examples of a finite population are 2,842 Republicans in the precinct, 9,241 applications for medical school, and the 18 Pontiac Vibes currently in stock at North Charleston Pontiac.

Recall that one of the criteria for the binomial distribution is that the probability of success remains the same from trial to trial. Since the probability of success does not remain the same from trial to trial when sampling is from a relatively small population without replacement, the binomial distribution should not be used. Instead, the **hypergeometric distribution** is applied. Therefore, (1) if a sample is selected from a finite population without replacement and (2) if the size of the sample n is more than 5 percent of the size of the population N, then the hypergeometric distribution is used to determine the probability of a specified number of successes or failures. It is especially appropriate when the size of the population is small.

The formula for the hypergeometric distribution is:

HYPERGEOMETRIC DISTRIBUTION	$$P(x) = \frac{(_SC_x)(_{N-S}C_{n-x})}{_NC_n}$$	**[6–6]**

where:

N is the size of the population.
S is the number of successes in the population.
x is the number of successes in the sample. It may be 0, 1, 2, 3, ...
n is the size of the sample or the number of trials.
C is the symbol for a combination.

In summary, a hypergeometric probability distribution has these characteristics:

HYPERGEOMETRIC PROBABILITY EXPERIMENT
1. An outcome on each trial of an experiment is classified into one of two mutually exclusive categories—a success or a failure.
2. The random variable is the number of successes in a fixed number of trials.
3. The trials are *not independent.*
4. We assume that we sample from a finite population without replacement and $n/N > 0.05$. So, the probability of a success *changes* for each trial.

The following example illustrates the details of determining a probability using the hypergeometric distribution.

Example

PlayTime Toys, Inc., employs 50 people in the Assembly Department. Forty of the employees belong to a union and ten do not. Five employees are selected at random to form a committee to meet with management regarding shift starting times. What is the probability that four of the five selected for the committee belong to a union?

Solution

The population in this case is the 50 Assembly Department employees. An employee can be selected for the committee only once. Hence, the sampling is done without replacement. Thus, the probability of selecting a union employee, for example, changes from one trial to the next. The hypergeometric distribution is appropriate for determining the probability. In this problem,

N is 50, the number of employees.
S is 40, the number of union employees.
x is 4, the number of union employees selected.
n is 5, the number of employees selected.

We wish to find the probability 4 of the 5 committee members belong to a union. Inserting these values into formula (6–6):

$$P(4) = \frac{(_{40}C_4)(_{50-40}C_{5-4})}{_{50}C_5} = \frac{(91{,}390)(10)}{2{,}118{,}760} = .431$$

Thus, the probability of selecting 5 assembly workers at random from the 50 workers and finding 4 of the 5 are union members is .431.

Table 6–4 shows the hypergeometric probabilities of finding 0, 1, 2, 3, 4, and 5 union members on the committee.

TABLE 6–4 Hypergeometric Probabilities ($n = 5$, N $= 50$, and S $= 40$) for the Number of Union Members on the Committee

Union Members	Probability
0	.000
1	.004
2	.044
3	.210
4	.431
5	.311
	1.000

In order for you to compare the two probability distributions, Table 6–5 shows the hypergeometric and binomial probabilities for the PlayTime Toys, Inc., example. Because 40 of the 50 Assembly Department employees belong to the union, we let $\pi = .80$ for the binomial distribution. The binomial probabilities for Table 6–5 come from the binomial distribution with $n = 5$ and $\pi = .80$.

TABLE 6–5 Hypergeometric and Binomial Probabilities for PlayTime Toys, Inc., Assembly Department

Number of Union Members on Committee	Hypergeometric Probability, $P(x)$	Binomial Probability ($n = 5$ and $\pi = .80$)
0	.000	.000
1	.004	.006
2	.044	.051
3	.210	.205
4	.431	.410
5	.311	.328
	1.000	1.000

When the binomial requirement of a constant probability of success cannot be met, the hypergeometric distribution should be used. However, as Table 6–5 shows, under certain conditions the results of the binomial distribution can be used to approximate the hypergeometric. This leads to a rule of thumb:

> If selected items are not returned to the population, the binomial distribution can be used to closely approximate the hypergeometric distribution when $n < .05N$. In words, the binomial will suffice if the sample is less than 5 percent of the population.

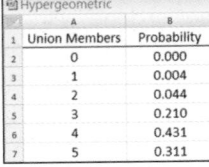

A hypergeometric distribution can be created using Excel. See the output on the left. The necessary steps are given in the Software Commands section.

Self-Review 6–5

Horwege Discount Brokers plans to hire 5 new financial analysts this year. There is a pool of 12 approved applicants, and George Horwege, the owner, decides to randomly select those who will be hired. There are 8 men and 4 women among the approved applicants. What is the probability that 3 of the 5 hired are men?

Exercises

25. A CD contains 10 songs; 6 are classical and 4 are rock and roll. In a sample of 3 songs, what is the probability that exactly 2 are classical? Assume the samples are drawn without replacement.

26. A population consists of 15 items, 10 of which are acceptable. In a sample of 4 items, what is the probability that exactly 3 are acceptable? Assume the samples are drawn without replacement.

27. Kolzak Appliance Outlet just received a shipment of 10 DVD players. Shortly after they were received, the manufacturer called to report that he had inadvertently shipped 3 defective units. Ms. Kolzak, the owner of the outlet, decided to test 2 of the 10 DVD players she received. What is the probability that neither of the 2 DVD players tested is defective? Assume the samples are drawn without replacement.

28. The Computer Systems Department has eight faculty, six of whom are tenured. Dr. Vonder, the chairman, wants to establish a committee of three department faculty members to review the curriculum. If she selects the committee at random:
   a. What is the probability all members of the committee are tenured?
   b. What is the probability that at least one member is not tenured? (Hint: For this question, use the complement rule.)

29. Keith's Florists has 15 delivery trucks, used mainly to deliver flowers and flower arrangements in the Greenville, South Carolina, area. Of these 15 trucks, 6 have brake problems. A sample of 5 trucks is randomly selected. What is the probability that 2 of those tested have defective brakes?

30. The game called Lotto sponsored by the Louisiana Lottery Commission pays its largest prize when a contestant matches all 6 of the 40 possible numbers. Assume there are 40 ping-pong balls each with a single number between 1 and 40. Any number appears only once, and the winning balls are selected without replacement.
   a. The commission reports that the probability of matching all the numbers are 1 in 3,838,380. What is this in terms of probability?
   b. Use the hypergeometric formula to find this probability.
   The lottery commission also pays if a contestant matches 4 or 5 of the 6 winning numbers. Hint: Divide the 40 numbers into two groups, winning numbers and nonwinning numbers.
   c. Find the probability, again using the hypergeometric formula, for matching 4 of the 6 winning numbers.
   d. Find the probability of matching 5 of the 6 winning numbers.

Poisson Probability Distribution

The **Poisson probability distribution** describes the number of times some event occurs during a specified interval. The interval may be time, distance, area, or volume.

The distribution is based on two assumptions. The first assumption is that the probability is proportional to the length of the interval. The second assumption is that the intervals are independent. To put it another way, the longer the interval, the larger the probability, and the number of occurrences in one interval does not affect the other intervals. This distribution is also a limiting form of the binomial distribution when the probability of a success is very small and n is large. It is often referred to as the "law of improbable events," meaning that the probability, π, of a particular event's happening is quite small. The Poisson distribution is a discrete probability distribution because it is formed by counting.

In summary, a Poisson probability distribution has these characteristics:

> **POISSON PROBABILITY EXPERIMENT**
> 1. The random variable is the number of times some event occurs during a defined interval.
> 2. The probability of the event is proportional to the size of the interval.
> 3. The intervals do not overlap and are independent.

This distribution has many applications. It is used as a model to describe the distribution of errors in data entry, the number of scratches and other imperfections in newly painted car panels, the number of defective parts in outgoing shipments, the number of customers waiting to be served at a restaurant or waiting to get into an attraction at Disney World, and the number of accidents on I–75 during a three-month period.

The Poisson distribution can be described mathematically by the formula:

POISSON DISTRIBUTION $$P(x) = \frac{\mu^x e^{-\mu}}{x!}$$ **[6–7]**

where:

μ (mu) is the mean number of occurrences (successes) in a particular interval.
e is the constant 2.71828 (base of the Napierian logarithmic system).
x is the number of occurrences (successes).
$P(x)$ is the probability for a specified value of x.

The mean number of successes, μ, can be determined by $n\pi$, where n is the total number of trials and π the probability of success.

MEAN OF A POISSON DISTRIBUTION $\mu = n\pi$ **[6–8]**

The variance of the Poisson is also equal to its mean. If, for example, the probability that a check cashed by a bank will bounce is .0003, and 10,000 checks are cashed, the mean and the variance for the number of bad checks is 3.0, found by $\mu = n\pi = 10,000(.0003) = 3.0$.

Recall that for a binomial distribution there is a fixed number of trials. For example, for a four-question multiple-choice test there can only be zero, one, two, three, or four successes (correct answers). The random variable, x, for a Poisson distribution, however, can assume an *infinite number of values*—that is, 0, 1, 2, 3, 4, 5, ... However, *the probabilities become very small after the first few occurrences* (successes).

To illustrate the Poisson probability computation, assume baggage is rarely lost by Northwest Airlines. Most flights do not experience any mishandled bags; some have one bag lost; a few have two bags lost; rarely a flight will have three lost bags; and so on. Suppose a random sample of 1,000 flights shows a total of 300 bags were lost. Thus, the arithmetic mean number of lost bags per flight is 0.3, found by 300/1,000. If the number of lost bags per flight follows a Poisson distribution with $\mu = 0.3$, we can compute the various probabilities using formula (6–7):

$$P(x) = \frac{\mu^x e^{-\mu}}{x!}$$

For example, the probability of not losing any bags is:

$$P(0) = \frac{(0.3)^0(e^{-0.3})}{0!} = 0.7408$$

Statistics in Action

Near the end of World War II, the Germans developed rocket bombs, which were fired at the city of London. The Allied military command didn't know whether these bombs were fired at random or whether they had an aiming device. To investigate, the city of London was divided into 586 square regions. The distribution of hits in each square was recorded as follows:

Hits	0	1	2	3	4	5
Regions	229	221	93	35	7	1

To interpret, the above chart indicates that 229 regions were not hit with one of the bombs. Seven regions were hit four times. Using the Poisson distribution, with a mean of 0.93 hits per region, the expected number of hits is as follows:

Hits	0	1	2	3	4	5 or more
Regions	231.2	215.0	100.0	31.0	7.2	1.6

Because the actual number of hits was close to the expected number of hits, the military command

(continued)

In other words, 74 percent of the flights will have no lost baggage. The probability of exactly one lost bag is:

$$P(1) = \frac{(0.3)^1(e^{-0.3})}{1!} = 0.2222$$

Thus, we would expect to find exactly one lost bag on 22 percent of the flights. Poisson probabilities can also be found in the table in Appendix B.5.

Example

Recall from the previous illustration that the number of lost bags follows a Poisson distribution with a mean of 0.3. Use Appendix B.5 to find the probability that no bags will be lost on a particular flight. What is the probability exactly one bag will be lost on a particular flight? When should the supervisor become suspicious that a flight is having too many lost bags?

Solution

Part of Appendix B.5 is repeated as Table 6–6. To find the probability of no lost bags, locate the column headed "0.3" and read down that column to the row labeled "0." The probability is .7408. That is the probability of no lost bags. The probability of one lost bag is .2222, which is in the next row of the table, in the same column. The probability of two lost bags is .0333, in the row below; for three lost bags it is .0033; and for four lost bags it is .0003. Thus, a supervisor should not be surprised to find one lost bag but should expect to see more than one lost bag infrequently.

TABLE 6–6 Poisson Table for Various Values of μ (from Appendix B.5)

x	μ								
	0.1	0.2	0.3	0.4	0.5	0.6	0.7	0.8	0.9
0	0.9048	0.8187	0.7408	0.6703	0.6065	0.5488	0.4966	0.4493	0.4066
1	0.0905	0.1637	0.2222	0.2681	0.3033	0.3293	0.3476	0.3595	0.3659
2	0.0045	0.0164	0.0333	0.0536	0.0758	0.0988	0.1217	0.1438	0.1647
3	0.0002	0.0011	0.0033	0.0072	0.0126	0.0198	0.0284	0.0383	0.0494
4	0.0000	0.0001	0.0003	0.0007	0.0016	0.0030	0.0050	0.0077	0.0111
5	0.0000	0.0000	0.0000	0.0001	0.0002	0.0004	0.0007	0.0012	0.0020
6	0.0000	0.0000	0.0000	0.0000	0.0000	0.0000	0.0001	0.0002	0.0003
7	0.0000	0.0000	0.0000	0.0000	0.0000	0.0000	0.0000	0.0000	0.0000

These probabilities can also be found using the MINITAB system. The commands necessary are reported at the end of the chapter.

	C1	C2	C3	C4	C5	C6
	Success	Probability				
1	0	0.740818				
2	1	0.222245				
3	2	0.033337				
4	3	0.003334				
5	4	0.000250				
6	5	0.000015				
7						

Worksheet 1 ***

Earlier in this section we mentioned that the Poisson probability distribution is a limiting form of the binomial. That is, we could estimate a binomial probability using the Poisson.

The Poisson probability distribution is characterized by the number of times an event happens during some interval or continuum. Examples include:

- The number of misspelled words per page in a newspaper.
- The number of calls per hour received by Dyson Vacuum Cleaner Company.
- The number of vehicles sold per day at Hyatt Buick GMC in Durham, North Carolina.
- The number of goals scored in a college soccer game.

In each of these examples there is some type of continuum—misspelled words per page, calls per hour, vehicles per day, or goals per game.

In the previous example we investigated the number of bags lost per flight, so the continuum was a "flight." We knew the mean number of bags of luggage lost per flight, but we did not know the number of passengers or the probability of a bag being lost. We suspected the number of passengers was fairly large and the probability of a passenger losing his or her bag of luggage was small. In the following example we use the Poisson distribution to estimate a binomial probability when n, the number of trials, is large and π, the probability of a success, small.

Example

Coastal Insurance Company underwrites insurance for beachfront properties along the Virginia, North and South Carolina, and Georgia coasts. It uses the estimate that the probability of a named Category III hurricane (sustained winds of more than 110 miles per hour) or higher striking a particular region of the coast (for example, St. Simons Island, Georgia) in any one year is .05. If a homeowner takes a 30-year mortgage on a recently purchased property in St. Simons, what is the likelihood that the owner will experience at least one hurricane during the mortgage period?

Solution

To use the Poisson probability distribution we begin by determining the mean or expected number of storms meeting the criterion hitting St. Simons during the 30-year period. That is:

$$\mu = n\pi = 30(.05) = 1.5$$

where:

n is the number of years, 30 in this case.
π is the probability a hurricane meeting the strength criteria comes ashore.
μ is the mean or expected number of storms in a 30-year period.

To find the probability of at least one storm hitting St. Simons Island, Georgia, we first find the probability of no storms hitting the coast and subtract that value from 1.

$$P(x \geq 1) = 1 - P(x = 0) = 1 - \frac{\mu^0 e^{-1.5}}{0!} = 1 - .2231 = .7769$$

We conclude that the likelihood a hurricane meeting the strength criteria will strike the beachfront property at St. Simons during the 30-year period when the mortgage is in effect is .7769. To put it another way, the probability St. Simons will be hit by a Category III or higher hurricane during the 30-year period is a little more than 75 percent.

We should emphasize that the continuum, as previously described, still exists. That is, there are expected to be 1.5 storms hitting the coast per 30-year period. The continuum is the 30-year period.

In the above case we are actually using the Poisson distribution as an estimate of the binomial. Note that we've met the binomial conditions outlined on page 192.

- There are only two possible outcomes: a hurricane hits the St. Simons area or it does not.
- There is a fixed number of trials, in this case 30 years.
- There is a constant probability of success; that is, the probability of a hurricane hitting the area is .05 each year.
- The years are independent. That means if a named storm strikes in the fifth year, that has no effect on any other year.

To find the probability of at least one storm striking the area in a 30-year period using the binomial distribution:

$$P(x \geq 1) = 1 - P(x = 0) = 1 - {}_{30}C_0(.05)^0 (.95)^{30} = 1 - (1)(1)(.2146) = .7854$$

The probability of at least one hurricane hitting the St. Simons area during the 30-year period using the binomial distribution is .7854.

Which answer is correct? Why should we look at the problem both ways? The binomial is the more "technically correct" solution. The Poisson can be thought of as an approximation for the binomial, when n, the number of trials is large, and π, the probability of a success, is small. We look at the problem using both distributions to emphasize the convergence of the two discrete distributions. In some instances using the Poisson may be the quicker solution, and as you see there is little practical difference in the answers. In fact, as n gets larger and π smaller, the differences between the two distributions gets smaller.

The Poisson probability distribution is always positively skewed and the random variable has no specific upper limit. The Poisson distribution for the lost bags illustration, where $\mu = 0.3$, is highly skewed. As μ becomes larger, the Poisson distribution becomes more symmetrical. For example, Chart 6–4 shows the distributions of the number of transmission services, muffler replacements, and oil changes per day at Avellino's Auto Shop. They follow Poisson distributions with means of 0.7, 2.0, and 6.0, respectively.

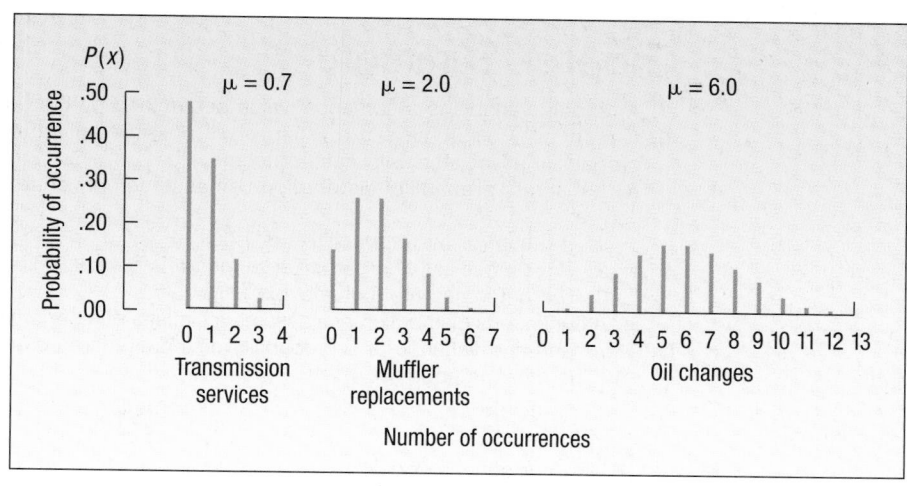

CHART 6–4 Poisson Probability Distributions for Means of 0.7, 2.0, and 6.0

Only μ needed to construct Poisson

In summary, the Poisson distribution is actually a family of discrete distributions. All that is needed to construct a Poisson probability distribution is the mean number of defects, errors, and so on—designated as μ.

Self-Review 6–6

From actuary tables Washington Insurance Company determined the likelihood that a man age 25 will die within the next year is .0002. If Washington Insurance sells 4,000 policies to 25-year-old men this year, what is the probability they will pay on exactly one policy?

Exercises

connect

31. In a Poisson distribution $\mu = 0.4$.
   a. What is the probability that $x = 0$?
   b. What is the probability that $x > 0$?
32. In a Poisson distribution $\mu = 4$.
   a. What is the probability that $x = 2$?
   b. What is the probability that $x \leq 2$?
   c. What is the probability that $x > 2$?
33. Ms. Bergen is a loan officer at Coast Bank and Trust. From her years of experience, she estimates that the probability is .025 that an applicant will not be able to repay his or her installment loan. Last month she made 40 loans.
   a. What is the probability that 3 loans will be defaulted?
   b. What is the probability that at least 3 loans will be defaulted?
34. Automobiles arrive at the Elkhart exit of the Indiana Toll Road at the rate of two per minute. The distribution of arrivals approximates a Poisson distribution.
   a. What is the probability that no automobiles arrive in a particular minute?
   b. What is the probability that at least one automobile arrives during a particular minute?
35. It is estimated that 0.5 percent of the callers to the Customer Service department of Dell, Inc., will receive a busy signal. What is the probability that of today's 1,200 callers at least 5 received a busy signal?
36. In the past, schools in Los Angeles County have closed an average of three days each year for weather emergencies. What is the probability that schools in Los Angeles County will close for four-days next year?

Chapter Summary

I. A random variable is a numerical value determined by the outcome of an experiment.
II. A probability distribution is a listing of all possible outcomes of an experiment and the probability associated with each outcome.
   A. A discrete probability distribution can assume only certain values. The main features are:
      1. The sum of the probabilities is 1.00.
      2. The probability of a particular outcome is between 0.00 and 1.00.
      3. The outcomes are mutually exclusive.
   B. A continuous distribution can assume an infinite number of values within a specific range.
III. The mean and variance of a probability distribution are computed as follows.
   A. The mean is equal to:

$$\mu = \Sigma[xP(x)] \qquad\qquad \textbf{[6–1]}$$

   B. The variance is equal to:

$$\sigma^2 = \Sigma[(x - \mu)^2 P(x)] \qquad\qquad \textbf{[6–2]}$$

IV. The binomial distribution has the following characteristics.
   A. Each outcome is classified into one of two mutually exclusive categories.
   B. The distribution results from a count of the number of successes in a fixed number of trials.

C. The probability of a success remains the same from trial to trial.
D. Each trial is independent.
E. A binomial probability is determined as follows:

$$P(x) = {}_nC_x \pi^x(1 - \pi)^{n-x}$$ [6–3]

F. The mean is computed as:

$$\mu = n\pi$$ [6–4]

G. The variance is

$$\sigma^2 = n\pi(1 - \pi)$$ [6–5]

V. The hypergeometric distribution has the following characteristics.
   A. There are only two possible outcomes.
   B. The probability of a success is not the same on each trial.
   C. The distribution results from a count of the number of successes in a fixed number of trials.
   D. It is used when sampling without replacement from a finite population.
   E. A hypergeometric probability is computed from the following equation:

$$P(x) = \frac{({}_SC_x)({}_{N-S}C_{n-x})}{({}_NC_n)}$$ [6–6]

VI. The Poisson distribution has the following characteristics.
   A. It describes the number of times some event occurs during a specified interval.
   B. The probability of a "success" is proportional to the length of the interval.
   C. Nonoverlapping intervals are independent.
   D. It is a limiting form of the binomial distribution when n is large and π is small.
   E. A Poisson probability is determined from the following equation:

$$P(x) = \frac{\mu^x e^{-\mu}}{x!}$$ [6–7]

F. The mean and the variance are:

$$\mu = n\pi$$ [6–8]

$$\sigma^2 = n\pi$$

Chapter Exercises

37. What is the difference between a random variable and a probability distribution?
38. For each of the following indicate whether the random variable is discrete or continuous.
   a. The length of time to get a haircut.
   b. The number of cars a jogger passes each morning while running.
   c. The number of hits for a team in a high school girls' softball game.
   d. The number of patients treated at the South Strand Medical Center between 6 and 10 P.M. each night.
   e. The distance your car traveled on the last fill-up.
   f. The number of customers at the Oak Street Wendy's who used the drive-through facility.
   g. The distance between Gainesville, Florida, and all Florida cities with a population of at least 50,000.
39. An investment will be worth $1,000, $2,000, or $5,000 at the end of the year. The probabilities of these values are .25, .60, and .15, respectively. Determine the mean and variance of the worth of the investment.
40. The personnel manager of Cumberland Pig Iron Company is studying the number of on-the-job accidents over a period of one month. He developed the following probability distribution. Compute the mean, variance, and standard deviation of the number of accidents in a month.

Number of Accidents	Probability
0	.40
1	.20
2	.20
3	.10
4	.10

41. Croissant Bakery, Inc., offers special decorated cakes for birthdays, weddings, and other occasions. It also has regular cakes available in its bakery. The following table gives the total number of cakes sold per day and the corresponding probability. Compute the mean, variance, and standard deviation of the number of cakes sold per day.

Number of Cakes Sold in a Day	Probability
12	.25
13	.40
14	.25
15	.10

42. The payouts for the Powerball lottery and their corresponding odds and probabilities of occurrence are shown below. The price of a ticket is $1.00. Find the mean and standard deviation of the payout. Hint: Don't forget to include the cost of the ticket and its corresponding probability.

Divisions	Payout	Odds	Probability
Five plus Powerball	$50,000,000	146,107,962	0.000000006844
Match 5	200,000	3,563,609	0.000000280614
Four plus Powerball	10,000	584,432	0.000001711060
Match 4	100	14,255	0.000070145903
Three plus Powerball	100	11,927	0.000083836351
Match 3	7	291	0.003424657534
Two plus Powerball	7	745	0.001340482574
One plus Powerball	4	127	0.007812500000
Zero plus Powerball	3	69	0.014285714286

43. In a recent survey 35 percent indicated chocolate was their favorite flavor of ice cream. Suppose we select a sample of ten people and ask them to name their favorite flavor of ice cream.
   a. How many of those in the sample would you expect to name chocolate?
   b. What is the probability exactly four of those in the sample name chocolate?
   c. What is the probability four or more name chocolate?
44. Thirty percent of the population in a southwestern community are Spanish-speaking Americans. A Spanish-speaking person is accused of killing a non-Spanish-speaking American and goes to trial. Of the first 12 potential jurors, only 2 are Spanish-speaking Americans, and 10 are not. The defendant's lawyer challenges the jury selection, claiming bias against her client. The government lawyer disagrees, saying that the probability of this particular jury composition is common. Compute the probability and discuss the assumptions.
45. An auditor for Health Maintenance Services of Georgia reports 40 percent of policyholders 55 years or older submit a claim during the year. Fifteen policyholders are randomly selected for company records.
   a. How many of the policyholders would you expect to have filed a claim within the last year?
   b. What is the probability that 10 of the selected policyholders submitted a claim last year?

    c. What is the probability that 10 or more of the selected policyholders submitted a claim last year?

    d. What is the probability that more than 10 of the selected policyholders submitted a claim last year?

46. Tire and Auto Supply is considering a 2-for-1 stock split. Before the transaction is finalized, at least two-thirds of the 1,200 company stockholders must approve the proposal. To evaluate the likelihood the proposal will be approved, the CFO selected a sample of 18 stockholders. He contacted each and found 14 approved of the proposed split. What is the likelihood of this event, assuming two-thirds of the stockholders approve?

47. A federal study reported that 7.5 percent of the U.S. workforce has a drug problem. A drug enforcement official for the State of Indiana wished to investigate this statement. In her sample of 20 employed workers:

    a. How many would you expect to have a drug problem? What is the standard deviation?

    b. What is the likelihood that *none* of the workers sampled has a drug problem?

    c. What is the likelihood *at least one* has a drug problem?

48. The Bank of Hawaii reports that 7 percent of its credit card holders will default at some time in their life. The Hilo branch just mailed out 12 new cards today.

    a. How many of these new cardholders would you expect to default? What is the standard deviation?

    b. What is the likelihood that *none* of the cardholders will default?

    c. What is the likelihood *at least one* will default?

49. Recent statistics suggest that 15 percent of those who visit a retail site on the World Wide Web make a purchase. A retailer wished to verify this claim. To do so, she selected a sample of 16 "hits" to her site and found that 4 had actually made a purchase.

    a. What is the likelihood of exactly four purchases?

    b. How many purchases should she expect?

    c. What is the likelihood that four or more "hits" result in a purchase?

50. In Chapter 19 we discuss the *acceptance sample.* Acceptance sampling is used to monitor the quality of incoming raw materials. Suppose a purchaser of electronic components allows 1 percent of the components to be defective. To ensure the quality of incoming parts, a purchaser or manufacturer normally samples 20 parts and allows 1 defect.

    a. What is the likelihood of accepting a lot that is 1 percent defective?

    b. If the quality of the incoming lot was actually 2 percent, what is the likelihood of accepting it?

    c. If the quality of the incoming lot was actually 5 percent, what is the likelihood of accepting it?

51. Colgate-Palmolive, Inc., recently developed a new toothpaste flavored with honey. It tested a group of ten people. Six of the group said they liked the new flavor, and the remaining four indicated they definitely did not. Four of the ten are selected to participate in an in-depth interview. What is the probability that of those selected for the in-depth interview two liked the new flavor and two did not?

52. Dr. Richmond, a psychologist, is studying the daytime television viewing habits of college students. She believes 45 percent of college students watch soap operas during the afternoon. To further investigate, she selects a sample of 10.

    a. Develop a probability distribution for the number of students in the sample who watch soap operas.

    b. Find the mean and the standard deviation of this distribution.

    c. What is the probability of finding exactly four watch soap operas?

    d. What is the probability less than half of the students selected watch soap operas?

53. A recent study conducted by Penn, Shone, and Borland, on behalf of LastMinute.com, revealed that 52 percent of business travelers plan their trips less than two weeks before departure. The study is to be replicated in the tri-state area with a sample of 12 frequent business travelers.

    a. Develop a probability distribution for the number of travelers who plan their trips within two weeks of departure.

    b. Find the mean and the standard deviation of this distribution.

    c. What is the probability exactly 5 of the 12 selected business travelers plan their trips within two weeks of departure?

    d. What is the probability 5 or fewer of the 12 selected business travelers plan their trips within two weeks of departure?

54. Suppose the Internal Revenue Service is studying the category of charitable contributions. A sample of 25 returns is selected from young couples between the ages of 20 and 35 who had an adjusted gross income of more than $100,000. Of these 25 returns five had charitable contributions of more than $1,000. Suppose four of these returns are selected for a comprehensive audit.

    a. Explain why the hypergeometric distribution is appropriate.

    b. What is the probability exactly one of the four audited had a charitable deduction of more than $1,000?

    c. What is the probability at least one of the audited returns had a charitable contribution of more than $1,000?

55. The law firm of Hagel and Hagel is located in downtown Cincinnati. There are 10 partners in the firm; 7 live in Ohio and 3 in northern Kentucky. Ms. Wendy Hagel, the managing partner, wants to appoint a committee of 3 partners to look into moving the firm to northern Kentucky. If the committee is selected at random from the 10 partners, what is the probability that:

    a. One member of the committee lives in northern Kentucky and the others live in Ohio?

    b. At least 1 member of the committee lives in northern Kentucky?

56. Recent information published by the U.S. Environmental Protection Agency indicates that Honda is the manufacturer of four of the top nine vehicles in terms of fuel economy.

    a. Determine the probability distribution for the number of Hondas in a sample of three cars chosen from the top nine.

    b. What is the likelihood that in the sample of three at least one Honda is included?

57. The position of chief of police in the city of Corry, Pennsylvania, is vacant. A search committee of Corry residents is charged with the responsibility of recommending a new chief to the city council. There are 12 applicants, 4 of which are either female or members of a minority. The search committee decides to interview all 12 of the applicants. To begin, they randomly select four applicants to be interviewed on the first day, and none of the four is female or a member of a minority. The local newspaper, the Corry *Press,* suggests discrimination in an editorial. What is the likelihood of this occurrence?

58. Listed below is the population by state for the 15 states with the largest population. Also included is whether that state's border touches the Gulf of Mexico, the Atlantic Ocean, or the Pacific Ocean (coastline).

Rank	State	Population	Coastline
1	California	36,553,215	Yes
2	Texas	23,904,380	Yes
3	New York	19,297,729	Yes
4	Florida	18,251,243	Yes
5	Illinois	12,852,548	No
6	Pennsylvania	12,432,792	No
7	Ohio	11,466,917	No
8	Michigan	10,071,822	No
9	Georgia	9,544,750	Yes
10	North Carolina	9,061,032	Yes
11	New Jersey	8,685,920	Yes
12	Virginia	7,712,091	Yes
13	Washington	6,468,424	Yes
14	Massachusetts	6,449,755	Yes
15	Indiana	6,345,289	No

Note that 5 of the 15 states do not have any coastline. Suppose three states are selected at random. What is the probability that:

    a. None of the states selected have any coastline?

    b. Exactly one of the selected states has a coastline.

    c. At least one of the selected states has a coastline.

59. The sales of Lexus automobiles in the Detroit area follow a Poisson distribution with a mean of 3 per day.
  a. What is the probability that no Lexus is sold on a particular day?
  b. What is the probability that for five consecutive days at least one Lexus is sold?

60. Suppose 1.5 percent of the antennas on new Nokia cell phones are defective. For a random sample of 200 antennas, find the probability that:
  a. None of the antennas is defective.
  b. Three or more of the antennas are defective.

61. A study of the checkout lines at the Safeway Supermarket in the South Strand area revealed that between 4 and 7 P.M. on weekdays there is an average of four customers waiting in line. What is the probability that you visit Safeway today during this period and find:
  a. No customers are waiting?
  b. Four customers are waiting?
  c. Four or fewer are waiting?
  d. Four or more are waiting?

62. An internal study by the Technology Services department at Lahey Electronics revealed company employees receive an average of two emails per hour. Assume the arrival of these emails is approximated by the Poisson distribution.
  a. What is the probability Linda Lahey, company president, received exactly 1 email between 4 P.M. and 5 P.M. yesterday?
  b. What is the probability she received 5 or more email during the same period?
  c. What is the probability she did not receive any email during the period?

63. Recent crime reports indicate that 3.1 motor vehicle thefts occur each minute in the United States. Assume that the distribution of thefts per minute can be approximated by the Poisson probability distribution.
  a. Calculate the probability exactly *four* thefts occur in a minute.
  b. What is the probability there are *no* thefts in a minute?
  c. What is the probability there is *at least one* theft in a minute?

64. New Process, Inc., a large mail-order supplier of women's fashions, advertises same-day service on every order. Recently the movement of orders has not gone as planned, and there were a large number of complaints. Bud Owens, director of customer service, has completely redone the method of order handling. The goal is to have fewer than five unfilled orders on hand at the end of 95 percent of the working days. Frequent checks of the unfilled orders at the end of the day reveal that the distribution of the unfilled orders follows a Poisson distribution with a mean of two orders.
  a. Has New Process, Inc., lived up to its internal goal? Cite evidence.
  b. Draw a histogram representing the Poisson probability distribution of unfilled orders.

65. The National Aeronautics and Space Administration (NASA) has experienced two disasters. The Challenger exploded over the Atlantic Ocean in 1986 and the Columbia exploded over East Texas in 2003. There have been a total of 123 space missions. Assume failures continue to occur at the same rate and consider the next 23 missions. What is the probability of exactly two failures? What is the probability of no failures?

66. According to the "January theory," if the stock market is up for the month of January, it will be up for the year. If it is down in January, it will be down for the year. According to an article in *The Wall Street Journal,* this theory held for 29 out of the last 34 years. Suppose there is no truth to this theory; that is, the probability it is either up or down is .50. What is the probability this could occur by chance? You will probably need a software package such as Excel or MINITAB.

67. During the second round of the 1989 U.S. Open golf tournament, four golfers scored a hole in one on the sixth hole. The odds of a professional golfer making a hole in one are estimated to be 3,708 to 1, so the probability is 1/3,709. There were 155 golfers participating in the second round that day. Estimate the probability that four golfers would score a hole in one on the sixth hole.

68. Suppose the National Hurricane Center forecasts that hurricanes will hit the strike area with a .95 probability. Answer the following questions:
  a. What probability distribution does this follow?
  b. What is the probability that 10 hurricanes reach landfall in the strike area?
  c. What is the probability at least one of 10 hurricanes reaches land outside the strike area?

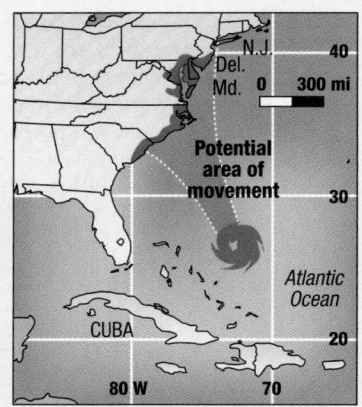

STORM CONTINUES NORTHWEST
Position : **27.8 N, 71.4 W**
Movement: **NNW at 8 mph**
Sustained winds: **105 mph**
As of 11 p.m. EDT Tuesday

━━━━ Hurricane watch
━━━━ Tropical storm watch

69. A recent CBS News survey reported that 67 percent of adults felt the U.S. Treasury should continue making pennies.

Suppose we select a sample of 15 adults.
a. How many of the 15 would we expect to indicate that the Treasury should continue making pennies? What is the standard deviation?
b. What is the likelihood that exactly 8 adults would indicate the Treasury should continue making pennies?
c. What is the likelihood at least 8 adults would indicate the Treasury should continue making pennies?

Data Set Exercises

70. Refer to the Real Estate data, which report information on homes sold in the Denver, Colorado, area last year.
a. Create a probability distribution for the number of bedrooms. Compute the mean and the standard deviation of this distribution.
b. Create a probability distribution for the number of bathrooms. Compute the mean and the standard deviation of this distribution.
71. Refer to the Baseball 2007 data, which contain information on the 2007 Major League Baseball season. There are 30 teams in the major leagues, and 3 of them have home fields with artificial playing surfaces. As part of the negotiations with the players' union, a study regarding injuries on grass versus artificial surfaces will be conducted. Five teams will be selected to participate in the study, and the teams will be selected at random. What is the likelihood that one of the five teams selected for study play their home games on artificial surfaces?

Software Commands

1. The MegaStat commands to create the binomial probability distribution on page 195 are:
   a. Select the **Add-Ins** tab in the top menu. On the far left, select the **MegaStat** pull-down menu.

   Click on **probability,** and **Discrete Probability Distributions.** Enter **n, number of trials,** and **p, probability of occurrence,** and click **OK.**

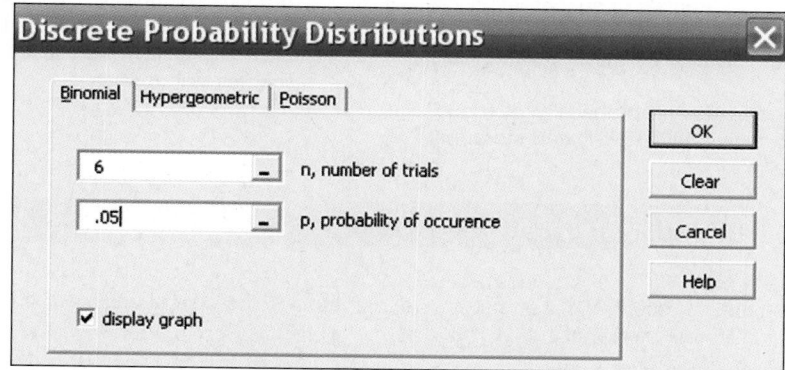

   b. In the dialog box select the **Binomial** tab. The number of trials is *6*, the probability of a success is *.05*. If you wish to see a graph, click on **display graph.**
2. The Excel commands necessary to determine the binomial probability distribution on page 196 are:
   a. On a blank Excel worksheet write the word *Success* in cell A1 and the word *Probability* in B1. In cells A2 through A17 write the integers *0* to *15*. Click on *B2* as the active cell.
   b. Click on the **Formulas** tab in the top menu, then, on the far left, select **Insert Function fx.**
   c. In the first dialog box select **Statistical** in the function category and **BINOMDIST** in the function name category, then click **OK.**
   d. In the second dialog box enter the four items necessary to compute a binomial probability.
      1. Enter *0* for the number of successes.
      2. Enter *40* for the number of trials.
      3. Enter *.09* for the probability of a success.
      4. Enter the word *false* or the number *0* for the individual probabilities and click on **OK.**

5. Excel will compute the probability of 0 successes in 40 trials, with a .09 probability of success. The result,.02299618, is stored in cell B2.
   e. To complete the probability distribution for successes of 1 through 15, double click on cell **B2.** The binomial function should appear. Replace the **0** to the right of the open parentheses with the cell reference **A2.**
   f. Move the mouse to the lower right corner of cell B2 till a solid black + symbol appears, then click and hold and highlight the B column to cell B17. The probability of a success for the various values of the random variable will appear.
3. The Excel commands necessary to determine the hypergeometric distribution on page 202 are:
   a. On a blank Excel worksheet write the word *Union Members* in cell A1 and the word *Probability* in B1. In cells A2 through A7 enter the numbers *0* through *5*. Click on cell **B2.**
   b. Click the **Formulas** tab in the top menu, then, on the far left, select **Insert Function fx.**

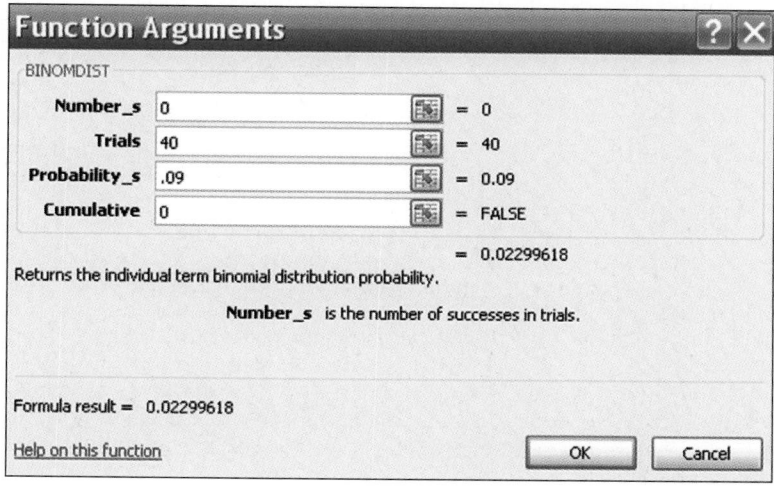

c. In the first dialog box select **Statistical** and **HYPGEOMDIST,** and then click **OK.**

d. In the second dialog box enter the four items necessary to compute a hypergeometric probability.
  1. Enter *0* for the number of successes.
  2. Enter *5* for the number of trials.
  3. Enter *40* for the number of successes in the population.
  4. Enter *50* for the size of the population and click **OK.**
  5. Excel will compute the probability of 0 successes in 5 trials (.000118937) and store that result in cell F9.

e. To complete the probability distribution for successes of 1 through 5, double click on cell **B2.** The hypergeometric function should appear. Replace the **0** to the right of the open parentheses with the cell reference **A2.**

f. Move the mouse to the lower right corner of cell F9 till a solid black + symbol appears, then click and hold and highlight the F column to cell F14. The probability of a success for the various outcomes will appear.

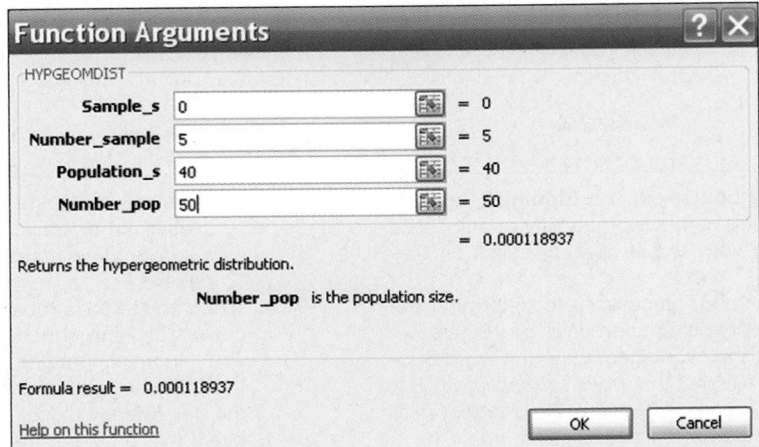

4. The MINITAB commands to generate the Poisson distribution on page 205 are:

a. Label column C1 as *Successes* and C2 as *Probability.* Enter the integers 0 though 5 in the first column.

b. Select **Calc,** then **Probability Distributions,** and **Poisson.**

c. In the dialog box click on **Probability,** set the mean equal to *.3,* and select *C1* as the Input column. Designate *C2* as Optional storage, and then click **OK.**

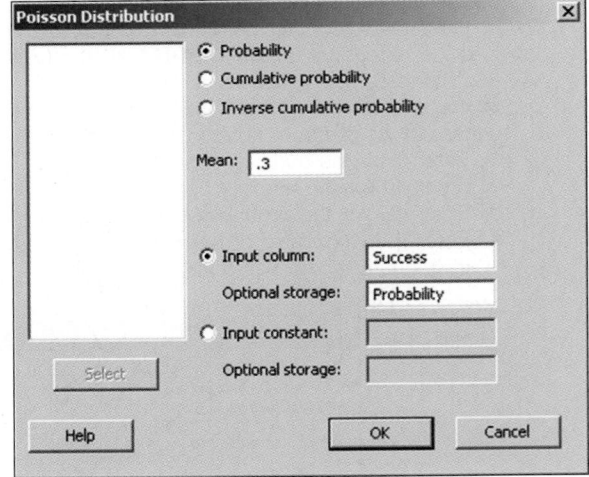

Chapter 6   Answers to Self-Review

6–1   **a.**

Number of Spots	Probability
1	$\frac{1}{6}$
2	$\frac{1}{6}$
3	$\frac{1}{6}$
4	$\frac{1}{6}$
5	$\frac{1}{6}$
6	$\frac{1}{6}$
Total	$\frac{6}{6} = 1.00$

b.

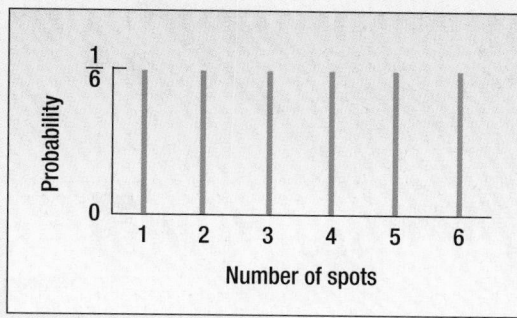

c. $\frac{6}{6}$ or 1.

6–2   **a.** It is discrete, because the value $0.80, $0.90, and $1.20 are clearly separated from each other. Also the sum of the probabilities is 1.00, and the outcomes are mutually exclusive.

b.

x	P(x)	xP(x)
$ .80	.30	0.24
.90	.50	0.45
1.20	.20	0.24
		0.93

The mean is 93 cents.

c.

x	P(x)	$(x - \mu)$	$(x - \mu)^2 P(x)$
$0.80	.30	−0.13	.00507
0.90	.50	−0.03	.00045
1.20	.20	0.27	.01458
			.02010

The variance is .02010, and the standard deviation is 14 cents.

6–3   **a.** It is reasonable because each employee either uses direct deposit or does not; employees are independent; the probability of using direct deposit is .80 for all; and we count the number using the service out of 7.

b. $P(7) = {}_7C_7 (.80)^7 (.20)^0 = .2097$

c. $P(4) = {}_7C_4 (.80)^4 (.20)^3 = .1147$

d. Answers are in agreement.

6–4 $n = 4, \pi = .60$

a. $P(x = 2) = .346$

b. $P(x \le 2) = .526$

c. $P(x > 2) = 1 - .526 = .474$

6–5 $P(3) = \dfrac{{}_8C_3 \, {}_4C_2}{{}_{12}C_5} = \dfrac{\left(\dfrac{8!}{3!5!}\right)\left(\dfrac{4!}{2!2!}\right)}{\dfrac{12!}{5!7!}}$

$\qquad = \dfrac{(56)(6)}{792} = .424$

6–6 $\mu = 4{,}000(.0002) = 0.8$

$P(1) = \dfrac{0.8^1 e^{-0.8}}{1!} = .3595$

7

Continuous Probability Distributions

Cruise ships of the Royal Viking line report that 80 percent of their rooms are occupied during September. For a cruise ship having 800 rooms, what is the probability that 665 or more are occupied in September? (Exercise 56, Goal 8)

Introduction

Chapter 6 began our study of probability distributions. We consider three *discrete* probability distributions: binomial, hypergeometric, and Poisson. These distributions are based on discrete random variables, which can assume only clearly separated values. For example, we select for study 10 small businesses that began operations during the year 2000. The number still operating in 2008 can be 0, 1, 2, . . . , 10. There cannot be 3.7, 12, or −7 still operating in 2008. In this example, only certain outcomes are possible and these outcomes are represented by clearly separated values. In addition, the result is usually found by counting the number of successes. We count the number of the businesses in the study that are still in operation in 2008.

In this chapter, we continue our study of probability distributions by examining *continuous* probability distributions. A continuous probability distribution usually results from measuring something, such as the distance from the dormitory to the classroom, the weight of an individual, or the amount of bonus earned by CEOs. Suppose we select five students and find the distance, in miles, they travel to attend class as 12.2, 8.9, 6.7, 3.6, and 14.6. When examining a continuous distribution we are usually interested in information such as the percent of students who travel less than 10 miles or the percent who travel more than 8 miles. In other words, for a continuous distribution we may wish to know the percent of observations that occur within a certain range. It is important to realize that a continuous random variable has an infinite number of values within a particular range. So you think of the probability a variable will have a value within a specified range, rather than the probability for a specific value.

We consider two families of continuous probability distributions, the **uniform probability distribution** and the **normal probability distribution.** These distributions describe the likelihood that a continuous random variable that has an infinite number of possible values will fall within a specified range. For example, suppose the time to access the McGraw-Hill Web page (www.mhhe.com) is uniformly distributed with a minimum time of 20 milliseconds and a maximum time of 60 milliseconds. Then we can determine the probability the page can be accessed in 30 milliseconds or less. The access time is measured on a continuous scale.

The second continuous distribution discussed in this chapter is the normal probability distribution. The normal distribution is described by its mean and standard deviation. For example, assume the operating life of an Energizer C-size battery follows a normal distribution with a mean of 45 hours and a standard deviation of 10 hours when used in a particular toy. We can determine the likelihood the battery will last more than 50 hours, between 35 and 62 hours, or less than 39 hours. The life of the battery is measured on a continuous scale.

The Family of Uniform Probability Distributions

The uniform probability distribution is perhaps the simplest distribution for a continuous random variable. This distribution is rectangular in shape and is defined by minimum and maximum values. Here are some examples that follow a uniform distribution.

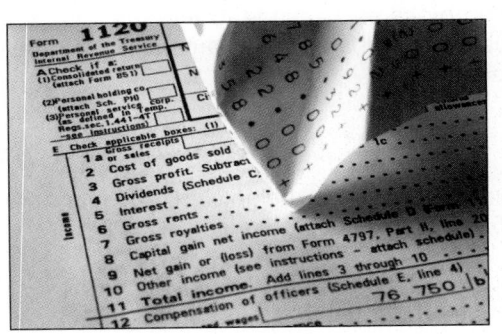

- The time to fly via a commercial airliner from Orlando, Florida, to Atlanta, Georgia, ranges from 60 minutes to 120 minutes. The random variable is the flight time within this interval. Note the variable of interest, flight time in minutes, is continuous in the interval from 60 minutes to 120 minutes.
- Volunteers at the Grand Strand Public Library prepare federal income tax forms. The time to prepare form 1040-EZ follows a uniform distribution over the interval between 10 minutes and 30 minutes. The random variable is the number of minutes to complete the form, and it can assume any value between 10 and 30.

A uniform distribution is shown in Chart 7–1. The distribution's shape is rectangular and has a minimum value of *a* and a maximum of *b*. Also notice in Chart 7–1 the height of the distribution is constant or uniform for all values between *a* and *b*.

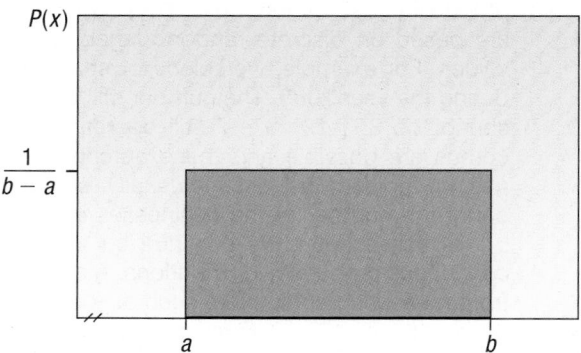

CHART 7–1 A Continuous Uniform Distribution

The mean of a uniform distribution is located in the middle of the interval between the minimum and maximum values. It is computed as:

> **MEAN OF THE UNIFORM DISTRIBUTION** $\mu = \dfrac{a + b}{2}$ **[7–1]**

The standard deviation describes the dispersion of a distribution. In the uniform distribution, the standard deviation is also related to the interval between the maximum and minimum values.

> **STANDARD DEVIATION OF THE UNIFORM DISTRIBUTION** $\sigma = \sqrt{\dfrac{(b - a)^2}{12}}$ **[7–2]**

The equation for the uniform probability distribution is:

> **UNIFORM DISTRIBUTION** $P(x) = \dfrac{1}{b - a}$ if $a \le x \le b$ and 0 elsewhere **[7–3]**

As described in Chapter 6, probability distributions are useful for making probability statements concerning the values of a random variable. For distributions describing a continuous random variable, areas within the distribution represent probabilities. In the uniform distribution, its rectangular shape allows us to apply the area formula for a rectangle. Recall we find the area of a rectangle by multiplying its length by its height. For the uniform distribution the height of the rectangle is $P(x)$, which is $1/(b - a)$. The length or base of the distribution is $b - a$. Notice that if we multiply the height of the distribution by its entire range to find the area, the result is always 1.00. To put it another way, the total area within a continuous probability distribution is equal to 1.00. In general

$$\text{Area} = (\text{height})(\text{base}) = \frac{1}{(b - a)}(b - a) = 1.00$$

So if a uniform distribution ranges from 10 to 15, the height is 0.20, found by $1/(15 - 10)$. The base is 5, found by $15 - 10$. The total area is:

$$\text{Area} = (\text{height})(\text{base}) = \frac{1}{(15 - 10)}(15 - 10) = 1.00$$

An example will illustrate the features of a uniform distribution and how we calculate probabilities using it.

Example

Southwest Arizona State University provides bus service to students while they are on campus. A bus arrives at the North Main Street and College Drive stop every 30 minutes between 6 A.M. and 11 P.M. during weekdays. Students arrive at the bus stop at random times. The time that a student waits is uniformly distributed from 0 to 30 minutes.

1. Draw a graph of this distribution.
2. Show that the area of this uniform distribution is 1.00.
3. How long will a student "typically" have to wait for a bus? In other words what is the mean waiting time? What is the standard deviation of the waiting times?
4. What is the probability a student will wait more than 25 minutes?
5. What is the probability a student will wait between 10 and 20 minutes?

Solution

In this case the random variable is the length of time a student must wait. Time is measured on a continuous scale, and the wait times may range from 0 minutes up to 30 minutes.

1. The graph of the uniform distribution is shown in Chart 7–2. The horizontal line is drawn at a height of .0333, found by 1/(30 − 0). The range of this distribution is 30 minutes.

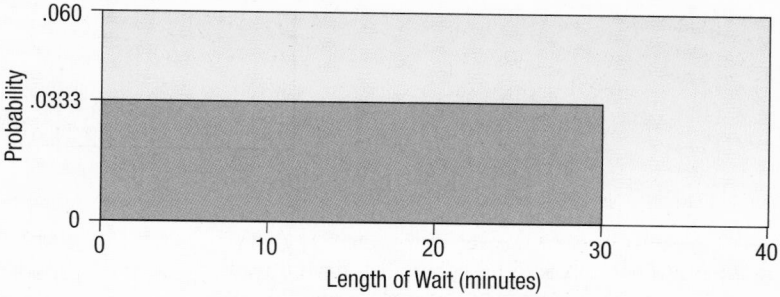

CHART 7–2 Uniform Probability Distribution of Student Waiting Times

2. The times students must wait for the bus is uniform over the interval from 0 minutes to 30 minutes, so in this case a is 0 and b is 30.

$$\text{Area} = (\text{height})(\text{base}) = \frac{1}{(30-0)}(30-0) = 1.00$$

3. To find the mean, we use formula (7–1).

$$\mu = \frac{a+b}{2} = \frac{0+30}{2} = 15$$

The mean of the distribution is 15 minutes, so the typical wait time for bus service is 15 minutes.
To find the standard deviation of the wait times, we use formula (7–2).

$$\sigma = \sqrt{\frac{(b-a)^2}{12}} = \sqrt{\frac{(30-0)^2}{12}} = 8.66$$

The standard deviation of the distribution is 8.66 minutes. This measures the variation in the student wait times.

4. The area within the distribution for the interval 25 to 30 represents this particular probability. From the area formula:

$$P(25 < \text{wait time} < 30) = (\text{height})(\text{base}) = \frac{1}{(30-0)}(5) = .1667$$

So the probability a student waits between 25 and 30 minutes is .1667. This conclusion is illustrated by the following graph.

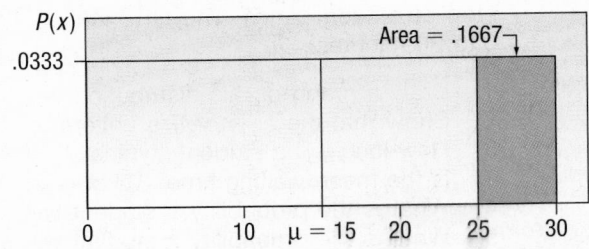

5. The area within the distribution for the interval 10 to 20 represents the probability.

$$P(10 < \text{wait time} < 20) = (\text{height})(\text{base}) = \frac{1}{(30 - 0)}(10) = .3333$$

We can illustrate this probability as follows.

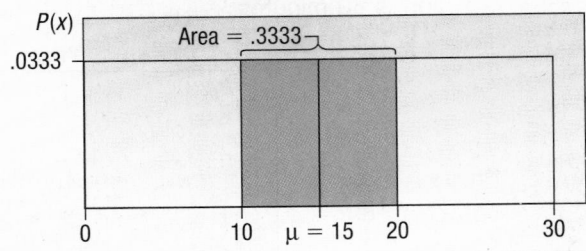

Self-Review 7–1

Australian sheepdogs have a relatively short life. The length of their life follows a uniform distribution between 8 and 14 years.
(a) Draw this uniform distribution. What are the height and base values?
(b) Show the total area under the curve is 1.00.
(c) Calculate the mean and the standard deviation of this distribution.
(d) What is the probability a particular dog lives between 10 and 14 years?
(e) What is the probability a dog will live less than 9 years?

Exercises

connect

1. A uniform distribution is defined over the interval from 6 to 10.
    a. What are the values for *a* and *b*?
    b. What is the mean of this uniform distribution?
    c. What is the standard deviation?
    d. Show that the total area is 1.00.
    e. Find the probability of a value more than 7.
    f. Find the probability of a value between 7 and 9.
2. A uniform distribution is defined over the interval from 2 to 5.
    a. What are the values for *a* and *b*?
    b. What is the mean of this uniform distribution?
    c. What is the standard deviation?
    d. Show that the total area is 1.00.
    e. Find the probability of a value more than 2.6.
    f. Find the probability of a value between 2.9 and 3.7.
3. The closing price of Schnur Sporting Goods, Inc., common stock is uniformly distributed between $20 and 30 per share. What is the probability that the stock price will be:
    a. More than $27?
    b. Less than or equal to $24?

4. According to the Insurance Institute of America, a family of four spends between $400 and $3,800 per year on all types of insurance. Suppose the money spent is uniformly distributed between these amounts.
  a. What is the mean amount spent on insurance?
  b. What is the standard deviation of the amount spent?
  c. If we select a family at random, what is the probability they spend less than $2,000 per year on insurance per year?
  d. What is the probability a family spends more than $3,000 per year?
5. The April rainfall in Flagstaff, Arizona, follows a uniform distribution between 0.5 and 3.00 inches.
  a. What are the values for *a* and *b*?
  b. What is the mean amount of rainfall for the month? What is the standard deviation?
  c. What is the probability of less than an inch of rain for the month?
  d. What is the probability of *exactly* 1.00 inch of rain?
  e. What is the probability of more than 1.50 inches of rain for the month?
6. Customers experiencing technical difficulty with their internet cable hookup may call an 800 number for technical support. It takes the technician between 30 seconds to 10 minutes to resolve the problem. The distribution of this support time follows the uniform distribution.
  a. What are the values for *a* and *b* in minutes?
  b. What is the mean time to resolve the problem? What is the standard deviation of the time?
  c. What percent of the problems take more than 5 minutes to resolve?
  d. Suppose we wish to find the middle 50 percent of the problem-solving times. What are the end points of these two times?

The Family of Normal Probability Distributions

Next we consider the normal probability distribution. Unlike the uniform distribution [see formula (7–3)] the normal probability distribution has a very complex formula.

NORMAL PROBABILITY DISTRIBUTION	$$P(x) = \frac{1}{\sigma\sqrt{2\pi}} e^{-\left[\frac{(X-\mu)^2}{2\sigma^2}\right]}$$	**[7–4]**

However, do not be bothered by how complex this formula looks. You are already familiar with many of the values. The symbols μ and σ refer to the mean and the standard deviation, as usual. The Greek symbol π is a natural mathematical constant and its value is approximately 22/7 or 3.1416. The letter *e* is also a mathematical constant. It is the base of the natural log system and is equal to 2.718. *X* is the value of a continuous random variable. So a normal distribution is based on—that is, it is defined by—its mean and standard deviation.

You will not need to make any calculations from formula (7–4). Instead you will be using a table, which is given as Appendix B.1, to look up the various probabilities.

The normal probability distribution has the following major characteristics.

1. It is **bell-shaped** and has a single peak at the center of the distribution. The arithmetic mean, median, and mode are equal and located in the center of the distribution. The total area under the curve is 1.00. Half the area under the normal curve is to the right of this center point and the other half to the left of it.
2. It is **symmetrical** about the mean. If we cut the normal curve vertically at the center value, the two halves will be mirror images.
3. It falls off smoothly in either direction from the central value. That is, the distribution is **asymptotic:** The curve gets closer and closer to the *X*-axis but never actually touches it. To put it another way, the tails of the curve extend indefinitely in both directions.
4. The location of a normal distribution is determined by the mean, μ. The dispersion or spread of the distribution is determined by the standard deviation, σ.

These characteristics are shown graphically in Chart 7–3.

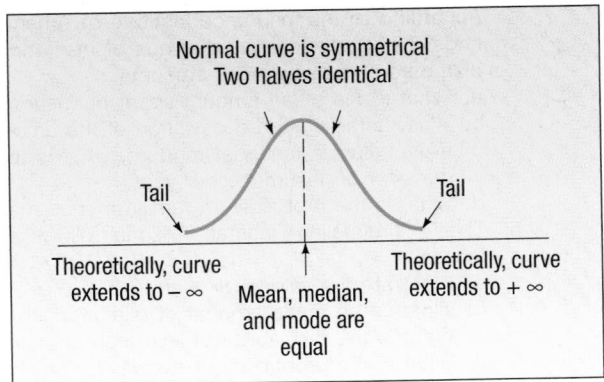

CHART 7–3 Characteristics of a Normal Distribution

There is not just one normal probability distribution, but rather a "family" of them. For example, in Chart 7–4 the probability distributions of length of employee service in three different plants can be compared. In the Camden plant, the mean is 20 years and the standard deviation is 3.1 years. There is another normal probability distribution for the length of service in the Dunkirk plant, where $\mu = 20$ years and $\sigma = 3.9$ years. In the Elmira plant, $\mu = 20$ years and $\sigma = 5.0$ years. Note that the means are the same but the standard deviations are different.

Equal means, unequal standard deviations

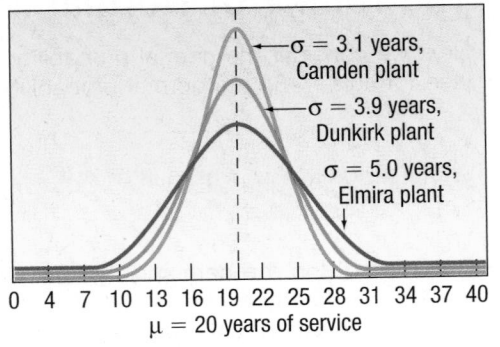

CHART 7–4 Normal Probability Distributions with Equal Means but Different Standard Deviations

Chart 7–5 shows the distribution of box weights of three different cereals. The weights follow a normal distribution with different means but identical standard deviations.

Unequal means, equal standard deviations

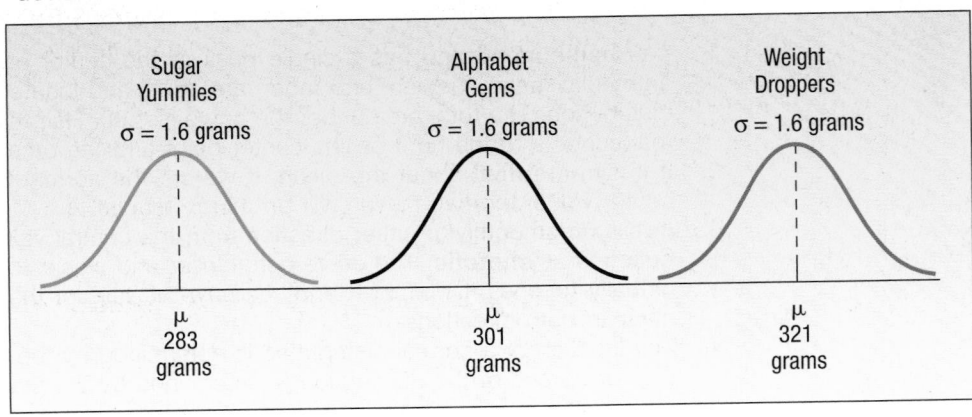

CHART 7–5 Normal Probability Distributions Having Different Means but Equal Standard Deviations

Finally, Chart 7–6 shows three normal distributions having different means and standard deviations. They show the distribution of tensile strengths, measured in pounds per square inch (psi), for three types of cables.

Unequal means, unequal standard deviations

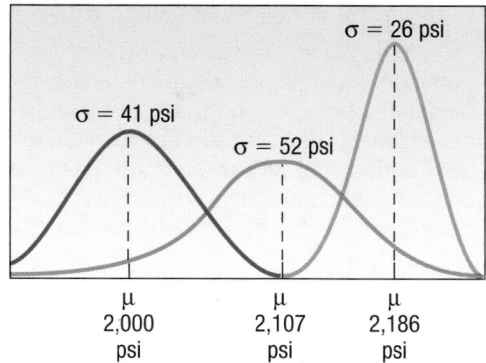

CHART 7–6 Normal Probability Distributions with Different Means and Standard Deviations

In Chapter 6, recall that discrete probability distributions show the specific likelihood a discrete value will occur. For example, on page 192, the binomial distribution is used to calculate the probability that none of the five flights arriving at the Bradford Pennsylvania Regional Airport would be late.

With a continuous probability distribution, areas below the curve define probabilities. The total area under the normal curve is 1.0. This accounts for all possible outcomes. Since a normal probability distribution is symmetric, the area under the curve to the left of the mean is 0.5, and the area under the curve to the right of the mean is 0.5. Apply this to the distribution of Sugar Yummies in Chart 7–5. It is normally distributed with a mean of 283 grams. Therefore, the probability of filling a box with more than 283 grams is 0.5 and the probability of filling a box with less than 283 grams is 0.5. We can also determine the probability that a box weighs between 280 and 286 grams. However, to determine this probability we need to know about the standard normal probability distribution.

The Standard Normal Probability Distribution

The number of normal distributions is unlimited, each having a different mean (μ), standard deviation (σ), or both. While it is possible to provide probability tables for discrete distributions such as the binomial and the Poisson, providing tables for the infinite number of normal distributions is impossible. Fortunately, one member of the family can be used to determine the probabilities for all normal probability distributions. It is called the **standard normal probability distribution,** and it is unique because it has a mean of 0 and a standard deviation of 1.

Any *normal probability distribution* can be converted into a *standard normal probability distribution* by subtracting the mean from each observation and dividing this difference by the standard deviation. The results are called **z values** or **z scores.**

> **z VALUE** The signed distance between a selected value, designated *X,* and the mean, μ, divided by the standard deviation, σ.

So, a z value is the distance from the mean, measured in units of the standard deviation.

In terms of a formula:

STANDARD NORMAL VALUE $\qquad\qquad z = \dfrac{X - \mu}{\sigma} \qquad\qquad$ **[7–5]**

where:

X is the value of any particular observation or measurement.
μ is the mean of the distribution.
σ is the standard deviation of the distribution.

As noted in the above definition, a z value expresses the distance or difference between a particular value of X and the arithmetic mean in units of the standard deviation. Once the normally distributed observations are standardized, the z values are normally distributed with a mean of 0 and a standard deviation of 1. So the z distribution has all the characteristics of any normal probability distribution. These characteristics are listed on page 223. The table in Appendix B.1 (also on the inside back cover) lists the probabilities for the standard normal probability distribution.

TABLE 7–1 Areas under the Normal Curve

z	0.00	0.01	0.02	0.03	0.04	0.05	...
1.3	0.4032	0.4049	0.4066	0.4082	0.4099	0.4115	
1.4	0.4192	0.4207	0.4222	0.4236	0.4251	0.4265	
1.5	0.4332	0.4345	0.4357	0.4370	0.4382	0.4394	
1.6	0.4452	0.4463	0.4474	0.4484	0.4495	0.4505	
1.7	0.4554	0.4564	0.4573	0.4582	0.4591	0.4599	
1.8	0.4641	0.4649	0.4656	0.4664	0.4671	0.4678	
1.9	0.4713	0.4719	0.4726	0.4732	0.4738	0.4744	
.							
.							
.							

To explain, suppose we wish to compute the probability that boxes of Sugar Yummies weigh between 283 and 285.4 grams. From Chart 7–5, we know that the box weight of Sugar Yummies follows the normal distribution with a mean of 283 grams and a standard deviation of 1.6 grams. We want to know the probability or area under the curve between the mean, 283 grams, and 285.4 grams. We can also express this problem using probability notation, similar to the style used in the previous chapter: $P(283 < \text{weight} < 285.4)$. To find the probability, it is necessary to convert both 283 grams and 285.4 grams to z values using formula (7–5). The z value corresponding to 283 is 0, found by $(283 - 283)/1.6$. The z value corresponding to 285.4 is 1.50 found by $(285.4 - 283)/1.6$. Next we go to the table in Appendix B.1. A portion of the table is repeated as Table 7–1. Go down the column of the table headed by the letter z to 1.5. Then move horizontally to the right and read the probability under the column headed 0.00. It is 0.4332. This means the area under the curve between 0.00 and 1.50 is 0.4332. This is the probability that a randomly selected box of Sugar Yummies will weigh between 283 and 285.4 grams. This is illustrated in the following graph.

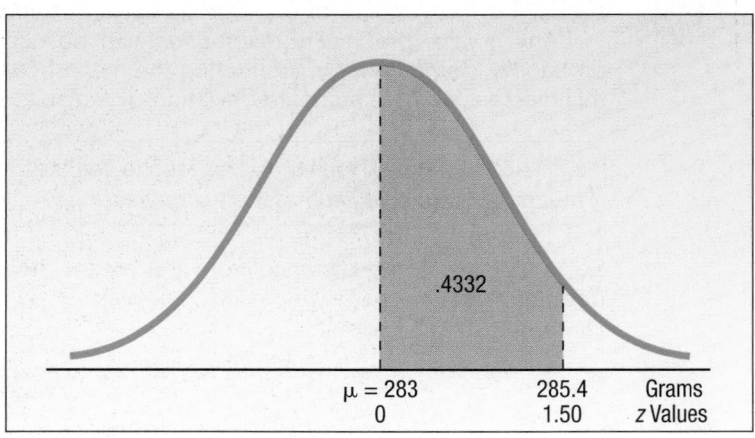

Applications of the Standard Normal Distribution

What is the area under the curve between the mean and X for the following z values? Check your answers against those given. Not all the values are available in Table 7–5. You will need to use Appendix B.1 or the table located on the inside back cover of the text.

Computed z Value	Area under Curve
2.84	.4977
1.00	.3413
0.49	.1879

Now we will compute the z value given the population mean, μ, the population standard deviation, σ, and a selected X.

Example

The weekly incomes of shift foremen in the glass industry follow the normal probability distribution with a mean of $1,000 and a standard deviation of $100. What is the z value for the income, let's call it X, of a foreman who earns $1,100 per week? For a foreman who earns $900 per week?

Solution

Using formula (7–5), the z values for the two X values ($1,100 and $900) are:

For $X = \$1,100$:

$$z = \frac{X - \mu}{\sigma}$$

$$= \frac{\$1,100 - \$1,000}{\$100}$$

$$= 1.00$$

For $X = \$900$:

$$z = \frac{X - \mu}{\sigma}$$

$$= \frac{\$900 - \$1,000}{\$100}$$

$$= -1.00$$

The z of 1.00 indicates that a weekly income of $1,100 is one standard deviation above the mean, and a z of -1.00 shows that a $900 income is one standard deviation below the mean. Note that both incomes ($1,100 and $900) are the same distance ($100) from the mean.

Self-Review 7–2

Using the information in the preceding example ($\mu = \$1,000$, $\sigma = \$100$), convert:
(a) The weekly income of $1,225 to a z value.
(b) The weekly income of $775 to a z value.

The Empirical Rule

Before examining further applications of the standard normal probability distribution, we will consider three areas under the normal curve that will be used extensively in the following chapters. These facts were called the Empirical Rule in Chapter 3, see page 83.

1. About 68 percent of the area under the normal curve is within one standard deviation of the mean. This can be written as $\mu \pm 1\sigma$.
2. About 95 percent of the area under the normal curve is within two standard deviations of the mean, written $\mu \pm 2\sigma$.
3. Practically all of the area under the normal curve is within three standard deviations of the mean, written $\mu \pm 3\sigma$.

This information is summarized in the following graph.

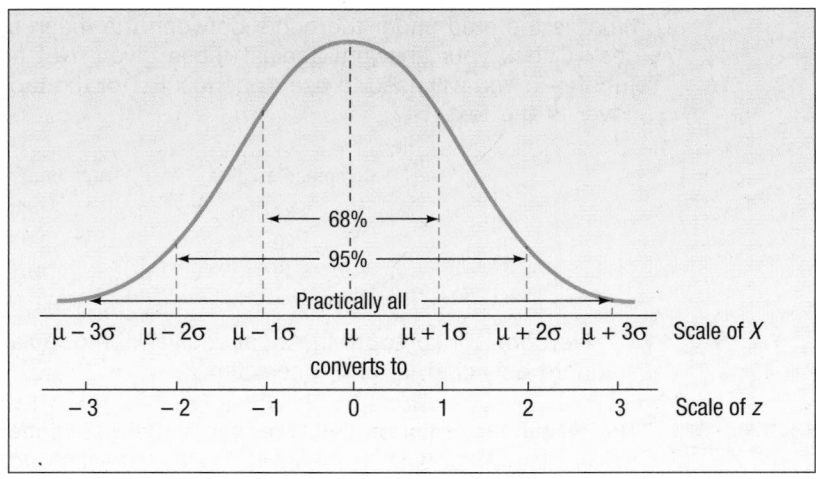

Transforming measurements to standard normal deviates changes the scale. The conversions are also shown in the graph. For example, $\mu + 1\sigma$ is converted to a z value of 1.00. Likewise, $\mu - 2\sigma$ is transformed to a z value of -2.00. Note that the center of the z distribution is zero, indicating no deviation from the mean, μ.

Example

As part of its quality assurance program, the Autolite Battery Company conducts tests on battery life. For a particular D-cell alkaline battery, the mean life is 19 hours. The useful life of the battery follows a normal distribution with a standard deviation of 1.2 hours. Answer the following questions.

1. About 68 percent of the batteries failed between what two values?
2. About 95 percent of the batteries failed between what two values?
3. Virtually all of the batteries failed between what two values?

Solution

We can use the results of the Empirical Rule to answer these questions.

1. About 68 percent of the batteries will fail between 17.8 and 20.2 hours, found by $19.0 \pm 1(1.2)$ hours.
2. About 95 percent of the batteries will fail between 16.6 and 21.4 hours, found by $19.0 \pm 2(1.2)$ hours.
3. Practically all failed between 15.4 and 22.6 hours, found by $19.0 \pm 3(1.2)$ hours.

This information is summarized on the following chart.

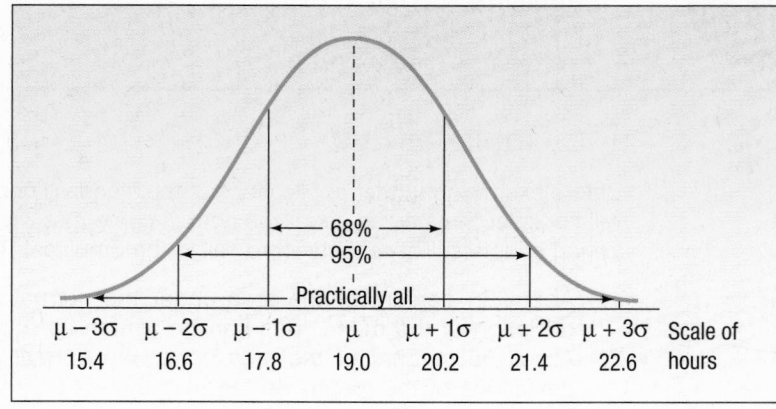

Self-Review 7–3

The distribution of the annual incomes of a group of middle-management employees at Compton Plastics approximates a normal distribution with a mean of $47,200 and a standard deviation of $800.
(a) About 68 percent of the incomes lie between what two amounts?
(b) About 95 percent of the incomes lie between what two amounts?
(c) Virtually all of the incomes lie between what two amounts?
(d) What are the median and the modal incomes?
(e) Is the distribution of incomes symmetrical?

Exercises

connect

7. Explain what is meant by this statement: "There is not just one normal probability distribution but a 'family' of them."
8. List the major characteristics of a normal probability distribution.
9. The mean of a normal probability distribution is 500; the standard deviation is 10.
   a. About 68 percent of the observations lie between what two values?
   b. About 95 percent of the observations lie between what two values?
   c. Practically all of the observations lie between what two values?
10. The mean of a normal probability distribution is 60; the standard deviation is 5.
   a. About what percent of the observations lie between 55 and 65?
   b. About what percent of the observations lie between 50 and 70?
   c. About what percent of the observations lie between 45 and 75?
11. The Kamp family has twins, Rob and Rachel. Both Rob and Rachel graduated from college 2 years ago, and each is now earning $50,000 per year. Rachel works in the retail industry, where the mean salary for executives with less than 5 years' experience is $35,000 with a standard deviation of $8,000. Rob is an engineer. The mean salary for engineers with less than 5 years' experience is $60,000 with a standard deviation of $5,000. Compute the z values for both Rob and Rachel and comment on your findings.
12. A recent article in the *Cincinnati Enquirer* reported that the mean labor cost to repair a heat pump is $90 with a standard deviation of $22. Monte's Plumbing and Heating Service completed repairs on two heat pumps this morning. The labor cost for the first was $75 and it was $100 for the second. Assume the distribution of labor costs follows the normal probability distribution. Compute z values for each and comment on your findings.

Finding Areas under the Normal Curve

The next application of the standard normal distribution involves finding the area in a normal distribution between the mean and a selected value, which we identify as X. The following example will illustrate the details.

Example

Recall in an earlier example (see page 227) we reported that the mean weekly income of a shift foreman in the glass industry is normally distributed with a mean of $1,000 and a standard deviation of $100. That is, μ = $1,000 and σ = $100. What is the likelihood of selecting a foreman whose weekly income is between $1,000 and $1,100? We write this question in probability notation as: P($1,000 < weekly income < $1,100).

Solution

We have already converted $1,100 to a z value of 1.00 using formula (7–5). To repeat:

$$z = \frac{X - \mu}{\sigma} = \frac{\$1,100 - \$1,000}{\$100} = 1.00$$

The probability associated with a *z* of 1.00 is available in Appendix B.1. A portion of Appendix B.1 follows. To locate the probability, go down the left column to 1.0, and then move horizontally to the column headed .00. The value is .3413.

z	0.00	0.01	0.02
.	.	.	.
.	.	.	.
.	.	.	.
0.7	.2580	.2611	.2642
0.8	.2881	.2910	.2939
0.9	.3159	.3186	.3212
1.0	.3413	.3438	.3461
1.1	.3643	.3665	.3686
.	.	.	.
.	.	.	.
.	.	.	.

The area under the normal curve between $1,000 and $1,100 is .3413. We could also say 34.13 percent of the shift foremen in the glass industry earn between $1,000 and $1,100 weekly, or the likelihood of selecting a foreman and finding his or her income is between $1,000 and $1,100 is .3413.

This information is summarized in the following diagram.

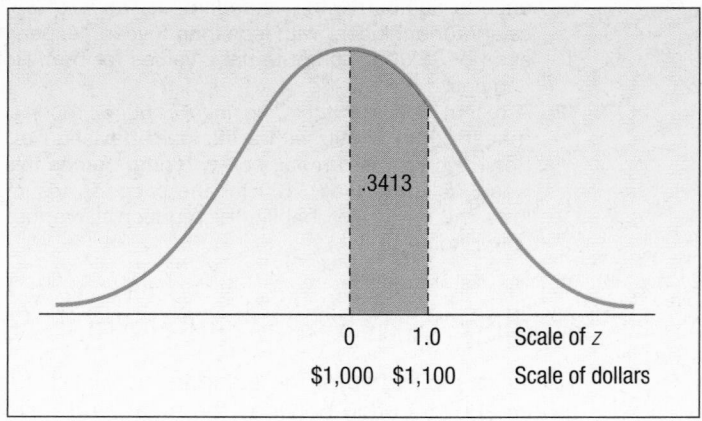

In the example just completed, we are interested in the probability between the mean and a given value. Let's change the question. Instead of wanting to know the probability of selecting at random a foreman who earned between $1,000 and $1,100, suppose we wanted the probability of selecting a foreman who earned less than $1,100. In probability notation we write this statement as P(weekly income < $1,100). The method of solution is the same. We find the probability of selecting a foreman who earns between $1,000, the mean, and $1,100. This probability is .3413. Next, recall that half the area, or probability, is above the mean and half is below. So the probability of selecting a foreman earning less than $1,000 is .5000. Finally, we add the two probabilities, so .3413 + .5000 = .8413. About 84 percent of the foremen in the glass industry earn less than $1,100 per month. See the following diagram.

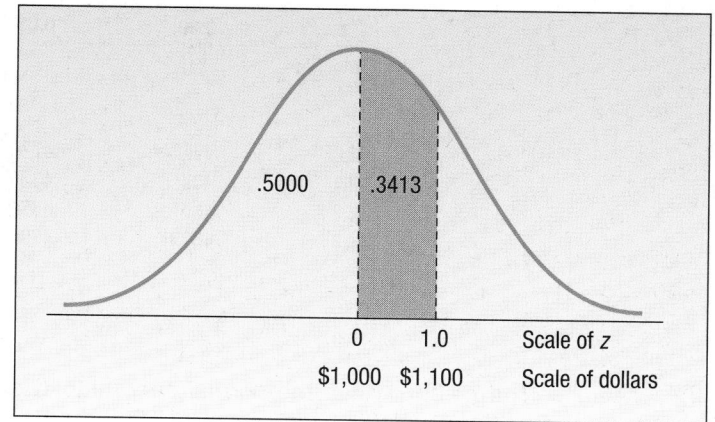

Excel will calculate this probability. The necessary commands are in the **Soft-ware Commands** section at the end of the chapter. The answer is .8413, the same as we calculated.

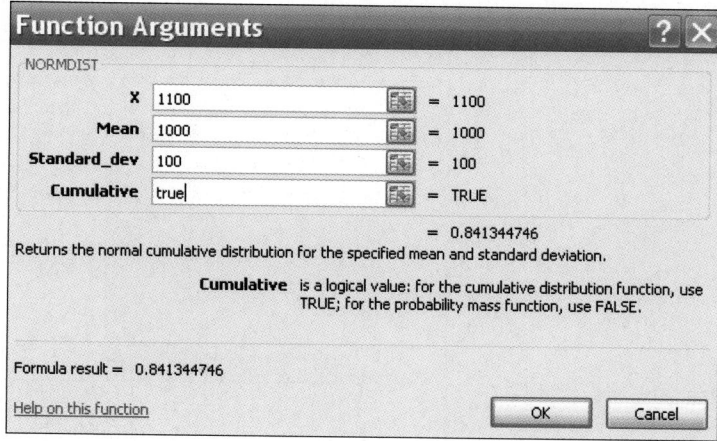

Example

Refer to the information regarding the weekly income of shift foremen in the glass industry. The distribution of weekly incomes follows the normal probability distribution, with a mean of $1,000 and a standard deviation of $100. What is the probability of selecting a shift foreman in the glass industry whose income is:

1. Between $790 and $1,000?
2. Less than $790?

Solution

We begin by finding the z value corresponding to a weekly income of $790. From formula (7–5):

$$z = \frac{X - \mu}{s} = \frac{\$790 - \$1,000}{\$100} = -2.10$$

See Appendix B.1. Move down the left margin to the row 2.1 and across that row to the column headed 0.00. The value is .4821. So the area under the standard normal curve corresponding to a z value of 2.10 is .4821. However, because the normal distribution is symmetric, the area between 0 and a negative z value is the same as that between 0 and the corresponding positive z value. The likelihood of finding a foreman earning between $790 and $1,000 is .4821. In probability notation we write $P(\$790 < \text{weekly income} < \$1000) = .4821$.

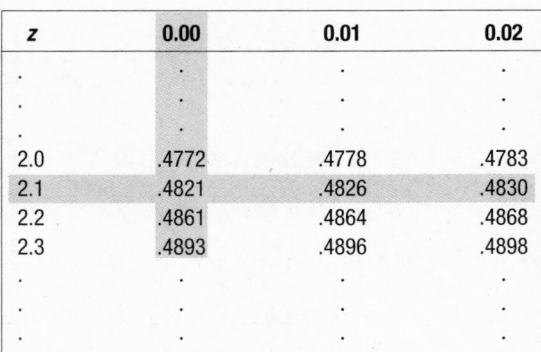

z	0.00	0.01	0.02
.	.	.	.
.	.	.	.
.	.	.	.
2.0	.4772	.4778	.4783
2.1	.4821	.4826	.4830
2.2	.4861	.4864	.4868
2.3	.4893	.4896	.4898
.	.	.	.
.	.	.	.
.	.	.	.

The mean divides the normal curve into two identical halves. The area under the half to the left of the mean is .5000, and the area to the right is also .5000. Because the area under the curve between $790 and $1,000 is .4821, the area below $790 is .0179, found by .5000 − .4821. In probability notation we write P(weekly income < $790) = .0179.

This means that 48.21 percent of the foremen have weekly incomes between $790 and $1,000. Further, we can anticipate that 1.79 percent earn less than $790 per week. This information is summarized in the following diagram.

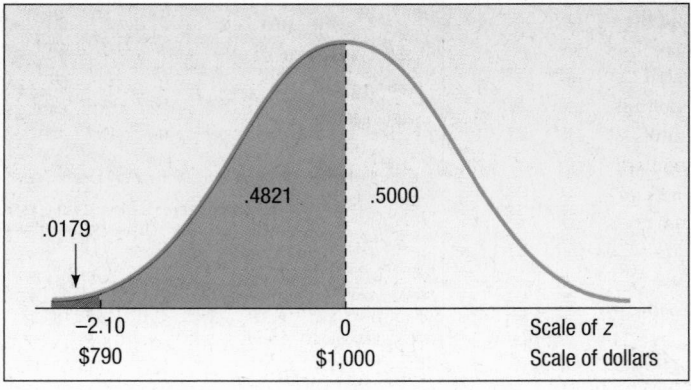

Self-Review 7–4

The employees of Cartwright Manufacturing are awarded efficiency ratings based on such factors as monthly output, attitude, and attendance. The distribution of the ratings follows the normal probability distribution. The mean is 400, the standard deviation 50.

(a) What is the area under the normal curve between 400 and 482? Write this area in probability notation.

(b) What is the area under the normal curve for ratings greater than 482? Write this area in probability notation.

(c) Show the facets of this problem in a chart.

Exercises

13. A normal population has a mean of 20.0 and a standard deviation of 4.0.
  a. Compute the z value associated with 25.0.
  b. What proportion of the population is between 20.0 and 25.0?
  c. What proportion of the population is less than 18.0?

14. A normal population has a mean of 12.2 and a standard deviation of 2.5.
  a. Compute the z value associated with 14.3.
  b. What proportion of the population is between 12.2 and 14.3?
  c. What proportion of the population is less than 10.0?

15. A recent study of the hourly wages of maintenance crew members for major airlines showed that the mean hourly salary was $20.50, with a standard deviation of $3.50. Assume the distribution of hourly wages follows the normal probability distribution. If we select a crew member at random, what is the probability the crew member earns:
   a. Between $20.50 and $24.00 per hour?
   b. More than $24.00 per hour?
   c. Less than $19.00 per hour?

16. The mean of a normal probability distribution is 400 pounds. The standard deviation is 10 pounds.
   a. What is the area between 415 pounds and the mean of 400 pounds?
   b. What is the area between the mean and 395 pounds?
   c. What is the probability of selecting a value at random and discovering that it has a value of less than 395 pounds?

Another application of the normal distribution involves combining two areas, or probabilities. One of the areas is to the right of the mean and the other to the left.

Example

Recall the distribution of weekly incomes of shift foremen in the glass industry. The weekly incomes follow the normal probability distribution, with a mean of $1,000 and a standard deviation of $100. What is the area under this normal curve between $840 and $1,200?

Solution

The problem can be divided into two parts. For the area between $840 and the mean of $1,000:

$$z = \frac{\$840 - \$1,000}{\$100} = \frac{-\$160}{\$100} = -1.60$$

For the area between the mean of $1,000 and $1,200:

$$z = \frac{\$1,200 - \$1,000}{\$100} = \frac{\$200}{\$100} = 2.00$$

The area under the curve for a z of -1.60 is .4452 (from Appendix B.1). The area under the curve for a z of 2.00 is .4772. Adding the two areas: .4452 + .4772 = .9224. Thus, the probability of selecting an income between $840 and $1,200 is .9224. In probability notation we write $P(\$840 < \text{weekly income} < \$1,200) = .4452 + .4772 = .9224$. To summarize, 92.24 percent of the foremen have weekly incomes between $840 and $1,200. This is shown in a diagram:

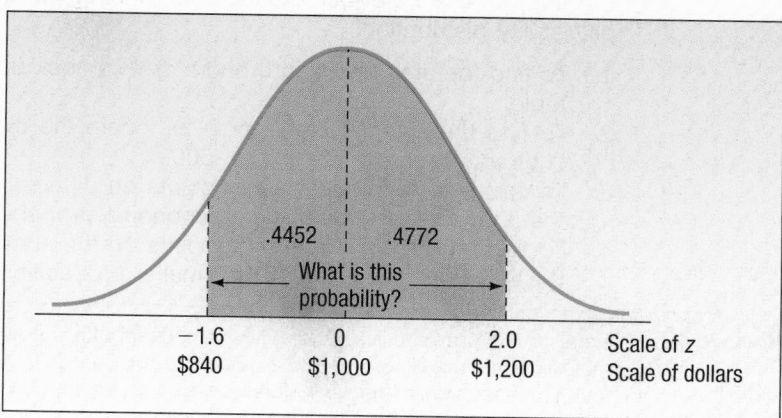

Another application of the normal distribution involves determining the area between values on the *same* side of the mean.

Example

Returning to the weekly income distribution of shift foremen in the glass industry (μ = $1,000, σ = $100), what is the area under the normal curve between $1,150 and $1,250?

Solution

The situation is again separated into two parts, and formula (7–5) is used. First, we find the z value associated with a weekly salary of $1,250:

$$z = \frac{\$1,250 - \$1,000}{\$100} = 2.50$$

Next we find the z value for a weekly salary of $1,150:

$$z = \frac{\$1,150 - \$1,000}{\$100} = 1.50$$

From Appendix B.1 the area associated with a z value of 2.50 is .4938. So the probability of a weekly salary between $1,000 and $1,250 is .4938. Similarly, the area associated with a z value of 1.50 is .4332, so the probability of a weekly salary between $1,000 and $1,150 is .4332. The probability of a weekly salary between $1,150 and $1,250 is found by subtracting the area associated with a z value of 1.50 (.4332) from that associated with a z of 2.50 (.4938). Thus, the probability of a weekly salary between $1,150 and $1,250 is .0606. In probability notation we write $P(\$1,150 < \text{weekly income} < \$1,250) = .4938 - .4332 = .0606$.

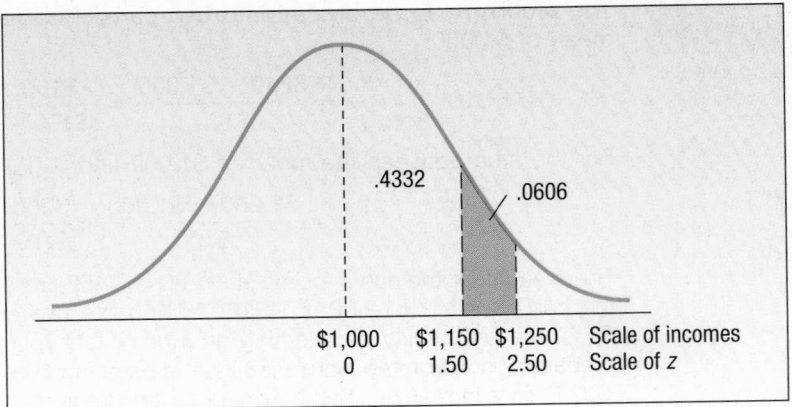

In brief, there are four situations for finding the area under the standard normal probability distribution.

1. To find the area between 0 and z or ($-z$), look up the probability directly in the table.
2. To find the area beyond z or ($-z$), locate the probability of z in the table and subtract that probability from .5000.
3. To find the area between two points on different sides of the mean, determine the z values and add the corresponding probabilities.
4. To find the area between two points on the same side of the mean, determine the z values and subtract the smaller probability from the larger.

Self-Review 7–5

Refer to the previous example, where the distribution of weekly incomes follows the normal distribution with a mean of $1,000 and the standard deviation is $100.
(a) What fraction of the shift foremen earn a weekly income between $750 and $1,225? Draw a normal curve and shade the desired area on your diagram.
(b) What fraction of the shift foremen earn a weekly income between $1,100 and $1,225? Draw a normal curve and shade the desired area on your diagram.

Exercises

17. A normal distribution has a mean of 50 and a standard deviation of 4.
   a. Compute the probability of a value between 44.0 and 55.0.
   b. Compute the probability of a value greater than 55.0.
   c. Compute the probability of a value between 52.0 and 55.0.
18. A normal population has a mean of 80.0 and a standard deviation of 14.0.
   a. Compute the probability of a value between 75.0 and 90.0.
   b. Compute the probability of a value 75.0 or less.
   c. Compute the probability of a value between 55.0 and 70.0.
19. According to the Internal Revenue Service, the mean tax refund for the year 2007 was $2,708. Assume the standard deviation is $650 and that the amounts refunded follow a normal probability distribution.
   a. What percent of the refunds are more than $3,000?
   b. What percent of the refunds are more than $3,000 but less than $3,500?
   c. What percent of the refunds are more than $2,500 but less than $3,500?
20. The number of viewers of *American Idol* has a mean of 29 million with a standard deviation of 5 million. Assume this distribution follows a normal distribution. What is the probability that next week's show will:
   a. Have between 30 and 34 million viewers?
   b. Have at least 23 million viewers?
   c. Exceed 40 million viewers?
21. WNAE, an all-news AM station, finds that the distribution of the lengths of time listeners are tuned to the station follows the normal distribution. The mean of the distribution is 15.0 minutes and the standard deviation is 3.5 minutes. What is the probability that a particular listener will tune in:
   a. More than 20 minutes?
   b. For 20 minutes or less?
   c. Between 10 and 12 minutes?
22. Among U.S. cities with a population of more than 250,000 the mean one-way commute to work is 24.3 minutes. The longest one-way travel time is New York City, where the mean time is 38.3 minutes. Assume the distribution of travel times in New York City follows the normal probability distribution and the standard deviation is 7.5 minutes.
   a. What percent of the New York City commutes are for less than 30 minutes?
   b. What percent are between 30 and 35 minutes?
   c. What percent are between 30 and 40 minutes?

Previous examples require finding the percent of the observations located between two observations or the percent of the observations above, or below, a particular observation *X*. A further application of the normal distribution involves finding the value of the observation *X* when the percent above or below the observation is given.

Example

Layton Tire and Rubber Company wishes to set a minimum mileage guarantee on its new MX100 tire. Tests reveal the mean mileage is 67,900 with a standard deviation of 2,050 miles and that the distribution of miles follows the normal probability distribution. Layton wants to set the minimum guaranteed mileage so that no more than 4 percent of the tires will have to be replaced. What minimum guaranteed mileage should Layton announce?

Solution

The facets of this case are shown in the following diagram, where *X* represents the minimum guaranteed mileage.

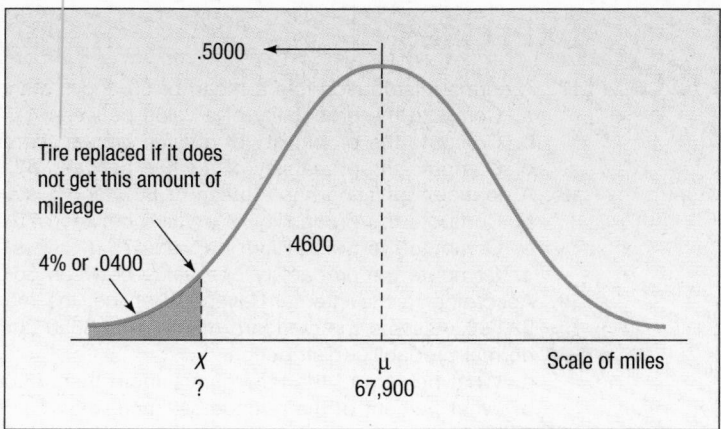

Inserting these values in formula (7–5) for z gives:

$$z = \frac{X - \mu}{\sigma} = \frac{X - 67{,}900}{2{,}050}$$

Notice that there are two unknowns, z and X. To find X, we first find z, and then solve for X. Notice the area under the normal curve to the left of μ is .5000. The area between μ and X is .4600, found by .5000 − .0400. Now refer to Appendix B.1. Search the body of the table for the area closest to .4600. The closest area is .4599. Move to the margins from this value and read the z value of 1.75. Because the value is to the left of the mean, it is actually −1.75. These steps are illustrated in Table 7–2.

TABLE 7–2   Selected Areas under the Normal Curve

z ...	.03	.04	.05	.06
.	.	.	.	.
.	.	.	.	.
.	.	.	.	.
1.5	.4370	.4382	.4394	.4406
1.6	.4484	.4495	.4505	.4515
1.7	.4582	.4591	.4599	.4608
1.8	.4664	.4671	.4678	.4686

Knowing that the distance between μ and X is -1.75σ or $z = -1.75$, we can now solve for X (the minimum guaranteed mileage):

$$z = \frac{X - 67{,}900}{2{,}050}$$

$$-1.75 = \frac{X - 67{,}900}{2{,}050}$$

$$-1.75(2{,}050) = X - 67{,}900$$

$$X = 67{,}900 - 1.75(2{,}050) = 64{,}312$$

So Layton can advertise that it will replace for free any tire that wears out before it reaches 64,312 miles, and the company will know that only 4 percent of the tires will be replaced under this plan.

Excel will also find the mileage value. See the following output. The necessary commands are given in the **Software Commands** section at the end of the chapter.

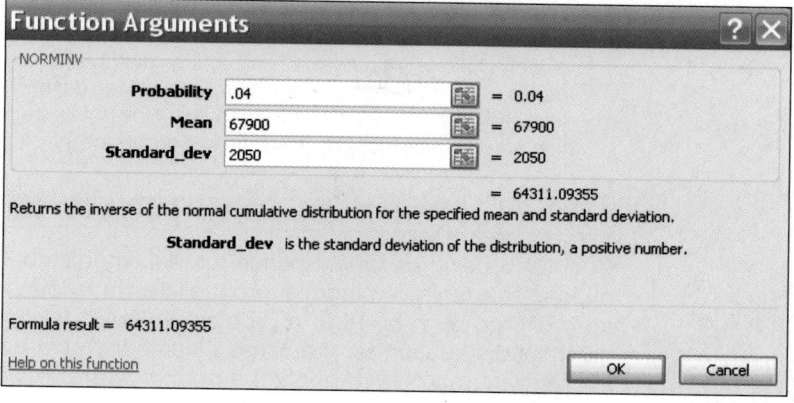

Excel

Self-Review 7–6

An analysis of the final test scores for Introduction to Business reveals the scores follow the normal probability distribution. The mean of the distribution is 75 and the standard deviation is 8. The professor wants to award an A to students whose score is in the highest 10 percent. What is the dividing point for those students who earn an A and those earning a B?

Exercises

connect

23. A normal distribution has a mean of 50 and a standard deviation of 4. Determine the value below which 95 percent of the observations will occur.

24. A normal distribution has a mean of 80 and a standard deviation of 14. Determine the value above which 80 percent of the values will occur.

25. Assume that the mean hourly cost to operate a commercial airplane follows the normal distribution with a mean of $2,100 per hour and a standard deviation of $250. What is the operating cost for the lowest 3 percent of the airplanes?

26. The monthly sales of mufflers in the Richmond, Virginia, area follow the normal distribution with a mean of 1,200 and a standard deviation of 225. The manufacturer would like to establish inventory levels such that there is only a 5 percent chance of running out of stock. Where should the manufacturer set the inventory levels?

27. According to media research, the typical American listened to 195 hours of music in the last year. This is down from 290 hours four years earlier. Dick Trythall is a big country and western music fan. He listens to music while working around the house, reading, and riding in his truck. Assume the number of hours spent listening to music follows a normal probability distribution with a standard deviation of 8.5 hours.
    a. If Dick is in the top 1 percent in terms of listening time, how many hours does he listen per year?
    b. Assume that the distribution of times four years earlier also follows the normal probability distribution with a standard deviation of 8.5 hours. How many hours did the 1 percent who listen to the *least* music actually listen?

28. For the most recent year available the mean annual cost to attend a private university in the United States was $26,889. Assume the distribution of annual costs follows a normal probability distribution and the standard deviation is $4,500. Ninety-five percent of all students at private universities pay less than what amount?

29. The newsstand at the corner of East 9th Street and Euclid Avenue in downtown Cleveland sells the daily edition of the *Cleveland Plain Dealer*. The number of papers sold each day follows a normal probability distribution with a mean of 200 copies and a standard deviation of 17 copies. How many copies should the owner of the newsstand order, so that he only runs out of papers on 20 percent of the days?

30. The manufacturer of a laser printer reports the mean number of pages a cartridge will print before it needs replacing is 12,200. The distribution of pages printed per cartridge closely follows the normal probability distribution and the standard deviation is 820 pages. The manufacturer wants to provide guidelines to potential customers as to how long they can expect a cartridge to last. How many pages should the manufacturer advertise for each cartridge if it wants to be correct 99 percent of the time?

The Normal Approximation to the Binomial

Chapter 6 describes the binomial probability distribution, which is a discrete distribution. The table of binomial probabilities in Appendix B.9 goes successively from an n of 1 to an n of 15. If a problem involved taking a sample of 60, generating a binomial distribution for that large a number would be very time consuming. A more efficient approach is to apply the *normal approximation to the binomial*.

Using the normal distribution (a continuous distribution) as a substitute for a binomial distribution (a discrete distribution) for large values of n seems reasonable because, as n increases, a binomial distribution gets closer and closer to a normal distribution. Chart 7–7 depicts the change in the shape of a binomial distribution with $\pi = .50$ from an n of 1, to an n of 3, to an n of 20. Notice how the case where $n = 20$ approximates the shape of the normal distribution. That is, compare the case where $n = 20$ to the normal curve in Chart 7–3 on page 224.

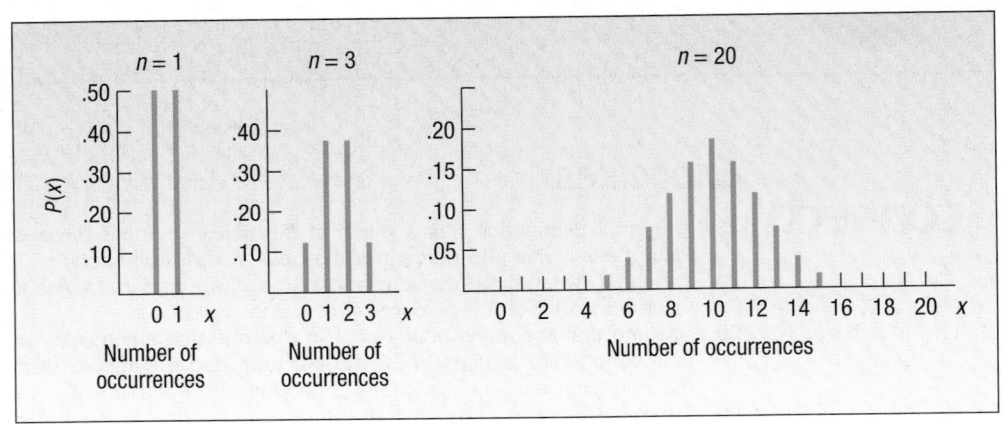

CHART 7–7 Binomial Distributions for an n of 1, 3, and 20, Where $\pi = .50$

When to use the normal approximation

When can we use the normal approximation to the binomial? The normal probability distribution is a good approximation to the binomial probability distribution when $n\pi$ and $n(1 - \pi)$ are both at least 5. However, before we apply the normal approximation, we must make sure that our distribution of interest is in fact a binomial distribution. Recall from Chapter 6 that four criteria must be met:

1. There are only two mutually exclusive outcomes to an experiment: a "success" and a "failure."
2. The distribution results from counting the number of successes in a fixed number of trials.
3. The probability of a success, π, remains the same from trial to trial.
4. Each trial is independent.

Continuity Correction Factor

To show the application of the normal approximation to the binomial and the need for a correction factor, suppose the management of the Santoni Pizza Restaurant found that 70 percent of its new customers return for another meal. For a week

in which 80 new (first-time) customers dined at Santoni's, what is the probability that 60 or more will return for another meal?

Notice the binomial conditions are met: (1) There are only two possible outcomes—a customer either returns for another meal or does not return. (2) We can count the number of successes, meaning, for example, that 57 of the 80 customers return. (3) The trials are independent, meaning that if the 34th person returns for a second meal, that does not affect whether the 58th person returns. (4) The probability of a customer returning remains at .70 for all 80 customers.

Therefore, we could use the binomial formula (6–3) described on page 192.

$$P(x) = {}_nC_x \, (\pi)^x \, (1 - \pi)^{n-x}$$

To find the probability 60 or more customers return for another pizza, we need to first find the probability exactly 60 customers return. That is:

$$P(x = 60) = {}_{80}C_{60} \, (.70)^{60} \, (1 - .70)^{20} = .063$$

Next we find the probability that exactly 61 customers return. It is:

$$P(x = 61) = {}_{80}C_{61} \, (.70)^{61} \, (1 - .70)^{19} = .048$$

We continue this process until we have the probability that all 80 customers return. Finally, we add the probabilities from 60 to 80. Solving the above problem in this manner is tedious. We can also use a computer software package such as MINITAB or Excel to find the various probabilities. Listed below are the binomial probabilities for $n = 80$, $\pi = .70$, and x, the number of customers returning, ranging from 43 to 68. The probability of any number of customers less than 43 or more than 68 returning is less than .001. We can assume these probabilities are 0.000.

Number Returning	Probability	Number Returning	Probability
43	.001	56	.097
44	.002	57	.095
45	.003	58	.088
46	.006	59	.077
47	.009	60	.063
48	.015	61	.048
49	.023	62	.034
50	.033	63	.023
51	.045	64	.014
52	.059	65	.008
53	.072	66	.004
54	.084	67	.002
55	.093	68	.001

We can find the probability of 60 or more returning by summing .063 + .048 + · · · + .001, which is .197. However, a look at the plot on the following page shows the similarity of this distribution to a normal distribution. All we need do is "smooth out" the discrete probabilities into a continuous distribution. Furthermore, working with a normal distribution will involve far fewer calculations than working with the binomial.

The trick is to let the discrete probability for 56 customers be represented by an area under the continuous curve between 55.5 and 56.5. Then let the probability for 57 customers be represented by an area between 56.5 and 57.5 and so on. This is just the opposite of rounding off the numbers to a whole number.

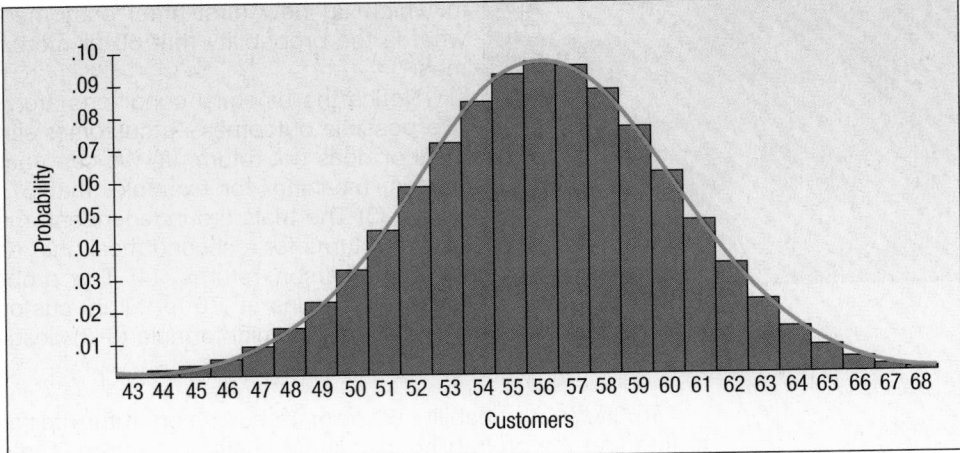

Because we use the normal distribution to determine the binomial probability of 60 or more successes, we must subtract, in this case, .5 from 60. The value .5 is called the **continuity correction factor.** This small adjustment must be made because a continuous distribution (the normal distribution) is being used to approximate a discrete distribution (the binomial distribution). Subtracting, $60 - .5 = 59.5$.

> **CONTINUITY CORRECTION FACTOR** The value .5 subtracted or added, depending on the question, to a selected value when a discrete probability distribution is approximated by a continuous probability distribution.

How to Apply the Correction Factor

Only four cases may arise. These cases are:

1. For the probability *at least* X occurs, use the area *above* $(X - .5)$.
2. For the probability that *more than* X occurs, use the area *above* $(X + .5)$.
3. For the probability that X *or fewer* occurs, use the area *below* $(X + .5)$.
4. For the probability that *fewer than* X occurs, use the area *below* $(X - .5)$.

To use the normal distribution to approximate the probability that 60 or more first-time Santoni customers out of 80 will return, follow the procedure shown below.

Step 1. Find the z corresponding to an X of 59.5 using formula (7–5), and formulas (6–4) and (6–5) for the mean and the variance of a binomial distribution:

$$\mu = n\pi = 80(.70) = 56$$
$$\sigma^2 = n\pi(1 - \pi) = 80(.70)(1 - .70) = 16.8$$
$$\sigma = \sqrt{16.8} = 4.10$$
$$z = \frac{X - \mu}{\sigma} = \frac{59.5 - 56}{4.10} = 0.85$$

Step 2. Determine the area under the normal curve between a μ of 56 and an X of 59.5. From step 1, we know that the z value corresponding to 59.5 is 0.85. So we go to Appendix B.1 and read down the left margin to 0.8, and then we go horizontally to the area under the column headed by .05. That area is .3023.

As another example, the driver's seat in most vehicles is set to comfortably fit a person who is at least 159 cm (62.5 inches) tall. The distribution of heights of adult women is approximately a normal distribution with a mean of 161.5 cm and a standard deviation of 6.3 cm. Thus about 35 percent of adult women will not fit comfortably in the driver's seat.

Step 3. Calculate the area beyond 59.5 by subtracting .3023 from .5000 (.5000 − .3023 = .1977). Thus, .1977 is the probability that 60 or more first-time Santoni customers out of 80 will return for another meal. In probability notation $P(\text{customers} > 59.5) = .5000 - .3023 = .1977$. The facets of this problem are shown graphically:

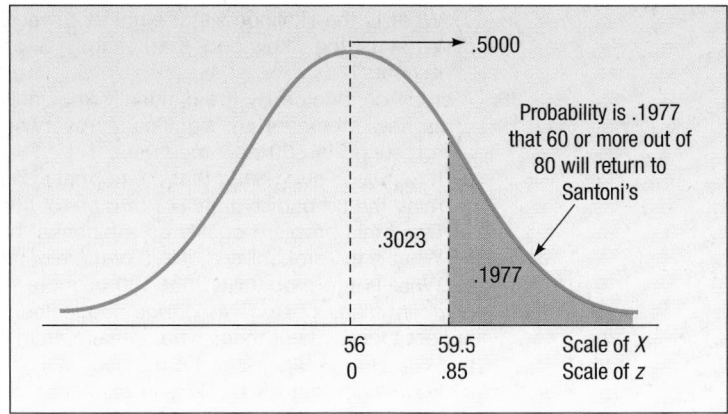

No doubt you will agree that using the normal approximation to the binomial is a more efficient method of estimating the probability of 60 or more first-time customers returning. The result compares favorably with that computed on page 239, using the binomial distribution. The probability using the binomial distribution is .197, whereas the probability using the normal approximation is .1977.

Self-Review 7–7

A study by Great Southern Home Insurance revealed that none of the stolen goods were recovered by the homeowners in 80 percent of reported thefts.
(a) During a period in which 200 thefts occurred, what is the probability that no stolen goods were recovered in 170 or more of the robberies?
(b) During a period in which 200 thefts occurred, what is the probability that no stolen goods were recovered in 150 or more robberies?

Exercises

31. Assume a binomial probability distribution with $n = 50$ and $\pi = .25$. Compute the following:
   a. The mean and standard deviation of the random variable.
   b. The probability that X is 15 or more.
   c. The probability that X is 10 or less.
32. Assume a binomial probability distribution with $n = 40$ and $\pi = .55$. Compute the following:
   a. The mean and standard deviation of the random variable.
   b. The probability that X is 25 or greater.
   c. The probability that X is 15 or less.
   d. The probability that X is between 15 and 25, inclusive.
33. Dottie's Tax Service specializes in federal tax returns for professional clients, such as physicians, dentists, accountants, and lawyers. A recent audit by the IRS of the returns she prepared indicated that an error was made on 7 percent of the returns she prepared last year. Assuming this rate continues into this year and she prepares 80 returns, what is the probability that she makes errors on:
   a. More than six returns?
   b. At least six returns?
   c. Exactly six returns?

34. Shorty's Muffler advertises it can install a new muffler in 30 minutes or less. However, the work standards department at corporate headquarters recently conducted a study and found that 20 percent of the mufflers were not installed in 30 minutes or less. The Maumee branch installed 50 mufflers last month. If the corporate report is correct:
  a. How many of the installations at the Maumee branch would you expect to take more than 30 minutes?
  b. What is the likelihood that fewer than eight installations took more than 30 minutes?
  c. What is the likelihood that eight or fewer installations took more than 30 minutes?
  d. What is the likelihood that exactly 8 of the 50 installations took more than 30 minutes?

35. A study conducted by the nationally known Taurus Health Club revealed that 30 percent of its new members are significantly overweight. A membership drive in a metropolitan area resulted in 500 new members.
  a. It has been suggested that the normal approximation to the binomial be used to determine the probability that 175 or more of the new members are significantly overweight. Does this problem qualify as a binomial problem? Explain.
  b. What is the probability that 175 or more of the new members are significantly overweight?
  c. What is the probability that 140 or more new members are significantly overweight?

36. A recent issue of *Bride Magazine* suggested that couples planning their wedding should expect two-thirds of those who are sent an invitation to respond that they will attend. Rich and Stacy are planning to be married later this year. They plan to send 197 invitations.
  a. How many guests would you expect to accept the invitation?
  b. What is the standard deviation?
  c. What is the probability 140 or more will accept the invitation?
  d. What is the probability exactly 140 will accept the invitation?

Chapter Summary

I. The uniform distribution is a continuous probability distribution with the following characteristics.
  A. It is rectangular in shape.
  B. The mean and the median are equal.
  C. It is completely described by its minimum value a and its maximum value b.
  D. It is also described by the following equation for the region from a to b:

$$P(x) = \frac{1}{b - a}$$ **[7–3]**

  E. The mean and standard deviation of a uniform distribution are computed as follows:

$$\mu = \frac{(a + b)}{2}$$ **[7–1]**

$$\sigma = \sqrt{\frac{(b - a)^2}{12}}$$ **[7–2]**

II. The normal probability distribution is a continuous distribution with the following characteristics.
  A. It is bell-shaped and has a single peak at the center of the distribution.
  B. The distribution is symmetric.
  C. It is asymptotic, meaning the curve approaches but never touches the X-axis.
  D. It is completely described by its mean and standard deviation.
  E. There is a family of normal probability distributions.
    1. Another normal probability distribution is created when either the mean or the standard deviation changes.
    2. The normal probability distribution is described by the following formula:

$$P(x) = \frac{1}{\sigma\sqrt{2\pi}} e^{-\left[\frac{(x - \mu)^2}{2\sigma^2}\right]}$$ **[7–4]**

III. The standard normal probability distribution is a particular normal distribution.
    A. It has a mean of 0 and a standard deviation of 1.
    B. Any normal probability distribution can be converted to the standard normal probability distribution by the following formula.

$$z = \frac{X - \mu}{\sigma}$$ **[7–5]**

    C. By standardizing a normal probability distribution, we can report the distance of a value from the mean in units of the standard deviation.
IV. The normal probability distribution can approximate a binomial distribution under certain conditions.
    A. $n\pi$ and $n(1 - \pi)$ must both be at least 5.
        1. n is the number of observations.
        2. π is the probability of a success.
    B. The four conditions for a binomial probability distribution are:
        1. There are only two possible outcomes.
        2. π remains the same from trial to trial.
        3. The trials are independent.
        4. The distribution results from a count of the number of successes in a fixed number of trials.
    C. The mean and variance of a binomial distribution are computed as follows:

$$\mu = n\pi$$
$$\sigma^2 = n\pi(1 - \pi)$$

    D. The continuity correction factor of .5 is used to extend the continuous value of X one-half unit in either direction. This correction compensates for approximating a discrete distribution by a continuous distribution.

Chapter Exercises

connect

37. The amount of cola in a 12-ounce can is uniformly distributed between 11.96 ounces and 12.05 ounces.
    a. What is the mean amount per can?
    b. What is the standard deviation amount per can?
    c. What is the probability of selecting a can of cola and finding it has less than 12 ounces?
    d. What is the probability of selecting a can of cola and finding it has more than 11.98 ounces?
    e. What is the probability of selecting a can of cola and finding it has more than 11.00 ounces?
38. A tube of Listerine Tartar Control toothpaste contains 4.2 ounces. As people use the toothpaste, the amount remaining in any tube is random. Assume the amount of toothpaste left in the tube follows a uniform distribution. From this information, we can determine the following information about the amount remaining in a toothpaste tube without invading anyone's privacy.
    a. How much toothpaste would you expect to be remaining in the tube?
    b. What is the standard deviation of the amount remaining in the tube?
    c. What is the likelihood there is less than 3.0 ounces remaining in the tube?
    d. What is the probability there is more than 1.5 ounces remaining in the tube?
39. Many retail stores offer their own credit cards. At the time of the credit application the customer is given a 10 percent discount on the purchase. The time required for the credit application process follows a uniform distribution with the times ranging from 4 minutes to 10 minutes.
    a. What is the mean time for the application process?
    b. What is the standard deviation of the process time?
    c. What is the likelihood a particular application will take less than 6 minutes?
    d. What is the likelihood an application will take more than 5 minutes?
40. The time patrons at the Grande Dunes Hotel in the Bahamas spend waiting for an elevator follows a uniform distribution between 0 and 3.5 minutes.
    a. Show that the area under the curve is 1.00.
    b. How long does the typical patron wait for elevator service?

c. What is the standard deviation of the waiting time?

d. What percent of the patrons wait for less than a minute?

e. What percent of the patrons wait more than 2 minutes?

41. The net sales and the number of employees for aluminum fabricators with similar characteristics are organized into frequency distributions. Both are normally distributed. For the net sales, the mean is $180 million and the standard deviation is $25 million. For the number of employees, the mean is 1,500 and the standard deviation is 120. Clarion Fabricators had sales of $170 million and 1,850 employees.

a. Convert Clarion's sales and number of employees to z values.

b. Locate the two z values.

c. Compare Clarion's sales and number of employees with those of the other fabricators.

42. The accounting department at Weston Materials, Inc., a national manufacturer of unattached garages, reports that it takes two construction workers a mean of 32 hours and a standard deviation of 2 hours to erect the Red Barn model. Assume the assembly times follow the normal distribution.

a. Determine the z values for 29 and 34 hours. What percent of the garages take between 32 hours and 34 hours to erect?

b. What percent of the garages take between 29 hours and 34 hours to erect?

c. What percent of the garages take 28.7 hours or less to erect?

d. Of the garages, 5 percent take how many hours or more to erect?

43. A recent report in *USA Today* indicated a typical family of four spends $490 per month on food. Assume the distribution of food expenditures for a family of four follows the normal distribution, with a mean of $490 and a standard deviation of $90.

a. What percent of the families spend more than $30 but less than $490 per month on food?

b. What percent of the families spend less than $430 per month on food?

c. What percent spend between $430 and $600 per month on food?

d. What percent spend between $500 and $600 per month on food?

44. A study of long-distance phone calls made from the corporate offices of Pepsi Bottling Group, Inc., in Somers, New York, revealed the length of the calls, in minutes, follows the normal probability distribution. The mean length of time per call was 4.2 minutes and the standard deviation was 0.60 minutes.

a. What fraction of the calls last between 4.2 and 5 minutes?

b. What fraction of the calls last more than 5 minutes?

c. What fraction of the calls last between 5 and 6 minutes?

d. What fraction of the calls last between 4 and 6 minutes?

e. As part of her report to the president, the director of communications would like to report the length of the longest (in duration) 4 percent of the calls. What is this time?

45. Shaver Manufacturing, Inc., offers dental insurance to its employees. A recent study by the human resource director shows the annual cost per employee per year followed the normal probability distribution, with a mean of $1,280 and a standard deviation of $420 per year.

a. What fraction of the employees cost more than $1,500 per year for dental expenses?

b. What fraction of the employees cost between $1,500 and $2,000 per year?

c. Estimate the percent that did not have any dental expense.

d. What was the cost for the 10 percent of employees who incurred the highest dental expense?

46. The annual commissions earned by sales representatives of Machine Products, Inc., a manufacturer of light machinery, follow the normal probability distribution. The mean yearly amount earned is $40,000 and the standard deviation is $5,000.

a. What percent of the sales representatives earn more than $42,000 per year?

b. What percent of the sales representatives earn between $32,000 and $42,000?

c. What percent of the sales representatives earn between $32,000 and $35,000?

d. The sales manager wants to award the sales representatives who earn the largest commissions a bonus of $1,000. He can award a bonus to 20 percent of the representatives. What is the cutoff point between those who earn a bonus and those who do not?

47. According to the South Dakota Department of Health, the mean number of hours of TV viewing per week is higher among adult women than men. A recent study showed women spent an average of 34 hours per week watching TV and men 29 hours per week. Assume that the distribution of hours watched follows the normal distribution for both groups, and that the standard deviation among the women is 4.5 hours and is 5.1 hours for the men.

    a. What percent of the women watch TV less than 40 hours per week?
    b. What percent of the men watch TV more than 25 hours per week?
    c. How many hours of TV do the one percent of women who watch the most TV per week watch? Find the comparable value for the men.

48. According to a government study among adults in the 25- to 34-year age group, the mean amount spent per year on reading and entertainment is $1,994. Assume that the distribution of the amounts spent follows the normal distribution with a standard deviation of $450.
    a. What percent of the adults spend more than $2,500 per year on reading and entertainment?
    b. What percent spend between $2,500 and $3,000 per year on reading and entertainment?
    c. What percent spend less than $1,000 per year on reading and entertainment?

49. Management at Gordon Electronics is considering adopting a bonus system to increase production. One suggestion is to pay a bonus on the highest 5 percent of production based on past experience. Past records indicate weekly production follows the normal distribution. The mean of this distribution is 4,000 units per week and the standard deviation is 60 units per week. If the bonus is paid on the upper 5 percent of production, the bonus will be paid on how many units or more?

50. Fast Service Truck Lines uses the Ford Super Duty F-750 exclusively. Management made a study of the maintenance costs and determined the number of miles traveled during the year followed the normal distribution. The mean of the distribution was 60,000 miles and the standard deviation 2,000 miles.
    a. What percent of the Ford Super Duty F-750s logged 65,200 miles or more?
    b. What percent of the trucks logged more than 57,060 but less than 58,280 miles?
    c. What percent of the Fords traveled 62,000 miles or less during the year?
    d. Is it reasonable to conclude that any of the trucks were driven more than 70,000 miles? Explain.

51. Best Electronics, Inc., offers a "no hassle" returns policy. The number of items returned per day follows the normal distribution. The mean number of customer returns is 10.3 per day and the standard deviation is 2.25 per day.
    a. In what percent of the days are there 8 or fewer customers returning items?
    b. In what percent of the days are between 12 and 14 customers returning items?
    c. Is there any chance of a day with no returns?

52. A recent report in *BusinessWeek* indicated that 20 percent of all employees steal from their company each year. If a company employs 50 people, what is the probability that:
    a. Fewer than 5 employees steal?
    b. More than 5 employees steal?
    c. Exactly 5 employees steal?
    d. More than 5 but fewer than 15 employees steal?

53. The *Orange County Register*, as part of its Sunday health supplement, reported that 64 percent of American men over the age of 18 consider nutrition a top priority in their lives. Suppose we select a sample of 60 men. What is the likelihood that:
    a. 32 or more consider nutrition important?
    b. 44 or more consider nutrition important?
    c. More than 32 but fewer than 43 consider nutrition important?
    d. Exactly 44 consider diet important?

54. It is estimated that 10 percent of those taking the quantitative methods portion of the CPA examination fail that section. Sixty students are taking the exam this Saturday.
    a. How many would you expect to fail? What is the standard deviation?
    b. What is the probability that exactly two students will fail?
    c. What is the probability at least two students will fail?

55. The Georgetown, South Carolina, Traffic Division reported 40 percent of high-speed chases involving automobiles result in a minor or major accident. During a month in which 50 high-speed chases occur, what is the probability that 25 or more will result in a minor or major accident?

56. Cruise ships of the Royal Viking line report that 80 percent of their rooms are occupied during September. For a cruise ship having 800 rooms, what is the probability that 665 or more are occupied in September?

57. The goal at U.S. airports handling international flights is to clear these flights within 45 minutes. Let's interpret this to mean that 95 percent of the flights are cleared in 45 minutes, so 5 percent of the flights take longer to clear. Let's also assume that the distribution is approximately normal.

    a. If the standard deviation of the time to clear an international flight is 5 minutes, what is the mean time to clear a flight?

    b. Suppose the standard deviation is 10 minutes, not the 5 minutes suggested in part (a). What is the new mean?

    c. A customer has 30 minutes from the time her flight lands to catch her limousine. Assuming a standard deviation of 10 minutes, what is the likelihood that she will be cleared in time?

58. The funds dispensed at the ATM machine located near the checkout line at the Kroger's in Union, Kentucky, follows a normal probability distribution with a mean of $4,200 per day and a standard deviation of $720 per day. The machine is programmed to notify the nearby bank if the amount dispensed is very low (less than $2,500) or very high (more than $6,000).

    a. What percent of the days will the bank be notified because the amount dispensed is very low?

    b. What percent of the time will the bank be notified because the amount dispensed is high?

    c. What percent of the time will the bank not be notified regarding the amount of funds dispersed?

59. The weights of canned hams processed at Henline Ham Company follow the normal distribution, with a mean of 9.20 pounds and a standard deviation of 0.25 pounds. The label weight is given as 9.00 pounds.

    a. What proportion of the hams actually weigh less than the amount claimed on the label?

    b. The owner, Glen Henline, is considering two proposals to reduce the proportion of hams below label weight. He can increase the mean weight to 9.25 and leave the standard deviation the same, or he can leave the mean weight at 9.20 and reduce the standard deviation from 0.25 pounds to 0.15. Which change would you recommend?

60. The *Cincinnati Enquirer*, in its Sunday business supplement, reported that the mean number of hours worked per week by those employed full time is 43.9. The article further indicated that about one-third of those employed full time work less than 40 hours per week.

    a. Given this information and assuming that number of hours worked follows the normal distribution, what is the standard deviation of the number of hours worked?

    b. The article also indicated that 20 percent of those working full time work more than 49 hours per week. Determine the standard deviation with this information. Are the two estimates of the standard deviation similar? What would you conclude?

61. Most four-year automobile leases allow up to 60,000 miles. If the lessee goes beyond this amount, a penalty of 20 cents per mile is added to the lease cost. Suppose the distribution of miles driven on four-year leases follows the normal distribution. The mean is 52,000 miles and the standard deviation is 5,000 miles.

    a. What percent of the leases will yield a penalty because of excess mileage?

    b. If the automobile company wanted to change the terms of the lease so that 25 percent of the leases went over the limit, where should the new upper limit be set?

    c. One definition of a low-mileage car is one that is 4 years old and has been driven less than 45,000 miles. What percent of the cars returned are considered low-mileage?

62. The price of shares of Bank of Florida at the end of trading each day for the last year followed the normal distribution. Assume there were 240 trading days in the year. The mean price was $42.00 per share and the standard deviation was $2.25 per share.

    a. What percent of the days was the price over $45.00? How many days would you estimate?

    b. What percent of the days was the price between $38.00 and $40.00?

    c. What was the stock's price on the *highest* 15 percent of days?

63. The annual sales of romance novels follow the normal distribution. However, the mean and the standard deviation are unknown. Forty percent of the time sales are more than 470,000, and 10 percent of the time sales are more than 500,000. What are the mean and the standard deviation?

64. In establishing warranties on HDTV sets, the manufacturer wants to set the limits so that few will need repair at the manufacturer's expense. On the other hand, the warranty period must be long enough to make the purchase attractive to the buyer. For a new HDTV the mean number of months until repairs are needed is 36.84 with a standard deviation of 3.34 months. Where should the warranty limits be set so that only 10 percent of the HDTVs need repairs at the manufacturer's expense?

65. DeKorte Tele-Marketing, Inc., is considering purchasing a machine that randomly selects and automatically dials telephone numbers. DeKorte Tele-Marketing makes most of its calls during the evening, so calls to business phones are wasted. The manufacturer of the machine claims that its programming reduces the calling to business phones to 15 percent of all calls. To test this claim the director of purchasing at DeKorte programmed the machine to select a sample of 150 phone numbers. What is the likelihood that more than 30 of the phone numbers selected are those of businesses, assuming the manufacturer's claim is correct?

Data Set Exercises

66. Refer to the Real Estate data, which report information on homes sold in the Denver, Colorado, area during the last year.

    a. The mean selling price (in $ thousands) of the homes was computed earlier to be $221.10, with a standard deviation of $47.11. Use the normal distribution to estimate the percent of homes selling for more than $280.0. Compare this to the actual results. Does the normal distribution yield a good approximation of the actual results?

    b. The mean distance from the center of the city is 14.629 miles with a standard deviation of 4.874 miles. Use the normal distribution to estimate the number of homes 18 or more miles but less than 22 miles from the center of the city. Compare this to the actual results. Does the normal distribution yield a good approximation of the actual results?

67. Refer to the Baseball 2007 data, which report information on the 30 Major League Baseball teams for the 2007 season.

    a. The mean attendance per team for the season was 2,650,000 with a standard deviation of 733,000. Use the normal distribution to estimate the number of teams with attendance of more than 3.5 million. Compare that estimate with the actual number. Comment on the accuracy of your estimate.

    b. The mean team salary was $83.16 million with a standard deviation of $33.47 million. Use the normal distribution to estimate the number of teams with a team salary of more than $50 million. Compare that estimate with the actual number. Comment on the accuracy of the estimate.

68. Refer to the CIA data, which report demographic and economic information on 46 countries.

    a. The mean of the GDP/capita variable is 16.58 with a standard deviation of 9.27. Use the normal distribution to estimate the percentage of countries with exports above 24. Compare this estimate with the actual proportion. Does the normal distribution appear accurate in this case? Explain.

    b. The mean of the exports is 116.3 with a standard deviation of 157.4. Use the normal distribution to estimate the percentage of countries with exports above 170. Compare this estimate with the actual proportion. Does the normal distribution appear accurate in this case? Explain.

Software Commands

1. The Excel commands necessary to produce the output on page 231 are:

    a. Click on the **Formulas** tab in the top menu, then, on the far left, select **Insert Function fx.** Then from the category box select **Statistical** and below that **NORMDIST** and click **OK.**

    b. In the dialog box put *1100* in the box for **X**, *1000* for the **Mean**, *100* for the **Standard_dev**, *True* in the **Cumulative** box, and click **OK.**

    c. The result will appear in the dialog box. If you click **OK,** the answer appears in your spreadsheet.

2. The Excel Commands necessary to produce the output on page 237 are:

    a. Click the **Formulas** tab in the top menu, then, on the far left, select **Insert Function fx.** Then from

the category box select **Statistical** and below that **NORMINV** and click **OK.**

    b. In the dialog box, set the **Probability** to *.04*, the **Mean** to *67900,* and the **Standard_dev** to *2050.*

    c. The results will appear in the dialog box. Note that the answer is different from page 236 because of rounding error. If you click **OK,** the answer also appears in your spreadsheet.

    d. Try entering a **Probability** of *.04*, a **Mean** of *0*, and a **Standard_dev** of *1*. The z value will be computed.

Chapter 7   Answers to Self-Review

7–1 **a.**

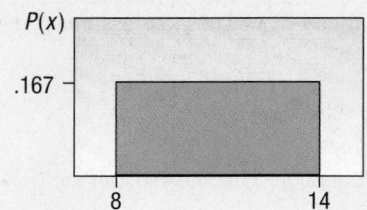

b. $P(x) = (\text{height})(\text{base})$

$$= \left(\frac{1}{14 - 8}\right)(14 - 8)$$

$$= \left(\frac{1}{6}\right)(6) = 1.00$$

c. $\mu = \dfrac{a + b}{2} = \dfrac{14 + 8}{2} = \dfrac{22}{2} = 11$

$\sigma = \sqrt{\dfrac{(b - a)^2}{12}} = \sqrt{\dfrac{(14 - 8)^2}{12}} = \sqrt{\dfrac{36}{12}} = \sqrt{3}$

$= 1.73$

d. $P(10 < x < 14) = (\text{height})(\text{base})$

$$= \left(\frac{1}{14 - 8}\right)(14 - 10)$$

$$= \frac{1}{6}(4)$$

$$= .667$$

e. $P(x < 9) = (\text{height})(\text{base})$

$$= \left(\frac{1}{14 - 8}\right)(9 - 8)$$

$$= 0.167$$

7–2 **a.** 2.25, found by:

$$z = \frac{\$1,225 - \$1,000}{\$100} = \frac{\$225}{\$100} = 2.25$$

b. -2.25, found by:

$$z = \frac{\$775 - \$1,000}{\$100} = \frac{-\$225}{\$100} = -2.25$$

7–3 **a.** $46,400 and $48,000, found by $47,200 ± 1($800).

b. $45,600 and $48,800, found by $47,200 ± 2($800).

c. $44,800 and $49,600, found by $47,200 ± 3($800).

d. $47,200. The mean, median, and mode are equal for a normal distribution.

e. Yes, a normal distribution is symmetrical.

7–4 **a.** Computing *z*:

$$z = \frac{482 - 400}{50} = +1.64$$

Referring to Appendix B.1, the area is .4495.
$P(400 < \text{rating} < 482) = .4495$

b. .0505, found by .5000 − .4495
$P(\text{rating} > 482) = .5000 - .4495 = .0505$

c.

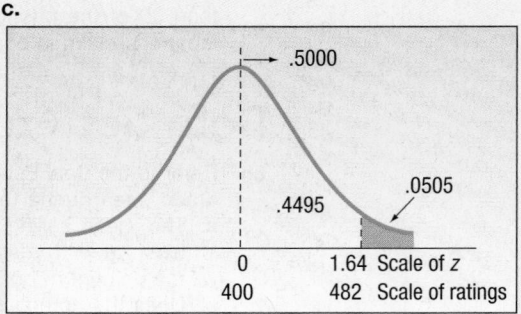

7–5 **a.** .9816, found by 0.4938 + 0.4878.

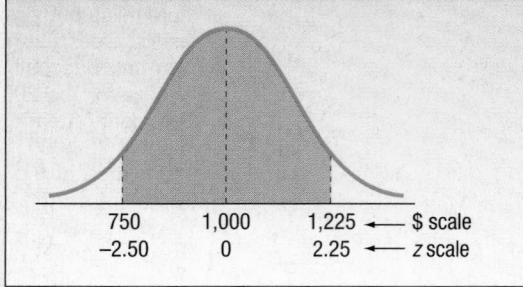

b. .1465, found by 0.4878 − 0.3413.

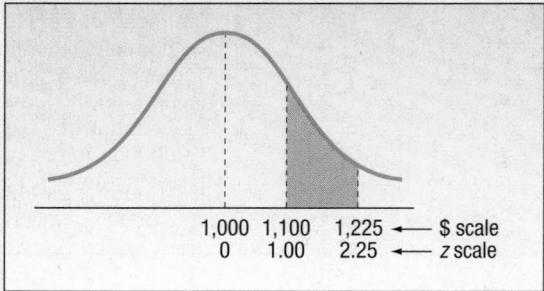

7–6 85.24 (instructor would no doubt make it 85). The closest area to .4000 is .3997; *z* is 1.28. Then:

$$1.28 = \frac{X - 75}{8}$$

$$10.24 = X - 75$$

$$X = 85.24$$

7–7 **a.** .0465, found by $\mu = n\pi = 200(.80) = 160$, and $\sigma^2 = n\pi(1 - \pi) = 200(.80)(1 - .80) = 32$. Then, $\sigma = \sqrt{32} = 5.66$

$$z = \frac{169.5 - 160}{5.66} = 1.68$$

Area from Appendix B.1 is .4535. Subtracting from .5000 gives .0465.

b. .9686, found by .4686 + .5000. First calculate *z*:

$$z = \frac{149.5 - 160}{5.66} = -1.86$$

Area from Appendix B.1 is .4686.

A Review of Chapters 5–7

This section is a review of the major concepts, terms, symbols, and equations introduced in Chapters 5, 6, and 7. These three chapters are concerned with methods of dealing with uncertainty. As an example of the uncertainty in business, consider the role of the quality assurance department in most mass-production firms. Usually, the department has neither the personnel nor the time to check, say, all 200 plug-in modules produced during a two-hour period. Standard operating procedure may call for selecting a sample of 5 modules and shipping all 200 modules if the 5 operate correctly. However, if 1 or more in the sample are defective, all 200 are checked. Assuming that all 5 function correctly, quality assurance personnel cannot be absolutely certain that their action (allowing shipment of the modules) will prove to be correct. The study of probability allows us to measure the uncertainty of shipping defective modules. Also, probability as a measurement of uncertainty comes into play when Gallup, Harris, and other pollsters predict that Jim Barstow will win the vacant senatorial seat in Georgia.

Chapter 5 notes that a *probability* is a value between 0 and 1, inclusive, that expresses the likelihood a particular event will occur. A weather forecaster might state that the probability of rain tomorrow is .20. The project director of a firm bidding on a subway station in Bangkok might assess the firm's chance of being awarded the contract at .50. We look at the ways probabilities can be combined using rules of addition and multiplication, some principles of counting, and the importance of Bayes' theorem.

Chapter 6 presents *discrete* probability distributions—the *binomial distribution*, the *hypergeometric distribution*, and the *Poisson distribution*. Other probability distributions will be discussed in forthcoming chapters (*t* distribution, chi-square distribution, etc.). Probability distributions are listings of all the possible outcomes of an experiment and the probability associated with each outcome.

Chapter 7 describes two continuous probability distributions—the *uniform probability distribution* and the *normal probability distribution*. The uniform probability distribution is rectangular in shape and is defined by a minimum and maximum value. The mean and the median of a uniform probability distribution are equal, and it does not have a mode.

A normal probability distribution is used to describe phenomena that follow a normal bell-shaped distribution, such as the tensile strength of wires and the weights or volumes of cans and bottles. Actually, there is a family of normal probability distributions—each with its own mean and standard deviation. There is a normal probability distribution, for example, for a mean of $100 and a standard deviation of $5, another for a mean of $149 and a standard deviation of $5.26, and so on. A normal probability distribution is symmetrical about its mean, and the tails of the normal curve extend in either direction infinitely.

There are an unlimited number of normal probability distributions, so the number of tables such as B.1 would be very large. Instead of using a large number of tables, we convert a normal distribution to a *standard normal probability distribution* by computing the *z value*. The standard normal probability distribution has a mean of 0 and a standard deviation of 1. It is useful because the probability for any event from a normal probability distribution can be computed using standard normal probability tables.

Glossary

Chapter 5

Bayes' theorem Developed by Reverend Bayes in the 1700s, it is designed to find the probability of one event, *A*, occurring, given that another event, *B*, has already occurred.

Classical probability Probability based on the assumption that each of the outcomes is equally likely. According to this concept of probability, if there are *n* possible outcomes, the probability of a particular outcome is $1/n$. Thus, on the toss of a coin, the probability of a head is $1/n = 1/2$.

Combination formula A formula to count the number of possible outcomes when the order of the outcomes is not important. If the order *a*, *b*, *c* is considered the same as *b*, *a*, *c*, or *c*, *b*, *a*, and so on, the number of arrangements is found by:

$$_nC_r = \frac{n!}{r!(n-r)!}$$

Conditional probability The likelihood that an event will occur given that another event has already occurred.

Empirical probability A concept of probability based on past experience. For example, Metropolitan Life Insurance Company reported that, during the year, 100.2 of every 100,000 persons in Wyoming died of accidental causes (motor vehicle accidents, falls, drowning, firearms, etc.). On the basis of this experience, Metropolitan can estimate the probability of accidental death for a particular person in Wyoming: $100.2/100,000 = .001002$.

Event A collection of one or more outcomes of an experiment. For example, an event is the collection of even numbers in the roll of a fair die.

Experiment An activity that is either observed or measured. An experiment may be counting the number of correct responses to a question, for example.

General rule of addition   Used to find the probabilities of complex events made up of A or B when the events are *not* mutually exclusive.

$$P(A \text{ or } B) = P(A) + P(B) - P(A \text{ and } B)$$

General rule of multiplication   Used to find the probabilities of events A and B both happening when the events are not independent. Example: It is known that there are 3 defective radios in a box containing 10 radios. What is the probability of selecting 2 defective radios on the first two selections from the box?

$$P(A \text{ and } B) = P(A)P(B \mid A) = \frac{3}{10} \times \frac{2}{9} = \frac{6}{90} = .067$$

where $P(B|A)$ is the conditional probability and means "the probability of B occurring given that A has already occurred."

Independent   The probability of one event has no effect on the probability of another event.

Multiplication formula   One of the formulas used to count the number of possible outcomes of an experiment. It states that if there are m ways of doing one thing and n ways of doing another, there are $m \times n$ ways of doing both. Example: A men's clothier offers two sport coats and three contrasting pants for $400. How many different outfits can there be? Answer: $m \times n = 2 \times 3 = 6$.

Mutually exclusive   The occurrence of one event means that none of the other events can occur at the same time.

Outcome   A particular observation or measurement of an experiment.

Permutation formula   A formula to count the number of possible outcomes when the order of the outcomes is important. If a, b, c is one arrangement, b, a, c another, c, a, b another, and so on, the total number of arrangements is determined by

$$_nP_r = \frac{n!}{(n - r)!}$$

Probability   A value between 0 and 1, inclusive, that reports the likelihood that a specific event will occur.

Special rule of addition   For this rule to apply, the events must be mutually exclusive. For two events, the probability of A or B occurring is found by:

$$P(A \text{ or } B) = P(A) + P(B)$$

Example: The probability of a one-spot or a two-spot occurring on the toss of one die.

$$P(A \text{ or } B) = \frac{1}{6} + \frac{1}{6} = \frac{2}{6} = \frac{1}{3}$$

Special rule of multiplication   If two events are not related—that is, they are independent—this rule is applied to determine the probability of their joint occurrence.

$$P(A \text{ and } B) = P(A)P(B)$$

Example: The probability of two heads on two tosses of a coin is:

$$P(A \text{ and } B) = P(A)P(B) = \frac{1}{2} \times \frac{1}{2} = \frac{1}{4}$$

Subjective probability   The chance of an event happening based on whatever information is available—hunches, personal opinion, opinions of others, rumors, and so on.

Chapter 6

Binomial probability distribution   A probability distribution based on a discrete random variable. Its major characteristics are:

1. Each outcome can be classified into one of two mutually exclusive categories.
2. The distribution is the result of counting the number of successes.
3. Each trial is independent, meaning that the answer to trial 1 (correct or wrong) in no way affects the answer to trial 2.
4. The probability of a success stays the same from trial to trial.

Continuous random variable   A random variable that may assume an infinite number of values within a given range.

Discrete random variable   A random variable that can assume only certain separate values.

Hypergeometric probability distribution   A probability distribution based on a discrete random variable. Its major characteristics are:

1. There is a fixed number of trials.
2. The probability of success is not the same from trial to trial.
3. There are only two possible outcomes.

Poisson distribution   A distribution often used to approximate binomial probabilities when n is large and π is small. What is considered "large" or "small" is not precisely defined, but a general rule is that n should be equal to or greater than 20 and π equal to or less than .05.

Probability distribution   A listing of the possible outcomes of an experiment and the probability associated with each outcome.

Random variable   A quantity obtained from an experiment that may, by chance, result in different values. For example, a count of the number of accidents (the experiment) on I-75 during a week might be 10, or 11, or 12, or some other number.

Chapter 7

Continuity correction factor   Used to improve the accuracy of the approximation of a discrete distribution by a continuous distribution.

Normal probability distribution   A continuous distribution that is bell-shaped, with the mean dividing the distribution into two equal parts. Further, the normal curve extends indefinitely in either direction, and it never touches the X-axis. The distribution is defined by its mean and standard deviation.

Uniform probability distribution   A continuous probability distribution that is rectangular in shape. It is completely described by using the minimum and maximum values of the distribution to compute the mean and standard deviation. Also, minimum and maximum values are used to compute the probability for any event.

z value   The distance between a selected value and the mean measured in units of the standard deviation.

Exercises

connect

Part I—Multiple Choice

1. Which of the following is *not* a correct statement about a probability?
   a. It must have a value between 0 and 1.
   b. It can be reported as a decimal or a fraction.
   c. A value near 0 means the event is not likely to happen.
   d. It is the collection of several experiments.
2. The collection of one or more outcomes from an experiment is called a/an
   a. Event.
   b. Probability.
   c. Random variable.
   d. *z* value.
3. If the occurrence of one event means that another cannot happen, the events are
   a. Independent.
   b. Mutually exclusive.
   c. Bayesian.
   d. Empirical.
4. Under which approach to probability are the outcomes equally likely?
   a. Classical.
   b. Subjective.
   c. Relative frequency.
   d. Independent.
5. To apply the special rule of addition, the events are always
   a. Independent.
   b. Mutually exclusive.
   c. Bayesian.
   d. Empirical.
6. A joint probability is
   a. The likelihood of two events happening.
   b. The likelihood of an event happening given another event has already happened.
   c. Based on two mutually exclusive events.
   d. Also called a prior probability.
7. To apply the special rule of multiplication, the events are always
   a. Independent.
   b. Mutually exclusive.
   c. Bayesian.
   d. Empirical.
8. A table used to classify sample observations according to two criteria is called a:
   a. Probability table.
   b. Contingency table.
   c. Bayesian table.
   d. Scatter diagram
9. A listing of the possible outcomes of an experiment and the corresponding probability is called a
   a. Random variable.
   b. Contingency table.
   c. Probability distribution.
   d. Frequency distribution.
10. Which of the following is *not* an example of a discrete probability distribution?
    a. The purchase price of a house.
    b. The number of bedrooms in a house.
    c. The number of bathrooms in a house.
    d. Whether or not a home has a swimming pool.
11. In a Poisson probability distribution
    a. The mean and variance of the distribution are equal.
    b. The probability of a success is always greater than .5.
    c. The number of trials is always less than 5.
    d. It always contains a contingency table.
12. Which of the following statements is *not* correct regarding the normal probability distribution?
    a. It is defined by its mean and standard deviation.
    b. The mean and median are equal.

c. It is symmetric.

d. It is based on only two observations.

Part II—Problems

13. It is claimed that Proactine, a new medicine for acne, is 80 percent effective. It is applied to the affected area of a sample of 15 people. What is the probability that:

   a. All 15 will show significant improvement?

   b. Fewer than 9 of 15 will show significant improvement?

   c. That 12 or more people will show significant improvement?

14. First National Bank thoroughly investigates its applicants for small home-improvement loans. Its default record is very impressive: The probability that a homeowner will default is only .005. The bank has approved 400 small home-improvement loans. Assuming the Poisson probability distribution applies to this problem:

   a. What is the probability that no homeowners out of the 400 will default?

   b. How many of the 400 are expected not to default?

   c. What is the probability that 3 or more homeowners will default on their small home-improvement loans?

15. A study of the attendance at the University of Alabama's basketball games revealed that the distribution of attendance is normally distributed with a mean of 10,000 and a standard deviation of 2,000.

   a. What is the probability a particular game has an attendance of 13,500 or more?

   b. What percent of the games have an attendance between 8,000 and 11,500?

   c. Ten percent of the games have an attendance of how many or less?

16. Daniel-James Insurance Company will insure an offshore Mobil Oil production platform against weather losses for one year. The president of Daniel-James estimates the following losses for that platform (in millions of dollars) with the accompanying probabilities:

Amount of Loss ($ millions)	Probability of Loss
0	.98
40	.016
300	.004

   a. What is the expected amount Daniel-James will have to pay to Mobil in claims?

   b. What is the likelihood that Daniel-James will actually lose less than the expected amount?

   c. Given that Daniel-James suffers a loss, what is the likelihood that it is for $300 million?

   d. Daniel-James has set the annual premium at $2.0 million. Does that seem like a fair premium?

   Will it cover its risk?

17. The distribution of the number of school-age children per family in the Whitehall Estates area of Boise, Idaho, is:

Number of children	0	1	2	3	4
Percent of families	40	30	15	10	5

   a. Determine the mean and standard deviation of the number of school-age children per family in Whitehall Estates.

   b. A new school is planned in Whitehall Estates. An estimate of the number of school-age children is needed. There are 500 family units. How many children would you estimate?

   c. Some additional information is needed about only the families having children. Convert the preceding distribution to one for families with children. What is the mean number of children among families that have children?

18. The following table shows a breakdown of the 110th U.S. Congress by party affiliation.

	Party		
	Democrats	**Republicans**	**Total**
House	236	199	435
Senate	48	52	100
Total	284	251	535

a. A member of Congress is selected at random. What is the probability of selecting a Republican?

b. Given that the person selected is a member of the House of Representatives, what is the probability he or she is a Republican?

c. What is the probability of selecting a member of the House of Representatives or a Democrat?

Cases

A. Century National Bank

Refer to the Century National Bank data. Is it reasonable that the distribution of checking account balances approximates a normal probability distribution? Determine the mean and the standard deviation for the sample of 60 customers. Compare the actual distribution with the theoretical distribution. Cite some specific examples and comment on your findings.

Divide the account balances into three groups, of about 20 each, with the smallest third of the balances in the first group, the middle third in the second group, and those with the largest balances in the third group. Next, develop a table that shows the number in each of the categories of the account balances by branch. Does it appear that account balances are related to the branch? Cite some examples and comment on your findings.

B. Elections Auditor

An item such as an increase in taxes, recall of elected officials, or an expansion of public services can be placed on the ballot if a required number of valid signatures are collected on the petition. Unfortunately, many people will sign the petition even though they are not registered to vote in that particular district, or they will sign the petition more than once.

Sara Ferguson, the elections auditor in Venango County, must certify the validity of these signatures after the petition is officially presented. Not surprisingly, her staff is overloaded, so she is considering using statistical methods to validate the pages of 200 signatures, instead of validating each individual signature. At a recent professional meeting, she found that, in some communities in the state, election officials were checking only five signatures on each page and rejecting the entire page if two or more signatures were invalid. Some people are concerned that five may not be enough to make a good decision. They suggest that you should check 10 signatures and reject the page if three or more are invalid.

In order to investigate these methods, Sara asks her staff to pull the results from the last election and sample 30 pages. It happens that the staff selected 14 pages from the Avondale district, 9 pages from the Midway district,

and 7 pages from the Kingston district. Each page had 200 signatures, and the data below show the number of invalid signatures on each.

Use the data to evaluate Sara's two proposals. Calculate the probability of rejecting a page under each of the approaches. Would you get about the same results by examining every single signature? Offer a plan of your own, and discuss how it might be better or worse than the two plans proposed by Sara.

Avondale	Midway	Kingston
9	19	38
14	22	39
11	23	41
8	14	39
14	22	41
6	17	39
10	15	39
13	20	
8	18	
8		
9		
12		
7		
13		

C. Geoff "Applies" His Education

Geoff Brown is the manager for a small telemarketing firm and is evaluating the sales rate of experienced workers in order to set minimum standards for new hires. During the past few weeks, he has recorded the number of successful calls per hour for the staff. These data appear below along with some summary statistics he worked out with a statistical software package. Geoff has been a student at the local community college and has heard of many different kinds of probability distributions (binomial, normal, hypergeometric, Poisson, etc.). Could you give Geoff some advice on which distribution to use to fit these data as well as possible and how to decide when a probationary employee should be accepted as having reached full production status? This is important because it means a pay raise for the employee, and there have been some probationary employees in the past who have quit because of discouragement that they would never meet the standard.

Successful sales calls per hour during the week of August 14:

4	2	3	1	4	5	5	2	3	2	2	4	5	2	5	3	3	0
1	3	2	8	4	5	2	2	4	1	5	5	4	5	1	2	4	

Descriptive statistics:

N	MEAN	MEDIAN	TRMEAN	STDEV	SEMEAN
35	3.229	3.000	3.194	1.682	0.284
MIN	MAX	Q1	Q3		
0.0	8.000	2.000	5.000		

Which distribution do you think Geoff should use for his analysis?

D. CNP Bank Card

Before banks issue a credit card, they usually rate or score the customer in terms of his or her projected probability of being a profitable customer. A typical scoring table appears below.

Age	Under 25 (12 pts.)	25–29 (5 pts.)	30–34 (0 pts.)	35+ (18 pts.)
Time at same address	<1 yr. (9 pts.)	1–2 yrs. (0 pts.)	3–4 yrs. (13 pts.)	5+ yrs. (20 pts.)
Auto age	None (18 pts.)	0–1yr. (12 pts.)	2–4 yrs. (13 pts.)	5+ yrs. (3 pts.)
Monthly car payment	None (15 pts.)	$1–$99 (6 pts.)	$100–$299 (4 pts.)	$300+ (0 pts.)
Housing cost	$1–$199 (0 pts.)	$200–$399 (10 pts.)	Owns (12 pts.)	Lives with relatives (24 pts.)
Checking/ savings accounts	Both (15 pts.)	Checking only (3 pts.)	Savings only (2 pts.)	Neither (0 pts.)

The score is the sum of the points on the six items. For example, Sushi Brown is under 25 years old (12 pts.), has lived at the same address for 2 years (0 pts.), owns a 4-year-old car (13 pts.), with car payments of $75 (6 pts.), housing cost of $200 (10 pts.), and a checking account (3 pts.). She would score 44.

A second chart is then used to convert scores into the probability of being a profitable customer. A sample chart of this type appears below.

Score	30	40	50	60	70	80	90
Probability	.70	.78	.85	.90	.94	.95	.96

Sushi's score of 44 would translate into a probability of being profitable of approximately .81. In other words 81 percent of customers like Sushi will make money for the bank card operations.

Here are the interview results for three potential customers.

Name	David Born	Edward Brendan	Ann McLaughlin
Age	42	23	33
Time at same address	9	2	5
Auto age	2	3	7
Monthly car payment	$140	$99	$175
Housing cost	$300	$200	Owns clear
Checking/savings accounts	Both	Checking only	Neither

1. Score each of these customers and estimate their probability of being profitable.
2. What is the probability that all three are profitable?
3. What is the probability that none of them are profitable?
4. Find the entire probability distribution for the number of profitable customers among this group of three.
5. Write a brief summary of your findings.

Practice Test

Part I—Objective

1. Under what conditions will a probability be greater than 1 or 100 percent?
   1. _____
2. An _____ is the observation of some activity or the act of taking some type of measurement.
   2. _____
3. An _____ is the collection of one or more outcomes to an experiment.
   3. _____
4. A _____ probability is the likelihood that two or more events will happen at the same time.
   4. _____

5. In a (5a) _____ the order in which the events are counted is important, but in a (5b) _____ it is not important.

                            5. a. _____

                            5. b. _____

6. In a discrete probability distribution, the sum of the possible outcomes is equal to _____.

                            6. _____

7. Which of the following is *NOT* a requirement of the binomial distribution? (constant probability of success, three or more outcomes, the result of counts)   **7.** _____

8. How many normal distributions are there? (1, 10, 30, 1,000, or infinite—pick one)

                            8. _____

9. How many standard normal distributions are there? (1, 10, 30, 1,000, or infinite—pick one)

                            9. _____

10. What is the probability of finding a z value between 0 and -0.76?

                            10. _____

11. What is the probability of finding a z value greater than 1.67?   **11.** _____

12. Two events are _____ if the occurrence of one event does not affect the occurrence of another event.

                            12. _____

13. Two event are _____ if by virtue of one event happening the other cannot happen.

                            13. _____

14. Which of the following is not true regarding the normal probability distribution? (asymptotic, family of distributions, only two outcomes, 50 percent of the observations greater than the mean)

                            14. _____

15. Which of the following statements best describes the shape of a normal probability distribution? (bell-shaped, uniform, V-shaped, no constant shape)   **15.** _____

Part II—Problems

1. Fred Frendly, CPA, has 20 tax returns to prepare before the April 15th deadline. It is late at night so he decides to do two more before going home. In his stack of accounts 12 are personal, 5 businesses, and 3 for charitable organizations. If he selects the two returns at random, what is the probability:
   a. Both are business?
   b. At least one is business?

2. The IRS reports that 15 percent of returns where the adjusted gross income is more than $1,000,000 will be subject to a computer audit. For the year 2008 Fred Friendly, CPA, completed 16 returns where the adjusted gross income was more than $1,000,000.
   a. What is the probability exactly one of these returns will be audited?
   b. What is the probability at least one will be audited?

3. Fred works in a tax office with five other CPAs. There are five parking spots beside the office. In how many different ways can the cars belonging to the CPAs be arranged in the five spots? Assume they all drive to work.

4. Fred decided to study the number of exemptions claimed on personal tax returns he prepared in 2007. The data are summarized in the following table.

Exemptions	Percent
1	20
2	50
3	20
4	10

   a. What is the mean number of exemptions per return?
   b. What is the variance of the number of exemptions per return?

5. In a memo to all those involved in tax preparation, the IRS indicated that the mean amount of refund was $1,600 with a standard deviation of $850. Assume the distribution of the amounts returned follows the normal distribution.
   a. What percent of the refunds were between $1,600 and $2,000?
   b. What percent of the refunds were between $900 and $2,000?
   c. According to the above information, what percent of the refunds were less than $0. That is, the taxpayer owed the IRS.

6. For the year 2008, Fred Friendly completed a total of 80 returns. He developed the following table summarizing the relationship between number of dependents and whether or not the client received a refund.

Refund	Dependents			Total
	1	2	3 or more	
Yes	20	20	10	50
No	10	20	0	30
Total	30	40	10	80

    a. What is the name given to this table?
    b. What is the probability of selecting a client who received a refund?
    c. What is the probability of selecting a client who received a refund or had one dependent?
    d. Given that the client received a refund, what is the probability he or she had one dependent?
    e. What is the probability of selecting a client who did *not* receive a refund and had one dependent?

7. The IRS offers taxpayers the choice of allowing the IRS to compute the amount of their tax refund. During the busy filing season, the number of returns received at the Springfield Service Center which request this service follows a Poisson distribution with a mean of three per day. What is the probability that on a particular day:
    a. There are no requests?
    b. Exactly three requests appear?
    c. Five or more requests take place?

Sampling Methods and the Central Limit Theorem

The Nike annual report says that the average American buys 6.5 pairs of sports shoes per year. Suppose the population standard deviation is 2.1 and that a sample of 81 customers will be examined next year. What is the standard error of the mean in this experiment? (See Goal 5 and Exercise 45.)

Introduction

Chapters 2 through 4 emphasize techniques to describe data. To illustrate these techniques, we organize the prices for the 80 vehicles sold last month at Whitner Autoplex into a frequency distribution and compute various measures of location and dispersion. Such measures as the mean and the standard deviation describe the typical selling price and the spread in the selling prices. In these chapters the emphasis is on describing the condition of the data. That is, we describe something that has already happened.

Chapter 5 starts to lay the foundation for statistical inference with the study of probability. Recall that in statistical inference our goal is to determine something about a *population* based only on the *sample*. The population is the entire group of individuals or objects under consideration, and the sample is a part or subset of that population. Chapter 6 extends the probability concepts by describing three discrete probability distributions: the binomial, the hypergeometric, and the Poisson. Chapter 7 describes the uniform probability distribution and the normal probability distribution. Both of these are continuous distributions. Probability distributions encompass all possible outcomes of an experiment and the probability associated with each outcome. We use probability distributions to evaluate the likelihood something occurs in the future.

This chapter begins our study of sampling. Sampling is a tool to infer something about a population. We begin this chapter by discussing methods of selecting a sample from a population. Next, we construct a distribution of the sample mean to understand how the sample means tend to cluster around the population mean. Finally, we show that for any population the shape of this sampling distribution tends to follow the normal probability distribution.

Sampling Methods

In Chapter 1, we said the purpose of inferential statistics is to find something about a population based on a sample. A sample is a portion or part of the population of interest. In many cases, sampling is more feasible than studying the entire population. In this section, we discuss the major reasons for sampling, and then several methods for selecting a sample.

Reasons to Sample

When studying characteristics of a population, there are many practical reasons why we prefer to select portions or samples of a population to observe and measure. Here are some of the reasons for sampling:

1. **To contact the whole population would be time consuming.** A candidate for a national office may wish to determine her chances for election. A sample poll using the regular staff and field interviews of a professional polling firm would take only 1 or 2 days. Using the same staff and interviewers and working 7 days a week, it would take nearly 200 years to contact all the voting population! Even if a large staff of interviewers could be assembled, the benefit of contacting all of the voters would probably not be worth the time.
2. **The cost of studying all the items in a population may be prohibitive.** Public opinion polls and consumer testing organizations, such as Gallup Polls and Harris Polls, usually contact fewer than 2,000 of the nearly 60 million families in the United States. One consumer panel–type organization charges about $40,000 to mail samples and tabulate responses in order to test a product (such as breakfast cereal, cat food, or perfume). The same product test using all 60 million families would cost about $1 billion.

3. **The physical impossibility of checking all items in the population.** Some populations are infinite. It would be impossible to check all the water in Lake Erie for bacterial levels, so we select samples at various locations. The populations of fish, birds, snakes, mosquitoes, and the like are large and are constantly moving, being born, and dying. Instead of even attempting to count all the ducks in Canada or all the fish in Lake Pontchartrain, we make estimates using various techniques—such as counting all the ducks on a pond picked at random, making creel checks, or setting nets at predetermined places in the lake.

4. **The destructive nature of some tests.** If the wine tasters at the Sutter Home Winery in California drank all the wine to evaluate the vintage, they would consume the entire crop, and none would be available for sale. In the area of industrial production, steel plates, wires, and similar products must have a certain minimum tensile strength. To ensure that the product meets the minimum standard, the Quality Assurance Department selects a sample from the current production. Each piece is stretched until it breaks and the breaking point (usually measured in pounds per square inch) recorded. Obviously, if all the wire or all the plates were tested for tensile strength, none would be available for sale or use. For the same reason, only a few seeds are tested for germination by Burpee Seeds, Inc., prior to the planting season.

5. **The sample results are adequate.** Even if funds were available, it is doubtful the additional accuracy of a 100 percent sample—that is, studying the entire population—is essential in most problems. For example, the federal government uses a sample of grocery stores scattered throughout the United States to determine the monthly index of food prices. The prices of bread, beans, milk, and other major food items are included in the index. It is unlikely that the inclusion of all grocery stores in the United States would significantly affect the index, since the prices of milk, bread, and other major foods usually do not vary by more than a few cents from one chain store to another.

Simple Random Sampling

The most widely used type of sampling is a **simple random sample.**

> **SIMPLE RANDOM SAMPLE** A sample selected so that each item or person in the population has the same chance of being included.

To illustrate simple random sampling and selection, suppose a population consists of 845 employees of Nitra Industries. A sample of 52 employees is to be selected from that population. One way of ensuring that every employee in the population has the same chance of being chosen is to first write the name of each employee on a small slip of paper and deposit all of the slips in a box. After they have been thoroughly mixed, the first selection is made by drawing a slip out of the box without looking at it. This process is repeated until the sample of 52 employees is chosen.

A table of random numbers is an efficient way to select members of the sample.

A more convenient method of selecting a random sample is to use the identification number of each employee and a **table of random numbers** such as the one in Appendix B.6. As the name implies, these numbers have been generated by a random process (in this case, by a computer). For each digit of a number, the probability of 0, 1, 2, . . . , 9 is the same. Thus, the probability that employee

Statistics in Action

Is discrimination taking a bite out of your paycheck? Before you answer, consider a recent article in *Personnel Journal*. These findings indicate that attractive men and women earn about 5 percent more than average lookers, who in turn earn about 5 percent more than their plain counterparts. This is true for both men and women. It is also true for a wide range of occupations, from construction work to auto repair to telemarketing, occupations for which it would seem that looks would not matter.

number 011 will be selected is the same as for employee 722 or employee 382. By using random numbers to select employees, bias is eliminated from the selection process.

A portion of a table of random numbers is shown in the following illustration. To select a sample of employees, you first choose a starting point in the table. Any starting point will do. Suppose the time is 3:04. You might look at the third column and then move down to the fourth set of numbers. The number is 03759. Since there are only 845 employees, we will use the first three digits of a five-digit random number. Thus, 037 is the number of the first employee to be a member of the sample. Another way of selecting the starting point is to close your eyes and point at a number in the table. To continue selecting employees, you could move in any direction. Suppose you move right. The first three digits of the number to the right of 03759 are 447—the number of the employee selected to be the second member of the sample. The next three-digit number to the right is 961. You skip 961 because there are only 845 employees. You continue to the right and select employee 784, then 189, and so on.

5 0 5 2 5	5 7 4 5 4	2 8 4 5 5	6 8 2 2 6	3 4 6 5 6	3 8 8 8 4	3 9 0 1 8
7 2 5 0 7	5 3 3 8 0	5 3 8 2 7	4 2 4 8 6	5 4 4 6 5	7 1 8 1 9	9 1 1 9 9
3 4 9 8 6	7 4 2 9 7	0 0 1 4 4	3 8 6 7 6	8 9 9 6 7	9 8 8 6 9	3 9 7 4 4
6 8 8 5 1	2 7 3 0 5	0 3 7 5 9	4 4 7 2 3	9 6 1 0 8	7 8 4 8 9	1 8 9 1 0
0 6 7 3 8	6 2 8 7 9	0 3 9 1 0	1 7 3 5 0	4 9 1 6 9	0 3 8 5 0	1 8 9 1 0
1 1 4 4 8	1 0 7 3 4	0 5 8 3 7	2 4 3 9 7	1 0 4 2 0	1 6 7 1 2	9 4 4 9 6

| | | Starting point | Second employee | | Third employee | Fourth employee |

Most statistical software packages have available a routine that will select a simple random sample. The following example uses the Excel System to select a random sample.

Example

Jane and Joe Miley operate the Foxtrot Inn, a bed and breakfast in Tryon, North Carolina. There are eight rooms available for rent at this B&B. Listed below is the number of these eight rooms rented each day during June 2008. Use Excel to select a sample of five nights during the month of June.

June	Rentals	June	Rentals	June	Rentals
1	0	11	3	21	3
2	2	12	4	22	2
3	3	13	4	23	3
4	2	14	4	24	6
5	3	15	7	25	0
6	4	16	0	26	4
7	2	17	5	27	1
8	3	18	3	28	1
9	4	19	6	29	3
10	7	20	2	30	3

Solution

Excel will select the random sample and report the results. On the first sampled date there were four of the eight rooms rented. On the second sampled date in June, seven of the eight rooms were rented. The information is reported in column D of the Excel spreadsheet. The Excel steps are listed in the **Software Commands** section at the end of the chapter. The Excel system performs the sampling *with* replacement. This means it is possible for the same day to appear more than once in a sample.

	A	B	C	D	E
	June	Rentals		Sample	
1	June	Rentals		Sample	
2	1	0		4	
3	2	2		7	
4	3	3		4	
5	4	2		3	
6	5	3		1	
7	6	4			
8	7	2			
9	8	3			
10	9	4			
11	10	7			
12	11	3			
13	12	4			
14	13	4			
15	14	4			

Num 1 one sample

Self-Review 8–1

The following class roster lists the students enrolling in an introductory course in business statistics. Three students are to be randomly selected and asked various questions regarding course content and method of instruction.

(a) The numbers 00 through 45 are handwritten on slips of paper and placed in a bowl. The three numbers selected are 31, 7, and 25. Which students would be included in the sample?

(b) Now use the table of random digits, Appendix B.6, to select your own sample.

(c) What would you do if you encountered the number 59 in the table of random digits?

CSPM 264 01 BUSINESS & ECONOMIC STAT
8:00 AM 9:40 AM MW ST 118 LIND D

RANDOM NUMBER	NAME	CLASS RANK	RANDOM NUMBER	NAME	CLASS RANK
00	ANDERSON, RAYMOND	SO	23	MEDLEY, CHERYL ANN	SO
01	ANGER, CHERYL RENEE	SO	24	MITCHELL, GREG R	FR
02	BALL, CLAIRE JEANETTE	FR	25	MOLTER, KRISTI MARIE	SO
03	BERRY, CHRISTOPHER G	FR	26	MULCAHY, STEPHEN ROBERT	SO
04	BOBAK, JAMES PATRICK	SO	27	NICHOLAS, ROBERT CHARLES	JR
05	BRIGHT, M. STARR	JR	28	NICKENS, VIRGINIA	SO
06	CHONTOS, PAUL JOSEPH	SO	29	PENNYWITT, SEAN PATRICK	SO
07	DETLEY, BRIAN HANS	JR	30	POTEAU, KRIS E	JR
08	DUDAS, VIOLA	SO	31	PRICE, MARY LYNETTE	SO
09	DULBS, RICHARD ZALFA	JR	32	RISTAS, JAMES	SR
10	EDINGER, SUSAN KEE	SR	33	SAGER, ANNE MARIE	SO
11	FINK, FRANK JAMES	SR	34	SMILLIE, HEATHER MICHELLE	SO
12	FRANCIS, JAMES P	JR	35	SNYDER, LEISHA KAY	SR
13	GAGHEN, PAMELA LYNN	JR	36	STAHL, MARIA TASHERY	SO
14	GOULD, ROBYN KAY	SO	37	ST. JOHN, AMY J	SO
15	GROSENBACHER, SCOTT ALAN	SO	38	STURDEVANT, RICHARD K	SO
16	HEETFIELD, DIANE MARIE	SO	39	SWETYE, LYNN MICHELE	SO
17	KABAT, JAMES DAVID	JR	40	WALASINSKI, MICHAEL	SO
18	KEMP, LISA ADRIANE	FR	41	WALKER, DIANE ELAINE	SO
19	KILLION, MICHELLE A	SO	42	WARNOCK, JENNIFER MARY	SO
20	KOPERSKI, MARY ELLEN	SO	43	WILLIAMS, WENDY A	SO
21	KOPP, BRIDGETTE ANN	SO	44	YAP, HOCK BAN	SO
22	LEHMANN, KRISTINA MARIE	JR	45	YODER, ARLAN JAY	JR

Systematic Random Sampling

The simple random sampling procedure may be awkward in some research situations. For example, suppose the sales division of Computer Graphic, Inc., needs to quickly estimate the mean dollar revenue per sale during the past month. It finds that 2,000 sales invoices were recorded and stored in file drawers, and decides to select 100 invoices to estimate the mean dollar revenue. Simple random sampling requires the numbering of each invoice before using the random number table to select the 100 invoices. The numbering process would be a very time-consuming task. Instead, we use **systematic random sampling.**

> **SYSTEMATIC RANDOM SAMPLE** A random starting point is selected, and then every kth member of the population is selected.

First, k is calculated as the population size divided by the sample size. For Computer Graphic, Inc., we would select every 20th (2,000/100) invoice from the file drawers; in so doing the numbering process is avoided. If k is not a whole number, then round down.

Random sampling is used in the selection of the first invoice. For example, a number from a random number table between 1 and k, or 20, would be selected. Say the random number was 18. Then, starting with the 18th invoice, every 20th invoice (18, 38, 58, etc.) would be selected as the sample.

Before using systematic random sampling, we should carefully observe the physical order of the population. When the physical order is related to the population characteristic, then systematic random sampling should not be used. For example, if the invoices in the example were filed in order of increasing sales, systematic random sampling would not guarantee a random sample. Other sampling methods should be used.

Stratified Random Sampling

When a population can be clearly divided into groups based on some characteristic, we may use **stratified random sampling.** It guarantees each group is represented in the sample. The groups are also called **strata.** For example, college students can be grouped as full time or part time, male or female, or traditional or nontraditional. Once the strata are defined, we can apply simple random sampling within each group or stratum to collect the sample.

> **STRATIFIED RANDOM SAMPLE** A population is divided into subgroups, called strata, and a sample is randomly selected from each stratum.

For instance, we might study the advertising expenditures for the 352 largest companies in the United States. Suppose the objective of the study is to determine whether firms with high returns on equity (a measure of profitability) spent more of each sales dollar on advertising than firms with a low return or deficit. To make sure that the sample is a fair representation of the 352 companies, the companies are grouped on percent return on equity. Table 8–1 shows the strata and the relative frequencies. If simple random sampling was used, observe that firms in the 3rd and 4th strata have a high chance of selection (probability of 0.87) while firms in the other strata have a low chance of selection (probability of 0.13). We might not select any firms in stratum 1 or 5 *simply by chance*. However, stratified random sampling will guarantee that at least one firm in strata 1 and 5 are represented in the sample. Let's say that 50 firms are selected for intensive study. Then 1 (0.02 × 50) firm from stratum 1 would be randomly selected, 5 (0.10 × 50) firms from stratum 2 would be randomly selected, and so on. In this case, the number of firms sampled from each stratum is proportional to the stratum's relative frequency in the population. Stratified sampling has the advantage, in

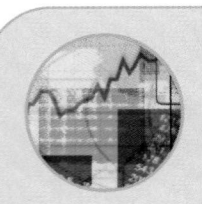

some cases, of more accurately reflecting the characteristics of the population than does simple random or systematic random sampling.

TABLE 8–1 Number Selected for a Proportional Stratified Random Sample

Stratum	Profitability (return on equity)	Number of Firms	Relative Frequency	Number Sampled
1	30 percent and over	8	0.02	1*
2	20 up to 30 percent	35	0.10	5*
3	10 up to 20 percent	189	0.54	27
4	0 up to 10 percent	115	0.33	16
5	Deficit	5	0.01	1
Total		352	1.00	50

*0.02 of 50 = 1, 0.10 of 50 = 5, etc.

Cluster Sampling

Another common type of sampling is **cluster sampling.** It is often employed to reduce the cost of sampling a population scattered over a large geographic area.

> **CLUSTER SAMPLE** A population is divided into clusters using naturally occurring geographic or other boundaries. Then, clusters are randomly selected and a sample is collected by randomly selecting from each cluster.

Suppose you want to determine the views of residents in Oregon about state and federal environmental protection policies. Selecting a random sample of residents in Oregon and personally contacting each one would be time consuming and very expensive. Instead, you could employ cluster sampling by subdividing the state into small units—either counties or regions. These are often called *primary units*.

Suppose you divided the state into 12 primary units, then selected at random four regions—2, 7, 4, and 12—and concentrated your efforts in these primary units. You could take a random sample of the residents in each of these regions and interview them. (Note that this is a combination of cluster sampling and simple random sampling.)

Many other sampling methods

The discussion of sampling methods in the preceding sections did not include all the sampling methods available to a researcher. Should you become involved in a major research project in marketing, finance, accounting, or other areas, you would need to consult books devoted solely to sample theory and sample design.

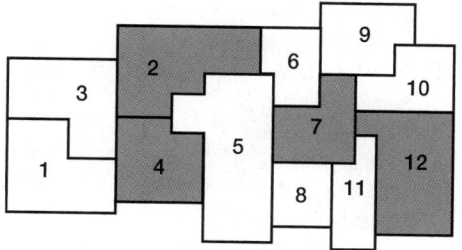

Self-Review 8–2

Refer to Self-Review 8–1 and the class roster on page 261. Suppose a systematic random sample will select every ninth student enrolled in the class. Initially, the fourth student on the list was selected at random. That student is numbered 03. Remembering that the random numbers start with 00, which students will be chosen to be members of the sample?

Exercises

connect™

1. The following is a list of Marco's Pizza stores in Lucas County. Also noted is whether the store is corporate-owned (C) or manager-owned (M). A sample of four locations is to be selected and inspected for customer convenience, safety, cleanliness, and other features.

ID No.	Address	Type	ID No.	Address	Type
00	2607 Starr Av	C	12	2040 Ottawa River Rd	C
01	309 W Alexis Rd	C	13	2116 N Reynolds Rd	C
02	2652 W Central Av	C	14	3678 Rugby Dr	C
03	630 Dixie Hwy	M	15	1419 South Av	C
04	3510 Dorr St	C	16	1234 W Sylvania Av	C
05	5055 Glendale Av	C	17	4624 Woodville Rd	M
06	3382 Lagrange St	M	18	5155 S Main	M
07	2525 W Laskey Rd	C	19	106 E Airport Hwy	C
08	303 Louisiana Av	C	20	6725 W Central	M
09	149 Main St	C	21	4252 Monroe	C
10	835 S McCord Rd	M	22	2036 Woodville Rd	C
11	3501 Monroe St	M	23	1316 Michigan Av	M

   a. The random numbers selected are 08, 18, 11, 54, 02, 41, and 54. Which stores are selected?
   b. Use the table of random numbers to select your own sample of locations.
   c. A sample is to consist of every seventh location. The number 03 is the starting point. Which locations will be included in the sample?
   d. Suppose a sample is to consist of three locations, of which two are corporate-owned and one is manager-owned. Select a sample accordingly.

2. The following is a list of hospitals in the Cincinnati (Ohio) and Northern Kentucky Region. Also included is whether the hospital is a general medical/surgical hospital (M/S) or a specialty hospital (S). We are interested in estimating the average number of full- and part-time nurses employed in the area hospitals.
   a. A sample of five hospitals is to be randomly selected. The random numbers are 09, 16, 00, 49, 54, 12, and 04. Which hospitals are included in the sample?
   b. Use a table of random numbers to develop your own sample of five hospitals.

ID Number	Name	Address	Type	ID Number	Name	Address	Type
00	Bethesda North	10500 Montgomery Cincinnati, Ohio 45242	M/S	10	Christ Hospital	2139 Auburn Avenue Cincinnati, Ohio 45219	M/S
01	Ft. Hamilton-Hughes	630 Eaton Avenue Hamilton, Ohio 45013	M/S	11	Deaconess Hospital	311 Straight Street Cincinnati, Ohio 45219	M/S
02	Jewish Hospital-Kenwood	4700 East Galbraith Rd. Cincinnati, Ohio 45236	M/S	12	Good Samaritan Hospital	375 Dixmyth Avenue Cincinnati, Ohio 45220	M/S
03	Mercy Hospital-Fairfield	3000 Mack Road Fairfield, Ohio 45014	M/S	13	Jewish Hospital	3200 Burnet Avenue Cincinnati, Ohio 45229	M/S
04	Mercy Hospital-Hamilton	100 Riverfront Plaza Hamilton, Ohio 45011	M/S	14	University Hospital	234 Goodman Street Cincinnati, Ohio 45267	M/S
05	Middletown Regional	105 McKnight Drive Middletown, Ohio 45044	M/S	15	Providence Hospital	2446 Kipling Avenue Cincinnati, Ohio 45239	M/S
06	Clermont Mercy Hospital	3000 Hospital Drive Batavia, Ohio 45103	M/S	16	St. Francis-St. George Hospital	3131 Queen City Avenue Cincinnati, Ohio 45238	M/S
07	Mercy Hospital-Anderson	7500 State Road Cincinnati, Ohio 45255	M/S	17	St. Elizabeth Medical Center, North Unit	401 E. 20th Street Covington, Kentucky 41014	M/S
08	Bethesda Oak Hospital	619 Oak Street Cincinnati, Ohio 45206	M/S	18	St. Elizabeth Medical Center, South Unit	One Medical Village Edgewood, Kentucky 41017	M/S
09	Children's Hospital Medical Center	3333 Burnet Avenue Cincinnati, Ohio 45229	M/S	19	St. Luke's Hospital West	7380 Turfway Drive Florence, Kentucky 41075	M/S

ID Number	Name	Address	Type	ID Number	Name	Address	Type
20	St. Luke's Hospital East	85 North Grand Avenue Ft. Thomas, Kentucky 41042	M/S	25	Drake Center Rehab— Long Term	151 W. Galbraith Road Cincinnati, Ohio 45216	S
21	Care Unit Hospital	3156 Glenmore Avenue Cincinnati, Ohio 45211	S	26	No. Kentucky Rehab Hospital—Short Term	201 Medical Village Edgewood, Kentucky	S
22	Emerson Behavioral Science	2446 Kipling Avenue Cincinnati, Ohio 45239	S	27	Shriners Burns Institute	3229 Burnet Avenue Cincinnati, Ohio 45229	S
23	Pauline Warfield Lewis Center for Psychiatric Treat.	1101 Summit Road Cincinnati, Ohio 45237	S	28	VA Medical Center	3200 Vine Cincinnati, Ohio 45220	S
24	Children's Psychiatric No. Kentucky	502 Farrell Drive Covington, Kentucky 41011	S				

    c. A sample is to consist of every fifth location. We select 02 as the starting point. Which hospitals will be included in the sample?

    d. A sample is to consist of four medical and surgical hospitals and one specialty hospital. Select an appropriate sample.

3. Listed below are the 35 members of the Metro Toledo Automobile Dealers Association. We would like to estimate the mean revenue from dealer service departments.

ID Number	Dealer	ID Number	Dealer	ID Number	Dealer
00	Dave White Acura	11	Thayer Chevrolet/Toyota	23	Kistler Ford, Inc.
01	Autofair Nissan	12	Spurgeon Chevrolet Motor Sales, Inc.	24	Lexus of Toledo
02	Autofair Toyota-Suzuki	13	Dunn Chevrolet	25	Mathews Ford Oregon, Inc.
03	George Ball's Buick GMC Truck	14	Don Scott Chevrolet-Pontiac	26	Northtowne Chevrolet
04	Yark Automotive Group	15	Dave White Chevrolet Co.	27	Quality Ford Sales, Inc.
05	Bob Schmidt Chevrolet	16	Dick Wilson Pontiac	28	Rouen Chrysler Jeep Eagle
06	Bowling Green Lincoln Mercury Jeep Eagle	17	Doyle Pontiac Buick	29	Saturn of Toledo
07	Brondes Ford	18	Franklin Park Lincoln Mercury	30	Ed Schmidt Pontiac Jeep Eagle
08	Brown Honda	19	Genoa Motors	31	Southside Lincoln Mercury
09	Brown Mazda	20	Great Lakes Ford Nissan	32	Valiton Chrysler
10	Charlie's Dodge	21	Grogan Towne Chrysler	33	Vin Divers
		22	Hatfield Motor Sales	34	Whitman Ford

    a. We want to select a random sample of five dealers. The random numbers are: 05, 20, 59, 21, 31, 28, 49, 38, 66, 08, 29, and 02. Which dealers would be included in the sample?

    b. Use the table of random numbers to select your own sample of five dealers.

    c. A sample is to consist of every seventh dealer. The number 04 is selected as the starting point. Which dealers are included in the sample?

4. Listed below are the 27 Nationwide Insurance agents in the Toledo, Ohio, metropolitan area. We would like to estimate the mean number of years employed with Nationwide.

ID Number	Agent	ID Number	Agent	ID Number	Agent
00	**Bly Scott** 3332 W Laskey Rd	10	**Heini Bernie** 7110 W Centra	19	**Riker Craig** 2621 N Reynolds Rd
01	**Coyle Mike** 5432 W Central Av	11	**Hinckley Dave** 14 N Holland Sylvania Rd	20	**Schwab Dave** 572 W Dussel Dr
02	**Denker Brett** 7445 Airport Hwy			21	**Seibert John H** 201 S Main
03	**Denker Rollie** 7445 Airport Hwy	12	**Joehlin Bob** 3358 Navarre Av	22	**Smithers Bob** 229 Superior St
04	**Farley Ron** 1837 W Alexis Rd	13	**Keisser David** 3030 W Sylvania Av	23	**Smithers Jerry** 229 Superior St
05	**George Mark** 7247 W Central Av	14	**Keisser Keith** 5902 Sylvania Av	24	**Wright Steve** 105 S Third St
06	**Gibellato Carlo** 6616 Monroe St	15	**Lawrence Grant** 342 W Dussel Dr	25	**Wood Tom** 112 Louisiana Av
07	**Glemser Cathy** 5602 Woodville Rd	16	**Miller Ken** 2427 Woodville Rd	26	**Yoder Scott** 6 Willoughby Av
08	**Green Mike** 4149 Holland Sylvania Rd	17	**O'Donnell Jim** 7247 W Central Av		
09	**Harris Ev** 2026 Albon Rd	18	**Priest Harvey** 5113 N Summit St		

a. We want to select a random sample of four agents. The random numbers are: 02, 59, 51, 25, 14, 29, 77, 69, and 18. Which dealers would be included in the sample?
b. Use the table of random numbers to select your own sample of four agents.
c. A sample is to consist of every seventh dealer. The number 04 is selected as the starting point. Which agents will be included in the sample?

Sampling "Error"

In the previous section we discussed sampling methods that are used to select a sample that is a fair and unbiased representation of the population. In each method, it is important to note that the selection of every possible sample of a specified size from a population has a known chance or probability. This is another way to describe an unbiased sampling method.

Samples are used to estimate population characteristics. For example, the mean of a sample is used to estimate the population mean. However, since the sample is a part or portion of the population, it is unlikely that the sample mean would be *exactly equal* to the population mean. Similarly, it is unlikely that the sample standard deviation would be *exactly equal* to the population standard deviation. We can therefore expect a difference between a *sample statistic* and its corresponding *population parameter*. This difference is called **sampling error.**

> **SAMPLING ERROR** The difference between a sample statistic and its corresponding population parameter.

The following example clarifies the idea of sampling error.

Example

Refer to the previous example on page 260 where we studied the number of rooms rented at the Foxtrot Inn bed and breakfast in Tryon, North Carolina. The population is the number of rooms rented each of the 30 days in June 2008. Find the mean of the population. Use Excel or other statistical software to select three random samples of five days. Calculate the mean of each sample and compare it to the population mean. What is the sampling error in each case?

Solution

During the month there were a total of 94 rentals. So the mean number of units rented per night is 3.13. This is the population mean. Hence we designate this value with the Greek letter μ.

$$\mu = \frac{\Sigma X}{N} = \frac{0 + 2 + 3 + \cdots + 3}{30} = \frac{94}{30} = 3.13$$

The first random sample of five nights resulted in the following number of rooms rented: 4, 7, 4, 3, and 1. The mean of this sample of five nights is 3.8 rooms, which we designate as $\overline{X}_1$. The bar over the X reminds us that it is a sample mean and the subscript 1 indicates it is the mean of the first sample.

$$\overline{X}_1 = \frac{\Sigma X}{n} = \frac{4 + 7 + 4 + 3 + 1}{5} = \frac{19}{5} = 3.80$$

The sampling error for the first sample is the difference between the population mean (3.13) and the first sample mean (3.80). Hence, the sampling error is $(\overline{X}_1 - \mu = 3.80 - 3.13 = 0.67)$. The second random sample of five days from the population of all 30 days in June revealed the following number of rooms rented: 3, 3, 2, 3, and 6. The mean of these five values is 3.4, found by

$$\overline{X}_2 = \frac{\Sigma X}{n} = \frac{3 + 3 + 2 + 3 + 6}{5} = 3.4$$

The sampling error is $(\overline{X}_2 - \mu = 3.4 - 3.13 = 0.27)$.

In the third random sample the mean was 1.8 and the sampling error was −1.33.

Each of these differences, 0.67, 0.27, and −1.33, is the sampling error made in estimating the population mean. Sometimes these errors are positive values, indicating that the sample mean overestimated the population mean; other times they are negative values, indicating the sample mean was less than the population mean.

Excel

Random Samples

	A	B	C	D	E	F	G	H
1	June	Rentals			Sample 1	Sample 2	Sample 3	
2	1	0			4	3	0	
3	2	2			7	3	0	
4	3	3			4	2	3	
5	4	2			3	3	3	
6	5	3			1	6	3	
7	6	4		Totals	19	17	9	
8	7	2		Sample means	3.8	3.4	1.8	
9	8	3						
10	9	4						
11	10	7						
12	11	3						
13	12	4						
14	13	4						
15	14	4						
16	15	7						

In this case where we have a population of 30 values and samples of 5 values there is a very large number of possible samples—142,506 to be exact! To find this value use the combination formula (5–10) on page 170. Each of the 142,506 different samples has the same chance of being selected. Each sample may have a different sample mean and therefore a different sampling error. The value of the sampling error is based on the particular one of the 142,506 different possible samples selected. Therefore, the sampling errors are random and occur by chance. If you were to determine the sum of these sampling errors over a large number of samples the result would be very close to zero. This is true because the sample mean is an *unbiased estimator* of the population mean.

Sampling Distribution of the Sample Mean

Now that we have discovered the possibility of a sampling error when sample results are used to estimate a population parameter, how can we make an accurate prediction about the possible success of a newly developed toothpaste or other product, based only on sample results? How can the quality-assurance department in a mass-production firm release a shipment of microchips based only on a sample of 10 chips? How can the CNN/*USA Today* or ABC News/*Washington Post* polling organizations make an accurate prediction about a presidential race based on a sample of 1,200 registered voters out of a voting population of nearly 90 million? To answer these questions, we first develop a *sampling distribution of the sample mean*.

Sample means vary from sample to sample.

The sample means in the previous example varied from one sample to the next. The mean of the first sample of 5 days was 3.80 rooms, and the second sample was 3.40 rooms. The population mean was 3.13 rooms. If we organized the means of all possible samples of 5 days into a probability distribution, the result is called the **sampling distribution of the sample mean.**

> **SAMPLING DISTRIBUTION OF THE SAMPLE MEAN** A probability distribution of all possible sample means of a given sample size.

The following example illustrates the construction of a sampling distribution of the sample mean.

Example

Tartus Industries has seven production employees (considered the population). The hourly earnings of each employee are given in Table 8–2.

TABLE 8–2 Hourly Earnings of the Production Employees of Tartus Industries

Employee	Hourly Earnings	Employee	Hourly Earnings
Joe	$7	Jan	$7
Sam	7	Art	8
Sue	8	Ted	9
Bob	8		

1. What is the population mean?
2. What is the sampling distribution of the sample mean for samples of size 2?
3. What is the mean of the sampling distribution?
4. What observations can be made about the population and the sampling distribution?

Solution

Here are the solutions to the questions.

1. The population mean is $7.71, found by:

$$\mu = \frac{\Sigma X}{N} = \frac{\$7 + \$7 + \$8 + \$8 + \$7 + \$8 + \$9}{7} = \$7.71$$

We identify the population mean with the Greek letter μ. Our policy, stated in Chapters 1, 3, and 4, is to identify population parameters with Greek letters.

2. To arrive at the sampling distribution of the sample mean, we need to select all possible samples of 2 without replacement from the population, then compute the mean of each sample. There are 21 possible samples, found by using formula (5–10) on page 170.

$$_NC_n = \frac{N!}{n!(N - n)!} = \frac{7!}{2!(7 - 2)!} = 21$$

where $N = 7$ is the number of items in the population and $n = 2$ is the number of items in the sample.

The 21 sample means from all possible samples of 2 that can be drawn from the population are shown in Table 8–3. These 21 sample means are used to construct a probability distribution. This is the sampling distribution of the sample mean, and it is summarized in Table 8–4.

TABLE 8–3 Sample Means for All Possible Samples of 2 Employees

Sample	Employees	Hourly Earnings	Sum	Mean	Sample	Employees	Hourly Earnings	Sum	Mean
1	Joe, Sam	$7, $7	$14	$7.00	12	Sue, Bob	$8, $8	$16	$8.00
2	Joe, Sue	7, 8	15	7.50	13	Sue, Jan	8, 7	15	7.50
3	Joe, Bob	7, 8	15	7.50	14	Sue, Art	8, 8	16	8.00
4	Joe, Jan	7, 7	14	7.00	15	Sue, Ted	8, 9	17	8.50
5	Joe, Art	7, 8	15	7.50	16	Bob, Jan	8, 7	15	7.50
6	Joe, Ted	7, 9	16	8.00	17	Bob, Art	8, 8	16	8.00
7	Sam, Sue	7, 8	15	7.50	18	Bob, Ted	8, 9	17	8.50
8	Sam, Bob	7, 8	15	7.50	19	Jan, Art	7, 8	15	7.50
9	Sam, Jan	7, 7	14	7.00	20	Jan, Ted	7, 9	16	8.00
10	Sam, Art	7, 8	15	7.50	21	Art, Ted	8, 9	17	8.50
11	Sam, Ted	7, 9	16	8.00					

TABLE 8–4 Sampling Distribution of the Sample Mean for $n = 2$

Sample Mean	Number of Means	Probability
$7.00	3	.1429
7.50	9	.4285
8.00	6	.2857
8.50	3	.1429
	21	1.0000

3. The mean of the sampling distribution of the sample mean is obtained by summing the various sample means and dividing the sum by the number of samples. The mean of all the sample means is usually written $\mu_{\overline{X}}$. The μ reminds us that it is a population value because we have considered all possible samples. The subscript $\overline{X}$ indicates that it is the sampling distribution of the sample mean.

Population mean is equal to the mean of the sample means

$$\mu_{\overline{X}} = \frac{\text{Sum of all sample means}}{\text{Total number of samples}} = \frac{\$7.00 + \$7.50 + \cdots + \$8.50}{21}$$

$$= \frac{\$162}{21} = \$7.71$$

4. Refer to Chart 8–1, which shows both the population distribution and the distribution of the sample mean. These observations can be made:
   a. The mean of the distribution of the sample mean ($7.71) is equal to the mean of the population: $\mu = \mu_{\overline{X}}$.
   b. The spread in the distribution of the sample mean is less than the spread in the population values. The sample mean ranges from $7.00 to $8.50, while the population values vary from $7.00 up to $9.00. Notice, as we increase the size of the sample, the spread of the distribution of the sample mean becomes smaller.
   c. The shape of the sampling distribution of the sample mean and the shape of the frequency distribution of the population values are different. The distribution of the sample mean tends to be more bell-shaped and to approximate the normal probability distribution.

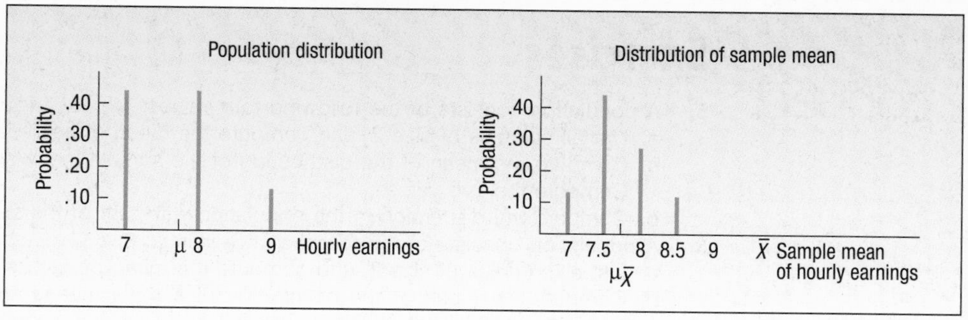

CHART 8–1 Distributions of Population Values and Sample Mean

In summary, we took all possible random samples from a population and for each sample calculated a sample statistic (the mean amount earned). This example illustrates important relationships between the population distribution and the sampling distribution of the sample mean:

1. The mean of the sample means is exactly equal to the population mean.
2. The dispersion of the sampling distribution of sample means is narrower than the population distribution.
3. The sampling distribution of sample means tends to become bell-shaped and to approximate the normal probability distribution.

Given a bell-shaped or normal probability distribution, we will be able to apply concepts from Chapter 7 to determine the probability of selecting a sample with a specified sample mean. In the next section, we will show the importance of sample size as it relates to the sampling distribution of sample means.

Self-Review 8–3

The lengths of service of all the executives employed by Standard Chemicals are:

Name	Years
Mr. Snow	20
Ms. Tolson	22
Mr. Kraft	26
Ms. Irwin	24
Mr. Jones	28

(a) Using the combination formula, how many samples of size 2 are possible?
(b) List all possible samples of 2 executives from the population and compute their means.
(c) Organize the means into a sampling distribution.
(d) Compare the population mean and the mean of the sample means.
(e) Compare the dispersion in the population with that in the distribution of the sample mean.
(f) A chart portraying the population values follows. Is the distribution of population values normally distributed (bell-shaped)?

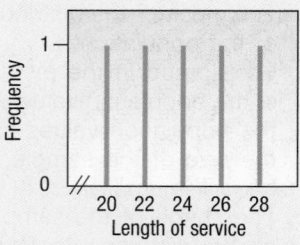

(g) Is the distribution of the sample mean computed in part (c) starting to show some tendency toward being bell-shaped?

Exercises

5. A population consists of the following four values: 12, 12, 14, and 16.
   a. List all samples of size 2, and compute the mean of each sample.
   b. Compute the mean of the distribution of the sample mean and the population mean. Compare the two values.
   c. Compare the dispersion in the population with that of the sample mean.
6. A population consists of the following five values: 2, 2, 4, 4, and 8.
   a. List all samples of size 2, and compute the mean of each sample.
   b. Compute the mean of the distribution of sample means and the population mean. Compare the two values.
   c. Compare the dispersion in the population with that of the sample means.
7. A population consists of the following five values: 12, 12, 14, 15, and 20.
   a. List all samples of size 3, and compute the mean of each sample.
   b. Compute the mean of the distribution of sample means and the population mean. Compare the two values.
   c. Compare the dispersion in the population with that of the sample means.
8. A population consists of the following five values: 0, 0, 1, 3, 6.
   a. List all samples of size 3, and compute the mean of each sample.
   b. Compute the mean of the distribution of sample means and the population mean. Compare the two values.
   c. Compare the dispersion in the population with that of the sample means.
9. In the law firm Tybo and Associates, there are six partners. Listed below is the number of cases each associate actually tried in court last month.

Associate	Number of Cases
Ruud	3
Wu	6
Sass	3
Flores	3
Wilhelms	0
Schueller	1

   a. How many different samples of 3 are possible?
   b. List all possible samples of size 3, and compute the mean number of cases in each sample.
   c. Compare the mean of the distribution of sample means to the population mean.
   d. On a chart similar to Chart 8–1, compare the dispersion in the population with that of the sample means.

10. There are five sales associates at Mid-Motors Ford. The five representatives and the number of cars they sold last week are:

Sales Representative	Cars Sold
Peter Hankish	8
Connie Stallter	6
Juan Lopez	4
Ted Barnes	10
Peggy Chu	6

   a. How many different samples of size 2 are possible?
   b. List all possible samples of size 2, and compute the mean of each sample.
   c. Compare the mean of the sampling distribution of sample means with that of the population.
   d. On a chart similar to Chart 8–1, compare the dispersion in sample means with that of the population.

The Central Limit Theorem

In this section, we examine the **central limit theorem.** Its application to the sampling distribution of the sample mean, introduced in the previous section, allows us to use the normal probability distribution to create confidence intervals for the population mean (described in Chapter 9) and perform tests of hypothesis (described in Chapter 10). The central limit theorem states that, for large random samples, the shape of the sampling distribution of the sample mean is close to the normal probability distribution. The approximation is more accurate for large samples than for small samples. This is one of the most useful conclusions in statistics. We can reason about the distribution of the sample mean with absolutely no information about the shape of the population distribution from which the sample is taken. In other words, the central limit theorem is true for all distributions.

A formal statement of the central limit theorem follows.

> **CENTRAL LIMIT THEOREM** If all samples of a particular size are selected from any population, the sampling distribution of the sample mean is approximately a normal distribution. This approximation improves with larger samples.

If the population follows a normal probability distribution, then for any sample size the sampling distribution of the sample mean will also be normal. If the population distribution is symmetrical (but not normal), you will see the normal shape of the distribution of the sample mean emerge with samples as small as 10. On the other hand, if you start with a distribution that is skewed or has thick tails, it may require samples of 30 or more to observe the normality feature. This concept is summarized in Chart 8–2

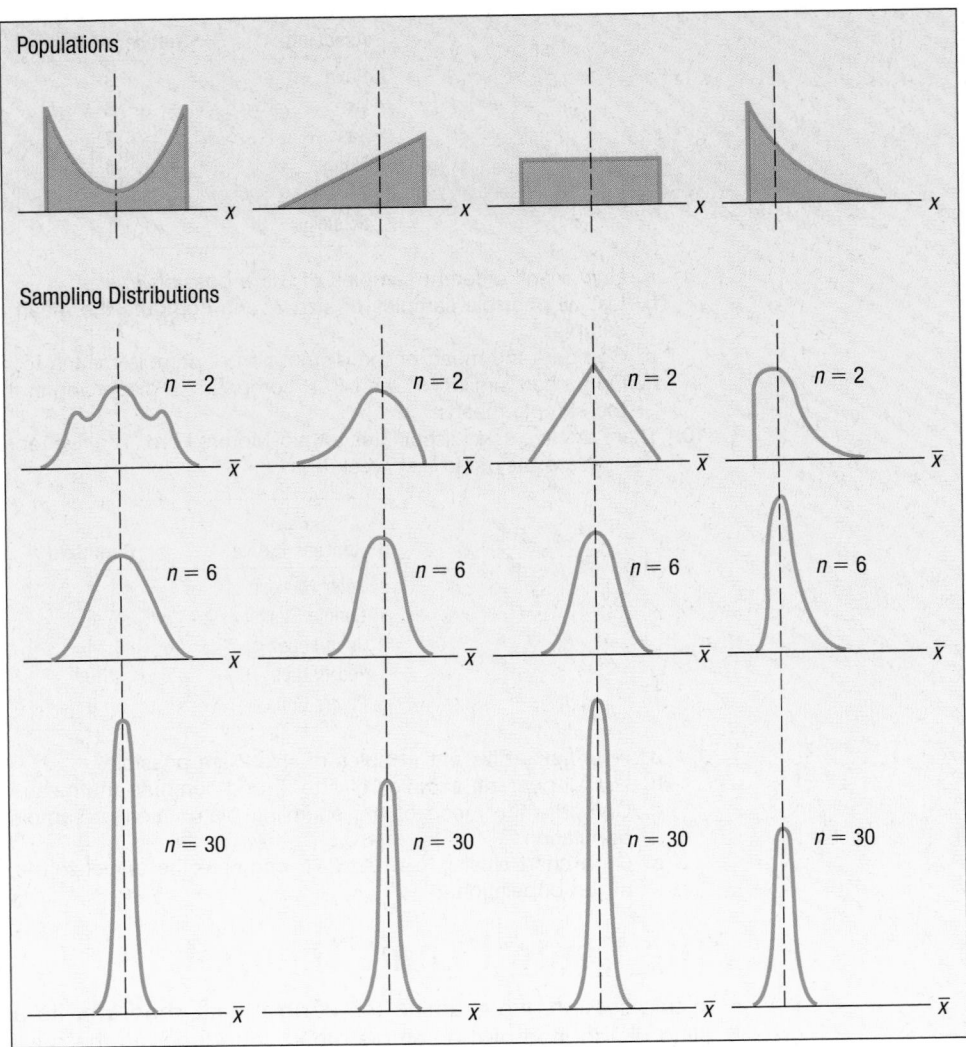

CHART 8–2 Results of the Central Limit Theorem for Several Populations

for various population shapes. Observe the convergence to a normal distribution regardless of the shape of the population distribution. Most statisticians consider a sample of 30 or more to be large enough for the central limit theorem to be employed.

The idea that the distribution of the sample means from a population that is not normal will converge to normality is illustrated in Charts 8–3, 8–4, and 8–5. We will discuss this example in more detail shortly, but Chart 8–3 is a graph of a discrete probability distribution that is positively skewed. There are many possible samples of 5 that might be selected from this population. Suppose we randomly select 25 samples of size 5 each and compute the mean of each sample. These results are shown in Chart 8–4. Notice that the shape of the distribution of sample means has changed from the shape of the original population even though we selected only 25 of the many possible samples. To put it another way, we selected 25 random samples of 5 each from a population that is positively skewed and found the distribution of sample means has changed from the shape of the population. As we take larger samples, that is, $n = 20$ instead of $n = 5$, we will find the distribution of the sample mean will approach the normal distribution. Chart 8–5 shows the results of 25 random samples of 20 observations each from the same population. Observe the clear trend toward the normal probability distribution. This is the point of the central limit theorem. The following example will underscore this condition.

Example

Ed Spence began his sprocket business 20 years ago. The business has grown over the years and now employs 40 people. Spence Sprockets, Inc., faces some major decisions regarding health care for these employees. Before making a final decision on what health care plan to purchase, Ed decides to form a committee of five representative employees. The committee will be asked to study the health care issue carefully and make a recommendation as to what plan best fits the employees' needs. Ed feels the views of newer employees toward health care may differ from those of more experienced employees. If Ed randomly selects this committee, what can he expect in terms of the mean years with Spence Sprockets for those on the committee? How does the shape of the distribution of years of experience of all employees (the population) compare with the shape of the sampling distribution of the mean? The lengths of service (rounded to the nearest year) of the 40 employees currently on the Spence Sprockets, Inc., payroll are as follows.

11	4	18	2	1	2	0	2	2	4
3	4	1	2	2	3	3	19	8	3
7	1	0	2	7	0	4	5	1	14
16	8	9	1	1	2	5	10	2	3

Solution

Chart 8–3 shows the distribution of the years of experience for the population of 40 current employees. This distribution of lengths of service is positively skewed because there are a few employees who have worked at Spence Sprockets for a longer period of time. Specifically, six employees have been with the company 10 years or more. However, because the business has grown, the number of employees has increased in the last few years. Of the 40 employees, 18 have been with the company two years or less.

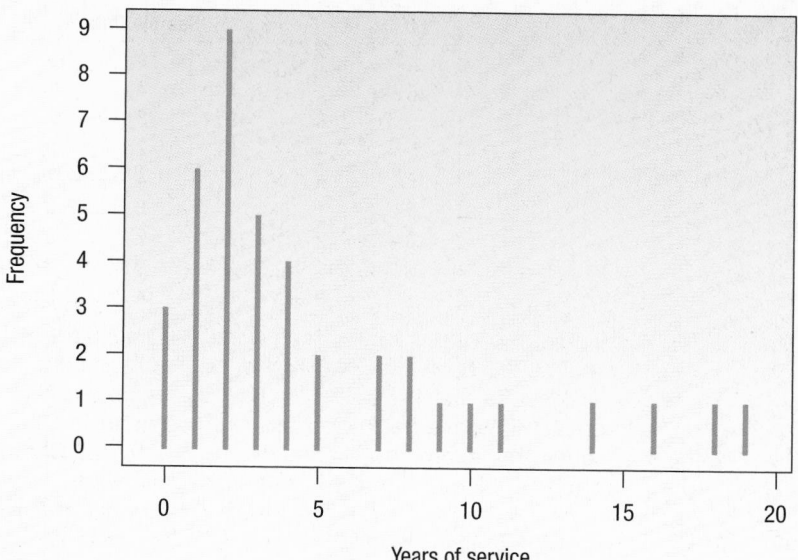

CHART 8–3 Length of Service for Spence Sprockets, Inc., Employees

Let's consider the first of Ed Spence's problems. He would like to form a committee of five employees to look into the health care question and suggest what type of health care coverage would be most appropriate for the majority of workers. How should he select the committee? If he selects the committee randomly, what might he expect in terms of mean length of service for those on the committee?

To begin, Ed writes the length of service for each of the 40 employees on pieces of paper and puts them into an old baseball hat. Next, he shuffles the pieces of paper around and randomly selects five slips of paper. The lengths of service for these five employees are 1, 9, 0, 19, and 14 years. Thus, the mean length of service for these five sampled employees is 8.60 years. How does that compare with the population mean? At this point Ed does not know the population mean, but the number of employees in the population is only 40, so he decides to calculate the mean length of service for *all* his employees. It is 4.8 years, found by adding the lengths of service for *all* the employees and dividing the total by 40.

$$\mu = \frac{11 + 4 + 18 + \cdots + 2 + 3}{40} = 4.80$$

The difference between the sample mean ($\overline{X}$) and the population mean (μ) is called **sampling error.** In other words, the difference of 3.80 years between the population mean of 4.80 and the sample mean of 8.60 is the sampling error. It is due to chance. Thus, if Ed selected these five employees to constitute the committee, their mean length of service would be larger than the population mean.

What would happen if Ed put the five pieces of paper back into the baseball hat and selected another sample? Would you expect the mean of this second sample to be exactly the same as the previous one? Suppose he selects another sample of five employees and finds the lengths of service in this sample to be 7, 4, 4, 1, and 3. This sample mean is 3.80 years. The result of selecting 25 samples of five employees each is shown in Table 8–5 and Chart 8–4. There are actually 658,008 possible samples of 5 from the population of 40 employees, found by the combination formula (5–10) for 40 things taken 5 at a time. Notice the difference in the shape of the population and

TABLE 8–5 Twenty-Five Random Samples of Five Employees

Sample I.D.	Sample Data					Sample Mean
A	1	9	0	19	14	8.6
B	7	4	4	1	3	3.8
C	8	19	8	2	1	7.6
D	4	18	2	0	11	7.0
E	4	2	4	7	18	7.0
F	1	2	0	3	2	1.6
G	2	3	2	0	2	1.8
H	11	2	9	2	4	5.6
I	9	0	4	2	7	4.4
J	1	1	1	11	1	3.0
K	2	0	0	10	2	2.8
L	0	2	3	2	16	4.6
M	2	3	1	1	1	1.6
N	3	7	3	4	3	4.0
O	1	2	3	1	4	2.2
P	19	0	1	3	8	6.2
Q	5	1	7	14	9	7.2
R	5	4	2	3	4	3.6
S	14	5	2	2	5	5.6
T	2	1	1	4	7	3.0
U	3	7	1	2	1	2.8
V	0	1	5	1	2	1.8
W	0	3	19	4	2	5.6
X	4	2	3	4	0	2.6
Y	1	1	2	3	2	1.8

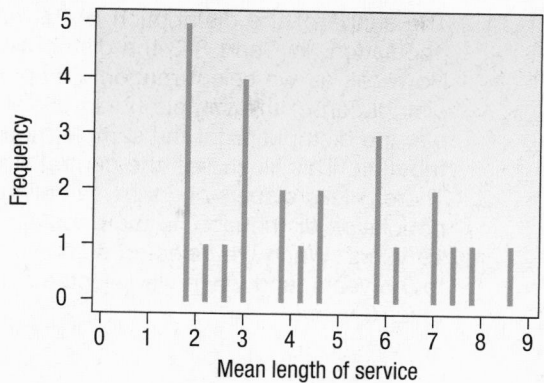

CHART 8–4 Histogram of Mean Lengths of Service for 25 Samples of Five Employees

the distribution of these sample means. The population of the lengths of service for employees (Chart 8–3) is positively skewed, but the distribution of these 25 sample means does not reflect the same positive skew. There is also a difference in the range of the sample means versus the range of the population. The population ranged from 0 to 19 years, whereas the sample means range from 1.6 to 8.6 years.

Table 8–6 reports the result of selecting 25 samples of 20 employees each and computing their sample means. These sample means are shown graphically in Chart 8–5. Compare the shape of this distribution to the population (Chart 8–3) and to the distribution of sample means where the sample is $n = 5$ (Chart 8–4). You should observe two important features:

TABLE 8–6 Random Samples and Sample Means of 25 Samples of 20 Spence Sprocket, Inc., Employees

Sample Number	Sample Data (Length of Service)																				Sample Mean
A	3	8	3	0	2	1	2	3	11	5	1	3	4	2	7	1	1	2	4	16	3.95
B	2	3	8	2	1	5	2	0	3	1	0	7	1	4	3	11	4	4	3	1	3.25
C	14	5	0	3	2	14	11	9	2	2	1	2	19	1	0	1	4	2	19	8	5.95
D	9	2	1	1	4	10	0	8	4	3	2	1	0	8	1	14	5	10	1	3	4.35
E	18	1	2	2	4	3	2	8	2	1	0	19	4	19	0	1	4	0	3	14	5.35
F	10	4	4	18	3	3	1	0	0	2	2	4	7	10	2	0	3	4	2	1	4.00
G	5	7	11	8	11	18	1	1	16	2	2	16	2	3	2	16	2	2	2	4	6.55
H	3	0	2	0	5	4	5	3	8	3	2	5	1	1	2	9	8	3	16	5	4.25
I	0	0	18	2	1	7	4	1	3	0	3	2	11	7	2	8	5	1	2	3	4.00
J	2	7	2	4	1	3	3	2	5	10	0	1	1	2	9	3	2	19	3	2	4.05
K	7	4	5	3	3	0	18	2	0	4	2	7	2	7	4	2	10	1	1	2	4.20
L	0	3	10	5	9	2	1	4	1	2	1	8	18	1	4	3	3	2	0	4	4.05
M	4	1	2	1	7	3	9	14	8	19	4	4	1	2	0	3	1	2	1	2	4.40
N	3	16	1	2	4	4	4	2	1	5	2	3	5	3	4	7	16	1	11	1	4.75
O	2	19	2	0	2	2	16	2	3	11	9	2	8	0	8	2	7	3	2	2	5.10
P	2	18	16	5	2	2	19	0	1	2	11	4	2	2	1	4	2	0	4	3	5.00
Q	3	2	3	11	10	1	1	5	19	16	7	10	3	1	1	1	2	2	3	1	5.10
R	2	3	1	2	7	4	3	19	9	2	2	1	1	2	2	2	1	8	0	2	3.65
S	2	14	19	1	19	2	8	4	2	2	14	2	8	16	4	7	2	9	0	7	7.10
T	0	1	3	3	2	2	3	1	1	0	3	2	3	5	2	10	14	4	2	0	3.05
U	1	0	1	2	16	1	1	2	5	1	4	1	2	2	2	2	2	8	9	3	3.25
V	1	9	4	4	2	8	7	1	14	18	1	5	10	11	19	0	3	7	2	11	6.85
W	8	1	9	19	3	19	0	5	2	1	5	3	3	4	1	5	3	1	8	7	5.35
X	4	2	0	3	1	16	1	11	3	3	2	18	2	0	1	5	0	7	2	5	4.30
Y	1	2	1	2	0	2	7	2	4	8	19	2	5	3	3	0	19	2	1	18	5.05

1. The shape of the distribution of the sample mean is different from that of the population. In Chart 8–3 the distribution of all employees is positively skewed. However, as we select random samples from this population, the shape of the distribution of the sample mean changes. As we increase the size of the sample, the distribution of the sample mean approaches the normal probability distribution. This illustrates the central limit theorem.

2. There is less dispersion in the sampling distribution of sample means than in the population distribution. In the population the lengths of service ranged from 0 to 19 years. When we selected samples of 5, the sample means ranged from 1.6 to 8.6 years, and when we selected samples of 20, the means ranged from 3.05 to 7.10 years.

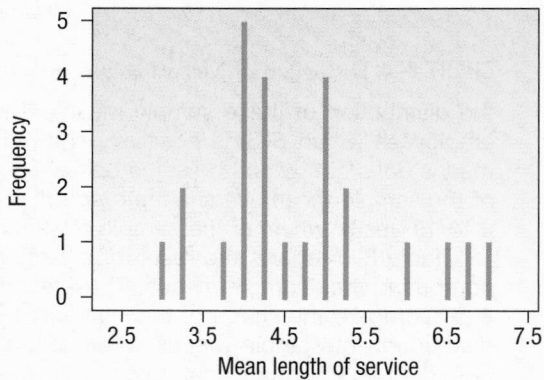

CHART 8–5 Histogram of Mean Lengths of Service for 25 Samples of 20 Employees

We can also compare the mean of the sample means to the population mean. The mean of the 25 samples of 20 employees reported in Table 8–6 is 4.676 years.

$$\mu_{\bar{X}} = \frac{3.95 + 3.25 + \cdots + 4.30 + 5.05}{25} = 4.676$$

We use the symbol $\mu_{\bar{X}}$ to identify the mean of the distribution of the sample mean. The subscript reminds us that the distribution is of the sample mean. It is read "mu sub X bar." We observe that the mean of the sample means, 4.676 years, is very close to the population mean of 4.80.

What should we conclude from this example? The central limit theorem indicates that, regardless of the shape of the population distribution, the sampling distribution of the sample mean will move toward the normal probability distribution. The larger the number of observations in each sample, the stronger the convergence. The Spence Sprockets, Inc., example shows how the central limit theorem works. We began with a positively skewed population (Chart 8–3). Next, we selected 25 random samples of 5 observations, computed the mean of each sample, and finally organized these 25 sample means into a graph (Chart 8–4). We observe a change in the shape of the sampling distribution of the sample mean from that of the population. The movement is from a positively skewed distribution to a distribution that has the shape of the normal probability distribution.

To further illustrate the effects of the central limit theorem, we increased the number of observations in each sample from 5 to 20. We selected 25 samples of 20 observations each and calculated the mean of each sample. Finally, we organized these sample means into a graph (Chart 8–5). The shape of the histogram in Chart 8–5 is clearly moving toward the normal probability distribution.

If you go back to Chapter 6 where several binomial distributions with a "success" proportion of .10 are shown in Chart 6–4, you can see yet another demonstration of the central limit theorem. Observe as n increases from 7 through 12 and 20 up to 40 that the profile of the probability distributions moves closer and closer to a normal probability distribution. Chart 8–5 on page 276 also shows the convergence to normality as n increases. This again reinforces the fact that, as more observations are sampled from any population distribution, the shape of the sampling distribution of the sample mean will get closer and closer to a normal distribution.

The central limit theorem itself (reread the definition on page 271) does not say anything about the dispersion of the sampling distribution of the sample mean or about the comparison of the mean of the sampling distribution of the sample mean to the mean of the population. However, in our Spence Sprockets example we did observe that there was less dispersion in the distribution of the sample mean than in the population distribution by noting the difference in the range in the population and the range of the sample means. We observe that the mean of the sample means is close to the mean of the population. It can be demonstrated that the mean of the sampling distribution is the population mean, i.e., $\mu_{\bar{X}} = \mu$, and if the standard deviation in the population is σ, the standard deviation of the sample means is $\sigma/\sqrt{n}$, where n is the number of observations in each sample. We refer to $\sigma/\sqrt{n}$ as the **standard error of the mean.** Its longer name is actually the *standard deviation of the sampling distribution of the sample mean*.

STANDARD ERROR OF THE MEAN	$\sigma_{\bar{X}} = \dfrac{\sigma}{\sqrt{n}}$	[8–1]

In this section we also came to other important conclusions.

1. The mean of the distribution of sample means will be *exactly* equal to the population mean if we are able to select all possible samples of the same size from a given population. That is:

$$\mu = \mu_{\bar{X}}$$

Even if we do not select all samples, we can expect the mean of the distribution of sample means to be close to the population mean.

2. There will be less dispersion in the sampling distribution of the sample mean than in the population. If the standard deviation of the population is σ, the standard deviation of the distribution of sample means is $\sigma/\sqrt{n}$. Note that when we increase the size of the sample the standard error of the mean decreases.

Self-Review 8–4

Refer to the Spence Sprockets, Inc., data on page 273. Select 10 random samples of 5 employees each. Use the methods described earlier in the chapter and the Table of Random Numbers (Appendix B.6) to find the employees to include in the sample. Compute the mean of each sample and plot the sample means on a chart similar to Chart 8–3. What is the mean of your 10 sample means?

Exercises

connect™

11. Appendix B.6 is a table of random numbers. Hence, each digit from 0 to 9 has the same likelihood of occurrence.
   a. Draw a graph showing the population distribution. What is the population mean?

b. Following are the first 10 rows of five digits from Appendix B.6. Assume that these are 10 random samples of five values each. Determine the mean of each sample and plot the means on a chart similar to Chart 8–3. Compare the mean of the sampling distribution of the sample means with the population mean.

0	2	7	1	1
9	4	8	7	3
5	4	9	2	1
7	7	6	4	0
6	1	5	4	5
1	7	1	4	7
1	3	7	4	8
8	7	4	5	5
0	8	9	9	9
7	8	8	0	4

12. Scrapper Elevator Company has 20 sales representatives who sell its product throughout the United States and Canada. The number of units sold last month by each representative is listed below. Assume these sales figures to be the population values.

2	3	2	3	3	4	2	4	3	2	2	7	3	4	5	3	3	3	3	5

   a. Draw a graph showing the population distribution.
   b. Compute the mean of the population.
   c. Select five random samples of 5 each. Compute the mean of each sample. Use the methods described in this chapter and Appendix B.6 to determine the items to be included in the sample.
   d. Compare the mean of the sampling distribution of the sample means to the population mean. Would you expect the two values to be about the same?
   e. Draw a histogram of the sample means. Do you notice a difference in the shape of the distribution of sample means compared to the shape of the population distribution?

13. Consider all of the coins (pennies, nickels, quarters, etc.) in your pocket or purse as a population. Make a frequency table beginning with the current year and counting backward to record the ages (in years) of the coins. For example, if the current year is 2009, then a coin with 2007 stamped on it is 2 years old.
   a. Draw a histogram or other graph showing the population distribution.
   b. Randomly select five coins and record the mean age of the sampled coins. Repeat this sampling process 20 times. Now draw a histogram or other graph showing the distribution of the sample means.
   c. Compare the shapes of the two histograms.

14. Consider the digits in the phone numbers on a randomly selected page of your local phone book a population. Make a frequency table of the final digit of 30 randomly selected phone numbers. For example, if a phone number is 555-9704, record a 4.
   a. Draw a histogram or other graph of this population distribution. Using the uniform distribution, compute the population mean and the population standard deviation.
   b. Also record the sample mean of the final four digits (9704 would lead to a mean of 5). Now draw a histogram or other graph showing the distribution of the sample means.
   c. Compare the shapes of the two histograms.

Using the Sampling Distribution of the Sample Mean

The previous discussion is important because most business decisions are made on the basis of sampling results. Here are some examples.

1. Arm and Hammer Company wants to ensure that its laundry detergent actually contains 100 fluid ounces, as indicated on the label. Historical summaries from

the filling process indicate the mean amount per container is 100 fluid ounces and the standard deviation is 2 fluid ounces. The quality technician in her 10 A.M. check of 40 containers finds the mean amount per container is 99.8 fluid ounces. Should the technician shut down the filling operation or is the sampling error reasonable?

2. A. C. Nielsen Company provides information to organizations advertising on television. Prior research indicates that adult Americans watch an average of 6.0 hours per day of television. The standard deviation is 1.5 hours. For a sample of 50 adults in the greater Boston area, would it be reasonable that we could randomly select a sample and find that they watch an average of 6.5 hours of television per day?

3. Haughton Elevator Company wishes to develop specifications for the number of people who can ride in a new oversized elevator. Suppose the mean weight for an adult is 160 pounds and the standard deviation is 15 pounds. However, the distribution of weights does not follow the normal probability distribution. It is positively skewed. What is the likelihood that for a sample of 30 adults their mean weight is 170 pounds or more?

In each of these situations we have a population about which we have some information. We take a sample from that population and wish to conclude whether the sampling error, that is, the difference between the population parameter and the sample statistic, is due to chance.

Using ideas discussed in the previous section, we can compute the probability that a sample mean will fall within a certain range. We know that the sampling distribution of the sample mean will follow the normal probability distribution under two conditions:

1. When the samples are taken from populations known to follow the normal distribution. In this case the size of the sample is not a factor.

2. When the shape of the population distribution is not known or the shape is known to be nonnormal, but our sample contains at least 30 observations. In this case, the central limit theorem guarantees the sampling distribution of the mean follows a normal distribution.

We can use formula (7–5) from the previous chapter to convert any normal distribution to the standard normal distribution. We also refer to this as a z value. Then we can use the standard normal table, Appendix B.1, to find the probability of selecting an observation that would fall within a specific range. The formula for finding a z value is:

$$z = \frac{X - \mu}{\sigma}$$

In this formula X is the value of the random variable, μ is the population mean, and σ the population standard deviation.

However, most business decisions refer to a sample—not just one observation. So we are interested in the distribution of $\overline{X}$, the sample mean, instead of X, the value of one observation. That is the first change we make in formula (7–5). The second is that we use the standard error of the mean of n observations instead of the population standard deviation. That is, we use $\sigma/\sqrt{n}$ in the denominator rather than σ. Therefore, to find the likelihood of a sample mean with a specified range, we first use the following formula to find the corresponding z value. Then we use Appendix B.1 to locate the probability.

FINDING THE z VALUE OF $\overline{X}$ WHEN THE POPULATION STANDARD DEVIATION IS KNOWN	$z = \dfrac{\overline{X} - \mu}{\sigma/\sqrt{n}}$	[8–2]

The following example will show the application.

The Quality Assurance Department for Cola, Inc., maintains records regarding the amount of cola in its Jumbo bottle. The actual amount of cola in each bottle is critical, but varies a small amount from one bottle to the next. Cola, Inc., does not wish to underfill the bottles, because it will have a problem with truth in labeling. On the other hand, it cannot overfill each bottle, because it would be giving cola away, hence reducing its profits. Its records indicate that the amount of cola follows the normal probability distribution. The mean amount per bottle is 31.2 ounces and the population standard deviation is 0.4 ounces. At 8 A.M. today the quality technician randomly selected 16 bottles from the filling line. The mean amount of cola contained in the bottles is 31.38 ounces. Is this an unlikely result? Is it likely the process is putting too much soda in the bottles? To put it another way, is the sampling error of 0.18 ounces unusual?

We can use the results of the previous section to find the likelihood that we could select a sample of 16 (n) bottles from a normal population with a mean of 31.2 (μ) ounces and a population standard deviation of 0.4 (σ) ounces and find the sample mean to be 31.38 ($\overline{X}$). We use formula (8–2) to find the value of z.

$$z = \frac{\overline{X} - \mu}{\sigma/\sqrt{n}} = \frac{31.38 - 31.20}{0.4/\sqrt{16}} = 1.80$$

The numerator of this equation, $\overline{X} - \mu = 31.38 - 31.20 = .18$, is the sampling error. The denominator, $\sigma/\sqrt{n} = 0.4/\sqrt{16} = 0.1$, is the standard error of the sampling distribution of the sample mean. So the z values express the sampling error in standard units, in other words, the standard error.

Next, we compute the likelihood of a z value greater than 1.80. In Appendix B.1 locate the probability corresponding to a z value of 1.80. It is .4641. The likelihood of a z value greater than 1.80 is .0359, found by .5000 − .4641.

What do we conclude? It is unlikely, less than a 4 percent chance, we could select a sample of 16 observations from a normal population with a mean of 31.2 ounces and a population standard deviation of 0.4 ounces and find the sample mean equal to or greater than 31.38 ounces. We conclude the process is putting too much cola in the bottles. The quality technician should see the production supervisor about reducing the amount of soda in each bottle. This information is summarized in Chart 8–6.

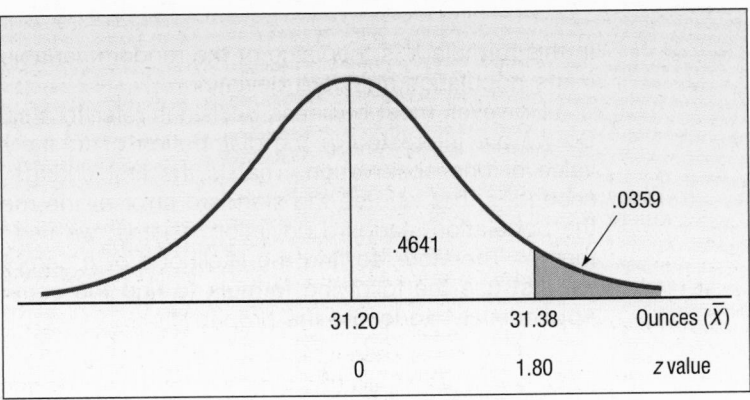

CHART 8–6 Sampling Distribution of the Mean Amount of Cola in a Jumbo Bottle

Self-Review 8–5

Refer to the Cola, Inc., information. Suppose the quality technician selected a sample of 16 Jumbo bottles that averaged 31.08 ounces. What can you conclude about the filling process?

Exercises

connect

15. A normal population has a mean of 60 and a standard deviation of 12. You select a random sample of 9. Compute the probability the sample mean is:
    a. Greater than 63.
    b. Less than 56.
    c. Between 56 and 63.

16. A normal population has a mean of 75 and a standard deviation of 5. You select a sample of 40. Compute the probability the sample mean is:
    a. Less than 74.
    b. Between 74 and 76.
    c. Between 76 and 77.
    d. Greater than 77.

17. The rent for a one-bedroom apartment in Southern California follows the normal distribution with a mean of $2,200 per month and a standard deviation of $250 per month. The distribution of the monthly costs does not follow the normal distribution. In fact, it is positively skewed. What is the probability of selecting a sample of 50 one-bedroom apartments and finding the mean to be at least $1,950 per month?

18. According to an IRS study, it takes a mean of 330 minutes for taxpayers to prepare, copy, and electronically file a 1040 tax form. This distribution of times follows the normal distribution and the standard deviation is 80 minutes. A consumer watchdog agency selects a random sample of 40 taxpayers.
    a. What is the standard error of the mean in this example?
    b. What is the likelihood the sample mean is greater than 320 minutes?
    c. What is the likelihood the sample mean is between 320 and 350 minutes?
    d. What is the likelihood the sample mean is greater than 350 minutes?

Chapter Summary

I. There are many reasons for sampling a population.
   A. The results of a sample may adequately estimate the value of the population parameter, thus saving time and money.
   B. It may be too time consuming to contact all members of the population.
   C. It may be impossible to check or locate all the members of the population.
   D. The cost of studying all the items in the population may be prohibitive.
   E. Often testing destroys the sampled item and it cannot be returned to the population.
II. In an unbiased or probability sample all members of the population have a chance of being selected for the sample. There are several probability sampling methods.
   A. In a simple random sample all members of the population have the same chance of being selected for the sample.
   B. In a systematic sample a random starting point is selected, and then every kth item thereafter is selected for the sample.
   C. In a stratified sample the population is divided into several groups, called strata, and then a random sample is selected from each stratum.
   D. In cluster sampling the population is divided into primary units, then samples are drawn from the primary units.

III. The sampling error is the difference between a population parameter and a sample statistic.

IV. The sampling distribution of the sample mean is a probability distribution of all possible sample means of the same sample size.

    A. For a given sample size, the mean of all possible sample means selected from a population is equal to the population mean.

    B. There is less variation in the distribution of the sample mean than in the population distribution.

    C. The standard error of the mean measures the variation in the sampling distribution of the sample mean. The standard error is found by:

$$\sigma_{\overline{X}} = \frac{\sigma}{\sqrt{n}} \qquad \text{[8–1]}$$

    D. If the population follows a normal distribution, the sampling distribution of the sample mean will also follow the normal distribution for samples of any size. Assume the population standard deviation is known. To determine the probability that a sample mean falls in a particular region, use the following formula.

$$z = \frac{\overline{X} - \mu}{\sigma/\sqrt{n}} \qquad \text{[8–2]}$$

Pronunciation Key

SYMBOL	MEANING	PRONUNCIATION
$\mu_{\overline{X}}$	Mean of the sampling distribution of the sample mean	*mu sub X bar*
$\sigma_{\overline{X}}$	Population standard error of the sample mean	*sigma sub X bar*

Chapter Exercises

connect

19. The retail stores located in the North Towne Square Mall are:

00	Elder-Beerman	09	Lion Store	18	County Seat
01	Sears	10	Bootleggers	19	Kid Mart
02	Deb Shop	11	Formal Man	20	Lerner
03	Frederick's of Hollywood	12	Leather Ltd.	21	Coach House Gifts
04	Petries	13	B Dalton Bookseller	22	Spencer Gifts
05	Easy Dreams	14	Pat's Hallmark	23	CPI Photo Finish
06	Summit Stationers	15	Things Remembered	24	Regis Hairstylists
07	E. B. Brown Opticians	16	Pearle Vision Express		
08	Kay-Bee Toy & Hobby	17	Dollar Tree		

    a. If the following random numbers are selected, which retail stores should be contacted for a survey? 11, 65, 86, 62, 06, 10, 12, 77, and 04

    b. Select a random sample of four retail stores. Use Appendix B.6.

    c. A systematic sampling procedure is to be used. The first store is to be contacted and then every third store. Which stores will be contacted?

20. Medical Mutual Insurance is investigating the cost of a routine office visit to family-practice physicians in the Rochester, New York, area. The following is a list of family-practice physicians in the region. Physicians are to be randomly selected and contacted regarding their charges. The 39 physicians have been coded from 00 to 38. Also noted is whether they are in practice by themselves (S), have a partner (P), or are in a group practice (G).

Number	Physician	Type of Practice	Number	Physician	Type of Practice
00	R. E. Scherbarth, M.D.	S	20	Gregory Yost, M.D.	P
01	Crystal R. Goveia, M.D.	P	21	J. Christian Zona, M.D.	P
02	Mark D. Hillard, M.D.	P	22	Larry Johnson, M.D.	P
03	Jeanine S. Huttner, M.D.	P	23	Sanford Kimmel, M.D.	P
04	Francis Aona, M.D.	P	24	Harry Mayhew, M.D.	S
05	Janet Arrowsmith, M.D.	P	25	Leroy Rodgers, M.D.	S
06	David DeFrance, M.D.	S	26	Thomas Tafelski, M.D.	S
07	Judith Furlong, M.D.	S	27	Mark Zilkoski, M.D.	G
08	Leslie Jackson, M.D.	G	28	Ken Bertka, M.D.	G
09	Paul Langenkamp, M.D.	S	29	Mark DeMichiei, M.D.	G
10	Philip Lepkowski, M.D.	S	30	John Eggert, M.D.	P
11	Wendy Martin, M.D.	S	31	Jeanne Fiorito, M.D.	P
12	Denny Mauricio, M.D.	P	32	Michael Fitzpatrick, M.D.	P
13	Hasmukh Parmar, M.D.	P	33	Charles Holt, D.O.	P
14	Ricardo Pena, M.D.	P	34	Richard Koby, M.D.	P
15	David Reames, M.D.	P	35	John Meier, M.D.	P
16	Ronald Reynolds, M.D.	G	36	Douglas Smucker, M.D.	S
17	Mark Steinmetz, M.D.	G	37	David Weldy, M.D.	P
18	Geza Torok, M.D.	S	38	Cheryl Zaborowski, M.D.	P
19	Mark Young, M.D.	P			

   a. The random numbers obtained from Appendix B.6 are: 31, 94, 43, 36, 03, 24, 17, and 09. Which physicians should be contacted?

   b. Select a random sample of four physicians using the random numbers of Appendix B.6.

   c. A sample is to consist of every fifth physician. The number 04 is selected as the starting point. Which physicians will be contacted?

   d. A sample is to consist of two physicians in solo practice (S), two in partnership (P), and one in group practice (G). Select a sample accordingly. Explain your procedure.

21. A population consists of the following three values: 1, 2, and 3.

   a. List all possible samples of size 2 (including possible repeats) and compute the mean of every sample.

   b. Find the means of the distribution of the sample mean and the population mean. Compare the two values.

   c. Compare the dispersion of the population with that of the sample mean.

   d. Describe the shapes of the two distributions.

22. In the Department of Education at UR University, student records suggest that the population of students spends an average of 5.5 hours per week playing organized sports. The population's standard deviation is 2.2 hours per week. Based on a sample of 121 students, Healthy Lifestyles Incorporated (HLI) would like to apply the central limit theorem to make various estimates.

   a. Compute the standard error of the sample mean.

   b. What is the chance HLI will find a sample mean between 5 and 6 hours?

   c. Calculate the probability that the sample mean will be between 5.3 and 5.7 hours.

   d. How strange would it be to obtain a sample mean greater than 6.5 hours?

23. The manufacturer of eMachines, an economy-priced computer, recently completed the design for a new laptop model. eMachine's top management would like some assistance in pricing the new laptop. Two market research firms were contacted and asked to prepare a pricing strategy. Marketing-Gets-Results tested the new eMachines laptop with 50 randomly selected consumers, who indicated they plan to purchase a laptop within the next year. The second marketing research firm, called Marketing-Reaps-Profits, test-marketed the new eMachines laptop with 200 current laptop owners. Which of the marketing research companies' test results will be more useful? Discuss why.

24. Answer the following questions in one or two well-constructed sentences.

   a. What happens to the standard error of the mean if the sample size is increased?

    b. What happens to the distribution of the sample means if the sample size in increased?

    c. When using the distribution of sample means to estimate the population mean, what is the benefit of using larger sample sizes?

25. There are 25 motels in Goshen, Indiana. The number of rooms in each motel follows:

90 72 75 60 75 72 84 72 88 74 105 115 68 74 80 64 104 82 48 58 60 80 48 58 100

    a. Using a table of random numbers (Appendix B.6), select a random sample of five motels from this population.

    b. Obtain a systematic sample by selecting a random starting point among the first five motels and then select every fifth motel.

    c. Suppose the last five motels are "cut-rate" motels. Describe how you would select a random sample of three regular motels and two cut-rate motels.

26. As a part of their customer-service program, United Airlines randomly selected 10 passengers from today's 9 A.M. Chicago–Tampa flight. Each sampled passenger is to be interviewed in depth regarding airport facilities, service, and so on. To identify the sample, each passenger was given a number on boarding the aircraft. The numbers started with 001 and ended with 250.

    a. Select 10 usable numbers at random using Appendix B.6.

    b. The sample of 10 could have been chosen using a systematic sample. Choose the first number using Appendix B.6, and then list the numbers to be interviewed.

    c. Evaluate the two methods by giving the advantages and possible disadvantages.

    d. In what other way could a random sample be selected from the 250 passengers?

27. Suppose your statistics instructor gave six examinations during the semester. You received the following grades (percent correct): 79, 64, 84, 82, 92, and 77. Instead of averaging the six scores, the instructor indicated he would randomly select two grades and compute the final percent correct based on the two percents.

    a. How many different samples of two test grades are possible?

    b. List all possible samples of size two and compute the mean of each.

    c. Compute the mean of the sample means and compare it to the population mean.

    d. If you were a student, would you like this arrangement? Would the result be different from dropping the lowest score? Write a brief report.

28. At the downtown office of First National Bank there are five tellers. Last week the tellers made the following number of errors each: 2, 3, 5, 3, and 5.

    a. How many different samples of 2 tellers are possible?

    b. List all possible samples of size 2 and compute the mean of each.

    c. Compute the mean of the sample means and compare it to the population mean.

29. The Quality Control Department employs five technicians during the day shift. Listed below is the number of times each technician instructed the production foreman to shut down the manufacturing process last week.

Technician	Shutdowns	Technician	Shutdowns
Taylor	4	Rousche	3
Hurley	3	Huang	2
Gupta	5		

    a. How many different samples of two technicians are possible from this population?

    b. List all possible samples of two observations each and compute the mean of each sample.

    c. Compare the mean of the sample means with the population mean.

    d. Compare the shape of the population distribution with the shape of the distribution of the sample means.

30. The Appliance Center has six sales representatives at its North Jacksonville outlet. Listed below is the number of refrigerators sold by each last month.

Sales Representative	Number Sold	Sales Representative	Number Sold
Zina Craft	54	Jan Niles	48
Woon Junge	50	Molly Camp	50
Ernie DeBrul	52	Rachel Myak	52

    a. How many samples of size 2 are possible?

    b. Select all possible samples of size 2 and compute the mean number sold.

    c. Organize the sample means into a frequency distribution.

    d. What is the mean of the population? What is the mean of the sample means?

    e. What is the shape of the population distribution?

    f. What is the shape of the distribution of the sample mean?

31. Mattel Corporation produces a remote-controlled car that requires three AA batteries. The mean life of these batteries in this product is 35.0 hours. The distribution of the battery lives closely follows the normal probability distribution with a standard deviation of 5.5 hours. As a part of its testing program Sony tests samples of 25 batteries.

    a. What can you say about the shape of the distribution of the sample mean?

    b. What is the standard error of the distribution of the sample mean?

    c. What proportion of the samples will have a mean useful life of more than 36 hours?

    d. What proportion of the sample will have a mean useful life greater than 34.5 hours?

    e. What proportion of the sample will have a mean useful life between 34.5 and 36.0 hours?

32. CRA CDs, Inc., wants the mean lengths of the "cuts" on a CD to be 135 seconds (2 minutes and 15 seconds). This will allow the disk jockeys to have plenty of time for commercials within each 10-minute segment. Assume the distribution of the length of the cuts follows the normal distribution with a population standard deviation of 8 seconds. Suppose we select a sample of 16 cuts from various CDs sold by CRA CDs, Inc.

    a. What can we say about the shape of the distribution of the sample mean?

    b. What is the standard error of the mean?

    c. What percent of the sample means will be greater than 140 seconds?

    d. What percent of the sample means will be greater than 128 seconds?

    e. What percent of the sample means will be greater than 128 but less than 140 seconds?

33. Recent studies indicate that the typical 50-year-old woman spends $350 per year for personal-care products. The distribution of the amounts spent follows a normal distribution with a standard deviation of $45 per year. We select a random sample of 40 women. The mean amount spent for those sampled is $335. What is the likelihood of finding a sample mean this large or larger from the specified population?

34. Information from the American Institute of Insurance indicates the mean amount of life insurance per household in the United States is $110,000. This distribution follows the normal distribution with a standard deviation of $40,000.

    a. If we select a random sample of 50 households, what is the standard error of the mean?

    b. What is the expected shape of the distribution of the sample mean?

    c. What is the likelihood of selecting a sample with a mean of at least $112,000?

    d. What is the likelihood of selecting a sample with a mean of more than $100,000?

    e. Find the likelihood of selecting a sample with a mean of more than $100,000 but less than $112,000.

35. The mean age at which men in the United States marry for the first time follows the normal distribution with a mean of 24.8 years. The standard deviation of the distribution is 2.5 years. For a random sample of 60 men, what is the likelihood that the age at which they were married for the first time is less than 25.1 years?

36. A recent study by the Greater Los Angeles Taxi Drivers Association showed that the mean fare charged for service from Hermosa Beach to Los Angeles International Airport is $18.00 and the standard deviation is $3.50. We select a sample of 15 fares.

    a. What is the likelihood that the sample mean is between $17.00 and $20.00?

    b. What must you assume to make the above calculation?

37. Crossett Trucking Company claims that the mean weight of its delivery trucks when they are fully loaded is 6,000 pounds and the standard deviation is 150 pounds. Assume that the population follows the normal distribution. Forty trucks are randomly selected and weighed. Within what limits will 95 percent of the sample means occur?

38. The mean amount purchased by a typical customer at Churchill's Grocery Store is $23.50 with a standard deviation of $5.00. Assume the distribution of amounts purchased follows the normal distribution. For a sample of 50 customers, answer the following questions.

    a. What is the likelihood the sample mean is at least $25.00?

    b. What is the likelihood the sample mean is greater than $22.50 but less than $25.00?

    c. Within what limits will 90 percent of the sample means occur?

39. The mean SAT score for Division I student-athletes is 947 with a standard deviation of 205. If you select a random sample of 60 of these students, what is the probability the mean is below 900?

40. Suppose we roll a fair die two times.
  a. How many different samples are there?
  b. List each of the possible samples and compute the mean.
  c. On a chart similar to Chart 8–1, compare the distribution of sample means with the distribution of the population.
  d. Compute the mean and the standard deviation of each distribution and compare them.

41. Following is a list of the 50 states with the numbers 0 through 49 assigned to them.

Number	State	Number	State
0	Alabama	25	Montana
1	Alaska	26	Nebraska
2	Arizona	27	Nevada
3	Arkansas	28	New Hampshire
4	California	29	New Jersey
5	Colorado	30	New Mexico
6	Connecticut	31	New York
7	Delaware	32	North Carolina
8	Florida	33	North Dakota
9	Georgia	34	Ohio
10	Hawaii	35	Oklahoma
11	Idaho	36	Oregon
12	Illinois	37	Pennsylvania
13	Indiana	38	Rhode Island
14	Iowa	39	South Carolina
15	Kansas	40	South Dakota
16	Kentucky	41	Tennessee
17	Louisiana	42	Texas
18	Maine	43	Utah
19	Maryland	44	Vermont
20	Massachusetts	45	Virginia
21	Michigan	46	Washington
22	Minnesota	47	West Virginia
23	Mississippi	48	Wisconsin
24	Missouri	49	Wyoming

  a. You wish to select a sample of eight from this list. The selected random numbers are 45, 15, 81, 09, 39, 43, 90, 26, 06, 45, 01, and 42. Which states are included in the sample?
  b. You wish to use a systematic sample of every sixth item and the digit 02 is chosen as the starting point. Which states are included?

42. Human Resource Consulting (HRC) is surveying a sample of 60 firms in order to study health care costs for a client. One of the items being tracked is the annual deductible that employees must pay. The state Bureau of Labor reports the mean of this distribution is $502 with a standard deviation of $100.
  a. Compute the standard error of the sample mean for HRC.
  b. What is the chance HRC finds a sample mean between $477 and $527?
  c. Calculate the likelihood that the sample mean is between $492 and $512.
  d. What is the probability the sample mean is greater that $550?

43. Over the past decade the mean number of members of the Information Systems Security Association who have experienced a denial-of-service attack each year is 510 with a standard deviation of 14.28 attacks. Suppose nothing in this environment changes.
  a. What is the likelihood this group will suffer an average of more than 600 attacks in the next 10 years?
  b. Compute the probability the mean number of attacks over the next 10 years is between 500 and 600.
  c. What is the possibility they will experience an average of less than 500 attacks over the next 10 years?

44. The Oil Price Information Center reports the mean price per gallon of regular gasoline is $3.79 with a population standard deviation of $0.18. Assume a random sample of 40 gasoline stations is selected and their mean cost for regular gasoline is computed.
    a. What is the standard error of the mean in this experiment?
    b. What is the probability that the sample mean is between $3.77 and $3.81?
    c. What is the probability that the difference between the sample mean and the population mean is less than 0.01?
    d. What is the likelihood the sample mean is greater than $3.87?
45. Nike's annual report says that the average American buys 6.5 pairs of sports shoes per year. Suppose the population standard deviation is 2.1 and that a sample of 81 customers will be examined next year.
    a. What is the standard error of the mean in this experiment?
    b. What is the probability that the sample mean is between 6 and 7 pairs of sports shoes?
    c. What is the probability that the difference between the sample mean and the population mean is less than 0.25 pairs?
    d. What is the likelihood the sample mean is greater than 7 pairs?

Data Set Exercises

46. Refer to the Real Estate data, which report information on the homes sold in the Denver, Colorado, area last year.
    a. Compute the mean and the standard deviation of the distribution of the selling prices for the homes. Assume this to be the population. Develop a histogram of the data. Would it seem reasonable from this histogram to conclude that the population of selling prices follows the normal distribution?
    b. Let's assume a normal population. Select a sample of 10 homes. Compute the mean and the standard deviation of the sample. Determine the likelihood of finding a sample mean this large or larger from the population.
47. Refer to the CIA data, which report demographic and economic information on 46 countries. Select a random sample of 10 countries. For this sample calculate the mean GDP/capita. Repeat this sampling and calculation process five more times. Then find the mean and standard deviation of your six sample means.
    a. How do this mean and standard deviation compare with the mean and standard deviation of the original "population" of 46 countries?
    b. Make a histogram of the six means and discuss whether the distribution is normal.
    c. Suppose the population distribution is normal. For the first sample mean you computed, determine the likelihood of finding a sample mean this large or larger from the population.

Software Commands

1. The Excel commands to select a simple random sample on page 261 are:
    a. Select the **Data** tab on the top of the menu. Then on the far right select **Data Analysis,** then **Sampling** and **OK.**
    b. For **Input Range** insert *B1:B31.* Since the column is named, click the **Labels** box. Select **Random,** and enter the sample size for the **Number of Samples,** in this case 5. Click on **Output Range** and indicate the place in the spreadsheet you want the sample information. Note that your sample results will differ from those in the text. Also recall that Excel samples with replacement, so it is possible for a population value to appear more than once in the sample.

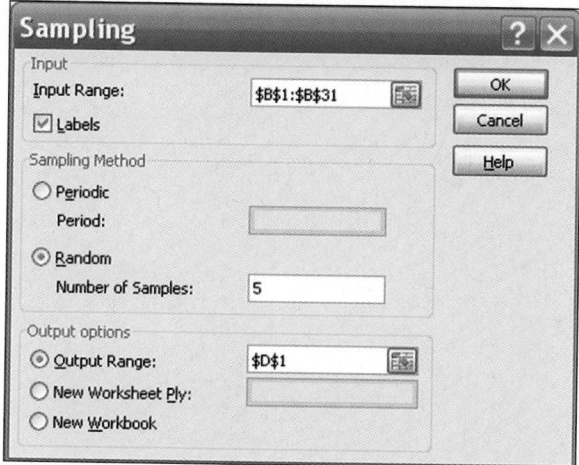

Chapter 8   Answers to Self-Review

8–1 **a.** Students selected are Price, Detley, and Molter.
b. Answers will vary.
c. Skip it and move to the next random number.

8–2 The students selected are Berry, Francis, Kopp, Poteau, and Swetye.

8–3 **a.** 10, found by:

$$_5C_2 = \frac{5!}{2!(5-2)!}$$

b.

	Service	Sample Mean
Snow, Tolson	20, 22	21
Snow, Kraft	20, 26	23
Snow, Irwin	20, 24	22
Snow, Jones	20, 28	24
Tolson, Kraft	22, 26	24
Tolson, Irwin	22, 24	23
Tolson, Jones	22, 28	25
Kraft, Irwin	26, 24	25
Kraft, Jones	26, 28	27
Irwin, Jones	24, 28	26

c.

Mean	Number	Probability
21	1	.10
22	1	.10
23	2	.20
24	2	.20
25	2	.20
26	1	.10
27	1	.10
	10	1.00

d. Identical: population mean, μ, is 24, and mean of sample means, $\mu_{\bar{X}}$, is also 24.
e. Sample means range from 21 to 27. Population values go from 20 to 28.
f. Nonnormal.
g. Yes.

8–4 The answers will vary. Here is one solution.

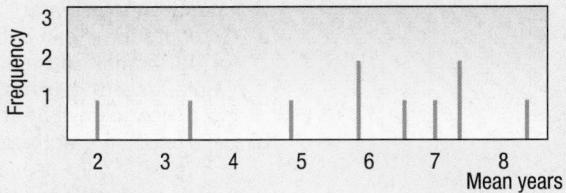

Sample Number										
	1	2	3	4	5	6	7	8	9	10
	8	2	2	19	3	4	0	4	1	2
	19	1	14	9	2	5	8	2	14	4
	8	3	4	2	4	4	1	14	4	1
	0	3	2	3	1	2	16	1	2	3
	2	1	7	2	19	18	18	16	3	7
Total	37	10	29	35	29	33	43	37	24	17
$\bar{X}$	7.4	2	5.8	7.0	5.8	6.6	8.6	7.4	4.8	3.4

Mean of the 10 sample means is 5.88.

8–5 $z = \dfrac{31.08 - 31.20}{0.4/\sqrt{16}} = -1.20$

The probability that z is greater than -1.20 is .5000 + .3849 = .8849. There is more than an 88 percent chance the filling operation will produce bottles with at least 31.08 ounces.

Estimation and Confidence Intervals

The American Restaurant Association collected information on the number of meals eaten outside the home per week by young married couples. A survey of 60 couples showed the sample mean number of meals eaten outside the home was 2.76 meals per week, with a standard deviation of 0.75 meals per week. Construct a 97 percent confidence interval for the population mean. (See Goal 3 and Exercise 36.)

Introduction

The previous chapter began our discussion of statistical inference. It introduced both the reasons for, and the methods of, sampling. The reasons for sampling were:

- To contact the entire population is too time consuming.
- The cost of studying all the items in the population is often too expensive.
- The sample results are usually adequate.
- Certain tests are destructive.
- Checking all the items is physically impossible.

There are several methods of sampling. Simple random sampling is the most widely used method. With this type of sampling, each member of the population has the same chance of being selected to be a part of the sample. Other methods of sampling include systematic sampling, stratified sampling, and cluster sampling.

Chapter 8 assumes information about the population, such as the mean, the standard deviation, or the shape of the population. In most business situations, such information is not available. In fact, the purpose of sampling may be to estimate some of these values. For example, you select a sample from a population and use the mean of the sample to estimate the mean of the population.

This chapter considers several important aspects of sampling. We begin by studying **point estimates.** A point estimate is a single value (point) derived from a sample and used to estimate a population value. For example, suppose we select a sample of 50 junior executives and ask each the number of hours they worked last week. Compute the mean of this sample of 50 and use the value of the sample mean as a point estimate of the unknown population mean. However, a point estimate is a single value. A more informative approach is to present a range of values in which we expect the population parameter to occur. Such a range of values is called a **confidence interval.**

Frequently in business we need to determine the size of a sample. How many voters should a polling organization contact to forecast the election outcome? How many products do we need to examine to ensure our quality level? This chapter also develops a strategy for determining the appropriate number of observations in the sample.

Point Estimates and Confidence Intervals for a Mean

We begin the study of point estimates and confidence intervals by studying estimates of the population mean. We will consider two cases, where

- The population standard deviation (σ) is known,
- The population standard deviation is unknown. In this case we substitute the sample standard deviation (s) for the population standard deviation (σ).

There are important distinctions in the assumptions between these two situations. We consider the case where σ is known first.

Population Standard Deviation, Known σ

In the previous chapter, the data on the length of service of Spence Sprockets employees, presented in the example on page 273, is a population because we present the length of service for all 40 employees. In that case we can easily compute the population mean. We have all the data and the population is not too large. In most situations, however, the population is large or it is difficult to identify all members of the population, so we need to rely on sample information. In other words, we do not know the population parameter and we therefore want to estimate the value from a sample statistic. Consider the following business situations.

1. Tourism is a major source of income for many Caribbean countries, such as Barbados. Suppose the Bureau of Tourism for Barbados wants an estimate of the mean amount spent by tourists visiting the country. It would not be feasible to contact each tourist. Therefore, 500 tourists are randomly selected as they depart the country and asked in detail about their spending while visiting the island. The mean amount spent by the sample of 500 tourists is an estimate of the unknown population parameter. That is, we let $\overline{X}$, the sample mean, serve as an estimate of μ, the population mean.

2. Centex Home Builders, Inc., builds quality homes in the southeastern region of the United States. One of the major concerns of new buyers is the date on which the home will be completed. In recent times Centex has been telling customers, "Your home will be completed 45 working days from the date we begin installing drywall." The customer relations department at Centex wishes to compare this pledge with recent experience. A sample of 50 homes completed this year revealed the mean number of working days from the start of drywall to the completion of the home was 46.7 days. Is it reasonable to conclude that the population mean is still 45 days and that the difference between the sample mean (46.7 days) and the proposed population mean is sampling error?

3. Recent medical studies indicate that exercise is an important part of a person's overall health. The director of human resources at OCF, a large glass manufacturer, wants an estimate of the number of hours per week employees spend exercising. A sample of 70 employees reveals the mean number of hours of exercise last week is 3.3. The sample mean of 3.3 hours estimates the unknown population mean, the mean hours of exercise for all employees.

A point estimate is a single statistic used to estimate a population parameter. Suppose Best Buy, Inc., wants to estimate the mean age of buyers of HD plasma televisions. They select a random sample of 50 recent purchasers, determine the age of each purchaser, and compute the mean age of the buyers in the sample. The mean of this sample is a point estimate of the mean of the population.

> **POINT ESTIMATE** The statistic, computed from sample information, which is used to estimate the population parameter.

The sample mean, $\overline{X}$, is a point estimate of the population mean, μ; p, a sample proportion, is a point estimate of π, the population proportion; and s, the sample standard deviation, is a point estimate of σ, the population standard deviation.

A point estimate, however, tells only part of the story. While we expect the point estimate to be close to the population parameter, we would like to measure how close it really is. A confidence interval serves this purpose.

> **CONFIDENCE INTERVAL** A range of values constructed from sample data so that the population parameter is likely to occur within that range at a specified probability. The specified probability is called the *level of confidence*.

For example, we estimate the mean yearly income for construction workers in the New York–New Jersey area is $65,000. The range of this estimate might be from $61,000 to $69,000. We can describe how confident we are that the population parameter is in the interval by making a probability statement. We might say, for instance, that we are 90 percent sure that the mean yearly income of construction workers in the New York–New Jersey area is between $61,000 and $69,000.

The information developed about the shape of a sampling distribution of the sample mean, that is, the sampling distribution of $\overline{X}$, allows us to locate an interval that has a specified probability of containing the population mean, μ. For a sample from a population that follows a normal distribution with σ known or a reasonably large sample from a population of any shape, the results of the central limit theorem allow us to state the following:

1. Ninety-five percent of the sample means selected from a population will be within 1.96 standard deviations of the population mean μ.
2. Ninety-nine percent of the sample means will lie within 2.58 standard deviations of the population mean.

The standard deviation discussed here is the standard deviation of the sampling distribution of the sample mean. It is usually called the *standard error*. Intervals computed in this fashion are called the **95 percent confidence interval** and the **99 percent confidence interval**. How are the values of 1.96 and 2.58 obtained? The *95 percent* and *99 percent* refer to the percent of similarly constructed intervals that would include the parameter being estimated. The *95 percent*, for example, refers to the middle 95 percent of the observations. Therefore, the remaining 5 percent are equally divided between the two tails. See the following diagram.

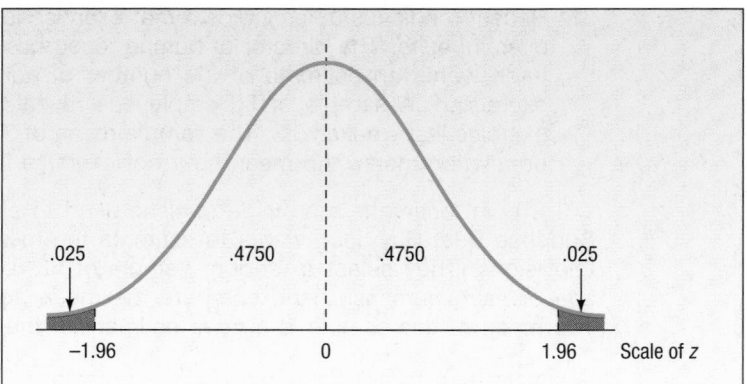

We use Appendix B.1 to find the appropriate z values. Locate .4750 in the body of the table. Read the corresponding row and column values. The value is 1.96. Thus, the probability of finding a z value between 0 and 1.96 is .4750. Likewise, the probability of being in the interval between −1.96 and 0 is also .4750. When we combine these two, the probability of being in the interval −1.96 to 1.96 is .9500. Following is a portion of Appendix B.1. The z value for the 90 percent level of confidence is determined in a similar manner. It is 1.65. For a 99 percent level of confidence the z value is 2.58.

z	0.00	0.01	0.02	0.03	0.04	0.05	0.06	0.07	0.08	0.09
⋮	⋮	⋮	⋮	⋮	⋮	⋮	⋮	⋮	⋮	⋮
1.5	0.4332	0.4345	0.4357	0.4370	0.4382	0.4394	0.4406	0.4418	0.4429	0.4441
1.6	0.4452	0.4463	0.4474	0.4484	0.4495	0.4505	0.4515	0.4525	0.4535	0.4545
1.7	0.4554	0.4564	0.4573	0.4582	0.4591	0.4599	0.4608	0.4616	0.4625	0.4633
1.8	0.4641	0.4649	0.4656	0.4664	0.4671	0.4678	0.4686	0.4693	0.4699	0.4706
1.9	0.4713	0.4719	0.4726	0.4732	0.4738	0.4744	0.4750	0.4756	0.4761	0.4767
2.0	0.4772	0.4778	0.4783	0.4788	0.4793	0.4798	0.4803	0.4808	0.4812	0.4817
2.1	0.4821	0.4826	0.4830	0.4834	0.4838	0.4842	0.4846	0.4850	0.4854	0.4857
2.2	0.4861	0.4864	0.4868	0.4871	0.4875	0.4878	0.4881	0.4884	0.4887	0.4890
2.3	0.4893	0.4896	0.4898	0.4901	0.4904	0.4906	0.4909	0.4911	0.4913	0.4916
2.4	0.4918	0.4920	0.4922	0.4925	0.4927	0.4929	0.4931	0.4932	0.4934	0.4936

How do we determine a 95 percent confidence interval? The width of the interval is determined by the level of confidence and the size of the standard error of the mean. We've described above how to find the z value for a particular level of confidence. Recall from the previous chapter (see formula 8–1 on page 277) the standard error of the mean reports the variation in the distribution of sample means. It is really the standard deviation of the distribution of sample means. The formula is repeated below:

$$\sigma_{\bar{x}} = \frac{\sigma}{\sqrt{n}}$$

where

$\sigma_{\bar{x}}$ is the symbol for the standard error of the mean. We use a Greek letter because it is a population value, and the subscript $\bar{x}$ reminds us that it refers to a sampling distribution of the sample means.

σ is the population standard deviation.

n is the number of observations in the sample.

The size of the standard error is affected by two values. The first is the standard deviation of the population. The larger the population standard deviation, σ, the larger $\sigma/\sqrt{n}$. If the population is homogenous, resulting in a small population standard deviation, the standard error will also be small. However, the standard error is also affected by the number of observations in the sample. A large number of observations in the sample will result in a small standard error of estimate, indicating that there is less variability in the sample means.

To explain these ideas, consider the following example. Del Monte Foods distributes diced peaches in 4-ounce plastic cups. To be sure each cup contains at least the

required amount Del Monte sets the filling operation to dispense 4.01 ounces of peaches and gel in each cup. So 4.01 is the population mean. Of course not every cup will contain exactly 4.01 ounces of peaches and gel. Some cups will have more and others less. Suppose the standard deviation of the process is .02 ounces. Let's also assume that the process follows the normal probability distribution. Now, we select a random sample of 16 cups and determine the sample mean. It is 4.015 ounces of peaches and gel. The 95 percent confidence interval for the population mean of this particular sample is:

$$4.015 \pm 1.96(.02/\sqrt{16}) = 4.015 \pm .0098$$

The 95 percent confidence interval is between 4.0052 and 4.0248. Of course in this case we observe that the population mean of 4.01 ounces is in this interval. But that will not always be the case. Theoretically, if we selected 100 samples of 16 cups from the population, calculated the sample mean, and developed a confidence interval based on each *sample* mean, we would expect to find the *population* mean in about 95 of the 100 intervals.

We can summarize the following calculations for a 95 percent confidence interval in the following formula:

$$\bar{X} \pm 1.96 \frac{\sigma}{\sqrt{n}}$$

Similarly a 99 percent confidence interval is computed as follows.

$$\bar{X} \pm 2.58 \frac{\sigma}{\sqrt{n}}$$

As we discussed earlier, the values 1.96 and 2.58 are z values corresponding to the middle 95 percent and the middle 99 percent of the observations, respectively.

We are not restricted to the 95 and 99 percent levels of confidence. We can select any confidence level between 0 and 100 percent and find the corresponding value for z. In general, a confidence interval for the population mean when the population standard deviation is known is computed by:

CONFIDENCE INTERVAL FOR POPULATION MEAN WITH σ KNOWN	$\bar{X} \pm z \dfrac{\sigma}{\sqrt{n}}$	[9–1]

where z depends on the level of confidence. Thus for a 92 percent level of confidence, the value of z in formula (9–1) is 1.75. The value of z is from Appendix B.1. This table is based on half the normal distribution, so .9200/2 = .4600. The closest value in the body of the table is .4599 and the corresponding z value is 1.75.

Frequently, we also use the 90 percent level of confidence. In this case, we want the area between 0 and z to be .4500, found by .9000/2. To find the z value for this level of confidence, move down the left column of Appendix B.1 to 1.6 and then over to the columns headed 0.04 and 0.05. The area corresponding to a z value of 1.64 is .4495, and for 1.65 it is .4505. To be conservative, we use 1.65. Try looking up the following levels of confidence and check your answers with the corresponding z values given on the right.

Confidence Level	Nearest Half Probability	z Value
80 percent	.3997	1.28
94 percent	.4699	1.88
96 percent	.4798	2.05

The following example shows the details for calculating a confidence interval and interpreting the result.

Example

The American Management Association wishes to have information on the mean income of store managers in the retail industry. A random sample of 256 managers reveals a sample mean of $45,420. The standard deviation of this population is $2,050. The association would like answers to the following questions:

1. What is the population mean?
2. What is a reasonable range of values for the population mean?
3. How do we interpret these results?

Solution

Generally, distributions of salary and income are positively skewed, because a few individuals earn considerably more than others, thus skewing the distribution in the positive direction. Fortunately, the central limit theorem stipulates that if we select a large sample, the distribution of the sample means will follow the normal distribution. In this instance, a sample of 256 store managers is large enough that we can assume that the sampling distribution will follow the normal distribution. Now to answer the questions posed in the example.

1. **What is the population mean?** In this case, we do not know. We do know the sample mean is $45,420. Hence, our best estimate of the unknown population value is the corresponding sample statistic. Thus the sample mean of $45,420 is a *point estimate* of the unknown population mean.

2. **What is a reasonable range of values for the population mean?** The association decides to use the 95 percent level of confidence. To determine the corresponding confidence interval we use formula (9–1).

$$\overline{X} \pm z\frac{\sigma}{\sqrt{n}} = \$45,420 \pm 1.96\frac{\$2,050}{\sqrt{256}} = \$45,420 \pm \$251$$

The usual practice is to round these endpoints to $45,169 and $45,671. These endpoints are called the *confidence limits*. The degree of confidence or the *level of confidence* is 95 percent and the confidence interval is from $45,169 to $45,671. The ±$251 is often referred to as the *margin of error*.

3. **How do we interpret these results?** Suppose we select many samples of 256 store managers, perhaps several hundred. For each sample, we compute the mean and then construct a 95 percent confidence interval, such as we did in the previous section. We could expect about 95 percent of these confidence intervals to contain the *population* mean. About 5 percent of the intervals would not contain the population mean annual income, which is μ. However, a particular confidence interval either contains the population parameter or it does not. The following diagram shows the results of selecting samples from the population of store managers in the retail industry, computing the mean of each and then, using formula (9–1), determining a 95 percent confidence interval for the population mean. Note that not all intervals include the population mean. Both the endpoints of the fifth sample are less than the population mean. We attribute this to sampling error, and it is the risk we assume when we select the level of confidence.

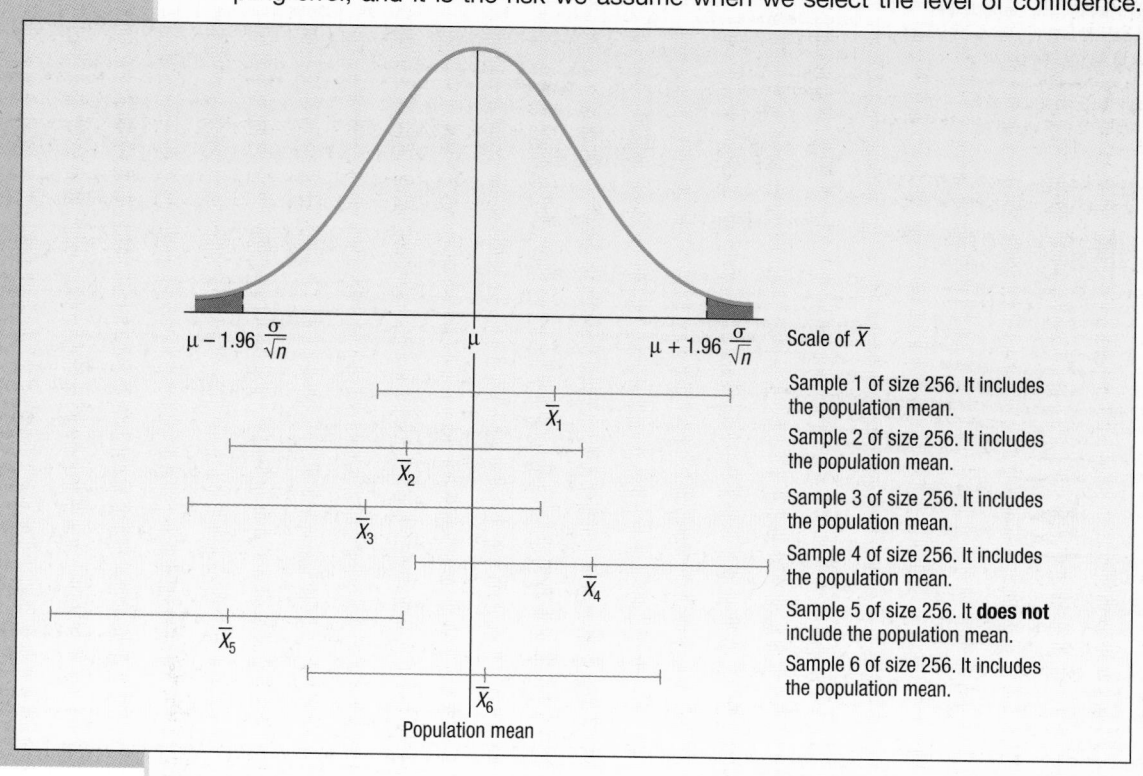

A Computer Simulation

With the aid of a computer, we can randomly select samples from a population, quickly compute the confidence interval, and show how confidence intervals usually, but not always, include the population parameter. The following example will help to explain.

Example

From many years in the automobile leasing business, Town Bank knows the mean distance driven on a four-year lease is 50,000 miles and the standard deviation is 5,000. These are population values. Suppose, using the MINITAB statistical software system, we want to find what proportion of the 95 percent confidence intervals will include the population mean of 50. To make the calculations easier to understand, we'll conduct the study in thousands of miles, instead of miles. We select 60 random samples of 30 observations from a population with a mean of 50 and a standard deviation of 5.

Solution

The results of 60 random samples of 30 automobiles each are summarized in the computer output below. Of the 60 confidence intervals with a 95 percent confidence level, 2, or 3.33 percent, did not include the population mean of 50. The intervals (C3 and C59) that do *not* include the population mean are highlighted. 3.33 percent is close to the estimate that 5 percent of the intervals will not include the population mean, and the 58 of 60, or 96.67 percent, is close to 95 percent.

To explain the first calculation in more detail: MINITAB began by selecting a random sample of 30 observations from a population with a mean of 50 and a standard deviation of 5. The mean of these 30 observations is 50.053. The sampling error is 0.053, found by $\overline{X} - \mu = 50.053 - 50.000$. The endpoints of the confidence interval are 48.264 and 51.842. These endpoints are determined by using formula (9–1):

$$\overline{X} \pm 1.96 \frac{\sigma}{\sqrt{n}} = 50.053 \pm 1.96 \frac{5}{\sqrt{30}} = 50.053 \pm 1.789$$

```
One-Sample Z:

The assumed sigma = 5

Variable     N        Mean      StDev     SE Mean        95.0% CI
C1          30       50.053     5.002      0.913     ( 48.264, 51.842)
C2          30       49.025     4.450      0.913     ( 47.236, 50.815)
C3          30       52.023     5.918      0.913     ( 50.234, 53.812)
C4          30       50.056     3.364      0.913     ( 48.267, 51.845)
C5          30       49.737     4.784      0.913     ( 47.948, 51.526)
C6          30       51.074     5.495      0.913     ( 49.285, 52.863)
C7          30       50.040     5.930      0.913     ( 48.251, 51.829)
C8          30       48.910     3.645      0.913     ( 47.121, 50.699)
C9          30       51.033     4.918      0.913     ( 49.244, 52.822)
C10         30       50.692     4.571      0.913     ( 48.903, 52.482)
C11         30       49.853     4.525      0.913     ( 48.064, 51.642)
C12         30       50.286     3.422      0.913     ( 48.497, 52.076)
C13         30       50.257     4.317      0.913     ( 48.468, 52.046)
C14         30       49.605     4.994      0.913     ( 47.816, 51.394)
C15         30       51.474     5.497      0.913     ( 49.685, 53.264)
C16         30       48.930     5.317      0.913     ( 47.141, 50.719)
C17         30       49.870     4.847      0.913     ( 48.081, 51.659)
C18         30       50.739     6.224      0.913     ( 48.950, 52.528)
C19         30       50.979     5.520      0.913     ( 49.190, 52.768)
C20         30       48.848     4.130      0.913     ( 47.059, 50.638)
C21         30       49.481     4.056      0.913     ( 47.692, 51.270)
C22         30       49.183     5.409      0.913     ( 47.394, 50.973)
C23         30       50.084     4.522      0.913     ( 48.294, 51.873)
C24         30       50.866     5.142      0.913     ( 49.077, 52.655)
C25         30       48.768     5.582      0.913     ( 46.979, 50.557)
C26         30       50.904     6.052      0.913     ( 49.115, 52.694)
C27         30       49.481     5.535      0.913     ( 47.691, 51.270)
C28         30       50.949     5.916      0.913     ( 49.160, 52.739)
C29         30       49.106     4.641      0.913     ( 47.317, 50.895)
C30         30       49.994     5.853      0.913     ( 48.205, 51.784)
C31         30       49.601     5.064      0.913     ( 47.811, 51.390)
C32         30       51.494     5.597      0.913     ( 49.705, 53.284)
C33         30       50.460     4.393      0.913     ( 48.671, 52.249)
C34         30       50.378     4.075      0.913     ( 48.589, 52.167)
C35         30       49.808     4.155      0.913     ( 48.019, 51.597)
C36         30       49.934     5.012      0.913     ( 48.145, 51.723)
```

Variable	N	Mean	StDev	SE Mean	95.0% CI
C37	30	50.017	4.082	0.913	(48.228, 51.806)
C38	30	50.074	3.631	0.913	(48.285, 51.863)
C39	30	48.656	4.833	0.913	(46.867, 50.445)
C40	30	50.568	3.855	0.913	(48.779, 52.357)
C41	30	50.916	3.775	0.913	(49.127, 52.705)
C42	30	49.104	4.321	0.913	(47.315, 50.893)
C43	30	50.308	5.467	0.913	(48.519, 52.097)
C44	30	49.034	4.405	0.913	(47.245, 50.823)
C45	30	50.399	4.729	0.913	(48.610, 52.188)
C46	30	49.634	3.996	0.913	(47.845, 51.424)
C47	30	50.479	4.881	0.913	(48.689, 52.268)
C48	30	50.529	5.173	0.913	(48.740, 52.318)
C49	30	51.577	5.822	0.913	(49.787, 53.366)
C50	30	50.403	4.893	0.913	(48.614, 52.192)
C51	30	49.717	5.218	0.913	(47.927, 51.506)
C52	30	49.796	5.327	0.913	(48.007, 51.585)
C53	30	50.549	4.680	0.913	(48.760, 52.338)
C54	30	50.200	5.840	0.913	(48.410, 51.989)
C55	30	49.138	5.074	0.913	(47.349, 50.928)
C56	30	49.667	3.843	0.913	(47.878, 51.456)
C57	30	49.603	5.614	0.913	(47.814, 51.392)
C58	30	49.441	5.702	0.913	(47.652, 51.230)
C59	30	47.873	4.685	0.913	(46.084, 49.662)
C60	30	51.087	5.162	0.913	(49.297, 52.876)

Self-Review 9–1

The Bun-and-Run is a franchise fast-food restaurant located in the Northeast specializing in half-pound hamburgers, fish sandwiches, and chicken sandwiches. Soft drinks and french fries are also available. The Planning Department of Bun-and-Run, Inc., reports that the distribution of daily sales for restaurants follows the normal distribution and that the standard deviation is $3,000. A sample of 40 showed the mean daily sales to be $20,000.
(a) What is the population mean?
(b) What is the best estimate of the population mean? What is this value called?
(c) Develop a 99 percent confidence interval for the population mean.
(d) Interpret the confidence interval.

Exercises

1. A sample of 49 observations is taken from a normal population with a standard deviation of 10. The sample mean is 55. Determine the 99 percent confidence interval for the population mean.
2. A sample of 81 observations is taken from a normal population with a standard deviation of 5. The sample mean is 40. Determine the 95 percent confidence interval for the population mean.
3. A sample of 10 observations is selected from a normal population for which the population standard deviation is known to be 5. The sample mean is 20.
   a. Determine the standard error of the mean.
   b. Explain why we can use formula (9–1) to determine the 95 percent confidence interval even though the sample is less than 30.
   c. Determine the 95 percent confidence interval for the population mean.
4. Suppose you want an 85 percent confidence level. What value would you use to multiply the standard error of the mean by?
5. A research firm conducted a survey to determine the mean amount steady smokers spend on cigarettes during a week. They found the distribution of amounts spent per week followed the normal distribution with a standard deviation of $5. A sample of 49 steady smokers revealed that $\overline{X}$ = $20.
   a. What is the point estimate of the population mean? Explain what it indicates.

b. Using the 95 percent level of confidence, determine the confidence interval for μ. Explain what it indicates.

6. Refer to the previous exercise. Suppose that 64 smokers (instead of 49) were sampled. Assume the sample mean remained the same.
   a. What is the 95 percent confidence interval estimate of μ?
   b. Explain why this confidence interval is narrower than the one determined in the previous exercise.

7. Bob Nale is the owner of Nale's Texaco GasTown. Bob would like to estimate the mean number of gallons of gasoline sold to his customers. Assume the number of gallons sold follows the normal distribution with a standard deviation of 2.30 gallons. From his records, he selects a random sample of 60 sales and finds the mean number of gallons sold is 8.60.
   a. What is the point estimate of the population mean?
   b. Develop a 99 percent confidence interval for the population mean.
   c. Interpret the meaning of part (b).

8. Dr. Patton is a professor of English. Recently she counted the number of misspelled words in a group of student essays. She noted the distribution of misspelled words per essay followed the normal distribution with a standard deviation of 2.44 words per essay. For her 10 A.M. section of 40 students, the mean number of misspelled words was 6.05. Construct a 95 percent confidence interval for the mean number of misspelled words in the population of student essays.

Population Standard Deviation, σ Unknown

In the previous section we assumed the population standard deviation was known. In the case involving Del Monte 4-ounce cups of peaches, there would likely be a long history of measurements in the filling process. Therefore, it is reasonable to assume the standard deviation of the population is available. However, in most sampling situations the population standard deviation (σ) is not known. Here are some examples where we wish to estimate the population means and it is unlikely we would know the population standard deviations. Suppose each of these studies involves students at West Virginia University.

- The Dean of the Business College wants to estimate the mean number of hours full-time students work at paying jobs each week. He selects a sample of 30 students, contacts each student and asks them how many hours they worked last week. From the sample information he can calculate the sample mean, but it is not likely he would know or be able to find the *population* (σ) standard deviation required in formula (9–1). He could calculate the standard deviation of the sample and use that as an estimate, but he would not likely know the population standard deviation.

- The Dean of Students wants to estimate the distance the typical commuter student travels to class. She selects a sample of 40 commuter students, contacts each, and determines the one-way distance from each student's home to the center of campus. From the sample data she calculates the mean travel distance, that is $\overline{X}$. It is unlikely the standard deviation of the population would be known or available, again making formula (9–1) unusable.

- The Director of Student Loans wants to know the mean amount owed on student loans at the time of his/her graduation. The director selects a sample of 20 graduating students and contacts each to find the information. From the sample information he can estimate the mean amount. However, to develop a confidence interval using formula (9–1), the population standard deviation is necessary. It is not likely this information is available.

Fortunately we can use the sample standard deviation to estimate the population standard deviation. That is, we use *s*, the sample standard deviation, to estimate σ, the population standard deviation. But in doing so, we cannot use formula

(9–1). Because we do not know σ we cannot use the *z* distribution. However, there is a remedy. We use the sample standard deviation and replace the *z* distribution with the *t* distribution.

The *t* distribution is a continuous probability distribution, with many similar characteristics to the *z* distribution. William Gosset, an English brewmaster, was the first to study the *t* distribution.

He was particularly concerned with the exact behavior of the distribution of the following statistic:

$$t = \frac{\overline{X} - \mu}{s/\sqrt{n}}$$

where *s* is an estimate of σ. He was especially worried about the discrepancy between *s* and σ when *s* was calculated from a very small sample. The *t* distribution and the standard normal distribution are shown graphically in Chart 9–1. Note particularly that the *t* distribution is flatter, more spread out, than the standard normal distribution. This is because the standard deviation of the *t* distribution is larger than the standard normal distribution.

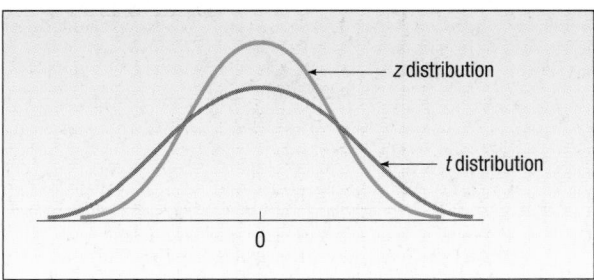

CHART 9–1 The Standard Normal Distribution and Student's *t* Distribution

The following characteristics of the *t* distribution are based on the assumption that the population of interest is normal, or nearly normal.

1. It is, like the *z* distribution, a continuous distribution.
2. It is, like the *z* distribution, bell-shaped and symmetrical.
3. There is not one *t* distribution, but rather a family of *t* distributions. All *t* distributions have a mean of 0, but their standard deviations differ according to the sample size, *n*. There is a *t* distribution for a sample size of 20, another for a sample size of 22, and so on. The standard deviation for a *t* distribution with 5 observations is larger than for a *t* distribution with 20 observations.
4. The *t* distribution is more spread out and flatter at the center than the standard normal distribution (see Chart 9–1). As the sample size increases, however, the *t* distribution approaches the standard normal distribution, because the errors in using *s* to estimate σ decrease with larger samples.

Because Student's *t* distribution has a greater spread than the *z* distribution, the value of *t* for a given level of confidence is larger in magnitude than the corresponding *z* value. Chart 9–2 shows the values of *z* for a 95 percent level of confidence and of *t* for the same level of confidence when the sample size is *n* = 5. How we obtained the actual value of *t* will be explained shortly. For now, observe that for the same level of confidence the *t* distribution is flatter or more spread out than the standard normal distribution.

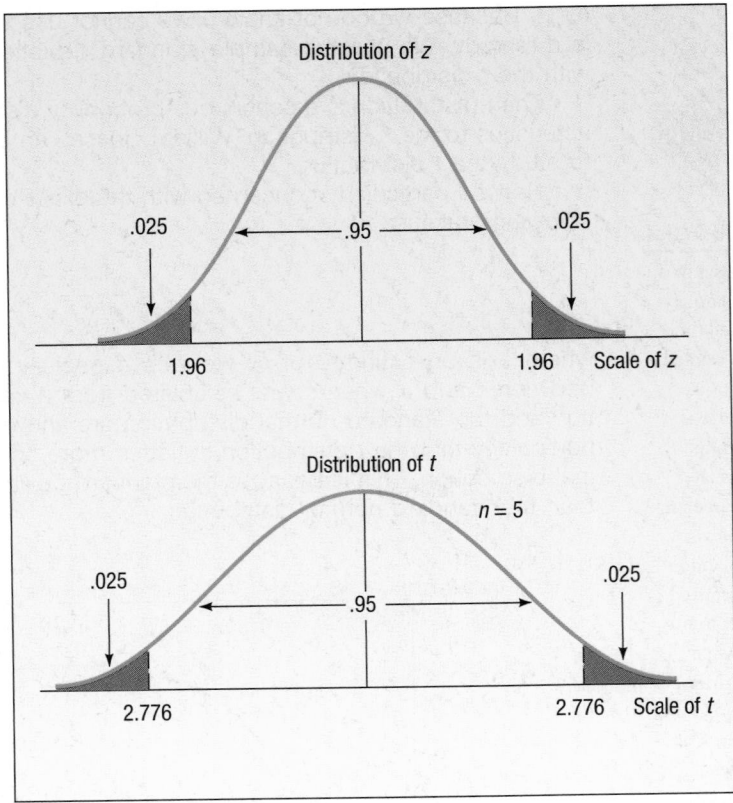

CHART 9–2 Values of z and t for the 95 Percent Level of Confidence

To develop a confidence interval for the population mean using the t distribution, we adjust formula (9–1) as follows.

CONFIDENCE INTERVAL FOR THE POPULATION MEAN, σ UNKNOWN	$\bar{X} \pm t\dfrac{s}{\sqrt{n}}$	[9–2]

To develop a confidence interval for the population mean with an unknown standard deviation we:

1. Assume the sampled population is either normal or approximately normal.
2. Estimate the population standard deviation (σ) with the sample standard deviation (s).
3. Use the t distribution rather than the z distribution.

We should be clear at this point. We base the decision on whether to use the t or the z on whether or not we know σ, the population standard deviation. If we know the population standard deviation, then we use z. If we do not know the population standard deviation, then we must use t. Chart 9–3 summarizes the decision-making process.

The following example will illustrate a confidence interval for a population mean when the population standard deviation is unknown and how to find the appropriate value of t in a table.

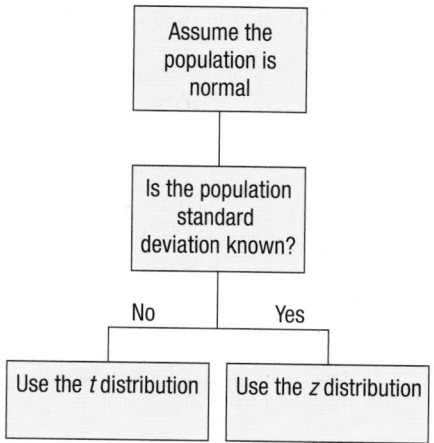

CHART 9–3 Determining When to Use the *z* Distribution or the *t* Distribution

Example

A tire manufacturer wishes to investigate the tread life of its tires. A sample of 10 tires driven 50,000 miles revealed a sample mean of 0.32 inch of tread remaining with a standard deviation of 0.09 inch. Construct a 95 percent confidence interval for the population mean. Would it be reasonable for the manufacturer to conclude that after 50,000 miles the population mean amount of tread remaining is 0.30 inches?

Solution

To begin, we assume the population distribution is normal. In this case, we don't have a lot of evidence, but the assumption is probably reasonable. We do not know the population standard deviation, but we know the sample standard deviation, which is .09 inches. We use formula (9–2):

$$\overline{X} \pm t\frac{s}{\sqrt{n}}$$

From the information given, $\overline{X} = 0.32$, $s = 0.09$, and $n = 10$. To find the value of *t* we use Appendix B.2, a portion of which is reproduced in Table 9–1. Appendix B.2 is also reproduced on the inside back cover of the text. The first step for locating *t* is to move across the columns identified for "Confidence Intervals" to the level of confidence requested. In this case we want the 95 percent level of confidence, so we move to the column headed "95%." The column on the left margin is identified as "*df.*" This refers to the number of degrees of freedom. The number of degrees of freedom is the number of observations in the sample minus the number of samples, written $n - 1$. In this case it is $10 - 1 = 9$. Why did we decide there were 9 degrees of freedom? When sample statistics are being used, it is necessary to determine the number of values that are *free to vary*.

To illustrate the meaning of degrees of freedom: assume that the mean of four numbers is known to be 5. The four numbers are 7, 4, 1, and 8. The deviations of these numbers from the mean must total 0. The deviations of +2, −1, −4, and +3 do total 0. If the deviations of +2, −1, and −4 are known, then the value of +3 is fixed (restricted) in order to satisfy the condition that the sum of the deviations must equal 0. Thus, 1 degree of freedom is lost in a sampling problem involving the standard deviation of the sample because one number (the arithmetic mean) is known. For a 95 percent level of confidence and 9 degrees of freedom, we select the row with 9 degrees of freedom. The value of *t* is 2.262.

TABLE 9–1 A Portion of the *t* Distribution

			Confidence Intervals		
	80%	90%	95%	98%	99%
		Level of Significance for One-Tailed Test			
df	0.10	0.05	0.025	0.010	0.005
		Level of Significance for Two-Tailed Test			
	0.20	0.10	0.05	0.02	0.01
1	3.078	6.314	12.706	31.821	63.657
2	1.886	2.920	4.303	6.965	9.925
3	1.638	2.353	3.182	4.541	5.841
4	1.533	2.132	2.776	3.747	4.604
5	1.476	2.015	2.571	3.365	4.032
6	1.440	1.943	2.447	3.143	3.707
7	1.415	1.895	2.365	2.998	3.499
8	1.397	1.860	2.306	2.896	3.355
9	1.383	1.833	2.262	2.821	3.250
10	1.372	1.812	2.228	2.764	3.169

To determine the confidence interval we substitute the values in formula (9–2).

$$\bar{X} \pm t \frac{s}{\sqrt{n}} = 0.32 \pm 2.262 \frac{0.09}{\sqrt{10}} = 0.32 \pm .064$$

The endpoints of the confidence interval are 0.256 and 0.384. How do we interpret this result? It is reasonable to conclude that the population mean is in this interval. The manufacturer can be reasonably sure (95 percent confident) that the mean remaining tread depth is between 0.256 and 0.384 inches. Because the value of 0.30 is in this interval, it is possible that the mean of the population is 0.30.

Here is another example to clarify the use of confidence intervals. Suppose an article in your local newspaper reported that the mean time to sell a residential property in the area is 60 days. You select a random sample of 20 homes sold in the last year and find the mean selling time is 65 days. Based on the sample data, you develop a 95 percent confidence interval for the population mean. You find that the endpoints of the confidence interval are 62 days and 68 days. How do you interpret this result? You can be reasonably confident the population mean is within this range. The value proposed for the population mean, that is, 60 days, is not included in the interval. It is not likely that the population mean is 60 days. The evidence indicates the statement by the local newspaper may not be correct. To put it another way, it seems unreasonable to obtain the sample you did from a population that had a mean selling time of 60 days.

The following example will show additional details for determining and interpreting a confidence interval. We used MINITAB to perform the calculations.

Example

The manager of the Inlet Square Mall, near Ft. Myers, Florida, wants to estimate the mean amount spent per shopping visit by customers. A sample of 20 customers reveals the following amounts spent.

$48.16	$42.22	$46.82	$51.45	$23.78	$41.86	$54.86
37.92	52.64	48.59	50.82	46.94	61.83	61.69
49.17	61.46	51.35	52.68	58.84	43.88	

What is the best estimate of the population mean? Determine a 95 percent confidence interval. Interpret the result. Would it be reasonable to conclude that the population mean is $50? What about $60?

Solution

The mall manager assumes that the population of the amounts spent follows the normal distribution. This is a reasonable assumption in this case. Additionally, the confidence interval technique is quite powerful and tends to commit any errors on the conservative side if the population is not normal. We should not make the normality assumption when the population is severely skewed or when the distribution has "thick tails." In Chapter 18 we present methods for handling this problem if we cannot make the normality assumption. In this case, the normality assumption is reasonable.

The population standard deviation is not known. Hence, it is appropriate to use the t distribution and formula (9–2) to find the confidence interval. We use the MINITAB system to find the mean and standard deviation of this sample. The results are shown below.

	C1	C
	Amount	
3	46.82	
4	51.45	
5	23.78	
6	41.86	
7	54.86	
8	37.92	
9	52.64	
10	48.59	
11	50.82	
12	46.94	

9-Shopping.MTW *

Session

Descriptive Statistics: Amount

Variable	N	N*	Mean	SE Mean	StDev	Minimum	Q1	Median	Q3	Maximum
Amount	20	0	49.35	2.02	9.01	23.78	44.62	50.00	54.31	61.83

One-Sample T: Amount

Variable	N	Mean	StDev	SE Mean	95% CI
Amount	20	49.35	9.01	2.02	(45.13, 53.57)

The mall manager does not know the population mean. The sample mean is the best estimate of that value. From the pictured MINITAB output, the mean is $49.35, which is the best estimate, the *point estimate,* of the unknown population mean.

We use formula (9–2) to find the confidence interval. The value of t is available from Appendix B.2. There are $n - 1 = 20 - 1 = 19$ degrees of freedom. We move across the row with 19 degrees of freedom to the column for the 95 percent confidence level. The value at this intersection is 2.093. We substitute these values into formula (9–2) to find the confidence interval.

$$\overline{X} \pm t \frac{s}{\sqrt{n}} = \$49.35 \pm 2.093 \frac{\$9.01}{\sqrt{20}} = \$49.35 \pm \$4.22$$

The endpoints of the confidence interval are $45.13 and $53.57. It is reasonable to conclude that the population mean is in that interval.

The manager of Inlet Square wondered whether the population mean could have been $50 or $60. The value of $50 is within the confidence interval. It is reasonable that the population mean could be $50. The value of $60 is not in the confidence interval. Hence, we conclude that the population mean is unlikely to be $60.

The calculations to construct a confidence interval are also available in Excel. The output follows. Note that the sample mean ($49.35) and the sample standard deviation ($9.01) are the same as those in the Minitab calculations. In the Excel information the last line of the output also includes the margin of error, which is the amount that is added and subtracted from the sample mean to form the endpoints of the confidence interval. This value is found from

$$t \frac{s}{\sqrt{n}} = 2.093 \frac{\$9.01}{\sqrt{20}} = \$4.22.$$

Excel

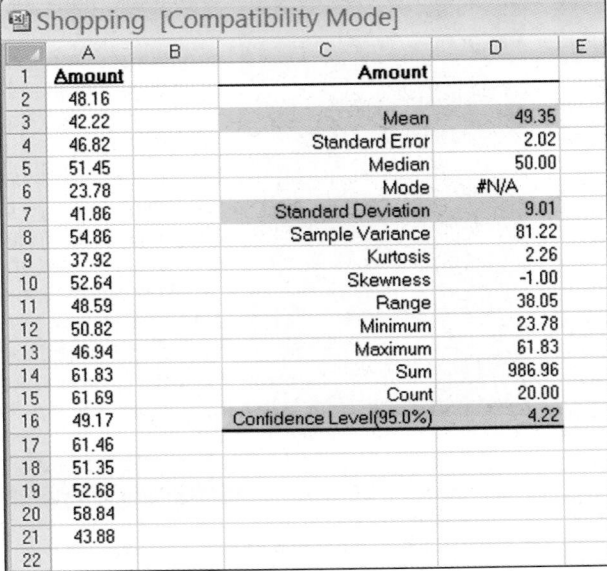

	A	B	C	D	E
	Shopping [Compatibility Mode]				
1	Amount		Amount		
2	48.16				
3	42.22		Mean	49.35	
4	46.82		Standard Error	2.02	
5	51.45		Median	50.00	
6	23.78		Mode	#N/A	
7	41.86		Standard Deviation	9.01	
8	54.86		Sample Variance	81.22	
9	37.92		Kurtosis	2.26	
10	52.64		Skewness	-1.00	
11	48.59		Range	38.05	
12	50.82		Minimum	23.78	
13	46.94		Maximum	61.83	
14	61.83		Sum	986.96	
15	61.69		Count	20.00	
16	49.17		Confidence Level(95.0%)	4.22	
17	61.46				
18	51.35				
19	52.68				
20	58.84				
21	43.88				
22					

Self-Review 9–2

Dottie Kleman is the "Cookie Lady." She bakes and sells cookies at 50 different locations in the Philadelphia area. Ms. Kleman is concerned about absenteeism among her workers. The information below reports the number of days absent for a sample of 10 workers during the last two-week pay period.

4	1	2	2	1	2	2	1	0	3

(a) Determine the mean and the standard deviation of the sample.
(b) What is the population mean? What is the best estimate of that value?
(c) Develop a 95 percent confidence interval for the population mean.
(d) Explain why the *t* distribution is used as a part of the confidence interval.
(e) Is it reasonable to conclude that the typical worker does not miss any days during a pay period?

Exercises

connect™

9. Use Appendix B.2 to locate the value of *t* under the following conditions.
   a. The sample size is 12 and the level of confidence is 95 percent.
   b. The sample size is 20 and the level of confidence is 90 percent.
   c. The sample size is 8 and the level of confidence is 99 percent.
10. Use Appendix B.2 to locate the value of *t* under the following conditions.
    a. The sample size is 15 and the level of confidence is 95 percent.
    b. The sample size is 24 and the level of confidence is 98 percent.
    c. The sample size is 12 and the level of confidence is 90 percent.
11. The owner of Britten's Egg Farm wants to estimate the mean number of eggs laid per chicken. A sample of 20 chickens shows they laid an average of 20 eggs per month with a standard deviation of 2 eggs per month.
    a. What is the value of the population mean? What is the best estimate of this value?
    b. Explain why we need to use the *t* distribution. What assumption do you need to make?
    c. For a 95 percent confidence interval, what is the value of *t*?
    d. Develop the 95 percent confidence interval for the population mean.

e. Would it be reasonable to conclude that the population mean is 21 eggs? What about 25 eggs?

12. The American Sugar Producers Association wants to estimate the mean yearly sugar consumption. A sample of 16 people reveals the mean yearly consumption to be 60 pounds with a standard deviation of 20 pounds.

    a. What is the value of the population mean? What is the best estimate of this value?

    b. Explain why we need to use the *t* distribution. What assumption do you need to make?

    c. For a 90 percent confidence interval, what is the value of *t*?

    d. Develop the 90 percent confidence interval for the population mean.

    e. Would it be reasonable to conclude that the population mean is 63 pounds?

13. Merrill Lynch Securities and Health Care Retirement, Inc., are two large employers in downtown Toledo, Ohio. They are considering jointly offering child care for their employees. As a part of the feasibility study, they wish to estimate the mean weekly child-care cost of their employees. A sample of 10 employees who use child care reveals the following amounts spent last week.

$107	$92	$97	$95	$105	$101	$91	$99	$95	$104

Develop a 90 percent confidence interval for the population mean. Interpret the result.

14. The Greater Pittsburgh Area Chamber of Commerce wants to estimate the mean time workers who are employed in the downtown area spend getting to work. A sample of 15 workers reveals the following number of minutes spent traveling.

29	38	38	33	38	21	45	34
40	37	37	42	30	29	35	

Develop a 98 percent confidence interval for the population mean. Interpret the result.

A Confidence Interval for a Proportion

The material presented so far in this chapter uses the ratio scale of measurement. That is, we use such variables as incomes, weights, distances, and ages. We now want to consider situations such as the following:

- The career services director at Southern Technical Institute reports that 80 percent of its graduates enter the job market in a position related to their field of study.
- A company representative claims that 45 percent of Burger King sales are made at the drive-through window.
- A survey of homes in the Chicago area indicated that 85 percent of the new construction had central air conditioning.
- A recent survey of married men between the ages of 35 and 50 found that 63 percent felt that both partners should earn a living.

These examples illustrate the nominal scale of measurement. When we measure with a nominal scale an observation is classified into one of two or more mutually exclusive groups. For example, a graduate of Southern Tech either entered the job market in a position related to his or her field of study or not. A particular Burger King customer either made a purchase at the drive-through window or did not make a purchase at the drive-through window. There are only two possibilities, and the outcome must be classified into one of the two groups.

> **PROPORTION** The fraction, ratio, or percent indicating the part of the sample or the population having a particular trait of interest.

As an example of a proportion, a recent survey indicated that 92 out of 100 surveyed favored the continued use of daylight savings time in the summer. The sample proportion is 92/100, or .92, or 92 percent. If we let p represent the sample proportion, X the number of "successes," and n the number of items sampled, we can determine a sample proportion as follows.

Statistics in Action

Many survey results reported in newspapers, in news magazines, and on TV use confidence intervals. For example, a recent survey of 800 TV viewers in Toledo, Ohio, found 44 percent watched the evening news on the local CBS affiliate. The article went on to indicate the margin of error was 3.4 percent. The margin of error is actually the amount that is added and subtracted from the point estimate to find the endpoints of a confidence interval. From formula (9–4) and the 95 percent level of confidence:

$$z\sqrt{\frac{p(1-p)}{n}}$$

$$= 1.96\sqrt{\frac{.44(1-.44)}{800}}$$

$$= 0.034$$

SAMPLE PROPORTION	$p = \dfrac{X}{n}$	**[9–3]**

The population proportion is identified by π. Therefore, π refers to the percent of successes in the population. Recall from Chapter 6 that π is the proportion of "successes" in a binomial distribution. This continues our practice of using Greek letters to identify population parameters and Roman letters to identify sample statistics.

To develop a confidence interval for a proportion, we need to meet the following assumptions.

1. The binomial conditions, discussed in Chapter 6, have been met. Briefly, these conditions are:
   a. The sample data is the result of counts.
   b. There are only two possible outcomes. (We usually label one of the outcomes a "success" and the other a "failure.")
   c. The probability of a success remains the same from one trial to the next.
   d. The trials are independent. This means the outcome on one trial does not affect the outcome on another.
2. The values $n\pi$ and $n(1 - \pi)$ should both be greater than or equal to 5. This condition allows us to invoke the central limit theorem and employ the standard normal distribution, that is, z, to complete a confidence interval.

Developing a point estimate for a population proportion and a confidence interval for a population proportion is similar to doing so for a mean. To illustrate, John Gail is running for Congress from the third district of Nebraska. From a random sample of 100 voters in the district, 60 indicate they plan to vote for him in the upcoming election. The sample proportion is .60, but the population proportion is unknown. That is, we do not know what proportion of voters in the *population* will vote for Mr. Gail. The sample value, .60, is the best estimate we have of the unknown population parameter. So we let p, which is .60, be an estimate of π, which is not known.

To develop a confidence interval for a population proportion, we use:

CONFIDENCE INTERVAL FOR A POPULATION PROPORTION	$p \pm z\sqrt{\dfrac{p(1-p)}{n}}$	**[9–4]**

An example will help to explain the details of determining a confidence interval and the result.

Example

The union representing the Bottle Blowers of America (BBA) is considering a proposal to merge with the Teamsters Union. According to BBA union bylaws, at least three-fourths of the union membership must approve any merger. A random sample of 2,000 current BBA members reveals 1,600 plan to vote for the merger proposal. What is the estimate of the population proportion? Develop a 95 percent confidence interval for the population proportion. Basing your decision on this sample information, can you conclude that the necessary proportion of BBA members favor the merger? Why?

Solution

First, calculate the sample proportion from formula (9–3). It is .80, found by

$$p = \frac{X}{n} = \frac{1,600}{2,000} = .80$$

Thus, we estimate that 80 percent of the population favor the merger proposal. We determine the 95 percent confidence interval using formula (9–4). The z value corresponding to the 95 percent level of confidence is 1.96.

$$p \pm z\sqrt{\frac{p(1-p)}{n}} = .80 \pm 1.96\sqrt{\frac{.80(1-.80)}{2,000}} = .80 \pm .018$$

The endpoints of the confidence interval are .782 and .818. The lower endpoint is greater than .75. Hence, we conclude that the merger proposal will likely pass because the interval estimate includes values greater than 75 percent of the union membership.

The interpretation of a confidence interval can be very useful in decision making and play a very important role especially on election night. For example, Cliff Obermeyer is running for Congress from the 6th District of New Jersey. Suppose 500 voters are contacted upon leaving the polls and 275 indicate they voted for Mr. Obermeyer. We will assume that the exit poll of 500 voters is a random sample of those voting in the 6th District. That means that 55 percent of those in the sample voted for Mr. Obermeyer. Based on formula (9–3):

$$p = \frac{X}{n} = \frac{275}{500} = .55$$

Now, to be assured of election, he must earn *more than* 50 percent of the votes in the population of those voting. At this point we know a point estimate, which is .55, of the population of voters that will vote for him. But we do not know the percent in the population that will vote for the candidate. So the question is could we take a sample of 500 voters from a population where 50 percent or less of the voters support Mr. Obermeyer and find that 55 percent of the sample support him? To put it another way, could the sampling error, which is $p - \pi = .55 - .50 = .05$ be due to chance, or is the population of voters who support Mr. Obermeyer greater than .50. If we develop a confidence interval for the sample proportion and find that .50 is *not* in the interval, then we conclude that the proportion of voters supporting Mr. Obermeyer is greater than .50. What does that mean? Well, it means he should be elected! What if .50 is in the interval? Then we conclude that it is possible that 50 percent or less of the voters support his candidacy and we cannot conclude that he will be elected based on the sample information. In this case using the 95 percent significance level and formula (9–4):

$$p \pm z\sqrt{\frac{p(1-p)}{n}} = .55 \pm 1.96\sqrt{\frac{.55(1-.55)}{500}} = .55 \pm .044$$

So the endpoints of the confidence interval are $.55 - .044 = .506$ and $.55 + .044 = .594$. The value of .50 is not in this interval. So we conclude that probably *more than 50 percent* of the voters support Mr. Obermeyer and that is enough to get him elected.

Is this procedure ever used? Yes! It is exactly the procedure used by television networks, news magazines, and polling organizations on election night.

Self-Review 9–3

A market survey was conducted to estimate the proportion of homemakers who would recognize the brand name of a cleanser based on the shape and the color of the container. Of the 1,400 homemakers sampled, 420 were able to identify the brand by name.
(a) Estimate the value of the population proportion.
(b) Develop a 99 percent confidence interval for the population proportion.
(c) Interpret your findings.

Exercises

connect™

15. The owner of the West End Kwick Fill Gas Station wishes to determine the proportion of customers who use a credit card or debit card to pay at the pump. He surveys 100 customers and finds that 80 paid at the pump.
    a. Estimate the value of the population proportion.
    b. Develop a 95 percent confidence interval for the population proportion.
    c. Interpret your findings.

16. Ms. Maria Wilson is considering running for mayor of the town of Bear Gulch, Montana. Before completing the petitions, she decides to conduct a survey of voters in Bear Gulch. A sample of 400 voters reveals that 300 would support her in the November election.
    a. Estimate the value of the population proportion.
    b. Develop a 99 percent confidence interval for the population proportion.
    c. Interpret your findings.

17. The Fox TV network is considering replacing one of its prime-time crime investigation shows with a new family-oriented comedy show. Before a final decision is made, network executives commission a sample of 400 viewers. After viewing the comedy, 250 indicated they would watch the new show and suggested it replace the crime investigation show.
    a. Estimate the value of the population proportion.
    b. Develop a 99 percent confidence interval for the population proportion.
    c. Interpret your findings.

18. Schadek Silkscreen Printing, Inc., purchases plastic cups on which to print logos for sporting events, proms, birthdays, and other special occasions. Zack Schadek, the owner, received a large shipment this morning. To ensure the quality of the shipment, he selected a random sample of 300 cups. He found 15 to be defective.
    a. What is the estimated proportion defective in the population?
    b. Develop a 95 percent confidence interval for the proportion defective.
    c. Zack has an agreement with his supplier that he is to return lots that are 10 percent or more defective. Should he return this lot? Explain your decision.

Finite-Population Correction Factor

The populations we have sampled so far have been very large or infinite. What if the sampled population is not very large? We need to make some adjustments in the way we compute the standard error of the sample means and the standard error of the sample proportions.

A population that has a fixed upper bound is *finite*. For example, there are 12,179 students enrolled at Eastern Illinois University, there are 40 employees at Spence Sprockets, Chrysler assembled 917 Jeep Wranglers at the Alexis Avenue plant yesterday, or there were 65 surgical patients at St. Rose Memorial Hospital in Sarasota yesterday. A finite population can be rather small; it could be all the students registered for this class. It can also be very large, such as all senior citizens living in Florida.

For a finite population, where the total number of objects or individuals is N and the number of objects or individuals in the sample is n, we need to adjust the standard errors in the confidence interval formulas. To put it another way, to find the confidence interval for the mean we adjust the standard error of the mean in formulas (9–1) and (9–2). If we are determining the confidence interval for a proportion, then we need to adjust the standard error of the proportion in formula (9–3).

This adjustment is called the **finite-population correction factor.** It is often shortened to *FPC* and is:

$$FPC = \sqrt{\frac{N - n}{N - 1}}$$

Why is it necessary to apply a factor, and what is its effect? Logically, if the sample is a substantial percentage of the population, the estimate is more precise. Note the effect of the term $(N - n)/(N - 1)$. Suppose the population is 1,000 and the sample is 100. Then this ratio is $(1{,}000 - 100)/(1{,}000 - 1)$, or 900/999. Taking the square root gives the correction factor, .9492. Multiplying this correction factor by the standard error *reduces* the standard error by about 5 percent $(1 - .9492 = .0508)$. This reduction in the size of the standard error yields a smaller range of values in estimating the population mean or the population proportion. If the sample is 200, the correction factor is .8949, meaning that the standard error has been reduced by more than 10 percent. Table 9–2 shows the effects of various sample sizes. Note that when the sample is less than about 5 percent of the population, the impact of the correction factor is quite small. The usual rule is if the ratio of n/N is less than .05, the correction factor is ignored.

TABLE 9–2 Finite-Population Correction Factor for Selected Samples When the Population Is 1,000

Sample Size	Fraction of Population	Correction Factor
10	.010	.9955
25	.025	.9879
50	.050	.9752
100	.100	.9492
200	.200	.8949
500	.500	.7075

So if we wished to develop a confidence interval for the mean from a finite population and the population standard deviation was unknown, we would adjust formula (9–2) as follows:

$$\bar{X} \pm t \frac{s}{\sqrt{n}} \left(\sqrt{\frac{N - n}{N - 1}} \right)$$

We would make a similar adjustment to formula (9–3) in the case of a proportion.

The following example summarizes the steps to find a confidence interval for the mean.

Example

There are 250 families in Scandia, Pennsylvania. A random sample of 40 of these families revealed the mean annual church contribution was $450 and the standard deviation of this was $75. Could the population mean be $445 or $425?

1. What is the population mean? What is the best estimate of the population mean?
2. Discuss why the finite-population correction factor should be used.

Solution

3. Develop a 90 percent confidence interval for the population mean. What are the endpoints of the confidence interval?
4. Interpret the confidence interval.

First, note the population is finite. That is, there is a limit to the number of people in Scandia, in this case 250.

1. We do not know the population mean. This is the value we wish to estimate. The best estimate we have of the population mean is the sample mean, which is $450.
2. The sample is 16 percent of the population, found by $n/N = 40/250 = .16$. Because the sample constitutes more than .05 of the population, we should use the *FPC* to adjust the standard error in determining the confidence interval.
3. The formula to find the confidence interval for a population mean follows.

$$\overline{X} \pm t \frac{s}{\sqrt{n}} \left(\sqrt{\frac{N - n}{N - 1}} \right)$$

In this case we know $\overline{X} = 450$, $s = 75$, $N = 250$, and that $n = 40$. We do not know the population standard deviation so we use the *t* distribution. To find the appropriate value of *t* we use Appendix B.2, and move across the top row to the column headed 90 percent. The degrees of freedom is $df = n - 1 = 40 - 1 = 39$, so we move to the cell where the *df* row of 39 intersects with the column headed 90 percent. The value is 1.685. Inserting these values in the formula:

$$\overline{X} \pm t \frac{s}{\sqrt{n}} \left(\sqrt{\frac{N - n}{N - 1}} \right)$$

$$= \$450 \pm 1.685 \frac{\$75}{\sqrt{40}} \left(\sqrt{\frac{250 - 40}{250 - 1}} \right) = \$450 \pm \$19.98 \sqrt{.8434} = \$450 \pm \$18.35$$

The endpoints of the confidence interval are $431.65 and $468.35.
4. It is likely that the population mean is more than $431.65 but less than $468.35. To put it another way, could the population mean be $445? Yes, but it is not likely that it is $425. Why is this so? Because the value $445 is within the confidence interval and $425 is not within the confidence interval.

Self-Review 9–4

The same study of church contributions in Scandia revealed that 15 of the 40 families sampled attend church regularly. Construct the 95 percent confidence interval for the proportion of families attending church regularly. Should the finite-population correction factor be used? Why or why not?

Exercises

connect

19. Thirty-six items are randomly selected from a population of 300 items. The sample mean is 35 and the sample standard deviation 5. Develop a 95 percent confidence interval for the population mean.
20. Forty-nine items are randomly selected from a population of 500 items. The sample mean is 40 and the sample standard deviation 9. Develop a 99 percent confidence interval for the population mean.
21. The attendance at the Savannah Colts minor league baseball game last night was 400. A random sample of 50 of those in attendance revealed that the mean number of soft

drinks consumed per person was 1.86 with a standard deviation of 0.50. Develop a 99 percent confidence interval for the mean number of soft drinks consumed per person.
22. There are 300 welders employed at Maine Shipyards Corporation. A sample of 30 welders revealed that 18 graduated from a registered welding course. Construct the 95 percent confidence interval for the proportion of all welders who graduated from a registered welding course.

Choosing an Appropriate Sample Size

A concern that usually arises when designing a statistical study is how many items should be in the sample. If a sample is too large, money is wasted collecting the data. Similarly, if the sample is too small, the resulting conclusions will be uncertain. The necessary sample size depends on three factors:

1. The level of confidence desired.
2. The margin of error the researcher will tolerate.
3. The variability in the population being studied.

The first factor is the *level of confidence*. Those conducting the study select the level of confidence. The 95 percent and the 99 percent levels of confidence are the most common, but any value between 0 and 100 percent is possible. The 95 percent level of confidence corresponds to a z value of 1.96, and a 99 percent level of confidence corresponds to a z value of 2.58. The higher the level of confidence selected, the larger the size of the corresponding sample.

The second factor is the *allowable error*. The maximum allowable error, designated as E, is the amount that is added and subtracted to the sample mean (or sample proportion) to determine the endpoints of the confidence interval. It is the amount of error those conducting the study are willing to tolerate. It is also one-half the width of the corresponding confidence interval. A small allowable error will require a larger sample. A large allowable error will permit a smaller sample.

The third factor in determining the size of a sample is the *population standard deviation*. If the population is widely dispersed, a large sample is required. On the other hand, if the population is concentrated (homogeneous), the required sample size will be smaller. However, it may be necessary to use an estimate for the population standard deviation. Here are three suggestions for finding that estimate.

1. **Use a comparable study.** Use this approach when there is an estimate of the dispersion available from another study. Suppose we want to estimate the number of hours worked per week by refuse workers. Information from certain state or federal agencies who regularly sample the workforce might be useful to provide an estimate of the standard deviation. If a standard deviation observed in a previous study is thought to be reliable, it can be used in the current study to help provide an approximate sample size.

2. **Use a range-based approach.** To use this approach we need to know or have an estimate of the largest and smallest values in the population. Recall from Chapter 3, where we described the Empirical Rule, that virtually all the observations could be expected to be within plus or minus 3 standard deviations of the mean, assuming that the distribution follows the normal distribution. Thus, the distance between the largest and the smallest values is 6 standard deviations. We could estimate the standard deviation as one-sixth of the range. For example, the director of operations at University Bank wants an estimate of the number of checks written per month by college students. She believes that the distribution of the number of checks written follows the normal distribution. The minimum number written per month is 2 and 50 is the most. The range of the number of checks written per month is 48, found by 50 − 2. The estimate of the standard deviation then would be 8 checks per month, 48/6.

3. **Conduct a pilot study.** This is the most common method. Suppose we want an estimate of the number of hours per week worked by students enrolled in

the College of Business at the University of Texas. To test the validity of our questionnaire, we use it on a small sample of students. From this small sample we compute the standard deviation of the number of hours worked and use this value to determine the appropriate sample size.

We can express the interaction among these three factors and the sample size in the following formula.

$$E = z \frac{\sigma}{\sqrt{n}}$$

Solving this equation for *n* yields the following result.

SAMPLE SIZE FOR ESTIMATING THE POPULATION MEAN	$n = \left(\dfrac{z\sigma}{E}\right)^2$	**[9–5]**

where:

    n is the size of the sample.
    z is the standard normal value corresponding to the desired level of confidence.
    σ is the population standard deviation.
    E is the maximum allowable error.

The result of this calculation is not always a whole number. When the outcome is not a whole number, the usual practice is to round up *any* fractional result. For example, 201.22 would be rounded up to 202.

Example

A student in public administration wants to determine the mean amount members of city councils in large cities earn per month as remuneration for being a council member. The error in estimating the mean is to be less than $100 with a 95 percent level of confidence. The student found a report by the Department of Labor that estimated the standard deviation to be $1,000. What is the required sample size?

Solution

The maximum allowable error, *E*, is $100. The value of *z* for a 95 percent level of confidence is 1.96, and the estimate of the standard deviation is $1,000. Substituting these values into formula (9–5) gives the required sample size as:

$$n = \left(\frac{z\sigma}{E}\right)^2 = \left(\frac{(1.96)(\$1,000)}{\$100}\right)^2 = (19.6)^2 = 384.16$$

The computed value of 384.16 is rounded up to 385. A sample of 385 is required to meet the specifications. If the student wants to increase the level of confidence, for example to 99 percent, this will require a larger sample. The *z* value corresponding to the 99 percent level of confidence is 2.58.

$$n = \left(\frac{z\sigma}{E}\right)^2 = \left(\frac{(2.58)(\$1,000)}{\$100}\right)^2 = (25.8)^2 = 665.64$$

We recommend a sample of 666. Observe how much the change in the confidence level changed the size of the sample. An increase from the 95 percent to the 99 percent level of confidence resulted in an increase of 281 observations. This could greatly increase the cost of the study, both in terms of time and money. Hence, the level of confidence should be considered carefully.

The procedure just described can be adapted to determine the sample size for a proportion. Again, three items need to be specified:

1. The desired level of confidence.
2. The margin of error in the population proportion.
3. An estimate of the population proportion.

The formula to determine the sample size of a proportion is:

| SAMPLE SIZE FOR THE POPULATION PROPORTION | $n = p(1 - p)\left(\dfrac{z}{E}\right)^2$ | [9–6] |

If an estimate of p is available from a pilot study or some other source, it can be used. Otherwise, .50 is used because the term $p(1 - p)$ can never be larger than when $p = .50$. For example, if $p = .30$, then $p(1 - p) = .3(1 - .3) = .21$, but when $p = .50$, $p(1 - p) = .5(1 - .5) = .25$

Example

The study in the previous example also estimates the proportion of cities that have private refuse collectors. The student wants the margin of error to be within .10 of the population proportion, the desired level of confidence is 90 percent, and no estimate is available for the population proportion. What is the required sample size?

Solution

The estimate of the population proportion is to be within .10, so $E = .10$. The desired level of confidence is .90, which corresponds to a z value of 1.65. Because no estimate of the population proportion is available, we use .50. The suggested number of observations is

$$n = (.5)(1 - .5)\left(\frac{1.65}{.10}\right)^2 = 68.0625$$

The student needs a random sample of 69 cities.

Self-Review 9–5

The registrar wants to estimate the arithmetic mean grade point average (GPA) of all graduating seniors during the past 10 years. GPAs range between 2.0 and 4.0. The mean GPA is to be estimated within plus or minus .05 of the population mean. The standard deviation is estimated to be 0.279. Use the 99 percent level of confidence. Will you assist the college registrar in determining how many transcripts to study?

Exercises

connect

23. A population is estimated to have a standard deviation of 10. We want to estimate the population mean within 2, with a 95 percent level of confidence. How large a sample is required?

24. We want to estimate the population mean within 5, with a 99 percent level of confidence. The population standard deviation is estimated to be 15. How large a sample is required?

25. The estimate of the population proportion is to be within plus or minus .05, with a 95 percent level of confidence. The best estimate of the population proportion is .15. How large a sample is required?

26. The estimate of the population proportion is to be within plus or minus .10, with a 99 percent level of confidence. The best estimate of the population proportion is .45. How large a sample is required?

27. A survey is being planned to determine the mean amount of time corporation executives watch television. A pilot survey indicated that the mean time per week is 12 hours, with a standard deviation of 3 hours. It is desired to estimate the mean viewing time within one-quarter hour. The 95 percent level of confidence is to be used. How many executives should be surveyed?

28. A processor of carrots cuts the green top off each carrot, washes the carrots, and inserts six to a package. Twenty packages are inserted in a box for shipment. To test the weight of the boxes, a few were checked. The mean weight was 20.4 pounds, the standard deviation 0.5 pounds. How many boxes must the processor sample to be 95 percent confident that the sample mean does not differ from the population mean by more than 0.2 pound?

29. Suppose the U.S. president wants an estimate of the proportion of the population who support his current policy toward revisions in the Social Security system. The president wants the estimate to be within .04 of the true proportion. Assume a 95 percent level of

confidence. The president's political advisors estimated the proportion supporting the current policy to be .60.
  a. How large of a sample is required?
  b. How large of a sample would be necessary if no estimate were available for the proportion supporting current policy?

30. Past surveys reveal that 30 percent of tourists going to Las Vegas to gamble during a weekend spend more than $1,000. Management wants to update this percentage.
  a. The new study is to use the 90 percent confidence level. The estimate is to be within 1 percent of the population proportion. What is the necessary sample size?
  b. Management said that the sample size determined above is too large. What can be done to reduce the sample? Based on your suggestion recalculate the sample size.

Chapter Summary

I. A point estimate is a single value (statistic) used to estimate a population value (parameter).

II. A confidence interval is a range of values within which the population parameter is expected to occur.
  A. The factors that determine the width of a confidence interval for a mean are:
    1. The number of observations in the sample, n.
    2. The variability in the population, usually estimated by the sample standard deviation, s.
    3. The level of confidence.
      a. To determine the confidence limits when the population standard deviation is known we use the z distribution. The formula is

$$\overline{X} \pm z \frac{\sigma}{\sqrt{n}} \tag{9–1}$$

      b. To determine the confidence limits when the population standard deviation is unknown we use the t distribution. The formula is

$$\overline{X} \pm t \frac{s}{\sqrt{n}} \tag{9–2}$$

III. The major characteristics of the t distribution are:
  A. It is a continuous distribution.
  B. It is mound-shaped and symmetrical.
  C. It is flatter, or more spread out, than the standard normal distribution.
  D. There is a family of t distributions, depending on the number of degrees of freedom.

IV. A proportion is a ratio, fraction, or percent that indicates the part of the sample or population that has a particular characteristic.
  A. A sample proportion is found by X, the number of successes, divided by n, the number of observations.
  B. We construct a confidence interval for a sample proportion from the following formula.

$$p \pm z \sqrt{\frac{p(1 - p)}{n}} \tag{9–4}$$

V. For a finite population, the standard error is adjusted by the factor $\sqrt{\frac{N - n}{N - 1}}$.

VI. We can determine an appropriate sample size for estimating both means and proportions.
  A. There are three factors that determine the sample size when we wish to estimate the mean.
    1. The desired level of confidence, which is usually expressed by z.
    2. The maximum allowable error, E.
    3. The variation in the population, expressed by s.
    4. The formula to determine the sample size for the mean is

$$n = \left(\frac{z\sigma}{E}\right)^2 \tag{9–5}$$

B. There are three factors that determine the sample size when we wish to estimate a proportion.
   1. The desired level of confidence, which is usually expressed by *z*.
   2. The maximum allowable error, *E*.
   3. An estimate of the population proportion. If no estimate is available, use .50.
   4. The formula to determine the sample size for a proportion is

$$n = p(1 - p)\left(\frac{z}{E}\right)^2$$

[9–6]

Chapter Exercises

connect

31. A random sample of 85 group leaders, supervisors, and similar personnel at General Motors revealed that, on the average, they spent 6.5 years on the job before being promoted. The standard deviation of the sample was 1.7 years. Construct a 95 percent confidence interval.

32. A state meat inspector in Iowa has been given the assignment of estimating the mean net weight of packages of ground chuck labeled "3 pounds." Of course, he realizes that the weights cannot be precisely 3 pounds. A sample of 36 packages reveals the mean weight to be 3.01 pounds, with a standard deviation of 0.03 pounds.
   a. What is the estimated population mean?
   b. Determine a 95 percent confidence interval for the population mean.

33. A recent study of 50 self-service gasoline stations in the Greater Cincinnati–Northern Kentucky metropolitan area revealed that the mean price of unleaded gas was $4.029 per gallon. The sample standard deviation was $0.03 per gallon.
   a. Determine a 99 percent confidence interval for the population mean price.
   b. Would it be reasonable to conclude that the population mean was $3.50? Why or why not?

34. A recent survey of 50 executives who were laid off from their previous position revealed it took a mean of 26 weeks for them to find another position. The standard deviation of the sample was 6.2 weeks. Construct a 95 percent confidence interval for the population mean. Is it reasonable that the population mean is 28 weeks? Justify your answer.

35. Marty Rowatti recently assumed the position of director of the YMCA of South Jersey. He would like some current data on how long current members of the YMCA have been members. To investigate, suppose he selects a random sample of 40 current members. The mean length of membership of those included in the sample is 8.32 years and the standard deviation is 3.07 years.
   a. What is the mean of the population?
   b. Develop a 90 percent confidence interval for the population mean.
   c. The previous director, in the summary report she prepared as she retired, indicated the mean length of membership was now "almost 10 years." Does the sample information substantiate this claim? Cite evidence.

36. The American Restaurant Association collected information on the number of meals eaten outside the home per week by young married couples. A survey of 60 couples showed the sample mean number of meals eaten outside the home was 2.76 meals per week, with a standard deviation of 0.75 meals per week. Construct a 97 percent confidence interval for the population mean.

37. The National Collegiate Athletic Association (NCAA) reported that the mean number of hours spent per week on coaching and recruiting by college football assistant coaches during the season was 70. A random sample of 50 assistant coaches showed the sample mean to be 68.6 hours, with a standard deviation of 8.2 hours.
   a. Using the sample data, construct a 99 percent confidence interval for the population mean.
   b. Does the 99 percent confidence interval include the value suggested by the NCAA? Interpret this result.
   c. Suppose you decided to switch from a 99 to a 95 percent confidence interval. Without performing any calculations, will the interval increase, decrease, or stay the same? Which of the values in the formula will change?

38. The Human Relations Department of Electronics, Inc., would like to include a dental plan as part of the benefits package. The question is: How much does a typical employee and his or her family spend per year on dental expenses? A sample of 45 employees reveals the mean amount spent last year was $1,820, with a standard deviation of $660.

a. Construct a 95 percent confidence interval for the population mean.

b. The information from part (a) was given to the president of Electronics, Inc. He indicated he could afford $1,700 of dental expenses per employee. Is it possible that the population mean could be $1,700? Justify your answer.

39. A student conducted a study and reported that the 95 percent confidence interval for the mean ranged from 46 to 54. He was sure that the mean of the sample was 50, that the standard deviation of the sample was 16, and that the sample was at least 30, but could not remember the exact number. Can you help him out?

40. A recent study by the American Automobile Dealers Association revealed the mean amount of profit per car sold for a sample of 20 dealers was $290, with a standard deviation of $125. Develop a 95 percent confidence interval for the population mean.

41. A study of 25 graduates of four-year colleges by the American Banker's Association revealed the mean amount owed by a student in student loans was $14,381. The standard deviation of the sample was $1,892. Construct a 90 percent confidence interval for the population mean. Is it reasonable to conclude that the mean of the population is actually $15,000? Tell why or why not.

42. An important factor in selling a residential property is the number of people who look through the home. A sample of 15 homes recently sold in the Buffalo, New York, area revealed the mean number looking through each home was 24 and the standard deviation of the sample was 5 people. Develop a 98 percent confidence interval for the population mean.

43. Warren County Telephone Company claims in its annual report that "the typical customer spends $60 per month on local and long-distance service." A sample of 12 subscribers revealed the following amounts spent last month.

$64	$66	$64	$66	$59	$62	$67	$61	$64	$58	$54	$66

a. What is the point estimate of the population mean?

b. Develop a 90 percent confidence interval for the population mean.

c. Is the company's claim that the "typical customer" spends $60 per month reasonable? Justify your answer.

44. The manufacturer of a new line of ink-jet printers would like to include as part of its advertising the number of pages a user can expect from a print cartridge. A sample of 10 cartridges revealed the following number of pages printed.

2,698	2,028	2,474	2,395	2,372	2,475	1,927	3,006	2,334	2,379

a. What is the point estimate of the population mean?

b. Develop a 95 percent confidence interval for the population mean.

45. Dr. Susan Benner is an industrial psychologist. She is currently studying stress among executives of Internet companies. She has developed a questionnaire that she believes measures stress. A score above 80 indicates stress at a dangerous level. A random sample of 15 executives revealed the following stress level scores.

94	78	83	90	78	99	97	90	97	90	93	94	100	75	84

a. Find the mean stress level for this sample. What is the point estimate of the population mean?

b. Construct a 95 percent confidence level for the population mean.

c. Is it reasonable to conclude that Internet executives have a mean stress level in the dangerous level, according to Dr. Benner's test?

46. As a condition of employment, Fashion Industries applicants must pass a drug test. Of the last 220 applicants 14 failed the test. Develop a 99 percent confidence interval for the proportion of applicants that fail the test. Would it be reasonable to conclude that more than 10 percent of the applicants are now failing the test? In addition to the testing of applicants, Fashion Industries randomly tests its employees throughout the year. Last year in the 400 random tests conducted, 14 employees failed the test. Would it be reasonable to conclude that less than 5 percent of the employees are not able to pass the random drug test?

47. There are 20,000 eligible voters in York County, South Carolina. A random sample of 500 York County voters revealed 350 plan to vote to return Louella Miller to the state senate. Construct a 99 percent confidence interval for the proportion of voters in the county who plan to vote for Ms. Miller. From this sample information, can you confirm she will be re-elected?

48. In a poll to estimate presidential popularity, each person in a random sample of 1,000 voters was asked to agree with one of the following statements:
  1. The president is doing a good job.
  2. The president is doing a poor job.
  3. I have no opinion.
  A total of 560 respondents selected the first statement, indicating they thought the president was doing a good job.
  a. Construct a 95 percent confidence interval for the proportion of respondents who feel the president is doing a good job.
  b. Based on your interval in part (a), is it reasonable to conclude that a majority (more than half) of the population believes the president is doing a good job?

49. Police Chief Edward Wilkin of River City reports 500 traffic citations were issued last month. A sample of 35 of these citations showed the mean amount of the fine was $54, with a standard deviation of $4.50. Construct a 95 percent confidence interval for the mean amount of a citation in River City.

50. The First National Bank of Wilson has 650 checking account customers. A recent sample of 50 of these customers showed 26 to have a Visa card with the bank. Construct the 99 percent confidence interval for the proportion of checking account customers who have a Visa card with the bank.

51. It is estimated that 60 percent of U.S. households subscribe to cable TV. You would like to verify this statement for your class in mass communications. If you want your estimate to be within 5 percentage points, with a 95 percent level of confidence, how large of a sample is required?

52. You need to estimate the mean number of travel days per year for outside salespeople. The mean of a small pilot study was 150 days, with a standard deviation of 14 days. If you must estimate the population mean within 2 days, how many outside salespeople should you sample? Use the 90 percent confidence level.

53. You are to conduct a sample survey to determine the mean family income in a rural area of central Florida. The question is, how many families should be sampled? In a pilot sample of 10 families, the standard deviation of the sample was $500. The sponsor of the survey wants you to use the 95 percent confidence level. The estimate is to be within $100. How many families should be interviewed?

54. *Families USA,* a monthly magazine that discusses issues related to health and health costs, surveyed 20 of its subscribers. It found that the annual health insurance premiums for a family with coverage through an employer averaged $10,979. The standard deviation of the sample was $1,000.
  a. Based on this sample information, develop a 90 percent confidence interval for the population mean yearly premium.
  b. How large a sample is needed to find the population mean within $250 at 99 percent confidence?

55. Passenger comfort is influenced by the amount of pressurization in an airline cabin. Higher pressurization permits a closer-to-normal environment and a more relaxed flight. A study by an airline user group recorded the corresponding air pressure on 30 randomly chosen flights. The study revealed a mean equivalent pressure of 8,000 feet with a standard deviation of 300 feet.
  a. Develop a 99 percent confidence interval for the population mean equivalent pressure.
  b. How large a sample is needed to find the population mean within 25 feet at 95 percent confidence?

56. A random sample of 25 people employed by the Florida state authority established they earned an average wage (including benefits) of $65.00 per hour. The sample standard deviation was $6.25 per hour.
  a. What is the population mean? What is the best estimate of the population mean?
  b. Develop a 99 percent confidence interval for the population mean wage (including benefits) for these employees.
  c. How large a sample is needed to assess the population mean with an allowable error of $1.00 at 95 percent confidence?

57. A film alliance used a random sample of 50 U.S. citizens to estimate that the typical American spent 78 hours watching videos and DVDs last year. The standard deviation of this sample was 9 hours.
  a. Develop a 95 percent confidence interval for the population mean number of hours spent watching videos and DVDs last year.
  b. How large a sample should be used to be 90 percent confident the sample mean is within 1.0 hour of the population mean?

58. Dylan Jones kept careful records of the fuel efficiency of his new car. After the first nine times he filled up the tank, he found the mean was 23.4 miles per gallon (mpg) with a sample standard deviation of 0.9 mpg.
  a. Compute the 95 percent confidence interval for his mpg.
  b. How many times should he fill his gas tank to obtain a margin of error below 0.1 mpg?
59. A survey of 36 randomly selected "iPhone" owners showed that the purchase price has a mean of $416 with a sample standard deviation of $180.
  a. Compute the standard error of the sample mean.
  b. Compute the 95 percent confidence interval for the mean.
  c. How large a sample is needed to estimate the population mean within $10?
60. You plan to conduct a survey to find what proportion of the workforce has two or more jobs. You decide on the 95 percent confidence level and state that the estimated proportion must be within 2 percent of the population proportion. A pilot survey reveals that 5 of the 50 sampled hold two or more jobs. How many in the workforce should be interviewed to meet your requirements?
61. The proportion of public accountants who have changed companies within the last three years is to be estimated within 3 percent. The 95 percent level of confidence is to be used. A study conducted several years ago revealed that the percent of public accountants changing companies within three years was 21.
  a. To update this study, the files of how many public accountants should be studied?
  b. How many public accountants should be contacted if no previous estimates of the population proportion are available?
62. Huntington National Bank, like most other large banks, found that using automatic teller machines (ATMs) reduces the cost of routine bank transactions. Huntington installed an ATM in the corporate offices of Fun Toy Company. The ATM is for the exclusive use of Fun's 605 employees. After several months of operation, a sample of 100 employees revealed the following use of the ATM machine by Fun employees in a month.

Number of Times ATM Used	Frequency
0	25
1	30
2	20
3	10
4	10
5	5

  a. What is the estimate of the proportion of employees who do not use the ATM in a month?
  b. Develop a 95 percent confidence interval for this estimate. Can Huntington be sure that at least 40 percent of the employees of Fun Toy Company will use the ATM?
  c. How many transactions does the average Fun employee make per month?
  d. Develop a 95 percent confidence interval for the mean number of transactions per month.
  e. Is it possible that the population mean is .7? Explain.
63. In a recent Zogby poll of 1,000 adults nationwide, 613 said they believe other forms of life exist elsewhere in the universe. Construct the 99 percent confidence interval for the population proportion of those believing life exists elsewhere in the universe. Does your result imply that a majority of Americans believe life exists outside of Earth?
64. As part of an annual review of its accounts, a discount brokerage selects a random sample of 36 customers. Their accounts are reviewed for total account valuation, which showed a mean of $32,000, with a sample standard deviation of $8,200. What is a 90 percent confidence interval for the mean account valuation of the population of customers?
65. The National Weight Control Registry tries to mine secrets of success from people who have lost at least 30 pounds and kept it off for at least a year. It reports that out of 2,700 registrants 459 were on low-carbohydrate diets (less than 90 grams a day).
  a. Develop a 95 percent confidence interval for this fraction.
  b. Is it possible that the population percentage is 18 percent?
  c. How large a sample is needed to estimate the proportion within 0.5 percent?
66. Near the time of an election, a cable news service performs an opinion poll of 1,000 probable voters. It shows that the Republican contender has an advantage of 52 percent to 48 percent.
  a. Develop a 95 percent confidence interval for the proportion favoring the Republican candidate.

b. Estimate the probability that the Democratic candidate is actually leading.

c. Repeat the above analysis based on a sample of 3,000 probable voters.

67. A sample of 352 subscribers to *Wired* magazine shows the mean time spent using the Internet is 13.4 hours per week, with a sample standard deviation of 6.8 hours. Find the 95 percent confidence interval for the mean time *Wired* subscribers spend on the Internet.

68. The Tennessee Tourism Institute (TTI) plans to sample information center visitors entering the state to learn the fraction of visitors who plan to camp in the state. Current estimates are that 35 percent of visitors are campers. How large a sample would you take to estimate at a 95 percent confidence level the population proportion with an allowable error of 2 percent?

Data Set Exercises

69. Refer to the Real Estate data, which report information on the homes sold in Denver, Colorado, last year.
   a. Develop a 95 percent confidence interval for the mean selling price of the homes.
   b. Develop a 95 percent confidence interval for the mean distance the home is from the center of the city.
   c. Develop a 95 percent confidence interval for the proportion of homes with an attached garage.

70. Refer to the Baseball 2007 data, which report information on the 30 Major League Baseball teams for the 2007 season.
   a. Develop a 95 percent confidence interval for the mean number of home runs per team.
   b. Develop a 95 percent confidence interval for the mean number of errors committed by each team.
   c. Develop a 95 percent confidence interval for the mean number of stolen bases for each team.

71. Refer to the Wage data, which report information on annual wages for a sample of 100 workers. Also included are variables relating to industry, years of education, and gender for each worker.
   a. Develop a 95 percent confidence interval for the mean wage of the workers. Is it reasonable to conclude that the population mean is $35,000?
   b. Develop a 95 percent confidence interval for the mean years of education. Is it reasonable to conclude that the population mean is 13 years?
   c. Develop a 95 percent confidence interval for the mean age of the workers. Could the mean age be 40 years?

72. Refer to the CIA data, which report demographic and economic information on 46 countries.
   a. Develop a 90 percent confidence interval for the mean percent of the population age 65 years or older.
   b. Develop a 90 percent confidence interval for the mean Gross Domestic Product (GDP) per capita.
   c. Develop a 90 percent confidence interval for the mean imports.

Software Commands

1. The MINITAB commands for the 60 columns of 30 random numbers used in the example/solution on page 296 are:
   a. Select **Calc, Random Data,** and then click on **Normal.**
   b. From the dialog box click in the **Generate** box and type *30* for the number of rows of data, **Store in column(s)** is *C1-C60*, **Mean** is *50*, **Standard deviation** is *5.0*, and finally click **OK.**

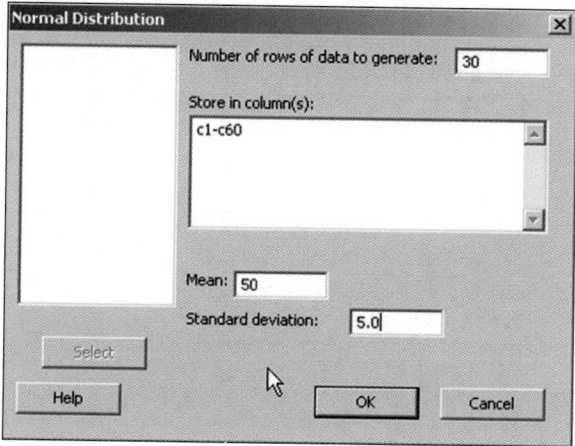

2. The MINITAB commands for the 60 confidence intervals on page 296 follow.
   a. Select **Stat, Basic Statistics,** and then click on **1-Sample Z.**
   b. In the dialog box indicate that the **Variables** are *C1-C60* and that **Standard Duration** is *5*. Next, click on **Options** in the lower right corner, and in the next dialog box indicate that the **Confidence level** is *95,* and then click **OK.** Click **OK** in the main dialog box.
3. The MINITAB commands for the descriptive statistics on page 303 follow. Enter the data in the first column and label this column *Amount*. On the Toolbar select **Stat, Basic Statistics,** and **Display Descriptive Statistics.** In the dialog box select *Amount* as the **Variable** and click **OK.**
4. The MINITAB commands for the confidence interval for the amount spent at the Inlet Square Mall on page 303 are:
   a. Enter the 20 amounts spent in column *C1* and name the variable *Amount,* or locate the data on the student data disk. It is named **Shopping** and is found in the folder for Chapter 9.
   b. On the Toolbar select **Stat, Basic Statistics,** and click on **1-Sample t.**
   c. Select **Samples in columns:** and select **Amount** and click **OK.**

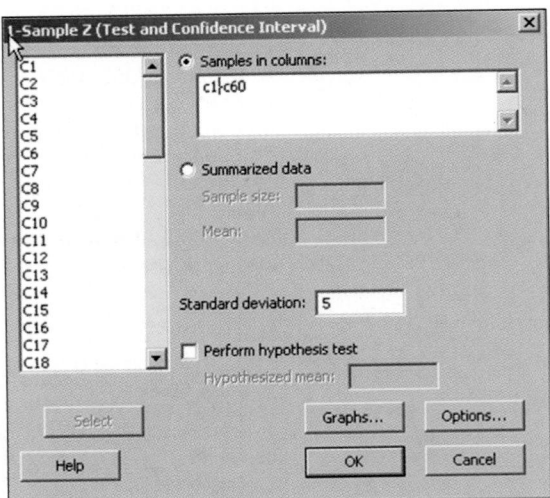

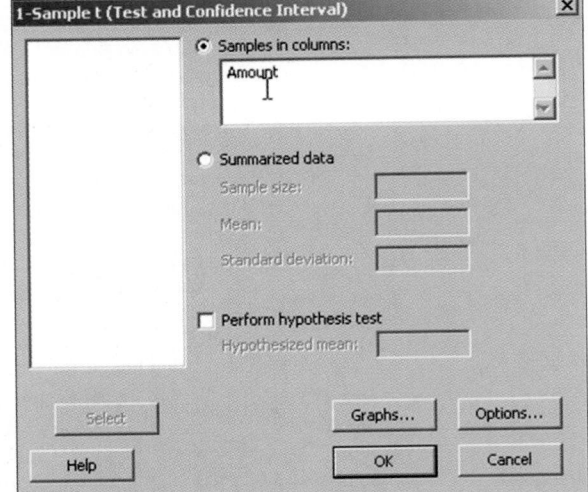

5. The Excel commands for the confidence interval for the amounts spent at the Inlet Square Mall on page 304 are:
   a. Select the **Data** tab on the top menu. Then, on the far right, select **Data Analysis,** and then **Descriptive Statistics** and click **OK.**
   b. For the **Input Range** type *A1:A21,* click on **Labels in first row,** type *C1* as the **Output Range,** click on **Summary statistics** and **Confidence Level for Mean,** and then on **OK.**

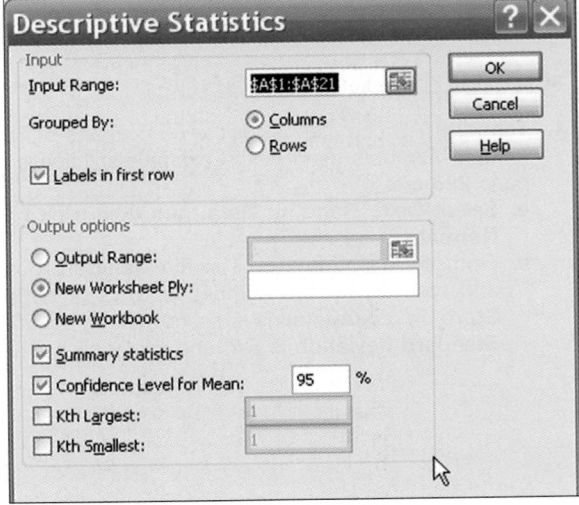

Chapter 9   Answers to Self-Review

9–1 **a.** Unknown. This is the value we wish to estimate.
   b. $20,000, point estimate.
   c. $20,000 \pm 2.58 \dfrac{\$3,000}{\sqrt{40}} = \$20,000 \pm \$1,224$
   d. The endpoints of the confidence interval are $18,776 and $21,224. About 99 percent of the intervals similarly constructed would include the population mean.

9–2 **a.** $\bar{X} = \dfrac{18}{10} = 1.8 \qquad s = \sqrt{\dfrac{11.6}{10-1}} = 1.1353$
   b. The population mean is not known. The best estimate is the sample mean, 1.8 days.
   c. $1.80 \pm 2.262 \dfrac{1.1353}{\sqrt{10}} = 1.80 \pm 0.81$
   The endpoints are 0.99 and 2.61
   d. t is used because the population standard deviation is unknown.
   e. The value of 0 is not in the interval. It is unreasonable to conclude that the mean number of days of work missed is 0 per employee.

9–3 **a.** $p = \dfrac{420}{1,400} = .30$
   b. $.30 \pm 2.58(.0122) = .30 \pm .03$
   c. The interval is between .27 and .33. About 99 percent of the similarly constructed intervals would include the population mean.

9–4 $.375 \pm 1.96 \sqrt{\dfrac{.375(1-.375)}{40}} \sqrt{\dfrac{250-40}{250-1}} =$
   $.375 \pm 1.96(.0765)(.9184) = .375 \pm .138$
   The correction factor should be applied because 40/250 > .05.

9–5 $n = \left(\dfrac{2.58(.279)}{.05}\right)^2 = 207.26.$ The sample should be rounded to 208.

A Review of Chapters 8 and 9

We began Chapter 8 by describing the reasons sampling is necessary. We sample because it is often impossible to study every item, or individual, in some populations. It would be too expensive and time consuming, for example, to contact and record the annual incomes of all U.S. bank officers. Also, sampling often destroys the product. A drug manufacturer cannot test the properties of each tablet manufactured, because there would be none left to sell. To estimate a population parameter, therefore, we select a sample from the population. A sample is a part of the population. Care must be taken to ensure that every member of our population has a chance of being selected; otherwise, the conclusions might be biased. A number of probability-type sampling methods can be used, including *simple random, systematic, stratified,* and *cluster sampling.*

Regardless of the sampling method selected, a sample statistic is seldom equal to the corresponding population parameter. For example, the mean of a sample is seldom exactly the same as the mean of the population. The difference between this sample statistic and the population parameter is the *sampling error.*

In Chapter 8 we demonstrated that, if we select all possible samples of a specified size from a population and calculate the mean of these samples, the result will be exactly equal to the population mean. We also showed that the dispersion in the distribution of the sample means is equal to the population standard deviation divided by the square root of the sample size. This result is called the standard error of the mean. There is less dispersion in the distribution of the sample means than in the population. In addition, as we increase the number of observations in each sample, we decrease the variation in the sampling distribution.

The central limit theorem is the foundation of statistical inference. It states that, if the population from which we select the samples follows the normal probability distribution, the distribution of the sample means will also follow the normal distribution. If the population is not normal, it will approach the normal probability distribution as we increase the size of the sample.

Our focus in Chapter 9 was point estimates and interval estimates. A point estimate is a single value used to estimate a population parameter. An interval estimate is a range of values within which we expect the population parameter to occur. For example, based on a sample, we estimate that the mean annual income of all professional house painters in Atlanta, Georgia (the population), is $45,300. That estimate is called a *point estimate.* If we state that the population mean is probably in the interval between $45,200 and $45,400, that estimate is called an *interval estimate.* The two endpoints ($45,200 and $45,400) are the *confidence limits* for the population mean. We described the procedure for establishing a confidence interval for both large and small sample means as well as for sample proportions. In this chapter we also provided a method to determine the necessary sample size based on the dispersion in the population, the level of confidence desired, and the desired precision of the estimate.

Glossary

Bias A possible consequence if certain members of the population are denied the chance to be selected for the sample. As a result, the sample may not be representative of the population.

Central limit theorem If the size of the sample is sufficiently large, the sampling distribution of the sample mean will approach a normal distribution regardless of the shape of the population.

Cluster sampling A method often used to lower the cost of sampling if the population is dispersed over a wide geographic area. The area is divided into smaller units (counties, precincts, blocks, etc.) called primary units. Then a few primary units are chosen, and a random sample is selected from each primary unit.

Finite-population correction factor (FPC) When sampling without replacement from a finite population, a correction term is used to reduce the standard error of the mean according to the relative size of the sample to the size of the population. The correction factor is used when the sample is more than 5 percent of a finite population.

Interval estimate The interval within which a population parameter probably lies, based on sample information. Example: According to sample data, the population mean is in the interval between 1.9 and 2.0 pounds.

Point estimate A single value computed from a sample and used to estimate a population parameter. Example: If the sample mean is 1,020 psi, it is the best estimate of the mean tensile strength of the population.

Probability sample A sample of items or individuals chosen so that each member of the population has a chance of being included in the sample.

Sampling distribution of the sample mean A probability distribution consisting of all possible means of samples of a given size selected from the population.

Sampling error The difference between a sample statistic and the corresponding population parameter. Example: The sample mean income is $22,100; the population mean is $22,000. The sampling error is $22,100 − $22,000 = $100. This error can be attributed to sampling, that is, chance.

Simple random sampling A sampling scheme such that each member of the population has the *same* chance of being selected as part of the sample.

Stratified random sampling A population is first divided into subgroups called strata. A sample is then chosen from each stratum. If, for example, the population of interest consisted of all undergraduate students, the sample design might call for sampling 62 freshmen, 51 sophomores, 40 juniors, and 39 seniors.

Systematic random sampling Assuming the population is arranged in some way, such as alphabetically, by height, or in a file drawer, a random starting point is selected, then every *k*th item becomes a member of the sample. If a sample design called for interviewing every ninth household on Main Street starting with 932 Main, the sample would consist of households at 932 Main, 941 Main, 950 Main, and so on.

Exercises

connect   Part I—Multiple Choice

1. The sampling error is:
   a. Equal to the population mean.
   b. A population parameter.
   c. Always positive.
   d. The difference between the sample statistic and the population parameter.
2. Which of the following are correct statements about confidence intervals?
   a. They cannot contain negative numbers.
   b. They are always based on the *z* distribution.
   c. They must always include the population parameter.
   d. None of the above are always correct.
3. The endpoints of a confidence interval are called:
   a. Confidence levels.
   b. The test statistics.
   c. The degrees of confidence.
   d. The confidence limits.
4. We compute the mean and the standard deviation from a sample of 16 observations. Assume the population follows a normal probability distribution. We wish to develop a confidence interval for the mean. Which of the following statements is correct?
   a. We cannot develop a confidence interval because we do not know the population standard deviation.
   b. We use the *z* distribution because we know the population standard deviation.

c. We can use the *t* distribution to develop the confidence interval.
d. None of the above statements are correct.

5. Which of the following is *not* a correct statement about the *t* distribution?
   a. It is positively skewed.
   b. It is a continuous distribution.
   c. It has a mean of 0.
   d. There is a family of *t* distributions.

6. As the number of degrees of freedom increases in the *t* distribution:
   a. It approaches the standard normal distribution.
   b. The level of confidence increases.
   c. It becomes a continuous distribution.
   d. It becomes flatter.

7. The degrees of freedom are:
   a. The total number of observations.
   b. The number of observations minus the number of samples.
   c. The number of samples.
   d. The number of samples minus one.

8. We select a sample of 15 observations from a normal population and wish to develop a 98 percent confidence interval for the mean. The appropriate value of *t* is:
   a. 2.947
   b. 2.977
   c. 2.624
   d. None of the above.

Part II—Problems

9. A recent study indicated that women took an average of 8.6 weeks of unpaid leave from their jobs after the birth of a child. Assume that this distribution follows the normal probability distribution with a standard deviation of 2.0 weeks. We select a sample of 35 women who recently returned to work after the birth of a child. What is the likelihood that the mean of this sample is at least 8.8 weeks?

10. The manager of Tee Shirt Emporium reports that the mean number of shirts sold per week is 1,210, with a standard deviation of 325. The distribution of sales follows the normal distribution. What is the likelihood of selecting a sample of 25 weeks and finding the sample mean to be 1,100 or less?

11. The owner of the Gulf Stream Café wished to estimate the mean number of lunch customers per day. A sample of 40 days revealed a mean of 160 per day, with a standard deviation of 20 per day. Develop a 98 percent confidence interval for the mean number of customers per day.

12. The manager of the local Hamburger Express wishes to estimate the mean time customers spend at the drive-through window. A sample of 20 customers experienced a mean waiting time of 2.65 minutes, with a standard deviation of 0.45 minutes. Develop a 90 percent confidence interval for the mean waiting time.

13. The office manager for a large company is studying the usage of its copy machines. A random sample of six copy machines revealed the following number of copies (reported in 000s) made yesterday.

| 826 | 931 | 1,126 | 918 | 1,011 | 1,101 |

Develop a 95 percent confidence interval for the mean number of copies per machine.

14. John Kleman is the host of KXYZ Radio 55 AM drive-time news in Denver. During his morning program, John asks listeners to call in and discuss current local and national news. This morning, John was concerned with the number of hours children under 12 years of age watch TV per day. The last 5 callers reported that their children watched the following number of hours of TV last night.

| 3.0 | 3.5 | 4.0 | 4.5 | 3.0 |

Would it be reasonable to develop a confidence interval from these data to show the mean number of hours of TV watched? If yes, construct an appropriate confidence interval and interpret the result. If no, why would a confidence interval not be appropriate?

15. Historically, Widgets Manufacturing, Inc., produces 250 widgets per day. Recently the new owner bought a new machine to produce more widgets per day. A sample of 16 days' production revealed a mean of 240 units with a standard deviation of 35. Construct a confidence interval for the mean number of widgets produced per day. Does it seem reasonable to conclude that the mean daily widget production has increased? Justify your conclusion.

16. The manufacturer of a power chip used in expensive stereo equipment wishes to estimate the useful life of the chip (in thousands of hours). The estimate is to be within 0.10 (100) hours. Assume a 95 percent level of confidence and that the standard deviation of the useful life of the chip is 0.90 (900 hours). Determine the required sample size.

17. The manager of a home improvement store wishes to estimate the mean amount of money spent in the store. The estimate is to be within $4.00 with a 95 percent level of confidence. The manager does not know the standard deviation of the amounts spent. However, he does estimate that the range is from $5.00 up to $155.00. How large of a sample is needed?

18. In a sample of 200 residents of Georgetown County, 120 reported they believed the county real estate taxes were too high. Develop a 95 percent confidence interval for the proportion of residents who believe the tax rate is too high. Would it be reasonable to conclude that the majority of the taxpayers feel that the taxes are too high?

19. In recent times, the percent of buyers purchasing a new vehicle via the Internet has been large enough that local automobile dealers are concerned about its impact on their business. The information needed is an estimate of the proportion of purchases via the Internet. How large of a sample of purchasers is necessary for the estimate to be within 2 percentage points with a 98 percent level of confidence? Current thinking is that about 8 percent of the vehicles are purchased via the Internet.

20. Historically, the proportion of adults over the age of 24 who smoke has been .30. In recent years, much information has been published and aired on radio and TV that smoking is not good for one's health. A sample of 500 adults revealed only 25 percent of those sampled smoked. Develop a 98 percent confidence interval for the proportion of adults who currently smoke. Would you agree that the proportion is less than 30 percent?

21. The auditor of the State of Ohio needs an estimate of the proportion of residents who regularly play the state lottery. Historically, about 40 percent regularly play, but the auditor would like some current information. How large a sample is necessary for the estimate to be within 3 percentage points, with a 98 percent level of confidence?

Case

Century National Bank

Refer to the description of Century National Bank at the end of the Review of Chapters 1–4 on page 137. When Mr. Selig took over as president of Century several years ago, the use of debit cards was just beginning. He would like an update on the use of these cards. Develop a 95 percent confidence interval for the proportion of customers using these cards. On the basis of the confidence interval, is it reasonable to conclude that more than half of the customers use a debit card? Write a brief report interpreting the results.

Practice Test

Part I—Objective

1. If each item in the population has the same chance of being selected, this is called a _____.

   1. _____

2. The difference between the population mean and the sample mean is called the _____.

   2. _____

3. The _____ is the standard deviation of the distribution of sample means.

   3. _____

4. If the sample size is increased, the variance of the sample means will _____. (become smaller, become larger, not change)

   4. _____

5. A single value used to estimate a population parameter is called a _____.

   5. _____

6. A range of values within which the population parameter is expected to occur is called a _____.

   6. _____

7. Which of the following do *not* affect the width of a confidence interval? (sample size, variation in the population, level of confidence, size of population)   7. _____
8. The fraction of a population that has a particular characteristic is called a _____.
   8. _____
9. Which of the following is not a characteristic of the *t* distribution? (positively skewed, continuous, mean of zero, based on degrees of freedom)   9. _____
10. To determine the required sample size of a proportion when no estimate of the population proportion is available, what value is used?   10. _____

Part II—Problems

1. Americans spend an average (mean) of 12.2 minutes (per day) in the shower. The distribution of times follows the normal distribution with a population standard deviation of 2.3 minutes. What is the likelihood that the mean time per day for a sample of 12 Americans was 11 minutes or less?
2. A recent study of 26 Conway, SC, residents revealed they had lived at their current address an average of 9.3 years. The standard deviation of the sample was 2 years.
   a. What is the population mean?
   b. What is the best estimate of the population mean?
   c. What is the standard error of estimate?
   d. Develop a 90 percent confidence interval for the population mean.
3. A recent federal report indicated that 27 percent of children ages 2 to 5 ate a vegetable at least 5 times a week. How large a sample is needed to estimate the true population proportion within 2 percent with a 98 percent level of confidence? Be sure to use the information contained in the federal report.
4. The Philadelphia Area Transit Authority wishes to estimate the proportion of central city workers that use public transportation to get to work. A sample of 100 workers revealed that 64 used public transportation. Develop a 95 percent confidence interval for the population proportion.

10

GOALS

When you have completed this chapter you will be able to:

1 Define a *hypothesis* and *hypothesis testing.*

2 Describe the five-step hypothesis-testing procedure.

3 Distinguish between a *one-tailed* and a *two-tailed test of hypothesis.*

4 Conduct a test of hypothesis about a population mean.

5 Conduct a test of hypothesis about a population proportion.

6 Define *Type I* and *Type II errors.*

7 Compute the probability of a Type II error.

One-Sample Tests of Hypothesis

Dole Pineapple, Inc., is concerned that the 16-ounce can of sliced pineapple is being overfilled. Assume the standard deviation of the process is .03 ounces. The quality control department took a random sample of 50 cans and found that the arithmetic mean weight was 16.05 ounces. At the 5 percent level of significance, can we conclude that the mean weight is greater than 16 ounces? Determine the *p*-value. (Exercise 32, Goal 4)

Introduction

Chapter 8 began our study of statistical inference. We described how we could select a random sample and from this sample estimate the value of a population parameter. For example, we selected a sample of 5 employees at Spence Sprockets, found the number of years of service for each sampled employee, computed the mean years of service, and used the sample mean to estimate the mean years of service for all employees. In other words, we estimated a population parameter from a sample statistic.

Chapter 9 continued the study of statistical inference by developing a confidence interval. A confidence interval is a range of values within which we expect the population parameter to occur. In this chapter, rather than develop a range of values within which we expect the population parameter to occur, we develop a procedure to test the validity of a statement about a population parameter. Some examples of statements we might want to test are:

- The mean speed of automobiles passing milepost 150 on the West Virginia Turnpike is 68 miles per hour.
- The mean number of miles driven by those leasing a Chevy TrailBlazer for three years is 32,000 miles.
- The mean time an American family lives in a particular single-family dwelling is 11.8 years.
- The 2007 mean starting salary for a graduate of a four-year college with a degree in business administrative is $41,155.
- Thirty-five percent of retirees in the upper Midwest sell their home and move to a warm climate within 1 year of their retirement.
- Eighty percent of those who regularly play the state lotteries never win more than $100 in any one play.

This chapter and several of the following chapters are concerned with statistical hypothesis testing. We begin by defining what we mean by a statistical hypothesis and statistical hypothesis testing. Next, we outline the steps in statistical hypothesis testing. Then we conduct tests of hypothesis for means and proportions. In the last section of the chapter, we describe possible errors due to sampling in hypothesis testing.

What Is a Hypothesis?

A hypothesis is a statement about a population parameter.

A hypothesis is a statement about a population. Data are then used to check the reasonableness of the statement. To begin we need to define the word *hypothesis*. In the United States legal system, a person is innocent until proven guilty. A jury hypothesizes that a person charged with a crime is innocent and subjects this hypothesis to verification by reviewing the evidence and hearing testimony before reaching a verdict. In a similar sense, a patient goes to a physician and reports various symptoms. On the basis of the symptoms, the physician will order certain diagnostic tests, then, according to the symptoms and the test results, determine the treatment to be followed.

In statistical analysis we make a claim, that is, state a hypothesis, collect data, then use the data to test the assertion. We define a statistical hypothesis as follows.

> **HYPOTHESIS** A statement about a population parameter subject to verification.

In most cases the population is so large that it is not feasible to study all the items, objects, or persons in the population. For example, it would not be possible to contact every systems analyst in the United States to find his or her monthly income. Likewise, the quality assurance department at Cooper Tire cannot check each tire produced to determine whether it will last more than 60,000 miles.

As noted in Chapter 8, an alternative to measuring or interviewing the entire population is to take a sample from the population. We can, therefore, test a statement to determine whether the sample does or does not support the statement concerning the population.

What Is Hypothesis Testing?

The terms *hypothesis testing* and *testing a hypothesis* are used interchangeably. Hypothesis testing starts with a statement, or assumption, about a population parameter—such as the population mean. As noted, this statement is referred to as a *hypothesis*. A hypothesis might be that the mean monthly commission of sales associates in retail electronics stores, such as Circuit City, is $2,000. We cannot contact all these sales associates to ascertain that the mean is in fact $2,000. The cost of locating and interviewing every electronics sales associate in the United States would be exorbitant. To test the validity of the assumption ($\mu = \$2,000$), we must select a sample from the population of all electronics sales associates, calculate sample statistics, and based on certain decision rules accept or reject the hypothesis. A sample mean of $1,000 for the electronics sales associates would certainly cause rejection of the hypothesis. However, suppose the sample mean is $1,995. Is that close enough to $2,000 for us to accept the assumption that the population mean is $2,000? Can we attribute the difference of $5 between the two means to sampling error, or is that difference statistically significant?

> **HYPOTHESIS TESTING** A procedure based on sample evidence and probability theory to determine whether the hypothesis is a reasonable statement.

Five-Step Procedure for Testing a Hypothesis

There is a five-step procedure that systematizes hypothesis testing; when we get to step 5, we are ready to reject or not reject the hypothesis. However, hypothesis testing as used by statisticians does not provide proof that something is true, in the manner in which a mathematician "proves" a statement. It does provide a kind of "proof beyond a reasonable doubt," in the manner of the court system. Hence, there are specific rules of evidence, or procedures, that are followed. The steps are shown in the following diagram. We will discuss in detail each of the steps.

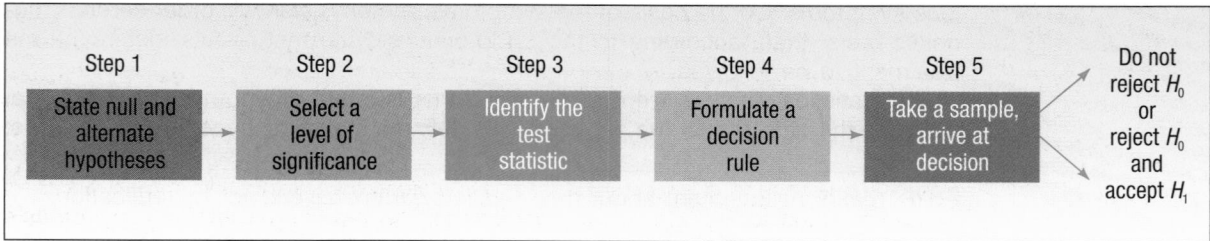

Step 1: State the Null Hypothesis (H_0) and the Alternate Hypothesis (H_1)

Five-step systematic procedure

The first step is to state the hypothesis being tested. It is called the **null hypothesis,** designated H_0, and read "*H sub zero.*" The capital letter H stands for hypothesis, and the subscript zero implies "no difference." There is usually a "not" or a "no" term in the null hypothesis, meaning that there is "no change." For example, the null hypothesis is that the mean number of miles driven on the steel-belted tire is not different from 60,000. The null hypothesis would be written H_0: $\mu = 60,000$. Generally speaking, the null hypothesis is developed for the purpose of testing. We either reject or fail to reject the null hypothesis. The null hypothesis is a statement that is not rejected unless our sample data provide convincing evidence that it is false.

We should emphasize that, if the null hypothesis is not rejected on the basis of the sample data, we cannot say that the null hypothesis is true. To put it another way, failing to reject the null hypothesis does not prove that H_0 is true, it means we have *failed to disprove* H_0. To prove without any doubt the null hypothesis is true, the population parameter would have to be known. To actually determine it, we would have to test, survey, or count every item in the population. This is usually not feasible. The alternative is to take a sample from the population.

State the null hypothesis and the alternative hypothesis.

It should also be noted that we often begin the null hypothesis by stating, "There is no *significant* difference between . . . ," or "The mean impact strength of the glass is not *significantly* different from. . . ." When we select a sample from a population, the sample statistic is usually numerically different from the hypothesized population parameter. As an illustration, suppose the hypothesized impact strength of a glass plate is 70 psi, and the mean impact strength of a sample of 12 glass plates is 69.5 psi. We must make a decision about the difference of 0.5 psi. Is it a true difference, that is, a significant difference, or is the difference between the sample statistic (69.5) and the hypothesized population parameter (70.0) due to chance (sampling)? As noted, to answer this question we conduct a test of significance, commonly referred to as a test of hypothesis. To define what is meant by a null hypothesis:

> **NULL HYPOTHESIS** A statement about the value of a population parameter developed for the purpose of testing numerical evidence.

The **alternate hypothesis** describes what you will conclude if you reject the null hypothesis. It is written H_1 and is read "*H sub one.*" It is also referred to as the research hypothesis. The alternate hypothesis is accepted if the sample data provide us with enough statistical evidence that the null hypothesis is false.

> **ALTERNATE HYPOTHESIS** A statement that is accepted if the sample data provide sufficient evidence that the null hypothesis is false.

The following example will help clarify what is meant by the null hypothesis and the alternate hypothesis. A recent article indicated the mean age of U.S. commercial aircraft is 15 years. To conduct a statistical test regarding this statement, the first step is to determine the null and the alternate hypotheses. The null hypothesis represents the current or reported condition. It is written H_0: $\mu = 15$. The alternate hypothesis is that the statement is not true, that is, H_1: $\mu \neq 15$. It is important to remember that no matter how the problem is stated, *the null hypothesis will always contain the equal sign.* The equal sign ($=$) will never appear in the alternate hypothesis. Why? Because the null hypothesis is the statement being tested, and we need a specific value to include in our calculations. We turn to the alternate hypothesis only if the data suggests the null hypothesis is untrue.

Step 2: Select a Level of Significance

After setting up the null hypothesis and alternate hypothesis, the next step is to state the level of significance.

> **LEVEL OF SIGNIFICANCE** The probability of rejecting the null hypothesis when it is true.

Select a level of significance or risk.

The level of significance is designated α, the Greek letter alpha. It is also sometimes called the level of risk. This may be a more appropriate term because it is the risk you take of rejecting the null hypothesis when it is really true.

There is no one level of significance that is applied to all tests. A decision is made to use the .05 level (often stated as the 5 percent level), the .01 level, the .10 level, or any other level between 0 and 1. Traditionally, the .05 level is selected for consumer research projects, .01 for quality assurance, and .10 for political polling. You, the researcher, must decide on the level of significance *before* formulating a decision rule and collecting sample data.

To illustrate how it is possible to reject a true hypothesis, suppose a firm manufacturing personal computers uses a large number of printed circuit boards. Suppliers

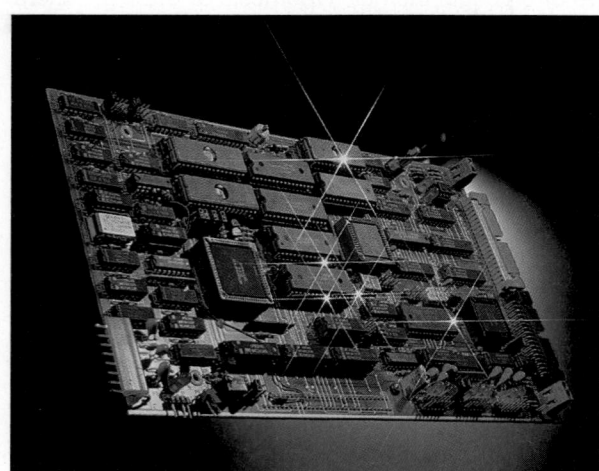

bid on the boards, and the one with the lowest bid is awarded a sizable contract. Suppose the contract specifies that the computer manufacturer's quality-assurance department will sample all incoming shipments of circuit boards. If more than 6 percent of the boards sampled are substandard, the shipment will be rejected. The null hypothesis is that the incoming shipment of boards contains 6 percent or less substandard boards. The alternate hypothesis is that more than 6 percent of the boards are defective.

A sample of 50 circuit boards received July 21 from Allied Electronics revealed that 4 boards, or 8 percent, were substandard. The shipment was rejected because it exceeded the maximum of 6 percent substandard printed circuit boards. If the shipment was actually substandard, then the decision to return the boards to the supplier was correct. However, suppose the 4 substandard printed circuit boards selected in the sample of 50 were the only substandard boards in the shipment of 4,000 boards. Then only $1/10$ of 1 percent were defective ($4/4,000 = .001$). In that case, less than 6 percent of the entire shipment was substandard and rejecting the shipment was an error. In terms of hypothesis testing, we rejected the null hypothesis that the shipment was not substandard when we should have accepted the null hypothesis. By rejecting a true null hypothesis, we committed a Type I error. The probability of committing a Type I error is α.

> **TYPE I ERROR** Rejecting the null hypothesis, H_0, when it is true.

The probability of committing another type of error, called a Type II error, is designated by the Greek letter beta (β).

> **TYPE II ERROR** Accepting the null hypothesis when it is false.

The firm manufacturing personal computers would commit a Type II error if, unknown to the manufacturer, an incoming shipment of printed circuit boards from Allied Electronics contained 15 percent substandard boards, yet the shipment was accepted. How could this happen? Suppose 2 of the 50 boards in the sample (4 percent) tested were substandard, and 48 of the 50 were good boards. According to the stated procedure, because the sample contained less than 6 percent substandard boards, the shipment was accepted. It could be that *by chance* the 48 good boards selected in the sample were the only acceptable ones in the entire shipment consisting of thousands of boards!

In retrospect, the researcher cannot study every item or individual in the population. Thus, there is a possibility of two types of error—a Type I error, wherein the null hypothesis is rejected when it should have been accepted, and a Type II error, wherein the null hypothesis is not rejected when it should have been rejected.

We often refer to the probability of these two possible errors as *alpha,* α, and *beta,* β. Alpha (α) is the probability of making a Type I error, and beta (β) is the probability of making a Type II error.

The following table summarizes the decisions the researcher could make and the possible consequences.

Null Hypothesis	Researcher	
	Does Not Reject H_0	Rejects H_0
H_0 is true	Correct decision	Type I error
H_0 is false	Type II error	Correct decision

Step 3: Select the Test Statistic

There are many test statistics. In this chapter we use both z and t as the test statistic. In later chapters we will use such test statistics as F and χ^2, called chi-square.

> **TEST STATISTIC** A value, determined from sample information, used to determine whether to reject the null hypothesis.

In hypothesis testing for the mean (μ) when σ is known, the test statistic z is computed by:

$$\text{TESTING A MEAN, } \sigma \text{ KNOWN} \qquad z = \frac{\overline{X} - \mu}{\sigma/\sqrt{n}} \qquad \text{[10–1]}$$

The z value is based on the sampling distribution of $\overline{X}$, which follows the normal distribution with a mean ($\mu_{\overline{x}}$) equal to μ, and a standard deviation $\sigma_{\overline{x}}$, which is equal to $\sigma/\sqrt{n}$. We can thus determine whether the difference between $\overline{X}$ and μ is statistically significant by finding the number of standard deviations $\overline{X}$ is from μ, using formula (10–1).

Step 4: Formulate the Decision Rule

The decision rule states the conditions when H_0 is rejected.

A decision rule is a statement of the specific conditions under which the null hypothesis is rejected and the conditions under which it is not rejected. The region or area of rejection defines the location of all those values that are so large or so small that the probability of their occurrence under a true null hypothesis is rather remote.

Chart 10–1 portrays the rejection region for a test of significance that will be conducted later in the chapter.

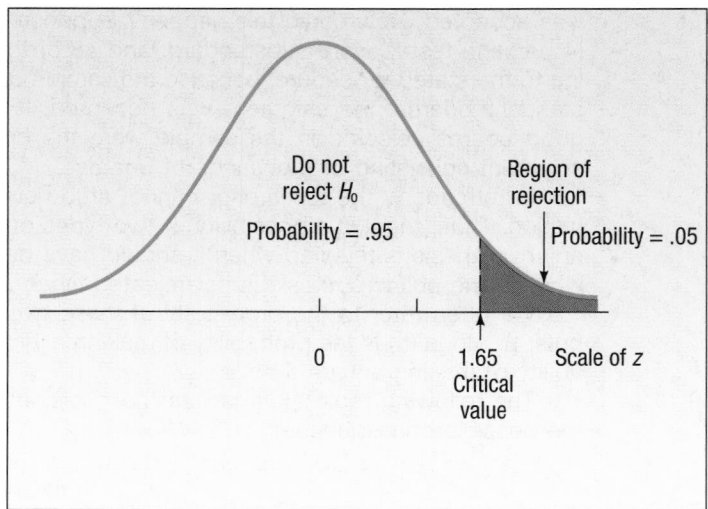

CHART 10–1 Sampling Distribution of the Statistic *z*, a Right-Tailed Test, .05 Level of Significance

Note in the chart that:

1. The area where the null hypothesis is not rejected is to the left of 1.65. We will explain how to get the 1.65 value shortly.
2. The area of rejection is to the right of 1.65.
3. A one-tailed test is being applied. (This will also be explained later.)
4. The .05 level of significance was chosen.
5. The sampling distribution of the statistic *z* follows the normal probability distribution.
6. The value 1.65 separates the regions where the null hypothesis is rejected and where it is not rejected.
7. The value 1.65 is the **critical value.**

> **CRITICAL VALUE** The dividing point between the region where the null hypothesis is rejected and the region where it is not rejected.

Step 5: Make a Decision

The fifth and final step in hypothesis testing is computing the test statistic, comparing it to the critical value, and making a decision to reject or not to reject the null hypothesis. Referring to Chart 10–1, if, based on sample information, *z* is computed to be 2.34, the null hypothesis is rejected at the .05 level of significance. The decision to reject H_0 was made because 2.34 lies in the region of rejection, that is, beyond 1.65. We would reject the null hypothesis, reasoning that it is highly improbable that a computed *z* value this large is due to sampling error (chance).

Had the computed value been 1.65 or less, say 0.71, the null hypothesis would not be rejected. It would be reasoned that such a small computed value could be attributed to chance, that is, sampling error.

As noted, only one of two decisions is possible in hypothesis testing—either accept or reject the null hypothesis. Instead of "accepting" the null hypothesis, H_0, some researchers prefer to phrase the decision as: "Do not reject H_0," "We fail to reject H_0," or "The sample results do not allow us to reject H_0."

It should be reemphasized that there is always a possibility that the null hypothesis is rejected when it should not be rejected (a Type I error). Also, there is a definable chance that the null hypothesis is accepted when it should be rejected (a Type II error).

> **SUMMARY OF THE STEPS IN HYPOTHESIS TESTING**
> 1. Establish the null hypothesis (H_0) and the alternate hypothesis (H_1).
> 2. Select the level of significance, that is α.
> 3. Select an appropriate test statistic.
> 4. Formulate a decision rule based on steps 1, 2, and 3 above.
> 5. Make a decision regarding the null hypothesis based on the sample information. Interpret the results of the test.

Before actually conducting a test of hypothesis, we will differentiate between a one-tailed test of significance and a two-tailed test.

One-Tailed and Two-Tailed Tests of Significance

Refer to Chart 10–1. It depicts a one-tailed test. The region of rejection is only in the right (upper) tail of the curve. To illustrate, suppose that the packaging department at General Foods Corporation is concerned that some boxes of Grape Nuts are significantly overweight. The cereal is packaged in 453-gram boxes, so the null hypothesis is H_0: $\mu \leq 453$. This is read, "the population mean (μ) is equal to or less than 453." The alternate hypothesis is, therefore, H_1: $\mu > 453$. This is read, "μ is greater than 453." Note that the inequality sign in the alternate hypothesis ($>$) points to the region of rejection in the upper tail. (See Chart 10–1.) Also note that the null hypothesis includes the equal sign. That is, H_0: $\mu \leq 453$. The equality condition always appears in H_0, never in H_1.

Chart 10–2 portrays a situation where the rejection region is in the left (lower) tail of the standard normal distribution. As an illustration, consider the problem of automobile manufacturers, large automobile leasing companies, and other organizations that purchase large quantities of tires. They want the tires to average, say, 60,000 miles of wear under normal usage. They will, therefore, reject a shipment of tires if tests reveal that the mean life of the tires is significantly below 60,000 miles. They gladly accept a shipment if the mean life is greater than 60,000 miles! They are not concerned with this possibility, however. They are concerned only if they have sample evidence to conclude that the tires will average less than 60,000 miles of useful life. Thus, the test is set up to satisfy the concern of the automobile manufacturers that *the mean life of*

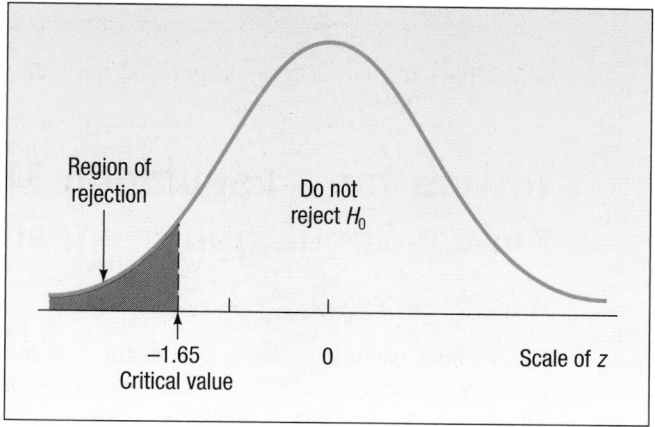

CHART 10–2 Sampling Distribution for the Statistic z, Left-Tailed Test, .05 Level of Significance

Test is one-tailed if H_1 states $\mu >$ or $\mu <$.

If H_1 states a direction, test is one-tailed.

the tires is no less than 60,000 miles. This statement appears in the alternate hypothesis. The null and alternate hypotheses in this case are written H_0: $\mu \geq 60{,}000$ and H_1: $\mu < 60{,}000$.

One way to determine the location of the rejection region is to look at the direction in which the inequality sign in the alternate hypothesis is pointing (either $<$ or $>$). In this problem it is pointing to the left, and the rejection region is therefore in the left tail.

In summary, a test is *one-tailed* when the alternate hypothesis, H_1, states a direction, such as:

H_0: The mean income of women stockbrokers is *less than or equal to* $65,000 per year.

H_1: The mean income of women stockbrokers is *greater than* $65,000 per year.

If no direction is specified in the alternate hypothesis, we use a *two-tailed* test. Changing the previous problem to illustrate, we can say:

H_0: The mean income of women stockbrokers is $65,000 per year.

H_1: The mean income of women stockbrokers is *not equal to* $65,000 per year.

If the null hypothesis is rejected and H_1 accepted in the two-tailed case, the mean income could be significantly greater than $65,000 per year or it could be significantly less than $65,000 per year. To accommodate these two possibilities, the 5 percent area of rejection is divided equally into the two tails of the sampling distribution (2.5 percent each). Chart 10–3 shows the two areas and the critical values. Note that the total area in the normal distribution is 1.0000, found by .9500 + .0250 + .0250.

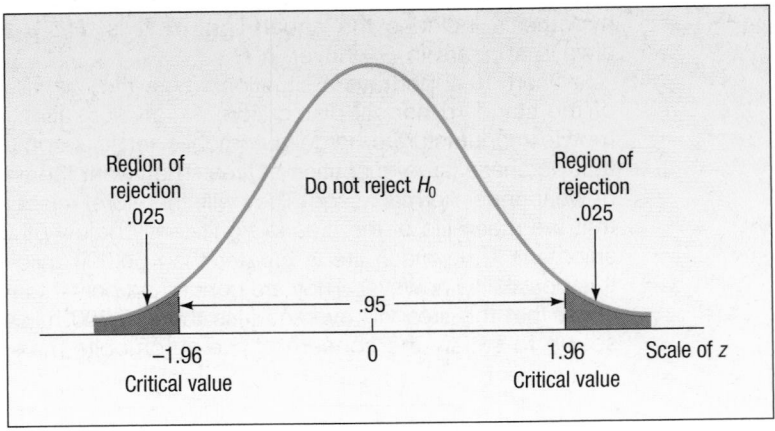

CHART 10–3 Regions of Nonrejection and Rejection for a Two-Tailed Test, .05 Level of Significance

Testing for a Population Mean: Known Population Standard Deviation

A Two-Tailed Test

An example will show the details of the five-step hypothesis testing procedure. We also wish to use a two-tailed test. That is, we are *not* concerned whether the sample results are larger or smaller than the proposed population mean. Rather, we are interested in whether it is *different from* the proposed value for the population mean. We begin, as we did in the previous chapter, with a situation in which we have historical information about the population and in fact know its standard deviation.

Example

Jamestown Steel Company manufactures and assembles desks and other office equipment at several plants in western New York State. The weekly production of the Model A325 desk at the Fredonia Plant follows a normal probability distribution with a mean of 200 and a standard deviation of 16. Recently, because of market expansion, new production methods have been introduced and new employees hired. The vice president of manufacturing would like to investigate whether there has been a *change* in the weekly production of the Model A325 desk. Is the mean number of desks produced at the Fredonia Plant *different from* 200 at the .01 significance level?

Solution

We use the statistical hypothesis testing procedure to investigate whether the production rate has changed from 200 per week.

Step 1: State the null hypothesis and the alternate hypothesis. The null hypothesis is "The population mean is 200." The alternate hypothesis is "The mean is different from 200" or "The mean is not 200." These two hypotheses are written:

$$H_0: \mu = 200$$

$$H_1: \mu \neq 200$$

This is a *two-tailed test* because the alternate hypothesis does not state a direction. In other words, it does not state whether the mean production is greater than 200 or less than 200. The vice president wants only to find out whether the production rate is different from 200.

Step 2: Select the level of significance. As noted, the .01 level of significance is used. This is α, the probability of committing a Type I error, and it is the probability of rejecting a true null hypothesis.

Step 3: Select the test statistic. The test statistic for a mean when σ is known is z. It was discussed at length in Chapter 7. Transforming the production data to standard units (z values) permits their use not only in this problem but also in other hypothesis-testing problems. Formula (10–1) for z is repeated below with the various letters identified.

[10–1]

Formula for the test statistic

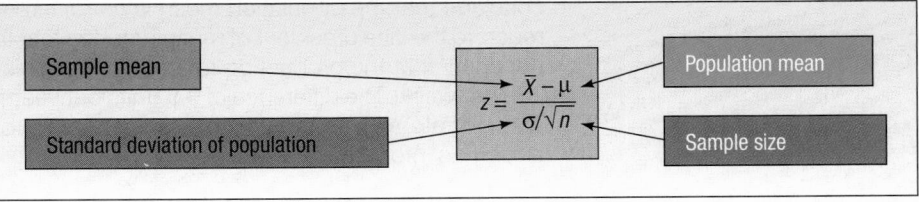

$$z = \frac{\bar{X} - \mu}{\sigma/\sqrt{n}}$$

Sample mean

Standard deviation of population

Population mean

Sample size

Step 4: Formulate the decision rule. The decision rule is formulated by finding the critical values of z from Appendix B.1. Since this is a two-tailed test, half of .01, or .005, is placed in each tail. The area where H_0 is not rejected, located between the two tails, is therefore .99. Appendix B.1 is based on half of the area under the curve, or .5000. Then, .5000 − .0050 is .4950, so .4950 is the area between 0 and the critical value. Locate .4950 in the body of the table. The value nearest to .4950 is .4951. Then read the critical value in the row and column corresponding to .4951. It is 2.58. For your convenience, Appendix B.1, Areas under the Normal Curve, is repeated in the inside back cover.

All the facets of this problem are shown in the diagram in Chart 10–4.

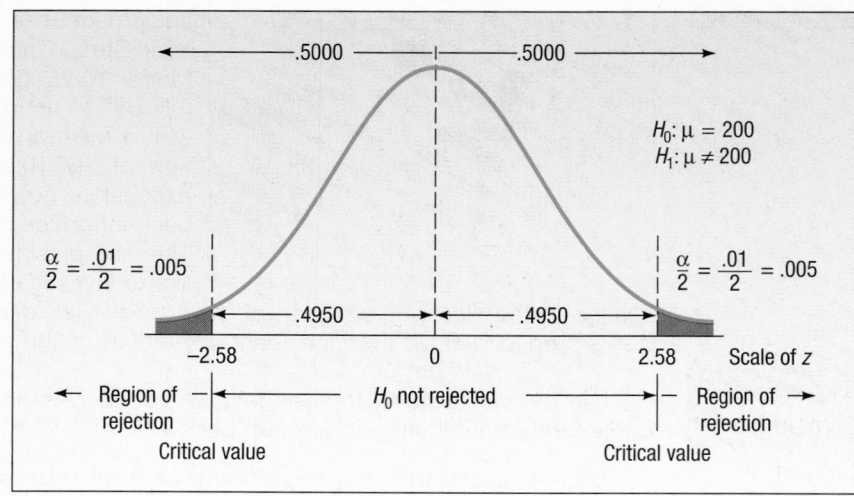

CHART 10–4 Decision Rule for the .01 Significance Level

The decision rule is, therefore: Reject the null hypothesis and accept the alternate hypothesis (which states that the population mean is not 200) if the computed value of z is not between −2.58 and +2.58. Do not reject the null hypothesis if z falls between −2.58 and +2.58.

Step 5: Make a decision and interpret the result. Take a sample from the population (weekly production), compute z, apply the decision rule, and arrive at a decision to reject H_0 or not to reject H_0. The mean number of desks produced last year (50 weeks, because the plant was shut down 2 weeks for vacation) is 203.5. The standard deviation of the population is 16 desks per week. Computing the z value from formula (10–1):

$$z = \frac{\overline{X} - \mu}{\sigma/\sqrt{n}} = \frac{203.5 - 200}{16/\sqrt{50}} = 1.55$$

Because 1.55 does not fall in the rejection region, H_0 is not rejected. We conclude that the population mean is *not* different from 200. So we would report to the vice president of manufacturing that the sample evidence does not show that the production rate at the Fredonia Plant has changed from 200 per week. The difference of 3.5 units between the historical weekly production rate and that last year can reasonably be attributed to sampling error. This information is summarized in the following chart.

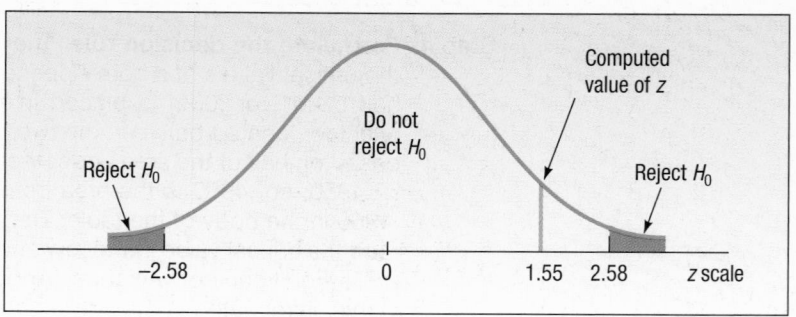

Did we prove that the assembly rate is still 200 per week? Not really. What we did, technically, was *fail to disprove the null hypothesis.* Failing to disprove the hypothesis that the population mean is 200 is not the same thing as proving it to be true. As we suggested in the chapter introduction, the conclusion is analogous to the American judicial system. To explain, suppose a person is accused of a crime but is acquitted by a jury. If a person is acquitted of a crime, the conclusion is that there was not enough evidence to prove the person guilty. The trial did not prove that the individual was innocent, only that there was not enough evidence to prove the defendant guilty. That is what we do in statistical hypothesis testing when we do not reject the null hypothesis. The correct interpretation is that we have failed to disprove the null hypothesis.

We selected the significance level, .01 in this case, before setting up the decision rule and sampling the population. This is the appropriate strategy. The significance level should be set by the investigator, but it should be determined *before* gathering the sample evidence and not changed based on the sample evidence.

Comparing confidence intervals and hypothesis testing.

How does the hypothesis testing procedure just described compare with that of confidence intervals discussed in the previous chapter? When we conducted the test of hypothesis regarding the production of desks we changed the units from desks per week to a z value. Then we compared the computed value of the test statistic (1.55) to that of the critical values (-2.58 and 2.58). Because the computed value was in the region where the null hypothesis was not rejected, we concluded that the population mean could be 200. To use the confidence interval approach, on the other hand, we would develop a confidence interval, based on formula (9–1). See page 294. The interval would be from 197.66 to 209.34, found by $203.5 \pm 2.58(16/\sqrt{50})$. Note that the proposed population value, 200, is within this interval. Hence, we would conclude that the population mean could reasonably be 200.

In general, H_0 is rejected if the confidence interval does not include the hypothesized value. If the confidence interval includes the hypothesized value, then H_0 is not rejected. So the "do not reject region" for a test of hypothesis is equivalent to the proposed population value occurring in the confidence interval. The primary difference between a confidence interval and the "do not reject" region for a hypothesis test is whether the interval is centered around the sample statistic, such as $\overline{X}$, as in the confidence interval, or around 0, as in the test of hypothesis.

Self-Review 10–1

Heinz, a manufacturer of ketchup, uses a particular machine to dispense 16 ounces of its ketchup into containers. From many years of experience with the particular dispensing machine, Heinz knows the amount of product in each container follows a normal distribution with a mean of 16 ounces and a standard deviation of 0.15 ounce. A sample of 50 containers filled last hour revealed the mean amount per container was 16.017 ounces. Does this evidence suggest that the mean amount dispensed is different from 16 ounces? Use the .05 significance level.

(a)   State the null hypothesis and the alternate hypothesis.
(b)   What is the probability of a Type I error?
(c)   Give the formula for the test statistic.
(d)   State the decision rule.
(e)   Determine the value of the test statistic.
(f)   What is your decision regarding the null hypothesis?
(g)   Interpret, in a single sentence, the result of the statistical test.

A One-Tailed Test

In the previous example, we emphasized that we were concerned only with reporting to the vice president whether there had been a change in the mean number of desks assembled at the Fredonia Plant. We were not concerned with whether the change was an increase or a decrease in the production.

To illustrate a one-tailed test, let's change the problem. Suppose the vice president wants to know whether there has been an *increase* in the number of units assembled. Can we conclude, because of the improved production methods, that the mean number of desks assembled in the last 50 weeks was more than 200? Look at the difference in the way the problem is formulated. In the first case we wanted to know whether there was a *difference* in the mean number assembled, but now we want to know whether there has been an *increase*. Because we are investigating different questions, we will set our hypotheses differently. The biggest difference occurs in the alternate hypothesis. Before, we stated the alternate hypothesis as "different from"; now we want to state it as "greater than." In symbols:

A two–tailed test:	A one–tailed test:
$H_0: \mu = 200$	$H_0: \mu \leq 200$
$H_1: \mu \neq 200$	$H_1: \mu > 200$

The critical values for a one-tailed test are different from a two-tailed test at the same significance level. In the previous example, we split the significance level in half and put half in the lower tail and half in the upper tail. In a one-tailed test we put all the rejection region in one tail. See Chart 10–5.

For the one-tailed test, the critical value is 2.33, found by: (1) subtracting .01 from .5000 and (2) finding the z value corresponding to .4900.

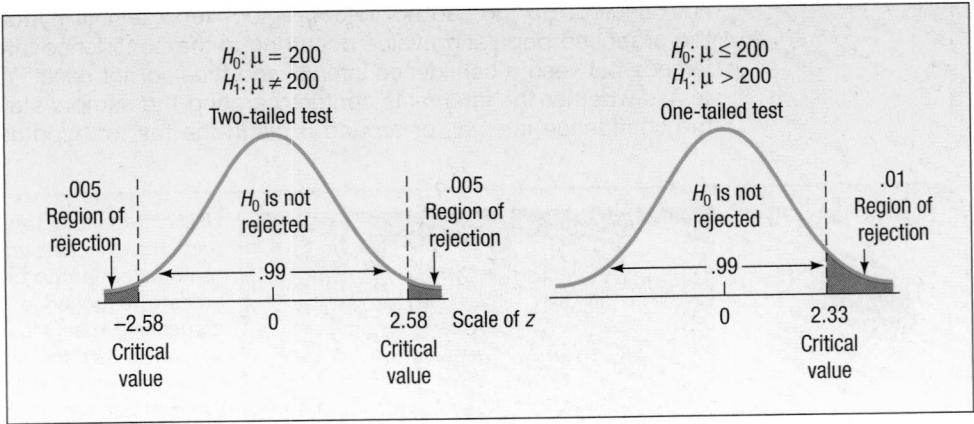

CHART 10–5 Rejection Regions for Two-Tailed and One-Tailed Tests, $\alpha = .01$

p-Value in Hypothesis Testing

In testing a hypothesis, we compare the test statistic to a critical value. A decision is made to either reject the null hypothesis or not to reject it. So, for example, if the critical value is 1.96 and the computed value of the test statistic is 2.19, the decision is to reject the null hypothesis.

In recent years, spurred by the availability of computer software, additional information is often reported on the strength of the rejection or acceptance. That is, how confident are we in rejecting the null hypothesis? This approach reports the

Statistics in Action

There is a difference between *statistically significant* and *practically significant*. To explain, suppose we develop a new diet pill and test it on 100,000 people. We conclude that the typical person taking the pill for two years lost one pound. Do you think many people would be interested in taking the pill to lose one pound? The results of using the new pill were statistically significant but not practically significant.

probability (assuming that the null hypothesis is true) of getting a value of the test statistic at least as extreme as the value actually obtained. This process compares the probability, called the **p-value,** with the significance level. If the p-value is smaller than the significance level, H_0 is rejected. If it is larger than the significance level, H_0 is not rejected.

> **p-VALUE** The probability of observing a sample value as extreme as, or more extreme than, the value observed, given that the null hypothesis is true.

Determining the p-value not only results in a decision regarding H_0, but it gives us additional insight into the strength of the decision. A very small p-value, such as .0001, indicates that there is little likelihood the H_0 is true. On the other hand, a p-value of .2033 means that H_0 is not rejected, and there is little likelihood that it is false.

How do we compute the p-value? To illustrate we will use the example in which we tested the null hypothesis that the mean number of desks produced per week at Fredonia was 200. We did not reject the null hypothesis, because the z value of 1.55 fell in the region between -2.58 and 2.58. We agreed not to reject the null hypothesis if the computed value of z fell in this region. The probability of finding a z value of 1.55 or more is .0606, found by $.5000 - .4394$. To put it another way, the probability of obtaining an $\overline{X}$ greater than 203.5 if $\mu = 200$ is .0606. To compute the p-value, we need to be concerned with the region less than -1.55 as well as the values greater than 1.55 (because the rejection region is in both tails). The two-tailed p-value is .1212, found by 2(.0606). The p-value of .1212 is greater than the significance level of .01 decided upon initially, so H_0 is not rejected. The details are shown in the following graph. In general, the area is doubled in a two-sided test. Then the p-value can easily be compared with the significance level. The same decision rule is used as in the one-sided test.

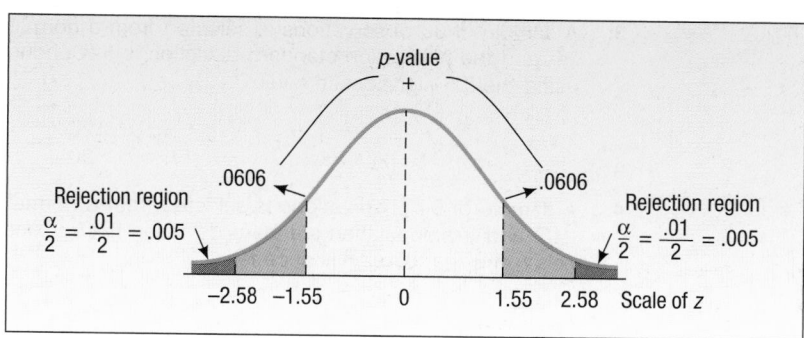

A p-value is a way to express the likelihood that H_0 is false. But how do we interpret a p-value? We have already said that if the p-value is less than the significance level, then we reject H_0; if it is greater than the significance level, then we do not reject H_0. Also, if the p-value is very large, then it is likely that H_0 is true. If the p-value is small, then it is likely that H_0 is not true. The following box will help to interpret p-values.

> **INTERPRETING THE WEIGHT OF EVIDENCE AGAINST H_0** If the p-value is less than
> (a) .10, we have *some* evidence that H_0 is not true.
> (b) .05, we have *strong* evidence that H_0 is not true.
> (c) .01, we have *very strong* evidence that H_0 is not true.
> (d) .001, we have *extremely strong* evidence that H_0 is not true.

Self-Review 10-2   Refer to Self-Review 10–1.

(a)   Suppose the next to the last sentence is changed to read: Does this evidence suggest that the mean amount dispensed is *more than* 16 ounces? State the null hypothesis and the alternate hypothesis under these conditions.

(b)   What is the decision rule under the new conditions stated in part (a)?

(c)   A second sample of 50 filled containers revealed the mean to be 16.040 ounces. What is the value of the test statistic for this sample?

(d)   What is your decision regarding the null hypothesis?

(e)   Interpret, in a single sentence, the result of the statistical test.

(f)   What is the *p*-value? What is your decision regarding the null hypothesis based on the *p*-value? Is this the same conclusion reached in part (d)?

Exercises

connect

For Exercises 1–4 answer the questions: (a) Is this a one- or two-tailed test? (b) What is the decision rule? (c) What is the value of the test statistic? (d) What is your decision regarding H_0? (e) What is the *p*-value? Interpret it.

1.   The following information is available.

$$H_0: \mu = 50$$
$$H_1: \mu \neq 50$$

The sample mean is 49, and the sample size is 36. The population standard deviation is 5. Use the .05 significance level.

2.   The following information is available.

$$H_0: \mu \leq 10$$
$$H_1: \mu > 10$$

The sample mean is 12 for a sample of 36. The population standard deviation is 3. Use the .02 significance level.

3.   A sample of 36 observations is selected from a normal population. The sample mean is 21, and the population standard deviation is 5. Conduct the following test of hypothesis using the .05 significance level.

$$H_0: \mu \leq 20$$
$$H_1: \mu > 20$$

4.   A sample of 64 observations is selected from a normal population. The sample mean is 215, and the population standard deviation is 15. Conduct the following test of hypothesis using the .03 significance level.

$$H_0: \mu \geq 220$$
$$H_1: \mu < 220$$

For Exercises 5–8: (a) State the null hypothesis and the alternate hypothesis. (b) State the decision rule. (c) Compute the value of the test statistic. (d) What is your decision regarding H_0? (e) What is the *p*-value? Interpret it.

5.   The manufacturer of the X-15 steel-belted radial truck tire claims that the mean mileage the tire can be driven before the tread wears out is 60,000 miles. The population standard deviation of the mileage is 5,000 miles. Crosset Truck Company bought 48 tires and found that the mean mileage for its trucks is 59,500 miles. Is Crosset's experience different from that claimed by the manufacturer at the .05 significance level?

6.   The MacBurger restaurant chain claims that the mean waiting time of customers is 3 minutes with a population standard deviation of 1 minute. The quality-assurance department found in a sample of 50 customers at the Warren Road MacBurger that the mean waiting time was 2.75 minutes. At the .05 significance level, can we conclude that the mean waiting time is less than 3 minutes?

7.   A recent national survey found that high school students watched an average (mean) of 6.8 DVDs per month with a population standard deviation of 0.5 hours. A random sample

of 36 college students revealed that the mean number of DVDs watched last month was 6.2. At the .05 significance level, can we conclude that college students watch fewer DVDs a month than high school students?

8. At the time she was hired as a server at the Grumney Family Restaurant, Beth Brigden was told, "You can average more than $80 a day in tips." Assume the standard deviation of the population distribution is $3.24. Over the first 35 days she was employed at the restaurant, the mean daily amount of her tips was $84.85. At the .01 significance level, can Ms. Brigden conclude that she is earning an average of more than $80 in tips?

Testing for a Population Mean: Population Standard Deviation Unknown

In the preceding example, we knew σ, the population standard deviation. In most cases, however, the population standard deviation is unknown. Thus, σ must be based on prior studies or estimated by the sample standard deviation, s. The population standard deviation in the following example is not known, so the sample standard deviation is used to estimate σ.

To find the value of the test statistic we use the t distribution and revise formula [10–1] as follows:

TESTING A MEAN, σ UNKNOWN	$t = \dfrac{\overline{X} - \mu}{s/\sqrt{n}}$	[10–2]

with $n - 1$ degrees of freedom, where:

$\overline{X}$ is the sample mean.
μ is the hypothesized population mean.
s is the sample standard deviation.
n is the number of observations in the sample.

We encountered this same situation when constructing confidence intervals in the previous chapter. See pages 298–304 in Chapter 9. We summarized this problem in Chart 9–3 on page 301. Under these conditions the correct statistical procedure is to replace the standard normal distribution with the t distribution. To review, the major characteristics of the t distribution are:

1. It is a continuous distribution.
2. It is bell-shaped and symmetrical.
3. There is a family of t distributions. Each time the degrees of freedom change, a new distribution is created.
4. As the number of degrees of freedom increases the shape of the t distribution approaches that of the standard normal distribution.
5. The t distribution is flatter, or more spread out, than the standard normal distribution.

The following example shows the details.

Example

The McFarland Insurance Company Claims Department reports the mean cost to process a claim is $60. An industry comparison showed this amount to be larger than most other insurance companies, so the company instituted cost-cutting measures. To evaluate the effect of the cost-cutting measures, the Supervisor of the Claims Department selected a random sample of 26 claims processed last month. The sample information is reported below.

$45	$49	$62	$40	$43	$61
48	53	67	63	78	64
48	54	51	56	63	69
58	51	58	59	56	57
38	76				

At the .01 significance level is it reasonable to conclude that mean cost to process a claim is now less than $60?

Solution

We will use the five-step hypothesis testing procedure.

Step 1: State the null hypothesis and the alternate hypothesis. The null hypothesis is that the population mean is at least $60. The alternate hypothesis is that the population mean is less than $60. We can express the null and alternate hypotheses as follows:

$$H_0: \mu \geq \$60$$

$$H_1: \mu < \$60$$

The test is *one*-tailed because we want to determine whether there has been a *reduction* in the cost. The inequality in the alternate hypothesis points to the region of rejection in the left tail of the distribution.

Step 2: Select the level of significance. We decided on the .01 significance level.

Step 3: Select the test statistic. The test statistic in this situation is the *t* distribution. Why? First it is reasonable to conclude that the distribution of the cost per claim follows the normal distribution. We can confirm this from the histogram in the center of the following MINITAB output. Observe the normal distribution superimposed on the frequency distribution.

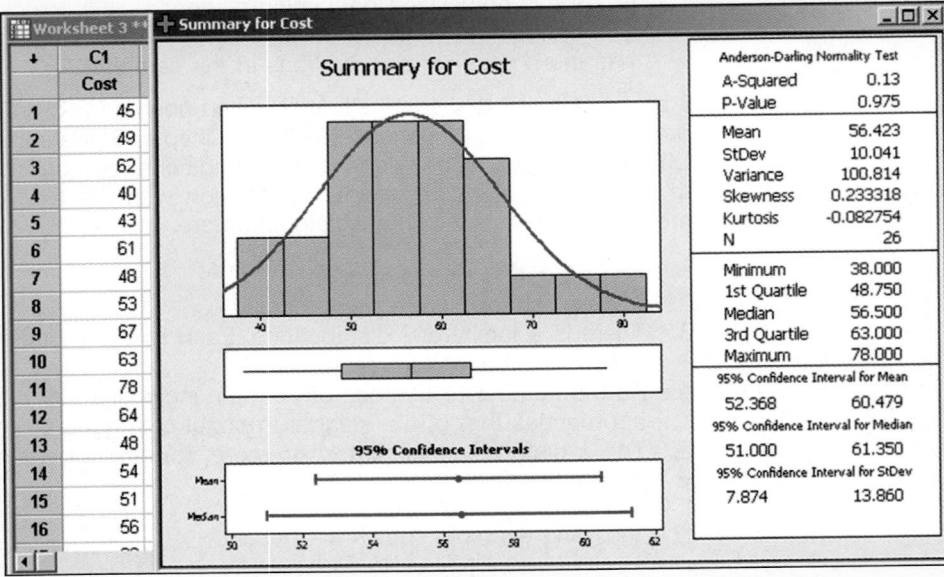

We do not know the standard deviation of the population. So we substitute the sample standard deviation. The value of the test statistic is computed by formula (10–2):

$$t = \frac{\overline{X} - \mu}{s/\sqrt{n}}$$

Step 4: Formulate the decision rule. The critical values of t are given in Appendix B.2, a portion of which is shown in Table 10–1. Appendix B.2 is also repeated in the back inside cover of the text. The far left column of the table is labeled "df" for degrees of freedom. The number of degrees of freedom is the total number of observations in the sample minus the number of populations sampled, written $n - 1$. In this case the number of observations in the sample is 26, and we sampled 1 population, so there are $26 - 1 = 25$ degrees of freedom. To find the critical value, first locate the row with the appropriate degrees of freedom. This row is shaded in Table 10–1. Next, determine whether the test is one-tailed or two-tailed. In this case, we have a one-tailed test, so find the portion of the table that is labeled "one-tailed." Locate the column with the selected significance level. In this example, the significance level is .01. Move down the column labeled "0.01" until it intersects the row with 25 degrees of freedom. The value is 2.485. Because this is a one-sided test and the rejection region is in the left tail, the critical value is negative. The decision rule is to reject H_0 if the value of t is less than -2.485.

TABLE 10–1 A Portion of the t Distribution Table

	\multicolumn{6}{c}{**Confidence Intervals**}
	80%	**90%**	**95%**	**98%**	**99%**	**99.9%**
	\multicolumn{6}{c}{**Level of Significance for One-Tailed Test, α**}
df	**0.10**	**0.05**	**0.025**	**0.01**	**0.005**	**0.0005**
	\multicolumn{6}{c}{**Level of Significance for Two-Tailed Test, α**}
	0.20	**0.10**	**0.05**	**0.02**	**0.01**	**0.001**
⋮	⋮	⋮	⋮	⋮	⋮	⋮
21	1.323	1.721	2.080	2.518	2.831	3.819
22	1.321	1.717	2.074	2.508	2.819	3.792
23	1.319	1.714	2.069	2.500	2.807	3.768
24	1.318	1.711	2.064	2.492	2.797	3.745
25	1.316	1.708	2.060	2.485	2.787	3.725
26	1.315	1.706	2.056	2.479	2.779	3.707
27	1.314	1.703	2.052	2.473	2.771	3.690
28	1.313	1.701	2.048	2.467	2.763	3.674
29	1.311	1.699	2.045	2.462	2.756	3.659
30	1.310	1.697	2.042	2.457	2.750	3.646

Step 5: Make a decision and interpret the result. From the MINITAB output, to the right of the histogram, the mean cost per claim for the sample of 26 observations is $56.42. The standard deviation of this sample is $10.04. We insert these values in formula (10–2) and compute the value of t:

$$t = \frac{\overline{X} - \mu}{s/\sqrt{n}} = \frac{\$56.42 - \$60}{\$10.04/\sqrt{26}} = -1.818$$

Because -1.818 lies in the region to the right of the critical value of -2.485, the null hypothesis is not rejected at the .01 significance level. We have not demonstrated that the cost-cutting measures reduced the mean cost per claim to less than $60. To put it another way, the difference of $3.58 ($56.42 $- $60) between the sample mean and the population mean could be due to sampling error. The computed value of t is shown in Chart 10–6. It is in the region where the null hypothesis is *not* rejected.

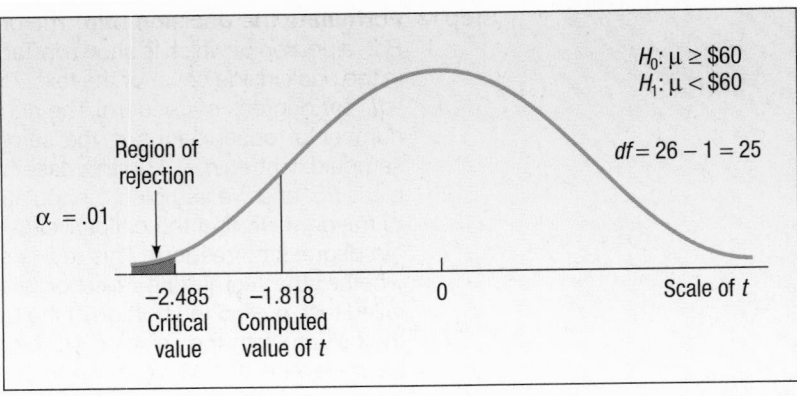

CHART 10–6 Rejection Region, t Distribution, .01 Significance Level

In the previous example the mean and the standard deviation were computed using MINITAB. The following example shows the details when the sample mean and sample standard deviation are calculated from sample data.

Example

The mean length of a small counterbalance bar is 43 millimeters. The production supervisor is concerned that the adjustments of the machine producing the bars have changed. He asks the Engineering Department to investigate. Engineering selects a random sample of 12 bars and measures each. The results are reported below in millimeters.

| 42 | 39 | 42 | 45 | 43 | 40 | 39 | 41 | 40 | 42 | 43 | 42 |

Is it reasonable to conclude that there has been a change in the mean length of the bars? Use the .02 significance level.

Solution

We begin by stating the null hypothesis and the alternate hypothesis.

$$H_0: \mu = 43$$
$$H_1: \mu \neq 43$$

The alternate hypothesis does not state a direction, so this is a two-tailed test. There are 11 degrees of freedom, found by $n - 1 = 12 - 1 = 11$. The t value is 2.718, found by referring to Appendix B.2 for a two-tailed test, using the .02 significance level, with 11 degrees of freedom. The decision rule is: Reject the null hypothesis if the computed t is to the left of -2.718 or to the right of 2.718. This information is summarized in Chart 10–7.

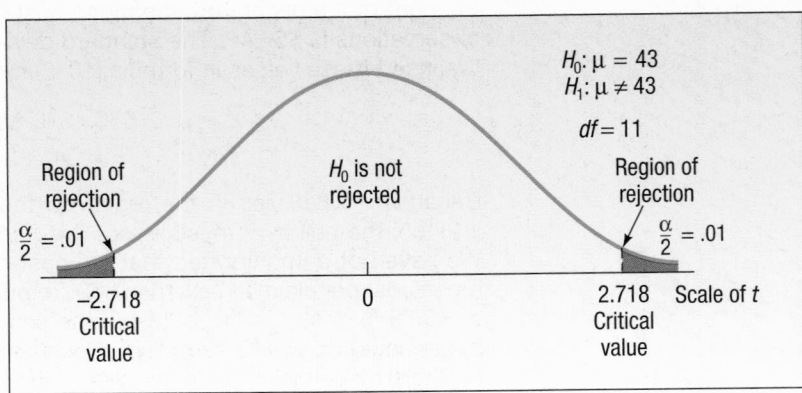

CHART 10–7 Regions of Rejection, Two-Tailed Test, Student's t Distribution, $\alpha = .02$

We calculate the standard deviation of the sample using formula (3–11). The mean, $\overline{X}$, is 41.5 millimeters, and the standard deviation, s, is 1.784 millimeters. The details are shown in Table 10–2.

TABLE 10–2 Calculations of the Sample Standard Deviation

X (mm)	X − X̄	(X − X̄)²
42	0.5	0.25
39	−2.5	6.25
42	0.5	0.25
45	3.5	12.25
43	1.5	2.25
40	−1.5	2.25
39	−2.5	6.25
41	−0.5	0.25
40	−1.5	2.25
42	0.5	0.25
43	1.5	2.25
42	0.5	0.25
498	0	35.00

$$\overline{X} = \frac{498}{12} = 41.5 \text{ mm}$$

$$s = \sqrt{\frac{\Sigma(X - \overline{X})^2}{n - 1}} = \sqrt{\frac{35}{12 - 1}} = 1.784$$

Now we are ready to compute the value of t, using formula (10–2).

$$t = \frac{\overline{X} - \mu}{s/\sqrt{n}} = \frac{41.5 - 43.0}{1.784/\sqrt{12}} = -2.913$$

The null hypothesis that the population mean is 43 millimeters is rejected because the computed t of −2.913 lies in the area to the left of −2.718. We accept the alternate hypothesis and conclude that the population mean is not 43 millimeters. The machine is out of control and needs adjustment.

Self-Review 10–3

The mean life of a battery used in a digital clock is 305 days. The lives of the batteries follow the normal distribution. The battery was recently modified to last longer. A sample of 20 of the modified batteries had a mean life of 311 days with a standard deviation of 12 days. Did the modification increase the mean life of the battery?
(a) State the null hypothesis and the alternate hypothesis.
(b) Show the decision rule graphically. Use the .05 significance level.
(c) Compute the value of t. What is your decision regarding the null hypothesis? Briefly summarize your results.

Exercises

9. Given the following hypothesis:

$$H_0: \mu \leq 10$$
$$H_1: \mu > 10$$

For a random sample of 10 observations, the sample mean was 12 and the sample standard deviation 3. Using the .05 significance level:
a. State the decision rule.
b. Compute the value of the test statistic.
c. What is your decision regarding the null hypothesis?

10. Given the following hypothesis:

$$H_0: \mu = 400$$
$$H_1: \mu \neq 400$$

For a random sample of 12 observations, the sample mean was 407 and the sample standard deviation 6. Using the .01 significance level:
a. State the decision rule.
b. Compute the value of the test statistic.
c. What is your decision regarding the null hypothesis?

11. The Rocky Mountain district sales manager of Rath Publishing, Inc., a college textbook publishing company, claims that the sales representatives make an average of 40 sales calls per week on professors. Several reps say that this estimate is too low. To investigate, a random sample of 28 sales representatives reveals that the mean number of calls made last week was 42. The standard deviation of the sample is 2.1 calls. Using the .05 significance level, can we conclude that the mean number of calls per salesperson per week is more than 40?

12. The management of White Industries is considering a new method of assembling its golf cart. The present method requires 42.3 minutes, on the average, to assemble a cart. The mean assembly time for a random sample of 24 carts, using the new method, was 40.6 minutes, and the standard deviation of the sample was 2.7 minutes. Using the .10 level of significance, can we conclude that the assembly time using the new method is faster?

13. A spark plug manufacturer claimed that its plugs have a mean life in excess of 22,100 miles. Assume the life of the spark plugs follows the normal distribution. A fleet owner purchased a large number of sets. A sample of 18 sets revealed that the mean life was 23,400 miles and the standard deviation was 1,500 miles. Is there enough evidence to substantiate the manufacturer's claim at the .05 significance level?

14. Most air travelers now use e-tickets. Electronic ticketing allows passengers to not worry about a paper ticket, and it costs the airline companies less to handle than paper ticketing. However, in recent times the airlines have received complaints from passengers regarding their e-tickets, particularly when connecting flights and a change of airlines were involved. To investigate the problem an independent watchdog agency contacted a random sample of 20 airports and collected information on the number of complaints the airport had with e-tickets for the month of March. The information is reported below.

| 14 | 14 | 16 | 12 | 12 | 14 | 13 | 16 | 15 | 14 |
| 12 | 15 | 15 | 14 | 13 | 13 | 12 | 13 | 10 | 13 |

At the .05 significance level can the watchdog agency conclude the mean number of complaints per airport is less than 15 per month?

a. What assumption is necessary before conducting a test of hypothesis?

b. Plot the number of complaints per airport in a frequency distribution or a dot plot. Is it reasonable to conclude that the population follows a normal distribution?

c. Conduct a test of hypothesis and interpret the results.

A Software Solution

The MINITAB statistical software system, used in earlier chapters and the previous section, provides an efficient way of conducting a one-sample test of hypothesis for a population mean. The steps to generate the following output are shown in the **Software Commands** section at the end of the chapter.

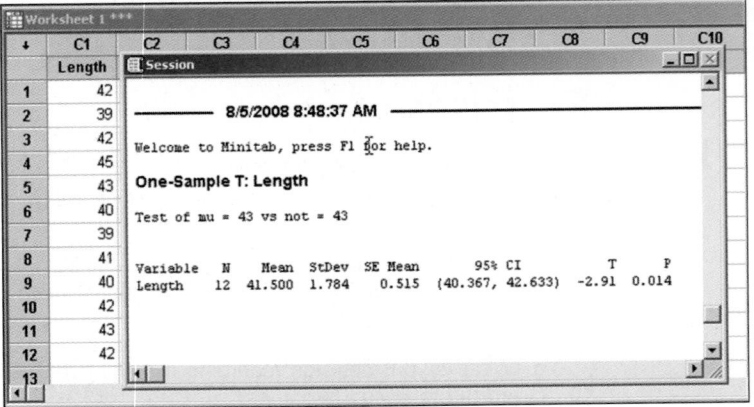

An additional feature of most statistical software packages is to report the *p*-value, which gives additional information on the null hypothesis. The *p*-value is the probability of a *t* value as extreme as that computed, given that the null hypothesis is true. Using the data from the previous counterbalance bar example, the *p*-value of .014 is the likelihood of a *t* value of −2.91 or less plus the likelihood of a *t* value of 2.91 or larger, given a population mean of 43. Thus, comparing the p-value to the significance level tells us whether the null hypothesis was close to being rejected, barely rejected, and so on.

To explain further, refer to the diagram below. The p-value of .014 is the darker or shaded area and the significance level is the total shaded area. Because the p-value of .014 is less than the significance level of .02, the null hypothesis is rejected. Had the p-value been larger than the significance level—say, .06, .19, or .57—the null hypothesis would not be rejected. If the significance level had initially been selected as .01, the null hypothesis would not be rejected.

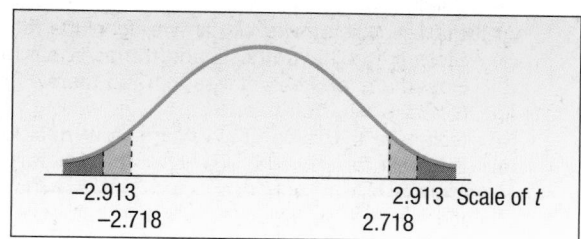

In the preceding example the alternate hypothesis was two-sided, so there were rejection areas in both the lower (left) tail and the upper (right) tail. To determine the p-value, it was necessary to determine the area to the left of -2.913 for a t distribution with 11 degrees of freedom and add to it the value of the area to the right of 2.913, also with 11 degrees of freedom.

What if we were conducting a one-sided test, so that the entire rejection region would be in either the upper or the lower tail? In that case, we would report the area from only the one tail. In the counterbalance example, if H_1 were stated as $\mu < 43$, the inequality would point to the left. Thus, we would have reported the p-value as the area to the left of -2.913. This value is .007, found by .014/2. Thus, the p-value for a one-tailed test would be .007.

How can we estimate a p-value without a computer? To illustrate, recall that, in the example regarding the length of a counterbalance, we rejected the null hypothesis that $\mu = 43$ and accepted the alternate hypothesis that $\mu \neq 43$. The significance level was .02, so logically the p-value is less than .02. To estimate the p-value more accurately, go to Appendix B.2 and find the row with 11 degrees of freedom. The computed t value of 2.913 is between 2.718 and 3.106. (A portion of Appendix B.2 is reproduced as Table 10–3.) The two-tailed significance level corresponding to 2.718

TABLE 10–3 A Portion of Student's t Distribution

	Confidence Intervals					
	80%	**90%**	**95%**	**98%**	**99%**	**99.9%**
	Level of Significance for One-Tailed Test, α					
df	**0.10**	**0.05**	**.0025**	**0.01**	**0.005**	**0.0005**
	Level of Significance for Two-Tailed Test, α					
	0.20	**0.10**	**0.05**	**0.02**	**0.01**	**0.001**
⋮	⋮	⋮	⋮	⋮	⋮	⋮
9	1.383	1.833	2.262	2.821	3.250	4.781
10	1.372	1.812	2.228	2.764	3.169	4.587
11	1.363	1.796	2.201	2.718	3.106	4.437
12	1.356	1.782	2.179	2.681	3.055	4.318
13	1.350	1.771	2.160	2.650	3.012	4.221
14	1.345	1.761	2.145	2.624	2.977	4.140
15	1.341	1.753	2.131	2.602	2.947	4.073

is .02, and for 3.106 it is .01. Therefore, the *p*-value is between .01 and .02. The usual practice is to report that the *p*-value is *less* than the larger of the two significance levels. So we would report, "the *p*-value is less than .02."

Self-Review 10–4

A machine is set to fill a small bottle with 9.0 grams of medicine. A sample of eight bottles revealed the following amounts (grams) in each bottle.

9.2	8.7	8.9	8.6	8.8	8.5	8.7	9.0

At the .01 significance level, can we conclude that the mean weight is less than 9.0 grams?
(a) State the null hypothesis and the alternate hypothesis.
(b) How many degrees of freedom are there?
(c) Give the decision rule.
(d) Compute the value of *t*. What is your decision regarding the null hypothesis?
(e) Estimate the *p*-value.

Exercises

connect

15. Given the following hypothesis:

$$H_0: \mu \geq 20$$
$$H_1: \mu < 20$$

A random sample of five resulted in the following values: 18, 15, 12, 19, and 21. Using the .01 significance level, can we conclude the population mean is less than 20?
a. State the decision rule.
b. Compute the value of the test statistic.
c. What is your decision regarding the null hypothesis?
d. Estimate the *p*-value.

16. Given the following hypothesis:

$$H_0: \mu = 100$$
$$H_1: \mu \neq 100$$

A random sample of six resulted in the following values: 118, 105, 112, 119, 105, and 111. Using the .05 significance level, can we conclude the mean is different from 100?
a. State the decision rule.
b. Compute the value of the test statistic.
c. What is your decision regarding the null hypothesis?
d. Estimate the *p*-value.

17. Experience raising New Jersey Red chickens revealed the mean weight of the chickens at five months is 4.35 pounds. The weights follow the normal distribution. In an effort to increase their weight, a special additive is added to the chicken feed. The subsequent weights of a sample of five-month-old chickens were (in pounds):

4.41	4.37	4.33	4.35	4.30	4.39	4.36	4.38	4.40	4.39

At the .01 level, has the special additive increased the mean weight of the chickens? Estimate the *p*-value.

18. The liquid chlorine added to swimming pools to combat algae has a relatively short shelf life before it loses its effectiveness. Records indicate that the mean shelf life of a 5-gallon jug of chlorine is 2,160 hours (90 days). As an experiment, Holdlonger was added to the chlorine to find whether it would increase the shelf life. A sample of nine jugs of chlorine had these shelf lives (in hours):

2,159	2,170	2,180	2,179	2,160	2,167	2,171	2,181	2,185

At the .025 level, has Holdlonger increased the shelf life of the chlorine? Estimate the *p*-value.

19. Wyoming fisheries contend that the mean number of cutthroat trout caught during a full day of fly-fishing on the Snake, Buffalo, and other rivers and streams in the Jackson Hole area is 4.0. To make their yearly update, the fishery personnel asked a sample of fly fishermen to keep a count of the number caught during the day. The numbers were: 4, 4, 3, 2, 6, 8, 7, 1, 9, 3, 1, and 6. At the .05 level, can we conclude that the mean number caught is greater than 4.0? Estimate the p-value.

20. Hugger Polls contends that an agent conducts a mean of 53 in-depth home surveys every week. A streamlined survey form has been introduced, and Hugger wants to evaluate its effectiveness. The number of in-depth surveys conducted during a week by a random sample of agents are:

53	57	50	55	58	54	60	52	59	62	60	60	51	59	56

At the .05 level of significance, can we conclude that the mean number of interviews conducted by the agents is more than 53 per week? Estimate the p-value.

Tests Concerning Proportions

In the previous chapter we discussed confidence intervals for proportions. We can also conduct a test of hypothesis for a proportion. Recall that a proportion is the ratio of the number of successes to the number of observations. We let X refer to the number of successes and n the number of observations, so the proportion of successes in a fixed number of trials is X/n. Thus, the formula for computing a sample proportion, p, is $p = X/n$. Consider the following potential hypothesis-testing situations.

- Historically, General Motors reports that 70 percent of leased vehicles are returned with less than 36,000 miles. A recent sample of 200 vehicles returned at the end of their lease showed 158 had less than 36,000 miles. Has the proportion increased?
- The American Association of Retired Persons (AARP) reports that 60 percent of retired people under the age of 65 would return to work on a full-time basis if a suitable job were available. A sample of 500 retirees under 65 revealed 315 would return to work. Can we conclude that more than 60 percent would return to work?
- Able Moving and Storage, Inc., advises its clients for long-distance residential moves that their household goods will be delivered in 3 to 5 days from the time they are picked up. Able's records show it is successful 90 percent of the time with this claim. A recent audit revealed it was successful 190 times out of 200. Can the company conclude its success rate has increased?

Some assumptions must be made and conditions met before testing a population proportion. To test a hypothesis about a population proportion, a random sample is chosen from the population. It is assumed that the binomial assumptions discussed in Chapter 6 are met: (1) the sample data collected are the result of counts; (2) the outcome of an experiment is classified into one of two mutually exclusive categories—a "success" or a "failure"; (3) the probability of a success is the same for each trial; and (4) the trials are independent, meaning the outcome of one trial does not affect the outcome of any other trial. The test we will conduct shortly is appropriate when both $n\pi$ and $n(1 - \pi)$ are at least 5. n is the sample size, and p is the population proportion. It takes advantage of the fact that a binomial distribution can be approximated by the normal distribution.

$n\pi$ and $n(1 - \pi)$ must be at least 5.

Example

Suppose prior elections in a certain state indicated it is necessary for a candidate for governor to receive at least 80 percent of the vote in the northern section of the state to be elected. The incumbent governor is interested in assessing his chances of returning to office and plans to conduct a survey of 2,000 registered voters in the northern section of the state.

Using the hypothesis-testing procedure, assess the governor's chances of reelection.

Solution

This situation regarding the governor's reelection meets the binomial conditions.

- There are only two possible outcomes. That is, a sampled voter will either vote or not vote for the governor.
- The probability of a success is the same for each trial. In this case the likelihood a particular sampled voter will support reelection is .80.
- The trials are independent. This means, for example, the likelihood the 23rd voter sampled will support reelection is not affected by what the 24th or 52nd voter does.
- The sample data is the result of counts. We are going to count the number of voters who support reelection in the sample of 2,000.

We can use the normal approximation to the binomial distribution, discussed in Chapter 7, because both $n\pi$ and $n(1 - \pi)$ exceed 5. In this case, $n = 2,000$ and $\pi = .80$ (π is the proportion of the vote in the northern part of the state, or 80 percent, needed to be elected). Thus, $n\pi = 2,000(.80) = 1,600$ and $n(1 - \pi) = 2,000(1 - .80) = 400$. Both 1,600 and 400 are greater than 5.

Step 1: State the null hypothesis and the alternate hypothesis. The null hypothesis, H_0, is that the population proportion π is .80 or larger. The alternate hypothesis, H_1, is that the proportion is less than .80. From a practical standpoint, the incumbent governor is concerned only when the proportion is less than .80. If it is equal to or greater than .80, he will have no problem; that is, the sample data would indicate he will probably be reelected. These hypotheses are written symbolically as:

$$H_0\text{: } \pi \geq .80$$
$$H_1\text{: } \pi < .80$$

H_1 states a direction. Thus, as noted previously, the test is one-tailed with the inequality sign pointing to the tail of the distribution containing the region of rejection.

Step 2: Select the level of significance. The level of significance is .05. This is the likelihood that a true hypothesis will be rejected.

Step 3: Select the test statistic. z is the appropriate statistic, found by:

TEST OF HYPOTHESIS, ONE PROPORTION

$$z = \frac{p - \pi}{\sqrt{\dfrac{\pi(1 - \pi)}{n}}}$$

[10–3]

where:
π is the population proportion.
p is the sample proportion.
n is the sample size.

Finding the critical value

Step 4: Formulate the decision rule. The critical value or values of z form the dividing point or points between the regions where H_0 is rejected and where it is not rejected. Since the alternate hypothesis states a direction, this is a one-tailed test. The sign of the inequality points to the left, so only the left side of the curve is used. (See Chart 10–8.) The significance level was given as .05 in step 2. This probability is in the left tail and determines the region of rejection. The area between zero and the critical value is .4500, found by .5000 − .0500. Referring to Appendix B.1 and searching for .4500, we find the critical value of z is 1.65. The decision rule is, therefore: Reject the null hypothesis and accept the alternate hypothesis if the computed value of z falls to the left of −1.65; otherwise do not reject H_0.

Select a sample and make a decision regarding H_0.

Step 5: Make a decision and interpret the result. Select a sample and make a decision about H_0. A sample survey of 2,000 potential voters in the northern part of the state revealed that 1,550 planned to vote for the incumbent governor. Is the sample proportion of .775 (found by 1,550/2,000)

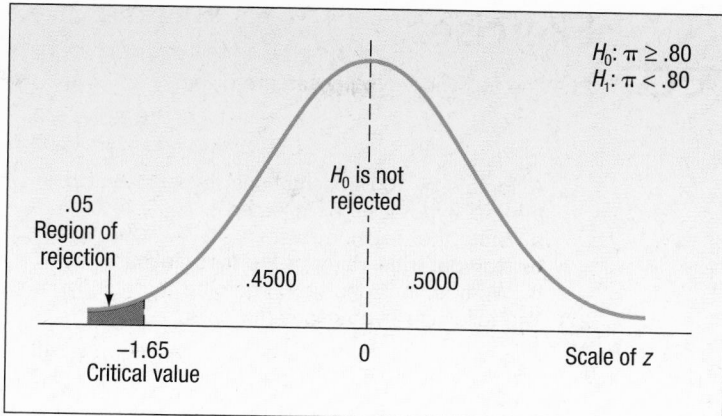

CHART 10–8 Rejection Region for the .05 Level of Significance, One-Tailed Test

close enough to .80 to conclude that the difference is due to sampling error? In this case:

p is .775, the proportion in the sample who plan to vote for the governor.

n is 2,000, the number of voters surveyed.

π is .80, the hypothesized population proportion.

z is a normally distributed test statistic when the hypothesis is true and the other assumptions are true.

Using formula (10–3) and computing z gives

$$z = \frac{p - \pi}{\sqrt{\dfrac{\pi(1 - \pi)}{n}}} = \frac{\dfrac{1,550}{2,000} - .80}{\sqrt{\dfrac{.80(1 - .80)}{2,000}}} = \frac{.775 - .80}{\sqrt{.00008}} = -2.80$$

The computed value of z (−2.80) is in the rejection region, so the null hypothesis is rejected at the .05 level. The difference of 2.5 percentage points between the sample percent (77.5 percent) and the hypothesized population percent in the northern part of the state necessary to carry the state (80 percent) is statistically significant. It is probably not due to sampling variation. To put it another way, the evidence at this point does not support the claim that the incumbent governor will return to the governor's mansion for another four years.

The p-value is the probability of finding a z value less than −2.80. From Appendix B.1, the probability of a z value between zero and −2.80 is .4974. So the p-value is .0026, found by .5000 − .4974. The governor cannot be confident of reelection because the p-value is less than the significance level.

Self-Review 10–5

A recent insurance industry report indicated that 40 percent of those persons involved in minor traffic accidents this year have been involved in a least one other traffic accident in the last five years. An advisory group decided to investigate this claim, believing it was too large. A sample of 200 traffic accidents this year showed 74 persons were also involved in another accident within the last five years. Use the .01 significance level.

(a) Can we use z as the test statistic? Tell why or why not.
(b) State the null hypothesis and the alternate hypothesis.
(c) Show the decision rule graphically.
(d) Compute the value of z and state your decision regarding the null hypothesis.
(e) Determine and interpret the p-value.

Exercises

21. The following hypotheses are given.

$$H_0: \pi \le .70$$
$$H_1: \pi > .70$$

A sample of 100 observations revealed that $p = .75$. At the .05 significance level, can the null hypothesis be rejected?
a. State the decision rule.
b. Compute the value of the test statistic.
c. What is your decision regarding the null hypothesis?

22. The following hypotheses are given.

$$H_0: \pi = .40$$
$$H_1: \pi \ne .40$$

A sample of 120 observations revealed that $p = .30$. At the .05 significance level, can the null hypothesis be rejected?
a. State the decision rule.
b. Compute the value of the test statistic.
c. What is your decision regarding the null hypothesis?

Note: It is recommended that you use the five-step hypothesis-testing procedure in solving the following problems.

23. The National Safety Council reported that 52 percent of American turnpike drivers are men. A sample of 300 cars traveling southbound on the New Jersey Turnpike yesterday revealed that 170 were driven by men. At the .01 significance level, can we conclude that a larger proportion of men were driving on the New Jersey Turnpike than the national statistics indicate?

24. A recent article in *USA Today* reported that a job awaits only one in three new college graduates. The major reasons given were an overabundance of college graduates and a weak economy. A survey of 200 recent graduates from your school revealed that 80 students had jobs. At the .02 significance level, can we conclude that a larger proportion of students at your school have jobs?

25. Chicken Delight claims that 90 percent of its orders are delivered within 10 minutes of the time the order is placed. A sample of 100 orders revealed that 82 were delivered within the promised time. At the .10 significance level, can we conclude that less than 90 percent of the orders are delivered in less than 10 minutes?

26. Research at the University of Toledo indicates that 50 percent of students change their major area of study after their first year in a program. A random sample of 100 students in the College of Business revealed that 48 had changed their major area of study after their first year of the program. Has there been a significant decrease in the proportion of students who change their major after the first year in this program? Test at the .05 level of significance.

Type II Error

Recall that the level of significance, identified by the symbol α, is the probability that the null hypothesis is rejected when it is true. This is called a Type I error. The most common levels of significance are .05 and .01 and are set by the researcher at the outset of the test.

In a hypothesis-testing situation there is also the possibility that a null hypothesis is not rejected when it is actually false. That is, we accept a false null hypothesis. This is called a Type II error. The probability of a Type II error is identified by the Greek letter beta (β). The following examples illustrate the details of determining the value of β.

Example

A manufacturer purchases steel bars to make cotter pins. Past experience indicates that the mean tensile strength of all incoming shipments is 10,000 psi and that the standard deviation, σ, is 400 psi.

In order to make a decision about incoming shipments of steel bars, the manufacturer set up this rule for the quality-control inspector to follow: "Take a sample of 100 steel bars. At the .05 significance level if the sample mean $(\overline{X})$ strength falls between 9,922 psi and 10,078 psi, accept the lot. Otherwise the lot is to be rejected." Refer to Chart 10–9, Region A. It shows the region where each lot is rejected and where it is not rejected. The mean of this distribution is designated μ_0. The tails of the curve represent the probability of making a Type I error, that is, rejecting the incoming lot of steel bars when in fact it is a good lot, with a mean of 10,000 psi.

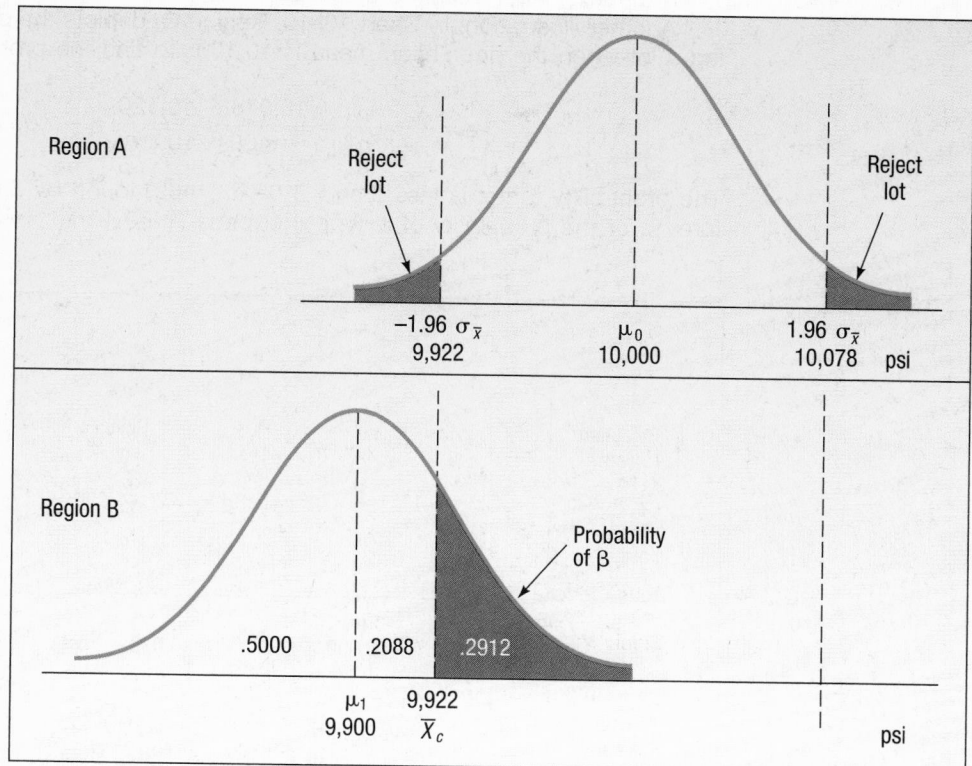

CHART 10–9 Charts Showing Type I and Type II Errors

Suppose the unknown population mean of an incoming lot, designated μ_1, is really 9,900 psi. What is the probability that the quality-control inspector will fail to reject the shipment (a Type II error)?

Solution

The probability of committing a Type II error, as represented by the shaded area in Chart 10–9, Region B, can be computed by determining the area under the normal curve that lies above 9,922 pounds. The calculation of the areas under the normal curve was discussed in Chapter 7. Reviewing briefly, it is necessary first to determine the probability of the sample mean falling between 9,900 and 9,922. Then this probability is subtracted from .5000 (which represents all the area beyond the mean of 9,900) to arrive at the probability of making a Type II error in this case.

The number of standard units (z value) between the mean of the incoming lot (9,900), designated by μ_1, and $\overline{X}_c$, representing the critical value for 9,922, is computed by:

TYPE II ERROR $\qquad\qquad z = \dfrac{\overline{X}_c - \mu_1}{\sigma/\sqrt{n}}$ $\qquad\qquad$ **[10–4]**

With $n = 100$ and $\sigma = 400$, the value of z is 0.55:

$$z = \frac{\overline{X}_c - \mu_1}{\sigma/\sqrt{n}} = \frac{9{,}922 - 9{,}900}{400/\sqrt{100}} = \frac{22}{40} = 0.55$$

The area under the curve between 9,900 and 9,922 (a z value of 0.55) is .2088. The area under the curve beyond 9,922 pounds is .5000 − .2088, or .2912; this is the probability of making a Type II error—that is, accepting an incoming lot of steel bars when the population mean is 9,900 psi.

Another illustration, in Chart 10–10, Region C, depicts the probability of accepting a lot when the population mean is 10,120. To find the probability:

$$z = \frac{\overline{X}_c - \mu_1}{\sigma/\sqrt{n}} = \frac{10{,}078 - 10{,}120}{400/\sqrt{100}} = -1.05$$

The probability that z is less than −1.05 is .1469, found by .5000 − .3531. Therefore, β, or the probability of a Type II error, is .1469.

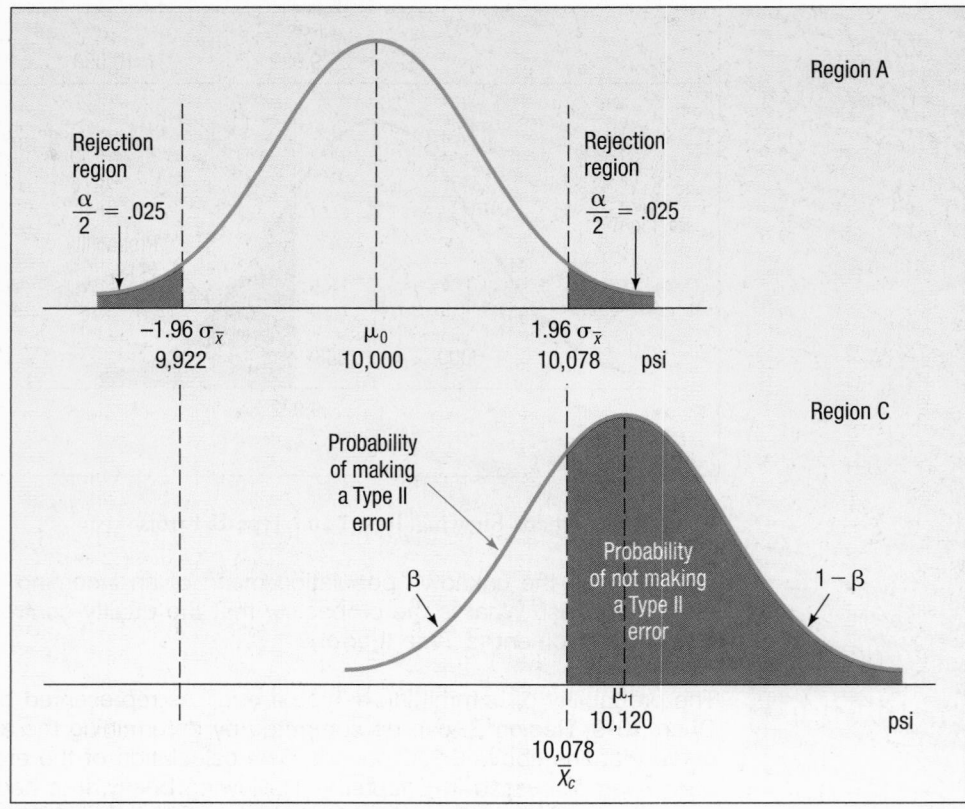

CHART 10–10 Type I and Type II Errors (Another Example)

Using the methods illustrated by Charts 10–9 Region B and 10-10 Region C, the probability of accepting a hypothesis as true when it is actually false can be determined for any value of μ_1.

Type II error probabilities are shown in the center column of Table 10–4 for selected values of μ, given in the left column. The right column gives the probability of not making a Type II error, which is also known as the power of a test.

TABLE 10–4 Probabilities of a Type II Error for $\mu_0 = 10,000$ Pounds and Selected Alternative Means, .05 Level of Significance

Selected Alternative Mean (pounds)	Probability of Type II Error (β)	Probability of Not Making a Type II Error ($1 - \beta$)
9,820	.0054	.9946
9,880	.1469	.8531
9,900	.2912	.7088
9,940	.6736	.3264
9,980	.9265	.0735
10,000	— *	—
10,020	.9265	.0735
10,060	.6736	.3264
10,100	.2912	.7088
10,120	.1469	.8531
10,180	.0054	.9946

*It is not possible to make a Type II error when $\mu = \mu_0$.

Self-Review 10–6

Refer to the previous Example. Suppose the true mean of an incoming lot of steel bars is 10,180 psi. What is the probability that the quality control inspector will accept the bars as having a mean of 10,000 psi? (It sounds implausible that steel bars will be rejected if the tensile strength is higher than specified. However, it may be that the cotter pin has a dual function in an outboard motor. It may be designed not to shear off if the motor hits a small object, but to shear off if it hits a rock. Therefore, the steel should not be *too* strong.)

The light area in Chart 10–10, Region C, represents the probability of falsely accepting the hypothesis that the mean tensile strength of the incoming steel is 10,000 psi. What is the probability of committing a Type II error?

Exercises

27. Refer to Table 10–4 and the example just completed. With $n = 100$, $\sigma = 400$, $\overline{X}_c = 9,922$, and $\mu_1 = 9,880$, verify that the probability of a Type II error is .1469.
28. Refer to Table 10–4 and the example just completed. With $n = 100$, $\sigma = 400$, $\overline{X}_c = 9,922$, and $\mu_1 = 9,940$, verify that the probability of a Type II error is .6736.

Chapter Summary

I. The objective of hypothesis testing is to check the validity of a statement about a population parameter.
II. The steps in conducting a test of hypothesis are:
   A. State the null hypothesis (H_0) and the alternate hypothesis (H_1).
   B. Select the level of significance.
      1. The level of significance is the likelihood of rejecting a true null hypothesis.
      2. The most frequently used significance levels are .01, .05, and .10, but any value between 0 and 1.00 is possible.
   C. Select the test statistic.
      1. A test statistic is a value calculated from sample information used to determine whether to reject the null hypothesis.
      2. Two test statistics were considered in this chapter.
         a. The standard normal distribution (the z distribution) is used when the population follows the normal distribution and the population standard deviation is known.

b. The t distribution is used when the population follows the normal distribution and the population standard deviation is unknown.

D. State the decision rule.

   1. The decision rule indicates the condition or conditions when the null hypothesis is rejected.

   2. In a two-tailed test, the rejection region is evenly split between the upper and lower tails.

   3. In a one-tailed test, all of the rejection region is in either the upper or the lower tail.

E. Select a sample, compute the value of the test statistic, make a decision regarding the null hypothesis, and interpret the results.

III. A p-value is the probability that the value of the test statistic is as extreme as the value computed, when the null hypothesis is true.

IV. When testing a hypothesis about a population mean:

A. If the population standard deviation, σ, is known, the test statistic is the standard normal distribution and is determined from:

$$z = \frac{\bar{X} - \mu}{\sigma/\sqrt{n}} \qquad \text{[10–1]}$$

B. If the population standard deviation is not known, s is substituted for σ. The test statistic is the t distribution, and its value is determined from:

$$t = \frac{\bar{X} - \mu}{s/\sqrt{n}} \qquad \text{[10–2]}$$

The major characteristics of the t distribution are:

   1. It is a continuous distribution.

   2. It is mound-shaped and symmetrical.

   3. It is flatter, or more spread out, than the standard normal distribution.

   4. There is a family of t distributions, depending on the number of degrees of freedom.

V. When testing about a population proportion:

A. The binomial conditions must be met.

B. Both $n\pi$ and $n(1 - \pi)$ must be at least 5.

C. The test statistic is

$$z = \frac{p - \pi}{\sqrt{\dfrac{\pi(1 - \pi)}{n}}} \qquad \text{[10–3]}$$

VI. There are two types of errors that can occur in a test of hypothesis.

A. A Type I error occurs when a true null hypothesis is rejected.

   1. The probability of making a Type I error is equal to the level of significance.

   2. This probability is designated by the Greek letter α.

B. A Type II error occurs when a false null hypothesis is not rejected.

   1. The probability of making a Type II error is designated by the Greek letter β.

   2. The likelihood of a Type II error is found by

$$z = \frac{\bar{X}_c - \mu_1}{\sigma/\sqrt{n}} \qquad \text{[10–4]}$$

Pronunciation Key

SYMBOL	MEANING	PRONUNCIATION
H_0	Null hypothesis	H sub zero
H_1	Alternate hypothesis	H sub one
$\alpha/2$	Two-tailed significance level	Alpha over 2
$\bar{X}_c$	Limit of the sample mean	X bar sub c
μ_0	Assumed population mean	mu sub zero

Chapter Exercises

connect

29. According to the local union president, the mean gross income of plumbers in the Salt Lake City area follows the normal probability distribution with a mean of $45,000 and a standard deviation of $3,000. A recent investigative reporter for KYAK TV found, for a sample of 120 plumbers, the mean gross income was $45,500. At the .10 significance level, is it reasonable to conclude that the mean income is not equal to $45,000? Determine the *p*-value.

30. Rutter Nursery Company packages its pine bark mulch in 50-pound bags. From a long history, the production department reports that the distribution of the bag weights follows the normal distribution and the standard deviation of this process is 3 pounds per bag. At the end of each day, Jeff Rutter, the production manager, weighs 10 bags and computes the mean weight of the sample. Below are the weights of 10 bags from today's production.

45.6	47.7	47.6	46.3	46.2	47.4	49.2	55.8	47.5	48.5

   a. Can Mr. Rutter conclude that the mean weight of the bags is less than 50 pounds? Use the .01 significance level.
   b. In a brief report, tell why Mr. Rutter can use the *z* distribution as the test statistic.
   c. Compute the *p*-value.

31. A new weight-watching company, Weight Reducers International, advertises that those who join will lose, on the average, 10 pounds the first two weeks with a standard deviation of 2.8 pounds. A random sample of 50 people who joined the new weight reduction program revealed the mean loss to be 9 pounds. At the .05 level of significance, can we conclude that those joining Weight Reducers on average will lose less than 10 pounds? Determine the *p*-value.

32. Dole Pineapple, Inc., is concerned that the 16-ounce can of sliced pineapple is being overfilled. Assume the standard deviation of the process is .03 ounces. The quality-control department took a random sample of 50 cans and found that the arithmetic mean weight was 16.05 ounces. At the 5 percent level of significance, can we conclude that the mean weight is greater than 16 ounces? Determine the *p*-value.

33. According to a recent survey, Americans get a mean of 7 hours of sleep per night. A random sample of 50 students at West Virginia University revealed the mean number of hours slept last night was 6 hours and 48 minutes (6.8 hours). The standard deviation of the sample was 0.9 hours. Is it reasonable to conclude that students at West Virginia sleep less than the typical American? Compute the *p*-value.

34. A statewide real estate sales agency, Farm Associates, specializes in selling farm property in the state of Nebraska. Its records indicate that the mean selling time of farm property is 90 days. Because of recent drought conditions, the agency believes that the mean selling time is now greater than 90 days. A statewide survey of 100 farms sold recently revealed that the mean selling time was 94 days, with a standard deviation of 22 days. At the .10 significance level, has there been an increase in selling time?

35. A cable news network, in a segment on the price of gasoline, reported that the mean price nationwide is $3.75 per gallon for self-serve regular unleaded. A random sample of 35 stations in the Milwaukee, Wisconsin, area revealed that the mean price was $3.77 per gallon and that the standard deviation was $0.05 per gallon. At the .05 significance level, can we conclude that the price of gasoline is higher in the Milwaukee area? Determine the *p*-value.

36. A recent article in *Vitality* magazine reported that the mean amount of leisure time per week for American men is 40.0 hours. You believe this figure is too large and decide to conduct your own test. In a random sample of 60 men, you find that the mean is 37.8 hours of leisure per week and that the standard deviation of the sample is 12.2 hours. Can you conclude that the information in the article is untrue? Use the .05 significance level. Determine the *p*-value and explain its meaning.

37. In recent years the interest rate on home mortgages has declined to less than 6.0 percent. However, according to a study by the Federal Reserve Board the rate charged on credit card debt is more than 14 percent. Listed below is the interest rate charged on a sample of 10 credit cards.

14.6	16.7	17.4	17.0	17.8	15.4	13.1	15.8	14.3	14.5

Is it reasonable to conclude the mean rate charged is greater than 14 percent? Use the .01 significance level.

38. A recent article in *The Wall Street Journal* reported that the 30-year mortgage rate is now less than 6 percent. A sample of eight small banks in the Midwest revealed the following 30-year rates (in percent):

4.8	5.3	6.5	4.8	6.1	5.8	6.2	5.6

At the .01 significance level, can we conclude that the 30-year mortgage rate for small banks is less than 6 percent? Estimate the *p*-value.

39. According to the Coffee Research Organization (http://www.coffeeresearch.org) the typical American coffee drinker consumes an average of 3.1 cups per day. A sample of 12 senior citizens revealed they consumed the following amounts of coffee, reported in cups, yesterday.

3.1	3.3	3.5	2.6	2.6	4.3	4.4	3.8	3.1	4.1	3.1	3.2

At the .05 significance level does this sample data suggest there is a difference between the national average and the sample mean from senior citizens?

40. The postanesthesia care area (recovery room) at St. Luke's Hospital in Maumee, Ohio, was recently enlarged. The hope was that with the enlargement the mean number of patients per day would be more than 25. A random sample of 15 days revealed the following numbers of patients.

25	27	25	26	25	28	28	27	24	26	25	29	25	27	24

At the .01 significance level, can we conclude that the mean number of patients per day is more than 25? Estimate the *p*-value and interpret it.

41. www.golfsmith.com receives an average of 6.5 returns per day from online shoppers. For a sample of 12 days, it received the following number of returns.

0	4	3	4	9	4	5	9	1	6	7	10

At the .01 significance level, can we conclude the mean number of returns is less than 6.5?

42. During recent seasons, Major League Baseball has been criticized for the length of the games. A report indicated that the average game lasts 3 hours and 30 minutes. A sample of 17 games revealed the following times to completion. (Note that the minutes have been changed to fractions of hours, so that a game that lasted 2 hours and 24 minutes is reported at 2.40 hours.)

2.98	2.40	2.70	2.25	3.23	3.17	2.93	3.18	2.80
2.38	3.75	3.20	3.27	2.52	2.58	4.45	2.45	

Can we conclude that the mean time for a game is less than 3.50 hours? Use the .05 significance level.

43. Watch Corporation of Switzerland claims that its watches on average will neither gain nor lose time during a week. A sample of 18 watches provided the following gains (+) or losses (−) in seconds per week.

−0.38	−0.20	−0.38	−0.32	+0.32	−0.23	+0.30	+0.25	−0.10
−0.37	−0.61	−0.48	−0.47	−0.64	−0.04	−0.20	−0.68	+0.05

Is it reasonable to conclude that the mean gain or loss in time for the watches is 0? Use the .05 significance level. Estimate the *p*-value.

44. Listed below is the rate of return for one year (reported in percent) for a sample of 12 mutual funds that are classified as taxable money market funds.

4.63	4.15	4.76	4.70	4.65	4.52	4.70	5.06	4.42	4.51	4.24	4.52

Using the .05 significance level is it reasonable to conclude that the mean rate of return is more than 4.50 percent?

45. Many grocery stores and large retailers such as Wal-Mart and Kmart have installed self-checkout systems so shoppers can scan their own items and cash out themselves. How do customers like this service and how often do they use it? Listed below is the number of customers using the service for a sample of 15 days at the Wal-Mart on Highway 544 in Surfside, South Carolina.

120	108	120	114	118	91	118	92	104	104
112	97	118	108	117					

Is it reasonable to conclude that the mean number of customers using the self-checkout system is more than 100 per day? Use the .05 significance level.

46. For a recent year the mean fare to fly from Charlotte, North Carolina, to Seattle, Washington, on a discount ticket was $267. A random sample of round-trip discount fares on this route last month gives:

$321	$286	$290	$330	$310	$250	$270	$280	$299	$265	$291	$275	$281

At the .01 significance level can we conclude that the mean fare has increased? What is the *p*-value?

47. The publisher of *Celebrity Living* claims that the mean sales for personality magazines that feature people such as Angelina Jolie or Paris Hilton are 1.5 million copies per week. A sample of 10 comparable titles shows a mean weekly sales last week of 1.3 million copies with a standard deviation of 0.9 million copies. Does this data contradict the publisher's claim? Use the 0.01 significance level.

48. A United Nations report shows the mean family income for Mexican migrants to the United States is $27,000 per year. A FLOC (Farm Labor Organizing Committee) evaluation of 25 Mexican family units reveals a mean to be $30,000 with a sample standard deviation of $10,000. Does this information disagree with the United Nations report? Apply the 0.01 significance level.

49. Traditionally, two percent of the citizens of the United States live in a foreign country because they are disenchanted with U.S. politics or social attitudes. In order to test if this proportion has increased since the September 11, 2001, terror attacks, U.S. consulates contacted a random sample of 400 of these expatriates. The sample yields 12 people who report they are living overseas because of political or social attitudes. Can you conclude this data shows the proportion of politically motivated expatriates has increased? Use the 0.05 significance level.

50. According to a study by the American Pet Food Dealers Association, 63 percent of U.S. households own pets. A report is being prepared for an editorial in the *San Francisco Chronicle.* As a part of the editorial a random sample of 300 households showed 210 own pets. Does this data disagree with the Pet Food Dealers Association data? Use a .05 level of significance.

51. Tina Dennis is the comptroller for Meek Industries. She believes that the current cash-flow problem at Meek is due to the slow collection of accounts receivable. She believes that more than 60 percent of the accounts are in arrears more than three months. A random sample of 200 accounts showed that 140 were more than three months old. At the .01 significance level, can she conclude that more than 60 percent of the accounts are in arrears for more than three months?

52. The policy of the Suburban Transit Authority is to add a bus route if more than 55 percent of the potential commuters indicate they would use the particular route. A sample of 70 commuters revealed that 42 would use a proposed route from Bowman Park to the downtown area. Does the Bowman-to-downtown route meet the STA criterion? Use the .05 significance level.

53. Past experience at the Crowder Travel Agency indicated that 44 percent of those persons who wanted the agency to plan a vacation for them wanted to go to Europe. During the most recent busy season, a sampling of 1,000 plans was selected at random from the files. It was found that 480 persons wanted to go to Europe on vacation. Has there been a significant shift upward in the percentage of persons who want to go to Europe? Test at the .05 significance level.

54. From past experience a television manufacturer found that 10 percent or less of its sets needed any type of repair in the first two years of operation. In a sample of 50 sets manufactured two years ago, 9 needed repair. At the .05 significance level, has the percent of sets needing repair increased? Determine the p-value.

55. An urban planner claims that, nationally, 20 percent of all families renting condominiums move during a given year. A random sample of 200 families renting condominiums in the Dallas Metroplex revealed that 56 had moved during the past year. At the .01 significance level, does this evidence suggest that a larger proportion of condominium owners moved in the Dallas area? Determine the p-value.

56. The cost of weddings in the United States has skyrocketed in recent years. As a result many couples are opting to have their weddings in the Caribbean. A Caribbean vacation resort recently advertised in *Bride Magazine* that the cost of a Caribbean wedding was less than $10,000. Listed below is a total cost in $000 for a sample of 8 Caribbean weddings.

9.7	9.4	11.7	9.0	9.1	10.5	9.1	9.8

At the .05 significance level is it reasonable to conclude the mean wedding cost is less than $10,000 as advertised?

57. The U.S. president's call for designing and building a missile defense system that ignores restrictions of the Anti-Ballistic Missile Defense System treaty (ABM) is supported by 483 of the respondents in a nationwide poll of 1,002 adults. Is it reasonable to conclude that the nation is evenly divided on the issue? Use the .05 significance level.

58. After a losing season there is a great uproar to fire the head football coach. In a random sample of 200 college alumni, 80 favor keeping the coach. Test at the .05 level of significance whether the proportion of alumni who support the coach is less than 50 percent.

59. During the 1990s the fatality rate for lung cancer was 80 per 100,000 people. After the turn of the century and the establishment of newer treatments and adjustment in public health advertising, a random sample of 10,000 people exhibits only six deaths due to lung cancer. Test at the .05 significance level whether that data is proof of a reduced fatality rate for lung cancer.

60. One of the major U.S. automakers wishes to review its warranty. The warranty covers the engine, transmission, and drivetrain of all new cars for up to two years or 24,000 miles, whichever comes first. The manufacturer's quality-assurance department believes that the mean number of miles driven by owners is more than 24,000. A sample of 35 cars revealed that the mean number of miles was 24,421, with a standard deviation of 1,944 miles.
   a. Conduct the following hypothesis test. Use the .05 significance level.

$$H_0: \mu \leq 24,000$$
$$H_1: \mu > 24,000$$

   b. What is the largest value for the sample mean for which H_0 is not rejected?
   c. Suppose the population mean shifts to 25,000 miles. What is the probability this change will not be detected?

61. A cola-dispensing machine is set to dispense 9.00 ounces of cola per cup, with a standard deviation of 1.00 ounces. The manufacturer of the machine would like to set the control limit in such a way that, for samples of 36, 5 percent of the sample means will be greater than the upper control limit, and 5 percent of the sample means will be less than the lower control limit.
   a. At what value should the control limit be set?
   b. What is the probability that if the population mean shifts to 8.9, this change will not be detected?
   c. What is the probability that if the population mean shifts to 9.3, this change will not be detected?

62. The owners of the Westfield Mall wished to study customer shopping habits. From earlier studies the owners were under the impression that a typical shopper spends 0.75 hours at the mall, with a standard deviation of 0.10 hours. Recently the mall owners added some specialty restaurants designed to keep shoppers in the mall longer. The consulting firm, Brunner and Swanson Marketing Enterprises, was hired to evaluate the

effects of the restaurants. A sample of 45 shoppers by Brunner and Swanson revealed that the mean time spent in the mall had increased to 0.80 hours.
  a. Develop a test of hypothesis to determine if the mean time spent in the mall is more than 0.75 hours. Use the .05 significance level.
  b. Suppose the mean shopping time actually increased from 0.75 hours to 0.77 hours. What is the probability this increase would not be detected?
  c. When Brunner and Swanson reported the information in part (b) to the mall owners, the owners were upset with the statement that a survey could not detect a change from 0.75 to 0.77 hours of shopping time. How could this probability be reduced?
63. The following null and alternate hypotheses are given.

$$H_0 : \mu \leq 50$$
$$H_1 : \mu > 50$$

Suppose the population standard deviation is 10. The probability of a Type I error is set at .01 and the probability of a Type II error at .30. Assume that the population mean shifts from 50 to 55. How large a sample is necessary to meet these requirements?
64. An insurance company, based on past experience, estimates the mean damage for a natural disaster in its area is $5,000. After introducing several plans to prevent loss, it randomly samples 200 policyholders and finds the mean amount per claim was $4,800 with a standard deviation of $1,300. Does it appear the prevention plans were effective in reducing the mean amount of a claim? Use the .05 significance level.
65. A national grocer's magazine reports the typical shopper spends eight minutes in line waiting to check out. A sample of 24 shoppers at the local Farmer Jack's showed a mean of 7.5 minutes with a standard deviation of 3.2 minutes. Is the waiting time at the local Farmer Jack's less than that reported in the national magazine? Use the .05 significance level.

Data Set Exercises

66. Refer to the Real Estate data, which report information on the homes sold in Denver, Colorado, last year.
  a. A recent article in the *Denver Post* indicated that the mean selling price of the homes in the area is more than $220,000. Can we conclude that the mean selling price in the Denver area is more than $220,000? Use the .01 significance level. What is the *p*-value?
  b. The same article reported the mean size was more than 2,100 square feet. Can we conclude that the mean size of homes sold in the Denver area is more than 2,100 square feet? Use the .01 significance level. What is the *p*-value?
  c. Determine the proportion of homes that have an attached garage. At the .05 significance level can we conclude that more than 60 percent of the homes sold in the Denver area had an attached garage? What is the *p*-value?
  d. Determine the proportion of homes that have a pool. At the .05 significance level, can we conclude that less than 40 percent of the homes sold in the Denver area had a pool? What is the *p*-value?
67. Refer to the Baseball 2007 data, which report information on the 30 Major League Baseball teams for the 2007 season.
  a. Conduct a test of hypothesis to determine whether the mean salary of the teams was different from $80.0 million. Use the .05 significance level.
  b. Conduct a test of hypothesis to determine whether the mean attendance was more than 2,000,000 per team.
68. Refer to the Wage data, which report information on the annual wages for a sample of 100 workers. Also included are variables relating to the industry, years of education, and gender for each worker.
  a. Conduct a test of hypothesis to determine if the mean annual wage is greater than $30,000. Use the .05 significance level. Determine the *p*-value and interpret the result.
  b. Conduct a test of hypothesis to determine if the mean years of experience is different from 20. Use the .05 significance level. Determine the *p*-value and interpret the result.
  c. Conduct a test of hypothesis to determine if the mean age is less than 40. Use the .05 significance level. Determine the *p*-value and interpret the result.
  d. Conduct a test of hypothesis to determine if the proportion of union workers is greater than 15 percent. Use the .05 significance level and report the *p*-value.

69. Refer to the CIA data, which report demographic and economic information on 46 different countries.

    a. Conduct a test of hypothesis to determine if the mean number of cell phones is greater than 4.0. Use the .05 significance level. What is the *p*-value?

    b. Conduct a test of hypothesis to determine if the mean size of the labor force is less than 50. Use the .05 significance level. What is the *p*-value?

Software Commands

1. The MINITAB commands for the histogram and the descriptive statistics on page 342 are:

    a. Enter the 26 sample observations in column *C1* and name the variable *Cost*.

    b. From the menu bar select **Stat, Basic Statistics,** and **Graphical Summary.** In the dialog box select **Cost** as the variable and click **OK.**

2. The MINITAB commands for the one-sample *t* test on page 346 are:

    a. Enter the sample data into column *C1* and name the variable *Length*.

    b. From the menu bar select **Stat, Basic Statistics,** and **1-Sample *t*** and then hit **Enter.**

    c. Select **Length** as the variable, select **Test mean,** insert the number *43* and click **OK.**

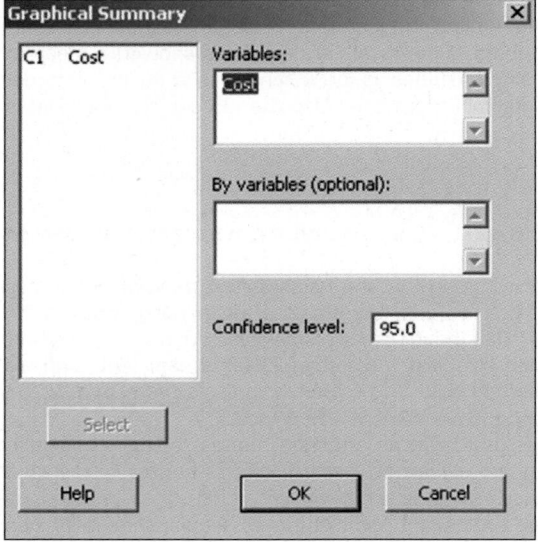

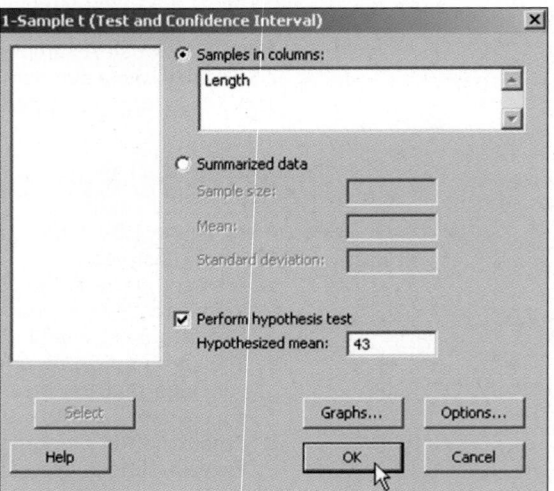

Chapter 10   Answers to Self-Review

10–1 a. $H_0: \mu = 16.0$; $H_1: \mu \neq 16.0$
  b. .05
  c. $z = \dfrac{\bar{X} - \mu}{\sigma/\sqrt{n}}$
  d. Reject H_0 if $z < -1.96$ or $z > 1.96$
  e. $z = \dfrac{16.017 - 16.0}{0.15/\sqrt{50}} = \dfrac{0.0170}{0.0212} = 0.80$
  f. Do not reject H_0
  g. We cannot conclude the mean amount dispensed is different from 16.0 ounces.

10–2 a. $H_0: \mu \leq 16.0$; $H_1: \mu > 16.0$
  b. Reject H_0 if $z > 1.65$
  c. $z = \dfrac{16.040 - 16.0}{0.15/\sqrt{50}} = \dfrac{.0400}{.0212} = 1.89$
  d. Reject H_0
  e. The mean amount dispensed is more than 16.0 ounces.
  f. p-value $= .5000 - .4706 = .0294$. The p-value is less than α (.05), so H_0 is rejected. It is the same conclusion as in part (d).

10–3 a. $H_0: \mu \leq 305$; $H_1: \mu > 305$.
  b. $df = n - 1 = 20 - 1 = 19$
  The decision rule is to reject H_0 if $t > 1.729$.

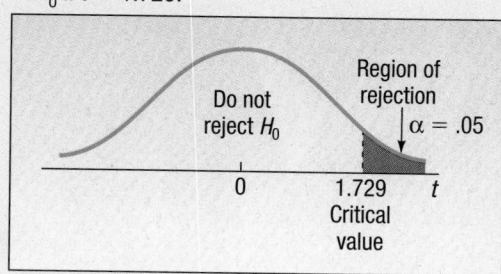

  c. $t = \dfrac{\bar{X} - \mu}{s/\sqrt{n}} = \dfrac{311 - 305}{12/\sqrt{20}} = 2.236$
  Reject H_0 because $2.236 > 1.729$. The modification increased the mean battery life to more than 305 days.

10–4 a. $H_0: \mu \geq 9.0$; $H_1: \mu < 9.0$.
  b. 7, found by $n - 1 = 8 - 1 = 7$.
  c. Reject H_0 if $t < -2.998$.

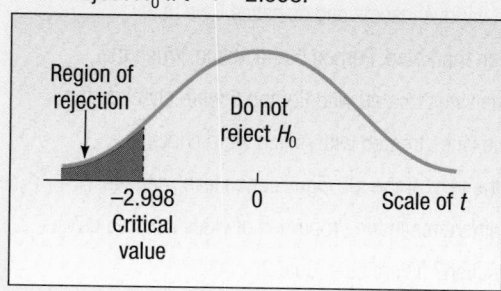

  d. $t = -2.494$, found by:
  $$s = \sqrt{\dfrac{0.36}{8 - 1}} = 0.2268$$
  $$\bar{X} = \dfrac{70.4}{8} = 8.8$$
  Then
  $$t = \dfrac{8.8 - 9.0}{0.2268/\sqrt{8}} = -2.494$$
  Since -2.494 lies to the right of -2.998, H_0 is not rejected. We have not shown that the mean is less than 9.0.
  e. The p-value is between .025 and .010.

10–5 a. Yes, because both $n\pi$ and $n(1 - \pi)$ exceed 5:
  $n\pi = 200(.40) = 80$, and
  $n(1 - \pi) = 200(.60) = 120$.
  b. $H_0: \pi \geq .40$
  $H_1: \pi < .40$
  c. Reject H_0 if $z < -2.33$

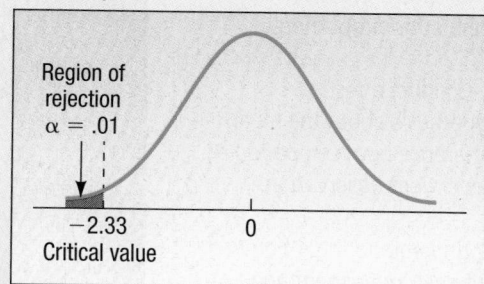

  d. $z = -0.87$, found by:
  $$z = \dfrac{.37 - .40}{\sqrt{\dfrac{.40(1 - .40)}{200}}} = \dfrac{-.03}{\sqrt{.0012}} = -0.87$$
  Do not reject H_0.
  e. The p-value is .1922, found by $.5000 - .3078$.

10–6 .0054, found by determining the area under the curve between 10,078 and 10,180.
  $$z = \dfrac{\bar{X}_c - \mu_1}{\sigma/\sqrt{n}}$$
  $$= \dfrac{10,078 - 10,180}{400/\sqrt{100}} = -2.55$$
  The area under the curve for a z of -2.55 is .4946 (Appendix B.1), and $.5000 - .4946 = .0054$.

11

GOALS

When you have completed this chapter, you will be able to:

1 Conduct a test of a hypothesis about the difference between two independent population means.

2 Conduct a test of a hypothesis about the difference between two population proportions.

3 Conduct a test of a hypothesis about the mean difference between *paired or dependent observations*.

4 Understand the difference between *dependent and independent samples*.

Two-Sample Tests of Hypothesis

The Damon family owns a large grape vineyard in western New York along Lake Erie. The grapevines must be sprayed at the beginning of the growing season to protect against various insects and diseases. Two new insecticides have just been marketed, Pernod 5 and Action. When the grapes ripened, 400 of the vines treated with Pernod 5 were checked for infestation, and 400 of the vines treated with Action were checked. Referring to the table in the text, at the .05 significance level, can we conclude that there is a difference in the proportion of vines infested using Pernod 5 as opposed to Action? (Exercise 9, Goal 2)

Introduction

Chapter 10 began our study of hypothesis testing. We described the nature of hypothesis testing and conducted tests of a hypothesis in which we compared the results of a single sample to a population value. That is, we selected a single random sample from a population and conducted a test of whether the proposed population value was reasonable. Recall, in Chapter 10 we selected a sample of the number of desks assembled per week at Jamestown Steel Company to determine whether there was a change in the production rate. Similarly, we sampled voters in one area of a particular state to determine whether the population proportion that

would support the governor for reelection was less than .80. In both of these cases, we compared the results of a *single* sample statistic to a population parameter.

In this chapter we expand the idea of hypothesis testing to two samples. That is, we select random samples from two different populations to determine whether the population means or proportions are equal. Some questions we might want to test are:

1. Is there a difference in the mean value of residential real estate sold by male agents and female agents in south Florida?
2. Is there a difference in the mean number of defects produced on the day and the afternoon shifts at Kimble Products?
3. Is there a difference in the mean number of days absent between young workers (under 21 years of age) and older workers (more than 60 years of age) in the fast-food industry?
4. Is there a difference in the proportion of Ohio State University graduates and University of Cincinnati graduates who pass the state Certified Public Accountant Examination on their first attempt?
5. Is there an increase in the production rate if music is piped into the production area?

We begin this chapter with the case in which we select random samples from two independent populations and wish to investigate whether these populations have the same mean.

Two-Sample Tests of Hypothesis: Independent Samples

A city planner in Florida wishes to know whether there is a difference in the mean hourly wage rate of plumbers and electricians in central Florida. A financial accountant wishes to know whether the mean rate of return for high yield mutual funds is different from the mean rate of return on global mutual funds. In each of these cases there are two independent populations. In the first case, the plumbers represent one population and the electricians the other. In the second case, high-yield mutual funds are one population and global mutual funds the other.

In each of these cases, to investigate the question, we would select a random sample from each population and compute the mean of the two samples. If the two

population means are the same, that is, the mean hourly rate is the same for the plumbers and the electricians, we would expect the *difference* between the two sam- ple means to be zero. But what if our sample results yield a difference other than zero? Is that difference due to chance or is it because there is a real difference in the hourly earnings? A two-sample test of means will help to answer this question.

We do need to return to the results of Chapter 8. Recall that we showed that a distribution of sample means would tend to approximate the normal distribution. We need to again assume that a distribution of sample means will follow the nor- mal distribution. It can be shown mathematically that the distribution of the differ- ences between sample means for two normal distributions is also normal.

We can illustrate this theory in terms of the city planner in Tampa, Florida. To begin, let's assume some information that is not usually available. Suppose that the popula- tion of plumbers has a mean of $30.00 per hour and a standard deviation of $5.00 per hour. The population of electricians has a mean of $29.00 and a standard deviation of $4.50. Now, from this information it is clear that the two population means are not the same. The plumbers actually earn $1.00 per hour more than the electricians. But we cannot expect to uncover this difference each time we sample the two populations.

Suppose we select a random sample of 40 plumbers and a random sample of 35 electricians and compute the mean of each sample. Then, we determine the difference between the sample means. It is this difference between the sample means that holds our interest. If the populations have the same mean, then we would expect the differ- ence between the two sample means to be zero. If there is a difference between the population means, then we expect to find a difference between the sample means.

To understand the theory, we need to take several pairs of samples, compute the mean of each, determine the difference between the sample means, and study the distribution of the differences in the sample means. Because of our study of the distribution of sample means in Chapter 8, we know that the distribution of the sam- ple means follows the normal distribution. If the two distributions of sample means follow the normal distribution, then we can reason that the distribution of their dif- ferences will also follow the normal distribution. This is the first hurdle.

The second hurdle refers to the mean of this distribution of differences. If we find the mean of this distribution is zero, that implies that there is no difference in the two populations. On the other hand, if the mean of the distribution of differ- ences is equal to some value other than zero, either positive or negative, then we conclude that the two populations do not have the same mean.

To report some concrete results, let's return to the city planner in Tampa, Florida. Table 11–1 shows the result of selecting 20 different samples of 40 plumbers and 35 electricians, computing the mean of each sample, and finding the difference between the two sample means. In the first case the sample of 40 plumbers has a mean of $29.80, and for the 35 electricians the mean is $28.76. The difference between the sample means is $1.04. This process was repeated 19 more times. Observe that in 17 of the 20 cases the mean of the plumbers is larger than the mean of the electricians.

Our final hurdle is that we need to know something about the *variability* of the distribution of differences. To put it another way, what is the standard deviation of this distribution of differences? Statistical theory shows that when we have inde- pendent populations, such as the case here, the distribution of the differences has a variance (standard deviation squared) equal to the sum of the two individual vari- ances. This means that we can add the variances of the two sampling distributions. To put it another way, the variance of the difference in sample means $(\bar{X}_1 - \bar{X}_2)$ is equal to the sum of the variance for the plumbers and the variance for the electricians.

| VARIANCE OF THE DISTRIBUTION OF DIFFERENCES IN MEANS | $\sigma^2_{\bar{X}_1 - \bar{X}_2} = \dfrac{\sigma^2_1}{n_1} + \dfrac{\sigma^2_2}{n_2}$ | **[11–1]** |

TABLE 11–1 The Means of Random Samples of Plumbers and Electricians

Sample	Plumbers	Electricians	Difference
1	$29.80	$28.76	$1.04
2	30.32	29.40	0.92
3	30.57	29.94	0.63
4	30.04	28.93	1.11
5	30.09	29.78	0.31
6	30.02	28.66	1.36
7	29.60	29.13	0.47
8	29.63	29.42	0.21
9	30.17	29.29	0.88
10	30.81	29.75	1.06
11	30.09	28.05	2.04
12	29.35	29.07	0.28
13	29.42	28.79	0.63
14	29.78	29.54	0.24
15	29.60	29.60	0.00
16	30.60	30.19	0.41
17	30.79	28.65	2.14
18	29.14	29.95	−0.81
19	29.91	28.75	1.16
20	28.74	29.21	−0.47

The term $\sigma^2_{\overline{X}_1-\overline{X}_2}$ looks complex but need not be difficult to interpret. The σ^2 portion reminds us that it is a variance, and the subscript $\overline{X}_1 - \overline{X}_2$ that it is a distribution of differences in the sample means.

We can put this equation in a more usable form by taking the square root, so that we have the standard deviation of the distribution or "standard error" of the differences. Finally, we standardize the distribution of the differences. The result is the following equation.

TWO-SAMPLE TEST OF MEANS—KNOWN σ

$$z = \frac{\overline{X}_1 - \overline{X}_2}{\sqrt{\dfrac{\sigma_1^2}{n_1} + \dfrac{\sigma_2^2}{n_2}}} \qquad \textbf{[11–2]}$$

Before we present an example, let's review the assumptions necessary for using formula (11–2).

Assumptions for testing independent sample means.

1. The two samples must be unrelated, that is, independent.
2. The standard deviations for both populations must be known.

The following example shows the details of the test of hypothesis for two population means.

Example

Customers at FoodTown Super Markets have a choice when paying for their groceries. They may check out and pay using the standard cashier-assisted checkout, or they may use the new Fast Lane procedure. In the standard procedure a FoodTown employee scans each item, puts it on a short conveyor where another employee puts it in a bag and then into the grocery cart. In the Fast Lane procedure the customer scans each item, bags it, and places the bags in the cart themselves.

The Fast Lane procedure is designed to reduce the time a customer spends in the checkout line.

The Fast Lane facility was recently installed at the Byrne Road FoodTown location. The store manager would like to know if the mean checkout time using the standard checkout method is longer than using the Fast Lane. She gathered the following sample information. The time is measured from when the customer enters the line until their bags are in the cart. Hence the time includes both waiting in line and checking out. What is the p-value?

Customer Type	Sample Mean	Population Standard Deviation	Sample Size
Standard	5.50 minutes	0.40 minutes	50
Fast Lane	5.30 minutes	0.30 minutes	100

Solution

We use the five-step hypothesis testing procedure to investigate the question.

Step 1: State the null hypothesis and the alternate hypothesis. The null hypothesis is that there is no difference in the mean checkout times for the two groups. In other words, the difference of 0.20 minutes between the mean checkout time for the standard method and the mean checkout time for Fast Lane is due to chance. The alternate hypothesis is that the mean checkout time is longer for those using the standard method. We will let μ_s refer to the mean checkout time for the population of standard customers and μ_f the mean checkout time for the Fast Lane customers. The null and alternative hypotheses are:

$$H_0: \mu_s \leq \mu_f$$
$$H_1: \mu_s > \mu_f$$

Step 2: Select the level of significance. The significance level is the probability that we reject the null hypothesis when it is actually true. This likelihood is determined prior to selecting the sample or performing any calculations. The .05 and .01 significance levels are the most common, but other values, such as .02 and .10, are also used. In theory, we may select any value between 0 and 1 for the significance level. In this case we selected the .01 significance level.

Step 3: Determine the test statistic. In Chapter 10 we used the standard normal distribution (that is z) and t as test statistics. In this case we use the z distribution as the test statistic because the standard deviations of both populations are known.

Step 4: Formulate a decision rule. The decision rule is based on the null and the alternate hypotheses (i.e., one-tailed or two-tailed test), the level of significance, and the test statistic used. We selected the .01 significance level and the z distribution as the test statistic, and we wish to determine whether the mean checkout time is longer using the standard method. We set the alternate hypothesis to indicate that the mean checkout time is longer for those using the standard method than the Fast Lane method. Hence, the rejection region is in the upper tail of the standard normal distribution (a one-tailed test). To find the critical value, place .01 of the total area in the upper tail. This means that .4900 (.5000 − .0100) of the area is located between the z value of 0 and the critical value. Next, we search the body of Appendix B.1 for a value located near .4900. It is 2.33, so our decision rule is to reject H_0 if the value computed from the test statistic exceeds 2.33. Chart 11–1 depicts the decision rule.

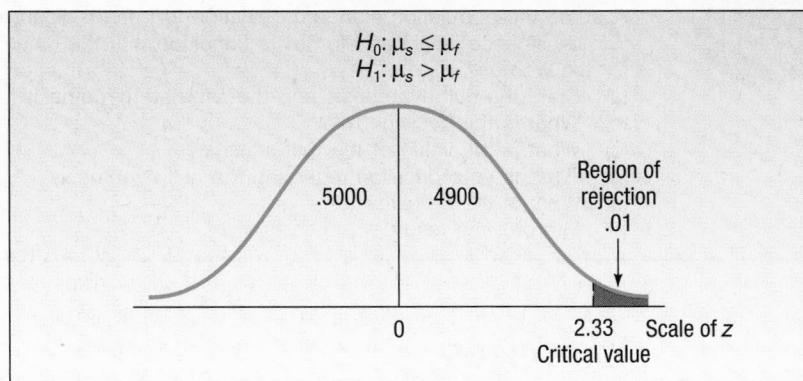

$H_0: \mu_s \leq \mu_f$
$H_1: \mu_s > \mu_f$

.5000   .4900   Region of rejection .01

0   2.33   Scale of z
Critical value

CHART 11–1 Decision Rule for One-Tailed Test at .01 Significance Level

Step 5: Make the decision regarding H_0 and interpret the result. We use formula (11–2) to compute the value of the test statistic.

$$z = \frac{\bar{X}_s - \bar{X}_f}{\sqrt{\dfrac{\sigma_s^2}{n_s} + \dfrac{\sigma_f^2}{n_f}}} = \frac{5.5 - 5.3}{\sqrt{\dfrac{0.40^2}{50} + \dfrac{0.30^2}{100}}} = \frac{0.2}{0.064} = 3.13$$

The computed value of 3.13 is larger than the critical value of 2.33. Our decision is to reject the null hypothesis and accept the alternate hypothesis. The difference of .20 minutes between the mean checkout time using the standard method is too large to have occurred by chance. To put it another way, we conclude the Fast Lane method is faster.

What is the p-value for the test statistic? Recall that the p-value is the probability of finding a value of the test statistic this extreme when the null hypothesis is true. To calculate the p-value we need the probability of a z value larger than 3.13. From Appendix B.1 we cannot find the probability associated with 3.13. The largest value available is 3.09. The area corresponding to 3.09 is .4990. In this case we can report that the p-value is less than .0010, found by .5000 − .4990. We conclude that there is very little likelihood that the null hypothesis is true!

In summary, the criteria for using formula (11–2) are:

1. *The samples are from independent populations.* This means, for example, that the checkout time for the Fast Lane customers is unrelated to the checkout time for the other customers. For example, Mr. Smith's checkout time does not affect any other customer's checkout time.
2. *Both population standard deviations are known.* In the FoodTown example, the population standard deviation of the Fast Lane times was 0.30 minutes. The standard deviation of the standard checkout times was 0.40 minutes. We use formula (11–2) to find the value of the test statistic.

Self-Review 11–1 Tom Sevits is the owner of the Appliance Patch. Recently Tom observed a difference in the dollar value of sales between the men and women he employs as sales associates. A sample of 40 days revealed the men sold a mean of $1,400 worth of appliances per day. For a sample of 50 days, the women sold a mean of $1,500 worth of appliances per day. Assume the population standard deviation for men is $200 and for women $250. At the .05 significance level can Mr. Sevits conclude that the mean amount sold per day is larger for the women?

(a) State the null hypothesis and the alternate hypothesis.
(b) What is the decision rule?
(c) What is the value of the test statistic?
(d) What is your decision regarding the null hypothesis?
(e) What is the *p*-value?
(f) Interpret the result.

Exercises

connect

1. A sample of 40 observations is selected from one population with a population standard deviation of 5. The sample mean is 102. A sample of 50 observations is selected from a second population with a population standard deviation of 6. The sample mean is 99. Conduct the following test of hypothesis using the .04 significance level.

$$H_0: \mu_1 = \mu_2$$
$$H_1: \mu_1 \neq \mu_2$$

   a. Is this a one-tailed or a two-tailed test?
   b. State the decision rule.
   c. Compute the value of the test statistic.
   d. What is your decision regarding H_0?
   e. What is the *p*-value?

2. A sample of 65 observations is selected from one population with a population standard deviation of 0.75. The sample mean is 2.67. A sample of 50 observations is selected from a second population with a population standard deviation of 0.66. The sample mean is 2.59. Conduct the following test of hypothesis using the .08 significance level.

$$H_0: \mu_1 \leq \mu_2$$
$$H_1: \mu_1 > \mu_2$$

   a. Is this a one-tailed or a two-tailed test?
   b. State the decision rule.
   c. Compute the value of the test statistic.
   d. What is your decision regarding H_0?
   e. What is the *p*-value?

Note: Use the five-step hypothesis testing procedure to solve the following exercises.

3. Gibbs Baby Food Company wishes to compare the weight gain of infants using its brand versus its competitor's. A sample of 40 babies using the Gibbs products revealed a mean weight gain of 7.6 pounds in the first three months after birth. For the Gibbs brand the population standard deviation of the sample is 2.3 pounds. A sample of 55 babies using the competitor's brand revealed a mean increase in weight of 8.1 pounds. The population standard deviation is 2.9 pounds. At the .05 significance level, can we conclude that babies using the Gibbs brand gained less weight? Compute the *p*-value and interpret it.

4. As part of a study of corporate employees, the director of human resources for PNC, Inc., wants to compare the distance traveled to work by employees at its office in downtown Cincinnati with the distance for those in downtown Pittsburgh. A sample of 35 Cincinnati employees showed they travel a mean of 370 miles per month. A sample of 40 Pittsburgh employees showed they travel a mean of 380 miles per month. The population standard deviation for the Cincinnati and Pittsburgh employees

are 30 and 26 miles, respectively. At the .05 significance level, is there a difference in the mean number of miles traveled per month between Cincinnati and Pittsburgh employees?

5. A financial analyst wants to compare the turnover rates, in percent, for shares of oil-related stocks versus other stocks, such as GE and IBM. She selected 32 oil-related stocks and 49 other stocks. The mean turnover rate of oil-related stocks is 31.4 percent and the population standard deviation 5.1 percent. For the other stocks, the mean rate was computed to be 34.9 percent and the population standard deviation 6.7 percent. Is there a significant difference in the turnover rates of the two types of stock? Use the .01 significance level.

6. Mary Jo Fitzpatrick is the vice president for Nursing Services at St. Luke's Memorial Hospital. Recently she noticed in the job postings for nurses that those that are unionized seem to offer higher wages. She decided to investigate and gathered the following information.

Group	Mean Wage	Population Standard Deviation	Sample Size
Union	$20.75	$2.25	40
Nonunion	$19.80	$1.90	45

Would it be reasonable for her to conclude that union nurses earn more? Use the .02 significance level. What is the *p*-value?

Two-Sample Tests about Proportions

In the previous section, we considered a test involving population means. However, we are often interested also in whether two sample proportions come from populations that are equal. Here are several examples.

- The vice president of human resources wishes to know whether there is a difference in the proportion of hourly employees who miss more than 5 days of work per year at the Atlanta and the Houston plants.
- General Motors is considering a new design for the Pontiac G6. The design is shown to a group of potential buyers under 30 years of age and another group over 60 years of age. Pontiac wishes to know whether there is a difference in the proportion of the two groups who like the new design.
- A consultant to the airline industry is investigating the fear of flying among adults. Specifically, the company wishes to know whether there is a difference in the proportion of men versus women who are fearful of flying.

In the above cases each sampled item or individual can be classified as a "success" or a "failure." That is, in the Pontiac G6 example each potential buyer is classified as "liking the new design" or "not liking the new design." We then compare the proportion in the under 30 group with the proportion in the over 60 group who indicated they liked the new design. Can we conclude that the differences are due to chance? In this study there is no measurement obtained, only classifying the individuals or objects. Then we assume the nominal scale of measurement.

To conduct the test, we assume each sample is large enough that the normal distribution will serve as a good approximation of the binomial distribution. The test statistic follows the standard normal distribution. We compute the value of *z* from the following formula:

| **TWO-SAMPLE TEST OF PROPORTIONS** | $$z = \frac{p_1 - p_2}{\sqrt{\dfrac{p_c(1 - p_c)}{n_1} + \dfrac{p_c(1 - p_c)}{n_2}}}$$ | **[11–3]** |

Formula (11–3) is formula (11–2) with the respective sample proportions replacing the sample means and $p_c(1 - p_c)$ replacing the two variances. In addition:

n_1 is the number of observations in the first sample.
n_2 is the number of observations in the second sample.
p_1 is the proportion in the first sample possessing the trait.
p_2 is the proportion in the second sample possessing the trait.
p_c is the pooled proportion possessing the trait in the combined samples. It is called the pooled estimate of the population proportion and is computed from the following formula.

POOLED PROPORTION	$$p_c = \frac{X_1 + X_2}{n_1 + n_2}$$	[11–4]

where:
X_1 is the number possessing the trait in the first sample.
X_2 is the number possessing the trait in the second sample.

The following example will illustrate the two-sample test of proportions.

Example

Manelli Perfume Company recently developed a new fragrance that it plans to market under the name Heavenly. A number of market studies indicate that Heavenly has very good market potential. The Sales Department at Manelli is particularly interested in whether there is a difference in the proportions of younger and older women who would purchase Heavenly if it were marketed. There are two independent populations, a population consisting of the younger women and a population consisting of the older women. Each sampled woman will be asked to smell Heavenly and indicate whether she likes the fragrance well enough to purchase a bottle.

Solution

We will use the usual five-step hypothesis-testing procedure.

Step 1: State H_0 and H_1. In this case the null hypothesis is: "There is no difference in the proportion of young women and older women who prefer Heavenly." We designate π_1 as the proportion of young women who would purchase Heavenly and π_2 as the proportion of older women who would purchase. The alternate hypothesis is that the two proportions are not equal.

$$H_0: \pi_1 = \pi_2$$
$$H_1: \pi_1 \neq \pi_2$$

Step 2: Select the level of significance. We choose the .05 significance level in this example.

Step 3: Determine the test statistic. The test statistic follows the standard normal distribution. The value of the test statistic can be computed from formula (11–3).

Step 4: Formulate the decision rule. Recall that the alternate hypothesis from **Step 1** does not state a direction, so this is a two-tailed test. To determine the critical value, we divide the significance level in half and place this amount in each tail of the z distribution. Next, we subtract this amount from the total area to the right of zero. That is .5000 − .0250 = .4750. Finally, we search the body of the z table (Appendix B.1) for the closest value. It is 1.96. The critical values are −1.96 and +1.96. As before, if the computed z value falls in the region between $+1.96$ and -1.96, the null hypothesis is not rejected. If that does occur, it is assumed that any difference between the two sample proportions is due to chance variation. This information is summarized in Chart 11–2.

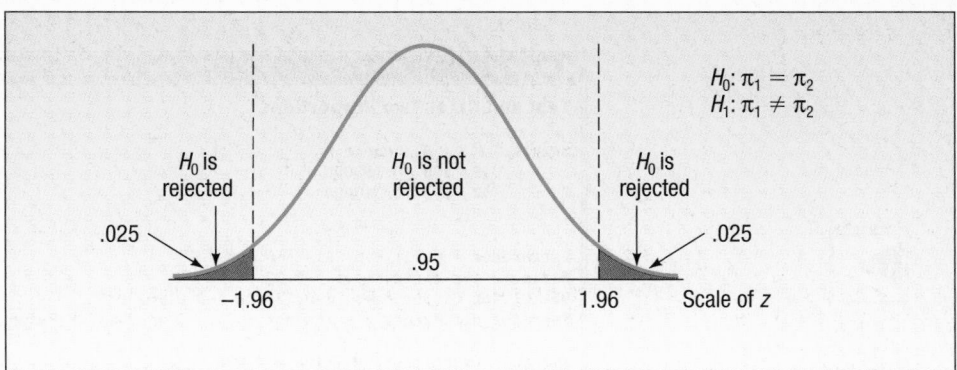

$$H_0: \pi_1 = \pi_2$$
$$H_1: \pi_1 \neq \pi_2$$

H_0 is rejected

H_0 is not rejected

H_0 is rejected

.025

.025

.95

-1.96 1.96   Scale of z

CHART 11–2 Decision Rules for Heavenly Fragrance Test, .05 Significance Level

Step 5: Select a sample and make a decision. A random sample of 100 young women revealed 19 liked the Heavenly fragrance well enough to purchase it. Similarly, a sample of 200 older women revealed 62 liked the fragrance well enough to make a purchase. We let p_1 refer to the young women and p_2 to the older women.

$$p_1 = \frac{X_1}{n_1} = \frac{19}{100} = .19 \qquad p_2 = \frac{X_2}{n_2} = \frac{62}{200} = .31$$

The research question is whether the difference of .12 in the two sample proportions is due to chance or whether there is a difference in the proportion of younger and older women who like the Heavenly fragrance.

Next, we combine or pool the sample proportions. We use formula (11–4).

$$p_c = \frac{X_1 + X_2}{n_1 + n_2} = \frac{19 + 62}{100 + 200} = \frac{81}{300} = 0.27$$

Note that the pooled proportion is closer to .31 than to .19 because more older women than younger women were sampled.

We use formula (11–3) to find the value of the test statistic.

$$z = \frac{p_1 - p_2}{\sqrt{\dfrac{p_c(1 - p_c)}{n_1} + \dfrac{p_c(1 - p_c)}{n_2}}} = \frac{.19 - .31}{\sqrt{\dfrac{.27(1 - .27)}{100} + \dfrac{.27(1 - .27)}{200}}} = -2.21$$

The computed value of -2.21 is in the area of rejection; that is, it is to the left of -1.96. Therefore, the null hypothesis is rejected at the .05 significance level. To put it another way, we reject the null hypothesis that the proportion of young women who would purchase Heavenly is equal to the proportion of older women who would purchase Heavenly. It is unlikely that the difference between the two sample proportions is due to chance. To find the p-value, go to Appendix B.1 and find the likelihood of a z value less than -2.21 or greater than 2.21. The z value corresponding to 2.21 is .4864. So the likelihood of finding the value of the test statistic to be less than -2.21 or greater than 2.21 is:

$$p\text{-value} = 2(.5000 - .4864) = 2(.0136) = .0272$$

The *p*-value of .0272 is less than the significance level of .05, so our decision is to reject the null hypothesis. Again, we conclude that there is a difference in the proportion of younger and older women who would purchase Heavenly.

The MINITAB system has a procedure to quickly determine the value of the test statistic and compute the *p*-value. The results follow.

```
Session                                                    _ □ ×

Test and CI for Two Proportions

Sample   X    N   Sample p             I
1       19  100   0.190000
2       62  200   0.310000


Difference = p (1) – p (2)
Estimate for difference:  –0.12
95% CI for difference:   (–0.220102, –0.0198978)
Test for difference = 0 (vs not = 0):   Z = –2.21   P-Value = 0.027

Fisher's exact test: P-Value = 0.028
```

Notice the MINITAB output includes the two sample proportions, the value of *z*, and the *p*-value.

Self-Review 11–2

Of 150 adults who tried a new peach-flavored Peppermint Patty, 87 rated it excellent. Of 200 children sampled, 123 rated it excellent. Using the .10 level of significance, can we conclude that there is a significant difference in the proportion of adults and the proportion of children who rate the new flavor excellent?
(a) State the null hypothesis and the alternate hypothesis.
(b) What is the probability of a Type I error?
(c) Is this a one-tailed or a two-tailed test?
(d) What is the decision rule?
(e) What is the value of the test statistic?
(f) What is your decision regarding the null hypothesis?
(g) What is the *p*-value? Explain what it means in terms of this problem.

Exercises

connect

7. The null and alternate hypotheses are:

$$H_0: \pi_1 \leq \pi_2$$
$$H_1: \pi_1 > \pi_2$$

A sample of 100 observations from the first population indicated that X_1 is 70. A sample of 150 observations from the second population revealed X_2 to be 90. Use the .05 significance level to test the hypothesis.
a. State the decision rule.
b. Compute the pooled proportion.
c. Compute the value of the test statistic.
d. What is your decision regarding the null hypothesis?

8. The null and alternate hypotheses are:

$$H_0: \pi_1 = \pi_2$$
$$H_1: \pi_1 \neq \pi_2$$

A sample of 200 observations from the first population indicated that X_1 is 170. A sample of 150 observations from the second population revealed X_2 to be 110. Use the .05 significance level to test the hypothesis.
a. State the decision rule.
b. Compute the pooled proportion.
c. Compute the value of the test statistic.
d. What is your decision regarding the null hypothesis?

Note: Use the five-step hypothesis-testing procedure in solving the following exercises.

9. The Damon family owns a large grape vineyard in western New York along Lake Erie. The grapevines must be sprayed at the beginning of the growing season to protect against various insects and diseases. Two new insecticides have just been marketed: Pernod 5 and Action. To test their effectiveness, three long rows were selected and sprayed with Pernod 5, and three others were sprayed with Action. When the grapes ripened, 400 of the vines treated with Pernod 5 were checked for infestation. Likewise, a sample of 400 vines sprayed with Action were checked. The results are:

Insecticide	Number of Vines Checked (sample size)	Number of Infested Vines
Pernod 5	400	24
Action	400	40

At the .05 significance level, can we conclude that there is a difference in the proportion of vines infested using Pernod 5 as opposed to Action?

10. The Roper Organization conducted identical surveys 5 years apart. One question asked of women was "Are most men basically kind, gentle, and thoughtful?" The earlier survey revealed that, of the 3,000 women surveyed, 2,010 said that they were. The later revealed 1,530 of the 3,000 women surveyed thought that men were kind, gentle, and thoughtful. At the .05 level, can we conclude that women think men are less kind, gentle, and thoughtful in the later survey compared with the earlier one?

11. A nationwide sample of influential Republicans and Democrats was asked as a part of a comprehensive survey whether they favored lowering environmental standards so that high-sulfur coal could be burned in coal-fired power plants. The results were:

	Republicans	Democrats
Number sampled	1,000	800
Number in favor	200	168

At the .02 level of significance, can we conclude that there is a larger proportion of Democrats in favor of lowering the standards? Determine the *p*-value.

12. The research department at the home office of New Hampshire Insurance conducts ongoing research on the causes of automobile accidents, the characteristics of the drivers, and so on. A random sample of 400 policies written on single persons revealed 120 had at least one accident in the previous three-year period. Similarly, a sample of 600 policies written on married persons revealed that 150 had been in at least one accident. At the .05 significance level, is there a significant difference in the proportions of single and married persons having an accident during a three-year period? Determine the *p*-value.

Comparing Population Means with Unknown Population Standard Deviations (the Pooled *t*-Test)

In the previous two sections we described conditions where the standard normal distribution, that is *z*, is used as the test statistic. In one case we were working with a variable (calculating the mean) and in the second an attribute (calculating a proportion). In the first case we wished to compare two sample means from independent populations to determine if they came from the same or equal populations. In that instance we assumed the population followed the normal probability distribution and that we knew the standard deviation of the population. In many cases, in fact in most cases, we do not know the population standard deviation. We can overcome this problem, as we did in the one sample case in the previous chapter, by substituting the sample standard deviation (s) for the population standard deviation (σ). See formula (10–2) on page 341.

This section describes another method for comparing the sample means of two independent populations to determine if the sampled populations could reasonably have the same mean. The method described does *not* require that we know the standard deviations of the populations. This gives us a great deal more flexibility when investigating the difference in sample means. There are two major differences in this test and the previous test described earlier in this chapter.

1. We assume the sampled populations have equal but unknown standard deviations. Because of this assumption we combine or "pool" the sample standard deviations.
2. We use the *t* distribution as the test statistic.

The formula for computing the value of the test statistic *t* is similar to (11–2), but an additional calculation is necessary. The two sample standard deviations are pooled to form a single estimate of the unknown population standard deviation. In essence we compute a weighted mean of the two sample standard deviations and use this value as an estimate of the unknown population standard deviation. The weights are the degrees of freedom that each sample provides. Why do we need to pool the sample standard deviations? Because we assume that the two populations have equal standard deviations, the best estimate we can make of that value is to combine or pool all the sample information we have about the value of the population standard deviation.

The following formula is used to pool the sample standard deviations. Notice that two factors are involved: the number of observations in each sample and the sample standard deviations themselves.

POOLED VARIANCE	$$s_p^2 = \frac{(n_1 - 1)s_1^2 + (n_2 - 1)s_2^2}{n_1 + n_2 - 2}$$	[11–5]

where:
s_1^2 is the variance (standard deviation squared) of the first sample.
s_2^2 is the variance of the second sample.

The value of *t* is computed from the following equation.

TWO-SAMPLE TEST OF MEANS—UNKNOWN σ'S	$$t = \frac{\overline{X}_1 - \overline{X}_2}{\sqrt{s_p^2\left(\dfrac{1}{n_1} + \dfrac{1}{n_2}\right)}}$$	[11–6]

where:
$\overline{X}_1$ is the mean of the first sample.
$\overline{X}_2$ is the mean of the second sample.
n_1 is the number of observations in the first sample.
n_2 is the number of observations in the second sample.
s_p^2 is the pooled estimate of the population variance.

The number of degrees of freedom in the test is the total number of items sampled minus the total number of samples. Because there are two samples, there are $n_1 + n_2 - 2$ degrees of freedom.

To summarize, there are three requirements or assumptions for the test.

1. The sampled populations follow the normal distribution.
2. The sampled populations are independent.
3. The standard deviations of the two populations are equal.

The following example/solution explains the details of the test.

Example

Owens Lawn Care, Inc., manufactures and assembles lawnmowers that are shipped to dealers throughout the United States and Canada. Two different procedures have been proposed for mounting the engine on the frame of the lawnmower. The question is: Is there a difference in the mean time to mount the engines on the frames of the lawnmowers? The first procedure was developed by longtime Owens employee Herb Welles (designated as procedure 1), and the other procedure was developed by Owens Vice President of Engineering William Atkins (designated as procedure 2). To evaluate the two methods, it was decided to conduct a time and motion study. A sample of five employees was timed using the Welles method and six using the Atkins method. The results, in minutes, are shown below. Is there a difference in the mean mounting times? Use the .10 significance level.

Welles (minutes)	Atkins (minutes)
2	3
4	7
9	5
3	8
2	4
	3

Solution

Following the five steps to test a hypothesis, the null hypothesis states that there is no difference in mean mounting times between the two procedures. The alternate hypothesis indicates that there is a difference.

$$H_0: \mu_1 = \mu_2$$
$$H_1: \mu_1 \neq \mu_2$$

The required assumptions are:

1. The observations in the Welles sample are *independent* of the observations in the Atkins sample.
2. The two populations follow the normal distribution.
3. The two populations have equal standard deviations.

Is there a difference between the mean assembly times using the Welles and the Atkins methods? The degrees of freedom are equal to the total number of items sampled minus the number of samples. In this case that is $n_1 + n_2 - 2$. Five assemblers used the Welles method and six the Atkins method. Thus, there are 9 degrees of freedom, found by $5 + 6 - 2$. The critical values of t, from Appendix B.2 for $df = 9$, a two-tailed test, and the .10 significance level, are -1.833 and 1.833. The decision rule is portrayed graphically in Chart 11–3. We do not reject the null hypothesis if the computed value of t falls between -1.833 and 1.833.

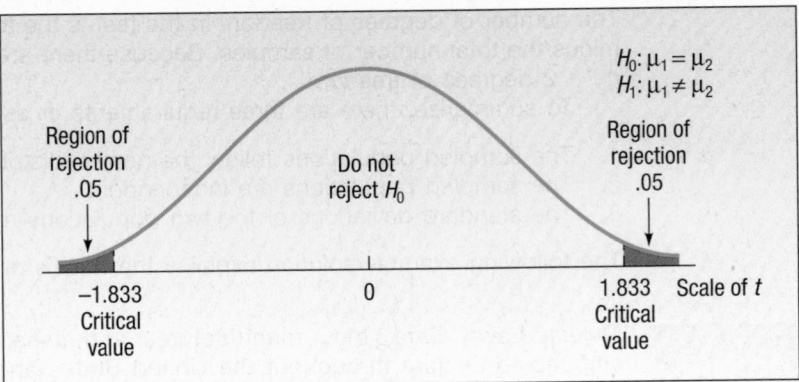

CHART 11–3 Regions of Rejection, Two-Tailed Test, $df = 9$, and .10 Significance Level

We use three steps to compute the value of t.

Step 1: Calculate the sample standard deviations. To compute the sample standard deviations, we use formula (3–11) from page 80. See the details below.

Welles Method		Atkins Method	
X_1	$(X_1 - \bar{X}_1)^2$	X_2	$(X_2 - \bar{X}_2)^2$
2	$(2 - 4)^2 = 4$	3	$(3 - 5)^2 = 4$
4	$(4 - 4)^2 = 0$	7	$(7 - 5)^2 = 4$
9	$(9 - 4)^2 = 25$	5	$(5 - 5)^2 = 0$
3	$(3 - 4)^2 = 1$	8	$(8 - 5)^2 = 9$
2	$(2 - 4)^2 = 4$	4	$(4 - 5)^2 = 1$
20	34	3	$(3 - 5)^2 = 4$
		30	22

$$\bar{X}_1 = \frac{\Sigma X_1}{n_1} = \frac{20}{5} = 4 \qquad\qquad \bar{X}_2 = \frac{\Sigma X_2}{n_2} = \frac{30}{6} = 5$$

$$s_1 = \sqrt{\frac{\Sigma(X_1 - \bar{X}_1)^2}{n_1 - 1}} = \sqrt{\frac{34}{5 - 1}} = 2.9155 \qquad s_2 = \sqrt{\frac{\Sigma(X_2 - \bar{X}_2)^2}{n_2 - 1}} = \sqrt{\frac{22}{6 - 1}} = 2.0976$$

Step 2: Pool the Sample Variances. We use formula (11–5) to pool the sample variances (standard deviations squared).

$$s_p^2 = \frac{(n_1 - 1)s_1^2 + (n_2 - 1)s_2^2}{n_1 + n_2 - 2} = \frac{(5 - 1)(2.9155)^2 + (6 - 1)(2.0976)^2}{5 + 6 - 2} = 6.2222$$

Step 3: Determine the value of t. The mean mounting time for the Welles method is 4.00 minutes, found by $\bar{X}_1 = 20/5$. The mean mounting time for the Atkins method is 5.00 minutes, found by $\bar{X}_2 = 30/6$. We use formula (11–6) to calculate the value of t.

$$t = \frac{\bar{X}_1 - \bar{X}_2}{\sqrt{s_p^2\left(\frac{1}{n_1} + \frac{1}{n_2}\right)}} = \frac{4.00 - 5.00}{\sqrt{6.2222\left(\frac{1}{5} + \frac{1}{6}\right)}} = -0.662$$

The decision is not to reject the null hypothesis, because -0.662 falls in the region between -1.833 and 1.833. We conclude that there is no difference in the mean times to mount the engine on the frame using the two methods.

We can also estimate the *p*-value using Appendix B.2. Locate the row with 9 degrees of freedom, and use the two-tailed test column. Find the *t* value, without regard to the sign, which is closest to our computed value of 0.662. It is 1.383, corresponding to a significance level of .20. Thus, even had we used the 20 percent significance level, we would not have rejected the null hypothesis of equal means. We can report that the *p*-value is greater than .20.

Excel has a procedure called "t-Test: Two Sample Assuming Equal Variances" that will perform the calculations of formulas (11–5) and (11–6) as well as find the sample means and sample variances. The details of the procedure are shown in the Software Commands section at the end of the chapter. The data are input in the first two columns of the Excel spreadsheet. They are labeled "Welles" and "Atkins." The output follows. The value of *t*, called the "t Stat," is −0.662, and the two-tailed *p*-value is .525. As we would expect, the *p*-value is larger than the significance level of .10. The conclusion is not to reject the null hypothesis.

	A	B	C	D	E	F	G
	welles and atkins						
1	Welles	Atkins		t-Test: Two-Sample Assuming Equal Variances			
2	2	3					
3	4	7			Welles	Atkins	
4	9	5		Mean	4.000	5.000	
5	3	8		Variance	8.500	4.400	
6	2	4		Observations	5.000	6.000	
7		3		Pooled Variance	6.222		
8				Hypothesized Mean Difference	0.000		
9				df	9.000		
10				t Stat	-0.662		
11				P(T<=t) one-tail	0.262		
12				t Critical one-tail	1.833		
13				P(T<=t) two-tail	0.525		
14				t Critical two-tail	2.262		
15							

Self-Review 11–3

The production manager at Bellevue Steel, a manufacturer of wheelchairs, wants to compare the number of defective wheelchairs produced on the day shift with the number on the afternoon shift. A sample of the production from 6 day shifts and 8 afternoon shifts revealed the following number of defects.

Day	5	8	7	6	9	7		
Afternoon	8	10	7	11	9	12	14	9

At the .05 significance level, is there a difference in the mean number of defects per shift?
(a) State the null hypothesis and the alternate hypothesis.
(b) What is the decision rule?
(c) What is the value of the test statistic?
(d) What is your decision regarding the null hypothesis?
(e) What is the *p*-value?
(f) Interpret the result.
(g) What are the assumptions necessary for this test?

Exercises

connect™

For Exercises 13 and 14: (a) state the decision rule, (b) compute the pooled estimate of the population variance, (c) compute the test statistic, (d) state your decision about the null hypothesis, and (e) estimate the *p*-value.

13. The null and alternate hypotheses are:

$$H_0: \mu_1 = \mu_2$$
$$H_1: \mu_1 \neq \mu_2$$

A random sample of 10 observations from one population revealed a sample mean of 23 and a sample deviation of 4. A random sample of 8 observations from another population revealed a sample mean of 26 and a sample standard deviation of 5. At the .05 significance level, is there a difference between the population means?

14. The null and alternate hypotheses are:

$$H_0: \mu_1 = \mu_2$$
$$H_1: \mu_1 \neq \mu_2$$

A random sample of 15 observations from the first population revealed a sample mean of 350 and a sample standard deviation of 12. A random sample of 17 observations from the second population revealed a sample mean of 342 and a sample standard deviation of 15. At the .10 significance level, is there a difference in the population means?

Note: Use the five-step hypothesis testing procedure for the following exercises.

15. A sample of scores on an examination given in Statistics 201 are:

Men	72	69	98	66	85	76	79	80	77
Women	81	67	90	78	81	80	76		

At the .01 significance level, is the mean grade of the women higher than that of the men?

16. A recent study compared the time spent together by single- and dual-earner couples. According to the records kept by the wives during the study, the mean amount of time spent together watching television among the single-earner couples was 61 minutes per day, with a standard deviation of 15.5 minutes. For the dual-earner couples, the mean number of minutes spent watching television was 48.4 minutes, with a standard deviation of 18.1 minutes. At the .01 significance level, can we conclude that the single-earner couples on average spend more time watching television together? There were 15 single-earner and 12 dual-earner couples studied.

17. Ms. Lisa Monnin is the budget director for Nexus Media, Inc. She would like to compare the daily travel expenses for the sales staff and the audit staff. She collected the following sample information.

Sales ($)	131	135	146	165	136	142	
Audit ($)	130	102	129	143	149	120	139

At the .10 significance level, can she conclude that the mean daily expenses are greater for the sales staff than the audit staff? What is the *p*-value?

18. The Tampa Bay (Florida) Area Chamber of Commerce wanted to know whether the mean weekly salary of nurses was larger than that of school teachers. To investigate, they collected the following information on the amounts earned last week by a sample of school teachers and nurses.

School Teachers ($)	845	826	827	875	784	809	802	820	829	830	842	832
Nurses ($)	841	890	821	771	850	859	825	829				

Is it reasonable to conclude that the mean weekly salary of nurses is higher? Use the .01 significance level. What is the *p*-value?

Comparing Population Means
with Unequal Standard Deviations

In the previous sections it was necessary to assume that the populations had equal standard deviations. To put it another way, we did not know the population standard deviations but we assumed they were equal. In many cases this is a reasonable assumption, but what if it is not? In the next chapter we present a formal method for testing this equal variance assumption.

If it is not reasonable to assume the population standard deviations are equal, then we use a statistic very much like formula [11–2]. The sample standard deviations, s_1 and s_2, are used in place of the respective population standard deviations. In addition, the degrees of freedom are adjusted downward by a rather complex approximation formula. The effect is to reduce the number of degrees of freedom in the test, which will require a larger value of the test statistic to reject the null hypothesis.

The formula for the t statistic is:

TEST STATISTIC FOR NO DIFFERENCE IN MEANS, UNEQUAL VARIANCES	$t = \dfrac{\overline{X}_1 - \overline{X}_2}{\sqrt{\dfrac{s_1^2}{n_1} + \dfrac{s_2^2}{n_2}}}$	**[11–7]**

The degrees of freedom statistic is found by:

DEGREES OF FREEDOM FOR UNEQUAL VARIANCE TEST	$df = \dfrac{[(s_1^2/n_1) + (s_2^2/n_2)]^2}{\dfrac{(s_1^2/n_1)^2}{n_1 - 1} + \dfrac{(s_2^2/n_2)^2}{n_2 - 1}}$	**[11–8]**

where n_1 and n_2 are the respective sample sizes and s_1 and s_2 are the respective sample standard deviations. If necessary, this fraction is rounded down to an integer value. An example will explain the details.

Example

Personnel in a consumer testing laboratory are evaluating the absorbency of paper towels. They wish to compare a set of store brand towels to a similar group of name brand ones. For each brand they dip a ply of the paper into a tub of fluid, allow the paper to drain back into the vat for two minutes, and then evaluate the amount of liquid the paper has taken up from the vat. A random sample of 9 store brand paper towels absorbed the following amounts of liquid in milliliters.

8	8	3	1	9	7	5	5	12

An independent random sample of 12 name brand towels absorbed the following amounts of liquid in milliliters:

12	11	10	6	8	9	9	10	11	9	8	10

Use the .10 significance level and test if there is a difference in the mean amount of liquid absorbed by the two types of paper towels.

Solution

To begin let's assume that the amounts of liquid absorbed follow the normal probability distribution for both the store brand and the name brand towels. We do not know either of the population standard deviations so we are going to use the *t* distribution as the test statistic. The assumption of equal population standard deviations does not appear reasonable. The amount of absorption in the store brand ranges from 1 ml to 12 ml. For the name brand, the amount of absorption ranges from 6 ml to 12 ml. That is, there is considerably more variation in the amount of absorption in the store brand than in the name brand. We observe the difference in the variation in the following dot plot provided by MINITAB. The software commands to create a MINITAB dot plot are given on page 129.

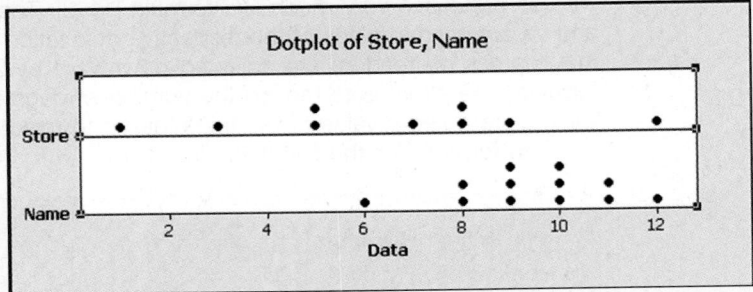

So we decide to use the *t* distribution and assume that the population standard deviations are not the same.

In the five-step hypothesis testing procedure the first step is to state the null hypothesis and the alternate hypothesis. The null hypothesis is that there is no difference in the mean amount of liquid absorbed between the two types of paper towels. The alternate hypothesis is that there is a difference.

$$H_0: \mu_1 = \mu_2$$
$$H_1: \mu_1 \neq \mu_2$$

The significance level is .10 and the test statistic follows the *t* distribution. Because we do not wish to assume equal population standard deviations, we adjust the degrees of freedom using formula (11–8). To do so we need to find the sample standard deviations. We can use the MINITAB system to quickly find these results. We will also find the mean absorption rate, which we will use shortly. The respective samples sizes are $n_1 = 9$ and $n_2 = 12$ and the respective standard deviations are 3.32 ml and 1.621 ml.

```
Descriptive Statistics: Store, Name

Variable     N      Mean      StDev
Store        9      6.44       3.32
Name        12     9.417      1.621
```

Inserting this information into formula (11–8):

$$df = \frac{[(s_1^2/n_1) + (s_2^2/n_2)]^2}{\dfrac{(s_1^2/n_1)^2}{n_1 - 1} + \dfrac{(s_2^2/n_2)^2}{n_2 - 1}} = \frac{[(3.32^2/9) + (1.621^2/12)]^2}{\dfrac{(3.32^2/9)^2}{9 - 1} + \dfrac{(1.621^2/12)^2}{12 - 1}} = \frac{1.4436^2}{.1875 + .0043} = 10.88$$

The usual practice is to round down to the integer, so we use 10 degrees of freedom. From Appendix B.2 with 10 degrees of freedom, a two-tailed test, and the .10 significance level, the critical *t* values are −1.812 and 1.812. Our decision rule is to reject the null hypothesis if the computed value of *t* is less than −1.812 or greater than 1.812.

To find the value of the test statistic we use formula (11–7). Recall from the MINITAB output above the mean amount of absorption for the store paper towels is 6.44 ml and 9.417 ml for the brand.

$$t = \frac{\bar{X}_1 - \bar{X}_2}{\sqrt{\dfrac{s_1^2}{n_1} + \dfrac{s_2^2}{n_2}}} = \frac{6.44 - 9.417}{\sqrt{\dfrac{3.32^2}{9} + \dfrac{1.621^2}{12}}} = -2.478$$

The computed value of t is less than the lower critical value, so our decision is to reject the null hypothesis. We conclude that the mean absorption rate for the two towels is not the same. The MINITAB output for this example follows.

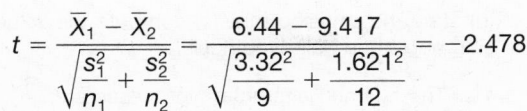

	C1	C2
↓	Store	Name
1	8	12
2	8	11
3	3	10
4	1	6
5	9	8
6	7	9
7	5	9
8	5	10
9	12	11
10		9
11		8
12		10

Session

Two-Sample T-Test and CI: Store, Name

Two-sample T for Store vs Name

```
        N   Mean   StDev   SE Mean
Store   9   6.44   3.32    1.1
Name    12  9.42   1.62    0.47
```

Difference = mu (Store) - mu (Name)
Estimate for difference: -2.97
95% CI for difference: (-5.65, -0.29)
T-Test of difference = 0 (vs not =):

T-Value = -2.47   P-Value = 0.033   DF = 10

Self-Review 11–4

It is often useful for companies to know who their customers are and how they became customers. A credit card company is interested in whether the owner of the card applied for the card on their own or was contacted by a telemarketer. The company obtained the following sample information regarding end-of-the-month balances for the two groups.

Source	Mean	Standard Deviation	Sample Size
Applied	$1,568	$356	10
Contacted	1,967	857	8

Is it reasonable to conclude the mean balance is larger for the credit card holders that were contacted by telemarketers than for those who applied on their own for the card? Assume the population standard deviations are not the same. Use the .05 significance level.
(a) State the null hypothesis and the alternate hypothesis.
(b) How many degrees of freedom are there?
(c) What is the decision rule?
(d) What is the value of the test statistic?
(e) What is your decision regarding the null hypothesis?
(f) Interpret the result.

Exercises

connect

For exercises 19 and 20 assume the sample populations do not have equal standard deviations and use the .05 significance level: (a) determine the number of degrees of freedom,

(b) state the decision rule, (c) compute the value of the test statistic, and (d) state your decision about the null hypothesis.

19. The null and alternate hypotheses are:

$$H_0: \mu_1 = \mu_2$$
$$H_1: \mu_1 \neq \mu_2$$

A random sample of 15 items from the first population showed a mean of 50 and a standard deviation of 5. A sample of 12 items for the second population showed a mean of 46 and a standard deviation of 15.

20. The null and alternate hypotheses are:

$$H_0: \mu_1 \leq \mu_2$$
$$H_1: \mu_1 > \mu_2$$

A random sample of 20 items from the first population showed a mean of 100 and a standard deviation of 15. A sample of 16 items for the second population showed a mean of 94 and a standard deviation of 8. Use the .05 significant level.

21. A recent article in *The Wall Street Journal* compared the cost of adopting children from China with that of Russia. For a sample of 16 adoptions from China the mean cost was $11,045 with a standard deviation of $835. For a sample of 18 adoptions from Russia the mean cost was $12,840 with a standard deviation of $1,545. Can we conclude the mean cost is larger for adopting children from Russia? Assume the two population standard deviations are not the same. Use the .05 significance level.

22. Suppose you are an expert on the fashion industry and wish to gather information to compare the amount earned per month by models featuring Liz Claiborne attire with those of Calvin Klein. The following is the amount ($000) earned per month by a sample of Claiborne models:

$5.0	$4.5	$3.4	$3.4	$6.0	$3.3	$4.5	$4.6	$3.5	$5.2
4.8	4.4	4.6	3.6	5.0					

The following is the amount ($000) earned by a sample of Klein models.

$3.1	$3.7	$3.6	$4.0	$3.8	$3.8	$5.9	$4.9	$3.6	$3.6
2.3	4.0								

Is it reasonable to conclude that Claiborne models earn more? Use the .05 significance level and assume the population standard deviations are not the same.

Two-Sample Tests of Hypothesis: Dependent Samples

On page 377, we tested the difference between the means from two independent samples. We compared the mean time required to mount an engine using the Welles method to the time to mount the engine using the Atkins method. The samples were *independent,* meaning that the sample of assembly times using the Welles method was in no way related to the sample of assembly times using the Atkins method.

There are situations, however, in which the samples are not independent. To put it another way, the samples are *dependent* or *related*. As an example, Nickel Savings and Loan employs two firms, Schadek Appraisals and Bowyer Real Estate, to appraise the value of the real estate properties on which it makes loans. It is important that these two firms be similar in their appraisal values. To review the consistency of the two appraisal firms, Nickel Savings randomly selects 10 homes and has both Schadek Appraisals and Bowyer Real Estate appraise the value of the selected homes. For each home, there will be a pair of appraisal values. That is, for

each home there will be an appraised value from both Schadek Appraisals and Bowyer Real Estate. The appraised values depend on, or are related to, the home selected. This is also referred to as a **paired sample.**

For hypothesis testing, we are interested in the distribution of the *differences* in the appraised value of each home. Hence, there is only one sample. To put it more formally, we are investigating whether the mean of the distribution of differences in the appraised values is 0. The sample is made up of the *differences* between the appraised values determined by Schadek Appraisals and the values from Bowyer Real Estate. If the two appraisal firms are reporting similar estimates, then sometimes Schadek Appraisals will be the higher value and sometimes Bowyer Real Estate will have the higher value. However, the mean of the distribution of differences will be 0. On the other hand, if one of the firms consistently reports the larger appraisal values, then the mean of the distribution of the differences will not be 0.

We will use the symbol μ_d to indicate the population mean of the distribution of differences. We assume the distribution of the population of differences follows the normal distribution. The test statistic follows the *t* distribution and we calculate its value from the following formula:

PAIRED *t* TEST	$$t = \frac{\bar{d}}{s_d/\sqrt{n}}$$	[11–9]

There are $n - 1$ degrees of freedom and

$\bar{d}$ is the mean of the difference between the paired or related observations.

s_d is the standard deviation of the differences between the paired or related observations.

n is the number of paired observations.

The standard deviation of the differences is computed by the familiar formula for the standard deviation (see formula 3–11), except d is substituted for X. The formula is:

$$s_d = \sqrt{\frac{\Sigma(d - \bar{d})^2}{n - 1}}$$

The following example illustrates this test.

Example

Recall that Nickel Savings and Loan wishes to compare the two companies it uses to appraise the value of residential homes. Nickel Savings selected a sample of 10 residential properties and scheduled both firms for an appraisal. The results, reported in $000, are:

Home	Schadek	Bowyer
1	235	228
2	210	205
3	231	219
4	242	240
5	205	198
6	230	223
7	231	227
8	210	215
9	225	222
10	249	245

At the .05 significance level, can we conclude there is a difference in the mean appraised values of the homes?

Solution

The first step is to state the null and the alternate hypotheses. In this case a two-tailed alternative is appropriate because we are interested in determining whether there is a *difference* in the appraised values. We are not interested in showing whether one particular firm appraises property at a higher value than the other. The question is whether the sample differences in the appraised values could have come from a population with a mean of 0. If the population mean of the differences is 0, then we conclude that there is no difference in the appraised values. The null and alternate hypotheses are:

$$H_0: \mu_d = 0$$
$$H_1: \mu_d \neq 0$$

There are 10 homes appraised by both firms, so $n = 10$, and $df = n - 1 = 10 - 1 = 9$. We have a two-tailed test, and the significance level is .05. To determine the critical value, go to Appendix B.2, move across the row with 9 degrees of freedom to the column for a two-tailed test and the .05 significance level. The value at the intersection is 2.262. This value appears in the box in Table 11–2. The decision rule is to reject the null hypothesis if the computed value of t is less than -2.262 or greater than 2.262. Here are the computational details.

Home	Schadek	Bowyer	Difference, d	$(d - \bar{d})$	$(d - \bar{d})^2$
1	235	228	7	2.4	5.76
2	210	205	5	0.4	0.16
3	231	219	12	7.4	54.76
4	242	240	2	-2.6	6.76
5	205	198	7	2.4	5.76
6	230	223	7	2.4	5.76
7	231	227	4	-0.6	0.36
8	210	215	-5	-9.6	92.16
9	225	222	3	-1.6	2.56
10	249	245	4	-0.6	0.36
			46	0	174.40

$$\bar{d} = \frac{\Sigma d}{n} = \frac{46}{10} = 4.60$$

$$s_d = \sqrt{\frac{\Sigma(d - \bar{d})^2}{n - 1}} = \sqrt{\frac{174.4}{10 - 1}} = 4.402$$

Using formula (11–9), the value of the test statistic is 3.305, found by

$$t = \frac{\bar{d}}{s_d/\sqrt{n}} = \frac{4.6}{4.402/\sqrt{10}} = 3.305$$

Because the computed t falls in the rejection region, the null hypothesis is rejected. The population distribution of differences does not have a mean of 0. We conclude that there is a difference in the mean appraised values of the homes. The largest difference of $12,000 is for Home 3. Perhaps that would be an appropriate place to begin a more detailed review.

To find the p-value, we use Appendix B.2 and the section for a two-tailed test. Move along the row with 9 degrees of freedom and find the values of t that are closest to our calculated value. For a .01 significance level, the value of t is 3.250.

The computed value is larger than this value, but smaller than the value of 4.781 corresponding to the .001 significance level. Hence, the *p*-value is less than .01. This information is highlighted in Table 11–2.

TABLE 11–2 A Portion of the *t* Distribution from Appendix B.2

	Confidence Intervals					
	80%	**90%**	**95%**	**98%**	**99%**	**99.9%**
	Level of Significance for One-Tailed Test					
df	**0.10**	**0.05**	**0.025**	**0.01**	**0.005**	**0.0005**
	Level of Significance for Two-Tailed Test					
	0.20	**0.10**	**0.05**	**0.02**	**0.01**	**0.001**
1	3.078	6.314	12.706	31.821	63.657	636.619
2	1.886	2.920	4.303	6.965	9.925	31.599
3	1.638	2.353	3.182	4.541	5.841	12.924
4	1.533	2.132	2.776	3.747	4.604	8.610
5	1.476	2.015	2.571	3.365	4.032	6.869
6	1.440	1.943	2.447	3.143	3.707	5.959
7	1.415	1.895	2.365	2.998	3.499	5.408
8	1.397	1.860	2.306	2.896	3.355	5.041
9	1.383	1.833	2.262	2.821	3.250	4.781
10	1.372	1.812	2.228	2.764	3.169	4.587

Excel has a procedure called "t-Test: Paired Two-Sample for Means" that will perform the calculations of formula (11–9). The output from this procedure is given below.

The computed value of *t* is 3.305, and the two-tailed *p*-value is .009. Because the *p*-value is less than .05, we reject the hypothesis that the mean of the distribution of the differences between the appraised values is zero. In fact, this *p*-value is between .01 and .001. There is a small likelihood that the null hypothesis is true.

	A	B	C	D	E	F	G
					paired t test		
1	Home	Schadek	Bowyer		t-Test: Paired Two Sample for Means		
2	1	235	228				
3	2	210	205			*Schadek*	*Bowyer*
4	3	231	219		Mean	226.800	222.200
5	4	242	240		Variance	208.844	204.178
6	5	205	198		Observations	10.000	10.000
7	6	230	223		Pearson Correlation	0.953	
8	7	231	227		Hypothesized Mean Difference	0.000	
9	8	210	215		df	9.000	
10	9	225	222		t Stat	3.305	
11	10	249	245		P(T<=t) one-tail	0.005	
12					t Critical one-tail	1.833	
13					P(T<=t) two-tail	0.009	
14					t Critical two-tail	2.262	
15							

Comparing Dependent and Independent Samples

Beginning students are often confused by the difference between tests for independent samples [formula (11–6)] and tests for dependent samples [formula (11–9)]. How do we tell the difference between dependent and independent samples? There are two types of dependent samples: (1) those characterized by a measurement, an intervention of some type, and then another measurement; and (2) a matching or pairing of the observations. To explain further:

1. The first type of dependent sample is characterized by a measurement followed by an intervention of some kind and then another measurement. This could be called a "before" and "after" study. Two examples will help to clarify. Suppose we want to show that, by placing speakers in the production area and playing soothing music, we are able to increase production. We begin by selecting a sample of workers and measuring their output under the current conditions. The speakers are then installed in the production area, and we again measure the output of the same workers. There are two measurements, before placing the speakers in the production area and after. The intervention is placing speakers in the production area.

   A second example involves an educational firm that offers courses designed to increase test scores and reading ability. Suppose the firm wants to offer a course that will help high school juniors increase their SAT scores. To begin, each student takes the SAT in the junior year in high school. During the summer between the junior and senior year, they participate in the course that gives them tips on taking tests. Finally, during the fall of their senior year in high school, they retake the SAT. Again, the procedure is characterized by a measurement (taking the SAT as a junior), an intervention (the summer workshops), and another measurement (taking the SAT during their senior year).

2. The second type of dependent sample is characterized by matching or pairing observations. Nickel Savings in the previous example is a dependent sample of this type. It selected a property for appraisal and then had two appraisals on the same property. As a second example, suppose an industrial psychologist wishes to study the intellectual similarities of newly married couples. She selects a sample of newlyweds. Next, she administers a standard intelligence test to both the man and woman to determine the difference in the scores. Notice the matching that occurred: comparing the scores that are paired or matched by marriage.

Why do we prefer dependent samples to independent samples? By using dependent samples, we are able to reduce the variation in the sampling distribution. To illustrate, we will use the Nickel Savings and Loan example just completed. Suppose we assume that we have two independent samples of real estate property for appraisal and conduct the following test of hypothesis, using formula (11–6). The null and alternate hypotheses are:

$$H_0: \mu_1 = \mu_2$$
$$H_1: \mu_1 \neq \mu_2$$

There are now two independent samples of 10 each. So the number of degrees of freedom is $10 + 10 - 2 = 18$. From Appendix B.2, for the .05 significance level, H_0 is rejected if t is less than -2.101 or greater than 2.101.

We use the same Excel commands as on page 97 in Chapter 3 to find the mean and the standard deviation of the two independent samples. We use the Excel commands on page 400 of this chapter to find the pooled variance and the value of the "t Stat." These values are highlighted in yellow.

Excel

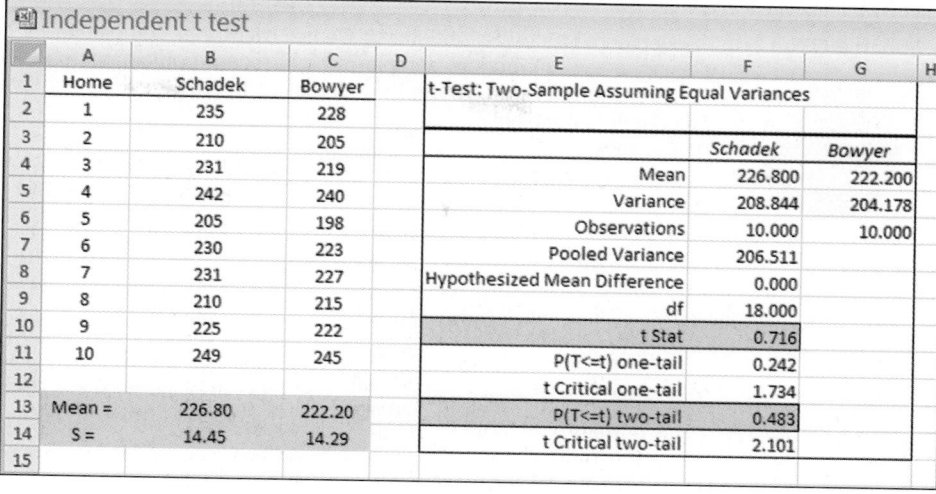

Independent t test

	A	B	C	D	E	F	G	H
1	Home	Schadek	Bowyer		t-Test: Two-Sample Assuming Equal Variances			
2	1	235	228					
3	2	210	205			Schadek	Bowyer	
4	3	231	219		Mean	226.800	222.200	
5	4	242	240		Variance	208.844	204.178	
6	5	205	198		Observations	10.000	10.000	
7	6	230	223		Pooled Variance	206.511		
8	7	231	227		Hypothesized Mean Difference	0.000		
9	8	210	215		df	18.000		
10	9	225	222		t Stat	0.716		
11	10	249	245		P(T<=t) one-tail	0.242		
12					t Critical one-tail	1.734		
13	Mean =	226.80	222.20		P(T<=t) two-tail	0.483		
14	S =	14.45	14.29		t Critical two-tail	2.101		
15								

The mean of the appraised value of the 10 properties by Schadek is $226,800, and the standard deviation is $14,500. For Bowyer Real Estate the mean appraised value is $222,200, and the standard deviation is $14,290. To make the calculations easier, we use $000 instead of $. The value of the pooled estimate of the variance from formula (11–5) is

$$s_p^2 = \frac{(n_1 - 1)s_1^2 + (n_2 - 1)s_2^2}{n_1 + n_2 - 2} = \frac{(10 - 1)(14.45^2) + (10 - 1)(14.29)^2}{10 + 10 - 2} = 206.50$$

From formula (11–6), t is 0.716.

$$t = \frac{\bar{X}_1 - \bar{X}_2}{\sqrt{s_p^2\left(\frac{1}{n_1} + \frac{1}{n_2}\right)}} = \frac{226.8 - 222.2}{\sqrt{206.50\left(\frac{1}{10} + \frac{1}{10}\right)}} = \frac{4.6}{6.4265} = 0.716$$

The computed t (0.716) is less than 2.101, so the null hypothesis is not rejected. We cannot show that there is a difference in the mean appraisal value. That is not the same conclusion that we got before! Why does this happen? The numerator is the same in the paired observations test (4.6). However, the denominator is smaller. In the paired test the denominator is 1.3920 (see the calculations on page 386). In the case of the independent samples, the denominator is 6.4265. There is more variation or uncertainty. This accounts for the difference in the t values and the difference in the statistical decisions. The denominator measures the standard error of the statistic. When the samples are *not* paired, two kinds of variation are present: differences between the two appraisal firms and the difference in the value of the real estate. Properties numbered 4 and 10 have relatively high values, whereas number 5 is relatively low. These data show how different the values of the property are, but we are really interested in the difference between the two appraisal firms.

The trick is to pair the values to reduce the variation among the properties. The paired test uses only the difference between the two appraisal firms for the same property. Thus, the paired or dependent statistic focuses on the variation between Schadek Appraisals and Bowyer Real Estate. Thus, its standard error is always smaller. That, in turn, leads to a larger test statistic and a greater chance of rejecting the null hypothesis. So whenever possible you should pair the data.

There is a bit of bad news here. In the paired observations test, the degrees of freedom are half of what they are if the samples are not paired. For the real estate example, the degrees of freedom drop from 18 to 9 when the observations are paired. However, in most cases, this is a small price to pay for a better test.

Self-Review 11–5

Advertisements by Sylph Fitness Center claim that completing its course will result in losing weight. A random sample of eight recent participants showed the following weights before and after completing the course. At the .01 significance level, can we conclude the students lost weight?

Name	Before	After
Hunter	155	154
Cashman	228	207
Mervine	141	147
Massa	162	157
Creola	211	196
Peterson	164	150
Redding	184	170
Poust	172	165

(a) State the null hypothesis and the alternate hypothesis.
(b) What is the critical value of t?
(c) What is the computed value of t?
(d) Interpret the result. What is the p-value?
(e) What assumption needs to be made about the distribution of the differences?

Exercises

connect

23. The null and alternate hypotheses are:

$$H_0: \mu_d \leq 0$$
$$H_1: \mu_d > 0$$

The following sample information shows the number of defective units produced on the day shift and the afternoon shift for a sample of four days last month.

	Day			
	1	**2**	**3**	**4**
Day shift	10	12	15	19
Afternoon shift	8	9	12	15

At the .05 significance level, can we conclude there are more defects produced on the afternoon shift?

24. The null and alternate hypotheses are:

$$H_0: \mu_d = 0$$
$$H_1: \mu_d \neq 0$$

The following paired observations show the number of traffic citations given for speeding by Officer Dhondt and Officer Meredith of the South Carolina Highway Patrol for the last five months.

	Day				
	May	**June**	**July**	**August**	**September**
Officer Dhondt	30	22	25	19	26
Officer Meredith	26	19	20	15	19

At the .05 significance level, is there a difference in the mean number of citations given by the two officers?

Note: Use the five-step hypothesis testing procedure to solve the following exercises.

25. The management of Discount Furniture, a chain of discount furniture stores in the Northeast, designed an incentive plan for salespeople. To evaluate this innovative plan, 12 salespeople were selected at random, and their weekly incomes before and after the plan were recorded.

Salesperson	Before	After
Sid Mahone	$320	$340
Carol Quick	290	285
Tom Jackson	421	475
Andy Jones	510	510
Jean Sloan	210	210
Jack Walker	402	500
Peg Mancuso	625	631
Anita Loma	560	560
John Cuso	360	365
Carl Utz	431	431
A. S. Kushner	506	525
Fern Lawton	505	619

Was there a significant increase in the typical salesperson's weekly income due to the innovative incentive plan? Use the .05 significance level. Estimate the *p*-value, and interpret it.

26. The federal government recently granted funds for a special program designed to reduce crime in high-crime areas. A study of the results of the program in eight high-crime areas of Miami, Florida, yielded the following results.

	A	B	C	D	E	F	G	H
	\multicolumn{8}{c}{**Number of Crimes by Area**}							
Before	14	7	4	5	17	12	8	9
After	2	7	3	6	8	13	3	5

Has there been a decrease in the number of crimes since the inauguration of the program? Use the .01 significance level. Estimate the *p*-value.

Chapter Summary

I. In comparing two population means we wish to know whether they could be equal.
   A. We are investigating whether the distribution of the difference between the means could have a mean of 0.
   B. The test statistic follows the standard normal distribution if the population standard deviations are known.
      1. No assumption about the shape of either population is required.
      2. The samples are from independent populations.
      3. The formula to compute the value of *z* is

$$z = \frac{\bar{X}_1 - \bar{X}_2}{\sqrt{\dfrac{\sigma_1^2}{n_1} + \dfrac{\sigma_2^2}{n_2}}}$$

[11–2]

II. We can also test whether two samples came from populations with an equal proportion of successes.

A. The two sample proportions are pooled using the following formula:

$$p_c = \frac{X_1 + X_2}{n_1 + n_2}$$ **[11–4]**

B. We compute the value of the test statistic from the following formula:

$$z = \frac{p_1 - p_2}{\sqrt{\dfrac{p_c(1 - p_c)}{n_1} + \dfrac{p_c(1 - p_c)}{n_2}}}$$ **[11–3]**

III. The test statistic to compare two means is the *t* distribution if the population standard deviations are not known.

A. Both populations must follow the normal distribution.

B. The populations must have equal standard deviations.

C. The samples are independent.

D. Finding the value of *t* requires two steps.

1. The first step is to pool the standard deviations according to the following formula:

$$s_p^2 = \frac{(n_1 - 1)s_1^2 + (n_2 - 1)s_2^2}{n_1 + n_2 - 2}$$ **[11–5]**

2. The value of *t* is computed from the following formula:

$$t = \frac{\overline{X}_1 - \overline{X}_2}{\sqrt{s_p^2\left(\dfrac{1}{n_1} + \dfrac{1}{n_2}\right)}}$$ **[11–6]**

3. The degrees of freedom for the test are $n_1 + n_2 - 2$.

IV. If we cannot assume the population standard deviations are equal, we adjust the degrees of freedom and the formula for finding *t*.

A. We determine the degrees of freedom based on the following formula.

$$df = \frac{[(s_1^2/n_1) + (s_2^2/n_2)]^2}{\dfrac{(s_1^2/n_1)^2}{n_1 - 1} + \dfrac{(s_2^2/n_2)^2}{n_2 - 1}}$$ **[11–8]**

B. The value of the test statistic is computed from the following formula.

$$t = \frac{\overline{X}_1 - \overline{X}_2}{\sqrt{\dfrac{s_1^2}{n_1} + \dfrac{s_2^2}{n_2}}}$$ **[11–7]**

V. For dependent samples, we assume the distribution of the paired differences between the populations has a mean of 0.

A. We first compute the mean and the standard deviation of the sample differences.

B. The value of the test statistic is computed from the following formula:

$$t = \frac{\overline{d}}{s_d/\sqrt{n}}$$ **[11–9]**

Pronunciation Key

SYMBOL	MEANING	PRONUNCIATION
p_c	Pooled proportion	p sub c
s_p^2	Pooled sample variance	s sub p squared
$\overline{X}_1$	Mean of the first sample	X bar sub 1
$\overline{X}_2$	Mean of the second sample	X bar sub 2
$\overline{d}$	Mean of the difference between dependent observations	d bar
s_d	Standard deviation of the difference between dependent observations	s sub d

Chapter Exercises

connect

27. A recent study focused on the number of times men and women who live alone buy take-out dinner in a month. The information is summarized below.

Statistic	Men	Women
Sample mean	24.51	22.69
Population standard deviation	4.48	3.86
Sample size	35	40

At the .01 significance level, is there a difference in the mean number of times men and women order take-out dinners in a month? What is the *p*-value?

28. Clark Heter is an industrial engineer at Lyons Products. He would like to determine whether there are more units produced on the night shift than on the day shift. Assume the population standard deviation for the number of units produced on the day shift is 21 and is 28 on the night shift. A sample of 54 day-shift workers showed that the mean number of units produced was 345. A sample of 60 night-shift workers showed that the mean number of units produced was 351. At the .05 significance level, is the number of units produced on the night shift larger?

29. Fry Brothers Heating and Air Conditioning, Inc., employs Larry Clark and George Murnen to make service calls to repair furnaces and air conditioning units in homes. Tom Fry, the owner, would like to know whether there is a difference in the mean number of service calls they make per day. Assume the population standard deviation for Larry Clark is 1.05 calls per day and 1.23 calls per day for George Murnen. A random sample of 40 days last year showed that Larry Clark made an average of 4.77 calls per day. For a sample of 50 days George Murnen made an average of 5.02 calls per day. At the .05 significance level, is there a difference in the mean number of calls per day between the two employees? What is the *p*-value?

30. A coffee manufacturer is interested in whether the mean daily consumption of regular-coffee drinkers is less than that of decaffeinated-coffee drinkers. Assume the population standard deviation for those drinking regular coffee is 1.20 cups per day and 1.36 cups per day for those drinking decaffeinated coffee. A random sample of 50 regular-coffee drinkers showed a mean of 4.35 cups per day. A sample of 40 decaffeinated-coffee drinkers showed a mean of 5.84 cups per day. Use the .01 significance level. Compute the *p*-value.

31. A cell phone company offers two plans to its subscribers. At the time new subscribers sign up, they are asked to provide some demographic information. The mean yearly income for a sample of 40 subscribers to Plan A is $57,000 with a standard deviation of $9,200. This distribution is positively skewed; the actual coefficient of skewness is 2.11. For a sample of 30 subscribers to Plan B the mean income is $61,000 with a standard deviation of $7,100. The distribution of Plan B subscribers is also positively skewed, but not as severely. The coefficient of skewness is 1.54. At the .05 significance level, is it reasonable to conclude the mean income of those selecting Plan B is larger? What is the *p*-value? Do the coefficients of skewness affect the results of the hypothesis test? Why?

32. A computer manufacturer offers a help line that purchasers can call for help 24 hours a day, 7 days a week. Clearing these calls for help in a timely fashion is important to the company's image. After telling the caller that resolution of the problem is important the caller is asked whether the issue is software or hardware related. The mean time it takes a technician to resolve a software issue is 18 minutes with a standard deviation of 4.2 minutes. This information was obtained from a sample of 35 monitored calls. For a study of 45 hardware issues, the mean time for the technician to resolve the problem was 15.5 minutes with a standard deviation of 3.9 minutes. This information was also obtained from monitored calls. At the .05 significance level does it take longer to resolve software issues? What is the *p*-value?

33. Suppose the manufacturer of Advil, a common headache remedy, recently developed a new formulation of the drug that is claimed to be more effective. To evaluate the new drug, a sample of 200 current users is asked to try it. After a one-month trial, 180 indicated the new drug was more effective in relieving a headache. At the same time a sample of 300 current Advil users is given the current drug but told it is the new formulation. From this group, 261 said it was an improvement. At the .05 significance level can we conclude that the new drug is more effective?

34. Each month the National Association of Purchasing Managers publishes the NAPM index. One of the questions asked on the survey to purchasing agents is: Do you think the economy is contracting? Last month, of the 300 responses, 160 answered yes to the question. This month, 170 of the 290 responses indicated they felt the economy was contracting. At the .05 significance level, can we conclude that a larger proportion of the agents believe the economy is contracting this month?

35. As part of a recent survey among dual-wage-earner couples, an industrial psychologist found that 990 men out of the 1,500 surveyed believed the division of household duties was fair. A sample of 1,600 women found 970 believed the division of household duties was fair. At the .01 significance level, is it reasonable to conclude that the proportion of men who believe the division of household duties is fair is larger? What is the *p*-value?

36. There are two major Internet providers in the Colorado Springs, Colorado, area, one called HTC and the other Mountain Communications. We want to investigate whether there is a difference in the proportion of times a customer is able to access the Internet. During a one-week period, 500 calls were placed at random times throughout the day and night to HTC. A connection was made to the Internet on 450 occasions. A similar one-week study with Mountain Communications showed the Internet to be available on 352 of 400 trials. At the .01 significance level, is there a difference in the percent of time that access to the Internet is successful?

37. In a poll recently conducted at Iowa State University, 68 out of 98 male students and 45 out of 85 female students expressed "at least some support" for implementing an "exit strategy" from Iraq. Test at the .05 significance level the null hypothesis that the population proportions are equal against the two-tailed alternative.

38. A study was conducted to determine if there was a difference in the humor content in British and American trade magazine advertisements. In an independent random sample of 270 American trade magazine advertisements, 56 were humorous. An independent random sample of 203 British trade magazines contained 52 humorous ads. Does this data provide evidence at the .05 significance level that there is a difference in the proportion of humorous ads in British versus American trade magazines?

39. Century Business Products tested 180 computers with 8-bit microcontrollers and found that 13 failed to perform adequately on a compliance test. The same test was applied to a sample of 67 32-bit CPUs and 7 of those failed. Use the 0.05 significance level to test if it is reasonable to conclude that the 32-bit machines are not performing as well as the 8-bit ones?

40. The National Basketball Association had 39 black top executives (presidents or vice presidents) among its 388 senior managers. Meanwhile Major League Baseball had only 11 blacks among its 307 top administrators. Test at the .05 significance level if this reveals the NBA has significantly more black participation in higher levels of management.

41. One of the music industry's most pressing questions is: Can paid download stores contend nose-to-nose with free peer-to-peer download services? Data gathered over the last 12 months show Apple's iTunes was used by an average of 1.65 million households with a sample standard deviation of 0.56 million family units. Over the same 12 months WinMX (a no-cost P2P download service) was used by an average of 2.2 million families with a sample standard deviation of 0.30 million. Assume the population standard deviations are not the same. Using a significance level of 0.05, test the hypothesis of no difference in the mean number of households picking either variety of service to download songs.

42. Businesses, particularly those in the food preparation industry such as General Mills, Kellogg, and Betty Crocker regularly use coupons as a brand allegiance builder to stimulate their retailing. There is uneasiness that the users of paper coupons are different from the users of e-coupons (coupons disseminated by means of the Internet). One survey recorded the age of each person who redeemed a coupon along with the type (either electronic or paper). The sample of 35 e-coupon users had a mean age of 33.6 years with a standard deviation of 10.9, while a similar sample of 25 traditional paper-coupon clippers had a mean age of 39.5 with a standard deviation of 4.8. Assume the population standard deviations are not the same. Using a significance level of 0.01, test the hypothesis of no difference in the mean ages of the two groups of coupon clients.

43. The owner of Bun 'N' Run Hamburgers wishes to compare the sales per day at two locations. The mean number sold for 10 randomly selected days at the Northside site was 83.55, and the standard deviation was 10.50. For a random sample of 12 days at the Southside location, the mean number sold was 78.80 and the standard deviation was 14.25. At the .05 significance level, is there a difference in the mean number of hamburgers sold at the two locations? What is the *p*-value?

44. The Engineering Department at Sims Software, Inc., recently developed two chemical solutions designed to increase the usable life of computer disks. A sample of disks treated with the first solution lasted 86, 78, 66, 83, 84, 81, 84, 109, 65, and 102 hours. Those treated with the second solution lasted 91, 71, 75, 76, 87, 79, 73, 76, 79, 78, 87, 90, 76, and 72 hours. Assume the population standard deviations are not the same. At the .10 significance level, can we conclude that there is a difference in the length of time the two types of treatment lasted?

45. The Willow Run Outlet Mall has two Haggar Outlet Stores, one located on Peach Street and the other on Plum Street. The two stores are laid out differently, but both store managers claim their layout maximizes the amounts customers will purchase on impulse. A sample of 10 customers at the Peach Street store revealed they spent the following amounts more than planned: $17.58, $19.73, $12.61, $17.79, $16.22, $15.82, $15.40, $15.86, $11.82, and $15.85. A sample of 14 customers at the Plum Street store revealed they spent the following amounts more than they planned: $18.19, $20.22, $17.38, $17.96, $23.92, $15.87, $16.47, $15.96, $16.79, $16.74, $21.40, $20.57, $19.79, and $14.83. At the .01 significance level, is there a difference in the mean amounts purchased on impulse at the two stores?

46. Grand Strand Family Medical Center is specifically set up to treat minor medical emergencies for visitors to the Myrtle Beach area. There are two facilities, one in the Little River Area and the other in Murrells Inlet. The Quality Assurance Department wishes to compare the mean waiting time for patients at the two locations. Samples of the waiting times, reported in minutes, follow:

Location	Waiting Time										
Little River	31.73	28.77	29.53	22.08	29.47	18.60	32.94	25.18	29.82	26.49	
Murrells Inlet	22.93	23.92	26.92	27.20	26.44	25.62	30.61	29.44	23.09	23.10	26.69	22.31

Assume the population standard deviations are not the same. At the .05 significance level, is there a difference in the mean waiting time?

47. Commercial Bank and Trust Company is studying the use of its automatic teller machines (ATMs). Of particular interest is whether young adults (under 25 years) use the machines more than senior citizens. To investigate further, samples of customers under 25 years of age and customers over 60 years of age were selected. The number of ATM transactions last month was determined for each selected individual, and the results are shown below. At the .01 significance level, can bank management conclude that younger customers use the ATMs more?

Under 25	10	10	11	15	7	11	10	9		
Over 60	4	8	7	7	4	5	1	7	4	10	5

48. Two boats, the *Prada* (Italy) and the *Oracle* (U.S.A.), are competing for a spot in the upcoming *America's Cup* race. They race over a part of the course several times. Below are the sample times in minutes. Assume the population standard deviations are not the same. At the .05 significance level, can we conclude that there is a difference in their mean times?

Boat	Time (minutes)										
Prada (Italy)	12.9	12.5	11.0	13.3	11.2	11.4	11.6	12.3	14.2	11.3	
Oracle (U.S.A.)	14.1	14.1	14.2	17.4	15.8	16.7	16.1	13.3	13.4	13.6	10.8	19.0

49. The manufacturer of an MP3 player wanted to know whether a 10 percent reduction in price is enough to increase the sales of its product. To investigate, the owner randomly selected eight outlets and sold the MP3 player at the reduced price. At seven randomly selected outlets, the MP3 player was sold at the regular price. Reported below is the number of units sold last month at the sampled outlets. At the .01 significance level, can the manufacturer conclude that the price reduction resulted in an increase in sales?

Regular price	138	121	88	115	141	125	96	
Reduced price	128	134	152	135	114	106	112	120

50. A number of minor automobile accidents occur at various high-risk intersections in Teton County despite traffic lights. The Traffic Department claims that a modification in the type of light will reduce these accidents. The county commissioners have agreed to a proposed experiment. Eight intersections were chosen at random, and the lights at those intersections were modified. The numbers of minor accidents during a six-month period before and after the modifications were:

	Number of Accidents							
	A	B	C	D	E	F	G	H
Before modification	5	7	6	4	8	9	8	10
After modification	3	7	7	0	4	6	8	2

At the .01 significance level is it reasonable to conclude that the modification reduced the number of traffic accidents?

51. Lester Hollar is vice president for human resources for a large manufacturing company. In recent years he has noticed an increase in absenteeism that he thinks is related to the general health of the employees. Four years ago, in an attempt to improve the situation, he began a fitness program in which employees exercise during their lunch hour. To evaluate the program, he selected a random sample of eight participants and found the number of days each was absent in the six months before the exercise program began and in the last six months. Below are the results. At the .05 significance level, can he conclude that the number of absences has declined? Estimate the p-value.

Employee	Before	After
1	6	5
2	6	2
3	7	1
4	7	3
5	4	3
6	3	6
7	5	3
8	6	7

52. The president of the American Insurance Institute wants to compare the yearly costs of auto insurance offered by two leading companies. He selects a sample of 15 families, some with only a single insured driver, others with several teenage drivers, and pays each family a stipend to contact the two companies and ask for a price quote. To make the data comparable, certain features, such as the deductible amount and limits of liability, are standardized. The sample information is reported below. At the .10 significance level, can we conclude that there is a difference in the amounts quoted?

Family	Progressive Car Insurance	GEICO Mutual Insurance
Becker	$2,090	$1,610
Berry	1,683	1,247
Cobb	1,402	2,327
Debuck	1,830	1,367
DuBrul	930	1,461
Eckroate	697	1,789
German	1,741	1,621
Glasson	1,129	1,914
King	1,018	1,956
Kucic	1,881	1,772
Meredith	1,571	1,375
Obeid	874	1,527
Price	1,579	1,767
Phillips	1,577	1,636
Tresize	860	1,188

53. Fairfield Homes is developing two parcels near Pigeon Fork, Tennessee. In order to test different advertising approaches, it uses different media to reach potential buyers. The mean annual family income for 15 people making inquiries at the first development is $150,000, with a standard deviation of $40,000. A corresponding sample of 25 people at the second development had a mean of $180,000, with a standard deviation of $30,000. Assume the population standard deviations are the same. At the .05 significance level, can Fairfield conclude that the population means are different?

54. The following data resulted from a taste test of two different chocolate bars. The first number is a rating of the taste, which could range from 0 to 5, with a 5 indicating the person liked the taste. The second number indicates whether a "secret ingredient" was present. If the ingredient was present a code of 1 was used and a 0 otherwise. Assume the population standard deviations are the same. At the .05 significance level, do these data show a difference in the taste ratings?

Rating	With/Without	Rating	With/Without
3	1	1	1
1	1	4	0
0	0	4	0
2	1	2	1
3	1	3	0
1	1	4	0

55. An investigation of the effectiveness of an antibacterial soap in reducing operating room contamination resulted in the accompanying table. The new soap was tested in a sample of eight operating rooms in the greater Seattle area during the last year.

	Operating Room							
	A	B	C	D	E	F	G	H
Before	6.6	6.5	9.0	10.3	11.2	8.1	6.3	11.6
After	6.8	2.4	7.4	8.5	8.1	6.1	3.4	2.0

At the 0.05 significance level, can we conclude the contamination measurements are lower after use of the new soap?

56. The following data on annual rates of return were collected from five stocks listed on the New York Stock Exchange ("the big board") and five stocks listed on NASDAQ. Assume the population standard deviations are the same. At the .10 significance level, can we conclude that the annual rates of return are higher on the big board?

NYSE	NASDAQ
17.16	15.80
17.08	16.28
15.51	16.21
8.43	17.97
25.15	7.77

57. The city of Laguna Beach operates two public parking lots. The one on Ocean Drive can accommodate up to 125 cars and the one on Rio Rancho can accommodate up to 130 cars. City planners are considering both increasing the size of the lots and changing the fee structure. To begin, the Planning Office would like some information on the number of cars in the lots at various times of the day. A junior planner officer is assigned the task of visiting the two lots at random times of the day and evening and counting the number of cars in the lots. The study lasted over a period of one month. Below is the number of cars in the lots for 25 visits of the Ocean Drive lot and 28 visits of the Rio Rancho lot. Assume the population standard deviations are equal.

Ocean Drive												
89	115	93	79	113	77	51	75	118	105	106	91	54
63	121	53	81	115	67	53	69	95	121	88	64	
Rio Rancho												
128	110	81	126	82	114	93	40	94	45	84	71	74
92	66	69	100	114	113	107	62	77	80	107	90	129
105	124											

Is it reasonable to conclude that there is a difference in the mean number of cars in the two lots? Use the .05 significance level.

58. The amount of income spent on housing is an important component of the cost of living. The total costs of housing for homeowners might include mortgage payments, property taxes, and utility costs (water, heat, electricity). An economist selected a sample of 20 homeowners in New England and then calculated these total housing costs as a percent of monthly income, five years ago and now. The information is reported below. Is it reasonable to conclude the percent is less now than five years ago?

Homeowner	Five Years Ago	Now	Homeowner	Five Years Ago	Now
1	17%	10%	11	35%	32%
2	20	39	12	16	32
3	29	37	13	23	21
4	43	27	14	33	12
5	36	12	15	44	40
6	43	41	16	44	42
7	45	24	17	28	22
8	19	26	18	29	19
9	49	28	19	39	35
10	49	26	20	22	12

59-60. Use this information to do exercises 59 and 60. The drivers, ages, odds against winning, row of their starting position, and car number for the 2008 Indianapolis 500 motorcar race are listed below. Use the .01 significance level.

Driver	Age	Odds	Row	Car Number	Driver	Age	Odds	Row	Car Number
Dixon	27	4	1	9	Hamilton	45	100	6	22
Wheldon	29	4	1	10	Lloyd	23	200	7	16
Briscoe	26	4	1	6	Hunter-Reay	27	100	7	17
Castroneves	33	4	2	3	Andretti, J	45	100	7	24
Patrick	26	8	2	7	Fisher	27	200	8	67
Kanaan	33	4	2	11	Power	27	100	8	8
Andretti, M	21	8	3	26	Simmons	31	200	8	41
Meira	31	25	3	4	Servia	33	150	9	5
Mutoh	25	20	3	27	Viso	23	200	9	33
Carpenter	27	50	4	20	Duno	36	200	9	23
Scheckter	27	45	4	12	Moraes	19	200	10	19
Bell	33	200	4	99	Bernoldi	29	200	10	36
Rahal	19	40	5	6	Camara	27	200	10	34
Manning	33	100	5	14	Foyt	24	150	11	2
Junqueira	31	75	5	18	Lazier	40	150	11	91
Wilson	29	50	6	2	Roth	49	300	11	25
Rice	32	50	6	15					

59. Is it reasonable to conclude that starting in the first five rows significantly reduces the odds against winning in contrast to the last four rows?

60. Does having a car number of 20 or below significantly change the odds of winning?

Data Set Exercises

61. Refer to the Real Estate data, which report information on the homes sold in Denver, Colorado, last year.

    a. At the .05 significance level, can we conclude that there is a difference in the mean selling price of homes with a pool and homes without a pool?

    b. At the .05 significance level, can we conclude that there is a difference in the mean selling price of homes with an attached garage and homes without an attached garage?

    c. At the .05 significance level, can we conclude that there is a difference in the mean selling price of homes in Township 1 and Township 2?

    d. Find the median selling price of the homes. Divide the homes into two groups, those that sold for more than (or equal to) the median price and those that sold for less. Is there a difference in the proportion of homes with a pool for those that sold at or above the median price versus those that sold for less than the median price? Use the .05 significance level.

62. Refer to the Baseball 2007 data, which report information on the 30 Major League Baseball teams for the 2007 season.

    a. At the .05 significance level, can we conclude that there is a difference in the mean salary of teams in the American League versus teams in the National League?

    b. At the .05 significance level, can we conclude that there is a difference in the mean home attendance of teams in the American League versus teams in the National League?

    c. Compute the mean and the standard deviation of the number of wins for the 10 teams with the highest salaries. Do the same for the 10 teams with the lowest salaries. At the .05 significance level is there a difference in the mean number of wins for the two groups?

63. Refer to the Wage data, which report information on annual wages for a sample of 100 workers. Also included are variables relating to industry, years of education, and gender for each worker.

    a. Conduct a test of hypothesis to determine if there is a difference in the mean annual wages of Southern residents versus non-Southern residents.

    b. Conduct a test of hypothesis to determine if there is a difference in the mean annual wages of white and non-white wage earners.

    c. Conduct a test of hypothesis to determine if there is a difference in the mean annual wages of Hispanic and non-Hispanic wage earners.

    d. Conduct a test of hypothesis to determine if there is a difference in the mean annual wages of female and male wage earners.

    e. Conduct a test of hypothesis to determine if there is a difference in the mean annual wages of married and nonmarried wage earners.

64. Refer to the CIA data, which report demographic and economic information on 46 countries. Conduct a test of hypothesis to determine whether the mean percent of the population over 65 years of age in G-20 countries is different from those that are not G-20 members.

Software Commands

1. The MINITAB commands for the two-sample test of proportions on page 374 are:

    a. From the toolbar, select **Stat, Basic Statistics,** and then **2 Proportions.**

    b. In the next dialog box select **Summarized data,** in the row labeled **First** enter *100* for **Trials** and *19* for **Events.** In the row labeled **Second** put *200* for **Trials** and *62* for **Events.** Then click on **Options** and select **Use pooled estimate of *p* for test,** finally click **OK** twice.

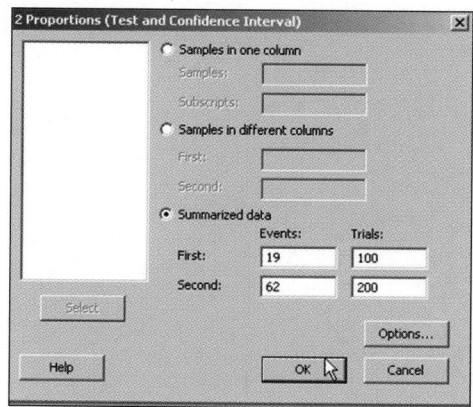

2. The Excel commands for the two-sample *t*-test on page 379 are:
   a. Enter the data into columns A and B (or any other columns) in the spreadsheet. Use the first row of each column to enter the variable name.
   b. Select the **Data** tab on the top menu. Then, on the far right, select **Data Analysis.** Select **t-Test: Two Sample Assuming Equal Variances,** then click **OK.**
   c. In the dialog box indicate that the range of **Variable 1** is from *A1* to *A6* and **Variable 2** from *B1* to *B7,* the **Hypothesized Mean Difference** is *0,* click **Labels, Alpha** is *0.05,* and the **Output Range** is *D1*. Click **OK.**

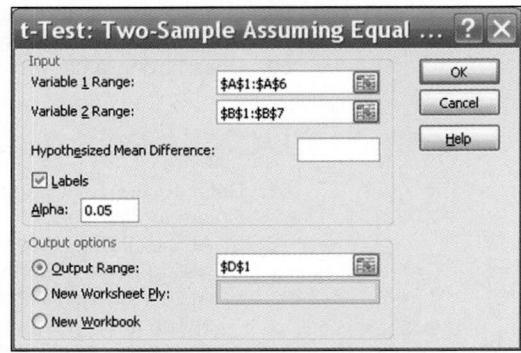

3. The MINITAB commands for the two-sample *t*-test on page 383 are:
   a. Put the amount absorbed by the Store brand in *C1* and the amount absorbed by the Name brand paper towel in *C2*.
   b. From the toolbar select **Stat, Basic Statistics,** and then **2-Sample** and click.
   c. In the next dialog box select **Samples in different columns,** select *C1* Store for the **First** column and *C2* Name of the **Second** and click **OK.**

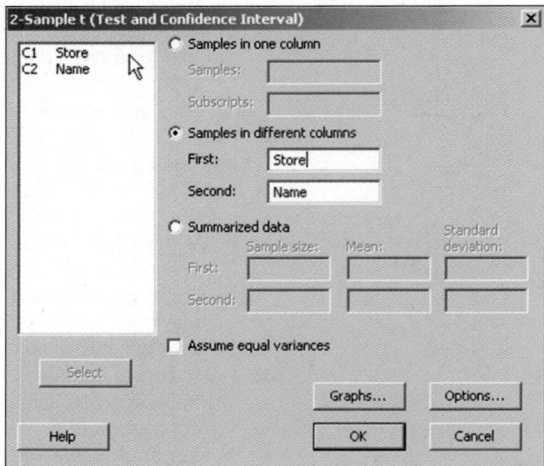

4. The Excel commands for the paired *t*-test on page 387 are:
   a. Enter the data into columns B and C (or any other two columns) in the spreadsheet, with the variable names in the first row.
   b. Select the **Data** tab on the top menu. Then, on the far right, select **Data Analysis.** Select **t-Test: Paired Two Sample for Means,** then click **OK.**
   c. In the dialog box indicate that the range of **Variable 1** is from *B1* to *B11* and **Variable 2** from *C1* to *C11,* the **Hypothesized Mean Difference** is *0,* click **Labels, Alpha** is *.05,* and the **Output Range** is *E1*. Click **OK.**

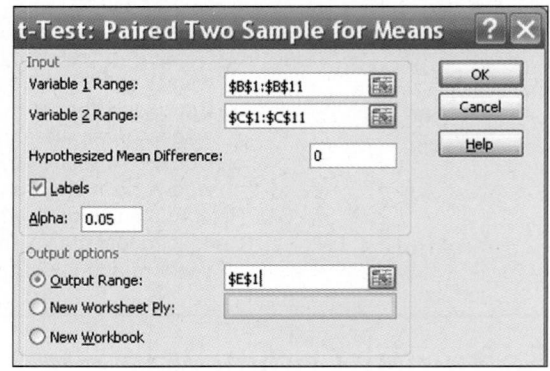

Chapter 11   Answers to Self-Review

11–1 **a.** $H_0: \mu_W \leq \mu_M$
$H_1: \mu_W > \mu_M$
The subscript W refers to the women and M to the men.
b. Reject H_0 if $z > 1.65$
c. $z = \dfrac{\$1{,}500 - \$1{,}400}{\sqrt{\dfrac{(\$250)^2}{50} + \dfrac{(\$200)^2}{40}}} = 2.11$
d. Reject the null hypothesis
e. $p\text{-value} = .5000 - .4826 = .0174$
f. The mean amount sold per day is larger for women.

11–2 **a.** $H_0: \pi_1 = \pi_2$
$H_1: \pi_1 \neq \pi_2$
b. .10
c. Two-tailed
d. Reject H_0 if z is less than -1.65 or greater than 1.65.
e. $p_c = \dfrac{87 + 123}{150 + 200} = \dfrac{210}{350} = .60$
$p_1 = \dfrac{87}{150} = .58 \qquad p_2 = \dfrac{123}{200} = .615$
$z = \dfrac{.58 - .615}{\sqrt{\dfrac{.60(.40)}{150} + \dfrac{.60(.40)}{200}}} = -0.66$
f. Do not reject H_0.
g. $p\text{-value} = 2(.5000 - .2454) = .5092$
There is no difference in the proportion of adults and children that liked the proposed flavor.

11–3 **a.** $H_0: \mu_d = \mu_a$
$H_1: \mu_d \neq \mu_a$
b. $df = 6 + 8 - 2 = 12$
Reject H_0 if t is less than -2.179 or t is greater than 2.179.
c. $\bar{X}_1 = \dfrac{42}{6} = 7.00 \quad s_1 = \sqrt{\dfrac{10}{6-1}} = 1.4142$
$\bar{X}_2 = \dfrac{80}{8} = 10.00 \quad s_2 = \sqrt{\dfrac{36}{8-1}} = 2.2678$
$s_p^2 = \dfrac{(6-1)(1.4142)^2 + (8-1)(2.2678)^2}{6+8-2}$
$= 3.8333$
$t = \dfrac{7.00 - 10.00}{\sqrt{3.8333\left(\dfrac{1}{6} + \dfrac{1}{8}\right)}} = -2.837$
d. Reject H_0 because -2.837 is less than the critical value.
e. The p-value is less than .02.
f. The mean number of defects is not the same on the two shifts.
g. Independent populations, populations follow the normal distribution, populations have equal standard deviations.

11–4 **a.** $H_0: \mu_c \geq \mu_a \qquad H_1: \mu_c < \mu_a$
b. $df = \dfrac{[(356^2/10) + (857^2/8)]^2}{\dfrac{(356^2/10)^2}{10-1} + \dfrac{(857^2/8)^2}{8-1}} = 8.93$
so $df = 8$
c. Reject H_0 if $t < -1.860$
d. $t = \dfrac{\$1{,}568 - \$1{,}967}{\sqrt{\dfrac{356^2}{10} + \dfrac{857^2}{8}}} = \dfrac{-399.00}{323.23} = -1.234$
e. Do not reject H_0.
f. There is no difference in the mean account balance of those who applied for their card or were contacted by a telemarketer.

11–5 **a.** $H_0: \mu_d \leq 0, H_1: \mu_d > 0$.
b. Reject H_0 if $t > 2.998$
c.

Name	Before	After	d	$(d - \bar{d})$	$(d - \bar{d})^2$
Hunter	155	154	1	−7.875	62.0156
Cashman	228	207	21	12.125	147.0156
Mervine	141	147	−6	−14.875	221.2656
Massa	162	157	5	−3.875	15.0156
Creola	211	196	15	6.125	37.5156
Peterson	164	150	14	5.125	26.2656
Redding	184	170	14	5.125	26.2656
Poust	172	165	7	−1.875	3.5156
			71		538.8750

$\bar{d} = \dfrac{71}{8} = 8.875$

$s_d = \sqrt{\dfrac{538.875}{8-1}} = 8.774$

$t = \dfrac{8.875}{8.774/\sqrt{8}} = 2.861$

d. Do not reject H_0. We cannot conclude that the students lost weight. The p-value is less than .025 but larger than .01.
e. The distribution of the differences must follow a normal distribution.

12

GOALS

When you have completed this chapter, you will be able to:

1 List the characteristics of the *F* distribution.

2 Conduct a test of hypothesis to determine whether the variances of two populations are equal.

3 Discuss the general idea of *analysis of variance*.

4 Organize data into a *one-way* and a *two-way ANOVA table*.

5 Conduct a test of hypothesis among three or more treatment means.

6 Develop confidence intervals for the difference in treatment means.

7 Conduct a test of hypothesis among treatment means using a blocking variable.

8 Conduct a two-way ANOVA with interaction.

Analysis of Variance

A computer manufacturer is about to unveil a new, faster personal computer. The new machine clearly is faster, but initial tests indicate there is more variation in the processing time, which depends on the program being run, and the amount of input and output data. A sample of 16 computer runs, covering a range of production jobs, showed that the standard deviation of the processing time was 22 (hundredths of a second) for the new machine and 12 (hundredths of a second) for the current machine. At the .05 significance level, can we conclude that there is more variation in the processing time of the new machine? (Exercise 24, Goal 2.)

Introduction

In this chapter we continue our discussion of hypothesis testing. Recall that in Chapters 10 and 11 we examined the general theory of hypothesis testing. We described the case where a sample was selected from the population. We used the z distribution (the standard normal distribution) or the t distribution to determine whether it was reasonable to conclude that the population mean was equal to a specified value. We tested whether two population means are the same. We also conducted both one- and two-sample tests for population proportions, using the standard normal distribution as the distribution of the test statistic. In this chapter we expand our idea of hypothesis tests. We describe a test for variances and then a test that simultaneously compares several means to determine if they came from equal populations.

The *F* Distribution

The probability distribution used in this chapter is the F distribution. It was named to honor Sir Ronald Fisher, one of the founders of modern-day statistics. The test statistic for several situations follows this probability distribution. It is used to test whether two samples are from populations having equal variances, and it is also applied when we want to compare several population means simultaneously. The simultaneous comparison of several population means is called **analysis of variance (ANOVA).** In both of these situations, the populations must follow a normal distribution, and the data must be at least interval-scale.

What are the characteristics of the F distribution?

Characteristics of the
F distribution

1. **There is a family of *F* distributions.** A particular member of the family is determined by two parameters: the degrees of freedom in the numerator and the degrees of freedom in the denominator. The shape of the distribution is illustrated by the following graph. There is one F distribution for the combination of 29 degrees of freedom in the numerator (df) and 28 degrees of freedom in the denominator. There is another F distribution for 19 degrees in the numerator and 6 degrees of freedom in the denominator. The final distribution shown has 6 degrees of freedom in the numerator and 6 degrees of freedom in the denominator. We will describe the concept of degrees of freedom later in the chapter. Note that the shapes of the distributions change as the degrees of freedom change.

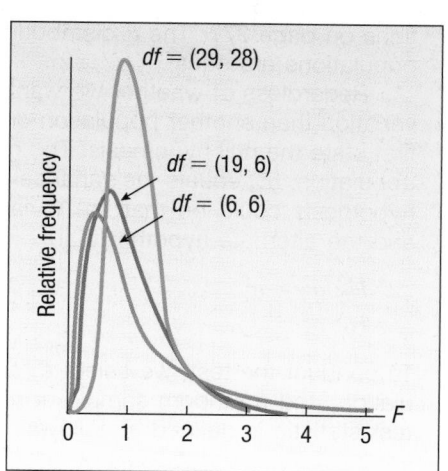

2. **The *F* distribution is continuous.** This means that it can assume an infinite number of values between zero and positive infinity.
3. **The *F* distribution cannot be negative.** The smallest value F can assume is 0.

4. **It is positively skewed.** The long tail of the distribution is to the right-hand side. As the number of degrees of freedom increases in both the numerator and denominator the distribution approaches a normal distribution.

5. **It is asymptotic.** As the values of X increase, the F distribution approaches the X-axis but never touches it. This is similar to the behavior of the normal probability distribution, described in Chapter 7.

Comparing Two Population Variances

The first application of the F distribution that we describe occurs when we test the hypothesis that the variance of one normal population equals the variance of another normal population. The following examples will show the use of the test:

- Two Barth shearing machines are set to produce steel bars of the same length. The bars, therefore, should have the same mean length. We want to ensure that in addition to having the same mean length they also have similar variation.

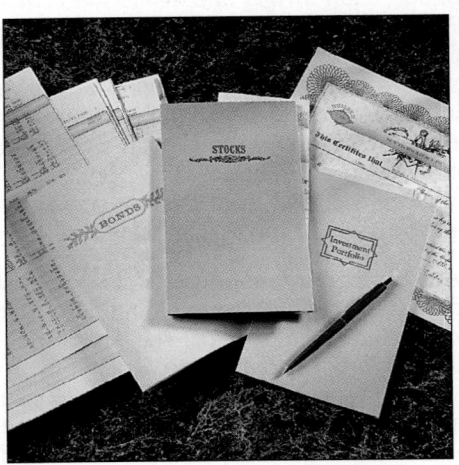

- The mean rate of return on two types of common stock may be the same, but there may be more variation in the rate of return in one than the other. A sample of 10 technology and 10 utility stocks shows the same mean rate of return, but there is likely more variation in the technology stocks.

- A study by the marketing department for a large newspaper found that men and women spent about the same amount of time per day surfing the Net. However, the same report indicated there was nearly twice as much variation in time spent per day among the men than the women.

The F distribution is also used to test assumptions for some statistical tests. Recall that in the previous chapter we used the t test to investigate whether the means of two independent populations differed. To employ that test, we sometimes assume that the variances of two normal populations are the same. See this list of assumptions on page 377. The F distribution is used to test if the variances of two normal populations are equal.

Regardless of whether we want to determine whether one population has more variation than another population or validate an assumption for a statistical test, we first state the null hypothesis. The null hypothesis is that the variance of one normal population, σ_1^2, equals the variance of the other normal population, σ_2^2. The alternate hypothesis could be that the variances differ. In this instance the null hypothesis and the alternate hypothesis are:

$$H_0: \sigma_1^2 = \sigma_2^2$$
$$H_1: \sigma_1^2 \neq \sigma_2^2$$

To conduct the test, we select a random sample of n_1 observations from one population, and a random sample of n_2 observations from the second population. The test statistic is defined as follows.

TEST STATISTIC FOR COMPARING TWO VARIANCES	$F = \dfrac{s_1^2}{s_2^2}$	[12–1]

The terms s_1^2 and s_2^2 are the respective sample variances. If the null hypothesis is true, the test statistic follows the F distribution with $n_1 - 1$ and $n_2 - 1$ degrees of freedom. In order to reduce the size of the table of critical values, the *larger* sample variance is placed in the numerator; hence, the tabled F ratio is always larger than 1.00. Thus, the right-tail critical value is the only one required. The critical value of F for a two-tailed test is found by dividing the significance level in half ($\alpha/2$) and then referring to the appropriate degrees of freedom in Appendix B.4. An example will illustrate.

Example

Lammers Limos offers limousine service from the city hall in Toledo, Ohio, to Metro Airport in Detroit. Sean Lammers, president of the company, is considering two routes. One is via U.S. 25 and the other via I-75. He wants to study the time it takes to drive to the airport using each route and then compare the results. He collected the following sample data, which is reported in minutes. Using the .10 significance level, is there a difference in the variation in the driving times for the two routes?

U.S. Route 25	Interstate 75
52	59
67	60
56	61
45	51
70	56
54	63
64	57
	65

Solution

The mean driving times along the two routes are nearly the same. The mean time is 58.29 minutes for the U.S. 25 route and 59.0 minutes along the I-75 route. However, in evaluating travel times, Mr. Lammers is also concerned about the variation in the travel times. The first step is to compute the two sample variances. We'll use formula (3–11) to compute the sample standard deviations. To obtain the sample variances, we square the standard deviations.

U.S. Route 25

$$\bar{X} = \frac{\Sigma X}{n} = \frac{408}{7} = 58.29 \qquad s = \sqrt{\frac{\Sigma(X - \bar{X})^2}{n - 1}} = \sqrt{\frac{485.43}{7 - 1}} = 8.9947$$

Interstate 75

$$\bar{X} = \frac{\Sigma X}{n} = \frac{472}{8} = 59.00 \qquad s = \sqrt{\frac{\Sigma(X - \bar{X})^2}{n - 1}} = \sqrt{\frac{134}{8 - 1}} = 4.3753$$

There is more variation, as measured by the standard deviation, in the U.S. 25 route than in the I-75 route. This is consistent with his knowledge of the two routes; the U.S. 25 route contains more stoplights, whereas I-75 is a limited-access interstate highway. However, the I-75 route is several miles longer. It is important that the service offered be both timely and consistent, so he decides to conduct a statistical test to determine whether there really is a difference in the variation of the two routes.

The usual five-step hypothesis-testing procedure will be employed.

Step 1: We begin by stating the null hypothesis and the alternate hypothesis. The test is two-tailed because we are looking for a difference in the variation of the two routes. We are *not* trying to show that one route has more variation than the other.

$$H_0: \sigma_1^2 = \sigma_2^2$$
$$H_1: \sigma_1^2 \neq \sigma_2^2$$

Step 2: We selected the .10 significance level.

Step 3: The appropriate test statistic follows the F distribution.

Step 4: The critical value is obtained from Appendix B.4, a portion of which is reproduced as Table 12–1. Because we are conducting a two-tailed test, the tabled significance level is .05, found by $\alpha/2 = .10/2 = .05$. There are $n_1 - 1 = 7 - 1 = 6$ degrees of freedom in the numerator, and $n_2 - 1 = 8 - 1 = 7$ degrees of freedom in the denominator. To find the critical value, move horizontally across the top portion of the F table (Table 12–1 or Appendix B.4) for the .05 significance level to 6 degrees of freedom in the numerator. Then move down that column to the critical value opposite 7 degrees of freedom in the denominator. The critical value is 3.87. Thus, the decision rule is: Reject the null hypothesis if the ratio of the sample variances exceeds 3.87.

TABLE 12–1 Critical Values of the F Distribution, $\alpha = .05$

Degrees of Freedom for Denominator	Degrees of Freedom for Numerator			
	5	**6**	**7**	**8**
1	230	234	237	239
2	19.3	19.3	19.4	19.4
3	9.01	8.94	8.89	8.85
4	6.26	6.16	6.09	6.04
5	5.05	4.95	4.88	4.82
6	4.39	4.28	4.21	4.15
7	3.97	3.87	3.79	3.73
8	3.69	3.58	3.50	3.44
9	3.48	3.37	3.29	3.23
10	3.33	3.22	3.14	3.07

Step 5: The final step is to take the ratio of the two sample variances, determine the value of the test statistic, and make a decision regarding the null hypothesis. Note that formula (12–1) refers to the sample *variances* but we calculated the sample *standard deviations*. We need to square the standard deviations to determine the variances.

$$F = \frac{s_1^2}{s_2^2} = \frac{(8.9947)^2}{(4.3753)^2} = 4.23$$

The decision is to reject the null hypothesis, because the computed F value (4.23) is larger than the critical value (3.87). We conclude that there is a difference in the variation of the travel times along the two routes.

As noted, the usual practice is to determine the F ratio by putting the larger of the two sample variances in the numerator. This will force the F ratio to be at least 1.00. This allows us to always use the right tail of the F distribution, thus avoiding the need for more extensive F tables.

A logical question arises: Is it possible to conduct one-tailed tests? For example, suppose in the previous example we suspected that the variance of the times using the U.S. 25 route is *larger* than the variance of the times along the I-75 route. We would state the null and the alternate hypothesis as

$$H_0: \sigma_1^2 \le \sigma_2^2$$
$$H_1: \sigma_1^2 > \sigma_2^2$$

The test statistic is computed as s_1^2/s_2^2. Notice that we labeled the population with the suspected largest variance as population 1. So s_1^2 appears in the numerator. The F ratio will be larger than 1.00, so we can use the upper tail of the F distribution. Under these conditions, it is not necessary to divide the significance level in half. Because Appendix B.4 gives us only the .05 and .01 significance levels, we are restricted to these levels for one-tailed tests and .10 and .02 for two-tailed tests unless we consult a more complete table or use statistical software to compute the F statistic.

The Excel software system has a procedure to perform a test of variances. Below is the output. The computed value of F is the same as determined by using formula (12–1).

	A	B	C	D	E	F	G	H
1	U. S. 25	Interstate 75		F-Test Two-Sample for Variances				
2	52	59			U. S. 25	Interstate 75		
3	67	60		Mean	58.29	59.00		
4	56	61		Variance	80.90	19.14		
5	45	51		Observations	7.00	8.00		
6	70	56		df	6.00	7.00		
7	54	63		F	4.23			
8	64	57		P(F<=f) one-tail	0.04			
9		65		F Critical one-tail	3.87			
10								
11								

Sheet1   Sheet2   Sheet3

Self-Review 12–1   Steele Electric Products, Inc., assembles electrical components for cell phones. For the last 10 days Mark Nagy has averaged 9 rejects, with a standard deviation of 2 rejects per day. Debbie Richmond averaged 8.5 rejects, with a standard deviation of 1.5 rejects, over the same period. At the .05 significance level, can we conclude that there is more variation in the number of rejects per day attributed to Mark?

Exercises

connect

1. What is the critical F value for a sample of six observations in the numerator and four in the denominator? Use a two-tailed test and the .10 significance level.
2. What is the critical F value for a sample of four observations in the numerator and seven in the denominator? Use a one-tailed test and the .01 significance level.

3. The following hypotheses are given.

$$H_0: \sigma_1^2 = \sigma_2^2$$
$$H_1: \sigma_1^2 \neq \sigma_2^2$$

   A random sample of eight observations from the first population resulted in a standard deviation of 10. A random sample of six observations from the second population resulted in a standard deviation of 7. At the .02 significance level, is there a difference in the variation of the two populations?

4. The following hypotheses are given.

$$H_0: \sigma_1^2 \leq \sigma_2^2$$
$$H_1: \sigma_1^2 > \sigma_2^2$$

   A random sample of five observations from the first population resulted in a standard deviation of 12. A random sample of seven observations from the second population showed a standard deviation of 7. At the .01 significance level, is there more variation in the first population?

5. Arbitron Media Research, Inc., conducted a study of the iPod listening habits of men and women. One facet of the study involved the mean listening time. It was discovered that the mean listening time for men was 35 minutes per day. The standard deviation of the sample of the 10 men studied was 10 minutes per day. The mean listening time for the 12 women studied was also 35 minutes, but the standard deviation of the sample was 12 minutes. At the .10 significance level, can we conclude that there is a difference in the variation in the listening times for men and women?

6. A stockbroker at Critical Securities reported that the mean rate of return on a sample of 10 oil stocks was 12.6 percent with a standard deviation of 3.9 percent. The mean rate of return on a sample of 8 utility stocks was 10.9 percent with a standard deviation of 3.5 percent. At the .05 significance level, can we conclude that there is more variation in the oil stocks?

ANOVA Assumptions

Another use of the F distribution is the analysis of variance (ANOVA) technique in which we compare three or more population means to determine whether they could be equal. To use ANOVA, we assume the following:

1. The populations follow the normal distribution.
2. The populations have equal standard deviations (σ).
3. The populations are independent.

When these conditions are met, F is used as the distribution of the test statistic.

Why do we need to study ANOVA? Why can't we just use the test of differences in population means discussed in the previous chapter? We could compare the population means two at a time. The major reason is the unsatisfactory buildup of Type I error. To explain further, suppose we have four different methods (A, B, C, and D) of training new recruits to be firefighters. We randomly assign each of the 40 recruits in this year's class to one of the four methods. At the end of the training program, we administer to the four groups a common test to measure understanding of firefighting techniques. The question is: Is there a difference in the mean test scores among the four groups? An answer to this question will allow us to compare the four training methods.

Using the *t* distribution leads to a buildup of Type I error.

Using the *t* distribution to compare the four population means, we would have to conduct six different *t* tests. That is, we would need to compare the mean scores for the four methods as follows: A versus B, A versus C, A versus D, B versus C, B versus D, and C versus D. If we set the significance level at .05, the probability of a correct statistical decision is .95, found by 1 − .05. Because we conduct six separate (independent) tests the probability that we do *not* make an incorrect decision due to sampling error in any of the six independent tests is:

$$P(\text{All correct}) = (.95)(.95)(.95)(.95)(.95)(.95) = .735$$

To find the probability of at least one error due to sampling, we subtract this result from 1. Thus, the probability of at least one incorrect decision due to sampling is $1 - .735 = .265$. To summarize, if we conduct six independent tests using the t distribution, the likelihood of rejecting a true null hypothesis because of sampling error is increased from .05 to an unsatisfactory level of .265. It is obvious that we need a better method than conducting six t tests. ANOVA will allow us to compare the treatment means simultaneously and avoid the buildup of Type I error.

ANOVA was first developed for applications in agriculture, and many of the terms related to that context remain. In particular the term *treatment* is used to identify the different populations being examined. For example, treatment refers to how a plot of ground was treated with a particular type of fertilizer. The following illustration will clarify the term *treatment* and demonstrate an application of ANOVA.

Example

Joyce Kuhlman manages a regional financial center. She wishes to compare the productivity, as measured by the number of customers served, among three employees. Four days are randomly selected and the number of customers served by each employee is recorded. The results are:

Wolfe	White	Korosa
55	66	47
54	76	51
59	67	46
56	71	48

Solution

Is there a difference in the mean number of customers served? Chart 12–1 illustrates how the populations would appear if there were a difference in the treatment means. Note that the populations follow the normal distribution and the variation in each population is the same. However, the means are *not* the same.

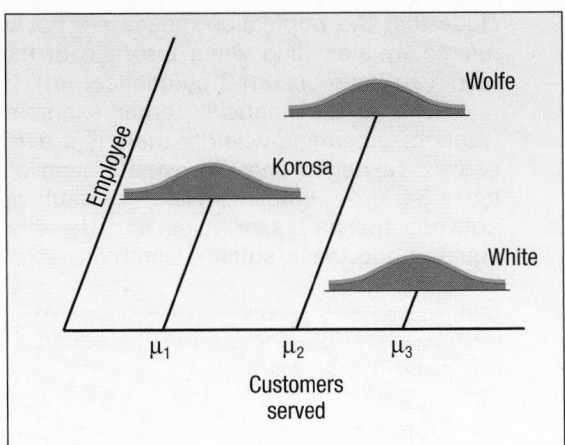

CHART 12–1 Case Where Treatment Means Are Different

Suppose the populations are the same. That is, there is no difference in the (treatment) means. This is shown in Chart 12–2. This would indicate that the population means are the same. Note again that the populations follow the normal distribution and the variation in each of the populations is the same.

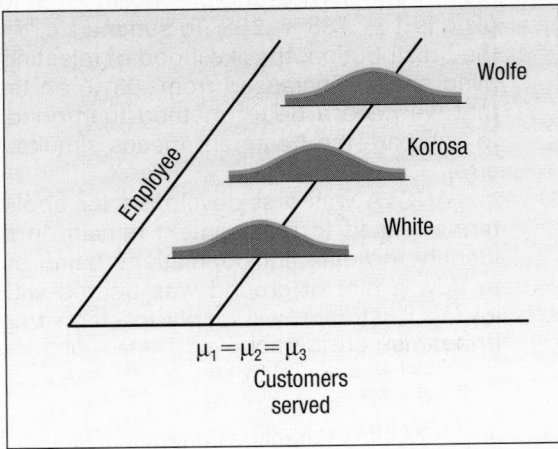

CHART 12–2 Case Where Treatment Means Are the Same

The ANOVA Test

How does the ANOVA test work? Recall that we want to determine whether the various sample means came from a single population or populations with different means. We actually compare these sample means through their variances. To explain, on page 408 we listed the assumptions required for ANOVA. One of those assumptions was that the standard deviations of the various normal populations had to be the same. We take advantage of this requirement in the ANOVA test. The underlying strategy is to estimate the population variance (standard deviation squared) two ways and then find the ratio of these two estimates. If this ratio is about 1, then logically the two estimates are the same, and we conclude that the population means are the same. If the ratio is quite different from 1, then we conclude that the population means are not the same. The F distribution serves as a referee by indicating when the ratio of the sample variances is too much greater than 1 to have occurred by chance.

Refer to the financial center example in the previous section. The manager wants to determine whether there is a difference in the mean number of customers served. To begin, find the overall mean of the 12 observations. It is 58, found by $(55 + 54 + \cdots + 48)/12$. Next, for each of the 12 observations find the difference between the particular value and the overall mean. Each of these differences is squared and these squares summed. This term is called the **total variation.**

> **TOTAL VARIATION** The sum of the squared differences between each observation and the overall mean.

In our example the total variation is 1,082, found by $(55 - 58)^2 + (54 - 58)^2 + \cdots + (48 - 58)^2$.

Next, break this total variation into two components: that which is due to the **treatments** and that which is **random.** To find these two components, determine the mean of each of the treatments. The first source of variation is due to the treatments.

> **TREATMENT VARIATION** The sum of the squared differences between each treatment mean and the grand or overall mean.

In the example, the variation due to the treatments is the sum of the squared differences between the mean number of customers served by each employee and the overall mean. This term is 992. To calculate it we first find the mean of each of the three treatments. The mean for Wolfe is 56 customers, found by $(55 + 54 + 59 + 56)/4$. The other means are 70 and 48, respectively. The sum of the squares due to the treatments is:

$$(56 - 58)^2 + (56 - 58)^2 + \cdots + (48 - 58)^2 = 4(56 - 58)^2 + 4(70 - 58)^2 + 4(48 - 58)^2$$
$$= 992$$

If there is considerable variation among the treatment means, it is logical that this term will be large. If the treatment means are similar, this term will be a small value. The smallest possible value would be zero. This would occur when all the treatment means are the same.

The other source of variation is referred to as the **random** component, or the error component.

> **RANDOM VARIATION** The sum of the squared differences between each observation and its treatment mean.

In the example this term is the sum of the squared differences between each value and the mean for that particular employee. The error variation is 90.

$$(55 - 56)^2 + (54 - 56)^2 + \cdots + (48 - 48)^2 = 90$$

We determine the test statistic, which is the ratio of the two estimates of the population variance, from the following equation.

$$F = \frac{\text{Estimate of the population variance based on the differences among the sample means}}{\text{Estimate of the population variance based on the variation within the sample}}$$

Our first estimate of the population variance is based on the treatments, that is, the difference *between* the means. It is 992/2. Why did we divide by 2? Recall from Chapter 3, to find a sample variance [see formula (3–11)], we divide by the number of observations minus one. In this case there are three treatments, so we divide by 2. Our first estimate of the population variance is 992/2.

The variance estimate *within* the treatments is the random variation divided by the total number of observations less the number of treatments. That is $90/(12 - 3)$. Hence, our second estimate of the population variance is 90/9. This is actually a generalization of formula (11–5), where we pooled the sample variances from two populations.

The last step is to take the ratio of these two estimates.

$$F = \frac{992/2}{90/9} = 49.6$$

Because this ratio is quite different from 1, we can conclude that the treatment means are not the same. There is a difference in the mean number of customers served by the three employees.

Here's another example, which deals with samples of different sizes.

Example

Recently airlines have cut services, such as meals and snacks during flights, and started charging extra for some services such as accommodating overweight luggage, last-minute flight changes, and pets traveling in the cabin. However, they are still very concerned about service. Recently a group of four carriers (we have used historical names for confidentiality) hired Brunner Marketing Research, Inc., to survey recent passengers regarding their level of satisfaction with a recent flight. The survey included questions on ticketing, boarding, in-flight service, baggage handling, pilot communication, and so forth. Twenty-five questions offered a range of possible answers: excellent, good, fair, or poor. A response of excellent was given a score of 4, good a 3, fair a 2, and poor a 1. These responses were then totaled, so the total score was an indication of the satisfaction with the flight. The greater the score, the higher the level of satisfaction with the service. The highest possible score was 100.

Brunner randomly selected and surveyed passengers from the four airlines. Below is the sample information. Is there a difference in the mean satisfaction level among the four airlines? Use the .01 significance level.

Eastern	TWA	Allegheny	Ozark
94	75	70	68
90	68	73	70
85	77	76	72
80	83	78	65
	88	80	74
		68	65
		65	

Solution

We will use the five-step hypothesis testing procedure.

Step 1: State the null hypothesis and the alternate hypothesis. The null hypothesis is that the mean scores are the same for the four airlines.

$$H_0: \mu_1 = \mu_2 = \mu_3 = \mu_4$$

The alternate hypothesis is that the mean scores are not all the same for the four airlines.

H_1: The mean scores are not all equal.

We can also think of the alternate hypothesis as "at least two mean scores are not equal."

If the null hypothesis is not rejected, we conclude that there is no difference in the mean scores for the four airlines. If H_0 is rejected, we conclude that there is a difference in at least one pair of mean scores, but at this point we do not know which pair or how many pairs differ.

Step 2: Select the level of significance. We selected the .01 significance level.

Step 3: Determine the test statistic. The test statistic follows the F distribution.

Step 4: Formulate the decision rule. To determine the decision rule, we need the critical value. The critical value for the F statistic is found in Appendix B.4. The critical values for the .05 significance level are found on the first page and the .01 significance level on the second page. To use this table we need to know the degrees of freedom in the numerator and the denominator. The degrees of freedom in the numerator equals the number of treatments, designated as k, minus 1. The degrees of freedom in the denominator is the total number of observations, n, minus the number of treatments. For this problem there are four treatments and a total of 22 observations.

Degrees of freedom in the numerator = $k - 1 = 4 - 1 = 3$

Degrees of freedom in the denominator = $n - k = 22 - 4 = 18$

Refer to Appendix B.4 and the .01 significance level. Move horizontally across the top of the page to 3 degrees of freedom in the numerator. Then move down that column to the row with 18 degrees of freedom. The value at this intersection is 5.09. So the decision rule is to reject H_0 if the computed value of F exceeds 5.09.

Step 5: Select the sample, perform the calculations, and make a decision. It is convenient to summarize the calculations of the F statistic in an **ANOVA table.** The format for an ANOVA table is as follows. Statistical software packages also use this format.

ANOVA Table				
Source of Variation	**Sum of Squares**	**Degrees of Freedom**	**Mean Square**	**F**
Treatments	SST	$k - 1$	$SST/(k - 1) = MST$	MST/MSE
Error	SSE	$n - k$	$SSE/(n - k) = MSE$	
Total	SS total	$n - 1$		

There are three values, or sum of squares, used to compute the test statistic F. You can determine these values by obtaining SS total and SSE, then finding SST by subtraction. The SS total term is the total variation, SST is the variation due to the treatments, and SSE is the variation within the treatments or the random error.

We usually start the process by finding SS total. This is the sum of the squared differences between each observation and the overall mean. The formula for finding SS total is:

$$SS\ total = \Sigma(X - \overline{X}_G)^2 \qquad \textbf{[12–2]}$$

where:

X is each sample observation.
$\overline{X}_G$ is the overall or grand mean.

Next determine SSE or the sum of the squared errors. This is the sum of the squared differences between each observation and its respective treatment mean. The formula for finding SSE is:

$$SSE = \Sigma(X - \overline{X}_c)^2 \qquad \textbf{[12–3]}$$

where:
$\overline{X}_c$ is the sample mean for treatment c.

The detailed calculations of SS total and SSE for this example follow. To determine the values of SS total and SSE we start by calculating the overall or grand mean. There are 22 observations and the total is 1,664, so the grand mean is 75.64.

$$\overline{X}_G = \frac{1,664}{22} = 75.64$$

	Eastern	TWA	Allegheny	Ozark	Total
	94	75	70	68	
	90	68	73	70	
	85	77	76	72	
	80	83	78	65	
		88	80	74	
			68	65	
			65		
Column total	349	391	510	414	1,664
n	4	5	7	6	22
Mean	87.25	78.20	72.86	69.00	75.64

Next we find the deviation of each observation from the grand mean, square those deviations, and sum this result for all 22 observations. For example, the first sampled passenger had a score of 94 and the overall or grand mean is 75.64. So $(X - \overline{X}_G) = 94 - 75.64 = 18.36$. For the last passenger $(X - \overline{X}_G) = 65 - 75.64 = -10.64$. The calculations for all other passengers follow.

Eastern	TWA	Allegheny	Ozark
18.36	−0.64	−5.64	−7.64
14.36	−7.64	−2.64	−5.64
9.36	1.36	0.36	−3.64
4.36	7.36	2.36	−10.64
	12.36	4.36	−1.64
		−7.64	−10.64
		−10.64	

Then square each of these differences and sum all the values. Thus for the first passenger:

$$(X - \overline{X}_G)^2 = (94 - 75.64)^2 = (18.36)^2 = 337.09.$$

Finally, sum all the squared differences as formula (12–2) directs. Our SS total value is 1,485.10.

	Eastern	TWA	Allegheny	Ozark	Total
	337.09	0.41	31.81	58.37	
	206.21	58.37	6.97	31.81	
	87.61	1.85	0.13	13.25	
	19.01	54.17	5.57	113.21	
		152.77	19.01	2.69	
			58.37	113.21	
			113.21		
Total	649.92	267.57	235.07	332.54	1,485.10

To compute the term SSE find the deviation between each observation and its treatment mean. In the example the mean of the first treatment (that is, the passengers on Eastern Airlines) is 87.25, found by $\overline{X}_E = 349/4$. The subscript E refers to Eastern Airlines.

The first passenger rated Eastern a 94, so $(X - \overline{X}_E) = (94 - 87.25) = 6.75$. The first passenger in the TWA group responded with a total score of 75, so $(X - \overline{X}_{TWA}) = (75 - 78.20) = -3.2$. The detail for all the passengers follows.

Eastern	TWA	Allegheny	Ozark
6.75	−3.2	−2.86	−1
2.75	−10.2	0.14	1
−2.25	−1.2	3.14	3
−7.25	4.8	5.14	−4
	9.8	7.14	5
		−4.86	−4
		−7.86	

Statistics in Action

Have you ever waited in line for a telephone and it seemed like the person using the phone talked on and on? There is evidence that people actually talk longer on public telephones when someone is waiting. In a recent survey, researchers measured the length of time that 56 shoppers in a mall spent on the phone (1) when they were alone, (2) when a person was using the adjacent phone, and (3) when a person was using an adjacent phone and someone was waiting to use the phone. The study, using the one-way ANOVA technique, showed that the mean time using the telephone was significantly less when the person was alone.

Each of these values is squared and then summed for all 22 observations. The values are shown in the following table.

	Eastern	TWA	Allegheny	Ozark	Total
	45.5625	10.24	8.18	1	
	7.5625	104.04	0.02	1	
	5.0625	1.44	9.86	9	
	52.5625	23.04	26.42	16	
		96.04	50.98	25	
			23.62	16	
			61.78		
Total	110.7500	234.80	180.86	68	594.41

So the SSE value is 594.41. That is $\Sigma(X - \overline{X}_c)^2 = 594.41$.

Finally we determine SST, the sum of the squares due to the treatments, by subtraction.

$$SST = SS\ total - SSE \qquad \text{[12–4]}$$

For this example:

$$SST = SS\ total - SSE = 1{,}485.10 - 594.41 = 890.69.$$

To find the computed value of F, work your way across the ANOVA table. The degrees of freedom for the numerator and the denominator are the same as in step 4 on page 412 when we were finding the critical value of F. The term **mean square** is another expression for an estimate of the variance. The mean square for treatments is SST divided by its degrees of freedom. The result is the **mean square for treatments** and is written MST. Compute the **mean square error** in a similar fashion. To be precise, divide SSE by its degrees of freedom. To complete the process and find F, divide MST by MSE.

Insert the particular values of F into an ANOVA table and compute the value of F as follows.

Source of Variation	Sum of Squares	Degrees of Freedom	Mean Square	F
Treatments	890.69	3	296.90	8.99
Error	594.41	18	33.02	
Total	1,485.10	21		

The computed value of F is 8.99, which is greater than the critical value of 5.09, so the null hypothesis is rejected. We conclude the population means are not all equal. The mean scores are not the same for the four airlines. It is likely that the passenger scores are related to the particular airline. At this point we can only conclude there is a difference in the treatment means. We cannot determine which treatment groups differ or how many treatment groups differ.

As noted in the previous example, the calculations are tedious if the number of observations in each treatment is large. There are many software packages that will perform the calculations and output the results. Following is the Excel output in the form of an ANOVA table for the previous example involving airlines and passenger ratings. There are some slight differences between the software output and the previous calculations. These differences are due to rounding.

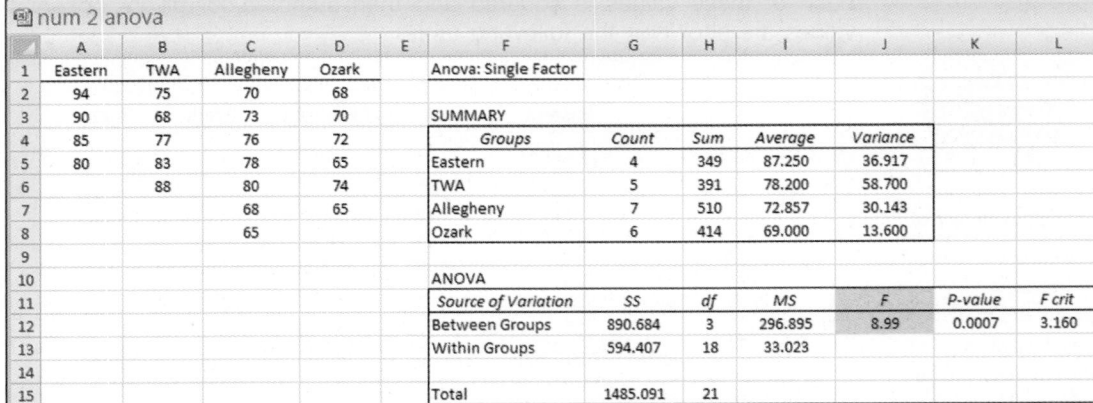

Notice Excel uses the term "Between Groups" for treatments and "Within Groups" for error. However, they have the same meanings. The *p*-value is .0007. This is the probability of finding a value of the test statistic this large or larger when the null hypothesis is true. To put it another way, it is the likelihood of calculating an *F* value larger than 8.99 with 3 degrees of freedom in the numerator and 18 degrees of freedom in the denominator. So when we reject the null hypothesis in this instance there is a very small likelihood of committing a Type I error!

Following is the MINITAB output from the airline passenger ratings example, which is similar to the Excel output. The output is also in the form of an ANOVA table. In addition, MINITAB provides information about the differences between means. This is discussed in the next section.

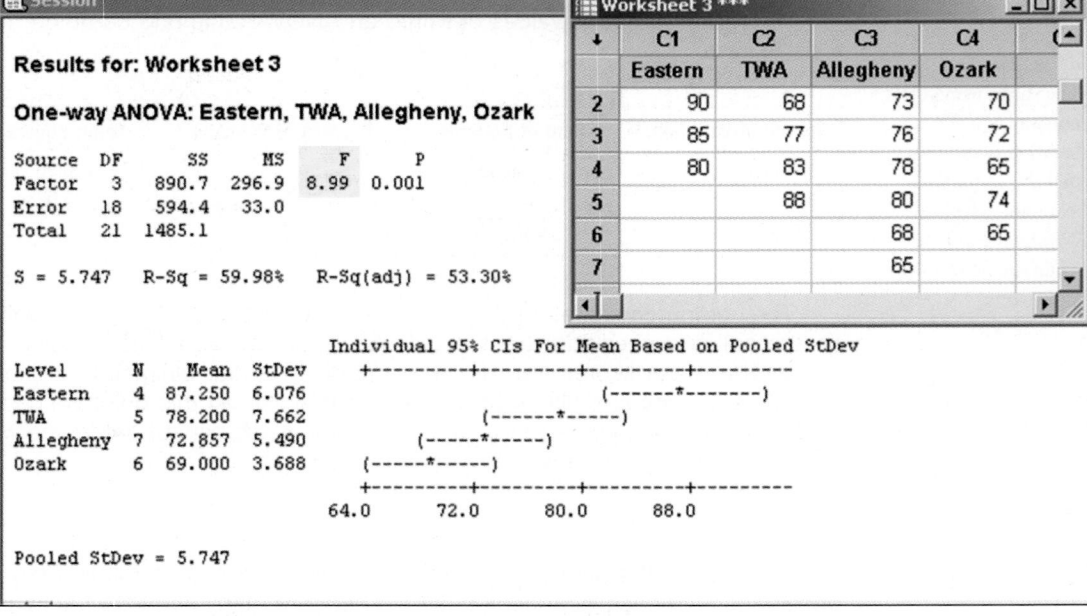

The MINITAB system uses the term "Factor" instead of *treatment,* with the same intended meaning.

Self-Review 12–2  Citrus Clean is a new all-purpose cleaner being test-marketed by placing displays in three different locations within various supermarkets. The number of 12-ounce bottles sold from each location within the supermarket is reported below.

Near bread	18	14	19	17
Near beer	12	18	10	16
Other cleaners	26	28	30	32

At the .05 significance level, is there a difference in the mean number of bottles sold at the three locations?
(a)   State the null hypothesis and the alternate hypothesis.
(b)   What is the decision rule?
(c)   Compute the values of SS total, SST, and SSE.
(d)   Develop an ANOVA table.
(e)   What is your decision regarding the null hypothesis?

Exercises

connect

7. The following is sample information. Test the hypothesis that the treatment means are equal. Use the .05 significance level.

Treatment 1	Treatment 2	Treatment 3
8	3	3
6	2	4
10	4	5
9	3	4

  a. State the null hypothesis and the alternate hypotheses.
  b. What is the decision rule?
  c. Compute SST, SSE, and SS total.
  d. Complete an ANOVA table.
  e. State your decision regarding the null hypothesis.
8. The following is sample information. Test the hypothesis at the .05 significance level that the treatment means are equal.

Treatment 1	Treatment 2	Treatment 3
9	13	10
7	20	9
11	14	15
9	13	14
12		15
10		

  a. State the null hypothesis and the alternate hypotheses.
  b. What is the decision rule?
  c. Compute SST, SSE, and SS total.
  d. Complete an ANOVA table.
  e. State your decision regarding the null hypothesis.

9. A real estate developer is considering investing in a shopping mall on the outskirts of Atlanta, Georgia. Three parcels of land are being evaluated. Of particular importance is the income in the area surrounding the proposed mall. A random sample of four families is selected near each proposed mall. Following are the sample results. At the .05 significance level, can the developer conclude there is a difference in the mean income? Use the usual five-step hypothesis testing procedure.

Southwyck Area ($000)	Franklin Park ($000)	Old Orchard ($000)
64	74	75
68	71	80
70	69	76
60	70	78

10. The manager of a computer software company wishes to study the number of hours senior executives by type of industry spend at their desktop computers. The manager selected a sample of five executives from each of three industries. At the .05 significance level, can she conclude there is a difference in the mean number of hours spent per week by industry?

Banking	Retail	Insurance
12	8	10
10	8	8
10	6	6
12	8	8
10	10	10

Inferences about Pairs of Treatment Means

Suppose we carry out the ANOVA procedure and make the decision to reject the null hypothesis. This allows us to conclude that all the treatment means are not the same. Sometimes we may be satisfied with this conclusion, but in other instances we may want to know which treatment means differ. This section provides the details for such a test.

Recall that in the Brunner Research example regarding airline passenger ratings there was a difference in the treatment means. That is, the null hypothesis was rejected and the alternate hypothesis accepted. If the passenger ratings do differ, the question is: Between which groups do the treatment means differ?

Several procedures are available to answer this question. The simplest is through the use of confidence intervals, that is, formula (9–2). From the computer output of the previous example (see page 416), note that the sample mean score for those passengers rating Eastern's service is 87.25, and for those rating Ozark's service the sample mean score is 69.00. Is there enough disparity to justify the conclusion that there is a significant difference in the mean satisfaction scores of the two airlines?

The t distribution, described in Chapters 10 and 11, is used as the basis for this test. Recall that one of the assumptions of ANOVA is that the population variances are the same for all treatments. This common population value is the

mean square error, or MSE, and is determined by $SSE/(n - k)$. A confidence interval for the difference between two populations is found by:

CONFIDENCE INTERVAL FOR THE DIFFERENCE IN TREATMENT MEANS	$(\bar{X}_1 - \bar{X}_2) \pm t\sqrt{MSE\left(\dfrac{1}{n_1} + \dfrac{1}{n_2}\right)}$	**[12–5]**

where

$\bar{X}_1$ is the mean of the first sample.

$\bar{X}_2$ is the mean of the second sample.

t is obtained from Appendix B.2. The degrees of freedom is equal to $n - k$.

MSE is the mean square error term obtained from the ANOVA table $[SSE/(n - k)]$.

n_1 is the number of observations in the first sample.

n_2 is the number of observations in the second sample.

How do we decide whether there is a difference in the treatment means? If the confidence interval includes zero, there is *not* a difference between the treatment means. For example, if the left endpoint of the confidence interval has a negative sign and the right endpoint has a positive sign, the interval includes zero and the two means do not differ. So if we develop a confidence interval from formula (12–5) and find the difference in the sample means was 5.00, that is, if $\bar{X}_1 - \bar{X}_2 = 5$ and $t\sqrt{MSE\left(\dfrac{1}{n_1} + \dfrac{1}{n_2}\right)} = 12$, the confidence interval would range from -7.00 up to 17.00. To put it in symbols:

$$(\bar{X}_1 - \bar{X}_2) \pm t\sqrt{MSE\left(\frac{1}{n_1} + \frac{1}{n_2}\right)} = 5.00 \pm 12.00 = -7.00 \text{ up to } 17.00$$

Note that zero is included in this interval. Therefore, we conclude that there is no significant difference in the selected treatment means.

On the other hand, if the endpoints of the confidence interval have the same sign, this indicates that the treatment means differ. For example, if $\bar{X}_1 - \bar{X}_2 = -0.35$ and $t\sqrt{MSE\left(\dfrac{1}{n_1} + \dfrac{1}{n_2}\right)} = 0.25$, the confidence interval would range from -0.60 up to -0.10. Because -0.60 and -0.10 have the same sign, both negative, zero is not in the interval and we conclude that these treatment means differ.

Using the previous airline example let us compute the confidence interval for the difference between the mean scores of passengers on Eastern and Ozark Airlines. With a 95 percent level of confidence, the endpoints of the confidence interval are 10.46 and 26.04.

$$(\bar{X}_E - \bar{X}_O) \pm t\sqrt{MSE\left(\frac{1}{n_E} + \frac{1}{n_O}\right)} = (87.25 - 69.00) \pm 2.101\sqrt{33.0\left(\frac{1}{4} + \frac{1}{6}\right)}$$

$$= 18.25 \pm 7.79$$

where

$\bar{X}_E$ is 87.25.

$\bar{X}_O$ is 69.00.

t is 2.101: from Appendix B.2 with $(n - k) = 22 - 4 = 18$ degrees of freedom.

MSE is 33.0: from the ANOVA table with $SSE/(n - k) = 594.4/18$.

n_E is 4.

n_O is 6.

The 95 percent confidence interval ranges from 10.46 up to 26.04. Both endpoints are positive; hence, we can conclude these treatment means differ significantly.

That is, passengers on Eastern rated service significantly different from those on Ozark.

Approximate results can also be obtained directly from the MINITAB output. Following is the lower portion of the output from page 416. On the left side is the number of observations, the mean, and the standard deviation for each treatment. Seven passengers on Allegheny rated the service as 72.857 with a standard deviation of 5.490.

```
                                 Individual 95% CIs For Mean
                                 Based on Pooled StDev
Level       N    Mean   StDev    +---------+---------+---------+---------
Eastern     4   87.250  6.076                              (------*-----)
TWA         5   78.200  7.662                    (-----*-----)
Allegheny   7   72.857  5.490                 (-----*-----)
Ozark       6   69.000  3.688      (-----*-----)
                                 +---------+---------+---------+---------
                                 64.0      72.0      80.0      88.0
```

On the right side of the printout is a confidence interval for each treatment mean. The asterisk (*) indicates the location of the treatment mean and the open parenthesis and close parenthesis, the endpoints of the confidence interval. In those instances where the intervals overlap, the treatment means may not differ. If there is no common area in the confidence intervals, that pair of means differ.

The endpoints of a 95 percent confidence interval for mean passenger scores for Allegheny are about 69 and 77. For Ozark the endpoints of the 95 percent confidence interval for the mean passenger score are about 64 and 73. There is common area between these points, so we conclude this pair of means does not differ. In other words, there is no significant difference between the mean passenger ratings for Allegheny and Ozark. The difference in the mean scores is due to chance.

There are two pairs of means that differ. The mean scores of passengers on Eastern Airlines are significantly different from the mean ratings of passengers on Allegheny and on Ozark. There is no common area between these two pairs of confidence intervals.

We should emphasize that this investigation is a step-by-step process. The initial step is to conduct the ANOVA test. Only if the null hypothesis that the treatment means are equal is rejected should any analysis of the individual treatment means be attempted.

Self-Review 12–3

The following data are the semester tuition charges ($000) for a sample of private colleges in various regions of the United States. At the .05 significance level, can we conclude there is a difference in the mean tuition rates for the various regions?

Northeast ($000)	Southeast ($000)	West ($000)
10	8	7
11	9	8
12	10	6
10	8	7
12		6

(a) State the null and the alternate hypotheses.
(b) What is the decision rule?
(c) Develop an ANOVA table. What is the value of the test statistic?
(d) What is your decision regarding the null hypothesis?
(e) Could there be a significant difference between the mean tuition in the Northeast and that of the West? If so, develop a 95 percent confidence interval for that difference.

Exercises

connect™

11. Given the following sample information, test the hypothesis that the treatment means are equal at the .05 significance level.

Treatment 1	Treatment 2	Treatment 3
8	3	3
11	2	4
10	1	5
	3	4
	2	

a. State the null hypothesis and the alternate hypothesis.
b. What is the decision rule?
c. Compute SST, SSE, and SS total.
d. Complete an ANOVA table.
e. State your decision regarding the null hypothesis.
f. If H_0 is rejected, can we conclude that treatment 1 and treatment 2 differ? Use the 95 percent level of confidence.

12. Given the following sample information, test the hypothesis that the treatment means are equal at the .05 significance level.

Treatment 1	Treatment 2	Treatment 3
3	9	6
2	6	3
5	5	5
1	6	5
3	8	5
1	5	4
	4	1
	7	5
	6	
	4	

a. State the null hypothesis and the alternate hypothesis.
b. What is the decision rule?
c. Compute SST, SSE, and SS total.
d. Complete an ANOVA table.
e. State your decision regarding the null hypothesis.
f. If H_0 is rejected, can we conclude that treatment 2 and treatment 3 differ? Use the 95 percent level of confidence.

13. A senior accounting major at Midsouth State University has job offers from four CPA firms. To explore the offers further, she asked a sample of recent trainees how many months each worked for the firm before receiving a raise in salary. The sample information is submitted to MINITAB with the following results:

```
Analysis of Variance
Source    DF      SS      MS      F       P
Factor     3   32.33   10.78   2.36   0.133
Error     10   45.67    4.57
Total     13   78.00
```

At the .05 level of significance, is there a difference in the mean number of months before a raise was granted among the four CPA firms?

14. A stock analyst wants to determine whether there is a difference in the mean rate of return for three types of stock: utility, retail, and banking stocks. The following output is obtained:

```
Analysis  of  Variance
Source      DF        SS       MS        F         P
Factor       2      86.49    43.25    13.09     0.001
Error       13      42.95     3.30
Total       15     129.44
                                      Individual  95%  CIs  For  Mean
                                      Based  on  Pooled  StDev
Level        N      Mean     StDev    ----------+---------+---------+------
Utility      5     17.400    1.916                       (------*------)
Retail       5     11.620    0.356    (------*------)
Banking      6     15.400    2.356              (------*------)
                                      ----------+---------+---------+------
Pooled  StDev  =  1.818                  12.0      15.0      18.0
```

a. Using the .05 level of significance, is there a difference in the mean rate of return among the three types of stock?

b. Suppose the null hypothesis is rejected. Can the analyst conclude there is a difference between the mean rates of return for the utility and the retail stocks? Explain.

Two-Way Analysis of Variance

In the airline passenger ratings example, we divided the total variation into two categories: the variation between the treatments and the variation within the treatments. We also called the variation within the treatments the error or the random variation. To put it another way, we considered only two sources of variation, that due to the treatments and the random differences. In the airline passenger ratings example there may be other causes of variation. These factors might include, for example, the season of the year, the particular airport, or the number of passengers on the flight.

The benefit of considering other factors is that we can reduce the error variance. That is, if we can reduce the denominator of the F statistic (reducing the error variance or, more directly, the SSE term), the value of F will be larger, causing us to reject the hypothesis of equal treatment means. In other words, if we can explain more of the variation, then there is less "error." An example will clarify the reduction in the error variance.

Example

WARTA, the Warren Area Regional Transit Authority, is expanding bus service from the suburb of Starbrick into the central business district of Warren. There are four routes being considered from Starbrick to downtown Warren: (1) via U.S. 6, (2) via the West End, (3) via the Hickory Street Bridge, and (4) via Route 59. WARTA conducted several tests to determine whether there was a difference in the mean travel times along the four routes. Because there will be many different drivers, the test was set up so each driver drove along each of the four routes. Below is the travel time, in minutes, for each driver–route combination.

Driver	Travel Time From Starbrick to Warren (minutes)			
	U.S. 6	West End	Hickory St.	Rte. 59
Deans	18	17	21	22
Snaverly	16	23	23	22
Ormson	21	21	26	22
Zollaco	23	22	29	25
Filbeck	25	24	28	28

At the .05 significance level, is there a difference in the mean travel time along the four routes? If we remove the effect of the drivers, is there a difference in the mean travel time?

Solution

To begin, we conduct a test of hypothesis using a one-way ANOVA. That is, we consider only the four routes. Under this condition the variation in travel times is either due to the treatments or it is random. The null hypothesis and the alternate hypothesis for comparing the mean travel time along the four routes are:

H_0: $\mu_1 = \mu_2 = \mu_3 = \mu_4$
H_1: Not all treatment means are the same.

There are four routes, so for the numerator the degrees of freedom is $k - 1 = 4 - 1 = 3$. There are 20 observations, so the degrees of freedom in the denominator is $n - k = 20 - 4 = 16$. From Appendix B.4, with the .05 significance level, the critical value of F is 3.24. The decision rule is to reject the null hypothesis if the computed value of F is greater than 3.24.

We use Excel to perform the calculations and output the results. The computed value of F is 2.482, so our decision is to not reject the null hypothesis. We conclude there is no difference in the mean travel time along the four routes. There is no reason to select one of the routes as faster than the other.

Excel

num 3 anova

	A	B	C	D	E	F	G	H	I	J	K	L	M
1													
2													
3	Driver	US 6	West End	Hickory St.	Rte. 59		Anova: Single Factor						
4	Deans	18	17	21	22								
5	Snaverly	16	23	23	22		SUMMARY						
6	Ormson	21	21	26	22		Groups	Count	Sum	Average	Variance		
7	Zollaco	23	22	29	25		US 6	5	103	20.6	13.3		
8	Filbeck	25	24	28	28		West End	5	107	21.4	7.3		
9							Hickory St.	5	127	25.4	11.3		
10							Rte. 59	5	119	23.8	7.2		
11													
12													
13				Treatments			ANOVA						
14				(Route)			Source of Variation	SS	df	MS	F	P-value	F crit
15							Between Groups	72.8	3	24.267	2.483	0.098	3.239
16							Within Groups	156.4	16	9.775			
17				Error									
18							Total	229.2	19				

From the above Excel output the mean travel times along the routes were: 20.6 minutes along U.S. 6, 21.4 minutes along the West End route, 25.4 minutes using Hickory Street, and 23.8 minutes using Route 59. We conclude these differences could reasonably be attributed to chance. From the ANOVA table we note: SST is 72.8, SSE is 156.4, and SS total is 229.2.

In the above example we considered the variation due to the treatments (routes) and took all the remaining variation to be random. If we could consider the effect of the several drivers, this would allow us to reduce the SSE term, which would lead to a larger value of F. The second treatment variable, the drivers in this case, is referred to as a **blocking variable.**

> **BLOCKING VARIABLE** A second treatment variable that when included in the ANOVA analysis will have the effect of reducing the SSE term.

In this case we let the drivers be the blocking variable, and removing the effect of the drivers from the SSE term will change the F ratio for the treatment variable. First, we need to determine the sum of squares due to the blocks.

In a two-way ANOVA, the sum of squares due to blocks is found by the following formula.

$$SSB = k\Sigma(\overline{X}_b - \overline{X}_G)^2 \qquad \textbf{[12–6]}$$

where
k is the number of treatments.
b is the number of blocks.
$\overline{X}_b$ is the sample mean of block b.
$\overline{X}_G$ is the overall or grand mean.

From the calculations below, the means for the respective drivers are 19.5 minutes, 21 minutes, 22.5 minutes, 24.75 minutes, and 26.25 minutes. The overall mean is 22.8 minutes, found by adding the travel time for all 20 drives (456 minutes) and dividing by 20.

Travel Time From Starbrick to Warren (minutes)						
Driver	**U.S. 6**	**West End**	**Hickory St.**	**Rte. 59**	**Driver Sums**	**Driver Means**
Deans	18	17	21	22	78	19.5
Snaverly	16	23	23	22	84	21
Ormson	21	21	26	22	90	22.5
Zollaco	23	22	29	25	99	24.75
Filbeck	25	24	28	28	105	26.25

Substituting this information into formula (12–6) we determine SSB, the sum of squares due to the drivers (the blocking variable), is 119.7.

$$SSB = k\Sigma(\overline{X}_b - \overline{X}_G)^2$$
$$= 4(19.5 - 22.8)^2 + 4(21.0 - 22.8)^2 + 4(22.5 - 22.8)^2$$
$$+ 4(24.75 - 22.8)^2 + 4(26.25 - 22.8)^2$$
$$= 119.7$$

The same format is used in the two-way ANOVA table as in the one-way case, except there is an additional row for the blocking variable. SS total and SST are calculated as before, and SSB is found from formula (12–6). The SSE term is found by subtraction.

SUM OF SQUARES ERROR, TWO-WAY $\qquad$ SSE = SS total − SST − SSB $\qquad$ **[12–7]**

The values for the various components of the ANOVA table are computed as follows.

Source of Variation	Sum of Squares	Degrees of Freedom	Mean Square	F
Treatments	SST	$k - 1$	$SST/(k - 1) = MST$	MST/MSE
Blocks	SSB	$b - 1$	$SSB/(b - 1) = MSB$	MSB/MSE
Error	SSE	$(k - 1)(b - 1)$	$SSE/(k - 1)(b - 1) = MSE$	
Total	SS total	$n - 1$		

SSE is found by formula (12–7).

$$SSE = SS\ total - SST - SSB = 229.2 - 72.8 - 119.7 = 36.7$$

Source of Variation	(1) Sum of Squares	(2) Degrees of Freedom	(3) Mean Square (1)/(2)
Treatments	72.8	3	24.27
Blocks	119.7	4	29.93
Error	36.7	12	3.06
Total	229.2	19	

There is disagreement at this point. If the purpose of the blocking variable (the drivers in this example) was only to reduce the error variation, we should not conduct a test of hypothesis for the difference in block means. That is, if our goal was to reduce the MSE term, then we should not test a hypothesis regarding the blocking variable. On the other hand, we may wish to give the blocks the same status as the treatments and conduct a test of hypothesis. In the latter case, when the blocks are important enough to be considered as a second factor, we refer to this as a **two-factor experiment.** In many cases the decision is not clear. In our example we are concerned about the difference in the travel time for the different drivers, so we will conduct the test of hypothesis. The two sets of hypotheses are:

1. H_0: The treatment means are the same ($\mu_1 = \mu_2 = \mu_3 = \mu_4$).
    H_1: The treatment means are not the same.
2. H_0: The block means are the same ($\mu_1 = \mu_2 = \mu_3 = \mu_4 = \mu_5$).
    H_1: The block means are not the same.

First, we will test the hypothesis concerning the treatment means. There are $k - 1 = 4 - 1 = 3$ degrees of freedom in the numerator and $(b - 1)(k - 1) = (5 - 1)(4 - 1) = 12$ degrees of freedom in the denominator. Using the .05 significance level, the critical value of F is 3.49. The null hypothesis that the mean times for the four routes are the same is rejected if the F ratio exceeds 3.49.

$$F = \frac{MST}{MSE} = \frac{24.27}{3.06} = 7.93$$

The null hypothesis is rejected and the alternate accepted. We conclude that the mean travel time is not the same for all routes. WARTA will want to conduct some tests to determine which treatment means differ.

Next, we test to find whether the travel time is the same for the various drivers. The degrees of freedom in the numerator for blocks is $b - 1 = 5 - 1 = 4$. The degrees of freedom for the denominator are the same as before: $(b - 1)(k - 1) = (5 - 1)(4 - 1) = 12$. The null hypothesis that the block means are the same is rejected if the F ratio exceeds 3.26.

$$F = \frac{MSB}{MSE} = \frac{29.93}{3.06} = 9.78$$

The null hypothesis is rejected, and the alternate is accepted. The mean time is not the same for the various drivers. Thus, WARTA management can conclude, based on the sample results, that there is a difference in the routes and in the drivers.

The Excel spreadsheet has a two-factor ANOVA procedure. The output for the WARTA example just completed follows. The results are the same as reported earlier. In addition the Excel output reports the p-values. The p-value for the null hypothesis regarding the drivers is .001 and .004 for the routes. These p-values confirm that the null hypotheses for treatments and blocks should both be rejected because the p-value is less than the significance level.

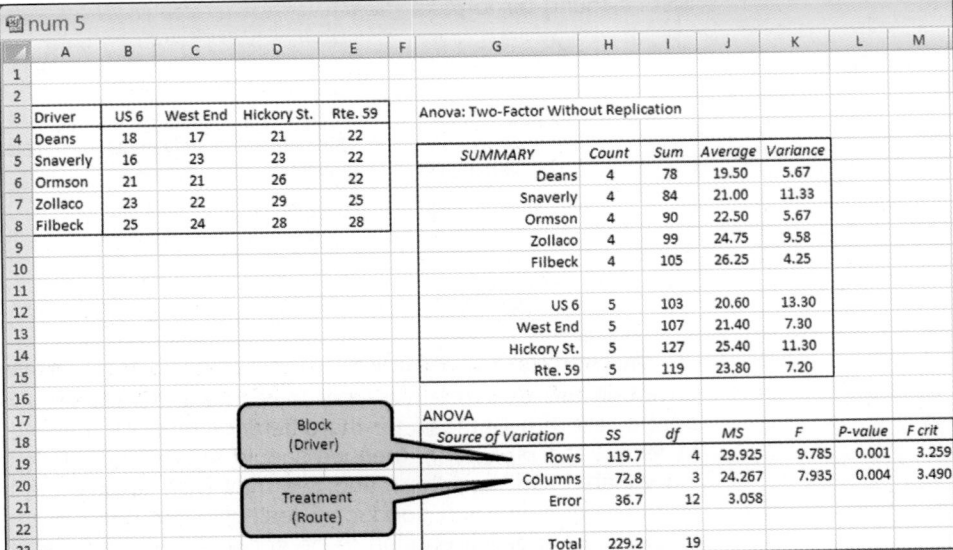

	A	B	C	D	E	F	G	H	I	J	K	L	M
1													
2													
3	Driver	US 6	West End	Hickory St.	Rte. 59		Anova: Two-Factor Without Replication						
4	Deans	18	17	21	22								
5	Snaverly	16	23	23	22		SUMMARY	Count	Sum	Average	Variance		
6	Ormson	21	21	26	22		Deans	4	78	19.50	5.67		
7	Zollaco	23	22	29	25		Snaverly	4	84	21.00	11.33		
8	Filbeck	25	24	28	28		Ormson	4	90	22.50	5.67		
9							Zollaco	4	99	24.75	9.58		
10							Filbeck	4	105	26.25	4.25		
11													
12							US 6	5	103	20.60	13.30		
13							West End	5	107	21.40	7.30		
14							Hickory St.	5	127	25.40	11.30		
15							Rte. 59	5	119	23.80	7.20		
16													
17							ANOVA						
18							Source of Variation	SS	df	MS	F	P-value	F crit
19							Rows	119.7	4	29.925	9.785	0.001	3.259
20							Columns	72.8	3	24.267	7.935	0.004	3.490
21							Error	36.7	12	3.058			
22													
23							Total	229.2	19				

Block (Driver) → Rows

Treatment (Route) → Columns

Self-Review 12–4

Rudduck Shampoo sells three shampoos, one each for dry, normal, and oily hair. Sales, in millions of dollars, for the past five months are given in the following table. Using the .05 significance level, test whether the mean sales differ for the three types of shampoo or by month.

Month	Sales ($ million)		
	Dry	**Normal**	**Oily**
June	7	9	12
July	11	12	14
August	13	11	8
September	8	9	7
October	9	10	13

Exercises

For exercises 15 and 16, conduct a test of hypothesis to determine whether the block or the treatment means differ. Using the .05 significance level: (a) state the null and alternate hypotheses for treatments; (b) state the decision rule for treatments; and (c) state the null and alternate hypotheses for blocks. Also, state the decision rule for blocks, then: (d) compute SST, SSB, SS total, and SSE; (e) complete an ANOVA table; and (f) give your decision regarding the two sets of hypotheses.

15. The following data are given for a two-factor ANOVA.

	Treatment	
Block	**1**	**2**
A	46	31
B	37	26
C	44	35

16. The following data are given for a two-factor ANOVA.

Block	Treatment 1	2	3
A	12	14	8
B	9	11	9
C	7	8	8

17. Chapin Manufacturing Company operates 24 hours a day, five days a week. The workers rotate shifts each week. Management is interested in whether there is a difference in the number of units produced when the employees work on various shifts. A sample of five workers is selected and their output recorded on each shift. At the .05 significance level, can we conclude there is a difference in the mean production rate by shift or by employee?

Employee	Units Produced Day	Afternoon	Night
Skaff	31	25	35
Lum	33	26	33
Clark	28	24	30
Treece	30	29	28
Morgan	28	26	27

18. There are three hospitals in the Tulsa, Oklahoma, area. The following data show the number of outpatient surgeries performed at each hospital last week. At the .05 significance level, can we conclude there is a difference in the mean number of surgeries performed by hospital or by day of the week?

Day	Number of Surgeries Performed St. Luke's	St. Vincent	Mercy
Monday	14	18	24
Tuesday	20	24	14
Wednesday	16	22	14
Thursday	18	20	22
Friday	20	28	24

Two-Way ANOVA with Interaction

In the previous section, we studied the separate or independent effects of two variables, routes into the city and drivers, on mean travel time. The sample results indicated differences in mean time among the routes. Perhaps this is simply related to differences in the distance among the routes. The results also indicated differences in the mean drive time among the several drivers. Perhaps this difference is explained by differing average speeds by the drivers regardless of the route. There is another effect that may influence travel time. This is called an **interaction effect** between route and driver on travel time. For example, is it possible that one of the drivers is especially good driving one or more of the routes? Perhaps one driver knows how to effectively time the traffic lights or how to avoid heavily congested intersections for one or more of the routes. In this case, the combined effect of driver and route may also explain differences in mean travel time. To measure interaction effects it is necessary to have at least two observations in each cell.

When we use a two-way ANOVA to study interaction, instead of using the terms treatments and blocks, we now call the two variables **factors.** So in this method there is a route factor, a driver factor, and an interaction of the two factors. That is, there is an *effect* for the routes, for the driver, and for the interaction of drivers and routes.

Interaction occurs if the combination of two factors has some effect on the variable under study, in addition to each factor alone. We refer to the variable being studied as the **response** variable. An everyday illustration of interaction is the effect of diet and exercise on weight. It is generally agreed that a person's weight (the response variable) can be controlled with two factors, diet and exercise. Research shows that weight is affected by diet alone and that weight is affected by exercise alone. However, the general recommended method to control weight is based on the combined or *interaction* effect of diet and exercise.

> **INTERACTION** The effect of one factor on a response variable differs depending on the value of another factor.

Interaction Plots

One way to study interaction is by plotting factor means in a graph called an interaction plot. Consider the bus driver example in the previous section. WARTA, the Warren Area Regional Transit Authority, wants to study the mean travel time for different routes and drivers. To complete the study, we should also explore the prospect of interaction between driver and route. We begin by graphing the mean travel times on each route for each driver and connect the points. We compute Deans' mean travel times for each route and plot them in a graph of mean travel times versus route. We repeat this process for each of the drivers. The interaction plot follows.

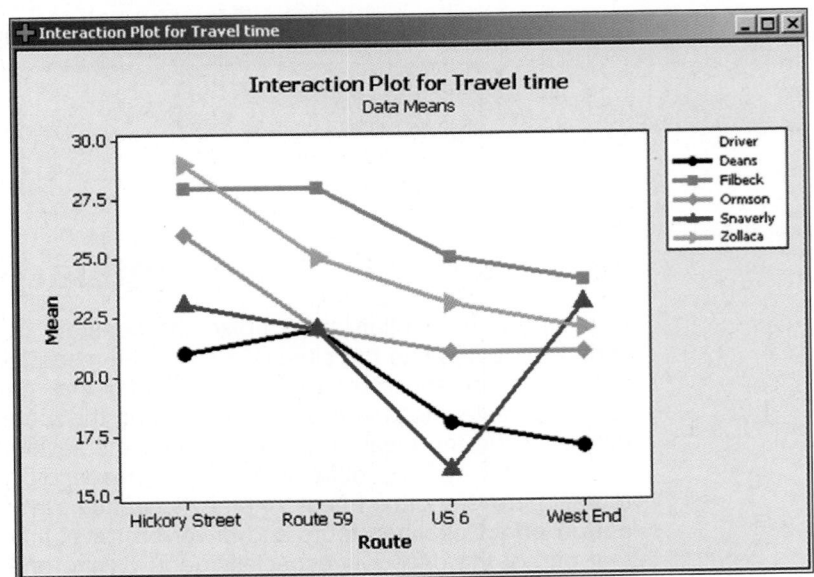

This plot helps us understand the interaction between the effects of drivers and routes on travel time. If the line segments for the drivers appear essentially parallel, then there is probably no interaction. On the other hand, if the line segments *do not*

seem to be parallel or cross, this suggests an interaction between the factors. The above plot suggests interaction because:

- The line segments for Zollaco and Filbeck cross over each other.
- Snaverly's line segment from U.S. 6 to West End crosses over three other line segments.

These observations suggest an interaction between driver and route.

Hypothesis Test for Interaction

The next step is to conduct statistical tests to further investigate the possible interaction effects. In summary, our study of travel times has several questions:

- Is there an interaction between routes and drivers?
- Are the travel times for drivers the same?
- Are the travel times for the routes the same?

Of the three questions, we are most interested in the test for interactions.

We can investigate these questions statistically by extending the two-way ANOVA procedure presented in the previous section. We add another source of variation, namely, the interaction. However, in order to estimate the "error" sum of squares, we need at least two measurements for each driver/route combination. So suppose the experiment reported on page 422 is repeated by measuring two more travel times for each driver and route combination. So, we **replicate** the experiment. Now we have three observations for each driver/route combination. Using the mean of three travel times for each driver/route combination we get a more reliable measure of the mean travel time. The results of replicating the experiment are in the following Excel table. Note that the data should be entered in this exact format so we can use statistical software.

Excel

Two Way Anova with Interactions

		US 6	West End	Hickory St	Route 59	
1						
2		US 6	West End	Hickory St	Route 59	
3	Deans	18	14	20	19	
4	Deans	15	17	21	22	
5	Deans	21	20	22	25	
6	Snaverly	19	20	24	24	
7	Snaverly	15	24	23	22	
8	Snaverly	14	25	22	20	
9	Ormson	19	23	25	23	
10	Ormson	21	21	29	23	
11	Ormson	23	19	24	20	
12	Zollaco	24	20	30	26	
13	Zollaco	20	24	28	25	
14	Zollaco	25	22	29	24	
15	Filbeck	27	24	28	28	
16	Filbeck	25	24	28	30	
17	Filbeck	23	24	28	26	
18						

To explain the spreadsheet, consider the "20, 21, 22" for the rows labeled "Deans" and column labeled "Hickory St." These are the three travel time measurements for Deans to drive the Hickory Street route. Specifically, Deans drove the Hickory Street route the first time in 20 minutes, 21 minutes on the second trip, and 22 minutes on the third trip.

The ANOVA now has three sets of hypotheses to test:

1. H_0: There is no interaction between drivers and routes.
   H_1: There is interaction between drivers and routes.
2. H_0: The driver means are the same.
   H_1: The driver means are *not* the same.
3. H_0: The route means are the same.
   H_1: The route means are *not* the same.

Note that we will label the route effect as **Factor A** and the driver effect as **Factor B.**

Each of these hypotheses is tested using the familiar F statistic. We can use a decision rule for each of the above tests or we can use the p-values for each test. In this case we will use the .05 significance level and compare the p-value generated by the statistical software with the significance level. So the various null hypotheses are rejected if the computed p-value is less than .05. Instead of computing treatment and block sum of squares, we compute factor and interaction sum of squares. The computations for the factor sum of squares are very similar to the SST and SSB as computed before. See formulas (12–4) and (12–6). The sum of squares due to possible interaction is:

$$\text{SSI} = (k - 1)(b - 1)\Sigma\Sigma\,(\overline{X}_{ij} - \overline{X}_{i.} - \overline{X}_{.j} + \overline{X}_G)^2 \qquad \textbf{[12–8]}$$

where
> i is a subscript or label representing a route.
> j is a subscript or label representing a driver.
> k is the number of Factor A (route effect) levels.
> b is the number of Factor B (driver effect) levels.
> n is the number of observations.
> $\overline{X}_{ij}$ is the mean travel time on a route, i, for driver, j. Note these are the means that we plotted in the graph on page 428.
> $\overline{X}_{i.}$ is the mean travel time for route i. Note the dot shows that the mean is calculated over all drivers. These are the route means that we compared on page 425.
> $\overline{X}_{.j}$ is the mean travel time for driver j. Note the dot shows that the mean is calculated over all routes. These are the driver means that we compared on page 425.
> $\overline{X}_G$ is the grand mean.

Once you have SSI, then SSE is found as:

$$\text{SSE} = \text{SS total} - \text{SS Factor A} - \text{SS Factor B} - \text{SSI} \qquad \textbf{[12–9]}$$

The complete ANOVA table including interactions is:

Source	Sum of Squares	df	Mean Square	F
Route	Factor A	$k - 1$	$\text{SSA}/(k - 1) = \text{MSA}$	MSA/MSE
Driver	Factor B	$b - 1$	$\text{SSB}/(b - 1) = \text{MSB}$	MSB/MSE
Interaction	SSI	$(k - 1)(b - 1)$	$\text{SSI}/[(k - 1)(b - 1)] = \text{MSI}$	MSI/MSE
Error	SSE	$n - kb$	$\text{SSE}/(n - kb) = \text{MSE}$	
Total	SS total	$n - 1$		

The resulting Excel output shows the summary descriptive statistics for each driver and an ANOVA table.

Two Way Anova with Interactions

Anova: Two-Factor With Replication

SUMMARY	US 6	West End	Hickory St	Route 59	Total
Deans					
Count	3	3	3	3	12.00
Sum	54	51	63	66	234.00
Average	18	17	21	22	19.50
Variance	9.00	9.00	1.00	9.00	9.73
Snaverly					
Count	3	3	3	3	12.00
Sum	48	69	69	66	252.00
Average	16	23	23	22	21.00
Variance	7.00	7.00	1.00	4.00	12.73
Ormson					
Count	3	3	3	3	12.00
Sum	63	63	78	66	270.00
Average	21	21	26	22	22.50
Variance	4	4	7	3	7.91

ANOVA

Source of Variation	SS	df	MS	F	P-value	F crit
Sample	359.10	4	89.78	20.88	0.000	2.61
Columns	218.40	3	72.80	16.93	0.000	2.84
Interaction	110.10	12	9.17	2.13	0.036	2.00
Within	172.00	40	4.30			
Total	859.60	59				

Route   Driver

The *p*-value for interactions of 0.036 (noted in yellow), is less than our significance level of 0.05. So our decision is to reject the null hypothesis of no interaction and conclude that the combination of route and driver has a significant effect on the response variable travel time.

Interaction effects provide information about the combined effects of variables. If interaction is present, then you should conduct a one-way ANOVA to test differences in the factor means for each level of the other factor. This analysis requires some time and work to complete but the results are usually enlightening.

We will continue the analysis by conducting a one-way ANOVA for each driver testing the hypothesis: H_0: Route travel times are equal. The results follow.

Deans: H_0: Route travel times are equal.

Source	DF	SS	MS	F	P
Dean RTE	3	51.00	17.00	2.43	0.140
Error	8	56.00	7.00		
Total	11	107.00			

Snaverly: H_0: Route travel times are equal.

Source	DF	SS	MS	F	P
SN RTE	3	102.00	34.00	7.16	0.012
Error	8	38.00	4.75		
Total	11	140.00			

Ormson: H_0: Route travel times are equal.

Source	DF	SS	MS	F	P
Ormson RTE	3	51.00	17.00	3.78	0.059
Error	8	36.00	4.50		
Total	11	87.00			

Zollaco: H_0: Route travel times are equal.

Source	DF	SS	MS	F	P
Z-RTE	3	86.25	28.75	8.85	0.006
Error	8	26.00	3.25		
Total	11	112.25			

Filbeck: H_0: Route travel times are equal.

Source	DF	SS	MS	F	P
Filbeck RTE	3	38.25	12.75	6.38	0.016
Error	8	16.00	2.00		
Total	11	54.25			

Recall the results from the two-way ANOVA without interaction on page 425. In that analysis, the results clearly showed that the factor "route" had a significant effect on travel time. However, now that we include the interaction effect, the results show that conclusion is not generally true. As we review the *p*-values for the five one-way ANOVAs above (reject the null if the *p*-value is less than 0.05), we know that route mean travel times are different for three drivers: Filbeck, Snaverly, and Zollaco. However, for Deans and Ormson, their mean route travel times are not significantly different.

Now that we know this new and interesting information, we would want to know why these differences exist. Further investigation of the driving habits of the five drivers is required.

In review, our presentation of two-way ANOVA with interaction shows the power of statistical analysis. In this analysis, we were able to test the combined effect of driver and route on travel time, and to show that different drivers evidently behave differently as they travel their routes. Gaining understanding of interaction effects is extremely important in many applications, from scientific areas such as agriculture and quality control to managerial fields like human resource management and gender equality in salary and performance ratings.

Self-Review 12–5   See the following ANOVA table.

ANOVA					
Source of Variation	**SS**	**df**	**MS**	**F**	**p-value**
Factor A	6.41	3	2.137	3.46	0.0322
Factor B	5.01	2	2.507	4.06	0.0304
Interaction	33.15	6	5.525	8.94	0.0000
Error	14.83	24	0.618		
Total	59.41	35			

Use the .05 significance level to answer the following questions.
(a) How many levels does Factor A have? Is there a significant difference among the Factor A means? How do you know?
(b) How many levels does Factor B have? Is there a significant difference among the Factor B means? How do you know?
(c) How many observations are there in each cell? Is there a significant interaction between Factor A and Factor B on the response variable? How do you know?

Exercises

connect

19. Consider the following sample data for a two-factor ANOVA experiment:

		Factor A		
		Level 1	**Level 2**	**Level 3**
Factor B	Level 1	23	20	11
		21	32	20
		25	26	20
	Level 2	13	20	11
		32	17	23
		17	15	8

Use the .05 significance level to answer the following questions.
a. Is there a difference in the Factor A means?
b. Is there a difference in the Factor B means?
c. Do Factors A and B have a significant interaction?

20. Consider the following partially completed two-way ANOVA table. Suppose there are four levels of Factor A and three levels of Factor B. The number of replications per cell is 5. Complete the table and test to determine if there is a significant difference in Factor A means, Factor B means, or the interaction means. Use the .05 significance level. (Hint: estimate the values from the F table.)

ANOVA				
Source	**SS**	**df**	**MS**	**F**
Factor A	75			
Factor B	25			
Interaction	300			
Error	600			
Total	1000			

21. The distributor of the *Wapakoneta Daily News,* a regional newspaper serving western Ohio, is considering three types of dispensing machines or "racks." Management wants to know if the different machines affect sales. These racks are designated as J-1000, D-320, and UV-57. Management also wants to know if the placement of the racks either inside or outside supermarkets affects sales. Each of six similar stores was randomly assigned a machine and location combination. The data below is the number of papers sold over four days.

Position/Machine	J-1000	D-320	UV-57
Inside	33, 40, 30, 31	29, 28, 33, 33	47, 39, 39, 45
Outside	43, 36, 41, 40	48, 45, 40, 44	37, 32, 36, 35

a. Draw the interaction graph. Based on your observations, is there an interaction effect? Based on the graph, describe the interaction effect of machine and position.
b. Use the 0.05 level to test for position, machine, and interaction effects on sales. Report the statistical results.
c. Compare the inside and outside mean sales for each machine using statistical techniques. What do you conclude?

22. A large company is organized into three functional areas: manufacturing, marketing, and research and development. The employees claim that the company pays women less than men for similar jobs. The company randomly selected four males and four females in each area and recorded their weekly salaries in dollars.

Area/Gender	Female	Male
Manufacturing	1016, 1007, 875, 968	978, 1056, 982, 748
Marketing	1045, 895, 848, 904	1154, 1091, 878, 876
Research and Development	770, 733, 844, 771	926, 1055, 1066, 1088

a. Draw the interaction graph. Based on your observations, is there an interaction effect? Based on the graph, describe the interaction effect of gender and area on salary.
b. Use the 0.05 level to test for gender, area, and interaction effects on salary. Report the statistical results.
c. Compare the male and female mean sales for each area using statistical techniques. What do you recommend to the distributor?

Chapter Summary

I. The characteristics of the F distribution are:
  A. It is continuous.
  B. Its values cannot be negative.
  C. It is positively skewed.
  D. There is a family of F distributions. Each time the degrees of freedom in either the numerator or the denominator changes, a new distribution is created.
II. The F distribution is used to test whether two population variances are the same.
  A. The sampled populations must follow the normal distribution.
  B. The larger of the two sample variances is placed in the numerator, forcing the ratio to be at least 1.00.
  C. The value of F is computed using the following equation:

$$F = \frac{s_1^2}{s_2^2}$$ [12–1]

III. A one-way ANOVA is used to compare several treatment means.
  A. A treatment is a source of variation.
  B. The assumptions underlying ANOVA are:
    1. The samples are from populations that follow the normal distribution.
    2. The populations have equal standard deviations.
    3. The samples are independent.
  C. The information for finding the value of F is summarized in an ANOVA table.
    1. The formula for SS total, the sum of squares total, is:

$$\text{SS total} = \Sigma(X - \overline{X}_G)^2$$ [12–2]

  2. The formula for SSE, the sum of squares error, is:

$$\text{SSE} = \Sigma(X - \overline{X}_c)^2$$ [12–3]

  3. The formula for the SST, the sum of squares treatment, is found by subtraction.

$$\text{SST} = \text{SS total} - \text{SSE}$$ [12–4]

  4. This information is summarized in the following table and the value of F determined.

Source of Variation	Sum of Squares	Degrees of Freedom	Mean Square	F
Treatments	SST	$k - 1$	$\text{SST}/(k - 1) = \text{MST}$	MST/MSE
Error	SSE	$n - k$	$\text{SSE}/(n - k) = \text{MSE}$	
Total	SS total	$n - 1$		

IV. If a null hypothesis of equal treatment means is rejected, we can identify the pairs of means that differ from the following confidence interval.

$$(\overline{X}_1 - \overline{X}_2) \pm t\sqrt{\text{MSE}\left(\frac{1}{n_1} + \frac{1}{n_2}\right)}$$ [12–5]

V. In a two-way ANOVA we consider a second treatment variable.
  A. The second treatment variable is called the blocking variable.
  B. It is determined using the following equation:

$$\text{SSB} = k\Sigma(\overline{X}_b - \overline{X}_G)^2$$ [12–6]

  C. The SSE term, or sum of squares error, is found from the following equation.

$$\text{SSE} = \text{SS total} - \text{SST} - \text{SSB}$$ [12–7]

D. The F statistics for the treatment variable and the blocking variable are determined in the following table.

Source of Variation	Sum of Squares	Degrees of Freedom	Mean Square	F
Treatments	SST	$k - 1$	$SST/(k - 1) = MST$	MST/MSE
Blocks	SSB	$b - 1$	$SSB/(b - 1) = MSB$	MSB/MSE
Error	SSE	$[(k - 1)(b - 1)]$	$SSE/[(k - 1)(b - 1)] = MSE$	
Total	SS total	$n - 1$		

VI. In a two-way ANOVA with repeated observations we consider two treatment variables and the possible interaction between the variables.

A. The sum of squares due to possible interactions is found by:

$$SSI = (k - 1)(b - 1) \sum \sum (\overline{X}_{ij} - \overline{X}_{i.} - \overline{X}_{j} + \overline{X}_{G})^2 \qquad \text{[12–8]}$$

B. The SSE term is found by subtraction.

$$SSE = SS\ total - SSA - SSB - SSI \qquad \text{[12–9]}$$

C. The complete ANOVA table including interactions is:

Source	Sum of Squares	df	Mean Square	F
Factor A	SSA	$k - 1$	$SSA/(k - 1) = MSA$	MSA/MSE
Factor B	SSB	$b - 1$	$SSB/(b - 1) = MSB$	MSB/MSE
Interaction	SSI	$(k - 1)(b - 1)$	$SSI/[(k - 1)(b - 1)] = MSI$	MSI/MSE
Error	SSE	$n - kb$	$SSE/(n - kb) = MSE$	
Total	SS total	$n - 1$		

Pronunciation Key

SYMBOL	MEANING	PRONUNCIATION
SS total	Sum of squares total	*S S total*
SST	Sum of squares treatment	*S S T*
SSE	Sum of squares error	*S S E*
MSE	Mean square error	*M S E*
SSB	Block sum of squares	*S S B*
SSI	Sum of squares interaction	*S S I*

Chapter Exercises

connect

23. A real estate agent in the coastal area of Georgia wants to compare the variation in the selling price of homes on the oceanfront with those one to three blocks from the ocean. A sample of 21 oceanfront homes sold within the last year revealed the standard deviation of the selling prices was $45,600. A sample of 18 homes, also sold within the last year, that were one to three blocks from the ocean revealed that the standard deviation was $21,330. At the .01 significance level, can we conclude that there is more variation in the selling prices of the oceanfront homes?

24. A computer manufacturer is about to unveil a new, faster personal computer. The new machine clearly is faster, but initial tests indicate there is more variation in the processing time. The processing time depends on the particular program being run, the amount of input data, and the amount of output. A sample of 16 computer runs, covering a range of production jobs, showed that the standard deviation of the processing time was 22 (hundredths of a second) for the new machine and 12 (hundredths of a second) for the current machine. At the .05 significance level can we conclude that there is more variation in the processing time of the new machine?

25. There are two Chevrolet dealers in Jamestown, New York. The mean monthly sales at Sharkey Chevy and Dave White Chevrolet are about the same. However, Tom Sharkey, the owner of Sharkey Chevy, believes his sales are more consistent. Below is the number of new cars sold at Sharkey in the last seven months and for the last eight months at Dave White. Do you agree with Mr. Sharkey? Use the .01 significance level.

Sharkey	98	78	54	57	68	64	70	
Dave White	75	81	81	30	82	46	58	101

26. Random samples of five were selected from each of three populations. The sum of squares total was 100. The sum of squares due to the treatments was 40.
    a. Set up the null hypothesis and the alternate hypothesis.
    b. What is the decision rule? Use the .05 significance level.
    c. Complete the ANOVA table. What is the value of F?
    d. What is your decision regarding the null hypothesis?

27. In an ANOVA table MSE was equal to 10. Random samples of six were selected from each of four populations, where the sum of squares total was 250.
    a. Set up the null hypothesis and the alternate hypothesis.
    b. What is the decision rule? Use the .05 significance level.
    c. Complete the ANOVA table. What is the value of F?
    d. What is your decision regarding the null hypothesis?

28. The following is a partial ANOVA table.

Source	Sum of Squares	df	Mean Square	F
Treatment		2		
Error			20	
Total	500	11		

Complete the table and answer the following questions. Use the .05 significance level.
    a. How many treatments are there?
    b. What is the total sample size?
    c. What is the critical value of F?
    d. Write out the null and alternate hypotheses.
    e. What is your conclusion regarding the null hypothesis?

29. A consumer organization wants to know whether there is a difference in the price of a particular toy at three different types of stores. The price of the toy was checked in a sample of five discount stores, five variety stores, and five department stores. The results are shown below. Use the .05 significance level.

Discount	Variety	Department
$12	$15	$19
13	17	17
14	14	16
12	18	20
15	17	19

30. A physician who specializes in weight control has three different diets she recommends. As an experiment, she randomly selected 15 patients and then assigned 5 to each diet.

After three weeks the following weight losses, in pounds, were noted. At the .05 significance level, can she conclude that there is a difference in the mean amount of weight loss among the three diets?

Plan A	Plan B	Plan C
5	6	7
7	7	8
4	7	9
5	5	8
4	6	9

31. The City of Maumee comprises four districts. Chief of Police Andy North wants to determine whether there is a difference in the mean number of crimes committed among the four districts. He recorded the number of crimes reported in each district for a sample of six days. At the .05 significance level, can the chief of police conclude there is a difference in the mean number of crimes?

Number of Crimes			
Rec Center	Key Street	Monclova	Whitehouse
13	21	12	16
15	13	14	17
14	18	15	18
15	19	13	15
14	18	12	20
15	19	15	18

32. A study of the effect of television commercials on 12-year-old children measured their attention span, in seconds. The commercials were for clothes, food, and toys. At the .05 significance level is there a difference in the mean attention span of the children for the various commercials? Are there significant differences between pairs of means? Would you recommend dropping one of the three commercial types?

Clothes	Food	Toys
26	45	60
21	48	51
43	43	43
35	53	54
28	47	63
31	42	53
17	34	48
31	43	58
20	57	47
	47	51
	44	51
	54	

33. When only two treatments are involved, ANOVA and the Student t test (Chapter 11) result in the same conclusions. Also, $t^2 = F$. As an example, suppose that 14 randomly selected students were divided into two groups, one consisting of 6 students and the other of 8. One group was taught using a combination of lecture and programmed instruction, the other using a combination of lecture and television. At the end of the course, each group was given a 50-item test. The following is a list of the number correct for each of the two groups.

Lecture and Programmed Instruction	Lecture and Television
19	32
17	28
23	31
22	26
17	23
16	24
	27
	25

a. Using analysis of variance techniques, test H_0 that the two mean test scores are equal; $\alpha = .05$.

b. Using the t test from Chapter 11, compute t.

c. Interpret the results.

34. There are four auto body shops in Bangor, Maine, and all claim to promptly serve customers. To check if there is any difference in service, customers are randomly selected from each repair shop and their waiting times in days are recorded. The output from a statistical software package is:

Summary				
Groups	Count	Sum	Average	Variance
Body Shop A	3	15.4	5.133333	0.323333
Body Shop B	4	32	8	1.433333
Body Shop C	5	25.2	5.04	0.748
Body Shop D	4	25.9	6.475	0.595833

ANOVA					
Source of Variation	SS	df	MS	F	p-value
Between Groups	23.37321	3	7.791069	9.612506	0.001632
Within Groups	9.726167	12	0.810514		
Total	33.09938	15			

Is there evidence to suggest a difference in the mean waiting times at the four body shops? Use the .05 significance level.

35. The fuel efficiencies for a sample of 27 compact, midsize, and large cars are entered into a statistical software package. Analysis of variance is used to investigate if there is a difference in the mean mileage of the three cars. What do you conclude? Use the .01 significance level.

Summary				
Groups	Count	Sum	Average	Variance
Compact	12	268.3	22.35833	9.388106
Midsize	9	172.4	19.15556	7.315278
Large	6	100.5	16.75	7.303

Additional results are shown below.

ANOVA					
Source of Variation	**SS**	**df**	**MS**	**F**	**p-value**
Between Groups	136.4803	2	68.24014	8.258752	0.001866
Within Groups	198.3064	24	8.262766		
Total	334.7867	26			

36. Three assembly lines are used to produce a certain component for an airliner. To examine the production rate, a random sample of six hourly periods is chosen for each assembly line and the number of components produced during these periods for each line is recorded. The output from a statistical software package is:

Summary				
Groups	**Count**	**Sum**	**Average**	**Variance**
Line A	6	250	41.66667	0.266667
Line B	6	260	43.33333	0.666667
Line C	6	249	41.5	0.7

ANOVA					
Source of Variation	**SS**	**df**	**MS**	**F**	**p-value**
Between Groups	12.33333	2	6.166667	11.32653	0.001005
Within Groups	8.166667	15	0.544444		
Total	20.5	17			

a. Use a .01 level of significance to test if there is a difference in the mean production of the three assembly lines.
b. Develop a 99 percent confidence interval for the difference in the means between Line B and Line C.

37. The postal service groups first-class mail as letters, cards, flats, or parcels. Over a period of three weeks, one item of each kind was sent from a particular postal administrative center. The total time in transit was recorded. A statistical software package was then used to perform the analysis. The results follow.

```
Source     DF         SS       MS       F        P
Factor      3      13.82     4.61     2.72     0.051
Error      68     115.17     1.69
Total      71     128.99

S = 1.301        R-Sq = 10.71%      R-Sq(adj) = 6.77%


                                   Individual 95% CIs for Mean Based on
                                   Pooled StDev
Level      N    Mean    StDev    ------+---------+---------+---------+---
Letters   18   1.444    1.097    (---------*---------)
Cards     18   1.667    1.455       (---------*---------)
Flats     18   2.444    1.617                  (---------*---------)
Parcels   18   2.389    0.916                 .(---------*---------)
                                   ------+---------+---------+---------+---
                                       1.20      1.80      2.40      3.00
```

Use the .05 significance level to test if this evidence suggests a difference in the means for the different types of first-class mail.

38. For your email you use a filter to block spam from your inbox. The number of items blocked by day of week is recorded and a statistical software system is used to perform the analysis that follows. Here are the results:

```
Source      DF        SS        MS        F         P
Factor       6     1367.8     228.0     5.72     0.000
Error       48     1913.2      39.9
Total       54     3281.0

S = 6.313        R-Sq = 41.69%      R-Sq(adj) = 34.40%

                                   Individual 95% CIs for Mean Based on
                                   Pooled StDev
Level        N     Mean   StDev   ----+---------+---------+---------+-----
Monday      10   74.000   6.164                          (-----*------)
Tuesday      9   66.111   7.288              (------*------)
Wednesday    7   74.143   2.268                     (-------*-------)
Thursday     8   62.375   5.041   (-------*------)
Friday       8   75.125   4.454                        (------*-------)
Saturday     5   63.200   7.259   (--------*---------)
Sunday       8   72.375   9.164                 (-------*------)
                                   ----+---------+---------+---------+-----
                                     60.0      66.0      72.0      78.0
```

Use the .05 significance level to test if this evidence suggests a difference in the means for the different days of the week.

39. Shank's, Inc., a nationwide advertising firm, wants to know whether the size of an advertisement and the color of the advertisement make a difference in the response of magazine readers. A random sample of readers is shown ads of four different colors and three different sizes. Each reader is asked to give the particular combination of size and color a rating between 1 and 10. Assume that the ratings follow the normal distribution. The rating for each combination is shown in the following table (for example, the rating for a small red ad is 2).

Size of Ad	Color of Ad			
	Red	Blue	Orange	Green
Small	2	3	3	8
Medium	3	5	6	7
Large	6	7	8	8

Is there a difference in the effectiveness of an advertisement by color and by size? Use the .05 level of significance.

40. There are four McBurger restaurants in the Columbus, Georgia, area. The numbers of burgers sold at the respective restaurants for each of the last six weeks are shown below. At the .05 significance level, is there a difference in the mean number sold among the four restaurants, when the factor of week is considered?

Week	Restaurant			
	Metro	Interstate	University	River
1	124	160	320	190
2	234	220	340	230
3	430	290	290	240
4	105	245	310	170
5	240	205	280	180
6	310	260	270	205

a. Is there a difference in the treatment means?
b. Is there a difference in the block means?

41. The city of Tucson, Arizona, employs people to assess the value of homes for the purpose of establishing real estate tax. The city manager sends each assessor to the same five homes and then compares the results. The information is given below, in thousands of dollars. Can we conclude that there is a difference in the assessors, at $\alpha = .05$?

Home	Assessor			
	Zawodny	Norman	Cingle	Holiday
A	$53.0	$55.0	$49.0	$45.0
B	50.0	51.0	52.0	53.0
C	48.0	52.0	47.0	53.0
D	70.0	68.0	65.0	64.0
E	84.0	89.0	92.0	86.0

a. Is there a difference in the treatment means?
b. Is there a difference in the block means?

42. Martin Motors has in stock three cars of the same make and model. The president would like to compare the gas consumption of the three cars (labeled car A, car B, and car C) using four different types of gasoline. For each trial, a gallon of gasoline was added to an empty tank, and the car was driven until it ran out of gas. The following table shows the number of miles driven in each trial.

Types of Gasoline	Distance (miles)		
	Car A	Car B	Car C
Regular	22.4	20.8	21.5
Super regular	17.0	19.4	20.7
Unleaded	19.2	20.2	21.2
Premium unleaded	20.3	18.6	20.4

Using the .05 level of significance:
a. Is there a difference among types of gasoline?
b. Is there a difference in the cars?

43. A research firm wants to compare the miles per gallon of unleaded regular, mid-grade, and super premium gasolines. Because of differences in the performance of different automobiles, seven different automobiles were selected and treated as blocks. Therefore, each brand of gasoline was tested with each type of automobile. The results of the trials, in miles per gallon, are shown in the following table. At the .05 significance level, is there a difference in the gasolines or automobiles?

Automobile	Regular	Mid-grade	Super Premium
1	21	23	26
2	23	22	25
3	24	25	27
4	24	24	26
5	26	26	30
6	26	24	27
7	28	27	32

44. Three supermarket chains in the Denver area each claim to have the lowest overall prices. As part of an investigative study on supermarket advertising, the *Denver Daily News* conducted a study. First, a random sample of nine grocery items was selected. Next, the price of each selected item was checked at each of the three chains on the same day.

At the .05 significance level, is there a difference in the mean prices at the supermarkets or for the items?

Item	Super$	Ralph's	Lowblaws
1	$1.12	$1.02	$1.07
2	1.14	1.10	1.21
3	1.72	1.97	2.08
4	2.22	2.09	2.32
5	2.40	2.10	2.30
6	4.04	4.32	4.15
7	5.05	4.95	5.05
8	4.68	4.13	4.67
9	5.52	5.46	5.86

45. Listed below are the weights (in grams) of a sample of M&M's Plain candies, classified according to color. Use a statistical software system to determine whether there is a difference in the mean weights of candies of different colors. Use the .05 significance level.

Red	Orange	Yellow	Brown	Tan	Green
0.946	0.902	0.929	0.896	0.845	0.935
1.107	0.943	0.960	0.888	0.909	0.903
0.913	0.916	0.938	0.906	0.873	0.865
0.904	0.910	0.933	0.941	0.902	0.822
0.926	0.903	0.932	0.838	0.956	0.871
0.926	0.901	0.899	0.892	0.959	0.905
1.006	0.919	0.907	0.905	0.916	0.905
0.914	0.901	0.906	0.824	0.822	0.852
0.922	0.930	0.930	0.908		0.965
1.052	0.883	0.952	0.833		0.898
0.903		0.939			
0.895		0.940			
		0.882			
		0.906			

46. There are four radio stations in Midland. The stations have different formats (hard rock, classical, country/western, and easy listening), but each is concerned with the number of minutes of music played per hour. From a sample of 10 hours from each station, the following sample means were offered.

$$\bar{X}_1 = 51.32 \qquad \bar{X}_2 = 44.64 \qquad \bar{X}_3 = 47.2 \qquad \bar{X}_4 = 50.85$$

$$\text{SS total} = 650.75$$

a. Determine SST.
b. Determine SSE.
c. Complete an ANOVA table.
d. At the .05 significance level, is there a difference in the treatment means?
e. Is there a difference in the mean amount of music time between station 1 and station 4? Use the .05 significance level.

We recommend you complete the following exercises using a statistical software package such as Excel, MegaStat, or MINITAB.

47. The American Accounting Association recently conducted a study to compare the weekly wages of men and women employed in either the public or private sector of accounting.

Gender	Sector	
	Public	**Private**
Men	$ 978	$1,335
	1,035	1,167
	964	1,236
	996	1,317
	1,117	1,192
Women	$ 863	$1,079
	975	1,160
	999	1,063
	1,019	1,110
	1,037	1,093

At the .05 significance level:
a. Draw an interaction plot of men and women means by sector.
b. Test the interaction effect of gender and sector on wages.
c. Based on your results in part (b), conduct the appropriate tests of hypotheses for differences in factor means.
d. Interpret the results in a brief report.

48. Robert Altoff is vice president for engineering for a manufacturer of household washing machines. As part of new product development, he wishes to determine the optimal length of time for the washing cycle. A part of the development is to study the relationship between the detergent used (four brands) and the length of the washing cycle (18, 20, 22, or 24 minutes). In order to run the experiment 32 standard household laundry loads (having equal amounts of dirt and the same total weights) are randomly assigned to the 16 detergent–washing cycle combinations. The results (in pounds of dirt removed) are shown below.

Detergent Brand	Cycle Time (min)			
	18	**20**	**22**	**24**
A	0.13	0.12	0.19	0.15
	0.11	0.11	0.17	0.18
B	0.14	0.15	0.18	0.20
	0.10	0.14	0.17	0.18
C	0.16	0.15	0.18	0.19
	0.17	0.14	0.19	0.21
D	0.09	0.12	0.16	0.15
	0.13	0.13	0.16	0.17

At the .05 significance level:
a. Draw an interaction plot of the detergent means by cycle time.
b. Test the interaction effect of brand and cycle time on "dirt removed."
c. Based on your results in part (b), conduct the appropriate tests of hypotheses for differences in factor means.
d. Interpret the results in a brief report.

Data Set Exercises

49. Refer to the Real Estate data, which report information on the homes sold in the Denver, Colorado, area last year.
a. At the .02 significance level, is there a difference in the variability of the selling prices of the homes that have a pool versus those that do not have a pool?
b. At the .02 significance level, is there a difference in the variability of the selling prices of the homes with an attached garage versus those that do not have an attached garage?

    c. At the .05 significance level, is there a difference in the mean selling price of the homes among the five townships?

50. Refer to the Baseball 2007 data, which report information on the 30 Major League Baseball teams for the 2007 season.

    a. At the .10 significance level, is there a difference in the variation in team salary among the American and National league teams?

    b. Create a variable that classifies a team's total attendance into three groups: less than 2.0 (million), 2.0 up to 3.0, and 3.0 or more. At the .05 significance level, is there a difference in the mean number of games won among the three groups? Use the .01 significance level.

    c. Using the same attendance variable developed in part (b), is there a difference in the mean team batting average? Use the .01 significance level.

    d. Using the same attendance variable developed in part (b), is there a difference in the mean salary of the three groups? Use the .01 significance level.

51. Refer to the Wage data, which report information on annual wages for a sample of 100 workers. Also included are variables relating to industry, years of education, and gender for each worker.

    a. Conduct a test of hypothesis to determine if there is a difference in the mean annual wages for workers in the three industries. If there is a difference in the means, which pair or pairs of means differ? Use the .05 significance level.

    b. Conduct a test of hypothesis to determine if there is a difference in the mean annual wages for workers in the six different occupations. If there is a difference in the means, which pair or pairs of means differ? Use the .05 significance level.

Software Commands

1. The Excel commands for the test of variances on page 407 are:

    a. Enter the data for U.S. 25 in column A and for I-75 in column B. Label the two columns.

    b. Select the **Data** tab on the top menu. Then, on the far right, select **Data Analysis.** Select **F-Test: Two-Sample for Variances,** then click **OK.**

    c. The range of the first variable is *A1:A8,* and *B1:B9* for the second. Click on **Labels,** enter *0.05* for **Alpha,** select *D1* for the **Output Range,** and click **OK.**

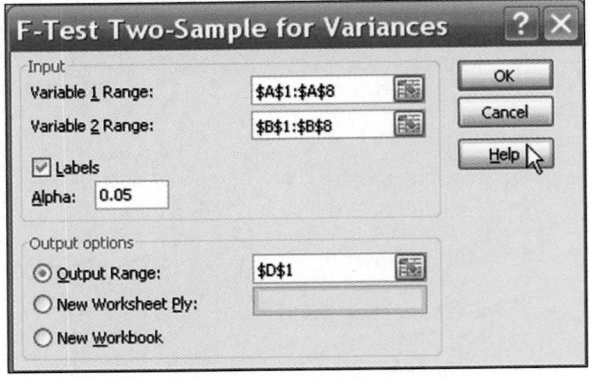

2. The Excel commands for the one-way ANOVA on page 416 are:

    a. Key in data into four columns labeled: *Eastern, TWA, Allegheny,* and *Ozark.*

    b. Select the **Data** tab on the top menu. Then, on the far right, select **Data Analysis.** Select **ANOVA: Single Factor,** then click **OK.**

    c. In the subsequent dialog box make the input range *A1:D8,* click on **Grouped by Columns,** click on **Labels in first row,** the **Alpha** text box is *.05,* and finally select **Output Range** as *F1* and click **OK.**

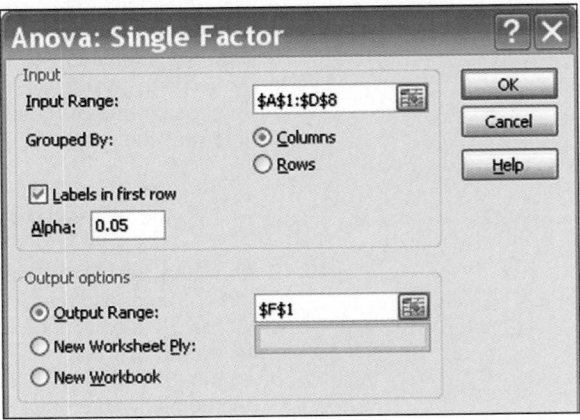

3. The MINITAB commands for the one-way ANOVA on page 416 are:
   a. Input the data into four columns and identify the columns as *Eastern, TWA, Allegheny,* and *Ozark.*
   b. Select **Stat, ANOVA,** and **One-way (Unstacked),** select the data in columns C1 to C4, check on **Select** in the lower left, and then click **OK.**

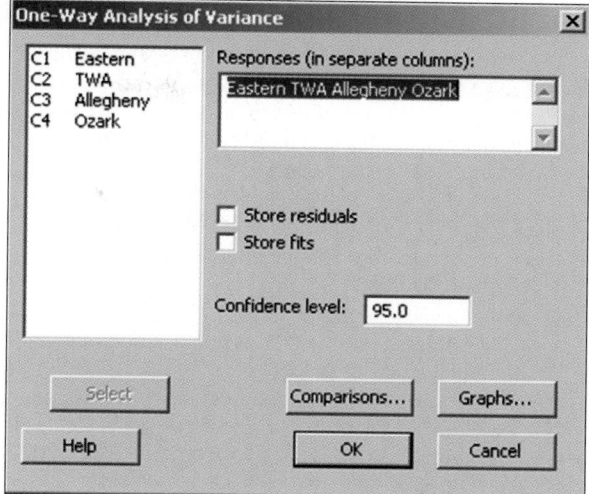

4. The Excel commands for the two-way ANOVA on page 426 are:
   a. In the first row of the first column write the word *Driver,* then list the five drivers in the first column. In the first row of the next four columns enter the name of the routes. Enter the data under each route name.
   b. Select the **Data** tab on the top menu. Then, on the far right, select **Data Analysis.** Select **ANOVA: Two-Factor Without Replication,** then click **OK.**
   c. In the dialog box, the **Input Range** is *A3:E8,* click on **Labels,** select G3 for the **Output Range,** and then click **OK.**

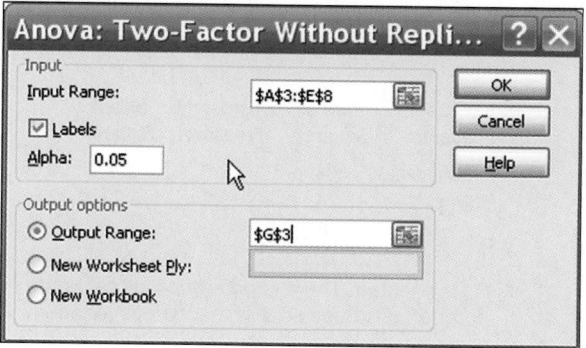

5. The Excel commands for the two-way ANOVA with interaction on page 431 are:
   a. Enter the data into Excel as shown on page 429.
   b. Select the **Data** tab on the top menu. Then, on the far right, select **Data Analysis.** Select **ANOVA: Two-Factor With Replication,** then click **OK.**
   c. In the dialog box, enter the **Input Range** as *B2:F17,* enter **Rows per sample** as *3,* select **New Worksheet Ply,** and then click **OK.**

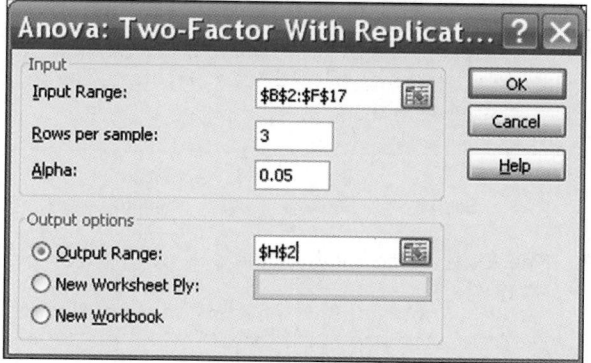

Chapter 12   Answers to Self-Review

12–1 Let Mark's assemblies be population 1, then
$H_0: \sigma_1^2 \le \sigma_2^2$; $H_1: \sigma_1^2 > \sigma_2^2$; $df_1 = 10 - 1 = 9$; and
df_2 also equals 9. H_0 is rejected if $F > 3.18$.

$$F = \frac{(2.0)^2}{(1.5)^2} = 1.78$$

H_0 is not rejected. The variation is the same for both employees.

12–2 a. $H_0: \mu_1 = \mu_2 = \mu_3$
   H_1: At least one treatment mean is different.
b. Reject H_0 if $F > 4.26$
c. $\overline{X} = \dfrac{240}{12} = 20$

    SS total $= (18 - 20)^2 + \cdots + (32 - 20)^2$
                $= 578$
       SSE $= (18 - 17)^2 + (14 - 17)^2 + \cdots +$
                $(32 - 29)^2$
            $= 74$
       SST $= 578 - 74 = 504$

d.

Source	Sum of Squares	Degrees of Freedom	Mean Square	F
Treatment	504	2	252	30.65
Error	74	9	8.22	
Total	578	11		

e. H_0 is rejected. There is difference in the mean number of bottles sold at the various locations.

12–3 a. $H_0: \mu_1 = \mu_2 = \mu_3$
   H_1: Not all means are equal.
b. H_0 is rejected if $F > 3.98$.
c. $\overline{X}_G = 8.86$, $\overline{X}_1 = 11$, $\overline{X}_2 = 8.75$, $\overline{X}_3 = 6.8$
    SS total $= 53.71$
        SST $= 44.16$
        SSE $= 9.55$

Source	Sum of Squares	df	Mean Square	F
Treatment	44.16	2	22.08	25.43
Error	9.55	11	0.8682	
Total	53.71	13		

d. H_0 is rejected. The treatment means differ.
e. $(11.0 - 6.8) \pm 2.201 \sqrt{0.8682(\frac{1}{6} + \frac{1}{5})} =$
    $4.2 \pm 1.30 = 2.90$ and 5.50
    These treatment means differ because both endpoints of the confidence interval are of the same sign—positive in this problem.

12–4 For types:

    $H_0: \mu_1 = \mu_2 = \mu_3$
    H_1: The treatment means are not equal.

Reject H_0 if $F > 4.46$.
For months:

    $H_0: \mu_1 = \mu_2 = \mu_3 = \mu_4 = \mu_5$
    H_1: The block means are not equal.

Reject H_0 if $F > 3.84$.
    The analysis of variance table is as follows:

Source:	df	SS	MS	F
Types	2	3.60	1.80	0.39
Months	4	31.73	7.93	1.71
Error	8	37.07	4.63	
Total	14	72.40		

The null hypotheses cannot be rejected for either types or months. There is no difference in the mean sales among types or months.

12–5 a. There are four levels of Factor A. The p-value is less than .05, so Factor A means differ.
b. There are three levels of Factor B. The p-value is less than .05, so the Factor B means differ.
c. There are three observations in each cell. There is an interaction between Factor A and Factor B means, because the p-value is less than .05.

A Review of Chapters 10–12

This section is a review of the major concepts and terms introduced in Chapters 10, 11, and 12. Chapter 10 began our study of hypothesis testing. A hypothesis is a statement about the value of a population parameter. In statistical hypothesis testing, we begin by making a statement about the value of the population parameter in the null hypothesis. We establish the null hypothesis for the purpose of testing. When we complete the testing, our decision is either to reject or to fail to reject the null hypothesis. If we reject the null hypothesis, we conclude that the alternate hypothesis is true. The alternate hypothesis is "accepted" only if we show that the null hypothesis is false. We also refer to the alternate hypothesis as the research hypothesis. Most of the time we want to prove the alternate hypothesis.

In Chapter 10 we selected random samples from a single population and tested whether it was reasonable that the population parameter under study equaled a particular value. For example, we wish to investigate whether the mean tenure time of those holding the position of CEO in large firms is 12 years. We select a sample of CEOs, compute the sample mean, and compare the mean of the sample to the population. The single population under consideration is the length of tenure of CEOs of large firms. We described methods for conducting the test when the population standard deviation was available and when it was not available. Also, in Chapter 10 we conducted tests of hypothesis about a population proportion. A proportion is the fraction of individuals or objects possessing a certain characteristic. For example, industry records indicate that 70 percent of gasoline sales for automobiles are for the regular grade of gasoline. A sample of the 100 sales from last month at the Pantry in Conway revealed 76 were for the regular grade. Can the owners conclude that more than 70 percent of their customers purchase the regular grade?

In Chapter 11 we extended the idea of hypothesis testing to whether two independent random samples came from populations having the same or equal population means. For example, St. Mathews Hospital operates an urgent care facility on both the north and south sides of Knoxville, Tennessee. The research question is: Is the mean waiting time for patients visiting the two facilities the same? To investigate, we select a random sample from each of the facilities and compute the sample means. We test the null hypothesis that the mean waiting time is the same at the two facilities. The alternate hypothesis is that the mean waiting time is not the same for the two facilities. If the population standard deviations are known, we use the z distribution as the distribution of the test statistic. If the population standard deviations are not known, the test statistic follows the t distribution.

Our discussion in Chapter 11 also concerned dependent samples. The test statistic is the t distribution and we assume that the distribution of differences follows the normal distribution. One typical paired sample problem calls for recording an individual's blood pressure before administering medication and then again afterward in order to evaluate the effectiveness of the medication. We also considered the case of testing two population proportions. For example, the production manager wished to compare the proportion of defects on the day shift with that of the second shift.

Chapter 11 dealt with the difference between two population means. Chapter 12 presented tests for variances and a procedure called the *analysis of variance,* or *ANOVA.* ANOVA is used to simultaneously determine whether several independent normal populations have the same mean. This is accomplished by comparing the variances of the random samples selected from these populations. We apply the usual hypothesis-testing procedure, but we use the F distribution as the test statistic. Often the calculations are tedious, so a software package is recommended.

As an example of analysis of variance, a test could be conducted to resolve whether there is any difference in effectiveness among five fertilizers on the weight of popcorn ears. This type of analysis is referred to as *one-factor ANOVA* because we are able to draw conclusions about only one factor, called a *treatment.* If we want to draw conclusions about the simultaneous effects of more than one factor or variable, we use the *two-factor ANOVA* technique. Both the one-factor and two-factor tests use the *F distribution* as the distribution of the test statistic. The F distribution is also the distribution of the test statistic used to find whether one normal population has more variation than another.

Two-factor analysis of variance is further complicated by the possibility that interactions may exist between the factors. There is an *interaction* if the response to one of the factors depends on the level of the other factor. Fortunately, the ANOVA technique is easily extended to include a test for interactions.

Glossary

Chapter 10

Alpha The probability of a Type I error or the level of significance. Its symbol is the Greek letter α.

Alternate hypothesis The conclusion we accept when we demonstrate that the null hypothesis is false. It is also called the research hypothesis.

Critical value   A value that is the dividing point between the region where the null hypothesis is not rejected and the region where it is rejected.

Degrees of freedom   The number of items in a sample that are free to vary. Suppose there are two items in a sample, and we know the mean. We are free to specify only one of the two values, because the other value is automatically determined (since the two values total twice the mean). Example: If the mean is $6, we are free to choose only one value. Choosing $4 makes the other value $8 because $4 + $8 = 2($6). So there is 1 degree of freedom in this illustration. We can determine the degrees of freedom by $n - 1 = 2 - 1 = 1$. If n is 4, then there are 3 degrees of freedom, found by $n - 1 = 4 - 1 = 3$.

Hypothesis   A statement or claim about the value of a population parameter. Examples: 40.7 percent of all persons 65 years old or older live alone. The mean number of people in a car is 1.33.

Hypothesis testing   A statistical procedure, based on sample evidence and probability theory, used to determine whether the statement about the population parameter is reasonable.

Null hypothesis   A statement about the value of a population parameter, H_0 that is developed for testing in the face of numerical evidence.

One-tailed test   Used when the alternate hypothesis states a direction, such as H_1: $\mu > 40$, read "the population mean is greater than 40." Here the rejection region is only in one tail (the right tail).

Proportion   A fraction or percentage of a sample or a population having a particular trait. If 5 out of 50 in a sample liked a new cereal, the proportion is 5/50, or .10.

p-value   The probability of computing a value of the test statistic at least as extreme as the one found in the sample data when the null hypothesis is true.

Significance level   The probability of rejecting the null hypothesis when it is true.

Two-tailed test   Used when the alternate hypothesis does not state a direction, such as H_1: $\mu \neq 75$, read "the population mean is not equal to 75." There is a region of rejection in each tail.

Type I error   Occurs when a true H_0 is rejected.

Type II error   Occurs when a false H_0 is accepted.

Chapter 11

Dependent samples   Dependent samples are characterized by a measurement, then some type of intervention, followed by another measurement. Paired samples are also dependent because the same individual or item is a member of both samples. Example: Ten participants in a marathon were weighed prior to and after competing in the race. We wish to study the mean amount of weight loss.

Independent samples   The samples chosen at random are not related to each other. We wish to study the mean

age of the inmates at the Auburn and Allegheny prisons. We select a random sample of 28 inmates from the Auburn prison and a sample of 19 inmates at the Allegheny prison. A person cannot be an inmate in both prisons. The samples are independent, that is, unrelated.

Pooled estimate of the population variance   A weighted average of s_1^2 and s_2^2 used to estimate the common variance, σ^2, when using small samples to test the difference between two population means.

t distribution   Investigated and reported by William S. Gossett in 1908 and published under the pseudonym *Student*. It is similar to the standard normal distribution presented in Chapter 7. The major characteristics of t are:

1. It is a continuous distribution.
2. It can assume values between minus infinity and plus infinity.
3. It is symmetrical about its mean of zero. However, it is more spread out and flatter at the apex than the standard normal distribution.
4. It approaches the standard normal distribution as n gets larger.
5. There is a family of t distributions. One t distribution exists for a sample of 15 observations, another for 25, and so on.

Chapter 12

Analysis of variance (ANOVA)   A technique used to test simultaneously whether the means of several populations are equal. It uses the F distribution as the distribution of the test statistic.

Block   A second source of variation, in addition to treatments.

F distribution   It is used as the test statistic for ANOVA problems, as well as others. The major characteristics of the F distribution are:

1. It is never negative.
2. It is a continuous distribution approaching the X-axis but never touching it.
3. It is positively skewed.
4. It is based on two sets of degrees of freedom.
5. Like the t distribution, there is a family of F distributions. There is one distribution for 17 degrees of freedom in the numerator and 9 degrees of freedom in the denominator, there is another F distribution for 7 degrees of freedom in the numerator and 12 degrees of freedom in the denominator, and so on.

Interaction   Two variables interact if the effect that one factor has on the variable being studied is different for different levels of the other factor.

Treatment   A source of variation. It identifies the several populations being examined.

Exercises

connect   **Part I—Multiple Choice**

1. In a one-tailed test using the z distribution as the test statistic and the .01 significance level, the critical value is either
   a. -1.96 or $+1.96$.
   b. -1.65 or $+1.65$.
   c. -2.58 or $+2.58$.

  d. 0 or 1.
  e. None of these is correct.
2. A Type II error is committed if we:
  a. Reject a true null hypothesis.
  b. Accept a true alternate hypothesis.
  c. Reject a true alternate hypothesis.
  d. Accept both the null and alternate hypotheses at the same time.
  e. None of these is correct.
3. The hypotheses are H_0: $\mu = 240$ pounds of pressure and H_1: $\mu \neq 240$ pounds of pressure.
  a. A one-tailed test is being applied.
  b. A two-tailed test is being applied.
  c. A three-tailed test is being applied.
  d. The wrong test is being applied.
  e. None of these is correct.
4. The .01 significance level is used in a one-tailed test of hypothesis with the rejection region in the lower tail. The computed value of z is -1.8. This indicates:
  a. H_0 should not be rejected.
  b. We should reject H_0 and accept H_1.
  c. We should take a larger sample.
  d. We should have used the .05 level of significance.
  e. None of these is correct.
5. The test statistic for testing a hypothesis for sample means when the population standard deviation is not known is:
  a. z.
  b. t.
  c. F.
  d. χ^2.
6. We want to test a hypothesis for the difference between two population means. The null and alternate hypotheses are stated as

  H_0: $\mu_1 = \mu_2$
  H_1: $\mu_1 \neq \mu_2$

  a. A left-tailed test should be applied.
  b. A two-tailed test should be applied.
  c. A right-tailed test should be applied.
  d. We cannot determine whether a left-, right-, or two-tailed test should be applied based on the information given.
  e. None of these is correct.
7. To conduct a paired difference test, the samples must be:
  a. Infinitely large.
  b. Equal to ANOVA.
  c. Independent.
  d. Dependent.
  e. None of these is correct.
8. An ANOVA test was conducted with respect to the population mean. The null hypothesis was rejected. This indicates:
  a. There were too many degrees of freedom.
  b. There is no difference between the population means.
  c. There is a difference between at least two population means.
  d. A larger sample should be selected.
  e. None of these is correct.

Part II—Problems

For problems 9–16, state: (a) the null and the alternate hypothesis, (b) the decision rule, and (c) the decision regarding the null hypothesis, (d) then interpret the result.
9. A machine is set to produce tennis balls so the mean bounce is 36 inches when the ball is dropped from a platform of a certain height. The production supervisor suspects that the mean bounce has changed and is less than 36 inches. As an experiment a sample of 12 balls was dropped from the platform and the mean height of the bounce was 35.5 inches, with a standard deviation of 0.9 inches. At the .05 significance level, can the supervisor conclude that the mean bounce height is less than 36 inches?

10. Research by First Bank of Illinois revealed that 8 percent of its customers wait more than five minutes to do their banking when not using the drive-through facility. Management considers this reasonable and will not add more tellers unless the proportion becomes larger than 8 percent. The branch manager at the Litchfield Branch believes that the wait is longer than the standard at her branch and requested additional part-time tellers. To support her request she found that, in a sample of 100 customers, 10 waited more than five minutes. At the .01 significance level, is it reasonable to conclude that more than 8 percent of the customers wait more than five minutes?

11. It was hypothesized that road construction workers do not engage in productive work 20 minutes on the average out of every hour. Some claimed the nonproductive time is greater than 20 minutes. An actual study was conducted at a construction site, using a stopwatch and other ways of checking the work habits. A random check of workers revealed the following unproductive times, in minutes, during a one-hour period (exclusive of regularly scheduled breaks):

10	25	17	20	28	30	18	23	18

Using the .05 significance level, is it reasonable to conclude the mean unproductive time is greater than 20 minutes?

12. A test is to be conducted involving the mean holding power of two glues designed for plastic. First, a small plastic hook was coated at one end with Epox glue and fastened to a sheet of plastic. After it dried, weight was added to the hook until it separated from the sheet of plastic. The weight was then recorded. This was repeated until 12 hooks were tested. The same procedure was followed for Holdtite glue, but only 10 hooks were used. The sample results, in pounds, were:

	Epox	Holdtite
Sample mean	250	252
Sample standard deviation	5	8
Sample size	12	10

At the .01 significance level, is there a difference between the mean holding power of Epox and that of Holdtite?

13. Pittsburgh Paints wishes to test an additive formulated to increase the life of paints used in the hot and arid conditions of the Southwest. The top half of a piece of wood was painted using the regular paint. The bottom half was painted with the paint including the additive. The same procedure was followed for a total of 10 pieces. Then each piece was subjected to brilliant light. The data, the number of hours each piece lasted before it faded beyond a certain point, follow:

Number of Hours by Sample									
	A	B	C	D	E	F	G	H	I	J
Without additive	325	313	320	340	318	312	319	330	333	319
With additive	323	313	326	343	310	320	313	340	330	315

Using the .05 significance level, determine whether the additive is effective in prolonging the life of the paint.

14. A Buffalo, New York, cola distributor is featuring a super-special sale on 12-packs. She wonders where in the grocery store to place the cola for maximum attention. Should it be near the front door of the grocery stores, in the cola section, at the checkout registers, or near the milk and other dairy products? Four stores with similar total sales cooperated in an experiment. In one store the 12-packs were stacked near the front door, in

another they were placed near the checkout registers, and so on. Sales were checked at specified times in each store for exactly four minutes. The results were:

Cola at the Door	In Soft Drink Section	Near Registers	Dairy Section
$6	$ 5	$ 7	$10
8	10	10	9
3	12	9	6
7	4	4	11
	9	5	
		7	

The Buffalo distributor wants to find out whether there is a difference in the mean sales for cola stacked at the four locations in the store. Use the .05 significance level.

15. Williams Corporation is investigating the effects of educational background on employee performance. A potential relevant variable in this case is the self-rated social status of the employee. The company has recorded the annual sales volumes (in $000) achieved by sales employees in each of the categories below. Perform a complete two-way analysis of variance (including the possibility of interactions) on the data and describe what your results suggest.

	School Type		
Self-Rated Social Status	**Ivy League**	**State-supported**	**Small Private**
Low	62, 61	68, 64	70, 70
Medium	68, 64	74, 68	62, 65
High	70, 71	57, 60	57, 56

16. A school supervisor is reviewing initial wages of former students (in $000). Samples were taken over three years for four different majors (accounting, administration, finance, and marketing).

Major/Year	2003	2004	2005
Accounting	75.4, 69.8, 62.3	73.9, 78.8, 62.0	64.2, 80.8, 68.2
Administration	61.5, 59.9, 62.1	63.9, 57.6, 66.5	74.2, 67.5, 58.1
Finance	63.6, 70.2, 72.2	69.2, 72.5, 67.2	74.7, 66.4, 77.9
Marketing	71.3, 69.2, 66.4	74.0, 67.6, 61.7	60.0, 61.3, 62.5

a. Here is an interaction plot of the information. What does it reveal?

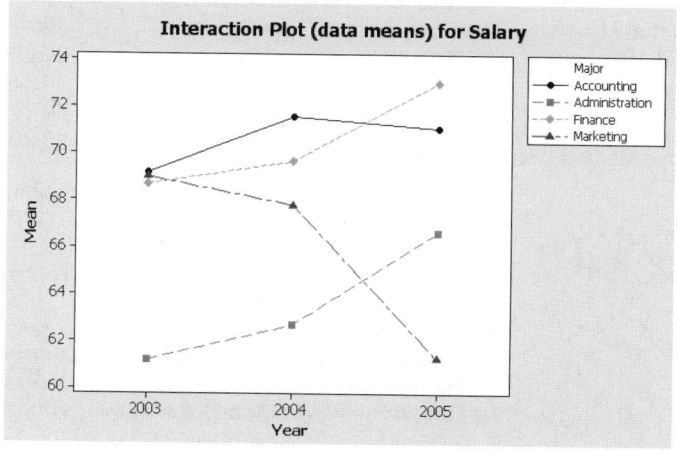

b. Write out all of the pairs of null and alternative hypotheses you would apply for a two-way ANOVA.

c. Here is the statistical software output. Use the 0.05 level to check for interactions.

Source	DF	SS	MS	F	P
Major	3	329.20	109.732	3.39	0.034
Year	2	7.32	3.659	0.11	0.894
Interaction	6	183.57	30.595	0.94	0.482
Error	24	777.29	32.387		
Total	35	1297.37			

d. If proper, test the other hypotheses at the 0.05 significance level. If it is not appropriate, describe why you should not do the tests.

Cases

A. Century National Bank

Refer to the description of Century National Bank at the end of the Review of Chapters 1–4 on page 138.

With many other options available, customers no longer let their money sit in a checking account. For many years the mean checking balance has been $1,600. Does the sample data indicate that the mean account balance has declined from this value?

Recent years have also seen an increase in the use of ATM machines. When Mr. Selig took over the bank, the mean number of transactions per month per customer was 8; now he believes it has increased to more than 10. In fact, the advertising agency that prepares TV commercials for Century would like to use this on the new commercial being designed. Is there sufficient evidence to conclude that the mean number of transactions per customer is more than 10 per month? Could the advertising agency say the mean is more than 9 per month?

The bank has branch offices in four different cities: Cincinnati, Ohio; Atlanta, Georgia; Louisville, Kentucky; and Erie, Pennsylvania. Mr. Selig would like to know whether there is a difference in the mean checking account balances among the four branches. If there are differences, between which branches do these differences occur?

Mr. Selig is also interested in the bank's ATMs. Is there a difference in ATM use among the branches? Also, do customers who have debit cards tend to use ATMs differently from those who do not have debit cards? Is there a difference in ATM use by those with checking accounts that pay interest versus those that do not? Prepare a report for Mr. Selig answering these questions.

B. Bell Grove Medical Center

Ms. Gene Dempsey manages the emergency care center at Bell Grove Medical Center. One of her responsibilities is to have enough nurses so that incoming patients needing service can be handled promptly. It is stressful for patients to wait a long time for emergency care even when their care needs are not life threatening. Ms. Dempsey gathered the following information regarding the number of patients over the last several weeks. The center is not open on weekends. Does it appear that there are any differences in the number of patients served by the day of the week? If there are differences, which days seem to be the busiest? Write a brief report summarizing your findings.

Date	Day	Patients
9-29-06	Monday	38
9-30-06	Tuesday	28
10-1-06	Wednesday	28
10-2-06	Thursday	30
10-3-06	Friday	35
10-6-06	Monday	35
10-7-06	Tuesday	25
10-8-06	Wednesday	22
10-9-06	Thursday	21
10-10-06	Friday	32
10-13-06	Monday	37
10-14-06	Tuesday	29
10-15-06	Wednesday	27
10-16-06	Thursday	28
10-17-06	Friday	35
10-20-06	Monday	37
10-21-06	Tuesday	26
10-22-06	Wednesday	28
10-23-06	Thursday	23
10-24-06	Friday	33

Practice Test

Part I—Objective

1. A statement about the value of a population parameter that always includes the equal sign is called the _____.

2. The likelihood of rejecting a true null hypothesis is called the _____.

1. _____

2. _____

3. When conducting a test of hypothesis about a population proportion, the value $n\pi$ should be at least _____.   **3.** _____
4. When conducting a test of hypothesis about a single population mean, the z distribution is used as the test statistic only when the _____ is known.   **4.** _____
5. In a two-sample test of hypothesis for means, the population standard deviations are not known and we must assume what about the shape of the populations?

                                                                                       5. _____

6. A value calculated from sample information used to determine whether to reject the null hypothesis is called the _____.   **6.** _____
7. In a two-tailed test the rejection region is _____. (all in the upper tail, all in the lower tail, split evenly between the two tails, none of these—pick one)   **7.** _____
8. Which of the following is not a characteristic of the F distribution? (continuous, positively skewed, range from $-\infty$ to ∞, family of distributions)   **8.** _____
9. To perform a one-way ANOVA, the treatments must be _____. (independent, mutually exclusive, continuous)   **9.** _____
10. In a one-way ANOVA there are four treatments and six observations in each treatment. What are the degrees of freedom for the F distribution?   **10.** _____

Part II—Problems

For problems 1 and 2 state the null and alternate hypotheses and the decision rule, make a decision regarding the null hypothesis, and interpret the result.

1. The Park Manager at Fort Fisher State Park in North Carolina believes the typical summer visitor spends more than 90 minutes in the park. A sample of 18 visitors during the months of June, July, and August of 2008 revealed the mean time in the park for visitors was 96 minutes, with a standard deviation of 12 minutes. At the .01 significance level is it reasonable to conclude the mean time in the park is greater than 90 minutes?

2. Is there a difference in the mean miles traveled per week by each of two taxi cab companies operating in the Grand Strand area? The *Sun News,* the local paper, is investigating and obtained the following sample information. At the .05 significance level is it reasonable to conclude there is a difference in the mean miles traveled? Assume equal population variances.

Variable	Yellow Cab	Horse and Buggy Cab Company
Mean miles	837	797
Standard deviation	30	40
Sample size	14	12

3. The results of a one-way ANOVA are reported below. Use the .05 significance level.

ANOVA				
Source of Variation	SS	df	MS	F
Between groups	6.892202	2	3.446101	4.960047
Within groups	12.50589	18	0.694772	
Total	19.3981	20		

Answer the following questions.
a. How many treatments are in the study?
b. What is the total sample size?
c. What is the critical value of F?
d. Write out the null hypothesis and the alternate hypothesis.
e. What is your decision regarding the null hypothesis?
f. Can we conclude the treatment means differ?

13

GOALS

When you have completed this chapter, you will be able to:

1 Understand and interpret the terms *dependent* and *independent variable.*

2 Calculate and interpret the *coefficient of correlation,* the *coefficient of determination,* and the *standard error of estimate.*

3 Conduct a test of hypothesis to determine whether the coefficient of correlation in the population is zero.

4 Calculate the least squares regression line.

5 Construct and interpret confidence and prediction intervals for the dependent variable.

Linear Regression and Correlation

Exercise 61 lists the movies with the largest world box office sales and their world box office budget. Find the correlation between world box office budget and world box office sales. Comment on the association between the two variables. (See Goal 2.)

Introduction

Chapters 2 through 4 dealt with *descriptive statistics*. We organized raw data into a frequency distribution, and computed several measures of location and measures of dispersion to describe the major characteristics of the data. Chapter 5 started the study of *statistical inference*. The main emphasis was on inferring something about a population parameter, such as the population mean, on the basis of a sample. We tested for the reasonableness of a population mean or a population proportion, the difference between two population means, or whether several population means were equal. All of these tests involved just *one* interval- or ratio-level variable, such as the weight of a plastic soft drink bottle, the income of bank presidents, or the number of patients admitted to a particular hospital.

We shift the emphasis in this chapter to the study of two variables. Recall in Chapter 4 we introduced the idea of showing the relationship between *two* variables with a scatter diagram. We plotted the price of vehicles sold at Whitner Autoplex on the vertical axis and the age of the buyer on the horizontal axis. See the statistical software output on page 120. In that case we observed that, as the age of the buyer increased, the amount spent for the vehicle also increased. In this chapter we carry this idea further. That is, we develop numerical measures to express the relationship between two variables. Is the relationship strong or weak, is it direct or inverse? In addition, we develop an equation to express the relationship between variables. This will allow us to estimate one variable on the basis of another. Here are some examples.

- Is there a relationship between the amount Healthtex spends per month on advertising and its sales in the month?
- Can we base an estimate of the cost to heat a home in January on the number of square feet in the home?
- Is there a relationship between the miles per gallon achieved by large pickup trucks and the size of the engine?
- Is there a relationship between the number of hours that students studied for an exam and the score earned?

Note in each of these cases there are two variables observed for each sampled observation. For the last example, we find, for each student selected for the sample, the hours studied and the score earned.

We begin this chapter by examining the meaning and purpose of **correlation analysis.** We continue our study by developing a mathematical equation that will allow us to estimate the value of one variable based on the value of another. This is called **regression analysis.** We will (1) determine the equation of the line that best fits the data, (2) use the equation to estimate the value of one variable based on another, (3) measure the error in our estimate, and (4) establish confidence and prediction intervals for our estimate.

Statistics in Action

The space shuttle *Challenger* exploded on January 28, 1986. An investigation of the cause examined four contractors: Rockwell International for the shuttle and engines, Lockheed Martin for ground support, Martin Marietta for the external fuel tanks, and Morton Thiokol for the solid fuel booster rockets. After several months, the investigation blamed the explosion on defective O-rings produced by Morton Thiokol. A study of the contractor's stock prices showed an interesting happenstance. On the day of the crash, Morton Thiokol stock was down 11.86% and the stock of the other three lost only 2 to 3%. Can we conclude that financial markets predicted the outcome of the investigation?

What Is Correlation Analysis?

Correlation analysis is the study of the relationship between variables. To explain, suppose the sales manager of Copier Sales of America, which has a large sales force throughout the United States and Canada, wants to determine whether there is a relationship between the number of sales calls made in a month and the number of copiers sold that month. The manager selects a random sample of 10 representatives and determines the number of sales calls each representative made last month and the number of copiers sold. The sample information is shown in Table 13–1.

TABLE 13–1 Number of Sales Calls and Copiers Sold for 10 Salespeople

Sales Representative	Number of Sales Calls	Number of Copiers Sold
Tom Keller	20	30
Jeff Hall	40	60
Brian Virost	20	40
Greg Fish	30	60
Susan Welch	10	30
Carlos Ramirez	10	40
Rich Niles	20	40
Mike Kiel	20	50
Mark Reynolds	20	30
Soni Jones	30	70

By reviewing the data we observe that there does seem to be some relationship between the number of sales calls and the number of units sold. That is, the salespeople who made the most sales calls sold the most units. However, the relationship is not "perfect" or exact. For example, Soni Jones made fewer sales calls than Jeff Hall, but she sold more units.

Instead of talking in generalities as we did in Chapter 4 and have so far in this chapter, we will develop some statistical measures to portray more precisely the relationship between the two variables, sales calls and copiers sold. This group of statistical techniques is called **correlation analysis.**

> **CORRELATION ANALYSIS** A group of techniques to measure the association between two variables.

The basic idea of correlation analysis is to report the association between two variables. The usual first step is to plot the data in a **scatter diagram.** An example will show how a scatter diagram is used.

Example

Copier Sales of America sells copiers to businesses of all sizes throughout the United States and Canada. Ms. Marcy Bancer was recently promoted to the position of national sales manager. At the upcoming sales meeting, the sales representatives from all over the country will be in attendance. She would like to impress upon them the importance of making that extra sales call each day. She decides to gather some information on the relationship between the number of sales calls and the number of copiers sold. She selects a random sample of 10 sales representatives and determines the number of sales calls they made last month and the number of copiers they sold. The sample information is reported in Table 13–1. What observations can you make about the relationship between the number of sales calls and the number of copiers sold? Develop a scatter diagram to display the information.

Solution

Based on the information in Table 13–1, Ms. Bancer suspects there is a relationship between the number of sales calls made in a month and the number of copiers sold. Soni Jones sold the most copiers last month, and she was one of three representatives making 30 or more sales calls. On the other hand, Susan Welch and

Carlos Ramirez made only 10 sales calls last month. Ms. Welch, along with two others, had the lowest number of copiers sold among the sampled representatives.

The implication is that the number of copiers sold is related to the number of sales calls made. As the number of sales calls increases, it appears the number of copiers sold also increases. We refer to number of sales calls as the **independent variable** and number of copiers sold as the **dependent variable.**

> **DEPENDENT VARIABLE** The variable that is being predicted or estimated. It is scaled on the *Y*-axis.
>
> **INDEPENDENT VARIABLE** The variable that provides the basis for estimation. It is the predictor variable. It is scaled on the *X*-axis.

It is common practice to scale the dependent variable (copiers sold) on the vertical or *Y*-axis and the independent variable (number of sales calls) on the horizontal or *X*-axis. To develop the scatter diagram of the Copier Sales of America sales information, we begin with the first sales representative, Tom Keller. Tom made 20 sales calls last month and sold 30 copiers, so $X = 20$ and $Y = 30$. To plot this point, move along the horizontal axis to $X = 20$, then go vertically to $Y = 30$ and place a dot at the intersection. This process is continued until all the paired data are plotted, as shown in Chart 13–1.

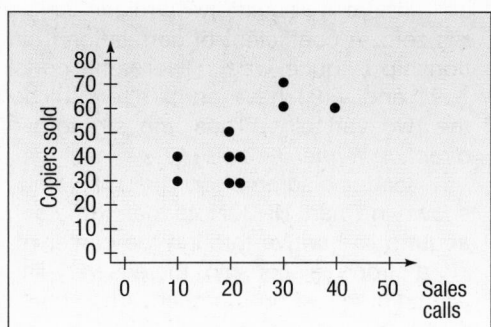

CHART 13–1 Scatter Diagram Showing Sales Calls and Copiers Sold

The scatter diagram shows graphically that the sales representatives who make more calls tend to sell more copiers. It is reasonable for Ms. Bancer, the national sales manager at Copier Sales of America, to tell her salespeople that, the more sales calls they make, the more copiers they can expect to sell. Note that, while there appears to be a positive relationship between the two variables, all the points do not fall on a line. In the following section you will measure the strength and direction of this relationship between two variables by determining the coefficient of correlation.

The Coefficient of Correlation

Interval- or ratio-level data are required.

Originated by Karl Pearson about 1900, the **coefficient of correlation** describes the strength of the relationship between two sets of interval-scaled or ratio-scaled variables. Designated *r,* it is often referred to as *Pearson's r* and as the *Pearson product-moment correlation coefficient*. It can assume any value from −1.00 to +1.00 inclusive. A correlation coefficient of −1.00 or +1.00 indicates *perfect correlation*. For example, a correlation coefficient for the preceding example computed to be +1.00 would indicate that the number of sales calls and the number of copiers sold are perfectly related in a positive linear sense. A computed value of −1.00 reveals that sales calls and the number of copiers sold are

Characteristics of r

perfectly related in an inverse linear sense. How the scatter diagram would appear if the relationship between the two sets of data were linear and perfect is shown in Chart 13–2.

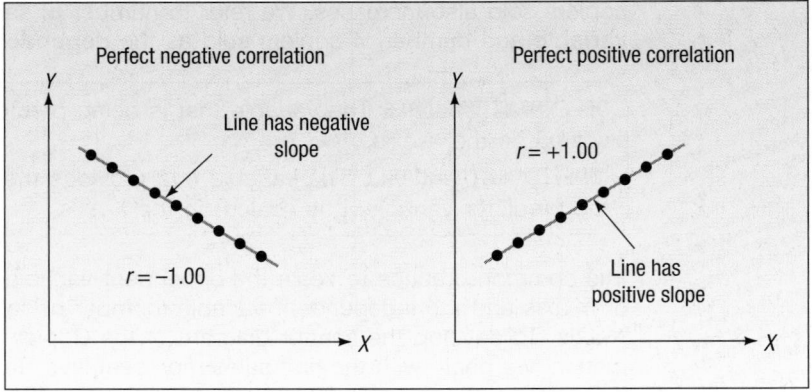

CHART 13–2 Scatter Diagrams Showing Perfect Negative Correlation and Perfect Positive Correlation

If there is absolutely no relationship between the two sets of variables, Pearson's *r* is zero. A coefficient of correlation *r* close to 0 (say, .08) shows that the linear relationship is quite weak. The same conclusion is drawn if *r* = −.08. Coefficients of −.91 and +.91 have equal strength; both indicate very strong correlation between the two variables. Thus, *the strength of the correlation does not depend on the direction (either − or +)*.

Scatter diagrams for *r* = 0, a weak *r* (say, −.23), and a strong *r* (say, +.87) are shown in Chart 13–3. Note that, if the correlation is weak, there is considerable scatter about a line drawn through the center of the data. For the scatter diagram representing a strong relationship, there is very little scatter about the line. This indicates, in the example shown on the chart, that hours studied is a good predictor of exam score.

Examples of degrees of correlation

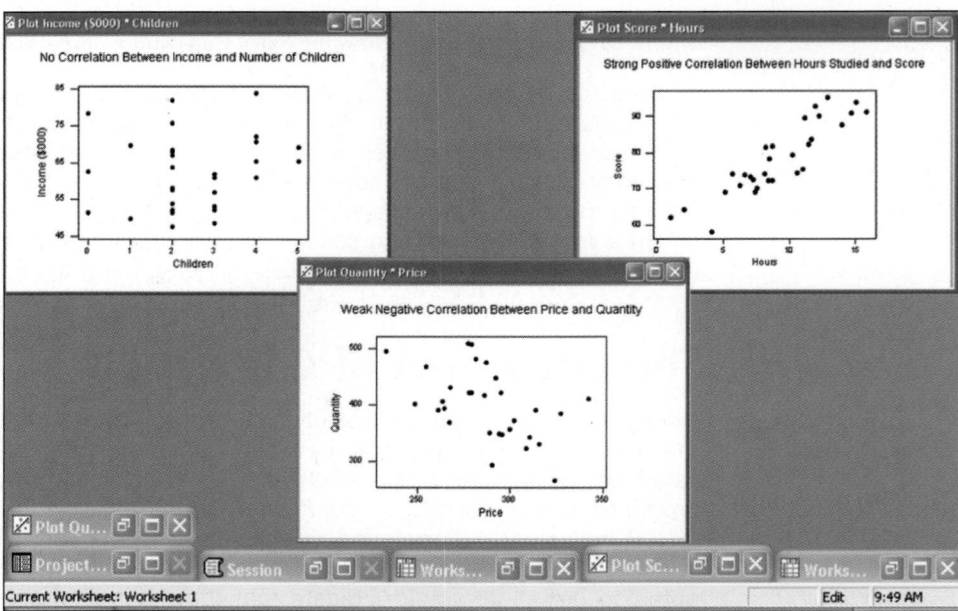

CHART 13–3 Scatter Diagrams Depicting Zero, Weak, and Strong Correlation

The following drawing summarizes the strength and direction of the coefficient of correlation.

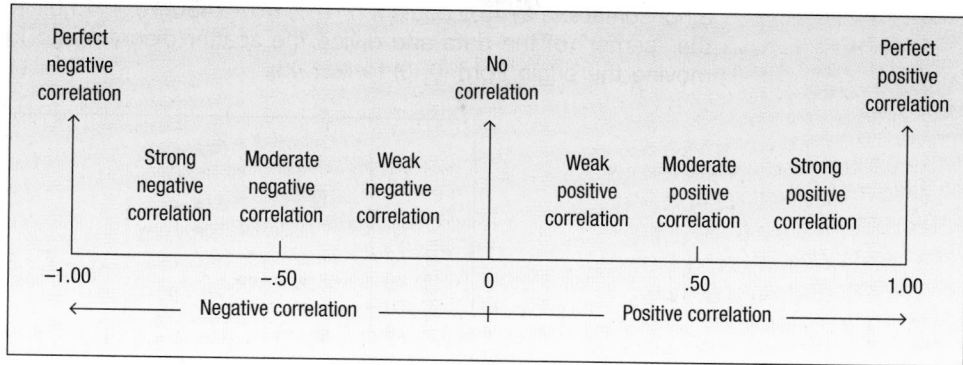

> **COEFFICIENT OF CORRELATION** A measure of the strength of the linear relationship between two variables.

The characteristics of the coefficient of correlation are summarized below.

> **CHARACTERISTICS OF THE COEFFICIENT OF CORRELATION**
> 1. The sample coefficient of correlation is identified by the lower-case letter r.
> 2. It shows the direction and strength of the linear (straight line) relationship between two interval- or ratio-scale variables.
> 3. It ranges from -1 up to and including $+1$.
> 4. A value near 0 indicates there is little association between the variables.
> 5. A value near 1 indicates a direct or positive association between the variables.
> 6. A value near -1 indicates inverse or negative association between the variables.

How is the value of the coefficient of correlation determined? We will use the Copier Sales of America data, which are reported in Table 13–2, as an example. We begin

TABLE 13–2 Sales Calls and Copiers Sold for 10 Salespeople

Sales Representative	Sales Calls, (X)	Copiers Sold, (Y)
Tom Keller	20	30
Jeff Hall	40	60
Brian Virost	20	40
Greg Fish	30	60
Susan Welch	10	30
Carlos Ramirez	10	40
Rich Niles	20	40
Mike Kiel	20	50
Mark Reynolds	20	30
Soni Jones	30	70
Total	220	450

with a scatter diagram, similar to Chart 13–2. Draw a vertical line through the data values at the mean of the X-values and a horizontal line at the mean of the Y-values. In Chart 13–4 we've added a vertical line at 22.0 calls ($\bar{X} = \Sigma X/n = 220/10 = 22$) and a horizontal line at 45.0 copiers ($\bar{Y} = \Sigma Y/n = 450/10 = 45.0$). These lines pass through the "center" of the data and divide the scatter diagram into four quadrants. Think of moving the origin from (0, 0) to (22, 45).

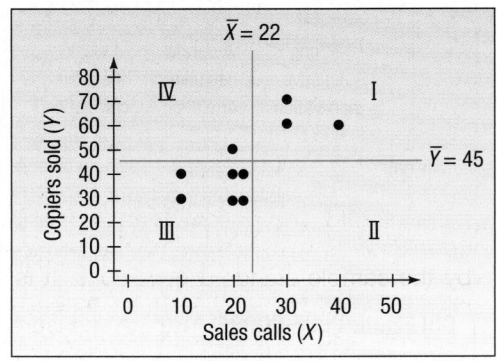

CHART 13–4 Computation of the Coefficient of Correlation

Two variables are positively related when the number of copiers sold is above the mean and the number of sales calls is also above the mean. These points appear in the upper-right quadrant (labeled Quadrant I) of Chart 13–4. Similarly, when the number of copiers sold is less than the mean, so is the number of sales calls. These points fall in the lower-left quadrant of Chart 13–4 (labeled Quadrant III). For example, the last person on the list in Table 13–2, Soni Jones, made 30 sales calls and sold 70 copiers. These values are above their respective means, so this point is located in Quadrant I which is in the upper-right quadrant. She made 8 ($X - \bar{X} = 30 - 22$) more sales calls than the mean and sold 25 ($Y - \bar{Y} = 70 - 45$) more copiers than the mean. Tom Keller, the first name on the list in Table 13–2, made 20 sales calls and sold 30 copiers. Both of these values are less than their respective mean; hence this point is in the lower-left quadrant. Tom made 2 less sales calls and sold 15 less copiers than the respective means. The deviations from the mean number of sales calls and for the mean number of copiers sold are summarized in Table 13–3 for the 10 sales representatives. The sum of the products of the deviations from the respective means is 900. That is, the term $\Sigma(X - \bar{X})(Y - \bar{Y}) = 900$.

In both the upper-right and the lower-left quadrants, the product of $(X - \bar{X})(Y - \bar{Y})$ is positive because both of the factors have the same sign. In our example this

TABLE 13–3 Deviations from the Mean and Their Products

Sales Representative	Calls, X	Sales, Y	$X - \bar{X}$	$Y - \bar{Y}$	$(X - \bar{X})(Y - \bar{Y})$
Tom Keller	20	30	−2	−15	30
Jeff Hall	40	60	18	15	270
Brian Virost	20	40	−2	−5	10
Greg Fish	30	60	8	15	120
Susan Welch	10	30	−12	−15	180
Carlos Ramirez	10	40	−12	−5	60
Rich Niles	20	40	−2	−5	10
Mike Kiel	20	50	−2	5	−10
Mark Reynolds	20	30	−2	−15	30
Soni Jones	30	70	8	25	200
					900

happens for all sales representatives except Mike Kiel. We can therefore expect the coefficient of correlation to have a positive value.

If the two variables are inversely related, one variable will be above the mean and the other below the mean. Most of the points in this case occur in the upper-left and lower-right quadrants, that is Quadrant II and IV. Now $(X - \overline{X})$ and $(Y - \overline{Y})$ will have opposite signs, so their product is negative. The resulting correlation coefficient is negative.

What happens if there is no linear relationship between the two variables? The points in the scatter diagram will appear in all four quadrants. The negative products of $(X - \overline{X})(Y - \overline{Y})$ offset the positive products, so the sum is near zero. This leads to a correlation coefficient near zero. So, the term $\Sigma(X - \overline{X})(Y - \overline{Y})$ drives the strength as well as the sign of the relationship between the two variables.

The correlation coefficient also needs to be unaffected by the units of the two variables. For example, if we had used hundreds of copiers sold instead of the number sold, the coefficient of correlation would be the same. The coefficient of correlation is independent of the scale used if we divide the term $\Sigma(X - \overline{X})(Y - \overline{Y})$ by the sample standard deviations. It is also made independent of the sample size and bounded by the values $+1.00$ and -1.00 if we divide by $(n - 1)$.

This reasoning leads to the following formula:

CORRELATION COEFFICIENT	$r = \dfrac{\Sigma(X - \overline{X})(Y - \overline{Y})}{(n - 1)s_x s_y}$	[13–1]

To compute the coefficient of correlation, we use the standard deviations of the sample of 10 sales calls and 10 copiers sold. We could use formula (3–12) to calculate the sample standard deviations or we could use a software package. For the specific Excel and MINITAB commands see the **Software Commands** section at the end of Chapter 3. The following is the Excel output. The standard deviation of the number of sales calls is 9.189 and of the number of copiers sold 14.337.

Excel

	A	B	C	D	E	F	G	H	I
	\<\>			num 1 dstats [Compatibility Mode]					
1	Calls	Sales		Calls			Sales		
2	20	30		Mean	22.000		Mean	45.000	
3	40	60		Standard Error	2.906		Standard Error	4.534	
4	20	40		Median	20.000		Median	40.000	
5	30	60		Mode	20.000		Mode	30.000	
6	10	30		Standard Deviation	9.189		Standard Deviation	14.337	
7	10	40		Sample Variance	84.444		Sample Variance	205.556	
8	20	40		Kurtosis	0.396		Kurtosis	-1.001	
9	20	50		Skewness	0.601		Skewness	0.566	
10	20	30		Range	30.000		Range	40.000	
11	30	70		Minimum	10.000		Minimum	30.000	
12				Maximum	40.000		Maximum	70.000	
13				Sum	220.000		Sum	450.000	
14				Count	10.000		Count	10.000	
15									

We now insert these values into formula (13–1) to determine the coefficient of correlation:

$$r = \frac{\Sigma(X - \overline{X})(Y - \overline{Y})}{(n - 1)s_x s_y} = \frac{900}{(10 - 1)(9.189)(14.337)} = 0.759$$

How do we interpret a correlation of 0.759? First, it is positive, so we conclude there is a direct relationship between the number of sales calls and the number of copiers sold. This confirms our reasoning based on the scatter diagram,

Chart 13–4. The value of 0.759 is fairly close to 1.00, so we conclude that the association is strong.

We must be careful with the interpretation. The correlation of 0.759 indicates a strong positive association between the variables. Ms. Bancer would be correct to encourage the sales personnel to make that extra sales call, because the number of sales calls made is related to the number of copiers sold. However, does this mean that more sales calls *cause* more sales? No, we have not demonstrated cause and effect here, only that the two variables—sales calls and copiers sold—are related.

The Coefficient of Determination

In the previous example regarding the relationship between the number of sales calls and the units sold, the coefficient of correlation, 0.759, was interpreted as being "strong." Terms such as *weak, moderate,* and *strong,* however, do not have precise meaning. A measure that has a more easily interpreted meaning is the **coefficient of determination.** It is computed by squaring the coefficient of correlation. In the example, the coefficient of determination, r^2, is 0.576, found by $(0.759)^2$. This is a proportion or a percent; we can say that 57.6 percent of the variation in the number of copiers sold is explained, or accounted for, by the variation in the number of sales calls.

> **COEFFICIENT OF DETERMINATION** The proportion of the total variation in the dependent variable Y that is explained, or accounted for, by the variation in the independent variable X.

Further discussion of the coefficient of determination is found later in the chapter.

Correlation and Cause

If there is a strong relationship (say, .91) between two variables, we are tempted to assume that an increase or decrease in one variable *causes* a change in the other variable. For example, it can be shown that the consumption of Georgia peanuts and the consumption of aspirin have a strong correlation. However, this does not indicate that an increase in the consumption of peanuts *caused* the consumption of aspirin to increase. Likewise, the incomes of professors and the number of inmates in mental institutions have increased proportionately. Further, as the population of donkeys has decreased, there has been an increase in the number of doctoral degrees granted. Relationships such as these are called **spurious correlations.** What we can conclude when we find two variables with a strong correlation is that there is a relationship or association between the two variables, not that a change in one causes a change in the other.

Self-Review 13–1

Haverty's Furniture is a family business that has been selling to retail customers in the Chicago area for many years. The company advertises extensively on radio, TV, and the Internet, emphasizing low prices and easy credit terms. The owner would like to review the relationship between sales and the amount spent on advertising. Below is information on sales and advertising expense for the last four months.

Month	Advertising Expense ($ million)	Sales Revenue ($ million)
July	2	7
August	1	3
September	3	8
October	4	10

(a) The owner wants to forecast sales on the basis of advertising expense. Which variable is the dependent variable? Which variable is the independent variable?

12. The Student Government Association at Middle Carolina University wanted to demonstrate the relationship between the number of beers a student drinks and their blood alcohol content (BAC). A random sample of 18 students participated in a study in which each participating student was randomly assigned a number of 12-ounce cans of beer to drink. Thirty minutes after consuming their assigned number of beers a member of the local sheriff's office measured their blood alcohol content. The sample information is reported below.

Student	Beers	BAC	Student	Beers	BAC
1	6	0.10	10	3	0.07
2	7	0.09	11	3	0.05
3	7	0.09	12	7	0.08
4	4	0.10	13	1	0.04
5	5	0.10	14	4	0.07
6	3	0.07	15	2	0.06
7	3	0.10	16	7	0.12
8	6	0.12	17	2	0.05
9	6	0.09	18	1	0.02

Use a statistical software package to answer the following questions.

a. Develop a scatter diagram for the number of beers consumed and BAC. Comment on the relationship. Does it appear to be strong or weak? Does it appear to be direct or inverse?

b. Determine the coefficient of correlation.

c. Determine the coefficient of determination.

d. At the .01 significance level is it reasonable to conclude that there is a positive relationship in the population between the number of beers consumed and the BAC? What is the *p*-value?

Regression Analysis

In the previous section we developed measures to express the strength and the direction of the linear relationship between two variables. In this section we wish to develop an equation to express the *linear* (straight line) relationship between two variables. In addition we want to be able to estimate the value of the dependent variable Y based on a selected value of the independent variable X. The technique used to develop the equation and provide the estimates is called **regression analysis.**

In Table 13–1 we reported the number of sales calls and the number of units sold for a sample of 10 sales representatives employed by Copier Sales of America. Chart 13–1 portrayed this information in a scatter diagram. Now we want to develop a linear equation that expresses the relationship between the number of sales calls and the number of units sold. The equation for the line used to estimate Y on the basis of X is referred to as the **regression equation.**

> **REGRESSION EQUATION** An equation that expresses the linear relationship between two variables.

Least Squares Principle

The scatter diagram in Chart 13–1 is reproduced in Chart 13–6, with a line drawn with a ruler through the dots to illustrate that a straight line would probably fit the data. However, the line drawn using a straight edge has one disadvantage: Its position is based in part on the judgment of the person drawing the line. The hand-drawn lines in Chart 13–7 represent the judgments of four people. All the lines except line *A* seem to be reasonable. However, each would result in a different estimate of units sold for a particular number of sales calls.

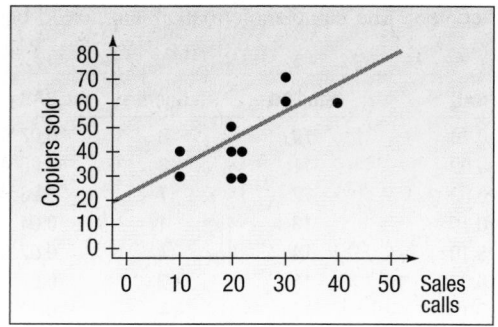

CHART 13–6 Sales Calls and Copiers Sold for 10 Sales Representatives

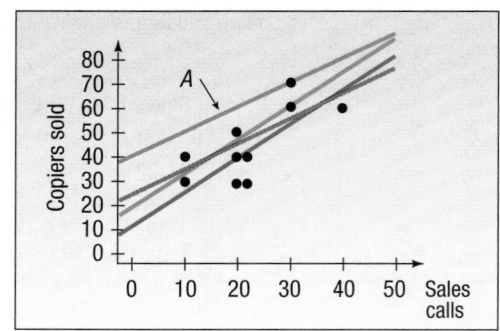

CHART 13–7 Four Lines Superimposed on the Scatter Diagram

Least squares line gives "best" fit; subjective method is unreliable.

Judgment is eliminated by determining the regression line using a mathematical method called the **least squares principle.** This method gives what is commonly referred to as the "best-fitting" line.

> **LEAST SQUARES PRINCIPLE** Determining a regression equation by minimizing the sum of the squares of the vertical distances between the actual *Y* values and the predicted values of *Y*.

To illustrate this concept, the same data are plotted in the three charts that follow. The regression line in Chart 13–8 was determined using the least squares method. It is the best-fitting line because the sum of the squares of the vertical deviations about it is at a minimum. The first plot ($X = 3$, $Y = 8$) deviates by 2 from the line, found by $10 - 8$. The deviation squared is 4. The squared deviation for the plot $X = 4$, $Y = 18$ is 16. The squared deviation for the plot $X = 5$, $Y = 16$ is 4. The sum of the squared deviations is 24, found by $4 + 16 + 4$.

Assume that the lines in Charts 13–9 and 13–10 were drawn with a straight edge. The sum of the squared vertical deviations in Chart 13–9 is 44. For Chart 13–10

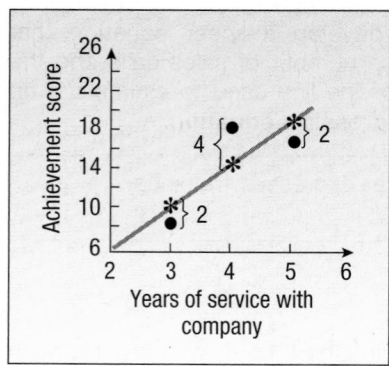

CHART 13–8 The Least Squares Line

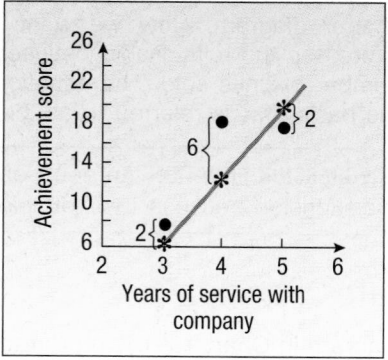

CHART 13–9 Line Drawn with a Straight Edge

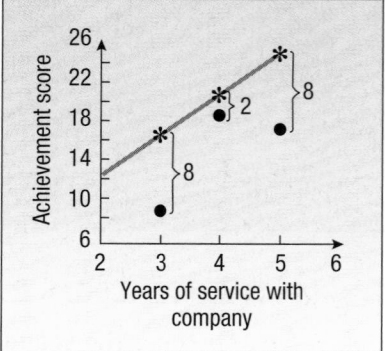

CHART 13–10 Different Line Drawn with a Straight Edge

it is 132. Both sums are greater than the sum for the line in Chart 13–8, found by using the least squares method.

The equation of a straight line has the form

> **GENERAL FORM OF LINEAR REGRESSION EQUATION** $\hat{Y} = a + bX$ **[13–3]**

where

$\hat{Y}$, read Y hat, is the estimated value of the Y variable for a selected X value.

a is the Y-intercept. It is the estimated value of Y when $X = 0$. Another way to put it is: a is the estimated value of Y where the regression line crosses the Y-axis when X is zero.

b is the slope of the line, or the average change in $\hat{Y}$ for each change of one unit (either increase or decrease) in the independent variable X.

X is any value of the independent variable that is selected.

The formulas for a and b are:

> **SLOPE OF THE REGRESSION LINE** $b = r\dfrac{s_y}{s_x}$ **[13–4]**

where

r is the correlation coefficient.

s_y is the standard deviation of Y (the dependent variable).

s_x is the standard deviation of X (the independent variable).

> **Y-INTERCEPT** $a = \overline{Y} - b\overline{X}$ **[13–5]**

where

$\overline{Y}$ is the mean of Y (the dependent variable).

$\overline{X}$ is the mean of X (the independent variable).

Example

Recall the example involving Copier Sales of America. The sales manager gathered information on the number of sales calls made and the number of copiers sold for a random sample of 10 sales representatives. As a part of her presentation at the upcoming sales meeting, Ms. Bancer, the sales manager, would like to offer specific information about the relationship between the number of sales calls and the number of copiers sold. Use the least squares method to determine a linear equation to express the relationship between the two variables. What is the expected number of copiers sold by a representative who made 20 calls?

Solution

The first step in determining the regression equation is to find the slope of the least squares regression line. That is, we need the value of b. On page 461, we determined the correlation coefficient r (.759). In the Excel output on the same page, we determined the standard deviation of the independent variable X (9.189) and the standard deviation of the dependent variable Y (14.337). The values are inserted in formula 13–4.

$$b = r\left(\frac{s_y}{s_x}\right) = .759\left(\frac{14.337}{9.189}\right) = 1.1842$$

Next we need to find the value of a. To do this we use the value for b that we just calculated as well as the means for the number of sales calls and the number of copiers sold. These means are also available in the Excel printout on page 461. From formula (13–5):

$$a = \overline{Y} - b\overline{X} = 45 - 1.1842(22) = 18.9476$$

Thus, the regression equation is $\hat{Y} = 18.9476 + 1.1842X$. So if a salesperson makes 20 calls, he or she can expect to sell 42.6316 copiers, found by $\hat{Y} = 18.9476 + 1.1842X = 18.9476 + 1.1842(20)$. The b value of 1.1842 indicates that for each additional sales call made the sales representative can expect to increase the number of copiers sold by about 1.2. To put it another way, five additional sales calls in a month will result in about six more copiers being sold, found by 1.1842(5) = 5.921.

The a value of 18.9476 is the point where the equation crosses the Y-axis. A literal translation is that if no sales calls are made, that is, $X = 0$, 18.9476 copiers will be sold. Note that $X = 0$ is outside the range of values included in the sample and, therefore, should not be used to estimate the number of copiers sold. The sales calls ranged from 10 to 40, so estimates should be limited to that range.

Statistics in Action

In finance, investors are interested in the trade-off between returns and risk. One technique to quantify risk is a regression analysis of a company's stock price (dependent variable) and an average measure of the stock market (independent variable). Often the Standard and Poor's (S&P) 500 Index is used to estimate the market. The regression coefficient, called beta in finance, shows the change in a company's stock price for a one-unit change in the S&P Index. For example, if a stock has a beta of 1.5, then when the S&P index *(continued)*

Drawing the Regression Line

The least squares equation, $\hat{Y} = 18.9476 + 1.1842X$, can be drawn on the scatter diagram. The first sales representative in the sample is Tom Keller. He made 20 calls. His estimated number of copiers sold is $\hat{Y} = 18.9476 + 1.1842(20) = 42.6316$. The plot $X = 20$ and $Y = 42.6316$ is located by moving to 20 on the X-axis and then going vertically to 42.6316. The other points on the regression equation can be determined by substituting the particular value of X into the regression equation. All the points are connected to give the line. See Chart 13–11.

Sales Representative	Sales Calls (X)	Estimated Sales ($\hat{Y}$)	Sales Representative	Sales Calls (X)	Estimated Sales ($\hat{Y}$)
Tom Keller	20	42.6316	Carlos Ramirez	10	30.7896
Jeff Hall	40	66.3156	Rich Niles	20	42.6316
Brian Virost	20	42.6316	Mike Kiel	20	42.6316
Greg Fish	30	54.4736	Mark Reynolds	20	42.6316
Susan Welch	10	30.7896	Soni Jones	30	54.4736

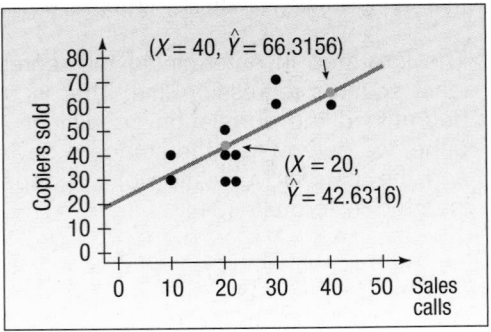

CHART 13–11 The Line of Regression Drawn on the Scatter Diagram

increases by 1%, the stock price will increase by 1.5%. The opposite is also true. If the S&P decreases by 1%, the stock price will decrease by 1.5%. If the beta is 1.0, then a 1% change in the index should show a 1% change in a stock price. If the beta is less than 1.0, then a 1% change in the index shows less than a 1% change in the stock price.

Excel

The least squares regression line has some interesting and unique features. First, it will always pass through the point $(\overline{X}, \overline{Y})$. To show this is true, we can use the mean number of sales calls to predict the number of copiers sold. In this example the mean number of sales calls is 22.0, found by $\overline{X} = 220/10$. The mean number of copiers sold is 45.0, found by $\overline{Y} = 450/10 = 45$. If we let $X = 22$ and then use the regression equation to find the estimated value for $\hat{Y}$, the result is:

$$\hat{Y} = 18.9476 + 1.1842(22) = 45$$

The estimated number of copies sold is exactly equal to the mean number of copies sold. This simple example shows the regression line will pass through the point represented by the two means. In this case the regression equation will pass through the point $X = 22$ and $Y = 45$.

Second, as we discussed earlier in this section, there is no other line through the data where the sum of the squared deviations is smaller. To put it another way, the term $\Sigma(Y - \hat{Y})^2$ is smaller for the least squares regression equation than for any other equation. We use the Excel system to demonstrate this condition.

Regression Table 13.1 [Compatibility Mode]

	A	B	C	D	E	F	G	H	I	J	K
1	Sales	Calls	Sales	Estimates Sales							
2	Representative	(X)	(Y)	$\hat{y}$	$(Y - \hat{y})$	$(Y - \hat{y})^2$	Y^*	$(Y - Y^*)^2$	Y^{**}	$(Y - Y^{**})^2$	
3	Tom Keller	20	30	42.6316	-12.6316	159.55731856	43	169	40	100	
4	Jeff Hall	40	60	66.3156	-6.3156	39.88680336	67	49	60	0	
5	Brian Virost	20	40	42.6316	-2.6316	6.92531856	43	9	40	0	
6	Greg Fish	30	60	54.4736	5.5264	30.54109696	55	25	50	100	
7	Susan Welch	10	30	30.7896	-0.7896	0.62346816	31	1	30	0	
8	Carlos Ramirez	10	40	30.7896	9.2104	84.83146816	31	81	30	100	
9	Rich Niles	20	40	42.6316	-2.6316	6.92531856	43	9	40	0	
10	Mike Kiel	20	50	42.6316	7.3684	54.29331856	43	49	40	100	
11	Mark Reynolds	20	30	42.6316	-12.6316	159.55731856	43	169	40	100	
12	Soni Jones	30	70	54.4736	15.5264	241.06909696	55	225	50	400	
13			Sum of		0.00	784.21052640		786		900	
14			Residuals								
15											
16				Least Squares							
17				Value							

In Columns A, B, and C in the Excel spreadsheet above we duplicated the sample information on sales and copiers sold from Table 13–1. In column D we provide the estimated sales values, the $\hat{Y}$ values, as calculated above.

In column E we calculate the **residuals,** or the error values. This is the difference between the actual values and the predicted values. That is, column E is $(Y - \hat{Y})$. For Soni Jones,

$$\hat{Y} = 18.9476 + 1.1842(30) = 54.4736$$

Her actual value is 70. So the residual, or error of estimate, is

$$(Y - \hat{Y}) = (70 - 54.4736) = 15.5264$$

This value reflects the amount the predicted value of sales is "off" from the actual sales value.

Next in Column F we square the residuals for each of the sales representatives and total the result. The total is 784.2105.

$$\Sigma(Y - \hat{Y})^2 = 159.5573 + 39.8868 + \cdots + 241.0691 = 784.2105$$

This is the sum of the squared differences or the least squares value. There is no other line through these 10 data points where the sum of the squared differences is smaller.

We can demonstrate the least squares criterion by choosing two arbitrary equations that are close to the least squares equation and determining the sum of the squared differences for these equations. In column G we use the equation $Y^* = 19 + 1.2X$ to find the predicted value. Notice this equation is very similar to the least squares equation. In Column H we determine the residuals and square these residuals. For the first sales representative, Tom Keller,

$$Y^* = 19 + 1.2(20) = 43$$

$$(Y - Y^*)^2 = (43 - 30)^2 = 169$$

This procedure is continued for the other nine sales representatives and the squared residuals totaled. The result is 786. This is a larger value (786 versus 784.2105) than the residuals for the least squares line.

In columns I and J on the output we repeat the above process for yet another equation $Y^{**} = 20 + X$. Again, this equation is similar to the least squares equation. The details for Tom Keller are:

$$Y^{**} = 20 + X = 20 + 20 = 40$$

$$(Y - Y^{**})^2 = (30 - 40)^2 = 100$$

This procedure is continued for the other nine sales representatives and the residuals totaled. The result is 900, which is also larger than the least squares values.

What have we shown with the example? The sum of the squared residuals $[\Sigma(Y - \hat{Y})^2]$ for the least squares equation is smaller than for other selected lines. The bottom line is you will not be able to find a line passing through these data points where the sum of the squared residuals is smaller.

Self-Review 13–3   Refer to Self-Review 13–1, where the owner of Haverty's Furniture Company was studying the relationship between sales and the amount spent on advertising. The sales information for the last four months is repeated below.

Month	Advertising Expense ($ million)	Sales Revenue ($ million)
July	2	7
August	1	3
September	3	8
October	4	10

(a) Determine the regression equation.
(b) Interpret the values of a and b.
(c) Estimate sales when $3 million is spent on advertising.

Exercises

connect

13. The following sample observations were randomly selected.

X:	4	5	3	6	10
Y:	4	6	5	7	7

  a. Determine the regression equation.
  b. Determine the value of $\hat{Y}$ when X is 7.
14. The following sample observations were randomly selected.

X:	5	3	6	3	4	4	6	8
Y:	13	15	7	12	13	11	9	5

a. Determine the regression equation.
b. Determine the value of $\hat{Y}$ when X is 7.

15. Bradford Electric Illuminating Company is studying the relationship between kilowatt-hours (thousands) used and the number of rooms in a private single-family residence. A random sample of 10 homes yielded the following.

Number of Rooms	Kilowatt-Hours (thousands)	Number of Rooms	Kilowatt-Hours (thousands)
12	9	8	6
9	7	10	8
14	10	10	10
6	5	5	4
10	8	7	7

a. Determine the regression equation.
b. Determine the number of kilowatt-hours, in thousands, for a six-room house.

16. Mr. James McWhinney, president of Daniel-James Financial Services, believes there is a relationship between the number of client contacts and the dollar amount of sales. To document this assertion, Mr. McWhinney gathered the following sample information. The X column indicates the number of client contacts last month, and the Y column shows the value of sales ($ thousands) last month for each client sampled.

Number of Contacts, X	Sales ($ thousands), Y	Number of Contacts, X	Sales ($ thousands), Y
14	24	23	30
12	14	48	90
20	28	50	85
16	30	55	120
46	80	50	110

a. Determine the regression equation.
b. Determine the estimated sales if 40 contacts are made.

17. A recent article in *BusinessWeek* listed the "Best Small Companies." We are interested in the current results of the companies' sales and earnings. A random sample of 12 companies was selected and the sales and earnings, in millions of dollars, are reported below.

Company	Sales ($ millions)	Earnings ($ millions)	Company	Sales ($ millions)	Earnings ($ millions)
Papa John's International	$89.2	$4.9	Checkmate Electronics	$17.5	$ 2.6
Applied Innovation	18.6	4.4	Royal Grip	11.9	1.7
Integracare	18.2	1.3	M-Wave	19.6	3.5
Wall Data	71.7	8.0	Serving-N-Slide	51.2	8.2
Davidson & Associates	58.6	6.6	Daig	28.6	6.0
Chico's FAS	46.8	4.1	Cobra Golf	69.2	12.8

Let sales be the independent variable and earnings be the dependent variable.
a. Draw a scatter diagram.
b. Compute the coefficient of correlation.
c. Compute the coefficient of determination.
d. Interpret your findings in parts (b) and (c).
e. Determine the regression equation.
f. For a small company with $50.0 million in sales, estimate the earnings.

18. We are studying mutual bond funds for the purpose of investing in several funds. For this particular study, we want to focus on the assets of a fund and its five-year performance. The question is: Can the five-year rate of return be estimated based on the assets of the

fund? Nine mutual funds were selected at random, and their assets and rates of return are shown below.

Fund	Assets ($ millions)	Return (%)	Fund	Assets ($ millions)	Return (%)
AARP High Quality Bond	$622.2	10.8	MFS Bond A	$494.5	11.6
Babson Bond L	160.4	11.3	Nichols Income	158.3	9.5
Compass Capital Fixed Income	275.7	11.4	T. Rowe Price Short-term	681.0	8.2
Galaxy Bond Retail	433.2	9.1	Thompson Income B	241.3	6.8
Keystone Custodian B-1	437.9	9.2			

   a. Draw a scatter diagram.
   b. Compute the coefficient of correlation.
   c. Compute the coefficient of determination.
   d. Write a brief report of your findings for parts (b) and (c).
   e. Determine the regression equation. Use assets as the independent variable.
   f. For a fund with $400.0 million in sales, determine the five-year rate of return (in percent).
19. Refer to Exercise 5.
   a. Determine the regression equation.
   b. Estimate the number of crimes for a city with 20 police.
   c. Interpret the regression equation.
20. Refer to Exercise 6.
   a. Determine the regression equation.
   b. Estimate the selling price of a 10-year-old car.
   c. Interpret the regression equation.

The Standard Error of Estimate

Note in the preceding scatter diagram (Chart 13–11) all of the points do not lie exactly on the regression line. If they all were on the line, there would be no error in estimating the number of units sold. To put it another way, if all the points were on the regression line, units sold could be predicted with 100 percent accuracy. Thus, there would be no error in predicting the Y variable based on an X variable. This is true in the following hypothetical case (see Chart 13–12). Theoretically, if $X = 4$, then an exact Y of 100 could be predicted with 100 percent confidence. Or if $X = 12$, then $Y = 300$. Because there is no difference between the observed values and the predicted values, there is no error in this estimate.

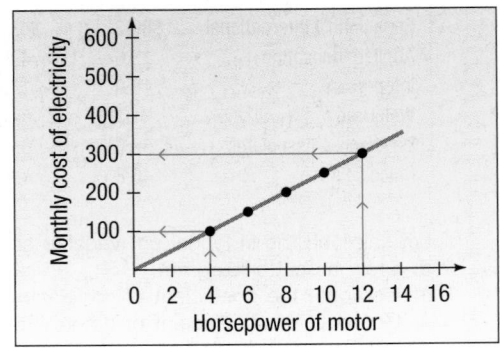

CHART 13–12 Example of Perfect Prediction: Horsepower and Cost of Electricity

Perfect prediction
unrealistic in business

    Perfect prediction in economics and business is practically impossible. For example, the revenue for the year from gasoline sales (Y) based on the number of automobile registrations (X) as of a certain date could no doubt be approximated fairly closely, but the prediction would not be exact to the nearest dollar, or probably even to the nearest thousand dollars. Even predictions of tensile strength of steel wires based on the outside diameters of the wires are not always exact due to slight differences in the composition of the steel.

What is needed, then, is a measure that describes how precise the prediction of Y is based on X or, conversely, how inaccurate the estimate might be. This measure is called the **standard error of estimate.** The standard error of estimate, symbolized by $s_{y \cdot x}$, is the same concept as the standard deviation discussed in Chapter 3. The standard deviation measures the dispersion around the mean. The standard error of estimate measures the dispersion about the regression line.

> **STANDARD ERROR OF ESTIMATE** A measure of the dispersion, or scatter, of the observed values around the line of regression.

The standard error of estimate is found using the following formula, (13–6). Note the following important features:

1. It is similar to the standard deviation in that it is based on squared deviations. The numerator of the standard deviation as we calculated in formula (3–11) on page 80 is based on squared deviations from the mean. The numerator of the standard error is based on squared deviations from the regression line.
2. The sum of the squared deviations is the least squares value used to find the best fitting regression line. Recall in the previous section we described how to find the least squares value (see Column F of the Excel spreadsheet on page 471). We compared the least squares value to values generated from other lines plotted through the data.
3. The denominator of the equation is $n - 2$. As usual, n is the number of observations. We lose two degrees of freedom because we are estimating two parameters. So the values of b, the slope of the line, and a, the Y-intercept, are sample values we use to estimate their corresponding population values. We are sampling from a population and are estimating the slope of the line and the intercept with the Y-axis. Hence the denominator is $n - 2$.

> **STANDARD ERROR OF ESTIMATE** $\qquad s_{y \cdot x} = \sqrt{\dfrac{\Sigma(Y - \hat{Y})^2}{n - 2}}$ **[13–6]**

If $s_{y \cdot x}$ is small, this indicates that the data are relatively close to the regression line and the regression equation can be used to predict Y with little error. If $s_{y \cdot x}$ is large, this indicates that the data are widely scattered around the regression line and the regression equation will not provide a precise estimate Y.

Example

Recall the example involving Copier Sales of America. The sales manager determined the least squares regression equation to be $\hat{Y} = 18.9476 + 1.1842X$, where $\hat{Y}$ refers to the predicted number of copiers sold and X the number of sales calls made. Determine the standard error of estimate as a measure of how well the values fit the regression line.

Solution

To find the standard error, we begin by finding the difference between the value, Y, and the value estimated from the regression equation, $\hat{Y}$. Next we square this difference, that is, $(Y - \hat{Y})^2$. We do this for each of the n observations and sum the results. That is, we compute $\Sigma(Y - \hat{Y})^2$, which is the numerator of formula (13–6). Finally, we divide by the number of observations minus 2. The details of the calculations are summarized in Table 13–4.

TABLE 13–4 Computations Needed for the Standard Error of Estimate

Sales Representative	Actual Sales, (Y)	Estimated Sales, ($\hat{Y}$)	Deviation, ($Y - \hat{Y}$)	Deviation Squared, ($Y - \hat{Y}$)^2
Tom Keller	30	42.6316	−12.6316	159.557
Jeff Hall	60	66.3156	−6.3156	39.887
Brian Virost	40	42.6316	−2.6316	6.925
Greg Fish	60	54.4736	5.5264	30.541
Susan Welch	30	30.7896	−0.7896	0.623
Carlos Ramirez	40	30.7896	9.2104	84.831
Rich Niles	40	42.6316	−2.6316	6.925
Mike Kiel	50	42.6316	7.3684	54.293
Mark Reynolds	30	42.6316	−12.6316	159.557
Soni Jones	70	54.4736	15.5264	241.069
			0.0000	784.211

The standard error of estimate is 9.901, found by using formula (13–6).

$$s_{y \cdot x} = \sqrt{\frac{\Sigma(Y - \hat{Y})^2}{n - 2}} = \sqrt{\frac{784.211}{10 - 2}} = 9.901$$

The deviations $(Y - \hat{Y})$ are the vertical deviations from the regression line. To illustrate, the 10 deviations from Table 13–4 are shown in Chart 13–13. Note in Table 13–4 that the sum of the signed deviations is zero. This indicates that the positive deviations (above the regression line) are offset by the negative deviations (below the regression line).

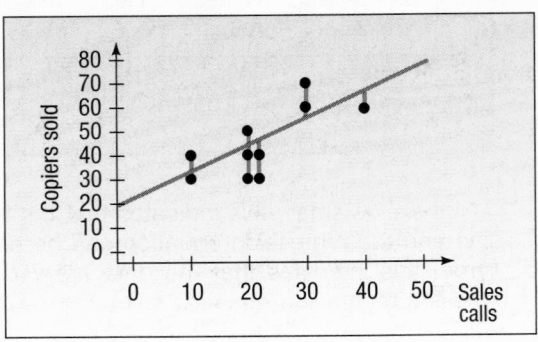

CHART 13–13 Sales Calls and Copiers Sold for 10 Salespeople

Statistical software eases computation when you are finding the least squares equation, the standard error of estimate, and the coefficient of correlation as well as other regression statistics. A portion of the Excel output for the Copier Sales of America example is included below. The intercept and slope values are cells F13 and F14, the standard error of estimate is in F8, and the coefficient of correlation (called Multiple R) is in cell F5.

Regression analysis [Compatibility Mode]

	A	B	C	D	E	F	G
1	Sales Representative	Calls	Sales				
2	Tom Keller	20	30		SUMMARY OUTPUT		
3	Jeff Hall	40	60				
4	Brian Virost	20	40		*Regression Statistics*		
5	Greg Fish	30	60		Multiple R	0.759014109	
6	Susan Welch	10	30		R Square	0.576102418	
7	Carlos Ramirez	10	40		Adjusted R Square	0.52311522	
8	Rich Niles	20	40		Standard Error	9.900823995	
9	Mike Kiel	20	50		Observations	10	
10	Mark Reynolds	20	30				
11	Soni Jones	30	70				
12						*Coefficients*	
13					Intercept	18.94736842	
14					Calls	1.184210526	
15							

Thus far we have presented linear regression only as a descriptive tool. In other words it is a simple summary ($\hat{Y} = a + bX$) of the relationship between the dependent Y variable and the independent X variable. When our data are a sample taken from a population, we are doing inferential statistics. Then we need to recall the distinction between population parameters and sample statistics. In this case, we "model" the linear relationship in the population by the equation:

$$Y = \alpha + \beta X$$

where
  Y is any value of the dependent variable.
  α is the Y-intercept (the value of Y when $X = 0$) in the population.
  β is the slope (the amount by which Y changes when X increases by one unit) of the population line.
  X is any value of the independent variable.

Now α and β are population parameters and a and b, respectively, are estimates of those parameters. They are computed from a particular sample taken from the population. Fortunately, the formulas given earlier in the chapter for a and b do not change when we move from using regression as a descriptive tool to regression in statistical inference.

It should be noted that the linear regression equation for the sample of salespeople is only an estimate of the relationship between the two variables for the population. Thus, the values of a and b in the regression equation are usually referred to as the **estimated regression coefficients,** or simply the **regression coefficients.**

Assumptions Underlying Linear Regression

To properly apply linear regression, several assumptions are necessary. Chart 13–14 illustrates these assumptions.

1. For each value of X, there are corresponding Y values. These Y values follow the normal distribution.
2. The means of these normal distributions lie on the regression line.
3. The standard deviations of these normal distributions are all the same. The best estimate we have of this common standard deviation is the standard error of estimate ($s_{y \cdot x}$).

Statistics in Action

Studies indicate that for both men and women, those who are considered good looking earn higher wages than those who are not. In addition, for men there is a correlation between height and salary. For each additional inch of height, a man can expect to earn an additional $250 per year. So a man 6′6″ tall receives a $3,000 "stature" bonus over his 5′6″ counterpart. Being overweight or underweight is also related to earnings, particularly among women. A study of young women showed the heaviest 10 percent earned about 6 percent less than their lighter counterparts.

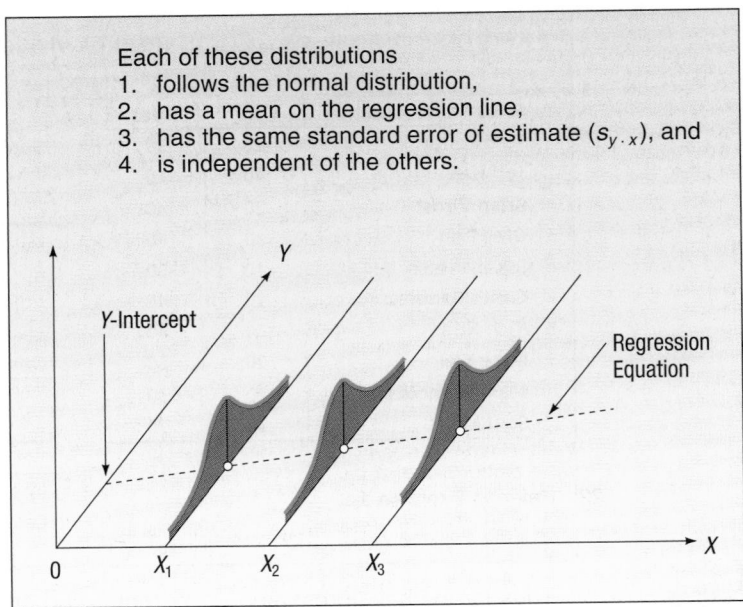

Each of these distributions
1. follows the normal distribution,
2. has a mean on the regression line,
3. has the same standard error of estimate ($s_{y \cdot x}$), and
4. is independent of the others.

CHART 13–14 Regression Assumptions Shown Graphically

4. The Y values are statistically independent. This means that in selecting a sample a particular X does not depend on any other value of X. This assumption is particularly important when data are collected over a period of time. In such situations, the errors for a particular time period are often correlated with those of other time periods.

Recall from Chapter 7 that if the values follow a normal distribution, then the mean plus or minus one standard deviation will encompass 68 percent of the observations, the mean plus or minus two standard deviations will encompass 95 percent of the observations, and the mean plus or minus three standard deviations will encompass virtually all of the observations. The same relationship exists between the predicted values $\hat{Y}$ and the standard error of estimate ($s_{y \cdot x}$).

1. $\hat{Y} \pm s_{y \cdot x}$ will include the middle 68 percent of the observations.
2. $\hat{Y} \pm 2s_{y \cdot x}$ will include the middle 95 percent of the observations.
3. $\hat{Y} \pm 3s_{y \cdot x}$ will include virtually all the observations.

We can now relate these assumptions to Copier Sales of America, where we studied the relationship between the number of sales calls and the number of copiers sold. Assume that we took a much larger sample than $n = 10$, but that the standard error of estimate was still 9.901. If we drew a parallel line 9.901 units above the regression line and another 9.901 units below the regression line, about 68 percent of the points would fall between the two lines. Similarly, a line 19.802 [$2s_{y \cdot x} = 2(9.901)$] units above the regression line and another 19.802 units below the regression line should include about 95 percent of the data values.

As a rough check, refer to the second column from the right in Table 13–4 on page 476, i.e., the column headed "Deviation." Three of the 10 deviations exceed one standard error of estimate. That is, the deviation of −12.6316 for Tom Keller, −12.6316 for Mark Reynolds, and +15.5264 for Soni Jones all exceed the value of 9.901, which is one standard error from the regression line. All of the values are within 19.802 units of the regression line. To put it another way, 7 of the 10 deviations in the sample are within one standard error of the regression line and all are within two—a good result for a relatively small sample.

Self-Review 13–4

Refer to Self-Reviews 13–1 and 13–3, where the owner of Haverty's Furniture was studying the relationship between sales and the amount spent on advertising. Determine the standard error of estimate.

Exercises

connect

21. Refer to Exercise 13.
  a. Determine the standard error of estimate.
  b. Suppose a large sample is selected (instead of just five). About 68 percent of the predictions would be between what two values?
22. Refer to Exercise 14.
  a. Determine the standard error of estimate.
  b. Suppose a large sample is selected (instead of just eight). About 95 percent of the predictions would be between what two values?
23. Refer to Exercise 15.
  a. Determine the standard error of estimate.
  b. Suppose a large sample is selected (instead of just 10). About 95 percent of the predictions regarding kilowatt-hours would occur between what two values?
24. Refer to Exercise 16.
  a. Determine the standard error of estimate.
  b. Suppose a large sample is selected (instead of just 10). About 95 percent of the predictions regarding sales would occur between what two values?
25. Refer to Exercise 5. Determine the standard error of estimate.
26. Refer to Exercise 6. Determine the standard error of estimate.

Confidence and Prediction Intervals

The standard error of estimate is also used to establish confidence intervals when the sample size is large and the scatter around the regression line approximates the normal distribution. In our example involving the number of sales calls and the number of copiers sold, the sample size is small; hence, we need a correction factor to account for the size of the sample. In addition, when we move away from the mean of the independent variable, our estimates are subject to more variation, and we also need to adjust for this.

We are interested in providing interval estimates of two types. The first, which is called a **confidence interval,** reports the *mean* value of *Y* for a given *X*. The second type of estimate is called a **prediction interval,** and it reports the *range of values of Y* for a *particular* value of *X*. To explain further, suppose we estimate the salary of executives in the retail industry based on their years of experience. If we want an interval estimate of the mean salary of *all* retail executives with 20 years of experience, we calculate a confidence interval. If we want an estimate of the salary of Curtis Bender, a *particular* retail executive with 20 years of experience, we calculate a prediction interval.

To determine the confidence interval for the mean value of *Y* for a given *X*, the formula is:

| CONFIDENCE INTERVAL FOR THE MEAN OF *Y*, GIVEN *X* | $\hat{Y} \pm t(s_{y \cdot x}) \sqrt{\dfrac{1}{n} + \dfrac{(X - \bar{X})^2}{\Sigma(X - \bar{X})^2}}$ | **[13–7]** |

where
$\hat{Y}$ is the predicted value for any selected X value.
X is any selected value of X.
$\overline{X}$ is the mean of the Xs, found by $\Sigma X/n$.
n is the number of observations.
$s_{y \cdot x}$ is the standard error of estimate.
t is the value of t from Appendix B.2 with $n - 2$ degrees of freedom.

We first described the t distribution in Chapter 9. In review the concept of t was developed by William Gossett in the early 1900s. He noticed that $\overline{X} \pm zs_{\bar{x}}$ was not precisely correct for small samples. He observed, for example, for degrees of freedom of 120, that 95 percent of the items fell within $\overline{X} \pm 1.98s$ instead of $\overline{X} \pm 1.96s_{\bar{x}}$. This difference is not too critical, but note what happens as the sample size becomes smaller:

df	t
120	1.980
60	2.000
21	2.080
10	2.228
3	3.182

This is logical. The smaller the sample size, the larger the possible error. The increase in the t value compensates for this possibility.

Example

We return to the Copier Sales of America illustration. Determine a 95 percent confidence interval for all sales representatives who make 25 calls and a prediction interval for Sheila Baker, a West Coast sales representative who made 25 calls.

Solution

We use formula (13–7) to determine a confidence interval. Table 13–5 includes the necessary totals and a repeat of the information of Table 13–2 on page 459.

TABLE 13–5 Calculations Needed for Determining the Confidence Interval and Prediction Interval

Sales Representative	Sales Calls, (X)	Copier Sales, (Y)	($X - \overline{X}$)	($X - \overline{X}$)^2
Tom Keller	20	30	−2	4
Jeff Hall	40	60	18	324
Brian Virost	20	40	−2	4
Greg Fish	30	60	8	64
Susan Welch	10	30	−12	144
Carlos Ramirez	10	40	−12	144
Rich Niles	20	40	−2	4
Mike Kiel	20	50	−2	4
Mark Reynolds	20	30	−2	4
Soni Jones	30	70	8	64
			0	760

The first step is to determine the number of copiers we expect a sales representative to sell if he or she makes 25 calls. It is 48.5526, found by $\hat{Y} = 18.9476 + 1.1842X = 18.9476 + 1.1842(25)$.

To find the *t* value, we need to first know the number of degrees of freedom. In this case the degrees of freedom is $n - 2 = 10 - 2 = 8$. We set the confidence level at 95 percent. To find the value of *t*, move down the left-hand column of Appendix B.2 to 8 degrees of freedom, then move across to the column with the 95 percent level of confidence. The value of *t* is 2.306.

In the previous section we calculated the standard error of estimate to be 9.901. We let $X = 25$, $\overline{X} = \Sigma X/n = 220/10 = 22$, and from Table 13–5 $\Sigma(X - \overline{X})^2 = 760$. Inserting these values in formula (13–7), we can determine the confidence interval.

$$\text{Confidence Interval} = \hat{Y} \pm ts_{y \cdot x}\sqrt{\frac{1}{n} + \frac{(X - \overline{X})^2}{\Sigma(X - \overline{X})^2}}$$

$$= 48.5526 \pm 2.306(9.901)\sqrt{\frac{1}{10} + \frac{(25 - 22)^2}{760}}$$

$$= 48.5526 \pm 7.6356$$

Thus, the 95 percent confidence interval for all sales representatives who make 25 calls is from 40.9170 up to 56.1882. To interpret, let's round the values. If a sales representative makes 25 calls, he or she can expect to sell 48.6 copiers. It is likely those sales will range from 40.9 to 56.2 copiers.

To determine the prediction interval for a particular value of *Y* for a given *X*, formula (13–7) is modified slightly: A 1 is added under the radical. The formula becomes:

PREDICTION INTERVAL FOR *Y*, GIVEN *X*	$\hat{Y} \pm ts_{y \cdot x}\sqrt{1 + \dfrac{1}{n} + \dfrac{(X - \overline{X})^2}{\Sigma(X - \overline{X})^2}}$	**[13–8]**

Suppose we want to estimate the number of copiers sold by Sheila Baker, who made 25 sales calls. The 95 percent prediction interval is determined as follows:

$$\text{Prediction Interval} = \hat{Y} \pm ts_{y \cdot x}\sqrt{1 + \frac{1}{n} + \frac{(X - \overline{X})^2}{\Sigma(X - \overline{X})^2}}$$

$$= 48.5526 \pm 2.306(9.901)\sqrt{1 + \frac{1}{10} + \frac{(25 - 22)^2}{760}}$$

$$= 48.5526 \pm 24.0746$$

Thus, the interval is from 24.478 up to 72.627 copiers. We conclude that the number of copiers sold will be between about 24 and 73 for a particular sales representative who makes 25 calls. This interval is quite large. It is much larger than the confidence interval for all sales representatives who made 25 calls. It is logical, however, that there should be more variation in the sales estimate for an individual than for a group.

The following MINITAB graph shows the relationship between the regression line (in the center), the confidence interval (shown in crimson), and the prediction interval (shown in green). The bands for the prediction interval are always further from the regression line than those for the confidence interval. Also, as the values of *X* move away from the mean number of calls (22) in either the positive or the negative direction, the confidence interval and prediction interval bands widen. This is caused by the numerator of the right-hand term under the radical in formulas (13–7) and (13–8). That is, as the term $(X - \overline{X})^2$ increases, the widths of the confidence interval and the prediction interval also increase. To put it another way, there is less precision in our estimates as we move away, in either direction, from the mean of the independent variable.

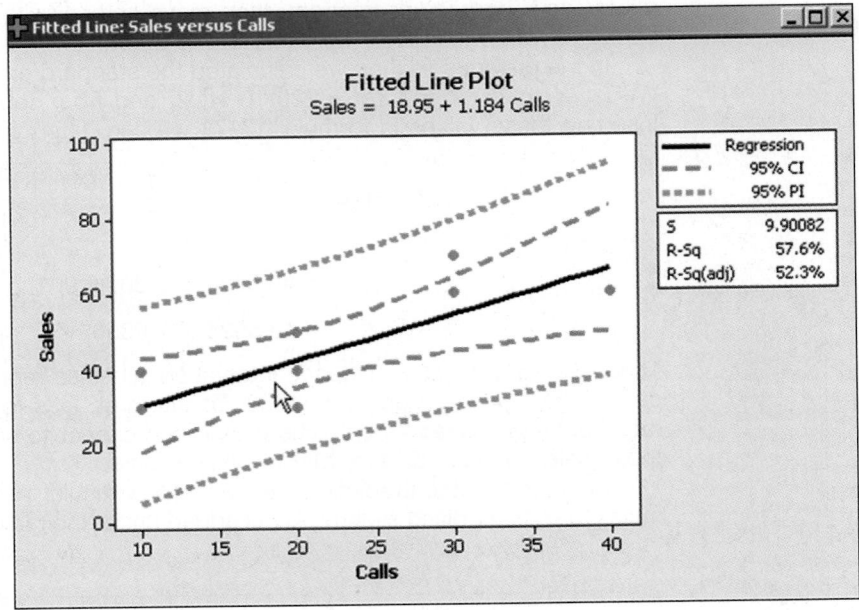

We wish to emphasize again the distinction between a confidence interval and a prediction interval. A confidence interval refers to all cases with a given value of X and is computed by formula (13–7). A prediction interval refers to a particular case for a given value of X and is computed using formula (13–8). The prediction interval will always be wider because of the extra 1 under the radical in the second equation.

Self-Review 13–5

Refer to the sample data in Self-Reviews 13–1, 13–3, and 13–4, where the owner of Haverty's Furniture was studying the relationship between sales and the amount spent on advertising. The sales information for the last four months is repeated below.

Month	Advertising Expense ($ million)	Sales Revenue ($ million)
July	2	7
August	1	3
September	3	8
October	4	10

The regression equation was computed to be $\hat{Y} = 1.5 + 2.2X$, and the standard error 0.9487. Both variables are reported in millions of dollars. Determine the 90 percent confidence interval for the typical month in which $3 million was spent on advertising.

Exercises

27. Refer to Exercise 13.
　a. Determine the .95 confidence interval for the mean predicted when $X = 7$.
　b. Determine the .95 prediction interval for an individual predicted when $X = 7$.
28. Refer to Exercise 14.
　a. Determine the .95 confidence interval for the mean predicted when $X = 7$.
　b. Determine the .95 prediction interval for an individual predicted when $X = 7$.

29. Refer to Exercise 15.
    a. Determine the .95 confidence interval, in thousands of kilowatt-hours, for the mean of all six-room homes.
    b. Determine the .95 prediction interval, in thousands of kilowatt-hours, for a particular six-room home.

30. Refer to Exercise 16.
    a. Determine the .95 confidence interval, in thousands of dollars, for the mean of all sales personnel who make 40 contacts.
    b. Determine the .95 prediction interval, in thousands of dollars, for a particular sales-person who makes 40 contacts.

More on the Coefficient of Determination

Earlier in the chapter, on page 462, we defined the coefficient of determination as the percent of the variation in the dependent variable that is accounted for by the independent variable. We indicated it is the square of the coefficient of correlation and that it is written r^2.

To further examine the basic concept of the coefficient of determination, suppose there is interest in the relationship between years on the job, X, and weekly production, Y. Sample data revealed:

Employee	Years on Job, X	Weekly Production, Y
Gordon	14	6
James	7	5
Ford	3	3
Salter	15	9
Artes	11	7

The sample data were plotted in a scatter diagram. Since the relationship between X and Y appeared to be linear, a line was drawn through the plots (see Chart 13–15). The equation is $\hat{Y} = 2 + 0.4X$.

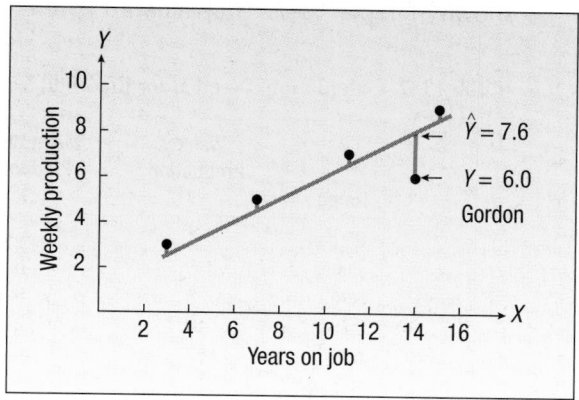

CHART 13–15 Observed Data and the Least Squares Line

Note in Chart 13–15 that, if we were to use that line to predict weekly production for an employee, in no case would our prediction be exact. That is, there would be some error in each of our predictions. As an example, for Gordon, who has been with the company 14 years, we would predict weekly production to be 7.6 units; however, he produces only 6 units.

To measure the overall error in our prediction, every deviation from the line is squared and the squares summed. The predicted point on the line is designated $\hat{Y}$, read Y hat, and the observed point is designated Y. For Gordon, $(Y - \hat{Y})^2 = (6 - 7.6)^2 = (-1.6)^2 = 2.56$. Logically, this variation cannot be explained by the independent variable, so it is referred to as the *unexplained variation.* Specifically, we cannot explain why Gordon's production of 6 units is 1.6 units below his predicted production of 7.6 units, based on the number of years he has been on the job.

Unexplained variation

The sum of the squared deviations, $\Sigma(Y - \hat{Y})^2$, is 4.00. (See Table 13–6.) The term $\Sigma(Y - \hat{Y})^2 = 4.00$ is the variation in Y (production) that cannot be predicted from X. It is the "unexplained" variation in Y.

TABLE 13–6 Computations Needed for the Unexplained Variation

	X	Y	$\hat{Y}$	$Y - \hat{Y}$	$(Y - \hat{Y})^2$
Gordon	14	6	7.6	−1.6	2.56
James	7	5	4.8	0.2	0.04
Ford	3	3	3.2	−0.2	0.04
Salter	15	9	8.0	1.0	1.00
Artes	11	7	6.4	0.6	0.36
Total	50	30		0.0*	4.00

*Must be 0.

Now suppose *only* the Y values (weekly production, in this problem) are known and we want to predict production for every employee. The actual production figures for the employees are 6, 5, 3, 9, and 7 (from Table 13–6). To make these predictions, we could assign the mean weekly production (6 units, found by $\Sigma Y/n = 30/5 = 6$) to each employee. This would keep the sum of the squared prediction errors at a minimum. (Recall from Chapter 3 that the sum of the squared deviations from the arithmetic mean for a set of numbers is smaller than the sum of the squared deviations from any other value, such as the median.) Table 13–7 shows the necessary calculations. The sum of the squared deviations is 20, as shown in Table 13–7. The value 20 is referred to as the *total variation in Y.*

Total variation in Y

TABLE 13–7 Calculations Needed for the Total Variation in Y

Name	Weekly Production, Y	Mean Weekly Production, $\bar{Y}$	$Y - \bar{Y}$	$(Y - \bar{Y})^2$
Gordon	6	6	0	0
James	5	6	−1	1
Ford	3	6	−3	9
Salter	9	6	3	9
Artes	7	6	1	1
Total			0*	20

*Must be 0.

What we did to arrive at the total variation in Y is shown diagrammatically in Chart 13–16.

Logically, the total variation in Y can be subdivided into unexplained variation and explained variation. To arrive at the explained variation, since we know the total variation and unexplained variation, we simply subtract: Explained variation = Total variation − Unexplained variation. Dividing the explained variation by the total

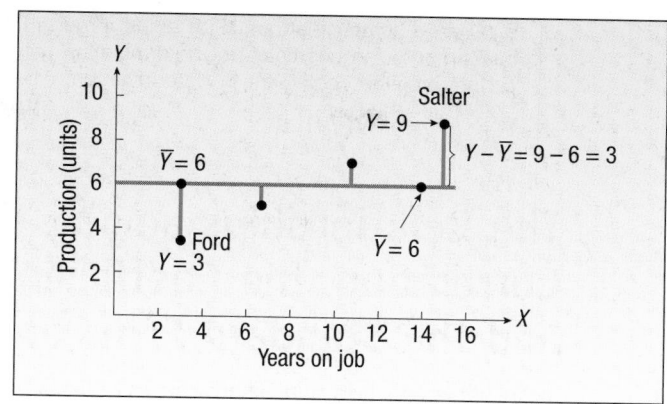

CHART 13–16 Plots Showing Deviations from the Mean of Y

variation gives the coefficient of determination, r^2, which is a proportion. In terms of a formula:

COEFFICIENT OF DETERMINATION	$r^2 = \dfrac{\text{Total variation} - \text{Unexplained variation}}{\text{Total variation}}$ $= \dfrac{\Sigma(Y - \overline{Y})^2 - \Sigma(Y - \hat{Y})^2}{\Sigma(Y - \overline{Y})^2}$	**[13–9]**

In this problem:

$$r^2 = \frac{20 - 4}{20} = \frac{16}{20}$$

Table 13–7
Table 13–6
Explained variation
Total variation

$$= .80$$

As mentioned, .80 is a proportion. We say that 80 percent of the variation in weekly production, Y, is determined, or accounted for, by its linear relationship with X (years on the job).

As a check, formula (13–1) for the coefficient of correlation could be used. Squaring r gives the coefficient of determination, r^2. Exercise 31 offers a check on the preceding problem.

Exercises

31. Using the preceding problem, involving years on the job and weekly production, verify that the coefficient of determination is in fact .80.
32. The number of shares of Icom, Inc., turned over during a month, and the price at the end of the month, are listed in the following table. Also given are the $\hat{Y}$ values.

Turnover (thousands of shares), X	Actual Price, Y	Estimated Price, $\hat{Y}$
4	$2	$2.7
1	1	0.6
5	4	3.4
3	2	2.0
2	1	1.3

a. Draw a scatter diagram. Plot a line through the dots.
b. Compute the coefficient of determination using formula (13–10).
c. Interpret the coefficient of determination.

The Relationships among the Coefficient of Correlation, the Coefficient of Determination, and the Standard Error of Estimate

In an earlier section, we discussed the standard error of estimate, which measures how close the actual values are to the regression line. When the standard error is small, it indicates that the two variables are closely related. In the calculation of the standard error, the key term is $\Sigma(Y - \hat{Y})^2$. If the value of this term is small, then the standard error will also be small.

The correlation coefficient measures the strength of the linear association between two variables. When the points on the scatter diagram appear close to the line, we note that the correlation coefficient tends to be large. Thus, the standard error of estimate and the coefficient of correlation relate the same information but use a different scale to report the strength of the association. However, both measures involve the term $\Sigma(Y - \hat{Y})^2$.

We also noted that the square of the correlation coefficient is the coefficient of determination. The coefficient of determination measures the percent of the variation in Y that is explained by the variation in X.

A convenient vehicle for showing the relationship among these three measures is an ANOVA table. This table is similar to the analysis of variance table developed in Chapter 12. In that chapter, the total variation was divided into two components: that due to the *treatments* and that due to *random error.* The concept is similar in regression analysis. The total variation, $\Sigma(Y - \overline{Y})^2$, is divided into two components: (1) that explained by the *regression* (explained by the independent variable) and (2) the *error,* or unexplained variation. These two categories are identified in the first column of the ANOVA table that follows. The column headed "*df*" refers to the degrees of freedom associated with each category. The total number of degrees of freedom is $n - 1$. The number of degrees of freedom in the regression is 1, since there is only one independent variable. The number of degrees of freedom associated with the error term is $n - 2$. The term "SS" located in the middle of the ANOVA table refers to the sum of squares—the variation. The terms are computed as follows:

$$\text{Regression} = SSR = \Sigma(\hat{Y} - \overline{Y})^2$$

$$\text{Error variation} = SSE = \Sigma(Y - \hat{Y})^2$$

$$\text{Total variation} = SS \text{ total} = \Sigma(Y - \overline{Y})^2$$

The format for the ANOVA table is:

Source	df	SS	MS
Regression	1	SSR	SSR/1
Error	$n - 2$	SSE	SSE/$(n - 2)$
Total	$n - 1$	SS total*	

*SS total = SSR + SSE.

The coefficient of determination, r^2, can be obtained directly from the ANOVA table by:

> **COEFFICIENT OF DETERMINATION** $\quad r^2 = \dfrac{\text{SSR}}{\text{SS total}} = 1 - \dfrac{\text{SSE}}{\text{SS total}}$ **[13–10]**

The term "SSR/SS total" is the proportion of the variation in Y *explained* by the independent variable, X. Note the effect of the SSE term on r^2. As SSE decreases, r^2 will increase. To put it another way, as the standard error decreases, the r^2 term increases.

The standard error of estimate can also be obtained from the ANOVA table using the following equation:

> **STANDARD ERROR OF ESTIMATE** $\quad s_{y \cdot x} = \sqrt{\dfrac{\text{SSE}}{n - 2}}$ **[13–11]**

The Copier Sales of America example is used to illustrate the computations of the coefficient of determination and the standard error of estimate from an ANOVA table.

Example

In the Copier Sales of America example we studied the relationship between the number of sales calls made and the number of copiers sold. Use a computer software package to determine the least squares regression equation and the ANOVA table. Identify the regression equation, the standard error of estimate, and the coefficient of determination on the computer output. From the ANOVA table on the computer output, determine the coefficient of determination and the standard error of estimate using formulas (13–10) and (13–11).

Solution

The output from Excel follows.

Excel

Regression analysis

	A	B	C	D	E	F	G	H	I	J
1	Sales Representative	Calls	Sales							
2	Tom Keller	20	30		ANOVA					
3	Jeff Hall	40	60			df	SS	MS	F	
4	Brian Virost	20	40		Regression	1	1065.8	1065.79	10.87	
5	Greg Fish	30	60		Residual	8	784.2	98.03		
6	Susan Welch	10	30		Total	9	1850.0			
7	Carlos Ramirez	10	40							
8	Rich Niles	20	40							
9	Mike Kiel	20	50							
10	Mark Reynolds	20	30							
11	Soni Jones	30	70							

From formula (13–10) the coefficient of determination is .576, found by

$$r^2 = \frac{\text{SSR}}{\text{SS total}} = \frac{1{,}065.8}{1{,}850} = .576$$

This is the same value we computed earlier in the chapter, when we found the coefficient of determination by squaring the coefficient of correlation. Again, the interpretation is that the independent variable, Calls, explains 57.6 percent of the variation in the number of copiers sold. If we needed the coefficient of correlation, we could find it by taking the square root of the coefficient of determination:

$$r = \sqrt{r^2} = \sqrt{.576} = .759$$

A problem does remain, and that involves the sign for the coefficient of correlation. Recall that the square root of a value could have either a positive or a negative sign. The sign of the coefficient of correlation will always be the same as that of the slope. That is, b and r will always have the same sign. In this case the sign of the regression coefficient (b) is positive, so the coefficient of correlation is .759.

To find the standard error of estimate, we use formula (13–11):

$$s_{y \cdot x} = \sqrt{\frac{SSE}{n - 2}} = \sqrt{\frac{784.2}{10 - 2}} = 9.901$$

Again, this is the same value calculated earlier in the chapter. These values are identified on the Excel computer output.

Transforming Data

The coefficient of correlation describes the strength of the *linear* relationship between two variables. It could be that two variables are closely related, but their relationship is not linear. Be cautious when you are interpreting the coefficient of correlation. A value of r may indicate there is no linear relationship, but it could be there is a relationship of some other nonlinear or curvilinear form.

To explain, below is a listing of 22 professional golfers, the number of events in which they participated, the amount of their winnings, and their mean score. In golf, the objective is to play 18 holes in the least number of strokes. So, we would expect that those golfers with the lower mean scores would have the larger winnings. In other words, score and winnings should be inversely related.

Tiger Woods played in a total of 19 events, earned $5,365,472, and had a mean score per round of 69.04. Fred Couples played in 16 events, earned $1,396,109, and had a mean score per round of 70.92. The data for the 22 golfers follows.

Player	Events	Winnings	Score
Vijay Singh	29	$10,905,166	68.84
Ernie Els	16	5,787,225	68.98
Phil Mickelson	22	5,784,823	69.16
Tiger Woods	19	5,365,472	69.04
Davis Love III	24	3,075,092	70.13
Chris DiMarco	27	2,971,842	70.28
John Daly	22	2,359,507	70.82
Charles Howell III	30	1,703,485	70.77
Kirk Triplett	24	1,566,426	70.31
Fred Couples	16	1,396,109	70.92
Tim Petrovic	32	1,193,354	70.91
Briny Baird	30	$1,156,517	70.79
Hank Kuehne	30	816,889	71.36

continued

Player	Events	Winnings	Score
J. L. Lewis	32	807,345	71.21
Aaron Baddeley	27	632,876	71.61
Craig Perks	27	423,748	71.75
David Frost	26	402,589	71.75
Rich Beem	28	230,499	71.76
Dicky Pride	23	230,329	72.91
Len Mattiace	25	213,707	72.03
Esteban Toledo	36	115,185	72.36
David Gossett	25	21,250	75.01

The correlation between the variables Winnings and Score is −0.782. This is a fairly strong inverse relationship. However, when we plot the data on a scatter diagram the relationship does not appear to be linear; it does not seem to follow a straight line. See the scatter diagram on the right-hand side of the following MINITAB output. The data points for the lowest score and the highest score seem to be well away from the regression line. In addition, for the scores between 70 and 72, the winnings are below the regression line. If the relationship were linear, we would expect these points to be both above and below the line.

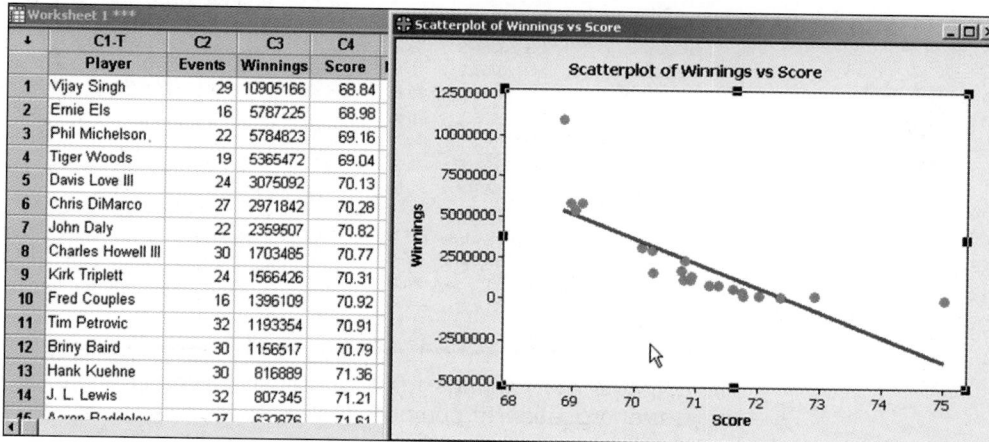

What can we do to explore other (nonlinear) relationships? One possibility is to transform one of the variables. For example, instead of using Y as the dependent variable, we might use its log, reciprocal, square, or square root. Another possibility is to transform the independent variable in the same way. There are other transformations, but these are the most common.

In the golf winnings example, changing the scale of the dependent variable is effective. We determine the log of each golfer's winnings and then find the correlation between the log of winnings and score. That is, we find the log to the base 10 of Tiger Woods' earnings of $5,365,472, which is 6.72961. Next we find the log to the base 10 of each golfer's winnings and then determine the correlation between log of winnings and the score. The correlation coefficient increases from −0.782 to −0.969. This means that the coefficient of determination is .939 [$r^2 = (-0.969)^2 = .939$]. That is, 93.9 percent of the variation in the log of winnings is accounted for by the independent variable score.

We have determined an equation that fits the data more closely than the straight line did. Clearly, as the mean score for a golfer increases, he can expect his winnings to decrease. It no longer appears that some of the data points are different from the regression line, as we found when using winnings instead of the log of winnings as the dependent variable. Also note the points between 70 and 72 in particular are now randomly distributed above and below the regression line.

	C1-T	C2	C3	C4	C5
	Player	Events	Winnings	Score	Log-Winnings
1	Vijay Singh	29	10905166	68.84	7.03763
2	Ernie Els	16	5787225	68.98	6.76247
3	Phil Michelson	22	5784823	69.16	6.76229
4	Tiger Woods	19	5365472	69.04	6.72961
5	Davis Love III	24	3075092	70.13	6.48786
6	Chris DiMarco	27	2971842	70.28	6.47303
7	John Daly	22	2359507	70.82	6.37282
8	Charles Howell III	30	1703485	70.77	6.23134
9	Kirk Triplett	24	1566426	70.31	6.19491
10	Fred Couples	16	1396109	70.92	6.14492
11	Tim Petrovic	32	1193354	70.91	6.07677
12	Briny Baird	30	1156517	70.79	6.06315
13	Hank Kuehne	30	816889	71.36	5.91216
14	J. L. Lewis	32	807345	71.21	5.90706

Fitted Line Plot
Log-Winnings = 37.20 - 0.4394 Score

S	0.162479
R-Sq	94.0%
R-Sq(adj)	93.7%

We can also estimate the amount of winnings based on the score. Following is the MINITAB regression output using score as the independent variable and the log of winnings as the dependent variable.

	C1-T	C2	C3	C4	C5
	Player	Events	Winnings	Score	Log-Winnings
1	Vijay Singh	29	10905166	68.84	7.03763
2	Ernie Els	16	5787225	68.98	6.76247
3	Phil Michelson	22	5784823	69.16	6.76229
4	Tiger Woods	19	5365472	69.04	6.72961
5	Davis Love III	24	3075092	70.13	6.48786
6	Chris DiMarco	27	2971842	70.28	6.47303
7	John Daly	22	2359507	70.82	6.37282
8	Charles Howell III	30	1703485	70.77	6.23134
9	Kirk Triplett	24	1566426	70.31	6.19491
10	Fred Couples	16	1396109	70.92	6.14492
11	Tim Petrovic	32	1193354	70.91	6.07677
12	Briny Baird	30	1156517	70.79	6.06315
13	Hank Kuehne	30	816889	71.36	5.91216
14	J. L. Lewis	32	807345	71.21	5.90706
15	Aaron Baddeley	27	632876	71.61	5.80132

Regression Analysis: Log-Winnings versus Score

```
The regression equation is
Log-Winnings = 37.2 - 0.439 Score

Predictor      Coef   SE Coef      T      P
Constant     37.198     1.766  21.07  0.000
Score       -0.43944   0.02485 -17.68  0.000

S = 0.162479   R-Sq = 94.0%   R-Sq(adj) = 93.7%

Analysis of Variance

Source          DF      SS       MS       F      P
Regression       1  8.2521   8.2521  312.59  0.000
Residual Error  20  0.5280   0.0264
Total           21  8.7801
```

To compute the earnings for a golfer with a mean score of 70, we first use the regression equation to compute the log of earnings.

$$\hat{Y} = 37.198 - .43944X = 37.198 - .43944(70) = 6.4372$$

The value 6.4372 is the log to the base 10 of winnings. The antilog of 6.4372 is 2,736,528. So a golfer that had a mean score of 70 could expect to earn $2,736,528. We can also evaluate the change in scores. The above golfer had a mean score of 70 and estimated earnings of $2,736,528. How much less would a golfer expect to win if his mean score was 71? Again solving the regression equation:

$$\hat{Y} = 37.198 - .43944X = 37.198 - .43944(71) = 5.99776$$

The antilog of this value is $994,855. So based on the regression analysis, there is a large financial incentive for a professional golfer to reduce his mean score by even one stroke. Those of you that play golf or know a golfer understand how difficult that change would be! That one stroke is worth over $1,700,000.

Exercises

33. Given the following ANOVA table:

```
SOURCE        DF        SS          MS          F
Regression     1     1000.0     1000.00      26.00
Error         13      500.0       38.46
Total         14     1500.0
```

a. Determine the coefficient of determination.

b. Assuming a direct relationship between the variables, what is the coefficient of correlation?

c. Determine the standard error of estimate.

34. On the first statistics exam the coefficient of determination between the hours studied and the grade earned was 80 percent. The standard error of estimate was 10. There were 20 students in the class. Develop an ANOVA table.

35. Given the following sample observations, develop a scatter diagram. Compute the coefficient of correlation. Does the relationship between the variables appear to be linear? Try squaring the X-variable and then determine the correlation coefficient.

X	−8	−16	12	2	18
Y	58	247	153	3	341

36. According to basic economics, as the demand for a product increases, the price will decrease. Listed below is the number of units demanded and the price.

Demand	Price
2	$120.0
5	90.0
8	80.0
12	70.0
16	50.0
21	45.0
27	31.0
35	30.0
45	25.0
60	21.0

a. Determine the correlation between price and demand. Plot the data in a scatter diagram. Does the relationship seem to be linear?

b. Transform the price to a log to the base 10. Plot the log of the price and the demand. Determine the correlation coefficient. Does this seem to improve the relationship between the variables?

Chapter Summary

I. A scatter diagram is a graphic tool to portray the relationship between two variables.
  A. The dependent variable is scaled on the Y-axis and is the variable being estimated.
  B. The independent variable is scaled on the X-axis and is the variable used as the estimator.

II. The coefficient of correlation measures the strength of the linear association between two variables.
  A. Both variables must be at least the interval scale of measurement.
  B. The coefficient of correlation can range from −1.00 up to 1.00.
  C. If the correlation between two variables is 0, there is no association between them.
  D. A value of 1.00 indicates perfect positive correlation, and −1.00 perfect negative correlation.
  E. A positive sign means there is a direct relationship between the variables, and a negative sign means there is an inverse relationship.
  F. It is designated by the letter r and found by the following equation:

$$r = \frac{\Sigma(X - \bar{X})(Y - \bar{Y})}{(n-1)s_x s_y}$$

[13–1]

  G. The following equation is used to determine whether the correlation in the population is different from 0.

$$t = \frac{r\sqrt{n-2}}{\sqrt{1-r^2}} \quad \text{with } n - 2 \text{ degrees of freedom}$$

[13–2]

III. The coefficient of determination is the fraction of the variation in one variable that is explained by the variation in the other variable.

A. It ranges from 0 to 1.0.

B. It is the square of the coefficient of correlation.

IV. In regression analysis we estimate one variable based on another variable.

   A. The variable being estimated is the dependent variable.

   B. The variable used to make the estimate is the independent variable.

   1. The relationship between the variables must be linear.

   2. Both the independent and the dependent variables must be interval or ratio scale.

   3. The least squares criterion is used to determine the regression equation.

V. The least squares regression line is of the form $\hat{Y} = a + bX$.

   A. $\hat{Y}$ is the estimated value of Y for a selected value of X.

   B. a is the constant or intercept.

   1. It is the value of $\hat{Y}$ when $X = 0$.

   2. a is computed using the following equation.

$$a = \overline{Y} - b\overline{X} \qquad \text{[13–5]}$$

   C. b is the slope of the fitted line.

   1. It shows the amount of change in $\hat{Y}$ for a change of one unit in X.

   2. A positive value for b indicates a direct relationship between the two variables, and a negative value an inverse relationship.

   3. The sign of b and the sign of r, the coefficient of correlation, are always the same.

   4. b is computed using the following equation.

$$b = r\left(\frac{s_y}{s_x}\right) \qquad \text{[13–4]}$$

   D. X is the value of the independent variable.

VI. The standard error of estimate measures the variation around the regression line.

   A. It is in the same units as the dependent variable.

   B. It is based on squared deviations from the regression line.

   C. Small values indicate that the points cluster closely about the regression line.

   D. It is computed using the following formula.

$$s_{y \cdot x} = \sqrt{\frac{\Sigma(Y - \hat{Y})^2}{n - 2}} \qquad \text{[13–6]}$$

VII. Inference about linear regression is based on the following assumptions.

   A. For a given value of X, the values of Y are normally distributed about the line of regression.

   B. The standard deviation of each of the normal distributions is the same for all values of X and is estimated by the standard error of estimate.

   C. The deviations from the regression line are independent, with no pattern to the size or direction.

VIII. There are two types of interval estimates.

   A. In a confidence interval the mean value of Y is estimated for a given value of X.

   1. It is computed from the following formula.

$$\hat{Y} \pm t(s_{y \cdot x}) \sqrt{\frac{1}{n} + \frac{(X - \overline{X})^2}{\Sigma(X - \overline{X})^2}} \qquad \text{[13–7]}$$

   2. The width of the interval is affected by the level of confidence, the size of the standard error of estimate, and the size of the sample, as well as the value of the independent variable.

   B. In a prediction interval the individual value of Y is estimated for a given value of X.

   1. It is computed from the following formula.

$$\hat{Y} \pm ts_{y \cdot x} \sqrt{1 + \frac{1}{n} + \frac{(X - \overline{X})^2}{\Sigma(X - \overline{X})^2}} \qquad \text{[13–8]}$$

   2. The difference between formulas (13–7) and (13–8) is the 1 under the radical.

   a. The prediction interval will be wider than the confidence interval.

   b. The prediction interval is also based on the level of confidence, the size of the standard error of estimate, the size of the sample, and the value of the independent variable.

Pronunciation Key

SYMBOL	MEANING	PRONUNCIATION
ΣXY	Sum of the products of X and Y	Sum X Y
ρ	Coefficient of correlation in the population	Rho
$\hat{Y}$	Estimated value of Y	Y hat
$s_{y \cdot x}$	Standard error of estimate	s sub y dot x
r^2	Coefficient of determination	r square

Chapter Exercises

connect

37. A regional commuter airline selected a random sample of 25 flights and found that the correlation between the number of passengers and the total weight, in pounds, of luggage stored in the luggage compartment is 0.94. Using the .05 significance level, can we conclude that there is a positive association between the two variables?

38. A sociologist claims that the success of students in college (measured by their GPA) is related to their family's income. For a sample of 20 students, the coefficient of correlation is 0.40. Using the 0.01 significance level, can we conclude that there is a positive correlation between the variables?

39. An Environmental Protection Agency study of 12 automobiles revealed a correlation of 0.47 between engine size and emissions. At the .01 significance level, can we conclude that there is a positive association between these variables? What is the *p*-value? Interpret.

40. A suburban hotel derives its gross income from its hotel and restaurant operations. The owners are interested in the relationship between the number of rooms occupied on a nightly basis and the revenue per day in the restaurant. Below is a sample of 25 days (Monday through Thursday) from last year showing the restaurant income and number of rooms occupied.

Day	Income	Occupied	Day	Income	Occupied
1	$1,452	23	14	$1,425	27
2	1,361	47	15	1,445	34
3	1,426	21	16	1,439	15
4	1,470	39	17	1,348	19
5	1,456	37	18	1,450	38
6	1,430	29	19	1,431	44
7	1,354	23	20	1,446	47
8	1,442	44	21	1,485	43
9	1,394	45	22	1,405	38
10	1,459	16	23	1,461	51
11	1,399	30	24	1,490	61
12	1,458	42	25	1,426	39
13	1,537	54			

Use a statistical software package to answer the following questions.

a. Does the breakfast revenue seem to increase as the number of occupied rooms increases? Draw a scatter diagram to support your conclusion.

b. Determine the coefficient of correlation between the two variables. Interpret the value.

c. Is it reasonable to conclude that there is a positive relationship between revenue and occupied rooms? Use the .10 significance level.

d. What percent of the variation in revenue in the restaurant is accounted for by the number of rooms occupied?

41. The table below shows the number of cars (in millions) sold in the United States for various years and the percent of those cars manufactured by GM.

Year	Cars Sold (millions)	Percent GM	Year	Cars Sold (millions)	Percent GM
1950	6.0	50.2	1980	11.5	44.0
1955	7.8	50.4	1985	15.4	40.1
1960	7.3	44.0	1990	13.5	36.0
1965	10.3	49.9	1995	15.5	31.7
1970	10.1	39.5	2000	17.4	28.6
1975	10.8	43.1	2005	16.9	26.9

Use a statistical software package to answer the following questions.
   a. Is the number of cars sold directly or indirectly related to GM's percent of the market? Draw a scatter diagram to show your conclusion.
   b. Determine the coefficient of correlation between the two variables. Interpret the value.
   c. Is it reasonable to conclude that there is a negative association between the two variables? Use the .01 significance level.
   d. How much of the variation in GM's market share is accounted for by the variation in cars sold?

42. For a sample of 32 large U.S. cities, the correlation between the mean number of square feet per office worker and the mean monthly rental rate in the central business district is −.363. At the .05 significance level, can we conclude that there is a negative association in the population between the two variables?

43. What is the relationship between the amount spent per week on recreation and the size of the family? Do larger families spend more on recreation? A sample of 10 families in the Chicago area revealed the following figures for family size and the amount spent on recreation per week.

Family Size	Amount Spent on Recreation	Family Size	Amount Spent on Recreation
3	$ 99	3	$111
6	104	4	74
5	151	4	91
6	129	5	119
6	142	3	91

   a. Compute the coefficient of correlation.
   b. Determine the coefficient of determination.
   c. Can we conclude that there is a positive association between the amount spent on recreation and family size? Use the .05 significance level.

44. A sample of 12 homes sold last week in St. Paul, Minnesota, is selected. Can we conclude that, as the size of the home (reported below in thousands of square feet) increases, the selling price (reported in $ thousands) also increases?

Home Size (thousands of square feet)	Selling Price ($ thousands)	Home Size (thousands of square feet)	Selling Price ($ thousands)
1.4	100	1.3	110
1.3	110	0.8	85
1.2	105	1.2	105
1.1	120	0.9	75
1.4	80	1.1	70
1.0	105	1.1	95

   a. Compute the coefficient of correlation.
   b. Determine the coefficient of determination.
   c. Can we conclude that there is a positive association between the size of the home and the selling price? Use the .05 significance level.

45. The manufacturer of Cardio Glide exercise equipment wants to study the relationship between the number of months since the glide was purchased and the length of time the equipment was used last week.

Person	Months Owned	Hours Exercised	Person	Months Owned	Hours Exercised
Rupple	12	4	Massa	2	8
Hall	2	10	Sass	8	3
Bennett	6	8	Karl	4	8
Longnecker	9	5	Malrooney	10	2
Phillips	7	5	Veights	5	5

a. Plot the information on a scatter diagram. Let hours of exercise be the dependent variable. Comment on the graph.
b. Determine the coefficient of correlation. Interpret.
c. At the .01 significance level, can we conclude that there is a negative association between the variables?

46. The following regression equation was computed from a sample of 20 observations:

$$\hat{Y} = 15 - 5X$$

SSE was found to be 100 and SS total 400.
a. Determine the standard error of estimate.
b. Determine the coefficient of determination.
c. Determine the coefficient of correlation. (Caution: Watch the sign!)

47. City planners believe that larger cities are populated by older residents. To investigate the relationship, data on population and median age in ten large cities were collected.

City	Population (in millions)	Median age
Chicago, IL	2.833	31.5
Dallas, TX	1.233	30.5
Houston, TX	2.144	30.9
Los Angeles, CA	3.849	31.6
New York, NY	8.214	34.2
Philadelphia, PA	1.448	34.2
Phoenix, AZ	1.513	30.7
San Antonio, TX	1.297	31.7
San Diego, CA	1.257	32.5
San Jose, CA	0.930	32.6

a. Plot this data on a scatter diagram with median age as the dependent variable.
b. Find the correlation coefficient.
c. A regression analysis was performed and the resulting regression equation is Median age = 31.4 + 0.272 population. Interpret the meaning of the slope.
d. Estimate the median age for a city of 2.5 million people.
e. Here is a portion of the regression software output. What does it tell you?

```
Predictor        Coef     SE Coef        T         P
Constant      31.3672      0.6158     50.94     0.000
Population     0.2722      0.1901      1.43     0.190
```

f. Test at the .10 significance level whether there is a significant relationship between these two variables.

48. Emily Smith decides to buy a fuel-efficient used car. Here are several vehicles she is considering with the estimated cost to purchase and the age of the vehicle.

Vehicle	Estimated Cost	Age
Honda Insight	$5,555	8
Toyota Prius	$17,888	3
Toyota Prius	$9,963	6
Toyota Echo	$6,793	5
Honda Civic Hybrid	$10,774	5
Honda Civic Hybrid	$16,310	2
Chevrolet Prizm	$2,475	8
Mazda Protege	$2,808	10
Toyota Corolla	$7,073	9
Acura Integra	$8,978	8
Scion xB	$11,213	2
Scion xA	$9,463	3
Mazda3	$15,055	2
Mini Cooper	$20,705	2

a. Plot this data on a scatter diagram with estimated cost as the dependent variable.
b. Find the correlation coefficient.
c. A regression analysis was performed and the resulting regression equation is Estimated Cost = 18358 − 1534 age. Interpret the meaning of the slope.
d. Estimate the cost of a five-year-old car.
e. Here is a portion of the regression software output. What does it tell you?

```
Predictor        Coef    SE Coef        T        P
Constant        18358       1817    10.10    0.000
Age           -1533.6      306.3    -5.01    0.000
```

f. Test at the .10 significance level whether there is a significant relationship between these two variables.

49. The National Highway Association is studying the relationship between the number of bidders on a highway project and the winning (lowest) bid for the project. Of particular interest is whether the number of bidders increases or decreases the amount of the winning bid.

Project	Number of Bidders, X	Winning Bid ($ millions), Y	Project	Number of Bidders, X	Winning Bid ($ millions), Y
1	9	5.1	9	6	10.3
2	9	8.0	10	6	8.0
3	3	9.7	11	4	8.8
4	10	7.8	12	7	9.4
5	5	7.7	13	7	8.6
6	10	5.5	14	7	8.1
7	7	8.3	15	6	7.8
8	11	5.5			

a. Determine the regression equation. Interpret the equation. Do more bidders tend to increase or decrease the amount of the winning bid?
b. Estimate the amount of the winning bid if there were seven bidders.
c. A new entrance is to be constructed on the Ohio Turnpike. There are seven bidders on the project. Develop a 95 percent prediction interval for the winning bid.
d. Determine the coefficient of determination. Interpret its value.

50. Mr. William Profit is studying companies going public for the first time. He is particularly interested in the relationship between the size of the offering and the price per share. A sample of 15 companies that recently went public revealed the following information.

Company	Size ($ millions), X	Price per Share, Y	Company	Size ($ millions), X	Price per Share, Y
1	9.0	10.8	9	160.7	11.3
2	94.4	11.3	10	96.5	10.6
3	27.3	11.2	11	83.0	10.5
4	179.2	11.1	12	23.5	10.3
5	71.9	11.1	13	58.7	10.7
6	97.9	11.2	14	93.8	11.0
7	93.5	11.0	15	34.4	10.8
8	70.0	10.7			

a. Determine the regression equation.
b. Determine the coefficient of determination. Do you think Mr. Profit should be satisfied with using the size of the offering as the independent variable?

51. Bardi Trucking Co., located in Cleveland, Ohio, makes deliveries in the Great Lakes region, the Southeast, and the Northeast. Jim Bardi, the president, is studying the relationship between the distance a shipment must travel and the length of time, in days, it takes the shipment to arrive at its destination. To investigate, Mr. Bardi selected a random sample of 20 shipments made last month. Shipping distance is the independent variable, and shipping time is the dependent variable. The results are as follows:

Shipment	Distance (miles)	Shipping Time (days)	Shipment	Distance (miles)	Shipping Time (days)
1	656	5	11	862	7
2	853	14	12	679	5
3	646	6	13	835	13
4	783	11	14	607	3
5	610	8	15	665	8
6	841	10	16	647	7
7	785	9	17	685	10
8	639	9	18	720	8
9	762	10	19	652	6
10	762	9	20	828	10

a. Draw a scatter diagram. Based on these data, does it appear that there is a relationship between how many miles a shipment has to go and the time it takes to arrive at its destination?
b. Determine the coefficient of correlation. Can we conclude that there is a positive correlation between distance and time? Use the .05 significance level.
c. Determine and interpret the coefficient of determination.
d. Determine the standard error of estimate.

52. Super Markets, Inc., is considering expanding into the Scottsdale, Arizona, area. You as director of planning, must present an analysis of the proposed expansion to the operating committee of the board of directors. As a part of your proposal, you need to include information on the amount people in the region spend per month for grocery items. You would also like to include information on the relationship between the amount spent for grocery items and income. Your assistant gathered the following sample information. The data are available on the data disk supplied with the text.

Household	Amount Spent	Monthly Income
1	$ 555	$4,388
2	489	4,558
⋮	⋮	⋮
39	1,206	9,862
40	1,145	9,883

a. Let the amount spent be the dependent variable and monthly income the independent variable. Create a scatter diagram, using a software package.

b. Determine the regression equation. Interpret the slope value.

c. Determine the coefficient of correlation. Can you conclude that it is greater than 0?

53. Below is information on the price per share and the dividend for a sample of 30 companies. The sample data are available on the data disk supplied with the text.

Company	Price per Share	Dividend
1	$20.00	$ 3.14
2	22.01	3.36
⋮	⋮	⋮
29	77.91	17.65
30	80.00	17.36

a. Calculate the regression equation using selling price based on the annual dividend. Interpret the slope value.

b. Determine the coefficient of determination. Interpret its value.

c. Determine the coefficient of correlation. Can you conclude that it is greater than 0 using the .05 significance level?

54. A highway employee performed a regression analysis of the relationship between the number of construction work-zone fatalities and the number of unemployed people in a state. The regression equation is Fatalities = 12.7 + 0.000114 (Unemp). Some additional output is:

```
Predictor          Coef        SE Coef        T         P
Constant         12.726          8.115      1.57     0.134
Unemp       0.00011386     0.00002896      3.93     0.001

Analysis of Variance
Source           DF         SS         MS       F         P
Regression        1      10354      10354   15.46     0.001
Residual Error   18      12054        670
Total            19      22408
```

a. How many states were in the sample?

b. Determine the standard error of estimate.

c. Determine the coefficient of determination.

d. Determine the coefficient of correlation.

e. At the .05 significance level does the evidence suggest there is a positive association between fatalities and the number unemployed?

55. A regression analysis relating the current market value in dollars to the size in square feet of homes in Greene County, Tennessee, follows. The regression equation is: Value = −37,186 + 65.0 Size.

```
Predictor      Coef     SE Coef        T          P
Constant     -37186        4629     -8.03      0.000
Size         64.993       3.047     21.33      0.000

Analysis of Variance
Source          DF              SS             MS          F        P
Regression       1     13548662082    13548662082     454.98    0.000
Residual Error  33       982687392       29778406
Total           34     14531349474
```

a. How many homes were in the sample?

b. Compute the standard error of estimate.

c. Compute the coefficient of determination.

d. Compute the coefficient of correlation.

e. At the .05 significance level does the evidence suggest a positive association between the market value of homes and the size of the home in square feet?

56. The following table shows the mean annual percent return on capital (profitability) and the mean annual percentage sales growth for eight aerospace and defense companies.

Company	Profitability	Growth
Alliant Techsystems	23.1	8.0
Boeing	13.2	15.6
General Dynamics	24.2	31.2
Honeywell	11.1	2.5
L-3 Communications	10.1	35.4
Northrop Grunmman	10.8	6.0
Rockwell Collins	27.3	8.7
United Technologies	20.1	3.2

a. Compute the coefficient of correlation. Conduct a test of hypothesis to determine if it is reasonable to conclude that the population correlation is greater than zero. Use the .05 significance level.
b. Develop the regression equation for profitability based on growth. Comment on the slope value.
c. Use a software package to determine the residual for each observation. Which company has the largest residual?

57. The following data show the retail price for 12 randomly selected laptop computers along with their corresponding processor speeds in gigahertz.

Computers	Speed	Price	Computers	Speed	Price
1	2.0	$2,017	7	2.0	$2,197
2	1.6	922	8	1.6	1,387
3	1.6	1,064	9	2.0	2,114
4	1.8	1,942	10	1.6	2,002
5	2.0	2,137	11	1.0	937
6	1.2	1,012	12	1.4	869

a. Develop a linear equation that can be used to describe how the price depends on the processor speed.
b. Based on your regression equation, is there one machine that seems particularly over- or underpriced?
c. Compute the correlation coefficient between the two variables. At the .05 significance level conduct a test of hypothesis to determine if the population correlation could be greater than zero.

58. A consumer buying cooperative tested the effective heating area of 20 different electric space heaters with different wattages. Here are the results.

Heater	Wattage	Area	Heater	Wattage	Area
1	1,500	205	11	1,250	116
2	750	70	12	500	72
3	1,500	199	13	500	82
4	1,250	151	14	1,500	206
5	1,250	181	15	2,000	245
6	1,250	217	16	1,500	219
7	1,000	94	17	750	63
8	2,000	298	18	1,500	200
9	1,000	135	19	1,250	151
10	1,500	211	20	500	44

    a. Compute the correlation between the wattage and heating area. Is there a direct or an indirect relationship?

    b. Conduct a test of hypothesis to determine if it is reasonable that the coefficient is greater than zero. Use the .05 significance level.

    c. Develop the regression equation for effective heating based on wattage.

    d. Which heater looks like the "best buy" based on the size of the residual?

59. A dog trainer is exploring the relationship between the size of the dog (weight in pounds) and its daily food consumption (measured in standard cups). Below is the result of a sample of 18 observations.

Dog	Weight	Consumption	Dog	Weight	Consumption
1	41	3	10	91	5
2	148	8	11	109	6
3	79	5	12	207	10
4	41	4	13	49	3
5	85	5	14	113	6
6	111	6	15	84	5
7	37	3	16	95	5
8	111	6	17	57	4
9	41	3	18	168	9

    a. Compute the correlation coefficient. Is it reasonable to conclude that the correlation in the population is greater than zero? Use the .05 significance level.

    b. Develop the regression equation for cups based on the dog's weight. How much does each additional cup change the estimated weight of the dog?

    c. Is one of the dogs a big undereater or overeater?

60. Waterbury Insurance Company wants to study the relationship between the amount of fire damage and the distance between the burning house and the nearest fire station. This information will be used in setting rates for insurance coverage. For a sample of 30 claims for the last year, the director of the actuarial department determined the distance from the fire station (X) and the amount of fire damage, in thousands of dollars (Y). The MegaStat output is reported below. (You can find the actual data in the data set on the CD as prb13-60.)

```
ANOVA table
Source                  SS      df           MS          F
Regression       1,864.5782    1     1,864.5782      38.83
Residual         1,344.4934   28        48.0176
Total            3,209.0716   29


Regression output
Variables      Coefficients    Std. Error    t(df = 28)
Intercept           12.3601        3.2915         3.755
Distance-X           4.7956        0.7696         6.231
```

Answer the following questions.

    a. Write out the regression equation. Is there a direct or indirect relationship between the distance from the fire station and the amount of fire damage?

    b. How much damage would you estimate for a fire 5 miles from the nearest fire station?

    c. Determine and interpret the coefficient of determination.

    d. Determine the coefficient of correlation. Interpret its value. How did you determine the sign of the correlation coefficient?

    e. Conduct a test of hypothesis to determine if there is a significant relationship between the distance from the fire station and the amount of damage. Use the .01 significance level and a two-tailed test.

61. Listed below are the movies with the largest world box office sales and their world box office budget (total amount available to spend making the picture).

Rank	Movie	Year	World Box Office ($ million)	Adjusted Budget ($ million)
1	Titanic	1997	$1,835.0	$789.3
2	LOTR: The Return of the King	2003	1,129.2	377
3	Pirates of the Caribbean: Dead Man's Chest	2006	1,060.6	321.4
4	Harry Potter and the Sorcerer's Stone	2001	968.7	338.3
5	Pirates of the Caribbean: At World's End	2007	958.4	308.9
6	Harry Potter and the Order of the Phoenix	2007	937.0	306.3
7	Star Wars: Episode I—The Phantom Menace	1999	925.5	511.7
8	The Lord of the Rings: The Two Towers	2002	920.5	354
9	Jurassic Park	1993	920	513.8
10	Shrek 2	2004	912	436.5
11	Harry Potter and the Goblet of Fire	2005	892.2	300.8
12	Spider-Man 3	2007	885.4	354
13	Harry Potter and the Chamber of Secrets	2002	866.4	272.4
14	The Lord of the Rings: The Fellowship of the Ring	2001	860.7	334.3
15	Finding Nemo	2003	853.2	339.7
16	Star Wars: Episode III—Revenge of the Sith	2005	848.5	278
17	Independence Day	1996	813.1	417.5
18	Spider-Man	2002	806.7	419.7
19	Star Wars	1977	797.9	1,084.3
20	Harry Potter and the Prisoner of Azkaban	2004	789.8	249.4
21	Spider-Man 2	2004	784.0	373.4
22	The Lion King	1994	771.9	446.2
23	E.T.	1982	757	860.6
24	The Matrix: Reloaded	2003	735.7	281.5
25	Forrest Gump	1994	680	470.2
26	The Sixth Sense	1999	661.5	348.4
27	Pirates of the Caribbean	2003	653.2	305.4
28	Star Wars: Episode II—Attack of the Clones	2002	648.3	323
29	The Incredibles	2004	631.2	261.4
30	The Lost World	1997	614.4	301
31	The Passion of the Christ	2004	611.8	370.3
32	Men In Black	1997	587.2	328.6
33	Return of the Jedi	1983	573	563.1
34	Mission: Impossible 2	2000	545.4	241
35	The Empire Strikes Back	1980	533.9	586.8
36	Home Alone	1990	533.8	401.6
37	Monsters, Inc.	2001	524.2	272.6
38	Ghost	1990	517.6	306.6
39	Meet the Fockers	2004	511.9	279.2
40	Aladdin	1992	502.4	311.7
41	Twister	1996	495	329.7
42	Toy Story 2	1999	485.7	291.8
43	Saving Private Ryan	1998	479.3	278.1
44	Jaws	1975	471	782.7
45	Shrek	2001	469.7	285.1
46	Bruce Almighty	2003	459	242.6
47	Cast Away	2000	424.3	261.4
48	Mrs. Doubtfire	1993	423.2	315.6
49	Batman	1989	413	375.2
50	Signs	2002	408	237
51	Raiders of the Lost Ark	1981	384	519.7
52	My Big Fat Greek Wedding	2002	356.5	251
53	Dr. Seuss' How the Grinch Stole Christmas	2000	340	290.9
54	Rush Hour 2	2001	329.1	240.9
55	Beverly Hills Cop	1984	316.4	416.4
56	Ghostbusters	1984	291.6	391.7

Find the correlation between the world box office budget and world box office sales. Comment on the association between the two variables. Does it appear that the movies with large budgets result in large box office revenues?

Data Set Exercises

62. Refer to the Real Estate data, which report information on homes sold in Denver, Colorado, last year.

   a. Let selling price be the dependent variable and size of the home the independent variable. Determine the regression equation. Estimate the selling price for a home with an area of 2,200 square feet. Determine the 95 percent confidence interval and the 95 percent prediction interval for the selling price of a home with 2,200 square feet.

   b. Let selling price be the dependent variable and distance from the center of the city the independent variable. Determine the regression equation. Estimate the selling price of a home 20 miles from the center of the city. Determine the 95 percent confidence interval and the 95 percent prediction interval for homes 20 miles from the center of the city.

   c. Can you conclude that the independent variables "distance from the center of the city" and "selling price" are negatively correlated and that the area of the home and the selling price are positively correlated? Use the .05 significance level. Report the *p*-value of the test.

63. Refer to the Baseball 2007 data, which report information on the 2007 Major League Baseball season.

   a. Let the games won be the dependent variable and total team salary, in millions of dollars, be the independent variable. Can you conclude that there is a positive association between the two variables? Determine the regression equation. Interpret the slope, that is, the value of *b*. How many additional wins will an additional $5 million in salary bring?

   b. Determine the correlation between games won and ERA and between games won and team batting average. Which has the stronger correlation? Can we conclude that there is a positive correlation between wins and team batting and a negative correlation between wins and ERA? Use the .05 significance level.

   c. Assume the number of games won is the dependent variable and attendance the independent variable. Can we conclude that the correlation between these two variables is greater than 0? Use the .05 significance level.

64. Refer to the Wage data, which report information on annual wages for a sample of 100 workers. Also included are variables relating to industry, years of education, and gender for each worker.

   a. Determine the correlation between the annual wage and the years of education. At the .05 significance level can we conclude there is a positive correlation between the two variables?

   b. Determine the correlation between the annual wage and the years of work experience. At the .05 significance level can we conclude there is a positive correlation between the two variables?

65. Refer to the CIA data, which report demographic and economic information on 46 countries.

   a. You wish to use the labor force variable as the independent variable to predict the unemployment rate. Interpret the slope value. Use the appropriate linear regression equation to predict unemployment in the United Arab Emirates.

   b. Find the correlation coefficient between the levels of exports and imports. Use the .05 significance level to test whether there is a positive correlation between these two variables.

   c. Does there appear to be a relationship between the percentage of the population over 65 and the literacy percentage? Support your answer with statistical evidence. Conduct an appropriate test of hypothesis and interpret the result.

Software Commands

1. The MINITAB commands for the output showing the coefficient of correlation on page 466 are:
   a. Enter the sales representative's name in *C1,* the number of calls in *C2,* and the sales in *C3.*
   b. Select **Stat, Basic Statistics,** and **Correlation.**
   c. Select *Calls* and *Units Sold* as the variables, click on **Display p-values,** and then click **OK.**

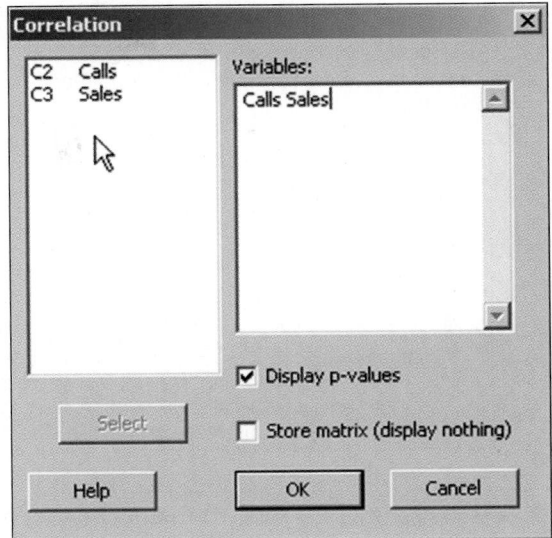

2. The computer commands for the Excel output on page 477 are:
   a. Enter the variable names in row 1 of columns A, B, and C. Enter the data in rows 2 through 11 in the same columns.
   b. Select the **Data** tab on the top of the menu. Then, on the far right, select **Data Analysis.** Select **Regression,** then click **OK.**
   c. For our spreadsheet we have *Calls* in column B and *Sales* in column C. The **Input Y-Range** is *C1:C11* and the **Input X-Range** is *B1:B11.* Click on **Labels,** select *E1* as the **Output Range,** and click **OK.**

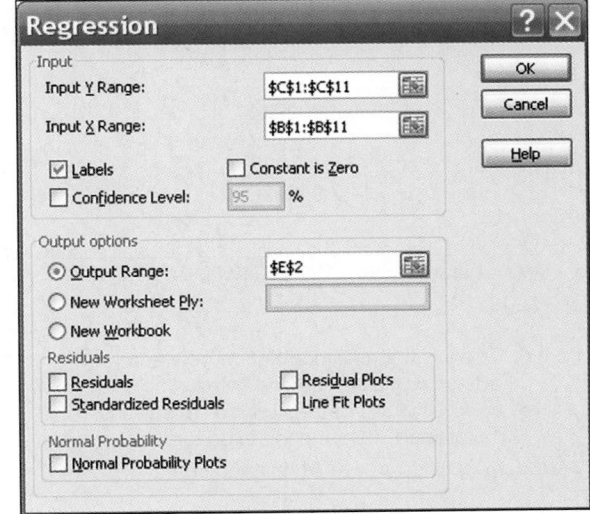

3. The MINITAB commands to the confidence intervals and prediction intervals on page 482 are:
   a. Select **Stat, Regression,** and **Fitted line plot.**
   b. In the next dialog box the **Response (Y)** is Sales and **Predictor (X)** is Calls. Select **Linear** for the type of regression model and then click on **Options.**
   c. In the **Options** dialog box click on **Display confidence and prediction bands,** use the **95.0 for confidence level,** type an appropriate heading in the **Title** box, then click **OK** and then **OK** again.

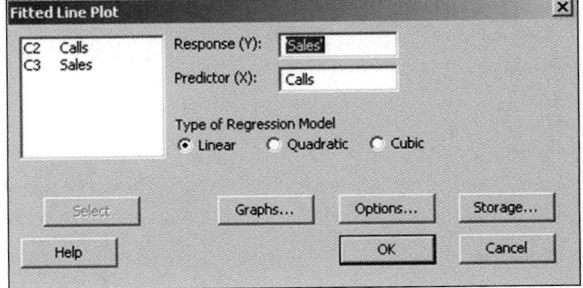

Chapter 13   Answers to Self-Review

13–1   **a.** Advertising expense is the independent variable, and sales revenue is the dependent variable.

     b.

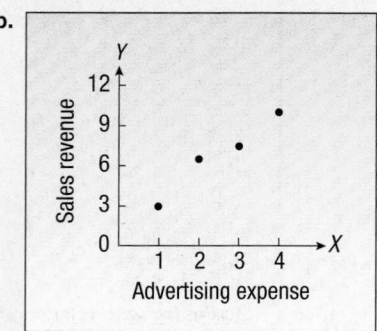

     c.

X	Y	$(X - \bar{X})$	$(X - \bar{X})^2$	$(Y - \bar{Y})$	$(Y - \bar{Y})^2$	$(X - \bar{X})(Y - \bar{Y})$
2	7	−0.5	.25	0	0	0
1	3	−1.5	2.25	−4	16	6
3	8	0.5	.25	1	1	0.5
4	10	1.5	2.25	3	9	4.5
10	28		5.00		26	11

$$\bar{X} = \frac{10}{4} = 2.5 \qquad \bar{Y} = \frac{28}{4} = 7$$

$$s_x = \sqrt{\frac{5}{3}} = 1.2909944$$

$$s_y = \sqrt{\frac{26}{3}} = 2.9439203$$

$$r = \frac{\Sigma(X - \bar{X})(Y - \bar{Y})}{(n - 1)s_x s_y} = \frac{11}{(4 - 1)(1.2909944)(2.9439203)}$$

$$= 0.9648$$

     d. There is a strong correlation between the advertising expense and sales.

     e. $r^2 = .93$, 93% of the variation in sales is "explained" by variation in advertising.

13–2 $H_0: \rho \leq 0$, $H_1: \rho > 0$. H_0 is rejected if $t > 1.714$.

$$t = \frac{.43\sqrt{25 - 2}}{\sqrt{1 - (.43)^2}} = 2.284$$

H_0 is rejected. There is a positive correlation between the percent of the vote received and the amount spent on the campaign.

13–3   **a.** See the calculations in Self-Review 13–1, part (c).

$$b = \frac{rs_y}{s_x} = \frac{(0.9648)(2.9439)}{1.2910} = 2.2$$

$$a = \frac{28}{4} - 2.2\left(\frac{10}{4}\right) = 7 - 5.5 = 1.5$$

     b. The slope is 2.2. This indicates that an increase of $1 million in advertising will result in an increase of $2.2 million in sales. The intercept is 1.5. If there was no expenditure for advertising, sales would be $1.5 million.

     c. $\hat{Y} = 1.5 + 2.2(3) = 8.1$

13–4   0.9487, found by:

Y	$\hat{Y}$	$(Y - \hat{Y})$	$(Y - \hat{Y})^2$
7	5.9	1.1	1.21
3	3.7	−0.7	.49
8	8.1	−0.1	.01
10	10.3	−0.3	.09
			1.80

$$s_{y \cdot x} = \sqrt{\frac{\Sigma(Y - \hat{Y})^2}{n - 2}}$$

$$= \sqrt{\frac{1.80}{4 - 2}} = .9487$$

13–5   6.58 and 9.62, since $\hat{Y}$ for an X of 3 is 8.1, found by $\hat{Y} = 1.5 + 2.2(3) = 8.1$, then $\bar{X} = 2.5$ and $\Sigma(X - \bar{X})^2 = 5$.

t from Appendix B.2 for $4 - 2 = 2$ degrees of freedom at the .10 level is 2.920.

$$\hat{Y} \pm t(s_{y \cdot x})\sqrt{\frac{1}{n} + \frac{(X - \bar{X})^2}{\Sigma(X - \bar{X})^2}}$$

$$= 8.1 \pm 2.920(0.9487)\sqrt{\frac{1}{4} + \frac{(3 - 2.5)^2}{5}}$$

$$= 8.1 \pm 2.920(0.9487)(0.5477)$$

$$= 6.58 \text{ and } 9.62 \text{ (in \$ millions)}$$

Multiple Regression and Correlation Analysis

A mortgage department of a large bank is studying its recent loans. A random sample of 25 recent loans is obtained and searched for factors such as the value of the home, education level of borrower, age, monthly mortgage payment and gender relate to the family income. Are these variables effective predictors of the income of the household? (See Exercise 26 and Goal 1.)

GOALS

When you have completed this chapter you will be able to:

1 Describe the relationship between several independent variables and a dependent variable using *multiple regression analysis*.

2 Set up, interpret, and apply an ANOVA table.

3 Compute and interpret the *multiple standard error of estimate*, the *coefficient of multiple determination*, and the *adjusted coefficient of multiple determination*.

4 Conduct a test of hypothesis to determine whether a set of regression coefficients differ from zero.

5 Conduct a test of hypothesis on each of the regression coefficients.

6 Use residual analysis to evaluate the assumptions of multiple regression analysis.

7 Evaluate the effects of correlated independent variables.

8 Use and understand qualitative independent variables.

9 Understand and interpret the *stepwise regression method*.

10 Understand and interpret possible interaction among independent variables.

Introduction

In Chapter 13 we described the relationship between a pair of interval- or ratio-scaled variables. We began the chapter by studying the coefficient of correlation, which measures the strength of the relationship. A coefficient near plus or minus 1.00 ($-.88$ or $.78$, for example) indicates a very strong linear relationship, whereas a value near 0 ($-.12$ or $.18$, for example) means that the relationship is weak. Next we developed a procedure to determine a linear equation to express the relationship between the two variables. We referred to this as a *regression line.* This line describes the relationship between the variables. It also describes the overall pattern of a dependent variable (Y) to a single independent or explanatory variable (X).

In multiple linear correlation and regression we use additional independent variables (denoted $X_1, X_2, \ldots,$ and so on) that help us better explain or predict the dependent variable (Y). Almost all of the ideas we saw in simple linear correlation and regression extend to this more general situation. However, the additional independent variables do lead to some new considerations. Multiple regression analysis can be used either as a descriptive or as an inferential technique.

Multiple Regression Analysis

The general descriptive form of a multiple linear equation is shown in formula (14–1). We use k to represent the number of independent variables. So k can be any positive integer.

GENERAL MULTIPLE REGRESSION EQUATION	$\hat{Y} = a + b_1X_1 + b_2X_2 + b_3X_3 + \cdots + b_kX_k$	[14–1]

where

a is the intercept, the value of Y when all the X's are zero.

b_j is the amount by which Y changes when that particular X_j increases by one unit, with the values of all other independent variables held constant. The subscript j is simply a label that helps to identify each independent variable; it is not used in any calculations. Usually the subscript is an integer value between 1 and k, which is the number of independent variables. However, the subscript can also be a short or abbreviated label. For example, age could be used as a subscript.

In Chapter 13, the regression analysis described and tested the relationship between a dependent variable, $\hat{Y}$, and a single independent variable, X. The relationship between $\hat{Y}$ and X was graphically portrayed by a line. When there are two independent variables, the regression equation is

$$\hat{Y} = a + b_1X_1 + b_2X_2$$

Because there are two independent variables, this relationship is graphically portrayed as a plane and is shown in Chart 14–1. The chart shows the residuals as the difference between the actual Y and the fitted $\hat{Y}$ on the plane. If a multiple regression analysis includes more than two independent variables, we cannot use a graph to illustrate the analysis since graphs are limited to three dimensions.

To illustrate the interpretation of the intercept and the two regression coefficients, suppose a vehicle's mileage per gallon of gasoline is directly related to the octane rating of the gasoline being used (X_1) and inversely related to the weight of the automobile (X_2). Assume that the regression equation, calculated using statistical software, is:

$$\hat{Y} = 6.3 + 0.2X_1 - 0.001X_2$$

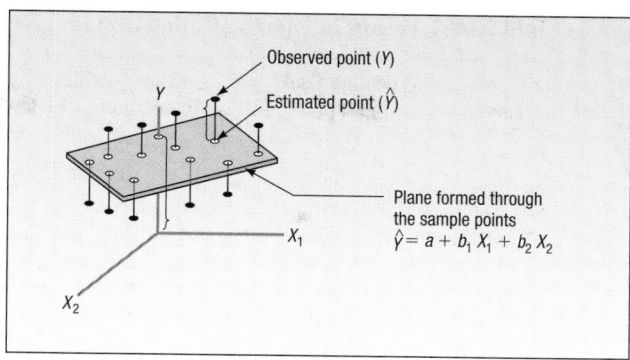

CHART 14–1 Regression Plane with 10 Sample Points

The intercept value of 6.3 indicates the regression equation intersects the Y-axis at 6.3 when both X_1 and X_2 are zero. Of course, this does not make any physical sense to own an automobile that has no (zero) weight and to use gasoline with no octane. It is important to keep in mind that a regression equation is not generally used outside the range of the sample values.

The b_1 of 0.2 indicates that for each increase of 1 in the octane rating of the gasoline, the automobile would travel 2/10 of a mile more per gallon, *regardless of the weight of the vehicle*. The b_2 value of -0.001 reveals that for each increase of one pound in the vehicle's weight, the number of miles traveled per gallon decreases by 0.001, *regardless of the octane of the gasoline being used*.

As an example, an automobile with 92-octane gasoline in the tank and weighing 2,000 pounds would travel an average 22.7 miles per gallon, found by:

$$\hat{Y} = a + b_1X_1 + b_2X_2 = 6.3 + 0.2(92) - 0.001(2,000) = 22.7$$

The values for the coefficients in the multiple linear equation are found by using the method of least squares. Recall from the previous chapter that the least squares method makes the sum of the squared differences between the fitted and actual values of Y as small as possible, that is, the term $\Sigma(Y - \hat{Y})^2$ is minimized. The calculations are very tedious, so they are usually performed by a statistical software package, such as Excel or MINITAB.

In the following example, we show a multiple regression analysis using three independent variables using Excel and MINITAB. Both packages report a standard set of statistics and reports. However, MINITAB also provides advanced regression analysis techniques that we will use later in the chapter.

Example

Salsberry Realty sells homes along the east coast of the United States. One of the questions most frequently asked by prospective buyers is: If we purchase this home, how much can we expect to pay to heat it during the winter? The research department at Salsberry has been asked to develop some guidelines regarding heating costs for single-family homes. Three variables are thought to relate to the heating costs: (1) the mean daily outside temperature, (2) the number of inches of insulation in the attic, and (3) the age in years of the furnace. To investigate, Salsberry's research department selected a random sample of 20 recently sold homes. It determined the cost to heat each home last January, as well as the January outside temperature in the region, the number of inches of insulation in the attic, and the age of the furnace. The sample information is reported in Table 14–1.

TABLE 14–1 Factors in January Heating Cost for a Sample of 20 Homes

Home	Heating Cost ($)	Mean Outside Temperature (°F)	Attic Insulation (inches)	Age of Furnace (years)
1	$250	35	3	6
2	360	29	4	10
3	165	36	7	3
4	43	60	6	9
5	92	65	5	6
6	200	30	5	5
7	355	10	6	7
8	290	7	10	10
9	230	21	9	11
10	120	55	2	5
11	73	54	12	4
12	205	48	5	1
13	400	20	5	15
14	320	39	4	7
15	72	60	8	6
16	272	20	5	8
17	94	58	7	3
18	190	40	8	11
19	235	27	9	8
20	139	30	7	5

Statistics in Action

Many studies indicate a woman will earn about 70 percent of what a man would for the same work. Researchers at the University of Michigan Institute for Social Research found that about one-third of the difference can be explained by such social factors as differences in education, seniority, and work interruptions. The remaining two-thirds is not explained by these social factors.

The data in Table 14–1 is available in both Excel and MINITAB formats on the student CD. The basic instructions for using Excel and MINITAB for this data are in the Software Commands section at the end of this chapter.

Determine the multiple regression equation. Which variables are the independent variables? Which variable is the dependent variable? Discuss the regression coefficients. What does it indicate if some coefficients are positive and some coefficients are negative? What is the intercept value? What is the estimated heating cost for a home if the mean outside temperature is 30 degrees, there are 5 inches of insulation in the attic, and the furnace is 10 years old?

Solution

We begin the analysis by defining the dependent and independent variables. The dependent variable is the January heating cost. It is represented by Y. There are three independent variables:

- The mean outside temperature in January, represented by X_1.
- The number of inches of insulation in the attic, represented by X_2.
- The age in years of the furnace, represented by X_3.

Given these definitions, the general form of the multiple regression equation follows. The value $\hat{Y}$ is used to estimate the value of Y.

$$\hat{Y} = a + b_1X_1 + b_2X_2 + b_3X_3.$$

Now that we have defined the regression equation, we are ready to use either Excel or MINITAB to compute all the statistics needed for the analysis. The outputs from the two software systems are shown below.

To use the regression equation to predict the January heating cost, we need to know the values of the regression coefficients, b_j. These are highlighted in the software reports. Note that the software used the variable names or labels associated with each independent variable. The regression equation intercept, a, is labeled as "constant" in the MINITAB output and "intercept" in the Excel output.

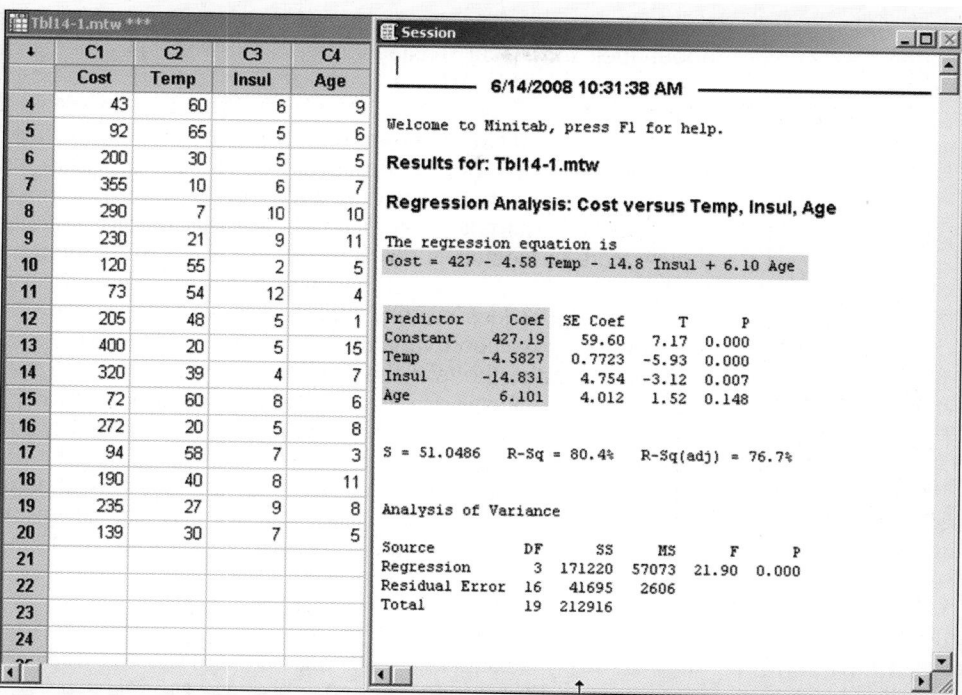

Excel

	A	B	C	D	F	G	H	I	J	K	L
1	Cost	Temp	Insul	Age		SUMMARY OUTPUT					
2	250	35	3	6							
3	360	29	4	10		*Regression Statistics*					
4	165	36	7	3		Multiple R	0.897				
5	43	60	6	9		R Square	0.804				
6	92	65	5	6		Adjusted R Square	0.767				
7	200	30	5	5		Standard Error	51.049				
8	355	10	6	7		Observations	20				
9	290	7	10	10							
10	230	21	9	11		ANOVA					
11	120	55	2	5							
12	73	54	12	4			df	SS	MS	F	Significance F
13	205	48	5	1		Regression	3	171220.473	57073.491	21.901	0.000
14	400	20	5	15		Residual	16	41695.277	2605.955		
15	320	39	4	7		Total	19	212915.750			
16	72	60	8	6							
17	272	20	5	8			Coefficients	Standard Error	t Stat	P-value	
18	94	58	7	3		Intercept	427.194	59.601	7.168	0.000	
19	190	40	8	11		Temp	-4.583	0.772	-5.934	0.000	
20	235	27	9	8		Insul	-14.831	4.754	-3.119	0.007	
21	139	30	7	5		Age	6.101	4.012	1.521	0.148	

In this case the estimated regression equation is:

$$\hat{Y} = 427.194 - 4.583X_1 - 14.831X_2 + 6.101X_3$$

We can now estimate or predict the January heating cost for a home if we know the mean outside temperature, the inches of insulation, and the age of the furnace. For an example home, the mean outside temperature for the month is 30 degrees (X_1), there are 5 inches of insulation in the attic (X_2), and the furnace is 10 years old (X_3). By substituting the values for the independent variables:

$$\hat{Y} = 427.194 - 4.583(30) - 14.831(5) + 6.101(10) = 276.56$$

The estimated January heating cost is $276.56.

The regression coefficients, and their algebraic signs, also provide information about their individual relationships with the January heating cost. The regression coefficient for mean outside temperature is −4.583. The coefficient is negative and shows an inverse relationship between heating cost and temperature. This is not surprising. As the outside temperature increases, the cost to heat the home decreases. The numeric value of the regression coefficient provides more information. If we increase temperature by 1 degree and hold the other two independent variables constant, we can estimate a decrease of $4.583 in monthly heating cost. So if the mean temperature in Boston is 25 degrees and it is 35 degrees in Philadelphia, all other things being the same (insulation and age of furnace), we expect the heating cost would be $45.83 less in Philadelphia.

The attic insulation variable also shows an inverse relationship: the more insulation in the attic, the less the cost to heat the home. So the negative sign for this coefficient is logical. For each additional inch of insulation, we expect the cost to heat the home to decline $14.83 per month, holding the outside temperature and the age of the furnace constant.

The age of the furnace variable shows a direct relationship. With an older furnace, the cost to heat the home increases. Specifically, for each additional year older the furnace is, we expect the cost to increase $6.10 per month.

Self-Review 14–1

There are many restaurants in northeastern South Carolina. They serve beach vacationers in the summer, golfers in the fall and spring, and snowbirds in the winter. Bill and Joyce Tuneall manage several restaurants in the North Jersey area and are considering moving to Myrtle Beach, SC, to open a new restaurant. Before making a final decision they wish to investigate existing restaurants and what variables seem to be related to profitability. They gather sample information where profit (reported in $000) is the dependent variable and the independent variables are:

X_1 the number of parking spaces near the restaurant.
X_2 the number of hours the restaurant is open per week.
X_3 the distance from the Hard Rock Park, a landmark in Myrtle Beach.
X_4 the number of servers employed.
X_5 the number of years the current owner has owned the restaurant.

The following is part of the output obtained using statistical software.

Predictor	Coef	SE Coef	T
Constant	2.50	1.50	1.667
X_1	3.00	1.500	2.000
X_2	4.00	3.000	1.333
X_3	−3.00	0.20	−15.00
X_4	0.20	.05	4.00
X_5	1.00	1.50	0.667

(a) What is the amount of profit for a restaurant with 40 parking spaces and that is open 72 hours per week, is 10 miles from the Pavilion, has 20 servers, and has been open 5 years?
(b) Interpret the values of b_2 and b_3 in the multiple regression equation.

Exercises

connect

1. The director of marketing at Reeves Wholesale Products is studying monthly sales. Three independent variables were selected as estimators of sales: regional population, per capita income, and regional unemployment rate. The regression equation was computed to be (in dollars):

$$\hat{Y} = 64{,}100 + 0.394X_1 + 9.6X_2 - 11{,}600X_3$$

    a. What is the full name of the equation?

    b. Interpret the number 64,100.

    c. What are the estimated monthly sales for a particular region with a population of 796,000, per capita income of $6,940, and an unemployment rate of 6.0 percent?

2. Thompson Photo Works purchased several new, highly sophisticated processing machines. The production department needed some guidance with respect to qualifications needed by an operator. Is age a factor? Is the length of service as an operator (in years) important? In order to explore further the factors needed to estimate performance on the new processing machines, four variables were listed:

$$X_1 = \text{Length of time an employee was in the industry.}$$
$$X_2 = \text{Mechanical aptitude test score.}$$
$$X_3 = \text{Prior on-the-job rating.}$$
$$X_4 = \text{Age}$$

Performance on the new machine is designated Y.

    Thirty employees were selected at random. Data were collected for each, and their performances on the new machines were recorded. A few results are:

Name	Performance on New Machine, Y	Length of Time in Industry, X_1	Mechanical Aptitude Score, X_2	Prior On-the-Job Performance, X_3	Age, X_4
Mike Miraglia	112	12	312	121	52
Sue Trythall	113	2	380	123	27

The equation is:

$$\hat{Y} = 11.6 + 0.4X_1 + 0.286X_2 + 0.112X_3 + 0.002X_4$$

    a. What is this equation called?

    b. How many dependent variables are there? Independent variables?

    c. What is the number 0.286 called?

    d. As age increases by one year, how much does estimated performance on the new machine increase?

    e. Carl Knox applied for a job at Photo Works. He has been in the business for six years, and scored 280 on the mechanical aptitude test. Carl's prior on-the-job performance rating is 97, and he is 35 years old. Estimate Carl's performance on the new machine.

3. A sample of General Mills employees was studied to determine their degree of satisfaction with their present life. A special index, called the index of satisfaction, was used to measure satisfaction. Six factors were studied, namely, age at the time of first marriage (X_1), annual income (X_2), number of children living (X_3), value of all assets (X_4), status of health in the form of an index (X_5), and the average number of social activities per week—such as bowling and dancing (X_6). Suppose the multiple regression equation is:

$$\hat{Y} = 16.24 + 0.017X_1 + 0.0028X_2 + 42X_3 + 0.0012X_4 + 0.19X_5 + 26.8X_6$$

    a. What is the estimated index of satisfaction for a person who first married at 18, has an annual income of $26,500, has three children living, has assets of $156,000, has an index of health status of 141, and has 2.5 social activities a week on the average?

    b. Which would add more to satisfaction, an additional income of $10,000 a year or two more social activities a week?

4. Cellulon, a manufacturer of home insulation, wants to develop guidelines for builders and consumers on how the thickness of the insulation in the attic of a home and the outdoor temperature affect natural gas consumption. In the laboratory it varied the insulation thickness and temperature. A few of the findings are:

Monthly Natural Gas Consumption (cubic feet), Y	Thickness of Insulation (inches), X_1	Outdoor Temperature (°F), X_2
30.3	6	40
26.9	12	40
22.1	8	49

On the basis of the sample results, the regression equation is:

$$\hat{Y} = 62.65 - 1.86X_1 - 0.52X_2$$

a. How much natural gas can homeowners expect to use per month if they install 6 inches of insulation and the outdoor temperature is 40 degrees F?

b. What effect would installing 7 inches of insulation instead of 6 have on the monthly natural gas consumption (assuming the outdoor temperature remains at 40 degrees F)?

c. Why are the regression coefficients b_1 and b_2 negative? Is this logical?

How Well Does the Equation Fit the Data?

Once you have the multiple regression equation, it is natural to ask "how well does the equation fit the data?" In linear regression, discussed in the previous chapter, you used summary statistics such as the standard error of estimate and the coefficient of determination to describe how effectively a single independent variable explained the variation of the dependent variable. The same procedures, broadened to additional independent variables, are used in multiple regression.

Multiple Standard Error of Estimate

We begin with the **multiple standard error of estimate.** Recall that the standard error of estimate is comparable to the standard deviation. The standard deviation uses squared deviations from the mean, $(Y - \overline{Y})^2$, whereas the standard error of estimate utilizes squared deviations from the regression line, $(Y - \hat{Y})^2$. To explain the details of the standard error of estimate, refer to the first sampled home in Table 14–1 in the previous example on page 508. The actual heating cost for the first observation, Y, is $250, the outside temperature, X_1, is 35 degrees, the depth of insulation, X_2, is 3 inches, and the age of the furnace, X_3, is 6 years. Using the regression equation developed in the previous section, the estimated heating cost for this home is:

$$\hat{Y} = 427.194 - 4.583X_1 - 14.831X_2 + 6.101X_3$$

$$= 427.194 - 4.583(35) - 14.831(3) + 6.101(6)$$

$$= 258.90$$

So we would estimate that a home with a mean January outside temperature of 35 degrees, 3 inches of insulation, and a 6-year-old furnace would cost $258.90 to heat. The actual heating cost was $250, so the residual—which is the difference between the actual value and the estimated value—is $Y - \hat{Y} = 250 - 258.90 = -8.90$. This difference of $8.90 is the random or unexplained error for the first home sampled. Our next step is to square this difference, that is find $(Y - \hat{Y})^2 = (250 - 258.90)^2 = (-8.90)^2 = 79.21$. We repeat these operations for the other 19 observations and total these squared values. This value is the numerator of the multiple standard error of estimate. The denominator is the degrees of freedom, that is $n - (k + 1)$. The formula for the standard error is:

MULTIPLE STANDARD ERROR OF ESTIMATE	$s_{Y.123...k} = \sqrt{\dfrac{\Sigma(Y - \hat{Y})^2}{n - (k + 1)}}$	[14–2]

where

Y is the actual observation.

$\hat{Y}$ is the estimated value computed from the regression equation.

n is the number of observations in the sample.

k is the number of independent variables.

In this example $n = 20$ and $k = 3$ (three independent variables) and we use the Excel software system to find the term $\Sigma(Y - \hat{Y})^2$. Note: There are small discrepancies due to rounding.

Excel

reg with predition and residuals [Compatibility Mode]

	A	B	C	D	F	G	H	I	J
1	Cost	Temp	Insul	Age	$\hat{Y}$	$Y - \hat{Y}$	$(Y - \hat{Y})^2$		
2	250	35	3	6	258.91	-8.91	79.46		
3	360	29	4	10	295.98	64.02	4098.12		
4	165	36	7	3	176.71	-11.71	137.01		
5	43	60	6	9	118.16	-75.16	5648.75		
6	92	65	5	6	91.77	0.23	0.05		
7	200	30	5	5	246.06	-46.06	2121.96		
8	355	10	6	7	335.09	19.91	396.44		
9	290	7	10	10	307.82	-17.82	317.44		
10	230	21	9	11	264.59	-34.59	1196.57		
11	120	55	2	5	175.99	-55.99	3134.97		
12	73	54	12	4	26.16	46.84	2193.63		
13	205	48	5	1	139.17	65.83	4333.23		
14	400	20	5	15	352.90	47.10	2218.25		
15	320	39	4	7	231.85	88.15	7769.76		
16	72	60	8	6	70.19	1.81	3.26		
17	272	20	5	8	310.19	-38.19	1458.82		
18	94	58	7	3	75.89	18.11	328.10		
19	190	40	8	11	192.35	-2.35	5.53		
20	235	27	9	8	218.79	16.21	262.69		
21	139	30	7	5	216.40	-77.40	5991.23		
22							41695.28		

$\Sigma(Y - \hat{Y})^2$

Since we have 3 independent variables, we identify the multiple standard error as $s_{Y.123}$. The subscripts indicate that three independent variables are being used to estimate Y.

$$s_{Y.123} = \sqrt{\frac{\Sigma(Y - \hat{Y})^2}{n - (k + 1)}} = \sqrt{\frac{41,695.28}{20 - (3 + 1)}} = 51.05$$

How do we interpret the standard error of estimate of 51.05? It is the typical "error" when we use this equation to predict the cost. First, the units are the same as the dependent variable, so the standard error is in dollars, $51.05. Second, we expect the residuals to be approximately normally distributed, so about 68 percent of the residuals will be within ±$51.05 and about 95 percent within ±2(51.05) = ±$102.10. Refer to column F of the Excel output, headed $Y - \hat{Y}$. Of the 20 values in this column, 14 (or 70 percent) are less than ±$51.05 and all are within ±$102.10, which is very close to the guidelines of 68 percent and 95 percent.

The ANOVA Table

As we said before, the multiple regression computations are long. Luckily, many statistical software systems are available to perform the detailed calculations. Most of them report the results in a standard format. The outputs from Excel and MINITAB on page 509 are typical. In particular, they include an analysis of variance (ANOVA) table. The output from MINITAB is repeated here.

↓	C1	C2	C3	C4
	Cost	Temp	Insul	Age
4	43	60	6	9
5	92	65	5	6
6	200	30	5	5
7	355	10	6	7
8	290	7	10	10
9	230	21	9	11
10	120	55	2	5
11	73	54	12	4
12	205	48	5	1
13	400	20	5	15
14	320	39	4	7
15	72	60	8	6
16	272	20	5	8
17	94	58	7	3
18	190	40	8	11
19	235	27	9	8
20	139	30	7	5
21				
22				
23				
24				

Regression Analysis: Cost versus Temp, Insul, Age

```
The regression equation is
Cost = 427 - 4.58 Temp - 14.8 Insul + 6.10 Age


Predictor    Coef  SE Coef      T      P
Constant   427.19    59.60   7.17  0.000
Temp      -4.5827   0.7723  -5.93  0.000
Insul     -14.831    4.754  -3.12  0.007
Age         6.101    4.012   1.52  0.148


S = 51.0486    R-Sq = 80.4%    R-Sq(adj) = 76.7%


Analysis of Variance

Source           DF      SS     MS      F      P
Regression        3  171220  57073  21.90  0.000
Residual Error   16   41695   2606
Total            19  212916


Source  DF  Seq SS
Temp     1  140215
Insul    1   24980
Age      1    6026
```

Focus on the analysis of variance table. It is similar to the ANOVA table used in Chapter 12. In that chapter the variation was divided into two components: variation due to the *treatments* and variation due to *random error.* Here total variation is also separated into two components:

- Variation in the dependent variable explained by the *regression* model (the independent variables).
- The *residual or error* variation. This is the random error due to sampling.

Incidentally, the term *residual error* will sometimes be called *random error* or just *error.*

There are three categories identified in the first or Source column in the ANOVA table; namely, the regression or explained variation, the residual or unexplained variation, and the total variation.

The second column is labeled *df* in the ANOVA table. It is the degrees of freedom. The degrees of freedom in the "Regression" row is the number of independent variables. We let k represent the number of independent variables, so $k = 3$. The degrees of freedom in the "Error" is $n - (k + 1) = 20 - (3 + 1) = 16$. In this example, there are 20 observations so $n = 20$. The total degrees of freedom is $n - 1 = 20 - 1 = 19$.

The heading SS in the third column of the ANOVA table is the sum of squares or the variation.

$$\text{Total variation} = \text{SS total} = \Sigma(Y - \overline{Y})^2 = 212{,}916$$

$$\text{Residual error or error variance} = \text{SSE} = \Sigma(Y - \hat{Y})^2 = 41{,}695$$

$$\text{Regression variation} = \text{SSR} = \Sigma(\hat{Y} - \bar{Y})^2 = \text{SS total} - \text{SSE}$$

$$= 212{,}916 - 41{,}695 = 171{,}220$$

(There is a small "round off" difference of one unit, which will have no effect on later calculations.)

The fourth column heading, MS or mean square, is obtained by dividing the SS quantity by the matching *df*. Thus MSR, the mean square regression, is equal to SSR/k. Similarly, MSE, the mean square error, is SSE/$(n - (k + 1))$.

The following ANOVA table summarizes the process.

Source	*df*	SS	MS	F
Regression	k	SSR	MSR = SSR/k	MSR/MSE
Residual or error	$n - (k + 1)$	SSE	MSE = SSE/$(n - (k + 1))$	
Total	$n - 1$	SS total		

Each value in the ANOVA table plays an important role in the evaluation and interpretation of a multiple regression equation. Notice, for example, that the standard error of estimate can very easily be computed from the ANOVA table.

$$s_{Y.123} = \sqrt{\text{MSE}} = \sqrt{2{,}606} = 51.05$$

Coefficient of Multiple Determination

Next, let's look at the coefficient of multiple determination. Recall from the previous chapter the coefficient of determination is defined as the percent of variation in the dependent variable explained, or accounted for, by the independent variable. In the multiple regression case we extend this definition as follows.

> **COEFFICIENT OF MULTIPLE DETERMINATION** The percent of variation in the dependent variable, Y, explained by the set of independent variables, X_1, X_2, X_3, . . . X_k.

The characteristics of the coefficient of multiple determination are:

1. **It is symbolized by a capital R squared.** In other words, it is written as R^2 because it behaves like the square of a correlation coefficient.
2. **It can range form 0 to 1.** A value near 0 indicates little association between the set of independent variables and the dependent variable. A value near 1 means a strong association.
3. **It cannot assume negative values.** Any number that is squared or raised to the second power cannot be negative.
4. **It is easy to interpret.** Because R^2 is a value between 0 and 1 it is easy to interpret, compare, and understand.

We can calculate the coefficient of determination from the information found in the ANOVA table. We look in the sum of squares column, which is labeled SS in the MINITAB output, and use the regression sum of squares, SSR, then divide by the total sum of squares, SS total.

COEFFICIENT OF MULTIPLE DETERMINATION	$R^2 = \dfrac{\text{SSR}}{\text{SS total}}$	[14–3]

The ANOVA portion of the MINITAB output in the heating cost example is repeated below.

```
Analysis of Variance
Source           DF        SS        MS         F        P
Regression        3    171220     57073     21.90    0.000
Residual Error   16     41695      2606
Total            19    212916
```

Use formula (14–3) to calculate the coefficient of multiple determination.

$$R^2 = \frac{\text{SSR}}{\text{SS total}} = \frac{171{,}220}{212{,}916} = .804$$

How do we interpret this value? We conclude that the independent variables (outside temperature, amount of insulation, and age of furnace) explain, or account for, 80.4 percent of the variation in heating cost. To put it another way, 19.6 percent of the variation is due to other sources, such as random error or variables not included in the analysis. Using the ANOVA table, 19.6 percent is the error sum of squares divided by the total sum of squares. Knowing that the SSR + SSE = SS total, the following relationship is true.

$$1 - R^2 = 1 - \frac{\text{SSR}}{\text{SS total}} = \frac{\text{SSE}}{\text{SS total}} = \frac{41{,}695}{212{,}916} = .196$$

Adjusted Coefficient of Determination

The number of independent variables in a multiple regression equation makes the coefficient of determination larger. Each new independent variable causes the predictions to be more accurate. That, in turn, makes SSE smaller and SSR larger. Hence, R^2 increases only because of the total number of independent variables and not because the added independent variable is a good predictor of the dependent variable. In fact, if the number of variables, k, and the sample size, n, are equal, the coefficient of determination is 1.0. In practice, this situation is rare and would also be ethically questionable. To balance the effect that the number of independent variables has on the coefficient of multiple determination, statistical software packages use an *adjusted* coefficient of multiple determination.

ADJUSTED COEFFICIENT OF DETERMINATION	$R^2_{adj} = 1 - \dfrac{\dfrac{\text{SSE}}{n - (k + 1)}}{\dfrac{\text{SS total}}{n - 1}}$	[14–4]

The error and total sum of squares are divided by their degrees of freedom. Notice especially the degrees of freedom for the error sum of squares includes k, the number of independent variables. For the cost of heating example, the adjusted coefficient of determination is:

$$R^2_{adj} = 1 - \frac{\dfrac{41{,}695}{20 - (3 + 1)}}{\dfrac{212{,}916}{20 - 1}} = 1 - \frac{2{,}606}{11{,}206.0} = 1 - .23 = .77$$

If we compare the R^2 (0.80) to the adjusted R^2 (0.77), the difference in this case is small.

Self-Review 14–2

Refer to Self-Review 14–1 on the subject of restaurants in Myrtle Beach. The ANOVA portion of the regression output is presented below.

```
Analysis of Variance
Source            DF    SS    MS
Regression         5   100    20
Residual Error    20    40     2
Total             25   140
```

(a) How large was the sample?
(b) How many independent variables are there?
(c) How many dependent variables are there?
(d) Compute the standard error of estimate. About 95 percent of the residuals will be between what two values?
(e) Determine the coefficient of multiple determination. Interpret this value.
(f) Find the coefficient of multiple determination, adjusted for the degrees of freedom.

Exercises

connect

5. Consider the ANOVA table that follows.

```
Analysis of Variance
Source            DF      SS         MS       F      P
Regression         2    77.907    38.954    4.14   0.021
Residual Error    62   583.693     9.414
Total             64   661.600
```

a. Determine the standard error of estimate. About 95 percent of the residuals will be between what two values?
b. Determine the coefficient of multiple determination. Interpret this value.
c. Determine the coefficient of multiple determination, adjusted for the degrees of freedom.

6. Consider the ANOVA table that follows.

```
Analysis of Variance
Source            DF      SS         MS       F
Regression         5   3710.00    742.00    12.89
Residual Error    46   2647.38     57.55
Total             51   6357.38
```

a. Determine the standard error of estimate. About 95 percent of the residuals will be between what two values?
b. Determine the coefficient of multiple determination. Interpret this value.
c. Determine the coefficient of multiple determination, adjusted for the degrees of freedom.

Inferences in Multiple Linear Regression

Thus far, multiple regression analysis has been viewed only as a way to describe the relationship between a dependent variable and several independent variables. However, the least squares method also has the ability to draw inferences or generalizations about the relationship for an entire population. Recall that when you create confidence intervals or perform hypothesis tests as a part of inferential statistics, you view the data as a random sample taken from some population.

In the multiple regression setting, we assume there is an unknown population regression equation that relates the dependent variable to the k independent variables. This is sometimes called a **model** of the relationship. In symbols we write:

$$\hat{Y} = \alpha + \beta_1 X_1 + \beta_2 X_2 + \cdots + \beta_k X_k$$

This equation is analogous to formula (14–1) except the coefficients are now reported as Greek letters. We use the Greek letters to denote *population parameters*. Then under a certain set of assumptions, which will be discussed shortly, the computed values of a and b_j are sample statistics. These sample statistics are point estimates of the corresponding population parameters α and β_j. For example, the sample regression coefficient b_2 is a point estimate of the population parameter β_2. The sampling distribution of these point estimates follows the normal probability distribution. These sampling distributions are each centered at their respective parameter values. To put it another way, the means of the sampling distributions are equal to the parameter values to be estimated. Thus, by using the properties of the sampling distributions of these statistics, inferences about the population parameters are possible.

Global Test: Testing the Multiple Regression Model

We can test the ability of the independent variables $X_1, X_2, \ldots, X_k$ to explain the behavior of the dependent variable Y. To put this in question form: Can the dependent variable be estimated without relying on the independent variables? The test used is referred to as the **global test.** Basically, it investigates whether it is possible all the independent variables have zero regression coefficients.

To relate this question to the heating cost example, we will test whether the independent variables (amount of insulation in the attic, mean daily outside temperature, and age of furnace) effectively estimate home heating costs. In testing a hypothesis, we first state the null hypothesis and the alternate hypothesis. In the heating cost example, there are three independent variables. Recall that b_1, b_2, and b_3 are sample regression coefficients. The corresponding coefficients in the population are given the symbols β_1, β_2, and β_3. We now test whether the regression coefficients in the population are all zero. The null hypothesis is:

$$H_0: \beta_1 = \beta_2 = \beta_3 = 0$$

The alternate hypothesis is:

$$H_1: \text{Not all the } \beta_i\text{'s are 0.}$$

If the null hypothesis is true, it implies the regression coefficients are all zero and, logically, are of no use in estimating the dependent variable (heating cost). Should that be the case, we would have to search for some other independent variables—or take a different approach—to predict home heating costs.

To test the null hypothesis that the multiple regression coefficients are all zero, we employ the F distribution introduced in Chapter 12. We will use the .05 level of significance. Recall these characteristics of the F distribution:

1. **There is a family of F distributions.** Each time the degrees of freedom in either the numerator or the denominator changes a new F distribution is created.
2. **The F distribution cannot be negative.** The smallest possible value is 0.
3. **It is a continuous distribution.** The distribution can assume an infinite number of values between 0 and positive infinity.
4. **It is positively skewed.** The long tail of the distribution is to the right-hand side. As the number of degrees of freedom increases in both the numerator and the denominator, the distribution approaches the normal probability distribution. That is, the distribution will move toward a symmetric distribution.
5. **It is asymptotic.** As the values of X increase, the F curve will approach the horizontal axis, but will never touch it.

The degrees of freedom for the numerator and the denominator may be found in the Excel ANOVA table that follows. The ANOVA output is highlighted in light green. The top number in the column marked "df" is 3, indicating there are 3 degrees of freedom in the numerator. This value corresponds to the number of independent variables. The middle number in the "df" column (16) indicated there are 16 degrees of freedom in the denominator. The number 16 is found by $(n - (k + 1)) = 20 - (3 + 1) = 16$.

Excel

	A	B	C	D	F	G	H	I	J	K	L
						SUMMARY OUTPUT					
1	Cost	Temp	Insul	Age							
2	250	35	3	6							
3	360	29	4	10		*Regression Statistics*					
4	165	36	7	3		Multiple R	0.897				
5	43	60	6	9		R Square	0.804				
6	92	65	5	6		Adjusted R Square	0.767				
7	200	30	5	5		Standard Error	51.049				
8	355	10	6	7		Observations	20				
9	290	7	10	10							
10	230	21	9	11		ANOVA					
11	120	55	2	5			*df*	*SS*	*MS*	*F*	*Significance F*
12	73	54	12	4		Regression	3	171220.473	57073.491	21.901	0.000
13	205	48	5	1		Residual	16	41695.277	2605.955		
14	400	20	5	15		Total	19	212915.750			
15	320	39	4	7							
16	72	60	8	6			*Coefficients*	*Standard Error*	*t Stat*	*P-value*	
17	272	20	5	8		Intercept	427.194	59.601	7.168	0.000	
18	94	58	7	3		Temp	-4.583	0.772	-5.934	0.000	
19	190	40	8	11		Insul	-14.831	4.754	-3.119	0.007	
20	235	27	9	8		Age	6.101	4.012	1.521	0.148	
21	139	30	7	5							

The critical value of F is found in Appendix B.4. Using the table for the .05 significance level, move horizontally to 3 degrees of freedom in the numerator, then down to 16 degrees of freedom in the denominator, and read the critical value. It is 3.24. The region where H_0 is not rejected and the region where H_0 is rejected are shown in the following diagram.

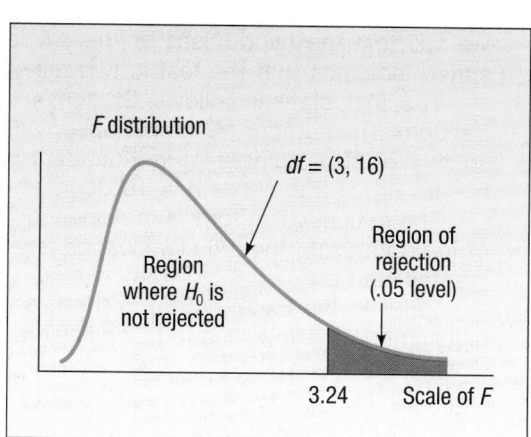

Continuing with the global test, the decision rule is: Do not reject the null hypothesis that all the regression coefficients are 0 if the computed value of F is less than or equal to 3.24. If the computed F is greater than 3.24, reject H_0 and accept the alternate hypothesis, H_1.

The value of F is found from the following equation.

GLOBAL TEST
$$F = \frac{SSR/k}{SSE/[n - (k + 1)]}$$
[14–5]

SSR is the sum of the squares regression, SSE the sum of squares error, n the number of observations, and k the number of independent variables. Inserting the heating cost example values in formula (14–5) gives:

$$F = \frac{SSR/k}{SSE/[n - (k + 1)]} = \frac{171{,}220/3}{41{,}695/[20 - (3 + 1)]} = 21.90$$

The computed value of F is 21.90, which is in the rejection region. The null hypothesis that all the multiple regression coefficients are zero is therefore rejected. This means that some of the independent variables (amount of insulation, etc.) do have the ability to explain the variation in the dependent variable (heating cost). We expected this decision. Logically, the outside temperature, the amount of insulation, and age of the furnace have a great bearing on heating costs. The global test assures us that they do.

Evaluating Individual Regression Coefficients

So far we have shown that at least one, but not necessarily all, of the regression coefficients are not equal to zero and thus useful for predictions. The next step is to test the independent variables *individually* to determine which regression coefficients may be 0 and which are not.

Why is it important to know if any of the β_i's equal 0? If a β could equal 0, it implies that this particular independent variable is of no value in explaining any variation in the dependent value. If there are coefficients for which H_0 cannot be rejected, we may want to eliminate them from the regression equation.

We will now conduct three separate tests of hypothesis—for temperature, for insulation, and for the age of the furnace.

For temperature:	For insulation:	For furnace age:
$H_0: \beta_1 = 0$	$H_0: \beta_2 = 0$	$H_0: \beta_3 = 0$
$H_1: \beta_1 \neq 0$	$H_1: \beta_2 \neq 0$	$H_1: \beta_3 \neq 0$

We will test the hypotheses at the .05 level. The way the alternate hypothesis is stated indicates that the test is two-tailed.

The test statistic follows Student's t distribution with $n - (k + 1)$ degrees of freedom. The number of sample observations is n. There are 20 homes in the study, so $n = 20$. The number of independent variables is k, which is 3. Thus, there are $n - (k + 1) = 20 - (3 + 1) = 16$ degrees of freedom.

The critical value for t is in Appendix B.2. For a two-tailed test with 16 degrees of freedom using the .05 significance level, H_0 is rejected if t is less than -2.120 or greater than 2.120.

Refer to the Excel output in the previous section. (See page 519.) The column highlighted in yellow, headed Coefficients, shows the values for the multiple regression equation:

$$\hat{Y} = 427.194 - 4.583X_1 - 14.831X_2 + 6.101X_3$$

Interpreting the term $-4.583X_1$ in the equation: For each degree the temperature increases, it is expected that the heating cost will decrease about \$4.58, holding the two other variables constant.

The column on the Excel output labeled Standard Error indicates the standard error of the sample regression coefficient. Recall that Salsberry Realty selected a sample of 20 homes along the east coast of the United States. If it was to select a second random sample and compute the regression coefficients of that sample, the values would not be exactly the same. If it repeated the sampling process many times, however, we could design a sampling distribution of these regression coefficients. The column labeled Standard Error estimates the variability of these regression coefficients. The sampling distribution of Coefficients/Standard Error follows the t distribution with $n - (k + 1)$ degrees of freedom. Hence, we are able to test the independent variables individually to determine whether the net regression coefficients differ from zero. The computed t ratio is -5.934 for temperature and -3.119 for insulation. Both of these t values are in the rejection region to the left of -2.120. Thus, we conclude that the regression coefficients for the temperature and insulation variables are *not* zero. The computed t for the age of the furnace is 1.521, so we conclude that b_3 could equal 0. The independent variable age of the furnace is not a significant predictor of heating cost. It can be dropped from the analysis. We can test individual regression coefficients using the t distribution. The formula is:

TESTING INDIVIDUAL REGRESSION COEFFICIENTS
$$t = \frac{b_i - 0}{s_{b_i}}$$
[14–6]

The b_i refers to any one of the regression coefficients and s_{b_i} refers to standard deviation of that distribution of the regression coefficient. We include 0 in the equation because the null hypothesis is $\beta_i = 0$.

To illustrate this formula, refer to the test of the regression coefficient for the independent variable temperature. We let b_1 refer to the regression coefficient. From the computer output on page 519 it is -4.583. s_{b_i} is the standard deviation of the sampling distribution of the regression coefficient for the independent variable temperature. Again, from the same computer output, it is 0.772. Inserting these values in formula (14–6):

$$t = \frac{b_1 - 0}{s_{b_1}} = \frac{-4.583 - 0}{0.772} = -5.936$$

This is the value found in the t Stat column of the Excel output. [There is a slight difference due to rounding.]

At this point we need to develop a strategy for deleting independent variables. In the Salsberry Realty case there were three independent variables, and one (the age of the furnace) had a regression coefficient that did not differ from 0. It is clear that we should drop that variable and rerun the regression equation. Below is the MINITAB output where heating cost is the dependent variable and outside temperature and amount of insulation are the independent variables.

	C1	C2	C3
	Cost	Temp	Insul
1	250	35	3
2	360	29	4
3	165	36	7
4	43	60	6
5	92	65	5
6	200	30	5
7	355	10	6
8	290	7	10
9	230	21	9
10	120	55	2
11	73	54	12
12	205	48	5
13	400	20	5
14	320	39	4
15	72	60	8
16	272	20	5
17	94	58	7
18	190	40	8

Regression Analysis: Cost versus Temp, Insul

The regression equation is
Cost = 490 - 5.15 Temp - 14.7 Insul

Predictor	Coef	SE Coef	T	P
Constant	490.29	44.41	11.04	0.000
Temp	-5.1499	0.7019	-7.34	0.000
Insul	-14.718	4.934	-2.98	0.008

S = 52.9824   R-Sq = 77.6%   R-Sq(adj) = 74.9%

Analysis of Variance

Source	DF	SS	MS	F	P
Regression	2	165195	82597	29.42	0.000
Residual Error	17	47721	2807		
Total	19	212916			

Source	DF	Seq SS
Temp	1	140215
Insul	1	24980

Summarizing the results from this new MINITAB output:

1. The new regression equation is:

$$\hat{Y} = 490.29 - 5.1499X_1 - 14.718X_2$$

    Notice that the regression coefficients for outside temperature (X_1) and amount of insulation (X_2) are similar to but not exactly the same as when we included the independent variable age of the furnace. Compare the above equation to that in the Excel output on page 519. Both of the regression coefficients are negative as in the earlier equation.

2. The details of the global test are as follows:

$$H_0: \beta_1 = \beta_2 = 0$$
$$H_1: \text{Not all of the } \beta_i\text{'s} = 0$$

    The F distribution is the test statistic and there are $k = 2$ degrees of freedom in the numerator and $n - (k + 1) = 20 - (2 + 1) = 17$ degrees of freedom in the denominator. Using the .05 significance level and Appendix B.4, the decision rule is to reject H_0 if F is greater than 3.59. We compute the value of F as follows:

$$F = \frac{\text{SSR}/k}{\text{SSE}/(n - (k + 1))} = \frac{165,195/2}{47,721/(20 - (2 + 1))} = 29.42$$

    Because the computed value of F (29.42) is greater than the critical value (3.59), the null hypothesis is rejected and the alternate accepted. We conclude that at least one of the regression coefficients is different from 0.

3. The next step is to conduct a test of the regression coefficients individually. We want to find out if one or both of the regression coefficients are different from 0. The null and alternate hypotheses for each of the independent variables are:

Outside Temperature	Insulation
$H_0: \beta_1 = 0$	$H_0: \beta_2 = 0$
$H_1: \beta_1 \neq 0$	$H_1: \beta_2 \neq 0$

    The test statistic is the t distribution with $n - (k + 1) = 20 - (2 + 1) = 17$ degrees of freedom. Using the .05 significance level and Appendix B.2, the decision rule is to reject H_0 if the computed value of t is less than -2.110 or greater than 2.110.

Outside Temperature	Insulation
$t = \dfrac{b_1 - 0}{s_{b_1}} = \dfrac{-5.1499 - 0}{0.7019} = -7.34$	$t = \dfrac{b_2 - 0}{s_{b_2}} = \dfrac{-14.718 - 0}{4.934} = -2.98$

In both tests we reject H_0 and accept H_1. We conclude that each of the regression coefficients is different from 0. Both outside temperature and amount of insulation are useful variables in explaining the variation in heating costs.

In the heating cost example, it was clear which independent variable to delete. However, in some instances which variable to delete may not be as clear-cut. To explain, suppose we develop a multiple regression equation based on five independent variables. We conduct the global test and find that some of the regression coefficients are different from zero. Next, we test the regression coefficients individually and find that three are significant and two are not. The preferred procedure is to drop the single independent variable with the *smallest absolute t value* or *largest p-value* and rerun the regression equation with the four remaining variables, then, on the new regression equation with four independent variables, conduct the individual tests. If there are still regression coefficients that are not significant, again drop the variable with the smallest absolute t value. To describe the process in another way, we should delete only one variable at a time. Each time we delete a variable, we need to rerun the regression equation and check the remaining variables.

This process of selecting variables to include in a regression model can be auto-mated, using Excel, MINITAB, MegaStat, or other statistical software. Most of the soft-ware systems include methods to sequentially remove and/or add independent variables and at the same time provide estimates of the percentage of variation ex-plained (the *R*-square term). Two of the common methods are **stepwise regression** and **best subset regression.** It may take a long time, but in the extreme we could compute every regression between the dependent variable and any possible subset of the independent variables.

Unfortunately, on occasion, the software may work "too hard" to find an equation that fits all the quirks of your particular data set. The suggested equation may not rep-resent the relationship in the population. A judgment is needed to choose among the equations presented. Consider whether the results are logical. They should have a sim-ple interpretation and be consistent with your knowledge of the application under study.

Self-Review 14–3

The regression output about eating places in Myrtle Beach is repeated below (see earlier self-reviews).

Predictor	Coef	SE Coef	T
Constant	2.50	1.50	1.667
X_1	3.00	1.500	2.000
X_2	4.00	3.000	1.333
X_3	−3.00	0.20	−15.00
X_4	0.20	.05	4.00
X_5	1.00	1.50	0.667

Analysis of Variance

Source	DF	SS	MS
Regression	5	100	20
Residual Error	20	40	2
Total	25	140	

(a) Perform a global test of hypothesis to check if any of the regression coefficients are different from 0. What do you decide? Use the .05 significance level.
(b) Do an individual test of each independent variable. Which variables would you consider eliminating? Use the .05 significance level.
(c) Outline a plan for possibly removing independent variables.

Exercises

connect

7. Given the following regression output,

Predictor	Coef	SE Coef	T	P
Constant	84.998	1.863	45.61	0.000
X_1	2.391	1.200	1.99	0.051
X_2	−0.4086	0.1717	−2.38	0.020

Analysis of Variance

Source	DF	SS	MS	F	P
Regression	2	77.907	38.954	4.14	0.021
Residual Error	62	583.693	9.414		
Total	64	661.600			

answer the following questions:
a. Write the regression equation.
b. If X_1 is 4 and X_2 is 11, what is the value of the dependent variable?
c. How large is the sample? How many independent variables are there?
d. Conduct a global test of hypothesis to see if any of the set of regression coefficients could be different from 0. Use the .05 significance level. What is your conclusion?
e. Conduct a test of hypothesis for each independent variable. Use the .05 significance level. Which variable would you consider eliminating?
f. Outline a strategy for deleting independent variables in this case.

8. The following regression output was obtained from a study of architectural firms. The dependent variable is the total amount of fees in millions of dollars.

Predictor	Coef	SE Coef	T
Constant	7.987	2.967	2.69
X_1	0.12242	0.03121	3.92
X_2	−0.12166	0.05353	−2.27
X_3	−0.06281	0.03901	−1.61
X_4	0.5235	0.1420	3.69
X_5	−0.06472	0.03999	−1.62

Analysis of Variance

Source	DF	SS	MS	F
Regression	5	3710.00	742.00	12.89
Residual Error	46	2647.38	57.55	
Total	51	6357.38		

X_1 is the number of architects employed by the company.
X_2 is the number of engineers employed by the company.
X_3 is the number of years involved with health care projects.
X_4 is the number of states in which the firm operates.
X_5 is the percent of the firm's work that is health care–related.

a. Write out the regression equation.
b. How large is the sample? How many independent variables are there?
c. Conduct a global test of hypothesis to see if any of the set of regression coefficients could be different from 0. Use the .05 significance level. What is your conclusion?
d. Conduct a test of hypothesis for each independent variable. Use the .05 significance level. Which variable would you consider eliminating?
e. Outline a strategy for deleting independent variables in this case.

Evaluating the Assumptions of Multiple Regression

In the previous section, we described the methods to statistically evaluate the multiple regression equation. The results of the test let us know if at least one of the coefficients was not equal to zero and we described a procedure of evaluating each regression coefficient. We also discussed the decision-making process for including and excluding independent variables in the multiple regression equation.

It is important to know that the validity of the statistical global and individual tests rely on several assumptions. That is, if the assumptions are not true, the results might be biased or misleading. It should be mentioned, however, that in practice strict adherence to the following assumptions is not always possible. Fortunately the statistical techniques discussed in this chapter appear to work well even when one or more of the assumptions are violated. Even if the values in the multiple regression equation are "off" slightly, our estimates using a multiple regression equation will be closer than any that could be made otherwise. Usually the statistical procedures are robust enough to overcome violations of some assumptions.

In Chapter 13 we listed the necessary assumptions for regression when we considered only a single independent variable. (See page 480.) The assumptions for multiple regression are similar.

1. **There is a linear relationship.** That is, there is a straight-line relationship between the dependent variable and the set of independent variables.

2. **The variation in the residuals is the same for both large and small values of $\hat{Y}$.** The put it another way, $(Y - \hat{Y})$ is unrelated to whether $\hat{Y}$ is large or small.
3. **The residuals follow the normal probability distribution.** Recall the residual is the difference between the actual value of Y and the estimated value $\hat{Y}$. So the term $(Y - \hat{Y})$ is computed for every observation in the data set. These residuals should approximately follow a normal probability distribution. In addition, the mean of the residuals should be 0.
4. **The independent variables should not be correlated.** That is, we would like to select a set of independent variables that are not themselves correlated.
5. **The residuals are independent.** This means that successive observations of the dependent variable are not correlated. This assumption is often violated when time is involved with the sampled observations.

In this section we present a brief discussion of each of these assumptions. In addition, we provide methods to validate these assumptions and indicate the consequences if these assumptions cannot be met. For those interested in additional discussion, Kutner, Nachtscheim, and Neter, *Applied Linear Regression Models,* 4th ed. (McGraw-Hill: 2004), is an excellent reference.

Linear Relationship

Let's begin with the linearity assumption. The idea is that the relationship between the set of independent variables and the dependent variable is linear. If we are considering two independent variables, we can visualize this assumption. The two independent variables and the dependent variable would form a three-dimensional space. The regression equation would then form a plane as shown on page 507. We can evaluate this assumption with scatter diagrams and residual plots.

Using Scatter Diagrams The evaluation of a multiple regression equation should always include a scatter diagram that plots the dependent variable against each independent variable. These graphs help us to visualize the relationships and provide some initial information about the direction (positive or negative), linearity, and strength of the relationship. For example, the scatter diagrams for the home heating example follow. The plots suggest a fairly strong negative, linear relationship between heating cost and temperature, and a negative relationship between heating cost and insulation.

Using Residual Plots Recall that a residual $(Y - \hat{Y})$ can be computed using the multiple regression equation for each observation in a data set. In Chapter 13, we

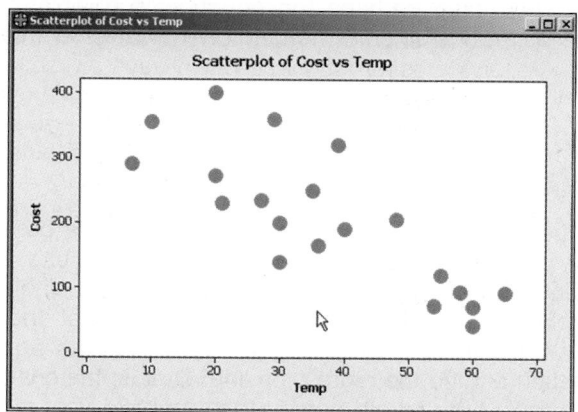

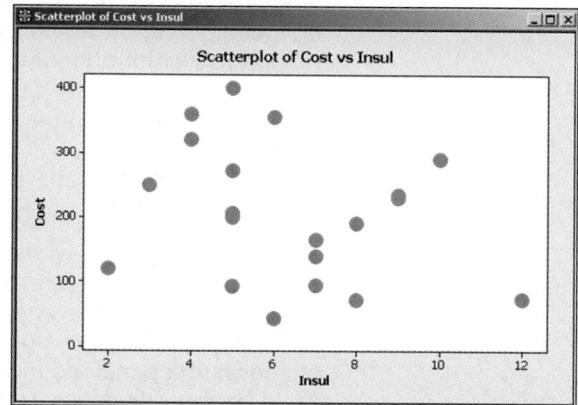

discussed the idea that the best regression line passed through the center of the data in a scatter plot. In this case, you would find a good number of the observations above the regression line (these residuals would have a positive sign), and a good number of the observations below the line (these residuals would have a negative sign). Further, the observations would be scattered above and below the line over the entire range of the independent variable.

The same concept is true for multiple regression, but we cannot graphically portray the multiple regression. However, plots of the residuals can help us evaluate the linearity of the multiple regression equation. To investigate, the residuals are plotted on the vertical axis against the predictor variable, $\hat{Y}$. The graph on the left below show the residual plots for the home heating cost example. Notice the following:

- The residuals are plotted on the vertical axis and are centered around zero. There are both positive and negative residuals.
- The residual plots show a random distribution of positive and negative values across the entire range of the variable plotted on the horizontal axis.
- The points are scattered and there is no obvious pattern, so there is no reason to doubt the linearity assumption.

This plot supports the assumption of linearity.

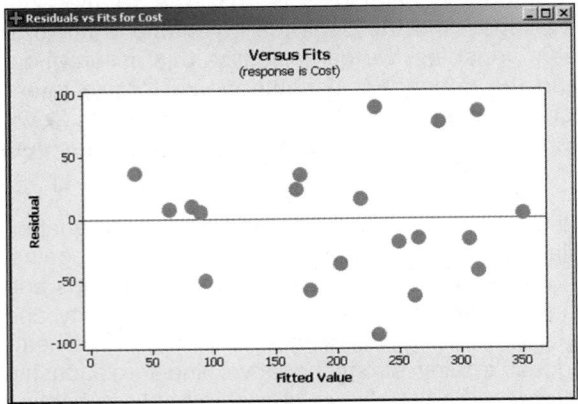
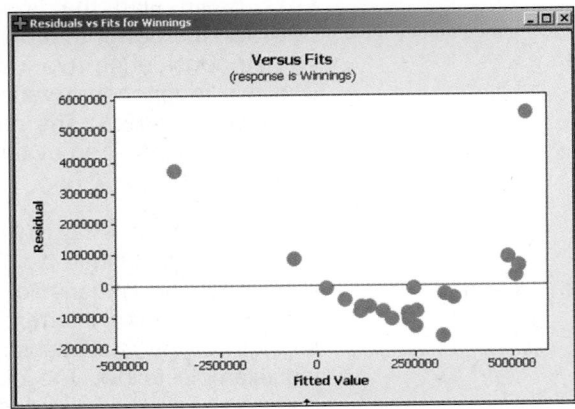

If there is a pattern to the points in the scatter plot, further investigation is necessary. The points in the graph on the right above show nonrandom residuals. See that the residual plot does *not* show a random distribution of positive and negative values across the entire range of the variable plotted on the horizontal axis. In fact, the graph shows a curvature to the residual plots. This indicates the relationship may not be linear. In this case perhaps the equation is quadratic, indicating that the square of one of the variables is needed. We discussed this possibility in Chapter 13.

Variation in Residuals Same for Large and Small $\hat{Y}$ Values

This requirement indicates that the variation about the predicted values is constant, regardless of whether the predicted values are large or small. To cite a specific example, which may violate the assumption, suppose we use the single independent variable age to explain the variation in income. We suspect that as age increases so does salary, but it also seems reasonable that as age increases there may be more variation around the regression line. That is, there will likely be more variation in income for a 50-year-old person than for a 35-year-old person. The requirement for constant variation around the regression line is called **homoscedasticity.**

> **HOMOSCEDASTICITY** The variation around the regression equation is the same for all of the values of the independent variables.

To check for homoscedasticity the residuals are plotted against the fitted values of Y. This is the same graph that we used to evaluate the assumption of linearity. (See page 526.) Based on the scatter diagram in that software output, it is reasonable to conclude that this assumption has not been violated.

Distribution of Residuals

To be sure that the inferences that we make in the global and individual hypotheses tests are valid, we evaluate the distribution of residuals. Ideally, the residuals should follow a normal probability distribution.

To evaluate this assumption, we can organize the residuals into a frequency distribution. The MINITAB histogram of the residuals is shown following on the left for the home heating cost example. Although it is difficult to show that the residuals follow a normal distribution with only 20 observations, it does appear the normality assumption is reasonable.

Both MINITAB and Excel offer another graph that helps to evaluate the assumption of normally distributed residuals. It is a called a **normal probability plot** and is shown to the right of the histogram. Without detailing the calculations, the normal probability plot supports the assumption of normally distributed residuals if the plotted points are fairly close to a straight line drawn from the lower left to the upper right of the graph.

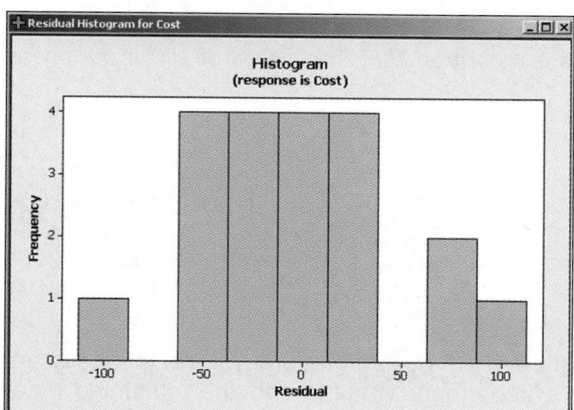

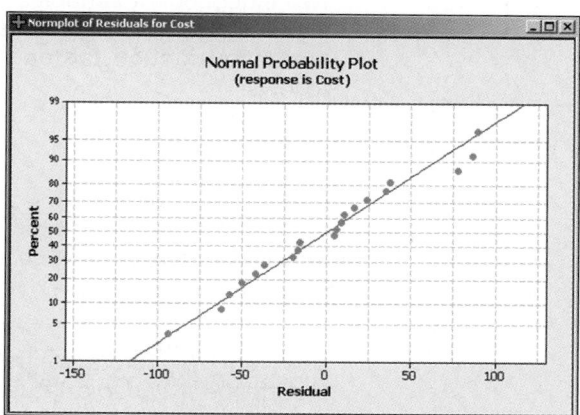

In this case, both graphs support the assumption that the residuals follow the normal probability distribution. Therefore, the inferences that we made based on the global and individual hypothesis tests are supported with the results of this evaluation.

Multicollinearity

Multicollinearity exists when independent variables are correlated. Correlated independent variables make it difficult to make inferences about the individual regression coefficients and their individual effects on the dependent variable. In practice, it is nearly impossible to select variables that are completely unrelated. To put it another way, it is nearly impossible to create a set of independent variables that are not correlated to some degree. However, a general understanding of the issue of multicollinearity is important.

First, we should point out that multicollinearity does not affect a multiple regression equation's ability to predict the dependent variable. However, when we are interested in evaluating the relationship between each independent variable and the dependent variable, multicollinearity may show unexpected results.

For example, if we use two highly multicollinear variables, high school GPA and high school class rank, to predict the GPA of incoming college freshmen (dependent variable), we would expect that both independent variables would be positively related to the dependent variable. However, because the independent variables are highly correlated, one of the independent variables may have an unexpected and inexplicable negative sign. In essence, these two independent variables are redundant in that they explain the same variation in the dependent variable.

A second reason for avoiding correlated independent variables is they may lead to erroneous results in the hypothesis tests for the individual independent variables. This is due to the instability of the standard error of estimate. Several clues that indicate problems with multicollinearity include the following:

1. An independent variable known to be an important predictor ends up having a regression coefficient that is not significant.
2. A regression coefficient that should have a positive sign turns out to be negative, or vice versa.
3. When an independent variable is added or removed, there is a drastic change in the values of the remaining regression coefficients.

In our evaluation of a multiple regression equation, an approach to reducing the effects of multicollinearity is to carefully select the independent variables that are included in the regression equation. A general rule is if the correlation between two independent variables is between -0.70 and 0.70 there likely is not a problem using both of the independent variables. A more precise test is to use the **variance inflation factor.** It is usually written *VIF*. The value of *VIF* is found as follows:

VARIANCE INFLATION FACTOR	$VIF = \dfrac{1}{1 - R_j^2}$	[14–7]

The term R_j^2 refers to the coefficient of determination, where the selected *independent variable* is used as a dependent variable and the remaining independent variables are used as independent variables. A *VIF* greater than 10 is considered unsatisfactory, indicating that the independent variable should be removed from the analysis. The following example will explain the details of finding the *VIF*.

Example

Refer to the data in Table 14–1, which relates the heating cost to the independent variables outside temperature, amount of insulation, and age of furnace. Develop a correlation matrix for all the independent variables. Does it appear there is a problem with multicollinearity? Find and interpret the variance inflation factor for each of the independent variables.

Solution

We begin by using the MINITAB system to find the correlation matrix for the dependent variable and the three independent variables. A portion of that output follows:

```
              Cost       Temp     Insul
Temp        -0.812
Insul       -0.257     -0.103
Age          0.537     -0.486     0.064

Cell Contents: Pearson correlation
```

The highlighted area indicates the correlation among the independent variables. None of the correlations among the independent variables exceed $-.70$ or $.70$, so we do not suspect problems with multicollinearity. The largest correlation among the independent variables is -0.486 between age and temperature.

To confirm this conclusion we compute the *VIF* for each of the three independent variables. We will consider the independent variable temperature first. We use MINITAB to find the multiple coefficient of determination with temperature as the *dependent variable* and amount of insulation and age of the furnace as independent variables. The relevant MINITAB output follows.

```
Regression Analysis: Temp versus Insul, Age

The regression equation is
Temp = 58.0 - 0.51 Insul - 2.51 Age

Predictor      Coef     SE Coef        T       P      VIF
Constant      57.99       12.35     4.70   0.000
Insul        -0.509       1.488    -0.34   0.737      1.0
Age          -2.509       1.103    -2.27   0.036      1.0

S = 16.0311   R-Sq = 24.1%   R-Sq(adj) = 15.2%

Analysis of Variance
Source           DF        SS       MS       F       P
Regression        2    1390.3    695.1    2.70   0.096
Residual Error   17    4368.9    257.0
Total            19    5759.2
```

The coefficient of determination is .241, so inserting this value into the *VIF* formula:

$$VIF = \frac{1}{1 - R_1^2} = \frac{1}{1 - .241} = 1.32$$

The *VIF* value of 1.32 is less than the upper limit of 10. This indicates that the independent variable temperature is not strongly correlated with the other independent variables.

Again, to find the *VIF* for insulation we would develop a regression equation with insulation as the *dependent variable* and temperature and age of furnace as independent variables. For this equation we would determine the coefficient of determination. This would be the value for R_2^2. We would substitute this value in equation 14–7, and solve for *VIF*.

Fortunately, MINITAB will generate the *VIF* values for each of the independent variables. These values are reported in the right-hand column under the heading *VIF* of the MINITAB output. Both of these values are 1.0, hence we conclude there is not a problem with multicollinearity in this example.

Independent Observations

The fifth assumption about regression and correlation analysis is that successive residuals should be independent. This means that there is not a pattern to the residuals, the residuals are not highly correlated, and there are not long runs of positive or negative residuals. When successive residuals are correlated we refer to this condition as **autocorrelation.**

Autocorrelation frequently occurs when the data are collected over a period of time. For example, we wish to predict yearly sales of Ages Software, Inc., based on the time and the amount spent on advertising. The dependent variable is yearly sales and the independent variables are time and amount spent on advertising. It is likely that for a period of time the actual points will be above the regression plane (remember there are two independent variables) and then for a period of time the points will be below the regression plane. The graph below shows the residuals plotted on the vertical axis and the fitted values $\hat{Y}$ on the horizontal axis. Note the run of residuals above the mean of the residuals, followed by a run below the mean. A scatter plot such as this would indicate possible autocorrelation.

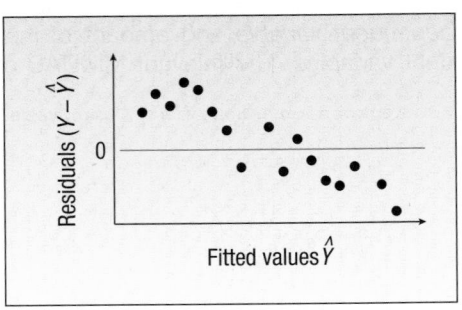

There is a test for autocorrelation, called the Durbin-Watson. We present the details of this test in Chapter 16.

Qualitative Independent Variables

In the previous example regarding heating cost, the two independent variables outside temperature and insulation were quantitative; that is, numerical in nature. Frequently we wish to use nominal-scale variables—such as gender, whether the home has a swimming pool, or whether the sports team was the home or the visiting team—in our analysis. These are called **qualitative variables** because they describe a particular quality, such as male or female. To use a qualitative variable in regression analysis, we use a scheme of **dummy variables** in which one of the two possible conditions is coded 0 and the other 1.

> **DUMMY VARIABLE** A variable in which there are only two possible outcomes. For analysis, one of the outcomes is coded a 1 and the other a 0.

For example, we might be interested in estimating an executive's salary on the basis of years of job experience and whether he or she graduated from college. "Graduation from college" can take on only one of two conditions: yes or no. Thus, it is considered a qualitative variable.

Suppose in the Salsberry Realty example that the independent variable "garage" is added. For those homes without an attached garage, 0 is used; for homes with an attached garage, a 1 is used. We will refer to the "garage" variable as X_4. The data from Table 14–2 are entered into the MINITAB system.

TABLE 14–2 Home Heating Costs, Temperature, Insulation, and Presence of a Garage for a Sample of 20 Homes

Cost, Y	Temperature, X_1	Insulation, X_2	Garage, X_4
$250	35	3	0
360	29	4	1
165	36	7	0
43	60	6	0
92	65	5	0
200	30	5	0
355	10	6	1
290	7	10	1
230	21	9	0
120	55	2	0
73	54	12	0
205	48	5	1
400	20	5	1
320	39	4	1
72	60	8	0
272	20	5	1
94	58	7	0
190	40	8	1
235	27	9	0
139	30	7	0

The output from MINITAB is:

↓	C1	C2	C3	C5
	Cost	Temp	Insul	Garage
4	43	60	6	0
5	92	65	5	0
6	200	30	5	0
7	355	10	6	1
8	290	7	10	1
9	230	21	9	0
10	120	55	2	0
11	73	54	12	0
12	205	48	5	1
13	400	20	5	1
14	320	39	4	1
15	72	60	8	0
16	272	20	5	1
17	94	58	7	0
18	190	40	8	1
19	235	27	9	0
20	139	30	7	0
21				
22				
23				

```
Regression Analysis: Cost versus Temp, Insul, Garage

The regression equation is
Cost = 394 - 3.96 Temp - 11.3 Insul + 77.4 Garage


Predictor    Coef   SE Coef      T      P
Constant   393.67     45.00   8.75  0.000
Temp      -3.9628    0.6527  -6.07  0.000
Insul     -11.334     4.002  -2.83  0.012
Garage      77.43     22.78   3.40  0.004


S = 41.6184   R-Sq = 87.0%   R-Sq(adj) = 84.5%


Analysis of Variance

Source          DF      SS     MS      F      P
Regression       3  185202  61734  35.64  0.000
Residual Error  16   27713   1732
Total           19  212916


Source  DF  Seq SS
Temp     1  140215
Insul    1   24980
Garage   1   20008
```

What is the effect of the garage variable? Should it be included in the analysis? To show the effect of the variable, suppose we have two houses exactly alike next to each other in Buffalo, New York; one has an attached garage, and the other does not. Both homes have 3 inches of insulation, and the mean January temperature in Buffalo is 20 degrees. For the house without an attached garage, a 0 is substituted for X_4 in the regression equation. The estimated heating cost is $280.90, found by:

$$\hat{Y} = 394 - 3.96X_1 - 11.3X_2 + 77.4X_4$$

$$= 394 - 3.96(20) - 11.3(3) + 77.4(0) = 280.90$$

For the house with an attached garage, a 1 is substituted for X_4 in the regression equation. The estimated heating cost is $358.30, found by:

$$\hat{Y} = 394 - 3.96X_1 - 11.3X_2 + 77.4X_4$$

$$= 394 - 3.96(20) - 11.3(3) + 77.4(1) = 358.30$$

The difference between the estimated heating costs is $77.40 ($358.30 − $280.90). Hence, we can expect the cost to heat a house with an attached garage to be $77.40 more than the cost for an equivalent house without a garage.

We have shown the difference between the two types of homes to be $77.40, but is the difference significant? We conduct the following test of hypothesis.

$$H_0: \beta_4 = 0$$

$$H_1: \beta_4 \neq 0$$

The information necessary to answer this question is on the MINITAB output above. The net regression coefficient for the independent variable garage is 77.43, and the standard deviation of the sampling distribution is 22.78. We identify this as the fourth independent variable, so we use a subscript of 4. Finally, we insert these values in formula (14–6).

$$t = \frac{b_4 - 0}{s_{b_4}} = \frac{77.43 - 0}{22.78} = 3.40$$

There are three independent variables in the analysis, so there are $n - (k + 1) = 20 - (3 + 1) = 16$ degrees of freedom. The critical value from Appendix B.2 is 2.120. The decision rule, using a two-tailed test and the .05 significance level, is to reject H_0 if the computed t is to the left of −2.120 or to the right of 2.120. Since the computed value of 3.40 is to the right of 2.120, the null hypothesis is rejected. It is concluded that the regression coefficient is not zero. The independent variable garage should be included in the analysis.

Is it possible to use a qualitative variable with more than two possible outcomes? Yes, but the coding scheme becomes more complex and will require a series of dummy variables. To explain, suppose a company is studying its sales as they relate to advertising expense by quarter for the last 5 years. Let sales be the dependent variable and advertising expense be the first independent variable, X_1. To include the qualitative information regarding the quarter, we use three additional independent variables. For the variable X_2, the five observations referring to the first quarter of each of the 5 years are coded 1 and the other quarters 0. Similarly, for X_3 the five observations referring to the second quarter are coded 1 and the other quarters 0. For X_4 the five observations referring to the third quarter are coded 1 and the other quarters 0. An observation that does not refer to any of the first three quarters must refer to the fourth quarter, so a distinct independent variable referring to this quarter is not necessary.

Self-Review 14–4   A study by the American Realtors Association investigated the relationship between the commissions earned by sales associates last year and the number of months since the associates earned their real estate licenses. Also of interest in the study is the gender of the sales associate. Below is a portion of the regression output. The dependent variable is commissions, which is reported in $000, and the independent variables are months since the license was earned and gender (female = 1 and male = 0).

```
Regression Analysis
        R²  0.642
Adjusted R²  0.600                 n    20
        R   0.801                  k    2
Std. Error  3.219      Dep. Var.  Commissions

ANOVA table
Source              SS      df       MS       F     p-value
Regression     315.9291     2    157.9645   15.25    .0002
Residual       176.1284    17     10.3605
Total          492.0575    19

Regression output
Variables    coefficients   std. error    t (df = 17)   p-value   95% lower   95% upper
Intercept        15.7625       3.0782         5.121      .0001      9.2680      22.2570
   Months         0.4415       0.0839         5.263      .0001      0.2645       0.6186
   Gender         3.8598       1.4724         2.621      .0179      0.7533       6.9663
```

(a) Write out the regression equation. How much commission would you expect a female agent to make who earned her license 30 months ago?

(b) Do the female agents on the average make more or less than the male agents? How much more?

(c) Conduct a test of hypothesis to determine if the independent variable gender should be included in the analysis. Use the 0.05 significance level. What is your conclusion?

Stepwise Regression

In our heating cost example (see sample information in Table 14–1 and Table 14–2) we considered four independent variables: the mean outside temperature, the amount of insulation in the home, the age of the furnace, and whether or not there was an attached garage. To obtain the equation, we first ran a global or "all at once" test to determine if any of the regression coefficients were significant. When we found at least one to be significant, we tested the regression coefficients individually to determine which were important. We left out the independent variables that did not have significant regression coefficients and kept the others. By retaining the independent variables with significant coefficients, we found the regression equation that used the fewest independent variables. This made the regression equation easy to interpret and explained as much variation in the dependent variable as possible.

We are now going to describe a technique called **stepwise regression,** which is more efficient in building the regression equation.

> **STEPWISE REGRESSION** A step-by-step method to determine a regression equation that begins with a single independent variable and adds or deletes independent variables one by one. Only independent variables with nonzero regression coefficients are included in the regression equation.

In the stepwise method, we develop a sequence of equations. The first equation contains only one independent variable. However, this independent variable is the one from the set of proposed independent variables that explains the most variation in the dependent variable. Stated differently, if we compute all the simple correlations between each independent variable and the dependent variable, the stepwise method first selects the independent variable with the strongest correlation with the dependent variable.

Next, the stepwise method looks at the remaining independent variables and then selects the one that will explain the largest percentage of the variation yet unexplained. We continue this process until all the independent variables with significant regression coefficients are included in the regression equation. The advantages to the stepwise method are:

1. Only independent variables with significant regression coefficients are entered into the equation.

2. The steps involved in building the regression equation are clear.
3. It is efficient in finding the regression equation with only significant regression coefficients.
4. The changes in the multiple standard error of estimate and the coefficient of determination are shown.

The stepwise MINITAB output for the heating cost problem follows. Note that the final equation, which is reported in the column labeled 3 includes the independent variables temperature, garage, and insulation. These are the same independent variables that were included in our equation using the global test and the test for individual independent variables. (See page 531.) The independent variable age, for age of the furnace, is not included because it is not a significant predictor of cost.

Tbl14-1.mtw ***				
↓	C1	C2	C3	C5
	Cost	Temp	Insul	Garage
4	43	60	6	0
5	92	65	5	0
6	200	30	5	0
7	355	10	6	1
8	290	7	10	1
9	230	21	9	0
10	120	55	2	0
11	73	54	12	0
12	205	48	5	1
13	400	20	5	1
14	320	39	4	1
15	72	60	8	0
16	272	20	5	1
17	94	58	7	0
18	190	40	8	1
19	235	27	9	0
20	139	30	7	0
21				
22				
23				

Session

Stepwise Regression: Cost versus Temp, Insul, Age, Garage

Alpha-to-Enter: 0.15   Alpha-to-Remove: 0.15

Response is Cost on 4 predictors, with N = 20

Step	1	2	3
Constant	388.8	300.3	393.7
Temp	-4.93	-3.56	-3.96
T-Value	-5.89	-4.70	-6.07
P-Value	0.000	0.000	0.000
Garage		93	77
T-Value		3.56	3.40
P-Value		0.002	0.004
Insul			-11.3
T-Value			-2.83
P-Value			0.012
S	63.6	49.5	41.6
R-Sq	65.85	80.46	86.98
R-Sq(adj)	63.96	78.16	84.54
Mallows Cp	26.8	10.5	4.3

Reviewing the steps and interpreting output:

1. The stepwise procedure selects the independent variable temperature first. This variable explains more of the variation in heating cost than any of the other three proposed independent variables. Temperature explains 65.85 percent of the variation in heating cost. The regression equation is:

$$\hat{Y} = 388.8 - 4.93X_1$$

    There is an inverse relationship between heating cost and temperature. For each degree the temperature increases, heating cost is reduced by \$4.93.

2. The next independent variable to enter the regression equation is garage. When this variable is added to the regression equation, the coefficient of determination is increased from 65.85 percent to 80.46 percent. That is, by adding garage as an independent variable, we increase the coefficient of determination by 14.61 percent. The regression equation after step 2 is:

$$\hat{Y} = 300.3 - 3.56X_1 + 93.0X_2$$

    Usually the regression coefficients will change from one step to the next. In this case the coefficient for temperature retained its negative sign, but it changed from −4.93 to −3.56. This change is reflective of the added influence of the independent variable garage. Why did the stepwise method select the independent variable garage instead of either insulation or age? The increase in R^2, the coefficient of determination, is larger if garage is included rather than either of the other two variables.

3. At this point there are two unused variables remaining, insulation and age. Notice on the third step the procedure selects insulation and then stops. This indicates the variable insulation explains more of the remaining variation in heating cost than the age variable does. After the third step, the regression equation is:

$$\hat{Y} = 393.7 - 3.96X_1 + 77.0X_2 - 11.3X_3$$

At this point 86.98 percent of the variation in heating cost is explained by the three independent variables temperature, garage, and insulation. This is the same R^2 value and regression equation we found on page 531 except for rounding differences.

4. At this point the stepwise procedure stops. This means the independent variable age does not add significantly to the coefficient of determination.

The stepwise method developed the same regression equation, selected the same independent variables, and found the same coefficient of determination as the global and individual tests described earlier in the chapter. The advantages to the stepwise method is that it is more direct than using a combination of the global and individual procedures.

Other methods of variable selection are available. The stepwise method is also called the **forward selection method** because we begin with no independent variables and add one independent variable to the regression equation at each iteration. There is also the **backward elimination method,** which begins with the entire set of variables and eliminates one independent variable at each iteration.

The methods described so far look at one variable at a time and decide whether to include or eliminate that variable. Another approach is the **best-subset regression.** With this method we look at the best model using one independent variable, the best model using two independent variables, the best model with three and so on. The criterion is to find the model with the largest R^2 value, regardless of the number of independent variables. Also, each independent variable does not necessarily have a nonzero regression coefficient. Since each independent variable could either be included or not included, there are $2^k - 1$ possible models, where k refers to the number of independent variables. In our heating cost example we considered four independent variables so there are 15 possible regression models, found by $2^4 - 1 = 16 - 1 = 15$. We would examine all regression models using one independent variable, all combinations using two variables, all combinations using three independent variables, and the possibility of using all four independent variables. The advantages to the best-subset method is it may examine combinations of independent variables not considered in the stepwise method. The process is available in MINITAB and MegaStat.

Regression Models with Interaction

In Chapter 12 we discussed interaction among independent variables. To explain, suppose we are studying weight loss and assume, as the current literature suggests, that diet and exercise are related. So the dependent variable is amount of change in weight and the independent variables are: diet (yes or no) and exercise (none, moderate, significant). We are interested in whether there is interaction among the independent variables. That is, if those studied maintain their diet and exercise significantly, will that increase the mean amount of weight lost? Is total weight loss more than the sum of the loss due to the diet effect and the loss due to the exercise effect?

We can expand on this idea. Instead of having two nominal-scale variables, diet and exercise, we can examine the effect (interaction) of several ratio-scale variables. For example, suppose we want to study the effect of room temperature (68, 72, 76, or 80 degrees Fahrenheit) and noise level (60, 70, or 80 decibels) on the number of units produced. To put it another way, does the combination of noise level in the room and the temperature of the room have an effect on the productivity of the workers? Would the workers in a quiet, cool room produce more units than those in a hot, noisy room?

In regression analysis, interaction can be examined as a separate independent variable. An interaction prediction variable can be developed by multiplying the data values in one independent variable by the values in another independent variable, thereby creating a new independent variable. A two-variable model that includes an interaction term is:

$$Y = \alpha + \beta_1 X_1 + \beta_2 X_2 + \beta_3 X_1 X_2$$

The term $X_1 X_2$ is the *interaction term.* We create this variable by multiplying the values of X_1 and X_2 to create the third independent variable. We then develop a regression equation using the three independent variables and test the significance of the third independent variable using the individual test for independent variables, described earlier in the chapter. An example will illustrate the details.

Example

Refer to the heating cost example and the data in Table 14–1. Is there an interaction between the outside temperature and the amount of insulation? If both variables are increased, is the effect on heating cost greater than the sum of savings from warmer temperature and the savings from increased insulation separately?

Solution

The information from Table 14–1 for the independent variables temperature and insulation is repeated below. We create the interaction variable by multiplying the temperature variable by the insulation. For the first sampled home the value temperature is 35 degrees and insulation is 3 inches so the value of the interaction variable is $35 \times 3 = 105$. The values of the other interaction products are found in a similar fashion.

regression with interaction [Compatibility Mode]

	A	B	C	D	E	F	G	H	I	J	K
1	Cost	Temp	Insul	Temp X Insul		SUMMARY OUTPUT					
2	250	35	3	105							
3	360	29	4	116		*Regression Statistics*					
4	165	36	7	252		Multiple R	0.893				
5	43	60	6	360		R Square	0.798				
6	92	65	5	325		Adjusted R Square	0.760				
7	200	30	5	150		Standard Error	51.846				
8	355	10	6	60		Observations	20				
9	290	7	10	70							
10	230	21	9	189		ANOVA					
11	120	55	2	110			*df*	*SS*	*MS*	*F*	*Significance F*
12	73	54	12	648		Regression	3	169908.452	56636.151	21.070	0.000
13	205	48	5	240		Residual	16	43007.298	2687.956		
14	400	20	5	100		Total	19	212915.750			
15	320	39	4	156							
16	72	60	8	480			*Coefficients*	*Standard Error*	*t Stat*	*P-value*	
17	272	20	5	100		Intercept	598.070	92.265	6.482	0.000	
18	94	58	7	406		Temp	-7.811	2.124	-3.678	0.002	
19	190	40	8	320		Insul	-30.161	12.621	-2.390	0.030	
20	235	27	9	243		Temp X Insul	0.385	0.291	1.324	0.204	
21	139	30	7	210							

We find the multiple regression using temperature, insulation, and the interaction of temperature and insulation as independent variables. The regression equation is reported below.

$$\hat{Y} = 598.070 - 7.811 X_1 - 30.161 X_2 + 0.385 X_1 X_2$$

The question we wish to answer is whether the interaction variable is significant. We will use the .05 significance level. In terms of a hypothesis:

$$H_0: \beta_3 = 0$$
$$H_1: \beta_3 \neq 0$$

There is $n - (k + 1) = 20 - (3 + 1) = 16$ degrees of freedom. Using the .05 significance level and a two-tailed test, the critical values of t are -2.120 and 2.120. We reject the null hypothesis if t is less than -2.120 or t is greater than 2.120. From the output, $b_3 = 0.385$ and $s_{b_3} = 0.291$. To find the value of t we use formula (14–6).

$$t = \frac{b_3 - 0}{s_{b_3}} = \frac{0.385 - 0}{0.291} = 1.324$$

Because the computed value of 1.324 is less than the critical value of 2.120, we do not reject the null hypothesis. We conclude that there is not a significant interaction between temperature and insulation.

There are other situations that can occur when studying interaction among independent variables.

1. It is possible to have a three-way interaction among the independent variables. In our heating example, we might have considered the three-way interaction between temperature, insulation, and age of the furnace.
2. It is possible to have an interaction where one of the independent variables is nominal scale. In our heating cost example, we could have studied the interaction between temperature and garage.

Studying all possible interactions can become very complex. However, careful consideration to possible interactions among independent variables can often provide useful insight into the regression models.

Exercises

connect

9. The production manager of High Point Sofa and Chair, a large furniture manufacturer located in North Carolina, is studying the job performance ratings of a sample of 15 electrical repairmen employed by the company. An aptitude test is required by the human resources department to become an electrical repairman. The production manager was able to get the score for each repairman in the sample. In addition, he determined which of the repairmen were union members (code = 1) and which were not (code = 0). The sample information is reported below.

Worker	Job Performance Score	Aptitude Test Score	Union Membership
Abbott	58	5	0
Anderson	53	4	0
Bender	33	10	0
Bush	97	10	0
Center	36	2	0
Coombs	83	7	0
Eckstine	67	6	0
Gloss	84	9	0
Herd	98	9	1
Householder	45	2	1
Iori	97	8	1
Lindstrom	90	6	1
Mason	96	7	1
Pierse	66	3	1
Rohde	82	6	1

a. Use a statistical software package to develop a multiple regression equation using the job performance score as the dependent variable and aptitude test score and union membership as independent variables.

b. Comment on the regression equation. Be sure to include the coefficient of determination and the effect of union membership. Are these two variables effective in explaining the variation in job performance?

c. Conduct a test of hypothesis to determine if union membership should be included as an independent variable.

d. Repeat the analysis considering possible interaction terms.

10. Cincinnati Paint Company sells quality brands of paints through hardware stores throughout the United States. The company maintains a large sales force whose job it is to call on existing customers as well as look for new business. The national sales manager is investigating the relationship between the number of sales calls made and the miles driven by the sales representative. Also, do the sales representatives who drive the most miles and make the most calls necessarily earn the most in sales commissions? To investigate, the vice president of sales selected a sample of 25 sales representatives and determined:

- The amount earned in commissions last month (Y)
- The number of miles driven last month (X_1)
- The number of sales calls made last month (X_2)

The information is reported below.

Commissions ($000)	Calls	Driven	Commissions ($000)	Calls	Driven
22	139	2,371	38	146	3,290
13	132	2,226	44	144	3,103
33	144	2,731	29	147	2,122
38	142	3,351	38	144	2,791
23	142	2,289	37	149	3,209
47	142	3,449	14	131	2,287
29	138	3,114	34	144	2,848
38	139	3,342	25	132	2,690
41	144	2,842	27	132	2,933
32	134	2,625	25	127	2,671
20	135	2,121	43	154	2,988
13	137	2,219	34	147	2,829
47	146	3,463			

Develop a regression equation including an interaction term. Is there a significant interaction between the number of sales calls and the miles driven?

11. An art collector is studying the relationship between the selling price of a painting and two independent variables. The two independent variables are the number of bidders at the particular auction and the age of the painting, in years. A sample of 25 paintings revealed the following sample information.

Painting	Auction Price	Bidders	Age	Painting	Auction Price	Bidders	Age
1	3,470	10	67	14	4,020	6	79
2	3,500	8	56	15	4,190	4	83
3	3,700	7	73	16	4,130	3	71
4	3,860	4	71	17	4,130	9	89
5	3,920	12	99	18	4,370	5	103
6	3,900	10	87	19	4,450	3	106
7	3,830	11	78	20	4,390	8	93
8	3,940	8	83	21	4,380	8	88
9	3,880	13	90	22	4,540	4	96
10	3,940	13	98	23	4,660	5	94
11	4,200	0	91	24	4,710	3	88
12	4,060	7	93	25	4,880	1	84
13	4,200	2	97				

a. Develop a multiple regression equation using the independent variables number of bidders and age of painting to estimate the dependent variable auction price. Discuss the equation. Does it surprise you that there is an inverse relationship between the number of bidders and the price of the painting?

b. Create an interaction variable and include it in the regression equation. Explain the meaning of the interaction. Is this variable significant?

c. Use the stepwise method and the independent variables for the number of bidders, the age of the painting, and the interaction between the number of bidders and the age of the painting. Which variables would you select?

12. A real estate developer wishes to study the relationship between the size of home a client will purchase (in square feet) and other variables. Possible independent variables include the family income, family size, whether there is a senior adult parent living with the family (1 for yes, 0 for no), and the total years of education beyond high school for the husband and wife. The sample information is reported below.

Family	Square Feet	Income (000s)	Family Size	Senior Parent	Education
1	2,240	60.8	2	0	4
2	2,380	68.4	2	1	6
3	3,640	104.5	3	0	7
4	3,360	89.3	4	1	0
5	3,080	72.2	4	0	2
6	2,940	114	3	1	10
7	4,480	125.4	6	0	6
8	2,520	83.6	3	0	8
9	4,200	133	5	0	2
10	2,800	95	3	0	6

Develop an appropriate multiple regression equation. Which independent variables would you include in the final regression equation? Use the stepwise method.

Chapter Summary

I. The general form of a multiple regression equation is:

$$\hat{Y} = a + b_1X_1 + b_2X_2 + \cdots + b_kX_k \qquad \text{[14–1]}$$

where a is the Y-intercept when all X's are zero, b_j refers to the sample regression coefficients, and X_j refers to the value of the various independent variables.

A. There can be any number of independent variables.

B. The least squares criterion is used to develop the regression equation.

C. A statistical software package is needed to perform the calculations.

II. There are two measures of the effectiveness of the regression equation.

A. The multiple standard error of estimate is similar to the standard deviation.

1. It is measured in the same units as the dependent variable.

2. It is based on squared deviations from the regression equation.

3. It ranges from 0 to plus infinity.

4. It is calculated from the following equation.

$$s_{Y.123...k} = \sqrt{\frac{\Sigma(Y - \hat{Y})^2}{n - (k + 1)}} \qquad \text{[14–2]}$$

B. The coefficient of multiple determination reports the percent of the variation in the dependent variable explained by the set of independent variables.

1. It may range from 0 to 1.

2. It is also based on squared deviations from the regression equation.

3. It is found by the following equation.

$$R^2 = \frac{\text{SSR}}{\text{SS total}}$$ [14–3]

4. When the number of independent variables is large, we adjust the coefficient of determination for the degrees of freedom as follows.

$$R^2_{\text{adj}} = 1 - \frac{\dfrac{\text{SSE}}{n - (k + 1)}}{\dfrac{\text{SS total}}{n - 1}}$$ [14–4]

III. An ANOVA table summarizes the multiple regression analysis.
   A. It reports the total amount of the variation in the dependent variable and divides this variation into that explained by the set of independent variables and that not explained.
   B. It reports the degrees of freedom associated with the independent variables, the error variation, and the total variation.
IV. A correlation matrix shows all possible simple correlation coefficients between pairs of variables.
   A. It shows the correlation between each independent variable and the dependent variable.
   B. It shows the correlation between each pair of independent variables.
V. A global test is used to investigate whether any of the independent variables have significant regression coefficients.
   A. The null hypothesis is: All the regression coefficients are zero.
   B. The alternate hypothesis is: At least one regression coefficient is not zero.
   C. The test statistic is the F distribution with k (the number of independent variables) degrees of freedom in the numerator and $n - (k + 1)$ degrees of freedom in the denominator, where n is the sample size.
   D. The formula to calculate the value of the test statistic for the global test is:

$$F = \frac{\text{SSR}/k}{\text{SSE}/[n - (k + 1)]}$$ [14–5]

VI. The test for individual variables determines which independent variables have nonzero regression coefficients.
   A. The variables that have zero regression coefficients are usually dropped from the analysis.
   B. The test statistic is the t distribution with $n - (k + 1)$ degrees of freedom.
   C. The formula to calculate the value of the test statistic for the individual test is:

$$t = \frac{b_i - 0}{s_{b_i}}$$ [14–6]

VII. Dummy variables are used to represent qualitative variables and can assume only one of two possible outcomes.
VIII. There are five assumptions to use multiple regression analysis.
   A. The relationship between the dependent variable and the set of independent variables must be linear.
      1. To verify this assumption develop a scatter diagram and plot the residuals on the vertical axis and the fitted values on the horizontal axis.
      2. If the plots appear random, we conclude the relationship is linear.
   B. The variation is the same for both large and small values of $\hat{Y}$.
      1. Homoscedasticity means the variation is the same for all fitted values of the dependent variable.
      2. This condition is checked by developing a scatter diagram with the residuals on the vertical axis and the fitted values on the horizontal axis.
      3. If there is no pattern to the plots—that is, they appear random—the residuals meet the homoscedasticity requirement.

C. The residuals follow the normal probability distribution.
   1. This condition is checked by developing a histogram of the residuals to see if they follow a normal distribution.
   2. The mean of the distribution of the residuals is 0.
D. The independent variables are not correlated.
   1. A correlation matrix will show all possible correlations among independent variables. Signs of trouble are correlations larger than 0.70 or less than −0.70.
   2. Signs of correlated independent variables include when an important predictor variable is found insignificant, when an obvious reversal occurs in signs in one or more of the independent variables, or when a variable is removed from the solution, there is a large change in the regression coefficients.
   3. The variance inflation factor is used to identify correlated independent variables.

$$VIF = \frac{1}{1 - R_j^2}$$ [14–7]

E. Each residual is independent of other residuals.
   1. Autocorrelation occurs when successive residuals are correlated.
   2. When autocorrelation exists, the value of the standard error will be biased and will return poor results for tests of hypothesis regarding the regression coefficients.
IX. Several techniques help build a regression model.
   A. A dummy or qualitative independent variable can assume one of two possible outcomes.
      1. A value of 1 is assigned to one outcome and 0 the other.
      2. Use formula (14–6) to determine if the dummy variable should remain in the equation.
   B. Stepwise regression is a step-by-step process to find the regression equation.
      1. Only independent variables with nonzero regression coefficients enter the equation.
      2. Independent variables are added one at a time to the regression equation.
   C. Interaction is the case in which one independent variable (such as X_2) affects the relationship with another independent variable (X_1) and the dependent variable (Y).

Pronunciation Key

SYMBOL	MEANING	PRONUNCIATION
b_1	Regression coefficient for the first independent variable	b sub 1
b_k	Regression coefficient for any independent variable	b sub k
$s_{Y.123...k}$	Multiple standard error of estimate	s sub Y dot 1, 2, 3 . . . k

Chapter Exercises

connect

13. A multiple regression equation yields the following partial results.

Source	Sum of Squares	df
Regression	750	4
Error	500	35

a. What is the total sample size?
b. How many independent variables are being considered?
c. Compute the coefficient of determination.
d. Compute the standard error of estimate.
e. Test the hypothesis that none of the regression coefficients is equal to zero. Let $\alpha = .05$.

14. In a multiple regression equation two independent variables are considered, and the sample size is 25. The regression coefficients and the standard errors are as follows.

$$b_1 = 2.676 \qquad s_{b_1} = 0.56$$

$$b_2 = -0.880 \qquad s_{b_2} = 0.71$$

Conduct a test of hypothesis to determine whether either independent variable has a coefficient equal to zero. Would you consider deleting either variable from the regression equation? Use the .05 significance level.

15. The following output was obtained.

```
Analysis of variance

SOURCE          DF         SS         MS
Regression       5        100         20
Error           20         40          2
Total           25        140

Predictor      Coef      StDev    t-ratio
Constant       3.00       1.50       2.00
    X1         4.00       3.00       1.33
    X2         3.00       0.20      15.00
    X3         0.20       0.05       4.00
    X4        -2.50       1.00      -2.50
    X5         3.00       4.00       0.75
```

a. What is the sample size?
b. Compute the value of R^2.
c. Compute the multiple standard error of estimate.
d. Conduct a global test of hypothesis to determine whether any of the regression coefficients are significant. Use the .05 significance level.
e. Test the regression coefficients individually. Would you consider omitting any variable(s)? If so, which one(s)? Use the .05 significance level.

16. In a multiple regression equation $k = 5$ and $n = 20$, the MSE value is 5.10, and SS total is 519.68. At the .05 significance level, can we conclude that any of the regression coefficients are not equal to 0?

17. The district manager of Jasons, a large discount electronics chain, is investigating why certain stores in her region are performing better than others. She believes that three factors are related to total sales: the number of competitors in the region, the population in the surrounding area, and the amount spent on advertising. From her district, consisting of several hundred stores, she selects a random sample of 30 stores. For each store she gathered the following information.

Y = total sales last year (in \$ thousands)
X_1 = number of competitors in the region
X_2 = population of the region (in millions)
X_3 = advertising expense (in \$ thousands)

The sample data were run on MINITAB, with the following results.

```
Analysis of variance

SOURCE          DF          SS          MS
Regression       3     3050.00     1016.67
Error           26     2200.00       84.62
Total           29     5250.00

Predictor      Coef      StDev    t-ratio
Constant      14.00       7.00       2.00
    X1        -1.00       0.70      -1.43
    X2        30.00       5.20       5.77
    X3         0.20       0.08       2.50
```

a. What are the estimated sales for the Bryne store, which has four competitors, a regional population of 0.4 (400,000), and advertising expense of 30 ($30,000)?
b. Compute the R^2 value.
c. Compute the multiple standard error of estimate.
d. Conduct a global test of hypothesis to determine whether any of the regression coefficients are not equal to zero. Use the .05 level of significance.
e. Conduct tests of hypotheses to determine which of the independent variables have significant regression coefficients. Which variables would you consider eliminating? Use the .05 significance level.

18. Suppose that the sales manager of a large automotive parts distributor wants to estimate as early as April the total annual sales of a region. On the basis of regional sales, the total sales for the company can also be estimated. If, based on past experience, it is found that the April estimates of annual sales are reasonably accurate, then in future years the April forecast could be used to revise production schedules and maintain the correct inventory at the retail outlets.

Several factors appear to be related to sales, including the number of retail outlets in the region stocking the company's parts, the number of automobiles in the region registered as of April 1, and the total personal income for the first quarter of the year. Five independent variables were finally selected as being the most important (according to the sales manager). Then the data were gathered for a recent year. The total annual sales for that year for each region were also recorded. Note in the following table that for region 1 there were 1,739 retail outlets stocking the company's automotive parts, there were 9,270,000 registered automobiles in the region as of April 1 and so on. The sales for that year were $37,702,000.

Annual Sales ($ millions), Y	Number of Retail Outlets, X_1	Number of Automobiles Registered (millions), X_2	Personal Income ($ billions), X_3	Average Age of Automobiles (years), X_4	Number of Supervisors, X_5
37.702	1,739	9.27	85.4	3.5	9.0
24.196	1,221	5.86	60.7	5.0	5.0
32.055	1,846	8.81	68.1	4.4	7.0
3.611	120	3.81	20.2	4.0	5.0
17.625	1,096	10.31	33.8	3.5	7.0
45.919	2,290	11.62	95.1	4.1	13.0
29.600	1,687	8.96	69.3	4.1	15.0
8.114	241	6.28	16.3	5.9	11.0
20.116	649	7.77	34.9	5.5	16.0
12.994	1,427	10.92	15.1	4.1	10.0

a. Consider the following correlation matrix. Which single variable has the strongest correlation with the dependent variable? The correlations between the independent variables outlets and income and between cars and outlets are fairly strong. Could this be a problem? What is this condition called?

	sales	outlets	cars	income	age
outlets	0.899				
cars	0.605	0.775			
income	0.964	0.825	0.409		
age	−0.323	−0.489	−0.447	−0.349	
bosses	0.286	0.183	0.395	0.155	0.291

b. The output for all five variables is on the following page. What percent of the variation is explained by the regression equation?

```
The regression equation is
sales = -19.7 - 0.00063 outlets + 1.74 cars + 0.410 income
          + 2.04 age - 0.034 bosses

          Predictor            Coef            StDev         t-ratio
          Constant          -19.672            5.422           -3.63
          outlets         -0.000629         0.002638           -0.24
          cars              1.7399           0.5530            3.15
          income           0.40994          0.04385            9.35
          age              2.0357           0.8779            2.32
          bosses          -0.0344           0.1880           -0.18

Analysis of Variance
     SOURCE          DF           SS             MS
     Regression       5       1593.81         318.76
     Error            4          9.08           2.27
     Total            9       1602.89
```

c. Conduct a global test of hypothesis to determine whether any of the regression coefficients are not zero. Use the .05 significance level.
d. Conduct a test of hypothesis on each of the independent variables. Would you consider eliminating "outlets" and "bosses"? Use the .05 significance level.
e. The regression has been rerun below with "outlets" and "bosses" eliminated. Compute the coefficient of determination. How much has R^2 changed from the previous analysis?

```
The regression equation is
sales = -18.9 + 1.61 cars + 0.400 income + 1.96 age

          Predictor            Coef            StDev         t-ratio
          Constant          -18.924            3.636           -5.20
          cars              1.6129           0.1979            8.15
          income           0.40031          0.01569           25.52
          age              1.9637           0.5846            3.36

Analysis of Variance
     SOURCE          DF           SS             MS
     Regression       3       1593.66         531.22
     Error            6          9.23           1.54
     Total            9       1602.89
```

f. Following is a histogram and a stem-and-leaf chart of the residuals. Does the normality assumption appear reasonable?

```
Histogram of residual N = 10        Stem-and-leaf of residual N = 10
                                    Leaf Unit = 0.10

Midpoint Count
   -1.5    1    *                   1   -1   7
   -1.0    1    *                   2   -1   2
   -0.5    2    **                  2   -0
   -0.0    2    **                  5   -0   440
    0.5    2    **                  5    0   24
    1.0    1    *                   3    0   68
    1.5    1    *                   1    1
                                    1    1   7
```

g. Following is a plot of the fitted values of Y (i.e., $\hat{Y}$) and the residuals. Do you see any violations of the assumptions?

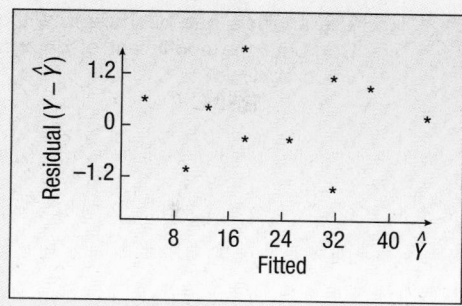

19. The administrator of a new paralegal program at Seagate Technical College wants to estimate the grade point average in the new program. He thought that high school GPA, the verbal score on the Scholastic Aptitude Test (SAT), and the mathematics score on the SAT would be good predictors of paralegal GPA. The data on nine students are:

Student	High School GPA	SAT Verbal	SAT Math	Paralegal GPA
1	3.25	480	410	3.21
2	1.80	290	270	1.68
3	2.89	420	410	3.58
4	3.81	500	600	3.92
5	3.13	500	490	3.00
6	2.81	430	460	2.82
7	2.20	320	490	1.65
8	2.14	530	480	2.30
9	2.63	469	440	2.33

a. Consider the following correlation matrix. Which variable has the strongest correlation with the dependent variable? Some of the correlations among the independent variables are strong. Does this appear to be a problem?

```
            legal        gpa        verbal
gpa        0.911
verbal     0.616        0.609
math       0.487        0.636       0.599
```

b. Consider the following output. Compute the coefficient of multiple determination.

```
The regression equation is
legal = -0.411 + 1.20 gpa + 0.00163 verbal - 0.00194 math

Predictor           Coef            StDev          t-ratio
Constant         -0.4111          0.7823          -0.53
gpa               1.2014          0.2955           4.07
verbal            0.001629        0.002147         0.76
math             -0.001939        0.002074        -0.94

Analysis of Variance
SOURCE           DF              SS              MS
Regression        3             4.3595          1.4532
Error             5             0.7036          0.1407
Total             8             5.0631
```

c. Conduct a global test of hypothesis from the preceding output. Does it appear that any of the regression coefficients are not equal to zero?
d. Conduct a test of hypothesis on each independent variable. Would you consider eliminating the variables "verbal" and "math"? Let $\alpha = .05$.

e. The analysis has been rerun without "verbal" and "math." See the following output. Compute the coefficient of determination. How much has R^2 changed from the previous analysis?

```
The regression equation is
legal = -0.454 + 1.16 gpa

   Predictor          Coef        StDev      t-ratio
   Constant        -0.4542       0.5542        -0.82
   gpa              1.1589       0.1977         5.86

Analysis of Variance
SOURCE            DF          SS          MS
Regression         1      4.2061      4.2061
Error              7      0.8570      0.1224
Total              8      5.0631
```

f. Following are a histogram and a stem-and-leaf diagram of the residuals. Does the normality assumption for the residuals seem reasonable?

```
Histogram of residual N = 9

Midpoint              Count
     -0.4               1   *
     -0.2               3   ***
      0.0               3   ***
      0.2               1   *
      0.4               0
      0.6               1   *

Stem-and-leaf of residual N = 9
Leaf unit = 0.10
   1     -0    4
   2     -0    2
  (3)    -0    110
   4      0    00
   2      0
   1      0
   1      0    6
```

g. Following is a plot of the residuals and the $\hat{Y}$ values. Do you see any violation of the assumptions?

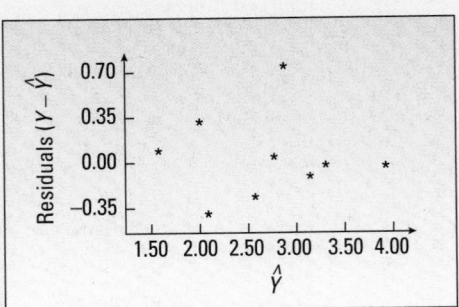

20. Mike Wilde is president of the teachers' union for Otsego School District. In preparing for upcoming negotiations, he would like to investigate the salary structure of classroom teachers in the district. He believes there are three factors that affect a teacher's salary: years of experience, a rating of teaching effectiveness given by the principal, and whether the teacher has a master's degree. A random sample of 20 teachers resulted in the following data.

Salary ($ thousands), Y	Years of Experience, X_1	Principal's Rating, X_2	Master's Degree,* X_3
31.1	8	35	0
33.6	5	43	0
29.3	2	51	1
43.0	15	60	1
38.6	11	73	0
45.0	14	80	1
42.0	9	76	0
36.8	7	54	1
48.6	22	55	1
31.7	3	90	1
25.7	1	30	0
30.6	5	44	0
51.8	23	84	1
46.7	17	76	0
38.4	12	68	1
33.6	14	25	0
41.8	8	90	1
30.7	4	62	0
32.8	2	80	1
42.8	8	72	0

*1 = yes, 0 = no.

a. Develop a correlation matrix. Which independent variable has the strongest correlation with the dependent variable? Does it appear there will be any problems with multicollinearity?

b. Determine the regression equation. What salary would you estimate for a teacher with five years' experience, a rating by the principal of 60, and no master's degree?

c. Conduct a global test of hypothesis to determine whether any of the regression coefficients differ from zero. Use the .05 significance level.

d. Conduct a test of hypothesis for the individual regression coefficients. Would you consider deleting any of the independent variables? Use the .05 significance level.

e. If your conclusion in part (d) was to delete one or more independent variables, run the analysis again without those variables.

f. Determine the residuals for the equation of part (e). Use a stem-and-leaf chart or a histogram to verify that the distribution of the residuals is approximately normal.

g. Plot the residuals computed in part (f) in a scatter diagram with the residuals on the Y-axis and the $\hat{Y}$ values on the X-axis. Does the plot reveal any violations of the assumptions of regression?

21. A consumer analyst collected the following data on the screen sizes of popular LCD televisions sold recently at a large retailer:

Manufacturer	Screen	Price	Manufacturer	Screen	Price
Sharp	46	$1473.00	Sharp	37	$1314.50
Samsung	52	2300.00	Sharp	32	853.50
Samsung	46	1790.00	Sharp	52	2778.00
Sony	40	1250.00	Samsung	40	1749.50
Sharp	42	1546.50	Sharp	32	1035.00
Samsung	46	1922.50	Samsung	52	2950.00
Samsung	40	1372.00	Sony	40	1908.50
Sharp	37	1149.50	Sony	52	3103.00
Sharp	46	2000.00	Sony	46	2606.00
Sony	40	1444.50	Sony	46	2861.00
Sony	52	2615.00	Sony	52	3434.00
Samsung	32	747.50			

a. Does there appear to be a linear relationship between the screen size and the price?
b. Which variable is the "dependent" variable?
c. Using statistical software determine the regression equation. Interpret the value of the slope in the regression equation.
d. Include the manufacturer in a multiple linear regression analysis using a "dummy" variable. Does it appear that some manufacturers can command a premium price? *Hint:* You will need to use a set of indicator variables.
e. Test each of the individual coefficients to see if they are significant.
f. Make a plot of the residuals and comment on whether they appear to follow a normal distribution.
g. Plot the residuals versus the fitted values. Do they seem to have the same amount of variation?

22. A regional planner is studying the demographics in a region of a particular state. She has gathered the following data on nine counties.

County	Median Income	Median Age	Coastal
A	$48,157	57.7	1
B	48,568	60.7	1
C	46,816	47.9	1
D	34,876	38.4	0
E	35,478	42.8	0
F	34,465	35.4	0
G	35,026	39.5	0
H	38,599	65.6	0
J	33,315	27.0	0

a. Is there a linear relationship between the median income and median age?
b. Which variable is the "dependent" variable?
c. Use statistical software to determine the regression equation. Interpret the value of the slope in a simple regression equation.
d. Include the aspect that the county is "coastal" or not in a multiple linear regression analysis using a "dummy" variable. Does it appear to be a significant influence on incomes?
e. Test each of the individual coefficients to see if they are significant.
f. Make a plot of the residuals and comment on whether they appear to follow a normal distribution.
g. Plot the residuals versus the fitted values. Do they seem to have the same amount of variation?

23. Great Plains Roofing and Siding Company, Inc., sells roofing and siding products to home repair retailers, such as Lowe's and Home Depot, and commercial contractors. The owner is interested in studying the effects of several variables on the value of shingles sold ($000). The marketing manager is arguing that the company should spend more money on advertising, while a market researcher suggests it should focus more on making its brand and product more distinct from its competitors.

The company has divided the United States into 26 marketing districts. In each district it collected information on the following variables: volume of sales (in thousands of dollars), advertising dollars (in thousands), number of active accounts, number of competing brands, and a rating of district potential.

Sales (000s)	Advertising Dollars (000s)	Number of Accounts	Number of Competitors	Market Potential
79.3	5.5	31	10	8
200.1	2.5	55	8	6
163.2	8.0	67	12	9

continued

Sales (000s)	Advertising Dollars (000s)	Number of Accounts	Number of Competitors	Market Potential
200.1	3.0	50	7	16
146.0	3.0	38	8	15
177.7	2.9	71	12	17
30.9	8.0	30	12	8
291.9	9.0	56	5	10
160.0	4.0	42	8	4
339.4	6.5	73	5	16
159.6	5.5	60	11	7
86.3	5.0	44	12	12
237.5	6.0	50	6	6
107.2	5.0	39	10	4
155.0	3.5	55	10	4
291.4	8.0	70	6	14
100.2	6.0	40	11	6
135.8	4.0	50	11	8
223.3	7.5	62	9	13
195.0	7.0	59	9	11
73.4	6.7	53	13	5
47.7	6.1	38	13	10
140.7	3.6	43	9	17
93.5	4.2	26	8	3
259.0	4.5	75	8	19
331.2	5.6	71	4	9

Conduct a multiple regression analysis to find the best predictors of sales.

a. Draw a scatter diagram comparing sales volume with each of the independent variables. Comment on the results.

b. Develop a correlation matrix. Do you see any problems? Does it appear there are any redundant independent variables?

c. Develop a regression equation. Conduct the global test. Can we conclude that some of the independent variables are useful in explaining the variation in the dependent variable?

d. Conduct a test of each of the independent variables. Are there any that should be dropped?

e. Refine the regression equation so the remaining variables are all significant.

f. Develop a histogram of the residuals and a normal probability plot. Are there any problems?

g. Determine the variance inflation factor for each of the independent variables. Are there any problems?

24. The *Times-Observer* is a daily newspaper in Metro City. Like many city newspapers, the *Times-Observer* is suffering through difficult financial times. The circulation manager is studying other papers in similar cities in the United States and Canada. She is particularly interested in what variables relate to the number of subscriptions to the paper. She is able to obtain the following sample information on 25 newspapers in similar cities. The following notation is used:

Sub = Number of subscriptions (in thousands)
Popul = The metropolitan population (in thousands)
Adv = The advertising budget of the paper (in $ hundreds)
Income = The median family income in the metropolitan area (in $ thousands)

Paper	Sub	Popul	Adv	Income	Paper	Sub	Popul	Adv	Income
1	37.95	588.9	13.2	35.1	3	37.55	566.3	19.8	34.8
2	37.66	585.3	13.2	34.7	4	38.78	642.9	17.6	35.1

continued

Paper	Sub	Popul	Adv	Income	Paper	Sub	Popul	Adv	Income
5	37.67	624.2	17.6	34.6	16	39.15	611.1	24.2	35.0
6	38.23	603.9	15.4	34.8	17	38.29	643.3	17.6	35.3
7	36.90	571.9	11.0	34.7	18	38.09	635.6	19.8	34.8
8	38.28	584.3	28.6	35.3	19	37.83	598.9	15.4	35.1
9	38.95	605.0	28.6	35.1	20	39.37	657.0	22.0	35.3
10	39.27	676.3	17.6	35.6	21	37.81	595.2	15.4	35.1
11	38.30	587.4	17.6	34.9	22	37.42	520.0	19.8	35.1
12	38.84	576.4	22.0	35.4	23	38.83	629.6	22.0	35.3
13	38.14	570.8	17.6	35.0	24	38.33	680.0	24.2	34.7
14	38.39	586.5	15.4	35.5	25	40.24	651.2	33.0	35.8
15	37.29	544.0	11.0	34.9					

a. Determine the regression equation.
b. Conduct a global test of hypothesis to determine whether any of the regression coefficients are not equal to zero.
c. Conduct a test for the individual coefficients. Would you consider deleting any coefficients?
d. Determine the residuals and plot them against the fitted values. Do you see any problems?
e. Develop a histogram of the residuals. Do you see any problems with the normality assumption?

25. How important is GPA in determining the starting salary of recent business school graduates? Does graduating from a business school increase the starting salary? The director of undergraduate studies at a major university wanted to study these questions. She gathered the following sample information on 15 graduates last spring to investigate these questions.

Student	Salary	GPA	Business	Student	Salary	GPA	Business
1	$31.5	3.245	0	9	$34.7	3.355	1
2	33.0	3.278	0	10	32.5	3.080	0
3	34.1	3.520	1	11	31.5	3.025	0
4	35.4	3.740	1	12	32.2	3.146	0
5	34.2	3.520	1	13	34.0	3.465	1
6	34.0	3.421	1	14	32.8	3.245	0
7	34.5	3.410	1	15	31.8	3.025	0
8	35.0	3.630	1				

The salary is reported in $000, GPA on the traditional 4-point scale. A 1 indicates the student graduated from a school of business; a 0 indicates that the student graduated from one of the other schools.
a. Develop a correlation matrix. Do you see any problems with multicollinearity?
b. Determine the regression equation. Discuss the regression equation. How much does graduating from a college of business add to a starting salary? What starting salary would you estimate for a student with a GPA of 3.00 who graduated from a college of business?
c. What is the value of R^2? Can we conclude that this value is greater than 0?
d. Would you consider deleting either of the independent variables?
e. Plot the residuals in a histogram. Is there any problem with the normality assumption?
f. Plot the fitted values against the residuals. Does this plot indicate any problems with homoscedasticity?

26. A mortgage department of a large bank is studying its recent loans. Of particular interest is how such factors as the value of the home (in thousands of dollars), education level of the head of the household, age of the head of the household, current monthly mortgage payment (in dollars), and gender of the head of the household (male = 1, female = 0) relate to the family income. Are these variables effective predictors of the income of the household? A random sample of 25 recent loans is obtained.

Income ($ thousands)	Value ($ thousands)	Years of Education	Age	Mortgage Payment	Gender
$40.3	$190	14	53	$230	1
39.6	121	15	49	370	1
40.8	161	14	44	397	1
40.3	161	14	39	181	1
40.0	179	14	53	378	0
38.1	99	14	46	304	0
40.4	114	15	42	285	1
40.7	202	14	49	551	0
40.8	184	13	37	370	0
37.1	90	14	43	135	0
39.9	181	14	48	332	1
40.4	143	15	54	217	1
38.0	132	14	44	490	0
39.0	127	14	37	220	0
39.5	153	14	50	270	1
40.6	145	14	50	279	1
40.3	174	15	52	329	1
40.1	177	15	47	274	0
41.7	188	15	49	433	1
40.1	153	15	53	333	1
40.6	150	16	58	148	0
40.4	173	13	42	390	1
40.9	163	14	46	142	1
40.1	150	15	50	343	0
38.5	139	14	45	373	0

a. Determine the regression equation.
b. What is the value of R^2? Comment on the value.
c. Conduct a global hypothesis test to determine whether any of the independent variables are different from zero.
d. Conduct individual hypothesis tests to determine whether any of the independent variables can be dropped.
e. If variables are dropped, recompute the regression equation and R^2.

27. Fred G. Hire is the manager of human resources at Crescent Tool and Die, Inc. As part of his yearly report to the CEO, he is required to present an analysis of the salaried employees. Because there are over 1,000 employees, he does not have the staff to gather information on each salaried employee, so he selects a random sample of 30. For each employee, he records monthly salary; service at Crescent, in months; gender (1 = male, 0 = female); and whether the employee has a technical or clerical job. Those working technical jobs are coded 1, and those who are clerical 0.

Sampled Employee	Monthly Salary	Length of Service	Age	Gender	Job
1	$1,769	93	42	1	0
2	1,740	104	33	1	0
3	1,941	104	42	1	1
4	2,367	126	57	1	1
5	2,467	98	30	1	1
6	1,640	99	49	1	1
7	1,756	94	35	1	0
8	1,706	96	46	0	1
9	1,767	124	56	0	0
10	1,200	73	23	0	1

continued

Sampled Employee	Monthly Salary	Length of Service	Age	Gender	Job
11	$1,706	110	67	0	1
12	1,985	90	36	0	1
13	1,555	104	53	0	0
14	1,749	81	29	0	0
15	2,056	106	45	1	0
16	1,729	113	55	0	1
17	2,186	129	46	1	1
18	1,858	97	39	0	1
19	1,819	101	43	1	1
20	1,350	91	35	1	1
21	2,030	100	40	1	0
22	2,550	123	59	1	0
23	1,544	88	30	0	0
24	1,766	117	60	1	1
25	1,937	107	45	1	1
26	1,691	105	32	0	1
27	1,623	86	33	0	0
28	1,791	131	56	0	1
29	2,001	95	30	1	1
30	1,874	98	47	1	0

a. Determine the regression equation, using salary as the dependent variable and the other four variables as independent variables.
b. What is the value of R^2? Comment on this value.
c. Conduct a global test of hypothesis to determine whether any of the independent variables are different from 0.
d. Conduct an individual test to determine whether any of the independent variables can be dropped.
e. Rerun the regression equation, using only the independent variables that are significant. How much more does a man earn per month than a woman? Does it make a difference whether the employee has a technical or a clerical job?

28. Many regions along the coast in North and South Carolina and Georgia have experienced rapid population growth over the last 10 years. It is expected that the growth will continue over the next 10 years. This has motivated many of the large grocery store chains building new stores in the region. The Kelley's Super Grocery Stores, Inc., chain is no exception. The director of planning for Kelley's Super Grocery Stores wants to study adding more stores in this region. He believes there are two main factors that indicate the amount families spend on groceries. The first is their income and the other is the number of people in the family. The director gathered the following sample information.

Family	Food	Income	Size	Family	Food	Income	Size
1	$5.04	$ 73.98	4	14	$4.92	$ 171.36	2
2	4.08	54.90	2	15	6.60	82.08	9
3	5.76	94.14	4	16	5.40	141.30	3
4	3.48	52.02	1	17	6.00	36.90	5
5	4.20	65.70	2	18	5.40	56.88	4
6	4.80	53.64	4	19	3.36	71.82	1
7	4.32	79.74	3	20	4.68	69.48	3
8	5.04	68.58	4	21	4.32	54.36	2
9	6.12	165.60	5	22	5.52	87.66	5
10	3.24	64.80	1	23	4.56	38.16	3
11	4.80	138.42	3	24	5.40	43.74	7
12	3.24	125.82	1	25	4.80	48.42	5
13	6.60	77.58	7				

Food and income are reported in thousands of dollars per year, and the variable size refers to the number of people in the household.

a. Develop a correlation matrix. Do you see any problems with multicollinearity?

b. Determine the regression equation. Discuss the regression equation. How much does an additional family member add to the amount spent on food?

c. What is the value of R^2? Can we conclude that this value is greater than 0?

d. Would you consider deleting either of the independent variables?

e. Plot the residuals in a histogram. Is there any problem with the normality assumption?

f. Plot the fitted values against the residuals. Does this plot indicate any problems with homoscedasticity?

29. An investment advisor is studying the relationship between a common stock's price to earnings (P/E) ratio and factors that she thinks would influence it. She has the following data on the earnings per share (EPS) and the dividend percentage (Yield) for a sample of 20 stocks.

Stock	P/E	EPS	Yield	Stock	P/E	EPS	Yield
1	20.79	$2.46	1.42	11	1.35	$2.93	2.59
2	3.03	2.69	4.05	12	25.43	2.07	1.04
3	44.46	−0.28	4.16	13	22.14	2.19	3.52
4	41.72	−0.45	1.27	14	24.21	−0.83	1.56
5	18.96	1.60	3.39	15	30.91	2.29	2.23
6	18.42	2.32	3.86	16	35.79	1.64	3.36
7	34.82	0.81	4.56	17	18.99	3.07	1.98
8	30.43	2.13	1.62	18	30.21	1.71	3.07
9	29.97	2.22	5.10	19	32.88	0.35	2.21
10	10.86	1.44	1.17	20	15.19	5.02	3.50

a. Develop a multiple linear regression with P/E as the dependent variable.

b. Are either of the two independent variables an effective predictor of P/E?

c. Interpret the regression coefficients.

d. Do any of these stocks look particularly undervalued?

e. Plot the residuals and check the normality assumption. Plot the fitted values against the residuals.

f. Does there appear to be any problems with homoscedasticity?

g. Develop a correlation matrix. Do any of the correlations indicate multicollinearity?

30. The Conch Café, located in Gulf Shores, Alabama, features casual lunches with a great view of the Gulf of Mexico. To accommodate the increase in business during the summer vacation season, Fuzzy Conch, the owner, hires a large number of servers as seasonal help. When he interviews a prospective server he would like to provide data on the amount a server can earn in tips. He believes that the amount of the bill and the number of diners are both related to the amount of the tip. He gathered the following sample information.

Customer	Amount of Tip	Amount of Bill	Number of Diners	Customer	Amount of Tip	Amount of Bill	Number of Diners
1	$7.00	$48.97	5	16	$3.30	$23.59	2
2	4.50	28.23	4	17	3.50	22.30	2
3	1.00	10.65	1	18	3.25	32.00	2
4	2.40	19.82	3	19	5.40	50.02	4
5	5.00	28.62	3	20	2.25	17.60	3
6	4.25	24.83	2	21	5.50	44.47	4
7	0.50	6.24	1	22	3.00	20.27	2
8	6.00	49.20	4	23	1.25	19.53	2
9	5.00	43.26	3	24	3.25	27.03	3
10	4.75	31.36	4	25	3.00	21.28	2
11	5.25	32.87	4	26	6.25	43.38	4
12	6.00	34.99	3	27	5.60	28.12	4
13	4.00	33.91	4	28	2.50	26.25	2
14	3.35	23.06	2	29	9.25	56.81	5
15	0.75	4.65	1	30	8.25	50.65	5

a. Develop a multiple regression equation with the amount of tips as the dependent variable and the amount of the bill and the number of diners as independent variables. Write out the regression equation. How much does another diner add to the amount of the tips?

b. Conduct a global test of hypothesis to determine if at least one of the independent variables is significant. What is your conclusion?

c. Conduct an individual test on each of the variables. Should one or the other be deleted?

d. Use the equation developed in part (c) to determine the coefficient of determination. Interpret the value.

e. Plot the residuals. Is it reasonable to assume they follow the normal distribution?

f. Plot the residuals against the fitted values. Is it reasonable to conclude they are random?

31. The president of Blitz Sales Enterprises sells kitchen products through television commercials, often called infomercials. He gathered data from the last 15 weeks of sales to determine the relationship between sales and the number of infomercials.

Infomercials	Sales ($000s)	Infomercials	Sales ($000s)
20	3.2	22	2.5
15	2.6	15	2.4
25	3.4	25	3.0
10	1.8	16	2.7
18	2.2	12	2.0
18	2.4	20	2.6
15	2.4	25	2.8
12	1.5		

a. Determine the regression equation. Are the sales predictable from the number of commercials?

b. Determine the residuals and plot a histogram. Does the normality assumption seem reasonable?

32. The director of special events for Sun City believed that the amount of money spent on fireworks displays on the 4th of July was predictive of attendance at the Fall Festival held in October. She gathered the following data to test her suspicion.

4th of July ($000)	Fall Festival (000)	4th of July ($000)	Fall Festival (000)
10.6	8.8	9.0	9.5
8.5	6.4	10.0	9.8
12.5	10.8	7.5	6.6
9.0	10.2	10.0	10.1
5.5	6.0	6.0	6.1
12.0	11.1	12.0	11.3
8.0	7.5	10.5	8.8
7.5	8.4		

Determine the regression equation. Is the amount spent on fireworks related to attendance at the Fall Festival? Conduct a hypothesis test to determine if there is a problem with autocorrelation.

33. You are a new hire at Laurel Woods Real Estate which specializes in selling foreclosed homes via public auction. Your boss has asked you to use the following data (mortgage balance, monthly payments, payments made before default, and final auction price) on a random sample of recent sales in order to estimate what the actual auction price will be.

Loan	Monthly Payments	Payments Made	Auction Price	Loan	Monthly Payments	Payments Made	Auction Price
$ 85,600	$ 985.87	1	$16,900	$105,200	$ 915.24	34	$52,600
115,300	902.56	33	75,800	105,900	905.67	38	51,900
103,100	736.28	6	43,900	94,700	810.70	25	43,200
84,600	945.45	9	16,600	105,600	891.33	20	52,600
97,600	821.07	24	40,700	104,100	864.38	7	42,700

continued

Loan	Monthly Payments	Payments Made	Auction Price	Loan	Monthly Payments	Payments Made	Auction Price
$104,400	$ 983.27	26	$63,100	$ 85,700	$1074.73	30	$22,200
113,800	1075.54	19	72,600	113,600	871.61	24	77,000
116,400	1087.16	35	72,300	119,400	1021.23	58	69,000
100,000	900.01	33	58,100	90,600	836.46	3	35,600
92,800	683.11	36	37,100	104,500	1056.37	22	63,000

    a. Carry out a global test of hypothesis to verify if any of the regression coefficients are different from zero.

    b. Do an individual test of the independent variables. Would you remove any of the variables?

    c. If it seems one or more of the independent variables is not needed, remove it and work out the revised regression equation.

34. Think about the figures from the previous exercise. Add a new variable that describes the potential interaction between the loan amount and the number of payments made. Then do a test of hypothesis to check if the interaction is significant.

Data Set Exercises

35. Refer to the Real Estate data, which report information on homes sold in the Denver, Colorado, area during the last year. Use the selling price of the home as the dependent variable and determine the regression equation with number of bedrooms, size of the house, whether there is a pool, whether there is an attached garage, distance from the center of the city, and number of bathrooms as independent variables.

    a. Write out the regression equation. Discuss each of the variables. For example, are you surprised that the regression coefficient for distance from the center of the city is negative? How much does a garage or a swimming pool add to the selling price of a home?

    b. Determine the value of R^2. Interpret.

    c. Develop a correlation matrix. Which independent variables have strong or weak correlations with the dependent variable? Do you see any problems with multicollinearity?

    d. Conduct the global test on the set of independent variables. Interpret.

    e. Conduct a test of hypothesis on each of the independent variables. Would you consider deleting any of the variables? If so, which ones?

    f. Rerun the analysis until only significant regression coefficients remain in the analysis. Identify these variables.

    g. Develop a histogram or a stem-and-leaf display of the residuals from the final regression equation developed in part (f). Is it reasonable to conclude that the normality assumption has been met?

    h. Plot the residuals against the fitted values from the final regression equation developed in part (f) against the fitted values of Y. Plot the residuals on the vertical axis and the fitted values on the horizontal axis.

36. Refer to the Baseball 2007 data, which report information on the 30 Major League Baseball teams for the 2007 season. Let the number of games won be the dependent variable and the following variables be independent variables: team batting average, number of stolen bases, number of errors committed, team ERA, number of home runs, and whether the team's home field is natural grass or artificial turf.

    a. Write out the regression equation. Discuss each of the variables. For example, are you surprised that the regression coefficient for ERA is negative? How many wins does playing on natural grass for a home field add to or subtract from the total wins for the season?

    b. Determine the value of R^2. Interpret.

    c. Develop a correlation matrix. Which independent variables have strong or weak correlations with the dependent variable? Do you see any problems with multicollinearity?

    d. Conduct a global test on the set of independent variables. Interpret.

    e. Conduct a test of hypothesis on each of the independent variables. Would you consider deleting any of the variables? If so, which ones?

    f. Rerun the analysis until only significant net regression coefficients remain in the analysis. Identify these variables.

    g. Develop a histogram or a stem-and-leaf display of the residuals from the final regression equation developed in part (f). Is it reasonable to conclude that the normality assumption has been met?

    h. Plot the residuals against the fitted values from the final regression equation developed in part (f) against the fitted values of Y. Plot the residuals on the vertical axis and the fitted values on the horizontal axis.

37. Refer to the Wage data, which report information on annual wages for a sample of 100 workers. Also included are variables relating to industry, years of education, and gender for each worker. Determine the regression equation using annual wage as the dependent variable and years of education, gender, years of work experience, age in years, and whether or not the worker is a union member.

    a. Write out the regression equation. Discuss each variable.

    b. Determine and interpret the R^2 value.

    c. Develop a correlation matrix. Which independent variables have strong or weak correlations with the dependent variable? Do you see any problems with multicollinearity?

    d. Conduct a global test of hypothesis on the set of independent variables. Interpret your findings. Is it reasonable to continue with the analysis or should you stop here?

    e. Conduct a test of hypothesis on each of the independent variables. Would you consider deleting any of these variables? If so, which ones?

    f. Rerun the analysis deleting any of the independent variables that are not significant. Delete the variables one at a time.

    g. Develop a histogram or a stem-and-leaf chart of the residuals from the final regression equation. Is it reasonable to conclude that the normality assumption has been met?

    h. Plot the residuals against the fitted values from the final regression equation. Plot the residuals on the vertical axis and the fitted values on the horizontal axis.

38. Refer to the CIA data, which report demographic and economic information on 46 countries. Let unemployment be the dependent variable and percent of the population over 65, life expectancy, and literacy be the independent variables.

    a. Determine the regression equation using a software package. Write out the regression equation.

    b. What is the value of the coefficient of determination?

    c. Check the independent variables for multicollinearity.

    d. Conduct a global test on the set of independent variables.

    e. Test each of the independent variables to determine if they differ from zero.

    f. Would you delete any of the independent variables? If so, rerun the regression analysis and report the new equation.

    g. Make a histogram of the residuals from your final regression equation. Is it reasonable to conclude that the residuals follow a normal distribution?

    h. Plot the residuals versus the fitted values and check. Are there any problems?

Software Commands

Note: We do not show steps for all the statistical software used in this chapter. Below are the first two, which show the basic steps.

  1. The MINITAB commands for the multiple regression output on page 509 are:

    a. Import the data from the CD. The file name is **Tbl14–1.**

    b. Select **Stat, Regression,** and then click on **Regression.**

    c. Select *Cost* as the **Response** variable, and *Temp, Insul,* and *Age* as the **Predictors,** then click on **OK.**

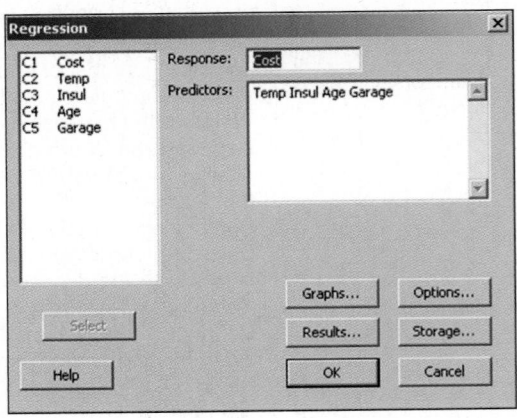

2. The Excel commands to produce the multiple regression output on page 509 are:
   a. Import the data from the CD. The file name is **Tbl14**.
   b. Select the **Data** tab on the top menu. Then on the far right, select **Data analysis**. Select **Regression** and click **OK**.
   c. Make the **Input Y Range** *A1:A21*, the **Input X Range** *B1:D21*, check the **Labels** box, the **Output Range** is *G1*, then click **OK**.

Chapter 14   Answers to Self-Review

14–1 a. $389,500 or 389.5 (in $000); found by
$$2.5 + 3(40) + 4(72) - 3(10) + .2(20) + 1(5)$$
$$= 3895$$
   b. The b_2 of 4 shows profit will go up $4,000 for each extra hour the restaurant is open (if none of the other variables change). The b_3 of -3 implies profit will fall $3,000 for each added mile away from the central area (if none of the other variables change).

14–2 a. The total degrees of freedom $(n - 1)$ is 25. So the sample size is 26.
   b. There are 5 independent variables.
   c. There is only 1 dependent variable (profit).
   d. $S_{Y.12345} = 1.414$, found by $\sqrt{2}$ Ninety-five percent of the residuals will be between -2.828 and 2.828, found by $\pm 2(1.414)$.
   e. $R^2 = .714$, found by $100/140$. 71.4% of the deviation in profit is accounted for by these five variables.
   f. $R_{adj}^2 = .643$, found by
$$1 - \left[\frac{40}{(26 - (5 + 1))} \right] \Big/ \left[\frac{140}{(26 - 1)} \right]$$

14–3 a. $H_0: \beta_1 = \beta_2 = \beta_3 = \beta_4 = \beta_5 = 0$
   H_1: Not all of the β's are 0.
   The decision rule is to reject H_0 if $F > 2.71$. The computed value of F is 10, found by $20/2$. So, you reject H_0, which indicates at least one of the regression coefficients is different from zero.

   b. For variable 1: $H_0: \beta_1 = 0$ and $H_1: \beta_1 \neq 0$
   The decision rule is: Reject H_0 if $t < -2.086$ or $t > 2.086$. Since 2.000 does not go beyond either of those limits. We fail to reject the null hypothesis. This regression coefficient could be zero. We can consider dropping this variable. By parallel logic the null hypothesis is rejected for variables 3 and 4.
   c. We should consider dropping variables 1, 2 and 5. Variable 5 has the smallest absolute value of t. So delete it first and refigure the regression analysis.

14–4 a. $\hat{Y} = 15.7625 + 0.4415X_1 + 3.8598X_2$
   $\hat{Y} = 15.7625 + 0.4415(30) + 3.8598(1)$
   $= 32.87$
   b. Female agents make $3,860 more than male agents.
   c. $H_0: \beta_3 = 0$
   $H_1: \beta_3 \neq 0$
   $df = 17$, reject H_0 if $t < -2.110$ or $t > 2.110$
   $$t = \frac{3.8598 - 0}{1.4724} = 2.621$$
   Reject H_0. Gender should be included in the regression equation.

A Review of Chapters 13 and 14

Simple regression and correlation examine the relationship between two variables.

This section is a review of the major concepts and terms introduced in Chapters 13 and 14. Chapter 13 noted that the strength of the relationship between the independent variable and the dependent variable can be measured by the *coefficient of correlation*. The coefficient of correlation is designated by the letter *r*. It can assume any value between −1.00 and +1.00 inclusive. Coefficients of −1.00 and +1.00 indicate perfect relationship, and 0 indicates no relationship. A value near 0, such as −.14 or .14, indicates a weak relationship. A value near −1 or +1, such as −.90 or +.90, indicates a strong relationship. Squaring *r* gives the *coefficient of determination,* also called r^2. It indicates the proportion of the total variation in the dependent variable explained by the independent variable.

Multiple regression and correlation is concerned with relationship between two or more independent variables and the dependent variable.

Likewise, the strength of the relationship between several independent variables and a dependent variable is measured by the *coefficient of multiple determination, R^2*. It measures the proportion of the variation in Y explained by two or more independent variables.

The linear relationship in the simple case involving one independent variable and one dependent variable is described by the equation $\hat{Y} = a + bx$. For three independent variables, X_1, X_2, and X_3, the same multiple regression equation is

$$\hat{Y} = a + b_1X_1 + b_2X_2 + \cdots + b_kX_k$$

Computer invaluable in multiple regression and correlation.

Solving for $b_1, b_2, \cdots, b_k$ would involve tedious calculations. Fortunately, this type of problem can be quickly solved using one of the many statistical software packages and spreadsheet packages. Various measures, such as the coefficient of determination, the multiple standard error of estimate, the results of the global test, and the test of the individual variables, are reported in the output of most computer software programs.

Glossary

Chapter 13
Coefficient of correlation A measure of the strength of association between two variables.

Coefficient of determination The proportion of the total variation in the dependent variable that is explained by the independent variable. It can assume any value between 0 and +1.00 inclusive. This coefficient is computed by squaring the coefficient of correlation, *r*.

Correlation analysis A group of statistical techniques used to measure the strength of the relationship between two variables.

Dependent variable The variable that is being predicted or estimated.

Independent variable A variable that provides the basis for estimation.

Least squares method A technique used to arrive at the regression equation by minimizing the sum of the squares of the vertical distances between the actual Y values and the predicted Y values.

Linear regression equation A mathematical equation that defines the relationship between two variables. It has the form $\hat{Y} = a + bX$. It is used to predict Y based on a selected X value. Y is the dependent variable and X the independent variable.

Scatter diagram A chart that visually depicts the relationship between two variables.

Standard error of estimate Measures the dispersion of the actual Y values about the regression line. It is reported in the same units as the dependent variable.

t test of significance of *r* A formula to answer the question: Is the correlation in the population from which the sample was selected zero? The test statistic is *t*, and the number of degrees of freedom is $n − 2$.

$$t = \frac{r\sqrt{n - 2}}{\sqrt{1 - r^2}} \qquad \textbf{[13–2]}$$

Chapter 14
Autocorrelation Correlation of successive residuals. This condition frequently occurs when time is involved in the analysis.

Correlation matrix A listing of all possible simple coefficients of correlation. A correlation matrix includes the correlations between each of the independent variables and the dependent variable, as well as those among all the independent variables.

Dummy variable A qualitative variable. It can assume only one of two possible outcomes.

Global test A test used to determine if any of the set of independent variables have regression coefficients different from zero.

Homoscedasticity The standard error of estimate is the same for all fitted values of the dependent variable.

Individual test A test to determine if a particular independent variable has a regression coefficient different from zero.

Interaction The case in which one independent variable (such as X_2) affects the relationship between another independent variable (X_1) and the dependent variable (Y).

Multicollinearity A condition that occurs in multiple regression analysis if the independent variables are themselves correlated.

Multiple regression equation The relationship in the form of a mathematical equation between several independent variables and a dependent variable. The general form is $\hat{Y} = a + b_1X_1 + b_2X_2 + b_3X_3 + \cdots + b_kX_k$. It is used to estimate Y given k independent variables, X_i.

Qualitative variables A nominal-scale variable that is coded to assume only one of two possible outcomes. For example, a person is considered either employed or unemployed.

Residual The difference between the actual value of the dependent variable and the estimated value of the dependent variable, that is, $Y - \hat{Y}$.

Stepwise regression A step-by-step process for finding the regression equation. Only independent variables with nonzero regression coefficients enter the regression equation. Independent variables are added one at a time to the regression equation.

Variance inflation factor A test used to detect correlation among independent variables.

Exercises

connect **Part I—Multiple Choice**

1. The strength of the association between a set of independent variables X and a dependent variable Y is measured by the
   a. Coefficient of correlation.
   b. Coefficient of determination.
   c. Standard error of estimate.
   d. All of the above.

2. The percent of total variation of the dependent variable Y explained by the set of independent variables X is measured by the
   a. Coefficient of correlation.
   b. Coefficient of determination.
   c. Standard error of estimate.
   d. Multicollinearity.

3. A coefficient of correlation is computed to be −0.90. This result means:
   a. The relationship between two variables is weak.
   b. The relationship between two variables is strong and positive.
   c. The relationship between two variables is strong and negative.
   d. The relationship between four variables is strong.

4. The coefficient of determination was computed to be .38 in a problem involving one independent variable and one dependent variable. This result means
   a. The relationship between the two variables is negative.
   b. The correlation coefficient is also .38.
   c. 38 percent of the total variation is explained by the independent variable.
   d. 38 percent of the total variation is explained by the dependent variable.

5. What is the relationship between the coefficient of correlation and the coefficient of determination?
   a. They are unrelated.
   b. The coefficient of determination is the coefficient of correlation squared.
   c. The coefficient of determination is the square root of the coefficient of correlation.
   d. They are equal.

6. Multicollinearity exists when
   a. Independent variables are correlated less than −0.70 or more than 0.70.
   b. An independent variable is strongly associated with a dependent variable.
   c. There is only one independent variable.
   d. The relationship between the dependent and independent variables is nonlinear.

7. If "time" is used as the independent variable in a simple linear regression analysis, which of the following assumptions could be violated?
   a. There is a linear relationship between the independent and dependent variables.
   b. The residual variation is the same for all fitted values of Y.
   c. The residuals are normally distributed.
   d. Successive observations of the dependent variable are uncorrelated.

8. In multiple regression, when the global test of significance is rejected, we can conclude:
   a. All of the net sample regression coefficients are equal to zero.
   b. All of the sample regression coefficients are not equal to zero.
   c. At least one sample regression coefficient is not equal to zero.
   d. The regression equation intersects the Y-axis at zero.

9. A residual is defined as:
   a. $Y - \hat{Y}$.
   b. Error sum of squares.
   c. Regression sum of squares.
   d. Type I error.

10. What test statistic is used for a global test of significance?
  a. z statistic.
  b. t statistic.
  c. Chi-square statistic.
  d. F statistic.

Part II—Problems

11. The accounting department at Crate and Barrel wishes to estimate the profit for each of the chain's many stores on the basis of the number of employees in the store, overhead costs, average markup, and theft loss. A few statistics from the stores are:

Store	Net Profit ($ thousands)	Number of Employees	Overhead Cost ($ thousands)	Average Markup (percent)	Theft Loss ($ thousands)
1	$846	143	$79	69%	$52
2	513	110	64	50	45

  a. The dependent variable is _____.
  b. The general equation for this problem is _____.
  c. The multiple regression equation was computed to be $\hat{Y} = 67 + 8X_1 - 10X_2 + 0.004X_3 - 3X_4$. What are predicted sales for a store with 112 employees, an overhead cost of $65,000, a markup rate of 50 percent, and a loss from theft of $50,000?
  d. Suppose R^2 was computed to be .86. Explain.
  e. Suppose that the multiple standard error of estimate was 3 (in $ thousands). Explain what this means in this problem.

12. Quick-print firms in a large downtown business area spend most of their advertising dollars on displays on bus benches. A research project involves predicting monthly sales based on the annual amount spent on placing ads on bus benches. A sample of quick-print firms revealed these advertising expenses and sales:

Firm	Annual Bus Bench Advertising ($ thousands)	Monthly Sales ($ thousands)
A	2	10
B	4	40
C	5	30
D	7	50
E	3	20

  a. Draw a scatter diagram.
  b. Determine the coefficient of correlation.
  c. What is the coefficient of determination?
  d. Compute the regression equation.
  e. Estimate the monthly sales of a quick-print firm that spends $4,500 on bus bench advertisements.
  f. Summarize your findings.

13. The following ANOVA output is given.

```
SOURCE        Sum of Squares      DF        MS
Regression         1050.8          4      262.70
Error                83.8         20        4.19
Total              1134.6         24

   Predictor            Coef    St.Dev.    t-ratio
   Constant            70.06       2.13      32.89
      X₁                0.42       0.17       2.47
      X₂                0.27       0.21       1.29
      X₃                0.75       0.30       2.50
      X₄                0.42       0.07       6.00
```

a. Compute the coefficient of determination.
b. Compute the multiple standard error of estimate.
c. Conduct a test of hypothesis to determine whether any of the regression coefficients are different from zero.
d. Conduct a test of hypothesis on the individual regression coefficients. Can any of the variables be deleted?

Cases

A. The Century National Bank

Refer to the Century National Bank data. Using checking account balance as the dependent variable and using as independent variables the number of ATM transactions, the number of other services used, whether the individual has a debit card, and whether interest is paid on the particular account, write a report indicating which of the variables seem related to the account balance and how well they explain the variation in account balances. Should all of the independent variables proposed be used in the analysis or can some be dropped?

B. Terry and Associates:
The Time to Deliver Medical Kits

Terry and Associates is a specialized medical testing center in Denver, Colorado. One of the firm's major sources of revenue is a kit used to test for elevated amounts of lead in the blood. Workers in auto body shops, those in the lawn care industry, and commercial house painters are exposed to large amounts of lead and thus must be randomly tested. It is expensive to conduct the test, so the kits are delivered on demand to a variety of locations throughout the Denver area.

Kathleen Terry, the owner, is concerned about setting appropriate costs for each delivery. To investigate, Ms. Terry gathered information on a random sample of 50 recent deliveries. Factors thought to be related to the cost of delivering a kit were:

Prep   The time in minutes between when the customized order is phoned into the company and when it is ready for delivery.

Delivery   The actual travel time in minutes from Terry's plant to the customer.

Mileage   The distance in miles from Terry's plant to the customer.

Sample Number	Cost	Prep	Delivery	Mileage
1	$32.60	10	51	20
2	23.37	11	33	12
3	31.49	6	47	19
4	19.31	9	18	8
5	28.35	8	88	17
6	22.63	9	20	11
7	22.63	9	39	11
8	21.53	10	23	10
9	21.16	13	20	8
10	21.53	10	32	10
11	28.17	5	35	16

Sample Number	Cost	Prep	Delivery	Mileage
12	$20.42	7	23	9
13	21.53	9	21	10
14	27.55	7	37	16
15	23.37	9	25	12
16	17.10	15	15	6
17	27.06	13	34	15
18	15.99	8	13	4
19	17.96	12	12	4
20	25.22	6	41	14
21	24.29	3	28	13
22	22.76	4	26	10
23	28.17	9	54	16
24	19.68	7	18	8
25	25.15	6	50	13
26	20.36	9	19	7
27	21.16	3	19	8
28	25.95	10	45	14
29	18.76	12	12	5
30	18.76	8	16	5
31	24.29	7	35	13
32	19.56	2	12	6
33	22.63	8	30	11
34	21.16	5	13	8
35	21.16	11	20	8
36	19.68	5	19	8
37	18.76	5	14	7
38	17.96	5	11	4
39	23.37	10	25	12
40	25.22	6	32	14
41	27.06	8	44	16
42	21.96	9	28	9
43	22.63	8	31	11
44	19.68	7	19	8
45	22.76	8	28	10
46	21.96	13	18	9
47	25.95	10	32	14
48	26.14	8	44	15
49	24.29	8	34	13
50	24.35	3	33	12

1. Develop a multiple linear regression equation that describes the relationship between the cost of delivery and the other variables. Do these three variables explain a reasonable amount of the variation in the

dependent variable? Estimate the delivery cost for a kit that takes 10 minutes for preparation, takes 30 minutes to deliver, and must cover a distance of 14 miles.
2. Test to determine that at least one net regression coefficient differs from zero. Also test to see whether any of

the variables can be dropped from the analysis. If some of the variables can be dropped, rerun the regression equation until only significant variables are included.
3. Write a brief report interpreting the final regression equation.

Practice Test

Part I—Objective

1. In a scatter diagram the dependent variable is always scaled on which axis?

   1. _____

2. What level of measurement is required to compute the coefficient of correlation?

   2. _____

3. If there is no correlation between two variables, what is the value of the coefficient of correlation?

   3. _____

4. Which of the following values indicates the strongest correlation between two variables? (0.65, −0.77, 0, −.12)

   4. _____

5. Under what conditions will the coefficient of determination assume a value greater than 1?

   5. _____

Given the following regression equation, $\hat{Y} = 7 - .5X$, and that the coefficient of determination is 0.81, answer questions 7, 8 and 9.

6. At what point does the regression equation cross the Y-axis?　　6. _____

7. An increase of 1 unit in the independent variable will result in what amount of an increase or decrease in the dependent variable?

   7. _____

8. What is the coefficient of correlation? (Be careful of the sign.)　　8. _____

9. If all the data points in a scatter diagram were on the regression line, what would be the value of the standard error of estimate?

   9. _____

10. In a multiple regression equation, what is the maximum number of independent variables allowed? (2, 10, 30, unlimited)

    10. _____

11. In multiple regression analysis we assume what type of relationship between the dependent variable and the set of independent variables? (linear, multiple, curved, none of these)

    11. _____

12. The difference between Y and $\hat{Y}$ is called a _____.　　12. _____

13. For a particular dummy variable, such as gender, how many different outcomes are possible?

    13. _____

14. What is the term given to a table that shows all possible coefficients of correlation between the dependent variable and all the independent variables and among all the independent variables?

    14. _____

15. If there is a linear relationship between the dependent variable and the set of independent variables a graph of the residuals will show what type of distribution?

    15. _____

Part II—Problems

1. Given the following software output.

Regression Analysis

ANOVA Table					
Source	SS	df	MS	F	p-value
Regression	129.7275	1	129.7275	14.50	.0007
Residual	250.4391	28	8.9443		
Total	380.1667	29			

Regression Output			
Variables	Coefficients	Standard Error	t (df = 28)
Intercept	90.6190	1.5322	59.141
Slope	−0.9401	0.2468	−3.808

  a. What is the sample size?
  b. Write out the regression equation. Interpret the slope and intercept values.
  c. If the value of the independent variable is 10, what is the value of the dependent variable?
  d. Calculate the coefficient of determination. Interpret this value.
  e. Calculate the coefficient of correlation. Conduct a test of hypothesis to determine if there is a significant negative association between the variables.
2. Given the following software output.

Regression Analysis

		ANOVA Table		
Source	**SS**	**df**	**MS**	**F**
Regression	227.0928	4	56.7732	9.27
Residual	153.0739	25	6.1230	
Total	380.1667	29		

		Regression Output	
Variables	**Coefficients**	**Standard Error**	**$t\,(df = 25)$**
Intercept	68.3366	8.9752	7.614
X1	0.8595	0.3087	2.784
X2	−0.3380	0.8381	−0.403
X3	−0.8179	0.2749	−2.975
X4	−0.5824	0.2541	−2.292

  a. How large is the sample size?
  b. How many independent variables are in the study?
  c. Determine the coefficient of determination.
  d. Conduct a global test of hypothesis. Can you conclude at least one of the independent variables does not equal zero? Use the .01 significance level.
  e. Conduct an individual test of hypothesis on each of the independent variables. Would you consider dropping any of the independent variables? If so, which variable or variables would you drop? Use the .01 significance level.

15

Index Numbers

Information for food items for the years 2000 and 2008 are provided in Exercise 27. Compute a simple price index for each of the four items, using 2000 as the base period. (Exercise 27, Goal 2)

Introduction

In this chapter we will examine a useful descriptive tool called an **index.** An index expresses the relative change in a value from one period to another. No doubt you are familiar with indexes such as the **Consumer Price Index,** which is released monthly by the U.S. Department of Labor. There are many other indexes, such as the **Dow Jones Industrial Average** (DJIA), **Nasdaq, NIKKEI 225,** and **Standard & Poor's 500 Stock Average.** Indexes are published on a regular basis by the federal government, by business publications such as *BusinessWeek* and *Forbes,* in most daily newspapers, and on the Internet.

Of what importance is an index? Why is the Consumer Price Index so important and so widely reported? As the name implies, it measures the change in the price of a large group of items consumers purchase. The Federal Reserve Board,

consumer groups, unions, management, senior citizens organizations, and others in business and economics are very concerned about changes in prices. These groups closely monitor the Consumer Price Index as well as the **Producer Price Index,** which measures price fluctuations at all stages of production. To combat sharp price increases, the Federal Reserve often raises the interest rate to "cool down" the economy. Likewise, the Dow Jones Industrial Average, which is updated continuously during the business day, describes the overall change in common stock prices of 30 large companies.

A few stock market indexes appear daily in the financial section of most newspapers. Many are reported in real time such as in the business section of *USA Today*'s website (http://www.usatoday.com/money/default.htm). Shown below are the Dow Jones Industrial Average, Nasdaq, and S&P 500 from the *USA Today* website.

Market Summary				
Latest Market Numbers				
Index	Last	Change	% change	YTD
DOW	11,268.92	▲ 38.19	0.34%	-15.05%
NASDAQ	2,228.70	▲ 18.89	0.85%	-15.97%
S&P 500	1,232.04	▲ 7.53	0.61%	-16.09%
Quotes as of 4:04 PM ET				© BigCharts

Stock Indexes
■ Dow Jones
Nasdaq
S&P 500
USA TODAY Internet 50

11,400
11,350
11,300
11,250
11,200
10 11 12 1 2 3

Simple Index Numbers

What is an index number? An index or index number measures the change in a particular item (typically a product or service) between two time periods.

> **INDEX NUMBER** A number that expresses the relative change in price, quantity, or value compared to a base period.

If the index number is used to measure the relative change in just one variable, such as hourly wages in manufacturing, we refer to this as a simple index. It is the ratio of two variables and that ratio converted to a percentage. The following four examples will serve to illustrate the use of index numbers. As noted in the definition, the main use of an index number in business is to show the percent change in one or more items from one time period to another.

Example

According to the Bureau of Labor Statistics, in January 2000 the average hourly earnings of production workers was $13.75. In March 2008 it was $17.87. What is the index of hourly earnings of production workers for March 2008 based on January 2000?

Solution

It is 129.96, found by:

$$P = \frac{\text{Average hourly earnings in March 2008}}{\text{Average hourly earnings in January 2000}}(100)$$

$$= \frac{\$17.87}{\$13.75}(100) = 129.96$$

Thus, the hourly earnings in March 2008 compared to January 2000 were 129.96 percent. This means there was a 29.96 percent increase in hourly earnings during the period, found by 129.96 − 100.0 = 29.96.

You can check the latest information on wages, the Consumer Price Indexes, and other business-related values at the Bureau of Labor Statistics (BLS) website, http://www.bls.gov. The following chart shows some statistics from the BLS.

Example

An index can also compare one item with another. The population of the Canadian province of British Columbia in 2007 was 4,352,798 and for Ontario it was 12,753,702. What is the population index of British Columbia compared to Ontario?

Solution

The index of population for British Columbia is 34.1, found by:

$$P = \frac{\text{Population of British Columbia}}{\text{Population of Ontario}}(100) = \frac{4,352,798}{12,753,702}(100) = 34.1$$

This indicates that the population of British Columbia is 34.1 percent (about one-third) of the population of Ontario, or the population of British Columbia is 65.9 percent less than the population of Ontario (100 − 34.1 = 65.9).

Example	The following Excel output shows the number of passengers (in millions) for the five largest airports in the United States in 2007. What is the index for Atlanta, Chicago, Los Angeles, and Dallas/Ft. Worth compared to John F. Kennedy International in New York?

Airport Indices

	A	B	C	D	E	F	G	H	I	J
1	Airport	Number of Passengers	Index							
2	Hartsfield_Jackson Atlanta Internationat Airport (ATL)	89.4	150.0							
3	O'Hare International Airport (ORD)	76.1	127.7							
4	Los Angeles International Airport (LAX)	61.9	103.9							
5	Dallas-Fort Worth International Airport (DFW)	59.9	100.5							
6	John F. Kennedy International Airport (JFK)	59.6	100.0							
7										
8										
9										
10										
11										

Number of Passengers at the Five Busiest US Airports

[Excel]

Solution	To find the four indexes, we divide the passengers for Atlanta, Chicago, Los Angeles, and Dallas/Ft. Worth by the number at JFK. We conclude that Atlanta had 50.0 percent more passengers than JFK, Chicago 27.7 percent more, Los Angeles 3.9 percent more, and Dallas/Ft. Worth 0.5 percent more.

Airport	Number of Passengers (millions)	Index	Found by
Hartsfield-Jackson Atlanta International Airport (ATL)	89.4	150.0	(89.4/59.6)(100)
O'Hare International Airport (ORD)	76.1	127.7	(76.1/59.6)(100)
Los Angeles International Airport (LAX)	61.9	103.9	(61.9/59.6)(100)
Dallas/Fort Worth International Airport (DFW)	59.9	100.5	(59.9/59.6)(100)
John F. Kennedy International Airport (JFK)	59.6	100.0	(59.6/59.6)(100)

Note from the previous discussion that:

1. The index of average hourly earnings of production workers (129.96), is a percent but the percent symbol is usually omitted.
2. Each index has a **base period.** In the example regarding the average hourly earnings of production workers, we used January 2000 as the base period. The base period for the Consumer Price Index is 1993–95. The parity ratio, which is the ratio of the prices received by farmers to the prices paid by farmers, still has 1910–14 as the base period. See http://agriculture.house.gov/info/glossary/p.htm.
3. Most business and economic indexes are computed to the nearest whole number, such as 214 or 96, or to the nearest tenth of a percent, such as 83.4 or 118.7.

Why Convert Data to Indexes?

Indexes allow us to express a change in price, quantity, or value as a percent.

Compiling index numbers is not a recent innovation. An Italian, G. R. Carli, is credited with originating index numbers in 1764. They were incorporated in a report he made regarding price fluctuations in Europe from 1500 to 1750. No systematic approach to collecting and reporting data in index form was evident in the United States until about 1900. The cost-of-living index (now called the Consumer Price Index) was introduced in 1913, and a long list of indexes has been compiled since then.

Why convert data to indexes? An index is a convenient way to express a change in a diverse group of items. The Consumer Price Index (CPI), for example, encompasses about 400 items—including golf balls, lawn mowers, hamburgers, funeral services, and dentists' fees. Prices are expressed in dollars per pound, box, yard, and many other different units. Only by converting the prices of these many diverse goods and services to one index number can the federal government and others concerned with inflation keep informed of the overall movement of consumer prices.

Converting data to indexes also makes it easier to assess the trend in a series composed of exceptionally large numbers. For example, the estimate of U.S. retail e-commerce sales for the fourth quarter of 2007, adjusted for seasonal variation, was $36,200,000. e-Commerce sales for the fourth quarter of 2006 was $30,700,000. This is an increase of $5,500,000. If e-commerce sales for the fourth quarter of 2007 are expressed as an index based on the fourth quarter of 2006, the increase is 17.9 percent.

$$\frac{\text{4th qtr 2007 e-commerce sales}}{\text{4th qtr 2006 e-commerce sales}} (100) = \frac{\$36,200,000}{\$30,700,000} (100) = 117.9$$

Construction of Index Numbers

We already discussed the construction of a simple price index. The price in a selected year (such as 2008) is divided by the price in the base year. The base-period price is designated as p_0, and a price other than the base period is often referred to as the *given period* or *selected period* and designated p_t. To calculate the simple price index P using 100 as the base value for any given period use the formula:

SIMPLE INDEX	$P = \dfrac{p_t}{p_0} \times 100$	[15–1]

Suppose the price of a fall weekend package (including lodging and all meals) at Tryon Mountain Lodge in western North Carolina in 2000 was $450. The price rose to $795 in 2008. What is the price index for 2008 using 2000 as the base period and 100 as the base value? It is 176.7, found by:

$$P = \frac{p_t}{p_0} (100) = \frac{\$795}{\$450} (100) = 176.7$$

Interpreting this result, the price of the fall weekend package increased 76.7 percent from 2000 to 2008.

The base period need not be a single year. Note in Table 15–1 that if we use 2000–01 = 100, the base price for the stapler would be $21 [found by determining the mean price of 2000 and 2001, ($20 + $22)/2 = $21]. The prices $20, $22, and $23 are averaged if 2000–02 is selected as the base. The mean price would be $21.67. The indexes constructed using the three different base periods are presented in Table 15–1. (Note that when 2000–02 = 100, the index numbers for 2000, 2001, and 2002 average 100.0, as we would expect.) Logically, the index numbers for 2008 using the three different bases are not the same.

TABLE 15–1 Prices of a Benson Automatic Stapler, Model 3, Converted to Indexes Using Three Different Base Periods

Year	Price of Stapler	Price Index (2000 = 100)	Price Index (2000–01 = 100)	Price Index (2000–02 = 100)
1995	$18	90.0	$\frac{18}{21} \times 100 = 85.7$	$\frac{18}{21.67} \times 100 = 83.1$
2000	20	100.0	$\frac{20}{21} \times 100 = 95.2$	$\frac{20}{21.67} \times 100 = 92.3$
2001	22	110.0	$\frac{22}{21} \times 100 = 104.8$	$\frac{22}{21.67} \times 100 = 101.5$
2002	23	115.0	$\frac{23}{21} \times 100 = 109.5$	$\frac{23}{21.67} \times 100 = 106.1$
2008	38	190.0	$\frac{38}{21} \times 100 = 181.0$	$\frac{38}{21.67} \times 100 = 175.4$

Self-Review 15–1

1. Listed below are the top steel-producing nations, in millions of tons, for the year 2008. Express the amount produced by China, the European Union, Japan, and Russia as an index, using the United States as a base. What percent more steel does China produce than the United States?

Nation	Amount (millions of tons)
China	197
European Union	144
Japan	103
United States	78
Russia	52

2. The average hourly earnings of production workers for January of selected years are given below.

Year	Average Hourly Earnings
1995	$11.47
2000	13.73
2003	15.19
2005	15.88
2006	16.40
2008	17.87

(a) Using 1995 as the base period and 100 as the base value, determine the indexes for the other years. Interpret the index.
(b) Use the average of 1995 and 2000 as the base and determine indexes for the other years. Interpret the index.

Exercises

connect

1. PNC Bank, Inc., which has its headquarters in Pittsburgh, Pennsylvania, reported $17,446 (million) in commercial loans in 1995, $19,989 in 1997, $21,468 in 1999, $21,685 in 2000, $15,922 in 2002 and $18,375 for 2004. Using 1995 as the base, develop a simple index

for the change in the amount of commercial loans for the years 1997, 1999, 2000, 2002 and 2004, based on 1995.

2. The table below reports the earnings per share of common stock for Home Depot Inc. for recent years. Develop an index, with 2001 as the base, for the change in earnings per share over the period.

Year	Earnings per Share	Year	Earnings per Share
2001	$1.29	2005	$2.72
2002	1.56	2006	2.63
2003	1.88	2007	2.55
2004	2.26	2008	2.27

3. Listed below are the net sales for Blair Corporation, a mail-order retailer located in Warren, Pennsylvania, for the years 1997 to 2006. In 2007 Blair became a subsidiary of Appleseed's Topco. Its website is www.blair.com. Use the mean sales for the earliest three years to determine a base and then find the index for 2003 and 2006. By how much have net sales increased from the base period?

Year	Sales (millions)	Year	Sales (millions)
1997	$486.6	2002	$568.5
1998	506.8	2003	581.9
1999	522.2	2004	496.1
2000	574.6	2005	456.6
2001	580.7	2006	433.3

4. In January 1994 the price for a whole fresh chicken was $0.899 per pound. In July 2008 the price for the same chicken was $1.989 per pound. Use the January 1994 price as the base period and 100 as the base value to develop a simple index. By what percent has the cost of chicken increased?

Unweighted Indexes

In many situations we wish to combine several items and develop an index to compare the cost of this aggregation of items in two different time periods. For example, we might be interested in an index for items that relate to the expense of operating and maintaining an automobile. The items in the index might include tires, oil changes, and gasoline prices. Or we might be interested in a college student index. This index might include the cost of books, tuition, housing, meals, and entertainment. There are several ways we can combine the items to determine the index.

Simple Average of the Price Indexes

Table 15–2 on the next page reports the prices for several food items for the years 1999 and 2009. We would like to develop an index for this group of food items for 2009, using 1999 as the base. This is written in the abbreviated code 1999 = 100.

We could begin by computing a **simple average of the price indexes** for each item, using 1999 as the base year and 2009 as the given year. The simple index for bread is 147.1, found by using formula (15–1).

$$P = \frac{p_t}{p_0}(100) = \frac{1.28}{.87}(100) = 147.1$$

We compute the simple index for the other items in Table 15–2 similarly. The largest price increase was for eggs, 106.7 percent, and bread was second with 47.1 percent.

TABLE 15–2 Computation of Index for Food Price 2009, 1999 = 100

Item	1999 Price	2009 Price	Simple Index
Bread, white, cost per pound	$ 0.87	$ 1.28	147.1
Eggs, dozen	1.05	2.17	206.7
Milk, gallon, white	2.94	3.87	131.6
Apples, Red Delicious, 1 pound	0.86	1.16	134.9
Orange Juice, 12 oz concentrate	1.75	2.54	145.1
Coffee, 100% ground roast, 1 pound	3.43	3.68	107.3
Total	$10.90	$14.70	

The price of coffee increased 7.3 percent found by 107.3 − 100 = 7.3. Then it would be natural to average the simple indexes. The formula is:

$$\text{SIMPLE AVERAGE OF THE PRICE RELATIVES} \qquad P = \frac{\Sigma P_i}{n} \qquad [15\text{–}2]$$

where P_i refers to the simple index for each of the items and n the number of items. In our example the index is 145.5, found by:

$$P = \frac{\Sigma P_i}{n} = \frac{147.1 + \cdots + 107.3}{6} = \frac{872.7}{6} = 145.5$$

This indicates that the mean of the group of indexes increased 45.5 percent from 1999 to 2009.

A positive feature of the simple average of price indexes is that we would obtain the same value for the index regardless of the units of measure. In the above index, if apples were priced in tons, instead of pounds, the impact of apples on the combined index would not change. That is, the commodity "apples" represents one of six items in the index, so the impact of the item is not related to the units. A negative feature of this index is that it fails to consider the relative importance of the items included in the index. For example, milk and eggs receive the same weight, even though a typical family might spend far more over the year on milk than on eggs.

Simple Aggregate Index

A second possibility is to sum the prices (rather than the indexes) for the two periods and then determine the index based on the totals. The formula is:

$$\text{SIMPLE AGGREGATE INDEX} \qquad P = \frac{\Sigma p_t}{\Sigma p_0} \times 100 \qquad [15\text{–}3]$$

This is called a **simple aggregate index.** The index for the above food items is found by summing the prices in 1999 and 2009. The sum of the prices for the base period is $10.90 and for the given period it is $14.70. The simple aggregate index is 134.9. This means that the aggregate group of prices had increased 34.9 percent in the 10-year period.

$$P = \frac{\Sigma p_t}{\Sigma p_0}(100) = \frac{\$14.70}{\$10.90}(100) = 134.9$$

Because the value of a simple aggregate index can be influenced by the units of measurement, it is not used frequently. In our example the value of the index would differ significantly if we were to report the price of apples in tons rather than pounds.

Also, note the effect of coffee on the total index. For both the current year and the base year, coffee is a significant contributor to the total index, so a change in the price of coffee will drive the index much more than any other item. So we need a way to appropriately "weight" the items according to their relative importance.

Weighted Indexes

Two methods of computing a **weighted price index** are the **Laspeyres** method and the **Paasche** method. They differ only in the period used for weighting. The Laspeyres method uses *base-period weights;* that is, the original prices and quantities of the items bought are used to find the percent change over a period of time in either price or quantity consumed, depending on the problem. The Paasche method uses *current-year weights.*

Laspeyres Price Index

Etienne Laspeyres developed a method in the latter part of the 18th century to determine a weighted price index using base-period quantities as weights. Applying his method, a weighted price index is computed by:

LASPEYRES PRICE INDEX	$P = \dfrac{\Sigma p_t q_0}{\Sigma p_0 q_0} \times 100$	[15–4]

where
  P is the price index.
  p_t is the current price.
  p_0 is the price in the base period.
  q_0 is the quantity used in the base period.

Example

The prices for the six food items from Table 15–2 are repeated below in Table 15–3. Also included is the number of units of each consumed by a typical family in 1999 and 2009.

TABLE 15–3 Price and Quantity of Food Items in 1999 and 2009

Item	1999 Price	1999 Quantity	2009 Price	2009 Quantity
Bread, white, cost per pound	$0.87	50	$1.28	55
Eggs, dozen	1.05	26	2.17	20
Milk, gallon, white	2.94	102	3.87	130
Apples, Red Delicious, 1 pound	0.86	30	1.16	40
Orange Juice, 12 oz concentrate	1.75	40	2.54	41
Coffee, 100% ground roast, 1 pound	3.43	12	3.68	12

Determine a weighted price index using the Laspeyres method. Interpret the result.

Solution

First we determine the total amount spent for the six items in the base period, 1999. To find this value we multiply the base period price for bread ($0.87) by the base period quantity of 50. The result is $43.50. This indicates that a total of $43.50 was spent in the base period on bread. We continue that for all items and total the results. The base period total is $507.64. The current period total is computed in a similar fashion. For the first item, bread, we multiply the quantity in 1999 by the price of bread in 2009, that is, $1.28(50). The result is $64.00. We make the same calculation for each item and total the result. The total is $695.72. Because of the repetitive nature of these calculations, a spreadsheet is effective for carrying out the calculations. Following is a copy of the Excel output.

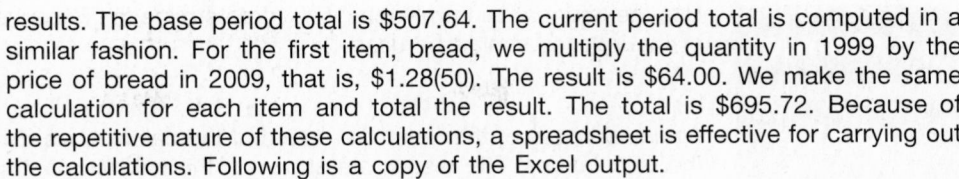

	A	B	C	D	E	F	G	H	I
					Laspeyres Index				
1									
2	Item	1999 Price	1999 Quantity		99 Price * '99 Quantity		2009 price		09 Price * '99 Quantity
3	Bread, white, cost per pound	$ 0.87	50		$ 43.50		$ 1.28		$ 64.00
4	Eggs, dozen	$ 1.05	26		$ 27.30		$ 2.17		$ 56.42
5	Milk, gallon, white	$ 2.94	102		$ 299.88		$ 3.87		$ 394.74
6	Apples, Red Delicious, 1 pound	$ 0.86	30		$ 25.80		$ 1.16		$ 34.80
7	Orange Juice, 12 oz concentrate	$ 1.75	40		$ 70.00		$ 2.54		$ 101.60
8	Coffee, 100% ground roast, 1 pound	$ 3.43	12		$ 41.16		$ 3.68		$ 44.16
9					$ 507.64				$ 695.72
10							P = 137.0		
11									

Excel

The weighted price index for 2009 is 137.0, found by

$$P = \frac{\Sigma p_t q_0}{\Sigma p_0 q_0}(100) = \frac{\$695.72}{\$507.64}(100) = 137.0$$

Based on this analysis we conclude that the price of this group of items has increased 37.0 percent in the ten-year period. The advantage of this method over the simple aggregate index is that the weight of each of the items is considered. In the simple aggregate index coffee had about 40 percent of the weight in determining the index. In the Laspeyres index the item with the most weight is milk, because the product of the price and the units sold is the largest.

Paasche Price Index

The major disadvantage of the Laspeyres index is it assumes that the base-period quantities are still realistic in the given period. That is, the quantities used for the six items are about the same in 1999 as 2009. In this case notice that the quantity of eggs purchased declined by 23 percent, the quantity of milk increased by nearly 28 percent, and the quantity of apples increased by 33 percent.

The Paasche index is an alternative. The procedure is similar, but instead of using base-period quantities as weights, we use current-period quantities as weights. We use the sum of the products of the 1999 prices and the 2009 quantities. This has the advantage of using the more recent quantities. If there has been a change in the quantities consumed since the base period, such a change is reflected in the Paasche index.

PAASCHE PRICE INDEX	$P = \dfrac{\Sigma p_t q_t}{\Sigma p_0 q_t} \times 100$	[15–5]

Example

Use the information from Table 15–3 to determine the Paasche index. Discuss which of the indexes should be used.

Solution

Again, because of the repetitive nature of the calculations, Excel is used to perform the calculations. The results are shown in the following output.

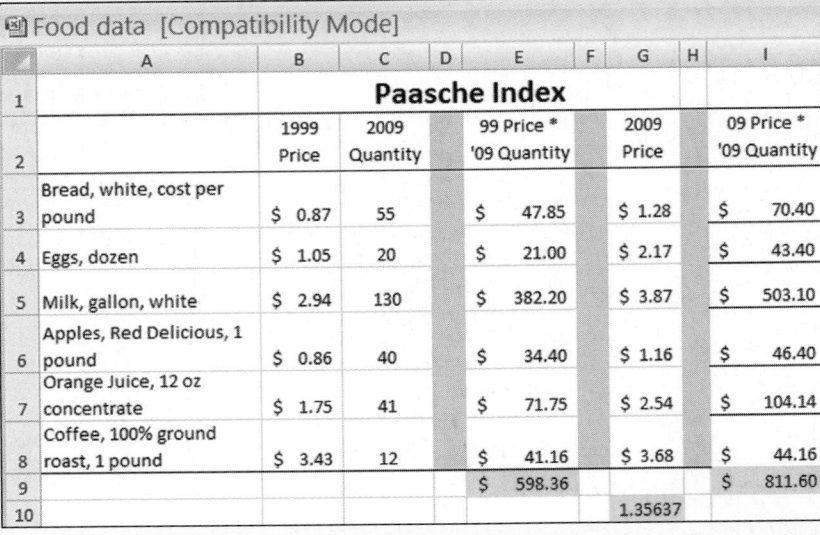

	1999 Price	2009 Quantity	99 Price * '09 Quantity	2009 Price	09 Price * '09 Quantity
Bread, white, cost per pound	$ 0.87	55	$ 47.85	$ 1.28	$ 70.40
Eggs, dozen	$ 1.05	20	$ 21.00	$ 2.17	$ 43.40
Milk, gallon, white	$ 2.94	130	$ 382.20	$ 3.87	$ 503.10
Apples, Red Delicious, 1 pound	$ 0.86	40	$ 34.40	$ 1.16	$ 46.40
Orange Juice, 12 oz concentrate	$ 1.75	41	$ 71.75	$ 2.54	$ 104.14
Coffee, 100% ground roast, 1 pound	$ 3.43	12	$ 41.16	$ 3.68	$ 44.16
			$ 598.36		$ 811.60
				1.35637	

The Paasche index is 135.6, found by

$$P = \frac{\Sigma p_t q_t}{\Sigma p_0 q_t}(100) = \frac{\$811.60}{\$598.36}(100) = 135.6$$

This result indicates that there has been an increase of 35.6 percent in the price of this "market basket" of goods between 1999 and 2009. That is, it costs 35.6 percent more to purchase these items in 2009 than it did in 1999. The Laspeyres index is more widely used because there are fewer pieces of data to update each period. The Consumer Price Index, the most widely reported index, is an example of a Laspeyres index.

How do we decide which index to use? When is Laspeyres most appropriate and when is Paasche the better choice?

Laspeyres

Advantages   Requires quantity data from only the base period. This allows a more meaningful comparison over time. The changes in the index can be attributed to changes in the price.

Disadvantages   Does not reflect changes in buying patterns over time. Also, it may overweight goods whose prices increase.

Paasche

Advantages   Because it uses quantities from the current period, it reflects current buying habits.

Disadvantages   It requires quantity data for the current year. Because different quantities are used each year, it is impossible to attribute changes in the index to changes in price alone. It tends to overweight the goods whose prices have declined. It requires the prices to be recomputed each year.

Fisher's Ideal Index

As noted above, Laspeyres' index tends to overweight goods whose prices have increased. Paasche's index, on the other hand, tends to overweight goods whose prices have gone down. In an attempt to offset these shortcomings, Irving Fisher, in his book *The Making of Index Numbers,* published in 1922, proposed an index called **Fisher's ideal index.** It is the geometric mean of the Laspeyres and Paasche indexes. We described the geometric mean in Chapter 3. It is determined by taking the kth root of the product of k positive numbers.

$$\text{Fisher's ideal index} = \sqrt{(\text{Laspeyres' index})(\text{Paasche's index})} \qquad \textbf{[15–6]}$$

Fisher's index seems to be theoretically ideal because it combines the best features of both Laspeyres' and Paasche's. That is, it balances the effects of the two indexes. However, it is rarely used in practice because it has the same basic set of problems as the Paasche index. It requires that a new set of quantities be determined for each period.

Example

Determine Fisher's ideal index for the data in Table 15–3.

Solution

Fisher's ideal index is 136.3.

$$\text{Fisher's ideal index} = \sqrt{(\text{Laspeyres' index})(\text{Paasche's index})}$$
$$= \sqrt{(137.0)(135.6)} = 136.3$$

Self-Review 15–2

An index of clothing prices for 2009 based on 2000 is to be constructed. The clothing items considered are shoes and dresses. The prices and quantities for both years is given below. Use 2000 as the base period and 100 as the base value.

Item	2000		2009	
	Price	Quantity	Price	Quantity
Dress (each)	$75	500	$85	520
Shoes (pair)	40	1,200	45	1,300

(a) Determine the simple average of the price indexes.
(b) Determine the aggregate price index for the two years.
(c) Determine Laspeyres' price index.
(d) Determine the Paasche price index.
(e) Determine Fisher's ideal index.

Exercises

connect

For exercises 5–8:
  a. Determine the simple price indexes.
  b. Determine the simple aggregate price index for the two years.
  c. Determine Laspeyres' price index.

  d. Determine the Paasche price index.
  e. Determine Fisher's ideal index.

5. Below are the prices of toothpaste (9 oz), shampoo (7 oz), cough tablets (package of 100), and antiperspirant (2 oz) for August 2000 and August 2008. Also included are the quantity purchased. Use August 2000 as the base.

	August 2000		August 2008	
Item	Price	Quantity	Price	Quantity
Toothpaste	$2.49	6	$3.35	6
Shampoo	3.29	4	4.49	5
Cough tablets	1.59	2	4.19	3
Antiperspirant	1.79	3	2.49	4

6. Fruit prices and the amounts consumed for 2000 and 2008 are below. Use 2000 as the base.

	2000		2008	
Fruit	Price	Quantity	Price	Quantity
Bananas (pound)	$0.23	100	$0.69	120
Grapefruit (each)	0.29	50	1.00	55
Apples (pound)	0.35	85	1.89	85
Strawberries (basket)	1.02	8	3.79	10
Oranges (bag)	0.89	6	2.99	8

7. The prices and the numbers of various items produced by a small machine and stamping plant are reported below. Use 2000 as the base.

	2000		2008	
Item	Price	Quantity	Price	Quantity
Washer	$0.07	17,000	$0.10	20,000
Cotter pin	0.04	125,000	0.03	130,000
Stove bolt	0.15	40,000	0.15	42,000
Hex nut	0.08	62,000	0.10	65,000

8. Following are the quantities and prices for the years 2000 and 2008 for Kinzua Valley Geriatrics. Use 2000 as the base period.

	2000		2008	
Item	Price	Quantity	Price	Quantity
Syringes (dozen)	$ 6.10	1,500	$ 6.83	2,000
Thermometers	8.10	10	9.35	12
Advil (bottle)	4.00	250	4.62	250
Patient record forms (box)	6.00	1,000	6.85	900
Computer paper (box)	12.00	30	13.65	40

Value Index

Value index measures percent change in value

A **value index** measures changes in both the price and quantities involved. A value index, such as the index of department store sales, considers the base-year prices, the base-year quantities, the present-year prices, and the present-year quantities for its construction. Its formula is:

> **VALUE INDEX** $$V = \frac{\Sigma p_t q_t}{\Sigma p_0 q_0} \times 100$$ [15–7]

Example

The prices and quantities sold at the Waleska Clothing Emporium for various items of apparel for May 2000 and May 2009 are:

Item	2000 Price, p_0	2000 Quantity Sold (thousands), q_0	2009 Price, p_t	2009 Quantity Sold (thousands), q_t
Ties (each)	$ 1	1,000	$ 2	900
Suits (each)	30	100	40	120
Shoes (pair)	10	500	8	500

What is the index of value for May 2009 using May 2000 as the base period?

Solution

Total sales in May 2009 were $10,600,000, and the comparable figure for 2000 is $9,000,000. (See Table 15–4.) Thus, the value index for May 2009 using 2000 = 100 is 117.8. The value of apparel sales in 2009 was 117.8 percent of the 2000 sales. To put it another way, the value of apparel sales increased 17.8 percent from May 2000 to May 2009.

$$V = \frac{\Sigma p_t q_t}{\Sigma p_0 q_0}(100) = \frac{\$10,600,000}{\$9,000,000}(100) = 117.8$$

TABLE 15–4 Construction of a Value Index for 2009 (2000 = 100)

Item	2000 Price, p_0	2000 Quantity Sold (thousands), q_0	$p_0 q_0$ ($ thousands)	2009 Price, p_t	2009 Quantity Sold (thousands), q_t	$p_t q_t$ ($ thousands)
Ties (each)	$ 1	1,000	$1,000	$ 2	900	$ 1,800
Suits (each)	30	100	3,000	40	120	4,800
Shoes (pair)	10	500	5,000	8	500	4,000
			$9,000			$10,600

Self-Review 15–3

The number of items produced by Houghton Products for 1996 and 2009 and the wholesale prices for the two periods are:

Item Produced	Price 1996	Price 2009	Number Produced 1996	Number Produced 2009
Shear pins (box)	$ 3	$4	10,000	9,000
Cutting compound (pound)	1	5	600	200
Tie rods (each)	10	8	3,000	5,000

(a) Find the value index of production for 2009 using 1996 as the base period.
(b) Interpret the index.

Exercises

connect™

9. The prices and production of grains for August 1995 and August 2008 are listed on the following page.

Grain	1995 Price	1995 Quantity Produced (millions of bushels)	2008 Price	2008 Quantity Produced (millions of bushels)
Oats	$1.52	200	$5.95	214
Wheat	2.10	565	9.80	489
Corn	1.48	291	6.00	203
Barley	3.05	87	3.29	106

Using 1995 as the base period, find the value index of grains produced for August 2008.

10. Johnson Wholesale Company manufactures a variety of products. The prices and quantities produced for April 1994 and April 2008 are:

Product	1994 Price	2008 Price	1994 Quantity Produced	2008 Quantity Produced
Small motor (each)	$23.60	$28.80	1,760	4,259
Scrubbing compound (gallon)	2.96	3.08	86,450	62,949
Nails (pound)	0.40	0.48	9,460	22,370

Using April 1994 as the base period, find the value index of goods produced for April 2008.

Special-Purpose Indexes

Many important indexes are prepared and published by private organizations. J. D. Power & Associates surveys automobile purchasers to determine how satisfied customers are with their vehicle after one year of ownership. This special index is called the *Consumer Satisfaction Index.* Financial institutions, utility companies, and university research centers often prepare indexes on employment, factory hours and wages, and retail sales for the regions they serve. Many trade associations prepare indexes of price and quantity that are vital to their particular area of interest. How are these special indexes prepared? An example, simplified of course, will help to explain some of the details.

Example

The Seattle Chamber of Commerce wants to develop a measure of general business activity for the northwest portion of the United States. The director of economic development has been assigned to develop the index. It will be called the *General Business Activity Index of the Northwest.*

Solution

After considerable thought and research, the director has concluded that four factors should be considered: the regional department store sales (which are reported in $ millions), the regional employment index (which has a 2000 base and is reported by the State of Washington), the freight car loadings (reported in millions), and exports for the Seattle Harbor (reported in thousands of tons). Recent information on these variables is reported in Table 15–5.

TABLE 15–5 Data for the Computation of the General Business Activity Index of the Northwest

Year	Department Store Sales	Index of Employment	Freight Car Loadings	Exports
1999	20	100	50	500
2004	41	110	30	900
2009	44	125	18	700

After review and consultation the director assigned weights of 40 percent to department store sales, 30 percent to employment, 10 percent to freight car loadings, and 20 percent to exports.

To develop the General Business Activity Index of the Northwest for 2009 using 1999 = 100, each 2009 value is expressed as a percentage, with the base-period value as the denominator. For illustration, department store sales for 2009 are converted to a percentage by ($44/$20)(100) = 220. This means that department store sales have increased 120 percent in the period. This percentage is then multiplied by the appropriate weight. For the department store sales this is (220)(.40) = 88.0. The details of the calculations for the years 2004 and 2009 are shown below.

	2004			2009	
Department store sales	($41/$20)(100)(.40) =	82.0		($44/$20)(100)(.40) =	88.0
Employment	(110/100)(100)(.30) =	33.0		(125/100)(100)(.30) =	37.5
Freight car loadings	(30/50)(100)(.10) =	6.0		(18/50)(100)(.10) =	3.6
Exports	(900/500)(100)(.20) =	36.0		(700/500)(100)(.20) =	28.0
Total		157.0			157.1

The General Business Activity Index of the Northwest for 2004 is 157.0 and for 2009 it is 157.1. Interpreting, business activity has increased 57.0 percent from 1999 to 2004 and 57.1 percent from the base period of 1999 to 2009.

As we stated at the start of the section, there are many special-purpose indexes. Here are a few examples.

Consumer Price Index

The U.S. Bureau of Labor Statistics reports this index monthly. It describes the changes in prices from one period to another for a "market basket" of goods and services. We discuss its history in detail and present some applications in the next section. You can access this information by going to www.bls.gov, then under **Inflation and Consumer Spending** select **Consumer Price Index,** then click on **Get Detailed CPI Statistics,** then select **All Urban Consumers (Current Series),** and then click on **U.S. all items 1982–84 = 100.** You may elect to include different periods. Following is a recent summary report.

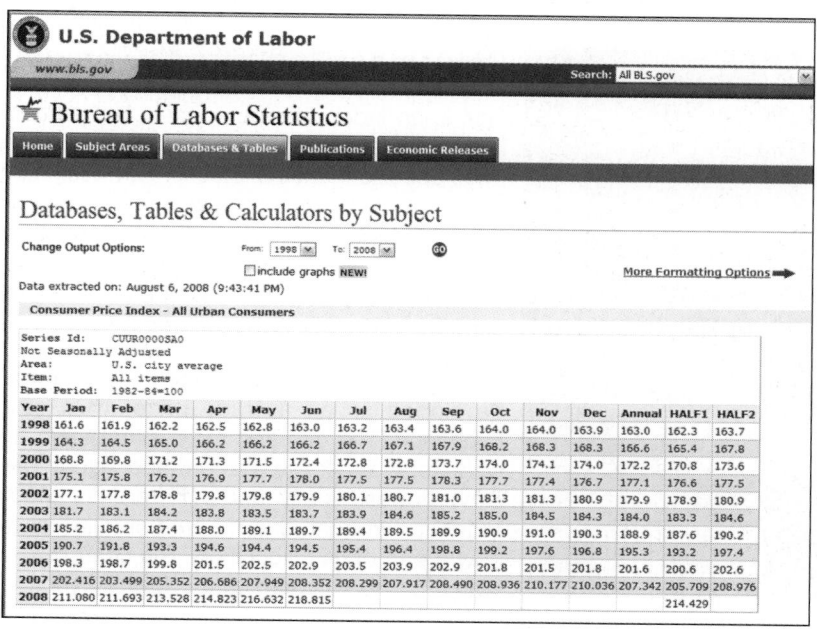

Year	Jan	Feb	Mar	Apr	May	Jun	Jul	Aug	Sep	Oct	Nov	Dec	Annual	HALF1	HALF2
1998	161.6	161.9	162.2	162.5	162.8	163.0	163.2	163.4	163.6	164.0	164.0	163.9	163.0	162.3	163.7
1999	164.3	164.5	165.0	166.2	166.2	166.2	166.7	167.1	167.9	168.2	168.3	168.3	166.6	165.4	167.8
2000	168.8	169.8	171.2	171.3	171.5	172.4	172.8	172.8	173.7	174.0	174.1	174.0	172.2	170.8	173.6
2001	175.1	175.8	176.2	176.9	177.7	178.0	177.5	177.5	178.3	177.7	177.4	176.7	177.1	176.6	177.5
2002	177.1	177.8	178.8	179.8	179.8	179.9	180.1	180.7	181.0	181.3	181.3	180.9	179.9	178.9	180.9
2003	181.7	183.1	184.2	183.8	183.5	183.7	183.9	184.6	185.2	185.0	184.5	184.3	184.0	183.3	184.6
2004	185.2	186.2	187.4	188.0	189.1	189.7	189.4	189.5	189.9	190.9	191.0	190.3	188.9	187.6	190.2
2005	190.7	191.8	193.3	194.6	194.4	194.5	195.4	196.4	198.8	199.2	197.6	196.8	195.3	193.2	197.4
2006	198.3	198.7	199.8	201.5	202.5	202.9	203.5	203.9	202.9	201.8	201.5	201.8	201.6	200.6	202.6
2007	202.416	203.499	205.352	206.686	207.949	208.352	208.299	207.917	208.490	208.936	210.177	210.036	207.342	205.709	208.976
2008	211.080	211.693	213.528	214.823	216.632	218.815								214.429	

Producer Price Index

Formerly called the Wholesale Price Index, it dates back to 1890 and is also published by the U.S. Bureau of Labor Statistics. It reflects the prices of over 3,400 commodities. Price data are collected from the sellers of the commodities, and it usually refers to the first large-volume transaction for each commodity. It is a Laspeyres-type index. To access this information, go to www.bls.gov, then **Inflation and Consumer Spending, Producer Price Indexes, Get Detailed PPI Statistics,** then under **Most Requested Statistics,** select **Commodity Data,** and finally select **Finished Goods.** You may select to include different periods. Below is a recent output.

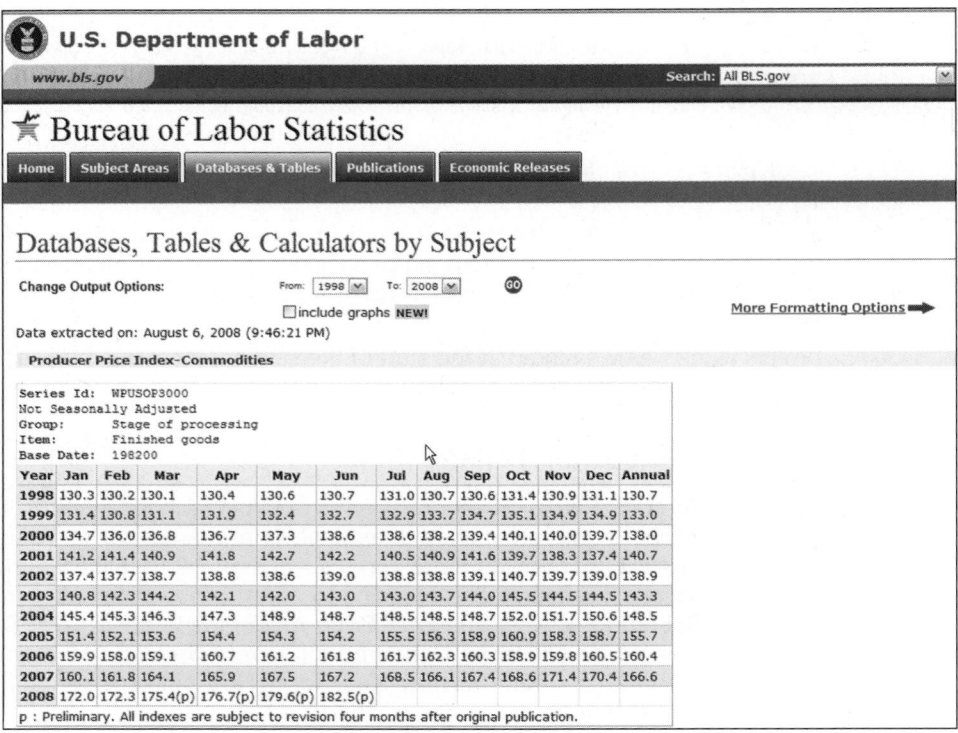

U.S. Department of Labor

www.bls.gov   Search: All BLS.gov

Bureau of Labor Statistics

Home | Subject Areas | Databases & Tables | Publications | Economic Releases

Databases, Tables & Calculators by Subject

Change Output Options: From: 1998   To: 2008   GO   More Formatting Options ➡
☐ include graphs **NEW!**

Data extracted on: August 6, 2008 (9:46:21 PM)

Producer Price Index-Commodities

```
Series Id:  WPUSOP3000
Not Seasonally Adjusted
Group:      Stage of processing
Item:       Finished goods
Base Date:  198200
```

Year	Jan	Feb	Mar	Apr	May	Jun	Jul	Aug	Sep	Oct	Nov	Dec	Annual
1998	130.3	130.2	130.1	130.4	130.6	130.7	131.0	130.7	130.6	131.4	130.9	131.1	130.7
1999	131.4	130.8	131.1	131.9	132.4	132.7	132.9	133.7	134.7	135.1	134.9	134.9	133.0
2000	134.7	136.0	136.8	136.7	137.3	138.6	138.6	138.2	139.4	140.1	140.0	139.7	138.0
2001	141.2	141.4	140.9	141.8	142.7	142.2	140.5	140.9	141.6	139.7	138.3	137.4	140.7
2002	137.4	137.7	138.7	138.8	138.6	139.0	138.8	138.8	139.1	140.7	139.7	139.0	138.9
2003	140.8	142.3	144.2	142.1	142.0	143.0	143.0	143.7	144.0	145.5	144.5	144.5	143.3
2004	145.4	145.3	146.3	147.3	148.9	148.7	148.5	148.5	148.7	152.0	151.7	150.6	148.5
2005	151.4	152.1	153.6	154.4	154.3	154.2	155.5	156.3	158.9	160.9	158.3	158.7	155.7
2006	159.9	158.0	159.1	160.7	161.2	161.8	161.7	162.3	160.3	158.9	159.8	160.5	160.4
2007	160.1	161.8	164.1	165.9	167.5	167.2	168.5	166.1	167.4	168.6	171.4	170.4	166.6
2008	172.0	172.3	175.4(p)	176.7(p)	179.6(p)	182.5(p)							

p : Preliminary. All indexes are subject to revision four months after original publication.

Dow Jones Industrial Average (DJIA)

This is an index of stock prices, but perhaps it would be better to say it is an "indicator" rather than an index. It is supposed to be the mean price of 30 specific industrial stocks. However, summing the 30 stock prices and dividing by 30 does not calculate its value. This is because of stock splits, mergers, and stocks being added or dropped. When changes occur, adjustments are made in the denominator used with the average. Today the DJIA is more of a psychological indicator than a representation of the general price movement on the New York Stock Exchange. The lack of representativeness of the stocks on the DJIA is one of the reasons for the development of the **New York Stock Exchange Index.** This index was developed as an average price of *all* stocks on the New York Stock Exchange. You can find more information about the DJIA by going to the website: www.dowjones.com and select **The Company** then select about **Dow Jones,** finally under Enterprise Media Group select **Dow Jones Indexes.** You can find its current value as well as the 30 stocks that are now a part of its calculation. The chart below summarizes the DJIA for one day. It can be located at the Merrill Lynch website: www.ml.com.

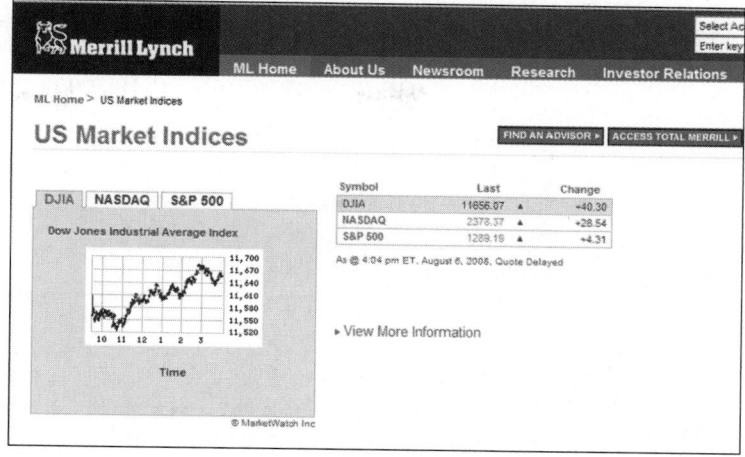

S&P 500 Index

The full name of this index is the Standard and Poor's Composite Index of Stock Prices. It is an aggregate price index of 500 common stocks. It, too, is probably a better reflection of the market than is the DJIA. You can access information about the S&P 500 from the Merrill Lynch website. Below is a recent summary.

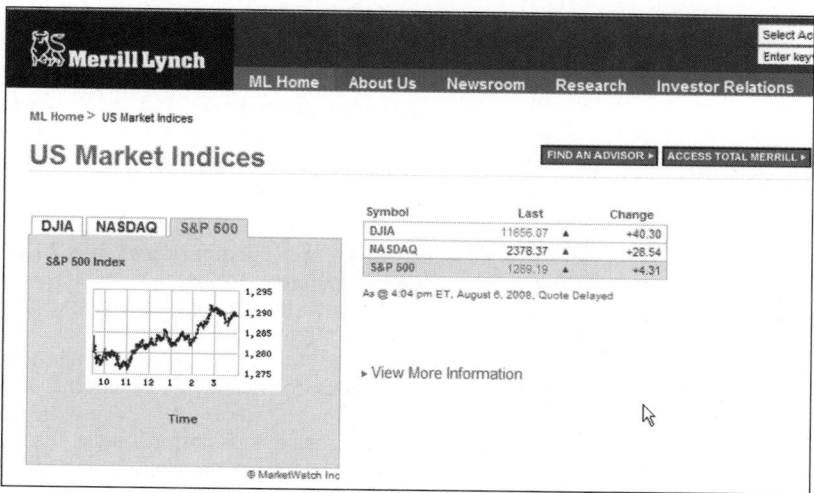

There are many other indexes that track business and economic behavior, such as the Nasdaq, the Russell 2000, and the Wilshire 5000.

Self-Review 15–4 As an intern in the Fulton County Economic Development Office, you have been asked to develop a special-purpose index for your county. Three economic series seem to hold promise as the basis of an index. These data are the price of cotton (per pound), the number of new automobiles sold in the county, and the rate of money turnover (published by the local bank). After discussing the project with your supervisor and the director, you decide that money turnover should have a weight of .60, the number of new automobiles sold a weight of .30, and the cotton price .10. The base period is 1999.

Year	Cotton Price	Automobiles Sold	Money Turnover
1999	$0.20	1,000	80
2004	0.25	1,200	90
2009	0.50	900	75

(a) Construct the index for 2004 and 2009.
(b) Interpret the index for 2004 and 2009.

Exercises

connect™

11. The index of leading economic indicators, compiled and published by the U.S. National Bureau of Economic Research, is composed of 12 time series, such as the average work hours of production in manufacturing, manufacturers' new orders, and money supply. This index and similar indexes are designed to move up or down before the economy begins to move the same way. Thus, an economist has statistical evidence to forecast future trends.

You want to construct a leading indicator for Erie County in upstate New York. The index is to be based on 2000 data. Because of the time and work involved, you decide to use only four time series. As an experiment, you select these four series: unemployment in the county, a composite index of county stock prices, the County Price Index, and retail sales. Here are the figures for 2000 and 2009.

	2000	2009
Unemployment rate (percent)	5.3	6.8
Composite county stocks	265.88	362.26
County Price Index (1982 = 100)	109.6	125.0
Retail sales ($ millions)	529,917.0	622,864.0

The weights you assign are: unemployment rate 20 percent, stock prices 40 percent, County Price Index 25 percent, and retail sales 15 percent.
a. Using 2000 as the base period, construct a leading economic indicator for 2009.
b. Interpret your leading index.

12. You are employed by the state bureau of economic development. There is a demand for a leading economic index to review past economic activity and to forecast future economic trends in the state. You decide that several key factors should be included in the index: number of new businesses started during the year, number of business failures, state income tax receipts, college enrollment, and the state sales tax receipts. Here are the data for 2000 and 2009.

	2000	2009
New businesses	1,088	1,162
Business failures	627	520
State income tax receipts ($ millions)	191.7	162.6
College student enrollment	242,119	290,841
State sales tax ($ millions)	41.6	39.9

a. Decide on the weights to be applied to each item in the leading index.
b. Compute the leading economic indicator for 2009.
c. Interpret the indexes.

Consumer Price Index

Frequent mention has been made of the Consumer Price Index (CPI) in the preceding pages. It measures the change in price of a fixed market basket of goods and services from one period to another. In January 1978 the Bureau of Labor Statistics began publishing CPIs for two groups of the population. One index, called the Consumer Price Index—All Urban Consumers, covers about 87 percent of the total population. The other index is for urban wage earners and clerical workers and covers about 32 percent of the population.

In brief, the CPI serves several major functions. It allows consumers to determine the degree to which their purchasing power is being eroded by price increases. In that respect, it is a yardstick for revising wages, pensions, and other income payments to keep pace with changes in prices. Equally important, it is an economic indicator of the rate of inflation in the United States.

The index includes about 400 items, and about 250 agents collect price data monthly. Prices are collected from more than 21,000 retail establishments and 60,000 housing units in 91 urban areas across the country. The prices of baby cribs, bread, beer, cigars, gasoline, haircuts, mortgage interest rates, physicians' fees, taxes, and operating-room charges are just a few of the items included in what is often termed a typical "market basket" of goods and services that you purchase.

The CPI originated in 1913 and has been published regularly since 1921. The standard reference period (the base period) has been updated periodically. The current base period is 1982–84. The earlier base periods were: 1967, 1957–59, 1947–49, 1935–39, and 1925–29. Why is it necessary to change the base? Our expenditure patterns change dramatically, and these changes must be reflected in the index. The most recent revision includes consumer items, such as VCRs, home computers, and cell phones. Earlier versions of the CPI did not include these items. By changing the base, the CPI captures the most recent expenditure patterns. You may want to go to www.bls.gov, click on the **Consumer Price Index,** and read more about it.

The CPI is actually not just one index. There are Consumer Price Indexes for New York, Chicago, Seattle, and Atlanta, as well as a number of other large cities. There are also price indexes for food, apparel, medical care, and other items. A few of them are shown below, 1982–84 = 100, for May 2008.

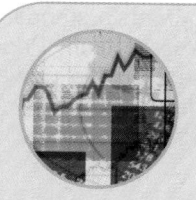

Item	CPI-U
All items	216.632
Food and beverage	212.251
Apparel	120.752
Transportation	205.262
Medical care	363.396
Housing	215.809

A perusal of this listing shows that a weighted index of all items has increased 116.632 percent since 1982–84; medical care has increased the most, 263.396 percent; and apparel went up the least, 20.752 percent.

Special Uses of the Consumer Price Index

In addition to measuring changes in the prices of goods and services, both consumer price indexes have a number of other applications. The CPI is used to determine real disposable personal income, to deflate sales or other variables, to find the purchasing power of the dollar, and to establish cost-of-living increases. We first discuss the use of the CPI in determining **real income.**

Real income

Money income

Real Income As an example of the meaning and computation of *real income,* assume the Consumer Price Index is presently 200 with 1982–84 = 100. Also, assume that Ms. Watts earned $20,000 per year in the base period of 1982, 1983, and 1984. She has a current income of $40,000. Note that although her *money income* has doubled since the base period of 1982–84, the prices she paid for food, gasoline, clothing, and other items have also doubled. Thus, Ms. Watts's standard of living has remained the same from the base period to the present time. Price increases have exactly offset an increase in income, so her present buying power (real income) is still $20,000. (See Table 15–6 for computations.) In general:

$$\text{REAL INCOME} \qquad \text{Real income} = \frac{\text{Money income}}{\text{CPI}} \times 100 \qquad \textbf{[15–8]}$$

TABLE 15–6 Computation of Real Income for 1982–84 and Present Year

Year	Annual Money Income	Consumer Price Index (1982–84 = 100)	Computation of Real Income	Real Income
1982–84	$20,000	100	$\frac{\$20,000}{100}(100)$	$20,000
Present year	40,000	200	$\frac{\$40,000}{200}(100)$	20,000

Deflated income and real income are the same.

The concept of real income is sometimes called *deflated income,* and the CPI is called the *deflator.* Also, a popular term for deflated income is *income expressed in constant dollars.* Thus, in Table 15–6, to determine whether Ms. Watts's standard of living changed, her money income was converted to constant dollars. We found that her purchasing power, expressed in 1982–84 dollars (constant dollars), remained at $20,000.

Self-Review 15–5

The take-home pay of Jon Greene and the CPI for 2000 and 2009 are:

Year	Take-Home Pay	CPI (1982–84 = 100)
2000	$25,000	170.8
2009	41,200	215.0

(a) What was Jon's real income in 2000?
(b) What was his real income in 2009?
(c) Interpret your findings.

Deflated sales important for showing the trend in "real" sales

Deflating Sales
A price index can also be used to "deflate" sales or similar money series. Deflated sales are determined by

> **USING AN INDEX AS A DEFLATOR**
>
> $$\text{Deflated sales} = \frac{\text{Actual sales}}{\text{An appropriate index}} \times 100 \qquad \text{[15–9]}$$

Example

The sales of Hill Enterprises, a small injection molding company in upstate New York, increased from $875,000 in 1982 to $1,482,000 in 1995, $1,491,000 in 2000, $1,502,000 in 2004, and $1,515,000 in 2007. The owner, Harry Hill, realizes that the price of raw materials used in the process has also increased over the period, so Mr. Hill wants to deflate sales to account for the increase in raw material prices. What are the deflated sales for 1995, 2000, 2004, and 2007 based on 1982 dollars? That is, what are sales for 1995, 2000, 2004, and 2007 expressed in constant 1982 dollars?

Solution

The Producer Price Index (PPI) is an index released every month and published in the *Monthly Labor Review* and is also available at the Bureau of Labor Statistics website. The prices included in the PPI reflect the prices charged the manufacturer for the metals, rubber, and other items purchased. So the PPI seems an appropriate index to use to deflate the manufacturer's sales. The manufacturer's sales are listed in the second column of Table 15–7, and the PPI for each year is in the third column. The next column shows sales divided by the PPI. The right-hand column details the calculations. The results are shown in the following Excel output.

TABLE 15–7 Calculation of Deflated Sales for Hill Enterprises

Table 15-7
Calculation of Deflated Sales
for Hill Enterprises

Year	Sales	PPI	Constant Dollars	Found By
1982	$875,000.00	100.0	$875,000.00	($875,000/100.0)*100.0
1995	$1,482,000.00	127.9	$1,158,717.75	($1,482,000/127.9)*100.0
2000	$1,491,000.00	139.0	$1,072,661.87	($1,491000/139.0)*100.0
2004	$1,502,000.00	148.5	$1,011,447.81	($1,502,000/148.4)*100.0
2007	$1,515,000.00	166.6	$909,363.75	($1,515,000/166.6)*100

Excel

Sales increased from 1995 through 2007, but if we compare the sales in constant dollars, sales declined during the period. That is, deflated sales were $1,072,661.87 in 2000 but declined to $1,011,477.81 in 2004. Deflated sales declined even further to $909,363.75 in 2007. This is so because the prices Hill Enterprises paid for raw materials grew more rapidly than sales.

What has happened to the purchasing power of your dollar?

Purchasing Power of the Dollar
The Consumer Price Index is also used to determine the *purchasing power of the dollar*.

> **USING AN INDEX TO FIND PURCHASING POWER**
>
> $$\text{Purchasing power of dollar} = \frac{\$1}{\text{CPI}} \times 100 \qquad \text{[15–10]}$$

Example

Suppose the Consumer Price Index this month is 200.0 (1982–84 = 100). What is the purchasing power of the dollar?

Solution

From formula (15–10), it is 50 cents, found by:

$$\text{Purchasing power of dollar} = \frac{\$1}{200.0}(100) = \$0.50$$

The CPI of 200.0 indicates that prices have doubled from the years 1982–84 to this month. Thus, the purchasing power of a dollar has been cut in half. That is, a 1982–84 dollar is worth only 50 cents this month. To put it another way, if you lost $1,000 in the period 1982–84 and just found it, the $1,000 could only buy half of what it could have bought in the years 1982, 1983, and 1984.

CPI used to adjust wages, pensions, and so on

Cost-of-Living Adjustments   The Consumer Price Index (CPI) is also the basis for cost-of-living adjustments, or COLA, in many management–union contracts. The specific clause in the contract is often referred to as the "escalator clause." About 31 million Social Security beneficiaries, 2.5 million retired military and federal civil service employees and survivors, and 600,000 postal workers have their incomes or pensions pegged to the CPI.

The CPI is also used to adjust alimony and child support payments; attorneys' fees; workers' compensation payments; rentals on apartments, homes, and office buildings; welfare payments; and so on. In brief, say a retiree receives a pension of $500 a month and the CPI increases 5 points from 165 to 170. Suppose for each point that the CPI increases the pension benefits increase 1.0 percent, so the monthly increase in benefits will be $25, found by $500 (5 points)(.01). Now the retiree will receive $525 per month.

Self-Review 15–6

Suppose the Consumer Price Index for the latest month is 195.4 (1982–84 = 100). What is the purchasing power of the dollar? Interpret.

Shifting the Base

If two or more time series have the same base period, they can be compared directly. As an example, suppose we are interested in the trend in the prices of food and beverages, housing, medical care, and so on since the base period, 1982–84. Note in Table 15–8 that all of the consumer price indexes use the same base. Hence, we conclude that the price of all consumer items combined increased 107.342 percent from the base period (1982–84) to the year 2007. (Beginning with January 2007,

TABLE 15–8 Trend in Consumer Prices to 2007 (1982–84 = 100)

Year	All Items	Food and Beverages	Housing	Apparel and Upkeep	Medical Care
1982–84	100.0	100.0	100.0	100.0	100.0
1990	130.7	132.1	128.5	124.1	162.8
1995	152.4	148.9	148.5	132.0	220.5
2000	172.2	168.4	169.6	129.6	260.8
2004	188.9	186.6	189.5	120.4	310.1
2005	195.3	191.2	195.7	119.5	323.2
2007	207.392	203.300	209.586	118.257	369.302

the CPI is reported to three decimal places instead of one.) Likewise, housing prices increased 109.586 percent, medical care 269.302 percent, and so on.

A problem arises, however, when two or more series being compared do not have the same base period. The following example compares the two most widely reported business indexes, the DJIA and Nasdaq.

Example

We want to compare the price changes in the Dow Jones Industrial Average (DJIA) with the Nasdaq. The two indexes for selected periods since 1995 follow. The information is reported on July 1 of each year.

Date	DJIA	Nasdaq
1-Jul-95	4,708.47	1,001.21
1-Jul-00	10,521.98	3,766.99
1-Jul-01	10,522.81	2,027.13
1-Jul-02	8,736.59	1,328.26
1-Jul-03	9,233.80	1,735.02
1-Jul-04	10,139.71	1,887.36
1-Jul-05	10,640.91	2,184.83
1-Jul-06	11,228.02	2,190.43
1-Jul-07	13,535.43	2,632.30

Solution

From the information given, we are not sure the base periods are the same. Hence, a direct comparison is not appropriate. Because we want to compare the changes in the two business indexes, the logical approach is to let a particular year, say 1995, be the base for both indexes. For the DJIA the base is 4,708.47 and for the Nasdaq it is 1,001.21.

The calculation of the index for the DJIA in 2005 is:

$$Index = \frac{10,640.91}{4,708.47}(100) = 226.0$$

The following Excel output reports the complete set of indexes.

compare djia and nasdaq

	A	B	C	D	E	F	G
1							
2			Comparison of DJIA and NASDAQ				
3							
4		Date	DJIA	Index	NASDAQ	Index	
5		1-Jul-95	4708.47	100.0	1001.21	100.0	
6		1-Jul-00	10521.98	223.5	3766.99	376.2	
7		1-Jul-01	10522.81	223.5	2027.13	202.5	
8		1-Jul-02	8736.59	185.6	1328.26	132.7	
9		1-Jul-03	9233.8	196.1	1735.02	173.3	
10		1-Jul-04	10139.71	215.4	1887.36	188.5	
11		1-Jul-05	10640.91	226.0	2184.83	218.2	
12		1-Jul-06	11,228.02	238.5	2,190.43	218.8	
13		1-Jul-07	13,535.43	287.5	2,632.30	262.9	
14							

We conclude that both indexes have increased over the period. The DJIA has increased 187.5 percent and the Nasdaq 162.9 percent for the period from July 1, 1995, until July 1, 2007. Notice that both indexes reached a peak in 2000, declined to their lowest points in 2002 and have increased since.

The following chart, obtained from the financial section of Yahoo!, is a line graph of the DJIA and Nasdaq. The vertical axis shows the percent change from the base period of June 2003 for both indexes. From this graph we conclude that both indexes reached their largest percent increase in late 2007, then declined to a value about the same as early 2007. The second quarter of 2008 has seen increases in both indexes. Of course, if we select different periods as the base, the results may not be exactly the same.

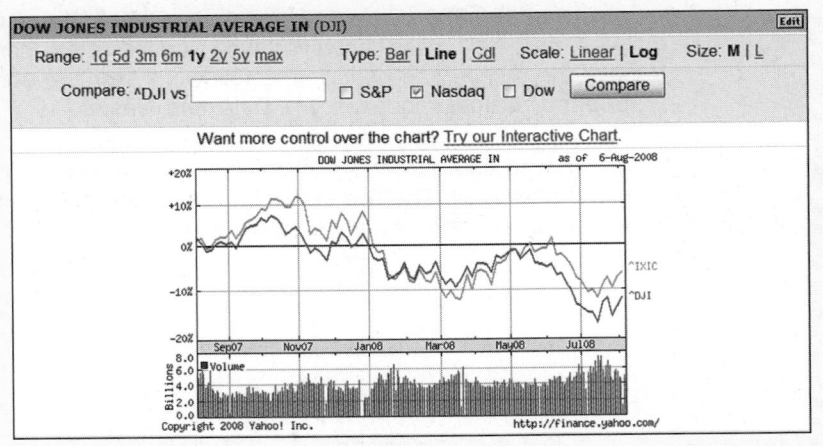

Self-Review 15–7   (a)   From the preceding example, verify that the DJIA price index for 2004, using 1995 as the base period, is 215.4.

(b)   The changes in industrial production and in the prices manufacturers paid for raw materials since 1982 are to be compared. Unfortunately, the index of industrial production, which measures changes in production, and the Producer Price Index, which measures the change in the prices of raw materials, have different base periods. The production index has a 1977 base period, and the Producer Price Index uses 1982 as the base period. Shift the base to 1982 and make the two series comparable. Interpret.

Year	Industrial Production Index (1977 = 100)	Producer Price Index (1982 = 100)
1982	115.3	100.0
1987	129.8	105.4
1994	142.8	119.2
1997	172.3	131.8
2000	185.6	138.0
2002	191.3	138.9
2004	194.7	143.3

Exercises

13. In April 2008 the mean salary for a nurse manager with a bachelor's degree was $89,673. The Consumer Price Index for April 2008 was 214.823 (1982–84 = 100). The mean annual salary for a nurse in the base period of 1982–84 was $19,800. What was the real income of the nurse in April 2008? How much had the mean salary increased?

14. The Trade Union Association of Orlando, Florida, maintains indexes on the hourly wages for a number of the trades. Unfortunately, the indexes do not all have the same base periods. Listed below is information on plumbers and electricians. Shift the base periods to 2000 and compare the hourly wage increases for the period from 2000 to 2006.

Year	Plumbers (1995 = 100)	Electricians (1998 = 100)
2000	133.8	126.0
2006	159.4	158.7

15. In 1995 the mean salary of classroom teachers in Tinora School District was $28,650. By 2004 the mean salary increased to $33,972, and further increased in 2008 to $37,382. The American Federation of Classroom Teachers maintains information on the trends throughout the United States in classroom teacher salaries. Its index, which has a base period of 1995, was 122.5 for 2004 and 136.9 for 2008. Compare the Tinora teachers to the national trends.

16. Sam Steward is a freelance Web page designer. Listed below are his yearly wages for several years between 2002 and 2008. Also included is an industry index for Web page designers that reports the rate of wage inflation in the industry. This index has a base period of 1995.

Year	Wage ($000)	Index (1995 = 100)
2002	134.8	160.6
2004	145.2	173.6
2006	156.6	187.9
2008	168.8	203.3

Compute Sam's real income for the selected years during the six-year period. Did his wages keep up with inflation, or did he lose ground?

Chapter Summary

I. An index number measures the relative change from one period to another.
   A. The major characteristics of an index are:
   1. It is a percentage, but the percent sign is usually omitted.
   2. It has a base period.
   3. Most indexes are reported to the nearest tenth of a percent, such as 153.1.
   4. The base of most indexes is 100.
   B. The reasons for computing an index are:
   1. It facilitates the comparison of unlike series.
   2. If the numbers are very large, often it is easier to comprehend the change of the index than the actual numbers.

II. There are two types of price indexes, unweighted and weighted.
   A. In an unweighted index we do not consider the quantities.
   1. In a simple index we compare the base period to the given period.

$$P = \frac{p_t}{p_0} \times 100 \qquad\qquad \textbf{[15–1]}$$

   where p_t refers to the price in the current period, and p_0 is the price in the base period.
   2. In the simple average of price indexes, we add the simple indexes for each item and divide by the number of items.

$$P = \frac{\Sigma P_i}{n} \qquad\qquad \textbf{[15–2]}$$

   3. In a simple aggregate price index the price of the items in the group are totaled for both periods and compared.

$$P = \frac{\Sigma p_t}{\Sigma p_0} \times 100 \qquad\qquad \textbf{[15–3]}$$

   B. In a weighted index the quantities are considered.
   1. In the Laspeyres method the base period quantities are used in both the base period and the given period.

$$P = \frac{\Sigma p_t q_0}{\Sigma p_0 q_0} \times 100 \qquad\qquad \textbf{[15–4]}$$

large as 500 million
marks. Stories are
told that workers
were paid daily, then
twice daily, so their
wives could shop for
necessities before the
wages became too
devalued.

2. In the Paasche method current period quantities are used.

$$P = \frac{\Sigma p_t q_t}{\Sigma p_0 q_t} \times 100 \qquad\qquad \textbf{[15–5]}$$

3. Fisher's ideal index is the geometric mean of Laspeyres' index and Paasche's index.

$$\text{Fisher's ideal index} = \sqrt{(\text{Laspeyres' index})(\text{Paasche's index})} \qquad \textbf{[15–6]}$$

C. A value index uses both base period and current period prices and quantities.

$$V = \frac{\Sigma p_t q_t}{\Sigma p_0 q_0} \times 100 \qquad\qquad \textbf{[15–7]}$$

III. The most widely reported index is the Consumer Price Index (CPI).
   A. It is often used to show the rate of inflation in the United States.
   B. It is reported monthly by the U.S. Bureau of Labor Statistics.
   C. The current base period is 1982–84.
   D. It is used by the Social Security system, so when the CPI changes, retirement benefits also change.

Chapter Exercises

connect

The following information was taken from Johnson & Johnson annual reports. The principal office of Johnson & Johnson is in New Brunswick, New Jersey. Its common stock is listed on the New York Stock Exchange, using the symbol JNJ.

Year	Domestic Sales ($ million)	International Sales ($ million)	Total Sales ($ million)	Employees (thousands)
2000	17,316	11,856	29,172	100.9
2001	19,825	12,492	32,317	101.8
2002	22,455	13,843	36,298	108.3
2003	25,274	16,588	41,862	110.6
2004	27,770	19,578	47,348	109.9
2005	28,377	22,137	50,514	115.6
2006	29,775	23,549	53,324	122.2
2007	32,444	28,651	61,095	119.2

17. Refer to the Johnson & Johnson data. Use 2000 as the base period and compute a simple index of domestic sales for each year from 2000 until 2007. Interpret the trend in domestic sales.

18. Refer to the Johnson & Johnson data. Use the period 2000–02 as the base period and compute a simple index of domestic sales for each year from 2003 to 2007.

19. Refer to the Johnson & Johnson data. Use 2000 as the base period and compute a simple index of international sales for each year from 2001 until 2007. Interpret the trend in international sales.

20. Refer to the Johnson & Johnson data. Use the period 2000–02 as the base period and compute a simple index of international sales for each year from 2003 to 2007.

21. Refer to the Johnson & Johnson data. Use 2000 as the base period and compute a simple index of the number of employees for each year from 2001 until 2007. Interpret the trend in the number of employees.

22. Refer to the Johnson & Johnson data. Use the period 2000–02 as the base period and compute a simple index of the number of employees for each year from 2003 to 2007.

The following information is from the General Electric Corporation annual report for 2004.

Year	Revenue ($ million)	Employees (000)	Year	Revenue ($ million)	Employees (000)
2000	130,385	90.0	2003	134,187	87.0
2001	126,416	91.0	2004	152,363	80.0
2002	132,210	96.0			

23. Compute a simple index for the revenue of GE. Use 2000 as the base period. What can you conclude about the change in revenue over the period?
24. Compute a simple index for the revenue of GE using the period 2000–02 as the base. What can you conclude about the change in revenue over the period?
25. Compute a simple index for the number of employees for GE. Use 2000 as the base period. What can you conclude about the change in the number of employees over the period?
26. Compute a simple index for the number of employees for GE using the period 2000–02 as the base. What can you conclude about the change in the number of employees over the period?

Below is information on food items for the years 2000 and 2008.

	2000		2008	
Item	**Price**	**Quantity**	**Price**	**Quantity**
Margarine (pound)	$0.81	18	$2.00	27
Shortening (pound)	0.84	5	1.88	9
Milk (½ gallon)	1.44	70	2.89	65
Potato chips	2.91	27	3.99	33

27. Compute a simple price index for each of the four items. Use 2000 as the base period.
28. Compute a simple aggregate price index. Use 2000 as the base period.
29. Compute Laspeyres' price index for 2008 using 2000 as the base period.
30. Compute Paasche's index for 2008 using 2000 as the base period.
31. Determine Fisher's ideal index using the values for the Laspeyres and Paasche indexes computed in the two previous problems.
32. Determine a value index for 2008 using 2000 as the base period.

Betts Electronics purchases three replacement parts for robotic machines used in its manufacturing process. Information on the price of the replacement parts and the quantity purchased is given below.

	Price		Quantity	
Part	**2000**	**2006**	**2000**	**2006**
RC-33	$0.50	$0.60	320	340
SM-14	1.20	0.90	110	130
WC50	0.85	1.00	230	250

33. Compute a simple price index for each of the three items. Use 2000 as the base period.
34. Compute a simple aggregate price index for 2006. Use 2000 as the base period.
35. Compute Laspeyres' price index for 2006 using 2000 as the base period.
36. Compute Paasche's index for 2006 using 2000 as the base period.
37. Determine Fisher's ideal index using the values for the Laspeyres and Paasche indexes computed in the two previous problems.
38. Determine a value index for 2006 using 2000 as the base period.

Prices for selected foods for 2000 and 2006 are given in the following table.

	Price		Quantity	
Item	**2000**	**2006**	**2000**	**2006**
Cabbage (pound)	$0.06	$0.05	2,000	1,500
Carrots (bunch)	0.10	0.12	200	200
Peas (quart)	0.20	0.18	400	500
Endive (bunch)	0.15	0.15	100	200

39. Compute a simple price index for each of the four items. Use 2000 as the base period.
40. Compute a simple aggregate price index. Use 2000 as the base period.
41. Compute Laspeyres' price index for 2006 using 2000 as the base period.
42. Compute Paasche's index for 2006 using 2000 as the base period.
43. Determine Fisher's ideal index using the values for the Laspeyres and Paasche indexes computed in the two previous problems.
44. Determine a value index for 2006 using 2000 as the base period.

The prices of selected items for 1990 and 2006 follow. Production figures for those two periods are also given.

	Price		Quantity	
Item	**1990**	**2006**	**1990**	**2006**
Aluminum (cents per pound)	$ 0.287	$ 0.76	1,000	1,200
Natural gas (1,000 cu. ft.)	0.17	2.50	5,000	4,000
Petroleum (barrel)	3.18	26.00	60,000	60,000
Platinum (troy ounce)	133.00	490.00	500	600

45. Compute a simple price index for each of the four items. Use 1990 as the base period.
46. Compute a simple aggregate price index. Use 1990 as the base period.
47. Compute Laspeyres' price index for 2006 using 1990 as the base period.
48. Compute Paasche's index for 2006 using 1990 as the base period.
49. Determine Fisher's ideal index using the values for the Laspeyres and Paasche indexes computed in the two previous problems.
50. Determine a value index for 2006 using 1990 as the base period.
51. A special-purpose index is to be designed to monitor the overall economy of the Southwest. Four key series were selected. After considerable deliberation it was decided to weight retail sales 20 percent, total bank deposits 10 percent, industrial production in the area 40 percent, and nonagricultural employment 30 percent. The data for 1996 and 2008 are:

Year	Retail Sales ($ millions)	Bank Deposits ($ billions)	Industrial Production (1990 = 100)	Employment
1996	1,159.0	87	110.6	1,214,000
2008	1,971.0	91	114.7	1,501,000

Construct a special-purpose index for 2008 using 1996 as the base period and interpret.
52. We are making a historical study of the American economy from 1950 to 1980. Data on prices, the labor force, productivity, and the GNP were collected. Note in the following table that the CPI has a base period of 1967, employment is in millions of persons, and so on. A direct comparison, therefore, is not feasible.
  a. Make whatever calculations are necessary to compare the trend in the four series from 1950 to 1980.
  b. Interpret.

Year	Consumer Price Index (1967 = 100)	Total Labor Force (millions)	Index of Productivity in Manufacturing (1967 = 100)	Gross National Product ($ billions)
1950	72.1	64	64.9	286.2
1967	100.0	81	100.0	789.6
1971	121.3	87	110.3	1,063.4
1975	161.2	95	114.9	1,516.3
1980	246.8	107	146.6	2,626.0

53. The management of Ingalls Super Discount stores, with several stores in the Oklahoma City area, wants to construct an index of economic activity for the metropolitan area. Management contends that, if the index reveals that the economy is slowing down, inventory should be kept at a low level.

    Three series seem to hold promise as predictors of economic activity—area retail sales, bank deposits, and employment. All of these data can be secured monthly from the U.S. government. Retail sales is to be weighted 40 percent, bank deposits 35 percent, and employment 25 percent. Seasonally adjusted data for the first three months of the year are:

Month	Retail Sales ($ millions)	Bank Deposits ($ billions)	Employment (thousands)
January	8.0	20	300
February	6.8	23	303
March	6.4	21	297

    Construct an index of economic activity for each of the three months, using January as the base period.

54. The following table gives information on the Consumer Price Index and the monthly take-home pay of Bill Martin, an employee at Jeep Corporation.

Year	Consumer Price Index (1982–84 = 100)	Mr. Martin's Monthly Take-Home Pay
1982–84	100.0	$ 600
2007	207.342	2,000

    a. What is the purchasing power of the dollar in 2007, based on the period 1982–84?
    b. Determine Mr. Martin's "real" monthly income for 2007.

55. Suppose that the Producer Price Index and the sales of Hoskin's Wholesale Distributors for 1995 and 2007 are:

Year	Producer Price Index	Sales
1995	127.9	$2,400,000
2007	169.0	3,500,000

    What are Hoskin's real sales (also called deflated sales) for the two years?

Software Commands

1. The Excel commands for the spreadsheet on page 573 are:
   a. Enter the data for the prices and quantities. We entered the label *Item* in cell A2, and the item names in cells A3 through A8. The label *1999 Price* was entered in B2, and the price data for 1999 in cells B3 through B8. The label *1999 Quantity* was entered in cell C2, with the 1999 quantities in cells C3 through C8. Cell E2 was labeled *1999 Price*1999 Quantity.*
   b. To determine the product of the 1999 prices and quantities, highlight the cell E3. Type = *B2*C2* in cell E3 and hit **Enter.** The value of 43.5 should

   appear. This is the product of the price of bread ($0.87) and the quantity of bread (50) sold in 1999.
   c. With cell E3 still highlighted, move the cursor to the bottom right corner of cell E3, hold the left mouse button and drag the cell down to cell E8. The remaining products should appear.
   d. Move to cell E9, click on Σ on the menu and hit **Enter.** The value of 507.64 will appear. This is the denominator for the Laspeyres price index. The other products and column totals are determined in a similar manner. The other Excel output in the chapter is computed similarly.

Chapter 15   Answers to Self-Review

15–1 1.

Nation	AMT	Index
China	197	252.6
EU	144	184.6
Japan	103	132.1
US	78	100.0
Russia	52	66.7

China produces 152.6 percent more steel than the United States.

2.

Year	Earnings	(a) Index*	(b) Index**
1995	$11.47	100.0	91.0
2000	13.73	119.7	109.0
2003	15.19	132.4	120.6
2005	15.88	138.4	126.0
2006	16.40	143.0	130.2
2008	17.87	155.8	141.8

*Base = 1995
**Base = 1995 and 2000
$\frac{(\$11.47 + \$13.73)}{2} = \$12.60$

15–2 a. $P_1 = (\$85/\$75)(100) = 113.3$
$P_2 = (\$45/\$40)(100) = 112.5$
$P = (113.3 + 112.5)/2 = 112.9$
  b. $P = (\$130/\$115)(100) = 113.0$
  c. $P = \dfrac{\$85(500) + \$45(1,200)}{\$75(500) + \$40(1,200)}(100)$
$= \dfrac{\$96,500}{85,500}(100) = 112.9$
  d. $P = \dfrac{\$85(520) + \$45(1,300)}{\$75(520) + \$40(1,300)}(100)$
$= \dfrac{\$102,700}{\$91,000}(100) = 112.9$
  e. $P = \sqrt{(112.9)(112.9)} = 112.9$

15–3 a. $P = \dfrac{\$4(9,000) + \$5(200) + \$8(5,000)}{\$3(10,000) + \$1(600) + \$10(3,000)}(100)$
$= \dfrac{\$77,000}{60,600}(100) = 127.1$
  b. The value of sales has gone up 27.1 percent from 1996 to 2009.

15–4 a.

For 2004	
Item	**Weight**
Cotton	($0.25/$0.20)(100)(.10) = 12.5
Autos	(1,200/1,000)(100)(.30) = 36.0
Money turnover	(90/80)(100)(.60) = 67.5
	116.0

For 2009	
Item	**Weight**
Cotton	($0.50/$0.20)(100)(.10) = 25.00
Autos	(900/1,000)(100)(.30) = 27.00
Money turnover	(75/80)(100)(.60) = 56.25
	108.25

  b. Business activity increased 16 percent from 1999 to 2004. It increased 8.25 percent from 1999 to 2009.

15–5 a. $14,637, found by ($25,000/170.8)(100).
  b. $19,163, found by ($41,200/215.0)(100).
  c. In terms of the base period, Jon's salary was $14,637 in 2000 and $19,163 in 2009. This indicates his take-home pay increased at a faster rate than the price paid for food, transportation, etc.

15–6 $0.51, found by ($1.00/195.4)(100). The purchasing power has declined by $0.49.

15–7 a. 215.4, found by (10,139.71/4,708.47)(100).
  b. With 1982 as the base period for both series:

	Industrial Production Index	Producer Price Index
1982	100.0	100.0
1987	112.6	105.4
1994	123.9	119.2
1997	149.4	131.8
2000	161.0	138.0
2002	165.9	138.9
2004	168.9	143.3

From the base of 1982, industrial production increased at a faster rate (68.9 percent) than prices (43.3 percent).

Time Series and Forecasting

Team Sports, Inc., sells sporting goods to high schools and colleges via a nationally distributed catalog. Management at Team Sports estimates it will sell 2,000 Wilson Model A2000 catcher's mitts next year. The deseasonalized sales are projected to be the same for each of the four quarters next year. The seasonal factor for the second quarter is 145. Determine the seasonally adjusted sales for the second quarter of next year. (Exercise 12, Goal 5)

Introduction

What is a time series?

The emphasis in this chapter is on time series analysis and forecasting. A **time series** is a collection of data recorded over a period of time—weekly, monthly, quarterly, or yearly. Two examples of time series are Microsoft Corporation sales by quarter since 1985 and the annual production of sulfuric acid since 1970. [The computer image in

the photo shows the volume of data traveling into the National Science Foundation network in one month. The colors represent traffic volume from zero bytes (purple) to 100 billion bytes (white).]

An analysis of history—a time series—can be used by management to make current decisions and plans based on long-term forecasting. We usually assume past patterns will continue into the future. Long-term forecasts extend more than 1 year into the future; 2-, 5-, and 10-year projections are common. Long-range predictions are essential to allow sufficient time for the procurement, manufacturing, sales, finance, and other departments of a company to develop plans for possible new plants, financing, development of new products, and new methods of assembling.

Forecasting the level of sales, both short-term and long-term, is practically dictated by the very nature of business organizations in the United States. Competition for the consumer's dollar, stress on earning a profit for the stockholders, a desire to procure a larger share of the market, and the ambitions of executives are some of the prime motivating forces in business. Thus, a forecast (a statement of the goals of management) is necessary to have the raw materials, production facilities, and staff to meet the projected demand.

This chapter deals with the use of data to forecast future events. First, we look at the components of a time series. Then, we examine some of the techniques used in analyzing data. Finally, we forecast future events.

Components of a Time Series

There are four components to a time series: the trend, the cyclical variation, the seasonal variation, and the irregular variation.

Secular Trend

The long-term trends of sales, employment, stock prices, and other business and economic series follow various patterns. Some move steadily upward, others decline, and still others stay the same over time.

> **SECULAR TREND** The smooth long-term direction of a time series.

The following are several examples of a secular trend.

- Home Depot was founded in 1978 and is the second largest retailer (Wal-Mart is the largest) in the United States. The following chart shows the number of employees at Home Depot, Inc. You can see this number has increased rapidly over the last 15 years. In 1993 there were just over 50,000 associates and by 2006 that number increased to 364,000, before declining to 331,000 in 2007.

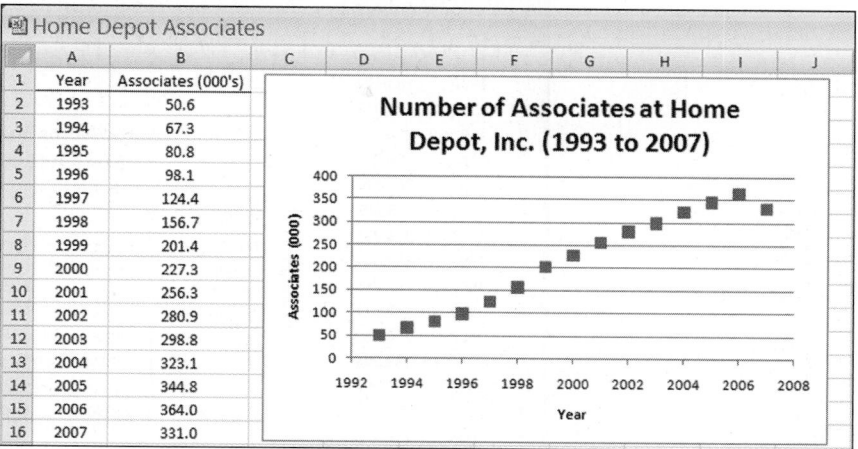

- The following chart shows the number of emergency medical service (EMS) calls in Horry County, South Carolina, since 1989. The number of calls for EMS has increased nearly 3.5 times from 12,269 in 1989 to 42,000 in 2008. Notice that the number of calls increased from 1989 to 1995. From 1995 to 2000 the number of calls stayed about the same, and then in 2000 it began another increase to over 40,000. The long-run direction of the trend is increasing.

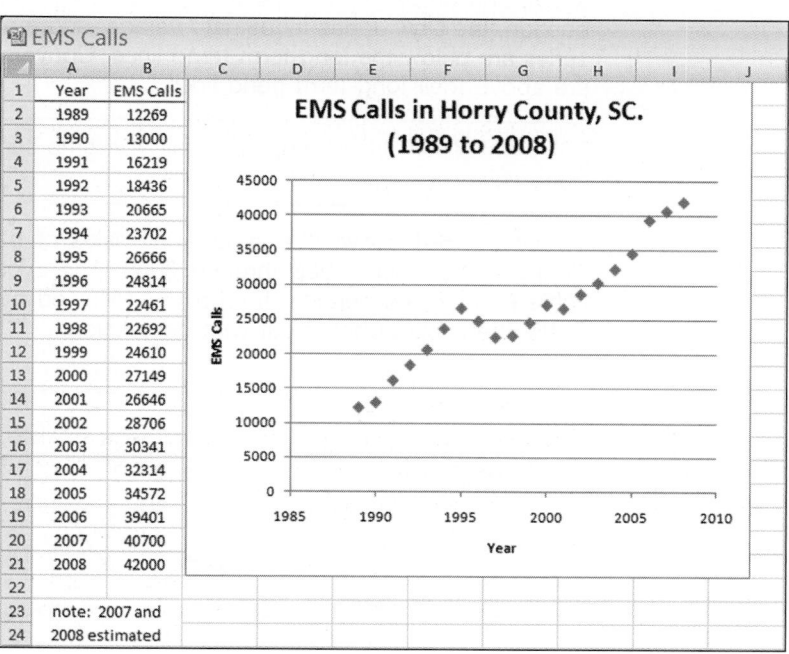

- The number of manufactured homes shipped in the United States showed a steady increase from 1990 to 1996, then remained about the same until 1999, when the number began to decline. By the year 2002 the number shipped was less than it had been in 1990 and continued to decline to 2007. This information is shown in the following chart.

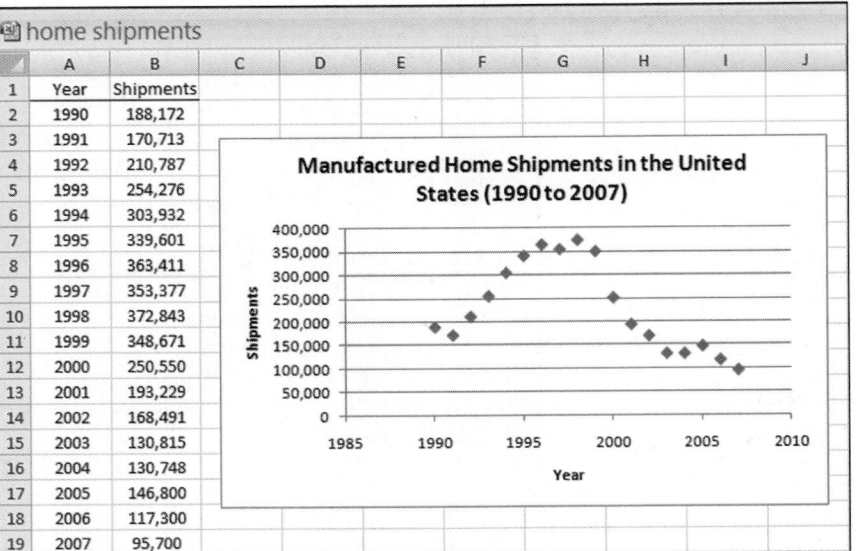

Cyclical Variation

The second component of a time series is cyclical variation. A typical business cycle consists of a period of prosperity followed by periods of recession, depression, and then recovery. There are sizable fluctuations unfolding over more than one year in time above and below the secular trend. In a recession, for example, employment, production, the Dow Jones Industrial Average, and many other business and economic series are below the long-term trend lines. Conversely, in periods of prosperity they are above their long-term trend lines.

> **CYCLICAL VARIATION** The rise and fall of a time series over periods longer than one year.

Chart 16–1 shows the annual unit sales of batteries sold by National Battery Retailers, Inc., from 1989 through 2008. The cyclical nature of business is highlighted. There are periods of recovery, followed by prosperity, then recession, and finally the cycle bottoms out with depression.

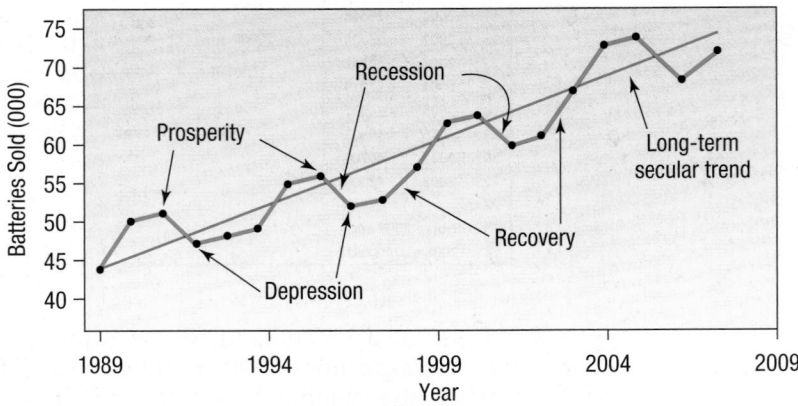

CHART 16–1 Batteries Sold by National Battery Retailers, Inc., from 1989 to 2008

Seasonal Variation

The third component of a time series is the **seasonal variation.** Many sales, production, and other series fluctuate with the seasons. The unit of time reported is either quarterly or monthly.

> **SEASONAL VARIATION** Patterns of change in a time series within a year. These patterns tend to repeat themselves each year.

Almost all businesses tend to have recurring seasonal patterns. Men's and boy's clothing, for example, has extremely high sales just prior to Christmas and relatively low sales just after Christmas and during the summer. Toy sales is another example with an extreme seasonal pattern. More than half of the business for the year is usually done in the months of November and December. The lawn care business is seasonal in the northeast and north-central states. Many businesses try to even out the seasonal effects by engaging in an offsetting seasonal business. In the Northeast you will see the operator of a lawn care business with a snowplow on the front of the truck in an effort to earn income in the off-season. At ski resorts throughout the country, you will often find golf courses nearby. The owners of the lodges try to rent to skiers in the winter and golfers in the summer. This is an effective method of spreading their fixed costs over the entire year rather than a few months.

Chart 16–2 shows the quarterly sales, in millions of dollars, of Hercher Sporting Goods, Inc. The Chicago area sporting goods company specializes in selling baseball and softball equipment to high schools, colleges, and youth leagues. It also has several retail outlets in some of the larger shopping malls. There is a distinct seasonal pattern to its business. Most of its sales are in the first and second quarters of the year, when schools and organizations are purchasing equipment for the upcoming season. During the early summer, it keeps busy by selling replacement equipment. It does some business during the holidays (fourth quarter). The late summer (third quarter) is its slow season.

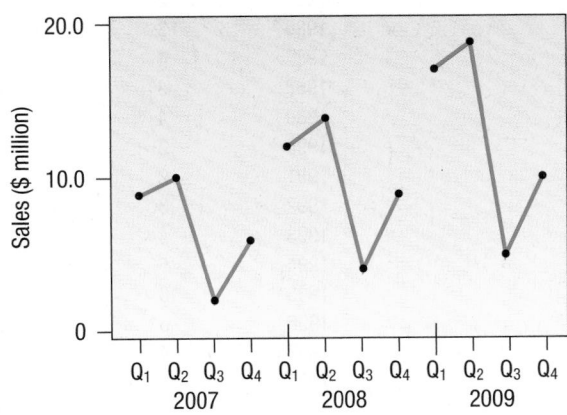

CHART 16–2 Sales of Baseball and Softball Equipment, Hercher Sporting Goods, 2007–2009 by Quarter

Irregular Variation

Many analysts prefer to subdivide the **irregular variation** into *episodic* and *residual* variations. Episodic fluctuations are unpredictable, but they can be identified. The initial impact on the economy of a major strike or a war can be identified, but a strike or war cannot be predicted. After the episodic fluctuations have been removed, the remaining variation is called the residual variation. The residual fluctuations, often called chance fluctuations, are unpredictable, and they cannot be identified. Of course, neither episodic nor residual variation can be projected into the future.

A Moving Average

Moving-average method smooths out fluctuations

A **moving average** is useful in smoothing a time series to see its trend. It is also the basic method used in measuring the seasonal fluctuation, described later in the chapter. In contrast to the least squares method, which expresses the trend in terms of a mathematical equation ($\hat{Y} = a + bt$), the moving-average method merely smooths the fluctuations in the data. This is accomplished by "moving" the arithmetic mean values through the time series.

To apply the moving average to a time series, the data should follow a fairly linear trend and have a definite rhythmic pattern of fluctuations (repeating, say, every three years). The data in the following example have three components—trend, cycle, and irregular, abbreviated T, C, and I. There is no seasonal variation, because the data are recorded annually. What the moving average accomplishes is to average out C and I. What is left is the trend.

If the duration of the cycles is constant, and if the amplitudes of the cycles are equal, the cyclical and irregular fluctuations are removed entirely using the moving average. The result is a line. For example, in the following time series the cycle repeats itself every seven years, and the amplitude of each cycle is 4; that is, there are exactly four units from the trough (lowest time period) to the peak. The seven-year moving average, therefore, averages out the cyclical and irregular fluctuations perfectly, and the residual is a linear trend.

Compute mean of first seven years

The first step in computing the seven-year moving average is to determine the seven-year moving totals. The total sales for the first seven years (1984–90 inclusive) are $22 million, found by $1 + 2 + 3 + 4 + 5 + 4 + 3$. (See Table 16–1.) The total

TABLE 16–1 The Computations for the Seven-Year Moving Average

Year	Sales ($ millions)	Seven-Year Moving Total	Seven-Year Moving Average
1984	$1		
1985	2		
1986	3		
1987	4	22	3.143
1988	5	23	3.286
1989	4	24	3.429
1990	3	25	3.571
1991	2	26	3.714
1992	3	27	3.857
1993	4	28	4.000
1994	5	29	4.143
1995	6	30	4.286
1996	5	31	4.429
1997	4	32	4.571
1998	3	33	4.714
1999	4	34	4.857
2000	5	35	5.000
2001	6	36	5.143
2002	7	37	5.286
2003	6	38	5.429
2004	5	39	5.571
2005	4	40	5.714
2006	5	41	5.857
2007	6		
2008	7		
2009	8		

of $22 million is divided by 7 to determine the arithmetic mean sales per year. The seven-year total (22) and the seven-year mean (3.143) are positioned opposite the middle year for that group of seven, namely, 1987, as shown in Table 16–1. Then the total sales for the next seven years (1985–91 inclusive) are determined. (A convenient way of doing this is to subtract the sales for 1984 [$1 million] from the first seven-year total [$22 million] and add the sales for 1991 [$2 million], to give the new total of $23 million.) The mean of this total, $3.286 million, is positioned opposite the middle year, 1988. The sales data and seven-year moving average are shown graphically in Chart 16–3.

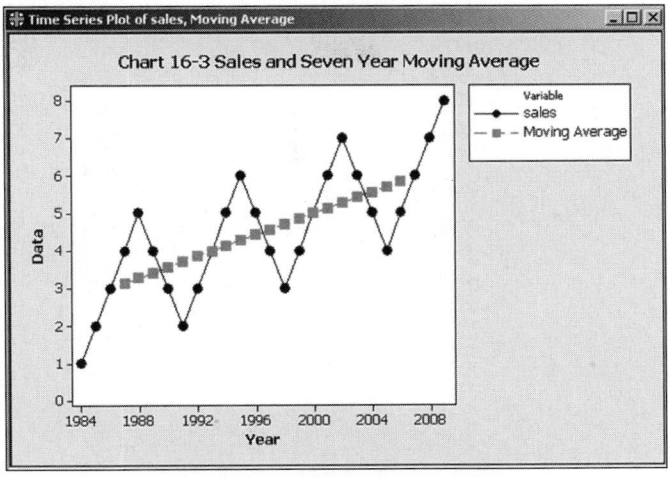

CHART 16–3 Sales and Seven-Year Moving Average

The number of data values to include in a moving average depends on the character of the data collected. If the data are quarterly, since there are four quarters in a year, then four terms might be typical. If the data are daily, since there are seven days in a week, then seven terms might be appropriate. You might also use trial and error to determine a number that best levels out the chance fluctuations.

A moving average can be easily computed in Excel. In fact, it requires only one command. If the original data are in locations D3 to D20 and you wish a three-period moving average, you can go to position E4 and type $= (D3+D4+D5)/3$ and then copy that same formula down to position E19.

A three-year and a five-year moving average for some production data are shown in Table 16–2 and depicted in Chart 16–4.

Sales, production, and other economic and business series usually do not have (1) periods of oscillation that are of equal length or (2) oscillations that have identical amplitudes. Thus, in practice, the application of a moving average does not result precisely in a line. For example, the production series in Table 16–2 repeats about every five years, but the amplitude of the data varies from one oscillation to another. The trend appears to be upward and somewhat linear. Both moving averages—the three-year and the five-year—seem to adequately describe the trend in production since 1991.

Determining a moving average for an even-numbered period, such as four years

Four-year, six-year, and other even-numbered-year moving averages present one minor problem regarding the centering of the moving totals and moving averages. Note in Table 16–3, on page 603, there is no center time period, so the moving totals are positioned *between* two time periods. The total for the first four years

TABLE 16–2 A Three-Year Moving Average and a Five-Year Moving Average

Year	Production, Y	Three-Year Moving Total	Three-Year Moving Average	Five-Year Moving Total	Five-Year Moving Average
1991	5				
1992	6	19	6.3		
1993	8	24	8.0	34	6.8
1994	10	23	7.7	32	6.4
1995	5	18	6.0	33	6.6
1996	3	15	5.0	35	7.0
1997	7	20	6.7	37	7.4
1998	10	29	9.7	43	8.6
1999	12	33	11.0	49	9.8
2000	11	32	10.7	55	11.0
2001	9	33	11.0	60	12.0
2002	13	37	12.3	66	13.2
2003	15	46	15.3	70	14.0
2004	18	48	16.0	72	14.4
2005	15	44	14.7	73	14.6
2006	11	40	13.3	75	15.0
2007	14	42	14.0	79	15.8
2008	17	53	17.7		
2009	22				

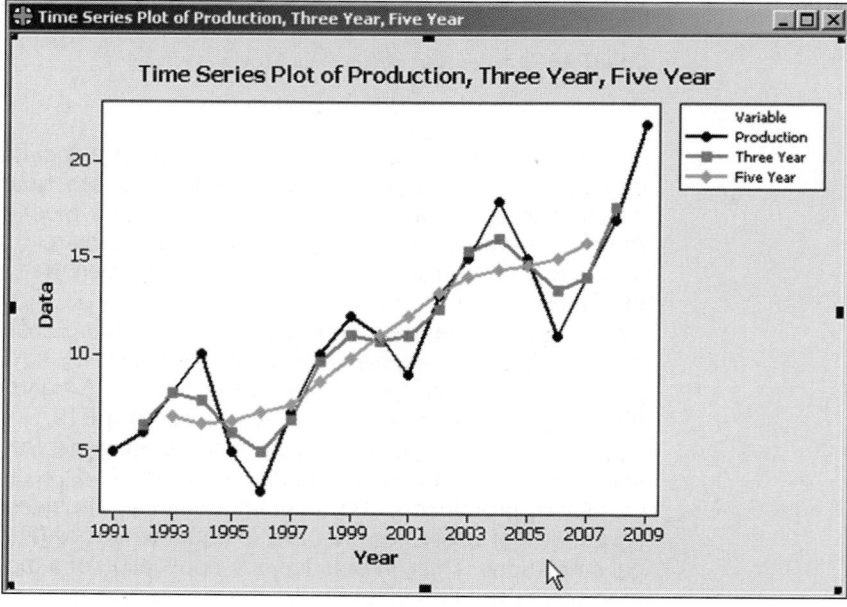

CHART 16–4 A Three-Year and Five-Year Moving Average 1991 to 2009

($42) is positioned between 2002 and 2003. The total for the next four years is $43. The averages of the first four years and the second four years ($10.50 and $10.75, respectively) are averaged, and the resulting figure is centered on 2003. This procedure is repeated until all possible four-year averages are computed.

TABLE 16–3 A Four-Year Moving Average

Year	Sales, Y	Four-Year Moving Total	Four-Year Moving Average	Centered Four-Year Moving Average
2001	$ 8			
2002	11			
		$42 (8 + 11 + 9 + 14)	$10.50 ($42 ÷ 4)	
2003	9			10.625
		43 (11 + 9 + 14 + 9)	10.75 ($43 ÷ 4)	
2004	14			10.625
		42	10.50	
2005	9			10.625
		43	10.75	
2006	10			10.000
		37	9.25	
2007	10			9.625
		40	10.00	
2008	8			
2009	12			

Weighted Moving Average

A moving average uses the same weight for each observation. For example, a three-year moving total is divided by the value 3 to yield the three-year moving average. To put it another way, each data value has a weight of one-third in this case. Similarly, you can see that for a five-year moving average each data value has a weight of one-fifth.

A natural extension of the weighted mean discussed in Chapter 3 is to compute a weighted moving average. This involves selecting a possibly different weight for each data value and then computing a weighted average of the most recent n values as the smoothed value. In the majority of applications we use the smoothed value as a forecast of the future. So, the most recent observation receives the most weight, and the weight decreases for older data values. Notice that for both the simple moving average and for the weighted moving average the sum of the weights is equal to 1.

Suppose, for example, we compute a two-year weighted moving average for the data in Table 16–3 giving twice as much weight to the most recent value. In other words give a weight of 2/3 to the last year and 1/3 to the value immediately before that. Then "forecast" sales for 2003 would be found by (1/3)($8) + (2/3)($11) = $10. The next moving average would be computed as (1/3)($11) + (2/3)($9) = $9.667. Proceeding in the same fashion, the final or 2010 weighted moving average would be (1/3)($8) + (2/3)($12) = $10.667. To summarize the technique of using moving averages, its purpose is to help identify the long-term trend in a time series (because it smooths out short-term fluctuations). It is used to reveal any cyclical and seasonal fluctuations.

Example

Cedar Fair operates seven amusement parks and five separately gated water parks. Its combined attendance (in thousands) for the last 15 years is given in the following table. A partner asks you to study the trend in attendance. Compute a three-year moving average and a three-year weighted moving average with weights of 0.2, 0.3, and 0.5 for successive years.

Year	Attendance (000)
1993	5,761
1994	6,148
1995	6,783
1996	7,445
1997	7,405
1998	11,450
1999	11,224
2000	11,703
2001	11,890
2002	12,380
2003	12,181
2004	12,557
2005	12,700
2006	19,300
2007	22,100

Solution

The three-year moving average is:

Year	Attendance (000)	Moving Average	Found by
1993	5,761		
1994	6,148	6,231	(5,761 + 6,148 + 6,783)/3
1995	6,783	6,792	(6,148 + 6,783 + 7,445)/3
1996	7,445	7,211	(6,783 + 7,445 + 7,405)/3
1997	7,405	8,767	(7,445 + 7,405 + 11,450)/3
1998	11,450	10,026	(7,405 + 11,450 + 11,224)/3
1999	11,224	11,459	(11,450 + 11,224 + 11,703)/3
2000	11,703	11,606	(11,224 + 11,703 + 11,890)/3
2001	11,890	11,991	(11,703 + 11,890 + 12,380)/3
2002	12,380	12,150	(11,890 + 12,380 + 12,181)/3
2003	12,181	12,373	(12,380 + 12,181 + 12,557)/3
2004	12,557	12,479	(12,181 + 12,557 + 12,700)/3
2005	12,700	14,852	(12,557 + 12,700 + 19,300)/3
2006	19,300	18,033	(12,700 + 19,300 + 22,100)/3
2007	22,100		

The three-year *weighted* moving average is:

Year	Attendance (000)	Weighted Moving Average	Found by
1993	5,761		
1994	6,148	6,388	.2(5,761) + .3(6,148) + .5(6,783)
1995	6,783	6,987	.2(6,148) + .3(6,783) + .5(7,445)
1996	7,445	7,293	.2(6,783) + .3(7,445) + .5(7,405)
1997	7,405	9,436	.2(7,445) + .3(7,405) + .5(11,450)
1998	11,450	10,528	.2(7,405) + .3(11,450) + .5(11,224)
1999	11,224	11,509	.2(11,450) + .3(11,224) + .5(11,703)
2000	11,703	11,701	.2(11,224) + .3(11,703) + .5(11,890)
2001	11,890	12,098	.2(11,703) + .3(11,890) + .5(12,380)
2002	12,380	12,183	.2(11,890) + .3(12,380) + .5(12,181)
2003	12,181	12,409	.2(12,380) + .3(12,181) + .5(12,557)
2004	12,557	12,553	.2(12,181) + .3(12,557) + .5(12,700)
2005	12,700	15,971	.2(12,557) + .3(12,700) + .5(19,300)
2006	19,300	19,380	.2(12,700) + .3(19,300) + .5(22,100)
2007	22,100		

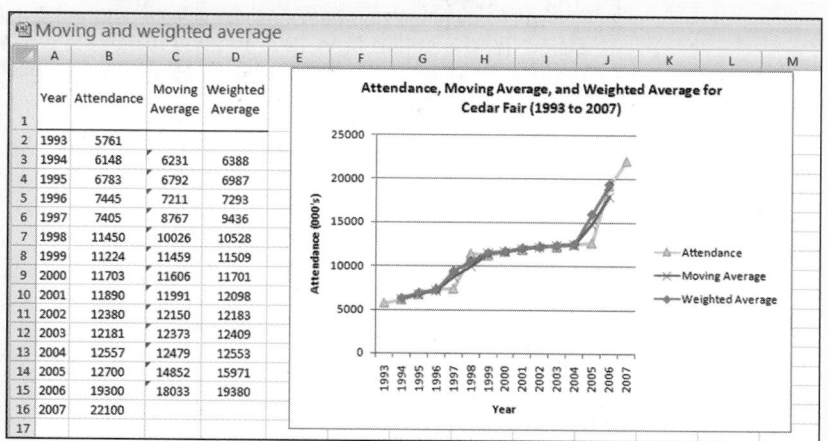

Study the graph carefully. You will see that the attendance trend is evenly upward with 360,000 added visitors each year. However, there is a "hop" of approximately 3 million per year between 1997 and 1998. That probably reflects the fact Cedar Fair acquired Knott's Berry Farm in late 1997, leading to a boost in attendance. A similar boost occurred in 2006 with the purchase of King's Island near Cincinnati. The weighted moving average follows the data more closely than the moving average. This reflects the additional influence given to the most recent period. In other words, the weighted method, where the most recent period is given the largest weight, won't be quite as smooth. However, it may be more accurate as a forecasting tool.

Self-Review 16–1

Determine a three-year moving average for the sales of Waccamaw Machine Tool, Inc. Plot both the original data and the moving average.

Year	Number Produced (thousands)	Year	Number Produced (thousands)
2003	2	2006	5
2004	6	2007	3
2005	4	2008	10

Exercises

connect

1. Calculate a four-quarter weighted moving average for the number of shares outstanding for the Boxley Box Company for the nine quarters of data. The data are reported in thousands. Apply weights of .1, .2, .3 and .4, respectively, for the quarters. In a few words describe the trend in the number of subscribers.

31-Mar-04	28,766	30-Jun-05	35,102
30-Jun-04	30,057	30-Sep-05	35,308
30-Sep-04	31,336	31-Dec-05	35,203
31-Dec-04	33,240	31-Mar-06	34,386
31-Mar-05	34,610		

2. Listed below is the number of movie tickets sold at the Library Cinema-Complex, in thousands, for the period from 1996 to 2008. Compute a five-year weighted moving average using weights of .1, .1, .2, .3, and .3, respectively. Describe the trend in yield.

1996	8.61	2003	6.61
1997	8.14	2004	5.58
1998	7.67	2005	5.87
1999	6.59	2006	5.94
2000	7.37	2007	5.49
2001	6.88	2008	5.43
2002	6.71		

Linear Trend

The long-term trend of many business series, such as sales, exports, and production, often approximates a straight line. If so, the equation to describe this growth is:

LINEAR TREND EQUATION	$\hat{Y} = a + bt$	[16–1]

where:

$\hat{Y}$ read Y hat, is the projected value of the Y variable for a selected value of t.

a is the Y-intercept. It is the estimated value of Y when $t = 0$. Another way to put it is: a is the estimated value of Y where the line crosses the Y-axis when t is zero.

Slope of trend line is b

b is the slope of the line, or the average change in $\hat{Y}$ for each increase of one unit in t.

t is any value of time that is selected.

To illustrate the meaning of $\hat{Y}$, a, b, and t in a time-series problem, a line has been drawn in Chart 16–5 to represent the typical trend of sales. Assume that this company started in business in 2001. This beginning year (2001) has been arbitrarily designated as year 1. Note that sales increased $2 million on the average every year; that is, based on the straight line drawn through the sales data, sales increased from $3 million in 2001 to $5 million in 2002, to $7 million in 2003, to $9 million in 2004, and so on. The slope, or b, is therefore 2. Note too that the line intercepts the Y-axis (when $t = 0$) at $1 million. This point is a. Another way of determining b is to locate the starting place of the straight line in year (1). It is 3 for 2001 in this

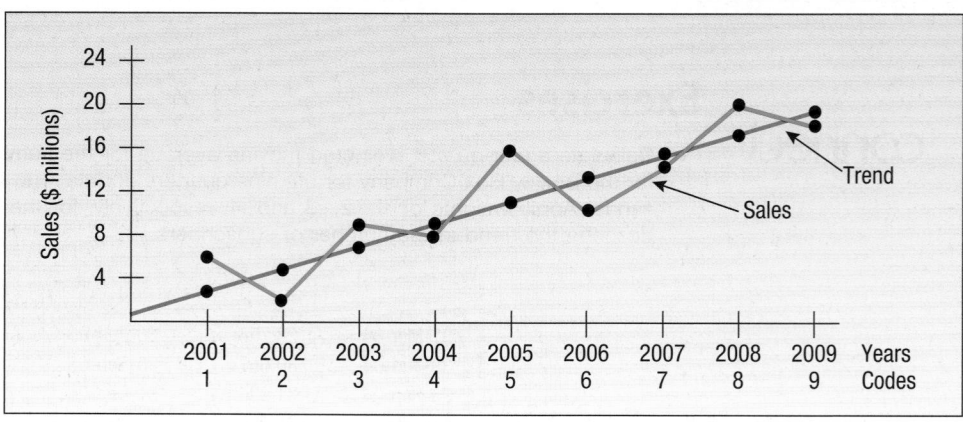

CHART 16–5 A Straight Line Fitted to Sales Data

problem. Then locate the value on the straight line for the last year. It is 19 for 2009. Sales went up $19 million − $3 million = $16 million, in eight years (2001 to 2009). Thus, 16 ÷ 8 = 2, which is the slope of the line, or b.

The equation for the line in Chart 16–5 is:

$$\hat{Y} = 1 + 2t$$

where

$\hat{Y}$ is sales in millions of dollars.

1 is the intercept with the Y-axis. It is also the sales in millions of dollars for year 0, or 2000.

t refers to the yearly increase in sales.

In Chapter 13 we drew a line through points on a scatter diagram to approximate the regression line. We stressed, however, that this method for determining the regression equation has a serious drawback—namely, the position of the line depends on the judgment of the individual who drew the line. Three people would probably draw three different lines through the scatter plots. Likewise, the line we drew through the sales data in Chart 16–5 might not be the best-fitting line. Because of the subjective judgment involved, this method should be used only when a quick approximation of the straight-line equation is needed, or to check the reasonableness of the least squares line, which is discussed next.

Least Squares Method

In the discussion of simple linear regression in Chapter 13, we showed how the least squares method is used to find the best linear relationship between two variables. In forecasting methods, time is the independent variable and the value of the time series is the dependent variable. Furthermore, we often code the independent variable time to make the equations easier to interpret. In other words, we let t be 1 for the first year, 2 for the second, and so on. If a time series includes the sales of General Electric for five years starting in 2002 and continuing through 2006, we would code the year 2002 as 1, 2003 as 2, and 2006 as 5.

Example

The sales of Jensen Foods, a small grocery chain located in southwest Texas, since 2005 are:

Year	Sales ($ million)
2005	7
2006	10
2007	9
2008	11
2009	13

Determine the regression equation. How much are sales increasing each year? What is the sales forecast for 2012?

Solution

To determine the trend equation we could use formula (13–4) to find the slope, or b value, and formula (13–5) to locate the intercept, or a value. We would substitute t, the coded values for the year, for X in these equations. Another approach is to use a software package, such as MINITAB or Excel. Chart 16–6 is output from MINITAB. The values for year, coded year, sales, and fitted sales are shown in the lower right portion of the output. The left half is a scatter plot of the data and the fitted regression line.

From the output the trend equation is $\hat{Y} = 6.1 + 1.3t$. How do we interpret this equation? The sales are in millions of dollars. So the value 1.3 tells us that sales

CHART 16–6 Sales and Trend Line, 2005–2009

Statistics in Action

Investors frequently use regression analysis to study the relationship between a particular stock and the general condition of the market. The dependent variable is the monthly percentage change in the value of the stock, and the independent variable is the monthly percentage change in a market index, such as the Standard & Poor's 500 Composite Index. The value of *b* in the regression equation is the particular stock's *beta coefficient* or just the *beta*. If *b* is greater than 1, the implication is that the stock is sensitive to market changes. If *b* is between 0 and 1, the implication is that the stock is not sensitive to market changes.

increased at a rate of 1.3 million dollars per year. The value 6.1 is the estimated value of sales in the year 0. That is the estimate for 2004, which is called the base year. For example, to determine the point on the line for 2008, insert the *t* value of 4 in the equation. Then $\hat{Y} = 6.1 + 1.3(4) = 11.3$.

If sales, production, or other data approximate a linear trend, the equation developed by the least squares technique can be used to estimate future values. It is reasonable that the sales for Jensen Foods follow a linear trend. So we can use the trend equation to forecast future sales.

See Table 16–4. The year 2005 is coded 1, the year 2007 is coded 3, and 2009 is coded 5. Logically we code 2011 as 7 and 2012 as 8. So we substitute 8 into the trend equation and solve for $\hat{Y}$.

$$\hat{Y} = 6.1 + 1.3t = 6.1 + 1.3(8) = 16.5$$

Thus, on the basis of past sales, the estimate for 2012 is $16.5 million.

TABLE 16–4 Calculations for Determining the Points on the Least Squares Line Using the Coded Values

Year	Sales ($ millions), Y	t	$\hat{Y}$	Found by
2005	7	1	7.4	6.1 + 1.3(1)
2006	10	2	8.7	6.1 + 1.3(2)
2007	9	3	10	6.1 + 1.3(3)
2008	11	4	11.3	6.1 + 1.3(4)
2009	13	5	12.6	6.1 + 1.3(5)

In this time series example, there were five years of sales data. Based on those five sales figures, we estimated sales for 2012. Many researchers suggest that we do not project sales, production, and other business and economic series more than $n/2$ time periods into the future where n is the number of data points. If, for example, there are 10 years of data, we would make estimates only up to 5 years into the future ($n/2 = 10/2 = 5$). Others suggest the forecast may be for no longer than 2 years, especially in rapidly changing economic times.

Self-Review 16–2   Annual production of king-size rockers by Wood Products, Inc., since 2002 follows.

Year	Production (thousands)	Year	Production (thousands)
2002	4	2006	11
2003	8	2007	9
2004	5	2008	11
2005	8	2009	14

(a)   Plot the production data.
(b)   Determine the least squares equation using a software package.
(c)   Determine the points on the line for 2002 and 2008. Connect the two points to arrive at the line.
(d)   Based on the linear trend equation, what is the estimated production for 2012?

Exercises

connect™

3. Listed below are the net sales for Schering-Plough Corporation (a pharmaceutical company) and its subsidiaries for the years from 1997 to 2007. The net sales are in millions of dollars.

Year	Net Sales	Year	Net Sales	Year	Net Sales
1997	$ 6,714	2001	$ 9,762	2005	$ 6,162
1998	7,991	2002	10,180	2006	6,897
1999	9,075	2003	8,334	2007	8,285
2000	9,775	2004	8,272		

Determine the least squares equation. According to this information, what are the estimated sales for 2008?

4. Listed below is the net sales in $ million for Home Depot, Inc., and its subsidiaries from 1993 to 2007.

Year	Net Sales	Year	Net Sales	Year	Net Sales
1993	9,239	1998	30,219	2003	64,816
1994	12,477	1999	38,434	2004	73,094
1995	15,470	2000	45,738	2005	81,511
1996	19,535	2001	53,553	2006	90,837
1997	24,156	2002	58,247	2007	77,349

Determine the least squares equation. On the basis of this information, what are the estimated sales for 2008 and 2009?

5. The following table lists the annual amounts of glass cullet produced by Kimble Glass Works, Inc.

Year	Code	Scrap (tons)
2002	1	2.0
2003	2	4.0
2004	3	3.0
2005	4	5.0
2006	5	6.0

Determine the least squares trend equation. Estimate the amount of scrap for the year 2008.

6. The amounts spent in vending machines in the United States, in billions of dollars, for the years 1999 through 2005 are given below. Determine the least squares trend equation, and estimate vending sales for 2007.

Year	Code	Vending Machine Sales ($ billions)
1999	1	17.5
2000	2	19.0
2001	3	21.0
2002	4	22.7
2003	5	24.5
2004	6	26.7
2005	7	27.3

Nonlinear Trends

The emphasis in the previous discussion was on a time series whose growth or decline approximated a line. A linear trend equation is used to represent the time series when it is believed that the data are increasing (or decreasing) by *equal amounts,* on the average, from one period to another.

Data that increase (or decrease) by *increasing amounts* over a period of time appear *curvilinear* when plotted on paper having an arithmetic scale. To put it another way, data that increase (or decrease) by *equal percents* or *proportions* over a period of time appear curvilinear on arithmetic paper. (See Chart 16–7.)

The trend equation for a time series that does approximate a curvilinear trend, such as the one portrayed in Chart 16–7, may be computed by using the logarithms of the data and the least squares method. The general equation for the logarithmic trend equation is:

LOG TREND EQUATION	$\log \hat{Y} = \log a + \log b(t)$	[16–2]

The logarithmic trend equation can be determined for the Gulf Shores Importers data in Chart 16–7 using Excel. The first step is to enter the data, then find the log base 10 of each year's imports. Finally, use the regression procedure to find the least squares equation. To put it another way, we take the log of each year's data, then use the logs as the dependent variable and the coded year as the independent variable.

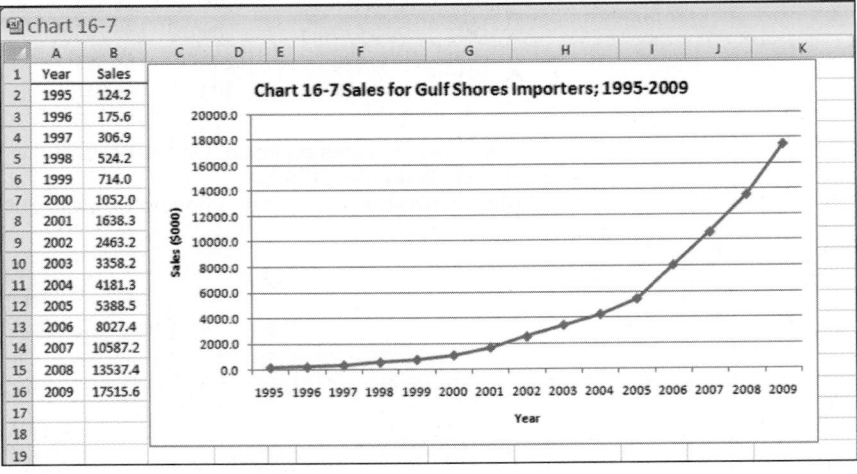

CHART 16–7 Sales for Gulf Shores Importers from 1995–2009

Excel

	A	B	C	D	E	F	G	H	I	J
						chart 16-7				
1	Year	Sales	Log-Sales	Code		SUMMARY OUTPUT				
2	1995	124.2	2.094122	1						
3	1996	175.6	2.244525	2		*Regression Statistics*				
4	1997	306.9	2.486997	3		Multiple R	0.994			
5	1998	524.2	2.719497	4		R Square	0.988			
6	1999	714.0	2.853698	5		Adjusted R Square	0.987			
7	2000	1052.0	3.022016	6		Standard Error	0.079			
8	2001	1638.3	3.214393	7		Observations	15			
9	2002	2463.2	3.3915	8						
10	2003	3358.2	3.526107	9		ANOVA				
11	2004	4181.3	3.621311	10			*df*	*SS*	*MS*	*F*
12	2005	5388.5	3.731468	11		Regression	1	6.585	6.585	1065.228
13	2006	8027.4	3.904575	12		Residual	13	0.080	0.006	
14	2007	10587.2	4.024781	13		Total	14	6.666		
15	2008	13537.4	4.131535	14						
16	2009	17515.6	4.243425	15			*Coefficients*	*Standard Error*	*t Stat*	*P-value*
17						Intercept	2.053805	0.0427	48.0741	0.0000
18						Code	0.153357	0.0047	32.6378	0.0000

The regression equation is $\hat{Y} = 2.053805 + 0.153357t$, which is the log form. We now have a trend equation in terms of percent of change. That is, the value 0.153357 is the percent of change in $\hat{Y}$ for each unit increase in t. This value is similar to the geometric mean described in Chapter 3.

The log of b is 0.153357 and its antilog or inverse is 1.423498. If we subtract 1 from this value, as we did in Chapter 3, the value 0.423498 indicates the geometric mean annual rate of increase from 1995 to 2009. We conclude that imports increased at a rate of 42.35 percent annually during the period.

We can also use the logarithmic trend equation to make estimates of future values. Suppose we want to estimate the imports in the year 2013. The first step is to determine the code for the year 2013, which is 19. How did we get 19? The year 2009 has a code of 15 and the year 2013 is four years later, so 15 + 4 = 19. The log of imports for the year 2013 is

$$\hat{Y} = 2.053805 + 0.153357t = 2.053805 + 0.153357(19) = 4.967588$$

To find the estimated imports for the year 2013, we need the antilog of 4.967588. It is 92,809. This is our estimate of the number of imports for 2013. Recall that the data were in thousands of dollars, so the estimate is $92,809,000.

Self-Review 16–3

Sales at Tomlin Manufacturing since 2005 are:

Year	Sales ($ millions)
2005	2.13
2006	18.10
2007	39.80
2008	81.40
2009	112.00

(a) Determine the logarithmic trend equation for the sales data.
(b) Sales increased by what percent annually from 2005 to 2009?
(c) What is the projected sales amount for 2010?

Exercises

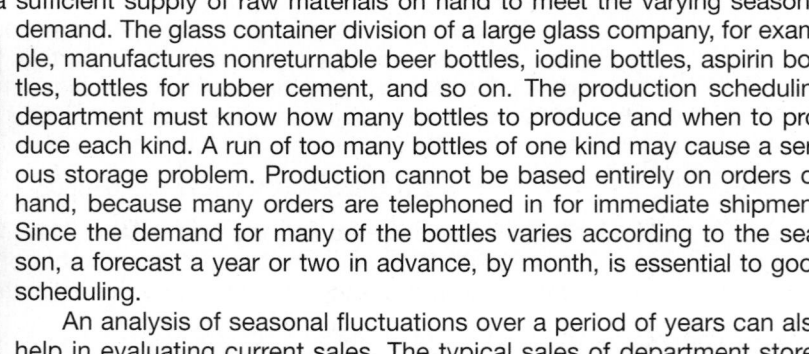

connect™

Year	Sales ($ millions)
2002	1.1
2003	1.5
2004	2.0
2005	2.4
2006	3.1

7. Sally's Software, Inc., is a rapidly growing supplier of computer software to the Sarasota area. Sales for the last five years are given on the left.
   a. Determine the logarithmic trend equation.
   b. By what percent did sales increase, on the average, during the period?
   c. Estimate sales for the year 2009.
8. It appears that the imports of carbon black have been increasing by about 10 percent annually.

Year	Imports of Carbon Black (thousands of tons)	Year	Imports of Carbon Black (thousands of tons)
1999	92.0	2003	135.0
2000	101.0	2004	149.0
2001	112.0	2005	163.0
2002	124.0	2006	180.0

   a. Determine the logarithmic trend equation.
   b. By what percent did imports increase, on the average, during the period?
   c. Estimate imports for the year 2009.

Seasonal Variation

We mentioned that *seasonal variation* is another of the components of a time series. Business series, such as automobile sales, shipments of soft-drink bottles, and residential construction, have periods of above-average and below-average activity each year.

In the area of production, one of the reasons for analyzing seasonal fluctuations is to have a sufficient supply of raw materials on hand to meet the varying seasonal demand. The glass container division of a large glass company, for example, manufactures nonreturnable beer bottles, iodine bottles, aspirin bottles, bottles for rubber cement, and so on. The production scheduling department must know how many bottles to produce and when to produce each kind. A run of too many bottles of one kind may cause a serious storage problem. Production cannot be based entirely on orders on hand, because many orders are telephoned in for immediate shipment. Since the demand for many of the bottles varies according to the season, a forecast a year or two in advance, by month, is essential to good scheduling.

An analysis of seasonal fluctuations over a period of years can also help in evaluating current sales. The typical sales of department stores in the United States, excluding mail-order sales, are expressed as indexes in Table 16–5. Each index represents the average sales for a period of several years. The actual sales for some months were above average (which is represented by an index over 100.0), and the sales for other months were below average. The index of 126.8 for December indicates that, typically, sales for December are 26.8 percent above an average month; the index of 86.0 for July indicates that department store sales for July are typically 14 percent below an average month.

TABLE 16–5 Typical Seasonal Indexes for U.S. Department Store Sales, Excluding Mail-Order Sales

January	87.0	July	86.0
February	83.2	August	99.7
March	100.5	September	101.4
April	106.5	October	105.8
May	101.6	November	111.9
June	89.6	December	126.8

Suppose an enterprising store manager, in an effort to stimulate sales during December, introduced a number of unique promotions, including bands of carolers strolling through the store singing holiday songs, large mechanical exhibits, and clerks dressed in Santa Claus costumes. When the index of sales was computed for that December, it was 150.0. Compared with the typical December sales of 126.8, it was concluded that the promotional program was a huge success.

Determining a Seasonal Index

Objective: To determine a set of "typical" seasonal indexes

A typical set of monthly indexes consists of 12 indexes that are representative of the data for a 12-month period. Logically, there are four typical seasonal indexes for data reported quarterly. Each index is a percent, with the average for the year equal to 100.0; that is, each monthly index indicates the level of sales, production, or another variable in relation to the annual average of 100.0. A typical index of 96.0 for January indicates that sales (or whatever the variable is) are usually 4 percent below the average for the year. An index of 107.2 for October means that the variable is typically 7.2 percent above the annual average.

Several methods have been developed to measure the typical seasonal fluctuation in a time series. The method most commonly used to compute the typical seasonal pattern is called the **ratio-to-moving-average method.** It eliminates the trend, cyclical, and irregular components from the original data (Y). In the following discussion, T refers to trend, C to cyclical, S to seasonal, and I to irregular variation. The numbers that result are called the *typical seasonal index.*

We will discuss in detail the steps followed in arriving at typical seasonal indexes using the ratio-to-moving-average method. The data of interest might be monthly or quarterly. To illustrate, we have chosen the quarterly sales of Toys International. First, we will show the steps needed to arrive at a set of typical quarterly indexes. Then we use MegaStat Excel and MINITAB software to calculate the seasonal indexes.

Example

Table 16–6 shows the quarterly sales for Toys International for the years 2004 through 2009. The sales are reported in millions of dollars. Determine a quarterly seasonal index using the ratio-to-moving-average method.

TABLE 16–6 Quarterly Sales of Toys International ($ millions)

Year	Winter	Spring	Summer	Fall
2004	6.7	4.6	10.0	12.7
2005	6.5	4.6	9.8	13.6
2006	6.9	5.0	10.4	14.1
2007	7.0	5.5	10.8	15.0
2008	7.1	5.7	11.1	14.5
2009	8.0	6.2	11.4	14.9

Solution

Chart 16–8 depicts the quarterly sales for Toys International over the six-year period. Notice the seasonal nature of the sales. For each year, the fourth-quarter sales are the largest and the second-quarter sales are the smallest. Also, there is a moderate increase in the sales from one year to the next. To observe this feature, look only at the six fourth-quarter sales values. Over the six-year period, the sales in the fourth quarter increased. If you connect these points in your mind, you can visualize fourth-quarter sales increasing for 2010.

There are six steps to determining the quarterly seasonal indexes.

> **Step 1:** For the following discussion, refer to Table 16–7. The first step is to determine the four-quarter moving total for 2004. Starting with the winter quarter of 2004, we add $6.7, $4.6, $10.0, and $12.7. The total is $34.0 (million). The four-quarter total is "moved along" by adding the spring,

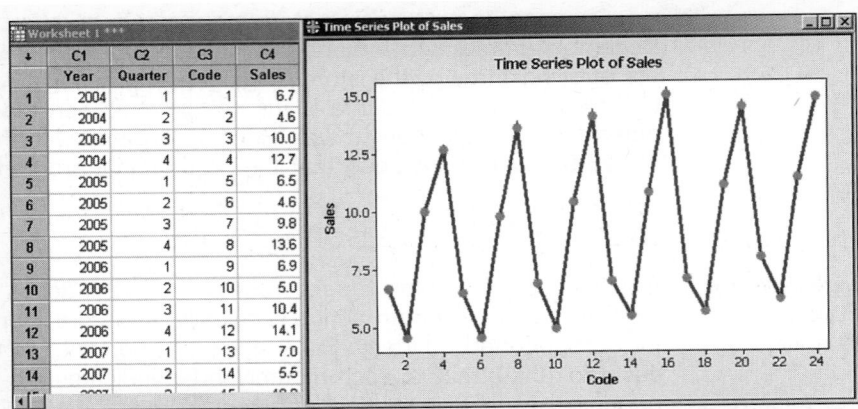

CHART 16–8 Quarterly Sales of Toys International 2004–2009

summer, and fall sales of 2004 to the winter sales of 2005. The total is $33.8 (million), found by 4.6 + 10.0 + 12.7 + 6.5. This procedure is continued for the quarterly sales for each of the six years. Column 2 of Table 16–7 shows all of the moving totals. Note that the moving total 34.0 is positioned between the spring and summer sales of 2004. The next moving total, 33.8, is positioned between sales for summer and fall 2004, and so on. Check the totals frequently to avoid arithmetic errors.

TABLE 16–7 Computations Needed for the Specific Seasonal Indexes

Year	Quarter	(1) Sales ($ millions)	(2) Four-Quarter Total	(3) Four-Quarter Moving Average	(4) Centered Moving Average	(5) Specific Seasonal
2004	Winter	6.7				
	Spring	4.6				
			34.0	8.500		
	Summer	10.0			8.475	1.180
			33.8	8.450		
	Fall	12.7			8.450	1.503
			33.8	8.450		
2005	Winter	6.5			8.425	0.772
			33.6	8.400		
	Spring	4.6			8.513	0.540
			34.5	8.625		
	Summer	9.8			8.675	1.130
			34.9	8.725		
	Fall	13.6			8.775	1.550
			35.3	8.825		
2006	Winter	6.9			8.900	0.775
			35.9	8.975		
	Spring	5.0			9.038	0.553
			36.4	9.100		

(continued)

Year	Quarter	(1) Sales ($ millions)	(2) Four-Quarter Total	(3) Four-Quarter Moving Average	(4) Centered Moving Average	(5) Specific Seasonal
	Summer	10.4			9.113	1.141
			36.5	9.125		
	Fall	14.1			9.188	1.535
			37.0	9.250		
2007	Winter	7.0			9.300	0.753
			37.4	9.350		
	Spring	5.5			9.463	0.581
			38.3	9.575		
	Summer	10.8			9.588	1.126
			38.4	9.600		
	Fall	15.0			9.625	1.558
			38.6	9.650		
2008	Winter	7.1			9.688	0.733
			38.9	9.725		
	Spring	5.7			9.663	0.590
			38.4	9.600		
	Summer	11.1			9.713	1.143
			39.3	9.825		
	Fall	14.5			9.888	1.466
			39.8	9.950		
2009	Winter	8.0			9.888	0.801
			40.1	10.025		
	Spring	6.2			10.075	0.615
			40.5	10.125		
	Summer	11.4				
	Fall	14.9				

Step 2: Each quarterly moving total in column 2 is divided by 4 to give the four-quarter moving average. (See column 3.) All the moving averages are still positioned between the quarters. For example, the first moving average (8.500) is positioned between spring and summer 2004.

Step 3: The moving averages are then centered. The first centered moving average is found by (8.500 + 8.450)/2 = 8.475 and centered opposite summer 2004. The second moving average is found by (8.450 + 8.450)/2 = 8.450. The others are found similarly. Note in column 4 that a centered moving average is positioned on a particular quarter.

Step 4: The **specific seasonal index** for each quarter is then computed by dividing the sales in column 1 by the centered moving average in column 4. The specific seasonal index reports the ratio of the original time series value to the moving average. To explain further, if the time series is represented by *TSCI* and the moving average by *TC*, then, algebraically, if we compute *TSCI/TC*, the result is the specified seasonal component *SI*. The specific seasonal index for the summer quarter of 2004 is 1.180, found by 10.0/8.475.

Step 5: The specific seasonal indexes are organized in Table 16–8. This table will help us locate the specific seasonals for the corresponding quarters. The values 1.180, 1.130, 1.141, 1.126, and 1.143 all represent estimates of the typical seasonal index for the summer quarter. A reasonable method to find a typical seasonal index is to average these values in order to eliminate the irregular component. So we find the typical index for the summer quarter by (1.180 + 1.130 + 1.141 + 1.126 + 1.143)/5 = 1.144. We used the arithmetic mean, but the median or a modified mean can also be used.

TABLE 16–8 Calculations Needed for Typical Quarterly Indexes

Year	Winter	Spring	Summer	Fall	
2004			1.180	1.503	
2005	0.772	0.540	1.130	1.550	
2006	0.775	0.553	1.141	1.535	
2007	0.753	0.581	1.126	1.558	
2008	0.733	0.590	1.143	1.466	
2009	0.801	0.615			
Total	3.834	2.879	5.720	7.612	
Mean	0.767	0.576	1.144	1.522	4.009
Adjusted	0.765	0.575	1.141	1.519	4.000
Index	76.5	57.5	114.1	151.9	

Step 6: The four quarterly means (0.767, 0.576, 1.144, and 1.522) should theoretically total 4.00 because the average is set at 1.0. The total of the four quarterly means may not exactly equal 4.00 due to rounding. In this problem the total of the means is 4.009. A *correction factor* is therefore applied to each of the four means to force them to total 4.00.

> **CORRECTION FACTOR FOR ADJUSTING QUARTERLY MEANS** $\qquad \text{Correction factor} = \dfrac{4.00}{\text{Total of four means}}$ **[16–3]**

In this example,

$$\text{Correction factor} = \frac{4.00}{4.009} = 0.997755$$

The adjusted winter quarterly index is, therefore, .767(.997755) = .765. Each of the means is adjusted downward so that the total of the four quarterly means is 4.00. Usually indexes are reported as percentages, so each value in the last row of Table 16–8 has been multiplied by 100. So the index for the winter quarter is 76.5 and for the fall it is 151.9. How are these values interpreted? Sales for the fall quarter are 51.9 percent above the typical quarter, and for winter they are 23.5 below the typical quarter (100.0 − 76.5). These findings should not surprise you. The period prior to Christmas (the fall quarter) is when toy sales are brisk. After Christmas (the winter quarter), sales of the toys decline drastically.

As we noted earlier there is software that will perform the calculations and output the results. The MegaStat Excel output is shown below. Use of software will greatly reduce the computational time and the chance of an error in arithmetic, but you should understand the steps in the process, as outlined earlier. There can be slight differences in the answers, due to the number of digits carried in the calculations.

Centered Moving Average and Deseasonalization

t	Year	Quarter	Sales	Centered Moving Average	Ratio to CMA	Seasonal Indexes	Sales Deseasonalized
1	2004	1	6.70			0.765	8.759
2	2004	2	4.60			0.575	8.004
3	2004	3	10.00	8.475	1.180	1.141	8.761
4	2004	4	12.70	8.450	1.503	1.519	8.361
5	2005	1	6.50	8.425	0.772	0.765	8.498
6	2005	2	4.60	8.513	0.540	0.575	8.004
7	2005	3	9.80	8.675	1.130	1.141	8.586
8	2005	4	13.60	8.775	1.550	1.519	8.953
							(continued)

Centered Moving Average and Deseasonalization

t	Year	Quarter	Sales	Centered Moving Average	Ratio to CMA	Seasonal Indexes	Sales Deseasonalized
9	2006	1	6.90	8.900	0.775	0.765	9.021
10	2006	2	5.00	9.038	0.553	0.575	8.700
11	2006	3	10.40	9.113	1.141	1.141	9.112
12	2006	4	14.10	9.188	1.535	1.519	9.283
13	2007	1	7.00	9.300	0.753	0.765	9.151
14	2007	2	5.50	9.463	0.581	0.575	9.570
15	2007	3	10.80	9.588	1.126	1.141	9.462
16	2007	4	15.00	9.625	1.558	1.519	9.875
17	2008	1	7.10	9.688	0.733	0.765	9.282
18	2008	2	5.70	9.663	0.590	0.575	9.918
19	2008	3	11.10	9.713	1.143	1.141	9.725
20	2008	4	14.50	9.888	1.466	1.519	9.546
21	2009	1	8.00	9.988	0.801	0.765	10.459
22	2009	2	6.20	10.075	0.615	0.575	10.788
23	2009	3	11.40			1.141	9.988
24	2009	4	14.90			1.519	9.809

 **MegaStat**

Calculation of Seasonal Indexes

	1	2	3	4	
2004			1.180	1.503	
2005	0.772	0.540	1.130	1.550	
2006	0.775	0.553	1.141	1.535	
2007	0.753	0.581	1.126	1.558	
2008	0.733	0.590	1.143	1.466	
2009	0.801	0.615			
Mean:	0.767	0.576	1.144	1.522	4.009
Adjusted:	0.765	0.575	1.141	1.519	4.000

Now we briefly summarize the reasoning underlying the preceding calculations. The original data in column 1 of Table 16–7 contain trend (T), cyclical (C), seasonal (S), and irregular (I) components. The ultimate objective is to remove seasonal (S) from the original sales valuation.

Columns 2 and 3 in Table 16–7 are concerned with deriving the centered moving average given in column 4. Basically, we "average out" the seasonal and irregular fluctuations from the original data in column 1. Thus, in column 4 we have only trend and cyclical (TC).

Next, we divide the sales data in column 1 ($TCSI$) by the centered fourth-quarter moving average in column 4 (TC) to arrive at the specific seasonals in column 5 (SI). In terms of letters, $TCSI/TC = SI$. We multiply SI by 100.0 to express the typical seasonal in index form.

Finally, we take the mean of all the winter typical indexes, all the spring indexes, and so on. This averaging eliminates most of the irregular fluctuations from the specific seasonals, and the resulting four indexes indicate the typical seasonal sales pattern.

Self-Review 16–4

Teton Village, Wyoming, near Grand Teton Park and Yellowstone Park, contains shops, restaurants, and motels. The village has two peak seasons—winter, for skiing on the 10,000-foot slopes, and summer, for tourists visiting the parks. The number of visitors (in thousands) by quarter for five years follows.

	Quarter			
Year	Winter	Spring	Summer	Fall
2005	117.0	80.7	129.6	76.1
2006	118.6	82.5	121.4	77.0
2007	114.0	84.3	119.9	75.0
2008	120.7	79.6	130.7	69.6
2009	125.2	80.2	127.6	72.0

(a) Develop the typical seasonal pattern for Teton Village using the ratio-to-moving-average method.
(b) Explain the typical index for the winter season.

Exercises

connect

9. Victor Anderson, the owner of Anderson Belts, Inc., is studying absenteeism among his employees. His workforce is small, consisting of only five employees. For the last three years he recorded the following number of employee absences, in days, for each quarter.

	Quarter			
Year	I	II	III	IV
2006	4	10	7	3
2007	5	12	9	4
2008	6	16	12	4

Determine a typical seasonal index for each of the four quarters.

10. Appliance Center sells a variety of electronic equipment and home appliances. For the last four years the following quarterly sales (in $ millions) were reported.

	Quarter			
Year	I	II	III	IV
2006	5.3	4.1	6.8	6.7
2007	4.8	3.8	5.6	6.8
2008	4.3	3.8	5.7	6.0
2009	5.6	4.6	6.4	5.9

Determine a typical seasonal index for each of the four quarters.

Deseasonalizing Data

A set of typical indexes is very useful in adjusting a sales series, for example, for seasonal fluctuations. The resulting sales series is called **deseasonalized sales** or **seasonally adjusted sales.** The reason for deseasonalizing the sales series is to remove the seasonal fluctuations so that the trend and cycle can be studied. To illustrate the procedure, the quarterly sales totals of Toys International from Table 16–6 are repeated in column 1 of Table 16–9.

To remove the effect of seasonal variation, the sales amount for each quarter (which contains trend, cyclical, irregular, and seasonal effects) is divided by the seasonal index for that quarter, that is, $TSCI/S$. For example, the actual sales for the first quarter of 2004 were $6.7 million. The seasonal index for the winter quarter is 76.5 percent, using the MegaStat results on page 616. The index of 76.5 indicates that sales for the first quarter are typically 23.5 percent below the average for a typical quarter. By dividing the actual sales of $6.7 million by 76.5 and multiplying the result by 100, we find the *deseasonalized sales* value—that is, removed the seasonal effect on sales—for the first quarter of 2004. It is $8,758,170, found by ($6,700,000/76.5)100.

TABLE 16–9 Actual and Deseasonalized Sales for Toys International

Year	Quarter	(1) Sales	(2) Seasonal Index	(3) Deseasonalized Sales
2004	Winter	6.7	0.765	8.76
	Spring	4.6	0.575	8.00
	Summer	10.0	1.141	8.76
	Fall	12.7	1.519	8.36
2005	Winter	6.5	0.765	8.50
	Spring	4.6	0.575	8.00
	Summer	9.8	1.141	8.59
	Fall	13.6	1.519	8.95
2006	Winter	6.9	0.765	9.02
	Spring	5.0	0.575	8.70
	Summer	10.4	1.141	9.11
	Fall	14.1	1.519	9.28
2007	Winter	7.0	0.765	9.15
	Spring	5.5	0.575	9.57
	Summer	10.8	1.141	9.47
	Fall	15.0	1.519	9.87
2008	Winter	7.1	0.765	9.28
	Spring	5.7	0.575	9.91
	Summer	11.1	1.141	9.73
	Fall	14.5	1.519	9.55
2009	Winter	8.0	0.765	10.46
	Spring	6.2	0.575	10.79
	Summer	11.4	1.141	9.99
	Fall	14.9	1.519	9.81

We continue this process for the other quarters in column 3 of Table 16–9, with the results reported in millions of dollars. Because the seasonal component has been removed (divided out) from the quarterly sales, the deseasonalized sales figure contains only the trend (T), cyclical (C), and irregular (I) components. Scanning the deseasonalized sales in column 3 of Table 16–9, we see that the sales of toys showed a moderate increase over the six-year period. Chart 16–9 shows both the actual sales and the deseasonalized sales. It is clear that removing the seasonal factor allows us to focus on the overall long-term trend of sales. We will also be able to determine the regression equation of the trend data and use it to forecast future sales.

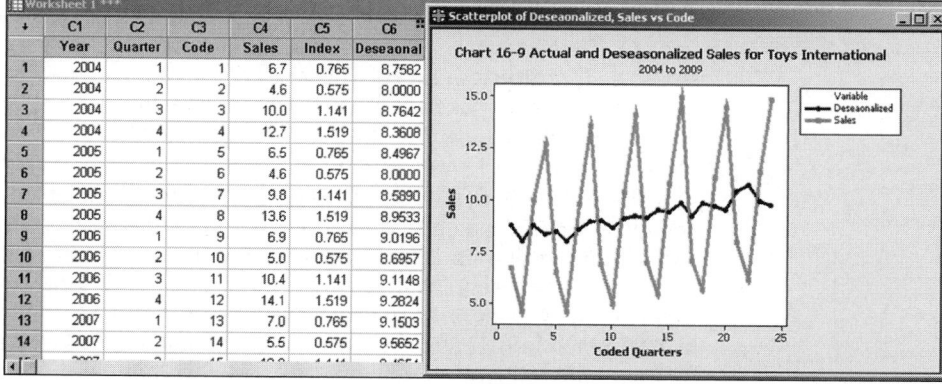

CHART 16–9 Actual and Deseasonalized Sales for Toys International from 2004–2009

Using Deseasonalized Data to Forecast

The procedure for identifying trend and the seasonal adjustments can be combined to yield seasonally adjusted forecasts. To identify the trend, we determine the least squares trend equation on the deseasonalized historical data. Then we project this trend into future periods, and finally we adjust these trend values to account for the seasonal factors. The following example will help to clarify.

Example

Toys International would like to forecast its sales for each quarter of 2010. Use the information in Table 16–9 to determine the forecast.

Solution

The deseasonalized data depicted in Chart 16–9 seems to follow a straight line. Hence it is reasonable to develop a linear trend equation based on these data. The deseasonalized trend equation is:

$$\hat{Y} = a + bt$$

where
$\hat{Y}$ is the estimated trend value for Toys International sales for the period t.
a is the intercept of the trend line at time 0.
b is the slope of the line.
t is the coded time period.

The winter quarter of 2004 is the first quarter, so it is coded 1, the spring quarter of 2004 is coded 2, and so on. The last quarter of 2009 is coded 24. A portion of these coded values are shown in the data section of the MINITAB output associated with Chart 16–9.

We use MINITAB to find the regression equation. The output follows. The output includes a scatter diagram of the coded time periods and the deseasonalized sales as well as the regression line.

The equation for the trend line is:

$$\hat{Y} = 8.109 + .08991t$$

The slope of the trend line is .08991. This shows that over the 24 quarters the deseasonalized sales increased at a rate of 0.08991 ($ million) per quarter, or $89,910 per quarter. The value of 8.109 is the intercept of the trend line on the Y-axis (i.e., for $t = 0$).

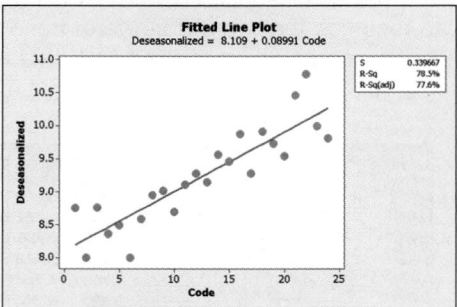

The MINITAB system also outputs the coefficient of determination. This value, called R^2, is 78.6 percent. It is shown in the upper right of the MINITAB output. We can use this value as an indication of the fit of the data. Because this is *not* sample information, technically we should not use R^2 for judging a regression equation. However, it will serve to quickly evaluate the fit of the deseasonalized sales data. In this instance, because R^2 is rather large, we conclude the deseasonalized sales of Toys International are effectively explained by a linear trend equation.

If we assume that the past 24 periods are a good indicator of future sales, we can use the trend equation to estimate future sales. For example, for the winter quarter of 2010 the value of t is 25. Therefore, the estimated sales of that period is 10.35675, found by

$$\hat{Y} = 8.109 + .08991t = 8.109 + .08991(25) = 10.35675$$

The estimated deseasonalized sales for the winter quarter of 2010 are $10,356,750. This is the sales forecast, before we consider the effects of seasonality.

We use the same procedure and an Excel spreadsheet to determine a forecast for each of the four quarters of 2010. A partial Excel output follows.

quarterly forecasts

	A	B	C	D	E	F	G
1			Quarterly Forecast for Toys International				
2				2010			
3							
4		Quarter	t value	Estimated Sales	Seasonal Index	Quarterly Forecast	
5		Winter	25	10.3565	0.765	7.923	
6		Spring	26	10.4464	0.575	6.007	
7		Summer	27	10.5363	1.141	12.022	
8		Fall	28	10.6262	1.519	16.141	
9							

Now that we have the forecasts for the four quarters of 2010, we can seasonally adjust them. The index for a winter quarter is 0.765. So we can seasonally adjust the forecast for the winter quarter of 2010 by 10.35675(0.765) = 7.923. The estimates for each of the four quarters of 2010 are in the right-hand column of the Excel output. Notice how the seasonal adjustments drastically increase the sales estimates for the last two quarters of the year.

Self-Review 16–5

Westberg Electric Company sells electric motors to customers in the Jamestown, New York, area. The monthly trend equation, based on five years of monthly data, is

$$\hat{Y} = 4.4 + 0.5t$$

The seasonal factor for the month of January is 120, and it is 95 for February. Determine the seasonally adjusted forecast for January and February of the sixth year.

Exercises

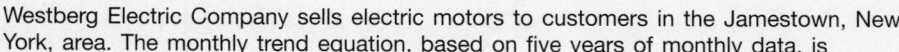

11. The planning department of Padget and Kure Shoes, the manufacturer of an exclusive brand of women's shoes, developed the following trend equation, in millions of pairs, based on five years of quarterly data.

$$\hat{Y} = 3.30 + 1.75t$$

The following table gives the seasonal factors for each quarter.

	Quarter			
	I	**II**	**III**	**IV**
Index	110.0	120.0	80.0	90.0

Determine the seasonally adjusted forecast for each of the four quarters of the sixth year.

12. Team Sports, Inc., sells sporting goods to high schools and colleges via a nationally distributed catalog. Management at Team Sports estimates it will sell 2,000 Wilson Model A2000 catcher's mitts next year. The deseasonalized sales are projected to be the same for each of the four quarters next year. The seasonal factor for the second quarter is 145. Determine the seasonally adjusted sales for the second quarter of next year.

13. Refer to Exercise 9, regarding the absences at Anderson Belts, Inc. Use the seasonal indexes you computed to determine the deseasonalized absences. Determine the linear trend equation based on the quarterly data for the three years. Forecast the seasonally adjusted absences for 2009.

14. Refer to Exercise 10, regarding sales at Appliance Center. Use the seasonal indexes you computed to determine the deseasonalized sales. Determine the linear trend equation based on the quarterly data for the four years. Forecast the seasonally adjusted sales for 2010.

The Durbin-Watson Statistic

Time series data or observations collected successively over a period of time present a particular difficulty when you use the technique of regression. One of the assumptions traditionally used in regression is that the successive residuals are independent. This means that there is not a pattern to the residuals, the residuals are not highly correlated, and there are not long runs of positive or negative residuals. In Chart 16–10 the residuals are scaled on the vertical axis and the $\hat{Y}$ values along the horizontal axis. Notice there are "runs" of residuals above and below the 0 line. If we computed the correlation between successive residuals, it is likely the correlation would be strong.

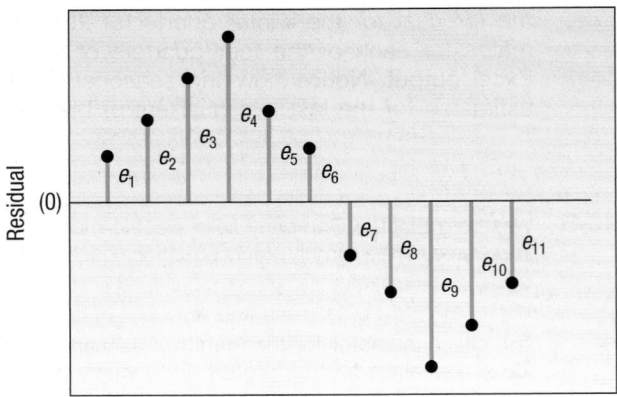

CHART 16–10 Correlated Residuals

This condition is called **autocorrelation** or serial correlation.

AUTOCORRELATION Successive residuals are correlated.

Successive residuals are correlated in time series data because an event in one time period often influences the event in the next period. To explain, the owner of a furniture store decides to have a sale this month and spends a large amount of money advertising the event. We would expect a correlation between sales and advertising expense, but all the results of the increase in advertising are not experienced this month. It is likely that some of the effect of the advertising carries over into next month. Therefore, we expect correlation among the residuals.

The regression relationship in a time series is written

$$Y_t = \alpha + \beta_1 X_t + \varepsilon_t$$

where the subscript t is used in place of i to suggest the data were collected over time.

If the residuals are correlated, problems occur when we try to conduct tests of hypotheses about the regression coefficients. Also, a confidence interval or a prediction interval, where the multiple standard error of estimate is used, may not yield the correct results.

The autocorrelation, reported as r, is the strength of the association among the residuals. The r has the same meaning as the coefficient of correlation. That is, values close to -1.00 or 1.00 indicate a strong association, and values near 0 indicate no association. Instead of directly conducting a hypothesis test on r, we use the **Durbin-Watson statistic.**

The Durbin-Watson statistic, identified by the letter d, is computed by first determining the residuals for each observation. That is, $e_t = (Y_t - \hat{Y_t})$. Next, we compute d using the following relationship.

DURBIN-WATSON STATISTIC	$$d = \dfrac{\sum\limits_{t=2}^{n}(e_t - e_{t-1})^2}{\sum\limits_{t=1}^{n}(e_t)^2}$$	**[16–4]**

To determine the numerator of formula (16–4), we lag each of the residuals one period and then square the difference between consecutive residuals. This may also be called finding the differences. This accounts for summing the observations from 2, rather than from 1, up to n. In the denominator we square the residuals and sum over all n observations.

The value of the Durbin-Watson statistic can range from 0 to 4. The value of d is 2.00 when there is no autocorrelation among the residuals. When the value of d gets close to 0, this indicates positive autocorrelation. Values beyond 2 indicate negative autocorrelation. Negative autocorrelation seldom exists in practice. To occur, successive residuals would tend to be large, but would have opposite signs.

To conduct a test for autocorrelation, the null and alternate hypotheses are:

H_0: No residual correlation ($\rho = 0$)
H_1: Positive residual correlation ($\rho > 0$)

Recall from the previous chapter that r refers to the sample correlation and that ρ is the correlation coefficient in the population. The critical values for d are reported in Appendix B.10. To determine the critical value, we need α (the significance level), n (the sample size), and k (the number of independent variables). The decision rule for the Durbin-Watson test is altered from what we are used to. As usual there is a range of values where the null hypothesis is rejected and a range where it is not rejected. However, there is also a range of values where d is inconclusive. That is, in the inconclusive range the null hypothesis is neither rejected nor not rejected. To state this more formally:

- Values less than d_l cause the rejection of the null hypothesis.
- Values greater then d_u will result in the null hypothesis not being rejected.
- Values of d between d_l and d_u yield inconclusive results.

The subscript l refers to the lower limit of d and the subscript u the upper limit.

How do we interpret the various decisions for the test for residual correlation? If the null hypothesis is not rejected, we conclude that autocorrelation is not present. The residuals are not correlated, there is no autocorrelation present, and the regression assumption has been met. There will not be any problem with the estimated value of the standard error of estimate. If the null hypothesis is rejected, then we conclude that autocorrelation is present.

The usual remedy for autocorrelation is to include another predictor variable that captures time order. For example, we might use the square root of Y instead of Y. This transformation will result in a change in the distribution of the residuals. If the result falls in the inconclusive range, more sophisticated tests are needed, or conservatively, we treat the conclusion as rejecting the null hypothesis.

An example will show the details of the Durbin-Watson test and how the results are interpreted.

Example

Banner Rocker Company manufactures and markets rocking chairs. The company developed a special rocker for senior citizens, which it advertises extensively on TV. Banner's market for the special chair is the Carolinas, Florida, and Arizona where there are many senior citizens and retired people. The president of Banner Rocker is studying the association between his advertising expense (X) and the number of rockers sold over the last 20 months (Y). He collected the following data. He would like to create a model to forecast sales, based on the amount spent on advertising, but is concerned that, because he gathered these data over consecutive months, there might be problems with autocorrelation.

Month	Sales (000)	Advertising ($ millions)	Month	Sales (000)	Advertising ($ millions)
1	153	$5.5	11	169	$6.3
2	156	5.5	12	176	5.9
3	153	5.3	13	176	6.1
4	147	5.5	14	179	6.2
5	159	5.4	15	184	6.2
6	160	5.3	16	181	6.5
7	147	5.5	17	192	6.7
8	147	5.7	18	205	6.9
9	152	5.9	19	215	6.5
10	160	6.2	20	209	6.4

Determine the regression equation. Is advertising a good predictor of sales? If the owner were to increase the amount spent on advertising by $1,000,000, how many additional chairs can he expect to sell? Investigate the possibility of autocorrelation.

Solution

The first step is to determine the regression equation.

```
Regression Analysis: Chairs (000) versus Advertising ($mil)

The regression equation is
Chairs (000) = −43.8 + 36.0 Advertising ($mil)

Predictor              Coef      SE Coef        T       P
Constant             −43.80        34.44    −1.27   0.220
Advertising ($mil)    35.950        5.746     6.26   0.000
```

```
S = 12.3474  R-Sq = 68.5%  R-Sq(adj) = 66.8%

Analysis of Variance

Source          DF      SS        MS       F        P
Regression       1    5967.7    5967.7    39.14    0.000
Residual Error  18    2744.3     152.5
```

The coefficient of determination is 68.5 percent. So we know there is a strong positive association between the variables. We conclude that, as we increase the amount spent on advertising, we can expect to sell more chairs. Of course this is what we had hoped.

How many more chairs can we expect to sell if we increase advertising by $1,000,000? We must be careful with the units of the data. Sales are in thousands of chairs and advertising expense is in millions of dollars. The regression equation is:

$$\hat{Y} = -43.80 + 35.950X$$

This equation indicates that an increase of 1 in X will result in an increase of 35.95 in Y. So an increase of $1,000,000 in advertising will increase sales by 35,950 chairs. To put it another way, it will cost $27.82 in additional advertising expense per chair sold, found by $1,000,000/35,950.

What about the potential problem with autocorrelation? Many software packages, such as MINITAB, will calculate the value of the Durbin-Watson test and output the results. To understand the nature of the test and to see the details of formula (16–4) we use an Excel spreadsheet.

Durbin Watson

	A	B	C	D	E	F	G	H	I
1		Chairs (000)	Advertising ($mil)	Predicted Chairs	Residuals	Lagged			
2	Month	Y	X	$\hat{Y}$	$e_1 = Y - \hat{Y}$	e_{i-1}	e^2_{i-1}	e^2_i	
3	1	153	5.5	153.92366	-0.9237			0.8531	
4	2	156	5.5	153.92366	2.0763	-0.9237	9.0000	4.3112	
5	3	153	5.3	146.7336221	6.2664	2.0763	17.5564	39.2675	
6	4	147	5.5	153.92366	-6.9237	6.2664	173.9771	47.9371	
7	5	159	5.4	150.328641	8.6714	-6.9237	243.2046	75.1925	
8	6	160	5.3	146.7336221	13.2664	8.6714	21.1142	175.9968	
9	7	147	5.5	153.92366	-6.9237	13.2664	407.6376	47.9371	
10	8	147	5.7	161.1136979	-14.1137	-6.9237	51.6966	199.1965	
11	9	152	5.9	168.3037358	-16.3037	-14.1137	4.7963	265.8118	
12	10	160	6.2	179.0887926	-19.0888	-16.3037	7.7565	364.3820	
13	11	169	6.3	182.6838116	-13.6838	-19.0888	29.2138	187.2467	
14	12	176	5.9	168.3037358	7.6963	-13.6838	457.1076	59.2325	
15	13	176	6.1	175.4937737	0.5062	7.6963	51.6966	0.2563	
16	14	179	6.2	179.0887926	-0.0888	0.5062	0.3540	0.0079	
17	15	184	6.2	179.0887926	4.9112	-0.0888	25.0000	24.1200	
18	16	181	6.5	189.8738495	-8.8738	4.9112	190.0278	78.7452	
19	17	192	6.7	197.0638874	-5.0639	-8.8738	14.5158	25.6430	
20	18	205	6.9	204.2539253	0.7461	-5.0639	33.7557	0.5566	
21	19	215	6.5	189.8738495	25.1262	0.7461	594.3881	631.3234	
22	20	209	6.4	186.2788305	22.7212	25.1262	5.7839	516.2515	
23							2338.583	2744.269	

To investigate the possible autocorrelation we need to determine the residuals for each observation. We find the fitted values, that is the $\hat{Y}$, for each of the 20 months. This information is shown in the fourth column, column D. Next we find the residual, which is the difference between the actual value and the fitted values. So for the first month:

$$\hat{Y} = -43.80 + 35.950X = -43.80 + 35.950(5.5) = 153.925$$

$$e_1 = Y_1 - \hat{Y}_1 = 153 - 153.925 = -0.925$$

The residual, reported in column E, is slightly different due to rounding in the software. Notice in particular the string of five negative residuals in rows 9 through 13. In column F we lag the residuals one period. In column G we find the difference between the current residual and the residual in the previous and square this difference. Using the values from the software:

$$(e_t - e_{t-1})^2 = (e_2 - e_{2-1})^2 = [2.0763 - (-0.9237)]^2 = (3.0000)^2 = 9.0000$$

The other values in column G are found the same way. The values in column H are the squares of those in column E.

$$(e_1)^2 = (-0.9237)^2 = 0.8531$$

To find the value of d we need the sums of columns G and H. These sums are noted in yellow in the spreadsheet.

$$d = \frac{\sum_{t=2}^{n} (e_t - e_{t-1})^2}{\sum_{t=1}^{n} (e_t)^2} = \frac{2338.583}{2744.269} = 0.8522$$

Now to answer the question as to whether there is significant autocorrelation. The null and the alternate hypotheses are stated as follows.

$$H_0: \text{No residual correlation}$$
$$H_1: \text{Positive residual correlation}$$

The critical value of d is found in Appendix B.10, a portion of which is shown below. There is one independent variable, so $k = 1$, the level of significance is 0.05, and the sample size is 20. We move to the .05 table, the columns where $k = 1$, and the row of 20. The reported values are $d_l = 1.20$ and $d_u = 1.41$. The null hypothesis is rejected if $d < 1.20$ and not rejected if $d > 1.41$. No conclusion is reached if d is between 1.20 and 1.41.

n	k 1		2	
	d_l	d_u	d_l	d_u
15	1.08	1.36	0.95	1.54
16	1.10	1.37	0.98	1.54
17	1.13	1.38	1.02	1.54
18	1.16	1.39	1.05	1.53
19	1.18	1.40	1.08	1.53
20	1.20	1.41	1.10	1.54
21	1.22	1.42	1.13	1.54
22	1.24	1.43	1.15	1.54
23	1.26	1.44	1.17	1.54
24	1.27	1.45	1.19	1.55
25	1.29	1.45	1.21	1.55

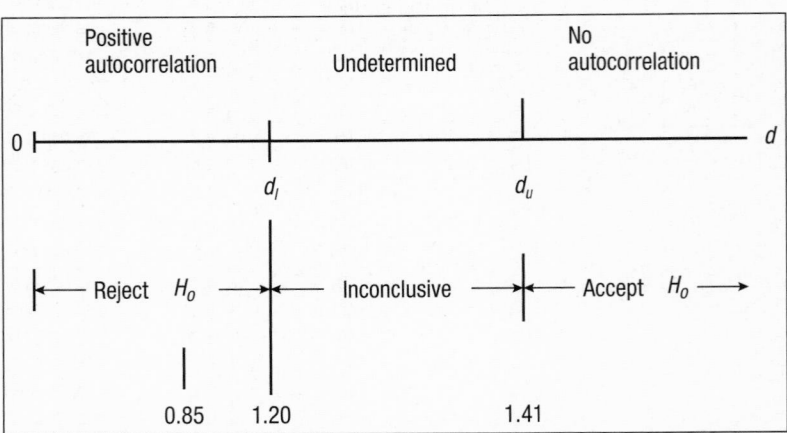

Because the computed value of d is 0.8522, which is less than the d_l, we reject the null hypothesis and accept the alternate hypothesis. We conclude that the residuals are autocorrelated. We have violated one of the regression assumptions. What do we do? The presence of autocorrelation usually means that the regression model has not been correctly specified. It is likely we need to add one or more independent variables that have some time-ordered effects on the dependent variable. The simplest independent variable to add is one that represents the time periods.

Exercises

connect™

15. Recall Exercise 9 from Chapter 14 and the regression equation to predict job performance. See page 537.
  a. Plot the residuals in the order in which the data are presented.
  b. Test for autocorrelation at the .05 significance level.

16. Consider the data in Exercise 10 from Chapter 14 and the regression equation to predict commissions earned. See page 538.
  a. Plot the residuals in the order in which the data are presented.
  b. Test for autocorrelation at the .01 significance level.

Chapter Summary

I. A time series is a collection of data over a period of time.
  A. The trend is the long-run direction of the time series.
  B. The cyclical component is the fluctuation above and below the long-term trend line over a longer period of time.
  C. The seasonal variation is the pattern in a time series within a year. These patterns tend to repeat themselves from year to year for most businesses.
  D. The irregular variation is divided into two components.
    1. The episodic variations are unpredictable, but they can usually be identified. A flood is an example.
    2. The residual variations are random in nature.
II. A moving average is used to smooth the trend in a time series.
III. The linear trend equation is $\hat{Y} = a + bt$, where a is the Y-intercept, b is the slope of the line, and t is the coded time.
  A. We use least squares to determine the trend equation.
  B. If the trend is not linear, but rather the increases tend to be a constant percent, the Y values are converted to logarithms, and a least squares equation is determined using the logarithms.
IV. A seasonal factor can be estimated using the ratio-to-moving-average method.
  A. The six-step procedure yields a seasonal index for each period.
    1. Seasonal factors are usually computed on a monthly or a quarterly basis.
    2. The seasonal factor is used to adjust forecasts, taking into account the effects of the season.
V. The Durbin-Watson statistic [16–4] is used to test for autocorrelation.

$$d = \frac{\sum\limits_{t=2}^{n}(e_t - e_{t-1})^2}{\sum\limits_{t=1}^{n}(e_t)^2}$$

[16–4]

Chapter Exercises

connect™

17. Refer to the following diagram.

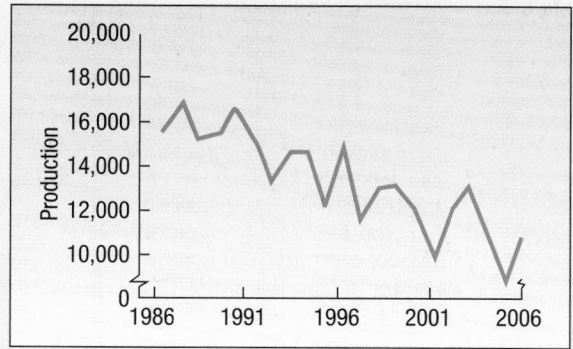

    a. Estimate the linear trend equation for the production series by drawing a straight line through the data.

    b. What is the average annual decrease in production?

    c. Based on the trend equation, what is the forecast for the year 2010?

18. Refer to the following diagram.

    a. Estimate the linear trend equation for the personal income series.

    b. What is the average annual increase in personal income?

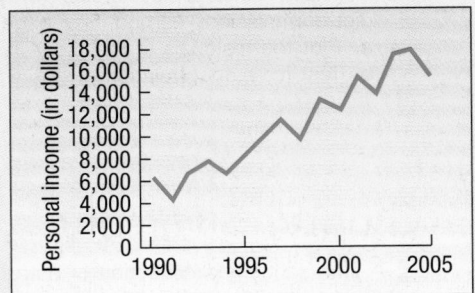

19. The asset turnovers, excluding cash and short-term investments, for RNC Company from 1996 to 2006 are:

1996	1997	1998	1999	2000	2001	2002	2003	2004	2005	2006
1.11	1.28	1.17	1.10	1.06	1.14	1.24	1.33	1.38	1.50	1.65

    a. Plot the data.

    b. Determine the least squares trend equation.

    c. Calculate the points on the trend line for 1999 and 2004, and plot the line on the graph.

    d. Estimate the asset turnover for 2011.

    e. How much did the asset turnover increase per year, on the average, from 1996 to 2006?

20. The sales, in billions of dollars, of Keller Overhead Door, Inc., for 2001 to 2006 are:

Year	Sales	Year	Sales
2001	7.45	2004	7.94
2002	7.83	2005	7.76
2003	8.07	2006	7.90

    a. Plot the data.

    b. Determine the least squares trend equation.

    c. Use the trend equation to calculate the points for 2003 and 2005. Plot them on the graph and draw the regression line.

    d. Estimate the net sales for 2009.

    e. By how much have sales increased (or decreased) per year on the average during the period?

21. The number of employees, in thousands, of Keller Overhead Door, Inc., for the years 2001 to 2006 are:

Year	Employees	Year	Employees
2001	45.6	2004	39.3
2002	42.2	2005	34.0
2003	41.1	2006	30.0

    a. Plot the data.

    b. Determine the least squares trend equation.

    c. Use the trend equation to calculate the points for 2003 and 2005. Plot them on the graph and draw the regression line.

    d. Estimate the number of employees in 2009.

    e. By how much has the number of employees increased (or decreased) per year on the average during the period?

22. Listed below is the selling price for a share of PepsiCo, Inc., at the close of each year.

Year	Price	Year	Price	Year	Price	Year	Price
1990	12.9135	1995	27.7538	2000	49.5625	2005	59.8500
1991	16.8250	1996	29.0581	2001	48.6800	2006	62.0000
1992	20.6125	1997	36.0155	2002	42.2200	2007	77.5100
1993	20.3024	1998	40.6111	2003	46.6200		
1994	18.3160	1999	35.0230	2004	52.2000		

a. Plot the data.
b. Determine the least squares trend equation.
c. Calculate the points for the years 1995 and 2000.
d. Estimate the selling price in 2008. Does this seem like a reasonable estimate based on the historical data?
e. By how much has the stock price increased or decreased (per year) on average during the period?

23. If plotted, the following sales series would appear curvilinear. This indicates that sales are increasing at a somewhat constant annual rate (percent). To fit the sales, therefore, a logarithmic equation should be used.

Year	Sales ($ millions)	Year	Sales ($ millions)
1998	8.0	2004	39.4
1999	10.4	2005	50.5
2000	13.5	2006	65.0
2001	17.6	2007	84.1
2002	22.8	2008	109.0
2003	29.3		

a. Determine the logarithmic equation.
b. Determine the coordinates of the points on the logarithmic straight line for 1995 and 2004.
c. By what percent did sales increase per year, on the average, during the period from 1996 to 2006?
d. Based on the equation, what are the estimated sales for 2007?

24. Reported below are the amounts spent on advertising ($ millions) by a large firm from 1996 to 2006.

Year	Amount	Year	Amount
1996	88.1	2002	132.6
1997	94.7	2003	141.9
1998	102.1	2004	150.9
1999	109.8	2005	157.9
2000	118.1	2006	162.6
2001	125.6		

a. Determine the logarithmic trend equation.
b. Estimate the advertising expenses for 2009.
c. By what percent per year did advertising expense increase during the period?

25. Listed below is the selling price for a share of Oracle, Inc., stock at the close of the year.

Year	Price	Year	Price	Year	Price	Year	Price
1990	0.1944	1995	3.1389	2000	29.0625	2005	12.2100
1991	0.3580	1996	4.6388	2001	13.8100	2006	19.11
1992	0.7006	1997	3.7188	2002	10.8000	2007	20.23
1993	1.4197	1998	7.1875	2003	13.2300		
1994	2.1790	1999	28.0156	2004	13.7200		

a. Plot the data.
b. Determine the least squares trend equation. Use both the actual stock price and the logarithm of the price. Which seems to yield a more accurate forecast?
c. Calculate the points for the years 1993 and 1998.
d. Estimate the selling price in 2009. Does this seem like a reasonable estimate based on the historical data?
e. By how much has the stock price increased or decreased (per year) on average during the period? Use your best answer from part (b).

26. The production of Reliable Manufacturing Company for 2007 and part of 2008 follows.

Month	2007 Production (thousands)	2008 Production (thousands)	Month	2007 Production (thousands)	2008 Production (thousands)
January	6	7	July	3	4
February	7	9	August	5	
March	12	14	September	14	
April	8	9	October	6	
May	4	5	November	7	
June	3	4	December	6	

a. Using the ratio-to-moving-average method, determine the specific seasonals for July, August, and September 2007.
b. Assume that the specific seasonal indexes in the following table are correct. Insert in the table the specific seasonals you computed in part (a) for July, August, and September 2007, and determine the 12 typical seasonal indexes.

Year	Jan.	Feb.	Mar.	Apr.	May	June	July	Aug.	Sept.	Oct.	Nov.	Dec.
2007							?	?	?	92.1	106.5	92.9
2008	88.9	102.9	178.9	118.2	60.1	43.1	44.0	74.0	200.9	90.0	101.9	90.9
2009	87.6	103.7	170.2	125.9	59.4	48.6	44.2	77.2	196.5	89.6	113.2	80.6
2010	79.8	105.6	165.8	124.7	62.1	41.7	48.2	72.1	203.6	80.2	103.0	94.2
2011	89.0	112.1	182.9	115.1	57.6	56.9						

c. Interpret the typical seasonal index.

27. The sales of Andre's Boutique for 2007 and part of 2008 are:

Month	2007 Sales (thousands)	2008 Sales (thousands)	Month	2007 Sales (thousands)	2008 Sales (thousands)
January	78	65	July	81	65
February	72	60	August	85	61
March	80	72	September	90	75
April	110	97	October	98	
May	92	86	November	115	
June	86	72	December	130	

a. Using the ratio-to-moving-average method, determine the specific seasonals for July, August, September, and October 2007.
b. Assume that the specific seasonals in the following table are correct. Insert in the table the specific seasonals you computed in part (a) for July, August, September, and October 2007, and determine the 12 typical seasonal indexes.

Year	Jan.	Feb.	Mar.	Apr.	May	June	July	Aug.	Sept.	Oct.	Nov.	Dec.
2007							?	?	?	?	123.6	150.9
2008	83.9	77.6	86.1	118.7	99.7	92.0	87.0	91.4	97.3	105.4	124.9	140.1
2009	86.7	72.9	86.2	121.3	96.6	92.0	85.5	93.6	98.2	103.2	126.1	141.7
2010	85.6	65.8	89.2	125.6	99.6	94.4	88.9	90.2	100.2	102.7	121.6	139.6
2011	77.3	81.2	85.8	115.7	100.3	89.7						

c. Interpret the typical seasonal index.

28. The quarterly production of pine lumber, in millions of board feet, by Northwest Lumber since 2004 is:

	Quarter			
Year	Winter	Spring	Summer	Fall
2004	7.8	10.2	14.7	9.3
2005	6.9	11.6	17.5	9.3
2006	8.9	9.7	15.3	10.1
2007	10.7	12.4	16.8	10.7
2008	9.2	13.6	17.1	10.3

   a. Determine the typical seasonal pattern for the production data using the ratio-to-moving-average method.
   b. Interpret the pattern.
   c. Deseasonalize the data and determine the linear trend equation.
   d. Project the seasonally adjusted production for the four quarters of 2009.
29. Work Gloves Corp. is reviewing its quarterly sales of Toughie, the most durable glove it produces. The numbers of pairs produced (in thousands) by quarter are:

	Quarter			
Year	I Jan.–Mar.	II Apr.–June	III July–Sept.	IV Oct.–Dec.
1999	142	312	488	208
2000	146	318	512	212
2001	160	330	602	187
2002	158	338	572	176
2003	162	380	563	200
2004	162	362	587	205

   a. Using the ratio-to-moving-average method, determine the four typical quarterly indexes.
   b. Interpret the typical seasonal pattern.
30. Sales of roof material, by quarter, since 2000 by Carolina Home Construction, Inc., are shown below (in $000).

	Quarter			
Year	I	II	III	IV
2000	210	180	60	246
2001	214	216	82	230
2002	246	228	91	280
2003	258	250	113	298
2004	279	267	116	304
2005	302	290	114	310
2006	321	291	120	320

   a. Determine the typical seasonal patterns for sales using the ratio-to-moving-average method.
   b. Deseasonalize the data and determine the trend equation.
   c. Project the sales for 2007, and then seasonally adjust each quarter.
31. Blueberry Farms Golf and Fish Club of Hilton Head, South Carolina, wants to find monthly seasonal indexes for package play, nonpackage play, and total play. The package play refers to golfers who visit the area as part of a golf package. Typically the greens fees, cart fees, lodging, maid service, and meals are included as part of a golfing package.

The course earns a certain percentage of this total. The nonpackage play includes play by local residents and visitors to the area who wish to play golf. The following data, beginning with July 2002, report the package and nonpackage play by month, as well as the total amount, in thousands of dollars.

Year	Month	Package	Local	Total	Year	Month	Package	Local	Total
2002	July	$ 18.36	$43.44	$ 61.80	2004	January	30.60	9.48	40.08
	August	28.62	56.76	85.38		February	63.54	30.96	94.50
	September	101.34	34.44	135.78		March	167.67	47.64	215.31
	October	182.70	38.40	221.10		April	299.97	59.40	359.37
	November	54.72	44.88	99.60		May	173.61	40.56	214.17
	December	36.36	12.24	48.60		June	64.98	63.96	128.94
2003	January	25.20	9.36	34.56		July	25.56	67.20	92.76
	February	67.50	25.80	93.30		August	31.14	52.20	83.34
	March	179.37	34.44	213.81		September	81.09	37.44	118.53
	April	267.66	34.32	301.98		October	213.66	62.52	276.18
	May	179.73	40.80	220.53		November	96.30	35.04	131.34
	June	63.18	40.80	103.98		December	16.20	33.24	49.44
	July	16.20	77.88	94.08	2005	January	26.46	15.96	42.42
	August	23.04	76.20	99.24		February	72.27	35.28	107.55
	September	102.33	42.96	145.29		March	131.67	46.44	178.11
	October	224.37	51.36	275.73		April	293.40	67.56	360.96
	November	65.16	25.56	90.72		May	158.94	59.40	218.34
	December	22.14	15.96	38.10		June	79.38	60.60	139.98

Using statistical software:

a. Develop a seasonal index for each month for the package sales. What do you note about the various months?

b. Develop a seasonal index for each month for the nonpackage sales. What do you note about the various months?

c. Develop a seasonal index for each month for the total sales. What do you note about the various months?

d. Compare the indexes for package sales, nonpackage sales, and total sales. Are the busiest months the same?

32. The following is the number of retirees receiving benefits from the State Teachers Retirement System of Ohio from 1991 until 2004.

Year	Service	Year	Service	Year	Service
1991	58,436	1996	70,448	2001	83,918
1992	59,994	1997	72,601	2002	86,666
1993	61,515	1998	75,482	2003	89,257
1994	63,182	1999	78,341	2004	92,574
1995	67,989	2000	81,111		

a. Plot the data.

b. Determine the least squares trend equation. Use a linear equation.

c. Calculate the points for the years 1993 and 1998.

d. Estimate the number of retirees that will be receiving benefits in 2006. Does this seem like a reasonable estimate based on the historical data?

e. By how much has the number of retirees increased or decreased (per year) on average during the period?

33. Ray Anderson, owner of Anderson Ski Lodge in upstate New York, is interested in forecasting the number of visitors for the upcoming year. The following data are available, by quarter, since 2000. Develop a seasonal index for each quarter. How many visitors would you expect for each quarter of 2007, if Ray projects that there will be a 10 percent increase from the total number of visitors in 2006? Determine the trend equation,

project the number of visitors for 2007, and seasonally adjust the forecast. Which forecast would you choose?

Year	Quarter	Visitors	Year	Quarter	Visitors
2000	I	86	2004	I	188
	II	62		II	172
	III	28		III	128
	IV	94		IV	198
2001	I	106	2005	I	208
	II	82		II	202
	III	48		III	154
	IV	114		IV	220
2002	I	140	2006	I	246
	II	120		II	240
	III	82		III	190
	IV	154		IV	252
2003	I	162			
	II	140			
	III	100			
	IV	174			

34. The enrollment in the College of Business at Midwestern University by quarter since 2001 is:

	Quarter			
Year	Winter	Spring	Summer	Fall
2001	2,033	1,871	714	2,318
2002	2,174	2,069	840	2,413
2003	2,370	2,254	927	2,704
2004	2,625	2,478	1,136	3,001
2005	2,803	2,668	—	—

Using the ratio-to-moving-average method:
a. Determine the four quarterly indexes.
b. Interpret the quarterly pattern of enrollment. Does the seasonal variation surprise you?
c. Compute the trend equation, and forecast the 2006 enrollment by quarter.

35. The Jamie Farr Kroger Classic is an LPGA (women's professional golf) tournament played in Toledo, Ohio, each year. Listed below are the total purse and the prize for the winner for the 22 years from 1987 through 2008. Develop a trend equation for both variables. Which variable is increasing at a faster rate? Project both the amount of the purse and the prize for the winner in 2010. Find the ratio of the winner's prize to the total purse. What do you find? Which variable can we estimate more accurately, the size of the purse or the winner's prize?

Year	Purse	Prize	Year	Purse	Prize
1987	$225,000	$33,750	1998	$ 800,000	$120,000
1988	275,000	41,250	1999	800,000	120,000
1989	275,000	41,250	2000	1,000,000	150,000
1990	325,000	48,750	2001	1,000,000	150,000
1991	350,000	52,500	2002	1,000,000	150,000
1992	400,000	60,000	2003	1,000,000	150,000
1993	450,000	67,500	2004	1,200,000	180,000
1994	500,000	75,000	2005	1,200,000	180,000
1995	500,000	75,000	2006	1,200,000	180,000
1996	575,000	86,250	2007	1,300,000	195,000
1997	700,000	105,000	2008	1,300,000	195,000

36. Go to the Bureau of Labor Statistics website, www.bls.gov, and click on the **Consumer Price Index** option, select **Consumer Price Index—All Urban Consumers (Current Series),** select **U.S. All items, 1982–84 = 100** and click **Retrieve data** at the bottom. Ask for the yearly output for the last 10 to 20 years. Develop a regression equation for the annual Consumer Price Index for the selected period. Use both the linear and the log approach. Which do you think is best?

37. Develop a trend line for a large or well-known company, such as GM, General Electric, or Microsoft, for the last 10 years. You could go to the company website. Most companies have a section called "Financial Information" or similar. Go to that location and look for sales over the last 10 years. If you do not know the website of the company, go to the financial section of Yahoo or *USA Today,* where there is a location for "symbol lookup." Type in the company name, which should then give you the symbol. Look up the company via the symbol, and you should find the information. The symbol for GM is just *GM,* the symbol for General Electric is *GE.* Comment on the trend line of the company you selected over the period. Is the trend increasing or decreasing? Does the trend follow a linear or log equation?

38. Select one of the major economic indicators, such as the Dow Jones Industrial Average, Nasdaq, or the S&P 500. Develop a trend line for the index over the last 10 years by using the value of the index at the end of the year, or for the last 30 days by selecting the closing value of the index for the last 30 days. You can locate this information in many places. For example, go to http://finance.yahoo.com, click on **Nasdaq** on the left hand, select **Historical Prices,** and a period of time, perhaps the last 30 days, and you will find the information. You should be able to download it directly to Excel to create your trend equation. Comment on the trend line you created. Is it increasing or decreasing? Does the trend line follow a linear or log equation?

Data Set Exercise

39. Refer to the Baseball 2007 data, which include information on the 2007 Major League Baseball season. The data include the mean player salary since 1989. Plot the information and develop a linear trend equation. Write a brief report on your findings.

Software Commands

1. The MegaStat commands for creating the seasonal indexes on page 617 are:

   a. Enter the coded time period and the value of the time series in two columns. You may also want to include information on the years and quarters.

   b. Select **MegaStat, Time Series/Forecasting,** and **Deseasonalization,** and hit **Enter.**

   c. Input the range of the data, indicate the data are in the first quarter, and click **OK.**

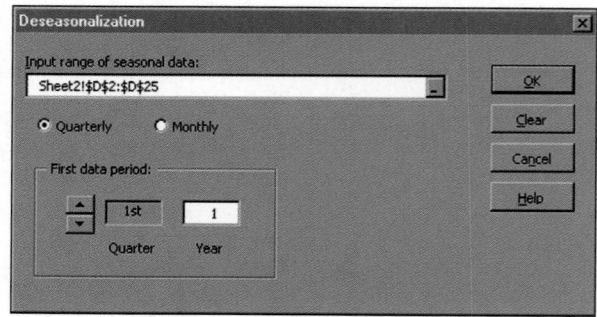

Chapter 16   Answers to Self-Review

16–1

Year	Production (thousands)	Three-Year Moving Total	Three-Year Moving Average
2003	2	—	—
2004	6	12	4
2005	4	15	5
2006	5	12	4
2007	3	18	6
2008	10	—	—

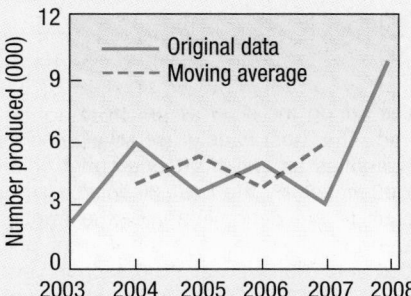

16–2 a.

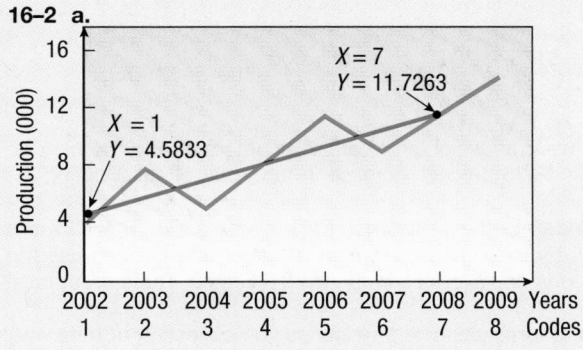

b. $\hat{Y} = a + bt = 3.3928 + 1.1905t$ (in thousands)

c. For 2002:

$$\hat{Y} = 3.3928 + 1.1905(1) = 4.5833$$

for 2008:

$$\hat{Y} = 3.3928 + 1.1905(7) = 11.7263$$

d. For 2012, $t = 11$, so

$$\hat{Y} = 3.3928 + 1.1905(11) = 16.4883$$

or 16,488 king-size rockers.

16–3 a.

Year	Y	log Y	t
2005	2.13	0.3284	1
2006	18.10	1.2577	2
2007	39.80	1.5999	3
2008	81.40	1.9106	4
2009	112.00	2.0492	5

$$b = 0.40945$$

$$a = 0.20081$$

b. About 156.7 percent. The antilog of 0.40945 is 2.567. Subtracting 1 yields 1.567.

c. About 454.5, found by $\hat{Y} = 0.20081 + .40945(6) = 2.65751$. The antilog of 2.65751 is 454.5.

16–4 a. The following values are from a software package. Due to rounding, your figures might be slightly different.

	Winter	Spring	Summer	Fall
Mean	119.35	81.66	125.31	74.24
Typical seasonal	119.18	81.55	125.13	74.13

The correction factor is 0.9986.

b. Total sales at Teton Village for the winter season are typically 19.18 percent above the annual average.

16–5 The forecast value for January of the sixth year is 34.9, found by

$$\hat{Y} = 4.4 + 0.5(61) = 34.9$$

Seasonally adjusting the forecast, $34.9(120)/100 = 41.88$. For February, $\hat{Y} = 4.4 + 0.5(62) = 35.4$. Then $(35.4)95/100 = 33.63$.

A Review of Chapters 15 and 16

Chapter 15 presents index numbers. An *index number* describes the relative change in value from one period, called the base period, to another called the given period. It is actually a percent, but the percent sign is usually omitted. Indexes are used to compare the change in unlike series over time. For example a company might wish to compare the change in sales with the change in the number of sales representatives employed over the same period of time. A direct comparison is not meaningful because the units for one set of data are dollars and the other people. Index numbers also facilitate the comparison of very large values, where the amount of change in the actual values is very large and therefore difficult to interpret.

There are two types of price indexes. In an *unweighted price index* the quantities are not considered. To form an unweighted index we divide the base period value into the current period (also called the given period) and report the percent change. So if sales were $12,000,000 in 2000 and $18,600,000 in 2006 the simple unweighted price index for 2006 is:

$$P = \frac{p_t}{p_0}(100) = \frac{\$18,600,000}{\$12,000,000}(100) = 155.0$$

We conclude there is a 55 percent increase in the sales during the six-year period.

In a *weighted price index quantities* are considered. The most widely used weighted index is the *Laspeyres Price Index*. It uses the base period quantities as weights to compare changes in prices. It is computed by multiplying the base period quantities by the base period price for each product considered and summing the result. This result is the denominator of the fraction. The numerator of the fraction is the product of the base period quantities and the current price. For example, an appliance store sold 50 computes at $1,000 and 200 DVDs at $150 each in year 2000. In 2008 the same store sold 60 computers at $1,200 and 230 DVDs at $175. The Laspeyres Price Index is:

$$P = \frac{\Sigma p_t q_0}{\Sigma p_0 q_0}(100) = \frac{\$1,200 \times 50 + \$175 \times 200}{\$1,000 \times 50 + \$150 \times 200}(100) = \frac{\$95,000}{\$80,000}(100) = 118.75$$

Notice the same base period quantities are used as weights in both the numerator and the denominator. The index indicates there has been an 18.75 percent increase in the value of sales during the six-year period.

The most widely used and reported index is the *Consumer Price Index (CPI)*. The CPI is a Laspeyres type index. It is reported monthly by the U.S. Department of Labor and is often used to report the rate of inflation in the prices of goods and services in the United States. The current base period is 1982–84.

In Chapter 16 we studied time series and forecasting. A *time series* is a collection of data over a period of time. The earnings per share of General Electric common stock over the last ten years is an example of a time series. There are four components to a time series: the trend, cyclic effects, seasonal effects, and irregular effects.

Trend is the long run direction of the time series. It can be either increasing or decreasing.

The *cyclical component* is the fluctuation above and below the trend line over a period of several years. Economic cycles are examples of the cyclical component. Most businesses shift between relative expansion and reduction periods over a cycle of several years.

Seasonal variation is the recurring pattern of the time series within a year. The consumption of many products and services is seasonal. Beach homes along the Gulf Coast are seldom rented during the winter and ski lodges in Wyoming are not used in the summer months. Hence we say the rental of beach front properties and ski lodges are seasonal.

The *irregular component* includes any unpredictable events. In other words, the irregular component includes events that cannot be forecast. There are two types of irregular components. Episodic variations are unpredictable, but can usually be identified. The Iowa floods in the summer of 2008 is an example. The residual variation is random in nature and not predicted or identified.

The linear trend for a time series is given by the equation $\hat{Y} = a + bt$, where $\hat{Y}$ is the estimated trend value, a is the intercept with the Y axis, b is the slope of the trend line (the rate of change), and t refers to the coded values for the time periods. We use the least squares method described in Chapter 13 to determine the trend line. Autocorrelation is often a problem when using the trend equation. Autocorrelation means that successive values of the time series are correlated.

Glossary

Chapter 15
Consumer Price Index An index reported monthly by the U.S. Department of Labor. It describes the change in a market basket of goods and services from the base period of 1982–84 to the present.

Simple index The value in the given period divided by the value in the base period. The result is usually multiplied by 100 and reported as a percent.

Weighted index The prices in the base period and the given period are multiplied by quantities (weights).

Chapter 16
Autocorrelation Successive residuals in a time series are correlated.

Cyclical variation The rise and fall of a time series over periods longer than one year.

Episodic variation It is variation that is random in nature, but a cause can be identified.

Irregular variation Variation in a times series that is random in nature and does not regularly repeat itself.

Residual variation It is variation that is random in nature and cannot be identified or predicted.

Seasonal variation Patterns of change in a time series within a year. These patterns of change repeat themselves each year.

Secular trend The smoothed long-term direction of a time series.

Exercises

connect™

Part I—Multiple Choice

1. An index number is
   a. Actually a percent but the percent sign is usually omitted.
   b. Useful for comparing data with different units.
   c. Useful for evaluating the change in very large numbers.
   d. All of the above.

2. The sales at Labate Sporting Goods in 2000 were $400,000. In 2008 the sales increased to $450,000.
   a. The index for 2008 is 112.5.
   b. There has been a 12.5 percent increase in sales during the 8-year period.
   c. The index is unweighted.
   d. All of the above are correct.

3. Which of the following weighted indexes uses current period or given period quantities to form the denominator of the index?
   a. Laspeyres' Price Index
   b. Paasche's Price Index
   c. Fisher's Ideal Index
   d. None of the above.

4. A major disadvantage of the Laspeyres price index is
   a. It does not reflect changes in buying habits over time.
   b. It is too sensitive to small changes during early periods.
   c. It requires the denominator to be recalculated each period.
   d. None of the above.

5. Which of the following are correct statements about the Consumer Price Index?
   a. It is reported monthly by the Bureau of Labor Statistics.
   b. It is often used to report the rate of inflation in the United States.
   c. The current base period of the index is 1982–84.
   d. All of the above.

6. The smoothed long-term direction of a time series is called the
   a. Cyclical variation.
   b. Seasonal variation.
   c. Trend.
   d. Irregular variation.

7. The rise and fall of a time series over periods longer than one year is called the
   a. Cyclical variation.
   b. Seasonal variation.
   c. Trend.
   d. Irregular variation.

8. Which of the following are correct statements about the seasonal component of a time series?
   a. It refers to changing patterns within a year.
   b. One of its components is the episodic variation.

   c. It is always greater than 100 percent.
   d. All of the above are correct.
9. The linear trend for the number of vehicles sold per year at Trythall Motor Sports, Inc. is given by the equation $\hat{Y} = 30 + 125t$. The base period, that is year 1, is 2000. Which of the following statements is correct?
   a. The estimated sales for 2008 are 1030.
   b. Sales are increasing at a rate of 125 per year.
   c. The estimated sales for 1999 would be 30.
   d. All of the above are correct.
10. If the rate of change from one period to the next is a constant *percent*
   a. A linear tend equation is used.
   b. A log transformation is used.
   c. The slope of the trend line will be negative.
   d. The episodic variation will always be less than 1.00.

Part II—Problems

11. Listed below is the consolidated revenue (in $ billions) for General Electric for the period from 2004 to 2008.

Year	Consolidated Revenues ($ billions)
2004	108
2005	114
2006	113
2007	134
2008	150

   a. Determine the index for 2008, using 2004 as the base period.
   b. Use the period 2004 to 2006 as the base period and find the index for 2008.
   c. With 2004 as the base year, use the least squares method to find the trend equation. What is the estimated consolidated revenue for 2011? What is the rate of increase per year?
12. The table below shows the unemployment rate and the available workforce for three counties in northwest Pennsylvania for the years 2005 and 2008.

County	2005 Labor Force	2005 Unemployed %	2008 Labor Force	2008 Unemployed %
Erie	141,500	6.7	141,800	5.6
Warren	22,700	5.8	21,300	5.3
McKean	22,200	6.0	21,900	5.7

   a. Find the overall unemployment rate for this region of northwest Pennsylvania for 2005?
   b. Use the data for this region of northwest Pennsylvania to create an unweighted index of percent unemployed for the year 2008.
   c. Use the data for this region of northwest Pennsylvania to create a weighted unemployment index using the Laspeyres method. Use the year 2008 as the base period.
13. Based on five years of monthly data (the period from January 2004 to December 2008) the trend equation for a small company is $\hat{Y} = 3.5 + 0.7t$. The seasonal index for January is 120 and for June it is 90. What is the seasonally adjusted sales forecast for January 2009 and June 2009?

Practice Test

Part I—Objective

1. To compute an index the base period is always in the _____. (numerator, denominator, can be in either, always 100)

1. _____

2. A number that measures the relative change from one period to another is called a/an
   _____.   2. _____
3. In a weighted index both the price and the _____ are considered.
                                                                        3. _____
4. In a Laspeyres index the _____ quantities are used in both the numerator and denominator. (base period, given period, oldest, newest—pick one)   4. _____
5. The current base period for the Consumer Price Index is _____.
                                                                        5. _____
6. The long-run direction of a time series is called the _____.   6. _____
7. One method used to smooth the trend in a time series is a _____.
                                                                        7. _____
8. When successive residuals are correlated this condition is called _____.
                                                                        8. _____
9. Irregular variation in a time series that is random in nature is called _____.
                                                                        9. _____
10. In a three-year moving average the weights given to each period are _____. (the same, oldest year has most weight, oldest year has the least weight)
                                                                        10. _____

Part II—Problems

1. Listed below are the sales at Roberta's Ice Cream Stand for the last five years.

Year	Sales
2005	$130,000
2006	145,000
2007	120,000
2008	170,000
2009	190,000

   a. Find the simple index for each year using 2005 as the base year.
   b. Find the simple index for each year using 2005–2006 as the base year.

2. Listed below are the price and quantity of several golf items purchased by members of the men's golf league at Indigo Creek Golf and Tennis Club.

	2005		2009	
	Price	Quantity	Price	Quantity
Driver	$250.00	5	$275.00	6
Putter	60.00	12	75.00	10
Irons	700.00	3	750.00	4

   a. Determine the simple aggregate price index, with 2005 as the base period.
   b. Determine a Laspeyres price index.
   c. Determine the Paasche price index.
   d. Determine a value index.

3. The monthly linear trend equation for the Hoopes ABC Beverage Store is:

   $$\hat{Y} = 5.50 + 1.25t$$

   The equation is based on four years of monthly data and is reported in thousands of dollars. The index for January is 105.0 and for February it is 98.3. Determine the seasonally adjusted forecast for January and February of the fifth year.

17

GOALS

When you have completed this chapter, you will be able to:

1 List the characteristics of the *chi-square distribution.*

2 Conduct a test of hypothesis comparing an observed set of frequencies to an expected distribution.

3 Conduct a test of hypothesis to determine whether two classification criteria are related.

Nonparametric Methods:

Chi-Square Applications

For many years, TV executives used the guideline that 30 percent of the audience were watching each of the traditional big three prime-time networks and 10 percent were watching cable stations on a weekday night. A random sample of 500 viewers in the Tampa–St. Petersburg, Florida, area last Monday night showed that 165 homes were tuned in to the ABC affiliate, 140 to the CBS affiliate, 125 to the NBC affiliate, and the remainder were viewing a cable station. At the .05 significance level, can we conclude that the guideline is still reasonable? (Exercise 12, Goal 2)

Introduction

Chapters 9 through 12 discuss data of interval or ratio scale, such as weights of steel ingots, incomes of minorities, and years of employment. We conducted hypothesis tests about a single population mean, two population means, and three or more population means. For these tests we assume the populations follow the normal probability distribution. However, there are tests available in which no assumption regarding the shape of the population is necessary. These tests are referred to as nonparametric. This means the assumption of a normal population is not necessary.

There are also tests exclusively for data of nominal scale of measurement. Recall from Chapter 1 that nominal data is the "lowest" or most primitive. For this type of measurement, data are classified into categories where there is no natural order. Examples include gender of Congressional representatives, state of birth of students, or brand of peanut butter purchased. In this chapter we introduce a new test statistic, the chi-square statistic. We use it for data measured with a nominal scale.

Goodness-of-Fit Test: Equal Expected Frequencies

The goodness-of-fit test is one of the most commonly used statistical tests. The first illustration of this test involves the case in which the expected cell frequencies are equal.

As the full name implies, the purpose of the goodness-of-fit test is to compare an observed distribution to an expected distribution. An example will describe the hypothesis-testing situation.

Example

Ms. Jan Kilpatrick is the marketing manager for a manufacturer of sports cards. She plans to begin selling a series of cards with pictures and playing statistics of former Major League Baseball players. One of the problems is the selection of the former players. At a baseball card show at Southwyck Mall last weekend, she set up a booth and offered cards of the following six Hall of Fame baseball players: Tom Seaver, Nolan Ryan, Ty Cobb, George Brett, Hank Aaron, and Johnny Bench. At the end of the day she sold a total of 120 cards. The number of cards sold for each old-time player is shown in Table 17–1. Can she conclude the sales are not the same for each player?

TABLE 17–1 Number of Cards Sold for Each Player

Player	Cards Sold
Tom Seaver	13
Nolan Ryan	33
Ty Cobb	14
George Brett	7
Hank Aaron	36
Johnny Bench	17
Total	120

If there is no significant difference in the popularity of the players, we would expect that the observed frequencies (f_o) would be equal—or nearly equal. That is, we would expect to sell as many cards for Tom Seaver as for Nolan Ryan. Thus, any discrepancy in the observed and expected frequencies could be attributed to sampling (chance).

What about the level of measurement in this problem? Notice when a card is sold, the "measurement" of the card is based on the player's name. There is no natural order to the players. No one player is assumed better than another. Therefore, a nominal scale is used to evaluate each observation.

Because there are 120 cards in the sample, we expect that 20 (f_e) cards, i.e., the expected frequency f_e, will fall in each of the six categories (Table 17–2). These categories are called **cells.** An examination of the set of observed frequencies in Table 17–1 indicates that the card for George Brett is sold rather infrequently, whereas the cards for Hank Aaron and Nolan Ryan are sold more often. Is the difference in sales due to chance, or can we conclude that there is a preference for the cards of certain players?

TABLE 17–2 Observed and Expected Frequencies for the 120 Cards Sold

Player	Cards Sold, f_o	Expected Number Sold, f_e
Tom Seaver	13	20
Nolan Ryan	33	20
Ty Cobb	14	20
George Brett	7	20
Hank Aaron	36	20
Johnny Bench	17	20
Total	120	120

Solution

We will use the same systematic five-step, hypothesis-testing procedure followed in previous chapters.

Step 1: State the null hypothesis and the alternate hypothesis. The null hypothesis, H_0, is that there is no difference between the set of observed frequencies and the set of expected frequencies; that is, any difference between the two sets of frequencies can be attributed to sampling (chance). The alternate hypothesis, H_1, is that there is a difference between the observed and expected sets of frequencies. If H_0 is rejected and H_1 is accepted, it means that sales are not equally distributed among the six categories (cells).

Step 2: Select the level of significance. We selected the .05 significance level. The probability is .05 that a true null hypothesis will be rejected.

Step 3: Select the test statistic. The test statistic follows the chi-square distribution, designated as χ^2:

CHI-SQUARE TEST STATISTIC $$\chi^2 = \Sigma \left[\frac{(f_o - f_e)^2}{f_e} \right]$$ [17–1]

with $k - 1$ degrees of freedom, where:

k is the number of categories.
f_o is an observed frequency in a particular category.
f_e is an expected frequency in a particular category.

We will examine the characteristics of the chi-square distribution in more detail shortly.

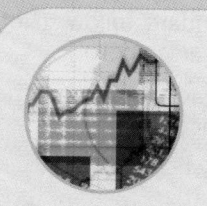
Step 4: Formulate the decision rule. Recall that the decision rule in hypothesis testing requires finding a number that separates the region where we do not reject H_0 from the region of rejection. This number is called the *critical value.* As we will soon see, the chi-square distribution is really a family of distributions. Each distribution has a slightly different shape, depending on the number of degrees of freedom. The number of degrees of freedom in this type of problem is found by $k - 1$, where k is the number of categories. In this particular problem there are six. Since there are six categories, there are $k - 1 = 6 - 1 = 5$ degrees of freedom. As noted, a category is called a *cell,* so there are six cells. The critical value for 5 degrees of freedom and the .05 level of significance is found in Appendix B.3. A portion of that table is shown in Table 17–3. The critical value is 11.070, found by locating 5 degrees of freedom in the left margin and then moving horizontally (to the right) and reading the critical value in the .05 column.

TABLE 17–3 A Portion of the Chi-Square Table

Degrees of Freedom df	Right-Tail Area			
	.10	.05	.02	.01
1	2.706	3.841	5.412	6.635
2	4.605	5.991	7.824	9.210
3	6.251	7.815	9.837	11.345
4	7.779	9.488	11.668	13.277
5	9.236	11.070	13.388	15.086

The decision rule is to reject H_0 if the computed value of chi-square is greater than 11.070. If it is less than or equal to 11.070, do not reject H_0. Chart 17–1 shows the decision rule.

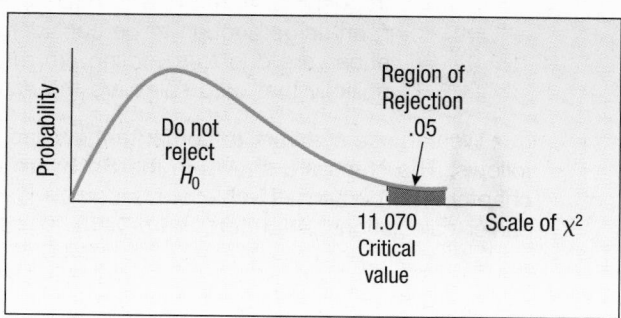

CHART 17–1 Chi-Square Probability Distribution for 5 Degrees of Freedom, Showing the Region of Rejection, .05 Level of Significance

The decision rule indicates that if there are large differences between the observed and expected frequencies, resulting in a computed χ^2 of more than 11.070, the null hypothesis should be rejected. However, if the differences between f_o and f_e are small, the computed χ^2 value will be 11.070 or less, and the null hypothesis should not be rejected. The reasoning is that such small differences between the observed and expected frequencies are probably due to chance. Remember, the 120 observations are a sample of the population.

Step 5: Compute the value of chi-square and make a decision. Of the 120 cards sold in the sample, we counted the number of times Tom Seaver and Nolan Ryan and each of the others were sold. The counts were reported in Table 17–1. The calculations for chi-square follow. (Note again that the expected frequencies are the same for each cell.)

Column 1: Determine the differences between each f_o and f_e. That is, $(f_o - f_e)$. The sum of these differences is zero.

Column 2: Square the difference between each observed and expected frequency, that is, $(f_o - f_e)^2$.

Column 3: Divide the result for each observation by the expected frequency. That is, $\dfrac{(f_o - f_e)^2}{f_e}$. Finally, sum these values. The result is the value of χ^2, which is 34.40.

Baseball Player	f_o	f_e	(1) $(f_o - f_e)$	(2) $(f_o - f_e)^2$	(3) $\dfrac{(f_o - f_e)^2}{f_e}$
Tom Seaver	13	20	−7	49	49/20 = 2.45
Nolan Ryan	33	20	13	169	169/20 = 8.45
Ty Cobb	14	20	−6	36	36/20 = 1.80
George Brett	7	20	−13	169	169/20 = 8.45
Hank Aaron	36	20	16	256	256/20 = 12.80
Johnny Bench	17	20	−3	9	9/20 = 0.45
			0		34.40

Must be ➚ χ^2 ➚

The computed χ^2 of 34.40 is in the rejection region beyond the critical value of 11.070. The decision, therefore, is to reject H_0 at the .05 level and to accept H_1. The difference between the observed and the expected frequencies is not due to chance. Rather, the differences between f_o and f_e are large enough to be considered significant. The chance these differences are due to sampling error is very small. So we conclude that it is unlikely that card sales are the same among the six players.

We can use software to compute the value of chi-square. The output of MegaStat follows. The steps are shown in the **Software Commands** section at the end of the chapter. The computed value of chi-square is 34.40, the same value obtained in our earlier calculations. Also note the p-value is much less than .05 (.00000198).

Goodness of Fit

	A	B	C	D	E	F	G
1							
2	Goodness of Fit Test						
3							
4		observed	expected	O - E	(O - E)² / E	% of chisq	
5		13	20.000	-7.000	2.450	7.12	
6		33	20.000	13.000	8.450	24.56	
7		14	20.000	-6.000	1.800	5.23	
8		7	20.000	-13.000	8.450	24.56	
9		36	20.000	16.000	12.800	37.21	
10		17	20.000	-3.000	0.450	1.31	
11		120	120.000	0.000	34.400	100.00	
12							
13		34.40	chi-square				
14		5	df				
15		1.98E-06	p-value				

The chi-square distribution, which is used as the test statistic in this chapter, has the following characteristics.

1. **Chi-square values are never negative.** This is because the difference between f_o and f_e is squared, that is, $(f_o - f_e)^2$.
2. **There is a family of chi-square distributions.** There is a chi-square distribution for 1 degree of freedom, another for 2 degrees of freedom, another for 3 degrees of freedom, and so on. In this type of problem the number of degrees of freedom is determined by $k - 1$, where k is the number of categories. Therefore, the shape of the chi-square distribution does *not* depend on the size of the sample, but on the number of categories used. For example, if 200 employees of an airline were classified into one of three categories—flight personnel, ground support, and administrative personnel—there would be $k - 1 = 3 - 1 = 2$ degrees of freedom.
3. **The chi-square distribution is positively skewed.** However, as the number of degrees of freedom increases, the distribution begins to approximate the normal probability distribution. Chart 17–2 shows the distributions for selected degrees of freedom. Notice that for 10 degrees of freedom the curve is approaching a normal distribution.

Shape of χ^2 distribution approaches normal distribution as *df* becomes larger

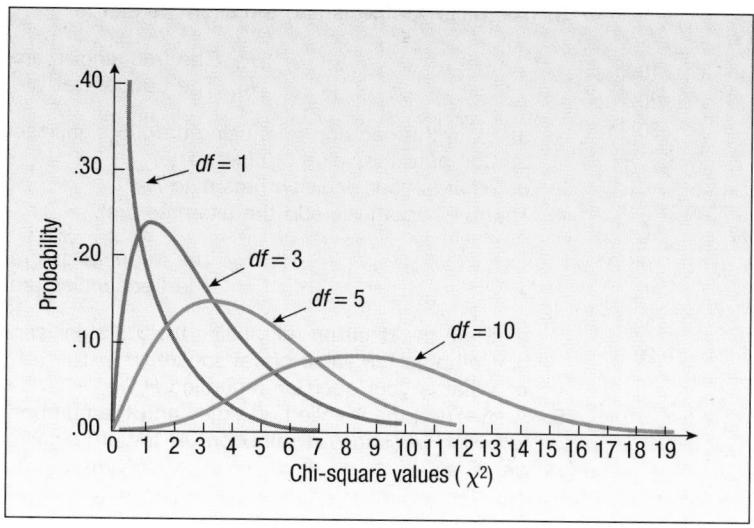

CHART 17–2 Chi-Square Distributions for Selected Degrees of Freedom

Self-Review 17–1

The human resources director at Georgetown Paper, Inc., is concerned about absenteeism among hourly workers. She decides to sample the company records to determine whether absenteeism is distributed evenly throughout the six-day work week. The hypotheses are:

H_0: Absenteeism is evenly distributed throughout the work week.
H_1: Absenteeism is *not* evenly distributed throughout the work week.

The sample results are:

	Number Absent		Number Absent
Monday	12	Thursday	10
Tuesday	9	Friday	9
Wednesday	11	Saturday	9

(a) What are the numbers 12, 9, 11, 10, 9, and 9 called?
(b) How many categories (cells) are there?
(c) What is the *expected* frequency for each day?
(d) How many degrees of freedom are there?
(e) What is the chi-square critical value at the 1 percent significance level?
(f) Compute the χ^2 test statistic.
(g) What is the decision regarding the null hypothesis?
(h) Specifically, what does this indicate to the human resources director?

Exercises

connect™

1. In a particular chi-square goodness-of-fit test there are four categories and 200 observations. Use the .05 significance level.
    a. How many degrees of freedom are there?
    b. What is the critical value of chi-square?
2. In a particular chi-square goodness-of-fit test there are six categories and 500 observations. Use the .01 significance level.
    a. How many degrees of freedom are there?
    b. What is the critical value of chi-square?
3. The null hypothesis and the alternate are:

    H_0: The frequencies are equal.
    H_1: The frequencies are not equal.

Category	f_o
A	10
B	20
C	30

   a. State the decision rule, using the .05 significance level.
   b. Compute the value of chi-square.
   c. What is your decision regarding H_0?

4. The null hypothesis and the alternate are:

    H_0: The frequencies are equal.
    H_1: The frequencies are not equal.

Category	f_o
A	10
B	20
C	30
D	20

   a. State the decision rule, using the .05 significance level.
   b. Compute the value of chi-square.
   c. What is your decision regarding H_0?

5. A six-sided die is rolled 30 times and the numbers 1 through 6 appear as shown in the following frequency distribution. At the .10 significance level, can we conclude that the die is fair?

Outcome	Frequency	Outcome	Frequency
1	3	4	3
2	6	5	9
3	2	6	7

6. Classic Golf, Inc., manages five courses in the Jacksonville, Florida, area. The director of golf wishes to study the number of rounds of golf played per weekday at the five courses. He gathered the following sample information shown to the left. At the .05 significance level, is there a difference in the number of rounds played by day of the week?

Day	Rounds
Monday	124
Tuesday	74
Wednesday	104
Thursday	98
Friday	120

7. A group of department store buyers viewed a new line of dresses and gave their opinions of them. The results were:

Opinion	Number of Buyers	Opinion	Number of Buyers
Outstanding	47	Good	39
Excellent	45	Fair	35
Very good	40	Undesirable	34

Because the largest number (47) indicated the new line is outstanding, the head designer thinks that this is a mandate to go into mass production of the dresses. The head sweeper (who somehow became involved in this) believes that there is not a clear mandate and claims that the opinions are evenly distributed among the six categories. He further states that the slight differences among the various counts are probably due to chance. Test the null hypothesis that there is no significant difference among the opinions of the buyers. Test at the .01 level of risk. Follow a formal approach; that is, state the null hypothesis, the alternate hypothesis, and so on.

8. The safety director of Honda USA took samples at random from company records of minor work-related accidents and classified them according to the time the accident took place.

Time	Number of Accidents	Time	Number of Accidents
8 up to 9 A.M.	6	1 up to 2 P.M.	7
9 up to 10 A.M.	6	2 up to 3 P.M.	8
10 up to 11 A.M.	20	3 up to 4 P.M.	19
11 up to 12 P.M.	8	4 up to 5 P.M.	6

Using the goodness-of-fit test and the .01 level of significance, determine whether the accidents are evenly distributed throughout the day. Write a brief explanation of your conclusion.

Goodness-of-Fit Test: Unequal Expected Frequencies

The expected frequencies (f_e) in the previous distribution involving baseball cards were all equal (20). According to the null hypothesis, it was expected that a picture of Tom Seaver would sell 20 times at random, a picture of Johnny Bench would sell 20 times out of 120 trials, and so on. The chi-square test can also be used if the expected frequencies are not equal.

Expected frequencies not equal in this problem

The following example illustrates the case of unequal frequencies and also gives a practical use of the chi-square goodness-of-fit test—namely, to find whether a local experience differs from the national experience.

Example

The American Hospital Administrators Association (AHAA) reports the following information concerning the number of times senior citizens are admitted to a hospital during a one-year period. Forty percent are not admitted; 30 percent are admitted once; 20 percent are admitted twice, and the remaining 10 percent are admitted three or more times.

A survey of 150 residents of Bartow Estates, a community devoted to active seniors located in central Florida, revealed 55 residents were not admitted during the last year, 50 were admitted to a hospital once, 32 were admitted twice, and the rest of those in the survey were admitted three or more times. Can we conclude the survey at Bartow Estates is consistent with the information suggested by the AHAA? Use the .05 significance level.

Solution

We begin by organizing the above information into Table 17–4. Clearly, we cannot compare percentages given in the study by the Hospital Administrators to the frequencies reported for the Bartow Estates. However, these percentages can be converted to expected frequencies, f_e. According to the Hospital Administrators, 40 percent of the Bartow residents in the survey did not require hospitalization. Thus, if there is no difference between the national experience and those of Bartow Estates, then 40

percent of the 150 seniors surveyed (60 residents) would not have been hospitalized. Further, 30 percent of those surveyed were admitted once (45 residents), and so on. The observed frequencies for Bartow residents and the expected frequencies based on the percents in the national study are given in Table 17–4.

TABLE 17–4 Summary of Study by AHAA and a Survey of Bartow Estates Residents

Number of Times Admitted	AHAA Percent of Total	Number of Bartow Residents (f_o)	Expected Number of Residents (f_e)
0	40	55	60
1	30	50	45
2	20	32	30
3 or more	10	13	15
Total	100	150	150

The null hypothesis and the alternate hypothesis are:

H_0: There is no difference between local and national experience for hospital admissions.
H_1: There is a difference between local and national experience for hospital admissions.

To find the decision rule we use Appendix B.3 and the .05 significance level. There are four admitting categories, so the degrees of freedom are $df = 4 - 1 = 3$. The critical value is 7.815. Therefore, the decision rule is to reject the null hypothesis if $\chi^2 > 7.815$. The decision rule is portrayed in Chart 17–3.

Now to compute the chi-square test statistic:

Number of Times Admitted	(f_o)	(f_e)	$f_o - f_e$	$(f_o - f_e)^2/f_e$
0	55	60	−5	0.4167
1	50	45	5	0.5556
2	32	30	2	0.1333
3 or more	13	15	−2	0.2667
Total	150	150	0	1.3723

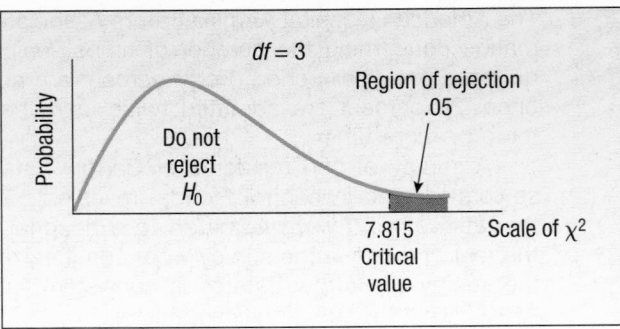

CHART 17–3 Decision Criteria for the Bartow Estates Research Study

The computed value of χ^2 (1.3723) lies to the left of 7.815. Thus, we cannot reject the null hypothesis. We conclude that there is no evidence of a difference between the local and national experience for hospital admissions.

Limitations of Chi-Square

Be careful in applying χ^2 to some problems.

If there is an unusually small expected frequency in a cell, chi-square (if applied) might result in an erroneous conclusion. This can happen because f_e appears in the denominator, and dividing by a very small number makes the quotient quite large! Two generally accepted policies regarding small cell frequencies are:

1. If there are only two cells, the *expected* frequency in each cell should be at least 5. The computation of chi-square would be permissible in the following problem, involving a minimum f_e of 6.

Individual	f_o	f_e
Literate	643	642
Illiterate	7	6

2. For more than two cells, chi-square should *not* be used if more than 20 percent of the f_e cells have expected frequencies less than 5. According to this policy, it would not be appropriate to use the goodness-of-fit test on the following data. Three of the seven cells, or 43 percent, have expected frequencies (f_e) of less than 5.

Level of Management	f_o	f_e
Foreman	30	32
Supervisor	110	113
Manager	86	87
Middle management	23	24
Assistant vice president	5	2
Vice president	5	4
Senior vice president	4	1
Total	263	263

To show the reason for the 20 percent policy, we conducted the goodness-of-fit test on the above data on the levels of management. The MegaStat output follows.

	A	B	C	D	E	F	G
16							
17	Goodness of Fit Test						
18							
19		observed	expected	O - E	(O - E)² / E	% of chisq	
20		30	32.000	-2.000	0.125	0.89	
21		110	113.000	-3.000	0.080	0.57	
22		86	87.000	-1.000	0.011	0.08	
23		23	24.000	-1.000	0.042	0.30	
24		5	2.000	3.000	4.500	32.12	
25		5	4.000	1.000	0.250	1.78	
26		4	1.000	3.000	9.000	64.25	
27		263	263.000	0.000	14.008	100.00	
28							
29		14.01	chi-square				
30		6	df				
31		.0295	p-value				

Goodness of Fit 2

For this test at the .05 significance level, H_0 is rejected if the computed value of chi-square is greater than 12.592. The computed value is 14.01, so we reject the null hypothesis that the observed frequencies represent a random sample from the population of the expected values. Examine the MegaStat output. More than 98 percent of the computed chi-square value is accounted for by the three vice president categories ($[4.500 + .250 + 9.000]/14.008 = 0.9815$). Logically, too much weight is being given to these categories.

The dilemma can be resolved by combining categories if it is logical to do so. In the above example we combine the three vice presidential categories, which satisfies the 20 percent policy.

Level of Management	f_o	f_e
Foreman	30	32
Supervisor	110	113
Manager	86	87
Middle management	23	24
Vice president	14	7
Total	263	263

The computed value of chi-square with the revised categories is 7.26. See the following MegaStat output. This value is less than the critical value of 9.488 for the .05 significance level. The null hypothesis is, therefore, not rejected at the .05 significance level. This indicates there is not a significant difference between the observed distribution and the expected distribution.

Goodness of Fit 3

	A	B	C	D	E	F	G
32							
33	Goodness of Fit Test						
34							
35		observed	expected	O - E	(O - E)² / E	% of chisq	
36		30	32.000	-2.000	0.125	1.72	
37		110	113.000	-3.000	0.080	1.10	
38		86	87.000	-1.000	0.011	0.16	
39		23	24.000	-1.000	0.042	0.57	
40		14	7.000	7.000	7.000	96.45	
41		263	263.000	0.000	7.258	100.00	
42							
43		7.26 chi-square					
44		4 df					
45		.1229 p-value					

Self-Review 17–2   The American Accounting Association classifies accounts receivable as "current," "late," and "not collectible." Industry figures show that 60 percent of accounts receivable are current, 30 percent are late, and 10 percent are not collectible. Massa and Barr, a law firm in Greenville, Ohio, has 500 accounts receivable: 320 are current, 120 are late, and 60 are not collectible. Are these numbers in agreement with the industry distribution? Use the .05 significance level.

Exercises

Category	f_o
A	30
B	20
C	10

9. The following hypotheses are given:

H_0: Forty percent of the observations are in category A, 40 percent are in B, and 20 percent are in C.

H_1: The distribution of the observations is not as described in H_0.

We took a sample of 60, with the results to the left.

a. State the decision rule using the .01 significance level.

b. Compute the value of chi-square.

c. What is your decision regarding H_0?

10. The chief of security for Mall of the Dakotas was directed to study the problem of missing goods. He selected a sample of 100 boxes that had been tampered with and ascertained that, for 60 of the boxes, the missing pants, shoes, and so on were attributed to shoplifting. For 30 other boxes employees had stolen the goods, and for the remaining 10 boxes he blamed poor inventory control. In his report to the mall management, can he say that shoplifting is *twice* as likely to be the cause of the loss as compared with either employee theft or poor inventory control and that employee theft and poor inventory control are equally likely? Use the .02 significance level.

11. The bank credit card department of Carolina Bank knows from experience that 5 percent of its card holders have had some high school, 15 percent have completed high school, 25 percent have had some college, and 55 percent have completed college. Of the 500 card holders whose cards have been called in for failure to pay their charges this month, 50 had some high school, 100 had completed high school, 190 had some college, and 160 had completed college. Can we conclude that the distribution of card holders who do not pay their charges is different from all others? Use the .01 significance level.

12. For many years TV executives used the guideline that 30 percent of the audience were watching each of the traditional big three prime-time networks and 10 percent were watching cable stations on a weekday night. A random sample of 500 viewers in the Tampa–St. Petersburg, Florida, area last Monday night showed that 165 homes were tuned in to the ABC affiliate, 140 to the CBS affiliate, 125 to the NBC affiliate, and the remainder were viewing a cable station. At the .05 significance level, can we conclude that the guideline is still reasonable?

Contingency Table Analysis

In Chapter 4 we discussed bivariate data, where we studied the relationship between two variables. We described a contingency table, which simultaneously summarizes two nominal-scale variables of interest. For example, a sample of students enrolled in the School of Business is classified by gender (male or female) and major (accounting, management, finance, marketing, or quantitative methods). This classification is based on the nominal scale, because there is no natural order to the classifications.

We discussed contingency tables in Chapter 5. On page 158, we illustrated the relationship between loyalty to a company and the length of employment and explored whether older employees were likely to be more loyal to the company.

We can use the chi-square statistic to formally test for a relationship between two nominal-scaled variables. To put it another way, Is one variable *independent* of the other? Here are some examples where we are interested in testing whether two variables are related.

- Ford Motor Company operates an assembly plant in Dearborn, Michigan. The plant operates three shifts per day, 5 days a week. The quality control manager wishes to compare the quality level on the three shifts. Vehicles are classified by quality level (acceptable, unacceptable) and shift (day, afternoon, night). Is there a difference in the quality level on the three shifts? That is, is the quality of the product related to the shift when it was manufactured? Or is the quality of the product independent of the shift on which it was manufactured?

- A sample of 100 drivers who were stopped for speeding violations was classified by gender and whether or not they were wearing a seat belt. For this sample, is wearing a seatbelt related to gender?
- Does a male released from federal prison make a different adjustment to civilian life if he returns to his hometown or if he goes elsewhere to live? The two variables are adjustment to civilian life and place of residence. Note that both variables are measured on the nominal scale.

Example

The Federal Correction Agency is investigating the last question cited above: Does a male released from federal prison make a different adjustment to civilian life if he returns to his hometown or if he goes elsewhere to live? To put it another way, is there a relationship between adjustment to civilian life and place of residence after release from prison? Use the .01 significance level.

Solution

As before, the first step in hypothesis testing is to state the null and alternate hypotheses.

H_0: There is no relationship between adjustment to civilian life and where the individual lives after being released from prison.

H_1: There is a relationship between adjustment to civilian life and where the individual lives after being released from prison.

The agency's psychologists interviewed 200 randomly selected former prisoners. Using a series of questions, the psychologists classified the adjustment of each individual to civilian life as outstanding, good, fair, or unsatisfactory. The classifications for the 200 former prisoners were tallied as follows. Joseph Camden, for example, returned to his hometown and has shown outstanding adjustment to civilian life. His case is one of the 27 tallies in the upper left box.

Residence after Release from Prison	Adjustment to Civilian Life			
	Outstanding	**Good**	**Fair**	**Unsatisfactory**
Hometown	ЖНІ ЖНІ ЖНІ ЖНІ ЖНІ ІІ	ЖНІ ЖНІ ЖНІ ЖНІ ЖНІ ЖНІ ЖНІ	ЖНІ ЖНІ ЖНІ ЖНІ ЖНІ ЖНІ ІІІ	ЖНІ ЖНІ ЖНІ ЖНІ ЖНІ
Not hometown	ЖНІ ЖНІ ІІІ	ЖНІ ЖНІ ЖНІ	ЖНІ ЖНІ ЖНІ ЖНІ ЖНІ ІІ	ЖНІ ЖНІ ЖНІ ЖНІ ЖНІ

Contingency table consists of count data.

The tallies in each box, or *cell,* were counted. The counts are given in the following **contingency table**. (See Table 17–5.) In this case, the Federal Correction Agency wondered whether adjustment to civilian life is *contingent on* where the prisoner goes after release from prison.

TABLE 17–5 Adjustment to Civilian Life and Place of Residence

Residence after Release from Prison	Adjustment to Civilian Life				Total
	Outstanding	Good	Fair	Unsatisfactory	
Hometown	27	35	33	25	120
Not hometown	13	15	27	25	80
Total	40	50	60	50	200

Once we know how many rows (2) and columns (4) there are in the contingency table, we can determine the critical value and the decision rule. For a chi-square test of significance where two traits are classified in a contingency table, the degrees of freedom are found by:

$$df = (\text{number of rows} - 1)(\text{number of columns} - 1) = (r - 1)(c - 1)$$

In this problem:

$$df = (r - 1)(c - 1) = (2 - 1)(4 - 1) = 3$$

To find the critical value for 3 degrees of freedom and the .01 level (selected earlier), refer to Appendix B.3. It is 11.345. The decision rule is to reject the null hypothesis if the computed value of χ^2 is greater than 11.345. The decision rule is portrayed graphically in Chart 17–4.

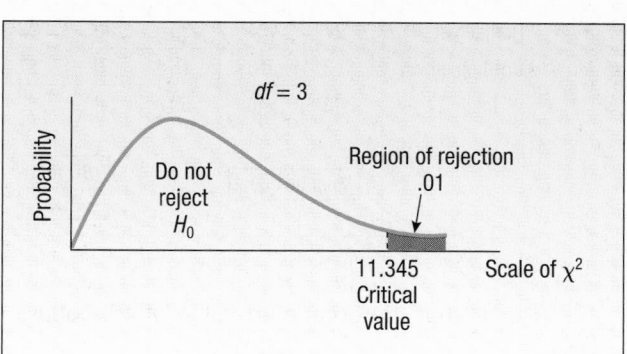

CHART 17–4 Chi-Square Distribution for 3 Degrees of Freedom

Next we find the computed value of χ^2. The observed frequencies, f_o, are shown in Table 17–5. How are the corresponding expected frequencies, f_e, determined? Note in the "Total" column of Table 17–5 that 120 of the 200 former prisoners (60 percent) returned to their hometowns. *If there were no relationship* between adjustment and residency after release from prison, we would expect 60 percent of the 40 ex-prisoners who made outstanding adjustment to civilian life to reside in their hometowns. Thus, the expected frequency f_e for the upper left cell is .60 × 40 = 24. Likewise, if there were no relationship between adjustment and present residence, we would expect 60 percent of the 50 ex-prisoners (30) who had "good" adjustment to civilian life to reside in their hometowns.

Further, notice that 80 of the 200 ex-prisoners studied (40 percent) did not return to their hometowns to live. Thus, of the 60 considered by the psychologists to have

made "fair" adjustment to civilian life, .40 × 60, or 24, would be expected not to return to their hometowns.

The expected frequency for any cell can be determined by

EXPECTED FREQUENCY $f_e = \dfrac{\text{(Row total)(Column total)}}{\text{Grand total}}$ **[17–2]**

From this formula, the expected frequency for the upper left cell in Table 17–5 is:

$$\text{Expected frequency} - \frac{\text{(Row total)(Column total)}}{\text{Grand total}} = \frac{(120)(40)}{200} = 24$$

The observed frequencies, f_o, and the expected frequencies, f_e, for all of the cells in the contingency table are listed in Table 17–6.

TABLE 17–6 Observed and Expected Frequencies

Residence after Release from Prison	Outstanding		Good		Fair		Unsatisfactory		Total	
	f_o	f_e	f_o	f_e	f_o	f_e	f_o	f_e	f_o	f_e
Hometown	27	24	35	30	33	36	25	30	120	120
Not hometown	13	16	15	20	27	24	25	20	80	80
Total	40	40	50	50	60	60	50	50	200	200

Must be equal $\dfrac{(80)(50)}{200}$ Must be equal

Recall that the computed value of chi-square using formula (17–1) is found by:

$$\chi^2 = \Sigma\left[\frac{(f_o - f_e)^2}{f_e}\right]$$

Starting with the upper left cell:

$$\chi^2 = \frac{(27-24)^2}{24} + \frac{(35-30)^2}{30} + \frac{(33-36)^2}{36} + \frac{(25-30)^2}{30}$$
$$+ \frac{(13-16)^2}{16} + \frac{(15-20)^2}{20} + \frac{(27-24)^2}{24} + \frac{(25-20)^2}{20}$$
$$= 0.375 + 0.833 + 0.250 + 0.833 + 0.563 + 1.250 + 0.375 + 1.250$$
$$= 5.729$$

Because the computed value of chi-square (5.729) lies in the region to the left of 11.345, the null hypothesis is not rejected at the .01 significance level. We conclude there is no evidence of a relationship between adjustment to civilian life and where the prisoner resides after being released from prison. For the Federal Correction Agency's advisement program, adjustment to civilian life is not related to where the ex-prisoner lives.

The following output is from the MINITAB system.

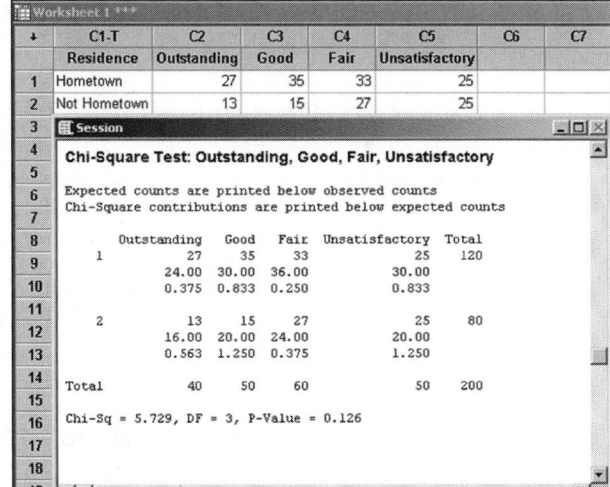

Observe that the value of chi-square is the same as that computed earlier. In addition, the *p*-value is reported, .126. So the probability of finding a value of the test statistic as large or larger is .126 when the null hypothesis is true. The *p*-value also results in the same decision, do not reject the null hypothesis.

Self-Review 17–3

A social scientist sampled 140 people and classified them according to income level and whether or not they played a state lottery in the last month. The sample information is reported below. Is it reasonable to conclude that playing the lottery is related to income level? Use the .05 significance level.

	Income			
	Low	**Middle**	**High**	**Total**
Played	46	28	21	95
Did not play	14	12	19	45
Total	60	40	40	140

(a) What is this table called?
(b) State the null hypothesis and the alternate hypothesis.
(c) What is the decision rule?
(d) Determine the value of chi-square.
(e) Make a decision on the null hypothesis. Interpret the result.

Exercises

13. The director of advertising for the *Carolina Sun Times*, the largest newspaper in the Carolinas, is studying the relationship between the type of community in which a subscriber resides and the section of the newspaper he or she reads first. For a sample of readers, she collected the sample information at the top of the next page.

	National News	Sports	Comics
City	170	124	90
Suburb	120	112	100
Rural	130	90	88

At the .05 significance level, can we conclude there is a relationship between the type of community where the person resides and the section of the paper read first?

14. Four brands of lightbulbs are being considered for use in the final assembly area of the Saturn plant in Spring Hill, Tennessee. The director of purchasing asked for samples of 100 from each manufacturer. The numbers of acceptable and unacceptable bulbs from each manufacturer are shown below. At the .05 significance level, is there a difference in the quality of the bulbs?

	Manufacturer			
	A	B	C	D
Unacceptable	12	8	5	11
Acceptable	88	92	95	89
Total	100	100	100	100

15. The quality control department at Food Town, Inc., a grocery chain in upstate New York, conducts a monthly check on the comparison of scanned prices to posted prices. The chart below summarizes the results of a sample of 500 items last month. Company management would like to know whether there is any relationship between error rates on regularly priced items and specially priced items. Use the .01 significance level.

	Regular Price	Advertised Special Price
Undercharge	20	10
Overcharge	15	30
Correct price	200	225

16. The use of cellular phones in automobiles has increased dramatically in the last few years. Of concern to traffic experts, as well as manufacturers of cellular phones, is the effect on accident rates. Is someone who is using a cellular phone more likely to be involved in a traffic accident? What is your conclusion from the following sample information? Use the .05 significance level.

	Had Accident in the Last Year	Did Not Have an Accident in the Last Year
Uses a cell phone	25	300
Does not use a cell phone	50	400

Chapter Summary

I. The characteristics of the chi-square distribution are:
  A. The value of chi-square is never negative.
  B. The chi-square distribution is positively skewed.
  C. There is a family of chi-square distributions.
    1. Each time the degrees of freedom change, a new distribution is formed.
    2. As the degrees of freedom increase, the distribution approaches a normal distribution.

II. A goodness-of-fit test will show whether an observed set of frequencies could have come from a hypothesized population distribution.
A. The degrees of freedom are $k - 1$, where k is the number of categories.
B. The formula for computing the value of chi-square is

$$\chi^2 = \Sigma \left[\frac{(f_o - f_e)^2}{f_e} \right]$$ **[17–1]**

III. A contingency table is used to test whether two traits or characteristics are related.
A. Each observation is classified according to two traits.
B. The expected frequency is determined as follows:

$$f_e = \frac{\text{(Row total)(Column total)}}{\text{Grand total}}$$ **[17–2]**

C. The degrees of freedom are found by:

$$df = (\text{Rows} - 1)(\text{Columns} - 1)$$

D. The usual hypothesis testing procedure is used.

Pronunciation Key

SYMBOL	MEANING	PRONUNCIATION
χ^2	Probability distribution	*ki square*
f_o	Observed frequency	*f sub oh*
f_e	Expected frequency	*f sub e*

Chapter Exercises

connect

17. Vehicles heading west on Front Street may turn right, left, or go straight ahead at Elm Street. The city traffic engineer believes that half of the vehicles will continue straight through the intersection. Of the remaining half, equal proportions will turn right and left. Two hundred vehicles were observed, with the following results. Can we conclude that the traffic engineer is correct? Use the .10 significance level.

	Straight	**Right Turn**	**Left Turn**
Frequency	112	48	40

18. The publisher of a sports magazine plans to offer new subscribers one of three gifts: a sweatshirt with the logo of their favorite team, a coffee cup with the logo of their favorite team, or a pair of earrings also with the logo of their favorite team. In a sample of 500 new subscribers, the number selecting each gift is reported below. At the .05 significance level, is there a preference for the gifts or should we conclude that the gifts are equally well liked?

Gift	Frequency
Sweatshirt	183
Coffee cup	175
Earrings	142

19. In a particular market there are three commercial television stations, each with its own evening news program from 6:00 to 6:30 P.M. According to a report in this morning's local newspaper, a random sample of 150 viewers last night revealed 53 watched the news on WNAE (channel 5), 64 watched on WRRN (channel 11), and 33 on WSPD (channel 13). At the .05 significance level, is there a difference in the proportion of viewers watching the three channels?

20. There are four entrances to the Government Center Building in downtown Philadelphia. The building maintenance supervisor would like to know if the entrances are equally utilized. To investigate, 400 people were observed entering the building. The number using each entrance is reported below. At the .01 significance level, is there a difference in the use of the four entrances?

Entrance	Frequency
Main Street	140
Broad Street	120
Cherry Street	90
Walnut Street	50
Total	400

21. The owner of a mail-order catalog would like to compare her sales with the geographic distribution of the population. According to the United States Bureau of the Census, 21 percent of the population lives in the Northeast, 24 percent in the Midwest, 35 percent in the South, and 20 percent in the West. Listed below is a breakdown of a sample of 400 orders randomly selected from those shipped last month. At the .01 significance level, does the distribution of the orders reflect the population?

Region	Frequency
Northeast	68
Midwest	104
South	155
West	73
Total	400

22. Banner Mattress and Furniture Company wishes to study the number of credit applications received per day for the last 300 days. The sample information is reported below.

Number of Credit Applications	Frequency (Number of Days)
0	50
1	77
2	81
3	48
4	31
5 or more	13

To interpret, there were 50 days on which no credit applications were received, 77 days on which only one application was received, and so on. Would it be reasonable to conclude that the population distribution is Poisson with a mean of 2.0? Use the .05 significance level. *Hint:* To find the expected frequencies use the Poisson distribution with a mean of 2.0. Find the probability of exactly one success given a Poisson distribution with a mean of 2.0. Multiply this probability by 300 to find the expected frequency for the number of days in which there was exactly one application. Determine the expected frequency for the other days in a similar manner.

23. Each of the digits in a raffle is thought to have the same chance of occurrence. The table shows the frequency of each digit for consecutive drawings in a California lottery. Perform the chi-square test to see if you reject the hypothesis at the .05 significance level that the digits are from a uniform population.

Digit	Frequency	Digit	Frequency
0	44	5	24
1	32	6	31
2	23	7	27
3	27	8	28
4	23	9	21

24. John Isaac, Inc., a designer and installer of industrial signs, employs 60 people. The company recorded the type of the most recent visit to a doctor by each employee. A national assessment conducted in 2004 found that 53 percent of all physician visits were to primary care physicians, 19 percent to medical specialists, 17 percent to surgical specialists and 11 percent to emergency departments. Test at the 0.01 significance level if Isaac employees differ significantly from the survey distribution. Here are their results:

Visit Type	Number of Visits
Primary care	29
Medical specialist	11
Surgical specialist	16
Emergency	4

25. A survey by *USA Today* investigated the public's attitude toward the federal deficit. Each sampled citizen was classified as to whether they felt the government should reduce the deficit, increase the deficit, or if they had no opinion. The sample results of the study by gender are reported below.

Gender	Reduce the Deficit	Increase the Deficit	No Opinion
Female	244	194	68
Male	305	114	25

At the .05 significance level, is it reasonable to conclude that gender is independent of a person's position on the deficit?

26. A study regarding the relationship between age and the amount of pressure sales personnel feel in relation to their jobs revealed the following sample information. At the .01 significance level, is there a relationship between job pressure and age?

| Age (years) | Degree of Job Pressure | | |
	Low	Medium	High
Less than 25	20	18	22
25 up to 40	50	46	44
40 up to 60	58	63	59
60 and older	34	43	43

27. The claims department at Wise Insurance Company believes that younger drivers have more accidents and, therefore, should be charged higher insurance rates. Investigating a sample of 1,200 Wise policyholders revealed the following breakdown on whether a claim had been filed in the last three years and the age of the policyholder. Is it reasonable to conclude that there is a relationship between the age of the policyholder and whether or not the person filed a claim? Use the .05 significance level.

Age Group	No Claim	Claim
16 up to 25	170	74
25 up to 40	240	58
40 up to 55	400	44
55 or older	190	24
Total	1,000	200

28. A sample of employees at a large chemical plant was asked to indicate a preference for one of three pension plans. The results are given in the following table. Does it seem that there is a relationship between the pension plan selected and the job classification of the employees? Use the .01 significance level.

	Pension Plan		
Job Class	Plan A	Plan B	Plan C
Supervisor	10	13	29
Clerical	19	80	19
Labor	81	57	22

29. Did you ever purchase a bag of M&M's candies and wonder about the distribution of colors? You can go to the website www.baking.m-ms.com and click the United States on the map, then click **About M&M's,** then **Products** and **Peanut** and find the percentage breakdown according to the manufacturer, as well as a brief history of the product. Did you know in the beginning they were all brown? For peanut M&M's 12 percent are brown, 15 percent yellow, 12 percent red, 23 percent blue, 23 percent orange, and 15 percent green. A 6-oz. bag purchased at the Book Store at Coastal Carolina University on November 1, 2008, had 12 blue, 14 brown, 13 yellow, 14 red, 7 orange, and 12 green. Is it reasonable to conclude that the actual distribution agrees with the expected distribution? Use the .05 significance level. Conduct your own trial. Be sure to share with your instructor.

Data Set Exercises

30. Refer to the Real Estate data, which report information on homes sold in the Denver, Colorado, area last year.
   a. Develop a contingency table that shows whether a home has a pool and the township in which the house is located. Is there an association between the variables pool and township? Use the .05 significance level.
   b. Develop a contingency table that shows whether a home has an attached garage and the township in which the home is located. Is there an association between the variables attached garage and township? Use the .05 significance level.
31. Refer to the Baseball 2007 data, which report information on the 30 Major League Baseball teams for the 2007 season. Set up a variable that divides the teams into two groups, those that had a winning season and those that did not. There are 162 games in the season, so define a winning season as having won 81 or more games. Next, divide the teams into two salary groups. Let the 15 teams with the largest salaries be in one group and the 15 teams with the smallest salaries in the other. At the .05 significance level is there a relationship between salaries and winning?

32. Refer to the Wage data, which report information on annual wages for a sample of 100 workers. Also included are variables relating to industry, years of education, and gender for each worker. Develop a table showing the industry of employment by gender. At the .05 significance level is it reasonable to conclude that industry of employment and gender are related?

33. Refer to the CIA data, which report demographic and economic information on 46 countries.
   a. Develop a contingency table that shows G-20 membership versus level of petroleum activity. Is there a significant association at the .05 level of significance between these variables?
   b. Group the countries into "young" (percent of population over 65 is less than 10) and "old" (percent of population over 65 is more than 10). Then develop a contingency table between this age variable and the level of petroleum activity. At the .05 level of significance can we conclude these variables are related?

Software Commands

1. The MegaStat commands to create the chi-square goodness-of-fit test on page 644 are:
   a. Enter the information from Table 17–2 into a worksheet as shown.
   b. Select **MegaStat, Chi-Square/Crosstabs,** and **Goodness of Fit Test** and hit **Enter.**
   c. In the dialog box select *B2:B7* as the **Observed values,** *C2:C7* as the **Expected values,** and enter *0* as the **Number of parameters estimated from the data.** Click on **OK.**

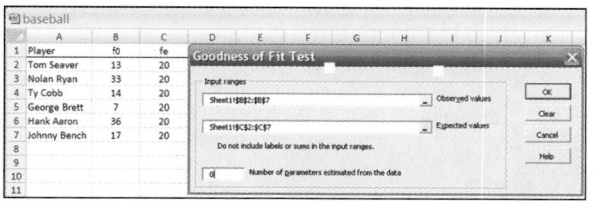

2. The MegaStat commands to create the chi-square goodness-of-fit tests on pages 649 and 650 are the same except for the number of items in the observed and expected frequency columns. Only one dialog box is shown.
   a. Enter the Levels of Management information shown on page 649.
   b. Select **MegaStat, Chi-Square/Crosstabs,** and **Goodness of Fit Test** and hit **Enter.**
   c. In the dialog box select *B2:B8* as the **Observed values,** *C2:C8* as the **Expected values,** and enter *0* as the **Number of parameters estimated from the data.** Click on **OK.**

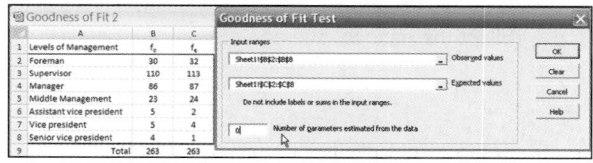

3. The MINITAB commands for the chi-square analysis on page 655 are:
   a. Enter the names of the variables in the first row and the data in the next two rows.
   b. Select **Stat, Table,** and then click on **Chi-Square Test** and hit **Enter.**
   c. In the dialog box select the columns labeled *Outstanding* to *Unsatisfactory* and click **OK.**

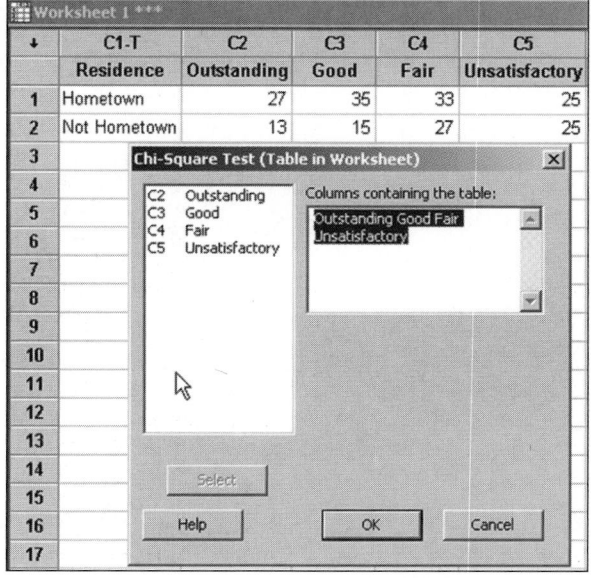

Chapter 17   Answers to Self-Review

17–1 a. Observed frequencies.
  b. Six (six days of the week).
  c. 10. Total observed frequencies ÷ 6 =
     60/6 = 10.
  d. 5; $k - 1 = 6 - 1 = 5$.
  e. 15.086 (from the chi-square table in
     Appendix B.3).
  f.

$$\chi^2 = \Sigma\left[\frac{(f_o - f_e)^2}{f_e}\right] = \frac{(12 - 10)^2}{10} + \cdots + \frac{(9 - 10)^2}{10} = 0.8$$

  g. Do not reject H_0.
  h. Absenteeism is distributed evenly throughout
     the week. The observed differences are due to
     sampling variation.

17–2 $H_0: P_C = .60, P_L = .30,$ and $P_U = .10$.
     $H_1:$ Distribution is not as above.
     Reject H_0 if $\chi^2 > 5.991$.

Category	f_o	f_e	$\dfrac{(f_o - f_e)^2}{f_e}$
Current	320	300	1.33
Late	120	150	6.00
Uncollectible	60	50	2.00
	500	500	9.33

Reject H_0. The accounts receivable data does not
reflect the national average.

17–3 a. Contingency table
  b. H_0: There is no relationship between income
     and whether the person played the lottery.
     H_1: There is a relationship between income and
     whether the person played the lottery.
  c. Reject H_0 if χ^2 is greater than 5.991.
  d.

$$\chi^2 = \frac{(46 - 40.71)^2}{40.71} + \frac{(28 - 27.14)^2}{27.14} + \frac{(21 - 27.14)^2}{27.14}$$
$$+ \frac{(14 - 19.29)^2}{19.29} + \frac{(12 - 12.86)^2}{12.86} + \frac{(19 - 12.86)^2}{12.86}$$
$$= 6.544$$

  e. Reject H_0. There is a relationship between
     income level and playing the lottery.

Nonparametric Methods:

Analysis of Ranked Data

Assembly workers at Computer Associates assemble one or two subassemblies and insert them in a frame. Executives at CA think that the employees would have more pride in their work if they assembled all components and tested the completed computer. A sample of 25 employees were selected to test the idea. Twenty liked assembling the entire unit and testing it. At the .05 level, can we conclude the employees preferred assembling the entire unit? (See Exercise 8 and Goal 1.)

Introduction

Chapter 17 introduced tests of hypothesis for *nominal-scale* variables. Recall from Chapter 1 that nominal level of measurement implies the data can only be classified into categories, and there is no particular order to the categories. The purpose of these tests is to determine whether an observed set of frequencies, f_o, is significantly different from a corresponding set of expected frequencies, f_e. Likewise, if you are interested in the relationship between two characteristics—such as the age of an individual and his or her music preference—you would tally the data into a contingency table and use the chi-square distribution as the test statistic. For both these types of problems, no assumptions need to be made about the shape of the population. We do not have to assume, for example, that the population of interest follows the normal distribution, as was done with tests of hypotheses in Chapters 10 through 12.

This chapter continues our discussion of hypothesis tests designed especially for nonparametric data. For these tests, we do not need to assume anything about the shape of the population distribution. Sometimes, we use the term distribution-free tests. These tests do require that the responses can be ranked or ordered. So the responses must be measured with an ordinal, interval, or ratio scale. An example of an ordinal scale is executive title. Corporate executives can be ranked as assistant vice president, vice president, senior vice president, and president. A vice president is ranked higher than an assistant vice president, a senior vice president is ranked higher than a vice president, and so on.

In this chapter we consider five distribution-free tests and the Spearman coefficient of rank correlation. The tests are: the sign test, the median test, the Wilcoxon signed-rank test, the Wilcoxon rank-sum test, and the Kruskal-Wallis analysis of variance by ranks.

The Sign Test

The **sign test** is based on the sign of a difference between two related observations. We usually designate a plus sign for a positive difference and a minus sign for a negative difference. For example, a dietitian wishes to see if a person's cholesterol level will decrease if the diet is supplemented by a certain mineral. She selects a sample of 20 production workers over the age of 40 and measures the workers' cholesterol level. After the 20 subjects take the mineral for 6 weeks, they are tested again. If the cholesterol level has dropped, a plus signed is recorded. If it has increased, a negative sign is recorded. If there is no change, a zero is recorded (and that person is dropped from the study). For a sign test, we are not concerned with the magnitude of the difference, only the direction of the difference.

The sign test has many applications. One is for "before/after" experiments. To illustrate, suppose an evaluation is to be made on a new tune-up program for automobiles. We record the number of miles traveled per gallon of gasoline before the tune-up and again after the tune-up. If the tune-up is not effective, that is, had no effect on performance, then about half of the automobiles tested would show an increase in miles per gallon and the other half a decrease. A "+" sign is assigned to an increase, a "−" sign to a decrease.

A product-preference experiment illustrates another use of the sign test. Taster's Choice markets two kinds of coffee in a 4-ounce jar: decaffeinated and regular. Its market research department wants to determine whether coffee drinkers prefer decaffeinated or regular coffee. Coffee drinkers are given two small, unmarked cups of coffee, and each is asked his or her preference. Preference for decaffeinated could be coded "+" and preference for regular "−." In a sense the data are ordinal level because the coffee drinkers give their preferred coffee the higher rank; they rank the other kind below it. Here again, if the population of consumers do not have a preference, we would expect half of the sample of coffee drinkers to prefer decaffeinated and the other half regular coffee.

We can best show the application of the sign test by an example. We will use a "before/after" experiment.

Example

The director of information systems at Samuelson Chemicals recommended that an in-plant training program be instituted for managers. The objective is to improve the knowledge of database usage in accounting, procurement, production, and so on. Some managers thought it would be a worthwhile program; others resisted it, saying it would be of no value. Despite these objections, it was announced that the training sessions would commence the first of the month.

A sample of 15 managers was selected at random. A panel of database experts determined the general level of competence of each manager with respect to using the database. Their competence and understanding were rated as being either outstanding, excellent, good, fair, or poor. (See Table 18–1.) After the three-month training program, the same panel of information systems experts rated each manager again. The two ratings (before and after) are shown along with the sign of the difference. A "+" sign indicates improvement, and a "−" sign indicates that the manager's competence using databases had declined after the training program.

TABLE 18–1 Competence Before and After the Training Program

	Name	Before	After	Sign of Difference
	T. J. Bowers	Good	Outstanding	+
	Sue Jenkins	Fair	Excellent	+
	James Brown	Excellent	Good	−
Dropped from analysis	Tad Jackson	Poor	Good	+
	~~Andy Love~~	~~Excellent~~	~~Excellent~~	0
	Sarah Truett	Good	Outstanding	+
	Antonia Aillo	Poor	Fair	+
	Jean Unger	Excellent	Outstanding	+
	Coy Farmer	Good	Poor	−
	Troy Archer	Poor	Good	+
	V. A. Jones	Good	Outstanding	+
	Juan Guillen	Fair	Excellent	+
	Candy Fry	Good	Fair	−
	Arthur Seiple	Good	Outstanding	+
	Sandy Gumpp	Poor	Good	+

We are interested in whether the in-plant training program effectively increased the competence of the managers using the company's database. That is, are the managers more competent after the training program than before?

Solution

We will use the five-step hypothesis-testing procedure.

Step 1: State the null hypothesis and the alternate hypothesis.

H_0: $\pi \leq .50$ There is no increase in competence as a result of the in-plant training program.

H_1: $\pi > .50$ The database competence of the managers has increased.

The symbol π refers to the proportion in the population with a particular characteristic. If we *do not reject* the null hypothesis, it will indicate the training program has produced no change in the level of competence, or that competence actually decreased. If we *reject* the null hypothesis, it will indicate that the competence of the managers has increased as a result of the training program.

The test statistic follows the binomial probability distribution. It is appropriate because the sign test meets all the binomial assumptions, namely:

1. There are only two outcomes: a "success" and a "failure." A manager either increased in database competence (a success) or did not.
2. For each trial the probability of success is assumed to be .50. Thus, the probability of a success is the same for all trials (managers in this case).
3. The total number of trials is fixed (15 in this experiment).
4. Each trial is independent. This means, for example, that Arthur Seiple's performance in the three-month course is unrelated to Sandy Gumpp's performance.

Step 2: Select a level of significance. We chose the .10 level.

Step 3: Decide on the test statistic. It is the *number of plus signs* resulting from the experiment.

Step 4: Formulate a decision rule. Fifteen managers were enrolled in the training course, but Andy Love showed no increase or decrease in competence. (See Table 18–1.) He was, therefore, eliminated from the study because he could not be assigned to either group, so $n = 14$. From the binomial probability distribution table in Appendix B.9, for an n of 14 and a probability of .50, we copied the binomial probability distribution in Table 18–2. The number of successes is in column 1, the probabilities of success in column 2, and the cumulative probabilities in column 3. To arrive at the cumulative probabilities, we *add* the probabilities of success in column 2 from the bottom. For illustration, to get the cumulative probability of 11 or more successes, we add .000 + .001 + .006 + .022 = .029.

This is a one-tailed test because the alternate hypothesis gives a direction. The inequality ($>$) points to the right. Thus, the region of rejection is in the upper tail. If the inequality sign pointed toward the left tail ($<$), the region of rejection would be in the lower tail. If that were the case, we would add the probabilities in column 2 *down* to get the cumulative probabilities in column 3.

Recall that we selected the .10 level of significance. To arrive at the decision rule for this problem, we go to the cumulative probabilities in Table 18–2, column 3. We read up from the bottom until we come to the *cumulative probability nearest to but not exceeding the level of significance* (.10). That cumulative probability is .090. The number of successes (plus signs) corresponding to .090 in column 1 is 10. Therefore, the decision rule is: If the number of pluses in the sample is 10 or more, the null hypothesis is rejected and the alternate hypothesis accepted.

To repeat: We add the probabilities up from the bottom because the direction of the inequality ($>$) is toward the right, indicating that the region of rejection is in the upper tail. If the number of plus signs in the sample is 10 or more, we reject the null hypothesis; otherwise, we do not reject H_0. The region of rejection is portrayed in Chart 18–1.

What procedure is followed for a two-tailed test? We combine (add) the probabilities of success in the two tails until we come as close to the

TABLE 18–2 Binomial Probability Distribution for $n = 14$, $\pi = .50$

(1) Number of Successes	(2) Probability of Success	(3) Cumulative Probability	
0	.000	1.000	
1	.001	.999	
2	.006	.998	
3	.022	.992	
4	.061	.970	
5	.122	.909	
6	.183	.787	
7	.209	.604	
8	.183	.395	
9	.122	.212	
10	.061	.090	
11	.022	.029	← .000 + .001 +
12	.006	.007	.006 + .022
13	.001	.001	Add up
14	.000	.000	

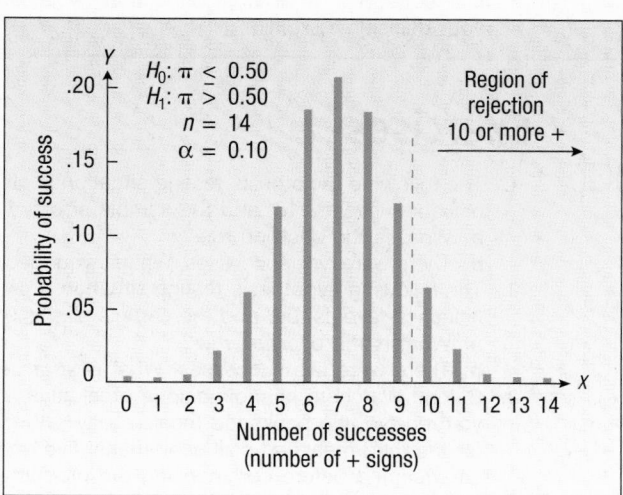

CHART 18–1 Binomial Distribution, $n = 14$, $\pi = .50$

desired level of significance (α) as possible without exceeding it. In this example α is .10. The probability of 3 or fewer successes is .029, found by .000 + .001 + .006 + .022. The probability of 11 or more successes is also .029. Adding the two probabilities gives .058. This is the closest we can come to .10 without exceeding it. Had we included the probabilities of 4 and 10 successes, the total would be .180, which exceeds .10. Hence, the decision rule for a two-tailed test would be to reject the null hypothesis if there are 3 or fewer plus signs, or 11 or more plus signs.

Step 5: Make a decision regarding the null hypothesis. Eleven out of the 14 managers in the training course increased their database competency. The number 11 is in the rejection region, which starts at 10, so H_0 is rejected. We conclude that the three-month training course was effective. It increased the database competency of the managers.

It should be noted again that if the alternate hypothesis does not give a direction—for example, H_0: $\pi = .50$ and H_1: $\pi \neq 50$—the test of hypothesis is *two-tailed*. In such cases there are two rejection regions—one in the lower tail and one in the upper tail. If $\alpha = .10$ and the test is two-tailed, the area in each tail is .05 ($\alpha/2 = .10/2 = .05$). Self-Review 18–1 illustrates this.

Self-Review 18–1

Recall the Taster's Choice example described on page 664, involving a consumer test to determine the preference for decaffeinated versus regular coffee. Use the .10 significance level. The null and alternate hypotheses are:

$$H_0: \pi = .50 \qquad n = 12$$
$$H_1: \pi \neq .50$$

(a) Is this a one-tailed or a two-tailed test of hypothesis?
(b) Show the decision rule in a chart.
(c) Letting consumer preference for decaffeinated coffee be a "+" and preference for regular coffee a "−," it was found that two customers preferred decaffeinated. What is your decision? Explain.

Exercises

connect

1. The following hypothesis-testing situation is given: H_0: $\pi \leq .50$ and H_1: $\pi > .50$. The significance level is .10, and the sample size is 12.
    a. What is the decision rule?
    b. There were nine successes. What is your decision regarding the null hypothesis? Explain.
2. The following hypothesis-testing situation is given: H_0: $\pi = .50$ and H_1: $\pi \neq .50$. The significance level is .05, and the sample size is 9.
    a. What is the decision rule?
    b. There were five successes. What is your decision regarding the null hypothesis?
3. Calorie Watchers has low-calorie breakfasts, lunches, and dinners. If you join the club, you receive two packaged meals a day. CW claims that you can eat anything you want for the third meal and still lose at least five pounds the first month. Members of the club are weighed before commencing the program and again at the end of the first month. The experiences of a random sample of 11 enrollees are:

Name	Weight Change	Name	Weight Change
Foster	Lost	Hercher	Lost
Taoka	Lost	Camder	Lost
Lange	Gained	Hinckle	Lost
Rousos	Lost	Hinkley	Lost
Stephens	No change	Justin	Lost
Cantrell	Lost		

We are interested in whether there has been a weight loss as a result of the Calorie Watchers program.
a. State H_0 and H_1.
b. Using the .05 level of significance, what is the decision rule?
c. What is your conclusion about the Calorie Watchers program?

4. Many new stockbrokers resist giving presentations to bankers and certain other groups. Sensing this lack of self-confidence, management arranged to have a confidence-building seminar for a sample of new stockbrokers and enlisted Career Boosters for a three-week course. Before the first session, Career Boosters measured the level of confidence of each participant. It was measured again after the three-week seminar. The before and after levels of self-confidence for the 14 in the course are shown below. Self-confidence was classified as being either negative, low, high, or very high.

Stockbroker	Before Seminar	After Seminar	Stockbroker	Before Seminar	After Seminar
J. M. Martin	Negative	Low	F. M. Orphey	Low	Very high
T. D. Jagger	Negative	Negative	C. C. Ford	Low	High
A. D. Hammer	Low	High	A. R. Utz	Negative	Low
T. A. Jones, Jr.	Very high	Low	M. R. Murphy	Low	High
B. G. Dingh	Low	High	P. A. Lopez	Negative	Low
D. A. Skeen	Low	High	B. K. Pierre	Low	High
C. B. Simmer	Negative	High	N. S. Walker	Low	Very high

The purpose of this study is to find whether Career Boosters was effective in raising the self-confidence of the new stockbrokers. That is, was the level of self-confidence higher after the seminar than before it? Use the .05 significance level.
a. State the null and alternate hypotheses.
b. Using the .05 level of significance, state the decision rule—either in words or in chart form.
c. Draw conclusions about the seminar offered by Career Boosters.

Using the Normal Approximation to the Binomial

If the number of observations in the sample is larger than 10, the normal distribution can be used to approximate the binomial. Recall in Chapter 6, we computed the mean of the binomial distribution from $\mu = n\pi$ and the standard deviation from $\sigma = \sqrt{n\pi(1 - \pi)}$. In this case $\pi = .50$, so the equations reduce to $\mu = .50n$ and $\sigma = .50\sqrt{n}$, respectively.

The test statistic z is

SIGN TEST, $n > 10$	$z = \dfrac{(X \pm .50) - \mu}{\sigma}$	[18–1]

If the number of pluses or minuses is *more than* $n/2$, we use the following form as the test statistic:

SIGN TEST, $n > 10$, + SIGNS MORE THAN $n/2$	$z = \dfrac{(X - .50) - \mu}{\sigma} = \dfrac{(X - .50) - .50n}{.50\sqrt{n}}$	[18–2]

If the number of pluses or minuses is *less than* $n/2$, the test statistic z is

SIGN TEST, $n > 10$, + SIGNS LESS THAN $n/2$	$z = \dfrac{(X + .50) - \mu}{\sigma} = \dfrac{(X + .50) - .50n}{.50\sqrt{n}}$	[18–3]

In the preceding formulas, X is the number of plus (or minus) signs. The value $+.50$ or $-.50$ is the *continuity correction factor,* discussed in Chapter 7. Briefly, it is applied when a continuous distribution such as the normal distribution (which we are using) is used to approximate a discrete distribution (the binomial).

The following example illustrates the details of the sign test when n is greater than 10.

Example

The market research department of Cola, Inc., has been given the assignment of testing a new soft drink. Two versions of the drink are considered—a rather sweet drink and a somewhat bitter one. A preference test is to be conducted consisting of a sample of 64 consumers. Each consumer will taste both the sweet cola (labeled A) and the bitter one (labeled B) and indicate a preference. Conduct a test of hypothesis to determine if there is a difference in the preference for the sweet and bitter tastes. Use the .05 significance level.

Solution

Step 1: State the null and alternate hypotheses.

H_0: $\pi = .50$ There is no preference.
H_1: $\pi \neq .50$ There is a preference.

Step 2: Select a level of significance. It is .05, which is stated in the problem.
Step 3: Select the test statistic. It is z, given in formula (18–1).

$$z = \frac{(X \pm .50) - \mu}{\sigma}$$

where $\mu = .50n$ and $\sigma = .50\sqrt{n}$.

Step 4: Formulate the decision rule. Referring to Appendix B.1, *Areas under the Normal Curve,* for a two-tailed test (because H_1 states that $\pi \neq .50$) and the .05 significance level, the critical values are +1.96 and −1.96. Recall from Chapter 10 that for a two-tailed test we split the rejection probability in half and place one half in each tail. That is, $\alpha/2 = .05/2 = .025$. Continuing, $.5000 - .0250 = .4750$. Searching for .4750 in the body of the table and reading the z value in the left margin gives 1.96, the critical value. Therefore, do not reject H_0 if the computed z value is between +1.96 and −1.96. Otherwise, reject H_0 and accept H_1.

Step 5: Compute z, compare the computed value with the critical value, and make a decision regarding H_0. Preference for cola A was given a "+" sign and preference for B a "−" sign. Out of the 64 in the sample, 42 preferred the sweet taste, which is cola A. Therefore, there are 42 pluses. Since 42 is *more than $n/2 = 64/2 = 32$,* we use formula (18–2) for z:

$$z = \frac{(X - .50) - .50n}{.50\sqrt{n}} = \frac{(42 - .50) - .50(64)}{.50\sqrt{64}} = 2.38$$

The computed z of 2.38 is beyond the critical value of 1.96. Therefore, the null hypothesis of no difference is rejected at the .05 significance level. There is evidence of a difference in consumer preference. That is, we conclude consumers prefer one cola over another.

The p-value is the probability of finding a z value larger than 2.38 or smaller than −2.38. From Appendix B.1, the probability of finding a z value greater than 2.38 is $.5000 - .4913 = .0087$. Thus, the two-tailed p-value is .0174. So the probability of obtaining a sample statistic this extreme when the null hypothesis is true is less than 2 percent.

Self-Review 18–2

The human resources department at Ford Motor Company began blood pressure screening and education for the 100 employees in the paint department at the first of the year. As a follow-up in July the same 100 employees were again screened for blood pressure and 80 showed a reduction. Can we conclude the screening was effective in reducing blood pressure readings?

(a) State the null hypothesis and the alternate hypothesis.
(b) What is the decision rule for a significance level of .05?
(c) Compute the value of the test statistic.
(d) What is your decision regarding the null hypothesis?
(e) Interpret your decision.

Exercises

connect™

5. A sample of 45 overweight men participated in an exercise program. At the conclusion of the program 32 had lost weight. At the .05 significance level, can we conclude the program is effective?
   a. State the null hypothesis and the alternate hypothesis.
   b. State the decision rule.
   c. Compute the value of the test statistic.
   d. What is your decision regarding the null hypothesis?

6. A sample of 60 college students was given a special training program designed to improve their time management skills. One month after completing the course the students were contacted and asked whether the skills learned in the program were effective. A total of 42 responded yes. At the .05 significance level, can we conclude the program is effective?
   a. State the null hypothesis and the alternate hypothesis.
   b. State the decision rule.
   c. Compute the value of the test statistic.
   d. What is your decision regarding the null hypothesis?

7. Pierre's Restaurant announced that on Thursday night the menu would consist of unusual gourmet items, such as squid, rabbit, snails from Scotland, and dandelion greens. As part of a larger survey, a sample of 81 regular customers was asked whether they preferred the regular menu or the gourmet menu. Forty-three preferred the gourmet menu. At the .02 level, can we conclude the customers preferred the gourmet menu?

8. Assembly workers at Computer Associates assemble just one or two subassemblies and insert them in a frame. The executives at CA think that the employees would have more pride in their work if they assembled all of the subassemblies and tested the complete computer. A sample of 25 employees was selected to experiment with the idea. After a training program, each was asked his or her preference. Twenty liked assembling the entire unit and testing it. At the .05 level, can we conclude the employees preferred assembling the entire unit? Explain the steps you used to arrive at your decision.

Testing a Hypothesis about a Median

Most of the tests of hypothesis we have conducted so far involved the population mean or a proportion. The sign test is one of the few tests that can be used to test the value of a median. Recall from Chapter 3 that the median is the value above which half of the observations lie and below which the other half lie. For hourly wages of $7, $9, $11, and $18, the median is $10. Half of the wages are above $10 an hour and the other half below $10.

To conduct a test of hypothesis, a value above the median is assigned a plus sign, and a value below the median is assigned a minus sign. If a value is the same as the median, it is dropped from further analysis.

Example

A study several years ago by the consumer research department of Superior Grocers found the median weekly amount spent on grocery items by young married couples was $123. The CEO would like to repeat the research to determine whether the median amount spent has changed. The department's new sample information showed that, in a random sample of 102 young adult married couples, 60 spent more than $123 last week on grocery items, 40 spent less, and 2 spent exactly $123. At the .10 significance level, is it reasonable to conclude that the median amount spent is not equal to $123?

Solution

If the population median is $123, then we expect about half the sampled couples to have spent more than $123 last week and about half less than $123. After discarding the two customers who spent exactly $123, we would expect 50 to be above the median and 50 to be below the median. Is this difference attributable to chance, or is the median some value other than $123? The statistical test for the median will help answer that question.

The null and the alternate hypotheses are:

$$H_0: \text{Median} = \$123$$
$$H_1: \text{Median} \neq \$123$$

This is a two-tailed test because the alternate hypothesis does not indicate a direction. That is, we are not interested in whether the median is less than or greater than $123, only that it is different from $123. The test statistic meets the binomial assumptions. That is:

1. An observation is either larger or smaller than the proposed median, so there are only two possible outcomes.
2. The probability of a success remains constant at .50. That is, $\pi = .50$.
3. The couples selected as part of the sample represent independent trials.
4. We count the number of successes in a fixed number of trials. In this case we consider 100 couples and count the number who spend more than $123 per week on grocery items.

The usable sample size is 100 and π is .50, so $n\pi = 100(.50) = 50$ and $n(1 - \pi) = 100(1 - .50) = 50$, which are both larger than 5, so we use the normal distribution to approximate the binomial. That is, we actually use the standard normal distribution as the test statistic. The significance level is .10, so $\alpha/2 = .10/2 = .05$ of the area is in each tail of a normal distribution. From Appendix B.1, which shows the areas under a normal curve, the critical values are -1.65 and 1.65. The decision rule is to reject H_0 if z is less than -1.65 or greater than 1.65.

We use formula (18–2) for z because 60 is greater than $n/2$ or $(100/2 = 50)$.

$$z = \frac{(X - .50) - .50n}{.50\sqrt{n}} = \frac{(60 - .5) - .50(100)}{.50\sqrt{100}} = 1.90$$

The null hypothesis is rejected because the computed value of 1.90 is greater than the critical value of 1.65. The sample evidence indicates that the median amount spent per week on grocery items by young couples is *not* $123. The *p*-value is .0574 found by 2(.5000 − .4713). The *p*-value is smaller than the significance level of .10 for this test.

Self-Review 18–3

After receiving the results regarding the weekly amount spent on grocery items for young couples from the consumer research department, the CEO of Superior Grocers wondered whether the same was true for senior citizen couples. In this case the CEO wants the consumer research department to investigate whether the median weekly amount spent per week by senior citizens is *greater than* $123. A sample of 64 senior citizen couples revealed 42 spent more than $123 per week on grocery items. Use the .05 significance level.

Exercises

connect

9. The median salary for a chiropractor in the United States is $81,500 per year, according to the U.S. Department of Labor. A group of recent graduates believe this amount is too low. In a random sample of 205 chiropractors who recently graduated, 170 began with a salary of more than $81,500 and five earned a salary of exactly $81,500.
    a. State the null and alternate hypotheses.
    b. State the decision rule. Use the .05 significance level.
    c. Do the necessary computations and interpret the results.
10. Central Airlines claims that the median price of a round-trip ticket from Chicago to Jackson Hole, Wyoming, is $503. This claim is being challenged by the Association of Travel Agents, who believe the median price is less than $503. A random sample of 400 round-trip tickets

from Chicago to Jackson Hole revealed 160 tickets were below $503. None of the tickets were exactly $503. Let $\alpha = .05$.

a. State the null and alternate hypotheses.

b. What is your decision regarding H_0? Interpret.

Wilcoxon Signed-Rank Test for Dependent Samples

The paired t test (page 384), described in Chapter 11, has two requirements. First, the samples must be dependent. Recall that dependent samples are characterized by a measurement, some type of intervention, and then another measurement. For example, a large company began a "wellness" program at the start of the year. Twenty workers were enrolled in the weight reduction portion of the program. To begin, all participants were weighed. Next they dieted, did the exercise, and so forth in an attempt to lose weight. At the end of the program, which lasted six months, all participants were weighed again. The difference in their weight between the start and the end of the program is the variable of interest. Note that there is a measurement, an intervention, and then another measurement.

The second requirement for the paired t test is that the distribution of the differences follow the normal probability distribution. In the company wellness example,

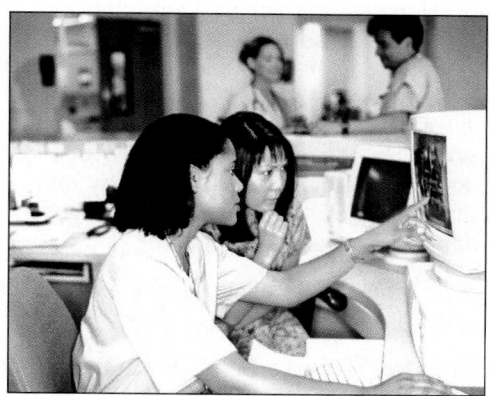

this would require that the differences in the weights of the 20 participants follow the normal probability distribution. In that case this assumption is reasonable. However, there are instances when we want to study the differences between dependent observations where we cannot assume that the distribution of the differences approximates a normal distribution. Frequently we encounter a problem with the normality assumption when the level of measurement in the samples is ordinal, rather than interval or ratio. For example, suppose there are 10 surgical patients on 3 East today. The nursing supervisor asks Nurse Benner and Nurse Jurris to rate each of the 10 patients on a scale of 1 to 10, according to the difficulty of patient care. The distribution of the differences in the ratings probably would not approximate the normal distribution, and, therefore, the paired t test would not be appropriate.

In 1945, Frank Wilcoxon developed a nonparametric test, based on the differences in dependent samples, where the normality assumption is not required. This test is called the **Wilcoxon signed-rank test.** The following example details its application.

Example

Fricker's is a family restaurant chain located primarily in the southeastern part of the United States. It offers a full dinner menu, but its specialty is chicken. Recently, Bernie Frick, the owner and founder, developed a new spicy flavor for the batter in which the chicken is cooked. Before replacing the current flavor, he wants to conduct some tests to be sure that patrons will like the spicy flavor better.

To begin, Bernie selects a random sample of 15 customers. Each sampled customer is given a small piece of the current chicken and asked to rate its overall taste on a scale of 1 to 20. A value near 20 indicates the participant liked the flavor, whereas a score near 0 indicates they did not like the flavor. Next, the same 15 participants are given a sample of the new chicken with the spicier flavor and again asked to rate its taste on a scale of 1 to 20. The results are reported below. Is it reasonable to conclude that the spicy flavor is preferred? Use the .05 significance level.

Participant	Spicy Flavor Score	Current Flavor Score	Participant	Spicy Flavor Score	Current Flavor Score
Arquette	14	12	Garcia	19	10
Jones	8	16	Sundar	18	10
Fish	6	2	Miller	16	13
Wagner	18	4	Peterson	18	2
Badenhop	20	12	Boggart	4	13
Hall	16	16	Hein	7	14
Fowler	14	5	Whitten	16	4
Virost	6	16			

Solution

The samples are dependent or related. That is, the participants are asked to rate both flavors of chicken. Thus, if we compute the difference between the rating for the spicy flavor and the current flavor, the resulting value shows the amount the participants favor one flavor over the other. If we choose to subtract the current flavor score from the spicy flavor score, a positive result is the "amount" the participant favors the spicy flavor. Negative difference scores indicate the participant favored the current flavor. Because of the somewhat subjective nature of the scores, we are not sure the distribution of the differences follows the normal distribution. We decide to use the nonparametric Wilcoxon signed-rank test.

As usual, we will use the five-step hypothesis-testing procedure. The null hypothesis is that there is no difference in the rating of the chicken flavors by the participants. That is, as many participants in the study rated the spicy flavor higher as rated the regular flavor higher. The alternate hypothesis is that the ratings are higher for the spicy flavor. More formally:

H_0: There is no difference in the ratings of the two flavors.
H_1: The spicy ratings are higher.

This is a one-tailed test. Why? Because Bernie Frick, the owner of Fricker's, will want to change his chicken flavor only if the sample participants show that the population of customers like the new flavor better. The significance level is .05, as stated above.

The steps to conduct the Wilcoxon signed-rank test are as follows.

1. Compute the difference between the spicy flavor score and the current flavor score for each participant. For example, Arquette's spicy flavor score was 14 and current flavor score was 12, so the amount of the difference is 2. For Jones, the difference is -8, found by $8 - 16$, and for Fish it is 4, found by $6 - 2$. The differences for all participants are shown in column 4 of Table 18–3.
2. Only the positive and negative differences are considered further. That is, if the difference in flavor scores is 0, that participant is dropped from further analysis and the number in the sample reduced. From Table 18–3, Hall, the sixth participant, scored both the spicy and the current flavor a 16. Hence, Hall is dropped from the study and the usable sample size reduced from 15 to 14.
3. Determine the absolute differences for the values computed in column 4. Recall that in an absolute difference we ignore the sign of the difference. The absolute differences are shown in column 5.
4. Next, rank the absolute differences from smallest to largest. Arquette, the first participant, scored the spicy chicken a 14 and the current a 12. The difference of 2 in the two taste scores is the smallest absolute difference, so it is given a ranking of 1. The next largest difference is 3, given by Miller, so it is given a

rank of 2. The other differences are ranked in a similar manner. There are three participants who rated the difference in the flavor as 8. That is, Jones, Badenhop, and Sundar each had a difference of 8 between their rating of the spicy flavor and the current flavor. To resolve this problem, we average the ranks involved and report the average rank for each. This situation involves the ranks 5, 6, and 7, so all three participants are assigned the rank of 6. The same situation occurs for those participants with a difference of 9. The ranks involved are 8, 9, and 10, so those participants are assigned a rank of 9.

TABLE 18–3 Flavor Rating for Current and Spicy Flavors

(1) Participant	(2) Spicy Score	(3) Current Score	(4) Difference in Score	(5) Absolute Difference	(6) Rank	(7) Signed Rank R^+	(7) Signed Rank R^-
Arquette	14	12	2	2	1	1	
Jones	8	16	−8	8	6		6
Fish	6	2	4	4	3	3	
Wagner	18	4	14	14	13	13	
Badenhop	20	12	8	8	6	6	
Hall	16	16	*	*	*	*	
Fowler	14	5	9	9	9	9	
Virost	6	16	−10	10	11		11
Garcia	19	10	9	9	9	9	
Sundar	18	10	8	8	6	6	
Miller	16	13	3	3	2	2	
Peterson	18	2	16	16	14	14	
Boggart	4	13	−9	9	9		9
Hein	7	14	−7	7	4		4
Whitten	16	4	12	12	12	12	
Total						75	30

5. Each assigned rank in column 6 is then given the same sign as the original difference, and the results are reported in column 7. For example, the second participant has a difference score of −8 and a rank of 6. This value is located in the R^- section of column 7.

6. The R^+ and R^- columns are totaled. The sum of the positive ranks is 75 and the sum of the negative ranks is 30. The smaller of the two rank sums is used as the test statistic and referred to as T.

The critical values for the Wilcoxon signed-rank test are located in Appendix B.7. A portion of that table is shown on the following page. The α row is used for one-tailed tests and the 2α row for two-tailed tests. In this case we want to show that customers like the spicy taste better, which is a one-tailed test, so we select the α row. We chose the .05 significance level, so move to the right to the column headed .05. Go down that column to the row where n is 14. (Recall that one person in the study rated the chicken flavors the same and was dropped from the study, making the usable sample size 14.) The value at the intersection is 25, so the critical value is 25. The decision rule is to reject the null hypothesis if the *smaller* of the rank sums is 25 or less. The value obtained from Appendix B.7 is the *largest value in the rejection region*. To put it another way, our decision rule is to reject H_0 if the smaller of the two rank sums is 25 or less. In this case the smaller rank sum is 30, so the decision is not to reject the null hypothesis. We cannot conclude there is a difference in the flavor ratings between the current and the spicy. Mr. Frick has not shown that customers prefer the new flavor. Likely, he would stay with the current flavor of chicken and not change to the more spicy flavor.

n	2α .15 α .075	.10 .05	.05 .025	.04 .02	.03 .015	.02 .01	.01 .005
4	0						
5	1	0					
6	2	2	0	0			
7	4	3	2	1	0	0	
8	7	5	3	3	2	1	0
9	9	8	5	5	4	3	1
10	12	10	8	7	6	5	3
11	16	13	10	9	8	7	5
12	19	17	13	12	11	9	7
13	24	21	17	16	14	12	9
14	28	25	21	19	18	15	12
15	33	30	25	23	21	19	15

Self-Review 18–4

The assembly area of Gotrac Products was recently redesigned. Installing a new lighting system and purchasing new workbenches were two features of the redesign. The production supervisor would like to know if the changes resulted in an improvement in worker productivity. To investigate she selected a sample of 11 workers and determined the production rate before and after the changes. The sample information is reported below.

Operator	Production Before	Production After	Operator	Production Before	Production After
S. M.	17	18	U. Z.	10	22
D. J.	21	23	Y. U.	20	19
M. D.	25	22	U. T.	17	20
B. B.	15	25	Y. H.	24	30
M. F.	10	28	Y. Y.	23	26
A. A.	16	16			

(a) How many usable pairs are there? That is, what is n?
(b) Use the Wilcoxon signed-rank test to determine whether the new procedures actually increased production. Use the .05 level and a one-tailed test.
(c) What assumption are you making about the distribution of the differences in production before and after redesign?

Exercises

11. An industrial psychologist selected a random sample of seven young urban professional couples who own their homes. The size of their home (square feet) is compared with that of their parents. At the .05 significance level, can we conclude that the professional couples live in larger homes than their parents?

Couple Name	Professional	Parent	Couple Name	Professional	Parent
Gordon	1,725	1,175	Kuhlman	1,290	1,360
Sharkey	1,310	1,120	Welch	1,880	1,750
Uselding	1,670	1,420	Anderson	1,530	1,440
Bell	1,520	1,640			

12. Toyota Motor Corporation is studying the effect of regular versus high-octane gasoline on fuel economy of its new high-performance, 3.5-liter, V6 engine. Ten executives are selected and asked to maintain records on the number of miles traveled per gallon of gas. The results are:

Executive	Miles per Gallon		Executive	Miles per Gallon	
	Regular	High-Octane		Regular	High-Octane
Bowers	25	28	Rau	38	40
Demars	33	31	Greolke	29	29
Grasser	31	35	Burns	42	37
DeToto	45	44	Snow	41	44
Kleg	42	47	Lawless	30	44

At the .05 significance level, is there a difference in the number of miles traveled per gallon between regular and high-octane gasoline?

13. A new assembly-line procedure to increase production has been suggested by Mr. Mump. To test whether the new procedure is superior to the old procedure, a random sample of 15 assembly line workers was selected. The number of units produced in an hour under the old procedure is determined, then the new Mump procedure was introduced. After an appropriate break-in period, their production was measured again. The results were:

Employee	Production		Employee	Production	
	Old System	Mump Method		Old System	Mump Method
A	60	64	I	87	84
B	40	52	J	80	80
C	59	58	K	56	57
D	30	37	L	21	21
E	70	71	M	99	108
F	78	83	N	50	56
G	43	46	O	56	62
H	40	52			

At the .05 significance level can we conclude the production is greater using the Mump method?
a. State the null and alternate hypotheses.
b. State the decision rule.
c. Arrive at a decision regarding the null hypothesis.

14. It has been suggested that daily production of a subassembly would be increased if better lighting were installed and background music and free coffee and doughnuts were provided during the day. Management agreed to try the scheme for a limited time. The number of subassemblies produced per week by a sample of employees follows.

Employee	Past Production Record	Production after Installing, Lighting, Music, etc.	Employee	Past Production Record	Production after Installing, Lighting, Music, etc.
JD	23	33	WWJ	21	25
SB	26	26	OP	25	22
MD	24	30	CD	21	23
RCF	17	25	PA	16	17
MF	20	19	RRT	20	15
UHH	24	22	AT	17	9
IB	30	29	QQ	23	30

Using the Wilcoxon signed-rank test, determine whether the suggested changes are worthwhile.
a. State the null hypothesis.
b. You decide on the alternate hypothesis.
c. You decide on the level of significance.
d. State the decision rule.
e. Compute T and arrive at a decision.
f. What did you assume about the distribution of the differences?

Wilcoxon Rank-Sum Test for Independent Samples

One test specifically designed to determine whether two *independent* samples came from equivalent populations is the **Wilcoxon rank-sum test.** This test is an alternative to the two-sample *t* test described in Chapter 11. Recall that the *t* test requires that the two populations follow the normal distribution and have equal population variances. These conditions are not required for the Wilcoxon rank-sum test.

The Wilcoxon rank-sum test is based on the sum of ranks. The data are ranked as if the observations were part of a single sample. If the null hypothesis is true, then the ranks will be about evenly distributed between the two samples, and the sum of the ranks for the two samples will be about the same. That is, the low, medium, and high ranks should be about equally divided between the two samples. If the alternate hypothesis is true, one of the samples will have more of the lower ranks and, thus, a smaller rank sum. The other sample will have more of the higher ranks and, therefore, a larger rank sum. If each of the samples contains *at least eight observations,* the standard normal distribution is used as the test statistic. The formula is:

Test using independent samples

| WILCOXON RANK-SUM TEST | $$z = \dfrac{W - \dfrac{n_1(n_1 + n_2 + 1)}{2}}{\sqrt{\dfrac{n_1 n_2(n_1 + n_2 + 1)}{12}}}$$ | [18–4] |

where
   n_1 is the number of observations from the first population.
   n_2 is the number of observations from the second population.
   W is the sum of the ranks from the first population.

Example

Dan Thompson, the president of CEO Airlines, recently noted an increase in the number of no-shows for flights out of Atlanta. He is particularly interested in determining whether there are more no-shows for flights that originate from Atlanta compared with flights leaving Chicago. A sample of nine flights from Atlanta and eight from Chicago are reported in Table 18–4. At the .05 significance level, can we conclude that there are more no-shows for the flights originating in Atlanta?

TABLE 18–4 Number of No-Shows for Scheduled Flights

Atlanta	Chicago	Atlanta	Chicago
11	13	20	9
15	14	24	17
10	10	22	21
18	8	25	
11	16		

Solution

If the populations of no-shows followed the normal probability distribution and had equal variances, the two-sample *t* test, discussed in Chapter 11, would be appropriate. In this case Mr. Thompson believes these two conditions cannot be met. Therefore, a nonparametric test, the Wilcoxon rank-sum test, is appropriate.

If the number of no-shows is the same for Atlanta and Chicago, then we expect the sum of the ranks for the two distributions to be about the same. Or to put it another way, the average rank of the two groups will be about the same. If the number of no-shows is not the same, we expect the average of ranks to be quite different.

Mr. Thompson believes there are more no-shows for Atlanta flights. Thus, a one-tailed test is appropriate, with the rejection region located in the upper tail. The null and alternate hypotheses are:

H_0: The population distribution of no-shows is the same or less for Atlanta and Chicago.

H_1: The population distribution of no-shows is larger for Atlanta than for Chicago.

The test statistic follows the standard normal distribution. At the .05 significance level, we find from Appendix B.1 the critical value of z is 1.65. The null hypothesis is rejected if the computed value of z is greater than 1.65.

The alternate hypothesis is that there are more no-shows in Atlanta, which means that distribution is located to the right of the Chicago distribution. The value of W is calculated for the Atlanta group and is found to be 96.5, which is the sum of the ranks for the no-shows for the Atlanta flights. The details of rank assignment are shown in Table 18–5. We rank the observations from *both* samples as if they were a single group. The Chicago flight with only 8 no-shows had the fewest, so it is assigned a rank of 1. The Chicago flight with 9 no-shows is ranked 2, and so on. The Atlanta flight with 25 no-shows is the highest, so it is assigned the largest rank, 17. There are also two instances of tied ranks. There are Atlanta and Chicago flights that each have 10 no-shows. There are also two Atlanta flights with 11 no-shows. How do we handle these ties? The solution is to average the ranks involved and assign the average rank to both flights. In the case involving 10 no-shows the ranks involved are 3 and 4. The mean of these ranks is 3.5, so a rank of 3.5 is assigned to both the Atlanta and the Chicago flights with 10 no-shows.

TABLE 18–5 Ranked Number of No-Shows for Scheduled Flights

Atlanta		Chicago	
No-Shows	**Rank**	**No-Shows**	**Rank**
11	5.5	13	7
15	9	14	8
10	3.5	10	3.5
18	12	8	1
11	5.5	16	10
20	13	9	2
24	16	17	11
22	15	21	14
25	17		
	96.5		56.5

Note from Table 18–5 that there are nine flights originating in Atlanta and eight in Chicago, so $n_1 = 9$ and $n_2 = 8$. Computing z from formula (18–4) gives:

$$z = \frac{W - \dfrac{n_1(n_1 + n_2 + 1)}{2}}{\sqrt{\dfrac{n_1 n_2(n_1 + n_2 + 1)}{12}}} = \frac{96.5 - \dfrac{9(9 + 8 + 1)}{2}}{\sqrt{\dfrac{9(8)(9 + 8 + 1)}{12}}} = 1.49$$

Because the computed z value (1.49) is less than 1.65, the null hypothesis is not rejected. The evidence does not show a difference in the distributions of the number of no-shows. That is, it appears that the number of no-shows is the same in Atlanta as in Chicago. The p-value is .0681, found by determining the area to the right of 1.49 (.5000 − .4319).

MegaStat software can produce the same results. The MegaStat p-value is .0742, which is close to the value we calculated. The difference is due to rounding in the system and correcting for ties.

	A	B	C	D	E	F	G
1							
2	Wilcoxon - Mann/Whitney Test						
3							
4		n	sum of ranks				
5		9	96.5	Atlanta			
6		8	56.5	Chicago			
7		17	153	total			
8							
9			81.00	expected value			
10			10.38	standard deviation			
11			1.45	z, corrected for ties			
12			.0742	p-value (one-tailed, upper)			
13							

Mann Whit1

In using the Wilcoxon rank-sum test, you may number the two populations in either order. However, once you have made a choice, W must be the sum of the ranks identified as population 1. If, in the no-show example, the population of Chicago was identified as number 1, the direction of the alternate hypothesis would be changed. The value of z would be the same but have the opposite sign.

H_0: The population distribution of no-shows is the same or larger for Chicago than for Atlanta.

H_1: The population distribution of no-shows is smaller for Chicago than for Atlanta.

The computed value of z is -1.49, found by:

$$z = \frac{W - \dfrac{n_1(n_1 + n_2 + 1)}{2}}{\sqrt{\dfrac{n_1 n_2(n_1 + n_2 + 1)}{12}}} = \frac{56.5 - \dfrac{8(8 + 9 + 1)}{2}}{\sqrt{\dfrac{8(9)(8 + 9 + 1)}{12}}} = -1.49$$

Our conclusion is the same as described earlier. There is no difference in the typical number of no-shows for Chicago and Atlanta.

Self-Review 18–5

The research director for Top Flite wants to know whether there is a difference in the distribution of the distances traveled by two of the company's golf balls. Eight of its XL-5000 brand and eight of its D2 brand balls were hit by an automatic fairway metal. The distances (in yards) were as follows:

XL-5000:	252, 263, 279, 273, 271, 265, 257, 280
D2:	262, 242, 256, 260, 258, 243, 239, 265

Do not assume the distributions of the distances traveled follow the normal probability distribution. At the .05 significance level, is there a difference between the two distributions?

Exercises

connect™

15. The following observations were randomly selected from populations that were not necessarily normally distributed. Use the .05 significance level, a two-tailed test, and the Wilcoxon rank-sum test to determine whether there is a difference between the two populations.

Population A:	38, 45, 56, 57, 61, 69, 70, 79
Population B:	26, 31, 35, 42, 51, 52, 57, 62

16. The following observations were randomly selected from populations that are not necessarily normally distributed. Use the .05 significance level, a two-tailed test, and the Wilcoxon rank-sum test to determine whether there is a difference between the two populations.

Population A:	12, 14, 15, 19, 23, 29, 33, 40, 51
Population B:	13, 16, 19, 21, 22, 33, 35, 43

17. Tucson State University offers two MBA programs. In the first program the students meet two nights per week at the university's main campus in downtown Tucson. In the second program students only communicate online with the instructor. The director of the MBA experience at Tucson wishes to compare the number of hours studied last week by the two groups of students. A sample of 10 on-campus students and 12 online students revealed the following information.

Campus	28, 16, 42, 29, 31, 22, 50, 42, 23, 25
Online	26, 42, 65, 38, 29, 32, 59, 42, 27, 41, 46, 18

Do not assume the two distributions of study times, which are reported in hours, follow a normal distribution. At the .05 significance level, can we conclude the online students study more?

18. In recent times, with mortgage rates at low levels, financial institutions have had to provide more customer convenience. One of the innovations offered by Coastal National Bank and Trust is online entry of mortgage applications. Listed below is the time, in minutes, to complete the application process for customers applying for a 15-year fixed-rate and a 30-year fixed-rate mortgage.

15 years, fixed rate	41, 36, 42, 39, 36, 48, 49, 38
30 years, fixed rate	21, 27, 36, 20, 19, 21, 39, 24, 22

At the .05 significance level, is it reasonable to conclude that it takes less time for those customers applying for the 30-year fixed-rate mortgage? Do not assume the distribution times follow a normal distribution for either group.

Kruskal-Wallis Test:
Analysis of Variance by Ranks

Kruskal-Wallis test less restrictive than ANOVA

The analysis of variance (ANOVA) procedure discussed in Chapter 12 was concerned with whether several population means were equal. The data were interval or ratio level. Also, it was assumed the populations followed the normal probability distribution and their standard deviations were equal. What if the data are ordinal scale and/or the populations do not follow a normal distribution? W. H. Kruskal and W. A. Wallis reported a nonparametric test in 1952 requiring only ordinal-level (ranked) data. No assumptions about the shape of the populations are required. The test is referred to as the **Kruskal-Wallis one-way analysis of variance by ranks.**

For the Kruskal-Wallis test to be applied, the samples selected from the populations must be *independent*. For example, if samples from three groups—executives, staff, and supervisors—are to be selected and interviewed, the responses of one group (say, the executives) must in no way influence the responses of the others.

To compute the Kruskal-Wallis test statistic, (1) all the samples are combined, (2) the combined values are ordered from low to high, and (3) the ordered values are *replaced by ranks, starting with 1 for the smallest value.* An example will clarify the details of the procedure.

Example

A management seminar consists of executives from manufacturing, finance, and engineering. Before scheduling the seminar sessions, the seminar leader is interested in whether the three groups are equally knowledgeable about management principles. Plans are to take samples of the executives in manufacturing, in finance, and in engineering and to administer a test to each executive. If there is no difference in the scores for the three groups, the seminar leader will conduct just one session. However, if there is a difference in the scores, separate sessions will be given.

We will use the Kruskal-Wallis test instead of ANOVA because the seminar leader is unwilling to assume that (1) the populations of scores for each group follow the normal distribution or (2) the population standard deviations are the same.

Solution

The usual first step in hypothesis testing is to state the null and the alternate hypotheses.

H_0: The population distributions of scores for executives in manufacturing, finance, and engineering are the same.
H_1: The population distributions are not all the same.

The seminar leader selected the .05 level of risk.

The test statistic used for the Kruskal-Wallis test is designated H. Its formula is:

KRUSKAL-WALLIS TEST
$$H = \frac{12}{n(n+1)}\left[\frac{(\Sigma R_1)^2}{n_1} + \frac{(\Sigma R_2)^2}{n_2} + \cdots + \frac{(\Sigma R_k)^2}{n_k}\right] - 3(n+1) \qquad \textbf{[18–5]}$$

with $k - 1$ degrees of freedom (k is the number of populations), where:

$\Sigma R_1, \Sigma R_2, \ldots, \Sigma R_k$ are the sums of the ranks of samples 1, 2, . . . , k, respectively.
$n_1, n_2, \ldots, n_k$ are the sizes of samples 1, 2, . . . , k, respectively.
n is the combined number of observations for all samples.

Chi-square used if every sample is at least 5

The distribution of the sample H statistic is very close to the chi-square distribution with $k - 1$ degrees of freedom *if each sample includes at least 5 observations.* Therefore, we will use the chi-square to formulate the decision rule. In this example there are three populations—a population of executives in manufacturing, another for executives in finance, and a third population of engineering executives. Thus, there are $k - 1$, or $3 - 1 = 2$ degrees of freedom. Refer to the chi-square table of critical values in Appendix B.3. The critical value for 2 degrees of freedom and the .05 level of significance is 5.991. Do not reject H_0 if the computed value of the test statistic H is less than or equal to 5.991. Reject H_0 if the computed value of H is greater than 5.991, and accept H_1.

The next step is to select random samples from the three populations. A sample of seven manufacturing, eight finance, and six engineering executives was selected. Their scores on the test are recorded in Table 18–6.

TABLE 18–6 Management Test Scores for Manufacturing, Finance, and Engineering Executives

Manufacturing Executives	Finance Executives	Engineering Executives
56	103	42
39	87	38 ←—— tie for next lowest
48	51	89
38 ←—— tie for next lowest	95	75
73	68	35 ←—— lowest
50	42	61
62	107 ←—— highest score	
	89	

Considering the scores as a single population, the engineering executive with a score of 35 is the lowest, so it is ranked 1. There are two scores of 38. To resolve this tie, each score is given a rank of 2.5, found by $(2 + 3)/2$. This process is continued for all scores. The highest score is 107, and that finance executive is given a rank of 21. The scores, the ranks, and the sum of the ranks for each of the three groups are given in Table 18–7.

TABLE 18–7 Scores, Ranks, and Sums of Ranks for Management Test Scores

Manufacturing Executives		Finance Executives		Engineering Executives	
Scores	Ranks (R_1)	Scores	Ranks (R_2)	Scores	Ranks (R_3)
56	10.0	103	20.0	42	5.5
39	4.0	87	16.0	38	2.5
48	7.0	51	9.0	89	17.5
38	2.5	95	19.0	75	15.0
73	14.0	68	13.0	35	1.0
50	8.0	42	5.5	61	11.0
62	12.0	107	21.0		
		89	17.5		
	$\Sigma R_1 = \overline{57.5}$		$\Sigma R_2 = \overline{121.0}$		$\Sigma R_3 = \overline{52.5}$

Solving for H gives

$$H = \frac{12}{n(n + 1)}\left[\frac{(\Sigma R_1)^2}{n_1} + \frac{(\Sigma R_2)^2}{n_2} + \frac{(\Sigma R_3)^2}{n_3}\right] - 3(n + 1)$$

$$= \frac{12}{21(21 + 1)}\left[\frac{57.5^2}{7} + \frac{121^2}{8} + \frac{52.5^2}{6}\right] - 3(21 + 1) = 5.736$$

Because the computed value of H (5.736) is less than the critical value of 5.991, the null hypothesis is not rejected. There is not enough evidence to conclude there is a difference among the executives from manufacturing, finance, and engineering with respect to their typical knowledge of management principles. From a practical standpoint, the seminar leader should consider offering only one session including executives from all areas.

The Kruskal-Wallis procedure can be done using MINITAB software. Output for the example regarding the knowledge of management principles of executives from several industries follows. The computed value of H is 5.74 and the p-value reported on the output is .057. This agrees with our earlier calculations.

↓	C1	C2	C3	C4	C5	C6	C7	C8	C9
	Scores	Group							
1	56	1							
2	39	1							
3	48	1							
4	38	1							
5	73	1							
6	50	1							
7	62	1							
8	103	2							
9	87	2							
10	51	2							
11	95	2							
12	68	2							
13	42	2							
14	107	2							
15	89	2							

Session

Kruskal-Wallis Test: Scores versus Group

Kruskal-Wallis Test on Scores

Group	N	Median	Ave Rank	Z
1	7	50.00	8.2	-1.45
2	8	88.00	15.1	2.39
3	6	51.50	8.8	-1.05
Overall	21		11.0	

H = 5.74 DF = 2 P = 0.057
H = 5.75 DF = 2 P = 0.057 (adjusted for ties)

Recall from Chapter 12 that, for the analysis of variance technique to apply, we assume: (1) the populations are normally distributed, (2) these populations have equal standard deviations, and (3) the samples are selected independently. If these assumptions are met, we use the F distribution as the test statistic. If these assumptions cannot be met, we apply the distribution-free test by Kruskal-Wallis. To highlight the similarities between the two approaches, we will solve the example regarding executive knowledge of management principles using the ANOVA technique.

To begin, we state the null and the alternate hypotheses for the three groups.

H_0: $\mu_1 = \mu_2 = \mu_3$
H_1: The treatment means are not all the same.

For the .05 significance level, with $k - 1 = 3 - 1 = 2$ degrees of freedom in the numerator and $n - k = 21 - 3 = 18$ degrees of freedom in the denominator, the critical value of F is 3.55. The decision rule is to reject the null hypothesis if the computed value of F is greater than 3.55. The output using Excel follows.

Excel

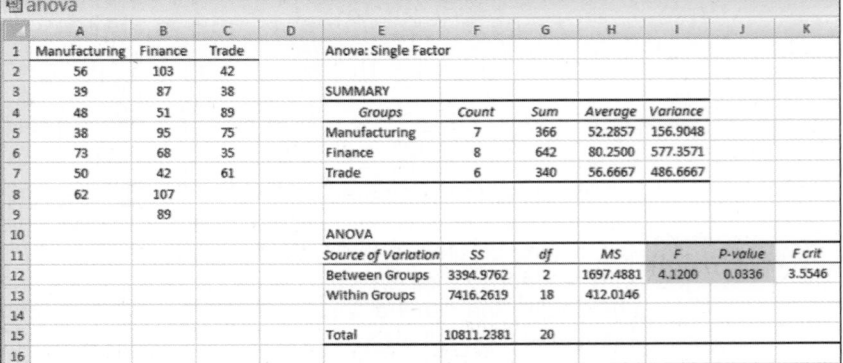

anova

	A	B	C	D	E	F	G	H	I	J	K
1	Manufacturing	Finance	Trade		Anova: Single Factor						
2	56	103	42								
3	39	87	38		SUMMARY						
4	48	51	89		Groups	Count	Sum	Average	Variance		
5	38	95	75		Manufacturing	7	366	52.2857	156.9048		
6	73	68	35		Finance	8	642	80.2500	577.3571		
7	50	42	61		Trade	6	340	56.6667	486.6667		
8	62	107									
9		89									
10					ANOVA						
11					Source of Variation	SS	df	MS	F	P-value	F crit
12					Between Groups	3394.9762	2	1697.4881	4.1200	0.0336	3.5546
13					Within Groups	7416.2619	18	412.0146			
14											
15					Total	10811.2381	20				
16											

From the previous output, the computed value of F is 4.12 and the p-value is .0336. Our decision is to reject the null hypothesis and accept the alternate hypothesis. Using this test we conclude that the treatment means are not the same. That is, the knowledge of management principles is different among the three executive groups.

We have contradictory conclusions on the same data. How can this happen? If we compare the results using p-values, the answers are similar. For the Kruskal-Wallis test the p-value was .057, which is only slightly more than the significance level of .05, but our decision was not to reject H_0. The p-value using ANOVA is .034, which is not far beyond the critical value into the rejection region. So, to summarize, we just missed rejecting H_0 with the Kruskal-Wallis test, and we were just in the rejection region using ANOVA. The difference in the p-values is .023. Thus, the results are actually quite close in terms of the p-values.

Self-Review 18–6

The regional bank manager of Statewide Financial Bank is interested in the turnover rate of personal checking accounts at four of the branches. (Turnover rate is the speed at which the money in an account is deposited and withdrawn. An extremely active account may have a rate of 300; if only one or two checks were written, the rate could be about 30.) The turnover rates of the samples selected from the four branch banks are shown in the table below. Using the .01 level and the Kruskal-Wallis test, determine whether there is a difference in the turnover rates of the personal checking accounts among the four branches.

Englewood Branch	West Side Branch	Great Northern Branch	Sylvania Branch
208	91	302	99
307	62	103	116
199	86	319	189
142	91	340	103
91	80	180	100
296			131

Exercises

connect

19. Under what conditions should the Kruskal-Wallis test be used instead of analysis of variance?
20. Under what conditions should the Kruskal-Wallis test be used instead of the Wilcoxon rank-sum test?
21. The following sample data were obtained from three populations that did not follow a normal distribution.

Sample 1	Sample 2	Sample 3
50	48	39
54	49	41
59	49	44
59	52	47
65	56	51
	57	

   a. State the null hypothesis.
   b. Using the .05 level of risk, state the decision rule.
   c. Compute the value of the test statistic.
   d. What is your decision on the null hypothesis?

22. The following sample data were obtained from three populations where the variances were not equal, and you wish to compare the populations.

Sample 1	Sample 2	Sample 3
21	15	38
29	17	40
35	22	44
45	27	51
56	31	53
71		

    a. State the null hypothesis.
    b. Using the .01 level of risk, state the decision rule.
    c. Compute the value of the test statistic.
    d. What is your decision on the null hypothesis?

23. Davis Outboard Motors, Inc., recently developed an epoxy painting process for corrosion protection on exhaust components. Bill Davis, the owner, wishes to determine whether the lengths of life for the paint are equal for three different conditions: saltwater, freshwater without weeds, and freshwater with a heavy concentration of weeds. Accelerated-life tests were conducted in the laboratory, and the number of hours the paint lasted before peeling was recorded.

Saltwater	Freshwater	Freshwater with Weeds
167.3	160.6	182.7
189.6	177.6	165.4
177.2	185.3	172.9
169.4	168.6	169.2
180.3	176.6	174.7

Use the Kruskal-Wallis test and the .01 level to determine whether the lasting quality of the paint is the same for the three water conditions.

24. The National Turkey Association wants to experiment with three different feed mixtures for very young turkeys. Since no experience exists regarding the three mixtures, no assumptions can be made about the distribution of weights. The Kruskal-Wallis test must be used to test whether the turkeys are equal in weight after eating the feed for a specified length of time. Five young turkeys were given feed A, six were given feed B, and five were given feed C. Test at the .05 level whether the mean weights of the turkeys who ate feed A, feed B, and feed C are equal.

Weight (in pounds)		
Feed Mixture A	Feed Mixture B	Feed Mixture C
11.2	12.6	11.3
12.1	10.8	11.9
10.9	11.3	12.4
11.3	11.0	10.6
12.0	12.0	12.0
	10.7	

Rank-Order Correlation

In Chapter 13, we discussed r, the sample coefficient of correlation. Recall that it measures the association between two interval- or ratio-scaled variables. For example, the coefficient of correlation reports the association between the salary of executives and their years of experience, or the association between the number of miles a shipment had to travel and the number of days it took to arrive at its destination.

Charles Spearman, a British statistician, introduced a measure of correlation for ordinal-level data. This measure allows us to describe the relationship between sets of ranked data. For example, two staff members in the Office of Research at the University of the Valley are asked to rank 10 faculty research proposals for funding purposes. We want to study the association between the ratings of the two staff members. That is, do the two staff members rate the same proposals as the most worthy and the least worthy of funding? Spearman's coefficient of rank correlation, denoted r_s, provides a measure of the association.

The coefficient of rank correlation is computed by the following formula.

SPEARMAN'S COEFFICIENT OF RANK CORRELATION	$r_s = 1 - \dfrac{6\Sigma d^2}{n(n^2 - 1)}$	[18–6]

where
  d is the difference between the ranks for each pair.
  n is the number of paired observations.

Like the coefficient of correlation, the coefficient of rank correlation can assume any value from -1.00 up to 1.00. A value of -1.00 indicates perfect negative correlation and a value of 1.00 perfect positive correlation among the ranks. A rank correlation of 0 indicates that there is no association among the ranks. Rank correlations of $-.84$ and $.80$ both indicate a strong association, but the former indicates an inverse relationship between the ranks and the latter a direct relationship.

Example

Lorrenger Plastics, Inc., recruits management trainees at colleges and universities throughout the United States. Each trainee is given a rating by the recruiter during the on-campus interview. This rating is an expression of future potential and may range from 0 to 15, with the higher score indicating more potential. The recent college graduate then enters an in-plant training program and is given another composite rating based on tests, opinions of group leaders, training officers, and so on. The on-campus rating and the in-plant training ratings are given in Table 18–8.

TABLE 18–8 Executive Ratings and In-Plant Training Ratings for a Sample of Recent College Graduates

Graduate	On-Campus Rating, X	Training Rating, Y	Graduate	On-Campus Rating, X	Training Rating, Y
A	8	4	G	11	9
B	10	4	H	7	6
C	9	4	I	8	6
D	4	3	J	13	9
E	12	6	K	10	5
F	11	9	L	12	9

Calculate the coefficient of rank correlation. Interpret its value.

Solution

It was decided to rank the variables from low to high. The lowest rating given by the on-campus recruiter was a 4 to graduate D, so it was ranked 1. The next lowest was a 7 to graduate H, so it was ranked 2. There were two graduates rated 8. The tie is resolved by giving each a rank of 3.5, which is the average of ranks 3 and 4. The same procedure is followed when there are more than two ratings tied. For example,

note that the lowest training rating is 3, and it is given a rank of 1. Then there are three ratings of 4. The average of the three tied ranks is 3, found by $(2 + 3 + 4)/3$. This is illustrated along with the necessary calculations for r_s in Table 18–9.

TABLE 18–9 Calculations Needed for r_s

Graduate	On-Campus Rating, X	Training Rating, Y	Rank		Difference between Ranks, d	Difference Squared, d^2
			On-Campus	Training		
A	8	4	3.5	3.0	0.5	0.25
B	10	4	6.5	3.0	3.5	12.25
C	9	4	5.0	3.0	2.0	4.00
D	4	3	1.0	1.0	0	0
E	12	6	10.5	7.0	3.5	12.25
F	11	9	8.5	10.5	−2.0	4.00
G	11	9	8.5	10.5	−2.0	4.00
H	7	6	2.0	7.0	−5.0	25.00
I	8	6	3.5	7.0	−3.5	12.25
J	13	9	12.0	10.5	1.5	2.25
K	10	5	6.5	5.0	1.5	2.25
L	12	9	10.5	10.5	0	0
					0.0	78.50

r_s is .726, found by:

$$r_s = 1 - \frac{6 \Sigma d^2}{n(n^2 - 1)} = 1 - \frac{6(78.50)}{12(143)} = .726$$

The value of .726 indicates a strong positive association between the ratings of the on-campus recruiter and the ratings of the training staff. The graduates that received high ratings from the on-campus recruiter also tended to be the ones that received high ratings from the training staff.

Testing the Significance of r_s

Testing whether
correlation in the
population is zero

In Chapter 13 we tested the significance of Pearson's r. For ranked data the question also arises whether the correlation in the population is actually zero. For instance, there were only 12 graduates sampled in the preceding example. In the solution to the example, the rank correlation coefficient of .726 indicates a rather strong relationship between the two sets of ranks. Is it possible that the correlation of .726 is due to chance and that the correlation among the ranks in the population is really 0? We will now conduct a test of significance to answer that question.

For a sample of 10 or more, the significance of r_s is determined by computing t using the following formula. The sampling distribution of r_s follows the t distribution with $n - 2$ degrees of freedom.

HYPOTHESES TEST, RANK CORRELATION	$t = r_s \sqrt{\dfrac{n - 2}{1 - r_s^2}}$	[18–7]

The null and the alternate hypotheses are:

H_0: The rank correlation in the population is zero.
H_1: There is a positive association among the ranks.

The decision rule is to reject H_0 if the computed value of t is greater than 1.812 (from Appendix B.2, .05 significance level, one-tailed test, and 10 degrees of freedom, found by $n - 2 = 12 - 2 = 10$).

The computed value of t is 3.338:

$$t = r_s\sqrt{\frac{n - 2}{1 - r_s^2}} = .726\sqrt{\frac{12 - 2}{1 - (.726)^2}} = 3.338$$

H_0 is rejected because the computed t of 3.338 is greater than 1.812. H_1 is accepted. There is evidence of a positive correlation between the ranks given by the on-campus recruiter and the ranks assigned during training.

Self-Review 18–7  A sample of individuals applying for factory positions at Davis Enterprises revealed the following scores on an eye perception test (X) and a mechanical aptitude test (Y):

Subject	Eye Perception	Mechanical Aptitude	Subject	Eye Perception	Mechanical Aptitude
001	805	23	006	810	28
002	777	62	007	805	30
003	820	60	008	840	42
004	682	40	009	777	55
005	777	70	010	820	51

(a) Compute the coefficient of rank correlation.
(b) At the .05 significance level, can we conclude that the correlation in the population is different from 0?

Exercises

connect

25. Do husbands and wives like the same TV shows? A recent study by Nielsen Media Research asked a young married couple to rank shows from 1 to 14. A rank of 1 indicates the best liked show and a rank of 14 the least liked show. The results for one married couple follow.

Program	Male Rating	Female Rating
60 Minutes	4	5
CSI—New York	6	4
Boston Legal	7	8
SportsCenter	2	7
Late Show with David Letterman	12	11
NBC Nightly News	8	6
Law and Order	5	3
Numbers	3	9
Survivor	13	2
Office	14	10
American Idol	1	1
Grey's Anatomy	9	13
House	10	12
Criminal Minds	11	14

a. Draw a scatter diagram. Place the male rankings on the horizontal axis and the female rankings on the vertical axis.
b. Compute the coefficient of rank correlation between the male and female rankings.
c. At the .05 significance level is it reasonable to conclude there is a positive association between the two rankings?

26. Far West University offers both day and evening classes in business administration. One question in a survey of students inquires how they perceive the prestige associated with certain careers. A day student was asked to rank the careers from 1 to 8, with 1 having the most prestige and 8 the least prestige. An evening student was asked to do the same. The results follow.

Career	Ranking by Day Student	Ranking by Evening Student	Career	Ranking by Day Student	Ranking by Evening Student
Accountant	6	3	Statistician	1	7
Computer programmer	7	2	Marketing researcher	4	8
Branch bank manager	2	6	Stock analyst	3	5
Hospital administrator	5	4	Production manager	8	1

Find Spearman's coefficient of rank correlation.

27. New representatives for Clark Sprocket and Chain, Inc., attended a brief training program before being assigned to a regional sales office. At the end of the training program, the representatives were ranked with respect to future sales potential by the vice president of sales. At the end of the first sales year, their rankings were paired with their first year sales:

Representative	Annual Sales ($ thousands)	Ranking in Training Program	Representative	Annual Sales ($ thousands)	Ranking in Training Program
Kitchen	319	3	Arden	300	10
Bond	150	9	Crane	280	5
Gross	175	6	Arthur	200	2
Arbuckle	460	1	Keene	190	7
Greene	348	4	Knopf	300	8

a. Compute and interpret the coefficient of rank correlation between first-year sales and rank after the training program.
b. At the .05 significance level, can we conclude that there is a positive association between first-year sales dollars and ranking in the training program?

28. Suppose Texas A & M University—Commerce has five scholarships available for the women's basketball team. The head coach provided the two assistant coaches with the names of 10 high school players with potential to play at the university. Each assistant coach attended three games and then ranked the 10 players with respect to potential. To explain, the first coach ranked Norma Tidwell as the best player among the 10 scouted and Jeannie Black the worst.

Player	Rank, by Assistant Coach Jean Cann	Rank, by Assistant Coach John Cannelli	Player	Rank, by Assistant Coach Jean Cann	Rank, by Assistant Coach John Cannelli
Cora Jean Seiple	7	5	Candy Jenkins	3	1
Bette Jones	2	4	Rita Rosinski	5	7
Jeannie Black	10	10	Anita Lockes	4	2
Norma Tidwell	1	3	Brenda Towne	8	9
Kathy Marchal	6	6	Denise Ober	9	8

a. Determine Spearman's rank correlation coefficient.
b. At the .05 significance level, can we conclude there is a positive association between the ranks?

Chapter Summary

I. The sign test is based on the sign difference between two related observations.
  A. No assumptions need be made about the shape of the two populations.
  B. It is based on paired or dependent samples.
  C. For small samples find the number of + or − signs and refer to the binomial distribution for the critical value.
  D. For a sample of 10 or more use the standard normal distribution and the following formula.

$$z = \frac{(X \pm .50) - .50n}{.50\sqrt{n}} \qquad \textbf{[18–2] [18–3]}$$

II. The median test is used to test a hypothesis about a population median.
  A. Find μ and σ for a binomial distribution.
  B. The z distribution is used as the test statistic.
  C. The value of z is computed from the following formula, where X is the number of observations above or below the median.

$$z = \frac{(X \pm .50) - \mu}{\sigma} \qquad \textbf{[18–1]}$$

III. The Wilcoxon signed-rank test is a nonparametric test where the normality assumption is not required.
  A. Data must be at least ordinal scale, and the samples must be dependent.
  B. The steps to conduct the test are:
    1. Rank absolute differences between the related observations.
    2. Apply the sign of the differences to the ranks.
    3. Sum negative ranks and positive ranks.
    4. The smaller of the two sums is the computed T value.
    5. Refer to Appendix B.7 for the critical value, and make a decision regarding H_0.
IV. The Wilcoxon rank-sum test is used to test whether two independent samples came from equal populations.
  A. No assumption about the shape of either population is required.
  B. The data must be at least ordinal scale.
  C. Each sample must contain at least eight observations.
  D. To determine the value of the test statistic W, the sample observations are ranked from low to high as if they were from a single group.
  E. The sum of ranks for each of the two samples is determined.
  F. W is used to compute z, where W is the sum of the ranks for population 1.

$$z = \frac{W - \dfrac{n_1(n_1 + n_2 + 1)}{2}}{\sqrt{\dfrac{n_1 n_2(n_1 + n_2 + 1)}{12}}} \qquad \textbf{[18–4]}$$

  G. The standard normal distribution, found in Appendix B.1, is the test statistic.
V. The Kruskal-Wallis one-way ANOVA by ranks is used to test whether several populations are the same.
  A. No assumption regarding the shape of any of the populations is required.
  B. The samples must be independent and at least ordinal scale.
  C. The sample observations are ranked from smallest to largest as though they were a single group.
  D. The test statistic follows the chi-square distribution, provided there are at least 5 observations in each sample.
  E. The value of the test statistic is computed from the following:

$$H = \frac{12}{n(n + 1)}\left[\frac{(\Sigma R_1)^2}{n_1} + \frac{(\Sigma R_2)^2}{n_2} + \cdots + \frac{(\Sigma R_k)^2}{n_k}\right] - 3(n + 1) \qquad \textbf{[18–5]}$$

VI. Spearman's coefficient of rank correlation is a measure of the association between two ordinal-scale variables.

A. It can range from -1 up to 1.

  1. A value of 0 indicates there is no association between the variables.

  2. A value of -1 indicates perfect negative correlation, and 1 perfect positive correlation.

B. The value of r_s is computed from the following formula.

$$r_s = 1 - \frac{6\Sigma d^2}{n(n^2 - 1)}$$ **[18–6]**

C. Provided the sample size is at least 10, we can conduct a test of hypothesis using the following formula:

$$t = r_s \sqrt{\frac{n - 2}{1 - r_s^2}}$$ **[18–7]**

  1. The test statistic follows the t distribution.

  2. There are $n - 2$ degrees of freedom.

Pronunciation Key

SYMBOL	MEANING	PRONUNCIATION
$(\Sigma R_1)^2$	Square of the total of the first column ranks	*Sigma R sub 1 squared*
r_s	Spearman's coefficient of rank correlation	*r sub s*

Chapter Exercises

connect

29. The vice president of programming at NBC is finalizing the prime-time schedule for the fall. She has decided to include a hospital drama but is unsure which of two possibilities to select. She has a pilot called "The Surgeon" and another called "Critical Care." To help her make a final decision, a sample of 20 viewers from throughout the United States was asked to watch the two pilots and indicate which show they prefer. The results were that 12 liked The Surgeon, 7 liked Critical Care, and one had no preference. Is there a preference for one of the two shows? Use the .10 significance level.

30. Merrill Lynch is going to award a contract for fine-line pens to be used nationally in its offices. Two suppliers, Bic and Pilot, have submitted bids. To determine the preference of office employees, brokers, and others, a personal preference test is to be conducted using a randomly selected sample of 20 employees. The .05 level of significance is to be used.

  a. If the alternate hypothesis states that Bic is preferred over Pilot, is the sign test to be conducted as a one-tailed or a two-tailed test? Explain.

  b. As each of the sample members told the researchers his or her preference, a "+" was recorded if it was Bic and a "−" if it was the Pilot fine-line pen. A count of the pluses revealed that 12 employees preferred Bic, 5 preferred Pilot, and 3 were undecided. What is n?

  c. What is the decision rule in words?

  d. What conclusion did you reach regarding pen preference? Explain.

31. Cornwall and Hudson, a large retail department store, wants to handle just one brand of high-quality CD player. The list has been narrowed to two brands: Sony and Panasonic. To help make a decision, a panel of 16 audio experts met. A passage using Sony components (labeled A) was played. Then the same passage was played using Panasonic components (labeled B). A "+" in the following table indicates an individual's preference for the Sony components, a "−" indicates preference for Panasonic, and a 0 signifies no preference.

Expert															
1	2	3	4	5	6	7	8	9	10	11	12	13	14	15	16
+	−	+	−	+	+	−	0	−	+	−	+	+	−	+	−

Conduct a test of hypothesis at the .10 significance level to determine whether there is a difference in preference between the two brands.

32. The South Carolina Real Estate Association claims that the median rental for three-bedroom condominiums in a metropolitan area is more than $1,200 a month. A random sample of 149 units showed 5 rented for exactly $1,200 a month, and 75 rented for more than $1,200. At the .05 level can we conclude that the median rental is more than $1,200?
   a. State H_0 and H_1.
   b. Give the decision rule.
   c. Do the necessary calculations, and arrive at a decision.
33. The Citrus Council of America wants to determine whether consumers prefer plain orange juice or juice with some orange pulp in it. A random sample of 212 consumers was selected. Each member of the sample tasted a small, unlabeled cup of one kind and then tasted the other kind. Twelve consumers said they had no preference, 40 preferred plain juice, and the remainder liked the juice with pulp better. Test at the .05 level that the preferences for plain juice and for orange juice with pulp are equal.
34. The objective of a community research project is to determine whether women are more community conscious before marriage or after five years of marriage. A test designed to measure community consciousness was administered to a sample of women before marriage, and the same test was given to them five years after marriage. The test scores are:

Name	Before Marriage	After Marriage	Name	Before Marriage	After Marriage
Beth	110	114	Carol	186	196
Jean	157	159	Lisa	116	116
Sue	121	120	Sandy	160	140
Cathy	96	103	Petra	149	142
Mary	130	139			

Test at the .05 level. H_0 is: There is no difference in community consciousness before and after marriage. H_1 is: There is a difference.
35. Is there a difference in the annual divorce rates in predominantly rural counties among three geographic regions, namely, the Southwest, the Southeast, and the Northwest? Test at the .05 level. Annual divorce rates per 1,000 population for randomly selected counties are:

Southwest:	5.9, 6.2, 7.9, 8.6, 4.6
Southeast:	5.0, 6.4, 7.3, 6.2, 8.1, 5.1
Northwest:	6.7, 6.2, 4.9, 8.0, 5.5

Day Shift	Evening Shift
92	96
103	114
116	80
81	82
89	88
	91

36. The production manager of MPS Audio Systems, Inc., is concerned about the idle time of workers. In particular he would like to know if there is a difference in the idle minutes for workers on the day shift and the evening shift. The information to the left is the number of idle minutes yesterday for the five day-shift workers and the six evening-shift workers. Use the .05 significance level.
37. Drs. Trythall and Kerns are studying the mobility of executives in selected industries. Their research measures mobility using a score based on the number of times an executive has moved, changed companies, or changed jobs within a company over the last 10 years. The highest number of points is awarded for moving and changing companies, the fewest for changing jobs within a company and not moving. The distribution of scores does not follow the normal probability distribution. Develop an appropriate test to determine if there is a difference in the mobility scores in the four industries. Use the .05 significance level.

Chemical	Retail	Internet	Space
4	3	62	30
17	12	40	38
8	40	81	46
20	17	96	40
16	31	76	21
	19		

38. A series of questions on sports and world events was asked of a randomly selected group of young adult naturalized citizens. The results were translated into a "knowledge" score. The scores were:

Citizen	Sports	World Events	Citizen	Sports	World Events
J. C. McCarthy	47	49	L. M. Zaugg	87	75
A. N. Baker	12	10	J. B. Simon	59	86
B. B. Beebe	62	76	J. Goulden	40	61
L. D. Gaucet	81	92	A. A. Fernandez	87	18
C. A. Jones	90	86	A. M. Carbo	16	75
J. N. Lopez	35	42	A. O. Smithy	50	51
A. F. Nissen	61	61	J. J. Pascal	60	61

a. Determine the degree of association between how the citizens ranked with respect to knowledge of sports and how they ranked on world events.

b. At the .05 significance level, is the rank correlation in the population greater than zero?

39. Early in the basketball season, 12 teams appeared to be outstanding. A panel of sportswriters and a panel of college basketball coaches were asked to rank the 12 teams. Their composite rankings were as follows.

Team	Coaches	Sportswriters	Team	Coaches	Sportswriters
Duke	1	1	Syracuse	7	10
UNLV	2	5	Georgetown	8	11
Indiana	3	4	Villanova	9	7
North Carolina	4	6	LSU	10	12
Louisville	5	3	St. Johns	11	8
Ohio State	6	2	Michigan	12	9

Determine the correlation between the rankings of the coaches and the sportswriters. At the .05 significance level, can we conclude there is a positive correlation between the rankings?

40. Professor Bert Forman believes the students who complete his examinations in the shortest time receive the highest grades and those who take the longest to complete them receive the lowest grades. To verify his suspicion, he assigns a rank to the order of finish and then grades the examinations. The results are shown below:

Student	Order of Completion	Score (50 possible)	Student	Order of Completion	Score (50 possible)
Gromney	1	48	Smythe	7	39
Bates	2	48	Arquette	8	30
MacDonald	3	43	Govito	9	37
Sosa	4	49	Gankowski	10	35
Harris	5	50	Bonfigilo	11	36
Cribb	6	47	Matsui	12	33

Convert the test scores to a rank and find the coefficient of rank correlation. At the .05 significance level, can Professor Forman conclude there is a positive association between the order of finish and the test scores?

Data Set Exercises

41. Refer to the Real Estate data, which report information on homes sold in the Denver, Colorado, area during the last year.

a. Use an appropriate nonparametric test to determine whether there is a difference in the typical selling price of the homes in the several townships. Assume the selling prices are not normally distributed. Use the .05 significance level.

    b. Combine the homes with 6 or more bedrooms into one group and determine whether there is a difference according to the number of bedrooms in the typical selling prices of the homes. Use the .05 significance level and assume the distribution of selling prices is not normally distributed.

    c. Assume that the distribution of the distance from the center of the city is positively skewed. That is, the normality assumption is not reasonable. Compare the distribution of the distance from the center of the city of the homes that have a pool with those that do not have a pool. Can we conclude there is a difference in the distributions? Use the .05 significance level.

42. Refer to the Baseball 2007 data, which report information on the 2007 Major League Baseball season.

    a. Rank the teams by the number of wins and their total team salary. Compute the coefficient of rank correlation between the two variables. At the .01 significance level, can you conclude that it is greater than zero?

    b. Assume that the distributions of team salaries for the American League and National League do not follow the normal distribution. Conduct a test of hypothesis to see if there is a difference in the two distributions.

    c. Rank the 30 teams by attendance and by team salary. Determine the coefficient of rank correlation between these two variables. At the .05 significance level is it reasonable to conclude the ranks of these two variables are related?

43. Refer to the Wage data set, which report information on annual wages for a sample of 100 workers. Also included are variables relating to industry, years of education, and gender for each worker.

    a. Conduct a test of hypothesis at the .05 significance level to determine if there is a difference in the median annual wages of union and nonunion members.

    b. Conduct a test of hypothesis at the .01 significance level to determine if there is a difference in the mean annual wages for workers in the three industries. Do not assume that the data follow a normal distribution. Compare the results with those of Exercise 47 in Chapter 12.

    c. Conduct a test of hypothesis at the .05 significance level to determine if there is a difference in the mean annual wages for workers in the six different occupations. Do not assume that the data follow a normal distribution.

44. Refer to the CIA data, which report demographic and economic information on 46 countries.

    a. Without assuming normal distributions, test at the .01 significance level whether there is a difference in the mean percent of the population over 65 years of age for countries with different levels of petroleum usage.

    b. Without assuming normal distributions, test at the .05 significance level whether there is a difference in the mean GDP per capita for countries with different levels of petroleum usage.

Software Commands

1. The MegaStat for Excel commands necessary for the Wilcoxon rank-sum test on page 680 are:

    a. Enter the number of no-shows for Atlanta in column A and for Chicago in column B.

    b. Select **MegaStat, Nonparametric Tests,** and **Wilcoxon-Mann/Whitney Test,** then hit **Enter.**

    c. For **Group 1** use the data on Atlanta flights (*B3:B11*) and for **Group 2** use the data on Chicago flights (*D3:D10*). Click on **Correct for ties** and **one-tailed,** and *less than* as the **alternative** then click on **OK.**

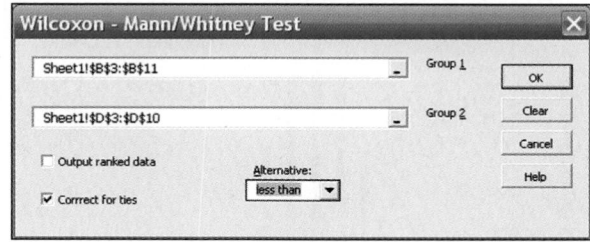

2. The MINITAB commands for the Kruskal-Wallis test on page 684 are:
   a. Enter the scores in column 1 and a code corresponding to their group in column 2. Name the variable in *C1 Scores* and the variable in *C2 Group.*
   b. From the menu bar select **Stat, Nonparametric,** and **Kruskal-Wallis,** and hit **Enter.**
   c. Select the variables *Scores* as the **Response** variable and *Group* as the **Factor.**

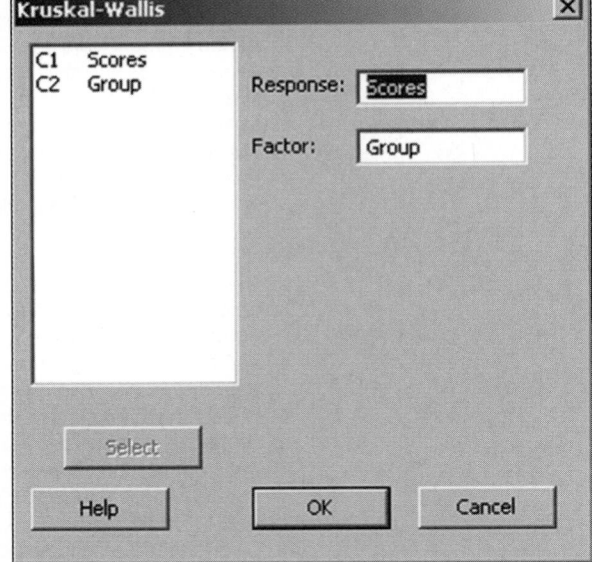

3. The Excel commands for the one-way ANOVA on page 684 are:
   a. Enter the names *Manufacturing, Finance,* and *Trade* in the first row and the data in the columns under them.
   b. Select the **Data** tab on the top of the menu. Then, on the far right, select **Data Analysis.** Select **ANOVA: Single Factor,** then click **OK.**
   c. In the dialog box the **Input Range** is *A1:C9,* click on **Labels in First Row,** and enter *E1* as the **Output Range,** then click **OK.**

Chapter 18   Answers to Self-Review

18–1 a. Two-tailed because H_1 does not state a direction.
   b.

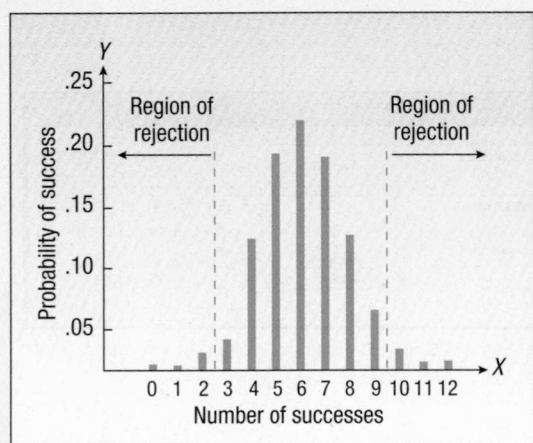

Adding down, .000 + .003 + .016 = .019. This is the largest cumulative probability up to but not exceeding .050, which is half the level of significance. The decision rule is to reject H_0 if the number of plus signs is 2 or less or 10 or more.
   c. Reject H_0; accept H_1. There is a preference.

18–2 a. H_0: $\pi \leq 0.50$, H_1: $\pi > 0.50$.
   b. Reject H_0 if $z > 1.65$.
   c. Since 80 is more than $n/2 = 100/2 = 50$, we use:

$$z = \frac{(80 - .50) - .50(100)}{.50\sqrt{100}} = \frac{29.5}{5} = 5.9$$

   d. H_0 is rejected.
   e. The screening was effective.

18–3 H_0: The median $\leq$ \$123, H_1: The median is more than \$123. The decision rule is to reject H_0 if $z > 1.65$.

$$z = \frac{(42 - .50) - 32}{.50\sqrt{64}} = \frac{9.5}{4} = 2.38$$

Reject H_0, because 2.38 is larger than 1.65. The median amount spent is more than \$123.

18–4 a. $n = 10$ (because there was no change for A.A.)
b.

Before	After	Difference	Absolute Difference	Rank	R^-	R^+
17	18	−1	1	1.5	1.5	
21	23	−2	2	3.0	3.0	
25	22	3	3	5.0		5.0
15	25	−10	10	8.0	8.0	
10	28	−18	18	10.0	10.0	
16	16	—	—	—	—	—
10	22	−12	12	9.0	9.0	
20	19	1	1	1.5		1.5
17	20	−3	3	5.0	5.0	
24	30	−6	6	7.0	7.0	
23	26	−3	3	5.0	5.0	
					48.5	6.5

H_0: Production is the same.
H_1: Production has increased.

The sum of the positive signed ranks is 6.5; the negative sum is 48.5. From Appendix B.7, one-tailed test, $n = 10$, the critical value is 10. Since 6.5 is less than 10, reject the null hypothesis and accept the alternate. New procedures did increase production.

c. No assumption regarding the shape of the distribution is necessary.

18–5 H_0: There is no difference in the distances traveled by the XL-5000 and by the D2.
H_1: There is a difference in the distances traveled by the XL-5000 and by the D2.

Do not reject H_0 if the computed z is between 1.96 and −1.96 (from Appendix B.1); otherwise, reject H_0 and accept H_1. $n_1 = 8$, the number of observations in the first sample.

XL-5000		D2	
Distance	**Rank**	**Distance**	**Rank**
252	4	262	9
263	10	242	2
279	15	256	5
273	14	260	8
271	13	258	7
265	11.5	243	3
257	6	239	1
280	16	265	11.5
Total	89.5		46.5

$W = 89.5$

$$z = \frac{89.5 - \dfrac{8(8 + 8 + 1)}{2}}{\sqrt{\dfrac{(8)(8)(8 + 8 + 1)}{12}}}$$

$$= \frac{21.5}{9.52} = 2.26$$

Reject H_0; accept H_1. There is evidence of a difference in the distances traveled by the two golf balls.

18–6

Ranks			
Englewood	**West Side**	**Great Northern**	**Sylvania**
17	5	19	7
20	1	9.5	11
16	3	21	15
13	5	22	9.5
5	2	14	8
18			12

$\Sigma R_1 = 89$	$\Sigma R_2 = 16$	$\Sigma R_3 = 85.5$	$\Sigma R_4 = 62.5$
$n_1 = 6$	$n_2 = 5$	$n_3 = 5$	$n_4 = 6$

H_0: The population distributions are identical.
H_1: The population distributions are not identical.

$$H = \frac{12}{22(22 + 1)}\left[\frac{(89)^2}{6} + \frac{(16)^2}{5} + \frac{(85.5)^2}{5} + \frac{(62.5)^2}{6}\right]$$
$$- 3(22 + 1)$$
$$= 13.635$$

The critical value of chi-square for $k - 1 = 4 - 1 = 3$ degrees of freedom is 11.345. Since the computed value of 13.635 is greater than 11.345, the null hypothesis is rejected. We conclude that the turnover rates are not the same.

18–7 a.

		Rank			
X	**Y**	**X**	**Y**	**d**	**d^2**
805	23	5.5	1	4.5	20.25
777	62	3.0	9	−6.0	36.00
820	60	8.5	8	0.5	0.25
682	40	1.0	4	−3.0	9.00
777	70	3.0	10	−7.0	49.00
810	28	7.0	2	5.0	25.00
805	30	5.5	3	2.5	6.25
840	42	10.0	5	5.0	25.00
777	55	3.0	7	−4.0	16.00
820	51	8.5	6	2.5	6.25
				0	193.00

$$r_s = 1 - \frac{6(193)}{10(99)} = -.170$$

b. H_0: $\rho = 0$; H_1: $\rho \neq 0$. Reject H_0 if $t < -2.306$ or $t > 2.306$.

$$t = -.170\sqrt{\frac{10 - 2}{1 - (-0.170)^2}} = -0.488$$

H_0 is not rejected. We have not shown a relationship between the two tests.

A Review of Chapters 17 and 18

In Chapters 17 and 18 we describe statistical methods to study data that is either the nominal or the ordinal scale of measurement. These methods are *nonparametric* or *distribution-free* statistics. They do not require assumptions regarding the shape of the population. Recall, for example, in Chapter 12 when investigating the means of several populations, we assume the populations follow the normal probability distribution.

In Chapter 17 we describe the chi-square distribution. We use this distribution to compare the observed set of frequencies in a random sample with the corresponding set of expected frequencies in the population. The level of measurement is the nominal scale. Recall when data is measured at the nominal level, the observations can only be classified according to some label, name, or characteristic.

In Chapter 17 we also studied the relationship between two variables in a contingency table. That is, we observe two characteristics of each sampled individual or object. For example, is there a relationship between the quality of the product (acceptable or unacceptable) and the shift on which it was manufactured (day, afternoon, or night)? The chi-square distribution is used as the test statistic.

In Chapter 18 we describe five nonparametric tests of hypothesis and the coefficient of rank correlation. Each of these tests requires at least the ordinal scale of measurement. That is, we are able to rank, or order, the variables of interest.

The *sign test* for dependent samples is based on the sign of the difference between related observations. The binomial distribution is the test statistic. In cases where the sample is greater than 10, the normal approximation to the binomial probability distribution serves as the test statistic.

The first step when using the *median test* is to count the number of observations above (or below) the proposed median. Next we use the standard normal distribution to determine if this number is reasonable or too large to have occurred by chance.

The *Wilcoxon signed-rank test* requires dependent samples. It is an extension of the sign test in that it makes use of both the direction and the magnitude of the difference between related values. It has its own sampling distribution, which is reported in Appendix B.7.

The *Wilcoxon ranked-sum test* assumes independent populations, but does not require the populations to follow the normal probability distribution. It is an alternative to the *t* test for independent samples described in Chapter 11. When there are at least eight observations in each sample, the test statistic is the standard normal distribution.

The *Kruskal-Wallis test* is an extension of the Wilcoxon ranked-sum test in that it handles more than two populations. It is an alternative to the one-way ANOVA method described in Chapter 12. It does not require the populations to follow the normal probability distribution or that the populations have equal standard deviations.

The statistic, *Spearman's coefficient of rank correlation,* is a special case of the Pearson coefficient of correlation, described in Chapter 13. It is based on the correlation between the *ranks* of related observations. It may range from −1.00 to 1.00, with 0 indicating no association between the ranks.

Glossary

Chapter 17
Chi-square distribution A distribution with these characteristics: (1) Its value can only be positive. (2) There is a family of chi-square distributions, a different one for each different degree of freedom. (3) The distributions are positively skewed, but as the number of degrees of freedom increases, the distribution approaches the normal distribution.

Chi-square goodness-of-fit test A test with the objective of determining how well an observed set of frequencies fits an expected set of frequencies. It is concerned with one nominal-scale variable, such as the color of a car.

Contingency table If two characteristics, such as gender and highest degree earned for a sample of stock brokers, are cross-classified into a table, the result is called a contingency table. The chi-square test statistic is used to investigate whether the two characteristics are related.

Nominal level of measurement The "lowest" level of measurement. Such data can only be classified into categories, and there is no particular order for the categories. For example, it makes no difference whether the categories "male" and "female" are listed in that order, or female first and male second. The categories are mutually exclusive—meaning, in this illustration, that a person cannot be a male and a female at the same time.

Nonparametric or distribution-free tests Hypothesis tests involving nominal- and ordinal-level data. No assumptions need be made about the shape of the population distribution; that is, we do not assume the population is normally distributed.

Chapter 18
Kruskal-Wallis one-way analysis of variance by ranks A test used when the assumptions for parametric analysis

of variance (ANOVA) cannot be met. Its purpose is to test whether several populations are equal. The data must be at least ordinal scale.

Sign test A test used for dependent samples. The sign test is used to find whether there is a brand preference for two products or to determine whether performance after an experiment is greater than before the experiment. Also, the sign test is used to test a hypothesis about the median.

Spearman's coefficient of rank correlation A measure of the association between the ranks of two variables. It can range from −1.00 to 1.00. A value of −1.00 indicates a perfect negative association among the ranks and a value of 1.00 a perfect positive association among the ranks. A value of 0 indicates no association among the ranks.

Wilcoxon rank-sum test A nonparametric test requiring independent samples. The data must be at least ordinal level. That is, the data must be capable of being ranked. The test is used when the assumptions for the parametric Student t test cannot be met. The objective of the test is to find whether two independent samples can be considered as coming from the same population.

Wilcoxon signed-rank test A nonparametric test requiring at least ordinal-level data and dependent samples. Its purpose is to find whether there is any difference between two sets of paired (related) observations. It is used if the assumptions required for the paired t test cannot be met.

Exercises

connect

Part I—Multiple Choice

1. Which of the following is not a characteristic of the chi-square distribution?
   a. It is positively skewed.
   b. It is based on the number of categories.
   c. It cannot assume negative values.
   d. It is based on at least 30 observations.

2. A sample of 50 nominal-scale observations is classified into four groups. The number of degrees of freedom for a chi-square test is:
   a. 49
   b. 4
   c. 3
   d. 12

3. The degrees of freedom for a chi-square test for independence with 6 rows and 3 columns are:
   a. 18
   b. 15
   c. 12
   d. 10

4. In a chi-square test with 10 categories and a significance level of .05, the critical value of chi-square is:
   a. 16.919
   b. 18.307
   c. 15.987
   d. 14.684

5. Which of the following statements is true regarding the sign test?
   a. It requires paired or dependent samples.
   b. The binomial distribution is the test statistic.
   c. It is based on counting the number of plus (or minus) signs.
   d. All of the above are true.

6. The median test
   a. Is based on ratio-scale data.
   b. Is an extension of the sign test.
   c. Requires a normal population.
   d. Uses the standard normal distribution as the test statistic.

7. Which of the following statements about the Wilcoxon signed-rank test are true?
   a. It requires dependent samples.
   b. It used the magnitude of the difference between related observations.
   c. The distribution of the difference does not have to follow a normal distribution.
   d. All the above are true.

8. Spearman's coefficient of rank correlation is applied when:
   a. The data are measured on the nominal scale.
   b. There are less than 5 observations in the sample.
   c. The observations are ranked.
   d. None of the above.

9. The Kruskal-Wallis test
   a. Investigates whether several populations are the same.
   b. Assumes independent samples.
   c. Does not require a normal population.
   d. All of the above are true.
10. Which of the following nonparametric tests require dependent samples?
    a. Sign test.
    b. Wilcoxon ranked-sum test.
    c. Kruskal-Wallis test.
    d. All of the above.

Part II—Problems

11. The owner of Beach Front Snow Cones, Inc., believes the median number of snow cones sold per day between Memorial Day and Labor Day is 60. Below is a sample of 20 days. Is it reasonable to conclude that the median is actually greater than 60? Use the .05 significance level.

65	70	65	64	66	54	68	61	62	67
65	50	64	55	74	57	67	72	66	65

12. The manufacturer of children's raincoats wants to know if there is a preference among children for any specific color. The information below is the color preference for a sample of 50 children between the ages 6 and 10. Use the .05 significance level to investigate.

Color	Frequency
Blue	17
Red	8
Green	12
Yellow	13

13. Is there a difference (in feet) of the length of suspension bridges in the northeast, southeast, and far west parts of the United States? Conduct an appropriate test of hypothesis on the following data. Do not assume the bridge lengths follow a normal probability distribution. Use the .05 significance level.

Northeast	Southeast	Far West
3,645	3,502	3,547
3,727	3,645	3,636
3,772	3,718	3,659
3,837	3,746	3,673
3,873	3,758	3,728
3,882	3,845	3,736
3,894	3,940	3,788
	4,070	3,802
	4,081	

Cases

A. Century National Bank

Is there a relationship between the location of the branch bank and whether the customer has a debit card? Based on the information available, develop a table that shows the relationship between these two variables. At the .05 significance level, can we conclude there is a relationship between the branch location and whether the customer uses a debit card?

B. Thomas Testing Labs

John Thomas, the owner of Thomas Testing, has for some time done contract work for insurance companies regarding drunk driving. To improve his research capabilities, he recently purchased the Rupple Driving Simulator. This device will allow a subject to take a "road test" and provide a score indicating the number of driving errors committed during the test drive. Higher scores indicate more driving errors. Driving errors would include: not coming to a complete stop at a stop sign, not using turning signals, not exercising caution on wet or snowy pavement, and so on. During the road test, problems appear at random and not all problems appear in each road test. These are major advantages to the Rupple Driving Simulator because subjects do not gain any advantage by taking the test several times.

With the new driving simulator, Mr. Thomas would like to study in detail the problem of drunk driving. He begins by selecting a random sample of 25 drivers. He asks each of the selected individuals to take the test drive on the Rupple Driving Simulator. The number of errors for each driver is recorded. Next, he has each of the individuals in the group drink three 16-ounce cans of beer in a 60-minute period and return to the Rupple Driving Simulator for another test drive. The number of driving errors after drinking the beer is also shown. The research question is: Does alcohol impair the driver's ability and, therefore, increase the number of driving errors?

Mr. Thomas believes the distribution of scores on the test drive does not follow a normal distribution and, therefore, a nonparametric test should be used. Because the observations are paired, he decides to use both the sign test and the Wilcoxon signed-rank test.

	Driving Errors			Driving Errors	
Subject	Without Alcohol	With Alcohol	Subject	Without Alcohol	With Alcohol
1	75	89	14	72	106
2	78	83	15	83	89
3	89	80	16	99	89
4	100	90	17	75	77
5	85	84	18	58	78
6	70	68	19	93	108
7	64	84	20	69	69
8	79	104	21	86	84
9	83	81	22	97	86
10	82	88	23	65	92
11	83	93	24	96	97
12	84	92	25	85	94
13	80	103			

a. Compare the results using these two procedures. Conduct an appropriate test of hypothesis to determine if alcohol is related to driving errors.

b. Write a report that summarizes your findings.

Practice Test

Part I—Objective

1. The _____ level of measurement is required for the chi-square goodness-of-fit test.
   1. _____

2. Which of the following is *not* a characteristic of the chi-square distribution? (positively skewed, based on degrees of freedom, cannot be negative, at least 30 observations)
   2. _____

3. In a contingency table how many traits are considered for each variable?
   3. _____

4. In a contingency table there are four rows and three columns; hence there are _____ degrees of freedom.
   4. _____

5. In a goodness-of-fit test the critical value of chi-square is based on _____. (sample size, number of categories, number of variables, or none of these.)
   5. _____

6. In a sign test are the samples dependent or independent?
   6. _____

7. In a sign test of eight paired observations, the test statistic is the _____ distribution. (binomial, z, t, or chi-square.)
   7. _____

8. What is the major difference between the Kruskal-Wallis test and the Wilcoxon rank-sum test? (one is based on dependent samples and the other independent samples, or one is for comparing two independent samples and the other two or more independent samples)
   8. _____

9. Under what conditions can the coefficient of rank correlation be less than −1.00?
   9. _____

10. The Kruskal-Wallis test is used in the place of ANOVA when which two of the following criteria are not met? (normal population, equal standard deviations, more than 12 items in the sample, the populations are independent)
    10. _____

Part II—Problems

Use the standard five-step hypothesis testing procedure.

1. A recent census report indicated that 65 percent of families have two parents present, 20 percent have only a mother present, 10 percent have only a father present,

and 5 percent have no parent present. A random sample of 200 children from a large rural school district revealed the following:

Two Parents	Mother Only	Father Only	No Parent	Total
120	40	30	10	200

Is there sufficient evidence to conclude that the proportion of families by type of parent present in this particular school district differs from those reported in the recent census?

2. A book publisher wants to investigate the type of books selected for recreational reading by men and women. A random sample provided the following information. At the .05 significance level, should we conclude that gender is related or unrelated to type of book selected?

	Mystery	Romance	Self-Help	Total
Men	250	100	190	540
Women	130	170	200	500

3. An instructor has three sections of basic statistics. Listed below are the grades on the first exam for each section. Assume that the distributions do not follow the normal probability distribution. At the .05 significance level is there a difference in the distributions of scores?

8 A.M.	10 A.M.	1:30 P.M.
68	59	67
84	59	69
75	63	75
78	62	76
70	78	79
77	76	83
88	80	86
71		86
		87

Statistical Process Control and Quality Management

A bicycle manufacturer randomly selects 10 frames each day and tests for defects. The number of defective frames found over the last 14 days is 3, 2, 1, 3, 2, 2, 8, 2, 0, 3, 5, 2, 0, and 4. Construct a control chart for this process and comment on whether the process is "in control." (See Exercise 11 and Goal 6.)

GOALS

When you have completed this chapter, you will be able to:

1 Discuss the role of quality control in production and service operations.

2 Define and understand the terms *chance cause, assignable cause, in control, out of control, attribute,* and *variable.*

3 Construct and interpret a *Pareto chart.*

4 Construct and interpret a *fishbone diagram.*

5 Construct and interpret *mean* and *range charts.*

6 Construct and interpret *percent defective* and *c-bar charts.*

7 Discuss *acceptance sampling.*

8 Construct an *operating characteristic curve* for various sampling plans.

Introduction

Throughout this text we present many applications of hypothesis testing. In Chapter 10 we describe methods for testing a hypothesis regarding a single population value. In Chapter 11 we describe methods for testing a hypothesis about two populations. In this chapter we present another, somewhat different application of hypothesis testing, called **statistical process control** or **SPC.**

Statistical process control is a collection of strategies, techniques, and actions taken by an organization to ensure it is producing a quality product or providing a quality service. SPC begins at the product planning stage, when we specify the attributes of the product or service. It continues through the production stage. Each attribute throughout the process contributes to the overall quality of the product. To effectively use quality control, measurable attributes and specifications are developed against which the actual attributes of the product or service are compared.

A Brief History of Quality Control

Prior to the 1900s U.S. industry was largely characterized by small shops making relatively simple products, such as candles or furniture. In these small shops the individual worker was generally a craftsman who was completely responsible for the quality of the work. The worker could ensure the quality through the personal selection of the materials, skillful manufacturing, and selective fitting and adjustment.

In the early 1900s factories sprang up, where people with limited training were formed into large assembly lines. Products became much more complex. The individual worker no longer had complete control over the quality of the product. A semi-professional staff, usually called the Inspection Department, became responsible for the quality of the product. The quality responsibility was usually fulfilled by a 100 percent inspection of all the important characteristics. If there were any discrepancies noted, these problems were handled by the manufacturing department supervisor. In essence, quality was attained by "inspecting the quality into the product."

During the 1920s Dr. Walter A. Shewhart, of Bell Telephone Laboratories, developed the concepts of statistical quality control. He introduced the concept of "controlling" the quality of a product as it was being manufactured, rather than inspecting the quality into the product after it was manufactured. For the purpose of controlling quality, Shewhart developed charting techniques for controlling in-process manufacturing operations. In addition, he introduced the concept of statistical sample inspection to estimate the quality of a product as it was being manufactured. This replaced the old method of inspecting each part after it was completed in the production operation.

Statistical quality control really came into its own during World War II. The need for mass-produced war-related items, such as bomb sights, accurate radar, and other electronic equipment, at the lowest possible cost hastened the use of statistical sampling and quality control charts. Since World War II these statistical techniques have been refined and sharpened. The use of computers has also widened the use of these techniques.

World War II virtually destroyed the Japanese production capability. Rather than retool their old production methods, the Japanese enlisted the aid of the late Dr. W. Edwards Deming, of the United States Department of Agriculture, to help them develop an overall plan. In a series of seminars with Japanese planners he stressed a philosophy that is known today as Deming's 14 points. These 14 points are listed on the following page. He emphasized that quality originates from improving the process, not from inspection, and that quality is determined by the customers. The manufacturer must be able, via market research, to anticipate the needs of customers. Senior management has the responsibility for long-term improvement. Another of his points, and one that the Japanese strongly endorsed, is that every member of the company must contribute to long-term improvement. To achieve this improvement, ongoing education and training are necessary.

Deming had some ideas that did not mesh with contemporary management philosophies in the United States. Two areas where Deming's ideas differed from U.S. management philosophy were with production quotas and merit ratings. He claimed these two practices, which are both common in the United States, are not productive and should be eliminated. He also pointed out that U.S. managers are mostly interested in good news. Good news, however, does not provide an opportunity for improvement. On the other hand, bad news opens the door for new products and allows for company improvement.

Listed below, in a condensed form, are Dr. Deming's 14 points. He was adamant that the 14 points needed to be adopted as a package in order to be successful. The underlying theme is cooperation, teamwork, and the belief that workers want to do their jobs in a quality fashion.

DEMING'S 14 POINTS

1. Create constancy of purpose for the continual improvement of products and service to society.
2. Adopt a philosophy that we can no longer live with commonly accepted levels of delays, mistakes, defective materials, and defective workmanship.
3. Eliminate the need for mass inspection as the way to achieve quality. Instead achieve quality by building the product correctly in the first place.
4. End the practice of awarding business solely on the basis of price. Instead, require meaningful measures of quality along with the price.
5. Improve constantly and forever every process for planning, production, and service.
6. Institute modern methods of training on the job for all employees, including managers. This will lead to better utilization of each employee.
7. Adopt and institute leadership aimed at helping people do a better job.
8. Encourage effective two-way communication and other means to drive out fear throughout the organization so that everyone may work more effectively and more productively for the company.
9. Break down barriers between departments and staff areas.
10. Eliminate the use of slogans, posters, and exhortations demanding zero defects and new levels of productivity without providing methods.
11. Eliminate work standards that prescribe quotas for the workforce and numerical goals for people in management. Substitute aids and helpful leadership in order to achieve continual improvement in quality and productivity.
12. Remove the barriers that rob hourly workers and the people in management of their right to pride of workmanship.
13. Institute a vigorous program of education and encourage self-improvement for everyone. What an organization needs is good people and people who are improving with education. Advancement to a competitive position will have its roots in knowledge.
14. Define clearly management's permanent commitment to ever-improving quality and productivity to implement all of these principles.

Deming's 14 points did not ignore statistical quality control, which is often abbreviated as SQC. The objective of statistical quality control is to monitor production through many stages of manufacturing. We use the tools of statistical quality control, such as X-bar and R charts, to monitor the quality of many processes and services. Control charts allow us to identify when a process or service is "out of control," that is, when the point in time is reached where an excessive number of defective units are being produced.

Interest in quality has accelerated dramatically in the United States since the late 1980s. Turn on the television and watch the commercials sponsored by Ford, Nissan, and GM to verify the emphasis on quality control on the assembly line. It is now one of the "in" topics in all facets of business. V. Daniel Hunt, a noted American Quality Control consultant, reports that in the United States 20 to 25 percent of the cost of production is currently spent finding and correcting mistakes. And, he added, the additional cost incurred in repairing or replacing faulty products in the field drives the total cost of poor quality to nearly 30 percent. In Japan, he indicated, this cost is about 3 percent!

In recent years companies have been motivated to improve quality by the challenge of being recognized for their quality achievements. The Malcolm Baldrige National Quality Award, established in 1988, is awarded annually to U.S. companies that demonstrate excellence in quality achievement and management. The award categories include manufacturing, service, small business, health care, and education. Past winners include Xerox, IBM, the University of Wisconsin–Stout, Ritz-Carlton Hotel Corporation, Federal Express, and Cadillac. The 2007 winners were:

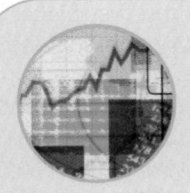

Statistics in Action

Does excellence in quality management lead to higher financial performance? Recent research compared the financial performance of companies that received the Baldrige National Quality Award to similar companies who did not receive the award. The research showed that the companies receiving the award had an average of 39 percent higher operating income and 26 percent higher sales, and were 1.22 percent lower in their cost per sales dollar.

- PRO-TEC Coating Company, established in 1990, was the winner in the small business category. PRO-TEC Coating is a joint venture between United States Steel Corporation and Kobe Steel Ltd. of Japan. They provide coated sheet steel primarily to the U.S. automotive industry for use in manufacturing cars, trucks, and sport utility vehicles. PRO-TEC's 236 employees, called "associates," work in a state-of-the-art 730,000-square-foot facility in the small town of Leipsic, Ohio. The location was chosen for its access to midwestern steel markets, its connection to rail and motor transportation, and its proximity to U.S. Steel's production facilities in Indiana and Pennsylvania.
- Mercy Health System, established in 1989, was the winner in the health care category. Mercy Health System (MHS) is a fully integrated health care system with three hospitals and a network of 64 facilities consisting of 39 multispecialty outpatient centers located in six counties throughout southern Wisconsin and northern Illinois. Mercy's nearly 4,000 employees, called "partners," include 285 physician partners who make up 80 percent of its medical staff. For the past six years, MHS has been ranked in the top 100 integrated health care networks, reaching number 11 on the list in 2008.
- Sharp HealthCare was another winner in the health care category. Sharp HealthCare is San Diego (CA) County's largest integrated health care delivery system, serving more than 27 percent of the county's 3 million plus residents—some 785,000 people—each year. A not-for-profit organization, Sharp has an annual net revenue of more than $1.9 billion; employs a workforce of more than 14,000 staff members and 2,600 affiliated physicians; operates 4 acute-care hospitals, 3 specialty hospitals, 3 affiliated medical groups, and 19 outpatient medical clinics; and manages its own health insurance plan.
- The city of Coral Springs, chartered in 1963, was the winner in the newly created category of state and local government. Coral Springs is located in Broward County in southern Florida. During the 1980s, the city was one of the fastest growing in the nation and now is home to about 132,000 people, making it the 13th largest city in the state of Florida. With an annual budget of $135 million, the city has a workforce of about 770 full-time employees and about 300 part-time and temporary employees as well as a large pool of more than 800 people who volunteer as needed for emergencies, special events, or other activities. The city delivers a broad array of products and services, including

police patrol, crime investigation, fire prevention and suppression, emergency medical services, parks maintenance, and economic development. Facilities include city hall, a public safety training and technology center, five fire stations, four police substations, regional and neighborhood parks, several sports and recreational centers, and a center for the arts.

- The U.S. Army Armament Research, Development and Engineering Center (ARDEC) is a specialized research, development, and engineering center within the U.S. Army Materiel Command. ARDEC develops 90 percent of the Army's armaments and ammunition including warheads, explosives, all sizes of firearms, battlefield sensors, and advanced weaponry. The center's annual net revenue is in excess of $1 billion. Of its nearly 3,000 employees, more than two-thirds are scientists and engineers. The ARDEC headquarters in Picatinny Arsenal, New Jersey, is home to 2,500 staff with the other employees located at ARDEC satellite offices and facilities in Illinois, Maryland, and New York.

You can obtain more information on these and other winners by visiting the website: http://www.quality.nist.gov.

Six Sigma

The Six Sigma program is designed to improve quality and performance throughout a company. It combines methodology, tools, software, and education to deliver a completely integrated approach to waste elimination and process capability improvement. The approach requires defining the process function; identifying, collecting, and analyzing data; creating and consolidating information into useful knowledge; and the communication and application of such knowledge to reduce variation.

Six Sigma gets its name from the normal distribution. The term sigma means standard deviation, and "plus or minus" three standard deviations gives a total range of six standard deviations. So Six Sigma means having no more than 3.4 defects per million opportunities in any process, product, or service. Through the application of statistical thinking it uncovers the relationship between variation and its effect on waste, operating cost, cycle time, profitability, and customer satisfaction.

General Electric, Motorola, and AlliedSignal (now a part of Honeywell) are large companies that have used Six Sigma methods and achieved significant quality improvement and cost savings. Even cities like Fort Wayne, Indiana have used six sigma techniques to improve their operations. The city is reported to have saved $10 million since 2000 and improved customer service at the same time. For example, the city cut missed trash pickups by 50 percent and cut the response time to repair potholes from 21 to 3 hours.

What is quality? There is no commonly agreed upon definition of quality. To cite a few diverse definitions: From Westinghouse, "Total quality is performance leadership in meeting the customer requirements by doing the right things right the first time." From AT&T, "Quality is meeting customer expectations." Historian Barbara W. Tuchman says, "Quality is achieving or reaching the highest standard as against being satisfied with the sloppy or fraudulent." You can learn more about Six Sigma ideas, methods, and training at www.6sigma.us.

Causes of Variation

No two products are *exactly* the same. There is always some variation. The weight of each McDonald's Quarter Pounder is not exactly 0.25 pounds. Some will weigh more than 0.25 pounds, others less. The standard time for the TARTA (Toledo Area Regional Transit Authority) bus run from downtown Toledo, Ohio, to Perrysburg is 25 minutes. However, each run does not take *exactly* 25 minutes. Some runs take longer. Other times the TARTA driver must wait in Perrysburg before returning to Toledo. In some cases there is a reason for the bus being late, an accident on the expressway or a snowstorm, for example. In other cases the driver may not "hit" the green lights or the traffic is unusually heavy and slow for no apparent reason. There are two general sources of variation in a process—chance and assignable.

> **CHANCE VARIATION** Variation that is random in nature. This type of variation cannot be completely eliminated unless there is a major change in the techniques, technologies, methods, equipment, or materials used in the process.

Internal machine friction, slight variations in material or process conditions (such as the temperature of the mold being used to make glass bottles), atmospheric conditions (such as temperature, humidity, and the dust content of the air), and vibrations transmitted to a machine from a passing forklift are a few examples of sources of chance variation.

If the hole drilled in a piece of steel is too large due to a dull drill, the drill may be sharpened or a new drill inserted. An operator who continually sets up the machine incorrectly can be replaced or retrained. If the roll of steel to be used in the process does not have the correct tensile strength, it can be rejected. These are examples of assignable variation.

> **ASSIGNABLE VARIATION** Variation that is not random. It can be eliminated or reduced by investigating the problem and finding the cause.

There are several reasons we should be concerned with variation.

1. It will change the shape, dispersion, and central location of the distribution of the product characteristic being measured.
2. Assignable variation is usually correctable, whereas chance variation usually cannot be corrected or stabilized economically.

Diagnostic Charts

There are a variety of diagnostic techniques available to investigate quality problems. Two of the more prominent of these techniques are **Pareto charts** and **fishbone diagrams.**

Pareto Charts

Pareto analysis is a technique for tallying the number and type of defects that happen within a product or service. The chart is named after a nineteenth-century Italian scientist, Vilfredo Pareto. He noted that most of the "activity" in a process is caused by relatively few of the "factors." His concept, often called the 80–20 rule, is that 80 percent of the activity is caused by 20 percent of the factors. By concentrating on 20 percent of the factors, managers can attack 80 percent of the problem. For example, Emily's Family Restaurant, located at the junction of Interstates 75 and 70, is investigating "customer complaints." The five complaints heard most frequently are: discourteous service, cold food, long wait for seating, few menu choices, and unruly young children. Suppose discourteous service was mentioned most frequently and cold food second. These two factors total more than 85 percent of the complaints and hence are the two that should be addressed first because this will yield the largest reduction in complaints.

To develop a Pareto chart, we begin by tallying the type of defects. Next, we rank the defects in terms of frequency of occurrence from largest to smallest. Finally, we produce a vertical bar chart, with the height of the bars corresponding to the frequency of each defect. The following example illustrates these ideas.

Example

The city manager of Grove City, Utah, is concerned with water usage, particularly in single family homes. She would like to develop a plan to reduce the water usage in Grove City. To investigate, she selects a sample of 100 homes and determines the typical daily water usage for various purposes. These sample results are as follows.

Reasons for Water Usage	Gallons per Day
Laundering	24.9
Watering lawn	143.7
Personal bathing	106.7
Cooking	5.1
Swimming pool	28.3
Dishwashing	12.3
Car washing	10.4
Drinking	7.9

What is the area of greatest usage? Where should she concentrate her efforts to reduce the water usage?

Solution

A Pareto chart is useful for identifying the major areas of water usage and focusing on those areas where the greatest reduction can be achieved. The first step is to convert each of the activities to a percent and then to order them from largest to smallest. The total water usage per day is 339.3 gallons, found by totaling the gallons used in the eight activities. The activity with the largest use is watering lawns. It accounts for 143.7 gallons of water per day, or 42.4 percent of the amount of water used. The next largest category is personal bathing, which accounts for 31.4 percent of the water used. These two activities account for 73.8 percent of the water usage.

Reasons for Water Usage	Gallons per Day	Percent
Laundering	24.9	7.3
Watering lawn	143.7	42.4
Personal bathing	106.7	31.4
Cooking	5.1	1.5
Swimming pool usage	28.3	8.3
Dishwashing	12.3	3.6
Car washing	10.4	3.1
Drinking	7.9	2.3
Total	339.3	100.0

To draw the Pareto chart, we begin by scaling the number of gallons used on the left vertical axis and the corresponding percent on the right vertical axis. Next we draw a vertical bar with the height of the bar corresponding to the activity with the largest number of occurrences. In the Grove City example, we draw a vertical bar for the activity watering lawns to a height of 143.7 gallons. (We call this the count.) We continue this procedure for the other activities, as shown in the MINITAB output in Chart 19–1.

Below the chart we list the activities, their frequency of occurrence, and the percent of the time each activity occurs. In the last row we list the cumulative percentage. This cumulative row will allow us to quickly determine which set of activities account for most of the activity. These cumulative percents are plotted above the

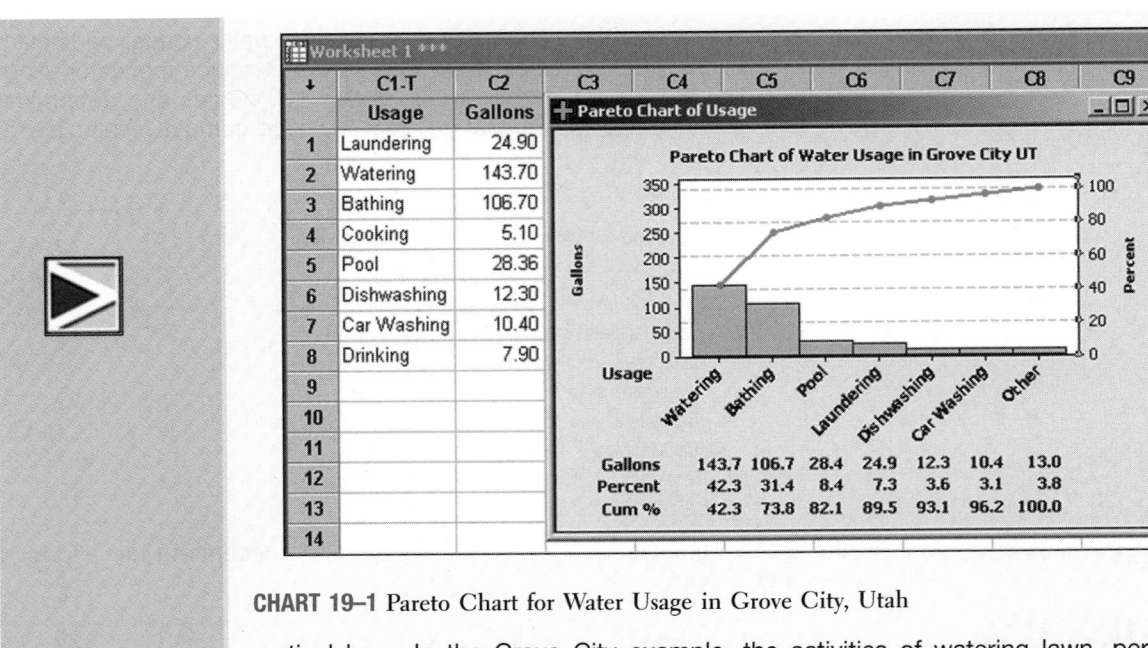

CHART 19–1 Pareto Chart for Water Usage in Grove City, Utah

vertical bars. In the Grove City example, the activities of watering lawn, personal bathing, and pools account for 82.1 percent of the water usage. The city manager can attain the greatest gain by looking to reduce the water usage in these three areas.

Fishbone Diagrams

Another diagnostic chart is a **cause-and-effect diagram** or a **fishbone diagram.** It is called a cause-and-effect diagram to emphasize the relationship between an effect and a set of possible causes that produce the particular effect. This diagram is useful to help organize ideas and to identify relationships. It is a tool that encourages open brainstorming for ideas. By identifying these relationships we can determine factors that are the cause of variability in our process. The name *fishbone* comes from the manner in which the various causes and effects are organized on the diagram. The effect is usually a particular problem, or perhaps a goal, and it is shown on the right-hand side of the diagram. The major causes are listed on the left-hand side of the diagram.

The usual approach to a fishbone diagram is to consider four problem areas, namely, methods, materials, equipment, and personnel. The problem, or the effect, is the head of the fish. See Chart 19–2.

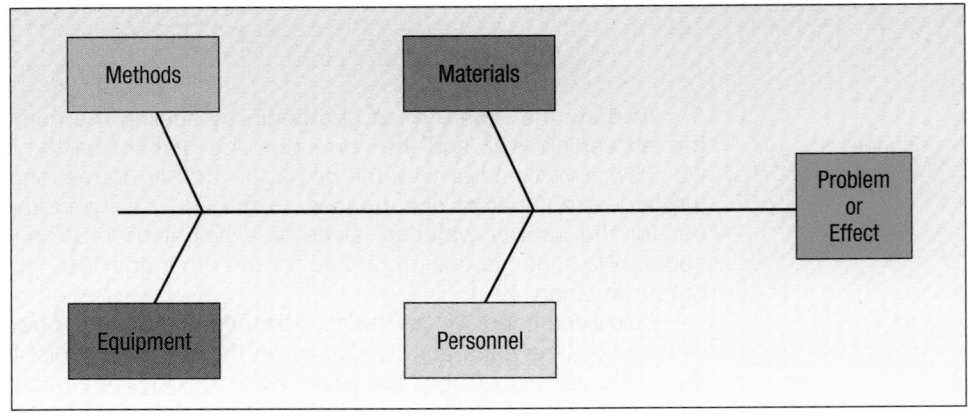

CHART 19–2 Fishbone Diagram

Under each of the possible causes are subcauses that are identified and investigated. The subcauses are factors that may be producing the particular effect. Information is gathered about the problem and used to fill in the fishbone diagram. Each of the subcauses is investigated and those that are not important eliminated, until the real cause of the problem is identified.

Chart 19–3 illustrates the details of a fishbone diagram. Suppose a family restaurant, such as those found along an interstate highway, has recently been experiencing complaints from customers that the food being served is cold. Notice each of the subcauses are listed as assumptions. Each of these subcauses must be investigated to find the real problem regarding the cold food. In a fishbone diagram there is no weighting of the subcauses.

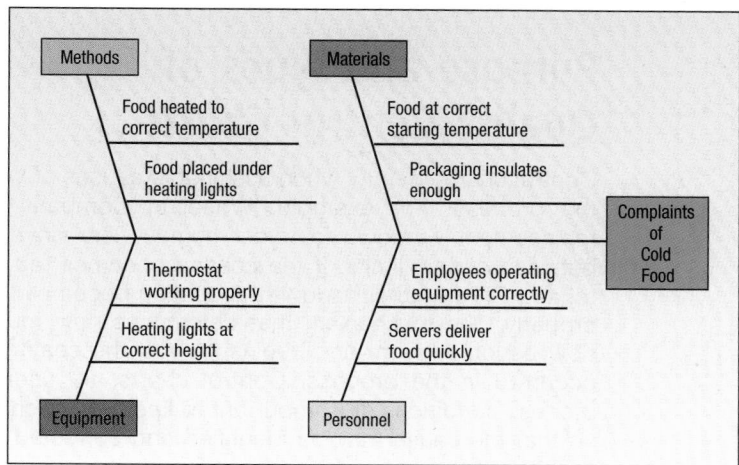

CHART 19–3 Fishbone Diagram for a Restaurant Investigation of Cold Food Complaints

---

Self-Review 19–1

The Rouse Home, located on the south side of Chicago, is a mental health facility. Recently there have been complaints regarding conditions at the home. The administrator would like to use a Pareto chart to investigate. When a patient or patient's relative has a complaint, they are asked to complete a complaint form. Listed below is a summary of the complaint forms received during the last 12 months.

Complaint	Number	Complaint	Number
Nothing to do	45	Dirty conditions	63
Poor care by staff	71	Poor quality of food	84
Medication error	2	Lack of respect by staff	35

Develop a Pareto chart. What complaints would you suggest the administrator work on first to achieve the most significant improvement?

Exercises

connect

1. Tom Sharkey is the owner of Sharkey Chevy, Buick, GMC, Isuzu. At the start of the year Tom instituted a customer opinion program to find ways to improve service. One week after the service is performed, Tom's administrative assistant calls the customer to find out whether the service was performed satisfactorily and how the service might be improved. Listed below is a summary of the complaints for the first six months.

Develop a Pareto chart. What complaints would you suggest that Tom work on to improve the quality of service?

Complaint	Frequency	Complaint	Frequency
Problem not corrected	38	Price too high	23
Error on invoice	8	Wait too long for service	10
Unfriendly atmosphere	12		

2. Out of 110 diesel engines tested, a rework and repair facility found 9 had leaky water pumps, 15 had faulty cylinders, 4 had ignition problems, 52 had oil leaks, and 30 had cracked blocks. Draw a Pareto chart to identify the key problem in the engines.

Purpose and Types of Quality Control Charts

Control charts identify when assignable causes of variation or changes have entered the process. For example, Wheeling Company makes vinyl-coated aluminum replacement windows for older homes. The vinyl coating must have a thickness between certain limits. If the coating becomes too thick, it will cause the windows to jam. On the other hand, if the coating becomes too thin, the window will not seal properly. The mechanism that determines how much coating is put on each window becomes worn and begins making the coating too thick. Thus, a change has occurred in the process. Control charts are useful for detecting the change in process conditions. It is important to know when changes have entered the process, so that the cause may be identified and corrected before a large number of unacceptable items are produced.

Control charts may be compared to the scoreboard in a baseball game. By looking at the scoreboard, the fans, coaches, and players can tell which team is winning the game. However, the scoreboard can do nothing to win or lose the game. Control charts provide a similar function. These charts indicate to the workers, group leaders, quality control engineers, production supervisor, and management whether the production of the part or service is "in control" or "out of control." If the production is "out of control," the control chart will not fix the situation; it is just a piece of paper with figures and dots on it. Instead, the person responsible will adjust the machine manufacturing the part or do what is necessary to return production to "in control."

There are two types of control charts. A **variable control chart** portrays measurements, such as the amount of cola in a two-liter bottle or the outside diameter of a piece of pipe. A variable control chart requires the interval or the ratio scale of measurement. An **attribute control chart** classifies a product or service as either acceptable or unacceptable. It is based on the nominal scale of measurement. The Marines stationed at Camp Lejeune are asked to rate the meals served as acceptable or unacceptable; bank loans are either repaid or they are defaulted.

Control Charts for Variables

To develop control charts for variables, we rely on the sampling theory discussed in connection with the central limit theorem in Chapter 8. Suppose a sample of five pieces is selected each hour from the production process and the mean of each sample computed. The sample means are $\overline{X}_1, \overline{X}_2, \overline{X}_3$, and so on. The mean of these sample means is denoted as $\overline{\overline{X}}$. We use k to indicate the number of sample means. The overall or grand mean is found by:

GRAND MEAN	$\overline{\overline{X}} = \dfrac{\Sigma \text{ of the sample means}}{\text{Number of sample means}} = \dfrac{\Sigma \overline{X}}{k}$	[19–1]

The standard error of the distribution of the sample means is designated by $s_{\overline{X}}$. It is found by:

STANDARD ERROR OF THE MEAN	$s_{\overline{X}} = \dfrac{s}{\sqrt{n}}$	[19–2]

These relationships allow limits to be established around the sample means to show how much variation can be expected for a given sample size. These expected limits are called the **upper control limit** (*UCL*) and the **lower control limit** (*LCL*). An example will illustrate the use of control limits and how the limits are determined.

Example

Statistical Software, Inc., offers a toll-free number where customers can call with problems involving the use of their products from 7 A.M. until 11 P.M. daily. It is impossible to have every call answered immediately by a technical representative, but it is important customers do not wait too long for a person to come on the line. Customers become upset when they hear the message "Your call is important to us. The next available representative will be with you shortly" too many times. To understand its process, Statistical Software decides to develop a control chart describing the total time from when a call is received until the representative answers the call and resolves the issue raised by the caller. Yesterday, for the 16 hours of operation, five calls were sampled each hour. This information is reported below, in minutes, until the issue was resolved.

		Sample Number				
Time		**1**	**2**	**3**	**4**	**5**
A.M.	7	8	9	15	4	11
	8	7	10	7	6	8
	9	11	12	10	9	10
	10	12	8	6	9	12
	11	11	10	6	14	11
P.M.	12	7	7	10	4	11
	1	10	7	4	10	10
	2	8	11	11	7	7
	3	8	11	8	14	12
	4	12	9	12	17	11
	5	7	7	9	17	13
	6	9	9	4	4	11
	7	10	12	12	12	12
	8	8	11	9	6	8
	9	10	13	9	4	9
	10	9	11	8	5	11

Based on this information, develop a control chart for the mean duration of the call. Does there appear to be a trend in the calling times? Is there any period in which it appears that customers wait longer than others?

Solution

A mean chart has two limits, an upper control limit (*UCL*) and a lower control limit (*LCL*). These upper and lower control limits are computed by:

> **CONTROL LIMITS FOR THE MEAN**
>
> $$UCL = \overline{\overline{X}} + 3\frac{s}{\sqrt{n}} \quad \text{and} \quad LCL = \overline{\overline{X}} - 3\frac{s}{\sqrt{n}}$$ **[19–3]**

where *s* is an estimate of the standard deviation of the population, σ. Notice that in the calculation of the upper and lower control limits the number 3 appears. It represents the 99.74 percent confidence limits. The limits are often called the 3-sigma limits. However, other levels of confidence (such as 90 or 95 percent) can be used.

This application was developed before computers were widely available, and computing standard deviations was difficult. Rather than calculate the standard deviation from each sample as a measure of variation, it is easier to use the range. For fixed sized samples there is a constant relationship between the range and the standard deviation, so we can use the following formulas to determine the 99.74 percent control limits for the mean. It can be demonstrated that the term $3(s/\sqrt{n})$ from formula (19–3) is equivalent to $A_2\overline{R}$ in the following formula.

> **CONTROL LIMITS FOR THE MEAN**
>
> $$UCL = \overline{\overline{X}} + A_2\overline{R} \qquad LCL = \overline{\overline{X}} - A_2\overline{R}$$ **[19–4]**

where

A_2 is a constant used in computing the upper and the lower control limits. It is based on the average range, $\overline{R}$. The factors for various sample sizes are available in Appendix B.8. (Note: *n* in this table refers to the number in the sample.) A portion of Appendix B.8 is shown below. To locate the A_2 factor for this problem, find the sample size for *n* in the left margin. It is 5. Then move horizontally to the A_2 column, and read the factor. It is 0.577.

n	*A₂*	*d₂*	*D₃*	*D₄*
2	1.880	1.128	0	3.267
3	1.023	1.693	0	2.575
4	0.729	2.059	0	2.282
5	0.577	2.326	0	2.115
6	0.483	2.534	0	2.004

$\overline{\overline{X}}$ is the mean of the sample means, computed by $\Sigma\overline{X}/k$, where *k* is the number of samples selected. In this problem a sample of 5 observations is taken each hour for 16 hours, so *k* = 16.

$\overline{R}$ is the mean of the ranges of the sample. It is $\Sigma R/k$. Remember the range is the difference between the largest and the smallest value in each sample.

It describes the variability occurring in that particular sample. (See Table 19–1.)

TABLE 19–1 Duration of 16 Samples of Five Help Sessions

Time		1	2	3	4	5	Mean	Range
A.M.	7	8	9	15	4	11	9.4	11
	8	7	10	7	6	8	7.6	4
	9	11	12	10	9	10	10.4	3
	10	12	8	6	9	12	9.4	6
	11	11	10	6	14	11	10.4	8
P.M.	12	7	7	10	4	11	7.8	7
	1	10	7	4	10	10	8.2	6
	2	8	11	11	7	7	8.8	4
	3	8	11	8	14	12	10.6	6
	4	12	9	12	17	11	12.2	8
	5	7	7	9	17	13	10.6	10
	6	9	9	4	4	11	7.4	7
	7	10	12	12	12	12	11.6	2
	8	8	11	9	6	8	8.4	5
	9	10	13	9	4	9	9.0	9
	10	9	11	8	5	11	8.8	6
Total							150.6	102

The centerline for the chart is $\overline{\overline{X}}$. It is 9.413 minutes, found by 150.6/16. The mean of the ranges $(\overline{R})$ is 6.375 minutes, found by 102/16. Thus, the upper control limit of the X bar chart is:

$$UCL = \overline{\overline{X}} + A_2\overline{R} = 9.413 + 0.577(6.375) = 13.091$$

The lower control limit of the X bar chart is:

$$LCL = \overline{\overline{X}} - A_2\overline{R} = 9.413 - 0.577(6.375) = 5.735$$

$\overline{\overline{X}}$, UCL, and LCL, and the sample means are portrayed in Chart 19–4. The mean, $\overline{\overline{X}}$, is 9.413 minutes, the upper control limit is located at 13.091 minutes, and the lower control limit is located at 5.735. There is some variation in the duration of the calls, but all sample means are within the control limits. Thus, based on 16 samples of 5 calls, we conclude that 99.74 percent of the time the mean length of a sample of 5 calls will be between 5.735 minutes and 13.091 minutes.

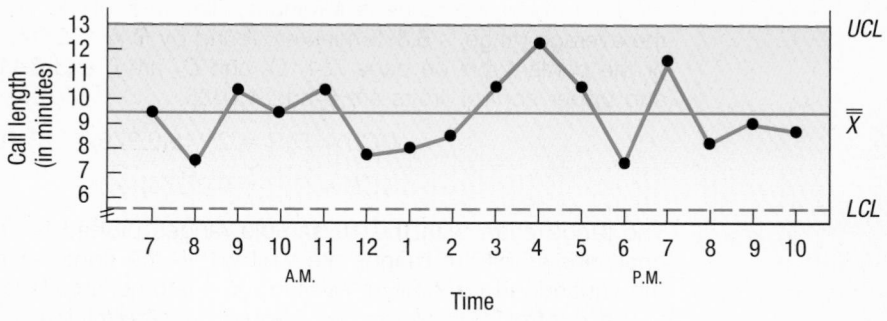

CHART 19–4 Control Chart for Mean Length of Customer Calls to Statistical Software, Inc.

Because the statistical theory is based on the normality of large samples, control charts should be based on a stable process, that is, a fairly large sample, taken over a long period of time. One rule of thumb is to design the chart after at least 25 samples have been selected.

Range Charts

In addition to the central location in a sample, we must also monitor the amount of variation from sample to sample. A **range chart** shows the variation in the sample ranges. If the points representing the ranges fall between the upper and the lower limits, it is concluded that the operation is in control. According to chance, about 997 times out of 1,000 the range of the samples will fall within the limits. If the range should fall above the limits, we conclude that an assignable cause affected the operation and an adjustment to the process is needed. Why are we not as concerned about the lower control limit of the range? For small samples the lower limit is often zero. Actually, for any sample of six or less, the lower control limit is 0. If the range is zero, then logically all the parts are the same and there is not a problem with the variability of the operation.

The upper and lower control limits of the range chart are determined from the following equations.

CONTROL CHART FOR RANGES	$UCL = D_4\overline{R} \qquad LCL = D_3\overline{R}$	[19–5]

The values for D_3 and D_4, which reflect the usual three σ (sigma) limits for various sample sizes, are found in Appendix B.8 or in the table on page 714.

Example

The length of time customers of Statistical Software, Inc., waited from the time their call was answered until a technical representative answered their question or solved their problem is recorded in Table 19–1. Develop a control chart for the range. Does it appear that there is any time when there is too much variation in the operation?

Solution

The first step is to find the mean of the sample ranges. The range for the five calls sampled in the 7 A.M. hour is 11 minutes. The longest call selected from that hour was 15 minutes and the shortest 4 minutes; the difference in the lengths is 11 minutes. In the 8 A.M. hour the range is 4 minutes. The total of the 16 ranges is 102 minutes, so the average range is 6.375 minutes, found by $\overline{R} = 102/16$. Referring to Appendix B.8 or the partial table on page 721, D_3 and D_4 are 0 and 2.115, respectively. The lower and upper control limits are 0 and 13.483.

$$UCL = D_4\overline{R} = 2.115(6.375) = 13.483$$

$$LCL = D_3\overline{R} = 0(6.375) = 0$$

The range chart with the 16 sample ranges plotted is shown in Chart 19–5. This chart shows all the ranges are well within the control limits. Hence, we conclude the variation in the time to service the customer's calls is within normal limits, that is, "in control." Of course, we should be determining the control limits based on one set of data and then applying them to evaluate future data, not the data we already know.

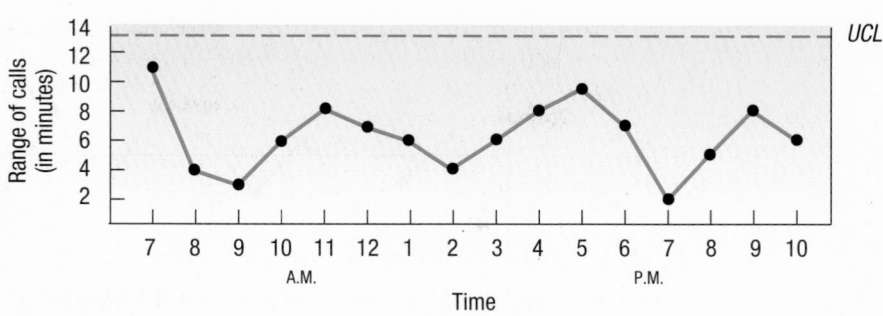

CHART 19–5 Control Chart for Ranges of Length of Customer Calls to Statistical Software, Inc.

MINITAB will draw a control chart for the mean and the range. Following is the output for the Statistical Software example. The data are in Table 19–1. The minor differences in the control limits are due to rounding.

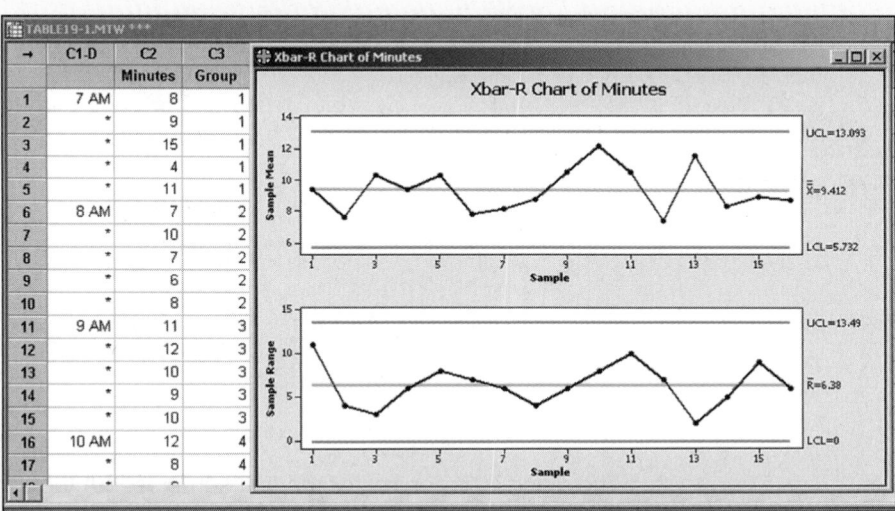

In-Control and Out-of-Control Situations

Three illustrations of in-control and out-of-control processes follow.

1. The mean chart and the range chart together indicate that the process is in control. Note the sample means and sample ranges are clustered close to the centerlines. Some are above and some below the centerlines, indicating the process is quite stable. That is, there is no visible tendency for the means and ranges to move toward the out-of-control areas.

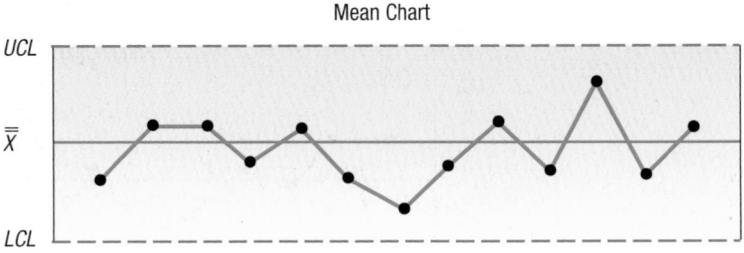

Mean Chart

Everything OK

Range Chart

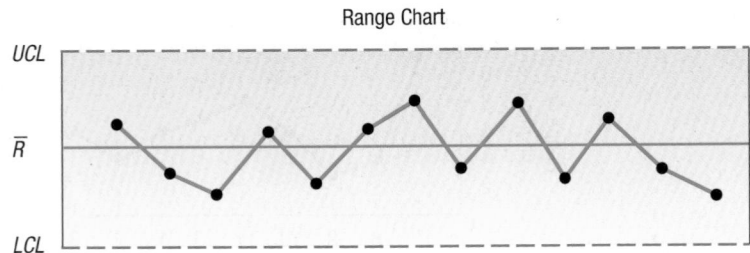

2. The sample means are in control, but the ranges of the last two samples are out of control. This indicates there is considerable variation in the samples. Some sample ranges are large; others are small. An adjustment in the process is probably necessary.

Mean Chart

Considerable variation in ranges

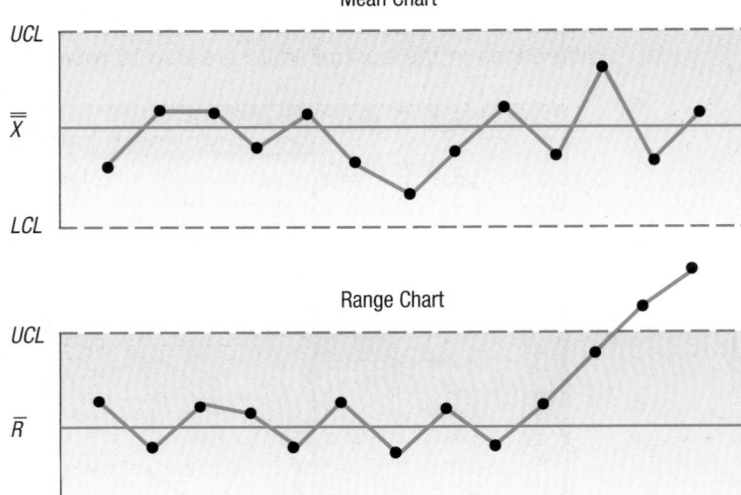

Range Chart

3. The mean is in control for the first samples, but there is an upward trend toward the *UCL*. The last two sample means are out of control. An adjustment in the process is indicated.

Mean Chart

Mean out of control

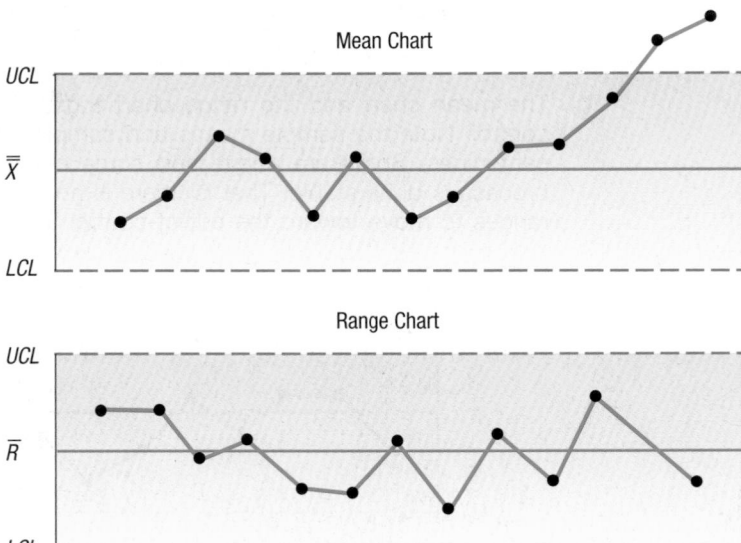

Range Chart

The above chart for the mean is an example of a control chart that offers some additional information. Note the direction of the last five observations of the mean. They are all above $\bar{\bar{X}}$ and increasing, and, in fact, the last two observations are out of control. The fact that the sample means were increasing for six consecutive observations is very improbable and another indication that the process is out of control.

Self-Review 19–2  The manager of River City McDonald's randomly selects four customers each hour. For these selected customers she determines the time, in minutes, between order entry and order delivery. The results are shown below.

	Sample Times			
Time	1	2	3	4
9 A.M.	1	4	5	2
10 A.M.	2	3	2	1
11 A.M.	1	7	3	5

(a) Compute the mean wait, the mean range, and determine the control limits for the mean and the range and chart them.
(b) Are the measurements within the control limits? Interpret the chart.

Exercises

3. Describe the difference between assignable variation and chance variation.
4. Describe the difference between an attribute control chart and a variable control chart.
5. Samples of size $n = 4$ are selected from a production line.
   a. What is the value of the A_2 factor used to determine the upper and lower control limits for the mean?
   b. What are the values of the D_3 and D_4 factors used to determine the lower and upper control limits for the range?
6. Samples of size 5 are selected from a manufacturing process. The mean of the sample ranges is .50. What is the estimate of the standard deviation of the population?
7. A new industrial oven has just been installed at Piatt Bakery. To develop experience regarding the oven temperature, an inspector reads the temperature at four different places inside the oven each half hour. The first reading, taken at 8:00 A.M., was 340 degrees Fahrenheit. (Only the last two digits are given in the following table to make the computations easier.)

	Reading			
Time	1	2	3	4
8:00 A.M.	40	50	55	39
8:30 A.M.	44	42	38	38
9:00 A.M.	41	45	47	43
9:30 A.M.	39	39	41	41
10:00 A.M.	37	42	46	41
10:30 A.M.	39	40	39	40

   a. On the basis of this initial experience, determine the control limits for the mean temperature. Determine the grand mean. Plot the experience on a chart.
   b. Interpret the chart. Does there seem to be a time when the temperature is out of control?
8. Refer to Exercise 7.
   a. On the basis of this initial experience, determine the control limits for the range. Plot the experience on a chart.
   b. Does there seem to be a time when there is too much variation in the temperature?

Attribute Control Charts

Often the data we collect are the result of counting rather than measuring. That is, we observe the presence or absence of some attribute. For example, the screw top on a bottle of shampoo either fits onto the bottle and does not leak (an "acceptable" condition) or does not seal and a leak results (an "unacceptable" condition), or a bank makes a loan to a customer and the loan is either repaid or it is not repaid. In other cases we are interested in the number of defects in a sample. British Airways might count the number of its flights arriving late per day at Gatwick Airport in London. In this section we discuss two types of attribute charts: the *p*-chart (percent defective) and the *c*-bar chart (number of defectives).

Percent Defective Charts

If the item recorded is the fraction of unacceptable parts made in a larger batch of parts, the appropriate control chart is the **percent defective chart.** This chart is based on the binomial distribution, discussed in Chapter 6, and proportions, discussed in Chapter 9. The centerline is at *p,* the mean proportion defective. The *p* replaces the $\overline{X}$ of the variable control chart. The mean proportion defective is found by:

$$\text{MEAN PROPORTION DEFECTIVE} \qquad p = \frac{\text{Total number defective}}{\text{Total number of items sampled}} \qquad \textbf{[19–6]}$$

The variation in the sample proportion is described by the standard error of a proportion. It is found by:

$$\text{STANDARD ERROR OF THE SAMPLE PROPORTION} \qquad s_p = \sqrt{\frac{p(1-p)}{n}} \qquad \textbf{[19–7]}$$

Hence, the upper control limit (*UCL*) and the lower control limit (*LCL*) are computed as the mean percent defective plus or minus three times the standard error of the percents (proportions). The formula for the control limits is:

$$\text{CONTROL LIMITS FOR PROPORTIONS} \qquad LCL, UCL = p \pm 3\sqrt{\frac{p(1-p)}{n}} \qquad \textbf{[19–8]}$$

An example will show the details of the calculations and the conclusions.

Example

Jersey Glass Company, Inc., produces small hand mirrors. Jersey Glass runs a day and evening shift each weekday. The quality assurance department (QA) monitors the quality of the mirrors twice during the day shift and twice during the evening shift. QA selects and carefully inspects a random sample of 50 mirrors once every 4 hours. Each mirror is classified as either acceptable or unacceptable. Finally QA counts the number of mirrors in the sample that do not conform to quality specifications. Listed below are the results of these checks over the last 10 business days.

Date	Number Sampled	Defects	Date	Number Sampled	Defects
10-Oct	50	1	17-Oct	50	7
	50	0		50	9
	50	9		50	0
	50	9		50	8
11-Oct	50	4	18-Oct	50	6
	50	4		50	9
	50	5		50	6
	50	3		50	1
12-Oct	50	9	19-Oct	50	4
	50	3		50	5
	50	10		50	2
	50	2		50	5
13-Oct	50	2	20-Oct	50	0
	50	4		50	0
	50	9		50	4
	50	4		50	7
14-Oct	50	6	21-Oct	50	5
	50	9		50	1
	50	2		50	9
	50	4		50	9

Construct a percent defective chart for this process. What are the upper and lower control limits? Interpret the results. Does it appear the process is out of control during the period?

Solution

The first step is to determine the mean proportion defective. We use formula (19–6).

$$\overline{p} = \frac{\text{Total number defective}}{\text{Total number of items sampled}} = \frac{196}{2,000} = .098$$

So we estimate that .098 of the mirrors produced during the period do not meet specifications.

Date	Number Sampled	Defects	Fraction Defective	Date	Number Sampled	Defects	Fraction Defective
10-Oct	50	1	0.02	17-Oct	50	7	0.14
	50	0	0.00		50	9	0.18
	50	9	0.18		50	0	0.00
	50	9	0.18		50	8	0.16
11-Oct	50	4	0.08	18-Oct	50	6	0.12
	50	4	0.08		50	9	0.18
	50	5	0.10		50	6	0.12
	50	3	0.06		50	1	0.02
12-Oct	50	9	0.18	19-Oct	50	4	0.08
	50	3	0.06		50	5	0.10
	50	10	0.20		50	2	0.04
	50	2	0.04		50	5	0.10
13-Oct	50	2	0.04	20-Oct	50	0	0.00
	50	4	0.08		50	0	0.00
	50	9	0.18		50	4	0.08
	50	4	0.08		50	7	0.14
14-Oct	50	6	0.12	21-Oct	50	5	0.10
	50	9	0.18		50	1	0.02
	50	2	0.04		50	9	0.18
	50	4	0.08		50	9	0.18
				Total	2000	196	

The upper and lower control limits are computed by using formula (19–8)

$$LCL, UCL = p \pm 3 \sqrt{\frac{p(1-p)}{n}} = .098 \pm 3 \sqrt{\frac{.098(1-.098)}{50}} = .098 \pm .1261$$

From the above calculations, the upper control limit is .2241, found by .098 + .1261. The lower control limit is 0. Why? The lower limit by the formula is .098 − .1261 = −0.0281. However, a negative proportion defective is not possible, so the smallest value is 0. We set the control limits at 0 and 0.2241. Any sample outside these limits indicates the quality level of the process has changed.

This information is summarized in Chart 19–6, which is output from the MINITAB system.

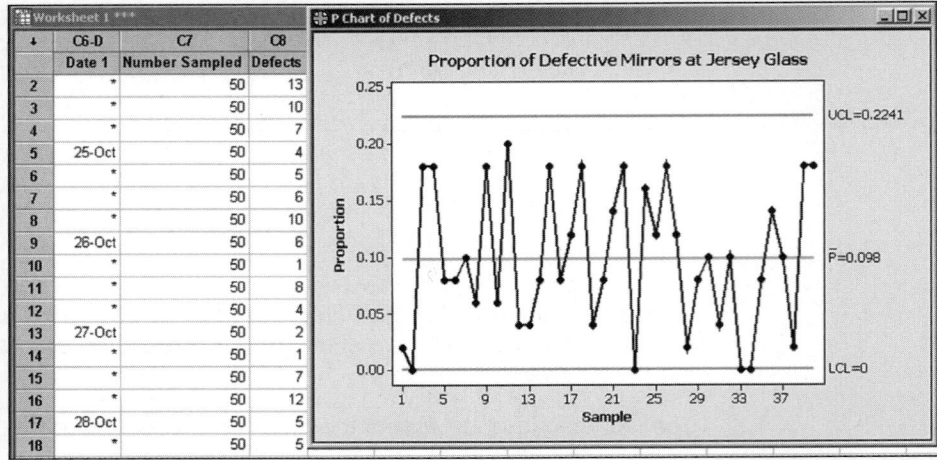

CHART 19–6 Percent Defective Chart for Mirrors at Jersey Glass

After establishing the limits the process is monitored for the next week, five days, two shifts per day, with two quality checks per shift. The results are shown below.

Date	Number Sampled	Defects	Fraction Defective	Date	Number Sampled	Defects	Fraction Defective
24-Oct	50	1	0.02	27-Oct	50	2	0.04
	50	13	0.26		50	1	0.02
	50	10	0.20		50	7	0.14
	50	7	0.14		50	12	0.24
25-Oct	50	4	0.08	28-Oct	50	5	0.10
	50	5	0.10		50	5	0.10
	50	6	0.12		50	10	0.20
	50	10	0.20		50	9	0.18
26-Oct	50	6	0.12				
	50	1	0.02				
	50	8	0.16				
	50	4	0.08				

The process was out of control on two occasions, on October 24 when the number of defects was 13 and again on October 27 when the number of defects was 12. QA should report this information to the production department for the appropriate action. The MINITAB output follows.

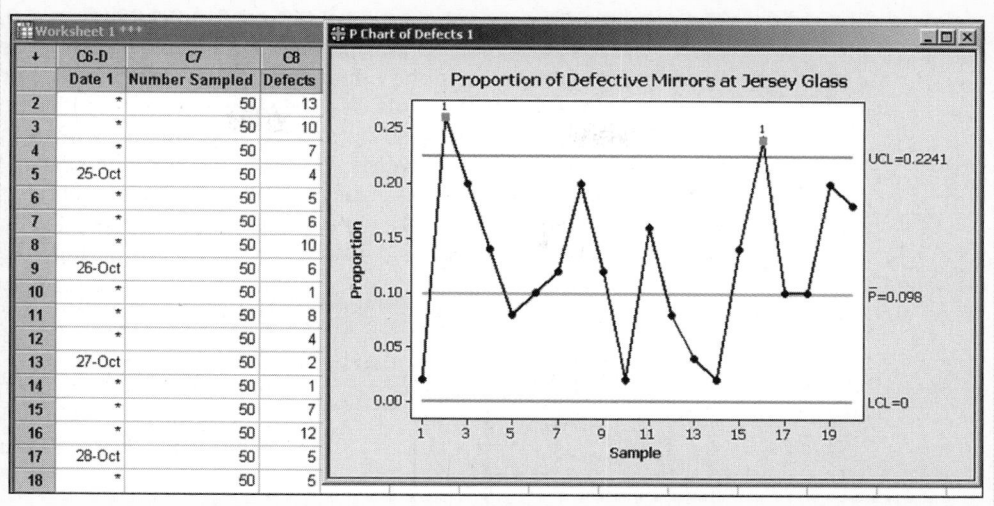

c-Bar Charts

The *c*-bar chart plots the number of defects or failures per unit. It is based on the Poisson distribution discussed in Chapter 6. The number of bags mishandled on a flight by Southwest Airlines might be monitored by a *c*-bar chart. The "unit" under consideration is the flight. On most flights there are no bags mishandled. On others there may be only one, on others two, and so on. The Internal Revenue Service might count and develop a control chart for the number of errors in arithmetic per tax return. Most returns will not have any errors, some returns will have a single error, others will have two, and so on. We let $\bar{c}$ be the mean number of defects per unit. Thus, $\bar{c}$ is the mean number of bags mishandled by Southwest Airlines per flight or the mean number of arithmetic errors per tax return. Recall from Chapter 6 that the standard deviation of a Poisson distribution is the square root of the mean. Thus, we can determine the 3-sigma, or 99.74 percent, limits on a *c*-bar chart by:

CONTROL LIMITS FOR THE NUMBER OF DEFECTS PER UNIT	$LCL, UCL = \bar{c} \pm 3\sqrt{\bar{c}}$	**[19–9]**

Example

The publisher of the *Oak Harbor Daily Telegraph* is concerned about the number of misspelled words in the daily newspaper. It does not print a paper on Saturday or Sunday. In an effort to control the problem and promote the need for correct spelling, a control chart will be used. The number of misspelled words found in the final edition of the paper for the last 10 days is: 5, 6, 3, 0, 4, 5, 1, 2, 7, and 4. Determine the appropriate control limits and interpret the chart. Were there any days during the period that the number of misspelled words was out of control?

Solution

During the 10-day period there were a total of 37 misspelled words. The mean number of misspelled words per edition is 3.7. The number of misspelled words per edition follows the Poisson probability distribution. The standard deviation is the square root of the mean.

$$\bar{c} = \frac{\Sigma X}{n} = \frac{5 + 6 + \cdots + 4}{10} = \frac{37}{10} = 3.7 \qquad s = \sqrt{\bar{c}} = \sqrt{3.7} = 1.924$$

To find the upper control limit we use formula (19–9). The lower control limit is zero.

$$UCL = \bar{c} + 3\sqrt{\bar{c}} = 3.7 + 3\sqrt{3.7} = 3.7 + 5.77 = 9.47$$

The computed lower control limit would be $3.7 - 3(1.924) = -2.07$. However, the number of misspelled words cannot be less than 0, so we use 0 as the lower limit. The lower control limit is 0 and the upper limit is 9.47. When we compare each of the data points to the value of 9.47, we see they are all less than the upper control limit; the number of misspelled words is "in control." Of course, newspapers are going to strive to eliminate all misspelled words, but control charting techniques offer a means of tracking daily results and determining whether there has been a change. For example, if a new proofreader was hired, her work could be compared with others. These results are summarized in Chart 19–7, which is output from the MINITAB system.

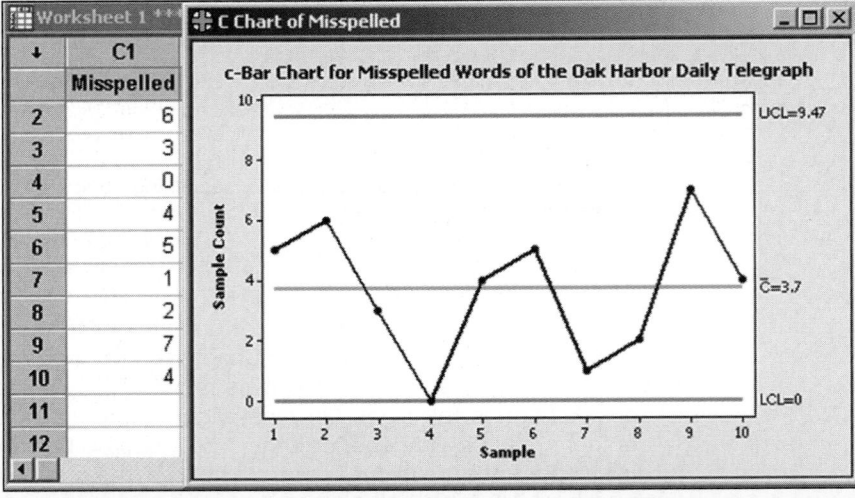

CHART 19–7 *c*-Bar Chart for Number of Misspelled Words per Edition of the *Oak Harbor Daily Telegraph*

Self-Review 19–3   Auto-Lite Company manufactures car batteries. At the end of each shift the quality assurance department selects a sample of batteries and tests them. The number of defective batteries found over the last 12 shifts is 2, 1, 0, 2, 1, 1, 7, 1, 1, 2, 6, and 1. Construct a control chart for the process and comment on whether the process is in control.

Exercises

connect

9. Below is a percent defective chart for a manufacturing process.

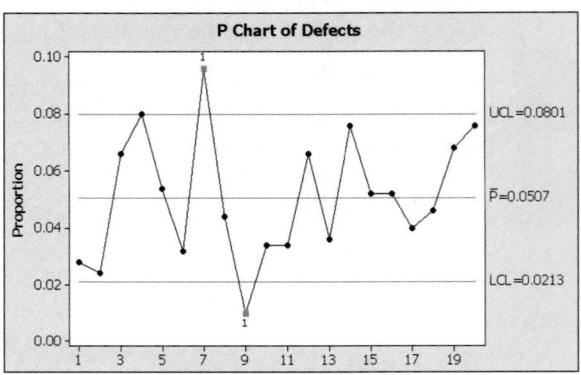

    a. What is the mean percent defective? What are the upper and lower control limits?

    b. Are there any sample observations that indicate the process is out of control? Which sample numbers are they?

    c. Does there seem to be any trend in the process? That is, does the process seem to be getting better, getting worse, or staying the same?

10. Inter State Moving and Storage Company is setting up a control chart to monitor the proportion of residential moves that result in written complaints due to late delivery, lost items, or damaged items. A sample of 50 moves is selected for each of the last 12 months. The number of written complaints in each sample is 8, 7, 4, 8, 2, 7, 11, 6, 7, 6, 8, and 12.

    a. Design a percent defective chart. Insert the mean percent defective, *UCL,* and *LCL.*

    b. Plot the proportion of written complaints in the last 12 months.

    c. Interpret the chart. Does it appear that the number of complaints is out of control for any of the months?

11. A bicycle manufacturer randomly selects 10 frames each day and tests for defects. The number of defective frames found over the last 14 days is 3, 2, 1, 3, 2, 2, 8, 2, 0, 3, 5, 2, 0, and 4. Construct a control chart for this process and comment on whether the process is "in control."

12. Scott Paper tests its toilet paper by subjecting 15 rolls to a wet stress test to see whether and how often the paper tears during the test. Following are the number of defectives found over the last 15 days: 2, 3, 1, 2, 2, 1, 3, 2, 2, 1, 2, 2, 1, 0, and 0. Construct a control chart for the process and comment on whether the process is "in control."

13. Sam's Supermarkets tests its checkout clerks by randomly examining the printout receipts for scanning errors. The following numbers are the number of errors on each receipt for October 27: 0, 1, 1, 0, 0, 1, 1, 0, 1, 1, 0. Construct a control chart for this process and comment on whether the process is "in control."

14. Dave Christi runs a car wash chain with outlets scattered throughout Chicago. He is concerned that some local managers are giving away free washes to their friends. He decides to collect data on the number of "voided" sales receipts. Of course, some of them are legitimate voids. Would the following data indicate a reasonable number of voids at his facilities: 3, 8, 3, 4, 6, 5, 0, 1, 2, 4? Construct a control chart for this process and comment on whether the process is "in control."

Statistics in Action

It was reported during the late 1980s that a Canadian firm ordered some parts from a Japanese company with instructions that there should be "no more than three defective parts per one thousand." When the parts arrived, there was a note attached that said, "Your three defective parts are wrapped separately in the upper left compartment of the shipment." This is a far cry from the days when "Made in Japan" meant cheap but not reliable.

Acceptance Sampling

The previous section was concerned with maintaining the *quality of the product as it is being produced.* In many business situations we are also concerned with the *quality of the incoming finished product.* What do the following cases have in common?

- Sims Software, Inc., purchases DVDs from DVD International. The normal purchase order is for 100,000 DVDs, packaged in lots of 1,000. Todd Sims, president, does not expect each DVD to be perfect. In fact, he has agreed to accept lots of 1,000 with up to 10 percent defective. He would like to develop a plan to inspect incoming lots, to ensure that the quality standard is met. The purpose of the inspection procedure is to separate the acceptable from the unacceptable lots.

- Zenith Electric purchases magnetron tubes from Bono Electronics for use in its new microwave oven. The tubes are shipped to Zenith in lots of 10,000. Zenith allows the incoming lots to contain up to 5 percent defective tubes. It would like to develop a sampling plan to determine which lots meet the criterion and which do not.

- General Motors purchases windshields from many suppliers. GM insists that the windshields be in lots of 1,000, and is willing to accept 50 or fewer defects in each lot, that is, 5 percent defective. They would like to develop a sampling procedure to verify that incoming shipments meet the criterion.

The common thread in these cases is a need to verify that an incoming product meets the stipulated requirements. The situation can be likened to a screen door, which allows the warm summer air to enter the room while keeping the bugs out. Acceptance sampling lets the lots of acceptable quality into the manufacturing area and screens out lots that are not acceptable.

Of course, the situation in modern business is more complex. The buyer wants protection against accepting lots that are below the quality standard. The best protection against inferior quality is 100 percent inspection. Unfortunately, the cost of 100 percent inspection is often prohibitive. Another problem with checking each item is that the test may be destructive. If all lightbulbs were tested until burning out before they were shipped, there would be none left to sell. Also, 100 percent inspection may not lead to the identification of all defects, because boredom might cause a loss of perception on the part of the inspectors. Thus, complete inspection is rarely employed in practical situations.

The usual procedure is to screen the quality of incoming parts by using a statistical sampling plan. According to this plan, a sample of *n* units is randomly selected from the lots of *N* units (the population). This is called **acceptance sampling.** The inspection will determine the number of defects in the sample. This number is compared with a predetermined number called the **critical number** or the **acceptance number.** The acceptance number is usually designated *c*. If the number of defects in the sample of size *n* is less than or equal to *c*, the lot is accepted. If the number of defects exceeds *c*, the lot is rejected and returned to the supplier, or perhaps submitted to 100 percent inspection.

Acceptance sampling is a decision-making process. There are two possible decisions: accept or reject the lot. In addition, there are two situations under which the decision is made: the lot is good or the lot is bad. These are the states of nature. If the lot is good and the sample inspection reveals the lot to be good, or if the lot is bad and the sample inspection indicates it is bad, then a correct decision is made. However, there are two other possibilities. The lot may actually contain more defects than it should, but it is accepted. This is called **consumer's risk.** Similarly, the lot may be within the agreed-upon limits, but it is rejected during the sample inspection. This is called the **producer's risk.** The following summary table for acceptance decisions shows these possibilities. Notice how this discussion is very similar to the ideas of Type I and Type II errors presented in Chapter 10. (See page 352.)

Acceptance sampling

Acceptance number

Consumer's risk

Producer's risk

	States of Nature	
Decision	**Good Lot**	**Bad Lot**
Accept lot	Correct	Consumer's risk
Reject lot	Producer's risk	Correct

OC curve

To evaluate a sampling plan and determine that it is fair to both the producer and the consumer, the usual procedure is to develop an **operating characteristic curve,** or an **OC curve** as it is usually called. An OC curve reports the percent defective along the horizontal axis and the probability of accepting that percent defective along the vertical axis. A smooth curve is usually drawn connecting all the possible levels of quality. The binomial distribution is used to develop the probabilities for an OC curve.

| Example | Sims Software, as mentioned earlier, purchases DVDs from DVD International. The DVDs are packaged in lots of 1,000 each. Todd Sims, president of Sims Software, has agreed to accept lots with 10 percent or fewer defective DVDs. Todd has directed his inspection department to select a random sample of 20 DVDs and examine them carefully. He will accept the lot if it has two or fewer defectives in the sample. Develop an OC curve for this inspection plan. What is the probability of accepting a lot that is 10 percent defective? |

| Solution | This type of sampling is called **attribute sampling** because the sampled item, a DVD in this case, is classified as acceptable or unacceptable. No "reading" or "measurement" is obtained on the DVD. Let π represent the actual proportion defective in the population. |

Attribute sampling

The lot is good if $\pi \leq .10$.
The lot is bad if $\pi > .10$.

Decision rule

Let X be the number of defects in the sample. The decision rule is:

Accept the lot if $X \leq 2$.
Reject the lot if $X \geq 3$.

Here the acceptable lot is one with 10 percent or fewer defective DVDs. If the lot is acceptable when it has exactly 10 percent defectives, it would be even more acceptable if it contained fewer than 10 percent defectives. Hence, it is the usual practice to work with the upper limit of the percent of defectives.

The binomial distribution is used to compute the various values on the OC curve. Recall that for us to use the binomial there are four requirements:

1. There are only two possible outcomes. Here the DVD is either acceptable or unacceptable.
2. There is a fixed number of trials. In this instance the number of trials is the sample size of 20.
3. There is a constant probability of success. A success is finding a defective DVD. The probability of success is assumed to be .10.
4. The trials are independent. The probability of obtaining a defective DVD on the third one selected is not related to the likelihood of finding a defect on the fourth DVD selected.

Appendix B.9 gives various binomial probabilities. However, the tables in Appendix B.9 go up to only 15, that is, $n = 15$. For this problem $n = 20$, so we will use Excel to compute the various binomial probabilities. The following Excel output shows the binomial probabilities for $n = 20$ when π equal to .05, .10, .15, .20, .25, and .30.

We need to convert the terms used in Chapter 6 to acceptance sampling vocabulary. We let π refer to the probability of finding a defect, c the number of defects allowed, and n the number of items sampled. In this case we will allow up to two defects, so $c = 2$. This means that we will allow 0, 1, or 2 of the 20 items sampled to be defective and still accept the incoming shipment of DVDs.

To begin we determine the probability of accepting a lot that is 5 percent defective. This means that $\pi = .05$, $c = 2$, and $n = 20$. From the Excel output, the likelihood of selecting a sample of 20 items from a shipment that contained 5 percent defective and finding exactly 0 defects is .358. The likelihood of finding exactly 1 defect is .377, and finding 2 is .189. Hence the likelihood of 2 or fewer defects is .924, found by .358 + .377 + .189. This result is usually written in shorthand notation as follows (recall that bar "|" means "given that").

$$P(x \leq 2 \mid \pi = .05 \text{ and } n = 20) = .358 + .377 + .189 = .924$$

Excel

	Number of Defects	\multicolumn{6}{c}{Probability}
		0.05	0.10	0.15	0.20	0.25	0.30
6	0	0.358	0.122	0.039	0.012	0.003	0.001
7	1	0.377	0.270	0.137	0.058	0.021	0.007
8	2	0.189	0.285	0.229	0.137	0.067	0.028
9	3	0.060	0.190	0.243	0.205	0.134	0.072
10	4	0.013	0.090	0.182	0.218	0.190	0.130
11	5	0.002	0.032	0.103	0.175	0.202	0.179
12	6	0.000	0.009	0.045	0.109	0.169	0.192
13	7	0.000	0.002	0.016	0.055	0.112	0.164
14	8	0.000	0.000	0.005	0.022	0.061	0.114
15	9	0.000	0.000	0.001	0.007	0.027	0.065
16	10	0.000	0.000	0.000	0.002	0.010	0.031
17	11	0.000	0.000	0.000	0.000	0.003	0.012
18	12	0.000	0.000	0.000	0.000	0.001	0.004
19	13	0.000	0.000	0.000	0.000	0.000	0.001
20	14	0.000	0.000	0.000	0.000	0.000	0.000
21	*	*	*	*	*	*	*
22	20	0.000	0.000	0.000	0.000	0.000	0.000

Continuing, the likelihood of accepting a lot that is actually 10 percent defective is .677. That is:

$$P(x \leq 2 \mid \pi = .10 \text{ and } n = 20) = .122 + .270 + .285 = .677$$

The complete OC curve in Chart 19–8 shows the smoothed curve for all values of π between 0 and about 30 percent. There is no need to show values larger than 30 percent because their probability is very close to 0. The likelihood of accepting lots of selected quality levels is shown in table form on the right-hand side of Chart 19–8. With the OC curve, the management of Sims Software will be able to quickly evaluate the probabilities of various quality levels.

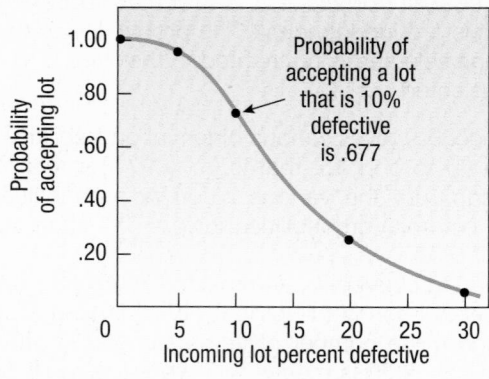

Lot percent defective	Probability of accepting lot
0	1.000
5	.924
10	.677
20	.207
30	.036

CHART 19–8 OC Curve for Sampling Plan ($n = 20$, $c = 2$)

Self-Review 19–4 Compute the probability of accepting a lot of DVDs that is actually 30 percent defective, using the sampling plan for Sims Software.

Exercises

15. Determine the probability of accepting lots that are 10 percent, 20 percent, 30 percent, and 40 percent defective using a sample of size 12 and an acceptance number of 2.
16. Determine the probability of accepting lots that are 10 percent, 20 percent, 30 percent, and 40 percent defective using a sample of size 14 and an acceptance number of 3.
17. Warren Electric manufactures fuses for many customers. To ensure the quality of the out-going product, it tests 10 fuses each hour. If no more than one fuse is defective, it packages the fuses and prepares them for shipment. Develop an OC curve for this sampling plan. Compute the probabilities of accepting lots that are 10 percent, 20 percent, 30 percent, and 40 percent defective. Draw the OC curve for this sampling plan using the four quality levels.
18. Grills Video Products purchases LCDs from Mira Electronics. According to his sampling plan, Art Grills, owner of Grills Video, will accept a shipment of LCDs if three or fewer are defective in a sample of 25. Develop an OC curve for these percents defective: 10 percent, 20 percent, 30 percent, and 40 percent. You will need a statistical software package.

Chapter Summary

I. The objective of statistical quality control is to monitor the quality of the product or service as it is being developed.
II. A Pareto chart is a technique for tallying the number and type of defects that happen within a product or service.
   A. This chart was named after an Italian scientist, Vilfredo Pareto.
   B. The concept of the chart is that 80 percent of the activity is caused by 20 percent of the factors.
III. A fishbone diagram emphasizes the relationship between a possible problem cause that will produce the particular effect.
   A. It is also called a cause-and-effect diagram.
   B. The usual approach is to consider four problem areas: methods, materials, equipment, and personnel.
IV. The purpose of a control chart is to monitor graphically the quality of a product or service.
   A. There are two types of control charts.
      1. A variable control chart is the result of a measurement.
      2. An attribute chart shows whether the product or service is acceptable or not acceptable.
   B. There are two sources of variation in the quality of a product or service.
      1. Chance variation is random in nature and cannot be controlled or eliminated.
      2. Assignable variation is not due to random causes and can be eliminated.
   C. Four control charts were considered in this chapter.
      1. A mean chart shows the mean of a variable, and a range chart shows the range of the variable.
         a. The upper and lower control limits are set at plus or minus 3 standard errors from the mean.
         b. The formulas for the upper and lower control limits for the mean are:

$$UCL = \overline{\overline{X}} + A_2\overline{R} \qquad LCL = \overline{\overline{X}} - A_2\overline{R} \qquad\qquad \text{[19–4]}$$

         c. The formulas for the upper and lower control limits for the range are:

$$UCL = D_4\overline{R} \qquad LCL = D_3\overline{R} \qquad\qquad \text{[19–5]}$$

      2. A percent defective chart is an attribute chart that shows the proportion of the product or service that does not conform to the standard.
         a. The mean percent defective is found by

$$p = \frac{\text{Total number defective}}{\text{Total number of items sampled}} \qquad\qquad \text{[19–6]}$$

         b. The control limits for the proportion defective are determined from the equation

$$LCL, UCL = p \pm 3\sqrt{\frac{p(1-p)}{n}} \qquad\qquad \text{[19–8]}$$

3. A *c*-bar chart refers to the number of defects per unit.
   a. It is based on the Poisson distribution.
   b. The mean number of defects per unit is $\bar{c}$.
   c. The control limits are determined from the following equation.

$$LCL, UCL = \bar{c} \pm 3\sqrt{\bar{c}} \qquad \text{[19–9]}$$

V. Acceptance sampling is a method to determine whether an incoming lot of a product meets specified standards.
   A. It is based on random sampling techniques.
   B. A random sample of *n* units is selected from a population of *N* units.
   C. *c* is the maximum number of defective units that may be found in the sample of *n* and the lot still considered acceptable.
   D. An OC (operating characteristic) curve is developed using the binomial probability distribution to determine the probability of accepting lots of various quality levels.

Pronunciation Key

SYMBOL	MEANING	PRONUNCIATION
$\bar{\bar{X}}$	Mean of the sample means	X double bar
$s_{\bar{X}}$	Standard error of the mean	s sub X bar
A_2	Constant used to determine the upper and lower control limit for the mean	A sub 2
$\bar{R}$	Mean of the sample ranges	R bar
D_4	Constant used to determine the upper control limit for the range	D sub 4
$\bar{c}$	Mean number of defects per unit	c bar

Chapter Exercises

connect

19. The production supervisor at Westburg Electric, Inc., noted an increase in the number of electric motors rejected at the time of final inspection. Of the last 200 motors rejected, 80 of the defects were due to poor wiring, 60 contained a short in the coil, 50 involved a defective plug, and 10 involved other defects. Develop a Pareto chart to show the major problem areas.

20. The manufacturer of running shoes conducted a study on its newly developed jogging shoe. Listed below are the type and frequency of the nonconformities and failures found. Develop a Pareto chart to show the major problem areas.

Type of Nonconformity	Frequency	Type of Nonconformity	Frequency
Sole separation	34	Lace breakage	14
Heel separation	98	Eyelet failure	10
Sole penetration	62	Other	16

21. Wendy's fills its soft drinks with an automatic machine whose operation is based on the weight of the soft drink. When the process is in control, the machine fills each cup so that the grand mean is 10.0 ounces and the mean range is 0.25 for samples of 5.
    a. Determine the upper and lower control limits for the process for both the mean and the range.
    b. The manager of the I-280 store tested five soft drinks served last hour and found that the mean was 10.16 ounces and the range was 0.35 ounces. Is the process in control? Should other action be taken?

22. A new machine has just been installed to cut and rough-shape large slugs. The slugs are then transferred to a precision grinder. One of the critical measurements is the outside diameter. The quality control inspector randomly selected five slugs each half-hour, measured the outside diameter, and recorded the results. The measurements (in millimeters) for the period 8:00 A.M. to 10:30 A.M. follow.

	Outside Diameter (millimeters)				
Time	1	2	3	4	5
8:00	87.1	87.3	87.9	87.0	87.0
8:30	86.9	88.5	87.6	87.5	87.4
9:00	87.5	88.4	86.9	87.6	88.2
9:30	86.0	88.0	87.2	87.6	87.1
10:00	87.1	87.1	87.1	87.1	87.1
10:30	88.0	86.2	87.4	87.3	87.8

a. Determine the control limits for the mean and the range.
b. Plot the control limits for the mean outside diameter and the range.
c. Are there any points on the mean or the range chart that are out of control? Comment on the chart.

23. Long Last Tire Company, as part of its inspection process, tests its tires for tread wear under simulated road conditions. Twenty samples of three tires each were selected from different shifts over the last month of operation. The tread wear is reported below in hundredths of an inch.

Sample	Tread Wear			Sample	Tread Wear		
1	44	41	19	11	11	33	34
2	39	31	21	12	51	34	39
3	38	16	25	13	30	16	30
4	20	33	26	14	22	21	35
5	34	33	36	15	11	28	38
6	28	23	39	16	49	25	36
7	40	15	34	17	20	31	33
8	36	36	34	18	26	18	36
9	32	29	30	19	26	47	26
10	29	38	34	20	34	29	32

a. Determine the control limits for the mean and the range.
b. Plot the control limits for the mean tread wear and the range.
c. Are there any points on the mean or the range chart that are "out of control"? Comment on the chart.

24. Charter National Bank has a staff of loan officers located in its branch offices throughout the Southwest. Robert Kerns, vice president of consumer lending, would like some information on the typical amount of loans and the range in the amount of the loans. A staff analyst of the vice president selected a sample of 10 loan officers and from each officer selected a sample of five loans he or she made last month. The data are reported below. Develop a control chart for the mean and the range. Do any of the officers appear to be "out of control"? Comment on your findings.

Officer	Loan Amount ($000)					Officer	Loan Amount ($000)				
	1	2	3	4	5		1	2	3	4	5
Weinraub	59	74	53	48	65	Bowyer	66	80	54	68	52
Visser	42	51	70	47	67	Kuhlman	74	43	45	65	49
Moore	52	42	53	87	85	Ludwig	75	53	68	50	31
Brunner	36	70	62	44	79	Longnecker	42	65	70	41	52
Wolf	34	59	39	78	61	Simonetti	43	38	10	19	47

25. The producer of a candy bar, called the "A Rod" Bar, reports on the package that the calorie content is 420 per 2-ounce bar. A sample of 5 bars from each of the last 10 days is sent for a chemical analysis of the calorie content. The results are shown below. Does it appear that there are any days where the calorie count is out of control? Develop an appropriate control chart and analyze your findings.

Sample	Calorie Count 1	2	3	4	5	Sample	Calorie Count 1	2	3	4	5
1	426	406	418	431	432	6	427	417	408	418	422
2	421	422	415	412	411	7	422	417	426	435	426
3	425	420	406	409	414	8	419	417	412	415	417
4	424	419	402	400	417	9	417	432	417	416	422
5	421	408	423	410	421	10	420	422	421	415	422

26. Early Morning Delivery Service guarantees delivery of small packages by 10:30 A.M. Of course, some of the packages are not delivered by 10:30 A.M. For a sample of 200 packages delivered each of the last 15 working days, the following number of packages were delivered after the deadline: 9, 14, 2, 13, 9, 5, 9, 3, 4, 3, 4, 3, 3, 8, and 4.
   a. Determine the mean proportion of packages delivered after 10:30 A.M.
   b. Determine the control limits for the proportion of packages delivered after 10:30 A.M. Were any of the sampled days out of control?
   c. If 10 packages out of 200 in the sample were delivered after 10:30 A.M. today, is this sample within the control limits?

27. An automatic machine produces 5.0-millimeter bolts at a high rate of speed. A quality control program has been initiated to control the number of defectives. The quality control inspector selects 50 bolts at random and determines how many are defective. The number of defectives in the first 10 samples is 3, 5, 0, 4, 1, 2, 6, 5, 7, and 7.
   a. Design a percent defective chart. Insert the mean percent defective, *UCL,* and *LCL.*
   b. Plot the percent defective for the first 10 samples on the chart.
   c. Interpret the chart.

28. Steele Breakfast Foods, Inc., produces a popular brand of raisin bran cereal. The package indicates it contains 25.0 ounces of cereal. To ensure the product quality, the Steele inspection department makes hourly checks on the production process. As a part of the hourly check, 4 boxes are selected and their contents weighed. The results are reported below.

Sample	Weights				Sample	Weights			
1	26.1	24.4	25.6	25.2	14	23.1	23.3	24.4	24.7
2	25.2	25.9	25.1	24.8	15	24.6	25.1	24.0	25.3
3	25.6	24.5	25.7	25.1	16	24.4	24.4	22.8	23.4
4	25.5	26.8	25.1	25.0	17	25.1	24.1	23.9	26.2
5	25.2	25.2	26.3	25.7	18	24.5	24.5	26.0	26.2
6	26.6	24.1	25.5	24.0	19	25.3	27.5	24.3	25.5
7	27.6	26.0	24.9	25.3	20	24.6	25.3	25.5	24.3
8	24.5	23.1	23.9	24.7	21	24.9	24.4	25.4	24.8
9	24.1	25.0	23.5	24.9	22	25.7	24.6	26.8	26.9
10	25.8	25.7	24.3	27.3	23	24.8	24.3	25.0	27.2
11	22.5	23.0	23.7	24.0	24	25.4	25.9	26.6	24.8
12	24.5	24.8	23.2	24.2	25	26.2	23.5	23.7	25.0
13	24.4	24.5	25.9	25.5					

Develop an appropriate control chart. What are the limits? Is the process out of control at any time?

29. An investor believes there is a 50–50 chance that a stock will increase or decrease on a particular day. To investigate this idea, for 30 consecutive trading days the investor selects a random sample of 50 stocks and counts the number that increase. The number of stocks in the sample that increased is reported below.

14	12	13	17	10	18	10	13	13	14
13	10	12	11	9	13	14	11	12	11
15	13	10	16	10	11	12	15	13	10

Develop a percent defective chart and write a brief report summarizing your findings. Based on these sample results, is it reasonable that the odds are 50–50 that a stock will increase? What percent of the stocks would need to increase in a day for the process to be "out of control"?

30. Lahey Motors specializes in selling cars to buyers with a poor credit history. Listed below is the number of cars that were repossessed from Lahey customers because they did not meet the payment obligations over each of the last 36 months.

6	5	8	20	11	10	9	3	9	9
15	12	4	11	9	9	6	18	6	8
9	7	13	7	11	8	11	13	6	14
13	5	5	8	10	11				

Develop a *c*-bar chart for the number repossessed. Were there any months when the number was out of control? Write a brief report summarizing your findings.

31. A process engineer is considering two sampling plans. In the first a sample of 10 will be selected and the lot accepted if 3 or fewer are found defective. In the second the sample size is 20 and the acceptance number is 5. Develop an OC curve for each. Compare the probability of acceptance for lots that are 5, 10, 20, and 30 percent defective. Which of the plans would you recommend if you were the supplier?

32. Christina Sanders is a member of the women's basketball team at Windy City College. Last season she made 55 percent of her free throw attempts. In an effort to improve this statistic, she attended a summer camp devoted to foul-shooting techniques. The next 20 days she shot 100 foul shots a day. She carefully recorded the number of attempts made each day. The results are reported below.

55	61	52	59	67	57	61	59	69	58
57	66	63	63	63	65	63	68	64	67

To interpret, the first day she made 55 out of 100, or 55 percent. The last day she made 67 out of 100 or 67 percent.

a. Develop a control chart for the proportion of shots made. Over the 20 days of practice, what percent of attempts did she make? What are the upper and lower control limits for the proportion of shots made?

b. Is there any trend in her proportion made? Does she seem to be improving, staying the same, or getting worse?

c. Find the percent of attempts made for the last five days of practice. Use the hypothesis testing procedure, formula (10–4), to determine if there is an improvement from 55 percent.

33. Eric's Cookie House sells chocolate chip cookies in shopping malls. Of concern is the number of chocolate chips in each cookie. Eric, the owner and president, would like to establish a control chart for the number of chocolate chips per cookie. He selects a sample of 15 cookies from today's production and counts the number of chocolate chips in each. The results are as follows: 6, 8, 20, 12, 20, 19, 11, 23, 12, 14, 15, 16, 12, 13, and 12.

a. Determine the centerline and the control limits.

b. Develop a control chart and plot the number of chocolate chips per cookie.

c. Interpret the chart. Does it appear that the number of chocolate chips is out of control in any of the cookies sampled?

34. The number of "near misses" recorded for the last 20 months at Lima International Airport is 3, 2, 3, 2, 2, 3, 5, 1, 2, 2, 4, 4, 2, 6, 3, 5, 2, 5, 1, and 3. Develop an appropriate control chart. Determine the mean number of misses per month and the limits on the number of misses per month. Are there any months where the number of near misses is out of control?

35. The following number of robberies was reported during the last 10 days to the robbery division of the Metro City Police: 10, 8, 8, 7, 8, 5, 8, 5, 4, and 7. Develop an appropriate control chart. Determine the mean number of robberies reported per day and determine the control limits. Are there any days when the number of robberies reported is out of control?

36. Seiko purchases watch stems for its watches in lots of 10,000. Seiko's sampling plan calls for checking 20 stems, and if 3 or fewer stems are defective, the lot is accepted.

a. Based on the sampling plan, what is the probability that a lot of 40 percent defective will be accepted?

b. Design an OC curve for incoming lots that have zero, 10 percent, 20 percent, 30 percent, and 40 percent defective stems.

37. Automatic Screen Door Manufacturing Company purchases door latches from a number of vendors. The purchasing department is responsible for inspecting the incoming latches. Automatic purchases 10,000 door latches per month and inspects 20 latches selected at random. Develop an OC curve for the sampling plan if three latches can be defective and the incoming lot is still accepted.

38. At the beginning of each football season Team Sports, the local sporting goods store, purchases 5,000 footballs. A sample of 25 balls is selected, and they are inflated, tested, and then deflated. If more than two balls are found defective, the lot of 5,000 is returned to the manufacturer. Develop an OC curve for this sampling plan.

    a. What are the probabilities of accepting lots that are 10 percent, 20 percent, and 30 percent defective?

    b. Estimate the probability of accepting a lot that is 15 percent defective.

    c. John Brennen, owner of Team Sports, would like the probability of accepting a lot that is 5 percent defective to be more than 90 percent. Does this appear to be the case with this sampling plan?

Software Commands

1. The MINITAB commands for the Pareto chart on page 710 are:

    a. Enter the reasons for water usage in column C1 and the gallons used in C2. Give the columns appropriate names.

    b. Click on **Stat, Quality Tools, Pareto Chart,** and then hit **Enter.**

    c. Select **Chart defects table,** indicate the location of the labels and frequencies, click on **Options** and type a chart title, and click **OK.**

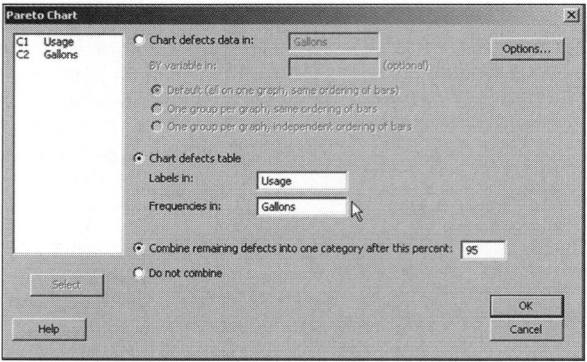

2. The MINITAB commands for the *X*-bar and *R* charts on page 717 are:

    a. Enter the information in Table 19–1 or from the CD. The file name is Table 19-1.

    b. Click on **Stat, Control Charts, Variables Charts for Subgroups, Xbar-R,** and hit **Enter.**

    c. Select **all observations for a chart are in one column.** Then in the box below, select the variable **minutes.**

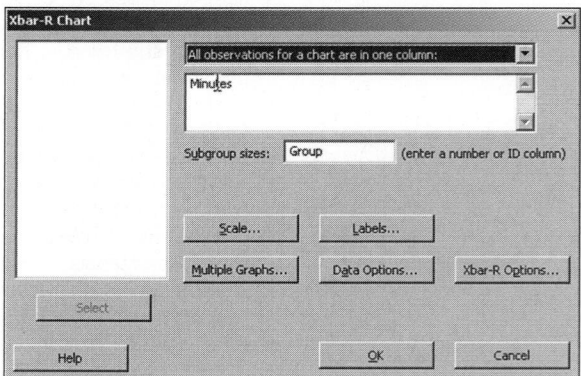

3. The MINITAB commands for the percent defective chart on page 722 are:

    a. Enter the data on the number of defects from page 721.

    b. Click on **Stat, Control Charts, Attribute Charts, P,** and hit **Enter.**

    c. Under **Variable,** select *Defects,* then enter *50* for **Subgroup sizes.** Click on **Labels,** type in the title, and click **OK** twice.

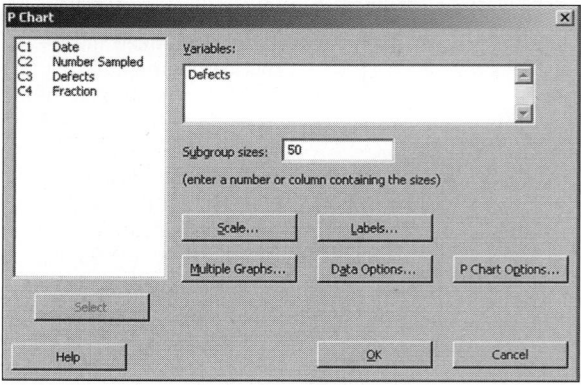

4. The MINITAB commands for the *c*-bar chart on page 724 are:

a. Enter the data on the number of misspelled words from page 723.

b. Click on **Stat, Control Charts, Attribute Charts, C,** and hit **Enter.**

c. Select the **Variable** indicating the number of misspelled words, then click on **Labels** and type the title in the space provided, and click **OK** twice.

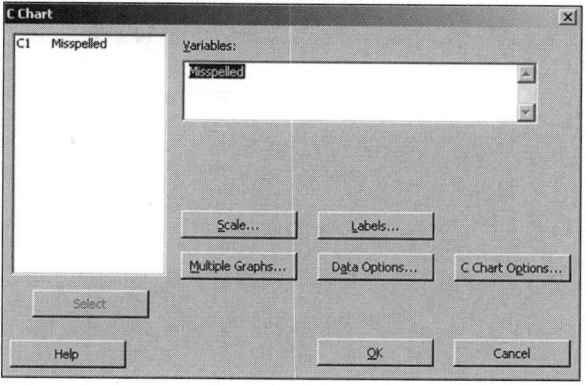

Chapter 19   Answers to Self-Review

19–1

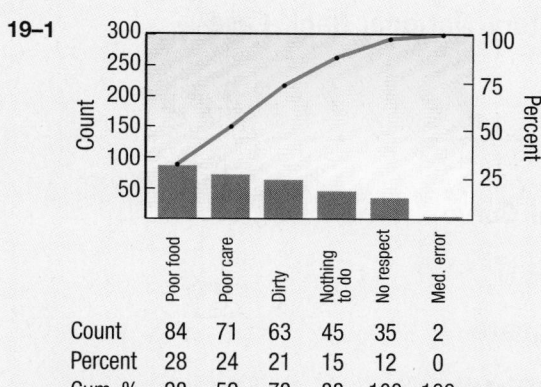

	Poor food	Poor care	Dirty	Nothing to do	No respect	Med. error
Count	84	71	63	45	35	2
Percent	28	24	21	15	12	0
Cum. %	28	52	73	88	100	100

Seventy-three percent of the complaints involve poor food, poor care, or dirty conditions. These are the factors the administrator should address.

19–2 a.

Sample Times						
1	2	3	4	**Total**	**Average**	**Range**
1	4	5	2	12	3	4
2	3	2	1	8	2	2
1	7	3	5	16	4	6
					9	12

$$\bar{\bar{X}} = \frac{9}{3} = 3 \qquad \bar{R} = \frac{12}{3} = 4$$

$$UCL \text{ and } LCL = \bar{\bar{X}} \pm A_2\bar{R}$$

$$= 3 \pm 0.729(4)$$

$$UCL = 5.916 \qquad LCL = 0.084$$

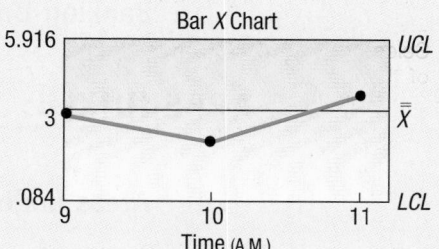

$$LCL = D_3\bar{R} = 0(4) = 0$$

$$UCL = D_4\bar{R} = 2.282(4) = 9.128$$

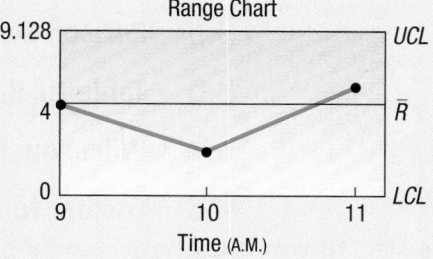

b. Yes. Both the mean chart and the range chart indicate that the process is in control.

19–3 $\bar{c} = \dfrac{25}{12} = 2.083$

$$UCL = 2.083 + 3\sqrt{2.083} = 6.413$$

$$LCL = 2.083 - 3\sqrt{2.083} = -2.247$$

Because *LCL* is a negative value, we set *LCL* = 0. The shift with 7 defects is out of control.

19–4 $P(X \le 2|\pi = .30 \text{ and } n = 20) = .036$

Appendixes

Appendix A: Data Sets

A.1 Data Set 1—Real Estate

Variables

x_1 = Selling price in $000
x_2 = Number of bedrooms
x_3 = Size of the home in square feet
x_4 = Pool (1 = yes, 0 = no)
x_5 = Distance from the center of the city in miles
x_6 = Township
x_7 = Garage attached (1 = yes, 0 = no)
x_8 = Number of bathrooms
105 homes sold

x_1	x_2	x_3	x_4	x_5	x_6	x_7	x_8
263.1	4	2,300	1	17	5	1	2.0
182.4	4	2,100	0	19	4	0	2.0
242.1	3	2,300	0	12	3	0	2.0
213.6	2	2,200	0	16	2	0	2.5
139.9	2	2,100	0	28	1	0	1.5
245.4	2	2,100	1	12	1	1	2.0
327.2	6	2,500	0	15	3	1	2.0
271.8	2	2,100	0	9	2	1	2.5
221.1	3	2,300	1	18	1	0	1.5
266.6	4	2,400	0	13	4	1	2.0
292.4	4	2,100	0	14	3	1	2.0
209.0	2	1,700	0	8	4	1	1.5
270.8	6	2,500	0	7	4	1	2.0
246.1	4	2,100	0	18	3	1	2.0
194.4	2	2,300	0	11	3	0	2.0
281.3	3	2,100	0	16	2	1	2.0
172.7	4	2,200	1	16	3	0	2.0
207.5	5	2,300	1	21	4	0	2.5
198.9	3	2,200	1	10	4	1	2.0
209.3	6	1,900	1	15	4	1	2.0
252.3	4	2,600	0	8	4	1	2.0
192.9	4	1,900	1	14	2	1	2.5
209.3	5	2,100	0	20	5	0	1.5
345.3	8	2,600	0	9	4	1	2.0
326.3	6	2,100	0	11	5	1	3.0
173.1	2	2,200	1	21	5	1	1.5
187.0	2	1,900	0	26	4	0	2.0
257.2	2	2,100	0	9	4	1	2.0
233.0	3	2,200	0	14	3	1	1.5
180.4	2	2,000	0	11	5	0	2.0
234.0	2	1,700	0	19	3	1	2.0
207.1	2	2,000	0	11	5	1	2.0
247.7	5	2,400	0	16	2	1	2.0
166.2	3	2,000	1	16	2	1	2.0
177.1	2	1,900	0	10	5	1	2.0

(continued)

Appendix A

A.1 Data Set 1—Real Estate (*continued*)

x_1	x_2	x_3	x_4	x_5	x_6	x_7	x_8
182.7	4	2,000	1	14	4	0	2.5
216.0	4	2,300	0	19	2	0	2.0
312.1	6	2,600	0	7	5	1	2.5
199.8	3	2,100	0	19	3	1	2.0
273.2	5	2,200	0	16	2	1	3.0
206.0	3	2,100	1	9	3	0	1.5
232.2	3	1,900	1	16	1	1	1.5
198.3	4	2,100	1	19	1	1	1.5
205.1	3	2,000	1	20	4	0	2.0
175.6	4	2,300	1	24	4	1	2.0
307.8	3	2,400	1	21	2	1	3.0
269.2	5	2,200	0	8	5	1	3.0
224.8	3	2,200	0	17	1	1	2.5
171.6	3	2,000	1	16	4	0	2.0
216.8	3	2,200	0	15	1	1	2.0
192.6	6	2,200	1	14	1	0	2.0
236.4	5	2,200	0	20	3	1	2.0
172.4	3	2,200	0	23	3	0	2.0
251.4	3	1,900	0	12	2	1	2.0
246.0	6	2,300	0	7	3	1	3.0
147.4	6	1,700	1	12	1	0	2.0
176.0	4	2,200	0	15	1	1	2.0
228.4	3	2,300	0	17	5	1	1.5
166.5	3	1,600	1	19	3	0	2.5
189.4	4	2,200	0	24	1	1	2.0
312.1	7	2,400	0	13	3	1	3.0
289.8	6	2,000	0	21	3	1	3.0
269.9	5	2,200	1	11	4	1	2.5
154.3	2	2,000	0	13	2	0	2.0
222.1	2	2,100	0	9	5	1	2.0
209.7	5	2,200	1	13	2	1	2.0
190.9	3	2,200	1	18	3	1	2.0
254.3	4	2,500	1	15	3	1	2.0
207.5	3	2,100	1	10	2	0	2.0
209.7	4	2,200	1	19	2	1	2.0
294.0	2	2,100	0	13	2	1	2.5
176.3	2	2,000	1	17	3	0	2.0
294.3	7	2,400	0	8	4	1	2.0
224.0	3	1,900	1	6	1	1	2.0
125.0	2	1,900	0	18	4	0	1.5
236.8	4	2,600	1	17	5	1	2.0
164.1	4	2,300	0	19	4	0	2.0
217.8	3	2,500	0	12	3	0	2.0
192.2	2	2,400	0	16	2	0	2.5
125.9	2	2,400	0	28	1	0	1.5

A.1 Data Set 1—Real Estate (*concluded*)

X_1	X_2	X_3	X_4	X_5	X_6	X_7	X_8
220.9	2	2,300	1	12	1	1	2.0
294.5	6	2,700	0	15	3	1	2.0
244.6	2	2,300	0	9	2	1	2.5
199.0	3	2,500	1	18	1	0	1.5
240.0	4	2,600	0	13	4	1	2.0
263.2	4	2,300	0	14	3	1	2.0
188.1	2	1,900	0	8	4	1	1.5
243.7	6	2,700	0	7	4	1	2.0
221.5	4	2,300	0	18	3	1	2.0
175.0	2	2,500	0	11	3	0	2.0
253.2	3	2,300	0	16	2	1	2.0
155.4	4	2,400	1	16	3	0	2.0
186.7	5	2,500	1	21	4	0	2.5
179.0	3	2,400	1	10	4	1	2.0
188.3	6	2,100	1	15	4	1	2.0
227.1	4	2,900	0	8	4	1	2.0
173.6	4	2,100	1	14	2	1	2.5
188.3	5	2,300	0	20	5	0	1.5
310.8	8	2,900	0	9	4	1	2.0
293.7	6	2,400	0	11	5	1	3.0
179.0	3	2,400	0	8	4	1	2.0
188.3	6	2,100	1	14	2	1	2.5
227.1	4	2,900	0	20	5	0	1.5
173.6	4	2,100	0	9	4	1	2.0
188.3	5	2,300	0	11	5	1	3.0

Appendix A

A.2 Data Set 2—Major League Baseball (2007)

Variables

x_1 = Team
x_2 = League (American = 1, National = 0)
x_3 = Built (year stadium was built)
x_4 = Size (stadium capacity)
x_5 = Surface (natural = 0, artificial = 1)
x_6 = Salary (total 2007 team salary $ Mil)
x_7 = Wins
x_8 = Attendance (total for team in Mil)
x_9 = Batting
x_{10} = ERA (earned run average)
x_{11} = HR (home runs)
x_{12} = Errors
x_{13} = SB (stolen bases)
x_{14} = Year
x_{15} = Average player salary ($)

Team, x_1	League, x_2	Built, x_3	Size, x_4	Surface, x_5	Salary, x_6	Wins, x_7	Attendance, x_8	Batting, x_9	ERA, x_{10}	HR, x_{11}	Errors, x_{12}	SB, x_{13}	Year, x_{14}	Average Player Salary, x_{15}
Baltimore	1	1992	48,262	0	93.6	69	2.16	0.272	5.17	142	79	144	1989	$ 512,930
Boston	1	1912	33,871	0	143	96	2.97	0.279	3.87	166	81	96	1990	578,930
Chicago	1	1991	44,321	0	108.7	72	2.68	0.246	4.77	190	108	78	1991	891,188
Cleveland	1	1994	43,368	0	61.7	96	2.28	0.268	4.05	178	92	72	1992	1,084,408
Detroit	1	2000	40,000	0	95.2	88	3.05	0.287	4.57	177	99	103	1993	1,120,254
Kansas City	1	1973	40,529	0	67.1	69	1.62	0.261	4.48	102	106	78	1994	1,188,679
Los Angeles Angels	1	1966	45,050	0	103.9	94	3.37	0.284	4.23	123	101	139	1995	1,071,029
Minnesota	1	1982	48,678	1	71.4	79	2.30	0.264	4.15	118	95	112	1996	1,176,967
New York	1	1923	57,746	0	189.6	94	4.27	0.290	4.49	201	88	123	1997	1,383,578
Oakland	1	1966	43,662	0	79.4	76	1.92	0.256	4.28	171	90	52	1998	1,441,406
Seattle	1	1999	45,611	0	106.5	88	2.67	0.287	4.73	153	90	81	1999	1,720,050
Tampa Bay	1	1990	44,027	1	24.1	66	1.39	0.268	5.53	187	117	131	2000	1,988,034
Texas	1	1994	52,000	0	68.3	75	2.35	0.263	4.75	179	124	88	2001	2,264,403
Toronto	1	1989	50,516	1	89.1	83	2.36	0.259	4	165	102	57	2002	2,383,235
Arizona	0	1998	49,075	0	66.2	90	2.32	0.25	3.54	171	106	109	2003	2,555,476
Atlanta	0	1993	50,062	0	87.3	84	2.75	0.275	3.46	176	107	64	2004	2,486,609
Chicago Cubs	0	1914	38,957	0	99.7	85	3.25	0.271	3.73	151	94	86	2005	2,632,655
Cincinnati	0	2003	42,059	0	68.9	72	2.06	0.267	4.56	204	95	97	2006	2,866,544
Colorado	0	1995	50,381	0	54.4	90	2.38	0.28	4.57	171	68	100	2007	2,944,556
Florida	0	1987	42,531	0	30.5	71	1.37	0.267	4.23	201	137	105	2008	3,154,845
Houston	0	2000	42,000	0	87.8	73	3.02	0.26	4.35	167	103	65		
Los Angeles Dodgers	0	1962	56,000	0	108.5	82	3.86	0.275	4.05	129	114	137		
Milwaukee	0	2001	42,400	0	71	83	2.87	0.262	4.56	231	109	96		
New York Mets	0	1964	55,775	0	115.2	88	3.85	0.275	4.1	177	101	200		
Philadelphia	0	2004	43,500	0	89.4	89	3.11	0.274	3.94	213	89	138		
Pittsburgh	0	2001	38,127	0	38.5	68	1.75	0.263	4.94	148	83	68		
San Diego	0	2004	42,445	0	58.1	89	2.79	0.251	4.4	171	92	55		
San Francisco	0	2000	40,800	0	90.2	71	3.22	0.254	4.4	131	88	119		
St. Louis	0	2006	46,861	0	90.3	78	3.55	0.274	3.95	141	121	56		
Washington	0	1961	56,000	0	37.3	73	1.96	0.256	4.5	123	109	69		

Appendix A

A.3 Data Set 3—Wages and Wage Earners

Variables

x_1 = Annual wage in dollars
x_2 = Industry (1 = manufacturing, 2 = construction, 0 = other)
x_3 = Occupation (1 = management, 2 = sales, 3 = clerical, 4 = service, 5 = professional, 0 = other)
x_4 = Years of education
x_5 = Southern resident (1 = yes, 0 = no)
x_6 = Nonwhite (1 = yes, 0 = no)
x_7 = Hispanic (1 = yes, 0 = no)
x_8 = Female (1 = yes, 0 = no)
x_9 = Years of work experience
x_{10} = Married (1 = yes, 0 = no)
x_{11} = Age in years
x_{12} = Union member (1 = yes, 0 = no)
100 observations

Row	Wage, x_1	Industry, x_2	Occupation, x_3	Education, x_4	South, x_5	Nonwhite, x_6	Hispanic, x_7	Female, x_8	Experience, x_9	Married, x_{10}	Age, x_{11}	Union, x_{12}
1	19,388	1	0	6	1	0	0	0	45	1	57	0
2	49,898	2	0	12	0	0	0	0	33	1	51	1
3	28,219	0	3	12	1	0	0	0	12	1	30	0
4	83,601	0	5	17	0	0	1	0	18	1	41	0
5	29,736	0	4	8	0	0	1	0	47	1	61	1
6	50,235	1	0	16	0	0	0	0	12	1	34	0
7	45,976	0	2	12	0	0	0	0	43	1	61	1
8	33,411	1	2	12	1	0	0	0	20	1	38	0
9	21,716	0	5	12	0	0	0	1	11	0	29	0
10	37,664	0	5	18	0	0	0	0	19	1	43	0
11	26,820	0	5	18	0	0	0	0	33	0	57	1
12	29,977	0	4	16	0	1	0	1	6	1	28	0
13	33,959	0	5	17	0	0	0	1	26	1	49	1
14	11,780	0	2	11	0	0	0	1	33	1	50	0
15	10,997	0	4	14	0	1	0	0	0	0	20	0
16	17,626	0	3	12	0	0	0	1	45	1	63	0
17	22,133	0	5	16	0	0	0	1	10	0	32	1
18	21,994	0	1	12	0	0	0	1	24	1	42	0
19	29,390	0	0	13	0	0	0	0	18	1	37	0
20	32,138	0	4	14	0	0	0	0	22	1	42	1
21	30,006	1	3	16	0	0	0	1	27	1	49	0
22	68,573	0	5	16	1	0	0	0	14	1	36	1
23	17,694	0	4	8	0	0	0	1	38	1	52	0
24	26,795	0	0	7	1	0	0	0	44	1	57	0
25	19,981	0	4	4	0	0	0	0	54	1	64	0
26	14,476	0	5	12	0	0	0	1	3	1	21	0
27	19,452	0	4	13	0	1	0	0	3	0	22	0
28	28,168	1	0	13	0	0	0	0	17	0	36	0
29	19,306	0	5	9	1	1	0	1	34	1	49	1
30	13,318	1	0	11	1	0	0	1	25	1	42	1

A.3 Data Set 3—Wages and Wage Earners (*continued*)

Row	Wage, x_1	Industry, x_2	Occupation, x_3	Education, x_4	South, x_5	Nonwhite, x_6	Hispanic, x_7	Female, x_8	Experience, x_9	Married, x_{10}	Age, x_{11}	Union, x_{12}
31	25,166	0	4	12	0	0	0	1	10	0	28	0
32	18,121	1	3	12	0	0	0	1	18	1	36	0
33	13,162	1	0	12	0	1	0	0	6	0	24	1
34	32,094	0	3	12	1	0	0	1	14	1	32	0
35	16,667	0	3	12	1	0	0	0	4	0	22	0
36	50,171	0	5	12	0	0	0	0	39	1	57	1
37	31,691	1	0	12	0	0	0	0	13	0	31	0
38	36,178	0	3	12	0	0	0	1	40	1	58	0
39	15,234	0	1	12	1	0	1	1	4	0	22	0
40	16,817	0	3	12	1	0	0	1	26	0	44	0
41	22,485	0	3	12	0	0	0	0	22	0	40	0
42	30,308	0	4	12	0	0	0	0	10	1	28	0
43	11,702	0	2	14	1	0	0	1	6	1	26	0
44	11,186	0	0	12	0	0	0	0	0	0	18	0
45	12,285	0	1	12	0	0	0	1	42	1	60	0
46	19,284	1	4	16	0	0	0	0	3	0	25	0
47	11,451	1	0	12	0	0	0	1	8	1	26	0
48	57,623	0	1	15	0	0	0	0	31	1	52	0
49	25,670	0	3	13	0	0	0	1	8	0	27	1
50	83,443	0	5	17	0	0	0	1	5	0	28	0
51	49,974	1	1	16	0	1	0	0	26	1	48	1
52	46,646	2	0	5	1	0	0	0	44	1	55	0
53	31,702	0	3	12	1	0	0	1	39	1	57	0
54	13,312	0	4	12	1	0	0	1	9	1	27	0
55	44,543	0	2	18	0	0	0	0	10	1	34	0
56	15,013	0	4	16	0	0	0	0	21	1	43	0
57	33,389	0	1	14	0	1	0	0	22	0	42	0
58	60,626	0	5	18	0	0	0	0	7	1	31	0
59	24,509	0	5	14	0	0	1	1	15	0	35	0
60	20,852	1	0	12	0	0	0	1	38	1	56	0
61	30,133	2	0	10	0	0	0	0	27	1	43	0
62	31,799	0	3	12	0	0	0	1	25	0	43	0
63	16,796	0	4	12	0	0	0	1	14	1	32	0
64	20,793	0	0	12	1	0	0	1	6	0	24	0
65	29,407	0	4	10	1	0	0	0	19	0	35	0
66	29,191	0	0	12	0	0	0	0	9	0	27	0
67	15,957	0	2	12	1	0	0	1	10	0	28	0
68	34,484	0	3	13	1	0	0	1	28	0	47	0
69	35,185	1	3	14	0	0	0	1	12	1	32	0
70	26,614	1	0	12	0	0	0	1	19	1	37	0
71	41,780	0	0	12	1	0	0	0	9	1	27	0
72	55,777	0	1	14	1	0	0	0	21	1	41	0
73	15,160	0	4	8	1	0	0	1	45	0	59	0
74	66,738	0	0	9	1	0	0	0	29	1	44	0
75	33,351	0	5	16	1	0	0	1	4	1	26	0

(continued)

Appendix A

A.3 Data Set 3—Wages and Wage Earners (*concluded*)

Row	Wage, x_1	Industry, x_2	Occupation, x_3	Education, x_4	South, x_5	Nonwhite, x_6	Hispanic, x_7	Female, x_8	Experience, x_9	Married, x_{10}	Age, x_{11}	Union, x_{12}
76	33,498	0	1	10	0	0	0	0	20	1	36	0
77	29,809	0	4	8	0	1	0	1	29	0	43	0
78	15,193	1	0	12	0	0	0	1	15	0	33	0
79	23,027	0	4	14	0	1	0	0	34	1	54	1
80	75,165	0	1	15	0	0	0	0	12	1	33	0
81	18,752	0	4	11	0	0	0	1	45	0	62	1
82	83,569	0	1	18	0	0	0	0	29	1	53	0
83	32,235	0	3	12	0	0	0	1	38	1	56	0
84	20,852	0	0	12	1	0	0	0	1	0	19	0
85	13,787	0	4	11	0	0	0	0	4	1	21	0
86	34,746	0	3	14	1	0	0	1	15	1	35	0
87	17,690	0	1	12	1	1	0	0	14	1	32	0
88	52,762	0	5	18	0	0	0	0	7	1	31	0
89	60,152	0	5	16	1	0	0	0	38	1	60	0
90	33,461	0	1	16	0	0	1	0	7	1	29	1
91	13,481	0	4	12	1	0	1	0	7	0	25	0
92	9,879	0	3	12	1	0	0	1	28	1	46	0
93	16,789	0	3	13	1	0	0	1	6	1	25	0
94	31,304	0	1	16	0	0	0	1	26	1	48	0
95	37,771	0	5	15	0	0	0	0	5	0	26	0
96	50,187	0	3	12	0	0	0	1	24	1	42	0
97	39,888	0	3	12	1	0	0	0	5	0	23	0
98	19,227	0	3	12	0	0	0	1	15	1	33	0
99	32,786	1	0	11	1	0	0	0	37	1	54	1
100	28,440	0	4	12	0	0	0	1	24	1	42	0

Appendix A

A.4 Data Set 4—CIA International Economic and Demographic Data

Variables

x_1 = Country name
x_2 = Total area (square kilometers)
x_3 = Member of the G-20, group of industrial nations to promote international financial stability (0 = nonmember, 1 = member)
x_4 = Country has petroleum as a natural resource [0 = no, 1 = petroleum is a natural resource, 2 = country is a member of OPEC (Organization of Petroleum Exporting Countries)]
x_5 = Population (expressed in thousands)
x_6 = Percent of population aged 65 years and over
x_7 = Life expectancy at birth
x_8 = Literacy: percent of population age 15 or more that can read and write
x_9 = Gross Domestic Product per capita expressed in thousands
x_{10} = Labor force (expressed in millions)
x_{11} = Percent unemployment
x_{12} = Exports expressed in billions of dollars
x_{13} = Imports expressed in billions of dollars
x_{14} = Number of mobile or cellular phones expressed in millions
46 Observations

Country, x_1	Area, x_2	G-20, x_3	Petroleum, x_4	Pop, x_5	65 & over, x_6	Life Expectancy, x_7
Algeria	2,381,740	0	2	31,736	4.07	69.95
Argentina	2,766,890	1	1	37,385	10.42	75.26
Australia	7,686,850	1	1	19,357	12.5	79.87
Austria	83,858	0	0	8,150	15.38	77.84
Belgium	30,510	0	0	10,259	16.95	77.96
Brazil	8,511,965	1	1	174,469	5.45	63.24
Canada	9,976,140	1	1	31,592	12.77	79.56
China	9,596,960	1	1	1,273,111	7.11	71.62
Czech Republic	79	0	0	10,264	13.92	74.73
Denmark	43,094	0	1	5,352	14.85	76.72
Finland	337,030	0	0	5,175	15.03	77.58
France	547,030	1	0	59,551	16.13	78.90
Germany	357,021	1	0	83,029	16.61	77.61
Greece	131,940	0	1	10,623	17.72	78.59
Hungary	93,030	0	0	10,106	14.71	71.63
Iceland	103,000	0	0	278	11.81	79.52
India	3,287,590	1	1	1,029,991	4.68	62.68
Indonesia	1,919,440	1	2	228,437	4.63	68.27
Iran	1,648,000	0	2	66,129	4.65	69.95
Iraq	437,072	0	2	23,332	3.08	66.95
Ireland	70,280	0	0	3,840	11.35	76.99
Italy	301,230	1	0	57,680	18.35	79.14
Japan	377,835	1	0	126,771	17.35	80.80
Kuwait	17,820	0	2	2,041	2.42	76.27
Libya	1,759,540	0	2	5,240	3.95	75.65

(continued)

Appendix A

A.4 Data Set 4—CIA International Economic and Demographic Data (*continued*)

Country, x_1	Area, x_2	G-20, x_3	Petroleum, x_4	Pop, x_5	65 & over, x_6	Life Expectancy, x_7
Luxembourg	2,586	0	0	443	14.06	77.30
Mexico	1,972,550	1	1	101,879	4.40	71.76
Netherlands	41,526	0	1	15,981	13.72	78.43
New Zealand	286,680	0	0	3,864	11.53	77.99
Nigeria	923,768	0	2	126,635	2.82	51.07
Norway	324,220	0	1	4,503	15.10	78.79
Poland	312,685	0	0	38,634	12.44	73.42
Portugal	92,391	0	0	10,066	15.62	75.94
Qatar	11,437	0	2	769	2.48	72.62
Russia	17,075,200	1	1	145,470	12.81	67.34
Saudi Arabia	1,960,582	1	2	22,757	2.68	68.09
South Africa	1,219,912	1	0	43,586	4.88	48.09
South Korea	98,480	1	0	47,904	7.27	74.65
Spain	504,782	0	0	40,038	17.18	78.93
Sweden	449,964	0	0	8,875	17.28	79.71
Switzerland	41,290	0	0	7,283	15.30	79.73
Turkey	780,580	1	0	66,494	6.13	71.24
United Arab Emirates	82,880	0	2	2,407	2.40	74.29
United Kingdom	244,820	1	1	59,648	15.70	77.82
United States	9,629,091	1	1	278,059	12.61	77.26
Venezuela	912,050	0	2	23,917	4.72	73.31

Appendix A

Country, x_1	Literacy %, x_8	GDP/cap, x_9	Labor Force, x_{10}	Unemployment, x_{11}	Exports, x_{12}	Imports, x_{13}	Cell Phones, x_{14}
Algeria	61.6	5.5	9.1	30.0	19.6	9.2	0.034
Argentina	96.2	12.9	15	15.0	26.5	25.2	3
Australia	100.0	23.2	9.5	6.4	69.0	77.0	6.4
Austria	98.0	25	3.7	5.4	63.2	65.6	4.5
Belgium	98.0	25.3	4.34	8.4	181.4	166.0	1
Brazil	83.3	6.5	79	7.1	55.1	55.8	4.4
Canada	97.0	24.8	16.1	6.8	272.3	238.2	4.2
China	81.5	3.6	700	10.0	232.0	197.0	65
Czech Republic	99.9	12.9	5.2	8.7	28.3	31.4	4.3
Denmark	100.0	25.5	2.9	5.3	50.8	43.6	1.4
Finland	100.0	22.9	2.6	9.8	44.4	32.7	2.2
France	99.0	24.4	25	9.7	325.0	320.0	11.1
Germany	99.0	23.4	40.5	9.9	578.0	505.0	15.3
Greece	95.0	17.2	4.32	11.3	15.8	33.9	0.937
Hungary	99.0	11.2	4.2	9.4	25.2	27.6	1.3
Iceland	100.0	24.8	0.16	2.7	2.0	2.2	0.066
India	52.0	2.2	*	*	43.1	60.8	2.93
Indonesia	83.8	2.9	99	17.5	64.7	40.4	1
Iran	72.1	6.3	17.3	14.0	25.0	15.0	0.265
Iraq	58.0	2.5	4.4	*	21.8	13.8	0
Ireland	98.0	21.6	1.82	4.1	73.5	45.7	2
Italy	98.0	22.1	23.4	10.4	241.1	231.4	20.5
Japan	99.0	24.9	67.7	4.7	450.0	355.0	63.9
Kuwait	78.6	15	1.3	1.8	23.2	7.6	0.21
Libya	76.2	8.9	1.5	30.0	13.9	7.6	0
Luxembourg	100.0	36.4	0.248	2.7	7.6	10.0	0.215
Mexico	89.6	9.1	39.8	2.2	168.0	176.0	2
Netherlands	99.0	24.4	7.2	2.6	210.3	201.2	4.1
New Zealand	99.0	17.7	1.88	6.3	14.6	14.3	0.6
Nigeria	57.1	0.95	66	28.0	22.2	10.7	0.027
Norway	100.0	27.7	2.4	3.0	59.2	35.2	2
Poland	99.0	8.5	17.2	12.0	28.4	42.7	1.8
Portugal	87.4	15.8	5	4.3	26.1	41.0	3
Qatar	79.0	20.3	0.233	*	9.8	3.8	0.043
Russia	98.0	7.7	66	10.5	105.1	44.2	2.5
Saudi Arabia	62.8	10.5	7	*	81.2	30.1	1
South Africa	81.1	8.5	17	30.0	30.8	27.6	2
South Korea	98.0	16.1	22	4.1	172.6	160.5	27
Spain	97.0	18	17	14.0	120.5	153.9	8.4
Sweden	99.0	22.2	4.4	6.0	95.5	80.0	3.8
Switzerland	99.0	28.6	3.9	1.9	91.3	91.6	2
Turkey	85.0	6.8	23	5.6	26.9	55.7	12.1
United Arab Emirates	79.2	22.8	1.4	*	46.0	34.0	1
United Kingdom	99.0	22.8	29.2	5.5	282.0	324.0	13
United States	97.0	36.2	140.9	4.0	776.0	1,223.0	69
Venezuela	91.1	6.2	9.9	14.0	32.8	14.7	2

Appendix A

A.5 Data Set 5—Whitner Autoplex

x_1 = Selling price in $
x_2 = Selling price in $000
x_3 = Age of buyer
x_4 = Domestic (0), Imported (1)
80 observations (Autos Sold)

Price, x_1	Price ($000), x_2	Age, x_3	Type, x_4	Price, x_1	Price ($000), x_2	Age, x_3	Type, x_4
23,197	23.197	46	0	20,642	20.642	39	1
23,372	23.372	48	0	21,981	21.981	43	1
20,454	20.454	40	1	24,052	24.052	56	0
23,591	23.591	40	0	25,799	25.799	44	0
26,651	26.651	46	1	15,794	15.794	30	1
27,453	27.453	37	1	18,263	18.263	39	1
17,266	17.266	32	1	35,925	35.925	53	0
18,021	18.021	29	1	17,399	17.399	29	1
28,683	28.683	38	1	17,968	17.968	30	1
30,872	30.872	43	0	20,356	20.356	44	0
19,587	19.587	32	0	21,442	21.442	41	1
23,169	23.169	47	0	21,722	21.722	41	0
35,851	35.851	56	0	19,331	19.331	35	1
19,251	19.251	42	1	22,817	22.817	51	1
20,047	20.047	28	1	19,766	19.766	44	1
24,285	24.285	56	0	20,633	20.633	51	1
24,324	24.324	50	1	20,962	20.962	49	1
24,609	24.609	31	1	22,845	22.845	41	1
28,670	28.670	51	1	26,285	26.285	44	0
15,546	15.546	26	1	27,896	27.896	37	0
15,935	15.935	25	1	29,076	29.076	42	1
19,873	19.873	45	1	32,492	32.492	51	0
25,251	25.251	56	1	18,890	18.890	31	1
25,277	25.277	47	0	21,740	21.740	39	0
28,034	28.034	38	1	22,374	22.374	53	0
24,533	24.533	51	0	24,571	24.571	55	1
27,443	27.443	39	0	25,449	25.449	40	0
19,889	19.889	44	1	28,337	28.337	46	0
20,004	20.004	46	1	20,642	20.642	35	1
17,357	17.357	28	1	23,613	23.613	47	1
20,155	20.155	33	1	24,220	24.220	58	1
19,688	19.688	35	1	30,655	30.655	51	0
23,657	23.657	35	0	22,442	22.442	41	1
26,613	26.613	42	1	17,891	17.891	33	1
20,895	20.895	35	0	20,818	20.818	46	1
20,203	20.203	36	1	26,237	26.237	47	0
23,765	23.765	48	0	20,445	20.445	34	1
25,783	25.783	53	1	21,556	21.556	43	1
26,661	26.661	46	1	21,639	21.639	37	1
32,277	32.277	55	0	24,296	24.296	47	0

A.6 Banking Data Set—Century National Bank Case (Review Sections)

x_1 = Account balance in $
x_2 = Number of ATM transactions in the month
x_3 = Number of other bank services used
x_4 = Has a debit card (1 = yes, 0 = no)
x_5 = Receives interest on the account (1 = yes, 0 = no)
x_6 = City where banking is done
60 Accounts

x_1	x_2	x_3	x_4	x_5	x_6	x_1	x_2	x_3	x_4	x_5	x_6
1,756	13	4	0	1	2	1,958	6	2	1	0	2
748	9	2	1	0	1	634	2	7	1	0	4
1,501	10	1	0	0	1	580	4	1	0	0	1
1,831	10	4	0	1	3	1,320	4	5	1	0	1
1,622	14	6	0	1	4	1,675	6	7	1	0	2
1,886	17	3	0	1	1	789	8	4	0	0	4
740	6	3	0	0	3	1,735	12	7	0	1	3
1,593	10	8	1	0	1	1,784	11	5	0	0	1
1,169	6	4	0	0	4	1,326	16	8	0	0	3
2,125	18	6	0	0	2	2,051	14	4	1	0	4
1,554	12	6	1	0	3	1,044	7	5	1	0	1
1,474	12	7	1	0	1	1,885	10	6	1	1	2
1,913	6	5	0	0	1	1,790	11	4	0	1	3
1,218	10	3	1	0	1	765	4	3	0	0	4
1,006	12	4	0	0	1	1,645	6	9	0	1	4
2,215	20	3	1	0	4	32	2	0	0	0	3
137	7	2	0	0	3	1,266	11	7	0	0	4
167	5	4	0	0	4	890	7	1	0	1	1
343	7	2	0	0	1	2,204	14	5	0	0	2
2,557	20	7	1	0	4	2,409	16	8	0	0	2
2,276	15	4	1	0	3	1,338	14	4	1	0	2
1,494	11	2	0	1	1	2,076	12	5	1	0	2
2,144	17	3	0	0	3	1,708	13	3	1	0	1
1,995	10	7	0	0	2	2,138	18	5	0	1	4
1,053	8	4	1	0	3	2,375	12	4	0	0	2
1,526	8	4	0	1	2	1,455	9	5	1	1	3
1,120	8	6	1	0	3	1,487	8	4	1	0	4
1,838	7	5	1	1	3	1,125	6	4	1	0	2
1,746	11	2	0	0	2	1,989	12	3	0	1	2
1,616	10	4	1	1	2	2,156	14	5	1	0	2

Appendix B: Tables

B.1 Areas under the Normal Curve

Example:
If $z = 1.96$, then
$P(0$ to $z) = 0.4750$.

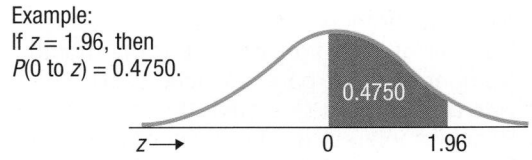

0.4750

$z \longrightarrow$ 0   1.96

z	0.00	0.01	0.02	0.03	0.04	0.05	0.06	0.07	0.08	0.09
0.0	0.0000	0.0040	0.0080	0.0120	0.0160	0.0199	0.0239	0.0279	0.0319	0.0359
0.1	0.0398	0.0438	0.0478	0.0517	0.0557	0.0596	0.0636	0.0675	0.0714	0.0753
0.2	0.0793	0.0832	0.0871	0.0910	0.0948	0.0987	0.1026	0.1064	0.1103	0.1141
0.3	0.1179	0.1217	0.1255	0.1293	0.1331	0.1368	0.1406	0.1443	0.1480	0.1517
0.4	0.1554	0.1591	0.1628	0.1664	0.1700	0.1736	0.1772	0.1808	0.1844	0.1879
0.5	0.1915	0.1950	0.1985	0.2019	0.2054	0.2088	0.2123	0.2157	0.2190	0.2224
0.6	0.2257	0.2291	0.2324	0.2357	0.2389	0.2422	0.2454	0.2486	0.2517	0.2549
0.7	0.2580	0.2611	0.2642	0.2673	0.2704	0.2734	0.2764	0.2794	0.2823	0.2852
0.8	0.2881	0.2910	0.2939	0.2967	0.2995	0.3023	0.3051	0.3078	0.3106	0.3133
0.9	0.3159	0.3186	0.3212	0.3238	0.3264	0.3289	0.3315	0.3340	0.3365	0.3389
1.0	0.3413	0.3438	0.3461	0.3485	0.3508	0.3531	0.3554	0.3577	0.3599	0.3621
1.1	0.3643	0.3665	0.3686	0.3708	0.3729	0.3749	0.3770	0.3790	0.3810	0.3830
1.2	0.3849	0.3869	0.3888	0.3907	0.3925	0.3944	0.3962	0.3980	0.3997	0.4015
1.3	0.4032	0.4049	0.4066	0.4082	0.4099	0.4115	0.4131	0.4147	0.4162	0.4177
1.4	0.4192	0.4207	0.4222	0.4236	0.4251	0.4265	0.4279	0.4292	0.4306	0.4319
1.5	0.4332	0.4345	0.4357	0.4370	0.4382	0.4394	0.4406	0.4418	0.4429	0.4441
1.6	0.4452	0.4463	0.4474	0.4484	0.4495	0.4505	0.4515	0.4525	0.4535	0.4545
1.7	0.4554	0.4564	0.4573	0.4582	0.4591	0.4599	0.4608	0.4616	0.4625	0.4633
1.8	0.4641	0.4649	0.4656	0.4664	0.4671	0.4678	0.4686	0.4693	0.4699	0.4706
1.9	0.4713	0.4719	0.4726	0.4732	0.4738	0.4744	0.4750	0.4756	0.4761	0.4767
2.0	0.4772	0.4778	0.4783	0.4788	0.4793	0.4798	0.4803	0.4808	0.4812	0.4817
2.1	0.4821	0.4826	0.4830	0.4834	0.4838	0.4842	0.4846	0.4850	0.4854	0.4857
2.2	0.4861	0.4864	0.4868	0.4871	0.4875	0.4878	0.4881	0.4884	0.4887	0.4890
2.3	0.4893	0.4896	0.4898	0.4901	0.4904	0.4906	0.4909	0.4911	0.4913	0.4916
2.4	0.4918	0.4920	0.4922	0.4925	0.4927	0.4929	0.4931	0.4932	0.4934	0.4936
2.5	0.4938	0.4940	0.4941	0.4943	0.4945	0.4946	0.4948	0.4949	0.4951	0.4952
2.6	0.4953	0.4955	0.4956	0.4957	0.4959	0.4960	0.4961	0.4962	0.4963	0.4964
2.7	0.4965	0.4966	0.4967	0.4968	0.4969	0.4970	0.4971	0.4972	0.4973	0.4974
2.8	0.4974	0.4975	0.4976	0.4977	0.4977	0.4978	0.4979	0.4979	0.4980	0.4981
2.9	0.4981	0.4982	0.4982	0.4983	0.4984	0.4984	0.4985	0.4985	0.4986	0.4986
3.0	0.4987	0.4987	0.4987	0.4988	0.4988	0.4989	0.4989	0.4989	0.4990	0.4990

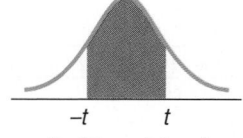
Confidence interval

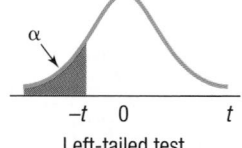
Left-tailed test

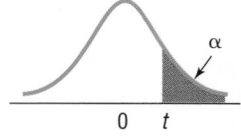
Right-tailed test

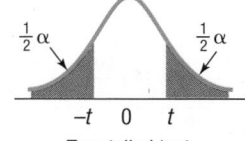
Two-tailed test

	Confidence Intervals, *c*								Confidence Intervals, *c*					
	80%	90%	95%	98%	99%	99.9%		80%	90%	95%	98%	99%	99.9%
	Level of Significance for One-Tailed Test, α							Level of Significance for One-Tailed Test, α					
df	0.10	0.05	0.025	0.01	0.005	0.0005	*df*	0.10	0.05	0.025	0.01	0.005	0.0005
	Level of Significance for Two-Tailed Test, α							Level of Significance for Two-Tailed Test, α					
	0.20	0.10	0.05	0.02	0.01	0.001		0.20	0.10	0.05	0.02	0.01	0.001
1	3.078	6.314	12.706	31.821	63.657	636.619	36	1.306	1.688	2.028	2.434	2.719	3.582
2	1.886	2.920	4.303	6.965	9.925	31.599	37	1.305	1.687	2.026	2.431	2.715	3.574
3	1.638	2.353	3.182	4.541	5.841	12.924	38	1.304	1.686	2.024	2.429	2.712	3.566
4	1.533	2.132	2.776	3.747	4.604	8.610	39	1.304	1.685	2.023	2.426	2.708	3.558
5	1.476	2.015	2.571	3.365	4.032	6.869	40	1.303	1.684	2.021	2.423	2.704	3.551
6	1.440	1.943	2.447	3.143	3.707	5.959	41	1.303	1.683	2.020	2.421	2.701	3.544
7	1.415	1.895	2.365	2.998	3.499	5.408	42	1.302	1.682	2.018	2.418	2.698	3.538
8	1.397	1.860	2.306	2.896	3.355	5.041	43	1.302	1.681	2.017	2.416	2.695	3.532
9	1.383	1.833	2.262	2.821	3.250	4.781	44	1.301	1.680	2.015	2.414	2.692	3.526
10	1.372	1.812	2.228	2.764	3.169	4.587	45	1.301	1.679	2.014	2.412	2.690	3.520
11	1.363	1.796	2.201	2.718	3.106	4.437	46	1.300	1.679	2.013	2.410	2.687	3.515
12	1.356	1.782	2.179	2.681	3.055	4.318	47	1.300	1.678	2.012	2.408	2.685	3.510
13	1.350	1.771	2.160	2.650	3.012	4.221	48	1.299	1.677	2.011	2.407	2.682	3.505
14	1.345	1.761	2.145	2.624	2.977	4.140	49	1.299	1.677	2.010	2.405	2.680	3.500
15	1.341	1.753	2.131	2.602	2.947	4.073	50	1.299	1.676	2.009	2.403	2.678	3.496
16	1.337	1.746	2.120	2.583	2.921	4.015	51	1.298	1.675	2.008	2.402	2.676	3.492
17	1.333	1.740	2.110	2.567	2.898	3.965	52	1.298	1.675	2.007	2.400	2.674	3.488
18	1.330	1.734	2.101	2.552	2.878	3.922	53	1.298	1.674	2.006	2.399	2.672	3.484
19	1.328	1.729	2.093	2.539	2.861	3.883	54	1.297	1.674	2.005	2.397	2.670	3.480
20	1.325	1.725	2.086	2.528	2.845	3.850	55	1.297	1.673	2.004	2.396	2.668	3.476
21	1.323	1.721	2.080	2.518	2.831	3.819	56	1.297	1.673	2.003	2.395	2.667	3.473
22	1.321	1.717	2.074	2.508	2.819	3.792	57	1.297	1.672	2.002	2.394	2.665	3.470
23	1.319	1.714	2.069	2.500	2.807	3.768	58	1.296	1.672	2.002	2.392	2.663	3.466
24	1.318	1.711	2.064	2.492	2.797	3.745	59	1.296	1.671	2.001	2.391	2.662	3.463
25	1.316	1.708	2.060	2.485	2.787	3.725	60	1.296	1.671	2.000	2.390	2.660	3.460
26	1.315	1.706	2.056	2.479	2.779	3.707	61	1.296	1.670	2.000	2.389	2.659	3.457
27	1.314	1.703	2.052	2.473	2.771	3.690	62	1.295	1.670	1.999	2.388	2.657	3.454
28	1.313	1.701	2.048	2.467	2.763	3.674	63	1.295	1.669	1.998	2.387	2.656	3.452
29	1.311	1.699	2.045	2.462	2.756	3.659	64	1.295	1.669	1.998	2.386	2.655	3.449
30	1.310	1.697	2.042	2.457	2.750	3.646	65	1.295	1.669	1.997	2.385	2.654	3.447
31	1.309	1.696	2.040	2.453	2.744	3.633	66	1.295	1.668	1.997	2.384	2.652	3.444
32	1.309	1.694	2.037	2.449	2.738	3.622	67	1.294	1.668	1.996	2.383	2.651	3.442
33	1.308	1.692	2.035	2.445	2.733	3.611	68	1.294	1.668	1.995	2.382	2.650	3.439
34	1.307	1.691	2.032	2.441	2.728	3.601	69	1.294	1.667	1.995	2.382	2.649	3.437
35	1.306	1.690	2.030	2.438	2.724	3.591	70	1.294	1.667	1.994	2.381	2.648	3.435

(continued)

Appendix B

B.2 Student's *t* Distribution (*concluded*)

	Confidence Intervals, *c*							Confidence Intervals, *c*					
	80%	90%	95%	98%	99%	99.9%		80%	90%	95%	98%	99%	99.9%
	Level of Significance for One-Tailed Test, α							Level of Significance for One-Tailed Test, α					
df	0.10	0.05	0.025	0.01	0.005	0.0005	*df*	0.10	0.05	0.025	0.01	0.005	0.0005
	Level of Significance for Two-Tailed Test, α							Level of Significance for Two-Tailed Test, α					
	0.20	0.10	0.05	0.02	0.01	0.001		0.20	0.10	0.05	0.02	0.01	0.001
71	1.294	1.667	1.994	2.380	2.647	3.433	89	1.291	1.662	1.987	2.369	2.632	3.403
72	1.293	1.666	1.993	2.379	2.646	3.431	90	1.291	1.662	1.987	2.368	2.632	3.402
73	1.293	1.666	1.993	2.379	2.645	3.429							
74	1.293	1.666	1.993	2.378	2.644	3.427	91	1.291	1.662	1.986	2.368	2.631	3.401
75	1.293	1.665	1.992	2.377	2.643	3.425	92	1.291	1.662	1.986	2.368	2.630	3.399
							93	1.291	1.661	1.986	2.367	2.630	3.398
76	1.293	1.665	1.992	2.376	2.642	3.423	94	1.291	1.661	1.986	2.367	2.629	3.397
77	1.293	1.665	1.991	2.376	2.641	3.421	95	1.291	1.661	1.985	2.366	2.629	3.396
78	1.292	1.665	1.991	2.375	2.640	3.420							
79	1.292	1.664	1.990	2.374	2.640	3.418	96	1.290	1.661	1.985	2.366	2.628	3.395
80	1.292	1.664	1.990	2.374	2.639	3.416	97	1.290	1.661	1.985	2.365	2.627	3.394
							98	1.290	1.661	1.984	2.365	2.627	3.393
81	1.292	1.664	1.990	2.373	2.638	3.415	99	1.290	1.660	1.984	2.365	2.626	3.392
82	1.292	1.664	1.989	2.373	2.637	3.413	100	1.290	1.660	1.984	2.364	2.626	3.390
83	1.292	1.663	1.989	2.372	2.636	3.412							
84	1.292	1.663	1.989	2.372	2.636	3.410	120	1.289	1.658	1.980	2.358	2.617	3.373
85	1.292	1.663	1.988	2.371	2.635	3.409	140	1.288	1.656	1.977	2.353	2.611	3.361
							160	1.287	1.654	1.975	2.350	2.607	3.352
86	1.291	1.663	1.988	2.370	2.634	3.407	180	1.286	1.653	1.973	2.347	2.603	3.345
87	1.291	1.663	1.988	2.370	2.634	3.406	200	1.286	1.653	1.972	2.345	2.601	3.340
88	1.291	1.662	1.987	2.369	2.633	3.405	∞	1.282	1.645	1.960	2.326	2.576	3.291

Appendix B

B.3 Critical Values of Chi-Square

This table contains the values of χ^2 that correspond to a specific right-tail area and specific number of degrees of freedom.

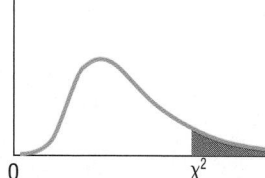

Example: With 17 *df* and a .02 area in the upper tail, $\chi^2 = 30.995$

Degrees of Freedom, *df*	Right-Tail Area			
	0.10	0.05	0.02	0.01
1	2.706	3.841	5.412	6.635
2	4.605	5.991	7.824	9.210
3	6.251	7.815	9.837	11.345
4	7.779	9.488	11.668	13.277
5	9.236	11.070	13.388	15.086
6	10.645	12.592	15.033	16.812
7	12.017	14.067	16.622	18.475
8	13.362	15.507	18.168	20.090
9	14.684	16.919	19.679	21.666
10	15.987	18.307	21.161	23.209
11	17.275	19.675	22.618	24.725
12	18.549	21.026	24.054	26.217
13	19.812	22.362	25.472	27.688
14	21.064	23.685	26.873	29.141
15	22.307	24.996	28.259	30.578
16	23.542	26.296	29.633	32.000
17	24.769	27.587	30.995	33.409
18	25.989	28.869	32.346	34.805
19	27.204	30.144	33.687	36.191
20	28.412	31.410	35.020	37.566
21	29.615	32.671	36.343	38.932
22	30.813	33.924	37.659	40.289
23	32.007	35.172	38.968	41.638
24	33.196	36.415	40.270	42.980
25	34.382	37.652	41.566	44.314
26	35.563	38.885	42.856	45.642
27	36.741	40.113	44.140	46.963
28	37.916	41.337	45.419	48.278
29	39.087	42.557	46.693	49.588
30	40.256	43.773	47.962	50.892

Appendix B

B.4 Critical Values of the F Distribution at a 5 Percent Level of Significance

		Degrees of Freedom for the Numerator														
	1	**2**	**3**	**4**	**5**	**6**	**7**	**8**	**9**	**10**	**12**	**15**	**20**	**24**	**30**	**40**
1	161	200	216	225	230	234	237	239	241	242	244	246	248	249	250	251
2	18.5	19.0	19.2	19.2	19.3	19.3	19.4	19.4	19.4	19.4	19.4	19.4	19.4	19.5	19.5	19.5
3	10.1	9.55	9.28	9.12	9.01	8.94	8.89	8.85	8.81	8.79	8.74	8.70	8.66	8.64	8.62	8.59
4	7.71	6.94	6.59	6.39	6.26	6.16	6.09	6.04	6.00	5.96	5.91	5.86	5.80	5.77	5.75	5.72
5	6.61	5.79	5.41	5.19	5.05	4.95	4.88	4.82	4.77	4.74	4.68	4.62	4.56	4.53	4.50	4.46
6	5.99	5.14	4.76	4.53	4.39	4.28	4.21	4.15	4.10	4.06	4.00	3.94	3.87	3.84	3.81	3.77
7	5.59	4.74	4.35	4.12	3.97	3.87	3.79	3.73	3.68	3.64	3.57	3.51	3.44	3.41	3.38	3.34
8	5.32	4.46	4.07	3.84	3.69	3.58	3.50	3.44	3.39	3.35	3.28	3.22	3.15	3.12	3.08	3.04
9	5.12	4.26	3.86	3.63	3.48	3.37	3.29	3.23	3.18	3.14	3.07	3.01	2.94	2.90	2.86	2.83
10	4.96	4.10	3.71	3.48	3.33	3.22	3.14	3.07	3.02	2.98	2.91	2.85	2.77	2.74	2.70	2.66
11	4.84	3.98	3.59	3.36	3.20	3.09	3.01	2.95	2.90	2.85	2.79	2.72	2.65	2.61	2.57	2.53
12	4.75	3.89	3.49	3.26	3.11	3.00	2.91	2.85	2.80	2.75	2.69	2.62	2.54	2.51	2.47	2.43
13	4.67	3.81	3.41	3.18	3.03	2.92	2.83	2.77	2.71	2.67	2.60	2.53	2.46	2.42	2.38	2.34
14	4.60	3.74	3.34	3.11	2.96	2.85	2.76	2.70	2.65	2.60	2.53	2.46	2.39	2.35	2.31	2.27
15	4.54	3.68	3.29	3.06	2.90	2.79	2.71	2.64	2.59	2.54	2.48	2.40	2.33	2.29	2.25	2.20
16	4.49	3.63	3.24	3.01	2.85	2.74	2.66	2.59	2.54	2.49	2.42	2.35	2.28	2.24	2.19	2.15
17	4.45	3.59	3.20	2.96	2.81	2.70	2.61	2.55	2.49	2.45	2.38	2.31	2.23	2.19	2.15	2.10
18	4.41	3.55	3.16	2.93	2.77	2.66	2.58	2.51	2.46	2.41	2.34	2.27	2.19	2.15	2.11	2.06
19	4.38	3.52	3.13	2.90	2.74	2.63	2.54	2.48	2.42	2.38	2.31	2.23	2.16	2.11	2.07	2.03
20	4.35	3.49	3.10	2.87	2.71	2.60	2.51	2.45	2.39	2.35	2.28	2.20	2.12	2.08	2.04	1.99
21	4.32	3.47	3.07	2.84	2.68	2.57	2.49	2.42	2.37	2.32	2.25	2.18	2.10	2.05	2.01	1.96
22	4.30	3.44	3.05	2.82	2.66	2.55	2.46	2.40	2.34	2.30	2.23	2.15	2.07	2.03	1.98	1.94
23	4.28	3.42	3.03	2.80	2.64	2.53	2.44	2.37	2.32	2.27	2.20	2.13	2.05	2.01	1.96	1.91
24	4.26	3.40	3.01	2.78	2.62	2.51	2.42	2.36	2.30	2.25	2.18	2.11	2.03	1.98	1.94	1.89
25	4.24	3.39	2.99	2.76	2.60	2.49	2.40	2.34	2.28	2.24	2.16	2.09	2.01	1.96	1.92	1.87
30	4.17	3.32	2.92	2.69	2.53	2.42	2.33	2.27	2.21	2.16	2.09	2.01	1.93	1.89	1.84	1.79
40	4.08	3.23	2.84	2.61	2.45	2.34	2.25	2.18	2.12	2.08	2.00	1.92	1.84	1.79	1.74	1.69
60	4.00	3.15	2.76	2.53	2.37	2.25	2.17	2.10	2.04	1.99	1.92	1.84	1.75	1.70	1.65	1.59
120	3.92	3.07	2.68	2.45	2.29	2.18	2.09	2.02	1.96	1.91	1.83	1.75	1.66	1.61	1.55	1.50
∞	3.84	3.00	2.60	2.37	2.21	2.10	2.01	1.94	1.88	1.83	1.75	1.67	1.57	1.52	1.46	1.39

Degrees of Freedom for the Denominator

Appendix B

		Degrees of Freedom for the Numerator														
	1	**2**	**3**	**4**	**5**	**6**	**7**	**8**	**9**	**10**	**12**	**15**	**20**	**24**	**30**	**40**
1	4052	5000	5403	5625	5764	5859	5928	5981	6022	6056	6106	6157	6209	6235	6261	6287
2	98.5	99.0	99.2	99.2	99.3	99.3	99.4	99.4	99.4	99.4	99.4	99.4	99.4	99.5	99.5	99.5
3	34.1	30.8	29.5	28.7	28.2	27.9	27.7	27.5	27.3	27.2	27.1	26.9	26.7	26.6	26.5	26.4
4	21.2	18.0	16.7	16.0	15.5	15.2	15.0	14.8	14.7	14.5	14.4	14.2	14.0	13.9	13.8	13.7
5	16.3	13.3	12.1	11.4	11.0	10.7	10.5	10.3	10.2	10.1	9.89	9.72	9.55	9.47	9.38	9.29
6	13.7	10.9	9.78	9.15	8.75	8.47	8.26	8.10	7.98	7.87	7.72	7.56	7.40	7.31	7.23	7.14
7	12.2	9.55	8.45	7.85	7.46	7.19	6.99	6.84	6.72	6.62	6.47	6.31	6.16	6.07	5.99	5.91
8	11.3	8.65	7.59	7.01	6.63	6.37	6.18	6.03	5.91	5.81	5.67	5.52	5.36	5.28	5.20	5.12
9	10.6	8.02	6.99	6.42	6.06	5.80	5.61	5.47	5.35	5.26	5.11	4.96	4.81	4.73	4.65	4.57
10	10.0	7.56	6.55	5.99	5.64	5.39	5.20	5.06	4.94	4.85	4.71	4.56	4.41	4.33	4.25	4.17
11	9.65	7.21	6.22	5.67	5.32	5.07	4.89	4.74	4.63	4.54	4.40	4.25	4.10	4.02	3.94	3.86
12	9.33	6.93	5.95	5.41	5.06	4.82	4.64	4.50	4.39	4.30	4.16	4.01	3.86	3.78	3.70	3.62
13	9.07	6.70	5.74	5.21	4.86	4.62	4.44	4.30	4.19	4.10	3.96	3.82	3.66	3.59	3.51	3.43
14	8.86	6.51	5.56	5.04	4.69	4.46	4.28	4.14	4.03	3.94	3.80	3.66	3.51	3.43	3.35	3.27
15	8.68	6.36	5.42	4.89	4.56	4.32	4.14	4.00	3.89	3.80	3.67	3.52	3.37	3.29	3.21	3.13
16	8.53	6.23	5.29	4.77	4.44	4.20	4.03	3.89	3.78	3.69	3.55	3.41	3.26	3.18	3.10	3.02
17	8.40	6.11	5.18	4.67	4.34	4.10	3.93	3.79	3.68	3.59	3.46	3.31	3.16	3.08	3.00	2.92
18	8.29	6.01	5.09	4.58	4.25	4.01	3.84	3.71	3.60	3.51	3.37	3.23	3.08	3.00	2.92	2.84
19	8.18	5.93	5.01	4.50	4.17	3.94	3.77	3.63	3.52	3.43	3.30	3.15	3.00	2.92	2.84	2.76
20	8.10	5.85	4.94	4.43	4.10	3.87	3.70	3.56	3.46	3.37	3.23	3.09	2.94	2.86	2.78	2.69
21	8.02	5.78	4.87	4.37	4.04	3.81	3.64	3.51	3.40	3.31	3.17	3.03	2.88	2.80	2.72	2.64
22	7.95	5.72	4.82	4.31	3.99	3.76	3.59	3.45	3.35	3.26	3.12	2.98	2.83	2.75	2.67	2.58
23	7.88	5.66	4.76	4.26	3.94	3.71	3.54	3.41	3.30	3.21	3.07	2.93	2.78	2.70	2.62	2.54
24	7.82	5.61	4.72	4.22	3.90	3.67	3.50	3.36	3.26	3.17	3.03	2.89	2.74	2.66	2.58	2.49
25	7.77	5.57	4.68	4.18	3.85	3.63	3.46	3.32	3.22	3.13	2.99	2.85	2.70	2.62	2.54	2.45
30	7.56	5.39	4.51	4.02	3.70	3.47	3.30	3.17	3.07	2.98	2.84	2.70	2.55	2.47	2.39	2.30
40	7.31	5.18	4.31	3.83	3.51	3.29	3.12	2.99	2.89	2.80	2.66	2.52	2.37	2.29	2.20	2.11
60	7.08	4.98	4.13	3.65	3.34	3.12	2.95	2.82	2.72	2.63	2.50	2.35	2.20	2.12	2.03	1.94
120	6.85	4.79	3.95	3.48	3.17	2.96	2.79	2.66	2.56	2.47	2.34	2.19	2.03	1.95	1.86	1.76
∞	6.63	4.61	3.78	3.32	3.02	2.80	2.64	2.51	2.41	2.32	2.18	2.04	1.88	1.79	1.70	1.59

Degrees of Freedom for the Denominator

Appendix B

B.5 Poisson Distribution

					μ				
x	0.1	0.2	0.3	0.4	0.5	0.6	0.7	0.8	0.9
0	0.9048	0.8187	0.7408	0.6703	0.6065	0.5488	0.4966	0.4493	0.4066
1	0.0905	0.1637	0.2222	0.2681	0.3033	0.3293	0.3476	0.3595	0.3659
2	0.0045	0.0164	0.0333	0.0536	0.0758	0.0988	0.1217	0.1438	0.1647
3	0.0002	0.0011	0.0033	0.0072	0.0126	0.0198	0.0284	0.0383	0.0494
4	0.0000	0.0001	0.0003	0.0007	0.0016	0.0030	0.0050	0.0077	0.0111
5	0.0000	0.0000	0.0000	0.0001	0.0002	0.0004	0.0007	0.0012	0.0020
6	0.0000	0.0000	0.0000	0.0000	0.0000	0.0000	0.0001	0.0002	0.0003
7	0.0000	0.0000	0.0000	0.0000	0.0000	0.0000	0.0000	0.0000	0.0000

					μ				
x	1.0	2.0	3.0	4.0	5.0	6.0	7.0	8.0	9.0
0	0.3679	0.1353	0.0498	0.0183	0.0067	0.0025	0.0009	0.0003	0.0001
1	0.3679	0.2707	0.1494	0.0733	0.0337	0.0149	0.0064	0.0027	0.0011
2	0.1839	0.2707	0.2240	0.1465	0.0842	0.0446	0.0223	0.0107	0.0050
3	0.0613	0.1804	0.2240	0.1954	0.1404	0.0892	0.0521	0.0286	0.0150
4	0.0153	0.0902	0.1680	0.1954	0.1755	0.1339	0.0912	0.0573	0.0337
5	0.0031	0.0361	0.1008	0.1563	0.1755	0.1606	0.1277	0.0916	0.0607
6	0.0005	0.0120	0.0504	0.1042	0.1462	0.1606	0.1490	0.1221	0.0911
7	0.0001	0.0034	0.0216	0.0595	0.1044	0.1377	0.1490	0.1396	0.1171
8	0.0000	0.0009	0.0081	0.0298	0.0653	0.1033	0.1304	0.1396	0.1318
9	0.0000	0.0002	0.0027	0.0132	0.0363	0.0688	0.1014	0.1241	0.1318
10	0.0000	0.0000	0.0008	0.0053	0.0181	0.0413	0.0710	0.0993	0.1186
11	0.0000	0.0000	0.0002	0.0019	0.0082	0.0225	0.0452	0.0722	0.0970
12	0.0000	0.0000	0.0001	0.0006	0.0034	0.0113	0.0263	0.0481	0.0728
13	0.0000	0.0000	0.0000	0.0002	0.0013	0.0052	0.0142	0.0296	0.0504
14	0.0000	0.0000	0.0000	0.0001	0.0005	0.0022	0.0071	0.0169	0.0324
15	0.0000	0.0000	0.0000	0.0000	0.0002	0.0009	0.0033	0.0090	0.0194
16	0.0000	0.0000	0.0000	0.0000	0.0000	0.0003	0.0014	0.0045	0.0109
17	0.0000	0.0000	0.0000	0.0000	0.0000	0.0001	0.0006	0.0021	0.0058
18	0.0000	0.0000	0.0000	0.0000	0.0000	0.0000	0.0002	0.0009	0.0029
19	0.0000	0.0000	0.0000	0.0000	0.0000	0.0000	0.0001	0.0004	0.0014
20	0.0000	0.0000	0.0000	0.0000	0.0000	0.0000	0.0000	0.0002	0.0006
21	0.0000	0.0000	0.0000	0.0000	0.0000	0.0000	0.0000	0.0001	0.0003
22	0.0000	0.0000	0.0000	0.0000	0.0000	0.0000	0.0000	0.0000	0.0001

Appendix B

02711	08182	75997	79866	58095	83319	80295	79741	74599	84379
94873	90935	31684	63952	09865	14491	99518	93394	34691	14985
54921	78680	06635	98689	17306	25170	65928	87709	30533	89736
77640	97636	37397	93379	56454	59818	45827	74164	71666	46977
61545	00835	93251	87203	36759	49197	85967	01704	19634	21898
17147	19519	22497	16857	42426	84822	92598	49186	88247	39967
13748	04742	92460	85801	53444	65626	58710	55406	17173	69776
87455	14813	50373	28037	91182	32786	65261	11173	34376	36408
08999	57409	91185	10200	61411	23392	47797	56377	71635	08601
78804	81333	53809	32471	46034	36306	22498	19239	85428	55721
82173	26921	28472	98958	07960	66124	89731	95069	18625	92405
97594	25168	89178	68190	05043	17407	48201	83917	11413	72920
73881	67176	93504	42636	38233	16154	96451	57925	29667	30859
46071	22912	90326	42453	88108	72064	58601	32357	90610	32921
44492	19686	12495	93135	95185	77799	52441	88272	22024	80631
31864	72170	37722	55794	14636	05148	54505	50113	21119	25228
51574	90692	43339	65689	76539	27909	05467	21727	51141	72949
35350	76132	92925	92124	92634	35681	43690	89136	35599	84138
46943	36502	01172	46045	46991	33804	80006	35542	61056	75666
22665	87226	33304	57975	03985	21566	65796	72915	81466	89205
39437	97957	11838	10433	21564	51570	73558	27495	34533	57808
77082	47784	40098	97962	89845	28392	78187	06112	08169	11261
24544	25649	43370	28007	06779	72402	62632	53956	24709	06978
27503	15558	37738	24849	70722	71859	83736	06016	94397	12529
24590	24545	06435	52758	45685	90151	46516	49644	92686	84870
48155	86226	40359	28723	15364	69125	12609	57171	86857	31702
20226	53752	90648	24362	83314	00014	19207	69413	97016	86290
70178	73444	38790	53626	93780	18629	68766	24371	74639	30782
10169	41465	51935	05711	09799	79077	88159	33437	68519	03040
81084	03701	28598	70013	63794	53169	97054	60303	23259	96196
69202	20777	21727	81511	51887	16175	53746	46516	70339	62727
80561	95787	89426	93325	86412	57479	54194	52153	19197	81877
08199	26703	95128	48599	09333	12584	24374	31232	61782	44032
98883	28220	39358	53720	80161	83371	15181	11131	12219	55920
84568	69286	76054	21615	80883	36797	82845	39139	90900	18172
04269	35173	95745	53893	86022	77722	52498	84193	22448	22571
10538	13124	36099	13140	37706	44562	57179	44693	67877	01549
77843	24955	25900	63843	95029	93859	93634	20205	66294	41218
12034	94636	49455	76362	83532	31062	69903	91186	65768	55949
10524	72829	47641	93315	80875	28090	97728	52560	34937	79548
68935	76632	46984	61772	92786	22651	07086	89754	44143	97687
89450	65665	29190	43709	11172	34481	95977	47535	25658	73898
90696	20451	24211	97310	60446	73530	62865	96574	13829	72226
49006	32047	93086	00112	20470	17136	28255	86328	07293	38809
74591	87025	52368	59416	34417	70557	86746	55809	53628	12000
06315	17012	77103	00968	07235	10728	42189	33292	51487	64443
62386	09184	62092	46617	99419	64230	95034	85481	07857	42510
86848	82122	04028	36959	87827	12813	08627	80699	13345	51695
65643	69480	46598	04501	40403	91408	32343	48130	49303	90689
11084	46534	78957	77353	39578	77868	22970	84349	09184	70603

Appendix B

B.7 Wilcoxon *T* Values

				2α			
	.15	.10	.05	.04	.03	.02	.01
				α			
n	.075	.050	.025	.020	.015	.010	.005
4	0						
5	1	0					
6	2	2	0	0			
7	4	3	2	1	0	0	
8	7	5	3	3	2	1	0
9	9	8	5	5	4	3	1
10	12	10	8	7	6	5	3
11	16	13	10	9	8	7	5
12	19	17	13	12	11	9	7
13	24	21	17	16	14	12	9
14	28	25	21	19	18	15	12
15	33	30	25	23	21	19	15
16	39	35	29	28	26	23	19
17	45	41	34	33	30	27	23
18	51	47	40	38	35	32	27
19	58	53	46	43	41	37	32
20	65	60	52	50	47	43	37
21	73	67	58	56	53	49	42
22	81	75	65	63	59	55	48
23	89	83	73	70	66	62	54
24	98	91	81	78	74	69	61
25	108	100	89	86	82	76	68
26	118	110	98	94	90	84	75
27	128	119	107	103	99	92	83
28	138	130	116	112	108	101	91
29	150	140	126	122	117	110	100
30	161	151	137	132	127	120	109
31	173	163	147	143	137	130	118
32	186	175	159	154	148	140	128
33	199	187	170	165	159	151	138
34	212	200	182	177	171	162	148
35	226	213	195	189	182	173	159
40	302	286	264	257	249	238	220
50	487	466	434	425	413	397	373
60	718	690	648	636	620	600	567
70	995	960	907	891	872	846	805
80	1,318	1,276	1,211	1,192	1,168	1,136	1,086
90	1,688	1,638	1,560	1,537	1,509	1,471	1,410
100	2,105	2,045	1,955	1,928	1,894	1,850	1,779

B.8 Factors for Control Charts

Number of Items in Sample,	Chart for Averages	Chart for Ranges		
	Factors for Control Limits	Factors for Central Line	Factors for Control Limits	
n	A_2	d_2	D_3	D_4
2	1.880	1.128	0	3.267
3	1.023	1.693	0	2.575
4	.729	2.059	0	2.282
5	.577	2.326	0	2.115
6	.483	2.534	0	2.004
7	.419	2.704	.076	1.924
8	.373	2.847	.136	1.864
9	.337	2.970	.184	1.816
10	.308	3.078	.223	1.777
11	.285	3.173	.256	1.744
12	.266	3.258	.284	1.716
13	.249	3.336	.308	1.692
14	.235	3.407	.329	1.671
15	.223	3.472	.348	1.652

SOURCE: Adapted from American Society for Testing and Materials, *Manual on Quality Control of Materials,* 1951, Table B2, p. 115. For a more detailed table and explanation, see J. Duncan Acheson, *Quality Control and Industrial Statistics,* 3d ed. (Homewood, Ill.: Richard D. Irwin, 1974), Table M, p. 927.

Appendix B

B.9 Binomial Probability Distribution

n = 1

x	Probability										
	0.05	0.10	0.20	0.30	0.40	0.50	0.60	0.70	0.80	0.90	0.95
0	0.950	0.900	0.800	0.700	0.600	0.500	0.400	0.300	0.200	0.100	0.050
1	0.050	0.100	0.200	0.300	0.400	0.500	0.600	0.700	0.800	0.900	0.950

n = 2

x	Probability										
	0.05	0.10	0.20	0.30	0.40	0.50	0.60	0.70	0.80	0.90	0.95
0	0.903	0.810	0.640	0.490	0.360	0.250	0.160	0.090	0.040	0.010	0.003
1	0.095	0.180	0.320	0.420	0.480	0.500	0.480	0.420	0.320	0.180	0.095
2	0.003	0.010	0.040	0.090	0.160	0.250	0.360	0.490	0.640	0.810	0.903

n = 3

x	Probability										
	0.05	0.10	0.20	0.30	0.40	0.50	0.60	0.70	0.80	0.90	0.95
0	0.857	0.729	0.512	0.343	0.216	0.125	0.064	0.027	0.008	0.001	0.000
1	0.135	0.243	0.384	0.441	0.432	0.375	0.288	0.189	0.096	0.027	0.007
2	0.007	0.027	0.096	0.189	0.288	0.375	0.432	0.441	0.384	0.243	0.135
3	0.000	0.001	0.008	0.027	0.064	0.125	0.216	0.343	0.512	0.729	0.857

n = 4

x	Probability										
	0.05	0.10	0.20	0.30	0.40	0.50	0.60	0.70	0.80	0.90	0.95
0	0.815	0.656	0.410	0.240	0.130	0.063	0.026	0.008	0.002	0.000	0.000
1	0.171	0.292	0.410	0.412	0.346	0.250	0.154	0.076	0.026	0.004	0.000
2	0.014	0.049	0.154	0.265	0.346	0.375	0.346	0.265	0.154	0.049	0.014
3	0.000	0.004	0.026	0.076	0.154	0.250	0.346	0.412	0.410	0.292	0.171
4	0.000	0.000	0.002	0.008	0.026	0.063	0.130	0.240	0.410	0.656	0.815

n = 5

x	Probability										
	0.05	0.10	0.20	0.30	0.40	0.50	0.60	0.70	0.80	0.90	0.95
0	0.774	0.590	0.328	0.168	0.078	0.031	0.010	0.002	0.000	0.000	0.000
1	0.204	0.328	0.410	0.360	0.259	0.156	0.077	0.028	0.006	0.000	0.000
2	0.021	0.073	0.205	0.309	0.346	0.313	0.230	0.132	0.051	0.008	0.001
3	0.001	0.008	0.051	0.132	0.230	0.313	0.346	0.309	0.205	0.073	0.021
4	0.000	0.000	0.006	0.028	0.077	0.156	0.259	0.360	0.410	0.328	0.204
5	0.000	0.000	0.000	0.002	0.010	0.031	0.078	0.168	0.328	0.590	0.774

B.9 Binomial Probability Distribution (*continued*)

n = 6
Probability

x	0.05	0.10	0.20	0.30	0.40	0.50	0.60	0.70	0.80	0.90	0.95
0	0.735	0.531	0.262	0.118	0.047	0.016	0.004	0.001	0.000	0.000	0.000
1	0.232	0.354	0.393	0.303	0.187	0.094	0.037	0.010	0.002	0.000	0.000
2	0.031	0.098	0.246	0.324	0.311	0.234	0.138	0.060	0.015	0.001	0.000
3	0.002	0.015	0.082	0.185	0.276	0.313	0.276	0.185	0.082	0.015	0.002
4	0.000	0.001	0.015	0.060	0.138	0.234	0.311	0.324	0.246	0.098	0.031
5	0.000	0.000	0.002	0.010	0.037	0.094	0.187	0.303	0.393	0.354	0.232
6	0.000	0.000	0.000	0.001	0.004	0.016	0.047	0.118	0.262	0.531	0.735

n = 7
Probability

x	0.05	0.10	0.20	0.30	0.40	0.50	0.60	0.70	0.80	0.90	0.95
0	0.698	0.478	0.210	0.082	0.028	0.008	0.002	0.000	0.000	0.000	0.000
1	0.257	0.372	0.367	0.247	0.131	0.055	0.017	0.004	0.000	0.000	0.000
2	0.041	0.124	0.275	0.318	0.261	0.164	0.077	0.025	0.004	0.000	0.000
3	0.004	0.023	0.115	0.227	0.290	0.273	0.194	0.097	0.029	0.003	0.000
4	0.000	0.003	0.029	0.097	0.194	0.273	0.290	0.227	0.115	0.023	0.004
5	0.000	0.000	0.004	0.025	0.077	0.164	0.261	0.318	0.275	0.124	0.041
6	0.000	0.000	0.000	0.004	0.017	0.055	0.131	0.247	0.367	0.372	0.257
7	0.000	0.000	0.000	0.000	0.002	0.008	0.028	0.082	0.210	0.478	0.698

n = 8
Probability

x	0.05	0.10	0.20	0.30	0.40	0.50	0.60	0.70	0.80	0.90	0.95
0	0.663	0.430	0.168	0.058	0.017	0.004	0.001	0.000	0.000	0.000	0.000
1	0.279	0.383	0.336	0.198	0.090	0.031	0.008	0.001	0.000	0.000	0.000
2	0.051	0.149	0.294	0.296	0.209	0.109	0.041	0.010	0.001	0.000	0.000
3	0.005	0.033	0.147	0.254	0.279	0.219	0.124	0.047	0.009	0.000	0.000
4	0.000	0.005	0.046	0.136	0.232	0.273	0.232	0.136	0.046	0.005	0.000
5	0.000	0.000	0.009	0.047	0.124	0.219	0.279	0.254	0.147	0.033	0.005
6	0.000	0.000	0.001	0.010	0.041	0.109	0.209	0.296	0.294	0.149	0.051
7	0.000	0.000	0.000	0.001	0.008	0.031	0.090	0.198	0.336	0.383	0.279
8	0.000	0.000	0.000	0.000	0.001	0.004	0.017	0.058	0.168	0.430	0.663

(*continued*)

Appendix B

B.9 Binomial Probability Distribution (*continued*)

n = 9

Probability

x	0.05	0.10	0.20	0.30	0.40	0.50	0.60	0.70	0.80	0.90	0.95
0	0.630	0.387	0.134	0.040	0.010	0.002	0.000	0.000	0.000	0.000	0.000
1	0.299	0.387	0.302	0.156	0.060	0.018	0.004	0.000	0.000	0.000	0.000
2	0.063	0.172	0.302	0.267	0.161	0.070	0.021	0.004	0.000	0.000	0.000
3	0.008	0.045	0.176	0.267	0.251	0.164	0.074	0.021	0.003	0.000	0.000
4	0.001	0.007	0.066	0.172	0.251	0.246	0.167	0.074	0.017	0.001	0.000
5	0.000	0.001	0.017	0.074	0.167	0.246	0.251	0.172	0.066	0.007	0.001
6	0.000	0.000	0.003	0.021	0.074	0.164	0.251	0.267	0.176	0.045	0.008
7	0.000	0.000	0.000	0.004	0.021	0.070	0.161	0.267	0.302	0.172	0.063
8	0.000	0.000	0.000	0.000	0.004	0.018	0.060	0.156	0.302	0.387	0.299
9	0.000	0.000	0.000	0.000	0.000	0.002	0.010	0.040	0.134	0.387	0.630

n = 10

Probability

x	0.05	0.10	0.20	0.30	0.40	0.50	0.60	0.70	0.80	0.90	0.95
0	0.599	0.349	0.107	0.028	0.006	0.001	0.000	0.000	0.000	0.000	0.000
1	0.315	0.387	0.268	0.121	0.040	0.010	0.002	0.000	0.000	0.000	0.000
2	0.075	0.194	0.302	0.233	0.121	0.044	0.011	0.001	0.000	0.000	0.000
3	0.010	0.057	0.201	0.267	0.215	0.117	0.042	0.009	0.001	0.000	0.000
4	0.001	0.011	0.088	0.200	0.251	0.205	0.111	0.037	0.006	0.000	0.000
5	0.000	0.001	0.026	0.103	0.201	0.246	0.201	0.103	0.026	0.001	0.000
6	0.000	0.000	0.006	0.037	0.111	0.205	0.251	0.200	0.088	0.011	0.001
7	0.000	0.000	0.001	0.009	0.042	0.117	0.215	0.267	0.201	0.057	0.010
8	0.000	0.000	0.000	0.001	0.011	0.044	0.121	0.233	0.302	0.194	0.075
9	0.000	0.000	0.000	0.000	0.002	0.010	0.040	0.121	0.268	0.387	0.315
10	0.000	0.000	0.000	0.000	0.000	0.001	0.006	0.028	0.107	0.349	0.599

n = 11

Probability

x	0.05	0.10	0.20	0.30	0.40	0.50	0.60	0.70	0.80	0.90	0.95
0	0.569	0.314	0.086	0.020	0.004	0.000	0.000	0.000	0.000	0.000	0.000
1	0.329	0.384	0.236	0.093	0.027	0.005	0.001	0.000	0.000	0.000	0.000
2	0.087	0.213	0.295	0.200	0.089	0.027	0.005	0.001	0.000	0.000	0.000
3	0.014	0.071	0.221	0.257	0.177	0.081	0.023	0.004	0.000	0.000	0.000
4	0.001	0.016	0.111	0.220	0.236	0.161	0.070	0.017	0.002	0.000	0.000
5	0.000	0.002	0.039	0.132	0.221	0.226	0.147	0.057	0.010	0.000	0.000
6	0.000	0.000	0.010	0.057	0.147	0.226	0.221	0.132	0.039	0.002	0.000
7	0.000	0.000	0.002	0.017	0.070	0.161	0.236	0.220	0.111	0.016	0.001
8	0.000	0.000	0.000	0.004	0.023	0.081	0.177	0.257	0.221	0.071	0.014
9	0.000	0.000	0.000	0.001	0.005	0.027	0.089	0.200	0.295	0.213	0.087
10	0.000	0.000	0.000	0.000	0.001	0.005	0.027	0.093	0.236	0.384	0.329
11	0.000	0.000	0.000	0.000	0.000	0.000	0.004	0.020	0.086	0.314	0.569

B.9 Binomial Probability Distribution (*continued*)

$n = 12$

Probability

x	0.05	0.10	0.20	0.30	0.40	0.50	0.60	0.70	0.80	0.90	0.95
0	0.540	0.282	0.069	0.014	0.002	0.000	0.000	0.000	0.000	0.000	0.000
1	0.341	0.377	0.206	0.071	0.017	0.003	0.000	0.000	0.000	0.000	0.000
2	0.099	0.230	0.283	0.168	0.064	0.016	0.002	0.000	0.000	0.000	0.000
3	0.017	0.085	0.236	0.240	0.142	0.054	0.012	0.001	0.000	0.000	0.000
4	0.002	0.021	0.133	0.231	0.213	0.121	0.042	0.008	0.001	0.000	0.000
5	0.000	0.004	0.053	0.158	0.227	0.193	0.101	0.029	0.003	0.000	0.000
6	0.000	0.000	0.016	0.079	0.177	0.226	0.177	0.079	0.016	0.000	0.000
7	0.000	0.000	0.003	0.029	0.101	0.193	0.227	0.158	0.053	0.004	0.000
8	0.000	0.000	0.001	0.008	0.042	0.121	0.213	0.231	0.133	0.021	0.002
9	0.000	0.000	0.000	0.001	0.012	0.054	0.142	0.240	0.236	0.085	0.017
10	0.000	0.000	0.000	0.000	0.002	0.016	0.064	0.168	0.283	0.230	0.099
11	0.000	0.000	0.000	0.000	0.000	0.003	0.017	0.071	0.206	0.377	0.341
12	0.000	0.000	0.000	0.000	0.000	0.000	0.002	0.014	0.069	0.282	0.540

$n = 13$

Probability

x	0.05	0.10	0.20	0.30	0.40	0.50	0.60	0.70	0.80	0.90	0.95
0	0.513	0.254	0.055	0.010	0.001	0.000	0.000	0.000	0.000	0.000	0.000
1	0.351	0.367	0.179	0.054	0.011	0.002	0.000	0.000	0.000	0.000	0.000
2	0.111	0.245	0.268	0.139	0.045	0.010	0.001	0.000	0.000	0.000	0.000
3	0.021	0.100	0.246	0.218	0.111	0.035	0.006	0.001	0.000	0.000	0.000
4	0.003	0.028	0.154	0.234	0.184	0.087	0.024	0.003	0.000	0.000	0.000
5	0.000	0.006	0.069	0.180	0.221	0.157	0.066	0.014	0.001	0.000	0.000
6	0.000	0.001	0.023	0.103	0.197	0.209	0.131	0.044	0.006	0.000	0.000
7	0.000	0.000	0.006	0.044	0.131	0.209	0.197	0.103	0.023	0.001	0.000
8	0.000	0.000	0.001	0.014	0.066	0.157	0.221	0.180	0.069	0.006	0.000
9	0.000	0.000	0.000	0.003	0.024	0.087	0.184	0.234	0.154	0.028	0.003
10	0.000	0.000	0.000	0.001	0.006	0.035	0.111	0.218	0.246	0.100	0.021
11	0.000	0.000	0.000	0.000	0.001	0.010	0.045	0.139	0.268	0.245	0.111
12	0.000	0.000	0.000	0.000	0.000	0.002	0.011	0.054	0.179	0.367	0.351
13	0.000	0.000	0.000	0.000	0.000	0.000	0.001	0.010	0.055	0.254	0.513

(*continued*)

B.9 Binomial Probability Distribution (*concluded*)

n = 14

Probability

x	0.05	0.10	0.20	0.30	0.40	0.50	0.60	0.70	0.80	0.90	0.95
0	0.488	0.229	0.044	0.007	0.001	0.000	0.000	0.000	0.000	0.000	0.000
1	0.359	0.356	0.154	0.041	0.007	0.001	0.000	0.000	0.000	0.000	0.000
2	0.123	0.257	0.250	0.113	0.032	0.006	0.001	0.000	0.000	0.000	0.000
3	0.026	0.114	0.250	0.194	0.085	0.022	0.003	0.000	0.000	0.000	0.000
4	0.004	0.035	0.172	0.229	0.155	0.061	0.014	0.001	0.000	0.000	0.000
5	0.000	0.008	0.086	0.196	0.207	0.122	0.041	0.007	0.000	0.000	0.000
6	0.000	0.001	0.032	0.126	0.207	0.183	0.092	0.023	0.002	0.000	0.000
7	0.000	0.000	0.009	0.062	0.157	0.209	0.157	0.062	0.009	0.000	0.000
8	0.000	0.000	0.002	0.023	0.092	0.183	0.207	0.126	0.032	0.001	0.000
9	0.000	0.000	0.000	0.007	0.041	0.122	0.207	0.196	0.086	0.008	0.000
10	0.000	0.000	0.000	0.001	0.014	0.061	0.155	0.229	0.172	0.035	0.004
11	0.000	0.000	0.000	0.000	0.003	0.022	0.085	0.194	0.250	0.114	0.026
12	0.000	0.000	0.000	0.000	0.001	0.006	0.032	0.113	0.250	0.257	0.123
13	0.000	0.000	0.000	0.000	0.000	0.001	0.007	0.041	0.154	0.356	0.359
14	0.000	0.000	0.000	0.000	0.000	0.000	0.001	0.007	0.044	0.229	0.488

n = 15

Probability

x	0.05	0.10	0.20	0.30	0.40	0.50	0.60	0.70	0.80	0.90	0.95
0	0.463	0.206	0.035	0.005	0.000	0.000	0.000	0.000	0.000	0.000	0.000
1	0.366	0.343	0.132	0.031	0.005	0.000	0.000	0.000	0.000	0.000	0.000
2	0.135	0.267	0.231	0.092	0.022	0.003	0.000	0.000	0.000	0.000	0.000
3	0.031	0.129	0.250	0.170	0.063	0.014	0.002	0.000	0.000	0.000	0.000
4	0.005	0.043	0.188	0.219	0.127	0.042	0.007	0.001	0.000	0.000	0.000
5	0.001	0.010	0.103	0.206	0.186	0.092	0.024	0.003	0.000	0.000	0.000
6	0.000	0.002	0.043	0.147	0.207	0.153	0.061	0.012	0.001	0.000	0.000
7	0.000	0.000	0.014	0.081	0.177	0.196	0.118	0.035	0.003	0.000	0.000
8	0.000	0.000	0.003	0.035	0.118	0.196	0.177	0.081	0.014	0.000	0.000
9	0.000	0.000	0.001	0.012	0.061	0.153	0.207	0.147	0.043	0.002	0.000
10	0.000	0.000	0.000	0.003	0.024	0.092	0.186	0.206	0.103	0.010	0.001
11	0.000	0.000	0.000	0.001	0.007	0.042	0.127	0.219	0.188	0.043	0.005
12	0.000	0.000	0.000	0.000	0.002	0.014	0.063	0.170	0.250	0.129	0.031
13	0.000	0.000	0.000	0.000	0.000	0.003	0.022	0.092	0.231	0.267	0.135
14	0.000	0.000	0.000	0.000	0.000	0.000	0.005	0.031	0.132	0.343	0.366
15	0.000	0.000	0.000	0.000	0.000	0.000	0.000	0.005	0.035	0.206	0.463

B.10A Critical Values for the Durbin–Watson d Statistic ($\alpha = .05$)

	$k = 1$		$k = 2$		$k = 3$		$k = 4$		$k = 5$	
n	$d_{L,.05}$	$d_{U,.05}$	$d_{L,.05}$	$d_{U,.05}$	$d_{L,.05}$	$d_{U,.05}$	$d_{L,.05}$	$d_{U,.05}$	$d_{L,.05}$	$d_{U,.05}$
15	1.08	1.36	0.95	1.54	0.82	1.75	0.69	1.97	0.56	2.21
16	1.10	1.37	0.98	1.54	0.86	1.73	0.74	1.93	0.62	2.15
17	1.13	1.38	1.02	1.54	0.90	1.71	0.78	1.90	0.67	2.10
18	1.16	1.39	1.05	1.53	0.93	1.69	0.82	1.87	0.71	2.06
19	1.18	1.40	1.08	1.53	0.97	1.68	0.86	1.85	0.75	2.02
20	1.20	1.41	1.10	1.54	1.00	1.68	0.90	1.83	0.79	1.99
21	1.22	1.42	1.13	1.54	1.03	1.67	0.93	1.81	0.83	1.96
22	1.24	1.43	1.15	1.54	1.05	1.66	0.96	1.80	0.86	1.94
23	1.26	1.44	1.17	1.54	1.08	1.66	0.99	1.79	0.90	1.92
24	1.27	1.45	1.19	1.55	1.10	1.66	1.01	1.78	0.93	1.90
25	1.29	1.45	1.21	1.55	1.12	1.66	1.04	1.77	0.95	1.89
26	1.30	1.46	1.22	1.55	1.14	1.65	1.06	1.76	0.98	1.88
27	1.32	1.47	1.24	1.56	1.16	1.65	1.08	1.76	1.01	1.86
28	1.33	1.48	1.26	1.56	1.18	1.65	1.10	1.75	1.03	1.85
29	1.34	1.48	1.27	1.56	1.20	1.65	1.12	1.74	1.05	1.84
30	1.35	1.49	1.28	1.57	1.21	1.65	1.14	1.74	1.07	1.83
31	1.36	1.50	1.30	1.57	1.23	1.65	1.16	1.74	1.09	1.83
32	1.37	1.50	1.31	1.57	1.24	1.65	1.18	1.73	1.11	1.82
33	1.38	1.51	1.32	1.58	1.26	1.65	1.19	1.73	1.13	1.81
34	1.39	1.51	1.33	1.58	1.27	1.65	1.21	1.73	1.15	1.81
35	1.40	1.52	1.34	1.58	1.28	1.65	1.22	1.73	1.16	1.80
36	1.41	1.52	1.35	1.59	1.29	1.65	1.24	1.73	1.18	1.80
37	1.42	1.53	1.36	1.59	1.31	1.66	1.25	1.72	1.19	1.80
38	1.43	1.54	1.37	1.59	1.32	1.66	1.26	1.72	1.21	1.79
39	1.43	1.54	1.38	1.60	1.33	1.66	1.27	1.72	1.22	1.79
40	1.44	1.54	1.39	1.60	1.34	1.66	1.29	1.72	1.23	1.79
45	1.48	1.57	1.43	1.62	1.38	1.67	1.34	1.72	1.29	1.78
50	1.50	1.59	1.46	1.63	1.42	1.67	1.38	1.72	1.34	1.77
55	1.53	1.60	1.49	1.64	1.45	1.68	1.41	1.72	1.38	1.77
60	1.55	1.62	1.51	1.65	1.48	1.69	1.44	1.73	1.41	1.77
65	1.57	1.63	1.54	1.66	1.50	1.70	1.47	1.73	1.44	1.77
70	1.58	1.64	1.55	1.67	1.52	1.70	1.49	1.74	1.46	1.77
75	1.60	1.65	1.57	1.68	1.54	1.71	1.51	1.74	1.49	1.77
80	1.61	1.66	1.59	1.69	1.56	1.72	1.53	1.74	1.51	1.77
85	1.62	1.67	1.60	1.70	1.57	1.72	1.55	1.75	1.52	1.77
90	1.63	1.68	1.61	1.70	1.59	1.73	1.57	1.75	1.54	1.78
95	1.64	1.69	1.62	1.71	1.60	1.73	1.58	1.75	1.56	1.78
100	1.65	1.69	1.63	1.72	1.61	1.74	1.59	1.76	1.57	1.78

Appendix B

B.10B Critical Values for the Durbin–Watson d Statistic ($\alpha = .025$)

n	$k=1$ $d_{L,.025}$	$d_{U,.025}$	$k=2$ $d_{L,.025}$	$d_{U,.025}$	$k=3$ $d_{L,.025}$	$d_{U,.025}$	$k=4$ $d_{L,.025}$	$d_{U,.025}$	$k=5$ $d_{L,.025}$	$d_{U,.025}$
15	0.95	1.23	0.83	1.40	0.71	1.61	0.59	1.84	0.48	2.09
16	0.98	1.24	0.86	1.40	0.75	1.59	0.64	1.80	0.53	2.03
17	1.01	1.25	0.90	1.40	0.79	1.58	0.68	1.77	0.57	1.98
18	1.03	1.26	0.93	1.40	0.82	1.56	0.72	1.74	0.62	1.93
19	1.06	1.28	0.96	1.41	0.86	1.55	0.76	1.72	0.66	1.90
20	1.08	1.28	0.99	1.41	0.89	1.55	0.79	1.70	0.70	1.87
21	1.10	1.30	1.01	1.41	0.92	1.54	0.83	1.69	0.73	1.84
22	1.12	1.31	1.04	1.42	0.95	1.54	0.86	1.68	0.77	1.82
23	1.14	1.32	1.06	1.42	0.97	1.54	0.89	1.67	0.80	1.80
24	1.16	1.33	1.08	1.43	1.00	1.54	0.91	1.66	0.83	1.79
25	1.18	1.34	1.10	1.43	1.02	1.54	0.94	1.65	0.86	1.77
26	1.19	1.35	1.12	1.44	1.04	1.54	0.96	1.65	0.88	1.76
27	1.21	1.36	1.13	1.44	1.06	1.54	0.99	1.64	0.91	1.75
28	1.22	1.37	1.15	1.45	1.08	1.54	1.01	1.64	0.93	1.74
29	1.24	1.38	1.17	1.45	1.10	1.54	1.03	1.63	0.96	1.73
30	1.25	1.38	1.18	1.46	1.12	1.54	1.05	1.63	0.98	1.73
31	1.26	1.39	1.20	1.47	1.13	1.55	1.07	1.63	1.00	1.72
32	1.27	1.40	1.21	1.47	1.15	1.55	1.08	1.63	1.02	1.71
33	1.28	1.41	1.22	1.48	1.16	1.55	1.10	1.63	1.04	1.71
34	1.29	1.41	1.24	1.48	1.17	1.55	1.12	1.63	1.06	1.70
35	1.30	1.42	1.25	1.48	1.19	1.55	1.13	1.63	1.07	1.70
36	1.31	1.43	1.26	1.49	1.20	1.56	1.15	1.63	1.09	1.70
37	1.32	1.43	1.27	1.49	1.21	1.56	1.16	1.62	1.10	1.70
38	1.33	1.44	1.28	1.50	1.23	1.56	1.17	1.62	1.12	1.70
39	1.34	1.44	1.29	1.50	1.24	1.56	1.19	1.63	1.13	1.69
40	1.35	1.45	1.30	1.51	1.25	1.57	1.20	1.63	1.15	1.69
45	1.39	1.48	1.34	1.53	1.30	1.58	1.25	1.63	1.21	1.69
50	1.42	1.50	1.38	1.54	1.34	1.59	1.30	1.64	1.26	1.69
55	1.45	1.52	1.41	1.56	1.37	1.60	1.33	1.64	1.30	1.69
60	1.47	1.54	1.44	1.57	1.40	1.61	1.37	1.65	1.33	1.69
65	1.49	1.55	1.46	1.59	1.43	1.62	1.40	1.66	1.36	1.69
70	1.51	1.57	1.48	1.60	1.45	1.63	1.42	1.66	1.39	1.70
75	1.53	1.58	1.50	1.61	1.47	1.64	1.45	1.67	1.42	1.70
80	1.54	1.59	1.52	1.62	1.49	1.65	1.47	1.67	1.44	1.70
85	1.56	1.60	1.53	1.63	1.51	1.65	1.49	1.68	1.46	1.71
90	1.57	1.61	1.55	1.64	1.53	1.66	1.50	1.69	1.48	1.71
95	1.58	1.62	1.56	1.65	1.54	1.67	1.52	1.69	1.50	1.71
100	1.59	1.63	1.57	1.65	1.55	1.67	1.53	1.70	1.51	1.72

SOURCE: J. Durbin and G. S. Watson, "Testing for Serial Correlation in Least Squares Regression, II," *Biometrika* 30 (1951), pp. 159–78. Reproduced by permission of the Biometrika Trustees.

B.10C Critical Values for the Durbin–Watson d Statistic ($\alpha = .01$)

n	$d_{L,.01}$ ($k=1$)	$d_{U,.01}$ ($k=1$)	$d_{L,.01}$ ($k=2$)	$d_{U,.01}$ ($k=2$)	$d_{L,.01}$ ($k=3$)	$d_{U,.01}$ ($k=3$)	$d_{L,.01}$ ($k=4$)	$d_{U,.01}$ ($k=4$)	$d_{L,.01}$ ($k=5$)	$d_{U,.01}$ ($k=5$)
15	0.81	1.07	0.70	1.25	0.59	1.46	0.49	1.70	0.39	1.96
16	0.84	1.09	0.74	1.25	0.63	1.44	0.53	1.66	0.44	1.90
17	0.87	1.10	0.77	1.25	0.67	1.43	0.57	1.63	0.48	1.85
18	0.90	1.12	0.80	1.26	0.71	1.42	0.61	1.60	0.52	1.80
19	0.93	1.13	0.83	1.26	0.74	1.41	0.65	1.58	0.56	1.77
20	0.95	1.15	0.86	1.27	0.77	1.41	0.68	1.57	0.60	1.74
21	0.97	1.16	0.89	1.27	0.80	1.41	0.72	1.55	0.63	1.71
22	1.00	1.17	0.91	1.28	0.83	1.40	0.75	1.54	0.66	1.69
23	1.02	1.19	0.94	1.29	0.86	1.40	0.77	1.53	0.70	1.67
24	1.04	1.20	0.96	1.30	0.88	1.41	0.80	1.53	0.72	1.66
25	1.05	1.21	0.98	1.30	0.90	1.41	0.83	1.52	0.75	1.65
26	1.07	1.22	1.00	1.31	0.93	1.41	0.85	1.52	0.78	1.64
27	1.09	1.23	1.02	1.32	0.95	1.41	0.88	1.51	0.81	1.63
28	1.10	1.24	1.04	1.32	0.97	1.41	0.90	1.51	0.83	1.62
29	1.12	1.25	1.05	1.33	0.99	1.42	0.92	1.51	0.85	1.61
30	1.13	1.26	1.07	1.34	1.01	1.42	0.94	1.51	0.88	1.61
31	1.15	1.27	1.08	1.34	1.02	1.42	0.96	1.51	0.90	1.60
32	1.16	1.28	1.10	1.35	1.04	1.43	0.98	1.51	0.92	1.60
33	1.17	1.29	1.11	1.36	1.05	1.43	1.00	1.51	0.94	1.59
34	1.18	1.30	1.13	1.36	1.07	1.43	1.01	1.51	0.95	1.59
35	1.19	1.31	1.14	1.37	1.08	1.44	1.03	1.51	0.97	1.59
36	1.21	1.32	1.15	1.38	1.10	1.44	1.04	1.51	0.99	1.59
37	1.22	1.32	1.16	1.38	1.11	1.45	1.06	1.51	1.00	1.59
38	1.23	1.33	1.18	1.39	1.12	1.45	1.07	1.52	1.02	1.58
39	1.24	1.34	1.19	1.39	1.14	1.45	1.09	1.52	1.03	1.58
40	1.25	1.34	1.20	1.40	1.15	1.46	1.10	1.52	1.05	1.58
45	1.29	1.38	1.24	1.42	1.20	1.48	1.16	1.53	1.11	1.58
50	1.32	1.40	1.28	1.45	1.24	1.49	1.20	1.54	1.16	1.59
55	1.36	1.43	1.32	1.47	1.28	1.51	1.25	1.55	1.21	1.59
60	1.38	1.45	1.35	1.48	1.32	1.52	1.28	1.56	1.25	1.60
65	1.41	1.47	1.38	1.50	1.35	1.53	1.31	1.57	1.28	1.61
70	1.43	1.49	1.40	1.52	1.37	1.55	1.34	1.58	1.31	1.61
75	1.45	1.50	1.42	1.53	1.39	1.56	1.37	1.59	1.34	1.62
80	1.47	1.52	1.44	1.54	1.42	1.57	1.39	1.60	1.36	1.62
85	1,48	1.53	1.46	1.55	1.43	1.58	1.41	1.60	1.39	1.63
90	1.50	1.54	1.47	1.56	1.45	1.59	1.43	1.61	1.41	1.64
95	1.51	1.55	1.49	1.57	1.47	1.60	1.45	1.62	1.42	1.64
100	1.52	1.56	1.50	1.58	1.48	1.60	1.46	1.63	1.44	1.65

SOURCE: J. Durbin and G. S. Watson, "Testing for Serial Correlation in Least Squares Regression, II," *Biometrika* 30 (1951), pp. 159–78. Reproduced by permission of the Biometrika Trustees.

Appendix C: Answers

Answers to Odd-Numbered Chapter Exercises

CHAPTER 1
1. **a.** Interval
   b. Ratio
   c. Nominal
   d. Nominal
   e. Ordinal
   f. Ratio
3. Answers will vary.
5. Qualitative data is not numerical, whereas quantitative data is numerical. Examples will vary by student.
7. A discrete variable may assume only certain values. A continuous variable may assume an infinite number of values within a given range. The number of traffic citations issued each day during February in Garden City Beach, South Carolina, is a discrete variable. The weight of commercial trucks passing the weigh station at milepost 195 on Interstate 95 in North Carolina is a continuous variable.
9. **a.** Ordinal
   b. Ratio
   c. The newer system provides information on the distance between exits.
11. If you were using the Ridgedale Mall store as typical of all Gap stores, then it would be sample data. However, if you were considering it as the only store of interest, then the data would be population data.
13.

	Discrete Variable	Continuous Variable
Qualitative	b. Gender d. Soft drink preference	
Quantitative	f. SAT scores g. Student rank in class h. Rating of a finance professor i. Number of home computers	a. Salary c. Sales volume of MP3 players e. Temperature

	Discrete	Continuous
Nominal	b. Gender	
Ordinal	d. Soft drink preference g. Student rank in class h. Rating of a finance professor	
Interval	f. SAT scores	e. Temperature
Ratio	i. Number of home computers	a. Salary c. Sales volume of MP3 players

15. According to the sample information, 120/300 or 40% would accept a job transfer.
17. **a.** Sales declined by 57,799 units or 5.8 percent.
   b. GM declined by 16.6 percent and Ford by 19.0 percent. Toyota increased by 9.5 percent and Nissan by 8.9 percent.

19. Earnings have increased every year over all previous years.
21. **a.** Grass or artificial turf field is a qualitative variable, the others are quantitative.
   b. Grass or artificial turf field is a nominal-level variable, the others are ratio-level variables.
23. **a.** All variables are quantitative except G-20 and petroleum.
   b. All variables are ratio except G-20 and petroleum, which are nominal.

CHAPTER 2
1. Answers will vary.
3.

Season	Frequency	Relative Frequency
Winter	100	.10
Spring	300	.30
Summer	400	.40
Fall	200	.20
	1,000	1.00

5. **a.** Frequency table
   b.

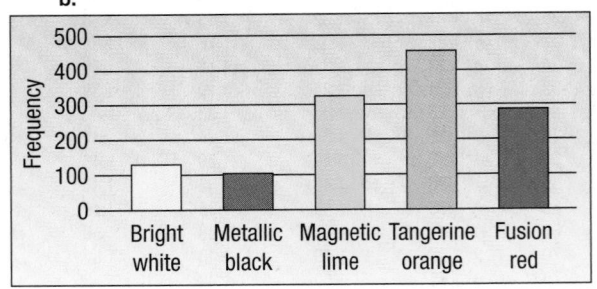

   c.

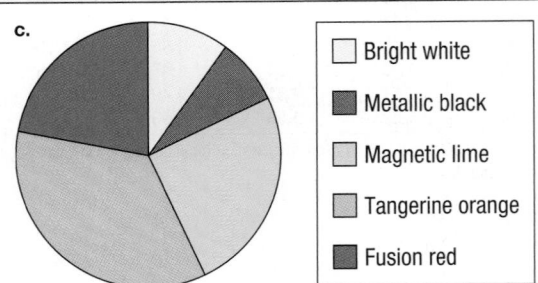

   d.

Color	Frequency	Relative Frequency	Production
Bright white	130	0.10	100,000
Metallic black	104	0.08	80,000
Magnetic lime	325	0.25	250,000
Tangerine orange	455	0.35	350,000
Fusion red	286	0.22	220,000
	1,300	1.00	1,000,000

Note: Production estimates are found by multiplying the relative frequency by the total production of 1,000,000 units.

7. $2^5 = 32$, $2^6 = 64$, therefore, 6 classes

9. $2^7 = 128$, $2^8 = 256$, suggests 8 classes

$i \geq \dfrac{567 - 235}{8} = 41$ Class intervals of 40, 45, or 50 all

would be acceptable.

11. **a.** $2^4 = 16$ Suggests 5 classes.

   b. $i \geq \dfrac{31 - 25}{5} = 1.2$ Use interval of 1.5.

   c. 24

   d.

Patients	f	Relative Frequency
24.0 up to 25.5	2	0.125
25.5 up to 27.0	4	0.250
27.0 up to 28.5	8	0.500
28.5 up to 30.0	0	0.000
30.0 up to 31.5	2	0.125
Total	16	1.000

   e. The largest concentration is in the 27.0 up to 28.5 class (8).

13. **a.**

Number of Visits	f
0 up to 3	9
3 up to 6	21
6 up to 9	13
9 up to 12	4
12 up to 15	3
15 up to 18	1
Total	51

   b. The largest group of shoppers (21) shop at the BiLo Supermarket 3, 4, or 5 times during a month period. Some customers visit the store only 1 time during the month, but others shop as many as 15 times.

   c.

Number of Visits	Percent of Total
0 up to 3	17.65
3 up to 6	41.18
6 up to 9	25.49
9 up to 12	7.84
12 up to 15	5.88
15 up to 18	1.96
Total	100.00

15. **a.** Histogram

   b. 100

   c. 5

   d. 28

   e. 0.28

   f. 12.5

   g. 13

17. **a.** 50

   b. 1.5 thousand miles, or 1,500 miles.

   c.

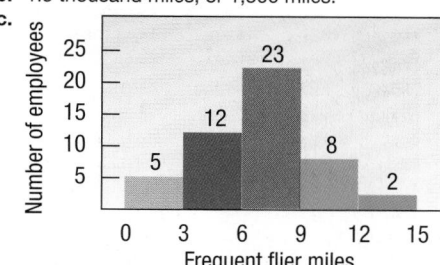

   d. $X = 1.5$, $Y = 5$

e.

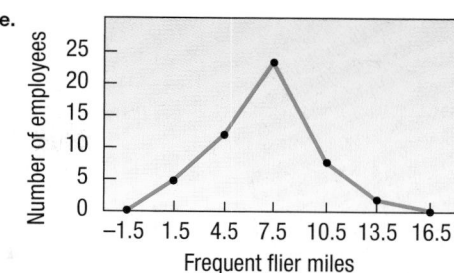

   f. For the 50 employees about half traveled between 6,000 and 9,000 miles. Five employees traveled less than 3,000 miles, and 2 traveled more than 12,000 miles.

19. **a.** 40

   b. 5

   c. 11 or 12

   d. About $18/hr

   e. About $9/hr

   f. About 75%

21. **a.** 5

   b.

Frequent Flier Miles	f	CF
0 up to 3	5	5
3 up to 6	12	17
6 up to 9	23	40
9 up to 12	8	48
12 up to 15	2	50

   c.

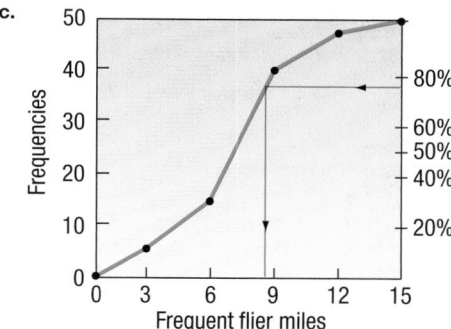

   d. About 8.7 thousand miles

23. **a.** A qualitative variable uses either the nominal or ordinal scale of measurement. It is usually the result of counts. Quantitative variables are either discrete or continuous. There is a natural order to the results for a quantitative variable. Quantitative variables can use the either the interval or ratio scale of measurement.

   b. Both types of variables can be used for samples and populations.

25. **a.** Frequency table

   b.

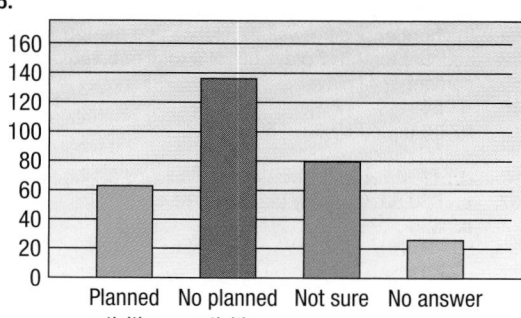

c.

☐	Planned Activities
■	No Planned Activities
▨	Not Sure
▨	No Answer

d. A pie chart would be better because it clearly shows that nearly half of the customers prefer no planned activities.

27. $2^6 = 64$ and $2^7 = 128$, suggest 7 classes

29. a. 5, because $2^4 = 16 < 25$ and $2^5 = 32 > 25$

b. $i \geq \dfrac{48 - 16}{5} = 6.4$ Use interval of 7.

c. 15

d.

Class	Frequency	
15 up to 22	III	3
22 up to 29	IIII III	8
29 up to 36	IIII II	7
36 up to 43	IIII	5
43 up to 50	II	2
		25

e. It is fairly symmetric, with most of the values between 22 and 36.

31. a. $2^5 = 32$, $2^6 = 64$, 6 classes recommended.

b. $i = \dfrac{10 - 1}{6} = 1.5$, use an interval of 2.

c. 0

d.

Class	Frequency
0 up to 2	1
2 up to 4	5
4 up to 6	12
6 up to 8	17
8 up to 10	8

e. The distribution is fairly symmetric or bell-shaped with a large peak in the middle of the two classes of 4 up to 8.

33.

Class	Frequency
0 up to 200	19
200 up to 400	1
400 up to 600	4
600 up to 800	1
800 up to 1000	2

This distribution is positively skewed with a large "tail" to the right or positive values. Notice that the top 7 tunes account for 4,342 plays out of a total of 5,968 or about 73 percent of all plays.

35. a. 56
b. 10 (found by $60 - 50$)
c. 55
d. 17

37. a. $30.50, found by ($265 − $82)/6.
b. $35

c.

$ 70 up to $105	4
105 up to 140	17
140 up to 175	14
175 up to 210	2
210 up to 245	6
245 up to 280	1

d. The purchases range from a low of about $70 to a high of about $280. The concentration is in the $105 up to $140 and $140 up to $175 classes.

39.

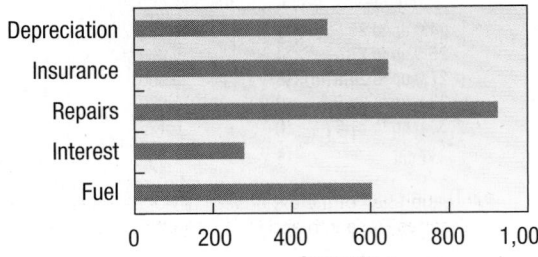

41.

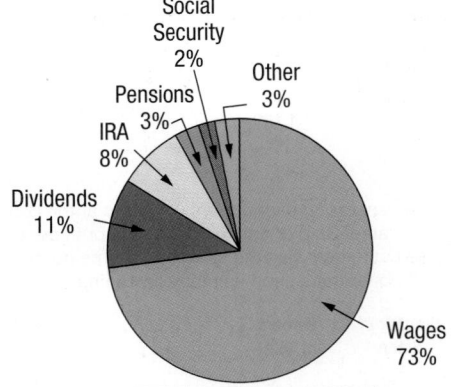

SC Income	Percent	Cumulative
Wages	73	73
Dividends	11	84
IRA	8	92
Pensions	3	95
Social Security	2	97
Other	3	100

By far the largest part of income in South Carolina is earned income. Almost three-fourths of the adjusted gross income comes from wages and salaries. Dividends and IRAs each contribute roughly another 10%.

43. a. Since $2^6 = 64 < 70 < 128 = 2^7$, 7 classes are recommended. The interval should be at least $(1,002.2 - 3.3)/7 = 142.7$. Use 150 as a convenient value.

b.

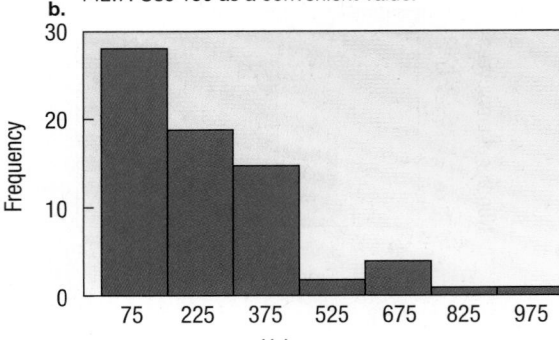

45.

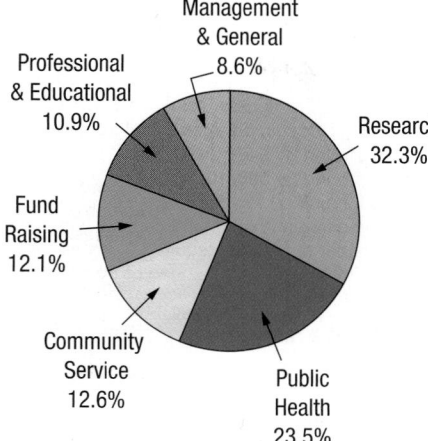

More than half of the expenses are concentrated in the categories Research and Public Health Education.

47.

Partner	Imports	Relative Frequency
Japan	9,550	0.52
United Kingdom	4,556	0.25
South Korea	2,441	0.13
China	1,182	0.06
Australia	618	0.03
	18,347	

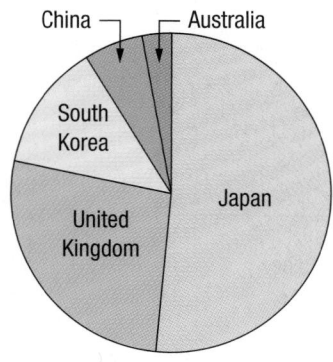

More than half of Canadian imports are from Japan. Japan and the United Kingdom make up more than 75 percent of Canadian imports.

49.

Color	Frequency
Brown	130
Yellow	98
Red	96
Blue	52
Orange	35
Green	33
	444

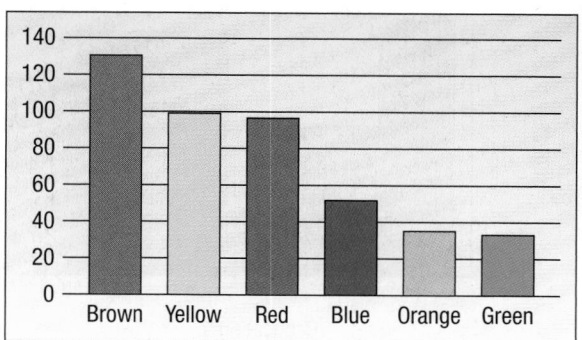

51. 25% market share

53. a.

Bedrooms	Frequency
2	24
3	26
4	26
5	11
6	14
7	2
8	2

1. A typical home had either 3 or 4 bedrooms. Seventy-two percent of the homes had 2, 3, or 4 bedrooms.
2. The fewest bedrooms was 2 and the most 8.

b. $i \geq \dfrac{345.3 - 125.0}{7} = 31.47$. Use interval of 35.

Selling Price ($000)	F	CF
110 up to 145	3	3
145 up to 180	19	22
180 up to 215	31	53
215 up to 250	25	78
250 up to 285	14	92
285 up to 320	10	102
320 up to 355	3	105

1. Most homes (53%) are in the 180 up to 250 range.
2. The largest value is near 355, the smallest near 110.

c.

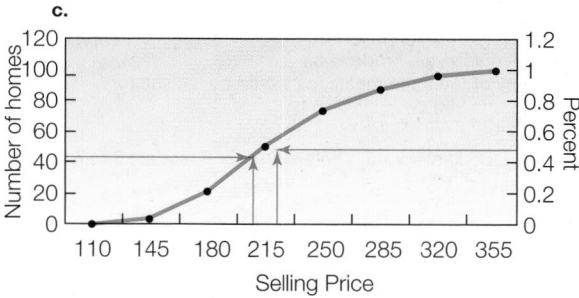

1. About 42 homes sold for less than 200.
2. About 55 percent of the homes sold for less than 220, so 45% sold for more.
3. Less than 1% of the homes sold for less than 125.
d. The selling price ranges from about $120,000 up to about $360,000. A typical home sold for about $210,000.

55.

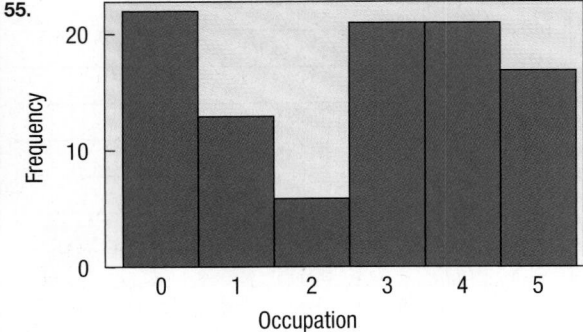

Occupational category 2 has the fewest members and most of the others are around 19.

CHAPTER 3

1. $\mu = 5.4$, found by 27/5
3. **a.** $\overline{X} = 7.0$, found by 28/4
   b. $(5 - 7) + (9 - 7) + (4 - 7) + (10 - 7) = 0$
5. $\overline{X} = 14.58$, found by 43.74/3.
7. **a.** 15.4, found by 154/10
   b. Population parameter, since it includes all the sales at Midtown Ford
9. **a.** $54.55, found by $1,091/20
   b. A sample statistic—assuming that the power company serves more than 20 customers
11. $\overline{X} = \dfrac{\Sigma X}{n}$ so
   $\Sigma X = \overline{X} \cdot n = (\$5430)(30) = \$162,900$
13. $22.91, found by $\dfrac{300(\$20) + 400(\$25) + 400(\$23)}{300 + 400 + 400}$
15. $17.75, found by ($400 + $750 + $2,400)/200
17. **a.** No mode
   b. The given value would be the mode.
   c. 3 and 4 bimodal
19. **a.** Mean = 3.25
   b. Median = 5,
   c. Mode = 5
21. **a.** Median = 2.9
   b. Mode = 2.9
23. $\overline{X} = \dfrac{647}{11} = 58.82$
   Median = 58, Mode = 58
   Any of the three measures would be satisfactory.
25. **a.** $\overline{X} = \dfrac{90.4}{12} = 7.53$
   b. Median = 7.45. There are several modes: 6.5, 7.3, 7.8, and 8.7
   c. $\overline{X} = \dfrac{33.8}{4} = 8.45,$
   Median = 8.7
   About 1 percentage point higher in Winter
27. 12.8 percent increase, found by
   $\sqrt[5]{(1.08)(1.12)(1.14)(1.26)(1.05)} = 1.128$
29. 12.28 percent increase, found by
   $\sqrt[5]{(1.094)(1.138)(1.117)(1.119)(1.147)} = 1.1228$
31. $GM = \sqrt[13]{\dfrac{210.2}{148.2}} - 1.00 = 1.0272 - 1.00 = .0272$
   Rate of increase is 2.72%.
33. $GM = \sqrt[21]{\dfrac{233,000,000}{340,213}} = 1.3647 - 1.00 = .3647$
   Rate of increase is 36.47 percent per year.

35. **a.** 7, found by 10 − 3.
   b. 6, found by 30/5.
   c. 2.4, found by 12/5.
   d. The difference between the highest number sold (10) and the smallest number sold (3) is 7. On average, the number of HDTV's sold deviates by 2.4 from the mean of 6.
37. **a.** 30, found by 54 − 24.
   b. 38, found by 380/10.
   c. 7.2, found by 72/10.
   d. The difference of 54 and 24 is 30. On average, the number of minutes required to install a door deviates 7.2 minutes from the mean of 38 minutes.
39.

State	Mean	Median	Range
California	33.10	34.0	32
Iowa	24.50	25.0	19

The mean and median ratings were higher, but there was also more variation in California.
41. **a.** 5
   b. 4.4, found by
$$\frac{(8 - 5)^2 + (3 - 5)^2 + (7 - 5)^2 + (3 - 5)^2 + (4 - 5)^2}{5}$$
43. **a.** $2.77
   b. 1.26, found by
$$\frac{(2.68 - 2.77)^2 + (1.03 - 2.77)^2 + (2.26 - 2.77)^2 + (4.30 - 2.77)^2 + (3.58 - 2.77)^2}{5}$$
45. **a.** Range: 7.3, found by 11.6 − 4.3. Arithmetic mean: 6.94, found by 34.7/5. Variance: 6.5944, found by 32.972/5. Standard deviation: 2.568, found by $\sqrt{6.5944}$.
   b. Dennis has a higher mean return (11.76 > 6.94). However, Dennis has greater spread in its returns on equity (16.89 > 6.59).
47. **a.** $\overline{X} = 4$
$$s^2 = \frac{(7 - 4)^2 + \cdots + (3 - 4)^2}{5 - 1} = 5.5$$
$$s^2 = \frac{22}{5 - 1} = 5.50$$
   b. $s = 2.3452$
49. **a.** $\overline{X} = 38$
$$s^2 = \frac{(28 - 38)^2 + \cdots + (42 - 38)^2}{10 - 1} = 82.667$$
$$s^2 = \frac{744}{10 - 1} = 82.667$$
   b. $s = 9.0921$
51. **a.** $\overline{X} = \dfrac{951}{10} = 95.1$
$$s^2 = \frac{(101 - 95.1)^2 + \cdots + (88 - 95.1)^2}{10 - 1}$$
$$= \frac{1,112.9}{9} = 123.66$$
   b. $s = \sqrt{123.66} = 11.12$
53. About 69%, found by $1 - 1/(1.8)^2$
55. **a.** About 95%
   b. 47.5%, 2.5%
57. Because the exact values in a frequency distribution are not known, the midpoint is used for every member of that class.
59.

Class	f	M	fM	$(M - \overline{X})$	$f(M - \overline{X})^2$
20 up to 30	7	25	175	−22.29	3,477.909
30 up to 40	12	35	420	−12.29	1,812.529
40 up to 50	21	45	945	−2.29	110.126
50 up to 60	18	55	990	7.71	1,069.994
60 up to 70	12	65	780	17.71	3,763.729
	70		3,310		10,234.287

$$\overline{X} = \frac{3,310}{70} = 47.29$$

$$s = \sqrt{\frac{10,234.287}{70 - 1}} = 12.18$$

61.

Number of Clients	f	M	fM	$(M - \overline{X})$	$f(M - \overline{X})^2$
20 up to 30	1	25	25	−19.8	392.04
30 up to 40	15	35	525	−9.8	1,440.60
40 up to 50	22	45	990	0.2	0.88
50 up to 60	8	55	440	10.2	832.32
60 up to 70	4	65	260	20.2	1,632.16
	50		2,240		4,298.00

$$\overline{X} = \frac{2,240}{50} = 44.8$$

$$s = \sqrt{\frac{4,298}{50 - 1}} = 9.37$$

63.
  a. Mean = 5, found by (6 + 4 + 3 + 7 + 5)/5.
Median is 5, found by rearranging the values and selecting the middle value.
  b. Population, because all partners were included
  c. $\Sigma(X - \mu) = (6 - 5) + (4 - 5) + (3 - 5) + (7 - 5) + (5 - 5) = 0$.

65. $\overline{X} = \frac{545}{16} = 34.06$

Median = 37.50

67. The data indicates that the communication industry favors older workers, the retail trade favors younger workers. The production workers showed the greatest difference in age. For communication, the distribution is skewed toward older workers. For retail trade, the ages are skewed toward younger workers.

69. $\overline{X}_w = \frac{\$5.00(270) + \$6.50(300) + \$8.00(100)}{270 + 300 + 100} = \$6.12$

71. $\overline{X}_w = \frac{[15,300(4.5) + 10,400(3.0) + 150,600(10.2)]}{176,300} = 9.28$

73. GM $= \sqrt[21]{\frac{6,286,800}{5,164,900}} - 1 = 1.0094 - 1.0 = .0094$

75.
  a. 55, found by 72 − 17
  b. 14.4, found by 144/10, where $\overline{X} = 43.2$
  c. 17.6245

77.
  a. Population
  b. 183.47

79.
  a. There were 13 flights, so all items are considered.
  b. $\mu = \frac{2,259}{13} = 173.77$

    Median = 195
  c. Range = 301 − 7 = 294

$$s = \sqrt{\frac{133,846}{13}} = 101.47$$

81.
  a. The mean is $717.20, found by $17,930/25. The median is $717.00 and there are two modes, $710 and $722.
  b. The range is $90, found by $771 − $681, and the standard deviation is $24.87, found by the square root of 14,850/24.
  c. From $667.46 up to $766.94, found by $717.20 ± 2($24.87).

83.
  a. The mean 0.8654, found by 17.309/2. The median is 0.86 and the mode is 0.792.
  b. The range is 0.269, found by 1.025 − 0.756 and the standard deviation is 0.0853, found by the square root of 0.138167/19.
  c. From 0.6948 up to 1.036, found by 0.8654 ± 2(0.0853).

85.
  a. $\overline{X} = \frac{273}{30} = 9.1$, Median = 9

  b. Range = 18 − 4 = 14
$$s = \sqrt{\frac{368.7}{30 - 1}} = 3.57$$

  c. $2^5 = 32$, so suggest 5 classes
$$i = \frac{18 - 4}{5} = 2.8. \quad \text{Use } i = 3$$

Class	M	f	fM	$M - \overline{X}$	$(M - \overline{X})^2$	$f(M - \overline{X})^2$
3.5 up to 6.5	5	10	50	−4	16	160
6.5 up to 9.5	8	6	48	−1	1	6
9.5 up to 12.5	11	9	99	2	4	36
12.5 up to 15.5	14	4	56	5	25	100
15.5 up to 18.5	17	1	17	8	64	64
			270			366

  d. $\overline{x} = \frac{270}{30} = 9.0$

$$s = \sqrt{\frac{366}{30 - 1}} = 3.552$$

The mean and standard deviation from grouped data are estimates of the mean and standard deviations of the actual values.

87.

Distance	f	M	fM	$f(M - \overline{X})^2$
0 up to 5	4	2.5	10.0	441.00
5 up to 10	15	7.5	112.5	453.75
10 up to 15	27	12.5	337.5	6.75
15 up to 20	18	17.5	315.0	364.50
20 up to 25	6	22.5	135.0	541.50
			910.0	1,807.50

$$\overline{X} = \frac{910}{70} = 13$$

$$s = \sqrt{\frac{1,807.5}{70 - 1}} = 5.118$$

89.
  a. The mean is $83,160,000. The median is $87,550,000. The standard deviation is $33,470,000.
  b. In 2009, the mean age is 26.87. The median age is 16.5. The standard deviation is 26.18.
  c. The mean is 45,820. The median is 44,174. The standard deviation is 5,856.

CHAPTER 4

1. In a histogram observations are grouped so their individual identity is lost. With a dot plot, identity of each observation is maintained.

3.
  a. Dot plot
  b. 15
  c. 1, 7
  d. 2 and 3

5.
  a. 620 to 629
  b. 5
  c. 621, 623, 623, 627, 629

7.
  a. 25
  b. One
  c. 38,106
  d. 60, 61, 63, 63, 65, 65, 69
  e. No values
  f. 9
  g. 9
  h. 76
  i. 16

9.

Stem	Leaves
0	5
1	28
2	
3	0024789
4	12366
5	2

There were a total of 16 calls studied. The number of calls ranged from 5 to 52. Seven of the 16 subscribers made between 30 and 39 calls.

11. Median = 53, found by $(11 + 1)(\frac{1}{2})$ ∴ 6th value in from lowest

$Q_1 = 49$, found by $(11 + 1)(\frac{1}{4})$ ∴ 3rd value in from lowest

$Q_3 = 55$, found by $(11 + 1)(\frac{3}{4})$ ∴ 9th value in from lowest

13. a. $Q_1 = 33.25$, $Q_3 = 50.25$

    b. $D_2 = 27.8$, $D_8 = 52.6$

    c. $P_{67} = 47$

15. a. 350

    b. $Q_1 = 175$, $Q_3 = 930$

    c. $930 - 175 = 755$

    d. Less than 0, or more than about 2,060

    e. There are no outliers.

    f. The distribution is positively skewed.

17.

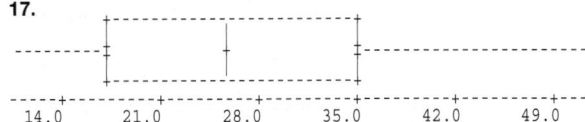

The distribution is somewhat positively skewed. Note that the dashed line above 35 is longer than below 18.

19. a. The mean is 30.8, found by 154/5. The median is 31.0, and the standard deviation is 3.96, found by

$$\sqrt{\frac{62.8}{4}}$$

    b. -0.15, found by $\dfrac{3(30.8 - 31.0)}{3.96}$

    c.

Salary	$\left(\dfrac{X - \overline{X}}{s}\right)$	$\left(\dfrac{X - \overline{X}}{s}\right)^3$
36	1.313131	2.264250504
26	−1.212121	−1.780894343
33	0.555556	0.171467764
28	−0.707071	−0.353499282
31	0.050505	0.000128826
		0.301453469

0.125, found by $[5/(4 \times 3)] \times 0.301$

21. a. The mean is 21.93, found by 328.9/15. The median is 15.8, and the standard deviation is 21.18, found by

$$\sqrt{\frac{6283}{14}}$$

    b. 0.868, found by $[3(21.93 - 15.8)]/21.18$

    c. 2.444, found by $[15/(14 \times 13)] \times 29.658$

23.

Scatter Diagram of Y versus X

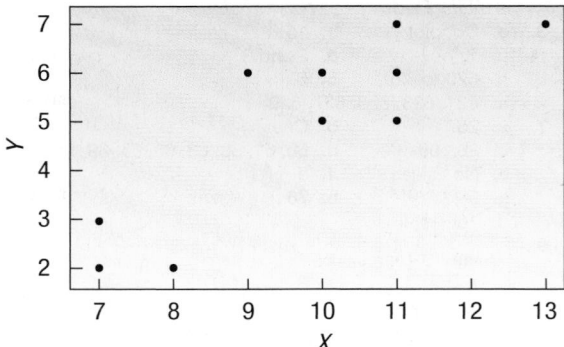

There is a positive relationship between the variables.

25. a. Both variables are nominal scale.

    b. Contingency table

    c. Men are about twice as likely to order a dessert. From the table 32 percent of the men ordered dessert, but only 15 percent of the women.

27. a. Dot plot

    b. 15

    c. 5

29. Stem-and-leaf $N = 23$

3	3	222
3	3	
5	3	77
5	3	
10	4	00000
11	4	2
11	4	
(6)	4	666666
6	4	
6	5	
6	5	222222

31. a. $L_{50} = (20 + 1)\frac{50}{100} = 10.50$

      Median $= \dfrac{83.7 + 85.6}{2} = 84.65$

      $L_{25} = (21)(.25) = 5.25$

      $Q_1 = 66.6 + .25(72.9 - 66.6) = 68.175$

      $L_{75} = 21(.75) = 15.75$

      $Q_3 = 87.1 + .75(90.2 - 87.1) = 89.425$

    b. $L_{26} = 21(.26) = 5.46$

      $P_{26} = 66.6 + .46(72.9 - 66.6) = 69.498$

      $L_{83} = 21(.83) = 17.43$

      $P_{83} = 93.3 + .43(98.6 - 93.3)$

           $= 95.579$

    c.

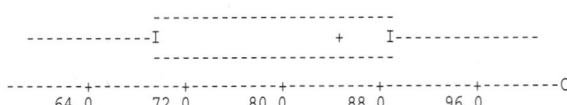

33. a. $Q_1 = 26.25$, $Q_3 = 35.75$, Median $= 31.50$

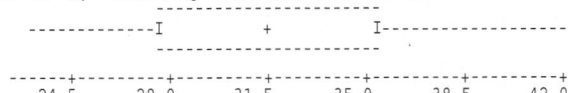

    b. $Q_1 = 33.25$, $Q_3 = 38.75$, Median $= 37.50$

    c. The median time for public transportation is about 6 minutes less. There is more variation in public transportation. The difference between Q_1 and Q_3 is 9.5 minutes for public transportation and 5.5 minutes for private transportation.

35. The distribution is positively skewed. The first quartile is approx. $20 and the third quartile is approx. $90. There is one outlier located at $255. The median is about $50.

37. a.

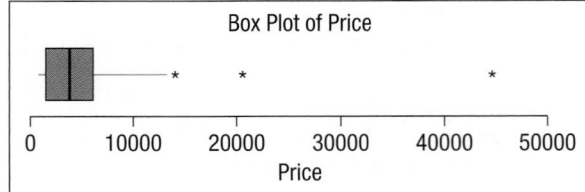

Median is 3373. First quartile is 1478. Third quartile is 6141. So prices over 13,135.5, found by 6141 + 1.5 (6141 − 1478), are outliers. There are three (13,925; 20,413 and 44,312).

b.

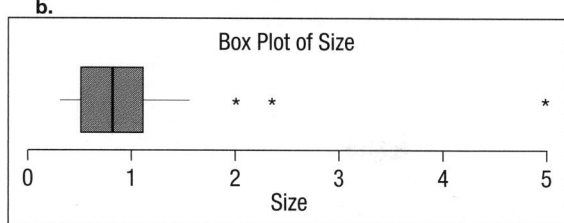

Box Plot of Size

Median is 0.84. First quartile is 0.515. Third quartile is 1.12. So sizes over 2.0275, found by 1.12 + 1.5 (1.12 − 0.515), are outliers. There are three (2.03, 2.35, and 5.03).

c.

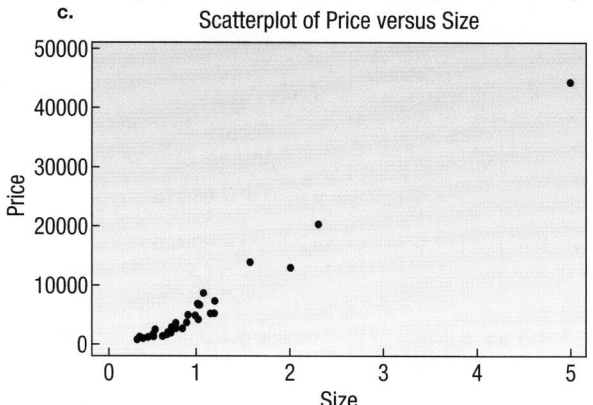

Scatterplot of Price versus Size

There is a direct association between them. The first observation is larger on both scales.

d.

Shape\Cut	Average	Good	Ideal	Premium	Ultra Ideal	All
Emerald	0	0	1	0	0	1
Marquise	0	2	0	1	0	3
Oval	0	0	0	1	0	1
Princess	1	0	2	2	0	5
Round	1	3	3	13	3	23
Total	2	5	6	17	3	33

The majority of the diamonds are round (23). Premium cut is most common (17). The Round Premium combination occurs most often (13).

39. $sk = 0.065$ or $sk = \dfrac{3(7.7143 - 8.0)}{3.9036} = -0.22$

41.

Scatterplot of Accidents versus Age

As age increases, the number of accidents decreases.

43.
  a. 139,340,000
  b. 5.4% unemployed, found by (7523/139,340)100
  c. Men = 5.64%
  Women = 5.12%
45.
  a. There are two outliers, Wrigley Field in Chicago and Fenway Park in Boston. Both of these stadiums are more than 90 years old.
  b. Q_1 = $65.08 million and Q_3 = $100.75 million. The distribution is positively skewed, with the New York Yankees an outlier.
  c. Higher salaries lead to more wins; lower salaries, fewer wins.
  d. The distribution is fairly uniform between 66 wins and 96 wins.
47.
  a. The first quartile is 71.5 years and the third is 78.5 years. The distribution is negatively skewed with two outliers (Nigeria and South Africa at 48 and 51, respectively).
  b. The first quartile is 8.3 and the third quartile is 24.4. The distribution is symmetric with no outliers.
  c. Stem-and-leaf of cell phones, $N = 46$, Leaf Unit = 1.0

(35)	0	00000000000111111122222222233344444
11	0	68
9	1	123
6	1	5
5	2	0
4	2	7
3	3	
3	3	
3	4	
3	4	
3	5	
3	5	
3	6	3
2	6	59

The distribution is extremely positively skewed. The median is 2 and the mean is around 8, which is above the third quartile of about 5.

CHAPTER 5
1.

Outcome	Person 1	Person 2
1	A	A
2	A	F
3	F	A
4	F	F

3.
  a. .176, found by $\dfrac{6}{34}$
  b. Empirical
5.
  a. Empirical
  b. Classical
  c. Classical
  d. Empirical, based on seismological data
7.
  a. The survey of 40 people about environmental issues
  b. 26 or more respond yes, for example
  c. 10/40 = .25
  d. Empirical
  e. The events are not equally likely, but they are mutually exclusive.
9.
  a. Answers will vary. Here are some possibilities: 123, 124, 125, 999
  b. $(1/10)^3$
  c. Classical
11. $P(A \text{ or } B) = P(A) + P(B) = .30 + .20 = .50$
  $P(\text{neither}) = 1 − .50 = .50$.
13.
  a. 102/200 = .51
  b. .49, found by 61/200 + 37/200 = .305 + .185. Special rule of addition.

15. $P(\text{above } C) = .25 + .50 = .75$

17. $P(A \text{ or } B) = P(A) + P(B) - P(A \text{ and } B)$
$= .20 + .30 - .15 = .35$

19. When two events are mutually exclusive, it means that if one occurs the other event cannot occur. Therefore, the probability of their joint occurrence is zero.

21. **a.** $P(P \text{ and } F) = 0.20$
   b. $P(P \text{ and } D) = 0.30$
   c. No
   d. Joint probability
   e. $P(P \text{ or } D \text{ or } F) = 1 - P(P \text{ and } D \text{ and } F)$
   $= 1 - .10 = .90$

23. $P(A \text{ and } B) = P(A) \times P(B|A) = .40 \times .30 = .12$

25. .90, found by $(.80 + .60) - .5.$
.10, found by $(1 - .90)$.

27. **a.** $P(A_1) = 3/10 = .30$
   b. $P(B_1|A_2) = 1/3 = .33$
   c. $P(B_2 \text{ and } A_3) = 1/10 = .10$

29. **a.** A contingency table
   b. .27, found by $300/500 \times 135/300$
   c. The tree diagram would appear as:

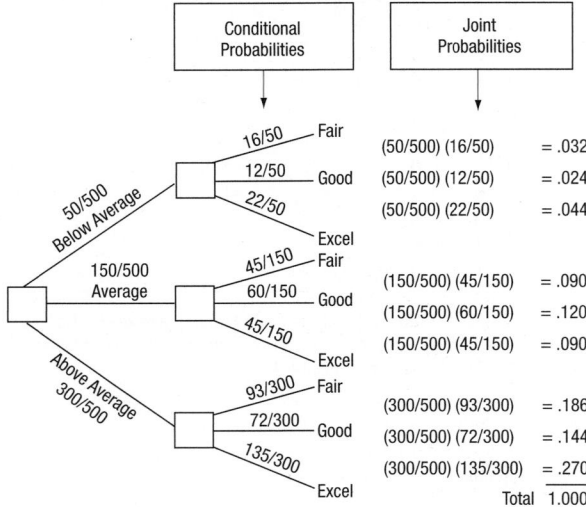

31. Probability the first presentation wins $= 3/5 = .60$
Probability the second presentation wins $= (2/5)(3/4) = .30$
Probability the third presentation wins $= (2/5)(1/4)(3/3) = .10$

33. $P(A_1|B_1) = \dfrac{P(A_1) \times P(B_1|A_1)}{P(A_1) \times P(B_1|A_1) + P(A_2) \times P(B_1|A_2)}$
$= \dfrac{.60 \times .05}{(.60 \times .05) + (.40 \times .10)} = .4286$

35. $P(\text{night}|\text{win}) = \dfrac{P(\text{night})P(\text{win}|\text{night})}{P(\text{night})P(\text{win}|\text{night}) + P(\text{day})P(\text{win}|\text{day})}$
$= \dfrac{(.70)(.50)}{[(.70)(.50)] + [(.30)(.90)]} = .5645$

37. $P(\text{cash or check} \mid > \$50)$
$= \dfrac{P(\text{cash or check}) \, P(> \$50 \mid \text{cash or check})}{\substack{P(\text{cash or check}) \, P(> \$50 \mid \text{cash or check}) \\ + P(\text{credit}) \, P(> \$50 \mid \text{credit}) \\ + P(\text{debit}) \, P(> \$50 \mid \text{debit})}}$
$= \dfrac{(.30)(.20)}{(.30)(.20) + (.30)(.90) + (.40)(.60)} = .1053$

39. **a.** 78,960,960
   b. 840, found by $(7)(6)(5)(4)$. That is $7!/3!$
   c. 10, found by $5!/3!2!$

41. 210, found by $(10)(9)(8)(7)/(4)(3)(2)$

43. 120, found by 5!

45. 10,897,286,400, found by
$_{15}P_{10} = (15)(14)(13)(12)(11)(10)(9)(8)(7)(6)$

47. **a.** Asking teenagers to compare their reactions to a newly developed soft drink.
   b. Answers will vary. One possibility is more than half of the respondents like it.

49. Subjective

51. **a.** 4/9, found by $(2/3) \cdot (2/3)$.
   b. 3/4, because $(3/4) \cdot (2/3) = 0.5$.

53. **a.** .8145, found by $(.95)^4$
   b. Special rule of multiplication
   c. $P(A \text{ and } B \text{ and } C \text{ and } D) = P(A) \times P(B) \times P(C) \times P(D)$

55. **a.** .08, found by $.80 \times .10$
   b. No; 90% of females attended college, 78% of males
   c.

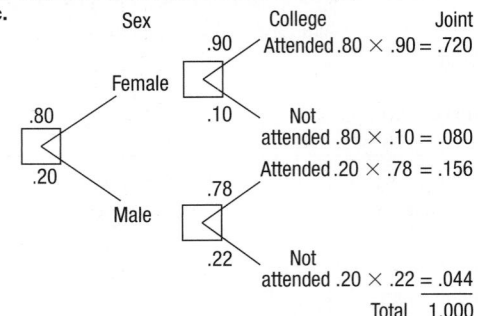

   d. Yes, because all the possible outcomes are shown on the tree diagram.

57. **a.** 0.57, found by 57/100
   b. 0.97, found by $(57/100) + (40/100)$
   c. Yes, because an employee cannot be both.
   d. 0.03, found by $1 - 0.97$

59. **a.** 0.4096, found by $(0.8)^4$
   b. 0.0016, found by $(0.2)^4$
   c. 0.9984, found by $1 - 0.0016$

61. **a.** 0.9039, found by $(0.98)^5$
   b. 0.0961, found by $1 - 0.9039$

63. **a.** 0.0333, found by $(4/10)(3/9)(2/8)$
   b. 0.1667, found by $(6/10)(5/9)(4/8)$
   c. 0.8333, found by $1 - 0.1667$
   d. Dependent

65. **a.** 0.3818, found by $(9/12)(8/11)(7/10)$
   b. 0.6182, found by $1 - 0.3818$

67. **a.** $P(S) \cdot P(R|S) = .60(.85) = 0.51$
   b. $P(S) \cdot P(PR|S) = .60(1 - .85) = 0.09$

69. **a.** $P(\text{not perfect}) = P(\text{bad sector}) + P(\text{defective})$
   $= \dfrac{112}{1,000} + \dfrac{31}{1,000} = .143$
   b. $P(\text{defective/not perfect}) = \dfrac{.031}{.143} = .217$

71. $P(\text{poor}|\text{profit}) = \dfrac{.10(.20)}{.10(.20) + .60(.80) + .30(.60)}$
$= .0294$

73. **a.** $P(P \text{ or } D) = (1/50)(9/10) + (49/50)(1/10) = 0.116$
   b. $P(\text{No}) = (49/50)(9/10) = 0.882$
   c. $P(\text{No on 3}) = (0.882)^3 = 0.686$
   d. $P(\text{at least one prize}) = 1 - 0.686 = 0.314$

75. Yes, 256 is found by 2^8

77. .9744, found by $1 - (.40)^4$

79. **a.** .185, found by $(.15)(.95) + (.05)(.85)$
   b. .0075, found by $(.15)(.05)$

81. a. $P(F$ and $>60) = .25$, found by solving with the general rule of multiplication:
$P(F) \cdot P(>60|F) = (.5)(.5)$
b. 0
c. .3333, found by 1/3

83. $26^4 = 456,976$

85. 1/3, 628,800

87. a. $P(D) = .20(.03) + .30(.04) + .25(.07) + .25(.065)$
$= .05175$

b. $P(\text{Tyson}|\text{defective}) = \dfrac{.20(.03)}{.20(.03) + .30(.04) + .25(.07) + .25(.065)} = .1159$

Supplier	Joint	Revised
Tyson	.00600	.1159
Fuji	.01200	.2319
Kirkpatricks	.01750	.3382
Parts	.01625	.3140
	.05175	1.0000

89. 0.512, found by $(0.8)^3$

91. .525, found by $1 - (.78)^3$

93. a.

Winning Season	Attendance			
	Low	Medium	High	Total
No	6	5	3	14
Yes	0	9	7	16
Total	6	14	10	30

1. $P(\text{win}) = \dfrac{16}{30} = .533$

2. $P(\text{win or high}) = \dfrac{16}{30} + \dfrac{10}{30} - \dfrac{7}{30} = .633$

3. $P(\text{win}|\text{high}) = \dfrac{7}{10} = .70$

4. $P(\text{lose and low}) = \dfrac{6}{30} = .200$

b.

Winning Season	Grass	Artificial	Total
No	12	2	14
Yes	15	1	16
Total	27	3	30

1. $P(\text{grass}) = \dfrac{27}{30} = 0.90$

2. $P(\text{win}|\text{grass}) = \dfrac{15}{27} = 0.556$

$P(\text{win}|\text{art}) = \dfrac{1}{3} = 0.333$

Teams playing on grass fields have higher winning percentage.

3. $P(\text{win or artificial}) = P(\text{win}) + P(\text{artificial})$
$- P(\text{win and artificial})$
$= \dfrac{16}{30} + \dfrac{3}{30} - \dfrac{1}{30} = 0.60$

CHAPTER 6

1. Mean = 1.3, variance = .81, found by:
$\mu = 0(.20) + 1(.40) + 2(.30) + 3(.10) = 1.3$
$\sigma^2 = (0 - 1.3)^2(.2) + (1 - 1.3)^2(.4)$
$+ (2 - 1.3)^2(.3) + (3 - 1.3)^2(.1)$
$= .81$

3. a. The second, or middle, one
b. 1. .2

2. .4
3. .9

c. $\mu = 14.5$, variance $= 27.25$, found by:
$\mu = 5(.1) + 10(.3) + 15(.2) + 20(.4) = 14.5$
$\sigma^2 = (5 - 14.5)^2(.1) + (10 - 14.5)^2(.3)$
$+ (15 - 14.5)^2(.2) + (20 - 14.5)^2(.4)$
$= 27.25$
$\sigma = 5.22$, found by $\sqrt{27.25}$

5. a.

Calls, x	Frequency	$P(x)$	$xP(x)$	$(x - \mu)^2 P(x)$
0	8	.16	0	.4624
1	10	.20	.20	.0980
2	22	.44	.88	.0396
3	9	.18	.54	.3042
4	1	.02	.08	.1058
	50		1.70	1.0100

b. Discrete distribution, because only certain outcomes are possible.
c. $\mu = \Sigma x \cdot P(x) = 1.70$
d. $\sigma = \sqrt{1.01} = 1.005$

7.

Amount	$P(x)$	$xP(x)$	$(x - \mu)^2 P(x)$
10	.50	5	60.50
25	.40	10	6.40
50	.08	4	67.28
100	.02	2	124.82
		21	259.00

a. $\mu = \Sigma xP(x) = 21$
b. $\sigma^2 = \Sigma(x - \mu)^2 P(x) = 259$
$\sigma = \sqrt{259} = 16.093$

9. a. $P(2) = \dfrac{4!}{2!(4 - 2)!}(.25)^2(.75)^{4-2} = .2109$

b. $P(3) = \dfrac{4!}{3!(4 - 3)!}(.25)^3(.75)^{4-3} = .0469$

11. a.

X	$P(X)$
0	.064
1	.288
2	.432
3	.216

b. $\mu = 1.8$
$\sigma^2 = 0.72$
$\sigma = \sqrt{0.72} = .8485$

13. a. .2668, found by $P(2) = \dfrac{9!}{(9 - 2)!2!}(.3)^2(.7)^7$

b. .1715, found by $P(4) = \dfrac{9!}{(9 - 4)!4!}(.3)^4(.7)^5$

c. .0404, found by $P(0) = \dfrac{9!}{(9 - 0)!0!}(.3)^0(.7)^9$

15. a. .2824, found by $P(0) = \dfrac{12!}{(12 - 0)!0!}(.10)^0(.9)^{12}$

b. .3765, found by $P(1) = \dfrac{12!}{(12 - 1)!1!}(.10)^1(.9)^{11}$

c. .2301, found by $P(2) = \dfrac{12!}{(12 - 2)!2!}(.10)^2(.9)^{10}$

d. $\mu = 1.2$, found by 12(.10)
$\sigma = 1.0392$, found by $\sqrt{1.08}$

17. a. 0.1858, found by $\dfrac{15!}{2!13!}(0.23)^2(0.77)^{13}$

b. 0.1416, found by $\dfrac{15!}{5!10!}(0.23)^5(0.77)^{10}$

c. 3.45, found by $(0.23)(15)$

19. a. 0.296, found by using Appendix B.9 with n of 8, π of 0.30, and x of 2

b. $P(x \le 2) = 0.058 + 0.198 + 0.296 = 0.552$

c. 0.448, found by $P(x \ge 3) = 1 - P(x \le 2) = 1 - 0.552$

21. a. 0.387, found from Appendix B.9 with n of 9, π of 0.90, and x of 9

b. $P(X < 5) = 0.001$

c. 0.992, found by $1 - 0.008$

d. 0.947, found by $1 - 0.053$

23. a. $\mu = 10.5$, found by $15(0.7)$ and $\sigma = \sqrt{15(0.7)(0.3)} = 1.7748$

b. 0.2061, found by $\dfrac{15!}{10!5!}(0.7)^{10}(0.3)^5$

c. 0.4247, found by $0.2061 + 0.2186$

d. 0.5154, found by
$0.2186 + 0.1700 + 0.0916 + 0.0305 + 0.0047$

25. $P(2) = \dfrac{[_6C_2][_4C_1]}{_{10}C_3} = \dfrac{15(4)}{120} = .50$

27. $P(0) = \dfrac{[_7C_2][_3C_0]}{[_{10}C_2]} = \dfrac{21(1)}{45} = .4667$

29. $P(2) = \dfrac{[_9C_3][_6C_2]}{[_{15}C_5]} = \dfrac{84(15)}{3003} = .4196$

31. a. .6703

b. .3297

33. a. .0613

b. .0803

35. $\mu = 6$

$P(X \ge 5) = .7149$
$= 1 - (.0025 + .0149 + .0446 + .0892 + .1339)$

37. A random variable is a quantitative or qualitative outcome that results from a chance experiment. A probability distribution also includes the likelihood of each possible outcome.

39. $\mu = \$1,000(.25) + \$2,000(.60) + \$5,000(.15) = \$2,200$
$\sigma^2 = (1,000 - 2,200)^2\,.25 + (\$2,000 - \$2,200)^2\,.60 +$
$(5,000 - 2,200)^2\,.15$
$= 1,560,000$

41. $\mu = 12(.25) + \cdots + 15(.1) = 13.2$
$\sigma^2 = (12 - 13.2)^2\,.25 + \cdots + (15 - 13.2)^2\,.10 = 0.86$
$\sigma = \sqrt{0.86} = .927$

43. a. $\mu = 10(.35) = 3.5$

b. $P(X = 4) = {}_{10}C_4\,(.35)^4\,(.65)^6 = 210(.0150)\,(.0754) = .2375$

c. $P(X \ge 4) = {}_{10}C_x\,(.35)^X\,(.65)^{10-X}$
$= .2375 + .1536 + \cdots + .0000 = .4862$

45. a. 6, found by 0.4×15

b. 0.0245, found by $\dfrac{15!}{10!5!}(0.4)^{10}(0.6)^5$

c. 0.0338, found by
$0.0245 + 0.0074 + 0.0016 + 0.0003 + 0.0000$

d. 0.0093, found by $0.0338 - 0.0245$

47. a. $\mu = 20(0.075) = 1.5$
$\sigma = \sqrt{20(0.075)(0.925)} = 1.1779$

b. 0.2103, found by $\dfrac{20!}{0!20!}(0.075)^0(0.925)^{20}$

c. 0.7897, found by $1 - 0.2103$

49. a. 0.1311, found by $\dfrac{16!}{4!12!}(0.15)^4(0.85)^{12}$

b. 2.4, found by $(0.15)(16)$

c. 0.2100, found by
$1 - 0.0743 - 0.2097 - 0.2775 - 0.2285$

51. $P(2) = \dfrac{[_6C_2][_4C_2]}{[_{10}C_4]} = \dfrac{(15)(6)}{210} = 0.4286$

53. a.

0	0.0002	7	0.2075
1	0.0019	8	0.1405
2	0.0116	9	0.0676
3	0.0418	10	0.0220
4	0.1020	11	0.0043
5	0.1768	12	0.0004
6	0.2234		

b. $\mu = 12(0.52) = 6.24$
$\sigma = \sqrt{12(0.52)(0.48)} = 1.7307$

c. 0.1768

d. 0.3343, found by $0.0002 + 0.0019 + 0.0116 + 0.0418 + 0.1020 + 0.1768$

55. a. $P(1) = \dfrac{[_7C_2][_3C_1]}{[_{10}C_3]} = \dfrac{(21)(3)}{120} = .5250$

b. $P(0) = \dfrac{[_7C_3][_3C_0]}{[_{10}C_3]} = \dfrac{(35)(1)}{120} = .2917$
$P(X \ge 1) = 1 - P(0) = 1 - .2917 = .7083$

57. $P(X = 0) = \dfrac{[_8C_4][_4C_0]}{[_{12}C_4]} = \dfrac{70}{495} = .141$

59. a. .0498

b. .7746, found by $(1 - .0498)^5$

61. $\mu = 4.0$, from Appendix B.5

a. .0183

b. .1954

c. .6289

d. .5665

63. a. 0.1733, found by $\dfrac{(3.1)^4 e^{-3.1}}{4!}$

b. 0.0450, found by $\dfrac{(3.1)^0 e^{-3.1}}{0!}$

c. 0.9550, found by $1 - 0.0450$

65. $\mu = n\pi = 23\left(\dfrac{2}{113}\right) = .407$

$P(2) = \dfrac{(.407)^2 e^{-.407}}{2!} = 0.0551$

$P(0) = \dfrac{(.407)^0 e^{-.407}}{0!} = 0.6656$

67. Let $\mu = n\pi = 155(1/3,709) = 0.042$

$P(5) = \dfrac{0.042^5 e^{-0.042}}{5!} = 0.000000001$

Very unlikely!

69. a. $\mu = n\pi = 15(.67) = 10.05$
$\sigma = \sqrt{n\pi(1 - \pi)} = \sqrt{15(.67)(.33)} = 1.8211$

b. $P(8) = {}_{15}C_8(.67)^8(.33)^7 = 6435(.0406)(.000426) = .1114$

c. $P(x \ge 8) = .1114 + .1759 + \cdots + .0025 = .9163$

71. $P(x = 1) = \dfrac{_{27}C_4\,_3C_1}{_{30}C_5} = \dfrac{(17,550)(3)}{142,506} = .3695$

CHAPTER 7

1. a. $b = 10, a = 6$

b. $\mu = \dfrac{6 + 10}{2} = 8$

c. $\sigma = \sqrt{\dfrac{(10 - 6)^2}{12}} = 1.1547$

d. Area $= \dfrac{1}{(10 - 6)} \cdot \dfrac{(10 - 6)}{1} = 1$

e. $P(X > 7) = \dfrac{1}{(10 - 6)} \cdot \dfrac{10 - 7}{1} = \dfrac{3}{4} = .75$

f. $P(7 \le x \le 9) = \dfrac{1}{(10 - 6)} \cdot \dfrac{(9 - 7)}{1} = \dfrac{2}{4} = .50$

3. a. 0.30, found by $(30 - 27)/(30 - 20)$
b. 0.40, found by $(24 - 20)/(30 - 20)$

5. a. $a = 0.5, b = 3.00$

b. $\mu = \dfrac{0.5 + 3.00}{2} = 1.75$

$\sigma = \sqrt{\dfrac{(3.00 - .50)^2}{12}} = .72$

c. $P(x < 1) = \dfrac{1}{(3.0 - 0.5)} \cdot \dfrac{1 - .5}{1} = \dfrac{.5}{2.5} = 0.2$

d. 0, found by $\dfrac{1}{(3.0 - 0.5)} \dfrac{(1.0 - 1.0)}{1}$

e. $P(x > 1.5) = \dfrac{1}{(3.0 - 0.5)} \cdot \dfrac{3.0 - 1.5}{1} = \dfrac{1.5}{2.5} = 0.6$

7. The actual shape of a normal distribution depends on its mean and standard deviation. Thus, there is a normal distribution, and an accompanying normal curve, for a mean of 7 and a standard deviation of 2. There is another normal curve for a mean of $25,000 and a standard deviation of $1,742, and so on.

9. a. 490 and 510, found by $500 \pm 1(10)$
b. 480 and 520, found by $500 \pm 2(10)$
c. 470 and 530, found by $500 \pm 3(10)$

11. $Z_{Rob} = \dfrac{\$50,000 - \$60,000}{\$5,000} = -2$

$Z_{Rachel} = \dfrac{\$50,000 - \$35,000}{\$8,000} = 1.875$

Adjusting for their industries, Rob is well below average and Rachel well above.

13. a. 1.25, found by $z = \dfrac{25 - 20}{4.0} = 1.25$

b. 0.3944, found in Appendix B.1

c. 0.3085, found by $z = \dfrac{18 - 20}{2.5} = -0.5$

Find 0.1915 in Appendix B.1 for $z = -0.5$, then $0.5000 - 0.1915 = 0.3085$

15. a. 0.3413, found by $z = \dfrac{\$24 - \$20.50}{\$3.50} = 1.00$,

then find 0.3413 in Appendix B.1 for $z = 1$
b. 0.1587, found by $0.5000 - 0.3413 = 0.1587$

c. 0.3336, found by $z = \dfrac{\$19.00 - \$20.50}{\$3.50} = -0.43$

Find 0.1664 in Appendix B.1, for $z = -0.43$, then $0.5000 - 0.1664 = 0.3336$

17. a. 0.8276: First find $z = -1.5$, found by $(44 - 50)/4$ and $z = 1.25 = (55 - 50)/4$. The area between -1.5 and 0 is 0.4332 and the area between 0 and 1.25 is 0.3944, both from Appendix B.1. Then adding the two areas we find that $0.4332 + 0.3944 = 0.8276$.
b. 0.1056, found by $0.5000 - .3944$, where $z = 1.25$
c. 0.2029: Recall that the area for $z = 1.25$ is 0.3944, and the area for $z = 0.5$, found by $(52 - 50)/4$, is 0.1915. Then subtract $0.3944 - 0.1915$ and find 0.2029.

19. a. 0.3264, found by $0.5000 - 0.1736$, where $z = 0.45$, found by $((3000 - 2708)/650)$.
b. 0.2152; the z-value for $3,500 is 1.22, found by $((3500 - 2708)/650)$, and the corresponding area is 0.3888, which leads to $0.3888 - 0.1736 = 0.2152$.
c. 0.5143; the z-value for $2,500 is -0.32, found by $((2,500 - 2,708)/650)$, and the corresponding area is 0.1255, which leads to $0.1255 + 0.3888 = 0.5143$.

21. a. 0.0764, found by $z = (20 - 15)/3.5 = 1.43$, then $0.5000 - 0.4236 = 0.0764$
b. 0.9236, found by $0.5000 + 0.4236$, where $z = 1.43$
c. 0.1185, found by $z = (12 - 15)/3.5 = -0.86$.

The area under the curve is 0.3051, then $z = (10 - 15)/3.5 = -1.43$. The area is 0.4236. Finally, $0.4236 - 0.3051 = 0.1185$.

23. $X = 56.60$, found by adding 0.5000 (the area left of the mean) and then finding a z value that forces 45 percent of the data to fall inside the curve. Solving for X: $1.65 = (X - 50)/4 = 56.60$.

25. $1,630, found by $2,100 - 1.88($250)

27. a. 214.8 hours: Find a z value where 0.4900 of area is between 0 and z. That value is $z = 2.33$. Then solve for X: $2.33 = (X - 195)/8.5$, so $X = 214.8$ hours.
b. 270.2 hours: Find a z value where 0.4900 of area is between 0 and $(-z)$. That value is $z = -2.33$. Then solve for X: $-2.33 = (X - 290)/8.5$, so $X = 270.2$ hours.

29. 214 copies: Find a z value where $0.3000(0.50 - 0.20)$ of area is between 0 and z. That value is 0.84. Then solve for X: $0.84 = (X - 200)/17$, so $X = 214$ copies.

31. a. $\mu = n\pi = 50(0.25) = 12.5$
$\sigma^2 = n\pi(1 - \pi) = 12.5(1 - 0.25) = 9.375$
$\sigma = \sqrt{9.375} = 3.0619$
b. 0.2578, found by $(14.5 - 12.5)/3.0619 = 0.65$. The area is 0.2422. Then $0.5000 - 0.2422 = 0.2578$.
c. 0.2578, found by $(10.5 - 12.5)/3.0619 = -0.65$. The area is 0.2422. Then $0.5000 - 0.2422 = 0.2578$.

33. a. $\mu = n\pi = 80(0.07) = 5.6$
$\sigma = \sqrt{5.208} = 2.2821$
0.3483, found from $z = (6.5 - 5.6)/2.2821 = 0.39$ with the corresponding area of 0.1517, then $0.5000 - 0.1517 = 0.3483$
b. 0.5160, found from $z = (5.5 - 5.6)/2.2821 = -0.04$ with the corresponding area of 0.0160, then $0.5000 + 0.0160 = 0.5160$
c. .1677, found by $.5160 - 0.3483$.

35. a. Yes. (1) There are two mutually exclusive outcomes: overweight and not overweight. (2) It is the result of counting the number of successes (overweight members). (3) Each trial is independent. (4) The probability of 0.30 remains the same for each trial.
b. 0.0084, found by
$\mu = 500(0.30) = 150$
$\sigma^2 = 500(.30)(.70) = 105$
$\sigma = \sqrt{105} = 10.24695$
$z = \dfrac{X - \mu}{\sigma} = \dfrac{174.5 - 150}{10.24695} = 2.39$
The area under the curve for 2.39 is 0.4916. Then $0.5000 - 0.4916 = 0.0084$.
c. 0.8461, found by $z = \dfrac{139.5 - 150}{10.24695} = -1.02$
The area between 139.5 and 150 is 0.3461. Adding $0.3461 + 0.5000 = 0.8461$.

37. a. $\mu = \dfrac{11.96 + 12.05}{2} = 12.005$

b. $\sigma = \sqrt{\dfrac{(12.05 - 11.96)^2}{12}} = .0260$

c. $P(X < 12) = \dfrac{1}{(12.05 - 11.96)} \dfrac{12.00 - 11.96}{1} = \dfrac{.04}{.09} = .44$

d. $P(X > 11.98) = \dfrac{1}{(12.05 - 11.96)} \left(\dfrac{12.05 - 11.98}{1} \right)$
$= \dfrac{.07}{.09} = .78$

e. All cans have more than 11.00 ounces, so the probability is 100%.

39. a. $\mu = \dfrac{4 + 10}{2} = 7$

b. $\sigma = \sqrt{\dfrac{(10 - 4)^2}{12}} = 1.732$

c. $P(X < 6) = \dfrac{1}{(10 - 4)} \cdot \left(\dfrac{6 - 4}{1}\right) = \dfrac{2}{6} = .33$

d. $P(X > 5) = \dfrac{1}{(10 - 4)} \cdot \left(\dfrac{10 - 5}{1}\right) = \dfrac{5}{6} = .83$

41. a. -0.4 for net sales, found by $(170 - 180)/25$.
2.92 for employees, found by $(1{,}850 - 1{,}500)/120$.

b. Net sales are 0.4 standard deviations below the mean. Employees is 2.92 standard deviations above the mean.

c. 65.54 percent of the aluminum fabricators have greater net sales compared with Clarion, found by $0.1554 + 0.5000$. Only 0.18 percent have more employees than Clarion, found by $0.5000 - 0.4982$.

43. a. 0.5000, because $z = \dfrac{30 - 490}{90} = -5.11$

b. 0.2514, found by $0.5000 - 0.2486$

c. 0.6374, found by $0.2486 + 0.3888$

d. 0.3450, found by $0.3888 - 0.0438$

45. a. 0.3015, found by $0.5000 - 0.1985$

b. 0.2579, found by $0.4564 - 0.1985$

c. 0.0011, found by $0.5000 - 0.4989$

d. 1,818, found by $1{,}280 + 1.28(420)$

47. a. 90.82%: First find $z = 1.33$ found by $(40 - 34)/4.5$. The area between 0 and 1.33 is 0.4082. Then add 0.5000 and 0.4082 and find 0.9082 or 90.82%.

b. 78.23%: First find $z = -0.78$ found by $(25 - 29)/5.1$. The area between 0 and (-0.78) is 0.2823. Then add 0.5000 and 0.2823 and find 0.7823 or 78.23%.

c. 44.5 hours/week for women: Find a z value where 0.4900 of the area is between 0 and z. That value is 2.33. Then solve for X: $2.33 = (X - 34)/4.5$, so $X = 44.5$ hours/week. 40.9 hours/week for men: $2.33 = (X - 29)/5.1$, so $X = 40.9$ hours/week.

49. About 4,099 units, found by solving for X.
$1.65 = (X - 4{,}000)/60$

51. a. 15.39%, found by $(8 - 10.3)/2.25 = -1.02$, then $0.5000 - 0.3461 = 0.1539$.

b. 17.31%, found by:
$z = (12 - 10.3)/2.25 = 0.76$. Area is 0.2764.
$z = (14 - 10.3)/2.25 = 1.64$. Area is 0.4495.
The area between 12 and 14 is 0.1731, found by $0.4495 - 0.2764$.

c. Yes, but it is rather remote. Reasoning: On 99.73% of the days, returns are between 3.55 and 17.05, found by $10.3 \pm 3(2.25)$. Thus, the chance of less than 3.55 returns is rather remote.

53. a. 0.9678, found by:
$\mu = 60(0.64) = 38.4$.
$\sigma^2 = 60(0.64)(0.36) = 13.824$
$\sigma = \sqrt{13.824} = 3.72$
Then $(31.5 - 38.4)/3.72 = -1.85$, for which the area is 0.4678.
Then $0.5000 + 0.4678 = 0.9678$.

b. 0.0853, found by $(43.5 - 38.4)/3.72 = 1.37$, for which the area is 0.4147. Then $0.5000 - 0.4147 = .0853$.

c. 0.8084, found by $0.4441 + 0.3643$.

d. 0.0348, found by $0.4495 - 0.4147$.

55. 0.0968, found by:
$\mu = 50(0.40) = 20$
$\sigma^2 = 50(0.40)(0.60) = 12$
$\sigma = \sqrt{12} = 3.46$
$z = (24.5 - 20)/3.46 = 1.30$.
The area is 0.4032. Then, for 25 or more, $0.5000 - 0.4032 = 0.0968$.

57. a. $1.65 = (45 - \mu)/5$ $\mu = 36.75$

b. $1.65 = (45 - \mu)/10$ $\mu = 28.5$

c. $z = (30 - 28.5)/10 = 0.15$, then $0.5000 + 0.0596 = 0.5596$

59. a. 21.19 percent found by $z = (9.00 - 9.20)/0.25 = -0.80$, so $0.5000 - 0.2881 = 0.2119$

b. Increase the mean. $z = (9.00 - 9.25)/0.25 = -1.00$, $P = 0.5000 - 0.3413 = 0.1587$.
Reduce the standard deviation. $\sigma = (9.00 - 9.20)/0.15 = -1.33$; $P = 0.5000 - 0.4082 = 0.0918$.
Reducing the standard deviation is better because a smaller percent of the hams will be below the limit.

61. a. $z = (52 - 60)/5 = 1.60$, so $0.5000 - 0.4452 = 0.0548$

b. Let $z = 0.67$, so $0.67 = (X - 52)/5$ and $X = 55.35$, set mileage at 55,350

c. $z = (45 - 52)/5 = -1.40$, so $0.5000 - 0.4192 = 0.0808$

63. $\dfrac{470 - \mu}{\sigma} = 0.25$ $\dfrac{500 - \mu}{\sigma} = 1.28$ $\sigma = 29{,}126$ and $\mu = 462{,}718$

65. $\mu = 150(0.15) = 22.5$ $\sigma = \sqrt{150(0.15)(0.85)} = 4.37$
$z = (29.5 - 22.5)/4.37 = 1.60$
$P(z > 1.60) = .05000 - 0.4452 = 0.0548$

67. a. 0.1230, found by $0.5000 - 0.3770$ with $z = (3500 - 2650)/733 = 1.16$; leads to 3.7 teams, found by $30(0.1230)$. Four teams actually had attendance of more than 3.5 million. So the estimate is fairly accurate.

b. 0.8389, found by $0.5000 + 0.3389$ with $z = (50 - 83.16)/33.47 = -0.99$; leads to 25.2 teams, found by $30(0.8389)$. Twenty-six teams actually had salaries of more than $50 million. So the estimate is accurate.

CHAPTER 8

1. a. 303 Louisiana, 5155 S. Main, 3501 Monroe, 2652 W. Central

b. Answers will vary.

c. 630 Dixie Hwy, 835 S. McCord Rd, 4624 Woodville Rd

d. Answers will vary.

3. a. Bob Schmidt Chevrolet
Great Lakes Ford Nissan
Grogan Towne Chrysler
Southside Lincoln Mercury
Rouen Chrysler Jeep Eagle

b. Answers will vary.

c. Yark Automotive
Thayer Chevrolet Toyota
Franklin Park Lincoln Mercury
Mathews Ford Oregon, Inc.
Valiton Chrysler

5. a.

Sample	Values	Sum	Mean
1	12, 12	24	12
2	12, 14	26	13
3	12, 16	28	14
4	12, 14	26	13
5	12, 16	28	14
6	14, 16	30	15

b. $\mu_{\bar{x}} = (12 + 13 + 14 + 13 + 14 + 15)/6 = 13.5$
$\mu = (12 + 12 + 14 + 16)/4 = 13.5$

c. More dispersion with population data compared to the sample means. The sample means vary from 12 to 15, whereas the population varies from 12 to 16.

7. a.

Sample	Values	Sum	Mean
1	12, 12, 14	38	12.66
2	12, 12, 15	39	13.00
3	12, 12, 20	44	14.66
4	14, 15, 20	49	16.33
5	12, 14, 15	41	13.66
6	12, 14, 15	41	13.66
7	12, 15, 20	47	15.66
8	12, 15, 20	47	15.66
9	12, 14, 20	46	15.33
10	12, 14, 20	46	15.33

b. $\mu_{\bar{X}} = \dfrac{(12.66 + \cdots + 15.33 + 15.33)}{10} = 14.6$

$\mu = (12 + 12 + 14 + 15 + 20)/5 = 14.6$

c. The dispersion of the population is greater than that of the sample means. The sample means vary from 12.66 to 16.33, whereas the population varies from 12 to 20.

9. a. 20, found by $_6C_3$

b.

Sample	Cases	Sum	Mean
Ruud, Wu, Sass	3, 6, 3	12	4.00
Ruud, Sass, Flores	3, 3, 3	9	3.00
⋮	⋮	⋮	⋮
Sass, Flores, Schueller	3, 3, 1	7	2.33

c. $\mu_{\bar{X}} = 2.67$, found by $\dfrac{53.33}{20}$.

$\mu = 2.67$, found by $(3 + 6 + 3 + 3 + 0 + 1)/6$. They are equal.

d.

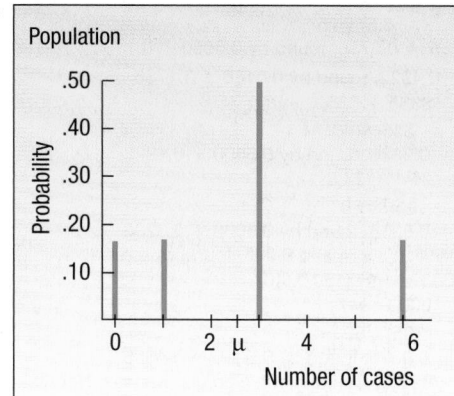

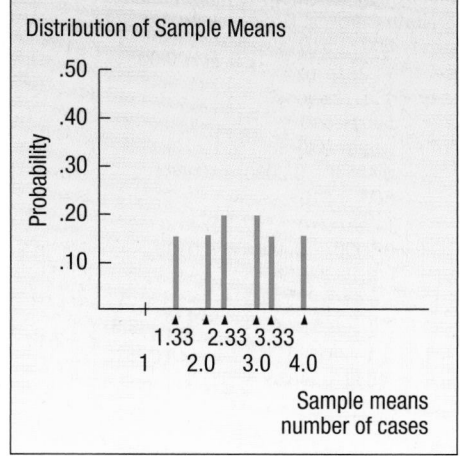

Sample Mean	Number of Means	Probability
1.33	3	.1500
2.00	3	.1500
2.33	4	.2000
3.00	4	.2000
3.33	3	.1500
4.00	3	.1500
	20	1.0000

The population has more dispersion than the sample means. The sample means vary from 1.33 to 4.0. The population varies from 0 to 6.

11. a.

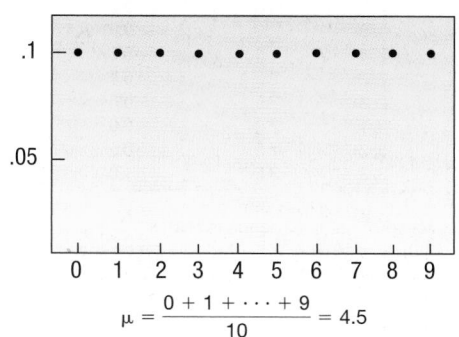

$\mu = \dfrac{0 + 1 + \cdots + 9}{10} = 4.5$

b.

Sample	Sum	$\bar{X}$
1	11	2.2
2	31	6.2
3	21	4.2
4	24	4.8
5	21	4.2
6	20	4.0
7	23	4.6
8	29	5.8
9	35	7.0
10	27	5.4

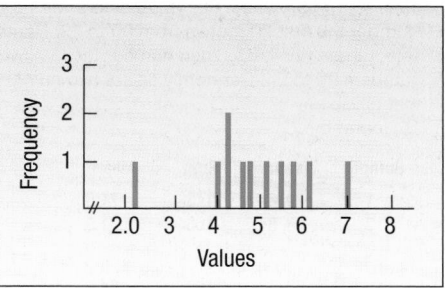

The mean of the 10 sample means is 4.84, which is close to the population mean of 4.5. The sample means range from 2.2 to 7.0, whereas the population values range from 0 to 9. From the above graph, the sample means tend to cluster between 4 and 5.

13. a.–c. Answers will vary depending on the coins in your possession.

15. a. $z = \dfrac{63 - 60}{12/\sqrt{9}} = 0.75$

$P = .2266$, found by $.5000 - .2734$

b. $z = \dfrac{56 - 60}{12/\sqrt{9}} = -1.00$

$P = .1587$, found by $.5000 - .3413$

c. $P = .6147$, found by $0.3413 + 0.2734$

17. $z = \dfrac{1{,}950 - 2{,}200}{250/\sqrt{50}} = -7.07$ $P = 1$, or virtually certain

19. **a.** Formal Man, Summit Stationers, Bootleggers, Leather Ltd, Petries

   b. Answers may vary.

   c. Elder-Beerman, Frederick's of Hollywood, Summit Stationers, Lion Store, Leather Ltd., Things Remembered, County Seat, Coach House Gifts, Regis Hairstylists

21. **a.**

Samples	Mean	Deviation from Mean	Square of Deviation
1, 1	1.0	−1.0	1.0
1, 2	1.5	−0.5	0.25
1, 3	2.0	0.0	0.0
2, 1	1.5	−0.5	0.25
2, 2	2.0	0.0	0.0
2, 3	2.5	0.5	0.25
3, 1	2.0	0.0	0.0
3, 2	2.5	0.5	0.25
3, 3	3.0	1.0	1.0

   b. Mean of sample means is $(1.0 + 1.5 + 2.0 + \cdots + 3.0)/9 = 18/9 = 2.0$. The population mean is $(1 + 2 + 3)/3 = 6/3 = 2$. They are the same value.

   c. Variance of sample means is $(1.0 + 0.25 + 0.0 + \cdots + 3.0)/9 = 18/9 = 2.0$. The population mean is $(1 + 1.0)/9 = 1/3$. Variance of the population values is $(1 + 0 + 1)/3 = 2/3$. The variance of the population is twice as large as that of the sample means.

   d. Sample means follow a triangular shape peaking at 2. The population is uniform between 1 and 3.

23. Larger samples provide narrower estimates of a population mean. So the company with 200 sampled customers can provide more precise estimates. In addition, they are selected consumers who are familiar with laptop computers and may be better able to evaluate the new computer.

25. **a.** We selected 60, 104, 75, 72, and 48. Answers will vary.

   b. We selected the third observation. So the sample consists of 75, 72, 68, 82, 48. Answers will vary.

   c. Number the first 20 motels from 00 to 19. Randomly select three numbers. Then number the last five numbers 20 to 24. Randomly select two numbers from that group.

27. **a.** 15, found by $_6C_2$

   b.

Sample	Value	Sum	Mean
1	79, 64	143	71.5
2	79, 84	163	81.5
⋮	⋮	⋮	⋮
15	92, 77	169	84.5
			1,195.0

   c. $\mu_{\bar{x}} = 79.67$, found by $1{,}195/15$.
   $\mu = 79.67$, found by $478/6$.
   They are equal.

   d. No. The student is not graded on all available information. He/she is as likely to get a lower grade based on the sample as a higher grade.

29. **a.** 10, found by $_5C_2$

b.

Number of Shutdowns	Mean	Number of Shutdowns	Mean
4, 3	3.5	3, 3	3.0
4, 5	4.5	3, 2	2.5
4, 3	3.5	5, 3	4.0
4, 2	3.0	5, 2	3.5
3, 5	4.0	3, 2	2.5

Sample Mean	Frequency	Probability
2.5	2	.20
3.0	2	.20
3.5	3	.30
4.0	2	.20
4.5	1	.10
	10	1.00

   c. $\mu_{\bar{x}} = (3.5 + 4.5 + \cdots + 2.5)/10 = 3.4$
   $\mu = (4 + 3 + 5 + 3 + 2)/5 = 3.4$
   The two means are equal.

   d. The population values are relatively uniform in shape. The distribution of sample means tends toward normality.

31. **a.** The distribution will be normal.

   b. $\sigma_{\bar{x}} = \dfrac{5.5}{\sqrt{25}} = 1.1$

   c. $z = \dfrac{36 - 35}{5.5/\sqrt{25}} = 0.91$
   $P = 0.1814$, found by $0.5000 - 0.3186$

   d. $z = \dfrac{34.5 - 35}{5.5/\sqrt{25}} = -0.45$
   $P = 0.6736$, found by $0.5000 + 0.1736$

   e. 0.4922, found by $0.3186 + 0.1736$

33. $z = \dfrac{\$335 - \$350}{\$45/\sqrt{40}} = -2.11$
   $P = 0.9826$, found by $0.5000 + 0.4826$

35. $z = \dfrac{25.1 - 24.8}{2.5/\sqrt{60}} = 0.93$
   $P = 0.8238$, found by $0.5000 + 0.3238$

37. Between 5,954 and 6,046, found by $6{,}000 \pm 1.96(150/\sqrt{40})$

39. $z = \dfrac{900 - 947}{205/\sqrt{60}} = -1.78$
   $P = 0.0375$, found by $0.5000 - 0.4625$

41. **a.** Alaska, Connecticut, Georgia, Kansas, Nebraska, South Carolina, Virginia, Utah

   b. Arizona, Florida, Iowa, Massachusetts, Nebraska, North Carolina, Rhode Island, Vermont

43. **a.** $z = \dfrac{600 - 510}{14.28/\sqrt{10}} = 19.9$, $P = 0.00$, or virtually never

   b. $z = \dfrac{500 - 510}{14.28/\sqrt{10}} = -2.21$,
   $P = 0.4864 + 0.5000 = 0.9864$

   c. $z = \dfrac{500 - 510}{14.28/\sqrt{10}} = -2.21$,
   $P = 0.5000 - 0.4864 = 0.0136$

45. **a.** $\sigma_{\bar{x}} = \dfrac{2.1}{\sqrt{81}} = 0.23$

   b. $z = \dfrac{7.0 - 6.5}{2.1/\sqrt{81}} = 2.14$, $z = \dfrac{6.0 - 6.5}{2.1/\sqrt{81}} = -2.14$,
   $P = .4838 + .4838 = .9676$

c. $z = \dfrac{6.75 - 6.5}{2.1/\sqrt{81}} = 1.07, z = \dfrac{6.25 - 6.5}{2.1/\sqrt{81}} = -1.07,$
$P = .3577 + .3577 = .7154$

d. .0162 found by .5000 − .4838

47. **a.–b.** Answers will vary.

CHAPTER 9

1. 51.314 and 58.686, found by $55 \pm 2.58(10/\sqrt{49})$
3. **a.** 1.581, found by $\sigma_{\overline{x}} = 5/\sqrt{10}$
   b. The population is normally distributed and the population variance is known.
   c. 16.901 and 23.099, found by 20 ± 3.099
5. **a.** $20. It is our best estimate of the population mean.
   b. $18.60 and $21.40, found by $20 \pm 1.96($5/\sqrt{49})$. About 95 percent of the intervals similarly constructed will include the population mean.
7. **a.** 8.60 gallons.
   b. 7.83 and 9.37, found by $8.60 \pm 2.58(2.30/\sqrt{60})$
   c. If 100 such intervals were determined, the population mean would be included in about 99 intervals.
9. **a.** 2.201
   b. 1.729
   c. 3.499
11. **a.** The population mean is unknown, but the best estimate is 20, the sample mean.
   b. Use the t distribution as the standard deviation is unknown. However, assume the population is normally distributed.
   c. 2.093
   d. Between 19.06 and 20.94, found by $20 \pm 2.093(2/\sqrt{20})$
   e. Neither value is reasonable, because they are not inside the interval.
13. Between 95.39 and 101.81, found by
   $98.6 \pm 1.833(5.54/\sqrt{10})$
15. **a.** 0.8, found by 80/100
   b. Between 0.72 and 0.88, found by
   $0.8 \pm 1.96\left(\sqrt{\dfrac{0.8(1 - 0.8)}{100}}\right)$
   c. We are reasonably sure the population proportion is between 72 and 88 percent.
17. **a.** 0.625, found by 250/400
   b. Between 0.563 and 0.687, found by
   $0.625 \pm 2.58\left(\sqrt{\dfrac{0.625(1 - 0.625)}{400}}\right)$
   c. We are reasonably sure the population proportion is between 56 and 69 percent.
19. 33.41 and 36.59, found by
   $35 \pm 2.030\left(\dfrac{5}{\sqrt{36}}\right)\sqrt{\dfrac{300 - 36}{300 - 1}}$
21. 1.683 and 2.037, found by
   $1.86 \pm 2.680\left(\dfrac{0.5}{\sqrt{50}}\right)\sqrt{\dfrac{400 - 50}{400 - 1}}$
23. 97, found by $n = \left(\dfrac{1.96 \times 10}{2}\right)^2 = 96.04$
25. 196, found by $n = 0.15(0.85)\left(\dfrac{1.96}{0.05}\right)^2 = 195.9216$
27. 554, found by $n = \left(\dfrac{1.96 \times 3}{0.25}\right)^2 = 553.19$
29. **a.** 577, found by $n = 0.60(0.40)\left(\dfrac{1.96}{0.04}\right)^2 = 576.24$
   b. 601, found by $n = 0.50(0.50)\left(\dfrac{1.96}{0.04}\right)^2 = 600.25$

31. 6.13 years to 6.87 years, found by $6.5 \pm 1.989(1.7/\sqrt{85})$
33. **a.** Between 4.018 and 4.040, found by
   $4.029 \pm 2.680\left(\dfrac{0.03}{\sqrt{50}}\right)$
   b. $3.50 is not reasonable, because it is outside the confidence interval.
35. **a.** The population mean is unknown.
   b. Between 7.50 and 9.14, found by
   $8.32 \pm 1.685(3.07/\sqrt{40})$
   c. 10 is not reasonable because it is outside the confidence interval.
37. **a.** 65.49 up to 71.71 hours, found by $68.6 \pm 2.680(8.2/\sqrt{50})$
   b. The value suggested by the NCAA is included in the confidence interval. Therefore, it is reasonable.
   c. Changing the confidence interval to 95 would reduce the width of the interval. The value of 2.680 would change to 2.010.
39. 61, found by $1.96(16/\sqrt{n}) = 4$
41. Between $13,734 up to $15,028, found by
   $14,381 \pm 1.711(1,892/\sqrt{25})$. 15,000 is reasonable because it is inside the confidence interval.
43. **a.** $62.583, found by $751/12
   b. Between $60.54 and $64.63, found by
   $62.583 \pm 1.796(3.94/\sqrt{12})$
   c. $60 is not reasonable, because it is outside the confidence interval.
45. **a.** 89.4667, found by 1,342/15
   b. Between 84.99 and 93.94, found by
   $89.4667 \pm 2.145(8.08/\sqrt{15})$
   c. Yes, because even the lower limit of the confidence interval is above 80.
47. Between 0.648 and 0.752, found by
   $.7 \pm 2.58\left(\sqrt{\dfrac{0.7(1 - 0.7)}{500}}\right)\left(\sqrt{\dfrac{20,000 - 500}{20,000 - 1}}\right)$
   Yes, because even the lower limit of the confidence interval is above 0.500.
49. $52.51 and $55.49, found by
   $54.00 \pm 2.032\dfrac{$4.50}{\sqrt{35}}\sqrt{\dfrac{(500 - 35)}{500 - 1}}$
51. 369, found by $n = 0.60(1 - 0.60)(1.96/0.05)^2$
53. 97, found by $[(1.96 \times 500)/100]^2$
55. **a.** Between 7,849 and 8,151, found by
   $8,000 \pm 2.756(300/\sqrt{30})$
   b. 554, found by $n = \left(\dfrac{(1.96)(300)}{25}\right)^2$
57. **a.** Between 75.44 and 80.56, found by $78 \pm 2.010(9/\sqrt{50})$
   b. 221, found by $n = \left(\dfrac{(1.65)(9)}{1.0}\right)^2$
59. **a.** 30, found by $180/\sqrt{36}$
   b. $355.10 and $476.90, found by $416 \pm 2.030\left(\dfrac{$180}{\sqrt{36}}\right)$
   c. About 1336, found by $\left(\dfrac{2,030(180)}{10}\right)^2$
61. **a.** 708.13, rounded up to 709, found by
   $0.21(1 - 0.21)(1.96/0.03)^2$
   b. 1,068, found by $0.50(0.50)(1.96/0.03)^2$
63. Between 0.573 and 0.653, found by
   $.613 \pm 2.58\left(\sqrt{\dfrac{0.613(1 - 0.613)}{1,000}}\right)$. Yes, because even the lower limit of the confidence interval is above 0.500.
65. **a.** Between 0.156 and 0.184, found by
   $0.17 \pm 1.96\sqrt{\dfrac{(0.17)(1 - 0.17)}{2700}}$

b. Yes, because 18 percent is inside the confidence interval.
c. 21,682; found by $0.17(1 - 0.17)[1.96/0.005]^2$

67. Between 12.69 and 14.11, found by $13.4 \pm 1.96 (6.8/\sqrt{352})$

69. **a.** For selling price: 211.99 up to 230.22, found by
$221.1 \pm (1.983)(47.11/\sqrt{105}) = 221.1 \pm 9.12$
b. For distance: 13.685 up to 15.572, found by
$14.629 \pm (1.983)(4.874/\sqrt{105}) = 14.629 \pm 0.943$
c. For garage: 0.5867 up to 0.7657, found by $0.6762 \pm$

$(1.96)\sqrt{\dfrac{0.6762(1 - 0.6762)}{105}} = 0.6762 \pm 0.0895$

71. **a.** $\$30,833 \pm 1.984 \dfrac{\$16,947}{\sqrt{100}} = \$30,833 \pm 3362$, so the

limits are $\$27,471$ and $\$34,196$. It is not reasonable that the population mean is $\$35,000$.

b. $12.73 \pm 1.984 \dfrac{\$2.792}{\sqrt{100}} = \$12.73 \pm 0.55$, so the limits

are 12.18 and 13.28. The population mean could be 13 years.

c. $39.11 \pm 1.984 \dfrac{12.57}{\sqrt{100}} = 39.11 \pm 2.49$, so the limits are

36.62 and 41.60. The mean age of the worker could be 40 years.

CHAPTER 10

1. **a.** Two-tailed
b. Reject H_0 when z does not fall in the region between -1.96 and 1.96.
c. -1.2, found by $z = (49 - 50)/(5/\sqrt{36}) = -1.2$
d. Fail to reject H_0
e. $p = .2302$, found by $2(.5000 - .3849)$. A 23.02% chance of finding a z value this large when H_0 is true.

3. **a.** One-tailed
b. Reject H_0 when $z > 1.65$.
c. 1.2, found by $z = (21 - 20)/(5/\sqrt{36}) = 1.2$
d. Fail to reject H_0 at the .05 significance level
e. $p = .1151$, found by $.5000 - .3849$. An 11.51 percent chance of finding a z value this large or larger.

5. **a.** $H_0: \mu = 60,000 \qquad H_1: \mu \neq 60,000$

b. Reject H_0 if $z < -1.96$ or $z > 1.96$.
c. -0.69, found by:

$$z = \frac{59,500 - 60,000}{(5,000/\sqrt{48})} = -0.69$$

d. Do not reject H_0
e. $p = .4902$, found by $2(.5000 - .2549)$. Crosset's experience is not different from that claimed by the manufacturer. If H_0 is true, the probability of finding a value more extreme than this is .4902.

7. **a.** $H_0: \mu \geq 6.8 \qquad H_1: \mu < 6.8$
b. Reject H_0 if $z < -1.65$
c. $z = \dfrac{6.2 - 6.8}{0.5/\sqrt{36}} = -7.2$

d. H_0 is rejected.
e. $p = 0$. The mean number of DVDs watched is less than 6.8 per month. If H_0 is true, there is virtually no chance of getting a statistic this small.

9. **a.** Reject H_0 when $t > 1.833$
b. $t = \dfrac{12 - 10}{(3/\sqrt{10})} = 2.108$

c. Reject H_0. The mean is greater than 10.

11. $H_0: \mu \leq 40 \qquad H_1: \mu > 40$

Reject H_0 if $t > 1.703$.

$$t = \frac{42 - 40}{(2.1/\sqrt{28})} = 5.040$$

Reject H_0 and conclude that the mean number of calls is greater than 40 per week.

13. $H_0: \mu \leq 22,100 \qquad H_1: \mu > 22,100$

Reject H_0 if $t > 1.740$

$$t = \frac{23,400 - 22,100}{(1,500/\sqrt{18})} = 3.680$$

Reject H_0 and conclude that the mean life of the spark plugs is greater than 22,100 miles.

15. **a.** Reject H_0 if $t < -3.747$

b. $\overline{X} = 17$ and $s = \sqrt{\dfrac{50}{5 - 1}} = 3.536$

$$t = \frac{17 - 20}{(3.536/\sqrt{5})} = -1.90$$

c. Do not reject H_0. We cannot conclude the population mean is less than 20.
d. Between .05 and .10, about .065

17. $H_0: \mu \leq 4.35 \qquad H_1: \mu > 4.35$

Reject H_0 if $t > 2.821$

$$t = \frac{4.368 - 4.35}{(0.0339/\sqrt{10})} = 1.68$$

Do not reject H_0. The additive did not increase the mean weight of the chickens. The p-value is between 0.10 and 0.05.

19. $H_0: \mu \leq 4.0 \qquad H_1: \mu > 4.0$

Reject H_0 if $t > 1.796$

$$t = \frac{4.50 - 4.0}{(2.68/\sqrt{12})} = 0.65$$

Do not reject H_0. The mean number of fish caught has not been shown to be greater than 4.0. The p-value is greater than 0.10.

21. **a.** H_0 is rejected if $z > 1.65$
b. 1.09, found by $z = (0.75 - 0.70)/\sqrt{(0.70 \times 0.30)/100}$
c. H_0 is not rejected

23. **a.** $H_0: \pi \leq 0.52 \qquad H_1: \pi > 0.52$
b. H_0 is rejected if $z > 2.33$
c. 1.62, found by $z = (.5667 - .52)/\sqrt{(0.52 \times 0.48)/300}$
d. H_0 is not rejected. We cannot conclude that the proportion of men driving on the Ohio Turnpike is larger than 0.52.

25. **a.** $H_0: \pi \geq 0.90 \qquad H_1: \pi < 0.90$
b. H_0 is rejected if $z < -1.28$
c. -2.67, found by $z = (0.82 - 0.90)/\sqrt{(0.90 \times 0.10)/100}$
d. H_0 is rejected. Fewer than 90 percent of the customers receive their orders in less than 10 minutes.

27. 1.05, found by $z = (9,992 - 9,880)/(400/\sqrt{100})$. Then $0.5000 - 0.3531 = 0.1469$, which is the probability of a Type II error.

29. $H_0: \mu = \$45,000 \qquad H_1: \mu \neq \$45,000$

Reject H_0 if $z < -1.65$ or $z > 1.65$

$$z = \frac{45,500 - 45,000}{\$3,000/\sqrt{120}} = 1.83$$

Reject H_0. We can conclude that the mean salary is not $\$45,000$. p-value 0.0672, found by $2(0.5000 - 0.4664)$.

31. $H_0: \mu \geq 10 \qquad H_1: \mu < 10$

Reject H_0 if $z < -1.65$

$$z = \frac{9.0 - 10.0}{2.8/\sqrt{50}} = -2.53$$

Reject H_0. The mean weight loss is less than 10 pounds. p-value $= 0.5000 - 0.4943 = 0.0057$

33. $H_0: \mu \geq 7.0 \qquad H_1: \mu < 7.0$

Assuming a 5% significance level, reject H_0 if $t < -1.677$.

$$t = \frac{6.8 - 7.0}{0.9/\sqrt{50}} = -1.57$$

Do not reject H_0. West Virginia students are not sleeping less than 6 hours. p-value is between .05 and .10.

35. $H_0: \mu \le \$3.75$ $\qquad$ $H_1: \mu > \$3.75$
Reject H_0 if $t > 1.691$

$$t = \frac{\$3.77 - \$3.75}{\$0.05/\sqrt{35}} = 2.37$$

Reject H_0. The mean price of gasoline is greater than $3.75 in Milwaukee. p-value: ($.025 > p$-value $> .01$)

37. $H_0: \mu \le 14$ $\qquad$ $H_1: \mu > 14$
Reject H_0 if $t > 2.821$
$\overline{X} = 15.66$ $\qquad$ $s = 1.544$

$$t = \frac{15.66 - 14.00}{1.544/\sqrt{10}} = 3.400$$

Reject H_0. The average rate is greater than 14 percent.

39. $H_0: \mu = 3.1$ $\qquad$ $H_1: \mu \ne 3.1$ Assume a normal population.
Reject H_0 if $t < -2.201$ or $t > 2.201$

$$\overline{X} = \frac{41.1}{12} = 3.425$$

$$s = \sqrt{\frac{4.0625}{12 - 1}} = .6077$$

$$t = \frac{3.425 - 3.1}{.6077/\sqrt{12}} = 1.853$$

Do not reject H_0. Cannot show a difference between senior citizens and the national average. p-value is about 0.09.

41. $H_0: \mu \ge 6.5$ $\qquad$ $H_1: \mu < 6.5$ Assume a normal population.
Reject H_0 if $t < -2.718$
$\overline{X} = 5.1667$ $\qquad$ $s = 3.1575$

$$t = \frac{5.1667 - 6.5}{3.1575/\sqrt{12}} = -1.463$$

Do not reject H_0. The p-value is greater than 0.05.

43. $H_0: \mu = 0$ $\qquad$ $H_1: \mu \ne 0$
Reject H_0 if $t < -2.110$ or $t > 2.110$
$\overline{X} = -0.2322$ $\qquad$ $s = 0.3120$

$$t = \frac{-0.2322 - 0}{0.3120/\sqrt{18}} = -3.158$$

Reject H_0. The mean gain or loss does not equal 0. The p-value is less than 0.01, but greater than 0.001.

45. $H_0: \mu \le 100$ $\qquad$ $H_1: \mu > 100$ Assume a normal population.
Reject H_0 if $t > 1.761$

$$\overline{X} = \frac{1,641}{15} = 109.4$$

$$s = \sqrt{\frac{1,389.6}{15 - 1}} = 9.9628$$

$$t = \frac{109.4 - 100}{9.9628/\sqrt{15}} = 3.654$$

Reject H_0. The mean number with the scanner is greater than 100. p-value is 0.001.

47. $H_0: \mu = 1.5$ $\qquad$ $H_1: \mu \ne 1.5$
Reject H_0 if $t > 3.250$ or $t < -3.250$

$$t = \frac{1.3 - 1.5}{0.9/\sqrt{10}} = -0.703$$

Fail to reject H_0

49. $H_0: \pi \le 0.02$ $\qquad$ $H_1: \pi > 0.02$
Reject H_0 if $z > 1.65$

$$z = \frac{0.03 - 0.02}{\sqrt{(0.02 \times 0.98)/400}} = 1.43$$

Fail to reject H_0

51. $H_0: \pi \le 0.60$ $\qquad$ $H_1: \pi > 0.60$

H_0 is rejected if $z > 2.33$

$$z = \frac{.70 - .60}{\sqrt{\dfrac{.60(.40)}{200}}} = 2.89$$

H_0 is rejected. Ms. Dennis is correct. More than 60 percent of the accounts are more than three months old.

53. $H_0: \pi \le 0.44$ $\qquad$ $H_1: \pi > 0.44$
H_0 is rejected if $z > 1.65$

$$z = \frac{0.480 - 0.44}{\sqrt{(0.44 \times 0.56)/1.000}} = 2.55$$

H_0 is rejected. We conclude that there has been an increase in the proportion of people wanting to go to Europe.

55. $H_0: \pi \le 0.20$ $\qquad$ $H_1: \pi > 0.20$
H_0 is rejected if $z > 2.33$

$$z = \frac{(56/200) - 0.20}{\sqrt{(0.20 \times 0.80)/200}} = 2.83$$

H_0 is rejected. More than 20 percent of the owners move during a particular year. p-value $= 0.5000 - 0.4977 = 0.0023$.

57. $H_0: \pi = 0.50$ $\qquad$ $H_1: \pi \ne 0.50$
Reject H_0 if z is not between -1.96 and 1.96

$$z = \frac{0.482 - 0.500}{\sqrt{(0.5)(0.5)/1,002}} = -1.14$$

Do not reject the null. The nation may be evenly divided.

59. $H_0: \pi \ge 0.0008$ $\qquad$ $H_1: \pi < 0.0008$
H_0 is rejected if $z < -1.645$

$$z = \frac{0.0006 - 0.0008}{\sqrt{\dfrac{0.0008\,(0.9992)}{10,000}}} = -0.707 \quad H_0 \text{ is not rejected.}$$

This data does not prove there is a reduced fatality rate.

61. a. $9.00 \pm 1.65(1/\sqrt{36}) = 9.00 \pm 0.275$
So the limits are 8.725 and 9.275.
b. $z = (8.725 - 8.900)/(1/\sqrt{36}) = -1.05$
$P(z > -1.05) = 0.5000 + 0.3531 = 0.8531$
c. $z = (9.275 - 9.300)/(1/\sqrt{36}) = -0.15$
$P(z < -0.15) = 0.5000 - 0.0596 = 0.4404$

63. $50 + 2.33\dfrac{10}{\sqrt{n}} = 55 - .525\dfrac{10}{\sqrt{n}}$ $\qquad$ $n = (5.71)^2 = 32.6$

Let $n = 33$

65. $H_0: \mu \ge 8$ $\qquad$ $H_1: \mu < 8$
Reject H_0 if $t < -1.714$

$$t = \frac{7.5 - 8}{3.2/\sqrt{24}} = -0.77$$

Do not reject the null hypothesis. The time is not less.

67. a. $H_0: \mu = 80$ $\qquad$ $H_1: \mu \ne 80$
Reject H_0 if t is not between -2.045 and 2.045.
$t = \dfrac{83.16 - 80}{33.47/\sqrt{30}} = 0.52$
Do not reject the null. The mean salary could be $80.0 million.
b. $H_0: \mu \le 2,000,000$ $\qquad$ $H_1: \mu > 2,000,000$
Reject H_0 if $t > 1.699$.

$$t = \frac{2,650,000 - 2,000,000}{733,000/\sqrt{30}} = 4.86$$

Reject the null. The mean attendance was more than 2,000,000.

69. a. $H_0: \mu \le 4.0$ $\qquad$ $H_1: \mu > 4.0$
Reject H_0 if $t > 1.679$

$$t = \frac{8.12 - 4.0}{16.43/\sqrt{46}} = 1.70$$

Reject H_0. The mean number of cell phones is greater than 4.0. p-value is less than .05

b. $H_0: \mu \geq 50$ $\quad$ $H_1: \mu < 50$

Reject H_0 if $t < -1.680$. Note there is one missing value, so $n = 45$.

$$t = \frac{36.0 - 50.0}{105.5/\sqrt{45}} = -0.89$$

Do not reject H_0. The mean size of the labor force is not less than 50.

CHAPTER 11

1. **a.** Two-tailed test

$\quad$ **b.** Reject H_0 if $z < -2.05$ or $z > 2.05$

$\quad$ **c.** $z = \dfrac{102 - 99}{\sqrt{\dfrac{5^2}{40} + \dfrac{6^2}{50}}} = 2.59$

$\quad$ **d.** Reject H_0

$\quad$ **e.** p-value = .0096, found by 2(.5000 − .4952)

3. **Step 1** $H_0: \mu_1 \geq \mu_2$ $\quad$ $H_1: \mu_1 < \mu_2$

$\quad$ **Step 2** The .05 significance level was chosen.

$\quad$ **Step 3** Reject H_0 if $z < -1.65$.

$\quad$ **Step 4** -0.94, found by:

$$z = \frac{7.6 - 8.1}{\sqrt{\dfrac{(2.3)^2}{40} + \dfrac{(2.9)^2}{55}}} = -0.94$$

$\quad$ **Step 5** Fail to reject H_0. Babies using the Gibbs brand did not gain less weight. p-value = .1736, found by .5000 − .3264.

5. Two-tailed test, because we are trying to show that a difference exists between the two means. Reject H_0 if $z < -2.58$ or $z > 2.58$.

$$z = \frac{31.4 - 34.9}{\sqrt{\dfrac{(5.1)^2}{32} + \dfrac{(6.7)^2}{49}}} = -2.66$$

Reject H_0 at the .01 level. There is a difference in the mean turnover rate. p-value = 2(.5000 − .4961) = .0078

7. **a.** H_0 is rejected if $z > 1.65$

$\quad$ **b.** 0.64, found by $p_c = \dfrac{70 + 90}{100 + 150}$

$\quad$ **c.** 1.61, found by

$$z = \frac{0.70 - 0.60}{\sqrt{[(0.64 \times 0.36)/100] + [(0.64 \times 0.36)/150]}}$$

$\quad$ **d.** H_0 is not rejected

9. **a.** $H_0: \pi_1 = \pi_2$ $\quad$ $H_1: \pi_1 \neq \pi_2$

$\quad$ **b.** H_0 is rejected if $z < -1.96$ or $z > 1.96$

$\quad$ **c.** $p_c = \dfrac{24 + 40}{400 + 400} = 0.08$

$\quad$ **d.** -2.09, found by

$$z = \frac{0.06 - 0.10}{\sqrt{[(0.08 \times 0.92)/400] + [(0.08 \times 0.92)/400]}}$$

$\quad$ **e.** H_0 is rejected. The proportion infested is not the same in the two fields.

11. $H_0: \pi_d \leq \pi_r$ $\quad$ $H_1: \pi_d > \pi_r$

H_0 is rejected if $z > 2.05$

$$p_c = \frac{168 + 200}{800 + 1,000} = 0.2044$$

$$z = \frac{0.21 - 0.20}{\sqrt{\dfrac{(0.2044)(0.7956)}{800} + \dfrac{(0.2044)(0.7956)}{1,000}}} = 0.52$$

H_0 is not rejected. We cannot conclude that a larger proportion of Democrats favor lowering the standards. p-value = 0.3015.

13. **a.** Reject H_0 if $t > 2.120$ or $t < -2.120$

$\quad$ $df = 10 + 8 - 2 = 16$

b. $s_p^2 = \dfrac{(10 - 1)(4)^2 + (8 - 1)(5)^2}{10 + 8 - 2} = 19.9375$

c. $t = \dfrac{23 - 26}{\sqrt{19.9375\left(\dfrac{1}{10} + \dfrac{1}{8}\right)}} = -1.416$

d. Do not reject H_0

e. p-value is greater than 0.10 and less than 0.20

15. $H_0: \mu_f \leq \mu_m$ $\quad$ $H_1: \mu_f > \mu_m$

$df = 9 + 7 - 2 = 14$

Reject H_0 if $t > 2.624$

$$s_p^2 = \frac{(7 - 1)(6.88)^2 + (9 - 1)(9.49)^2}{7 + 9 - 2} = 71.749$$

$$t = \frac{79 - 78}{\sqrt{71.749\left(\dfrac{1}{7} + \dfrac{1}{9}\right)}} = 0.234$$

Do not reject H_0. There is no difference in the mean grades.

17. $H_0: \mu_s \leq \mu_a$ $\quad$ $H_1: \mu_s > \mu_a$

$df = 6 + 7 - 2 = 11$

Reject H_0 if $t > 1.363$

$$s_p^2 = \frac{(6 - 1)(12.2)^2 + (7 - 1)(15.8)^2}{6 + 7 - 2} = 203.82$$

$$t = \frac{142.5 - 130.3}{\sqrt{203.82\left(\dfrac{1}{6} + \dfrac{1}{7}\right)}} = 1.536$$

Reject H_0. The mean daily expenses are greater for the sales staff. The p-value is between 0.05 and 0.10.

19. **a.** $df = \dfrac{\left(\dfrac{25}{15} + \dfrac{225}{12}\right)^2}{\dfrac{\left(\dfrac{25}{15}\right)^2}{15 - 1} + \dfrac{\left(\dfrac{225}{12}\right)^2}{12 - 1}} = \dfrac{416.84}{0.1984 + 31.9602}$

$\quad$ $= 12.96 \to 12df$

$\quad$ **b.** $H_0: \mu_1 = \mu_2$ $\quad$ $H_1: \mu_1 \neq \mu_2$

$\quad$ Reject H_0 if $t > 2.179$ or $t < -2.179$

$\quad$ **c.** $t = \dfrac{50 - 46}{\sqrt{\dfrac{25}{15} + \dfrac{225}{12}}} = 0.8852$

$\quad$ **d.** Fail to reject the null hypothesis.

21. **a.** $df = \dfrac{\left(\dfrac{697,225}{16} + \dfrac{2,387,025}{18}\right)^2}{\dfrac{\left(\dfrac{697,225}{16}\right)^2}{16 - 1} + \dfrac{\left(\dfrac{2,387,025}{18}\right)^2}{18 - 1}} = 26.7 \to 26df$

$\quad$ **b.** $H_0: \mu_{Russia} \leq \mu_{China}$ $\quad$ $H_1: \mu_{Russia} > \mu_{China}$

$\quad$ Reject H_0 if $t > 1.706$

$\quad$ **c.** $t = \dfrac{12,840 - 11,045}{\sqrt{\dfrac{2,387,025}{18} + \dfrac{697,225}{16}}} = 4.276$

$\quad$ **d.** Reject the null hypothesis. The mean adoption cost from Russia is greater than the mean adoption cost from China.

23. **a.** Reject H_0 if $t > 2.353$

$\quad$ **b.** $\bar{d} = \dfrac{12}{4} = 3.00$ $\quad$ $s_d = \sqrt{\dfrac{2}{3}} = 0.816$

$\quad$ **c.** $t = \dfrac{3.00}{0.816/\sqrt{4}} = 7.35$

$\quad$ **d.** Reject H_0. There are more defective parts produced on the day shift.

$\quad$ **e.** p-value is less than 0.005, but greater than 0.0005

25. $H_0: \mu_d \leq 0$ $\quad$ $H_1: \mu_d > 0$

$\bar{d} = 25.917$

$s_d = 40.791$

Reject H_0 if $t > 1.796$

$$t = \frac{25.917}{40.791/\sqrt{12}} = 2.20$$

Reject H_0. The incentive plan resulted in an increase in daily income. The p-value is about .025.

27. $H_0: \mu_M = \mu_W$ $H_1: \mu_M \neq \mu_W$

Reject H_0 if $df = 35 + 40 - 2, t < -2.645$ or $t > 2.645$

$$s_p^2 = \frac{(35-1)(4.48)^2 + (40-1)(3.86)^2}{35 + 40 - 2} = 17.3079$$

$$t = \frac{24.51 - 22.69}{\sqrt{17.3079\left(\frac{1}{35} + \frac{1}{40}\right)}} = 1.890$$

Do not reject H_0. There is no difference in the number of times men and women buy take-out dinner in a month. The p-value is between .05 and .10.

29. $H_0: \mu_1 = \mu_2$ $H_1: \mu_1 \neq \mu_2$

Reject H_0 if $z < -1.96$ or $z > 1.96$

$$z = \frac{4.77 - 5.02}{\sqrt{\frac{(1.05)^2}{40} + \frac{(1.23)^2}{50}}} = -1.04$$

H_0. is not rejected. There is no difference in the mean number of calls. p-value = 2(0.5000 − 0.3508) = 0.2984.

31. $H_0: \mu_B \leq \mu_A$ $H_1: \mu_B > \mu_A$

Reject H_0 if $t > 1.668$

$$t = \frac{\$61{,}000 - \$57{,}000}{\sqrt{\frac{(\$7{,}100)^2}{30} + \frac{(\$9{,}200)^2}{40}}} = \frac{\$4000.00}{\$1948.42} = 2.05$$

Reject H_0. The mean income is larger for Plan B. The p-value = .5000 − .4798 = .0202. The skewness does not matter because of the sample sizes.

33. $H_0: \pi_1 \leq \pi_2$ $H_1: \pi_1 > \pi_2$

Reject H_0 if $z > 1.65$

$$p_c = \frac{180 + 261}{200 + 300} = 0.882$$

$$z = \frac{0.90 - 0.87}{\sqrt{\frac{0.882(0.118)}{200} + \frac{0.882(0.118)}{300}}} = 1.019$$

H_0 is not rejected. There is no difference in the proportions that found relief with the new and the old drugs.

35. $H_0: \pi_1 \leq \pi_2$ $H_1: \pi_1 > \pi_2$

If $z > 2.33$, reject H_0.

$$p_c = \frac{990 + 970}{1{,}500 + 1{,}600} = 0.63$$

$$z = \frac{.6600 - .60625}{\sqrt{\frac{.63(.37)}{1{,}500} + \frac{.63(.37)}{1{,}600}}} = 3.10$$

Reject the null hypothesis. We can conclude the proportion of men who believe the division is fair is greater.

37. $H_0: \pi_m = \pi_f$ $H_1: \pi_m \neq \pi_f$

Reject H_0 if $z > 1.96$ or $z < -1.96$

$$p_c = \frac{68 + 45}{98 + 85} = 0.6175$$

$$z = \frac{0.6939 - 0.5294}{\sqrt{\frac{(0.6175)(0.3825)}{98} + \frac{(0.6175)(0.3875)}{85}}} = 2.28$$

Reject the null hypothesis. There is a difference of opinion.

39. $H_0: \pi_1 \geq \pi_2$ $H_1: \pi_1 < \pi_2$ If $z < -1.65$, reject H_0.

$$p_c = \frac{13 + 7}{180 + 67} = 0.081$$

$$z = \frac{0.07222 - 0.10448}{\sqrt{\frac{(0.081)(0.919)}{180} + \frac{(0.081)(0.919)}{67}}} = -0.826$$

Do not reject the null. We cannot determine the 32-bit machines are inferior to the 8-bit ones.

41. a. $df = \dfrac{\left(\dfrac{0.3136}{12} + \dfrac{0.0900}{12}\right)^2}{\dfrac{\left(\dfrac{0.3136}{12}\right)^2}{12 - 1} + \dfrac{\left(\dfrac{0.0900}{12}\right)^2}{12 - 1}}$

$= \dfrac{0.0011}{0.000062 + 0.0000051} = 16.37 \rightarrow 16df$

b. $H_0: \mu_a = \mu_w$ $H_1: \mu_a \neq \mu_w$

Reject H_0 if $t > 2.120$ or $t < -2.120$

c. $t = \dfrac{1.65 - 2.20}{\sqrt{\dfrac{0.3136}{12} + \dfrac{0.0900}{12}}} = -3.00$

d. Reject the null hypothesis. There is a difference.

43. Assume equal population standard deviations.

$H_0: \mu_n = \mu_s$ $H_1: \mu_n \neq \mu_s$

Reject H_0 if $t < -2.086$ or $t > 2.086$

$$s_p^2 = \frac{(10-1)(10.5)^2 + (12-1)(14.25)^2}{10 + 12 - 2} = 161.2969$$

$$t = \frac{83.55 - 78.8}{\sqrt{161.2969\left(\frac{1}{10} + \frac{1}{12}\right)}} = 0.874$$

p-value > 0.10. Do not reject H_0. There is no difference in the mean number of hamburgers sold at the two locations.

45. Assume equal population standard deviations.

$H_0: \mu_1 = \mu_2$ $H_1: \mu_1 \neq \mu_2$

Reject H_0 if $t > 2.819$ or $t < -2.819$

$$s_p^2 = \frac{(10-1)(2.33)^2 + (14-1)(2.55)^2}{10 + 14 - 2} = 6.06$$

$$t = \frac{15.87 - 18.29}{\sqrt{6.06\left(\frac{1}{10} + \frac{1}{14}\right)}} = -2.374$$

Do not reject H_0. There is no difference in the mean amount purchased.

47. Assume equal population standard deviations.

$H_0: \mu_1 \leq \mu_2$ $H_1: \mu_1 > \mu_2$ Reject H_0 if $t > 2.567$

$$s_p^2 = \frac{(8-1)(2.2638)^2 + (11-1)(2.4606)^2}{8 + 11 - 2} = 5.672$$

$$t = \frac{10.375 - 5.636}{\sqrt{5.672\left(\frac{1}{8} + \frac{1}{11}\right)}} = 4.28$$

Reject H_0. The mean number of transactions by the young adults is more than for the senior citizens.

49. $H_0: \mu_1 \leq \mu_2$ $H_1: \mu_1 > \mu_2$ Reject H_0 if $t > 2.650$

$\bar{X}_1 = 125.125$ $s_1 = 15.094$

$\bar{X}_2 = 117.714$ $s_2 = 19.914$

$$s_p^2 = \frac{(8-1)(15.094)^2 + (7-1)(19.914)^2}{8 + 7 - 2} = 305.708$$

$$t = \frac{125.125 - 117.714}{\sqrt{305.708\left(\frac{1}{8} + \frac{1}{7}\right)}} = 0.819$$

H_0 is not rejected. There is no difference in the mean number sold at the regular price and the mean number sold at the reduced price.

51. $H_0: \mu_d \leq 0$ $H_1: \mu_d > 0$ Reject H_0 if $t > 1.895$

$\bar{d} = 1.75$ $s_d = 2.9155$

$$t = \frac{1.75}{2.9155/\sqrt{8}} = 1.698$$

Do not reject H_0. There is no difference in the mean number of absences. The p-value is greater than 0.05 but less than .10.

53. $H_0: \mu_1 = \mu_2$ $H_1: \mu_1 \neq \mu_2$

Reject H_0 if $t < -2.024$ or $t > 2.204$.

$$s_p^2 = \frac{(15-1)(40)^2 + (25-1)(30)^2}{15+25-2} = 1157.89$$

$$t = \frac{150-180}{\sqrt{1157.89\left(\frac{1}{15} + \frac{1}{25}\right)}} = -2.699$$

Reject the null hypothesis. The population means are different.

55. $H_0: \mu_d \leq 0$ $H_1: \mu_d > 0$

Reject H_0 if $t > 1.895$

$\bar{d} = 3.11$ $s_d = 2.91$

$$t = \frac{3.11}{2.91/\sqrt{8}} = 3.02$$

Reject H_0. The mean is lower.

57. $H_0: \mu_O = \mu_R$, $H_1: \mu_O \neq \mu_R$

$df = 25 + 28 - 2 = 51$

Reject H_0 if $t < -2.008$ or $t > 2.008$

$\bar{X}_O = 86.24, s_O = 23.43$

$X_R = 92.04, s_R = 24.12$

$$s_p^2 = \frac{(25-1)(23.43)^2 + (28-1)(24.12)^2}{25+28-2} = 566.335$$

$$t = \frac{86.24 - 92.04}{\sqrt{566.335\left(\frac{1}{25} + \frac{1}{28}\right)}} = -0.886$$

Do not reject H_0. There is no difference in the mean number of cars in the two lots.

59. $H_0: \mu_F \geq \mu_B$ $H_1: \mu_F < \mu_B$

$$df = 24, \text{ found by } \frac{\left(\frac{53.2^2}{15} + \frac{48.3^2}{12}\right)^2}{\frac{\left(\frac{53.2^2}{15}\right)^2}{14} + \frac{\left(\frac{48.3^2}{12}\right)^2}{11}} = 24.546$$

Round down degrees of freedom.

Reject H_0 if $t < -2.492$.

$$t = \frac{39.4 - 187.5}{\sqrt{\frac{(53.2)^2}{15} + \frac{(48.3)^2}{12}}} = -7.57 \quad \text{Reject } H_0.$$

Starting in the first five rows (in contrast to the last four) lowers the odds.

61. **a.** $\mu_1 =$ with pool $\mu_2 =$ without pool

$H_0: \mu_1 = \mu_2$ $H_1: \mu_1 \neq \mu_2$

Reject H_0 if $t > 2.000$ or $t < -2.000$

$\bar{X}_1 = 202.8$ $s_1 = 33.7$ $n_1 = 38$

$\bar{X}_2 = 231.5$ $s_2 = 50.46$ $n_2 = 67$

$$s_p^2 = \frac{(38-1)(33.7)^2 + (67-1)(50.46)^2}{38+67-2} = 2,041.05$$

$$t = \frac{202.8 - 231.5}{\sqrt{2,041.05\left(\frac{1}{38} + \frac{1}{67}\right)}} = -3.12$$

Reject H_0. There is a difference in mean selling price for homes with and without a pool.

b. $\mu_1 =$ without attached garage $\mu_2 =$ with garage

$H_0: \mu_1 = \mu_2$ $H_1: \mu_1 \neq \mu_2$

Reject H_0 if $t > 2.000$ or $t < -2.000$

$\alpha = 0.05$ $df = 34 + 71 - 2 = 103$

$\bar{X}_1 = 185.45$ $s_1 = 28.00$

$\bar{X}_2 = 238.18$ $s_2 = 44.88$

$$s_p^2 = \frac{(34-1)(28.00)^2 + (71-1)(44.88)^2}{103} = 1,620.07$$

$$t = \frac{185.45 - 238.18}{\sqrt{1,620.07\left(\frac{1}{34} + \frac{1}{71}\right)}} = -6.28$$

Reject H_0. There is a difference in mean selling price for homes with and without an attached garage.

c. $H_0: \mu_1 = \mu_2$ $H_1: \mu_1 \neq \mu_2$

Reject H_0 if $t > 2.036$ or $t < -2.036$

$\bar{X}_1 = 196.91$ $s_1 = 35.78$ $n_1 = 15$

$\bar{X}_2 = 227.45$ $s_2 = 44.19$ $n_2 = 20$

$$s_p^2 = \frac{(15-1)(35.78)^2 + (20-1)(44.19)^2}{15+20-2} = 1,667.43$$

$$t = \frac{196.91 - 227.45}{\sqrt{1,667.43\left(\frac{1}{15} + \frac{1}{20}\right)}} = -2.19$$

Reject H_0. There is a difference in mean selling price for homes in Township 1 and Township 2.

d. $H_0: \pi_1 = \pi_2$ $H_1: \pi_1 \neq \pi_2$

If z is not between -1.96 and 1.96, reject H_0

$$p_c = \frac{24 + 43}{52 + 53} = 0.64$$

$$z = \frac{0.462 - 0.811}{\sqrt{0.64 \times 0.36/52 + 0.64 \times 0.36/53}} = -3.73$$

Reject the null hypothesis. There is a difference.

63. **a.** $H_0: \mu_s = \mu_{ns}$ $H_1: \mu_s \neq \mu_{ns}$

Reject H_0 if $t < -1,984$ or $t > 1.984$.

Answer worked in thousands.

$$s_p^2 = \frac{(67-1)(17.403)^2 + (33-1)(16.062)^2}{67+33-2} = 288.21$$

$$t = \frac{31.798 - 28.876}{\sqrt{288.21\left(\frac{1}{67} + \frac{1}{33}\right)}} = \frac{2.922}{3.610} = 0.803$$

Do not reject H_0. No difference in the mean wages.

b. $H_0: \mu_w = \mu_{nw}$ $H_1: \mu_w \neq \mu_{nw}$

Note, because one sample is less than 30, use t and pool variances. Also answer reported in $000.

Reject H_0 if $t < -1.984$ or $t > 1.984$.

$$s_p^2 = \frac{(90-1)(17.358)^2 + (10-1)(11.536)^2}{90+10-2} = 285.85$$

$$t = \frac{31.517 - 24.678}{\sqrt{285.85\left(\frac{1}{90} + \frac{1}{10}\right)}} = 1.214$$

Do not reject H_0. No difference in the mean wages.

c. $H_0: \mu_h = \mu_{nh}$ $H_1: \mu_h \neq \mu_{nh}$

Reject H_0 if $t < -1.984$ or $t > 1.984$.

Because one sample is less than 30, use t. Answer reported in $000.

$$s_p^2 = \frac{(94-1)(16.413)^2 + (6-1)(25.843)^2}{94+6-2} = 289.72$$

$$t = \frac{30.674 - 33.337}{\sqrt{289.72\left(\frac{1}{94} + \frac{1}{6}\right)}} = -0.37$$

Do not reject H_0. No difference in the mean wages.

d. $H_0: \mu_m = \mu_f$ $H_1: \mu_m \neq \mu_f$

Reject H_0 if $t < -1.984$ or $t > 1.984$

$$t = \frac{\$36,493 - \$24,452}{\sqrt{(15914.75)^2\left(\frac{1}{53} + \frac{1}{47}\right)}} = 3.776$$

Reject H_0. There is a difference in the mean wages for men and women.

e. $H_0: \mu_m = \mu_{nm}$ $H_1: \mu_m \neq \mu_{nm}$
Reject H_0 if $t < -1.984$ or $t > 1.984$.

$$t = \frac{24{,}864 - 33{,}773}{\sqrt{(16499.33)^2\left(\dfrac{1}{33} + \dfrac{1}{67}\right)}} = -2.539$$

Reject H_0. There is a difference in the mean wages of the two groups.

CHAPTER 12

1. 9.01, from Appendix B.4

3. Reject H_0 if $F > 10.5$, where degrees of freedom in the numerator are 7 and 5 in the denominator. Computed $F = 2.04$, found by:

$$F = \frac{s_1^2}{s_2^2} = \frac{(10)^2}{(7)^2} = 2.04$$

Do not reject H_0. There is no difference in the variations of the two populations.

5. $H_0: \sigma_1^2 = \sigma_2^2$ $H_1: \sigma_1^2 \neq \sigma_2^2$
Reject H_0 where $F > 3.10$. (3.10 is about halfway between 3.14 and 3.07.) Computed $F = 1.44$, found by:

$$F = \frac{(12)^2}{(10)^2} = 1.44$$

Do not reject H_0. There is no difference in the variations of the two populations.

7. a. $H_0: \mu_1 = \mu_2 = \mu_3$; H_1: Treatment means are not all the same.
   b. Reject H_0 if $F > 4.26$
   c & d.

Source	SS	df	MS	F
Treatment	62.17	2	31.08	21.94
Error	12.75	9	1.42	
Total	74.92	11		

   e. Reject H_0. The treatment means are not all the same.

9. $H_0: \mu_1 = \mu_2 = \mu_3$; H_1: Treatment means are not all the same. Reject H_0 if $F > 4.26$.

Source	SS	df	MS	F
Treatment	276.50	2	138.25	14.18
Error	87.75	9	9.75	

Reject H_0. The treatment means are not all the same.

11. a. $H_0: \mu_1 = \mu_2 = \mu_3$; H_1: Not all means are the same.
   b. Reject H_0 if $F > 4.26$
   c. SST = 107.20, SSE = 9.47, SS total = 116.67.
   d.

Source	SS	df	MS	F
Treatment	107.20	2	53.600	50.96
Error	9.47	9	1.052	
Total	116.67	11		

   e. Since $50.96 > 4.26$. H_0 is rejected. At least one of the means differs.
   f. $(\bar{X}_1 - \bar{X}_2) \pm t\sqrt{\text{MSE}(1/n_1 + 1/n_2)}$
   $= (9.667 - 2.20) \pm 2.262 \sqrt{1.052(1/3 + 1/5)}$
   $= 7.467 \pm 1.69$
   $= [5.777, 9.157]$
   Yes, we can conclude that treatments 1 and 2 have different means.

13. $H_0: \mu_1 = \mu_2 = \mu_3 = \mu_4$; H_1: Not all means are equal. H_0 is rejected if $F > 3.71$.

Source	SS	df	MS	F
Treatment	32.33	3	10.77	2.36
Error	45.67	10	4.567	
Total	78.00	13		

Because 2.36 is less than 3.71, H_0 is not rejected. There is no difference in the mean number of weeks.

15. a. $H_0: \mu_1 = \mu_2$; H_1: Not all treatment means are equal.
   b. Reject H_0 if $F > 18.5$
   c. $H_0: \mu_1 = \mu_2 = \mu_3$; H_1: Not all block means are equal. H_0 is rejected if $F > 19.0$.
   d. SS total $= (46.0 - 36.5)^2 + \cdots + (35 - 36.5)^2 = 289.5$
   SSE $= (46 - 42.3333)^2 + \cdots + (35 - 30.6667)^2$
   $= 85.3333$
   SST $= 289.5 - 85.3333 = 204.1667$
   SSB $= 2(38.5 - 36.5)^2 + 2(31.5 - 36.5)^2 +$
   $2(39.5 - 36.5)^2 = 8 + 50 + 18 = 76$
   SSE $= 289.50 - 204.1667 - 76 = 9.3333$
   e.

Source	SS	df	MS	F
Treatment	204.167	1	204.167	43.75
Blocks	76.000	2	38.000	8.14
Error	9.333	2	4.667	
Total	289.5000	5		

   f. $43.75 > 18.5$, so reject H_0. There is a difference in the treatments. $8.14 < 19.0$, so do not reject H_0 for blocks. There is no difference among blocks.

17. For treatment: For blocks:
   $H_0: \mu_1 = \mu_2 = \mu_3$ $H_0: \mu_1 = \mu_2 = \mu_3 = \mu_4 = \mu_5$
   H_1: Not all means equal H_1: Not all means equal
   Reject if $F > 4.46$ Reject if $F > 3.84$

Source	SS	df	MS	F
Treatment	62.53	2	31.2650	5.75
Blocks	33.73	4	8.4325	1.55
Error	43.47	8	5.4338	
Total	139.73			

There is a difference in shifts, but not by employee.

19.

Source	df	SS	MS	F	P
Factor B	1	98.000	98.0000	2.48	0.141
Factor A	2	156.333	78.1667	1.98	0.180
Interaction	2	36.333	18.1667	0.46	0.642
Error	12	473.333	39.4444		
Total	17	764.000			

   a. p-value > 0.05. Therefore, no difference in Factor A means.
   b. p-value > 0.05. Therefore, no difference in Factor B means.
   c. p-value > 0.05. Therefore, no interaction between Factor A and Factor B.

21. a.

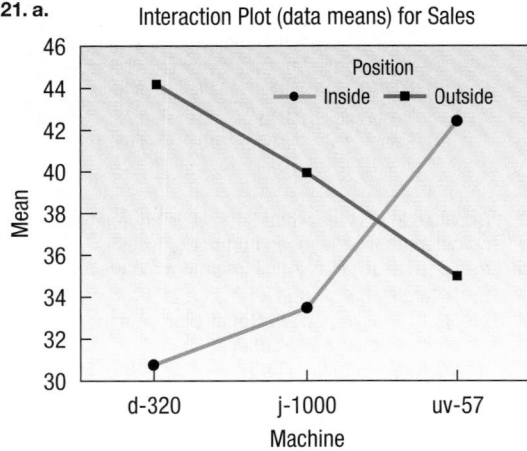

Interaction Plot (data means) for Sales

Yes, there appears to be an interaction effect. Sales are different based on machine position, either in inside or outside position.

b.

Two-way ANOVA: Sales versus Position, Machine				
Source	df	SS	MS	F	P
Position	1	104.167	104.167	9.12	0.007
Machine	2	16.333	8.167	0.72	0.502
Interaction	2	457.333	228.667	20.03	0.000
Error	18	205.500	11.417		
Total	23	783.333			

The position and the interaction of position and machine effects are significant. The effect of machine on sales is not significant.

c.

One-way ANOVA: D-320 Sales versus Position				
Source	df	SS	MS	F	P
Position	1	364.50	364.50	40.88	0.001
Error	6	53.50	8.92		
Total	7	418.00			

One-way ANOVA: J-1000 Sales versus Position				
Source	df	SS	MS	F	P
Position	1	84.5	84.5	5.83	0.052
Error	6	87.0	14.5		
Total	7	171.5			

One-way ANOVA: UV-57 Sales versus Position				
Source	df	SS	MS	F	P
Position	1	112.5	112.5	10.38	0.018
Error	6	65.0	10.8		
Total	7	177.5			

Recommendations using the statistical results and mean sales plotted in part (a): Position the D-320 machine outside. Statistically, the position of the J-1000 does not matter. Position the UV-57 machine inside.

23. $H_0: \sigma_1^2 \le \sigma_2^2; H_1: \sigma_1^2 > \sigma_2^2.$ $df_1 = 21 - 1 = 20;$ $df_2 = 18 - 1 = 17.$ H_0 is rejected if $F > 3.16.$

$$F = \frac{(45,600)^2}{(21,330)^2} = 4.57$$

Reject H_0. There is more variation in the selling price of oceanfront homes.

25. Sharkey: $n = 7$ $s_s = 14.79$
White: $n = 8$ $s_w = 22.95$

$H_0: \sigma_w^2 \le \sigma_s^2; H_1: \sigma_w^2 > \sigma_s^2.$ $df_s = 7 - 1 = 6;$
$df_w = 8 - 1 = 7.$ Reject H_0 if $F > 8.26.$

$$F = \frac{(22.95)^2}{(14.79)^2} = 2.41$$

Cannot reject H_0. There is no difference in the variation of the monthly sales.

27. a. $H_0: \mu_1 = \mu_2 = \mu_3 = \mu_4$
H_1: Treatment means are not all equal.
b. $\alpha = .05$ Reject H_0 if $F > 3.10.$
c.

Source	SS	df	MS	F
Treatment	50	$4 - 1 = 3$	50/3	1.67
Error	200	$24 - 4 = 20$	10	
Total	250	$24 - 1 = 23$		

d. Do not reject H_0

29. $H_0: \mu_1 = \mu_2 = \mu_3; H_1:$ Not all treatment means are equal.
H_0 is rejected if $F > 3.89.$

Source	SS	df	MS	F
Treatment	63.33	2	31.667	13.38
Error	28.40	12	2.367	
Total	91.73	14		

H_0 is rejected. There is a difference in the treatment means.

31. $H_0: \mu_1 = \mu_2 = \mu_3 = \mu_4; H_1:$ Not all means are equal.
H_0 is rejected if $F > 3.10.$

Source	SS	df	MS	F
Factor	87.79	3	29.26	9.12
Error	64.17	20	3.21	
Total	151.96	23		

Because computed F of $9.12 > 3.10$, the null hypothesis of no difference is rejected at the .05 level.

33. a. $H_0: \mu_1 = \mu_2; H_1: \mu_1 \ne \mu_2.$ Critical value of $F = 4.75.$

Source	SS	df	MS	F
Treatment	219.43	1	219.43	23.10
Error	114.00	12	9.5	
Total	333.43	13		

b. $t = \dfrac{19 - 27}{\sqrt{9.5\left(\dfrac{1}{6} + \dfrac{1}{8}\right)}} = -4.806$

Then $t^2 = F.$ That is $(-4.806)^2 = 23.10.$
c. H_0 is rejected. There is a difference in the mean scores.

35. The null hypothesis is rejected because the F statistic (8.26) is greater than the critical value (5.61) at the .01 significance level. The p-value (.0019) is also less than the significance level. The mean gasoline mileages are not the same.

37. $H_0: \mu_1 = \mu_2 = \mu_3 = \mu_4.$ H_1: At least one mean is different. Reject H_0 if $F > 2.7395.$ Since 2.72 is less than 2.7395, H_0 is not rejected. You can also see this conclusion from the p-value of 0.051, which is greater than 0.05. There is no difference in the means for the different types of first-class mail.

39. For color, the critical value of F is 4.76; for size, it is 5.14.

Source	SS	df	MS	F
Treatment	25.0	3	8.3333	5.88
Blocks	21.5	2	10.75	7.59
Error	8.5	6	1.4167	
Total	55.0	11		

H_0s for both treatment and blocks (color and size) are rejected. At least one mean differs for color and at least one mean differs for size.

41. a. Critical value of F is 3.49. Computed F is .668. Do not reject H_0.

b. Critical value of F is 3.26. Computed F value is 100.204. Reject H_0 for block means.

There is a difference in homes but not assessors.

43. For gasoline:

H_0: $\mu_1 = \mu_2 = \mu_3$; H_1: Mean mileage is not the same.
Reject H_0 if $F > 3.89$.

For automobile:

H_0: $\mu_1 = \mu_2 = \cdots = \mu_7$; H_1: Mean mileage is not the same.
Reject H_0 if $F > 3.00$.

ANOVA Table				
Source	SS	df	MS	F
Gasoline	44.095	2	22.048	26.71
Autos	77.238	6	12.873	15.60
Error	9.905	12	0.825	
Total	131.238	20		

There is a difference in both autos and gasoline.

45. H_0: $\mu_1 = \mu_2 = \mu_3 = \mu_4 = \mu_5 = \mu_6$; H_1: The treatment means are not equal. Reject H_0 if $F > 2.37$.

Source	SS	df	MS	F
Treatment	0.03478	5	0.00696	3.86
Error	0.10439	58	0.0018	
Total	0.13917	63		

H_0 is rejected. There is a difference in the mean weight of the colors.

47. a.

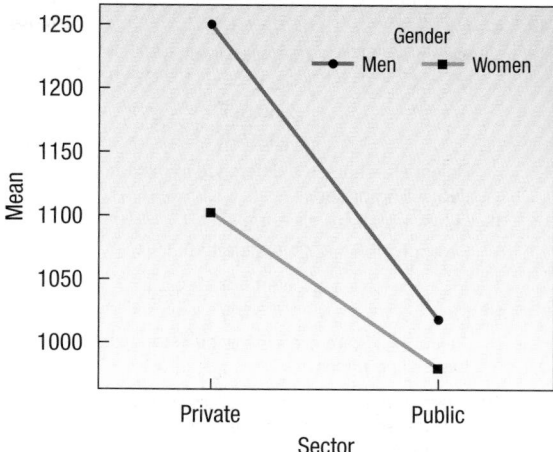

Interaction Plot (data means) for Wage

47. b. Two-way ANOVA: Wage versus Gender, Sector

```
Source        DF       SS       MS       F       P
Gender         1    44086    44086   11.44   0.004
Sector         1   156468   156468   40.61   0.000
Interaction    1    14851    14851    3.85   0.067
Error         16    61640     3853
Total         19   277046
```

There is no interaction effect of gender and sector on wages. However, there are significant differences in mean wages based on gender and significant differences in mean wages based on sector.

47. c. One-way ANOVA: Wage versus Sector

```
Source   DF       SS       MS       F       P
Sector    1   156468   156468   23.36   0.000
Error    18   120578     6699
Total    19   277046
```

```
s = 81.85   R-Sq = 56.48%   R-Sq(adj) = 54.06%
```

```
                              Individual 95% CIs For Mean Based on
                              Pooled StDev
Level     N    Mean   StDev   --+---------+---------+---------+-------
Private  10  1175.2    95.9                         (------*------)
Public   10   998.3    64.8   (------*------)
                              --+---------+---------+---------+-------
                              960      1040      1120      1200
```

One-way ANOVA: Wage versus Gender

```
Source   DF       SS       MS       F       P
Gender    1    44086    44086    3.41   0.081
Error    18   232960    12942
Total    19   277046
```

```
s = 113.8  R-Sq = 15.91%  R-Sq(adj) = 11.24%
```

```
                              Individual 95% CIs For Mean Based on
                              Pooled StDev
Level     N    Mean   StDev   --+---------+---------+---------+-------
Men      10  1133.7   137.9                 (----------*----------)
Women    10  1039.8    82.9   (----------*---------)
                              --+---------+---------+---------+-------
                              980      1050      1120      1190
```

d. The statistical results show that only sector, private or public, has a significant effect on the wages of accountants.

49. a. $H_0: \sigma_{np}^2 = \sigma_p^2$ $H_1: \sigma_{np}^2 \neq \sigma_p^2$.

Reject H_0 if $F > 2.05$ (estimated).
$df_1 = 67 - 1 = 66$; $df_2 = 38 - 1 = 37$.

$$F = \frac{(50.57)^2}{(33.71)^2} = 2.25$$

Reject H_0. There is a difference in the variance of the two selling prices.

b. $H_0: \sigma_g^2 = \sigma_{ng}^2$; $H_1: \sigma_g^2 \neq \sigma_{ng}^2$.

Reject H_0 if $F > 2.21$ (estimated).

$$F = \frac{(44.88)^2}{(28.00)^2} = 2.57$$

Reject H_0. There is a difference in the variance of the two selling prices.

c.

Source	SS	df	MS	F
Township	13,263	4	3,316	1.52
Error	217,505	100	2,175	
Total	230,768	104		

$H_0: \mu_1 = \mu_2 = \mu_3 = \mu_4 = \mu_5$; H_1: Not all treatment means are equal. Reject H_0 if $F > 2.46$.
Do not reject H_0. There is no difference in the mean selling prices in the five townships.

51. a. $H_0: \mu_1 = \mu_2 = \mu_3$; H_1: Treatment means are not equal. Reject H_0 if $F > 3.09$. The computed value of F is 1.30. We conclude there is no difference among the industries.

b. $H_0: \mu_1 = \mu_2 = \mu_3 = \mu_4 = \mu_5$; H_1: Treatment means are not equal.
Reject H_0 if $F > 2.31$. The computed value of F is 4.85. The treatment means differ. The MINITAB output follows.

```
Level   N    Mean    StDev
0       22   28921   14517
1       13   40074   22733
2       6    27228   16101
3       21   27619   9821
4       21   21510   6946
5       17   43002   22062

Pooled St Dev = 15507

Individual 95% CIs for Mean
Based on Pooled StDev
------+---------+---------+---------+
      (------*-----)
                  (------*-----)
  (---------*--------)
      (------*-----)
  (------*-----)
                      (------*-----)
------+---------+---------+---------+
  20000     30000     40000     50000
```

From this graph the following means differ: 0 and 5, 1 and 4, 3 and 5, and 4 and 5.

c. $H_0: \sigma_u^2 = \sigma_{nu}^2$; $H_1: \sigma_u^2 \neq \sigma_{nu}^2$; reject H_0 if $F > 1.99$.

Computed F is 1.36, found by $(17,413)^2/(14,940)^2$. There is no difference in the variation of union and nonunion members.

CHAPTER 13

1. $\Sigma(X - \bar{X})(Y - \bar{Y}) = 10.6$, $s_x = 2.7019$, $s_y = 1.3038$

$$r = \frac{10.6}{(5-1)(2.7019)(1.3038)} = 0.7522$$

The 0.7522 coefficient indicates a rather strong positive correlation between X and Y. The coefficient of determination is 0.5658, found by $(0.7522)^2$. More than 56 percent of the variation in Y is accounted for by X.

3. a. Sales.

b.

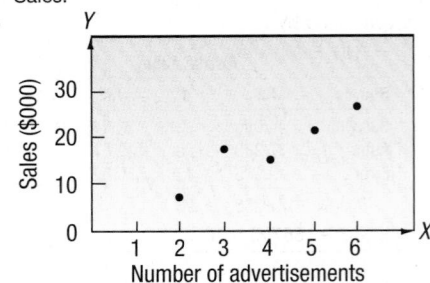

c. $\Sigma(X - \bar{X})(Y - \bar{Y}) = 36$, $n = 5$, $s_x = 1.5811$, $s_y = 6.1237$

$$r = \frac{36}{(5-1)(1.5811)(6.1237)} = 0.9295$$

d. The coefficient of determination is 0.8640, found by $(0.9295)^2$.

e. There is a strong positive association between the variables. About 86 percent of the variation in sales is explained by the number of airings.

5. a. Police is the independent variable, and crime is the dependent variable.

b.

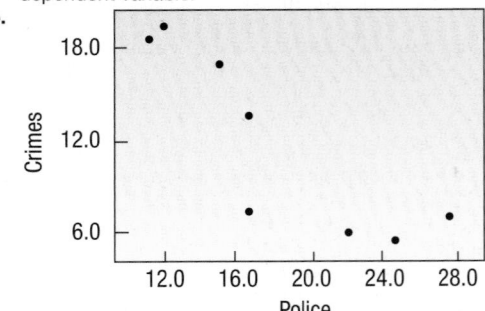

c. $n = 8$, $\Sigma(X - \bar{X})(Y - \bar{Y}) = -231.75$,
$s_x = 5.8737$, $s_y = 6.4462$

$$r = \frac{-231.75}{(8-1)(5.8737)(6.4462)} = -0.8744$$

d. 0.7646, found by $(-0.8744)^2$

e. Strong inverse relationship. As the number of police increases, the crime decreases.

7. Reject H_0 if $t > 1.812$

$$t = \frac{.32\sqrt{12 - 2}}{\sqrt{1 - (.32)^2}} = 1.068$$

Do not reject H_0

9. $H_0: \rho \leq 0$; $H_1: \rho > 0$. Reject H_0 if $t > 2.552$. $df = 18$.

$$t = \frac{.78\sqrt{20 - 2}}{\sqrt{1 - (.78)^2}} = 5.288$$

Reject H_0. There is a positive correlation between gallons sold and the pump price.

11. $H_0: \rho \leq 0$ $H_1: \rho > 0$
Reject H_0 if $t > 2.650$

$$t = \frac{0.667\sqrt{15-2}}{\sqrt{1-0.667^2}} = 3.228$$

Reject H_0. There is a positive correlation between the number of passengers and plane weight.

13. a. $\hat{Y} = 3.7778 + 0.3630X$

$$b = 0.7522\left(\frac{1.3038}{2.7019}\right) = 0.3630$$

$$a = 5.8 - 0.3630(5.6) = 3.7671$$

b. 6.3081, found by $\hat{Y} = 3.7671 + 0.3630(7)$

15. a. $\Sigma(X-\overline{X})(Y-\overline{Y}) = 44.6$, $s_x = 2.726$, $s_y = 2.011$

$$r = \frac{44.6}{(10-1)(2.726)(2.011)} = .904$$

$$b = .904\left(\frac{2.011}{2.726}\right) = 0.667$$

$$a = 7.4 - .677(9.1) = 1.333$$

b. $\hat{Y} = 1.333 + .667(6) = 5.335$

17. a.

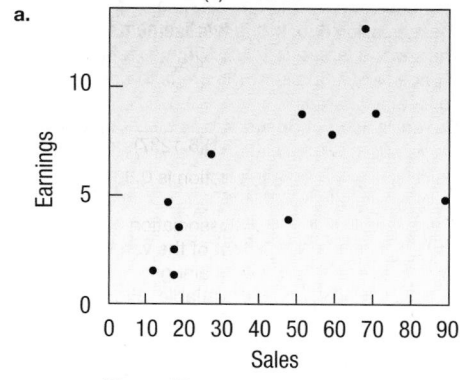

b. $\Sigma(X-\overline{X})(Y-\overline{Y}) = 629.64$, $s_x = 26.17$, $s_y = 3.248$

$$r = \frac{629.64}{(12-1)(26.17)(3.248)} = .6734$$

c. $r^2 = (0.673)^2 = 0.4529$

d. A strong positive association between the variables. About 45 percent of the variation in earnings is accounted for by sales.

e. $b = .6734\left(\frac{3.248}{26.170}\right) = 0.0836$

$$a = \frac{64.1}{12} - 0.0836\left(\frac{501.10}{12}\right) = 1.8507$$

f. $\hat{Y} = 1.8507 + 0.0836(50.0) = 6.0307$ ($ millions)

19. a. $b = -.8744\left(\frac{6.4462}{5.8737}\right) = -0.9596$

$$a = \frac{95}{8} - (-0.9596)\left(\frac{146}{8}\right) = 29.3877$$

b. 10.1957, found by $29.3877 - 0.9596(20)$

c. For each policeman added, crime goes down by almost one.

21. a. $\sqrt{\frac{2.958}{5-2}} = .993$

b. $\hat{Y} \pm .993$

23. a. $\sqrt{\frac{6.667}{10-2}} = 0.913$

b. $\hat{Y} \pm 1.826$

25. $\sqrt{\frac{68.4877}{8-2}} = 3.379$

27. a. $6.308 \pm (3.182)(.993)\sqrt{.2 + \frac{(7-5.6)^2}{29.2}}$

$$= 6.308 \pm 1.633$$
$$= [4.675, 7.941]$$

b. $6.308 \pm (3.182)(.993)\sqrt{1 + 1/5 + .0671}$
$$= [2.751, 9.865]$$

29. a. 4.2939, 6.3721

b. 2.9854, 7.6806

31. $\overline{X} = 10$, $\overline{Y} = 6$, $\Sigma(X-\overline{X})(Y-\overline{Y}) = 40$, $s_y = 2.2361$, $s_x = 5.0$

$$r = \frac{40}{(5-1)(2.2361)(5.0)} = .8944$$

Then, $(.8944)^2 = .80$, the coefficient of determination.

33. a. $r^2 = 1,000/1,500 = .667$

b. .82, found by $\sqrt{.667}$

c. 6.20, found by $s_{y\cdot x} = \sqrt{\frac{500}{15-2}}$

35. The correlation between the two variables is 0.298. By squaring X, the correlation increases to .998.

37. $H_0: \rho \leq 0$; $H_1: \rho > 0$. Reject H_0 if $t > 1.714$.

$$t = \frac{.94\sqrt{25-2}}{\sqrt{1-(.94)^2}} = 13.213$$

Reject H_0. There is a positive correlation between passengers and weight of luggage.

39. $H_0: \rho \leq 0$; $H_1: \rho > 0$. Reject H_0 if $t > 2.764$.

$$t = \frac{.47\sqrt{12-2}}{\sqrt{1-(.47)^2}} = 1.684$$

Do not reject H_0. There is not a positive correlation between engine size and performance. p-value is greater than .05, but less than .10.

41. a. The total number of cars sold decreases as the percent market share decreases. The relationship is inverse so as one increases, the other decreases.

b. $r = \frac{-305.19}{(12-1)(3.849)(8.185)} = -0.881$

The value of r indicates a fairly strong negative association between the variables.

c. $H_0: \rho \geq 0$ $H_1: \rho < 0$
Reject H_0 if $t < -2.764$

$$t = \frac{-0.881\sqrt{12-2}}{\sqrt{1-(-0.881)^2}} = -5.89$$

Reject H_0. There is a negative correlation.

d. 77.6 percent, found by $(-0.881)^2$, of the variation in market share is accounted for by variation in cars sold.

43. a. $r = 0.589$

b. $r^2 = (0.589)^2 = 0.3469$

c. $H_0: \rho \leq 0$; $H_1: \rho > 0$. Reject H_0 if $t > 1.860$.

$$t = \frac{0.589\sqrt{10-2}}{\sqrt{1-(.589)^2}} = 2.062$$

H_0 is rejected. There is a positive association between family size and the amount spent on food.

45. a.

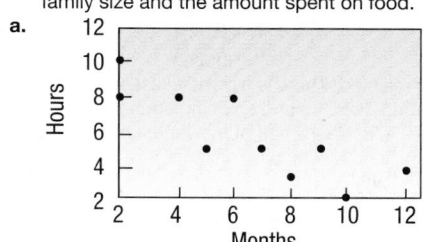

There is an inverse relationship between the variables. As the months owned increase, the number of hours exercised decreases.

b. $r = -0.827$

c. $H_0: \rho \geq 0$; $H_1: \rho < 0$. Reject H_0 if $t < -2.896$.

$$t = \frac{-0.827\sqrt{10-2}}{\sqrt{1-(-0.827)^2}} = -4.16$$

Reject H_0. There is a negative association between months owned and hours exercised.

47. a. Median age and population are directly related.

b. $r = \dfrac{11.93418}{(10-1)(2.207)(1.330)} = 0.452$

c. The slope of 0.272 indicates that for each increase of 1 million in the population, the median age increases on average by 0.272 years.

d. The median age is 32.08 years, found by $31.4 + 0.272(2.5)$.

e. The p-value (0.190) for the population variable is greater than, say 0.05. A test for significance of that coefficient would fail to be rejected. In other words, it is possible the population coefficient is zero.

f. $H_0: \rho = 0$ $H_1: \rho \neq 0$ Reject H_0 if t is not between -2.306 and 2.306.

$\text{df} = 8$ $t = \dfrac{0.452\sqrt{10-2}}{\sqrt{1-(0.452)^2}} = 1.433$ Do not reject H_0.

There may be no relationship between age and population.

49. a. $b = -0.4667$, $a = 11.2358$

b. $\hat{Y} = 11.2358 - 0.4667(7.0) = 7.9689$

c. $7.9689 \pm (2.160)(1.114)\sqrt{1 + \dfrac{1}{15} + \dfrac{(7-7.1333)^2}{73.7333}}$

$= 7.9689 \pm 2.4854$
$= [5.4835, 10.4543]$

d. $r^2 = 0.499$. Nearly 50 percent of the variation in the amount of the bid is explained by the number of bidders.

51. a.

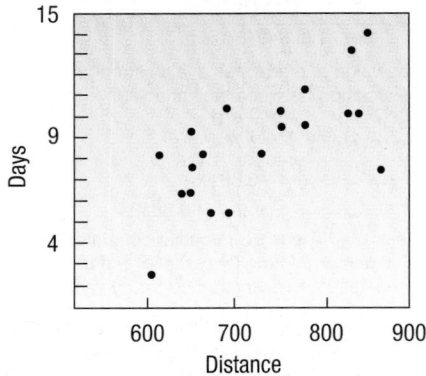

There appears to be a relationship between the two variables. As the distance increases, so does the shipping time.

b. $r = 0.692$

$H_0: \rho \leq 0$; $H_1: \rho > 0$. Reject H_0 if $t > 1.734$.

$$t = \frac{0.692\sqrt{20-2}}{\sqrt{1-(0.692)^2}} = 4.067$$

H_0 is rejected. There is a positive association between shipping distance and shipping time.

c. $r^2 = 0.479$. Nearly half of the variation in shipping time is explained by shipping distance.

d. $s_{y \cdot x} = 1.987$

53. a. $b = 2.41$
$a = 26.8$

The regression equation is: Price $= 26.8 + 2.41 \times$ Dividend. For each additional dollar of dividend, the price increases by $2.41.

b. $r^2 = \dfrac{5{,}057.6}{7{,}682.7} = 0.658$ Thus, 65.8 percent of the variation in price is explained by the dividend.

c. $r = \sqrt{.658} = 0.811$ $H_0: \rho \leq 0$ $H_1: \rho > 0$
At the 5 percent level, reject H_0 when $t > 1.701$.

$$t = \frac{0.811\sqrt{30-2}}{\sqrt{1-(0.811)^2}} = 7.34$$

Thus H_0 is rejected. The population correlation is positive.

55. a. 35

b. $s_{y \cdot x} = \sqrt{29{,}778{,}406} = 5{,}456.96$

c. $r^2 = \dfrac{13{,}548{,}662{,}082}{14{,}531{,}349{,}474} = 0.932$

d. $r = \sqrt{0.932} = 0.966$

e. $H_0: \rho \leq 0$, $H_1: \rho > 0$; reject H_0 if $t > 1.692$

$$t = \frac{.966\sqrt{35-2}}{\sqrt{1-(.966)^2}} = 21.46$$

Reject H_0. There is a direct relationship between size of the house and its market value.

57. a. The regression equation is Price $= -773 + 1{,}408$ Speed.

b. The second laptop (1.6, 922) with a residual of -557.60, is priced \$557.60 below the predicted price. That is a noticeable "bargain."

c. The correlation of Speed and Price is 0.835.
$H_0: \rho \leq 0$ $H_1: \rho > 0$ Reject H_0 if $t > 1.8125$

$$t = \frac{0.835\sqrt{12-2}}{\sqrt{1-(0.835)^2}} = 4.799$$

Reject H_0. It is reasonable to say the population correlation is positive.

59. a. $r = .987$, $H_0: \rho \leq 0$, $H_1: \rho > 0$. Reject H_0 if $t > 1.746$.

$$t = \frac{.987\sqrt{18-2}}{\sqrt{1-(.987)^2}} = 24.564$$

b. $\hat{Y} = -29.7 + 22.93X$; an additional cup increases the dog's weight by almost 23 pounds.

c. Dog number 4 is an overeater.

61. $r = 0.297$
$H_0: \rho \leq 0$ $H_1: \rho > 0$
Level of significance $= 0.05$
Reject H_0 if $t > 1.674$

$$t = \frac{0.297\sqrt{56-2}}{\sqrt{(1-0.297)^2}} = 2.292$$

Reject H_0. There is a positive correlation between movie sales and budget. "Big budget" movies do lead to large box office.

63. a. The correlation between wins and salary is 0.505.
$H_0: \rho \leq 0$, $H_1: \rho > 0$, at .05 significance level, reject H_0 if $t > 1.701$.

$$t = \frac{0.505\sqrt{30-2}}{\sqrt{1-(0.505)^2}} = 3.10$$

Reject H_0: Wins and salary are related.
$\hat{Y} = 69.4 + 0.140X$. An additional \$5 million would increase wins by 0.7, found by 0.140(5).

b. The correlation between games won and ERA is -0.542; and between games won and batting average 0.496. ERA has a stronger correlation. Critical values of t are -1.701 for ERA and 1.701 for batting average.

$$t = \frac{-0.542\sqrt{30-2}}{\sqrt{1-(-0.542)^2}} = -3.41$$

$$t = \frac{0.496\sqrt{30-2}}{\sqrt{1-(0.496)^2}} = 3.02$$

Both variables are significantly correlated with winning.

c. The correlation between wins and attendance is 0.562.
$H_0: \rho \leq 0$ $H_1: \rho > 0$ At the 5 percent level, reject H_0 if $t > 1.701$.

$$t = \frac{0.562\sqrt{30-2}}{\sqrt{1-(0.562)^2}} = 3.60$$

Reject H_0. The population correlation is positive.

65. a. The regression equation is: Unemployment $= 9.558 + 0.0020$ Labor force. The slope tells you one more person in the labor force will add 0.002 or 0.2% to unemployment. The predicted unemployment for the UAE is 9.5608, found by $9.558 + 0.002(1.4)$.

b. Pearson correlation of Exports and Imports $= 0.948$
$H_0: \rho \leq 0$ $H_1: \rho > 0$
At the 5% level, reject H_0 when $t > 1.680$.

$$t = \frac{0.948\sqrt{46-2}}{\sqrt{1-(0.948)^2}} = 19.758$$

Reject H_0. The population correlation is positive.

c. Pearson correlation of 65 & over and Literacy % $= 0.794$
$H_0: \rho \leq 0$ $H_1: \rho > 0$
At the 5% level, reject H_0 when $t > 1.680$.

$$t = \frac{0.794\sqrt{46-2}}{\sqrt{1-(0.794)^2}} = 8.66$$

Reject H_0. The population correlation is positive.

CHAPTER 14

1. a. Multiple regression equation
b. The Y-intercept
c. $\hat{Y} = 64{,}100 + 0.394(796{,}000) + 9.6(6{,}940) - 11{,}600(6.0) = \$374{,}748$

3. a. 497.736, found by
$\hat{Y} = 16.24 + 0.017(18)$
$+ 0.0028(26{,}500) + 42(3)$
$+ 0.0012(156{,}000)$
$+ 0.19(141) + 26.8(2.5)$

b. Two more social activities. Income added only 28 to the index; social activities added 53.6.

5. a. $s_{Y \cdot 12} = \sqrt{\dfrac{SSE}{n-(k+1)}} = \sqrt{\dfrac{583.693}{65-(2+1)}}$
$= \sqrt{9.414} = 3.068$

95% of the residuals will be between ± 6.136, found by $2(3.068)$

b. $R^2 = \dfrac{SSR}{SS\ total} = \dfrac{77.907}{661.6} = .118$

The independent variables explain 11.8% of the variation.

c. $R^2_{adj} = 1 - \dfrac{\dfrac{SSE}{n-(k+1)}}{\dfrac{SS\ total}{n-1}} = 1 - \dfrac{\dfrac{583.693}{65-(2+1)}}{\dfrac{661.6}{65-1}}$

$= 1 - \dfrac{9.414}{10.3375} = 1 - .911 = .089$

7. a. $\hat{Y} = 84.998 + 2.391X_1 - 0.4086X_2$
b. 90.0674, found by $\hat{Y} = 84.998 + 2.391(4) - 0.4086(11)$
c. $n = 65$ and $k = 2$
d. $H_0: \beta_1 = \beta_2 = 0$ $H_1:$ Not all β's are 0
Reject H_0 if $F > 3.15$
$F = 4.14$, reject H_0. Not all net regression coefficients equal zero.
e. For X_1 For X_2
$H_0: \beta_1 = 0$ $H_0: \beta_2 = 0$
$H_1: \beta_1 \neq 0$ $H_1: \beta_2 \neq 0$
$t = 1.99$ $t = -2.38$
Reject H_0 if $t > 2.0$ or $t < -2.0$.
Delete variable 1 and keep 2.

f. The regression analysis should be repeated with only X_2 as the independent variable.

9. a. The regression equation is: Performance $= 29.3 + 5.22$ Aptitude $+ 22.1$ Union

Predictor	Coef	SE Coef	T	P
Constant	29.28	12.77	2.29	0.041
Aptitude	5.222	1.702	3.07	0.010
Union	22.135	8.852	2.50	0.028

S = 16.9166   R-Sq = 53.3%   R-Sq (adj) = 45.5%

Analysis of Variance

Source	DF	SS	MS	F	P
Regression	2	3919.3	1959.6	6.85	0.010
Residual Error	12	3434.0	286.2		
Total	14	7353.3			

b. These variables are effective in predicting performance. They explain 45.5 percent of the variation in performance. In particular, union membership increases the typical performance by 22.1.

c. $H_0: \beta_2 = 0$ $H_1: \beta_2 \neq 0$
Reject H_0 if $t < -2.179$ or $t > 2.179$.
Since 2.50 is greater than 2.179, we reject the null hypothesis and conclude that union membership is significant and should be included.

d. When you consider the interaction variable, the regression equation is Performance $= 38.7 + 3.80$ Aptitude -0.1 Union $+ 3.61\ X_1X_2$

Predictor	Coef	SE Coef	T	P
Constant	38.69	15.62	2.48	0.031
Aptitude	3.802	2.179	1.74	0.109
Union	-0.10	23.14	-0.00	0.997
X_1X_2	3.610	3.473	1.04	0.321

The t value corresponding to the interaction term is 1.04. This is not significant. So we conclude there is no interaction between aptitude and union membership when predicting job performance.

11. a. The regression equation is
Price $= 3080 - 54.2$ Bidders $+ 16.3$ Age

Predictor	Coef	SE Coef	T	P
Constant	3080.1	343.9	8.96	0.000
Bidders	-54.19	12.28	-4.41	0.000
Age	16.289	3.784	4.30	0.000

The price decreases 54.2 as each additional bidder participates. Meanwhile the price increases 16.3 as the painting gets older. While one would expect older paintings to be worth more, it is unexpected that the price goes down as more bidders participate!

b. The regression equation is
Price $= 3{,}972 - 185$ Bidders $+ 6.35$ Age $+ 1.46\ X_1X_2$

Predictor	Coef	SE Coef	T	P
Constant	3971.7	850.2	4.67	0.000
Bidders	-185.0	114.9	-1.61	0.122
Age	6.353	9.455	0.67	0.509
X_1X_2	1.462	1.277	1.15	0.265

The t value corresponding to the interaction term is 1.15. This is not significant. So we conclude there is no interaction.

c. In the stepwise procedure, the number of bidders enters the equation first. Then the interaction term enters. The variable age would not be included as it is not significant. Response is Price on 3 predictors, with $N = 25$.

```
Step           1       2
Constant    4,507   4,540

Bidders       -57    -256
T-Value     -3.53   -5.59
P-Value     0.002   0.000

X₁X₂                 2.25
T-Value              4.49
P-Value              0.000

S             295     218
R-Sq        35.11   66.14
R-Sq(adj)   32.29   63.06
```

13. a. $n = 40$

b. 4

c. $R^2 = \dfrac{750}{1250} = .60$

d. $s_{y \cdot 1234} = \sqrt{500/35} = 3.7796$

e. $H_0: \beta_1 = \beta_2 = \beta_3 = \beta_4 = 0$
$H_1:$ Not all the βs equal zero.
H_0 is rejected if $F > 2.65$.
$$F = \frac{750/4}{500/35} = 13.125$$
H_0 is rejected. At least one β_i does not equal zero.

15. a. $n = 26$

b. $R^2 = 100/140 = .7143$

c. 1.4142, found by $\sqrt{2}$

d. $H_0: \beta_1 = \beta_2 = \beta_3 = \beta_4 = \beta_5 = 0$
$H_1:$ Not all the βs are 0.
H_0 is rejected if $F > 2.71$.
Computed $F = 10.0$. Reject H_0. At least one regression coefficient is not zero.

e. H_0 is rejected in each case if $t < -2.086$ or $t > 2.086$.
X_1 and X_5 should be dropped.

17. a. $28,000

b. $R^2 = \dfrac{SSR}{SS\ total} = \dfrac{3,050}{5,250} = .5809$

c. 9.199, found by $\sqrt{84.62}$

d. H_0 is rejected if $F > 2.97$ (approximately)
$$\text{Computed } F = \frac{1,016.67}{84.62} = 12.01$$
H_0 is rejected. At least one regression coefficient is not zero.

e. If computed t is to the left of -2.056 or to the right of 2.056, the null hypothesis in each of these cases is rejected. Computed t for X_2 and X_3 exceed the critical value. Thus, "population" and "advertising expenses" should be retained and "number of competitors," X_1, dropped.

19. a. The strongest correlation is between GPA and legal. No problem with multicollinearity.

b. $R^2 = \dfrac{4.3595}{5.0631} = .8610$

c. H_0 is rejected if $F > 5.41$
$$F = \frac{1.4532}{0.1407} = 10.328$$
At least one coefficient is not zero.

d. Any H_0 is rejected if $t < -2.571$ or $t > 2.571$. It appears that only GPA is significant. Verbal and math could be eliminated.

e. $R^2 = \dfrac{4.2061}{5.0631} = .8307$
R^2 has only been reduced .0303.

f. The residuals appear slightly skewed (positive), but acceptable.

g. There does not seem to be a problem with the plot.

21. a. The correlation of Screen and Price is 0.893. So there does appear to be a linear relationship between the two.

b. Price is the "dependent" variable.

c. The regression equation is Price $= -2484 + 101$ Screen. For each inch increase in screen size, the price increases $101 on average.

d. Using "dummy" indicator variables for Sharp and Sony, the regression equation is Price $= -2308 + 94.1$ Screen $+ 15$ Manufacturer Sharp $+ 381$ Manufacturer Sony. Sharp can obtain on average $15 more than Samsung and Sony can collect an additional benefit of $381 more than Samsung.

e. Here is some of the output.

```
Predictor            Coef  SE Coef      T      P
Constant          -2308.2    492.0  -4.69  0.000
Screen              94.12    10.83   8.69  0.000
Manufacturer_Sharp   15.1    171.6   0.09  0.931
Manufacturer_Sony   381.4    168.8   2.26  0.036
```

The p-value for Sharp is relatively large. A test of their coefficient would not be rejected. That means they may not have any real advantage over Samsung. On the other hand, the p-value for the Sony coefficient is quite small. That indicates that it did not happen by chance and there is some real advantage to Sony over Samsung.

f. A histogram of the residuals indicates they follow a normal distribution.

g. The residual variation may be increasing for larger fitted values.

23. a.

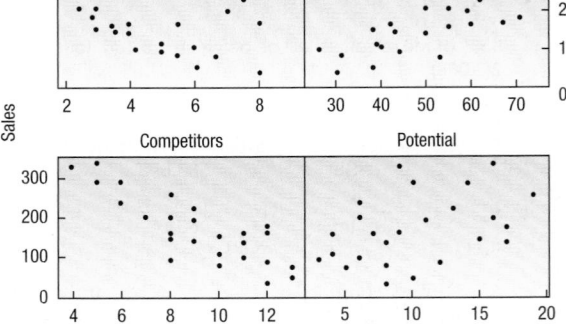

Scatter Diagram of Sales vs Advertising, Accounts, Competitors, Potential

Sales seem to fall with the number of competitors and rise with the number of accounts and potential.

b. Pearson correlations

```
              Sales  Advertising  Accounts  Competitors
Advertising   0.159
Accounts      0.783        0.173
Competitors  -0.833       -0.038    -0.324
Potential     0.407       -0.071     0.468      -0.202
```

The number of accounts and the market potential are moderately correlated.

c. The regression equation is:
Sales $= 178 + 1.81$ Advertising $+ 3.32$ Accounts $- 21.2$ Competitors $+ 0.325$ Potential

```
Predictor         Coef   SE Coef        T       P
Constant        178.32     12.96    13.76   0.000
Advertising      1.807     1.081     1.67   0.109
Accounts        3.3178    0.1629    20.37   0.000
Competitors   -21.1850    0.7879   -26.89   0.000
Potential       0.3245    0.4678     0.69   0.495

S = 9.60441  R-Sq = 98.9%  R-Sq(adj) = 98.7%

Analysis of Variance

Source           DF      SS     MS       F       P
Regression        4  176777  44194  479.10   0.000
Residual Error   21    1937     92
Total            25  178714
```

The computed F value is quite large. So we can reject the null hypothesis that all of the regression coefficients are zero. We conclude that some of the independent variables are effective in explaining sales.

d. Market potential and advertising have large p-values (0.495 and 0.109, respectively). You would probably drop them.

e. If you omit potential, the regression equation is:
Sales $= 180 + 1.68$ Advertising $+ 3.37$ Accounts $- 21.2$ Competitors

```
Predictor         Coef   SE Coef        T       P
Constant        179.84     12.62    14.25   0.000
Advertising      1.677     1.052     1.59   0.125
Accounts        3.3694    0.1432    23.52   0.000
Competitors   -21.2165    0.7773   -27.30   0.000
```

Now advertising is not significant. That would also lead you to cut out the advertising variable and report that the polished regression equation is:
Sales $= 187 + 3.41$ Accounts $- 21.2$ Competitors

```
Predictor         Coef  SE Coef        T       P
Constant        186.69    12.26    15.23   0.000
Accounts        3.4081   0.1458    23.37   0.000
Competitors   -21.1930   0.8028   -26.40   0.000
```

f.

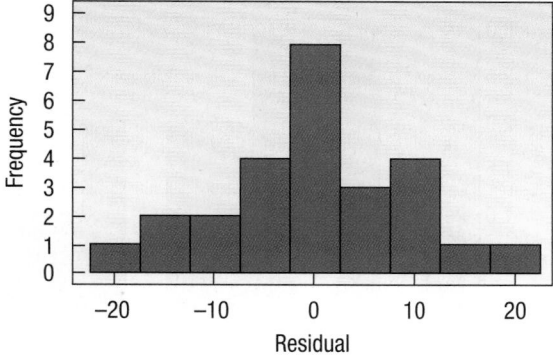

Histogram of the Residuals
(response is Sales)

The histogram looks to be normal. There are no problems shown in this plot.

g. The variance inflation factor for both variables is 1.1. They are less than 10. There are no troubles as this value indicates the independent variables are not strongly correlated with each other.

25. a. The correlation matrix is:

	Salary	GPA
GPA	0.902	
Business	0.911	0.851

The two independent variables are related. There may be multicollinearity.

b. The regression equation is: Salary $= 23.447 + 2.775$ GPA $+ 1.307$ Business. As GPA increases by one point, salary increases by \$2,775. The average business school graduate makes \$1,307 more than a corresponding nonbusiness graduate. Estimated salary is \$33,079, found by \$23,447 $+$ 2,775(3.00) $+$ 1,307(1).

c. $R^2 = \dfrac{21.182}{23.857} = 0.888$

To conduct the global test: $H_0: = \beta_1 = \beta_2 = 0$; H_1: Not all β_i's $= 0$
At the 0.05 significance level, H_0 is rejected if $F > 3.89$.

Source	SS	df	MS	F	p
Regression	21.182	2	10.591	47.50	0.000
Error	2.676	12	0.223		
Total	23.857	14			

The computed value of F is 47.50, so H_0 is rejected. Some of the regression coefficients are not zero.

d. Since the p-values are less than 0.05, there is no need to delete variables.

Predictor	Coef	SE Coef	T	P
Constant	23.447	3.490	6.72	0.000
GPA	2.775	1.107	2.51	0.028
Business	1.3071	0.4660	2.80	0.016

e. The residuals appear normally distributed.

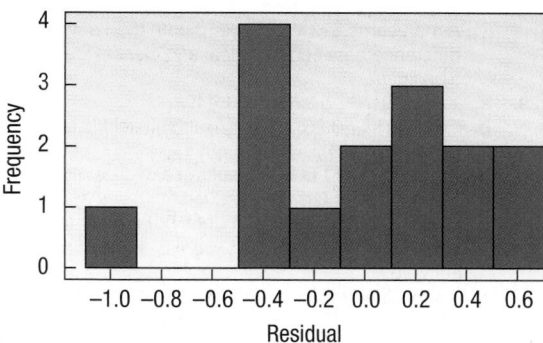

Histogram of the Residuals
(Response Is Salary)

f. The variance is the same as we move from small values to large. So there is no homoscedasticity problem.

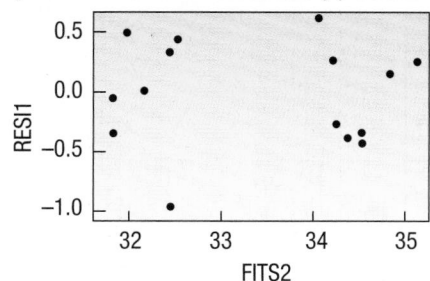

27. The computer output is:

Predictor	Coef	Stdev	t-ratio	p
Constant	651.9	345.3	1.89	0.071
Service	13.422	5.125	2.62	0.015
Age	−6.710	6.349	−1.06	0.301
Gender	205.65	90.27	2.28	0.032
Job	−33.45	89.55	−0.37	0.712

Analysis of Variance

SOURCE	DF	SS	MS	F	p
Regression	4	1066830	266708	4.77	0.005
Error	25	1398651	55946		
Total	29	2465481			

a. $\hat{Y} = 651.9 + 13.422X_1 − 6.710X_2 + 205.65X_3 − 33.45X_4$

b. $R^2 = .433$, which is somewhat low for this type of study.

c. $H_0: \beta_1 = \beta_2 = \beta_3 = \beta_4 = 0$; H_1: not all βs equal zero. Reject H_0 if $F > 2.76$.

$$F = \frac{1,066,830/4}{1,398,651/25} = 4.77$$

H_0 is rejected. Not all the β_i's equal 0.

d. Using the .05 significance level, reject the hypothesis that the regression coefficient is 0 if $t < −2.060$ or $t > 2.060$. Service and gender should remain in the analyses; age and job should be dropped.

e. Following is the computer output using the independent variables service and gender.

Predictor	Coef	Stdev	t-ratio	p
Constant	784.2	316.8	2.48	0.020
Service	9.021	3.106	2.90	0.007
Gender	224.41	87.35	2.57	0.016

Analysis of Variance

SOURCE	DF	SS	MS	F	p
Regression	2	998779	499389	9.19	0.001
Error	27	1466703	54322		
Total	29	2465481			

A man earns \$224 more per month than a woman. The difference between technical and clerical jobs is not significant.

29. a. $\hat{Y} = 29.913 − 5.324X_1 + 1.449X_2$

b. EPS is ($t = −3.26$, p-value = .005). Yield is not ($t = 0.81$, p-value = .431).

c. An increase of 1 in EPS results in a decline of 5.324 in P/E.

d. Stock number 2 is undervalued.

e. Below is a residual plot. It does *not* appear to follow the normal distribution.

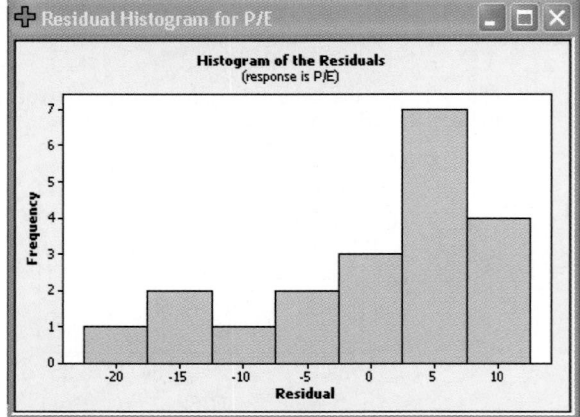

f. There does not seem to be a problem with the plot of the residuals versus the fitted values.

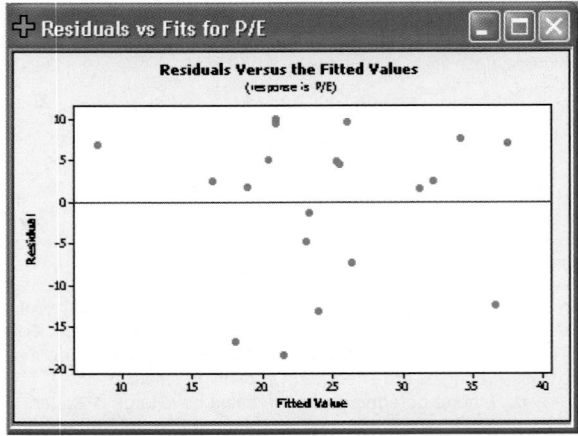

g. The correlation between yield and EPS is not a problem. No problem with multicollinearity.

	P/E	EPS
EPS	−0.602	
Yield	.054	.162

31. a. The regression equation is
Sales (000) = 1.02 + 0.0829 Informercials

Predictor	Coef	SE Coef	T	P
Constant	1.0188	0.3105	3.28	0.006
Informericals	0.08291	0.01680	4.94	0.000

Analysis of Variance

Source	DF	SS	MS	F	P
Regression	1	2.3214	2.3214	24.36	0.000
Residual Error	13	1.2386	0.0953		
Total	14	3.5600			

The global test demonstrates there is a relationship between sales and the number of infomercials.

b.

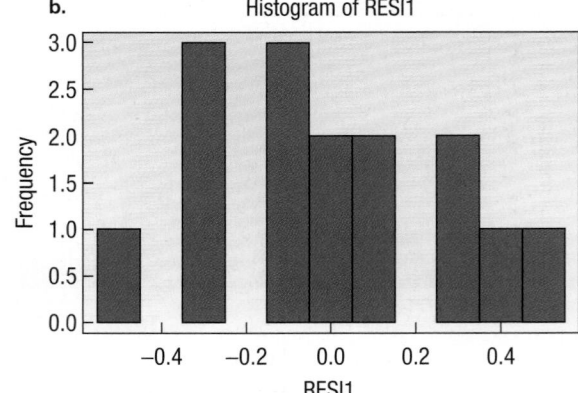

The residuals appear to follow the normal distribution.

33. a. The regression equation is
Auction Price = −118929 + 1.63 Loan + 2.1 Monthly Payment + 50 Payments Made

```
Analysis of Variance
Source       DF        SS          MS        F      P
Regression    3  5966725061  1988908354  39.83  0.000
Residual
  Error      16   798944439    49934027
Total        19  6765669500
```

The computed *F* is 39.83. It is much larger than the critical value 3.24. The *p* value is also quite small. Thus, the null hypothesis that all the regression coefficients are zero can be rejected. At least one of the multiple regression coefficients is different from zero.

b.

```
Predictor    Coef    SE Coef       T       P
Constant   -118929     19734    -6.03  0.000
Loan        1.6268    0.1809     8.99  0.000
Monthly
  Payment     2.06     14.95     0.14  0.892
Payments
  Made        50.3     134.9     0.37  0.714
```

The null hypothesis is that the coefficient is zero in the individual test. It would be rejected if *t* is less than −2.120 or more than 2.120. In this case the *t* value for the loan variable is larger than the critical value. Thus, it should not be removed. However, the monthly payment and payments made variables would likely be removed.

c. The revised regression equation is: Auction Price = −119893 + 1.67 Loan

35. The computer output is as follows:

```
Predictor    Coef    SE Coef       T       P
Constant    57.03     39.99      1.43  0.157
Bedrooms    7.118     2.551      2.79  0.006
Size        0.03800   0.01468    2.59  0.011
Pool       -18.321    6.999     -2.62  0.010
Distance   -0.9295    0.7279    -1.28  0.205
Garage     35.810     7.638      4.69  0.000
Baths      23.315     9.025      2.58  0.011

S = 33.21  R-Sq = 53.2%  R-Sq (adj) = 50.3%

Analysis of Variance
SOURCE           DF      SS      MS      F      P
Regression        6  122676   20446  18.54  0.000
Residual Error   98  108092    1103
Total           104  230768
```

a. Each additional bedroom adds about $7,000 to the selling price, each additional square foot adds $38, a pool reduces the value by $18,300, an attached garage increases the value by $35,800, and each mile the home is from the center of the city reduces the selling price by $929.

b. The *R*-square value is 0.532.

c. The correlation matrix is as follows:

	Price	Bedrooms	Size	Pool	Distance	Garage
Bedrooms	0.467					
Size	0.371	0.383				
Pool	-0.294	-0.005	-0.201			
Distance	-0.347	-0.153	-0.117	0.139		
Garage	0.526	0.234	0.083	-0.114	-0.359	
Baths	0.382	0.329	0.024	-0.055	-0.195	0.221

The independent variable *garage* has the strongest correlation with price. Distance is inversely related, as expected, and there does not seem to be a problem with correlation among the independent variables.

d. The results of the global test suggest that some of the independent variables have net regression coefficients different from zero.

e. We can delete *distance*.

f. The new regression output follows.

```
Predictor    Coef    SE Coef       T       P
Constant    36.12     36.59      0.99  0.326
Bedrooms     7.169     2.559     2.80  0.006
Size        0.03919   0.01470   -2.67  0.009
Pool       -19.110     6.994    -2.73  0.007
Garage     38.847      7.281     5.34  0.000
Baths      24.624      8.995     2.74  0.007

S = 33.32  R-Sq = 52.4%  R-Sq(adj) = 50.0%

Analysis of Variance
SOURCE           DF      SS      MS      F      P
Regression        5  120877   24175  21.78  0.000
Residual Error   99  109890    1110
Total           104  230768
```

In reviewing the *p*-values for the various regression coefficients, all are less than .05. We leave all the independent variables.

g. & h. Analysis of the residuals, not shown, indicates the normality assumption is reasonable. In addition, there is no pattern to the plots of the residuals and the fitted values of *Y*.

37. a. $\hat{Y} = -14,174 + 3,325X_1 - 11,675X_2 + 448X_3 - 5,355X_4$
Note age is dropped because of association with other variables. Women earn $11,675 less than men, and union members $5,355 less than nonunion workers. Wages increase $3,325 for each year of education and $448 for each year of experience.

b. $R^2 = .366$, which is rather low.

c. Education and gender have the strongest association with wages; age and experience have a nearly perfect association. Drop age.

d. The computed value of *F* is 13.69, so we conclude some of the regression coefficients are not equal to zero.

e. Drop the union variable, $t = -1.40$

f. Deleting union decreases R^2 to .352

g. & h. Analysis of the residuals, not shown, indicates the normality assumption is reasonable. In addition, there is no pattern to the plots of the residuals and the fitted values of *Y*.

CHAPTER 15

1. 114.6, found by ($19,989/$17,446)(100)
123.1, found by ($21,468/$17,446)(100)
124.3, found by ($21,685/$17,446)(100)
91.3, found by ($15,922/$17,446)(100)
105.3, found by ($18,375/$17,446)(100)

3. 2003: 115.2, found by (581.9/505.2)/(100)
2004: 98.2, found by (496.1/505.2)/(100)
2005: 90.4, found by (456.6/505.2)(100)
2006: 85.8, found by (433.3/505.2)(100)

5. a. $P_t = \dfrac{3.35}{2.49}(100) = 134.54 \qquad P_s = \dfrac{4.49}{3.29}(100) = 136.47$

$P_c = \dfrac{4.19}{1.59}(100) = 263.52 \qquad P_a = \dfrac{2.49}{1.79}(100) = 139.11$

b. $P = \dfrac{14.52}{9.16}(100) = 158.52$

c. $P = \dfrac{\$3.35(6) + 4.49(4) + 4.19(2) + 2.49(3)}{\$2.49(6) + 3.29(4) + 1.59(2) + 1.79(3)}(100) = 147.1$

d. $P = \dfrac{\$3.35(6) + 4.49(5) + 4.19(3) + 2.49(4)}{\$2.49(6) + 3.29(5) + 1.59(3) + 1.79(4)}(100) = 150.2$

e. $I = \sqrt{(147.1)(150.2)} = 148.64$

7. a. $P_W = \dfrac{0.10}{0.07}(100) = 142.9 \qquad P_C = \dfrac{0.03}{0.04}(100) = 75.0$

$P_S = \dfrac{0.15}{0.15}(100) = 100 \qquad P_H = \dfrac{0.10}{0.08}(100) = 125.0$

b. $P = \dfrac{0.38}{0.34}(100) = 111.8$

c.
$P = \dfrac{0.10(17,000) + 0.03(125,000) + 0.15(40,000) + 0.10(62,000)}{0.07(17,000) + 0.04(125,000) + 0.15(40,000) + 0.08(62,000)}$
$(100) = 102.92$

d.
$P = \dfrac{0.10(20,000) + 0.03(130,000) + 0.15(42,000) + 0.10(65,000)}{0.07(20,000) + 0.04(130,000) + 0.15(42,000) + 0.08(65,000)}$
$(100) = 103.32$

e. $P = \sqrt{102.92(103.32)} = 103.12$

9. $V = \dfrac{\$5.95(214) + 9.80(489) + 6.00(203) + 3.29(106)}{\$1.52(200) + 2.10(565) + 1.48(291) + 3.05(87)}(100)$
$= 349.06$

11. a. $I = \dfrac{6.8}{5.3}(0.20) + \dfrac{362.26}{265.88}(0.40) + \dfrac{125.0}{109.6}(0.25) + \dfrac{622,864}{529,917}$
$(0.15) = 1.263.$
Index is 126.3.

b. Business activity increased 26.3 percent from 2000 to 2005.

13. $X = (\$89,673)/2.14823 = \$41,743.$
"Real" salary increased $\$41,743 - \$19,800 = \$21,943.$

15.

Year	Tinora	Tinora	National Index
1995	$28,650	100.0	100
2000	$33,972	118.6	122.5
2004	$37,382	130.5	136.9

The Tinora teachers received smaller increases than the national average.

17. The index (2000 = 100) for selected years is:

Year	2001	2002	2003	2004	2005	2006	2007
Index	114.5	129.7	146.0	160.4	163.9	172.0	187.4

The domestic sales almost doubled between 2000 and 2007.

19. The index (2000 = 100) for selected years is:

Year	2001	2002	2003	2004	2005	2006	2007
Index	105.4	116.8	139.9	165.1	186.7	198.6	241.7

International sales grew by about 140 percent between 2000 and 2007.

21. The index (2000 = 100) for selected years is:

Year	2001	2002	2003	2004	2005	2006	2007
Index	100.9	107.3	109.6	108.9	114.6	121.1	118.1

The number of employees increased almost 20 percent between 2000 and 2007.

23. The index (2000 = 100) for selected years is:

Year	2001	2002	2003	2004
Index	97.0	101.4	102.9	116.9

Revenue increased about 17 percent over the period.

25. The index (2000 = 100) for selected years is:

Year	2001	2002	2003	2004
Index	101.1	106.7	96.7	88.9

The number of employees decreased about 11 percent between 2000 and 2004.

27. $P_{ma} = \dfrac{2.00}{0.81}(100) = 246.91 \qquad P_{sh} = \dfrac{1.88}{0.84}(100) = 223.81$

$P_{mi} = \dfrac{2.89}{1.44}(100) = 200.69 \qquad P_{po} = \dfrac{3.99}{2.91}(100) = 137.11$

29. $P = \dfrac{\$2.00(18) + 1.88(5) + 2.89(70) + 3.99(27)}{\$0.81(18) + 0.84(5) + 1.44(70) + 2.91(27)}(100) = 179.37$

31. $I = \sqrt{179.37(178.23)} = 178.80$

33. $P_R = \dfrac{0.60}{0.50}(100) = 120 \qquad P_S = \dfrac{0.90}{1.20}(100) = 75.0$

$P_W = \dfrac{1.00}{0.85}(100) = 117.65$

35. $P = \dfrac{0.60(320) + 0.90(110) + 1.00(230)}{0.50(320) + 1.20(110) + 0.85(230)}(100) = 106.87$

37. $P = \sqrt{(106.87)(106.04)} = 106.45$

39. $P_C = \dfrac{0.05}{0.06}(100) = 83.33 \qquad P_C = \dfrac{0.12}{0.10}(100) = 120$

$P_P = \dfrac{0.18}{0.20}(100) = 90 \qquad P_E = \dfrac{.015}{0.15}(100) = 100$

41. $P = \dfrac{0.05(2,000) + 0.12(200) + 0.18(400) + 0.15(100)}{0.06(2,000) + 0.10(200) + 0.20(400) + 0.15(100)}(100)$
$= 89.79$

43. $P = \sqrt{(89.79)(91.25)} = 90.52$

45. $P_A = \dfrac{0.76}{0.287}(100) = 264.8 \qquad P_N = \dfrac{2.50}{0.17}(100) = 1,470.59$

$P_P = \dfrac{26.00}{3.18}(100) = 817.61 \qquad P_P = \dfrac{490}{133}(100) = 368.42$

47. $P = \dfrac{0.76(1,000) + 2.50(5,000) + 26(60,000) + 490(500)}{0.287(1,000) + 0.17(5,000) + 3.18(60,000) + 133(500)}$
$(100) = 703.56$

49. $P = \sqrt{(703.56)(686.58)} = 695.02$

51. $I = 100\left[\dfrac{1,971.0}{1,159.0}(0.20) + \dfrac{91}{87}(0.10) + \dfrac{114.7}{110.6}(0.40)\right.$
$\left. + \dfrac{1,501}{1,214}(0.30)\right] = 123.05$

The economy is up 23.05 percent from 1996 to 2006.

53. February: $I = 100\left[\dfrac{6.8}{8.0}(0.40) + \dfrac{23}{20}(0.35) + \dfrac{303}{300}(0.25)\right]$
$= 99.50$

March: $I = 100\left[\dfrac{6.4}{8.0}(0.40) + \dfrac{21}{20}(0.35) + \dfrac{297}{300}(0.25)\right]$
$= 93.5$

55. For 1995 $1,876,466, found by $2,400,000/1.279.
For 2007 $2,071,006, found by $3,500,000/1.690.

CHAPTER 16

1. The weighted moving averages are: 31,584.8, 33,088.9, 34,205.4, 34,899.8, 35,155.0, 34,887.1

3. $\hat{Y} = 8842 - 88.1273t$
For 2008: $t = 12$, $\hat{Y} = 8842 - 88.1273(12) = 7784.47$

5. $\hat{Y} = 1.30 + 0.90t$
$\hat{Y} = 1.30 + 0.90(7) = 7.6$

7. a. $\hat{Y} = -0.0531997 + 0.1104057t$
b. 28.95%, found by $1.28945 - 1.0$
c. $\hat{Y} = -0.0531997 + 0.1104057(8) = .8300459.$
Antilog of .8300459 = 6.76

9.

Quarter	Average SI Component	Seasonal Index
1	0.6859	0.6911
2	1.6557	1.6682
3	1.1616	1.1704
4	0.4732	0.4768

11.

t	Estimated Pairs (millions)	Seasonal Index	Quarterly Forecast (millions)
21	40.05	110.0	44.055
22	41.80	120.0	50.160
23	43.55	80.0	34.840
24	45.30	90.0	40.770

13. $\hat{Y} = 5.1658 + .37805t$. The following are the sales estimates.

Estimate	Index	Seasonally Adjusted
10.080	0.6911	6.966
10.458	1.6682	17.446
10.837	1.1704	12.684
11.215	0.4768	5.343

15. **a.** The ordered residuals are: 2.61, 2.83, −48.50, 15.50, −3.72, 17.17, 6.39, 7.72, −0.41, −16.86, 3.81, 7.25, 8.03, −1.08, and −0.75.

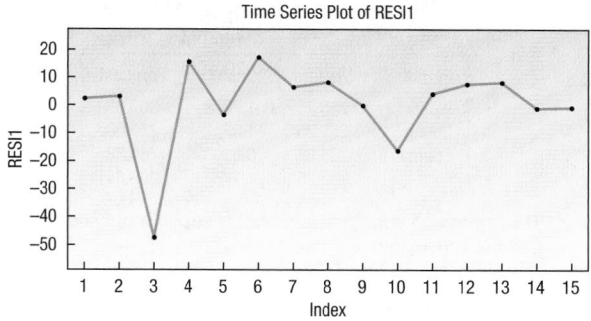

Time Series Plot of RESI1

b. There are 2 independent variables (k) and the sample size (n) is 15. For a significance level of 0.05 the upper value is 1.54. Since the computed value of the Durbin-Watson statistic is 2.48, which is above the upper limit, the null hypothesis is not rejected. There is no autocorrelation among these residuals.

17. **a.** $\hat{Y} = 18,000 − 400t$, assuming the line starts at 18,000 in 1986 and goes down to 10,000 in 2006.
b. 400
c. 8,000, found by 18,000 − 400(25).

19. **a.**

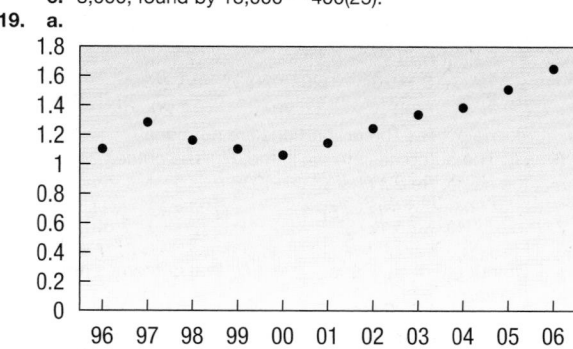

b. $\hat{Y} = 1.00455 + 0.04409t$, using $t = 1$ for 1996
c. For 1999, $\hat{Y} = 1.18091$, and for 2004, $\hat{Y} = 1.40136$
d. For 2011, $\hat{Y} = 1.70999$
e. Each asset turned over 0.044 times.

21. **a.**

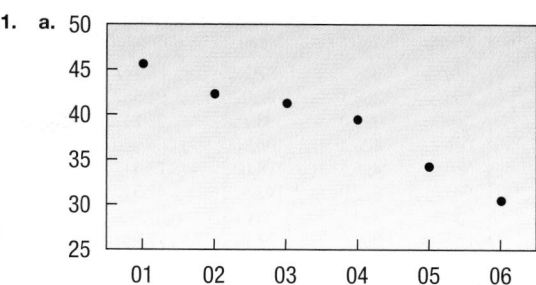

b. $\hat{Y} = 49.140 − 2.9829t$
c. For 2003, $\hat{Y} = 40.1913$. For 2005, $\hat{Y} = 34.2255$.
d. For 2009, $\hat{Y} = 22.2939$
e. The number of employees decreases at a rate of 2,983 per year.

23. **a.** Log $\hat{Y} = 0.790231 + .113669t$
b. Log $\hat{Y} = 0.790231$, found by $0.790231 + 0.113669(0)$, antilog is 6.169
Log $\hat{Y} = 1.813252$, found by $0.790231 + 0.113669(9)$, antilog is 65.051
c. 29.92, which is the antilog of .113669 minus 1
d. Log $\hat{Y} = 2.154258$, antilog is 142.65

25. **a.**

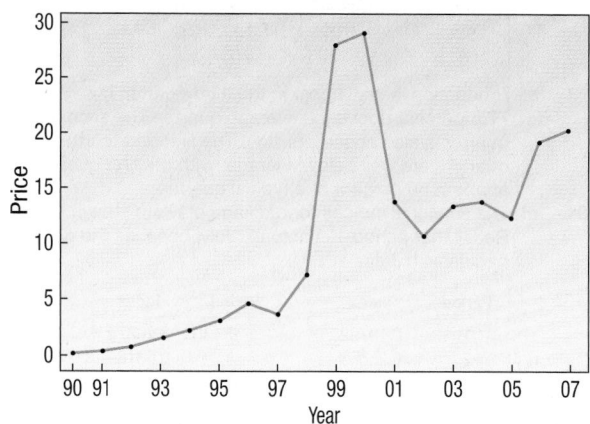

Oracle Share Price by Year

b. The equations are $\hat{Y} = −1.583 + 1.241t$ and/or log $\hat{Y} = −0.3056 + 0.1069t$. The equation using the logarithm appears better because R^2 is larger.
c. log $\hat{Y} = −0.3056 + 0.1069 (4) = 0.122$, antilog is 1.3243.
log $\hat{Y} = −0.3056 + 0.1069 (9) = 0.6565$, antilog is 4.5342.
d. log $\hat{Y} = −0.3056 + 0.1069 (20) = 1.8324$, antilog is 67.98.
It is reasonable if the price rises at the historical rate!
e. The annual rate of increase is 27.91 percent, found by the antilog of 0.1069 minus 1.

27. **a.** July 87.5; August 92.9; September 99.3; October 109.1

b.

Month	Total	Mean	Corrected
July	348.9	87.225	86.777
Aug.	368.1	92.025	91.552
Sept.	395.0	98.750	98.242
Oct.	420.4	105.100	104.560
Nov.	496.2	124.050	123.412
Dec.	572.3	143.075	142.340
Jan.	333.5	83.375	82.946
Feb.	297.5	74.375	73.993
March	347.3	86.825	86.379
April	481.3	120.325	119.707
May	396.2	99.050	98.541
June	368.1	92.025	91.552
		1,206.200	

Correction = 1,200/1,206.2 = 0.99486

c. April, November, and December are periods of high sales, while February's sales are lowest.

Note: The solution to Exercises 29 to 33 may vary due to rounding and the particular software package used.

29. a.

Seasonal Index by Quarter

Quarter	Average SI Component	Seasonal Index
1	0.5014	0.5027
2	1.0909	1.0936
3	1.7709	1.7753
4	0.6354	0.6370

b. Production is the largest in the third quarter. It is 77.5 percent above the average quarter. The second quarter is also above average. The first and fourth quarters are well below average, with the first quarter at about 50 percent of a typical quarter.

31. a. The seasonal indices for package play are shown below. Recall that period 1 is actually July, because the data begins with July.

Period	Index	Period	Index
1	0.19792	7	0.26874
2	0.25663	8	0.63189
3	0.87840	9	1.67943
4	2.10481	10	2.73547
5	0.77747	11	1.67903
6	0.18388	12	0.60633

Notice the 4th period (October) and the 10th period (April) are more than twice the average.

b. The seasonal indices for nonpackage play are:

Period	Index	Period	Index
1	1.73270	7	0.23673
2	1.53389	8	0.69732
3	0.94145	9	1.00695
4	1.29183	10	1.13226
5	0.66928	11	0.98282
6	0.52991	12	1.24486

These indices are more constant. Notice the very low values in the 6th (December) and 7th (January) periods.

c. The seasonal indices for total play are:

Period	Index	Period	Index
1	0.63371	7	0.25908
2	0.61870	8	0.65069
3	0.89655	9	1.49028
4	1.86415	10	2.28041
5	0.74353	11	1.48235
6	0.29180	12	0.78876

These indices show both the peaks in October (4th period) and April (10th period) and the valleys in December (6th period) and January (7th period).

d. Package play is relatively highest in April. Nonpackage play is relatively high in July. Since 70% of total play comes from package play, total play is very similar to package play.

33.

Seasonal Index by Quarter

Quarter	Average SI Component	Seasonal Index
1	1.1962	1.2053
2	1.0135	1.0212
3	0.6253	0.6301
4	1.1371	1.1457

The regression equation is: $\hat{Y} = 43.611 + 7.2153t$

Period	Visitors	Index	Forecast
29	252.86	1.2053	304.77
30	260.07	1.0212	265.58
31	267.29	0.6301	168.42
32	274.50	1.1457	314.50

In 2006 there were 928 visitors. A 10 percent increase in 2007 means there will be 1,021 visitors. The quarterly estimates are 1,021/4 = 255.25 visitors per quarter.

Period	Visitors	Index	Forecast
Winter	255.25	1.2053	307.65
Spring	255.25	1.0212	260.66
Summer	255.25	0.6301	160.83
Fall	255.25	1.1457	292.44

The regression approach is probably superior because the trend is considered.

35. Log-Prize = 1.5524 + 0.0377t
Log-Purse = 2.3763 + 0.0377t
The "slopes" are identical because the prize is always 15 percent of the purse. The projected purse for 2010 is $1.91 million, found as the antilog of 2.3763 + 0.0377(24) = 3.2811.

37. Answers will vary.

39. With 1988 as the base year, the regression equation is: $\hat{Y} = 317,958 + 138,508t$. Salary increased at a rate of $138,508 per year over the period.

CHAPTER 17

1. a. 3
b. 7.815
3. a. Reject H_0 if $\chi^2 > 5.991$
b. $\chi^2 = \dfrac{(10 - 20)^2}{20} + \dfrac{(20 - 20)^2}{20} + \dfrac{(30 - 20)^2}{20} = 10.0$
c. Reject H_0. The proportions are not equal.
5. H_0: The outcomes are the same; H_1: The outcomes are not the same. Reject H_0 if $\chi^2 > 9.236$

$$\chi^2 = \frac{(3 - 5)^2}{5} + \cdots + \frac{(7 - 5)^2}{5} = 7.60$$

Do not reject H_0. Cannot reject H_0 that outcomes are the same.

7. H_0: There is no difference in the proportions.
H_1: There is a difference in the proportions.
Reject H_0 if $\chi^2 > 15.086$.
$$\chi^2 = \frac{(47 - 40)^2}{40} + \cdots + \frac{(34 - 40)^2}{40} = 3.400$$
Do not reject H_0. There is no difference in the proportions.

9. a. Reject H_0 if $\chi^2 > 9.210$.
b. $\chi^2 = \frac{(30 - 24)^2}{24} + \frac{(20 - 24)^2}{24} + \frac{(10 - 12)^2}{12} = 2.50$
c. Do not reject H_0

11. H_0: Proportions are as stated; H_1: Proportions are not as stated. Reject H_0 if $\chi^2 > 11.345$.
$$\chi^2 = \frac{(50 - 25)^2}{25} + \cdots + \frac{(160 - 275)^2}{275} = 115.22$$
Reject H_0. The proportions are not as stated.

13. H_0: There is no relationship between community size and section read. H_1: There is a relationship. Reject H_0 if $\chi^2 > 9.488$.
$$\chi^2 = \frac{(170 - 157.50)^2}{157.50} + \cdots + \frac{(88 - 83.62)^2}{83.62} = 7.340$$
Do not reject H_0. There is no relationship between community size and section read.

15. H_0: No relationship between error rates and item type. H_1: There is a relationship between error rates and item type. Reject H_0 if $\chi^2 > 9.21$.
$$\chi^2 = \frac{(20 - 14.1)^2}{14.1} + \cdots + \frac{(225 - 225.25)^2}{225.25} = 8.033$$
Do not reject H_0. There is not a relationship between error rates and item type.

17. H_0: $\pi_s = 0.50$, $\pi_r = \pi_e = 0.25$
H_1: Distribution is not as given above.
$df = 2$. Reject H_0 if $\chi^2 > 4.605$.

Turn	f_o	f_e	$f_o - f_e$	$(f_o - f_e)^2/f_e$
Straight	112	100	12	1.44
Right	48	50	−2	0.08
Left	40	50	−10	2.00
Total	200	200		3.52

H_0 is not rejected. The proportions are as given in the null hypothesis.

19. H_0: There is no preference with respect to TV stations.
H_1: There is a preference with respect to TV stations.
$df = 3 - 1 = 2$. H_0 is rejected if $\chi^2 > 5.991$.

TV Station	f_o	f_e	$f_o - f_e$	$(f_o - f_e)^2$	$(f_o - f_e)^2/f_e$
WNAE	53	50	3	9	0.18
WRRN	64	50	14	196	3.92
WSPD	33	50	−17	289	5.78
	150	150	0		9.88

H_0 is rejected. There is a preference for TV stations.

21. H_0: $\pi_n = 0.21$, $\pi_m = 0.24$, $\pi_s = 0.35$, $\pi_w = 0.20$.
H_1: The distribution is not as given.
Reject H_0 if $\chi^2 > 11.345$.

Region	f_o	f_e	$f_o - f_e$	$(f_o - f_e)^2/f_e$
Northeast	68	84	−16	3.0476
Midwest	104	96	8	0.6667
South	155	140	15	1.6071
West	73	80	−7	0.6125
Total	400	400	0	5.9339

H_0 is not rejected. The distribution of order destinations reflects the population.

23. H_0: The proportions are the same.
H_1: The proportions are not the same.
Reject H_0 if $\chi^2 > 16.919$.

f_o	f_e	$f_o - f_e$	$(f_o - f_e)^2$	$(f_o - f_e)^2/f_e$
44	28	16	256	9.143
32	28	4	16	0.571
23	28	−5	25	0.893
27	28	−1	1	0.036
23	28	−5	25	0.893
24	28	−4	16	0.571
31	28	3	9	0.321
27	28	−1	1	0.036
28	28	0	0	0.000
21	28	−7	49	1.750
				14.214

Do not reject H_0. The digits are evenly distributed.

25. H_0: Gender and attitude toward the deficit are not related.
H_1: Gender and attitude toward the deficit are related.
Reject H_0 if $\chi^2 > 5.991$.
$$\chi^2 = \frac{(244 - 292.41)^2}{292.41} + \frac{(194 - 164.05)^2}{164.05}$$
$$+ \frac{(68 - 49.53)^2}{49.53} + \frac{(305 - 256.59)^2}{256.59}$$
$$+ \frac{(114 - 143.95)^2}{143.95} + \frac{(25 - 43.47)^2}{43.47} = 43.578$$
Since $43.578 > 5.991$, you reject H_0. A person's position on the deficit is influenced by his or her gender.

27. H_0: Whether a claim is filed and age are not related.
H_1: Whether a claim is filed and age are related.
Reject H_0 if $\chi^2 > 7.815$.
$$\chi^2 = \frac{(170 - 203.33)^2}{203.33} + \cdots + \frac{(24 - 35.67)^2}{35.67} = 53.639$$
Reject H_0. Age is related to whether a claim is filed.

29. H_0: $\pi_{BL} = \pi_O = .23$, $\pi_Y = \pi_G = .15$, $\pi_{BR} = \pi_R = .12$. H_1: The proportions are not as given. Reject H_0 if $\chi^2 > 15.086$.

Color	f_o	f_e	$(f_o - f_e)^2/f_e$
Blue	12	16.56	1.256
Brown	14	8.64	3.325
Yellow	13	10.80	0.448
Red	14	8.64	3.325
Orange	7	16.56	5.519
Green	12	10.80	0.133
Total	72		14.006

Do not reject H_0. The color distribution agrees with the manufacturer's information.

31. H_0: Salary and winning are not related.
H_1: Salary and winning are related.
Reject H_0 if $\chi^2 > 3.84$.

	Salary		
Winning	Lower Half	Top Half	Total
No	9	5	14
Yes	6	10	16
Total	15	15	

$$\chi^2 = \frac{(9 - 7)^2}{7} + \frac{(5 - 7)^2}{7} + \frac{(6 - 8)^2}{8} + \frac{(10 - 8)^2}{8} = 2.14$$
Do not reject H_0. Conclude that salary and winning may not be related.

33. a. H_0: Membership and petroleum activity are not related.
H_1: Membership and petroleum activity are related.
Reject H_0 if $\chi^2 > 5.991$

$$\chi^2 = \frac{(14 - 12.33)^2}{12.33} + \cdots + \frac{(2 - 4.54)^2}{4.54} = 8.217$$

Reject H_0. Membership and activity are related.

b. H_0: Age and activity are not related.
H_1: Age and activity are related.
Reject H_0 of $\chi^2 > 5.991$

$$\chi^2 = \frac{(3 - 8.22)^2}{8.22} + \cdots + \frac{(0 - 6.7)^2}{6.7} = 23.209$$

Reject H_0. Age and activity are related.

CHAPTER 18

1. a. If the number of pluses (successes) in the sample is 9 or more, reject H_0.

b. Reject H_0 because the cumulative probability associated with nine or more successes (.073) does not exceed the significance level (.10).

3. a. H_0: $\pi \le .50$; H_1: $\pi > .50$; $n = 10$

b. H_0 is rejected if there are nine or more plus signs. A "+" represents a loss.

c. Reject H_0. It is an effective program, because there were 9 people who lost weight.

5. a. H_0: $\pi \le .50$ (There is no change in weight.)
H_1: $\pi > .50$ (There is a loss of weight.)

b. Reject H_0 if $z > 1.65$

c. $z = \dfrac{(32 - .50) - .50(45)}{.50\sqrt{45}} = 2.68$

d. Reject H_0. The weight loss program is effective.

7. H_0: $\pi \le .50$, H_1: $\pi > .50$. H_0 is rejected if $z > 2.05$.

$$z = \frac{42.5 - 40.5}{4.5} = .44$$

Because $.44 < 2.05$, do not reject H_0. No preference.

9. a. H_0: Median $\le \$81,500$; H_1: Median $> \$81,500$

b. H_0 is rejected if $z > 1.65$

c. $z = \dfrac{170 - .50 - 100}{7.07} = 9.83$

H_0 is rejected. The median income is greater than $81,500.

11.

Couple	Difference	Rank
1	550	7
2	190	5
3	250	6
4	−120	3
5	−70	1
6	130	4
7	90	2

Sums: −4, +24. So $T = 4$ (the smaller of the two sums). From Appendix B.7, .05 level, one-tailed test, $n = 7$, the critical value is 3. Since the T of $4 > 3$, do not reject H_0 (one-tailed test). There is no difference in square footage. Professional couples do not live in larger homes.

13. a. H_0: The production is the same for the two systems.
H_1: Production using the Mump method is greater.

b. H_0 is rejected if $T \le 21$, $n = 13$.

c. The calculations for the first three employees are:

Employee	Old	Mump	d	Rank	R^+	R^-
A	60	64	4	6	6	
B	40	52	12	12.5	12.5	
C	59	58	−1	2		2

The sum of the negative ranks is 6.5. Since 6.5 is less than 21, H_0 is rejected. Production using the Mump method is greater.

15. H_0: The distributions are the same. H_1: The distributions are not the same. Reject H_0 if $z < -1.96$ or $z > 1.96$.

A		B	
Score	**Rank**	**Score**	**Rank**
38	4	26	1
45	6	31	2
56	9	35	3
57	10.5	42	5
61	12	51	7
69	14	52	8
70	15	57	10.5
79	16	62	13
	86.5		49.5

$$z = \frac{86.5 - \dfrac{8(8 + 8 + 1)}{2}}{\sqrt{\dfrac{8(8)(8 + 8 + 1)}{12}}} = 1.943$$

H_0 is not rejected. There is no difference in the two populations.

17. H_0: The distributions are the same. H_1: The distribution of Campus is to the right. Reject H_0 if $z > 1.65$.

Campus		Online	
Age	**Rank**	**Age**	**Rank**
26	6	28	8
42	16.5	16	1
65	22	42	16.5
38	13	29	9.5
29	9.5	31	11
32	12	22	3
59	21	50	20
42	16.5	42	16.5
27	7	23	4
41	14	25	5
46	19		94.5
18	2		
	158.5		

$$z = \frac{158.5 - \dfrac{12(12 + 10 + 1)}{2}}{\sqrt{\dfrac{12(10)(12 + 10 + 1)}{12}}} = 1.35$$

H_0 is not rejected. There is no difference in the distributions.

19. ANOVA requires that we have two or more populations, the data are interval- or ratio-level, the populations are normally distributed, and the population standard deviations are equal. Kruskal-Wallis requires only ordinal-level data, and no assumptions are made regarding the shape of the populations.

21. a. H_0: The three population distributions are equal. H_1: Not all of the distributions are the same.

b. Reject H_0 if $H > 5.991$

c.

Rank	Rank	Rank
8	5	1
11	6.5	2
14.5	6.5	3
14.5	10	4
16	12	9
64	13	19
	53	

$$H = \frac{12}{16(16+1)}\left[\frac{(64)^2}{5} + \frac{(53)^2}{6} + \frac{(19)^2}{5}\right] - 3(16+1)$$
$$= 59.98 - 51 = 8.98$$

d. Reject H_0 because $8.98 > 5.991$. The three distributions are not equal.

23. H_0: The distributions of the lengths of life are the same.
H_1: The distributions of the lengths of life are not the same.
H_0 is rejected if $H > 9.210$.

Salt		Fresh		Others	
Hours	Rank	Hours	Rank	Hours	Rank
167.3	3	160.6	1	182.7	13
189.6	15	177.6	11	165.4	2
177.2	10	185.3	14	172.9	7
169.4	6	168.6	4	169.2	5
180.3	12	176.6	9	174.7	8
	46		39		35

$$H = \frac{12}{15(16)}\left[\frac{(46)^2}{5} + \frac{(39)^2}{5} + \frac{(35)^2}{5}\right] - 3(16) = 0.62$$

H_0 is not rejected. There is no difference in the three distributions.

25. a.

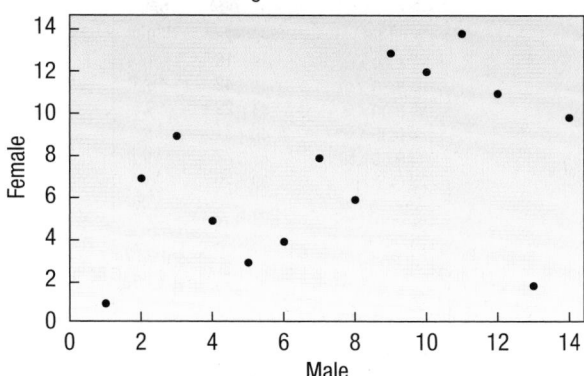

Scatter Diagram of Female versus Male

b.

Male	Female	d	d^2
4	5	−1	1
6	4	2	4
7	8	−1	1
2	7	−5	25
12	11	1	1
8	6	2	4
5	3	2	4
3	9	−6	36
13	2	11	121
14	10	4	16
1	1	0	0
9	13	−4	16
10	12	−2	4
11	14	−3	9
		Total	242

$$r_s = 1 - \frac{6(242)}{14(14^2 - 1)} = 0.47$$

c. H_0: No correlation among the ranks.
H_1: A positive correlation among the ranks.
Reject H_0 if $t > 1.782$.
$$t = 0.47\sqrt{\frac{14 - 2}{1 - (0.47)^2}} = 1.84$$
H_0 is rejected. We conclude the correlation in population among the ranks is positive. Husbands and wives generally like the same shows.

27.

Representative	Sales	Rank	Training Rank	d	d^2
1	319	3	3	0	0
2	150	10	9	1	1
3	175	9	6	3	9
4	460	1	1	0	0
5	348	2	4	−2	4
6	300	4.5	10	−5.5	30.25
7	280	6	5	1	1
8	200	7	2	5	25
9	190	8	7	1	1
10	300	4.5	8	−3.5	12.25
					83.50

a. $r_s = 1 - \dfrac{6(83.5)}{10(10^2 - 1)} = 0.494$

A moderate positive correlation.

b. H_0: No correlation among the ranks. H_1: A positive correlation among the ranks. Reject H_0 if $t > 1.860$.
$$t = 0.494\sqrt{\frac{10 - 2}{1 - (0.494)^2}} = 1.607$$
H_0 is not rejected. The correlation in population among the ranks could be 0.

29. H_0: $\pi = .50$; H_1: $\pi \neq .50$; Use a software package to develop the binomial probability distribution for $n = 19$ and $\pi = .50$. H_0 is rejected if there are either 5 or fewer "+" signs, or 14 or more. The total of 12 "+" signs falls in the acceptance region. H_0 is not rejected. There is no preference between the two shows.

31. H_0: $\pi = .50$ H_1: $\pi \neq .50$
H_0 is rejected if there are 12 or more or 3 or fewer plus signs. Because there are only 8 plus signs, H_0 is not rejected. There is no preference with respect to the two brands of components.

33. H_0: $\pi = .50$; H_1: $\pi \neq .50$. Reject H_0 if $z > 1.96$ or $z < -1.96$.
$$z = \frac{159.5 - 100}{7.071} = 8.415$$
Reject H_0: There is a difference in the preference for the two types of orange juice.

35. H_0: Rates are the same; H_1: The rates are not the same.
H_0 is rejected if $H > 5.991$. $H = .082$. Do not reject H_0.

37. H_0: The populations are the same. H_1: The populations differ.
Reject H_0 if $H > 7.815$. $H = 14.30$. Reject H_0.

39. $r_s = 1 - \dfrac{6(78)}{12(12^2 - 1)} = 0.727$

H_0: There is no correlation between the rankings of the coaches and of the sportswriters.
H_1: There is a positive correlation between the rankings of the coaches and of the sportswriters.
Reject H_0 if $t > 1.812$.
$$t = 0.727\sqrt{\frac{12 - 2}{1 - (.727)^2}} = 3.348$$

H_0 is rejected. There is a positive correlation between the sportswriters and the coaches.

41. a. H_0: There is no difference in the distributions of the selling prices in the five townships. H_1: There is a difference in the distributions of the selling prices of the five townships. H_0 is rejected if H is greater than 9.488. The computed value of H is 4.70, so the null hypothesis is not rejected. The sample data does not suggest a difference in the distributions of selling prices.

b. H_0: There is no difference in the distributions of the selling prices depending on the number of bedrooms. H_1: There is a difference in the distributions of the selling prices depending on the number of bedrooms. H_0 is rejected if H is greater than 9.448. The computed value of H is 16.34, so the null hypothesis is rejected. The sample data indicate there is a difference in the distributions of selling prices based on the number of bedrooms. Note: Combine 6 or more into a single group.

c. H_0: There is no difference in the distributions of the distance from the center of the city depending on whether the home had a pool or not. H_1: There is a difference in the distributions of the distances from the center of the city depending on whether the home has a pool or not. H_0 is rejected if H is greater than 3.84. The computed value of H is 3.37, so the null hypothesis is not rejected. The sample data do not suggest a difference in the distributions of the distances.

43. a. H_0: Median wages the same for union and nonunion workers.
H_1: Median wages not the same for union and nonunion workers.
Reject H_0 if $z < -1.96$ or $z > 1.96$.
$$z = \frac{4{,}037 - \dfrac{82(82 + 18 + 1)}{2}}{\sqrt{\dfrac{82(18)(82 + 18 + 1)}{12}}} = \frac{-104}{111.46} = -0.93$$
Do not reject H_0. There is no difference in the median wages of union and nonunion workers.

b. H_0: Median wages are the same for three industries.
H_1: Median wages are not the same for three industries.
Reject H_0 if $H > 9.21$.
$H = 2.97$
We do not reject H_0, the results are similar.

c. H_0: The wage distributions are the same in the occupations.
H_1: The wage distributions are not the same.
Reject H_0 if $\chi^2 > 11.070$.
$\chi^2 = 16.75$.
Reject H_0. The wage distributions are not the same for the various occupations.

CHAPTER 19

1.

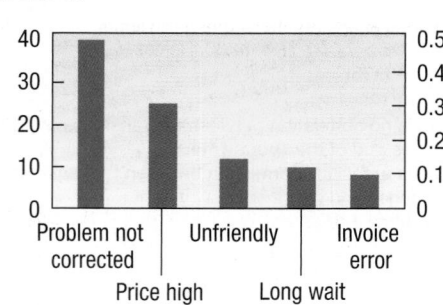

	Problem not corrected	Price high	Unfriendly	Long wait	Invoice error
Count	38	23	12	10	8
Percent	42	25	13	11	9
Cum %	42	67	80	91	100

About 67 percent of the complaints concern the problem not being corrected and the price being too high.

3. Chance variation is random in nature; because the cause is a variety of factors, it cannot be entirely eliminated. Assignable variation is not random; it is usually due to a specific cause and can be eliminated.

5. a. The A_2 factor is 0.729.

b. The value for D_3 is 0, and for D_4 it is 2.282.

7. a.

UCL — 46.78
$\overline{X}$ — 41.92
LCL — 37.06

8   8:30   9   9:30   10   10:30

	$\overline{X}$, Arithmetic Means	R, Range
Time		
8:00 A.M.	46	16
8:30 A.M.	40.5	6
9:00 A.M.	44	6
9:30 A.M.	40	2
10:00 A.M.	41.5	9
10:30 A.M.	39.5	1
	251.5	40

$$\overline{\overline{X}} = \frac{251.5}{6} = 41.92 \qquad \overline{R} = \frac{40}{6} = 6.67$$
$$UCL = 41.92 + 0.729(6.67) = 46.78$$
$$LCL = 41.92 - 0.729(6.67) = 37.06$$

b. Interpreting, the mean reading was 341.92 degrees Fahrenheit. If the oven continues operating as evidenced by the first six hourly readings, about 99.7 percent of the mean readings will lie between 337.06 degrees and 346.78 degrees.

9. a. The fraction defective is 0.0507. The upper control limit is 0.0801 and the lower control limit is 0.0213.

b. Yes, the 7th and 9th samples indicate the process is out of control.

c. The process appears to stay the same.

11. $\overline{c} = \dfrac{37}{14} = 2.64$
$2.64 \pm 3\sqrt{2.64}$
The control limits are 0 and 7.5. The process is out of control on the seventh day.

13. $\overline{c} = \dfrac{6}{11} = 0.545$
$0.545 \pm 3\sqrt{0.545} = 0.545 \pm 2.215$
The control limits are from 0 to 2.760, so there are no receipts out of control.

15.

Percent Defective	Probability of Accepting Lot
10	.889
20	.558
30	.253
40	.083

17. $P(X \leq 1 \mid n = 10, \pi = .10) = .736$
$P(X \leq 1 \mid n = 10, \pi = .20) = .375$
$P(X \leq 1 \mid n = 10, \pi = .30) = .149$
$P(X \leq 1 \mid n = 10, \pi = .40) = .046$

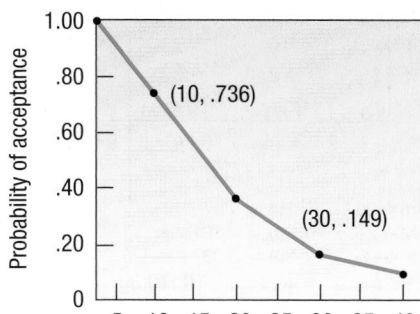

19.

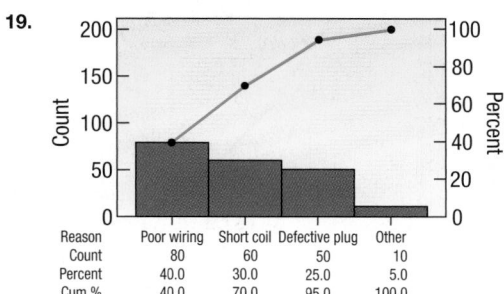

Reason	Poor wiring	Short coil	Defective plug	Other
Count	80	60	50	10
Percent	40.0	30.0	25.0	5.0
Cum %	40.0	70.0	95.0	100.0

21. **a.** $UCL = 10.0 + 0.577(0.25) = 10.0 + 0.14425$
$\qquad = 10.14425$
$\qquad LCL = 10.0 - 0.577(0.25) = 10.0 - 0.14425$
$\qquad = 9.85575$
$\qquad UCL = 2.115(0.25) = 0.52875$
$\qquad LCL = 0(0.25) = 0$

b. The mean is 10.16, which is above the upper control limit and is out of control. There is too much cola in the soft drinks. The process is in control for variation; an adjustment is needed.

23. **a.** $\overline{\overline{X}} = \dfrac{611.3333}{20} = 30.57$

$\qquad \overline{R} = \dfrac{312}{20} = 15.6$

$\qquad UCL = 30.5665 + (1.023)(15.6) = 46.53$
$\qquad LCL = 30.5665 - (1.023)(15.6) = 14.61$
$\qquad UCL = 2.575(15.6) = 40.17$

b.

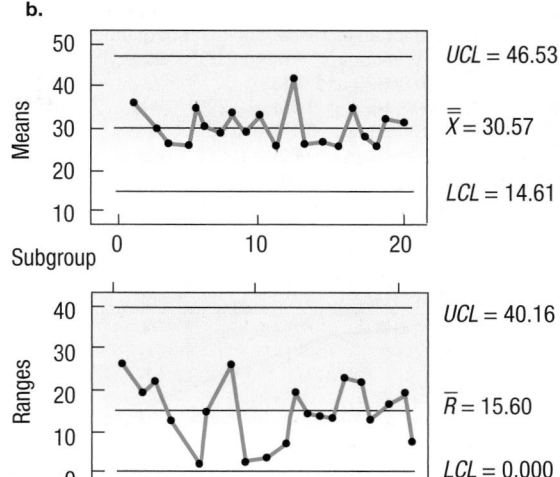

c. The points all seem to be within the control limits. No adjustments are necessary.

25. $\overline{\overline{X}} = \dfrac{4,183}{10} = 418.3$

$\qquad \overline{R} = \dfrac{162}{10} = 16.2$

$\qquad UCL = 418.3 + (0.577)(16.2) = 427.65$
$\qquad LCL = 418.3 - (0.577)(16.2) = 408.95$
$\qquad UCL = 2.115(16.2) = 34.26$
All the points are in control for both the mean and the range.

27. **a.** $p = \dfrac{40}{10(50)} = 0.08$

$\qquad 3\sqrt{\dfrac{0.08(0.92)}{50}} = 0.115$
$\qquad UCL = 0.08 + 0.115 = 0.195$
$\qquad LCL = 0.08 - 0.115 = 0$

b.

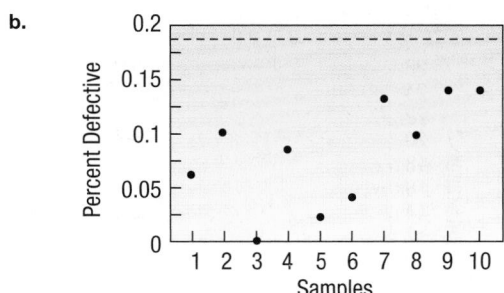

c. There are no points that exceed the limits.

29.
P Chart for C1

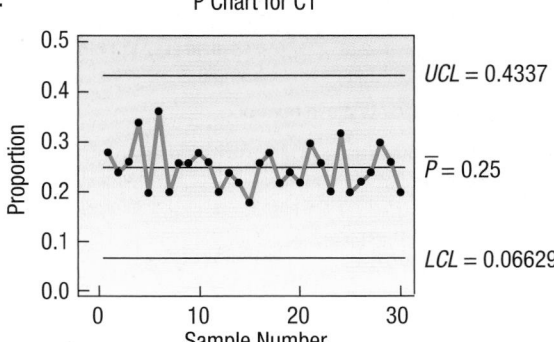

These sample results indicate that the odds are much less than 50-50 for an increase. The percent of stocks that increase is "in control" around 0.25, or 25%. The control limits are 0.06629 and 0.4337.

31. $P(X \le 3 | n = 10, \pi = 0.05) = 0.999$
$P(X \le 3 | n = 10, \pi = 0.10) = 0.987$
$P(X \le 3 | n = 10, \pi = 0.20) = 0.878$
$P(X \le 3 | n = 10, \pi = 0.30) = 0.649$

$P(X \le 5 | n = 20, \pi = 0.05) = 0.999$
$P(X \le 5 | n = 20, \pi = 0.10) = 0.989$
$P(X \le 5 | n = 20, \pi = 0.20) = 0.805$
$P(X \le 5 | n = 20, \pi = 0.30) = 0.417$

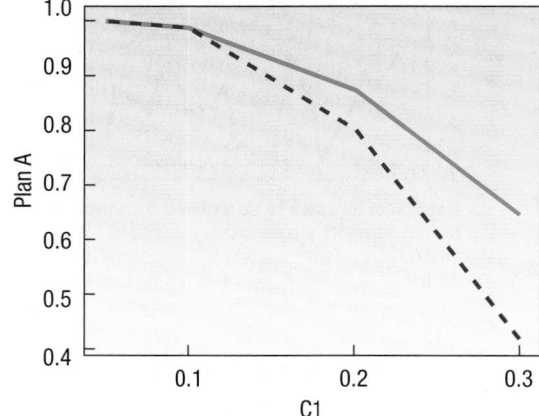

The solid line is the operating characteristic curve for the first plan, and the dashed line, the second. The supplier would prefer the first because the probability of acceptance is higher (above). However, if he is really sure of his quality, the second plan seems higher at the very low range of defect percentages and might be preferred.

33. a. $\bar{c} = \dfrac{213}{15} = 14.2; 3\sqrt{14.2} = 11.30$

$UCL = 14.2 + 11.3 = 25.5$
$LCL = 14.2 - 11.3 = 2.9$

b.

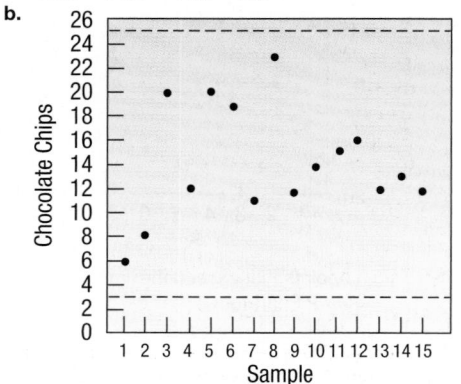

c. All the points are in control.

35. $\bar{c} = \dfrac{70}{10} = 7.0$

$UCL = 7.0 + 3\sqrt{7} = 14.9$
$LCL = 7.0 - 3\sqrt{7} = 0$

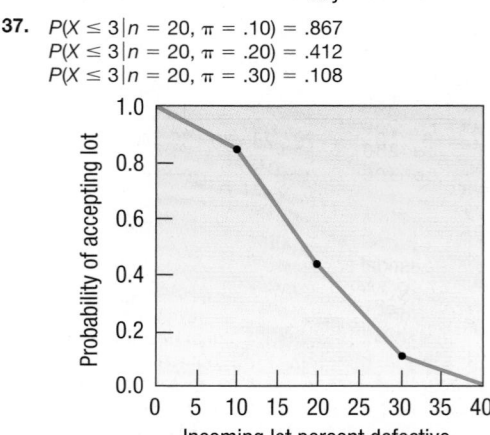

37. $P(X \le 3 | n = 20, \pi = .10) = .867$
$P(X \le 3 | n = 20, \pi = .20) = .412$
$P(X \le 3 | n = 20, \pi = .30) = .108$

Appendix C

Answers to Odd-Numbered Review Exercises

REVIEW OF CHAPTERS 1–4
PART I—MULTIPLE CHOICE
1. b
3. d
5. b
7. 10.24%
9. b

PART II—PROBLEMS

11. a. $2^6 = 64$, use 6 classes; $i = \dfrac{299 - 14}{6} = 47.5$, use $i = 50$

Amount	Frequency
$ 0 up to 50	3
50 up to 100	8
100 up to 150	15
150 up to 200	13
200 up to 250	7
250 up to 300	4

b. and c.

From statistical software:
$\overline{X} = 147.90$, Median = 148.50, $s = 69.24$, and range = 285
The distribution is fairly symmetrical because the mean ($147.90) and the median ($148.50) are quite close. The mean $\pm 2s$ indicates that the middle 95 percent of the deposits are between $147.90 \pm 2(\$69.24) = \$9.42$ and $286.38. Range = $299.00 - $14.00 = $285.00.

13. The typical age is about 55 years and half the presidents were between 51 and 58 years of age when they were inaugurated.

```
Stem-and-Leaf Display

    2    4 23
    2    4
    5    4 667
    8    4 899
   14    5 001111
   16    5 22
   (9)   5 444445555
   18    5 6667777
   11    5 8
   10    6 0111
    6    6 2
    5    6 445
    2    6
    2    6 89
```

```
Descriptive Statistics: years
Variable   N    Mean  StDev  Minimum     Q1  Median     Q3  Maximum
years     43  54.837  6.271   42.000  51.000  55.000  58.000   69.000

Dot plot not shown.
```

15.

Income	f
9.0 up to 11.0	4
11.0 up to 13.0	16
13.0 up to 15.0	17
15.0 up to 17.0	8
17.0 up to 19.0	5
19.0 up to 21.0	1
	51

$\overline{X} = 13.77$, Median = 13.6, $s = 2.305$, $Q_1 = 12.05$, $Q_3 = 15.10$, and $sk = 0.518$.

REVIEW OF CHAPTERS 5–7
PART I—MULTIPLE CHOICE
1. d **7.** a
3. b **9.** c
5. b **11.** a

PART II—PROBLEMS
13. a. .035
b. .018
c. .648
15. a. .0401
b. .6147
c. 7,440
17. a. $\mu = 1.10$
$\sigma = 1.18$
b. about 550
c. $\mu = 1.833$

REVIEW OF CHAPTERS 8 AND 9
PART I—MULTIPLE CHOICE
1. d **5.** a
3. d **7.** b

PART II—PROBLEMS

9. $z = \dfrac{8.8 - 8.6}{2.0/\sqrt{35}} = 0.59$, $.5000 - .2224 = .2776$

11. $160 \pm 2.426 \dfrac{20}{\sqrt{40}}$, 152.33 up to 167.67

13. $985.5 \pm 2.571 \dfrac{115.5}{\sqrt{6}}$, 864.27 up to 1,106.73

15. $240 \pm 2.131 \dfrac{35}{\sqrt{16}}$, 221.35 up to 258.65

Because 250 is in the interval, the evidence does *not* indicate an increase in production.

17. $n = \left[\dfrac{1.96(25)}{4}\right]^2 = 150$

19. $n = .08(.92)\left(\dfrac{2.33}{0.02}\right)^2 = 999$

21. $n = .4(.6)\left(\dfrac{2.33}{0.03}\right)^2 = 1,448$

REVIEW OF CHAPTERS 10–12
PART I—MULTIPLE CHOICE
1. e   5. b
3. b   7. d

PART II—PROBLEMS
9. $H_0: \mu \geq 36$; $H_1: \mu < 36$. Reject H_0 if $t < -1.683$

$$t = \frac{35.5 - 36.0}{0.9/\sqrt{42}} = -3.60$$

Reject H_0. The mean height is less than 36 inches.

11. $H_0: \mu \leq 20$, $H_1: \mu > 20$. Reject H_0 if $t > 1.860$.

$$t = \frac{21 - 20}{6.185/\sqrt{9}} = 0.485$$

H_0 is not rejected. The mean amount of unproductive time is not more than 20 minutes.

13. $H_0: \mu_d \leq 0$; $H_1: \mu_d > 0$. Reject H_0 if $t > 1.883$.

$$\bar{d} = 0.4 \qquad s_d = 6.11 \qquad t = \frac{0.4}{6.11/\sqrt{10}} = 0.21$$

H_0 is not rejected. There is no difference in the life of the paints.

15. For Social Status

H_0: The mean self-rated social status of the employees is the same.

H_1: The mean self-rated social status of the employees is not the same.

Reject H_0 if $F > 4.26$.

For Educational Background

H_0: The mean scores for school type is the same.

H_1: The mean scores for school type is not the same.

Reject H_0 if $F > 4.26$.

For Interaction

H_0: There is no interaction between social status and school type.

H_1: There is interaction between social status and school type.

Reject H_0 if $F > 3.63$.

Two-way ANOVA: Sales versus Social, School				
Source	**df**	**SS**	**MS**	**F**	**P**
Social	2	84.000	42.0000	8.49	0.008
School	2	22.333	11.1667	2.26	0.160
Interaction	4	337.667	84.4167	17.07	0.000
Error	9	44.500	4.9444		
Total	17	488.500			

There is a difference between the mean sales for social status but not for schools. There is an interaction between social status and schools.

REVIEW OF CHAPTERS 13 AND 14
PART I—MULTIPLE CHOICE
1. d   5. b   9. a
3. c   7. d

PART II—PROBLEMS
11. a. Profit
   b. $\hat{Y} = a + b_1 X_1 + b_2 X_2 + b_3 X_3 + b_4 X_4$

c. $163,200

d. About 86 percent of the variation in net profit is explained by the four variables.

e. About 68 percent of the net profits would be within $3,000 of the estimates; about 95% would be within 2($3,000), or $6,000, of the estimates; and virtually all would be within 3($3,000), or $9,000, of the estimates.

13. a. 0.9261

b. 2.0469, found by $\sqrt{83.8/20}$

c. $H_0: \beta_1 = \beta_2 = \beta_3 = \beta_4 = 0$

H_1: Not all coefficients are zero.

Reject if $F > 2.87$, computed $F = 62.697$, found by 162.70/4.19.

d. Could delete X_2 because t-ratio (1.29) is less than the critical t value of 2.086. Otherwise reject H_0 for X_1, X_3, and X_4 because all of those t-ratios are greater than 2.086.

REVIEW OF CHAPTERS 15 AND 16
PART I—MULTIPLE CHOICE
1. d   5. d   9. d
3. b   7. a

PART II PROBLEMS
11. a. $P = \dfrac{150}{108}(100) = 138.9$

b. $\bar{P} = \dfrac{108 + 114 + 113}{3} = 111.67$

$P = \dfrac{150}{111.67}(100) = 134.32$

c. $\hat{Y} = 92.6 + 10.4t$

$\hat{Y} = 92.6 + 10.4(8) = 175.8$

The rate of increase is 10.4 per year

13. $\hat{Y} = [3.5 + 0.7(61)]1.20 = [46.2][1.20] = 55.44$

$\hat{Y} = [3.5 + 0.7(66)]0.90 = (49.7)(0.90) = 44.73$

REVIEW OF CHAPTERS 17 AND 18
PART I—MULTIPLE CHOICE
1. d   5. d   9. d
3. d   7. d

PART II—PROBLEMS
11. H_0: Median ≤ 60

H_1: Median > 60

$\mu = 20(.5) = 10$

$\sigma = \sqrt{20(.5)(.5)} = 2.2361$

H_0 is rejected if $z > 1.65$. There are 16 observations greater than 60.

$$z = \frac{15.5 - 10.0}{2.2361} = 2.46$$

Reject H_0. The median sales per day is greater than 60.

13. H_0: The population lengths are the same.

H_1: The population lengths are not the same.

H_0 is rejected if H is > 5.991.

$$H = \frac{12}{24(24 + 1)}\left[\frac{(104.5)^2}{7} + \frac{(125.5)^2}{9} + \frac{(70)^2}{8}\right] - 3(24 + 1)$$

$$= 78.451 - 75 = 3.451$$

Do not reject H_0. The population lengths are the same.

Appendix C

Solutions to Practice Tests

PRACTICE TEST (AFTER CHAPTER 4)
Part I
1. statistics
2. descriptive statistics
3. population
4. quantitative and qualitative
5. discrete
6. nominal
7. nominal
8. zero
9. seven
10. 50
11. variance
12. never
13. median

PROBLEMS
1. $\sqrt[3]{(1.18)(1.04)(1.02)} = 1.0777$ *or* 7.77%
2. **a.** 30 thousands of dollars
   b. 105
   c. 52
   d. 0.19, found by 20/105
   e. 165
   f. 120 and 330
3. **a.** 70
   b. 71.5
   c. 67.8
   d. 28
   e. 9.34
4. $44.20, found by [(200)$36 + (300)$40 + (500)$50]/1,000
5. **a.** pie chart
   b. 11.1
   c. three times
   d. 65%

PRACTICE TEST (AFTER CHAPTER 7)
Part I
1. never
2. experiment
3. event
4. joint
5. **a.** permutation
   b. combination
6. one
7. three or more outcomes
8. infinite
9. one
10. 0.2764
11. 0.0475
12. independent
13. mutually exclusive
14. only two outcomes
15. bell-shaped

PROBLEMS
1. **a.** 0.0526, found by (5/20)(4/19)
   b. 0.4474, found by $1 - (15/20)(14/19)$
2. **a.** 0.2097, found by $16(.15)(.85)^{15}$
   b. 0.9257, found by $1 - (.85)^{16}$
3. 720, found by $6 \times 5 \times 4 \times 3 \times 2$
4. **a.** 2.2, found by .2(1) + .5(2) + .2(3) + .1(4)
   b. 0.76, found by .2(1.44) + .5(0.04) + .2(0.64) + .1(3.24)
5. **a.** 0.1808. The z value for $2,000 is 0.47, found by (2,000 − 1,600)/850.
   b. 0.4747, found by 0.2939 + 0.1808
   c. 0.0301, found by 0.5000 − 0.4699
6. **a.** contingency table
   b. 0.625, found by 50/80
   c. 0.75, found by 60/80
   d. 0.40, found by 20/50
   e. 0.125, found by 10/80
7. **a.** 0.0498, found by $\dfrac{3^0 e^{-3}}{0!}$
   b. 0.2240, found by $\dfrac{3^3 e^{-3}}{3!}$
   c. 0.1847, found by 1 − [0.0498 + 0.1494 + 0.2240 + 0.2240 + 0.1680]

PRACTICE TEST (AFTER CHAPTER 9)
PART I
1. random sample
2. sampling error
3. standard error
4. become smaller
5. point estimate
6. confidence interval
7. population size
8. proportion
9. positively skewed
10. 0.5

PART II
1. 0.0351, found by 0.5000 − 0.4649. The corresponding
   $$z = \frac{11 - 12.2}{2.3/\sqrt{12}} = -1.81$$
2. **a.** The population mean is unknown.
   b. 9.3 years, which is the sample mean
   c. 0.3922, found by $2/\sqrt{26}$
   d. The confidence interval is from 8.63 up to 9.97, found by $9.3 \pm 1.708\left(\dfrac{2}{\sqrt{26}}\right)$
3. 2675, found by $.27(1 - .27)\left(\dfrac{2.33}{.02}\right)^2$
4. The confidence interval is from 0.5459 up to 0.7341, found by $.64 \pm 1.96\sqrt{\dfrac{.64(1 - .64)}{100}}$

PRACTICE TEST (AFTER CHAPTER 12)
PART I
1. null hypothesis
2. significance level
3. five
4. standard deviation
5. normality
6. test statistic
7. split evenly between the two tails
8. range from negative infinity to positive infinity
9. independent
10. three and 20

PART II

1. $H_0: \mu \leq 90$ $H_1: \mu > 90$ If $t > 2.567$, reject H_0.

   $t = \dfrac{96 - 90}{12/\sqrt{18}} = 2.12$

   Do not reject the null. The mean time in the park could be 90 minutes.

2. $H_0: \mu_1 = \mu_2$ $H_1: \mu_1 \neq \mu_2$

   $df = 14 + 12 - 2 = 24$
   If $t < -2.064$ or $t > 2.064$, then reject H_0.

   $s_p^2 = \dfrac{(14-1)(30)^2 + (12-1)(40)^2}{14 + 12 - 2} = 1220.83$

   $t = \dfrac{837 - 797}{\sqrt{1220.83\left(\dfrac{1}{14} + \dfrac{1}{12}\right)}} = \dfrac{40.0}{13.7455} = 2.910$

   Reject the null hypothesis. There is a difference in the mean miles traveled.

3. **a.** three, because there are 2 df between groups.
   b. 21, found by the total degrees of freedom plus 1.
   c. If the significance level is 0.05, the critical value is 3.55.
   d. $H_0: \mu_1 = \mu_2 = \mu_3$ H_1: Treatment means are not all the same.
   e. At a 5 percent significance level, the null hypothesis is rejected.
   f. At a 5 percent significance level, we can conclude the treatment means differ.

PRACTICE TEST (AFTER CHAPTER 14)
PART I
1. vertical
2. interval
3. zero
4. -0.77
5. never
6. 7
7. decrease of .5
8. -0.9
9. zero
10. unlimited
11. linear
12. residual
13. two
14. correlation matrix
15. normal distribution

PART II
1. **a.** 30
   b. The regression equation is $\hat{Y} = 90.619X - 0.9401$. If X is zero, the line crosses the vertical axis at -0.9401. As the independent variable increases by one unit, the dependent variable increases by 90.619 units.
   c. 905.2499

d. 0.3412, found by 129.7275/380.1667. Thirty-four percent of the variation in the dependent variable is explained by the independent variable.
e. 0.5842, found by $\sqrt{0.3412}$ $H_0: p \geq 0$ $H_1: p < 0$
   Using a significance level of 0.01, reject H_0 if $t > 2.467$

   $t = \dfrac{0.5842\sqrt{30 - 2}}{\sqrt{1 - (0.5842)^2}} = 3.81$

   Reject H_0. There is a negative correlation between the variables.

2. **a.** 30
   b. 4
   c. 0.5974, found by 227.0928/380.1667
   d. $H_0: \beta_1 = \beta_2 = \beta_3 = \beta_4 = 0$ H_1: Not all β's are 0.
   Reject H_0 if $F > 4.18$ (using a 1 percent level of significance).
   Since the computed value of F is 9.27, reject H_0.
   Not all of the regression coefficients are zero.
   e. Reject H_0 if $t > 2.787$ or $t < -2.787$ (using a 1 percent level of significance). Drop variable 2 initially and then rerun. Perhaps you will delete variable(s) 1 or 4 also.

PRACTICE TEST (AFTER CHAPTER 16)
PART I
1. denominator
2. index
3. quantity
4. base period
5. 1982–1984
6. trend
7. moving average
8. autocorrelation
9. residual
10. same

PART II
1. **a.** 111.54, found by (145,000/130,000) × 100 for 2006
   92.31, found by (120,000/130,000) × 100 for 2007
   130.77, found by (170,000/130,000) × 100 for 2008
   146.15, found by (190,000/130,000) × 100 for 2009
   b. 87.27, found by (120,000/137,500) × 100 for 2007
   126.64, found by (170,000/137,500) × 100 for 2008
   138.18, found by (190,000/137,500) × 100 for 2009
2. **a.** 108.91, found by (1100/1010) × 100
   b. 111.18, found by (4525/4070) × 100
   c. 110.20, found by (5400/4900) × 100
   d. 110.69, found by the square root of (111.18) × (110.20)
3. For January of the fifth year, the seasonally adjusted forecast is 70.0875, found by 1.05 × [5.50 + 1.25(49)]
   For February of the fifth year, the seasonally adjusted forecast is 66.844, found by 0.983 × [5.50 + 1.25(50)]

PRACTICE TEST (AFTER CHAPTER 18)
PART I
1. nominal
2. at least 30 observations
3. two
4. 6
5. number of categories
6. dependent
7. binomial
8. comparing two or more independent samples
9. never
10. normal populations, equal standard deviations

PART II

1. H_0: The proportions are as stated. H_1: The proportions are not as stated.

   Using a significance level of 0.05, reject H_0 if $\chi^2 > 7.815$.

   $$\chi^2 = \frac{(120 - 130)^2}{130} + \frac{(40 - 40)^2}{40}$$
   $$+ \frac{(30 - 20)^2}{20} + \frac{(10 - 10)^2}{10} = 5.769$$

   Do not reject H_0. Proportions could be as declared.

2. H_0: No relationship between gender and book type.
   H_1: There is a relationship between gender and book type.
   Using a significance level of 0.01, reject H_0 if $\chi^2 > 9.21$.

   $$\chi^2 = \frac{(250 - 197.3)^2}{197.3} + \cdots + \left(\frac{200 - 187.5}{187.5}\right)^2 = 54.84$$

   Reject H_0. There is a relationship between gender and book type.

3. H_0: The distributions are the same.
   H_1: The distributions are not the same.
   H_0 is rejected if $H > 5.99$.

8:00 A.M. Ranks		10:00 A.M. Ranks		1:30 P.M. Ranks	
68	6	59	1.5	67	5
84	20	59	1.5	69	7
75	10.5	63	4	75	10.5
78	15.5	62	3	76	12.5
70	8	78	15.5	79	17
77	14	76	12.5	83	19
88	24	80	18	86	21.5
71	9			86	21.5
				87	23
Sums	107		56		137
Count	8		7		9

$$H = \frac{12}{24(25)}\left[\frac{107^2}{8} + \frac{56^2}{7} + \frac{137^2}{9}\right] - 3(25) = 4.29$$

H_0 is not rejected. There is no difference in the three distributions.

Photo Credits

Chapter 1
Page 1: Carl de Souza / AFP / Getty Images; **Page 2:** John A. Rizzo / Getty Images / DAL; **Page 5:** Image Source / PictureQuest / DAL; **Page 10:** Rachel Epstein / The Image Works; **Page 11:** Royalty Free / Corbis

Chapter 2
Page 20: Roy Zipstein / Bernstein & Andriulli, Courtesy Merrill Lynch; **Page 21:** Mark Elias / Bloomberg News / Landov; **Page 40:** PhotoDisc / Getty Images

Chapter 3
Page 55: Frank Vetere / Alamy; **Page 56:** McGraw Hill Companies, Inc. / Gary He, photographer / DAL; **Page 63:** Neil Beer / PhotoDisc / Getty Images / DAL; **Page 74:** Spencer Grant / Photoedit

Chapter 4
Page 99: Randy Faris / Corbis; **Page 105:** The Home Depot, Inc.; **Page 108:** Ryan McVay / Getty Images; **Page 118:** Steve Mason / Getty Images / DIL

Chapter 5
Page 140: Gavin Hellier / Corbis; **Page 141:** Digital Vision / Superstock; **Page 149:** Courtesy of Dean's Foods; **Page 152:** Tony Arruza / Corbis; **Page 164:** Courtesy Intel

Chapter 6
Page 182: Chemistry / Getty Images; **Page 188:** Thinkstock / Jupiter Images / DIL; **Page 191:** Royalty Free / Corbis **Page 201:** 2003 The LEGO Group. Used here with permission. All Rights Reserved.

Chapter 7
Page 218: Ilene MacDonald / Alamy; **Page 219:** C. Sherburne / Photolink / Getty Images / DIL; **Page 235:** The Goodyear Tire and Rubber Company; **Page 239:** Royalty Free / Corbis / DIL

Chapter 8
Page 257: AP Photo; **Page 259:** Comstock / PunchStock / DIL; **Page 279:** Terry Wild Stock, Inc.

Chapter 9
Page 289: Jack Hollingsworth / Photodisc / Getty Images; **Page 293:** Del Monte Corporation; **Page 303:** Photo Link / Getty Images / DIL; **Page 305:** AP Photo

Chapter 10
Page 326: Photo Source Hawaii / Alamy; **Page 327:** Russell Illig / Getty Images / DIL; **Page 330:** Tomi / PhotoLink / Getty Images / DIL; **Page 335:** AP Photo; **Page 337:** AP Photo

Chapter 11
Page 364: Charles O'Rear / Corbis; **Page 365:** Royalty Free / Corbis / DIL; **Page 368:** NCR Corporation; **Page 372:** Royalty Free / Corbis / DIL; **Page 385:** Photodisc / Getty Images / DIL

Chapter 12
Page 402: Image reprinted with permission from ViewSonic Corporation; **Page 404:** Photodisc / Getty Images / DIL; **Page 405:** PhotoLink / Getty Images / DIL; **Page 422:** John A. Rizzo / Getty Images / DIL

Chapter 13
Page 454: © Bureau L.A. Collection / Corbis Sygma; **Page 455:** The Coca-Cola Company; **Page 467:** ThinkStock / Superstock; **Page 488:** Tannen Maury / epa / Corbis

Chapter 14
Page 505: Keith Brofsky / Getty Images / DIL

Chapter 15
Page 564: Steve Cole / Photodisc / Getty Images; **Page 565:** © Digital Vision / PunchStock / DIL; **Page 580:** Image Ideas Inc. / PictureQuest / DIL

Chapter 16
Page 595: Bob Levey / Getty Images; **Page 596:** Digital Vision / Getty Images; **Page 604:** RF / Corbis / DIL; **Page 612:** PhotoLink / Getty Images / DIL; **Page 624:** Arthur Tilley / Getty Images

Chapter 17
Page 640: Najlah Feanny / Corbis; **Page 641:** AP Photos; **Page 651:** Scott Olson / Getty Images

Chapter 18
Page 663: Courtesy of Dell Inc; **Page 664:** Photo courtesy of Nestle; **Page 668:** © Corbis; **Page 673:** Ryan McVay / Getty Images / DIL

Chapter 19
Page 703: Jerry Lampen / Reuters / Landov; **Page 706:** Courtesy of the National Institute of Standards and Technology, Office of Quality Programs, Gaithersburg, MD; **Page 712:** Image by Christina Sanders, MHHE; **Page 725:** Gary Gladstone Studio, Inc. / Getty Images

Chapter 20 (on Student CD)
Page P20-1: Mark Horn / Getty Images; **Page P20-2:** AP Photo

Index

- Sum of squares, error

$$SSE = \Sigma(X - \overline{X}_c)^2 \qquad \text{[12–3]}$$

- Sum of squares, treatments

$$SST = SS\ total - SSE \qquad \text{[12–4]}$$

- Confidence interval for differences in treatment means

$$(\overline{X}_1 - \overline{X}_2) \pm t\,\sqrt{MSE\left(\frac{1}{n_1} + \frac{1}{n_2}\right)} \qquad \text{[12–5]}$$

- Sum of squares, blocks

$$SSB = k\Sigma(\overline{X}_b - \overline{X}_G)^2 \qquad \text{[12–6]}$$

- Sum of squares, two-way ANOVA

$$SSE = SS\ total - SST - SSB \qquad \text{[12–7]}$$

- Sum of squares, interaction

$$SSI = (k-1)(b-1)\Sigma\Sigma\,(\overline{X}_{ij} - \overline{X}_{i.} - \overline{X}_{.j} + \overline{X}_G)^2 \qquad \text{[12–8]}$$

- Sum of squares error, with interaction

$$SSE = SS\ total - SS\ factor\ A - SS\ factor\ B - SSI \qquad \text{[12–9]}$$

CHAPTER 13

- Coefficient of correlation

$$r = \frac{\Sigma(X - \overline{X})(Y - \overline{Y})}{(n-1)\,s_x s_y} \qquad \text{[13–1]}$$

- Test for significant correlation

$$t = \frac{r\sqrt{n-2}}{\sqrt{1-r^2}} \qquad \text{[13–2]}$$

- Linear regression equation

$$\hat{Y} = a + bX \qquad \text{[13–3]}$$

- Slope of the regression line

$$b = r\frac{s_y}{s_x} \qquad \text{[13–4]}$$

- Intercept of the regression line

$$a = \overline{Y} - b\overline{X} \qquad \text{[13–5]}$$

- Standard error of estimate

$$s_{y\cdot x} = \sqrt{\frac{\Sigma(Y - \hat{Y})^2}{n-2}} \qquad \text{[13–6]}$$

- Confidence interval

$$\hat{Y} \pm t(s_{y\cdot x})\,\sqrt{\frac{1}{n} + \frac{(X - \overline{X})^2}{\Sigma(X - \overline{X})^2}} \qquad \text{[13–7]}$$

- Prediction interval

$$\hat{Y} \pm t(s_{y\cdot x})\,\sqrt{1 + \frac{1}{n} + \frac{(X - \overline{X})^2}{\Sigma(X - \overline{X})^2}} \qquad \text{[13–8]}$$

- Coefficient of determination

$$r^2 = \frac{\Sigma(Y - \overline{Y})^2 - \Sigma(Y - \hat{Y})^2}{\Sigma(Y - \overline{Y})^2} \qquad \text{[13–9]}$$

$$= 1 - \frac{SSE}{SS\ total} \qquad \text{[13–10]}$$

- Standard error of estimate

$$s_{y\cdot x} = \sqrt{\frac{SSE}{n-2}} \qquad \text{[13–11]}$$

- Sample covariance

$$s_{xy} = \frac{SS_{xy}}{n-1} \qquad \text{[13–12]}$$

CHAPTER 14

- Multiple regression equation

$$\hat{Y} = a + b_1 X_1 + b_2 X_2 + \cdots + b_k X_k \qquad \text{[14–1]}$$

- Multiple standard error of estimate

$$s_{Y.123\ldots k} = \sqrt{\frac{\Sigma(Y - \hat{Y})^2}{n - (k+1)}} \qquad \text{[14–2]}$$

- Coefficient of multiple determination

$$R^2 = \frac{SSR}{SS\ total} \qquad \text{[14–3]}$$

- Adjusted coefficient of determination

$$R_{adj}^2 = 1 - \frac{\dfrac{SSE}{n - (k+1)}}{\dfrac{SS\ total}{n-1}} \qquad \text{[14–4]}$$

- Global test of hypothesis

$$F = \frac{SSR/k}{SSE/[n - (k+1)]} \qquad \text{[14–5]}$$

- Testing for a particular regression coefficient

$$t = \frac{b_i - 0}{s_{b_i}} \qquad \text{[14–6]}$$

- Variance inflation factor

$$VIF = \frac{1}{1 - R_j^2} \qquad \text{[14–7]}$$

CHAPTER 15

- Simple index

$$P = \frac{p_t}{p_0}\,(100) \qquad \text{[15–1]}$$

- Simple average of price relatives

$$P = \frac{\Sigma P_i}{n} \qquad \text{[15–2]}$$

- Simple aggregate index

$$P = \frac{\Sigma p_t}{\Sigma p_0}\,(100) \qquad \text{[15–3]}$$

- Laspeyres price index

$$P = \frac{\Sigma p_t q_0}{\Sigma p_0 q_0}\,(100) \qquad \text{[15–4]}$$

- Paasche price index

$$P = \frac{\Sigma p_t q_t}{\Sigma p_0 q_t}\,(100) \qquad \text{[15–5]}$$

- Fisher's ideal index

$$\sqrt{(\text{Laspeyres' price index})(\text{Paasche's price index})} \qquad \text{[15–6]}$$

- Value index

$$V = \frac{\Sigma p_t q_t}{\Sigma p_0 q_0}\,(100) \qquad \text{[15–7]}$$

Student's *t* Distribution (*concluded*)

(*continued*)

df (degrees of freedom)	Confidence Intervals, *c*					
	80%	90%	95%	98%	99%	99.9%
	Level of Significance for One-Tailed Test, α					
	0.10	0.05	0.025	0.01	0.005	0.0005
	Level of Significance for Two-Tailed Test, α					
	0.20	0.10	0.05	0.02	0.01	0.001
71	1.294	1.667	1.994	2.380	2.647	3.433
72	1.293	1.666	1.993	2.379	2.646	3.431
73	1.293	1.666	1.993	2.379	2.645	3.429
74	1.293	1.666	1.993	2.378	2.644	3.427
75	1.293	1.665	1.992	2.377	2.643	3.425
76	1.293	1.665	1.992	2.376	2.642	3.423
77	1.293	1.665	1.991	2.376	2.641	3.421
78	1.292	1.665	1.991	2.375	2.640	3.420
79	1.292	1.664	1.990	2.374	2.640	3.418
80	1.292	1.664	1.990	2.374	2.639	3.416
81	1.292	1.664	1.990	2.373	2.638	3.415
82	1.292	1.664	1.989	2.373	2.637	3.413
83	1.292	1.663	1.989	2.372	2.636	3.412
84	1.292	1.663	1.989	2.372	2.636	3.410
85	1.292	1.663	1.988	2.371	2.635	3.409
86	1.291	1.663	1.988	2.370	2.634	3.407
87	1.291	1.663	1.988	2.370	2.634	3.406
88	1.291	1.662	1.987	2.369	2.633	3.405
89	1.291	1.662	1.987	2.369	2.632	3.403
90	1.291	1.662	1.987	2.368	2.632	3.402
91	1.291	1.662	1.986	2.368	2.631	3.401
92	1.291	1.662	1.986	2.368	2.630	3.399
93	1.291	1.661	1.986	2.367	2.630	3.398
94	1.291	1.661	1.986	2.367	2.629	3.397
95	1.291	1.661	1.985	2.366	2.629	3.396
96	1.290	1.661	1.985	2.366	2.628	3.395
97	1.290	1.661	1.985	2.365	2.627	3.394
98	1.290	1.661	1.984	2.365	2.627	3.393
99	1.290	1.660	1.984	2.365	2.626	3.392
100	1.290	1.660	1.984	2.364	2.626	3.390
120	1.289	1.658	1.980	2.358	2.617	3.373
140	1.288	1.656	1.977	2.353	2.611	3.361
160	1.287	1.654	1.975	2.350	2.607	3.352
180	1.286	1.653	1.973	2.347	2.603	3.345
200	1.286	1.653	1.972	2.345	2.601	3.340
∞	1.282	1.645	1.960	2.326	2.576	3.291